Exploring Education

An Introduction to the Foundations of Education

ALAN R. SADOVNIK
Rutgers University

PETER W. COOKSON, JR.
Lewis and Clark College

SUSAN F. SEMEL
City College of New York and CUNY Graduate Center

PEARSON

Boston   New York   San Francisco
Mexico City   Montreal   Toronto   London   Madrid   Munich   Paris
Hong Kong   Singapore   Tokyo   Cape Town   Sydney

Executive Editor and Publisher: Stephen D. Dragin
Editorial Assistant: Meaghan Minnick
Marketing Manager: Tara Kelly
Production Editor: Annette Joseph
Editorial Production Coordinator: Holly Crawford
Editorial Production Service: Lynda Griffiths
Composition Buyer: Linda Cox
Manufacturing Buyer: Andrew Turso
Electronic Composition: Publishers' Design and Production Services, Inc.
Cover Administrator: Linda Knowles

For related titles and support materials, visit our online catalog at www.ablongman.com.

Copyright © 2006, 2001, 1994 Pearson Education, Inc.

All rights reserved. No part of the material protected by this copyright notice may be reproduced or utilized in any form or by any means, electronic or mechanical, including photocopying, recording, or by any information storage and retrieval system, without written permission from the copyright owner.

To obtain permission(s) to use material from this work, please submit a written request to Allyn and Bacon, Permissions Department, 75 Arlington Street, Boston, MA 02116 or fax your request to 617-848-7320.

Between the time website information is gathered and then published, it is not unusual for some sites to have closed. Also, the transcription of URLs can result in typographical errors. The publisher would appreciate notification where these errors occur so that they may be corrected in subsequent editions.

Library of Congress Cataloging-in-Publication Data
Sadovnik, Alan R.
    Exploring education: an introduction to the foundations of education / Alan R. Sadovnik, Peter W. Cookson, Susan F. Semel.—3rd ed.
        p.   cm.
    Includes bibliographical references and index.
    ISBN 0-205-47359-8
        1. Education—United States.   2. Educational sociology—United States.   3. Education—United States—Philosophy.   I. Cookson, Peter W.   II. Semel, Susan F.   III. Title.

    LA217.2.S23 2005
    370'.973—dc22

                                                            2005049154

Printed in the United States of America

10 9 8 7 6 5 4 3 2   10 09 08 07 06

Permission credits appear on the last page of this book, which constitutes a continuation of the copyright page.

For Our Children:
Sasha and Aram Cookson
and
Margaret and John Semel

And to the Memory of Carla Hernandez

Contents

Preface

Exploring Education: An Introduction to the Foundations of Education developed out of our dissatisfaction with the textbooks available for foundations of education courses. None of us is a strong advocate of traditional textbooks, as they often simplify complex material to the point of distortion and, more importantly, they do too much work for students. One of the reasons many undergraduate and graduate students cannot read in a critical and analytical mode is that they have been educated, in part, through reading textbooks that summarize everything for them. As firm believers in the use of primary sources, we have written a book that will provide students with material that will encourage them to read, write, and think critically.

Originally, we wanted to compile a reader on the foundations of education. Once we began, however, the project evolved into a combined text/reader in a number of ways. First, in testing the readings in our classes, we found that many of our students required a context to help them make sense of the readings. Thus, we concluded that a book that combined our own text with illustrative readings made more pedagogical sense. As we moved along, we began to realize that our writings should not simply be an introduction to the readings; rather, each chapter should include our own analysis of the material, with a set of readings at the end of each chapter to illuminate the major concepts. This formula, we believed, would provide the necessary balance between text and primary sources.

Moreover, in thinking about our own textual material, we concluded that we wanted to present our point of view about the value of the foundations of education and their application to understanding education. Further, we wanted to argue that a "foundations perspective," as we call it, is a useful tool in helping to improve schools and schooling.

Thus, the final product is the result of considerable thinking about the importance of the foundations of education for teachers and prospective teachers and about how best to present the foundations of education to students. Our book is nontraditional in that it combines our own analysis with primary source readings. We have chosen to include a smaller number of complete or near-complete readings, rather than a larger number of shorter, excerpted readings. We believe strongly that students need to read complete sources to develop their critical reading, writing, and thinking skills.

The purpose of *Exploring Education* is to provide prospective and practicing teachers with an introduction to the foundations of education: history, philosophy, politics, and sociology of education. We also draw on the research of anthropologists of education in a number of places. Chapters 1 through 5 provide a basic introduction to the value of the foundations perspective and to the politics, history, sociology, and philosophy of education. Chapters 6 through 10 apply the foundations of education to particular educational issues, including school organization and teaching, curriculum and pedagogic practices, education and inequality, and school reform and improvement.

Our approach is not meant to be exhaustive. Rather, we have attempted to provide a research- and theory-based approach that demonstrates the usefulness of the foundations lens for thinking critically about and, hopefully, solving educational problems.

This third edition continues to reflect these goals. We have eliminated some readings and added others based on responses from faculty, students, and reviewers. Additionally, the new readings often reflect more updated perspectives and data. At a time when foundations of education are marginalized in many teacher education programs and teacher education reform standards in favor of putatively more practical approaches in curriculum and instruction, we hope this book helps teachers and prospective teachers to think critically about the what and why as well as the how.

Exploring Education has truly been a collaborative effort. Although each of us was responsible for writing a number of chapters (Sadovnik: Chapters 2, 7, and 9; Cookson: Chapters 4, 6, and 8; Semel: Chapters 3 and 5; Sadovnik, Cookson, and Semel: Chapter 1; Semel, Cookson, and Sadovnik: Chapter 10), each of us edited all of the chapters, and the final product is the outcome of our joint efforts. We have attempted to create a consistency in style throughout.

Finally, we hope this book provides teachers and prospective teachers with a tool for understanding schools and a belief in their ability to help improve schooling. Although this book conveys a realistic portrayal of the societal and institutional factors that inhibit meaningful educational change, we believe that teachers, long the forgotten voice in educational reform, need to be part of such change. We believe that the foundations perspective is an important tool in school improvement and change, and hope our book provides its readers with both a realistic picture of educational problems and a sense of hope that they can contribute to change.

Acknowledgments

A number of individuals have contributed to the publication of this book. At Allyn and Bacon, Sean Wakely, our original editor, Virginia Lanigan, our editor for the first edition, Steve Dragin, our editor for the second and third editions, and Nicole DePalma, our editorial assistant, provided essential advice and support. Sean Wakely believed in this project from the outset and had the vision to sign a nontraditional textbook. Virginia Lanigan and Steve Dragin provided strong and sound guidance in the completion of the manuscript and production stages. Nicole DePalma provided assistance for the first edition, Bridget McSweeney for the second edition, and Meaghan Minnick for the third edition. Our thanks, again, to copyeditor Lynda Griffiths.

A number of individuals at Rutgers University provided secretarial and research assistance for the third edition: Bette Jenkins, LaChone McKenzie, Diana Soriel, and graduate assistants Chelsea Dullea and Erin Corbett.

Seven reviewers provided thoughtful, critical, and insightful comments on the original manuscript: They are Justine C. Baker (West Chester University), William M. Britt (University of North Carolina–Charlotte), Joseph C. Bronars (Queens College), Richard C. Jacobs (California State Polytechnic University–Pomona), John McFadden (California State University–Sacramento), David N. Mielke (Appalachian State University), and Harry White (State University of New York–New Paltz). Four additional reviewers provided similarly thoughtful comments on the second edition that were extremely helpful in our revisions: Michael J. Berson (The Citadel), Brigitte Boettiger (University of Colorado–Boulder), Donna L. Ferrara (Long Island University, Southampton), and Margaret A. Laughlin (University of Wisconsin–Green Bay). Four additional reviewers provided important comments on the third edition: Thomas J. Fiala (Arkansas State University), Lawrence D. Klein (Central Connecticut State University), David J. Magleby (Brigham Young University–Utah), and Michael C. Petrowsky (Glendale Community College).

In addition, Carole Shmurak of Central Connecticut State University and Diane Sawyer of Hofstra University provided detailed and helpful comments based on their use of the book. In particular, Professor Shmurak's inclusion of her students' comments proved invaluable. We hope the book reflects many of their suggestions and we believe it is a better book because of their input. We are, however, responsible for whatever shortcomings remain.

In July 1993, Carla A. Hernandez died; she was 24 years old. Carla was an undergraduate and graduate student of ours at Adelphi University; she was also our graduate assistant and, after graduation, was Peter W. Cookson, Jr.'s assistant. She was a gifted teacher and, at the time of her death, was the coordinator of Adelphi University's Off-Campus Education Program in Huntington, New York. Carla's contributions to this book and to our work were profound. She not only provided expert editorial assistance but also contributed many insights and observations about the nature of education and the possibilities of teaching. Carla was a lover of life and a true educator; few people have left such a deep impression in such a short period of time. We all still miss her greatly. Her spirit, however, lives on through the Carla A. Hernandez Memorial Award at Adelphi University, which was endowed by her family and friends. This award, given annually at commencement, provides a graduate assistantship for the graduating Adelphi senior most representative of Carla's life and values.

1 The Limits and Promises of Education

Toward Reflective Practitioners

Americans have always placed a great deal of faith in education. Schools have been viewed as providers of opportunities for social mobility, as places that nurture and develop the hearts and minds of children, as antidotes for ignorance and prejudice, and as solutions to myriad social problems. Throughout this country's history, countless Americans have regarded schools as a symbol of the American dream—that each successive generation, through hard work and initiative, could achieve more than their parents' generation.

This is not to say that Americans have not been critical of their educational system—quite the contrary! Throughout history, schools have been the subject of intense controversy and debate. Questions concerning teaching methods, politics, curricula, racial desegregation, equality of educational opportunity, and countless other issues have constantly defined the educational arena. It is precisely because Americans believe so passionately in education and expect so much from their schools that the educational system has never been free of disagreements and, at times, heated disputes.

Throughout the twentieth century, educational leaders, teachers, parents, and students disagreed about the fundamental goals of education and the educational practices occurring within classrooms. As the educational system steadily expanded and as the society of which it is a part became more complex, the role of schools also became more diverse, if not more diffuse. As prospective teachers, you are about to enter a profession that has both exciting possibilities and serious challenges. It is also a profession that is constantly subject to criticism and reform efforts. A look at the last 30 years provides a small but poignant glimpse of some of these reform movements.

Once again, today, there is a crisis in education. To historians of education, however, the existence of a crisis is by no means new and the meaning of *crisis* is by no means clear. In the early 1970s, *crisis in education* referred to the inequalities of educational opportunity, the allegedly authoritarian and oppressive nature of the schools, and the way in which classroom practices thwarted the personal development of students. The phrases of the day emphasized *relevance, equity, freedom,* and *individualism.* In the 1980s and 1990s, however, the emphasis shifted and the crisis was attributed to the decline of standards and authority, which was thought to be linked to the erosion of U.S. economic superiority in the world. The phrases of the day talked about *excellence, standards, back to basics,* and *cultural literacy.*

In these cycles of educational reform, teachers are often seen as both scapegoats and saviors. They are scapegoats in that if students do not know enough, it is because their teachers have not taught them enough or, worse still, do not know enough to teach them. Or, if children are not developing their individual creative abilities, it is because their teachers may have been more concerned with classroom control than individualized instruction. Teachers are saviors, on the other hand, in that they are mandated to implement the recommendations of each new wave of reforms.

As prospective teachers, you are thinking about a career in education for a variety of reasons. Some of them may include your love of children, the effects your own teachers had on you, the desire to make a difference and contribute to society, and your desire to help children develop both emotionally and intellectually. Some of you may have some less noble reasons, including the perception—however inaccurate—that teachers have easy schedules (home by 3:00 and summers off). Whatever your specific motives, we are sure that you are entering the profession to make a positive contribution to the lives of children and to gain internal satisfaction from witnessing educational success. Although we strongly believe that teachers can and do make a difference, we also recognize that you will be entering an educational system that has many problems. These problems often limit teachers in the fulfillment of their goals.

It is not our intention to depress you with pictures of educational problems nor to create an unrealistic portrait of an educational panacea that does not exist. Rather, we wish to produce a balanced tapestry of the world of schools—a world filled with both promise and limits, hope and despair. But most important, the purpose of this book is to help you understand this world of education: how it works, the factors that affect it, and your role as a teacher in making it better.

The following vignettes present the two poles of the teaching experience. The first, the poignant story of a teacher in an urban public school system, represents the underside of this country's schools and the frustration of a teacher caught in the middle of political, social, and educational problems that she alone cannot possibly solve:

> My experience as a school teacher, both as a high school English teacher and an elementary school teacher, has been one of disappointment, frustration, anger and anxiety. I chose secondary English for a number of reasons, two primary ones being my love of literature and my comfortable familiarity with the school setting. Nothing in my college training gave me even an inkling that literature would not be the focus of my teaching, or that my future students would have values, outlooks and attitudes that were totally unfamiliar to me. . . .
>
> Imagine my shock, then, when I walked into a classroom the following fall as a newly licensed teacher, and encountered surly, hostile, disinterested, below-grade-level students!. . . They had been reared on failure and low expectations, and consequently regarded school and teachers as enemies. . . .
>
> As shocked and repulsed as I was initially, I was still determined to make a difference in the lives of my students. I thought I could plough through the poverty, illness, abuse, neglect and defeatism of their lives and get them to respond to Shakespeare's language, to Hawthorne's characters, to Hardy's themes. How foolishly unrealistic I was. My successes were scant and infrequent, my failures numerous and daily. I rarely knew the feeling that some teachers profess to experience when they "reach even one child." I was too numbed by a sense of futility to feel any sense of success. . . .

Over the years, I became cynical and resentful and even contemptuous of some of my students. When colleagues praised my teaching and my management ability, I felt as though I were fooling the world—a guilty feeling. Why would people think I was a good teacher when I knew that most of my students were bored, that they were making little if any progress and that I was not being dynamic or even enthusiastic in my approach? The answer is that none of those things mattered. As long as there was order in the room and notes on the chalkboard, everyone was satisfied. Record-keeping and keeping control of the kids were all that seemed important to administrators. You clocked in and clocked out and got paid, regardless of what you did in the intervening hours. Good teachers got no more recognition than poor ones, and poor ones could not be weeded out once they were tenured. It all seemed so pointless and hopeless.

. . . My current school has classrooms that are converted closets, lacks paper and other integral supplies, employs an assistant principal whose job was given to him by a politician, allows hoards of children to simply watch cartoons in the auditorium and calls that a "media lesson," is overrun with mice and roaches, has gaping holes in ceilings and walls, has toilets and water fountains that are nonfunctioning, and promotes children who are practically illiterate. Security breeches abound, with intruders walking in and out of the building at will; instruction is interrupted sometimes ten or fifteen times in one hour by announcements blaring over the intercom; innovative ideas that certain teachers toil to create in an effort to improve the school are almost always ignored by a principal who is resistant to change. Teachers live for 3 o'clock dismissals, for holidays, for summer vacations. A snow storm that closes the school for a day is viewed as one of nature's blessings.

What happened to the joys and rewards of teaching and learning? After eighteen years of seeking the answer and trying to buck the system, I've given up. It's been said that one good teacher can influence a child's entire life. I've never seen that happen personally. I've seen students come back to visit favorite teachers, I've heard students thank and praise helpful teachers, and I've known students who'll work harder for one teacher than he has for others. But I've never met an inner-city student who claimed that the course of his life had been shaped by one particular teacher, or who was inspired enough by that teacher's values and ideals to rethink his own. Maybe I expected too much from the profession; maybe I should be satisfied when one or two children out of thirty improve their reading comprehension or math skills each year. But I'm not; it isn't enough for me! (Katz, 1988)

The difficulties experienced by this teacher are not representative of what all or even most teachers face, but they do indicate that the educational systems that you will enter are often beset with problems that are not solely educational.

On the other hand, this second vignette speaks passionately and lovingly about the positive effects of teachers and describes the kind of teacher we all want to be. Written by Fred Hechinger in the *New York Times* and entitled "Gift of a Great Teacher," this tribute captures the ways in which teachers make a significant difference in the lives of students:

Tessie is different from the other teachers, a 9-year-old boy told his parents. . . . When he was asked how she was different, he replied, "Tessie knows how we children think."

Tessie, the boy's fourth-grade teacher at [a school in New York City], was Theresa Ross, who taught elementary and middle school classes for nearly 60 years. . . .Last June Tessie, who was affectionately known by that name to children and adults alike, died at the age of 83. . . .

The only way to describe great teaching, a rare art, is to study great teachers like Tessie. When her pupils recognized that she knew how they thought, it did not mean that she herself thought childishly or indulgently about them. To write about her is not to celebrate a person but to try to define some qualities of exceptional teaching.

It has been said that education is what you remember when you have forgotten what you learned. Often, that means remembering one's great teachers more vividly than any particular lesson. Anyone who has never had at least one such teacher is truly deprived. To expect many is unreasonable. . . . As a teacher, [Tessie's] only doctrine was to make education come to life. When she taught history, her favorite subject, she took the children back with her into antiquity. She believed that even fourth-graders could deal with the universe.

[A former student teacher] in Tessie's class. . .recalls how Tessie used all the children's experiences to teach them—street games, the previous night's television programs, great myths.

She would do "weird" things. . . . To make children understand the evil consequences of a hostile invasion, she once had her pupils "invade" another classroom. As expected, the result was often bedlam, and she asked the children to report on the experience.

Great teachers are strong enough to dare being unconventional, even controversial, and this was an example. Actually,. . . Tessie had second thoughts about the experiment and never repeated it. Still, both she and the children had learned from the experience.

. . .Great teachers develop their own ways, without relying on prescribed lesson plans. Tessie said: "The child needs a framework within which to find himself; otherwise, he is an egg without a shell. The adult is there to guide and teach. If a child asks how to do something, you don't tell him just to go and find out; you say, 'Come, let's work it out together.'"

. . .Once, a picnic in the park that she and her fourth-graders had prepared was rained out, to universal groans. Tessie's response was to have the desks and chairs pushed aside, turning the classroom floor into a substitute picnic ground.

Tessie tried to get children to understand the nature of leadership without lecturing about it. She might start with baseball or with the news, and then move on to Julius Caesar.

. . .When Tessie died, even the youngest children who had known her sensed a sharp loss. Some felt guilty, said one teacher who met with them to talk about Tessie's life and to help them cope with her death. Perhaps, the teacher thought, as Tessie got older and a little forgetful, the children thought they might not have been sufficiently thoughtful and appreciative. A more plausible explanation may be that the children instinctively recognized an extraordinary teacher, and mourned the loss. (Hechinger, 1987)

How do you balance the extremes of these portraits? On the one hand, you see an educational system beset with insurmountable problems; on the other hand, you see a world in which individual teachers have the power to influence countless children in a positive way. Moreover, what is the relationship between the two? That is, how do the problems within schools limit teachers' abilities to make a difference? And how do teachers who do make a difference help solve some of the problems? Teacher number 1 was not a less effective teacher than teacher number 2. Rather, the social, political, and economic problems she encountered in her school made it almost impossible to be effective. Teacher number 2 worked in a setting without these problems and one far more conducive to teaching excellence. The important point is that teachers work within organizational contexts that have a profound impact on their lives in classrooms.

As a person entering the teaching profession, you will ultimately find yourself in a curious quandary—responsible for educational problems and their solutions, but often without out the necessary knowledge and perspective for understanding the complexity of these problems and the intricacies of their solutions. Furthermore, although teacher education programs do a respectable job at providing teachers with teaching methods, research on teacher education as well as a number of reform proposals indicates that programs are less effective in providing teachers with a social and intellectual context for understanding the educational world in which these methods will be employed. This understanding is crucial to the development of teachers, who must be an integral part of the problem-solving process if schools are to fulfill their promise.

In his classic book, *The Sociological Imagination,* C. Wright Mills (1959) outlined the value of a sociological perspective for understanding society. The sociological imagination, according to Mills, allows individuals to transcend the often narrow boundaries of their lives and to see the world from the broader context of history and society. Adopting the sociological imagination permits the user to connect his or her own life with the social, cultural, and historical events that have affected it, and ultimately enables the individual to understand how and why these forces are instrumental in shaping human existence. The promise of sociology, then, is its ability to provide a powerful understanding of society and oneself (Sadovnik et al., 1987, p. 3). In light of the significant social, political, economic, and moral questions of his time, Mills argued that "the sociological imagination [is] our most needed quality of mind" (Mills, 1959, p. 3).

In a similar vein, contemporary American education, as we have argued, is beset by problems. The following section provides a brief overview of some of these.

Educational Problems

During the 1980s and 1990s, educational problems became the focus of national attention. The issues of educational standards, excellence, and the decline of U.S. educational superiority in the international arena became central concerns. To a lesser extent, although of equal importance, the topic of equity, with particular attention to the crisis in urban education and the plight of children in the United States, received significant discussion. Although subsequent chapters will look at these issues more completely, this section briefly outlines a few of the significant educational problems today and some of the policies and programs aimed at treating them.

The Achievement Gaps

Since the 1960s, the achievement gaps based on social class, race, ethnicity, and gender have been the focus of educational policy. These gaps include group differences in achievement based on standardized tests and grades; attainment based on the number of years of schooling, high school and college attendance and graduation, dropout rates, and completion of honors and advanced placement courses; and opportunity based on access to qualified teachers, challenging curriculum placement in special education, and investments in education, including state and local funding. Beginning with the Elementary and Secondary Education Act of 1965 through President George W. Bush's reauthorization of the act, the No Child Left Behind Act of 2001, federal educational policy has attempted to reduce these gaps (Cross, 2004). In addition, beginning with the Coleman Report (1966), educational research has focused on the causes of inequalities of educational achievement, with a variety of factors both inside and outside schools seen as responsible for the gaps.

Trends.   The gaps include higher academic achievement by high-income students compared to low-income students; white and Asian American students compared to African American and Hispanic students, even when controlling for socioeconomic level; and male students compared to female students. There have been some improvements since the 1960s, with the gender gap closing dramatically and in some cases, women outperforming men. Until 1988, social class, race, and ethnic differences decreased, but since then these gaps have widened, despite continued educational policies aimed at reducing them. Data from the National Assessment of Education Progress (NAEP) illustrate these achievement gaps.

■ From 1970 to 1988, the gaps between African Americans and Hispanic Americans, as a group, and whites narrowed on the NAEP Reading for 17-year-olds; from 1973 to 1986, it narrowed on the NAEP Math for 13-year-olds. Between 1988 and 1990, this progress halted and gaps began to widen. In 1990, the gap between white and African American 17-year-olds on the NAEP Math was 20 points, and in 1999, it was 32 points; in 1988, the gap between white and African American 17-year-olds in NAEP Reading was 21 points, and in 1999, it was 31 points (U.S. Department of Education, National Center for Educational Statistics, NAEP Trends in Academic Progress, 2000).

■ On grade 4 Reading Achievement, 30 percent of all students were proficient or above, and 62 percent of all students were scored basic or above. Disaggregated by group, the scores are African American: 2 percent advanced, 11 percent proficient, 27 percent basic, and 61 percent below basic; Asian American: 11 percent advanced, 26 percent proficient, 32 percent basic, and 31 percent below basic; Hispanic American: 2 percent advanced, 12 percent proficient, 28 percent basic, and 57 percent below basic; Native American: 2 percent advanced, 14 percent proficient, 31 percent basic, and 53 percent below basic; white: 10 percent advanced, 30 percent proficient, 34 percent basic, and 26 percent below basic (The Education Trust, 2004, www.edtrust.org).

■ On grade 8 Mathematics Achievement, 27 percent of all students were proficient or above, and 67 percent of all students were basic or above. Disaggregated by group, the scores are African American: 0 percent advanced, 7 percent proficient, 32 percent basic, and 61 percent below basic; Asian American: 12 percent advanced, 30 percent proficient, 36 percent basic, and 23 percent below basic; Hispanic American: 1 percent advanced, 10 percent proficient, 35 percent basic, and 53 percent below basic; Native American: 2 percent advanced, 14 percent proficient, 38 percent basic, and 46 percent below basic; white: 7 percent advanced, 29 percent proficient, 43 percent basic, and 21 percent below basic (The Education Trust, 2004, www.edtrust.org).

■ With respect to social class differences, on grade 4 Reading Achievement, the average scale score of poor students was approximately 196, and for nonpoor students approximately 232. On grade 8 Mathematics Achievement, the average scale score for poor students was approximately 259, and for nonpoor students approximately 286 (The Education Trust, 2004, www.edtrust.org).

■ Based on 1999 NAEP data, African American and Hispanic American 17-year-olds did math at the same levels as white 13-year-olds, and African American and Hispanic American 17-year-olds read at the same levels as white 13-year-olds.

■ With respect to attainment, four-year high school graduation 2001 rates, by group, were: all students: 70 percent; African American: 51 percent; Asian American: 79 percent; Hispanic American: 52 percent; Native American: 54 percent; white: 72 percent (The Education Trust, 2004, www.edtrust.org). Four-year college graduation 2002 rates for students who began college as freshmen were: all students: 55 percent; African American: 40 percent; Asian American: 64 percent; Hispanic American: 36 percent; white: 59 percent. Based on longer-term graduation rates of six years or more, in 1998, group graduation rates were African American: 81 percent; Asian American: 94 percent; Hispanic American: 63 percent; white: 90 percent (U.S. Bureau of the Census, Current Population Reports, Educational Attainment in the United States, March 2002).

■ Of every 100 white kindergartners, by the age of 24, 93 graduate from high school, 65 complete some college, and 32 earn at least a bachelor's degree. Of every 100 African American kindergartners, by the age of 24, 87 graduate from high school, 51 complete some college, and 17 earn at least a bachelor's degree. Of every 100 Hispanic American kindergartners, by the age of 24, 63 graduate from high school, 32 complete some college, and 11 earn at least a bachelor's degree (U.S. Bureau of the Census, Current Population Reports, Educational Attainment in the United States, March 1998). Also, 60 percent of young people from high-income families graduate from college by the age of 26 as compared to 7 percent of young people from low-income families (Mortenson, 1997).

■ With respect to opportunity, in 1999–2000, 24 percent of all secondary classes were taught by teachers without a major or minor in their teaching field. In low-poverty schools it was 19 percent; in high-poverty schools it was 34 percent; in low-minority schools it was 21 percent; and in high-minority schools it was 29 percent (U.S. Department of Education, National Center for Education Statistics, 2004).

■ With respect to opportunity, in 2000, African Americans comprised 17 percent of all public school K–12 enrollment. They comprised 8 percent of enrollment in gifted and talented classes; 22 percent of enrollment in special education classes; and 34 percent of suspensions. Asian Americans comprised 4 percent of all public school K–12 enrollment. They comprised 7 percent of enrollment in gifted and talented classes; 2 percent of enrollment in special education classes; and 2 percent of suspensions. Hispanic Americans comprised 16 percent of all public school K–12 enrollment. They comprised 10 percent of enrollment in gifted and talented classes; 15 percent of enrollment in special education classes; and 15 percent of suspensions. Native Americans comprised 1 percent of all public school K–12 enrollment. They comprised 1 percent of enrollment in gifted and talented classes; 1 percent of enrollment in special education classes; and 1 percent of suspensions. Whites comprised 61 percent of all public school K–12 enrollment. They comprised 74 percent of enrollment in gifted and talented classes; 60 percent of enrollment in special education classes, and 48 percent of suspensions (NAEP, 2004).

■ With respect to investments, in 2001, the nation has an effective funding gap between highest and lowest poverty districts of $1,256 per student, $31,400 for a typical classroom of 25 students, and $502,392 for a typical elementary school of 400 students. These gaps vary by state, with some (e.g., Illinois, New York, and Pennsylvania) having large gaps and some (e.g., Delaware, Massachusetts, Minnesota, and New Jersey) providing more funding to high-poverty districts (The Education Trust, 2004, www .edtrust.org).

Policy Issues.   There is little agreement about the causes of the achievement gap or solutions aimed at eliminating it. Some researchers point to factors inside schools, including school funding, teacher quality, curriculum tracking, and teacher expectations; others blame outside school factors, including poverty, parental involvement, cultural differences, genetic differences in intelligence, and lack of economic opportunities. The policy issues aimed at reducing the achievement gap are discussed more fully in the next section on improving urban schools, where the various achievement gaps are most pronounced.

Programmatic Issues.   Consequently, there is also little agreement about programs aimed at eliminating the gaps. Some advocate programs that are aimed at reducing the school-based gaps in opportunity, including teacher quality and experience, unequal funding, access to rigorous curricula, and comprehensive whole-school reforms (The Education Trust, 2004, www.edtrust.org). No Child Left Behind (NCLB) is this type of programmatic reform. Others advocate programs that are aimed at reducing economic and cultural disadvantage as well as social, economic, and health disparities related to poverty (Anyon, 1997, 2005; Rothstein, 2004b). The programmatic issues aimed at reducing the achievement gap are discussed more fully in the next section on improving urban schools, where the programmatic debates have been most heated.

The Crisis in Urban Education

This nation's urban public schools continue to be in crisis. Over the past 40 years, as central cities have become increasingly poor and populated by minorities, the schools reflect the problems endemic to urban poverty. Although there are similar problems in rural schools and in many suburban schools, urban educational problems represent perhaps the nation's most serious challenge. A high proportion of urban schools are ineffective by most measures of school quality, a large percentage of urban students perform below national standards, and high school dropout rates in many large cities are over 40 percent. Despite these dismal data, there are policies and programs—including school restructuring programs, effective school models, and school choice and magnet programs—that many believe display significant potential for improvement. Clear national, state, and local policies are needed that emphasize excellence with equity and funding for programs.

Trends.   Urban schools reflect the demographic characteristics of the urban environment. As large cities have become increasingly poor and populated by minorities, their schools reflect the problems of urban poverty. Low student achievement, high dropout rates, and high levels of school ineffectiveness characterize many urban school districts.

■ The United States has witnessed a significant increase in the percentage of poor and minority children and youth living in the central cities of the country. In 1971, 17 percent of the children and youth between the ages of 6 and 17 in large central cities were both poor and minority; by 1983, this percentage increased to 28 percent and continued to increase throughout the 1980s, the 1990s, and into the twenty-first century (Anyon, 1997, 2005; Levine & Havighurst, 1989, p. 75).

■ Urban schools reflect social stratification and segregation. Due to the concentration of poor and minority populations in large urban areas, urban public schools have significantly higher percentages of low socioeconomic status (SES) and minority students than neighboring suburban school districts. In 1989, 48.6 percent of the children in New York City were from low-income families; 80.1 percent were black, Hispanic, or Asian. Increasingly, affluent white families in cities send their children to private schools (New York City Board of Education, 1989). This pattern continues in the twenty-first century.

In 2003, the enrollments of the seven largest city school districts in the United States were

1. New York: Asian American: 10.0 percent; African American: 36.1 percent; Hispanic American: 37.3 percent; white: 16.1 percent
2. Los Angeles: Asian American: 6.0 percent; African American: 12.9 percent; Hispanic American: 71.4 percent; white: 9.6 percent
3. Chicago: Asian American: 3.3 percent; African American: 50.9 percent; Hispanic American: 36.4 percent; white: 9.2 percent
4. Miami: Asian American: <2.0 percent; African American: 30.1 percent; Hispanic American: 57.2 percent; white: 10.6 percent
5. Houston: Asian American: 3.0 percent; African American: 30.5 percent; Hispanic American: 57.1 percent; white: 9.3 percent
6. Philadelphia: Asian American: 4.9 percent; African American: 65.3 percent; Hispanic American: 13.1 percent; white: 16.4 percent
7. Detroit: Asian American: 1.0 percent; African American: 90.1 percent; Hispanic American: 2.8 percent; white: 5.2 percent (Ladson-Billings, 2004).

■ In urban schools, the relationship between socioeconomic status and academic attainment and achievement reflects overall national patterns. Students from lower SES families attain lower levels of academic attainment and performance than students from higher SES backgrounds. For example, in New York City districts with 50 percent or more students from low-income families, less than 40 percent are reading at or above grade level; in districts with less than 50 percent of students from low-income families, almost 60 percent are reading at or above grade level (New York City Board of Education, 2003). In addition, urban school dropout rates reflect this pattern. For example, the dropout rate in East Los Angeles is 60 percent; Boston, 50 percent; and Washington, DC, 45 percent. In other cities, such as Detroit, Pittsburgh, Chicago, New York, Cleveland, and Baton Rouge, high school dropout rates are also very high (between 30 and 45 percent) (Levine & Havighurst, 1989, pp. 55–58). Again, these patterns continue in the twenty-first century (Anyon, 1997, 2005).

■ Many urban public schools do not provide their students with a minimally adequate education. For example, in New York City, 47.2 percent of the public schools were rated ineffective by New York State Department of Education standards. In addition, only 47.8 percent of its students were reading at or above grade level, and only 56.2 percent of its students were at or above grade level in mathematics. These data reflected national patterns for public schools in large urban areas (New York City Board of Education, 1989). In 2004, the largest percentage of schools labeled "in need of improvement" under NCLB are in urban areas (New York State Department of Education, 2004).

Policy Issues.   There is considerable disagreement among researchers and policy makers as to how to improve urban schools. There is little consensus about school choice (giving parents the right to choose their children's schools), desegregation, and school financing policies. What is clear, however, is that policies that are aimed at the schools alone, without addressing the significant social and economic problems of urban areas, are doomed to failure (Anyon, 1997, 2005; Rothstein, 2004b).

■ Inequities in school financing exacerbate the problems faced by urban school systems. Because school financing is based on state funding formulas and local property taxes, most urban districts spend significantly less per pupil than wealthier suburban districts. Recent lawsuits in New Jersey, New York, and other states have sought to remedy these inequalities with varying degrees of success. For example, *Abbott* v. *Burke* in New Jersey has provided funding for its 31 urban Abbott districts equal to its highest socioeconomic districts. Also the Campaign for Fiscal Equity lawsuit in New York is still being adjudicated, despite the state's highest court mandating an additional $5.6 billion per year for New York City students.

■ Demographic realities make urban schools increasingly segregated both by race and social class. Although the evidence on the effects of school desegregation on academic achievement is not conclusive, many policy makers argue that there are moral imperatives requiring school desegregation.

■ The difficult problems within urban schools have, in part, resulted in a crisis in staffing. Many urban school systems face a continual teacher shortage and witness significant teacher turnover. Most important, in many cities there is a crucial shortage of minority teachers to serve as role models for the increasingly minority student population (Educational Priorities Panel, 1987; Ingersoll, 2004; New York State Board of Regents, 1999).

■ Policy makers disagree about how to improve urban schools. Some studies propose a radical overhaul of public education, including a voucher system, a free market competition between public and private schools, and unlimited parental choice in school selection (Chubb & Moe, 1990). Other studies suggest that such policies will increase the ability of high-income families to improve their children's education and ultimately continue to penalize low-income families. In the 1990s, charter schools (public schools that are independent of local school districts) became increasingly popular (Bulkley & Wohlstetter, 2004; Wells et al., 1998).

Programmatic Issues.   Research suggests that there are programs that will improve urban schools. Effective school models, magnet programs (specialized schools), school choice programs, and parental community involvement all indicate promise. Funding for successful programs is needed to encompass a larger urban population.

■ Effective school research has indicated that there are programmatic ways to improve urban schools. For example, the following characteristics have been identified with unusually effective schools in general and in urban settings: a safe and orderly environment; a clear school mission; instructional leadership by a principal or school head; a climate of high expectations; a concentration on instructional tasks; monitoring of student progress; and positive home-school relations (cited in Gartner & Lipsky, 1987, p. 389). School restructuring efforts based on these principles suggest promise (www.edtrust.org; just4kids.org). For instance, the work of Deborah Meier, former principal of Central Park East Secondary School in New York City, and James Comer, at Yale Medical School, in the New Haven Schools, are striking examples. Meier successfully implemented progressive school restructuring in an urban school with a mostly black and Latino population. Comer sucessfully implemented a school-university cooperative program for mostly low-income black students.

■ Compensatory education programs (programs aimed at providing equality of opportunity for disadvantaged students) have resulted in academic improvement for children from low SES and disadvantaged backgrounds. Although the overall research on the effects of compensatory programs is mixed, there are studies that indicate that effective compensatory programs result in positive academic and social results (Natriello, McDill, & Pallas, 1990). Many policy makers believe that programs such as Head Start (a preschool program for children from low-income families), dropout prevention programs, and many bilingual education programs need to be funded, not eliminated (Lynch, 2004/2005).

■ School choice programs may help to improve the education of urban children. Although there is disagreement about the extent of parental choice, many researchers believe that some combination of school choice and magnet school programs will improve urban education problems. In a number of urban settings, such as Minneapolis and District 4 in New York City, there have been significant improvements. In addition, studies of magnet and charter schools indicate significant educational possibilities (Powers & Cookson, 1999; Tractenberg, Sadovnik, & Liss, 2004).

■ The paucity of minority teachers and the lack of multicultural curricula are significant problems in urban school systems. Many experts believe that given the student populations of most urban schools, it is imperative that programs are developed to attract and train minority teachers and to develop more multicultural curriculum projects.

The Decline of Literacy

Critics of U.S. public education have pointed to the failure of schools to teach children basic literacy skills in reading, writing, and mathematics and basic knowledge in history, literature, and the arts. Although there has been significant controversy over the value of such skills and knowledge, and whether such a decline is related to the decline in U.S. economic superiority, it is apparent that schools have become less effective in transmitting skills and knowledge.

Trends. During the 1990s and into the twenty-first century, educational reforms stressed standards, NCLB, and accountability. Goals 2000, an educational bill passed under the Clinton administration, and state-mandated curriculum standards and assessments resulted in some increases in educational achievement. Although there are some problems with using standardized tests, and despite some achievement increases of the 1990s, comparisons of U.S. students to students from other countries, SAT scores, and other data indicate continuing problems in literacy.

■ U.S. high school students performed less well than their counterparts in other industrialized nations in mathematics, science, history, and literature. Studies by the International Association for the Evaluation of Educational Achievement (IAEEA) reflect this trend. Although fourth-graders in the United States compare well, U.S. student performance declines in grades 8 and 12. U.S. fourth-graders scored above the 26-nation average in both mathematics and science. In science, only students in Korea outperformed U.S. fourth-graders, while in mathematics, U.S. fourth-graders outperformed their peers in 12 countries and scored below their peers in 7 countries. U.S. eighth-graders scored above the 41-nation average in science and below the international average in mathematics. In science, U.S. eighth-graders outperformed their peers in 15 countries and scored below their peers in 9 countries. In mathematics, eighth-graders in 20 countries outperformed U.S. eighth-graders. U.S. eighth-graders had higher scores than their peers in 7 countries. U.S. twelfth-graders scored below the 21-nation average in both mathematics and science. In science, U.S. twelfth-graders scored below students in the last year of secondary school in 11 countries. U.S. twelfth-graders outperformed their peers in 2 countries. In mathematics, U.S. students scored below their peers in 14 countries and outperformed their peers in 2 countries (U.S. Department of Education, National Center for Education Statistics, 1998). These patterns continued in the early part of the twenty-first century.

The belief that U.S. public schools are mediocre was not universally supported. David Berliner and Bruce Biddle argued in *The Manufactured Crisis* (1995) that the literacy and achievement crisis was largely a myth perpetuated by conservatives who supported tuition vouchers, school choice, and charter schools. They stated that the real crisis in education in the United States is the large achievement gap between affluent and poor students. Data from the Third International Mathematics and Science Study (TIMSS) indicated general improvement by U.S. students in science. The performance of U.S. students in mathematics remains a little below the international average (Baker & Smith, 1997). Recent TIMSS data in 2003 support those conclusions.

■ U.S. high school students scored lower on the SAT verbal and mathematic tests in the 1980s than in previous decades. For example, in 1967–1968, the average verbal SAT score was 466 and the average mathematics score was 492. In 1977–1978, the average scores were 429 and 468, respectively; in 1987–1988, the average scores were 428 and 476, respectively; in 1994–1995, the average scores were 428 and 482, respectively; and in 2002–2003, the average scores were 507 and 519, respectively (U.S. Department of Education, National Center for Education Statistics, 1989, 1997, 1989a, 1989b, 1997a, 1997b; U.S. Department of Education, Office of the Under Secretary and Office of Elementary and Secondary Education, 2004). Again, the validity of these scores is questionable, since more students attended college and thus took the SATs in the 1980s (therefore, a larger number of students from the lower achievement tracks in high school took the SATs), and the scores were recentered, creating higher scores in the post 1998 period, but these data point to problems in the U.S. schools. In addition, U.S. high school students do not score particularly well on standardized tests of culturally valued knowledge in history and literature. For example, in *What Do Our Seventeen Year Olds Know?* Ravitch and Finn (1987) argued that 17-year-old high school students have abysmal knowledge of basic information in history and literature. Although there is general controversy over the intrinsic value of such knowledge, New York State high school performance on these tests may indicate a problem in U.S. schools in transmitting this form of cultural knowledge to its students.

■ In the 1980s, critics argued that the curriculum in many public and private high schools was "watered down" and provided far too many elective courses of suspect value and too little of substance. The National Commission on Excellence report *(A Nation at Risk)* and other reports pointed to the absence of a core curriculum of required courses for all students. In addition, critics suggested that, because most states require only the fulfillment of credit hours (that is, four years of English, three years of mathematics, etc.), specific knowledge in curriculum areas is rarely uniformly required. In addition, some critics pointed to the absence of a national curriculum and standards, commonplace in many countries (e.g., France), as a major shortcoming in U.S. education. Although there was significant controversy over many of these claims, there was agreement that the curriculum in most U.S. high schools needs significant attention.

In the 1990s, although national curriculum standards did not emerge, curriculum standards set by national associations, such as the National Council of Teachers of Mathematics (NCTM) and the National Council of Social Studies (NCSS), as well as standards mandated by individual states often based on these, resulted in an increase in curriculum standards ("Quality Counts, 1999," 1999).

■ The U.S. literacy (and illiteracy rate) is shocking. Jonathan Kozol, in *Illiterate America* (1986), indicated that there are over 25 million functionally illiterate Americans. This record has not improved dramatically and continues to be well below the literacy rates of other industrialized nations and is a serious indictment of the nation's educational system.

Policy Issues.   There is little agreement about policy regarding standards and curriculum. Given the constitutional authority granted to states and localities for educational policies, many people argue against any federal governmental role. Others, such as Chester Finn, Jr., continue to propose the adoption of national standards in curriculum, knowledge, and skills (Finn, 1989). Finally, many are concerned with the need to balance higher standards with the guarantee that all students are given an equal opportunity to meet these standards.

■ The adoption of national standards in curriculum, knowledge, and skills is a controversial proposal. The creation of nationally prescribed norms of what should be taught, what students should learn and know, and what students should be able to do is favored by some and opposed by others. Those in opposition believe that such norms should be locally determined or that such norms are impossible to develop.

■ The balancing of higher standards and the ability of all students, particularly disadvantaged students, to meet these standards is an important issue. With dropout rates over 50 percent in many urban school districts, many fear that simply raising standards will exacerbate an already problematic situation.

■ The development of core curriculum for graduation from high school, which would include the same academic subjects and knowledge for all students, poses significant issues about what the curriculum would include. Proponents of core curriculum, such as Diane Ravitch, Chester Finn, Jr., and E. D. Hirsch, suggest that the curriculum should include the canons of Western civilization as its starting point. Critics of this view suggest that a more multicultural curriculum needs to be developed.

■ Policies aimed at raising standards and improving curriculum need to look at the effects of curriculum tracking policies. Curriculum tracking at the high school level and ability grouping (with the same or different curricula) at the K–12 level is a controversial policy. Proponents point to the functional necessity and benefits of homogeneous groups; critics, such as Jeannie Oakes (1985), point to the inequities of such arrangements. Because research is inconclusive, policies concerning tracking need to be carefully addressed.

Programmatic Issues.   In the past few years, all 50 states and most localities have implemented programs to raise academic achievement. At the federal level, the Goals 2000 legislation defined a national set of learning goals for all students, and NCLB mandated state testings in grades 3 through 8.

■ Programs at the state and local levels to define what students should know and be able to do were implemented in the 1990s. Taking their initial cue from the National Commission on Excellence report, *A Nation at Risk* (1983), many states and districts increased curriculum requirements for graduation and instituted core curriculum requirements. One fear is that such programmatic reforms may be artificial and raise scores simply by having teachers teach to tests. Another concern is that such standardization of curriculum may reduce innovation.

■ States initiated minimum performance requirements for promotion (grades 4, 8, 10) and graduation (grade 12). NCLB initiated mandated state testing as well as requiring states to label schools that did not meet standards, as In Need of Improvement. Schools labeled this way face significant sanctions, including restructuring or closure. There is a concern with the use of standardized tests as the inclusive evaluation tool, and many states and local districts are experimenting with portfolios and other more qualitative evaluations. However, NCLB has made such assessments difficult, if not impossible.

■ Effective school research indicates that schools that place student learning as the most important school goal are effective in improving learning. The application of effective school models, especially in urban areas, is necessary to ensure equity.

■ Compensatory education programs and dropout prevention programs are essential if higher standards are not to become one more barrier for disadvantaged students. With literacy rates lowest with at-risk children and poor adults, both in urban and rural settings, literacy programs aimed at these populations are required.

■ There have been increases in achievement due to these reforms. For example, from 1982 to 2003, the percentage of high school students taking the challenging academic courses recommended in *A Nation at Risk* increased significantly. Enrollments in Advanced Placement (AP) courses also increased significantly, and the number of students passing AP exams nearly tripled between 1982 and 2003. National Assessment of Educational Progress (NAEP) scores also increased. The average performance in mathematics improved substantially on the NAEP between 1978 and 2000. Among 9- and 13-year-olds, the improvement was the equivalent of at least one grade level. Performance in science was also higher in 2000 than in 1978 among all age groups, especially in general science knowledge and skills. These gains in academic performance, while significant, are not sufficient. The NAEP results in reading performance remain relatively unchanged, and the narrowed gap in performance between white and minority students remains unacceptably large (U.S. Department of Education, National Center for Education Statistics, 1998, 2000, 2003).

Assessment Issues

For both educational problems—the crisis in urban education and the decline of literacy—there are a number of assessment issues that need to be addressed. More empirical evidence on school effectiveness, especially qualitative studies on school processes, is needed. New assessment measures that eliminate class, racial, gender, and cultural bias must be developed.

■ Large-scale educational studies have provided important data on school and student outcomes. More studies on the process of schooling, including ethnographic studies, are needed to understand the factors within schools that affect student achievement.

■ Effective school research has provided significant understanding of the relationship between school organization and processes and academic achievement. Research that assesses the implementation of effective school models based on this research is needed.

■ More research on the relationship between family, culture, community, and school is needed. Although there are many theoretical analyses of these issues, far more empirical research is needed.

■ New assessment techniques are needed to evaluate teacher and student performance and curriculum design. Studies indicate that traditional assessment devices may be culturally and racially biased. In addition to different quantitative measures, many researchers and educators believe that qualitative approaches such as portfolios should be considered (Martin-Kniep & Kniep, 1992; "Quality Counts, 1999," 1999).

The preceding discussion is a brief overview of a few of the many problems addressed more fully in this book. The presentation of trends, policy issues, programmatic issues, and assessment issues provides only a glimpse into the complexity of the problems and their solutions. In subsequent chapters, the specific issues will be explored in greater detail. For our purposes here, it is important to recognize that, as teachers, you will face many of these problems and will need a perspective for grappling with them. We believe that the foundations perspective is an important tool in understanding and solving such difficult educational dilemmas.

Understanding Education: The Foundations Perspective

As you can see, there is no shortage of critiques and there are a plethora of reform proposals. New teachers need a quality of mind—the kind of perspective that the sociological imagination advocated by Mills (1959) offers—in order to place the educational system in a context. Such a context or framework is necessary to understand the schools and the teacher's place within them, to understand how the schools relate to other aspects of society, and to see how educational problems are related to larger societal dilemmas. Finally, seeing the schools in their context will enhance your understanding of how the schools today reflect the historical evolution of reform efforts as well as how current debates frame what the schools will look like for each successive generation of teachers and students.

What do we propose that you, as prospective teachers, need in order to understand and answer these questions? Quite simply, we call it a *foundations perspective.* The foundations perspective is a lens for viewing the schools analytically from a variety of approaches that, taken together, provide the viewer with an understanding of the connections between teacher, student, school, and society. The foundations perspective also serves to relate educational organization and processes, and educational theory and practice. Most important, it links the understanding of these relationships to meaningful activity—the improvement of this nation's schools.

The foundations perspective consists of four interrelated approaches: historical, philosophical, political, and the sociological. Through the use of the insights of the history of education, the philosophy of education, the politics of education, and the sociology of education, you will be better able to comprehend the educational system you are about to enter as teachers.

The history, philosophy, politics, and sociology of education, or what are commonly referred to as the *foundations of education,* are by no means separate and distinct perspectives. On one hand, they represent the unique vantage points of the separate disciplines of history, philosophy, political science, and sociology. On the other hand, historians, philosophers, political scientists, and sociologists rarely write from their own disciplines alone; more often than not, they tend to view the world from interdisciplinary and multidisciplinary perspectives. Therefore, although the following discussion presents the insights of each as a separate entity, please keep in mind that ultimately the foundations perspective seeks to combine all four disciplinary approaches and to look at the relationships between their central areas of concern. What, then, are the central areas of concern? And what is their value for teachers? We begin with the first question.

The History of Education

In *The Culture of Narcissism,* Christopher Lasch (1983) bemoaned what he termed the "waning of a sense of history." Lasch argued that contemporary Americans had lost their understanding of the past and therefore could neither understand the complexities of the present nor look to a better future. For Lasch, the historical perspective is essential not only because it gives one a grasp of one's heritage but also because it empowers one to envision the possibilities of the future.

All of you will enter an educational system that looks the way it does today because of historical processes and events. The debates, controversies, and reforms of the past are not unimportant footnotes for historians to mull over in their scholarly work. Rather, they are the pieces in the historical puzzle that comprise the educational world that you, as teachers, will inherit. Likewise, you in turn will become the next generation to place its stamp and have an impact on what the schools of tomorrow will be like.

In *The Eighteenth Brumaire of Louis Bonaparte,* Karl Marx (1963) wrote, "Men make their own history, but they do not make it just as they please; they do not make it under circumstances chosen by themselves, but under circumstances directly encountered, given, and transmitted from the past." History, then, provides people not only with a chronicle of the past but with a deep understanding of how and why the world has come to be. Such an understanding helps individuals to see both the limits and the possibilities for the future.

The schools look and work the way they do because of complex historical events and processes. To understand the educational problems of today, you must first have a perspective from which to comprehend these historical processes. This is the value and purpose of the history of education.

It is often said that people who do not understand history are doomed to repeat the mistakes of the past. Although we do not claim that the study of the history of education will make educators capable of eliminating mistakes altogether, and although the history of education suggests that people indeed tend to repeat some mistakes, we nonetheless believe that an ignorance of the past is a major barrier to educational improvement. Thus, the insights of the history of education are crucial to a foundations perspective.

This book will introduce you to the events that have defined the evolution of the U.S. educational system and to the significant debates between historians of education regarding the meaning of these events. First, you will look at the major historical periods in U.S. educational history: the colonial period, the common school era, the progressive era, and the modern era. Through an examination of what historians have written about each period, you will come to understand the relationship between each period and the debates and issues that characterized it, and you will be able to see how each educational reform set the stage for successive reform and reaction. Second, the readings in this book will also explore the controversies in the history of education about the interpretation of these events. That is, even when historians agree about the facts of educational development, they often passionately disagree about why things happened as they did. Over the past 30 years, for example, democratic liberal historians, who believe the history of U.S. education represents the increasing success of the schools in providing equality of opportunity for all citizens, and revisionist historians, who believe that the history of U.S. education represents a series of broken promises and the triumph of social and economic elites, have raised significant questions about the role of schools and the groups that have power to shape the educational system. Through an exploration of the views of historians from both of these perspectives, you may see that our schools are indeed the product of a variety of related factors and that the present debates are inherited from the past and influenced by its triumphs and defeats. To understand this is to understand the complexity of the present.

The Philosophy of Education

In order to comprehend fully the world of schooling, you, as future teachers, must possess a social and intellectual context (the foundations perspective). An understanding of the philosophy of education is essential in building this perspective.

Students often wonder why philosophy is considered to be an integral part of the foundations perspective, arguing that education is shaped by practice rather than by theory. They argue that teachers are called on to make situational decisions and that the methods employed by teachers at any given moment are based on their instincts or feelings. Students object to the study of philosophy on the grounds that it is an elite discipline that has little practical value. Why, then, do we contend that philosophy is an important component of both comprehending and negotiating the world of schooling?

We begin to answer this question by establishing the relationship between educational practices and philosophy. As is customary in the discipline of philosophy, issues are often resolved by posing questions and offering answers, which in turn usually lead to more questions. This method, established centuries ago by the ancient Greeks, is known as the *dialectic method*. Thus, we begin by posing the first of two questions to our students: What is your practice?—that is, What will you do with your own classes when you become practitioners? After our students describe, define, or clarify what they intend, we pose a second question: Why will you do what you have just described? By asking you to reflect on the "what" and "how" as you go about teaching in your classrooms, we may help you realize that your decisions and actions are shaped by a host of human experiences firmly rooted in our culture.

For example, why do some of you prefer informal classroom settings to formal ones? Why might some of you lean toward the adoption of the project method—an interdisciplinary curriculum approach developed during the progressive era? We suggest that your feelings might be articulated in the work of John Dewey, or that a preference for adopting the spiral curriculum may best be articulated through Jerome Bruner's work on curriculum. In other words, the choices that you, as prospective teachers, make and the preferences you have may best be clarified and expressed through the study of the philosophy of education.

As educators, we believe certain fundamentals exist within the human experience that color the choices we make as human beings and as teachers in the classroom. We suggest that as prospective teachers, you begin your reflective quest for these fundamentals by examining thought patterns and ideas within the discipline of philosophy.

This brings us to our second point: the uniqueness of the study of the philosophy of education, as distinct from philosophy. An interdisciplinary approach is called for in order to seek out the theoretical foundations upon which practice will be built. As students of the philosophy of education, it is important that you read selections from literature, psychology, sociology, and history, as well as philosophy. Through a thorough examination of thought patterns within the different disciplines, you will be sufficiently empowered to effect your own personal syntheses of the human experience, reflect on your world views, and make your own intensely personal choices as to what sort of practitioners you will be. Ultimately, the philosophy of education will allow you to examine *what ought to be* and thus enable you to envision the type of teachers you want to be and the types of schools that ought to exist.

The Politics of Education

Throughout history, schools have been the subject of considerable conflict about goals, methods, curriculum, and other important issues. Decisions about educational policies are rarely made in a smooth consensual manner, but rather are often the result of battles between various interest groups. U.S. schools are a contested terrain in which groups attempt to use political strategies to shape the educational system to best represent their interests and needs.

Political science helps educators understand power relations and the way interest groups use the political process to maximize their advantages within organizations. A political science perspective focuses on the politics of education—on power relations; on the relationship between the local, state, and federal governments and education; on school financing and law; and on the question of who controls the schools.

One of the major questions political scientists ask is How democratic are our schools?—that is, To what extent are educational policies shaped by the pluralistic input of many groups, or To what extent are they the result of domination by political elites? The political science approach to education will allow you to examine the complexities of questions such as these, while also providing important insights into education policy and change.

Another issue of importance, especially for teachers, is the organizational politics within schools. How do educational interest groups within schools—including administrators, teachers, students, and parents—arrive at policy? Which groups have the power to shape educational decisions for their own benefit? What are the patterns of political conflict and consensus? How do the relationships between these groups help define the educational debates of today? Through a close look at the politics of education, you will become aware of how these group interactions are essential for understanding schools and, more importantly, the ability of teachers to shape and change the educational system.

The Sociology of Education

The discipline of sociology developed at the end of the nineteenth century amid the turmoil and promise of industrialization, urbanization, and a growing faith in democracy and education. As more and more children were required to attend schools, questions arose about the relationship between school and society. As the institution of education grew, there was a perception among many thinkers that schools would help usher in a modern era in which merit and effort would replace privilege and inheritance as the criteria for social and occupational success.

Sociologists of education generally shared in this optimism. They began to explore the ways in which students were socialized for adult status, they examined the school as a social system, and they analyzed the effects of education on students' life chances. They believed that they could improve education through the application of social scientific theory and research. Because of their scientific orientation, sociologists of education are more apt to ask *what is* rather than *what ought to be.* They want to know what really goes on in schools and what the measurable effects of education are on individuals and on society. The hallmark of the sociological approach to education is empiricism, or the collection and analysis of social facts within a theoretical context that allows researchers to build a coherent set of findings. Thus, sociologists of education are interested in collecting data and they try to avoid abstract speculation.

The sociological method is particularly useful when educational practices are related to educational outcomes. For example, in a study of public, Catholic, and other private schools, sociologists Coleman, Hoffer, and Kilgore (1982) were able to compare learning outcomes in these three types of schools by using survey analysis techniques. A practitioner or policy maker interested in school improvement can have some confidence that these results are valid and generalizable, and not simply opinion or wishful thinking. Of course, results are always subject to interpretation because all knowledge is, in a sense, the result of competing interpretations of events and ideas.

In sum, the methods of sociology are useful tools for understanding how schools actually interact with society. Although social science has no monopoly on wisdom or knowledge, it is based on an honest attempt to be objective, scientific, and empirical. Like history, sociology grounds us in the social context and tempers our educational inquiries by contrasting the real with the ideal. The sociological approach is fundamental to the foundations perspective because it keeps one's observations focused and testable. Without knowing *what is,* one cannot make the *ought to be* a reality.

The Foundations Perspective: A Multidisciplinary and Interdisciplinary Approach

The history, philosophy, politics, and sociology of education are separate disciplines; they are rarely used in isolation and are most often combined to ask the type of questions we have discussed. Although the selections in this book are often written from one of the perspectives, they generally use more than one of the disciplinary approaches. In fact, they are usually multidisciplinary and/or interdisciplinary (i.e., integrating more than one discipline). Moreover, the foundations perspective is a way of viewing schools that uses each of the approaches—the historical, the philosophical, the political, and the sociological—in an integrative manner. Therefore, although Chapters 2 through 5 of this book are organized around each discipline, the remainder is thematically arranged. Each theme is looked at through a variety of foundations approaches, each reflecting the critical applications of a foundations perspective to education.

Critical Literacy and Empowerment: Toward the Active Voice of Teachers

Teachers' voices have long been silent in discussions of educational reform. On one hand, administrators, college professors, politicians, and other educational experts all write about what is wrong with schools, but often without the practical experiential foundation of what it is like in the classroom. On the other hand, teachers often criticize these writings because the experts lack an understanding of what is termed "life in the trenches." However, many teachers show the same kind of oversight when they criticize the experts—they sometimes believe that the voice of experience is sufficient to describe, understand, and change schools. What is needed is a perspective that relates theory and practice so that teachers can combine their experiential knowledge with a broader, more multidimensional analysis of the context in which their experiences occur. The foundations perspective provides a theoretical and empirical base, but it alone is similarly insufficient as a tool for optimal understanding and effective change. When combined with the experiential voice of teachers, however, the foundations perspective becomes a powerful tool for teachers in the development of their active voice about educational matters.

In the view of C. Wright Mills (1959), the individual does not have the ability to understand the complex social forces that affect him or her and make up a society simply by virtue of living in the society. Likewise, teachers, solely by virtue of their classroom experiences, do not have the tools to make sense of the world of education. In fact, some teachers are too close and subjectively involved to have the emotional distance that is required for critical analysis. We are not suggesting that a teacher's experience is unimportant. We are saying that the theoretical and empirical insights of the foundations of education must comprise a crucial part of a teacher's perspective on education and thereby contribute to critical literacy. *Critical literacy* in education is simply the ability to connect knowledge, theory, and research evidence to the everyday experiences of teaching. Through the use of a foundations perspective, teachers can develop this essential ability and become, in Donald Schön's (1983) words, "reflective practitioners."

Criticisms of teacher education programs suggest that teachers do not receive a sufficiently intellectually rigorous education. Reports by the Carnegie Task Force (1986), the Holmes Group (1986, 1995), and the National Commission on Teaching and America's Future (1996) state that teacher education programs, especially those at the undergraduate level, place too much emphasis on methodology and do not provide a solid knowledge base in the traditional disciplines that education students will eventually teach. The overemphasis on process at the expense of depth and breadth of knowledge and intellectual demands has, according to these critics, resulted in teachers who do not possess the intellectual tools needed to educate their students successfully. Thus, the cycle of educational decline in terms of knowledge and skills is reproduced. These reports propose the elimination of undergraduate education programs. In their place, the Commission recommends the requirement that prospective teachers complete professional training at the graduate level after attaining a liberal arts baccalaureate degree.

Although these criticisms are somewhat simplistic in that they often scapegoat teachers for educational problems that go well beyond the shortcomings of teacher education programs, we do believe that teachers should be more liberally and critically educated. The emphasis on knowledge, however, is not sufficient. The cultural literacy envisioned by the educational reformers of the 1980s and championed by writers such as E. D. Hirsch, Allan Bloom, and Diane Ravitch will not by itself provide teachers with the analytical and critical tools needed for understanding the schools. Although cultural literacy is important (even though the question of what constitutes the knowledge that teachers and students ought to have is a crucial dilemma), teachers need critical literacy in their ongoing attempt to make their voices heard and to effect meaningful change.

Students and teachers often ask us how critical literacy will help them solve problems. Are we suggesting that teachers equipped with the ability to understand the educational system will improve it easily? Of course not! Understanding the schools and improving them are two different matters. Without changes in the factors that affect the schools, as well as changes in the structure and processes within the schools, it is highly unlikely that large-scale change or even significant improvement will take place. What we are saying, however, is that teachers must be part of the ongoing dialogue focused on improving schools, and in order to contribute meaningfully to this dialogue they need more than their own experiences. They need the knowledge, confidence, and authority that are products of critical literacy.

Developing critical literacy is a first and necessary step toward bringing the active voice of teachers into the educational debates so that, together with other professionals, teachers can become intimately involved in the development of a better educational world. It will not be easy. As sociologists, philosophers, and historians of education, we do not pretend that the record suggests that we should be overly optimistic; neither does it suggest, however, that we should lose hope. It is our profound desire that the readings in this book will give you the tools to become part of this ongoing effort—the quest for better schools, better teachers, and a more humane and intelligent society!

2 The Politics of Education

Conservative, Liberal, and Radical Perspectives

Too often, teachers and prospective teachers look at educational issues within the narrow context of schools. That is, they treat what goes on inside classrooms and in the school at large as unrelated to the larger society of which it is a part. Schools are institutions that are rarely immune from external influences such as the economy, the political system, the family, and so on. Moreover, schools in every society exist for specific reasons, not all of which are educational. It is essential, then, that you understand the diverse and often conflicting purposes of schooling, as these goals are often at the heart of disagreements about education.

The terms *education* and *schooling* are sometimes used interchangeably when in fact they refer to somewhat different but related processes. Lawrence A. Cremin, the distinguished historian of U.S. education, defined *education* as

> the deliberate, systematic, and sustained effort to transmit, evoke, or acquire knowledge, attitudes, skills, or sensibilities, as well as any outcomes of that effort. . . . The definition projects us beyond the schools and colleges to the multiplicity of individuals and institutions that educate—parents, peers, siblings, and friends, as well as families, churches, synagogues, libraries, museums, summer camps, benevolent societies, agricultural fairs, settlement houses, factories, publishers, radio stations, and television networks. (1977, pp. 135–136)

Cremin's definition looks at education in the broadest possible sense to include all processes in a society that transmit knowledge, skills, and values, and educational institutions as all the places in which these activities occur.

Schooling is a more narrow process, as it is concerned with the activities that occur in schools. Therefore, where education is the most general societal activity, schooling is a particular example of the ways in which education occurs within the schools. Clearly from these definitions, schools are educational institutions. Why do they exist and what are their purposes?

In the broadest sense, schools have political, social, economic, and intellectual purposes. On a philosophical level, however, the purposes of education speak to what the political scientist Amy Gutmann refers to as "that portion of education most amenable to our influence; the conscious efforts of men and women to inform the intellect and to shape the character of less educated men and women. And we naturally begin by asking what the purposes of human education should be—what kind of people should human education create" (1987, p. 19). Therefore, the purposes of education, in general, and schooling, in particular, are concerned with the type of society people wish to live in and the type of people we wish to live in it. Ultimately, the purposes of education are directed at conceptions of what constitutes the "good life" and a "good person"—questions that have been at the center of philosophical inquiry from Plato to Aristotle, Marx, Freud, and Dewey.

As you will read throughout this book, there is little agreement about these difficult questions. Although men and women have different ideas about what society and individuals ought to look like, every society attempts to transmit its conception on these matters to its citizens. Education is crucial to this process.

The Purposes of Schooling

The specific purposes of schooling are intellectual, political, social, and economic (Bennett & LeCompte, 1990, pp. 5–21). These purposes refer to their role within any existing society—for our purposes, U.S. society. As you will read later in this chapter and in Chapter 4, one often must make the distinction between what the purposes of schooling are and what they ought to be. For example, those who support the goals of a society believe that schools should educate citizens to fit into that society; those who disagree with its goals believe that schools should educate citizens to change the society. As you can see, differing visions of education relate back to differing conceptions of what constitutes a good society.

The *intellectual* purposes of schooling are to teach basic cognitive skills such as reading, writing, and mathematics; to transmit specific knowledge (e.g., in literature, history, the sciences, etc.); and to help students acquire higher-order thinking skills such as analysis, evaluation, and synthesis.

The *political* purposes of schooling are to inculcate allegiance to the existing political order (patriotism); to prepare citizens who will participate in this political order (e.g., in political democracies); to help assimilate diverse cultural groups into a common political order; and to teach children the basic laws of the society.

The *social* purposes of schooling are to help solve social problems; to work as one of many institutions, such as the family and the church (or synagogue) to ensure social cohesion; and to socialize children into the various roles, behaviors, and values of the society. This process, referred to by sociologists as *socialization,* is a key ingredient to the stability of any society.

The *economic* purposes of schooling are to prepare students for their later occupational roles and to select, train, and allocate individuals into the division of labor. The degree to which schools directly prepare students for work varies from society to society, but most schools have at least an indirect role in this process.

As you will read in Chapter 4, these purposes sometimes contradict each other. For example, the following question underscores the clash between the intellectual and political purposes of the school: If it is the intellectual purpose of the school to teach higher-order thinking skills, such as critical thinking and evaluation, then can it simultaneously engender patriotism and conformity to society's rules? Lawrence A. Cremin pointed out:

> Schooling, like education in general—never liberates without at the same time limiting. It never empowers without at the same time constraining. It never frees without at the same time socializing. The question is not whether one or the other is occurring in isolation but what the balance is, and to what end, and in light of what alternatives. (1977, p. 37)

This dialectic, or the tension between schooling's role in maintaining the status quo and its potential to bring about change, is at the heart of differing conceptions of education and schooling. As we pointed out earlier, those who support the society tend to stress the school's role in helping to maintain it; those who believe the society is in need of improvement or change stress its role in either improving or transforming it. In the following sections, you will read about how different political perspectives on education view not only the purposes of schooling but a variety of related issues.

Political Perspectives

Debates about educational issues often focus on different views concerning the goals of schools and their place within society. From the inception of the U.S. republic through the present, there have been significantly different visions of U.S. education and the role of schools in society. Although many of the views are complex, it is helpful to simplify them through the use of a political typology. In its most simple form, the different visions of U.S. education can be discussed in terms of conservative, liberal, and radical perspectives. Although the nature of these approaches has changed over time, what follows is a contemporary model of how each perspective views a number of related educational issues. In the following sections, we will explore each perspective in terms of its view of U.S. society, its view of the role of the school in relation to equality and the "American dream," its explanation of student failure and under-achievement in schools, its definition of educational problems at the turn of the twenty-first century, and its educational policy and reform proposals.

General Issues: Conservative, Liberal, and Radical Perspectives

Political perspectives on education have rarely been used consistently. One of the problems in using labels or typologies is that there is often little agreement about what constitutes the basic principles of any particular perspective. Furthermore, there have been historical changes in the meanings of each of the approaches under consideration: the conservative, the liberal, and the radical. In addition, as many educators have used the terms *traditional* and *progressive* to denote similar approaches, there is often considerable confusion over matters of terminology. In this section, we will define each of the perspectives and relate them to progressive and traditional perspectives. In subsequent sections, the specific features of the conservative, liberal, and radial perspectives will be delineated.

A *perspective* is a general model for looking at something—in this case, a model for understanding, analyzing, and solving educational problems. As you will see throughout this book, there has been and continues to be little agreement about the nature, causes, and solutions to educational problems. In order to understand the ways in which various authors look at educational issues, it is necessary to understand how they approach the problems—that is, to understand where they are coming from (their perspective, its assumptions, etc.).

The conservative, liberal, and radical perspectives all look at educational issues and problems from distinctly different, although at times overlapping, vantage points. Although there are areas of agreement, they each have distinctly different views on education and its role in U.S. society. Moreover, they each have fundamentally different viewpoints on social problems and their solution in general, and their analysis of education is a particular application of this more general world view.

The Conservative Perspective.   The conservative view has its origins in nineteenth-century social Darwinist thought (see Gordon, 1977) that applied the evolutionary theories of Charles Darwin to the analysis of societies. This perspective, developed originally by the sociologist William Graham Sumner, looks at social evolution as a process that enables the strongest individuals and/or groups to survive, and looks at human and social evolution as adaptation to changes in the environment. From this point of view, individuals and groups must compete in the social environment in order to survive, and human progress is dependent on individual initiative and drive.

A second feature of the conservative viewpoint is the belief that the free market or market economy of capitalism is both the most economically productive economic system as well as the system that is most respectful of human needs (e.g., for competition and freedom). Based in part on the eighteenth-century writings of the British political economist Adam Smith and applied to twentieth-century economic policy by the Nobel laureate economist Milton Friedman, conservatism argues that free market capitalism allows for the maximization of economic growth and individual liberty with competition ensuring that potential abuses can be minimized. Central to this perspective is the view that individuals are rational actors who make decisions on a cost-benefit scale.

Thus, the conservative view of social problems places its primary emphasis on the individual and suggests that individuals have the capacity to earn or not earn their place within a market economy, and that solutions to problems should also be addressed at the individual level. The presidency of Ronald Reagan represented the political ascendancy of this viewpoint. Reagan championed a free market philosophy and argued that welfare state policies (government intervention in the economy) were at the heart of an American malaise. His presidency (1980–1988) was characterized by supply side economics (a form of free market capitalism), the elimination of many governmental regulations, and the curtailment of many social programs. The Reagan philosophy stressed individual initiative and portrayed the individual as the only one capable of solving his or her own problems. Whereas conservatives lauded Reagan's policies and credited him with restoring U.S. economic growth, both liberals and radicals were very critical.

The Liberal Perspective.   The liberal view has its origins in the twentieth century, in the works of the U.S. philosopher John Dewey, and, historically, in the progressive era of U.S. politics from the 1880s to the 1930s. Perhaps more important, the liberal view became politically dominant during the administration of Franklin Delano Roosevelt (1933–1945) and what is often referred to as the *New Deal era*.

The liberal perspective, although accepting the conservative belief in a market capitalist economy, believes that the free market, if left unregulated, is prone to significant abuses, particularly to those groups who are disadvantaged economically and politically. Moreover, the liberal view, based on the economic theories of John Maynard Keynes, believes that the capitalist market economy is prone to cycles of recession that must be addressed through government intervention. Thus, the liberal perspective insists that government involvement in the economic, political, and social arenas is necessary to ensure fair treatment of all citizens and to ensure a healthy economy. The impact of such liberal policies is evident throughout the twentieth century, from the New Deal initiatives of FDR (including the Social Security Act and the Works Progress Administration, a federally funded jobs program) to the New Frontier proposals of John F. Kennedy, to the Great Society programs of Lyndon Baines Johnson to (although he probably would take issue with this) George H. W. Bush's savings and loan bailout.

The liberal perspective, then, is concerned primarily with balancing the economic productivity of capitalism with the social and economic needs of the majority of people in the United States. Because liberals place a heavy emphasis on issues of equality, especially equality of opportunity, and because they believe that the capitalist system often gives unfair advantages to those with wealth and power, liberals assert that the role of the government is to ensure the fair treatment of all citizens, to ensure that equality of opportunity exists, and to minimize exceedingly great differences in the life chances and life outcomes of the country's richest and poorest citizens. Moreover, liberals believe that individual effort alone is sometimes insufficient and that the government must sometimes intercede on behalf of those in need. Finally, the liberal perspective on social problems stresses that groups rather than individuals are affected by the structure of society, so solutions to social problems must address group dynamics rather than individuals alone.

The Radical Perspective.   The radical perspective, in contrast to both the conservative and liberal perspectives, does not believe that free market capitalism is the best form of economic organization, but rather believes that democratic socialism is a fairer political-economic system. Based on the writings of the nineteenth-century German political economist and philosopher Karl Marx (1818–1883), the radical viewpoint suggests that the capitalist system, although undeniably the most productive form of economic organization, also produces fundamental contradictions that ultimately will lead to its transformation into socialism.

Although the economic analysis of these contradictions are complex and unnecessary to the level of understanding required here, it is important to note that the central contradiction pointed out by radicals is between the accumulation laws of capitalism (i.e., that wealth is both accumulated and controlled privately) and the general social welfare of the public. That is, radicals (Gordon, 1977; Bowles & Gintis, 1976, 1986) assert that, at this stage in capitalist development, U.S. society has the productive capacity to ensure a minimally acceptable standard of living, including food and shelter for all its citizens. Thus, radicals believe a socialist economy that builds on the democratic political system (and retains its political freedoms) would more adequately provide all citizens with a decent standard of living. What is essential to the radical perspective is the belief that social problems such as poverty and the educational problems of the poorest citizens are endemic to capitalism and cannot be solved under the present economic system. Rather, radicals assert that only a transformation of capitalism into democratic socialism will ensure that the social problems that disproportionately affect the disadvantaged in U.S. society will be addressed.

Radicals believe that the capitalist system is central to U.S. social problems. They also recognize that the capitalist system is not going to change easily and, furthermore, that most Americans fervently support it. Therefore, most radicals place their primary emphasis on the analysis of inequality under capitalism, the economic and power relationships that are central to the perpetuation of inequalities, and policies that seek to reduce these inequities under the existing capitalist system. Thus, while theoretically and politically supporting change, the radical perspective often agrees with those liberal programs aimed at issues concerning equity.

Finally, the radical perspective believes that social problems are structural in nature—that is, that they are caused by the structure of U.S. society and therefore the solutions must be addressed to this structure, not at individuals. To argue that social problems are caused by deficits in individuals or groups is to "blame the victim," according to the radical perspective (Ryan, 1971).

The collapse of the communist (state socialism) world in Eastern Europe and the former Soviet Union has resulted in serious challenges in the United States to the claims of the radical perspective. Conservatives and many liberals argue that the events in the former Soviet Union and Eastern Europe signal the death of communism, as well as socialism, and denote historical evidence for the superiority of capitalism. Although it is clear that state socialism as practiced in the former Soviet Union and Eastern Europe has failed, radicals do not agree that its failure denotes either the bankruptcy of socialism or the final moral victory of capitalism. Rather, radicals suggest that socialism failed in these cases for a number of reasons.

First, without a capitalist economic base to build on (a prerequisite for socialism in Marx's original theory), socialist economies in communist societies could not efficiently produce sufficient goods and services. Second, without a democratic political base, communist societies denied the necessary human freedoms essential to a healthy society. Furthermore, radicals suggest that the collapse of state socialist economies does not preclude the ability of socialism to succeed in democratic-capitalist societies. Finally, radicals argue that the collapse of communism in no way eliminates the problems endemic to Western capitalist societies, particularly those related to extremes of inequality. Therefore, although conservatives view these events with great satisfaction, radicals point to the social problems in U.S. society. Liberals, to some degree, believe that these events point to the power of their point of view: that the collapse of socialist economies in communist societies indicates the strength of the capitalist economy, while the significant social problems that remain in U.S. society suggest the importance of further liberal responses.

The three perspectives, then, have overlapping but distinctly different views on the nature of U.S. society and its social problems. The conservative perspective is a positive view of U.S. society and believes that capitalism is the best economic system, as it ensures maximum productivity with the greatest degree of individual freedom. Social problems, from its vantage point, are caused by individuals and groups, and it must be individuals and groups that solve them on their own, with little or no direct government intervention.

The liberal perspective is also positive about U.S. society, albeit with reservations. Liberals also believe that capitalism is indeed the most productive economic system, but they suggest that, if left unrestrained, capitalism often creates far too much political and economic disparity between citizens. Thus, liberals believe the state (government) must intercede to ensure the fair treatment of all and that social problems are often the result of societal rather than individual or group forces.

Finally, the radical perspective, unlike the other two, is negative about U.S. society. It recognizes the productive capacity of its capitalist economic system, but it argues that the society structurally creates vast and morally indefensible inequalities between its members. Radicals, who favor significantly greater equality of outcomes between citizens, believe that U.S. social problems cannot be solved under the existing economic system. They favor a movement toward democratic socialism: a society that, according to radicals, would combine democratic political principles (including representative government, civil liberties, and individual freedom) with a planned economic system—one that is planned for the satisfaction of the human needs of all of its citizens.

In the United Kingdom, under Tony Blair's New Labor party, which came to power in 1997, the government has supported a blend of liberal and radical policies. Based on British sociologist Anthony Giddens's (the director of the London School of Economics) concept of *the third way* (1999), New Labor believes that the strengths of market capitalism combined with welfare state socialism reflect the goals of social democracy.

Traditional and Progressive Visions of Education

Discussions of education often refer to *traditional* and *progressive* visions. Although these terms have a great deal in common with the conservative, liberal, and radical perspectives discussed earlier, they are sometimes used interchangeably or without clear definitions, and therefore there is often confusion concerning terminology. For our purposes, we will use the terms *traditional* and *progressive* as the most general representations of views about education. Traditional visions tend to view the schools as necessary to the transmission of the traditional values of U.S. society, such as hard work, family unity, individual initiative, and so on. Progressive visions tend to view the schools as central to solving social problems, as a vehicle for upward mobility, as essential to the development of individual potential, and as an integral part of a democratic society.

In a nutshell, traditionalists believe the schools should pass on the best of what was and what is, and progressives believe the schools should be part of the steady progress to make things better. In relation to the conservative, liberal, and radical perspectives, there is significant overlap. If we use a political continuum from left to right, with the left signifying the radical pole and the right the conservative pole (mirroring the political terminology of *left* and *right wing*), we suggest the following relationship:

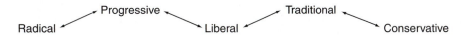

Thus, progressive visions encompass the left liberal to the radical spectrums; traditional vision encompass the right liberal to the conservative spectrums. Obviously, as with all typologies, this is somewhat of a simplification. Although many theories that we will discuss and illustrate in subsequent chapters may have significantly more overlap, this typology is, nonetheless, a useful tool for understanding different visions about education.

The discussion so far has concentrated on the general approach to U.S. society and social problems taken by each perspective. The next section looks specifically at how each perspective analyzes education and educational problems.

The Role of the School

The role of the school is a central focus of each of the perspectives and is at the heart of their differing analyses. The school's role in the broadest sense is directly concerned with the aims, purposes, and functions of education in a society.

The conservative perspective sees the role of the school as providing the necessary educational training to ensure that the most talented and hard-working individuals receive the tools necessary to maximize economic and social productivity. In addition, conservatives believe that schools socialize children into the adult roles necessary to the maintenance of the social order. Finally, they see the school's function as one of transmitting the cultural traditions through what is taught (the curriculum). Therefore, the conservative perspective views the role of the school as essential to both economic productivity and social stability.

The liberal perspective, while also stressing the training and socializing function of the school, sees these aims a little differently. In line with the liberal belief in equality of opportunity, it stresses the school's role in providing the necessary education to ensure that all students have an equal opportunity to succeed in society. Whereas liberals also point to the school's role in socializing children into societal roles, they stress the pluralistic nature of U.S. society and the school's role in teaching children to respect cultural diversity so that they understand and fit into a diverse society. On the political level, liberals stress the importance of citizenship and participation in a democratic society and the need for an educated citizenry in such a society. Finally, the liberal perspective stresses individual as well as societal needs and thus sees the school's role as enabling the individual to develop his or her talents, creativity, and sense of self.

Therefore, the liberal perspective sees the role of education as balancing the needs of society and the individual in a manner that is consistent with a democratic and meritocratic society. That is, liberals envision a society in which citizens participate in decision making, in which adult status is based on merit and achievement, and in which all citizens receive a fair and equal opportunity for economic wealth, political power, and social status.

Diane Ravitch, historian of education, eloquently summarizes the liberal view of education:

> To believe in education is to believe in the future, to believe in what may be accomplished through the disciplined use of intelligence, allied with cooperation and good will. If it seems naively American to put so much stock in schools, colleges, universities, and the endless prospect of self-improvement and social improvement, it is an admirable, and perhaps even a noble flaw. (1983, p. 330)

The radical perspective, given its vastly differing view on U.S. society, likewise has a significantly different view of what the school's role is. Although radicals believe schools ought to eliminate inequalities, they argue that the school's role is to reproduce the unequal economic conditions of the capitalist economy and to socialize individuals to accept the legitimacy of the society. Through what radicals term *social and cultural reproduction,* the school's role is to perpetuate the society and to serve the interests of those with economic wealth and political power. Most important, through a vastly unequal educational system, radicals believe that schools prepare children from different social backgrounds for different roles within the economic division of labor. The radical perspective, unlike the liberal, views equality of opportunity as an illusion and as no more than an ideology used to convince individuals that they have been given a fair chance, when in fact they have not. Therefore, the radical perspective argues that schools reproduce economic, social, and political inequality within U.S. society.

In Chapter 1, we discussed the U.S. belief in education and the view that schooling is an essential component of the American dream of social mobility and equality of opportunity. Conservatives, liberals, and radicals have differing views on the role of the school in meeting these goals.

The conservative perspective believes that schools should ensure that all students have the opportunity to compete individually in the educational marketplace and that schools should be meritocratic to the extent that individual effort is rewarded. Based on the belief that individuals succeed largely on their own accord, conservatives argue that the role of the school is to provide a place for individual merit to be encouraged and rewarded.

Liberals believe that schools should ensure that equality of opportunity exists and that inequality of results be minimized. Based on the historical record, the liberal perspective indicates that although schools have made a significant difference in the lives of countless Americans and have provided upward mobility for many individuals, there remain significant differences in the educational opportunities and achievement levels for rich and poor.

Radicals believe that schools should reduce inequality of educational results and provide upward social mobility, but that historically the schools have been ineffective in attaining these noble goals. Moreover, the radical perspective argues that under capitalism schools will remain limited, if not wholly unsuccessful, vehicles for addressing problems of inequality—problems that radicals suggest are structurally endemic to capitalism.

Explanations of Unequal Educational Performance

If, as radicals and many liberals suggest, schooling has not sufficiently provided a reduction in inequality of results, and as educational achievement is closely related to student socioeconomic backgrounds (as was indicated in Chapter 1), then the explanation of why certain groups, particularly from lower socioeconomic backgrounds, perform less well in school is a crucial one. Conservatives argue that individuals or groups of students rise and fall on their own intelligence, hard work, and initiative, and that achievement is based on hard work and sacrifice. The school system, from this vantage point, is designed to allow individuals the opportunity to succeed. If they do not, it may be because they are, as individuals, deficient in some manner or because they are members of a group that is deficient.

The liberal perspective argues that individual students or groups of students begin school with different life chances and therefore some groups have significantly more advantages than others. Therefore, society must attempt through policies and programs to equalize the playing field so that students from disadvantaged backgrounds have a better chance.

Radicals, like liberals, believe that students from lower socioeconomic backgrounds begin schools with unequal opportunities. Unlike liberals, however, radicals believe that the conditions that result in educational failure are caused by the economic system, not the educational system, and can only be ameliorated by changes in the political-economic structure.

Definition of Educational Problems

Until this point, we have focused on the role of the school and, in particular, its relationship to equality of opportunity and results. Although these are certainly significant issues, the ways in which each perspective addresses specific educational problems at the close of the twentieth century, and consequently how each sees solutions to these, is of the utmost importance. We will begin with a discussion of the definition of educational problems.

The conservative perspective argues the following points:

1. In their response to liberal and radical demands for greater equality in the 1960s and 1970s, schools systematically lowered academic standards and reduced educational quality. Conservatives often refer to this problem as the *decline of standards.*
2. In their response to liberal and radical demands for multicultural education (i.e., education that responds to the needs of all cultural groups), schools watered down the traditional curriculum and thus weakened the school's ability to pass on the heritage of American and Western civilizations to children. Conservatives often define this problem as the *decline of cultural literacy.*
3. In their response to liberal and radical demands for cultural relativism (i.e., that every culture's values and ideas are equally valid), schools lost their traditional role of teaching moral standards and values. Conservatives often refer to this problem as the *decline of values or of civilization.*
4. In their response to liberal and radical demands for individuality and freedom, schools lost their traditional disciplinary function and often became chaotic. Conservatives often refer to this problem as the *decline of authority.*
5. Because they are state controlled and are immune from the laws of a competitive free market, schools are stifled by bureaucracy and inefficiency.

Liberals have significantly different viewpoints on the major educational problems of our times. The liberal perspective argues the following points:

1. Schools have too often limited the life chances of poor and minority children and therefore the problem of underachievement by these groups is a critical problem.

2. Schools place too much emphasis on discipline and authority, thus limiting their role in helping students develop as individuals.
3. The differences in quality and climate between urban and suburban schools and, most specifically, between schools with students of low socioeconomic backgrounds and high socioeconomic backgrounds is a central problem related to inequalities of results.
4. The traditional curriculum leaves out the diverse cultures of the groups that comprise the pluralistic society.

The radical perspective, although often similar in its analysis to the liberal viewpoint, is quite different in its tone. The radical perspective argues the following points:

1. The educational system has failed the poor, minorities, and women through classist, racist, and sexist policies.
2. The schools have stifled critical understanding of the problems of American society through a curriculum and teaching practices that promote conformity.
3. The traditional curriculum is racist, sexist, and classist and leaves out the culture, history, and voices of the oppressed.
4. In general, the educational system promotes inequality of both opportunity and results.

Educational Policy and Reform

Defining educational problems is the first step toward the construction of solutions. During the 1980s and 1990s, proponents of each perspective supported specific educational reform and policy recommendations. The following brief discussion outlines the policies and programs of each without going into any detail. (A more detailed analysis will be provided in Chapters 3, 6, and 10.)

Conservatives support the following:

1. Return to basics (often referred to as *back to basics*), including the strengthening of literacy skills, such as reading and writing, and other forms of traditional learning.
2. Return to the traditional academic curriculum, including history, literature, and the canons of Western civilization.
3. Introduce accountability measures for students and schools, including minimum standards of performance and knowledge—that is, create minimum standards for what students should know and for the skills they should possess at specific grade levels (e.g., fourth, eighth, and twelfth grades).
4. Introduce free market mechanisms in the educational marketplace, including tuition tax credits and vouchers for parents who wish to send their children to private schools and public school choice programs, including charter schools (allowing parents to choose among different public schools). This is often referred to as *school privatization*.

Liberals support the following:

1. Policies should combine a concern for quality for all students with equality of opportunity for all. This is sometimes referred to as *quality with equality.*
2. Policies should lead to the improvement of failing schools, especially urban schools. Such programs should include school-based management and teacher empowerment (decentralized control of individual schools with teachers having a significant voice in decision making), effective school programs (programs that are based on what is called the *effective school research*—research that indicates "what works"), and public school choice programs. Whereas liberals support parental choice of public schools, they rarely support conservative proposals for complete privatization, tuition tax credits, and vouchers, as these are seen as threatening public education and creating increasingly unfair advantages for parents who are already economically advantaged.
3. Programs should enhance equality of opportunity for disadvantaged groups, including Head Start (a preschool program for students from lower socioeconomic backgrounds), affirmative action programs, compensatory higher education programs (college programs for disadvantaged students), and so forth.
4. A curriculum should balance the presentation of the traditions of Western civilization with the treatment of other groups within the culturally diverse society.
5. A balance should be maintained between setting acceptable performance standards and ensuring that all students can meet them.

Radicals support the following:

1. On a general level, radicals do not believe that educational reform alone will solve educational problems, as they see their causes outside the purview of the educational system. Short of what most radicals see is necessary but unrealistic large-scale societal change—they support most liberal reform programs as long as they lead to greater equality of educational results.
2. Programs should result in greater democratization of schools—that is, give teachers, parents, and students a greater voice in decision making. Examples of these are teacher empowerment, school-based management, school decentralization, and school-community cooperation efforts.
3. Curriculum and teaching methods should involve "critical pedagogy" (Giroux, 1988; Kincheloe & Steinberg, 1998)—that is, radicals support educational programs that enable teachers and students to understand social and educational problems and to see potential solutions (radical) to these.
4. Curriculum and teaching methods should be multicultural, antiracist, antisexist, and anticlassist—that is, radicals support educational programs that include curricular treatment of the diverse groups that comprise U.S. society and that are pedagogically aimed at sensitizing students to racism, sexism, and classism.

Radicals, although often supporting many of the liberal educational reform proposals, are less sanguine about their potential effectiveness. In fact, as Samuel Bowles pointed out, the failure of liberal reforms may prove successful in a very different political context:

Educational equality cannot be achieved through changes in the school system alone. Nonetheless, attempts at educational reform may move us closer to that objective if, in their failure, they lay bare the unequal nature of our school system and destroy the illusion of unimpeded mobility through education. Successful educational reforms—reducing racial and class disparities in schooling, for example, may also serve the cause of equality of education, for it seems likely that equalizing access in schooling will challenge the system to make good its promise of rewarding educational attainment or find ways of coping with mass disillusionment with the great panacea. (1977, p. 149)

Education and the American Dream

The next chapter will focus directly on the ways in which educational reform evolved in U.S. history. Although our discussion thus far has looked at the last 30 years, it is essential to understand that the present debates and crises are outcomes of a much longer historical time span in which the disagreements about educational issues helped shape the present educational system. It is also important to note that all three perspectives have different views on U.S. educational history, especially with regard to the school's success in living up to the democratic promise discussed in Chapter 1.

Conservatives argue that the U.S. schools have succeeded in providing a quality education for those who are capable and have taken advantage of it, and that, until the 1960s and 1970s, schools were responsible for U.S. superiority in economic and technological realms. On one hand, conservatives argue that the system has provided a meritocratic selection process that has ensured that the most talented and motivated individuals are rewarded by the schools and later in life. This mechanism historically has successfully guaranteed that the important roles and occupations are filled with those individuals capable of handling them. On the other hand, conservatives believe that the progressive reforms of the twentieth century (to be discussed in Chapter 3), especially those occurring in the 1960s and 1970s, eroded the quality of the schools, their curriculum, and what students learned. Thus, the U.S. educational system, from this point of view, is found wanting, especially in relation to its role in economic development and competitiveness.

The liberal perspective is more concerned with the social and political functions of schooling than the economic. As such, liberals believe that schools have been successful in extending public education to the masses and providing more opportunity for mobility than any other system in the world. Moreover, liberals believe that U.S. education has been essential in the long, slow, and flawed march toward a more democratic and meritocratic society—a society where one's individual achievement is more important than one's family background, a society that is more just and humane, and a society where tolerance of others who are different is an important value. Despite these successes, liberals argue that the educational system has been an imperfect panacea (Perkinson, 1995) and has yet to provide sufficient access, opportunity, and success for all citizens, and thus must continue to improve.

The radical perspective is far less optimistic about the historical success than either the liberal or conservative viewpoints. According to radicals, the U.S. schools have been unsuccessful in providing equality of opportunity or results to the majority of citizens. Although it is true that the United States has educated more people for longer periods of time than any other nation in the world, radicals believe the overall out-comes have reproduced rather than reduced social and economic inequalities. Accord-ing to this perspective, the historical record suggests that, although educational opportunities expanded throughout the twentieth century, students from different class backgrounds were offered different types of education (e.g., middle- and upper middle-class students in an academic program in the public high school and poor students in a vocational program; middle- and upper middle-class students in a four-year baccalau-reate college education and poor students in a two-year community college education). Therefore, according to radicals, the history of U.S. education has been the story of false promises and shattered dreams.

In the next chapter, you will have the opportunity to explore the events, conflicts, de-bates, and reforms that comprise this history and to judge for yourself the extent to which the history of U.S. education supports one or more of these political interpretations.

From Political Perspectives to the Politics of Education

As you have read, there is considerable disagreement among the three perspectives. In the world of education, these disagreements play themselves out in conflicts. These conflicts involve different groups, parents, teachers, administrators, legislators, busi-ness people, and so on, and are central to understanding educational decision making. As you will read in Chapter 3, the history of education in the United States has rarely been a smooth one. It has involved the conflict between groups with opposing values and interests, groups all seemingly interested in the same thing—the best education for the nation's children—but with significantly different perceptions of what that consti-tutes and how to go about it.

Sometimes these conflicts have been about curriculum and pedagogy (e.g., the conflicts about vocational versus academic education in the 1930s and 1940s or tradi-tional versus child-centered teaching at the turn of the twentieth century); sometimes they have been about values and morality (e.g., as in the textbook and book-banning controversies of the last 20 years or over the question of prayer in schools); and some-times they have been about civil rights and racial issues (e.g., the violent battles over school desegregation in Little Rock, Arkansas, in the late 1950s and in Boston, Mass-achusetts, in the 1970s).

Sometimes these conflicts are external to the school and involve the federal, state, and local governments, the courts, and the business community. Sometimes they are in-ternal to the schools and involve parents, teachers, and teacher unions or organizations, students, and administrators.

Whatever the specific nature of the conflicts, they all involve power and power re-lationships. Political scientists are concerned with understanding how power relation-ships (i.e., which groups have power and which do not) affect educational decision making and organizational outcomes. As our discussion in Chapter 3 about the history of education will reveal, struggles about education rarely involve equals, but rather in-volve groups with disparate degrees of power. Therefore, these struggles often involve the attempts to maximize political advantage and to minimize that of opposing groups.

Whereas political scientists are concerned with who controls our schools (Kirst, 1984), political philosophers are concerned with who ought to control them and for what end. In her brilliant book *Democratic Education,* Gutmann (1987) outlined the philosophical dimensions of this political question. She argued that there are four different conceptions of who should have the authority to determine educational matters: the family state, the state of families, the state of individuals, and the democratic state (pp. 19–47). Each perspective answers the question, Who should have the authority over educational decisions in a different manner?

The family state viewpoint is derived from Plato's theories of education (to be discussed more fully in Chapter 5). This approach sees the purpose of education as creating a socially stable society committed to the good life and justice. The definition of a just society, however, is determined by an elite—what Plato referred to as the *philosopher kings* (or in Gutmann's gender equal terminology, *philosopher queens*). It is this elite that defines the just society and it is through education that citizens learn to accept this view of society and are thereby able to contribute to its smooth functioning. In terms of educational authority, it is a small and hopefully just elite that should determine educational decisions.

The second viewpoint, the state of families, is derived from the eighteenth-century English political philosopher John Locke. Based on the Lockean view that parents are the best guardians of their children's rights and interests, it suggests that families should have the final authority in educational decision making.

The third position, the state of individuals, is derived from the work of the nineteenth-century British philosopher John Stuart Mill. Based on the nineteenth-century liberal notion that the state should not impose its will on individuals nor threaten their individual liberties, it suggests that educational authorities should not "bias the choices of children toward some disputed or controversial ways of life and away from others" (Gutmann, 1987, p. 34). Thus, educational authority ought to provide opportunity for choice among competing conceptions of the good life and neutrality among them (Gutmann, 1987, p. 34). In this manner, individuals have authority over educational matters to the extent that they are given the freedom to choose among the widest possible options about the kind of lives they wish to live.

Gutmann provided an exhaustive criticism of these three perspectives, suggesting that the family state leaves one at the tyranny of the state, the state of families at the tyranny of families, and the state of individuals without a clear way to reproduce what a society believes is responsible for its citizens. Each perspective, she argued, is flawed because it fails to provide a compelling rationale for either its view of a good society or who should define it.

Gutmann proposed a fourth perspective: the democratic state of education. In this view,

> Educational authority must be shared among parents, citizens, and professional educators even though such sharing does not guarantee that power will be wedded to knowledge (as in the family state), that parents can successfully pass their prejudices on to their children (as in the state of families), or that education will be neutral among competing conceptions of the good life (as in the state of individuals). (1987, p. 42)

Recognizing that a democratic state has built-in problems, including the tyranny of the many over the few, Gutmann argued that there must be two limitations on such a state: nonrepression and nondiscrimination. Nonrepression does not permit the state or groups to use the educational system for eliminating choice between different alternatives of a just society; nondiscrimination requires that all children receive an adequate education—one that will enable them to participate in the democratic deliberations of their society (1987, p. 46).

As you can see, the question of educational authority is a complex one and has been at the center of educational conflict. Throughout this book, you will read about different educational viewpoints and different recommendations for solutions to educational problems. In this chapter, we have tried to make you aware that such conflicts rest on different assumptions about society, the purposes of education, and who should determine these important matters.

In the following readings, the perspectives on education are illustrated. In the first article, "Lessons Learned from a Half-Century of Federal Policy Development," Christopher T. Cross discusses the lessons from 50 years of federal involvement in education. Cross, a former Assistant Secretary of Education, analyzes the limits and possibilities of federal involvement and the politics of educational policy.

The second article, "What 'Counts' as Educational Policy? Notes toward a New Paradigm," by educational researcher Jean Anyon, argues that the types of conservative and liberal educational policies discussed by Cross have had little impact on reducing the achievement gap. Anyon's article outlines a radical perspective in which she argues that liberal educational reforms must be tied to larger political, social, and economic reforms to be successful. Her article combines a radical critique of the excesses of free market capitalism with a view that liberal educational reforms are necessary under capitalism.

Lessons Learned from a Half-Century of Federal Policy Development

CHRISTOPHER T. CROSS

From the previous examination of the evolution of federal education policy some lessons have been learned that provide an understanding of what federal policy is today, as well as guidance with respect to future policy development. This chapter groups these lessons into four sections; the first deals with defining federal policy, the second with how policy works, the third with factors that make a difference, the fourth with other factors that affect federal policy development.

From Christopher Cross, "Lessons Learned from a Half-Century of Federal Policy Development," in Christopher Cross, *Political Education: National Policy Comes of Age,* Teachers College Press, 2003. Reprinted by permission.

What Is the Nation's Education Policy?

Several themes characterize the development of education policy in the 20th century, and these may provide important guidance for the further development of federal policy.

The Primary Federal Role Is to Ensure Equity

Although the definition of equity has changed over the years, it continues to be the key principle guiding federal aid. In the Great Society of the Johnson era, equity in education was seen in terms of both civil rights and resources. Getting resources to schools was the main objective. It was assumed that educators would do the right thing, and that education was the ticket out of poverty.

By the end of the 20th century, it had become clear that resources alone were not sufficient to ensure equity in education. Federal expectations have become quite specific and amenable to quantitative measurement. One objective is that all children will read at grade level by no later than the third grade, another is that there will be no achievement gap separating children by race, ethnicity, income, or language.

Federal Programs Are Now at the Core of Teaching and Learning

Whereas federal programs once provided only supplementary services, the 1994 ESEA reauthorization set federal policy in a new direction. Today, it encompasses policies at the core of teaching, assessment, professional development, teacher qualifications, and clear systems of accountability for all children.

In a perfect world, the federal government would decide whether its mission is to support the core, as in the Title I focus on teaching and learning, or supplemental programs, such as migrant education or charter schools. However, the political reality is that the government will support both core and supplementary programs, in large part because political support for the core is often obtained by also supporting smaller, supplementary programs. Whereas bipartisan majorities are required to enact core programs, supplemental programs are generally enacted (and, usually, minimally funded) by political logrolling—"I'll support your special interest, if you support mine."

Race and Religion Are Decisive Factors

The emotional, often divisive, issues of race and religion, though redefined over the years, remain. Although public services to children in parochial and private schools through Title I, while minor, are more extensive than ever, and the U.S. Supreme Court has upheld the use of vouchers for students in nonpublic schools, the battle continues. The coming set of battles will be in the states, as they consider voucher programs as a result of the Supreme Court ruling. However, the 2003–4 reauthorization of IDEA and the 2007 reauthorization of ESEA will rekindle this issue at the federal level. Private school enrollment is about 11% of students aged 5–17. Although this percentage is below what it was 40 years ago in the wake of the *Brown* decision, the parents of these 6 million children feel they deserve public support. The original ESEA law would not have been passed in 1965 had there been no compromise on this issue. Further major breakthroughs will require new accommodations and compromises.

Although the issue of race is no longer one of de jure segregation, the achievement gap between White and Asian children and those who are Black or of Hispanic origin will likely remain a major factor in education policy for decades. If our society is not able to raise the achievement levels of those for whom the system has not worked well, then the nation's economy will suffer and it will be unlikely that these children will live full and enriching lives.

The Quest for Excellence versus the Opportunity for a Second Chance

The notion that people should have a second chance to succeed is in the very fabric of the nation; after all, the United States was created by immigrants looking for a second chance.

Few of this country's competitors or allies in the industrialized world (Canada, Australia, and New Zealand, also nations founded by immigrants, are exceptions) have this "second chance" tradition. Most other countries channel students, usually by testing, into formal tracks that lead to specific career paths. In those countries, once a student finishes high school and goes into higher education or the labor force, the idea of changing one's mind, discovering new motivations, or simply wanting to go back to school to master a new skill is almost impossible to imagine.

The U.S. system, by contrast, offers students many opportunities, from a GED high school degree, to open-enrollment community colleges, to technology-based education and training programs. Second and third careers are commonplace.

How Does the Policy Work?

There are several factors that describe the way that federal policy works, as well as the importance of how the federal government is organized in the education arena.

The Federal System Is "Messy and Cumbersome," but Unlikely to Change

As Alan Ginsburg, a senior career official in the Department of Education, said, "The feds are very powerful, so a system that is messy and cumbersome is not a bad thing" (Alan Ginsburg, personal interview, October 11, 2002).

Many federal agencies have at least a toehold in education, ranging from the NSF, to NIH, to the Department of Defense. Their education functions are aligned with the respective agency's mission and consolidating them into one agency makes little sense. An example is the DOD school system, which was kept out of the Department of Education because of the strong relationship that exists between military commanders and the support systems that enable the schools to function on a military base.

Politically, consolidation into a single agency is almost inconceivable. Congress has a committee structure that ensures that coordination and consolidation are unnatural acts. Interest groups maintain the status quo, as evidenced by President Carter's attempts to move programs to create a new department. In fact, a recent proposal by President George W. Bush to transfer Head Start from Health and Human Services (HHS) to the Department of Education is generating opposition that repeats the arguments heard when Congress debated creation of the department more than 20 years ago.

The Federal Government Deserves a D in Implementing Programs, Building Capacity at the State and Local Level, and Getting Time Lines Right

As Barry White, now retired after a distinguished career in OMB, put it, when things fail, and they often do, it is almost always due to the lack of an implementation plan (Barry White, personal interview, May 7, 2002). A major factor in failure is that making national policy that will handle the differences in 50 states is very difficult.

When there is a major change in federal law, few, if any, resources are made available for technical assistance, training, and support. The political pressure is to add money for direct services, since that is the money that reaches constituents.

Although Frank Keppel and the Gardner Task Force understood and fought for building capacity in ESEA in 1965, funding for these activities is almost always eliminated or severely reduced. This problem plagues almost all human-service programs. How does a politician explain supporting the salaries of "bureaucrats" rather than expanding services, even if the quality of the services suffers from the lack of the capacity to deliver them?

Communications are a constant problem. The United States has more than 15,000 school districts and 80,000 public schools. The information pipeline is inefficient and, as in the old game of telephone, messages are often received—if at all—with the content distorted as it is passes from layer to layer, person to person.

States want to control the message to local districts; local districts want to control the message to schools. Each has its own set of procedures, its own time line. Some states have more than 1,000 school districts; Hawaii is a single district. Although there are a few states—such as Delaware, Maryland, and Nevada—where there are so few districts that all the superintendents meet together, for most states, the number of districts and policymakers makes communications, hence implementation, unmanageable.

At the federal level, surprisingly little is being done with electronic communications. Some federal Web sites have been set up and some are quite professional. However, these sites rely on someone seeking information ("pulling") rather than automatically sending ("pushing") it.

Time lines are equally problematic. In 1994, the time lines in ESEA were stretched out for years, yet states still sought, and usually received, waivers. In 2001, the time lines were so short that regulations were often issued after the dates when the law went into effect.

When bills are introduced, the time lines often seem fair; but by the time they are enacted, the time lines are often unachievable. In the fine art of political compromise when legislation is negotiated, all the time and energy goes into other issues; time lines rarely take into consideration when schools start, when staff is hired, or what state laws and local practices need to be enacted or amended to carry out federal law. The *New York Times* reported in mid-October 2002, 9 months after enactment, that states still had not informed schools of provisions in the No Child Left Behind Act that took effect about 2 months before the school year began ("Law on Overhaul," 2002, p. 1).

Factors That Make a Difference

As seen above, the development of federal education policy was minor and uneventful until after World War II. Only then did enough support emerge to permit the enactment of major legislation. A number of factors have facilitated or hindered the development of federal policy over the course of the years.

Although Presidential Involvement Is Not Essential, It Makes a Huge Difference

The bookends of current education policy, Lyndon Johnson and George W. Bush, illustrate the difference presidential involvement can make. Neither the landmark original Elementary and Secondary Education Act of 1965, nor the dramatic changes made in No Child Left Behind in 2001 would have been possible without the highly personal intervention of these two presidents.

The most important policy change that did not actively involve a president occurred in 1975 with the passage of the Education of All Handicapped Children Act (EHCA), now known as the Individuals with Disabilities Education Act (IDEA). Coming as it did on the heels of Watergate and addressing an issue around which a strong external civil-rights-oriented constituency had formed, this bill had exceptional external legitimacy and momentum. Few members in either house, or party, dared risk voting against children with special needs, and the issue was consistent with the equity mission established in 1965 for poor children.

Further substantial changes in federal policy will only happen if they are initiated by the White House and if the president is personally committed and involved.

Ideas Do Matter, and Powerful Ideas Succeed

Although federal programs seem to have a momentum of their own, new ideas can change the direction of policy. Three such examples are cited below.

Uniform Standards. The first idea came in 1988 from Marshall "Mike" Smith, then the dean of the School of Education at Stanford University, and Jennifer O'Day, a graduate student at Stanford. In their paper (Smith & O'Day, 1991, pp. 233–267), the concept of an aligned system (systemic reform) was laid out with the starting point of academic content standards. The Smith-O'Day paper influenced the 1988 reauthorization of ESEA, the 1989 Charlottesville Education Summit, policies of the Clinton Administration, and states' policies. One of these states was Texas, where Governor Bush incorporated this idea as a part of the theory of action that he brought to Washington in 2000. A powerful, yet relatively simple, idea changed the course of policy.

Charter Schools. In the early 1980s, Minnesota became the first state to have a charter school. Minnesota activists Ted Kolderie and Joe Nathan were among the driving forces behind this idea.

Although it took a decade, President Clinton incorporated support of charter schools in several of his education initiatives, as did many governors. Today there are federal programs to support charters and almost all states have authorized their creation. Charter schools have opened up the system, made it more flexible, and spurred many public systems to improve.

Closing the Achievement Gap. The top priority of the 2001 ESEA amendments is on closing the achievement gap between White and Asian students at one extreme, and African American and Hispanic students at the other, to improve equity in education. This goal was incorporated into the Bush Administration's first education proposals in 2001. The idea also had support from the left and the right, so it was an easy sell to the leadership of the House and Senate committees. Again, a simple yet powerful idea became the driving force behind a major redirection of federal policy.

The Inevitable Link between Social Issues and Education

Education bills have long been magnets for social issues, most of which are only tenuously related to federal education policy. Since almost everyone in society has a stake in schools, and since education touches almost every social issue—even if only remotely—that is unlikely ever to change. Unrelated social policy issues have killed education legislation in the past and will continue to do so. The political link between schools and societal issues is inevitable.

The Merits of the Issue and Strength of Leadership Outweigh External Political Pressure

It is relatively easy for an interest group to get a small categorical program enacted; dozens have been so created in the past 40 years. However, enactment does not guarantee even minimal funding. Virtually every major directional change in federal policy has been in the face of significant opposition from the organizations representing the K–12 education community, starting with Title I in 1965 and ending with the 2001 law that changed reading programs and created new accountability systems. In the end, sound ideas and political leadership matter more than externally generated political pressure.

More Often than We Might Wish to Know, Federal Law Is Shaped by Anecdotes

The power of a personal story, the presence of a wronged parent or child, an exposé of an injustice—all motivate political leaders. Often these stories are reported in the press or told by a witness at a hearing, but often they are the result of a lawmaker's personal experience. When research contradicts personal experience or political ideology, research usually loses. The recent experience with federal evaluations showing the ineffectiveness of programs aimed at drug abuse prevention illustrates this clash of ideology and evidence.

The quality of educational research has had a mostly negative reputation since the 1972 creation of the National Institute of Education. As a consequence, funding for research in both real and inflation adjusted dollars has decreased dramatically. Most of the current appropriation is committed to the support of research centers and regional labs; relatively little is available to fund long-term, quantitative research. As a result, research has little credibility, and personal experiences have great impact.

The Creation of the Department of Education Has Advanced the Education Agenda, but Not without Some Negatives

Patricia Gwaltney, who headed the Carter administration's OMB reorganization study, which led to the enactment of the department, said, "There would have never been a bully pulpit unless there had been a department" (Patricia [Gwaltney] McGinnis, personal interview, September 17, 2002). Although her reference was to Ted Bell and *A Nation at Risk,* it applies equally to the ability of any secretary or senior federal official to take on issues that must be addressed nationally.

Education was, literally, a "rounding error" in the HEW budget, and any potential education budget appeals to the president—only two or three were ever presented by a HEW secretary—were inevitably trumped by welfare, health, and social security issues. An education secretary may have to prioritize among his or her

"children," but everything that he or she considers before going to the White House is in that domain; trade-offs with other domestic programs are not an issue.

On the negative side, a separate education agency means that coordinating programs like Head Start in HHS and Title I and Early Reading in the Department of Education is even more difficult than it might have been under HEW.

Research on education and learning is now carried out by agencies as widely disbursed as the Office of Naval Research, the Defense Advanced Research and Projects Administration, the NIH, and NSF. Only a small amount of fundamental research in education is done by the Department of Education, and there are no viable mechanisms in place to coordinate how research in other agencies might be applied to benefit the education of children, despite the existence of 10 regional educational laboratories that are supported by the Department of Education. In recent years, the only exception is NIH's research on reading, but multiple bureaucratic and cultural barriers between agencies have mitigated the effective use of that research. This is a classic case of "if it's not invented here, it can't be that good."

Finally, and contrary to popular belief, the federal government does run schools. Operated by the DOD and the Department of Interior, these schools serve military dependents (primarily overseas), and children on Indian reservations. According to test data, the DOD schools are far more successful at educating a diverse student body than is almost every large stateside school district, as continually demonstrated by test score data.

Members of Congress from "Safe" Districts or States Have Most Successfully Taken on the Washington-Based Education Establishment

Some, like Carl Perkins, needed little campaign money; others refused to believe that laws should be written by lobbyists and stamped by Congress. Leaders like Jacob Javits, Al Quie, Claiborne Pell, George Miller, Gus Hawkins, and John Boehner all fall into this category.

With campaign costs skyrocketing, few elected officials can ignore the link between political support and campaign contributions. Although education organizations are not as skilled in making the link between lobbying and campaign contributions as unions and business organizations, more political action committees will be formed among education-interest groups, and pressure will continue for the support of certain positions in exchange for endorsements and campaign contributions.

Timing Is Crucial

As noted by former House education committee staff member Marty LaVor, the special education law that was enacted in 1975 could not have been enacted in the 1980s, or before the 1970s (Marty LaVor, personal interview, September 16, 2002), because the political circumstances were not right and neither was the timing. It is instructive to note that NDEA passed on the heels of a crisis in national defense. The passage of Title I was in part a tribute to assassinated President Kennedy, and the resignation of Nixon and the political furor over his pardon by Ford made a veto of the special education law unthinkable.

The circumstances and timing were also perfectly aligned in 2001, when Bush pushed No Child Left Behind through to enactment, and again in 2002 when the new federal education research bill became law. In both cases, the accumulation of events over time, along with having the right people in the right places, ensured the passage of new laws.

Outsiders Sometimes Play a Major Role, but Rarely Those Who Represent Membership Organizations

Although there are exceptions—the Council for Exceptional Children in the enactment of the 1975 special education act and the NEA in creation of the department—most organized groups of administrators, teachers, and school boards have fought against proposed changes, but they lose far more than they win.

Among the interest groups representing the major stakeholders, a pack mentality operates. That led, in the late 1990s, to the creation of the Education Leaders Council (ELC) by a group of chief state school officers and state board members who often did not agree with the positions of organizations such as the Council of Chief State School Officers and the National Association of State Boards of Education.

In contrast, some individuals and think tanks have had a substantial impact. In the case of No Child Left Behind, the Progressive Policy Institute, the Fordham Foundation, the Education Trust, and the Business Roundtable helped committee leaders gain enactment.

Federal Policy Often Follows State/Local Action

State laws for compensatory education and for disabled children existed before the federal laws were proposed.

The idea for individualized education plans came from a field visit made by a House subcommittee (Marty LaVor, personal interview, September 16, 2002). Bush's experience in Texas greatly influenced his 2001 education plan. The impetus for the national education goals emerged from the Southern Regional Education Board, a coalition of states.

Congressional hearings do matter, especially those that occur outside of Washington. In addition, every key elected official has a formal or informal kitchen cabinet of advisors on education, many of whom may not realize the potential influence of their informally expressed views. White House officials listen to governors, especially those in their own party, and are influenced by public opinion polls.

Federal Organization Matters, Whether in Congress or in the Executive Branch

Because several different Congressional subcommittees control federal education policy, there has never been an attempt to rationalize or integrate programs like compensatory and special education. Seven major organizational units in the U.S. Department of Education now deal with K–12 education: the Office of Elementary and Secondary Education, the Office of English Language Acquisition, the Office of Special Education and Vocational Rehabilitation, the Office of Vocational and Adult Education, the Institute of Educational Sciences, the Office of Innovation and Improvement, and the Office of Safe and Drug Free Schools. Each office has its programs, loyal staff, and relationships with interest groups and elected officials to protect those programs, creating the "issue networks" studied by political scientists, and the silos that maintain separation between programs.

The salaries of more than half the staff in state education agencies are paid with federal funds. That practice began in 1965 with ESEA as a way to both build state staffs and create loyalty to federal programs. In many states, staff members who work for major federal programs operate separately from the state superintendents and their staff. Most state agencies mirror major organizational units of the U.S. Department of Education. Therefore, states also usually deal with issues based on program fealty rather than from the perspective of a child or parent.

Until and unless the organization of Congress and the U.S. Department of Education changes, it is unlikely that the organization of most states and large school districts—and the way they view issues—will change. Even though new laws permit the transfer of funds among programs, inertia and fear of a federal audit finding, reigns supreme.

The Federal Government's Control Is Indirect, Because It Operates through State Agencies

Because the federal government operates through the state agencies, there are 50-plus opportunities for interpretation of laws and regulations. There are few tools that the federal government can use to enforce compliance. Cutting off financial support will hurt children more than the state or local bureaucracy and some states may be willing to accept a cutoff of administrative funds during a period of increasing federal support. Going to court takes forever, and often Congressional supporters will pressure a cabinet secretary or the White House to back off in return for support on another issue. Frank Keppel discovered this in the Johnson administration when he tried to force action on school desegregation in Chicago. He soon found himself in a new job with few powers, and even fewer staff.

Unless state agencies are effective in their roles with respect to federal programs, it is almost impossible for local school districts to "get it right." The regional educational laboratories supported by the federal government should be used much more effectively than they ever have been to assist states. That was, after all, part of the rationale for their creation in 1965.

What the Federal Bureaucracy Does Matters, and So Does That Federal Money!

In recalling the more than 20 interviews I conducted for this book, one keeps coming back to mind. Barry White tells of running into a longtime senior career person one day in 2001 outside the Department of Education. In talking about the change in administrations, the career person said, "This is the first time that someone has ever told us that what we do really matters" (Barry White, personal interview, May 7, 2002).

Whether it is writing regulations, talking with educators, or getting money to schools, the actions of federal staff are exceedingly important. Although the federal government contributes less than a dime of every dollar spent on K–12 education, the leverage those few cents have is immeasurable. Federal dollars are often the "leadership dollars" to ensure that needs are met, progress is made, and all children are served. Without federal leadership and federal dollars, it is un-

likely that we would see national attention directed to issues like the achievement gap between students of different races and economic conditions, the need to use reading programs based upon research, or the need for teacher aides to have some education beyond high school. Federal aid is no longer marginal.

The Consistency of the Federal Message Is Extremely Important

If the players on the federal policy scene send different messages, confusion is created at state and local levels, giving those who wish to do nothing, the opportunity to do so.

Following the negotiations and subsequent enactment of the No Child Left Behind Act of 2001, the key leaders were united and have remained so on policy issues, even if they differ on funding. The consistency of that message has made a marked impression on educators at all levels. The education systems in this nation are extremely complex and multilayered. Getting a clear message through the layers to the school principal and to teachers requires a Herculean effort. Multiple messages create confusion, confusion leads to uncertainty, uncertainty stifles improvement.

Other Observations

There are a number of other observations that can be made about federal policy and its development that do not neatly fit into a category.

The Power of the Federal Court System Is Immense and Underestimated

Although desegregation cases have clearly been the most important and prominent of the court actions, in recent years almost every U.S. Supreme Court docket has contained other education-related cases, ranging from prayer, to the privacy of student records, to the enforcement of laws on special education.

So prominent have these cases become that almost any potentially contentious law that passes today contains a severability clause, a provision stating that if one element of the law is overturned by court decision, the rest of the law remains in force.

These court decisions affect policy, but they also influence practice. The 2002 decision upholding the Cleveland, Ohio, voucher program may be the most significant in the long run in helping to open up delivery systems, even though its immediate impact was small because it merely permits the voucher program in Cleveland and, by implication, the one in Milwaukee, to stay in effect.

Political Party Distinctions on Education Have Become Less Clear

In many ways, No Child Left Behind represents the reemergence of conservative Republicans as progressive leaders. After World War II, it was Ohio Republican senator Robert Taft who shocked the body politic with his support for general federal aid, in much the same way that George W. Bush did in 2001 by proposing a law that was at odds with the right wing of his own party. Both parties now vie to see who can get credit for the largest increases in education funding. After the 1996 election, polls showed that the anti-education stance of the GOP was a negative for voters. Within 4 years, that stance has disappeared. Polls—and elections—make a difference!

Federal Programs Do Not Meet the Needs of the Brightest Students

Although there is a small program for gifted and talented students, it does not begin to meet the need. By design, the federal role focuses on those in greatest need, leaving to states the question of how to serve these students.

By focusing on issues of equity and on the need for an aligned system, schools often have no way to challenge students once they have mastered the required standards and demonstrated through the assessment system that they know and understand the material. Schools are, therefore, often doing a disservice to these students and the nation.

Advanced placement classes and dual enrollment in college courses can be used to serve these students, but care must be taken to ensure that federal law protects and encourages these options, without creating a system that is racially or economically segregated.

While Federal Policy Has Attempted to Deal with Parental Involvement and Student Motivation, Those Efforts Have Been Halfhearted, Unfocused, and Ineffective

We have learned from the success of other nations—Japan, Germany, Singapore, Korea—that parental involvement and student motivation are vital to creating a culture that values education, and one in which the need for personal improvement is readily understood.

Student motivation, especially at the high school level, is hard to sustain unless real consequences, such as college admission or a job, are at stake. Many other nations maintain that motivation through a sorting system that keeps parents involved and students motivated. Such a system seems contrary to the American value system.

What "Counts" as Educational Policy?
Notes toward a New Paradigm

JEAN ANYON

In my first article as a young PhD, which was published in the *Harvard Educational Review,* I argued that high school U.S. history curriculum, as represented in widely used textbooks, excises and thereby defines out of existence radical responses American workers have had to the problems they face on the job and in their communities (Anyon, 1979). This educational excision is one way that schooling mitigates against the development of working-class consciousness.

In empirical and theoretical work since then, I have investigated knowledge and pedagogical experiences made available to students in different social-class contexts (1980, 1981), and have attempted to understand the consequences of ways we conceptualize urban education, urban school reform, and neighborhood poverty. Recent arguments have aimed at unseating simplistic notions of the causes of urban poverty and low achievement in city districts, and explicating unexplored relations between urban education and movements for social change (e.g., 1995, 1997, 2005).

In this article I think about education policy over the seventy-five years of *Harvard Educational Review* publication. During these decades, many K–12 policies have been written and implemented by federal, state, and local governments. Some of these have aimed at improving education in America's cities and are my primary focus. Over the years, dominant strategies called upon to improve urban schools have included curricular, administrative, and funding reforms, as well as increases in educational opportunity and district/school accountability.

A historical examination of policies can inform decisions we make today. Policy failures, for example, may demonstrate that we need to rethink strategies we choose in our long-term attempts to solve the problems of school and student achievement in urban districts. Indeed, I will argue that the quality of education in city schools is a complex problem, and education policy as historically conceived has not been adequate to the task of increasing urban school achievement to acceptable levels. Academic learning in city schools is undoubtedly higher than in, say, 1900, yet there is still no large urban district that can demonstrate high achievement in even half its students or schools. Noting this failure of educational policy to render most urban schools high-quality institutions, I ask, what *should* count as educational policy? As in any attempt to resolve complex issues, workable solutions can only be generated by an understanding of underlying causes.

The diagnosis I provide is based on analyses completed for my book, *Radical Possibilities: Public Policy, Urban Education, and a New Social Movement* (Anyon, 2005). In this book I examine federal and regional mandates that affect economic and social opportunities available to the urban poor. I find that despite stated intentions, federal and metropolitan policies and arrangements generally restrict opportunities available to city residents and neighborhoods. I show how job, wage, housing, tax, and transportation policies maintain minority poverty in urban neighborhoods, and thereby create environments that overwhelm the potential of educational policy to create systemic, sustained improvements in the schools. For example, policies such as minimum wage statutes that

yield full-time pay below the poverty level, and affordable housing and transportation policies that segregate low-income workers of color in urban areas but industrial and other job development in far-flung suburbs where public transit routes do not reach, are all culpable.

In order to solve the systemic problems of urban education, then, I argue in the book—and will argue here—that we need not only better schools but also the reform of these public policies. Rules and regulations regarding teaching, curriculum, and assessment certainly are important, but policies to eliminate poverty-wage work and housing segregation (for example) should be part of the educational policy panoply as well, for these have consequences for urban education at least as profound as curriculum, pedagogy, and testing.

In the sections that follow I describe major K–12 education policies that have been implemented over the years to attempt to improve urban education, and then discuss several federal and metro-area policies and practices that limit the potential and success of these strategies. I also report hopeful new research suggesting that even modest income and other family supports typically improve low-income students' academic achievement. I end by arguing that, given this power of economic access to influence educational outcomes, strategies to support economic opportunity and development for urban residents and neighborhoods should be among the policies we consider in our attempts to improve urban schools and districts. Just as in affluent suburban districts where economic strength is the engine of educational reform, so it would be in urban districts where resident and neighborhood affluence would support and retool the schools. I begin with an overview of education policy as typically conceived.

Education Policies

Over the last seventy-five years or so, federal policies have attempted various strategies to improve city education. The first federal policy aimed at working-class populations was the Smith-Hughes Act of 1917, which provided funds to prepare students in industrialized areas for working-class jobs through vocational programs. Variants of this policy continued throughout the twentieth century, in the Vocational Education Acts of 1963, 1984, and 1998, and in the School-to-Work Opportunity Act of 1994 and the later federal legislation in which it was subsumed.

Some federal education policies have attempted to improve urban education by making funding available for increased curriculum materials and libraries, early childhood classes, and various types of programmatic innovations in city schools. Head Start in 1965, Follow Through in 1967, and, to a lesser extent, Title IX, which banned sex discrimination in 1972, brought and instigated new curricula and programs into city districts.[1] These policies were intended to increase student access and/or achievement by upgrading curricular resources and experiences.

Other federal K–12 policies have aimed specifically at increasing educational equity. The 1954 *Brown* decision (which committed the federal government to desegregation as a policy stance), the Elementary and Secondary Education Act of 1965 (ESEA), the Bilingual Act in 1968, Title IX in 1972, and the Education for All Handicapped Children Act in 1975 opened doors to academic experiences for previously underserved K–12 students. These policies are generally thought to have expanded urban students' educational opportunities.

More recent federal education policies to improve schooling—with urban students and teachers often a target—have called for increased academic standards and requirements, standardized testing, and professional development of teachers. These policies were recommended by the influential report *A Nation at Risk,* commissioned by President Ronald Reagan and published in 1983. The emphasis on increased academic standards was part of an effort to support business needs for well-prepared workers and employees. The report's recommendations for higher standards and increased testing were introduced as policy in 1994 and 1996 as part of the Goals 2000 legislation. In 2001 these goals were instantiated as federal mandates in the No Child Left Behind Act (NCLB). Privatization of education via nonpublic providers when K–12 schools fail is a subtextual education policy in NCLB (Conley, 2003; Cross, 2004; Stein, 2004).

It is important to note that federal education policies intended to improve urban schools did not take aim at the economic arrangements and practices that themselves produced the poverty in which city schools were embedded. Despite increases in educational opportunity, the effects of almost a century of educational policies on urban school and student achievement have, by most accounts, been disappointing.

The first state policies regarding the education of America's urban (and rural) poor emerged earlier than federal ones. What has counted as state education policy regarding poor students can be said to have begun with mid- to late-nineteenth century insertions into state constitutions of the right of all students to a free, "thorough," "efficient," or "useful" education (Odden & Picus, 1992). Following these insertions and until the 1970s, however, most state education policies did not focus specifically on urban education. State mandates typically set regulations and requirements for school systems, teacher and administrator preparation, and school funding (through property taxes). During the 1970s and 1980s, lawsuits challenging state education funding systems brought increased attention to city schools and districts. State urban education policy in these decades involved various kinds of efforts, including school-based management and basic skills mandates. In the 1990s, state policies attempted to align education standards and regulations with federal ones, mandated curriculum and teacher licensure reform, and closely monitored urban districts. As legal challenges to state systems have led to increased funding of city schools, states have imposed stricter academic and graduation requirements, as well as multigrade and multisubject standardized testing. Quasi-privatization policies supporting charter schools, vouchers, and other school choice programs have also been a state strategy to attempt to improve the education of urban children by offering them a choice of schools to attend (Conley, 2003).

Over the decades, federal and state policies codified an increasing number of requirements that urban schools and districts must meet. Local governments and educational bureaucracies have undertaken a plethora of programs to attempt to meet those guidelines. Local districts have also mounted school reform projects in response to local social conditions and political pressure from parents and communities. Most local initiatives have been curricular, pedagogical, and administrative.

During the Progressive Era, cities consolidated and professionalized their school systems and personnel, introduced programs like the Gary Plan to prepare students for the industrial experience, increased access to high school, organized educational opportunities for immigrant parents, and sometimes fed, bathed, and clothed poor children. During the decade of the Great Depression, most large cities retrenched and severely cut educational social service and academic programs, as local tax receipts plummeted and banks that offered loans demanded broad cuts in education. During the

1960s, many urban districts were weakened further as most remaining businesses and jobs moved to the suburbs, decimating the urban property tax base (Anyon, 1997; Ravitch, 2000; Tyack, 1974; Wrigley, 1982).

Since the 1970s, in response to federal, judicial, and state mandates, urban districts have bused students to meet racial integration guidelines, decentralized authority to increase community participation, and created magnet schools to attempt to attract middle-class parents. Other local policies that have been attempted to improve achievement are a multitude of reform programs or "school improvement projects," student retention services, privatization of educational offerings, vouchers and magnets, mayoral control, small schools, and curriculum standardization and evaluation through testing. The social context of these policies has included pressure to be accountable in the wake of increased funding, as well as community and corporate demands for better schools. None of the local policies has focused on the poverty of families or neighborhoods.

One way to evaluate this long run of education policy is to compare the achievement of urban students at the beginning of the twentieth and twenty-first centuries. Although achievement is higher now in that larger percentages of students remain in school past the elementary years than in 1900, I would argue that the improvement is relative and illusory. That is, while in the early twentieth century relatively few urban poor students went beyond fifth grade, the vast majority did not require further education to find employment in industries that could lead to middle-class income (Anyon, 1997; Ayres, 1909). Currently, relatively few urban poor students go past ninth grade: The graduation rates in large comprehensive inner-city high schools are abysmally low. In fourteen such New York City schools, for example, only 10 percent to 20 percent of ninth graders in 1996 graduated four years later (Fine, 2001; Greene, 2001; Miao & Haney, 2004).[2] Despite the fact that low-income individuals desperately need a college degree to find decent employment, only 7 percent obtain a bachelor's degree by age twenty-six (Education Trust, 2001; Mishel, Bernstein, & Schmitt, 2001). So, in relation to the needs of low-income students, urban districts fail their students with more egregious consequences now than in the early twentieth century.

Given the plethora of federal, state, and local education policies aimed at urban schools and the current widely acknowledged necessity of high-quality education for all, why have most urban schools and districts not been able to provide such an education for their students?

Barriers to High-Quality Public Education in Cities

There are multiple causes of low-quality schooling in urban areas, and education policies as heretofore conceived address only a few. Education policy has not addressed the neighborhood poverty that surrounds and invades urban schools with low expectations and cynicism. Education policy has not addressed the unemployment and joblessness of families who will have few if any resources for the further education of their children, even if they excel in K–12 classes.

And education policy—even in response to state financial challenges—has not addressed the political economy that largely determines low levels of city district funding. Taxes on wealthy families and corporations are among the lowest on record (Phillips, 2002). Business and government investment in affluent suburban job centers rather than urban areas continues to deprive poor neighborhoods of entry-level jobs and a tax base, and residents' poverty wages further diminish available funding sources (Anyon, 2005; Orfield, 2002; Rusk, 1999). These political-economic constraints on quality schooling are not challenged by current or past education policy. In most U.S. cities, the political leverage of urban parents has not been sufficient to force the funding necessary to overcome outdated buildings, broken computer labs, and overcrowded classrooms.

These economic and political conditions are the building blocks of formidable barriers to systemic, sustainable school quality. Indeed, even when urban school reform succeeds, it fails—when there are no decent jobs a diploma from a successfully reformed school or district will attract, and there is no government or familial funding sufficient for the vast majority of low-income graduates of even good urban high schools to obtain a bachelors degree.

Individual and neighborhood poverty builds walls around schools and classrooms that education policy does not penetrate or scale. In the following section I describe some of the federal and metro-area policies and arrangements that sustain these barriers.

Federal Policy

Analysts typically do not link federal policies to the maintenance of poverty, to the lack of jobs that bedevils American workers, or to the increasingly large portion of employment that pays poverty and near-poverty wages. Yet federal policy is determinative. To take a blatant example, Congress set the first minimum wage in 1938 at $3.05 (in 2000 dollars); it stands in 2005 at $5.15—a mere two dollars more. (Yearly income at this wage is $10,712.) This sum ensures that full-time, year-round, minimum-wage work will not raise people out of poverty (Mishel, Bernstein, & Boushey, 2003). Analysis in 2004 found that minimum-wage standards directly affect the wages of 8.9 percent of the workforce (9.9 million workers); when we include those making one dollar more an hour than the minimum wage, this legislation affects the wages of as much as 18 percent of the workforce (Economic Policy Institute, 2004). Contrary to the claims of those who oppose raising the minimum wage (that an increase will force employers to fire, or hire fewer of those affected by the increase), studies of the 1990–1991 and 1996–1997 minimum-wage increases failed to find any systematic, significant job losses associated with the increases and found no evidence of negative employment effects on small businesses (Economic Policy Institute, 2004).

Almost half the workforce earns what some economists call poverty-*zone* wages (and what I define as up to and including 125% of the official poverty level; Anyon, 2005). I analyzed figures provided by the Economic Policy Institute to calculate the overall percentage of people who work full-time year round yet make wages up to and including 125 percent of the official poverty threshold needed to support a family of four at the poverty level. The analysis demonstrates that in 1999, during a very strong economy, almost half of the people at work in the United States (41.3%) earned poverty-zone wages—in 1999, $10.24/hour ($21,299/year) or less, working full-time year round (Mishel et al., 2001). Two years later, in 2001, 38.4 percent earned poverty-zone wages working full-time year round (in 2001, 125% of the poverty line was a $10.88 hourly wage; Mishel et al., 2003). This suggests that the federal minimum-wage policy is an important determinant of poverty for many millions of U.S. families.

There are other macroeconomic policies that produce hardship. These especially penalize Blacks and Latinos, the majority of whom live in segregated, low-income urban neighborhoods. These policies include the following: job training as a predominant federal antipoverty policy when there have been too few jobs for graduates; ineffective federal implementation of policies that outlaw racial discrimination in hiring and housing; regressive income taxes that charge wealthy individuals less than half the rate charged the rich during most of the first sixty years of the twentieth century, yet substantially raise the payroll taxes paid by the working poor and middle class; and corporate tax policies in recent years that allow 60 percent of large U.S. corporations to pay no federal taxes at all (and in some cases to obtain millions in rebates; Citizens for Tax Justice, 2002; Lafer, 2002; Orfield, 2002; Rusk, 1999).

These federal policies and practices contribute to personal, neighborhood, and educational poverty because they lead to the following problems: There are not enough jobs for poor families who need them; low-income families of color are concentrated in low-resourced urban neighborhoods; and when the wealthy do not contribute equitably to public expenses, funding for services like education declines and the quality of the services tends to be low.

The effects of these policies are compounded by harsh union laws and lack of federal protection for labor organizing; Federal Reserve Bank pronouncements that ignore the portion of its mandate to maintain a high level of employment; and free-trade agreements that send thousands of corporations, and their job opportunities, to other countries. These policies hurt workers of all colors—and in most sectors of the economy—as existing jobs disappear and those remaining pay lower wages, in part because they are not unionized (Anyon, 2005; Citizens for Tax Justice, 2002; Economic Policy Institute, 2002, 2004; Galbraith, 1998; Lafer, 2002; Mishel et al., 2001).

However, there are federal policies we could create that would lower poverty by important margins—including a significantly raised minimum wage, comparable worth laws, and policies to enforce existing regulations that outlaw discrimination in hiring. A raise in the minimum wage that brought workers above poverty would improve the lives of at least a fifth of U.S. workers (Economic Policy Institute, 2004). Paying women the same amount men are paid for comparable work would, according to one analysis, reduce poverty by 40 percent, as such a large percentage of poor people are women in low-wage jobs (Lafer,

2002). And requiring employers to hire without discriminating against Blacks and Latinos would further open opportunities currently denied.

In addition, policies that worked against U.S. poverty in the past could be reinstated: U.S. government regulation of the minimum wage, which kept low-paid workers' income at the median of highly paid unionized workers in the decades after World War II; federal support for union organizing; a federal program of job creation in cities, as during the Great Depression of the 1930s; and federal programs for urban youth that would support further education, as such policies did for eight million men and women after World War II (Anyon, 2005; Galbraith, 1998). These national policies were important supports of the widespread prosperity of the United States' working and middle classes in the quarter century following 1945 (Galbraith, 1998).

Metropolitan Policy and Practice

Like current federal mandates, there are metro-area policies and practices that increase the problems of urban residents and neighborhoods. Metro areas are shaped by regional markets—for jobs, housing, investment, and production. Metro areas account for over 80 percent of national output and drive the economic performance of the nation as a whole. Each metro area is anchored by one or more cities (Dreier, Mollenkopf, & Swanstrom, 2001).

Today, metropolitan regions are characterized by population growth, extensive inequality, and segregation (Orfield, 2002; Rusk, 1999). The percentage of racial minorities in large metro areas who live in the suburbs jumped from 19 percent to 27 percent during the 1990s. However, a growing share of these families lives in fiscally stressed suburbs, with an increasing number of neighborhoods having poverty levels over 30 percent (Kingsley & Petit, 2003; Orfield, 2002). As in areas of concentrated poverty in the central city, low levels of taxable resources in these "urbanized" segregated suburbs leave services like education lacking in funds.

U.S. metropolitan areas are characterized by the following problems, all of which disadvantage urban minority families and communities: Most entry-level jobs for which adults with low to moderate education levels are qualified are increasingly located in suburbs, rather than in central cities, but public transit systems do not connect these suburban job centers to urban areas, where most low-income minorities live—thus preventing them from access to jobs there. State-allowed local zoning on the basis of income prevents affordable housing in most suburbs where entry-level jobs are located, which means there is little if any housing for low-income families near the suburban job centers. Indeed, as I have mentioned, the failure to enforce antiracial discrimination statutes in housing confines most Blacks and Latinos to housing sites in central cities and segregated suburbs. Finally, even though federal and state taxes are paid by residents throughout metro regions (including inner cities), most tax-supported development takes place in the affluent suburbs rather than in low-income areas. Thus, few jobs exist in most low-income urban neighborhoods (Anyon, 2005; Dreir et al., 2001; Orfield, 2002; Rusk, 1999). These inequitable regional arrangements and policies exacerbate federal wage and job mandates and contribute in important ways to joblessness and poverty in cities and urbanized suburbs, and to the low quality of investment in services such as education there.

Poverty

One consequence of federal and regional policies regarding work, wages, housing segregation, and transportation is that the numbers of poor people approach the figures of 1959—before massive urban poverty became a national issue. Although the percentages are lower now, the numbers are still staggering: There were about as many people officially poor in 1993 (39.2 million) as in 1959 (39.4 million; Harrington, 1963). And in 2003, 35.8 million were officially poor, only 3.5 million fewer than in 1959 (Mishel et al., 2003).

A more realistic measure of poverty than federal guidelines is that those earning incomes up to 200 percent of the official levels are considered poor (Bernstein, Brocht, & Spade-Aguilar, 2000; Citro & Michael, 1995; Short, Iceland, & Garner, 1999). This revised threshold is used by increasing numbers of social scientists. A calculation of the individuals who earned less than 200 percent of the poverty level in 2001 ($17.40/hour, or $36,192/year), demonstrates a much larger percentage of poor employees than is commonly acknowledged: *84 percent of Hispanic workers, 80 percent of Black workers, and 64.3 percent of White workers made wages at or under 200 percent of the official poverty line* (Mishel et al., 2001).

A calculation of *families* living with earnings up to 200 percent of the poverty line reveals that Black and Latino families face the greatest financial hurdles. More than 50 percent of Black and Latino families earn less than 200 percent of the poverty level, compared to only 20.3 percent of White families, even though White families constitute a slight majority (50.5%) of families that fall below 200 percent of the poverty level (Mishel et al., 2001). In sum, poverty in the United States is higher than commonly perceived and is maintained in urban areas by federal and metro-area policies and distributions.

Effects of Poverty on Urban Students

Macroeconomic policies that set wages below poverty levels, that train inner-city hopefuls for jobs that do not exist, that do not extract from the wealthy a fair share of social expenses, and that rarely enforce laws that would substantially decrease the economic discrimination of people of color all support persistent poverty and near-poverty among minority urban populations. This economic and social distress can prevent children from developing their full potential and can certainly dampen the enthusiasm, effort, and expectations with which urban children and their families approach K–12 education.

As I will report, a recent national study of young children confirms the potential of impoverished circumstances to prevent students' full cognitive growth before they enroll in kindergarten. Of countervailing power, however, is research demonstrating that when parents obtain better financial resources or better living conditions, the educational achievement of the children typically improves significantly. These findings empirically support the argument that for the urban poor, even with the right educational policies in place, school achievement may await a family's economic access.

I already presented adult poverty figures at the official threshold and noted the alarming increase in numbers when a more realistic assessment is made. The same disparities exist between federal and alternative counts of poor children. Sixteen percent of American children—almost 12 million—lived below the *official* federal poverty line in 2001. Almost half of those children (44%, or a little over 5 million) lived in *extreme* poverty (less than half the poverty line, or $7,400 for a family of three in 2001)—including nearly a million African American children. This was a 17

percent increase in the number of children in extreme poverty from 2000, at the end of the economic boom (Cauthen & Lu, 2001; Dillon, 2003; Lu, 2003).

When the more appropriate alternative poverty threshold criterion is applied, however, a full *38 percent* of American children are identified as poor—27 million who lived in families with income up to 200 percent of the official poverty line. These children live in poverty as well—although official statistics do not designate them as such. However, these families experience hardships that are almost as severe as those who are officially poor (Cauthen & Lu 2001; Lu, 2003). *By the revised measure—200 percent of the official poverty cutoff—a full 57 percent of African American children, 64 percent of Latino, and 34 percent of White children were poor in the United States in 2001* (Lu, 2003; Mishel et al., 2003).

It is only in the 1990s that empirical studies focused on why and how poverty affects cognitive development and school achievement. Researchers began to document the specific effects of poverty environments on children's development (Brooks-Gunn, Duncan, Leventhal, & Aber, 1997; Goering & Feins, 2003; Sampson, Morenoff, & Gannon-Rowley, 2002). This body of work documents the correlations between low income, child development, and educational achievement (see Duncan & Brooks-Gunn, 1997, for an overview of studies). For example, poverty has been found to have consistently negative effects on children's cognitive development (Duncan & Brooks-Gunn, 1997; Duncan, Brooks-Gunn, & Klebanov, 1994; McLoyd, 1998). Longitudinal studies that have been carried out also demonstrate that "family income consistently predicts children's academic and cognitive performance, even when other family characteristics are taken into account" (Duncan & Brooks-Gunn, 1997). Persistent and extreme poverty has been shown to be more detrimental to children than temporary poverty (Bolger & Patterson, 1995; Duncan et al., 1994). Family income may influence children through both lack of resources and parental emotional stress (Bradley, 1984; McLoyd & Jartayne, 1994; Smith, Brooks-Gunn, & Klebanov, 1997; Sugland, Zaslow, Brooks-Gunn, & Moore, 1995). Poor children have more health and behavior difficulties than those from more affluent families, which mitigates against educational success (Duncan & Brooks-Gunn, 1997; Houser, Brown, & Prosser, 1997; Klerman, 1991/2003; Korenman & Miller, 1997). Studies collected by Duncan and

Brooks-Gunn teased out some of the variables within the effects of income. In summarizing research reported in their 1997 volume *Consequences of Growing up Poor,* they point out the following:

1. Income matters for the cognitive development of preschoolers "because it is associated with the provision of a richer learning environment" (p. 601). This is true in part because family income is a "significant determinant of child care environments, including center-based childcare (p. 601). . . . Income allows parents to provide their children with safer, more stimulating home environments; to live in communities with better schools, parks, and libraries and more challenging peers; to afford tuition and other expenses associated with higher education; to purchase or otherwise gain access to higher-quality health care; and in many other ways to buy the things that promote the health and development of their children" (p. 14).

2. "A variety of income measures—income [relative to needs] . . . income loss, the ratio of debts to assets, and unstable work—are associated with family economic pressure" (p. 602). Economic pressure has been found to be associated with depression (and stress) in parents, which can affect parenting, and thus school achievement.

3. "Family income is usually a stronger predictor of ability and achievement outcomes than are measures of parental schooling or family structure [e.g., single parenthood]" (p. 603). Many studies have shown that children raised in low-income families score lower than children from more affluent families do on assessments of health, cognitive development, and positive behavior. "In general, the better the measure of family income and the longer the period over which it is measured, the stronger the association between the family's economic well-being and children's outcomes" (p. 14).

It is important to understand that these findings do not suggest that poor students are of low intelligence; rather, the studies point to the power of the economy—and of economic hardship—to place extremely high hurdles to full development in front of children who are poor. It is of course possible—although it is not the norm—that education over time mitigates the effects of SES (Hout, 1988; Jencks & Phillips, 1998).

In 2002, Valerie Lee and David Burkham published the results of a large-sample assessment of the effects of poverty on cognitive development. They utilized data from the United States Department of Education's early childhood longitudinal kindergarten cohort, which is a comprehensive dataset that provides a nationally representative portrait of kindergarten students. Lee and Burkham (2002) explored differences in young children's achievement scores in literacy and mathematics by race, ethnicity, and socioeconomic status (SES) as they began kindergarten. They also analyzed differences by social background in an array of children's homes and family activities.

The study demonstrates that inequalities in children's cognitive ability by SES are substantial even before children begin kindergarten and that poverty has a detrimental impact on early intellectual achievement. Importantly, it demonstrates that the disadvantages of being poor outweigh by far the race or family structure of children as causes of the cognitive disadvantages.

Details of the national assessment include the following:

1. Before children enter kindergarten, the average cognitive scores of children in the highest SES group are 60 percent above the scores of the lowest SES group.

2. Cognitive skills are much *less* closely related to race/ethnicity after accounting for SES. After taking racial differences into account, children from different SES groups achieve at different levels—before they begin kindergarten.

3. The impact of family structure on cognitive skills (e.g., being in a single-parent family) is much less than either race or SES.

4. Socioeconomic status is very strongly related to cognitive skills; SES accounts for more of the variation in cognitive scores than any other factor by far.

Lee and Burkham (2002) also found that disadvantaged children not only enter kindergarten with significantly lower cognitive skills than their advantaged peers, but also that low-SES children begin school (kindergarten) in systematically lower-quality elementary schools than their more advantaged counterparts. "However school quality is defined—in terms of higher student achievement, more school resources, more qualified teachers, more positive teacher attitudes, better neighborhood or school conditions, private vs. public schools—the least advantaged United States children begin their formal schooling in consistently lower-quality schools. This reinforces the inequalities that develop even before children reach school age" (p. 3; see also Entwistle & Alexander, 1997; Phillips, Brooks-Gunn, Duncan, Klevanov, & Crane, 1998; Phillips, Crouse, & Ralph, 1998; Stipic & Ryan, 1997; White, 1982).

In their review of studies of poverty's effects on individual development, Duncan and Brooks-Gunn (1997) conclude, "Taken together, [these studies] suggest that programs that raise the incomes of poor families will enhance the cognitive development of children and may improve their chance of success in [education and] the labor market during adulthood. Most important appears to be the elimination of deep and persistent poverty during a child's early years" (p. 608). I now turn to research suggesting that familial financial and other supports do indeed lead to increased educational achievement in children.

Evidence That Familial Supports Raise Educational Achievement

I have been examining relationships among education policy, the economy, and achievement in urban schools. First, I critiqued education policy for its lack of attention to urban poverty, which, I argued, is maintained by policies and decisions made at the federal and metropolitan levels. I provided evidence of some of the egregious consequences of federal and regional policies and practices for urban families, neighborhoods, students, and schools. In particular, I demonstrated that child poverty creates obstacles to full development and educational achievement, especially when low-income minority children attend low-resourced schools—which most do. In this section I provide indirect and direct research evidence that increased family supports such as financial resources and less segregated neighborhoods raise educational achievement.

Indirect evidence is present in a longitudinal study completed in 2003 that found that improving family income reduces the negative (aggressive) social behavior of children, which in turn is likely to lead to better school behavior and performance. For eight years, researchers studied a representative population sample of 1,420 children ages nine to thirteen in rural North Carolina. A quarter of the children were from a Cherokee reservation. Psychological tests were given at the start of the study and repeated each year (Costello, Compton, Keeler, & Angold, 2003; O'Connor, 2003).

When the study began, 68 percent of the children were living below the official poverty line. On average, the poorer children engaged in more vandalism, steal-

ing, bullying, stubbornness, and outbursts of anger than those who were not poor. But halfway through the study, a local casino began distributing a percentage of its profits to tribal families. Given to each tribal member over eighteen and put in a trust fund for younger members, the payment increased slightly each year, reaching about $6,000 per person for the year 2001. Psychiatric tests administered by researchers for the four years that the funds were being distributed demonstrated that the negative behaviors of children in families who were no longer poor dropped to the same levels found among children whose families had never been poor (decreasing by 40%). Parents who moved out of poverty reported having more time to spend with their children, and researchers identified better parenting behavior. Researchers also identified the psychological benefits of not being poor as important to both parents and children. Poverty puts stress on families, which can increase the likelihood of children developing behavioral problems. One parent in the study told researchers that "the jobs [produced by the casino] give people the chance to pull themselves up by their bootstraps and get out of poverty. That carries over into less juvenile crime, less domestic violence, and an overall better living experience for families" (O'Connor, 2003, p. 2).

Other research demonstrates that urban low-income parents are also able to practice more effective parenting strategies when some of the stress of poverty is eased by a higher income. And the reduction in stress in turn may positively affect the behavior and achievement of low-income children (see information below; also Jackson, Brooks-Gunn, Huang, & Glassman, 2000; Jeremiah, 2003; Seitz, Rosenbaum, & Apfel, 1985).

Direct evidence that income supports improved educational achievement is also available. In March 2001, the Manpower Demonstration Research Corporation (MDRC) published a synthesis of research on how welfare and work policies affect the children of single mothers (Morris, Huston, Duncan, Crosby, & Bos, 2001). This synthesis reviewed data from evaluations of five programs that provided income supplements to poverty-wage workers (Florida's Family Transition Program, the Minnesota Family Investment Program, the National Evaluation of Welfare-to-Work Strategies, Milwaukee's New Hope for Families and Children Program, and the Self-Sufficiency Project). These programs offered supports of differing kinds to poverty-wage workers—income supplements, earnings disregards (rules that allow working welfare recipients to keep more of their income when they go to work), subsidized health care, employment services, counseling, supervised afterschool activities for children and youth, and informal get-togethers with project staff.

MDRC's review of the studies found that even relatively small income supplements to working parents (amounting to about $4,000 per year) improved children's elementary school achievement by about 10 to 15 percent of the average variation in the control groups. These improvements were seen on test scores as well as on ratings by parents and/or teachers. The earning supplements had "consistently positive impacts on children's [school] achievement" (Morris et al., 2001, p. 63). The positive effects were small, but were statistically significant.

Longitudinal studies have found that the achievement and behavior problems of young children can have important implications for their well-being in adolescence and adulthood (Caspi, Wright, Moffit, & Silva, 1998; Masten & Coatsworth, 1995). Moreover, even small differences between children in school achievement early on can translate into larger differences later (Entwistle & Alexander, 1997). Therefore, as the authors of the research synthesis state, "a program's effects on children, even if the effects are small, may continue to have implications over the course of their lives" (Caspi et al., 1998, p. 25).

The earning supplements provided by four of these programs did not, however, bring the families above the poverty level. The improvements in children's school achievement and behavior from even these relatively meager cash supplements for working families suggest that if we were to increase family resources substantially, we could probably improve educational and social outcomes for children substantially.

Indeed, one program that did provide an earning supplement that brought the families above poverty level showed particularly impressive results for children's behavior and achievement. New Hope for Families and Children was run between 1994 and 1998 in two inner-city areas in Milwaukee. Candidates had to live in one of two targeted areas, be eighteen or older, be willing and able to work at least thirty hours per week, and have a household income at or below 150 percent of the federal poverty level (Huston et al., 2001). Almost 90 percent of the adults in the sample were single or separated mothers with children when they entered the study, and 80 percent were receiving public assistance. The program was conceived by a

nonprofit community-based organization and provided several benefits: the earnings supplement, subsidized health insurance, and subsidized child care. The program offered help in obtaining a job and provided a community-service job for up to one year for those not able to find work elsewhere, the advice and support of project staff were made available. The annual cost of providing these benefits was $5,300 per family.

New Hope was evaluated at two-year and five-year intervals using a random assignment research design. After conducting outreach in the communities to identify eligible people, the study enrolled over 1,300 low-income adults. Half the applicants were randomly assigned to a program group that received New Hope's benefits, and the other half were randomly assigned to a control group that was not eligible for the benefits.

Both evaluations showed positive results (Bos, Huston, Duncan, Brock, & McLoyd, 1996; Huston et al., 2001). Financial supplements in the New Hope program did reduce the number of families in poverty, but both program and control groups reported similar levels of hardship, such as food insecurity and financial insufficiency. Yet the program had positive effects on parents' well-being and coping skills. As Huston et al. (2003) explain:

> Parents in the New Hope group were more aware of available "helping" resources in the community, such as where to find assistance with energy costs or housing problems. More of them also knew about the [Earned Income Tax Credit] and its support, an important source of support for low-income workers. Ethnographic data suggest that a significant number of families intentionally used the Earned Income Tax Credits as a savings plan for making major purchases, reducing debt, and stabilizing rent and other payments. Parents in New Hope also reported better physical health and fewer symptoms associated with depression than did parents in the control group. At the two-year point, New Hope parents reported reduced stress, increased feelings of social support, and increased time pressure. The ethnographic study found that many parents had children with disabilities or behavioral difficulties; New Hope helped the parents achieve a difficult balance among work, services, and parenting. . . . The New Hope parents did report fewer problems controlling their children, and parents of adolescents reported more effective management (better control and less need for punishment). (p. 9)

New Hope improved children's school performance. "At both the two-year and the five-year points, children in the program performed better than control group children on several measures of academic achievement, particularly on reading and literacy tests. After five years, they scored higher on a standardized test of reading skills and their parents reported that they got higher grades in reading skills" (Huston et al., 2001, p. 13). These effects were slightly more pronounced for boys than for girls. Compared with their control group counterparts, boys in New Hope also received higher ratings of academic performance from their teachers and were more likely to expect to attend college at both the two-year and the five-year assessments. "New Hope adolescents reported more engagement with schools, feelings of efficacy, and expectations to finish college than did their control group counterparts" (pp. 13–14). New Hope's effects are consistent with the results of other programs that have improved children's outcomes by providing wage supplements and subsidized child care (Michalopoulos et al., 2002; Morris et al., 2001).

Indeed, the New Hope findings are in line with the increased educational achievement of students that has been identified in large-scale programs that assist low-income minority families by helping them move from inner-city neighborhoods to more affluent and/or less segregated metropolitan areas. The first of these "mobility programs" was the Gautreaux program in the Chicago metropolitan area.

As a result of a victorious lawsuit charging the Chicago Housing Authority with segregation in public housing, the court ordered the housing authority to move families who wanted to live in less segregated areas of the city and suburbs. The Gautreaux program moved over 7,000 families to higher-income areas of the Chicago metropolitan region between 1976 and 1998 (Rubinowitz & Rosenbaum, 2002). Although at first a disproportionate number of the children who moved were placed in classes for the learning disabled by their suburban schools, they ultimately were significantly more likely than their urban counterparts to be in college-bound tracks, in four-year colleges, and were subsequently more likely to be employed in jobs with higher pay and with benefits than children who stayed in the city (Rubinowitz & Rosenbaum, 2002).

The success of the Gautreaux program led to more than fifty other mobility programs, including the Moving To Opportunity program (MTO) begun by the U.S. Department of Housing and Urban Development (HUD) in 1994. The Housing and Community Development Act of 1992 authorized HUD to "assist very low-income families with children who reside in public housing or housing receiving project-based assistance under Section 8 of the Housing and Community Development Act of 1937 to move out of areas with high concentrations of persons living in poverty (40% or more) to areas with low concentrations of such persons (less than 10% in poverty)" (Goering & Feins, 2003, p. 6). Moving To Opportunity projects were carried out in five cities: Baltimore, Boston, Chicago, Los Angeles, and New York. Congress stipulated that HUD conduct evaluations of the program to determine its effects (Goering & Feins, 2003).

Overall, roughly 5,300 families volunteered to move within the metropolitan area of the city in which they lived. In total, 4,608 families were eligible. They were divided into three groups: the MTO "treatment" or experimental group, which received Section 8 certificates or vouchers that could only be used in areas where 10 percent or less of the residents lived below official poverty levels; they also received counseling assistance in finding private rental units. A second group was given Section 8 certificates with no special restrictions on where they were to move, and no counseling (Section 8–only group). An in-place control group continued to receive housing project assistance in the inner-city neighborhoods where they lived. The families in all three groups of the MTO program tended to be young single mothers (under age 35), African American, with a median income of $8,200. Most stated that their main reason for wanting to move was fear of gangs and violence in the neighborhoods in which they lived.

Social scientists conducted research at all five sites, using HUD data, baseline surveys, follow-up surveys of families, qualitative interviews, and data on juvenile crime, labor-market outcomes, and school performance. Among their findings are the following.

One to three years after the families in the experimental group moved, they lived in significantly more affluent and more racially mixed communities than families in the other two groups. In addition, those who were in the experimental group had median incomes that were 73 percent higher than the median incomes for the control group and 53 percent higher than the Section 8–only group. In 1997, three years after the program began, the MTO experimental group families in all five metropolitan areas lived in less-segregated neighborhoods than either of the other two groups.

Studies of adults in the experimental groups in New York and Boston reported significantly better health and emotional well-being than the Section

8–only and control groups in those cities. Mothers in both the experimental groups were much less likely to report being depressed or stressed. The parents provided more structure for their children's activities and used less restrictive parenting styles. By the third year, 10 percent fewer of the experimental group in New York City were receiving welfare. In Boston, public assistance for MTO families dropped by half, and employment in all MTO sites increased from 27 percent at the beginning of the program to 43 percent three years later. Employment in Boston increased by more than one-half.

The outcomes for children in these experimental groups were also encouraging. They attended schools that had higher pass rates, more affluent student bodies, and more resources than the schools attended by control group children. Ludwig, Duncan, and Ladd (2003) hypothesize that the peer groups in the new schools had more positive attitudes toward school than in the inner city, and this may also have contributed to good outcomes for the children.

Ludwig, Duncan, and Ladd report that young children in the experimental and Section 8–only groups "achieved higher test scores than the controls, and experienced fewer arrests for violent criminal behavior" (2003, p. 164). The authors report in some detail the assessments in Baltimore, and state that they are "largely consistent with evidence from the other MTO sites" (p. 163). Young children in the experimental and Section 8–only groups had Comprehensive Test of Basic Skills (CTBS) reading scores that were on average six to seven percentage points higher than those in the control group (i.e., in low-income urban schools). "This large effect is equal to around one-quarter of the control group mean of 25 percentile points and one-quarter of a standard deviation in the national CTBS math distribution" (p. 165). Children in the experimental group also raised their CTBS math scores about the same amount, and their pass rates on the Maryland Functional Tests' (MFT) reading test were almost double those in the inner-city schools.

High school students in the Baltimore experimental group had a more difficult transition. In the first three years of MTO, they had higher rates of grade retention, disciplinary action, and school dropout rates than the children of families in the other two groups. The authors suggest that these differences may be due to the enforcement of higher behavioral and/or educational standards in more affluent schools (Ludwig et al., 2003).

However, teens who moved from high- to low-poverty neighborhoods were arrested less often than teens in the other groups. For example, 2.7 percent of control group adolescents were arrested during an average three-month period, compared with only 1.4 percent of teens in the experimental group during the same period. Furthermore, there was a 50 percent reduction in the proportion of juveniles in the experimental group who were arrested for violent offenses. For example, in a given quarter, 3 percent of adolescents in the control group were arrested for violent crimes, compared with only 1.4 percent among the experimental group (Ludwig et al., 2003).

Research in the Boston MTO found significantly fewer behavioral and mental health problems among boys in both the experimental and Section 8-only groups, and experimental-group children were less likely to be injured or to experience asthma attacks. Among children with asthma, the number of attacks requiring medical attention fell significantly (Goering & Feins, 2003). Additionally, the children in the experimental group in Boston were less likely to engage in antisocial behavior (Ludwig et al., 2003).

In sum, these results are in general agreement with evaluations of other mobility programs, which have generally led to "substantial improvements in . . . neighborhood conditions, physical and mental health, safety, housing conditions, adult labor-market outcomes (although the findings here are mixed)" (Johnson, Ladd, & Ludwig, 2002, p. 185) and improvements in the children's behavior and educational outcomes of families who moved.

The success of even small family supports and of a move to places of increased opportunity suggests that we should provide a financial and opportunity base for urban families. This in itself will lay the foundation for fuller child development and educational achievement.

A New Education Policy Paradigm

I have outlined a number of federal and regional policies and practices that undermine urban school quality and potential by maintaining large poverty populations in urban neighborhoods. I have also provided evidence that this poverty works against the development and achievement of urban students. Importantly, however, we also see that even modest financial and social supports for poor families enable the children to achieve at higher levels in school. This suggests that policies to counter the devastating effects of macroeconomic and regional mandates and practices should "count" as policies we call on to create equity and quality in urban districts and schools.

As education policymakers and practitioners, we can acknowledge and act on the power of urban poverty, low-wage work, and housing segregation to dwarf most curricular, pedagogical, and other educational reforms. The effects of macroeconomic policies continually trump the effects of education policies.

To remove economic barriers to school quality and consequence, we can legislate a significantly higher living wage; we can create jobs in cities that offer career ladders and prepare low-income residents to fill them. And, like a number of European countries, we can tax wealthy families and corporations to pay for these and other investments. We should enforce federal antidiscrimination measures to integrate segregated housing and create public transit routes so low-income urban residents without cars are not denied access to jobs in the suburbs. Policies like these would create a social foundation on which high-quality schooling would rest. As has been the case in affluent suburbs, economic access creates the financial and political conditions in families and communities for educational commitment and reward.

In this new paradigm, education policies for which we press would take on the larger issues: Education funding reform would include the companion need for financing neighborhood jobs and decent wages. New small schools would be created as an important part of coordinated efforts at neighborhood revitalization for low-income residents. Vocational offerings in high school would link to living-wage campaigns and employers who support them. College graduation would be understood as a continuation of government's financial responsibility for public education. And lawsuits to racially integrate districts would acknowledge housing segregation as fundamental and target legal challenges accordingly.

Policies that set the standards schools must meet would identify the money, materials, teachers, courses, and neighborhood needs that must be filled in order to provide opportunities to learn at high levels. Educational accountability would be conceived as a public undertaking, centrally involving families, communities, and students, in consultation with district and government officials.

In this approach to urban school reform, "policy alignment" would not refer to the fit between education mandates issued by various levels of government and bureaucracy. The fit we would seek is between neighborhood, family, and student needs and the potential of education policies to contribute to their fulfillment.

However, economic strength and political leverage is not all that is required to transform urban education. Good schools require not only good neighborhoods, but—as equity-seeking educational reforms have promised—also the detracking of minority and working-class youth, a culture responsive to students, and assistance to teachers in their struggle to surmount the wall of resignation and defiance that separates many students from the educational enterprise.

A new paradigm of education policy is possible—one that promotes equity-seeking school change and that includes strategies to create conditions that will allow the educational improvements to take root, grow, and bear fruit in students' lives.

Notes

1. The 1958 National Defense Education Act (NDEA) funded and promoted curriculum materials, primarily in science, math, and foreign languages (e.g., the "New Math"), and some of these probably found their way into city districts and classrooms. But the NDEA was aimed at increasing the security and technological prowess of the United States, not at improving urban schools.

2. Graduation rates in large urban high schools are lower than is commonly believed. Jay P. Greene, senior fellow at the Manhattan Institute for Policy Research, calculated graduation rates in all states and large cities for major racial groups. For this calculation he first identified the eighth-grade public school enrollment for each jurisdiction and for each subgroup from the 1993 fall semester, adjusting for student movement into or out of an area. He then obtained counts of the number of regular high school diplomas awarded in the spring of 1998 when the eighth graders should have been graduating. (In calculating the 1998 graduation rate, he did not include later GED or other alternative diplomas, as the federal government does.) He found that the national graduation rate for the class of 1998 was 71 percent. For White students the rate was 78 percent, for African American students it was 56 percent, and for Latinos, 54 percent. In fifteen of forty-five large (mostly urban) districts for which there were data, fewer than 50 percent of African American students graduated; and in twenty-one of thirty-six large, mostly urban districts for which there were data, fewer than 50 percent of Latino students graduated (Greene, 2001, pp. 1–5).

References

Anyon, J. (1979). Ideology and U.S. history textbooks. *Harvard Educational Review, 49,* 361–386.

Anyon, J. (1980). Social class and the hidden curriculum of work. *Journal of Education, 162,* 7–92.

Anyon, J. (1981). Social class and school knowledge. *Curriculum Inquiry, 11,* 3–42.

Anyon, J. (1995). Race, social class, and educational reform in an inner city school. *Teachers College Record, 97,* 69–94.

Anyon, J. (1997). *Ghetto schooling: A political economy of urban educational reform.* New York: Teachers College Press.

Anyon, J. (in press). *Radical possibilities: Public policy, urban education, and a new social movement.* New York: Routledge.

Ayres, L. (1909). *Laggards in our schools: A study of retardation and elimination in city school systems.* New York: Russell Sage.

Bernstein, J., Brocht, C., & Spade-Aguilar, M. (2000). *How much is enough? Basic family budgets for working families.* Washington, DC: Economic Policy Institute.

Bolger, K., & Patterson, C. (1995). Psychosocial adjustment among children experiencing persistent and intermittent family economic hardship. *Child Development, 66,* 1107–1129.

Bradley, R. (1984). One hundred, seventy-four children: A study of the relation between the home environment and early cognitive development in the first 5 years. In A. Gottfried (Ed.), *The home environment and early cognitive development* (pp. 5–56). Orlando, FL: Academic Press.

Brooks-Gunn, J., Duncan, G., Leventhal, T., & Aber, L. (1997). Lessons learned and future directions for research on the neighborhoods in which children live. In J. Brooks-Gunn, G. Duncan, & L. Aber (Eds.), *Neighborhood poverty, volume 1: Contexts and consequences for children* (pp. 279–298). New York: Russell Sage.

Bos, J., Huston, A. C., Duncan, G .J., Brock, T., & McLoyd, V. (1996). *New hope for people with low incomes: Two-year results of a program to reduce poverty and reform welfare.* New York: Manpower Demonstration Research Corporation.

Caspi, A., Wright, B., Moffit, E., & Silva, T. (1998). Early failure in the labor market: Childhood and adolescent predictors of unemployment in the transition to adulthood. *American Sociological Review, 63,* 424–451.

Cauthen, N., & Lu, H. (2001, August). *Living on the edge: Employment alone is not enough for America's low-income children and families* (Research Brief No. 1, Mailman School of Public Health, National Center for Children in Poverty). New York: Columbia University.

Citizens for Tax Justice. (2002). *Surge in corporate tax welfare drives corporate tax payments down to near record low.* Washington, DC: Author.

Citro, C., & Michael, R. (Eds.). (1995). *Measuring poverty: A new approach.* Washington, DC: National Academy Press.

Conley, D. (2003). *Who governs our schools? Changing roles and responsibilities.* New York: Teachers College Press.

Costello, J., Compton, S., Keeler, G., & Angold, A. (2003). Relationships between poverty and psychopathology: A natural experiment. *Journal of the American Medical Association, 290,* 2023–2029.

Cross, C. (2004). *Political education: National policy comes of age.* New York: Teachers College Press.

Dillon, S. (2003, April 30). Report finds number of black children in deep poverty rising. *New York Times,* p. 18A.

Dreier, P., Mollenkopf, J., & Swanstrom, T. (2001). *Place matters: Metropolitics for the 21st century.* Lawrence: University Press of Kansas.

Duncan, G., & Brooks-Gunn, J. (Eds.). (1997). *Consequences of growing up poor.* New York: Russell Sage.

Duncan, G., Brooks-Gunn, J., & Klebanov, P. (1994). Economic deprivation and early childhood development. *Child Development, 65,* 296–318.

Economic Policy Institute. (2002). *Economic snapshots.* Washington, DC: Author.

Economic Policy Institute. (2004). *EPI issue guide: Minimum wage.* Washington, DC: Author.

Education Trust. (2001). *The funding gap: Low-income and minority students receive fewer dollars.* Washington, DC: Author.

Entwistle, D., & Alexander, K. (1997). *Children, schools, and inequality.* Boulder, CO: West-view Press.

Fine, M. (2001, May). *Comparative analysis of the organization of high schools 1996–97, NYC Board of Education.* Findings presented at the Spencer Conference, New York. Document available at www.nysed.gov.80/emsc/docs4-99NYStrategy.ppt.3.

Galbraith, J. (1998). *Created unequal: The crisis in American pay.* New York: Free Press.

Goering, J., & Feins, J. (Eds.). (2003). *Choosing a better life? Evaluating the Moving To Opportunity social experiment.* Washington, DC: Urban Institute Press.

Greene, J. (2001). *High school graduation rates in the United States.* Washington, DC: Black Alliance for Educational Options and the Manhattan Institute.

Harrington, M. (1963). *The other America: Poverty in the United States.* Baltimore: Penguin.

Houser, R. M., Brown, B. V., & Prosser, W. R. (1998). *Indicators of children's well-being.* New York: Russell Sage.

Hout, M. (1988). More universalism, less structural mobility: The American occupational structure in the 1980s. *American Journal of Sociology, 93,* 1358–1400.

Huston, A. C., Duncan, G. J., Granger, R., Bos, J., McLoyd, V. C., Mistry, R., Crosby, D. A., Gibson, C., Magnuson, K., Romich, J., & Ventura, A. (2001). Work-based anti-poverty programs for parents can enhance the school performance and social behavior of children. *Child Development, 72,* 318–336.

Huston, A. C., Miller, C., Richburg-Hayes, L., Duncan, G. J., Eldred, C. A., Weisner, T. S., Lowe, E., McLoyd, V. C., Crosby, D. A., Ripke, M. N., & Redcross, C. (2003). *Summary report, New Hope for families and children: Five-year results of a program to reduce poverty and reform welfare.* New York: Manpower Demonstration Research Corporation.

Jackson, A., Brooks-Gunn, J., Huang, C., & Glassman, M. (2000) Single mothers in low-wage jobs: Financial strain, parenting, and preschoolers' outcomes. *Child Development 71,* 1409–1423.

Jencks, C., & Phillips, M. (1998) *The Black/White test score gap.* Washington, DC: Brookings Institution Press.

Jeremiah, L. (2003). *Family support programs and academic achievement: Lessons for Seattle.* Unpublished manuscript. Available online at http://www.evans.washington.edu/research/psclinic/pdf/02-03dp/Jeremiahdp.pdf.

Johnson, M., Ladd, H., & Ludwig, J. (2002). The benefits and costs of residential mobility programs. *Housing Studies 17,* 125–138.

Kingsley, T., & Petit, K. (2003). *Concentrated poverty? A change in course.* Neighborhood change in urban America series. Washington, DC: Urban Institute.

Klerman, L. (1991; 2003 Reprint edition). The health of poor children: Problems and programs. In A. C. Huston (Ed.), *Children and poverty: Child development and public policy* (pp. 136–157). New York: Cambridge University Press.

Korenman, S., & Miller, J. (1997). Effects of long-term poverty on physical health of children in the national longitudinal survey of youth. In G. Duncan & J. Brooks-Gunn (Eds.), *Consequences of growing up poor* (pp. 70–99). New York: Russell Sage.

Lafer, G. (2002). *The job training charade.* Ithaca, NY: Cornell University Press.

Lee, V., & Burkham, D. (2002). *Inequality at the starting gate: Social background and achievement at kindergarten entry.* Washington, DC: Economic Policy Institute.

Lu, H. (2003). *Low-income children in the United States.* New York: Columbia University, Mailman School of Public Health.

Ludwig, J., Duncan, G., & Ladd, H. (2003). The effects of moving to opportunity on children and parents in Baltimore. In J. Goering & J. Feins (Eds.), *Choosing a better life?* (pp. 153–177). Washington, DC: Urban Institute Press.

Masten, A., & Coatsworth, D. (1995). The structure and coherence of competence from childhood through adolescence. *Child Development, 66,* 1635–1659.

McLoyd, V. (1998). Socioeconomic disadvantage and child development. *American Psychologist, 53,* 185–204.

McLoyd, V., & Jartayne, T. (1994). Unemployment and work interruption among African-American single mothers: Effects on parenting and adolescent socioemotional functioning. *Child Development, 65,* 562–589.

Miao, J., & Haney, W. (2004). High school graduation rates: Alternative methods and implications. *Education Policy Analysis Archives, 12*(55). Available online at http://epaa.asu.edu/epaa/v12n55.

Michaloupolos, C., Tattri, D., Miller, C., Robins, P. K., Morris, P., Gyarmati, D., Redcross, C., Foley, K., & Ford, R. (2002). *Making work pay: Final report on the self-sufficiency project for long-term welfare recipients.* New York: Manpower Demonstration Research Corporation.

Mishel, L., Bernstein, J., & Boushey, H. (2003). *The state of working America: 2002/2003.* Ithaca, NY: Cornell University Press.

Mishel, L., Bernstein, J., & Schmitt, J. (2001). *The state of working America: 2000/2001.* Ithaca, NY: Cornell University Press.

Morris, P., Huston, A.C., Duncan, G.J., Crosby, D., & Bos, J. (2001). *How welfare and work policies affect children: A synthesis of research.* Washington, DC: Manpower Demonstration Research Corporation.

O'Connor, A. (2003, October 21). Rise in income improves children's behavior. *New York Times,* p. F5.

Odden, A., & Picus, L. (1992). *School finance: A policy perspective.* New York: McGraw-Hill.

Orfield, M. (2002). *American metropolitics: The new suburban reality.* Washington, DC: Brookings Institute.

Phillips, K. (2002). *Wealth and democracy: A political history of the American rich.* New York: Broadway Books.

Phillips, M., Brooks-Gunn, J., Duncan, G., Klevanov, P., & Crane, J. (1998). Family background, parenting practices, and the Black/White test score gap. In C. Jencks & M. Phillips (Eds.), *The Black/White test score gap* (pp. 103–145). Washington, DC: Brookings Institution Press.

Phillips, M., Crouse, J., & Ralph, J. (1998). Does the Black/White test score gap widen after children enter school? In C. Jencks & M. Phillips (Eds.), *The Black/White test score gap* (pp. 229–272). Washington, DC: Brookings Institution Press.

Ravitch, D. (2000). *The great school wars: A history of the New York City public schools.* Baltimore: Johns Hopkins University Press.

Rubinowitz, L., & Rosenbaum, J. (2002). *Crossing the class and color line: From public housing to White suburbia.* Chicago: University of Chicago Press.

Rusk, D. (1999). *Inside game/outside game: Winning strategies for saving urban America.* Washington, DC: Brookings Institution.

Sampson, R., Morenoff, J., & Gannon-Rowley, T. (2002). Assessing "neighborhood effects:" Social processes and new directions in research. *Annual Review of Sociology, 28,* 443–478.

Seitz, V., Rosenbaum L., & Apfel, N. (1985). Effects of family support intervention: A ten-year follow-up. *Child Development 56,* 376–391.

Short, K., Iceland, J., & Garner, T. (1999). *Experimental poverty measures: 1998.* Washington, DC: U.S. Census Bureau.

Smith, J., Brooks-Gunn, J., and Klebanov, P. (1997). Consequences of living in poverty for young children's cognitive and verbal ability and early school achievement. In G. Duncan & J. Brooks-Gunn (Eds.), *Consequencs of growing up poor* (pp. 132–189). New York: Russell Sage Foundation.

Stein, S. (2004). *The culture of educational policy.* New York: Teachers College Press.

Stipic, D., & Ryan, R. (1997). Economically disadvantaged preschoolers: Ready to learn but further to go. *Developmental Psychology, 33,* 711–723.

Sugland, B., Zaslow, M., & Brooks-Gunn, J. (1995). The early childhood HOME inventory and HOME short form in differing socio-cultural groups: Are there differences in underlying structure, internal consistency of subcases, and patterns of prediction? *Journal of Family Issues, 16,* 632–663.

Tyack, D. (1974). *The one best system: A history of American urban education.* Cambridge, MA: Harvard University Press.

White, K. (1982). The relationship between socio-economic status and academic achievement. *Psychological Bulletin, 91,* 46–81.

Wrigley, J. (1982). *Class politics and public schools: Chicago 1900–1950.* New Brunswick, NJ: Rutgers University Press.

I would like to thank my colleague Tony Picciano for his thoughts.

3 | The History of Education

Our discussion of the history of education in the United States begins with the introduction of schooling in colonial America when Europeans settled in the colonies and began to devise systematic and deliberate forms of education for their children. Other forms of education existed in North America prior to European settlement. Native Americans educated their children within the structure of their communities and acculturated them into the rituals, obligations, and roles necessary for the maintenance and continuity of community life. Although such forms of education were extremely important, the development of U.S. schooling was heavily influenced by the European colonists as they adapted to life in North America.

There are many interpretations as to why education was so important to the early settlers and why it continues to be an important issue in contemporary society. Historians, such as Bernard Bailyn (1960), have attributed the use of the school to the failure of particular institutions such as the family, church, and community to provide the necessary tools demanded by the conditions of the new emerging society. Historian Merle Curti (1959/1971) attributed the use of formal schooling to the interests of the colonists in protecting freedoms such as thought, religion, and press—freedoms necessary for the maintenance of a democratic society. Regardless of the motives and intentions, it is important to look at the early versions of schools in order to understand how the present-day school evolved. What will become increasingly apparent are three ideas:

1. From its very inception, the school was charged with assuming roles that once were the province of family, church, and community.
2. The school continues to serve as a focal point in larger issues of societal needs.
3. There is little consensus on the motives for school reforms.

Old World and New World Education: The Colonial Era

Our discussion of the history of U.S. education begins with the settlers who brought their ideas about education to the New World. In general, the society of the Old World was highly stratified and the view most Europeans held was that only the sons of the rich required an education since they would be the future ruling class. Thus, early affluent settlers such as planters and townsmen, particularly in the southern colonies, hired tutors for their sons and sent their sons back to England, if they could afford it, for their university educations.

It is interesting to note, however, that many of the wealthy colonists' sons did remain in the United States for their higher education, since nine institutions of higher learning were founded prior to the American Revolution. These were Harvard University (1636), College of William and Mary (1693), Yale University (1701), University of Pennsylvania (1740), Princeton University (1746), Columbia University (1754), Brown University (1764), Rutgers University (1766), and Dartmouth College (1769). However, the colleges themselves were not at all revolutionary. They taught most of the same subjects found at Oxford or Cambridge, and Greek and Latin were required subjects.

What becomes increasingly apparent in the history of U.S. education is that even before education began to formalize and acquire certain specific patterns, there emerged distinctly different themes regarding the purpose of education. For example, as just noted, the upper-class planter aristocracy and wealthy merchants saw education as a means of perpetuating the ruling class. Religious, utilitarian, and civic motives also emerged over time.

The religious impetus to formalize instruction can best be exemplified by the Puritans in New England who, early in 1642 and 1647, passed school laws commonly referred to as the *Old Deluder Laws.* The first law chastised parents for not attending to their children's "ability to read and understand the principles of religion and capital laws of this country" and fined them for their children's "wanton" and "immodest" behavior. Thus, the first law pointed to a problem among the young, to which the parents failed to attend.

The second law was far more specific regarding formalized schooling. To keep the "old deluder" Satan away, the Massachusetts School Law of 1647 provided that every town that had "50 household" would appoint one person to teach all children, regardless of gender, to read and write. Furthermore, the town was required to pay the wages of the teacher. Towns that numbered "100 families or household" had to set up a grammar school (equivalent to a secondary school today) to prepare students for university studies. Towns that failed to comply were subject to fines. Thus, early in the nation's history, the theme of literacy as a means of teaching a Christian life was articulated.

The Old Deluder Law was not very popular throughout New England. Often, towns simply neglected to provide the education for their youth, as dictated by law. However, it remains a landmark in the history of U.S. education, for it established a precedent for public responsibility for education.

The theme of utilitarianism as the purpose of education can best be seen through an examination of the ideas of Benjamin Franklin, who, in 1749, published "Proposals Related to the Education of Youth in Pennsylvania." Franklin called for an education for youth based on secular and utilitarian courses of study rather than on the traditional studies of religion and classics. However, as Bailyn (1960) pointed out, Franklin did not define education along narrowly defined utilitarian principles. Rather, Franklin believed that "the purpose of schooling was to provide in systematic form what he had extemporized, haphazardly feeling his way" (p. 35). Thus, Franklin believed that students should pursue a course of study that would allow them mastery of process rather than rote learning. Reading, writing, public speaking, and art as a means of understanding creative expression would be integral components of the curriculum.

Utilitarian components of the curriculum would be practical aspects of mathematics, such as accounting and natural history (biology). Additionally, students would study history, geography, and political studies. Languages such as Latin and Greek would be available to students who wished to enter the ministry. Others, who sought commerce and trade as careers, might study more modern languages such as French, Italian, German, and Spanish.

Perhaps because of his own life experience, Benjamin Franklin fervently believed in the ability of people to better themselves. His faith in self-improvement through education and in an education that reflected practical concerns was not explored again until the nineteenth century. Franklin's proposal for an academy became the prototype for private secondary education in the United States. It was not until the second half of the nineteenth century, however, that public support for Franklin's ideas became a reality.

The civic motive for education is best illustrated through the ideas of the prominent American statesman, Thomas Jefferson, who fervently believed that the best safeguard for democracy was a literate population. It was Jefferson who proposed to the Virginia Legislature in 1779, a "Bill for the More General Diffusion of Knowledge," which would provide free education to *all* children for the first three years of elementary school. Jefferson, a product of enlightenment thinking, was optimistic enough to think that if citizens possessed enough education to read newspapers and thus inform themselves of pressing public issues, they would make intelligent, informed decisions at the polls.

Jefferson's bill also provided for a limited meritocracy within the educational structure. After the initial three years of reading, writing, and "common arithmetic," all students could advance to 1 of 20 grammar schools within the state of Virginia, contingent on their payment of tuition. However, Jefferson proposed that each elementary school send one scholarship student to a grammar school. After two to three years of rigorous, classical studies (Latin, Greek, English grammar, geography, mathematics), the most promising scholarship student from among this group of 20 students would be selected for another funded four years of study, while the remaining group would be dismissed.

Finally, each grammar school would have the task of selecting 10 of its best students who would receive three-year scholarships to the College of William and Mary. Thus, Jefferson set forth in his bill a proposal for an aristocracy of talent, which would be nurtured and supported through a statewide educational structure. Unfortunately, Jefferson was ahead of his time; the majority of the state legislators agreed that the state should not be involved in educating its inhabitants and that, in any event, Jefferson's proposal required funds far beyond those possessed by the state of Virginia at that time.

The schools that were established in the United States during the colonial period varied greatly in the quality of instruction. In Puritan New England, often an elderly housewife (usually a widow) heard lessons, which consisted of recitations. These schools became known as *dame schools*. Elementary education, in the New England *town school*, established by the Old Deluder Law, consisted of such basic subjects as reading, writing, and religion. Students were taught by learning the alphabet: letters first, syllables and words next, and then sentences. There were few supplies and textbooks, except for the famous *New England Primer*. This book, sometimes referred to as the "Little Bible of New England," combined the teaching of reading with religious education, obedience, and citizenship. For example, in teaching the first letter of the alphabet, children would be treated to an illustration of Adam and Eve, the latter holding an apple given to her by a serpent, wrapped around a tree that was separating the couple, with the accompanying words: "A: In Adam's Fall/We Sinned, All." This book, which appeared about 1690, sold more than 3,000,000 copies during the 1700s (Gutek, 1991).

Students were taught content mastery through memorization. They were taught writing skills by copying directly from the printed page or by taking dictation from the schoolmaster. Classes were ungraded; all students were housed in the same room and taught by a teacher who might have been either an indentured servant, a divinity student, or a village preacher. Strict disciplinary methods prevailed, which might be considered overly harsh by today's standards, perhaps influenced by the Puritan predilection to the "authoritarian temperament" of leadership (Button & Provenzano, 1989).

Secondary education, as it evolved in New England, was not coeducational, as was the elementary school; rather, it was for the sons of the elite who were usually tutored at home rather than receiving their primary schooling at the local town school. This school was called the *Latin Grammar School,* as the curriculum emphasized the teaching of Latin and Greek—languages of the educated elite in Europe. Ultimately, it served as a sorting device through which the newly formed Puritan elite in the United States could reproduce itself. Male students entered the Latin Grammar School at eight years of age and studied there for another eight years. They read classical texts, such as Cicero and Caesar in Latin, and Homer and Hesiod in Greek. Clearly, the emphasis here was not on a utilitarian education as later articulated by Franklin; rather, students were being "taught by example" from classical literature, which hopefully would enable them to function effectively as leaders in the Puritan oligarchy.

Education in the middle colonies was far more diverse than in Puritan New England, as the schools that emerged there reflected the vast religious and cultural differences of the region. Generally, education was the province of the colonies' numerous religious denominations, such as Dutch Reformed, Quaker, Roman Catholic, and Jewish. New York was dominated by the Dutch Reformed Church, which, like the Puritans, espoused the importance of literate congregations. When the English took over New York, they established charity schools, which were controlled by the Anglican Church. These schools emphasized reading, writing, arithmetic, catechism, and religion. In Pennsylvania, where English Quakers dominated the political and economic life of the colony, they also controlled education. However, in keeping with their humane attitude toward human life, the Quakers rejected the harsh treatment of children prevalent in the other colonies and paid more attention to individual children as they mastered reading, writing, arithmetic, and religion (Gutek, 1991).

Education in the South was largely confined to the upper class and took place at home on the plantation, since the vastness of these economic units made the construction of formal schools virtually impossible. Education was provided by tutors who might have been indentured servants, divinity students, impoverished second sons of European aristocrats, or convicts. Indeed, before the American Revolution, one observer reported that "two-thirds of the schoolmasters in Maryland were either indentured servants or convicts" (Wright, 1957, p. 101).

Both male and female children were educated on an aristocratic model: Classical studies were emphasized for boys, whereas dancing and music lessons were emphasized for girls. Although some southern women may have shared their brothers' tutors, learning to master the social graces took precedence over Caesar in aristocratic southern households. Occasionally, boys were sent away to school, most likely to England. Plantation management was learned by both sexes according to gender-specific roles. Girls were expected to master the domestic side of plantation management from their mothers, while boys learned the practical aspects from their fathers. Southern planters often sent their sons north to colonial colleges or to Europe to complete their education. However, by 1817, Jefferson wrote the "Rockfish Gap Report," the report of the Commission to establish a public university in Virginia, leading to the establishment of the University of Virginia in Charlottesville. The university was based on Jefferson's model of a natural aristocracy based on talent, or what later was called a *meritocracy*.

On the eve of the American Revolution, almost all of the African American population of one-half million were slaves. As Gutek (1991) observed, "In being uprooted from their native Africa, the blacks were torn from their own culture and thrust into an environment not merely inhospitable, but completely alien. As slaves the African blacks were undergoing induction into a society vastly different from that of their homeland" (p. 10). Few members of this group could read or write. Those who could, more often than not, had received their instruction outside of existing formal schools, for "it appears that only a handful attended school along with the whites" (Cremin, 1972, pp. 194–195). Schools that did exist for African Americans were usually sponsored by church groups, in particular Anglicans and Quakers (Button & Provenzano, 1989). Few slave owners were willing to support formal education for their slaves, since literacy was not directly connected to their work. Moreover, many feared that literate slaves would be more likely to lead insurrections. Although African Americans were kept illiterate as part of their subordinate position both on plantations and in the cities, some managed to learn skills as artisans, working as carpenters, coopers, wainwrights, farriers, coachmen, and skilled domestics.

Formal schooling for Native Americans was largely confined to missionary activities. In Virginia, the colonists at first attempted to establish "friendly" relations with their Native American neighbors. However, after hostilities broke out in 1622, they decided that "the way of conquering them is much more easy than of civilizing them by fair means" (Cremin, 1972, p. 194). There were some mildly successful educative endeavors in New England, particularly in Cambridge and Roxbury, which were directed by individual schoolmasters to prepare Native Americans for the Indian College that was established at Harvard University in approximately 1653. This Indian College, as Wright (1957) noted, was brought about largely due to the misguided belief held by some educated whites that "Indians were merely awaiting the opportunity to embrace classical scholarship and learn Cicero's orations" (p. 116). Ultimately, this experiment resulted in failure and was the first example of attempting to educate Native Americans by assimilating them into European culture. As in the case of African Americans, this period represents the beginning of the marginalization of Native Americans with respect to formal schooling.

The Age of Reform: The Rise of the Common School

Historians point to the period from 1820 to 1860 in the United States as one in which enormous changes took place with unprecedented speed. The Industrial Revolution, which began in the textile industry in England, crossed the Atlantic Ocean and brought its factory system with its new machinery to urban areas, particularly in the North. Urban clusters grew more dense as migrants from agricultural areas and immigrants from Europe flocked to the factories, looking for work. By 1850, these immigrants included a significant group of Roman Catholics who were escaping starvation in Ireland. Westward expansion, aided in part by the revolution in transportation and in part by the land hunger of pioneers, extended to settlements in Oregon and California by 1850.

By 1828, when Andrew Jackson was elected president, all men (except slaves and emotionally disturbed persons) had obtained the right to vote. Thus, the founding fathers' visions of a political democracy were increasingly becoming a reality.

In the decades following 1815, groups of reformers—quite different from such archetypes of rationalism as Franklin and Jefferson—emerged. These men and women often lacked higher education and did not hold public office but often articulated their ideas with the fervor of evangelical Christianity. However, their ultimate goals were secular in nature. America, once seen as the New Jerusalem by the Puritans, would become a secular paradise created by the new reformers.

Ralph Waldo Emerson, a New England essayist and philosopher, wrote of this age, "We are all a little wild here with numberless projects of social reform." Although the reform movement attempted to address such diverse societal problems as slavery, mental illness, intemperance, and pacifism, many reformers generally believed that the road to secular paradise was through education.

By 1820, it had become evident to those interested in education that the schools that had been established by the pre-war generation were not functioning effectively. Webster's *New England Primer* had been secularized so that the first line "In Adam's Fall/We Sinned, All" was replaced by "A was an Apple Pie made by the Cook" (Malone & Rauch, 1960, p. 491), but few children had access to the reader. The vast majority of Americans were, not surprisingly, illiterate. Even in New England, with its laws specifying common schools, towns neglected or evaded their duties. In other parts of the country, charity schools provided the only opportunities for disadvantaged children to obtain an education.

The struggle for free public education was led by Horace Mann of Massachusetts. Abandoning a successful career as a lawyer, Mann lobbied for a state board of education, and when the Massachusetts legislature created one in 1837, Horace Mann became its first secretary, an office he occupied for 11 years. His annual reports served as models for public school reforms throughout the nation and, partly due to Mann's efforts, the first state *normal school* (from the French écoles normal), or teacher training school was established in Lexington, Massachusetts, in 1839.

Mann's arguments for the establishment of the *common school,* or free publicly funded elementary schools, reflects both the concern for stability and order and the concern for social mobility—both of which were to be addressed through free public education. Admittedly, Mann could not have been immune to the waves of different immigrant groups that were changing the cultural composition of the cities. Nor could he fail to be immune to the goals of his audiences, often the wealthy factory owners, who had to be convinced to support public education. Thus, he spoke of school as preparation for citizenship as well as the "balance wheel"—"the great equalizer of the conditions of men."

Although many historians, particularly liberals and conservatives, view Mann as one of America's greatest educational reformers, radicals take issue with his arguments, pointing to the common school as a pernicious device for teaching skills such as hygiene, punctuality, and rudimentary skills that would create docile, willing workers. Whatever interpretation one chooses, Mann's belief that schools can change the social order and that education can foster social mobility are beliefs responsible for the faith and support many people give to U.S. public schools.

Opposition to Public Education

Not all groups subscribed to the idea of the common school. The same arguments made today by people without children or people who send their children to private schools in opposition to public support of schools were articulated against the common school Horace Mann envisioned. For example, taxation for public education was viewed as "unjust" by nonrecipients. Roman Catholics, who viewed the common school as dominated by a Protestant ethos, founded their own schools. However, by 1860, public support of elementary schools was becoming prevalent throughout the United States. Education beyond the elementary level, however, was primarily a province of private academies. Nonetheless, in 1862, Congress passed the Morrill Act, which authorized the use of public money to establish public land grant universities, resulting in the establishment of large state universities, espcially in the Midwest.

Education for Women and African Americans

Traditionally, the role of a woman in Western society has been that of helpmate or homemaker to the male, who assumed the role of provider. This role for women was vividly described by Jean-Jacques Rousseau in *Emile,* written in the eighteenth century. Rousseau, in his tract on education, created the female character, Sophie, who was to be the companion of the central male character, Emile, the recipient of a nontraditional but rigorous education. Sophie was encouraged to eat sweets, learn womanly arts, and be a supportive, loving helpmate to Emile.

This prescriptive role for women held sway throughout the nineteenth century and, for some, into the twentieth century as well. Generally, education for women was viewed as biologically harmful or too stressful. Thus, through the first half of the nineteenth century, educational opportunities for women were severely limited. Few females achieved an education other than rudimentary literacy and numeracy.

By the middle of the nineteenth century, however, a significant number of girls attended elementary schools and many were admitted to private academies, which functioned as secondary schools. By 1820, the movement for education for women in the United States was making important inroads.

In 1821, Emma Hart Willard opened the Troy Female Seminary in Troy, New York. The curriculum at this female seminary included so-called serious subjects of study, such as mathematics, science, history, and geography. Modeled on the curriculum of single-sex male academies, Troy Female Seminary sought to deliver an education to females that was similar to that of their male counterparts. In subsequent years, other female reformers dedicated to education for women, such as Catherine Esther Beecher and Mary Lyon, opened schools for females. A pioneer in postsecondary education for women, Mary Lyon founded Mount Holyoke Seminary in 1837. Entry requirements (with the exception of a foreign language) and level of instruction were the same for women as for men at their institutions of higher learning.

Higher education for women did not remain the exclusive domain of eastern reformers; the movement for female education spread quickly through the midwest. In 1833, Oberlin Collegiate Institute in Ohio opened its doors to women as well as African Americans. In 1856, the University of Iowa became the first state university to admit women. In 1865, Vassar College, the first of the Seven Sisters women's colleges, was founded in Poughkeepsie, New York. Shortly after, Wellesley College and Smith Colleges in Massachusetts were founded, and Mount Holyoke and Bryn Mawr Seminaries became colleges.

Although educational opportunities for women were expanding during the period preceding the Civil War, education for African Americans was severely limited. After Nat Turner's Revolt in 1831, southerners believed more than ever that literacy bred both insubordination and revolution. Thus, they forbade the teaching of reading and writing to the slave population. In the North, education for African Americans was usually of inferior quality and separate from the mainstream public school, if provided at all by the public.

This dismal picture of schooling for African Americans prompted African American Benjamin Roberts to file a legal suit in Boston in 1846 over the requirement that his daughter attend a segregated school. In a precedent-setting case, *Roberts* v. *City of Boston,* the court ruled that the local school committee had the right to establish separate educational facilities for whites and blacks. As a result of this ruling, African Americans were encouraged to establish their own schools. These were usually administered by their churches and aided in part through funds from abolitionists. During the Civil War, President Abraham Lincoln issued the Emancipation Proclamation in 1863, which announced the end of slavery in all states in rebellion against the Union. In 1865, several months after the end of the Civil War, congress passed the Thirteenth Ammendment to the Constitution, which freed four million slaves. In 1868, the Fourteenth Amendment to the Constitution was ratified, giving full citizenship to ex-slaves. Although this amendment and the Freedman's Bureau attempted to reconstruct the South's economy and include Blacks as full citizens, the Ku Klux Klan continued to spread racial hatred, and Jim Crow Laws and Black Codes in the South continued discrimination against Blacks. Its equal protection clause has been applied to important legal decisions regarding education. In 1868, the Freedman's Bureau helped to establish historically Black Colleges, including Howard University in Washington, D.C., and Hampton Institute in Virginia. However, the problem of equality of opportunity, in general, and school segregation, in particular, continued to be a significant issue throughout the remainder of the nineteenth and twentieth centuries (Andersen, 1988).

Urbanization and the Progressive Impetus

The beginning of the nineteenth century ushered in the First Industrial Revolution—immigration and urbanization of unprecedented proportions. Accordingly, the conditions created by these events were met with responses from social reformers whose concerns were far reaching and who attempted to address and redress the evils in U.S. life.

If the beginning of the nineteenth century seemed problematic to Americans, the close of the century must have been even more so. Again, there was a revolution in industry, referred to as the Second Industrial Revolution, this time involving steam-driven and electric-powered machinery. Factories had given way to gigantic corporations, under the control of such captains of industry as Andrew Carnegie, John D. Rockefeller, and Cornelius Vanderbilt. Significantly, immigrant labor played an essential role in this revolution.

At the beginning of the nineteenth century, the largest number of immigrants to the United States came from the northwestern part of Europe—namely, Great Britain, Scandinavia, Germany, and the Netherlands. After 1890, an increasingly large number of immigrants came from southern and eastern Europe. These immigrants' languages, customs, and living styles were dramatically different from those of the previous group. They settled in closely crowded substandard living quarters in urban areas and found work in factories. Thus, by the turn of the century, U.S. cities contained enormous concentrations of both wealth and poverty. Indeed, the gap between rich and poor had never been as great as it was at the close of the nineteenth century.

Thus far in this chapter, we have argued that the purpose of education has been seen in a variety of ways: religious, utilitarian, civic, and, with Mann, social mobility. The common school was born of an age of reform in this country that was unprecedented until the period between 1900 and 1914 in which a new reform movement, the Progressive Movement, would sweep the country. Progressive reformers insisted on government regulation of industry and commerce, as well as government regulation and conservation of the nation's natural resources. Moreover, progressive reformers insisted that government at national, state, and local levels be responsive to the welfare of its citizens rather than to the welfare of corporations. Significantly, progressive reforms had a sweeping agenda, ranging from secret ballot to schooling. As reformers, such as Horace Mann, in the nineteenth century had looked to schools as a means of addressing social problems, so reformers once again looked to schools as a means of preserving and promoting democracy within the new social order.

An important U.S. philosopher whose influence on schooling is still very much with us today was John Dewey (1859–1952). Dewey was a contemporary of such reformers as "Fighting Bob La Follette," governor of Wisconsin and architect of the "Wisconsin Idea," which harnessed the expertise of university professors to the mechanics of state government; settlement workers, such as Jane Addams and Lillian Wald; and municipal reformers and labor leaders, such as Henry Bruere and John Golden. Thus, progressive education, the movement with which John Dewey has become associated, can best be understood, as both historians Lawrence Cremin and Richard Hofstadter remind us, as part of "a broader program of social and political reform called the Progressive Movement" (Cremin, 1961, p. 88).

Just as the schools today are undergoing a transformation due in part to rapidly changing technology, altered life-styles, and new, massive waves of immigrants, it could be argued that the schools at the turn of the twentieth century were undergoing a similar transformation in their time. In 1909, for example, 57.8 percent of the children in schools in 37 of the largest cities in the United States were foreign born (Cremin, 1961, p. 72). Suddenly, teachers were faced with problems of putative uncleanliness (bathing became part of the school curriculum in certain districts), and teachers began to teach basic socialization skills. Just how these socialization skills have come to be interpreted, whether malevolently by radical historians or benevolently by liberal and conservative historians, is of little concern here. What is important is to consider how Dewey proposed to meet these challenges through education and how his ideas were interpreted by progressive disciples in such a way as to alter the course of schooling in this country.

John Dewey was born and raised in Vermont. By 1894, he had become thoroughly enmeshed in the problems of urbanization as a resident of Chicago and Chair of the Department of Philosophy, Psychology, and Pedagogy at the University of Chicago. Distressed with the abrupt dislocation of families from rural to urban environments, concerned with the loss of traditional ways of understanding the maintenance of civilization, and anxious about the effects unleashed individualism and rampant materialism would have on a democratic society, Dewey sought answers in pedagogic practice (see Westbrook, 1991, for an in-depth biography).

Dewey argued in *My Pedagogic Creed* (1897), *The School and Society* (1899), and *The Child and the Curriculum* (1902) for a restructuring of schools along the lines of "embryonic communities." He advocated the creation of a curriculum that would allow for the child's interests and developmental level while introducing the child to "the point of departure from which the child can trace and follow the progress of mankind in history, getting an insight also into the materials used and the mechanical principles involved" (Dworkin, 1959, p. 43).

Dewey believed that the result of education was growth, which was firmly posited within a democratic society. Thus, school for Dewey was "that form of community life in which all those agencies are concentrated that will be most effective in bringing the child to share in the inherited resources of the race, and to use his own powers for social ends" (Dworkin, 1959, p. 22).

To implement his ideas, Dewey created the Laboratory School at the University of Chicago. There, children studied basic subjects in an integrated curriculum, since, according to Dewey, "the child's life is an integral, a total one" and therefore the school should reflect the "completeness" and "unity" of "the child's own world" (Dworkin, 1959, p. 93). Dewey advocated active learning, starting with the needs and interests of the child; he emphasized the role of experience in education and introduced the notion of teacher as facilitator of learning rather than the font from which all knowledge flows. The school, according to Dewey, was a "miniature community, an embryonic society" (Dworkin, 1959, p. 41) and discipline was a tool that would develop "a spirit of social cooperation and community life" (Dworkin, 1959, p. 40).

That John Dewey made important contributions to both philosophy of education and pedagogic practice is undisputable, especially if one examines what happened to education in the wake of Dewey's early work. It is important to keep in mind just how rapidly education had expanded in this period. For example, in 1870, about 6.5 million children from ages 5 through 18 attended school; in 1880, about 15.5 million children attended school—a significant increase, indeed. No less than 31 states by 1900 had enacted compulsory education laws. Thus, what occurred in schools throughout this nation was to influence large numbers of Americans.

Although few can dispute Dewey's influence on educational reformers, many believe that Dewey was often misread, misunderstood, and misinterpreted. Thus, Dewey's emphasis on the child's impulses, feelings, and interests led to a form of progressive education that often became synonymous with permissiveness, and his emphasis on vocations ultimately led the way for "life adjustment" curriculum reformers.

Psychologists as well as philosophers became actively involved in educational reform. In fact, two distinctly different approaches to progressive educational reforms became apparent: the child-centered pedagogy of G. Stanley Hall and the social efficiency pedagogy of Edward L. Thorndike.

G. Stanley Hall (1844–1924), once referred to as "the Darwin of the mind" (Cremin, 1961, p. 101), believed that children, in their development, reflected the stages of development of civilization. Thus, according to Hall, schools should tailor their curriculums to the stages of child development. Hall argued that traditional schools stifled the child's natural impulses, and he suggested that schools individualize instruction and attend to the needs and interests of the children they educate. This strand of progressive reform became known as *child-centered reform.*

On the opposite side of child-centered reform was *social engineering reform,* proposed by Edward L. Thorndike. Thorndike (1874–1949) placed his emphasis on the organism's response to its environment. Working with animals in the laboratory, he came to the conclusion that human nature could be altered for better or worse, depending on the education to which it was subjected. Ultimately, Thorndike came to believe that schools could change human beings in a positive way and that the methods and aims of pedagogy to achieve this would be scientifically determined (Cremin, 1961, p. 114).

Thorndike's work, Frederick Winslow Taylor's work in scientific management, and that of other progressive thinkers encouraged educators to be "socially efficient" in the ways they went about educating students. In particular, this thinking led to a belief that schools should be a meaningful experience for students and that schools should prepare students to earn a living. It also suggested that schools might begin to educate students based on their abilities or talents. In particular, a leading proponent of this view was educational reformer Franklin Bobbitt. An issue of particular importance, although never resolved, was Bobbitt's scientific approach to curriculum design (a curriculum designer, according to Bobbitt, was like a "great engineer"). The purpose of curriculum design was to create a curriculum that would include the full range of human experience and prepare students for life.

Education for All: The Emergence of the Public High School

Prior to 1875, fewer than 25,000 students were enrolled in public high schools. Most adolescents who were engaged in some form of secondary education attended private academies that were either traditional, college preparatory schools or vocational schools (such as Franklin had proposed a century earlier). These academies taught not only academic subjects but also vocational ones. Yet, between 1880 and 1920, 2,382,542 students attended public high schools (Gutek, 1991, p. 122), probably outnumbering those who attended academies, and by 1940, about 6.5 million students attended public high school (U.S. Department of Education, National Center for Education Statistics, 1989b, p. 45). In a scant 40 years or so, a structure for the high school had to be put in place and debates had to be resolved regarding the purpose of secondary education.

One of the great changes that has affected high school attendance is that "whereas once it was altogether voluntary, and for this reason quite selective, it is now, at least for those sixteen and under, compulsory and unselective" (Hofstadter, 1966, p. 326). Compulsory school laws grew steadily. In 1890, 27 states had them; by 1918, all states followed suit, encouraged by court cases, such as the one in Kalamazoo, Michigan, in 1874, which paved the way for the school districts' right to levy taxes to support public high schools.

In examining the evolution of the high school, what becomes immediately apparent is the tension in society over the meaning and purpose of education—a debate that began with the ideas of Jefferson and Franklin, that was augmented by the arguments of Horace Mann, and that was made even more complex with the ideas of progressive educators.

Historian Diane Ravitch has pointed to four themes in particular that were troubling high school educators at the turn of the century. The first was the tension between classical subjects, such as Latin and Greek, and modern subjects, such as science, English literature, and foreign languages. The second was the problem of meeting college entrance requirements, since different colleges required different courses of study. The third involved educators who believed that students should study subjects that would prepare them for life, as opposed to traditional academic subjects. And the fourth, inextricably linked to the other three, was whether all students should pursue the same course of study or whether the course of study should be determined by the interests and abilities of the students (Ravitch, 1983, pp. 136–137).

In order to address the reality that by the 1890s "the high school curriculum had begun to resemble a species of academic jungle creeper, spreading thickly and quickly in many directions at once" (cited in Powell, Farrar, & Cohen, 1985, p. 240) and to clarify the purpose of a high school education, a Committee of Ten was formed by the National Education Association, headed by Harvard University President Charles Eliot. The committee issued its report in 1893, supporting the academic purpose of secondary education and dismissing curricula differentiation. It argued that the purpose of secondary education was to prepare students for "the duties of life" (quoted in Ravitch, 1983, p. 138). Furthermore, the committee recommended that modern academic subjects be awarded the same stature as traditional ones. It proposed five model curricula, including classical and modern languages, English, mathematics, history, and science—in essence, a liberal arts curriculum. Finally, the committee recommended that all students should be taught in the same manner; it was conspicuously silent on the subject of vocational education.

The Committee of Ten's recommendations were subsequently reinforced in two ways. The first was through the National Education Association's (NEA's) newly established committee on college entrance requirements, which recommended that all high school students study a core of academic subjects. The second was through the Carnegie Foundation for the Advancement of Teaching's adoption of the same core courses, which became known as *Carnegie units* and which were implemented in high schools throughout the country.

Not to be ignored was the progressive response to the Committee of Ten. In 1918, the NEA's Commission on the Reorganization of Secondary Schools made its report, which became known as the *Cardinal Principles of Secondary Education.* These principles, harkening back to the work of men such as G. Stanley Hall and supported by the "neutral measurement" work of Edward F. Thorndike, opened the door to a curriculum less academically demanding and far more utilitarian than the one proposed by Charles Eliot's Committee of Ten. Essentially, the Cardinal Principles, or the main goals of secondary education, were:

1. Health
2. Command of fundamental processes
3. Worthy home-membership
4. Vocation
5. Citizenship
6. Worthy use of leisure
7. Ethical character (Ravitch, 1983, p. 146)

For many educators, these Cardinal Principles helped to resolve the difficulty of educating students who were not college bound (at this time, only a small group of students in U.S. high schools expected to attend college). Educational historian David Cohen stated, "Americans quickly built a system around the assumption that most students didn't have what it took to be serious about the great issues of human life, and that even if they had the wit, they had neither the will nor the futures that would support heavy-duty study" (cited in Powell, Farrar, & Cohen, 1985, p. 245).

The final curriculum reform and a logical conclusion to the direction educational reform took during the period preceding the Second World War was the "Education for Life Adjustment" movement, first proposed in a lecture at Harvard University by Charles Prosser in 1939. Concerned with the failure of educators to effect any meaningful changes during the Depression years, Prosser proposed a curriculum for the nation's high schools, which addressed the practical concerns of daily living. Prosser's ideas were not entirely new; in fact, they could be said to be the logical conclusion of educators who believed, in the final analysis, that not all students were able to master serious academic subject matter.

However, Prosser and his apostles sought life adjustment courses, not just for those at the bottom of the educational ladder but for all high school students. As Hofstadter (1966) aptly observed, "American utility and American democracy would now be realized in the education of all youth" (p. 353). Students who once studied chemistry might study "the testing of detergents; not physics, but how to drive and service a car; not history, but the operation of the local gas works" (p. 356). As historians, Richard Hofstadter and David Cohen are quick to point out that this phase in educational reform exemplifies both the unbridled faith Americans have in education and the ambivalent feelings they harbor toward the life of the mind.

The Post–World War II Equity Era: 1945–1980

During the post–World War II period, the patterns that emerged during the Progressive Era were continued. First, the debate about the goals of education (i.e., academic, social, or both) and whether all children should receive the same education remained an important one. Second, the demand for the expansion of educational opportunity became perhaps the most prominent feature of educational reform. Whereas the Common School era opened access to elementary education and the Progressive Era to secondary education, the post–World War II years were concerned with expanding opportunities to the postsecondary level. They were also directed at finding ways to translate these expanded opportunities into more equal educational outcomes at all levels of education. As in the first half of the twentieth century, so too in the second half, the compatibility of expanded educational opportunity with the maintenance of educational standards would create significant problems. Thus, the tensions between equity and excellence became crucial in the debates of this period.

Cycles of Reform: Progressive and Traditional

The post–World War II years witnessed the continuation of the processes that defined the development of the comprehensive high school. The debates over academic issues, begun at the turn of the twentieth century, may be defined as the movement between pedagogical progressivism and pedagogical traditionalism. This movement focuses not only on the process of education but on its goals. At the center of these debates are the questions regarding the type of education children should receive and whether all children should receive the same education. Although many of these debates focused on curriculum and method, they ultimately were associated with the question of equity versus excellence.

Perhaps these debates can be best understood by examining reform cycles of the twentieth century that revolved between progressive and traditional visions of schooling. On one hand, traditionalists believed in knowledge-centered education, a traditional subject-centered curriculum, teacher-centered education, discipline and authority, and the defense of academic standards in the name of excellence. On the other hand, progressives believed in experiential education, a curriculum that responded to both the needs of students and the times, child-centered education, freedom and individualism, and the relativism of academic standards in the name of equity. Although these poles and educational practices rarely were in only one direction, the conflicts over educational policies and practices seemed to move back and forth between these two extremes. From 1945 to 1955, the progressive education of the previous decades was critically attacked.

These critics, including Mortimer Smith, Robert Hutchins, and Arthur Bestor, assailed progressive education for its sacrificing of intellectual goals to social ones. They argued that the life adjustment education of the period, combined with an increasingly antiintellectual curriculum, destroyed the traditional academic functions of schooling. Arthur Bestor, a respected historian and a graduate of the Lincoln School (one of the early progressive schools in New York City) argued that it was "regressive education," not progressive education, that had eliminated the school's primary role in teaching children to think (Ravitch, 1983, p. 76). Bestor, like the other critics, assailed the schools for destroying the democratic vision that all students should receive an education that was once reserved for the elite. He suggested that the social and vocational emphasis of the schools indicated a belief that all students could not learn academic material. In an ironic sense, many of the conservative critics were agreeing with the radical critique that the Progressive Era distorted the ideals of democratic education by tracking poor and working-class children into nonacademic vocational programs.

Throughout the 1950s, the debate between progressives who defended the social basis of the curriculum and critics who demanded a more academic curriculum raged on. What was often referred to as "the great debate" (Ravitch, 1983, p. 79) ended with the Soviet launching of the space satellite *Sputnik*. The idea that the Soviets would win the race for space resulted in a national commitment to improve educational standards in general and to increase mathematical and scientific literacy in particular. From 1957 through the mid-1960s, the emphasis shifted to the pursuit of excellence, and curriculum reformers attempted to redesign the curricula in ways that would lead to the return of academic standards (although many doubted that such a romantic age ever existed).

By the mid-1960s, however, the shift in educational priorities moved again toward the progressive side. This occurred in two distinct but overlapping ways. First, the Civil Rights movement, as we will discuss, led to an emphasis on equity issues. Thus, federal legislation, such as the Elementary and Secondary Education Act of 1965, emphasized the education of disadvantaged children. Second, in the context of the antiwar movement of the times, the general criticism of U.S. society, and the persistent failure of the schools to ameliorate problems of poverty and of racial minorities, a "new progressivism" developed that linked the failure of the schools to the problems in society. Ushered in by the publication of A. S. Neill's *Summerhill* in 1960—a book about an English boarding school with few, if any, rules and that was dedicated to the happiness of the child—the new progressivism provided an intellectual and pedagogical assault on the putative sins of traditional education, its authoritarianism, its racism, its misplaced values of intellectualism, and its failure to meet the emotional and psychological needs of children.

The new progressivism developed during one of the most turbulent decades in American history (Cavallo, 1999). Colleges and universities became sites of protests by the anti-Vietnam War and Civil Rights movements. In 1964, Students for a Democratic Society (SDS), a radical group of students headed by Tom Hayden at the University of Michigan, issued the *Port Huron Statement,* a radical critique of U.S. society and a call for action by U.S. students. In the same year, the University of California, Berkeley, Free Speech Movement, led by Mario Savio, protested university rules limiting assembly and demonstrations on campus. In 1968, African American students went on strike at San Francisco State University, resulting in the resignation of its president. Its new president, S. I. Hiyakawa, a law and order advocate, threatened to suspend anyone who interfered with the college. The strike ended after a number of months, with each side declaring victory. At the same time, African American students took over Willard Straight Hall at Cornell University. Faced with threats to take over the entire university by the African-American Society (AAS) and SDS, President James Perkins agreed to consider their demands without reprimands. Downstate, New York City police were called in to end a takeover of the Columbia University library. SDS-led students protesting the Vietnam War and the university's plan to build a gymnasium in the neighboring Morningside Heights section of Harlem were removed forcefully. Finally, on May 4, 1970, four students at Kent State University, protesting the U.S. invasion of Cambodia, were killed by the Ohio National Guard called in by Governor James Rhodes after protestors burned down the Army ROTC building. These killings, memorialized by Crosby, Stills, Nash, and Young's haunting words, "four dead in Ohio, four dead in Ohio" in their song *Ohio,* resulted in mass demonstrations at colleges and universities throughout the United States, but also in the beginning of the end of the antiwar movement. When students recognized that the government would kill them, the protests began to slowly subside.

Throughout the 1960s and early 1970s, a variety of books provided scathing criticism of U.S. education. These included Jonathon Kozol's *Death at an Early Age* (1967), which assailed the racist practices of the Boston public schools; Herbert Kohl's *36 Children* (1967), which demonstrated the pedagogical possibilities of open education; and Charles S. Silberman's *Crisis in the Classroom* (1969), which attacked the bureaucratic, stultifying mindlessness of U.S. education. These books, along with a series of articles by Joseph Featherstone and Beatrice and Ronald Gross on British progressive education (or open education), resulted in significant experimentation in some schools. Emphasis on individualism and relevant education, along with the challenge to the unquestioned authority of the teacher, resulted in alternative, free (or open) education—schooling that once again shifted attention away from knowledge (product) to process.

Although there is little evidence to suggest that the open classroom was a national phenomenon, and as the historian Larry Cuban noted in his history of teaching, *How Teachers Taught* (1984), there was surprisingly little variation in teaching methods during the twentieth century. (That is, despite the cycles of debate and reform, most secondary teachers still lectured more than they involved students.) Nonetheless, the period from the mid-1960s to the mid-1970s was a time of great turmoil in the educational arena. The time was marked by two simultaneous processes: (1) the challenge to traditional schooling and (2) the attempt to provide educational opportunity for the disadvantaged. In order to understand the latter, one must look back to the origins of the concerns for equity.

Equality of Opportunity

The demand for equality of opportunity, as we have noted, has been a central feature of U.S. history. From the Jeffersonian belief in a meritocratic elite, to Mann's vision of schooling as a "great equalizer," to Dewey's notion that the schools would be a "lever of social progress," U.S. reformers have pointed to the schools as capable of solving problems of inequality. More importantly, as Lawrence Cremin (1990) pointed out, Americans have expected their schools to solve social, political, and economic problems and have placed on the schools "all kinds of millennial hopes and expectations" (p. 92). While this has been true throughout America's history, the translation of this view into concrete policy has defined the postwar years and has helped explain the increasing politicization of the educational conflicts.

Immediately following the Second World War, the issue of access to educational opportunity became an important one. The GI Bill of Rights offered 16 million servicemen and -women the opportunity to pursue higher education. Ravitch (1983, pp. 12–13) pointed out that the GI Bill was the subject of considerable controversy over the question of access and excellence. On one hand, veterans groups, Congress, and other supporters believed the bill provided both a just reward for national service and a way to avoid massive unemployment in the postwar economy. Further, although aimed at veterans, it was part of the growing policy to provide access to higher education to those who, because of economic disadvantage and/or poor elementary and secondary preparation, had heretofore been denied the opportunity to attend college. On the other hand, critics such as Robert Maynard Hutchins, chancellor at the University of Chicago, and James Conant, president of Harvard University, feared that the policy would threaten the traditional meritocratic selection process and result in the lowering of academic standards (Ravitch, 1983, p. 13).

Despite these criticisms, the GI Bill, according to Ravitch (1983), was "the most ambitious venture in mass higher education that had ever been attempted by any society" (p. 14). Furthermore, she noted that the evidence does not suggest a decline in academic standards but rather a refreshing opening of the elite postsecondary education system. Historians and policy makers may disagree about the success of the GI Bill, but it is clear that it represented a building block in the post–World War II educational expansion. This expansion was similar to previous expansions, first in the Common School Era to compulsory elementary education, second in the Progressive Era to the high school, and in the post–World War II years to postsecondary education. The same types of questions left unresolved, especially from the Progressive Era, as to whether mass public education was possible, would become central points of controversy in the coming years.

Although the GI Bill set an important precedent, the issue of educational inequality for the poor and disadvantaged, in general, and for African Americans, in particular, became the focus of national attention and debate during this period. From the years immediately following the Second World War to the present, the questions of equality of opportunity at all levels have been significant areas of concern. In the late 1940s and 1950s, the relationships between race and education and the question of school segregation were at the forefront of political, educational, and moral conflicts.

Race, as much as any other single issue in U.S. history, has challenged the democratic ethos of the American dream. The ideals of equality of opportunity and justice have been contradicted by the actual practices concerning African Americans and other minorities. Although legally guaranteed equal protection by the Fourteenth Amendment, African Americans continue to experience vast inequities. Nowhere was this more evident than in education.

The post–Civil War Reconstruction period, despite the constitutional amendments enacted to guarantee equality of treatment before the law, had little positive effect on African Americans, especially in the South. During the latter years of the nineteenth century, the Supreme Court successfully blocked civil rights legislation. In the famous 1896 decision relating to education, *Plessy* v. *Ferguson,* the Court upheld a Louisiana law that segregated railway passengers by race. In what is commonly referred to as its "separate but equal" doctrine, the Court upheld the constitutionality of segregated facilities. In his famous dissenting opinion, Justice John Marshall Harlan stated:

> In view of the Constitution, in the eye of the law, there is in this country no superior, dominant, ruling class of citizens. There is no caste here. Our constitution is color blind, and neither knows nor tolerates classes among citizens. In respect of civil rights, all citizens are equal before the law. The humblest is the peer of the most powerful. The law regards man as man, and takes no account of his surroundings or of his color when his civil rights guaranteed by the supreme law of the land are involved. (cited in Ravitch, 1983, p. 120)

Despite Justice Harlan's interpretation that the Constitution guaranteed a color-blind treatment of all citizens, the *Plessy* v. *Ferguson* decision remained the precedent through the first half of the twentieth century. In the 1930s and 1940s, the National Association for the Advancement of Colored People (NAACP) initiated a campaign to overthrow the law, with school segregation a major component of its strategy.

The proper education of African Americans became a controversial subject for African American leaders. In 1895, Alabama Tuskegee Institute's Booker T. Washington gave his "Atlanta Compromise Speech" at the Atlanta Exposition, arguing that Blacks should be more thrifty and industrious and should pursue vocational education to prepare them for work in the new southern industrial economy. In 1903, W. E. B. DuBois, a Harvard Ph.D. and professor at Atlanta University, published *The Souls of Black Folk,* which criticized Booker T. Washington's vocational approach to education as assimilationist. DuBois called for academic education and Civil Rights protest against institutional racism.

The unequal and separate education of African Americans in the South became a focal point of the civil rights movements of the 1930s, 1940s, and 1950s. Although the *Plessy* decision supported separate and equal, it was apparent to civil rights advocates that the schools were anything but equal. Furthermore, in terms of both educational opportunities and results, African Americans in both the North and South received nothing approximating equal treatment.

After a series of victories, the advocates of civil rights won their major victory on May 17, 1954, when, in its landmark decision in *Brown* v. *Topeka Board of Education,* the Supreme Court ruled that state-imposed segregation of schools was unconstitutional. Chief Justice Earl Warren wrote, "It is doubtful that any child may reasonably be expected to succeed in life if he is denied the opportunity of education. Such an opportunity, where the state has undertaken to provide it, is a right that must be made available to all on equal terms" (cited in Ravitch, 1983, p. 127). Thus, the Supreme Court reversed the "separate but equal" doctrine enshrined in the *Plessy* case, and stated that separate educational institutions are unequal in and of themselves.

Although there would be considerable conflict in the implementation of the ruling, and although many legal scholars criticized both the basis and scope of the decision, the *Brown* decision marked both a symbolic and concrete affirmation of the ethos of democratic schooling. Although a compelling victory, *Brown* served to underscore the vast discrepancies between what Myrdal (1944) pointed to as the American belief in equality and the American reality of inequality. In the coming years, the fight for equality of opportunity for African Americans and other minorities would be a salient feature of educational reform. The *Brown* decision may have provided the legal foundation for equality, but the unequal results of schooling in the United States did not magically change in response to the law.

In the years following the 1955 *Brown II* decision, which ordered desegregation "with all deliberate speed," the battle for equality of opportunity was fought on a number of fronts with considerable conflict and resistance. The attempt to desegregate schools in the South first, and later in the North, resulted in confrontation and, at times, violence. For example, in Little Rock, Arkansas, President Eisenhower sent federal troops to enforce desegregation in 1957. When Arkansas Governor Orval Faubus responded to the Supreme Court's refusal to delay desegregation by closing Little Rock's high schools, the federal courts declared the Arkansas school closing laws unconstitutional. Thus, events in Little Rock made it clear that the federal government would not tolerate continued school segregation. Although protests continued in the South into the 1960s, it was apparent that the segregationists would lose their battle to defend a southern tradition.

The issue of school desegregation, however, was not an exclusively southern matter. In the northern cities and metropolitan area suburbs, where housing patterns resulted in segregated schools, the issue of *de jure* (segregation by law) segregation was often less clear. Where *de facto* segregation existed (that is, the schools were not segregated intentionally by law but by neighborhood housing patterns), the constitutional precedent for desegregation under *Brown* was shaky. Nonetheless, the evidence in the North of unequal educational opportunities based on race was clear. Thus, civil rights advocates pressed for the improvement of urban schools and for their desegregation.

The desegregation conflicts in Boston, every bit as embittered as in the South, demonstrated the degree to which the issue divided its citizens. As recently as the 1970s and early 1980s, the Boston School Committee was under judicial mandate to desegregate its schools. Judge Arthur Garrity ruled that the school committee knowingly, over a long period of time, conspired to keep schools segregated and thus limited the educational opportunity of African American children. For a period of over five years, the citizens of Boston were torn apart by the Garrity desegregation order. Groups of white parents opposed, sometimes violently, the forced busing that was imposed. As J. Anthony Lukas, in his Pulitzer prize–winning account *Common Ground* (1986) noted, the Boston situation became a symbol of frustration as it signified how a group of families, all committed to the best education for their children, could have such significantly different visions of what that meant. Judge Garrity stood resolute in his interpretation of the Constitution. Over time, the violence subsided. Many white Bostonians who could afford to do so either sent their children to private schools or moved to the suburbs. Thus, the Boston school system moved into an uneasy "cease fire" committed, at least publicly, to the improvement of education for all.

The Boston desegregation wars, like the conflicts a decade earlier in the South, revealed that U.S. society, although moving to ameliorate problems of racial inequality, was nonetheless a society in which racist attitudes changed slowly. Moreover, the Boston schools were a microcosm of the U.S. educational system—a system in which inequalities of race and class were salient features. Educational reforms of the 1960s and 1970s were directed at their elimination.

An important concurrent theme was the question of unequal educational outcomes based on socioeconomic position. From the late 1950s, the findings of social scientists, including James Coleman, author of the 1966 report *Equality of Educational Opportunity,* focused national attention on the relationship between socioeconomic position and unequal educational outcomes. Furthermore, as part of Presidents John F. Kennedy's and Lyndon Baines Johnson's social programs, Americans were sensitized to the idea of ameliorating poverty. Since schools were, in Horace Mann's vision, the lever of social reform, it was only natural that schools once again became the focal point.

During the 1960s and 1970s, a series of reform efforts were directed at providing equality of opportunity and increased access at all levels of education. Based on the Coleman report findings that unequal minority student educational achievement was caused more by family background than differences in the quality of schools attended, federally funded programs, such as Project Head Start, were aimed at providing early preschool educational opportunities for the disadvantaged. Although many radicals criticized the assumption of cultural deprivation implicit in these efforts, many reform efforts were aimed at the family and the school rather than the school itself.

In 1974, the U.S. Supreme Court in a 5–4 vote in *Milliken* v. *Bradley* ruled that the Detroit interdistrict city-suburb busing plan was unconstitutional. Based on this ruling and continuing opposition to forced busing for desegregation, educational reformers shifted their attention to improving education for often segregated inner-city school districts. From the 1970s on, school finance litigation attempted to equalize spending between high-income suburban and low-income urban and rural districts. In 1971, in *Serrano* v. *Priest,* the California Supreme Court ruled the state's system of unequal funding unconstitutional. However, in 1973, the U.S. Supreme Court ruled 5–4 in *San Antonio (Texas) Independent School District* v. *Rodriguez* that there was no constitutional guarantee to an equal education. In subsequent years, school finance cases had to be filed at the state level based on individual state constitutional provisions for equal education. Examples of successful cases are *Robinson* v. *Cahill* (1973) and *Abbott* v. *Burke* (1990) in New Jersey, *The Campaign for Fiscal Equity* v. *New York State* (2004), and *Williams* v. *The State of California* (2004). The Kentucky Education Reform Act (1988) represented one of the landmark legislative reforms to provide equal education.

Although these cases provided increased funding for low-income students, they did little to eliminate the de facto segregation in most northern urban districts, which by the fiftieth anniversary of *Brown* in 2004 were almost as segregated as southern districts before desegregation (Orfield & Lee, 2004; Harvard Civil Rights Project, 2004). Furthermore, court decisions such as the long-standing *Swann* v. *Charlotte-Mecklenberg (NC) School District* (2002), which ruled that busing was no longer necessary to achieve racial balance, resulted in the resegregation of many formerly integrated districts (Frankenberg & Lee, 2002; Frankenberg, Lee, & Orfield, 2003; Mickelson, 2002). Paul Tractenberg, founder of the Education Law Center in Newark, New Jersey, which has represented the state's low-income children in *Robinson* and in *Abbott,* noted that *Abbott* is more consistent with the separate but equal doctrine of *Plessy* than the separate is never equal doctrine of Brown (Tractenberg et al., 2002).

The fiftieth anniversary of *Brown* v. *Board of Education* in 2004 was marked by disagreements over whether the decision should be celebrated or commemorated. Advocates of celebration argued that the decision ended legally sanctioned segregation, marked the end of Jim Crow, and ushered in the Civil Rights movement. Advocates of commemoration argued that U.S. schools are still overwhelmingly segregated and that the continuing black-white achievement gap indicates that the decision never lived up to its promise.

Nowhere was the conflict over these liberal reforms more clearly demonstrated than in the area of higher education. During the 1960s, educational reformers placed significant emphasis on the need to open access to postsecondary education to students who were traditionally underrepresented at colleges and universities–namely, minority groups and the disadvantaged. Arguing that college was a key to social mobility and success, reformers concluded that college was a right rather than a privilege for all (see Lavin, Alba, & Silberstein, 1981). Defenders of the traditional admissions standards argued that postsecondary education would be destroyed if admissions standards were relaxed (see Sadovnik, 1994).

By the late 1960s, many colleges and universities adopted the policy of open enrollment. The City University of New York, long a symbol of quality education for the working class and poor, guaranteed a place for all graduating New York City high school students in either its four-year colleges (for students with high school averages of 80 and above) or its community college system (for students with averages below 80). Similar open admissions systems were introduced in other public university systems. Furthermore, federal financial aid funds were appropriated for students from low-income families. The results were a dramatic increase in the numbers of students participating in U.S. higher education and a growing debate over the efficacy of such liberal reforms.

Conservatives bemoaned the decline of standards and warned of the collapse of the intellectual foundations of Western civilization. Radicals suggested that more often than not students were given "false hopes and shattered dreams" as they were sometimes underprepared, given their unequal educational backgrounds, for the rigors of college education. Liberals, agreeing that the new students were often underprepared, suggested that it was now the role of the college to provide remedial services to turn access into success (see Sadovnik, 1994).

During the 1970s, colleges took on the task, however reluctantly, of providing remediation for the vast number of underprepared students, many of whom were first-generation college students. The City University of New York became perhaps the largest experiment in compensatory higher education. Its efforts symbolized both the hopes and frustrations of ameliorating unequal educational achievement. Although there is significant disagreement as to the success of these higher-education reforms (which we will examine more closely later in this book), it is important to recognize that this period did result in the significant expansion of higher education.

During this period, the coeducation movement at elite colleges and universities began. In 1969, all male–Ivy League Universities (Harvard, Yale, Princeton, Columbia, Brown, Pennsylvania, and Dartmouth) began to admit women. In response, in 1970, Vassar College became coeducational, leading to other women's colleges such as Connecticut College for Women and Skidmore College admitting men. Coeducation became the rule, with only some of the elite Seven Sisters (Smith, Mount Holyoke, Wellesley, and Bryn Mawr) and a few others still women's colleges in the year 2004.

We have looked at two related processes that define the post–World War II history of education. The first is the continued debate between progressives and traditionalists about the proper aims, content, and methods of schooling. The second is the struggle for equality of opportunity and the opening of access to higher education. The educational history of the 1980s and 1990s, as you will see, was characterized by the perceived failure of the reforms of this period, most particularly those of the 1960s and 1970s.

Educational Reaction and Reform and the Standards Era: 1980s–2005

By the late 1970s, conservative critics began to react to the educational reforms of the 1960s and 1970s. They argued that liberal reforms in pedagogy and curriculum and in the arena of educational opportunity had resulted in the decline of authority and standards. Furthermore, the critics argued that the preoccupation with using the schools to ameliorate social problems, however well intended, not only failed to do this but was part of an overall process that resulted in mass mediocrity. What was needed was nothing less than a complete overhaul of the U.S. educational system. While radical critics also pointed to the failure of the schools to ameliorate problems of poverty, they located the problem not so much in the schools but in the society at large. Liberals defended the reforms of the period by suggesting that social improvement takes a long time, and a decade and a half was scarcely sufficient to turn things around.

In 1983, the National Commission on Excellence (1983), founded by President Reagan's Secretary of Education, Terrel Bell, issued its now famous report, *A Nation at Risk*. This report provided a serious indictment of U.S. education and cited high rates of adult illiteracy, declining SAT scores, and low scores on international comparisons of knowledge by U.S. students as examples of the decline of literacy and standards. The committee stated that "the educational foundations of our society are presently being eroded by a rising tide of mediocrity that threatens our very future as a Nation and a people" (p. 5). As solutions, the commission offered five recommendations: (1) that all students graduating from high school complete what was termed the "new basics"—four years of English, three years of mathematics, three years of science, three years of social studies, and a half year of computer science; (2) that schools at all levels expect higher achievement from their students and that four-year colleges and universities raise their admissions requirements; (3) that more time be devoted to teaching the new basics; (4) that the preparation of teachers be strengthened and that teaching be made a more respected and rewarded profession; and (5) that citizens require their elected representatives to support and fund these reforms (cited in Cremin, 1990, p. 31).

The years following this report were characterized by scores of other reports that both supported the criticism and called for reform. During the 1980s and 1990s, and into the twenty-first century, significant attention was given to the improvement of curriculum, the tightening of standards, and a move toward the setting of academic goals and their assessment. A coalition of U.S. governors took on a leading role in setting a reform agenda; business leaders stressed the need to improve the nation's schools and proposed partnership programs; the federal government, through its Secretary of Education (under Ronald Reagan), William Bennett, took an active and critical role but continued to argue that it was not the federal government's role to fund such reform; and educators, at all levels, struggled to have a say in determining the nature of the reforms.

As we have pointed out in Chapter 2, the politics of the reform movement were complex and multidimensional. Conservatives wanted to restore both standards and the traditional curriculum; liberals demanded that the new drive for excellence not ignore the goals for equity; radicals believed it was another pendulum swing doomed to failure (one that sought to reestablish *excellence* as a code word for *elitism*).

In the 1990s and in the early part of the twenty-first century, the reforms initiated in the 1980s continued and expanded (see Tyack & Cuban, 1995). There are a number of reforms, including President Clinton's Goals 2000 in 1994 and President G. W. Bush's No Child Left Behind (NCLB) in 2001, that have the most visibility. Although they all purport to balance equity and excellence as their goal, it is not clear how effective they have been. In Chapter 10, we will discuss them more fully; in this section, we will describe them briefly.

First, school-based management is a reform that many believe holds promise. This reform shifts the control of schools from highly bureaucratic and centralized boards of education to the school itself, where teachers, parents, and administrators work cooperatively in decision making. Second, teacher empowerment, a reform closely related to school-based management, seeks to give teachers far more authority in decision making. Third, the school choice movement seeks to give parents the right to choose the public school to send their children, rather than the traditional method in which one's school was based on neighborhood zoning patterns (Cookson, 1994; Fuller, Elmore, & Orfield, 1996; Wells, 1993a, 1993b; Tractenberg, Sadovnik, & Liss, 2004). The choice movement is divided into those who support public school choice only (that is, giving parents the right to choose from public schools) to those who would include intersectional choice policies, including private schools. Such an intersectional choice program has been employed in Milwaukee where low-income parents receive tuition vouchers to send their children to private schools. There is significant controversy over this plan, with supporters stating it is the key to equity and critics arguing that it means the death of public education. The most important reform in this area is charter schools, which are independent of local district control, but receive public funding. By 1998, 33 states passed charter school legislation, resulting in more than 1,000 charter schools (Wells et al., 1998, p. 6).

It is perhaps too early to assess these reforms, but it is apparent that they are part of the recurring debate in U.S. educational history about the efficacy of mass public education and the compatibility of excellence and equity. Throughout history, these themes have been crucial as the preceding historical discussion delineates; the answer to the questions is a matter of both historical interpretation and empirical investigation.

Understanding the History of U.S. Education: Different Historical Interpretations

The history of education in the United States, as we have illustrated, has been one of conflict, struggle, and disagreement. It has also been marked by a somewhat ironic pattern of cycles of reform about the aims, goals, and purpose of education on one hand, and little change in actual classroom practice on the other (Cuban, 1984). Moreover, as we pointed out in Chapter 2, one's view of U.S. educational history and the effectiveness of the schools in meeting their democratic aspirations depends on one's interpretation of the historical trends and events. In the following sections, we outline the different schools of historical interpretation.

The different interpretations of U.S. educational history revolve around the tensions between equity and excellence, between the social and intellectual functions of schooling, and over differing responses to the questions, Education in whose interests? Education for whom? The U.S. school system has expanded to serve more students for longer periods of time than any other system in the modern world. This occurred, first, by extending primary school to all through compulsory education laws during the Common School Era; second, by extending high school education to the majority of adolescents by the end of the Progressive Era; and third, by extending postsecondary education to the largest number of high school graduates in the world by the 1990s. However, historians and sociologists of education disagree about whether this pattern of increased access means a pattern of educational success. Moreover, these disagreements concern the questions of the causes of educational expansion (that is, who supported the reforms), who benefited from them, and which types of goals have been met and/or sacrificed.

The Democratic-Liberal School

Democratic-liberals believe that the history of U.S. education involves the progressive evolution, albeit flawed, of a school system committed to providing equality of opportunity for all. Democratic-liberal historians suggest that each period of educational expansion involved the attempts of liberal reformers to expand educational opportunities to larger segments of the population and to reject the conservative view of schools as elite institutions for the meritorious (which usually meant the privileged). Historians such as Ellwood Cubberly, Merle Curti, and Lawrence A. Cremin are representative of this view. Both Cubberly (1934) and Curti (1959/1971) have portrayed the Common School Era as a victory for democratic movements and the first step in opening U.S education to all. Furthermore, both historians, in varying degrees, portray the early school reformers such as Horace Mann and Henry Barnard as reformers dedicated to egalitarian principles (Curti is more critical than Cubberly).

Lawrence A. Cremin, in his three-volume history of U.S. education (1972, 1980, 1988) and in a study of the Progressive Era (1961), portrays the evolution of U.S. education in terms of two related processes: popularization and multitudinousness (Cremin, 1988). For Cremin, educational history in the United States involved both the expansion of opportunity and purpose. That is, as more students from diverse backgrounds went to school for longer periods of time, the goals of education became more diverse, with social goals often becoming as or more important than intellectual ones. Although Cremin does not deny the educational problems and conflicts, and he notes the discrepancies between opportunity and results—particularly for the economically disadvantaged—he never relinquished his vision that the genius of U.S. education lies with its commitment to popularization and multitudinousness. In his final book, *Popular Education and Its Discontents* (1990), Cremin summarized this democratic liberal perspective as follows: "That kind of organization [referring to U.S. higher education] is part of the genius of American education—it provides a place for everyone who wishes one, and in the end yields one of the most educated populations in the world" (p. 46).

Although democratic-liberals tend to interpret U.S. educational history optimistically, the evolution of the nation's schools has been a flawed, often conflictual march toward increased opportunities. Thus, historians such as Cremin do not see equity and excellence as inevitably irreconcilable, but rather see the tensions between the two as resulting in necessary compromises. The ideals of equality and excellence are just that: ideals. Democratic-liberals believe that the U.S. educational system must continue to move closer to each, without sacrificing one or the other too dramatically.

The Radical-Revisionist School

Beginning in the 1960s, the optimistic vision of the democratic-liberal historians began to be challenged by radical historians, sociologists, and political economists of education. The radical-revisionist historians of education, as they have come to be called, revised the history of education in a more critical direction. These historians, including Michael Katz (1968), Joel Spring (1972), and Clarence Karier (1976), argue that the history of U.S. education is the story of expanded success for very different reasons and with very different results. Radical historians do not deny that the educational system has expanded; rather, they believe it expanded to meet the needs of the elites in society for the control of the working class and immigrants, and for economic efficiency and productivity. In addition, radicals suggest that expanded opportunity did not translate into more egalitarian results. Rather, they point out that each period of educational reform (the Common School Era, the Progressive Era, the Post–World War II) led to increasing stratification within the educational system, with working class, poor, and minority students getting the short end of the stick.

Let us examine the radical view on educational expansion and the question of whose interests it served. Michael Katz (1968) argued that it was the economic interests of nineteenth-century capitalists that more fully explain the expansion of schooling and that educational reformers stressed the ability of schools to train factory workers, to socialize immigrants into U.S. values, and to create stability in the newly expanding urban environments. Likewise, historians Joel Spring (1972) and Clarence Karier (1976) both advanced the thesis that the expansion of the schools in the late nineteenth and early twentieth centuries was done more so in the interests of social control than in the interests of equity. Spring argued that this perspective

> advances the idea that schools were shaped as instruments of the corporate liberal state for mainstreaming social control. . . . The public schools were seen as an important instrument used by the government to aid in the rationalization and minimization of conflict by selecting and training students for their future positions in the economy and by imbuing the population with a sense of cooperation and national spirit. (1986, p. 154)

One of the problems with this view, pointed out by radicals who generally agree with this interpretation, is that it views the expansion of education as imposed on the poor and working class from above and often against their will. Other radical historians, including David Hogan (1978) and Julia Wrigley (1982), suggest that the working class and labor unions actively supported the expansion of public education for their own interests. Thus, the explanation of educational expansion is a more conflictual one rather than a simplistic tale of elite domination.

Despite these historiographical disagreements, radical historians agree that the results of educational expansion rarely met their putative democratic aspirations. They suggest that each new expansion increased stratification of working-class and disadvantaged students within the system, with these students less likely to succeed educationally. For example, political economists Samuel Bowles and Herbert Gintis (1976) noted that the expansion of the high school resulted in a comprehensive secondary system that tracked students into vocational and academic curriculums with placement, more often than not, determined by social class background and race. Furthermore, the expansion of higher education in the post–World War II period often resulted in the stratification between community colleges that stressed vocational education and four-year colleges and universities that stressed the liberal arts and sciences. Once again, radicals argue that placement in the higher education system is based on social class and race. Studies by Kevin Dougherty (1987, 1994) and Steven Brint and Jerome Karabel (1989) give ample evidence to support the view that the expansion of higher education has not resulted in equality of opportunity.

Thus, the radical interpretation of U.S. educational history is a more pessimistic one. While acknowledging educational expansion, they suggest that this process has benefited the elites more than the masses and has not produced either equality of opportunity or results. Further, they view the debates about equity and excellence as a chimera, with those who bemoan the decline of standards seeking to reimpose excellence with little regard for equality.

Conservative Perspectives

In the 1980s, as we noted in Chapter 2, a rising tide of conservative criticism swept education circles. Although much of this criticism was political and, at times, ahistorical, it did have an implicit historical critique of the schools. Arguing that U.S. students knew very little and that U.S. schools were mediocre, the conservative critics such as William Bennett, Chester Finn, Jr., Diane Ravitch, E. D. Hirsch, Jr., and Allan Bloom all pointed to the failure of so-called progressive education to fulfill its lofty social goals without sacrificing academic quality. Although critics such as Ravitch and Hirsch supported the democratic-liberal goal of equality of opportunity and mobility through education, they believed that the historical pursuit of social and political objectives resulted in significant harm to the traditional academic goals of schooling.

Diane Ravitch (1977) provided a passionate critique of the radical-revisionist perspective and a defense of the democratic-liberal position. Yet, in the 1980s, Ravitch moved from this centrist position to a more conservative stance. In a series of essays and books, including *The Troubled Crusade* (1983), Ravitch argued that the preoccupation with using education to solve social problems has not solved these problems and, simultaneously, has led to the erosion of educational excellence. Although Ravitch remains faithful to the democratic-liberal belief that schools have expanded opportunities to countless numbers of the disadvantaged and immigrants, she has argued that the adjustment of the traditional curriculum to meet the needs of all of these groups has been a violation of the fundamental function of schooling, which is to develop the powers of intelligence (1985, p. 40). According to Ravitch, the progressive reforms of the twentieth century denigrated the traditional role of schools in passing on a common culture and produced a generation of students who know little, if anything, about their Western heritage. Although she believes the curriculum ought to be fair and nonracist, she has also argued that efforts at multiculturalism are often historically incorrect and neglect the fact that the heritage of our civilization, from a conservative vantage point, is Western.

Ravitch's conservatism is far more complex than that of other conservative critics such as Bennett, Bloom, Finn, and Hirsch. Where these authors, like Bloom in *The Closing of the American Mind* (1987) and Hirsch in *Cultural Literacy* (1987), never fully capture the complex relationship between educational reform and social and political milieu, Ravitch's *The Troubled Crusade* (1983) points to the putative decline of educational standards within the context of political movements to move us closer to a fair and just society. In fact, Ravitch has argued that the belief that all students learn a rigorous curriculum is not conservative, but rather consistent with her earlier liberal belief that all students be given an equal opportunity to succeed (Ravitch, 1994). Ravitch understands the conflictual nature of U.S. educational history and simultaneously praises the schools for being a part of large-scale social improvement while damning them for losing their academic standards in the process. Bloom blames the universities for watering down their curriculums; Hirsch blames the public schools for valuing skills over content; and Bennett, in his role as Secretary of Education during the Reagan administration, called for a return to a traditional Western curriculum. None of these conservatives has analyzed as Ravitch has (perhaps because she is the only historian among them) the historical tensions between equity and excellence that are crucial to understanding the problem. Nonetheless, what they all have in common is the vision that the evolution of U.S. education has resulted in the dilution of academic excellence.

Conclusion

As students of educational history, you may well be perplexed by the different interpretations of the history of U.S. education. How is it possible, you may ask, that given the same evidence, historians reach such vastly different conclusions? As we pointed out in Chapter 2, the interpretation of educational issues, including the interpretation of its history, depends to a large extent on one's perspective. Thus, each school of historical interpretation sees the events, data, and conflicts in different ways. We do not propose that there is one unified theory of the history of education, nor do we believe that the historical and sociological data support only one theory. Rather, we believe that there are patterns in the history of education and that the foundations perspective is a lens for looking at these patterns.

The history of U.S. education has involved a number of related patterns. First, it has been defined by the expansion of schooling to increasingly larger number of children for longer periods of time. Second, with this expansion has come the demand for equality of opportunity and ways to decrease inequality of results. Third is the conflict over goals, curriculum, and method, and the politization of these issues. Fourth is the conflict between education for a common culture, or a "distinctively American paideia, or self-conscious culture" (Cremin, 1990, p. 107) and education for the diversity of a pluralistic society. And fifth are the tensions between popularization and educational excellence. All of these processes speak to the fact that Americans have always asked a great deal, perhaps too much, from their schools, and that conflict and controversy are the definitive features of the evolution of the school.

The history of U.S. education is a complex story of conflict, compromise, and struggle (see Table 3.1). The disagreements over this history are summed up well by Diane Ravitch, defending the democratic-liberal tradition, and David Nassaw, arguing for a more radical interpretation. Ravitch (1977) stated:

> Education in a liberal society must sustain and balance ideals that exist in tension: equity and excellence. While different generations have emphasized one or the other, in response to the climate of the times, schools cannot make either ideal a reality, though they contribute to both. The schools are limited institutions which have certain general responsibilities and certain specific capacities; sometimes they have failed to meet realistic expectations, and at other times they have succeeded beyond realistic expectations in dispersing intelligence and opportunity throughout the community. In order to judge them by reasonable standards and in order to have any chance of improving their future performance, it is necessary to abandon the simplistic search for heroes and devils, scapegoats and panaceas. (p. 173)

Nassaw (1979), in a very different vein, stated:

> The public schools emerge in the end compromised by reform and resistance. They do not belong to the corporations and the state, but neither do they belong to their communities. They remain "contested" institutions with several agendas and several purposes. The reformers have not in the past made them into efficient agencies for social channeling and control. Their opponents will not, on the other hand, turn them into truly egalitarian institutions without at the same time effecting radical changes in the state and society that support them. The public schools will, in short, continue to be the social arena where the tension is reflected and the contest played out between the promise of democracy and the rights of class division. (p. 243)

Thus, from their very different vantage points, Ravitch and Nassaw agree that schools are imperfect institutions with conflicting goals that have been the center of struggle throughout our history. There have been no easy answers to the complex questions we have examined. As teachers, you will become a part of this ongoing history, and we believe only through reflective consideration of the issues will you be able to understand the many conflicts of which you will be a part, let alone resolve these conflicts and make a difference.

TABLE 3.1   Timeline of Historical Events in U.S. Education

Date	Event
1636	The first college in the American colonies, Harvard College, is founded in Newtown (later renamed Cambridge, MA). Its dual function was educating civic leaders and preparing a learned clergy.
1779	Thomas Jefferson writes his *Bill for a More General Diffusion of Knowledge,* outlining his views on the popularization of elementary and grammar school education.
1789	The Tenth Amendment to the U.S. Constitution provides for public education and delegates authority to the states. This has resulted in the absence of a national system of education or national curriculum, as exists in many other liberal-democratic societies.
1817	Thomas Jefferson writes the "Rockfish Gap Report," the report of the Commission to establish a public university in Virginia, leading to the establishment of the University of Virginia in Charlottesville. The university is based on Jefferson's model of a natural aristocracy based on talent, or what later was called a *meritocracy.*
1821	Troy Female Seminary in New York is founded by Emma Willard.
1833	Oberlin College in Ohio admits women, becoming the first coeducational college in the United States.
1837	Horace Mann becomes Secretary to the Massachusetts Board of Education, ushering in the Common School Era of compulsory primary education.
1837	Mount Holyoke Female Seminary (later, Mount Holyoke College) in Massachusetts is founded by Mary Lyon.
1848	Horace Mann, in his Twelfth (and final) Report to the Massachusetts Board of Education, states that "education is the great equalizer of the conditions of men . . . the balance wheel of the social machinery," which becomes the basis of an American democratic ideology of education.
1862	The Morrill Act is passed, authorizing the use of public money to establish public land grant universities, resulting in the establishment of large public universities, especially in the Midwest.
1863	During the Civil War, President Abraham Lincoln issues the Emancipation Proclamation, announcing the end of slavery in all states in rebellion against the Union.
1865	Several months after the end of the Civil War, Congress passes the Thirteenth Amendment to the Constitution, which freed four million slaves.
1865	Vassar College, the first of the Seven Sisters women's colleges, is founded in Poughkeepsie, NY. Shortly after, Wellesley College and Smith College in Massachusetts are founded, and Mount Holyoke and Bryn Mawr (PA) Seminaries become colleges.
1868	The Fourteenth Amendment to the Constitution is ratified, giving full citizenship to ex-slaves. Although this amendment and the Freedman's Bureau attempted to reconstruct the South's economy and include Blacks as full citizens, the Ku Klux Klan continued to spread racial hatred, and Jim Crow Laws and Black Codes in the South continued discrimination against Blacks. Its equal protection clause has been applied to important legal decisions regarding education.
1868	The Freedman's Bureau helps establish historically Black Colleges, including Howard University in Washington, D.C., and Hampton Institute in Virginia.
1891	Jane Addams founds Hull House in Chicago, a settlement house that provided cultural and educational programs for Chicago's immigrants and poor.
1893	The National Education Association's Committee of Ten, chaired by Harvard University President Charles Eliot, issues its report on secondary education, which reasserts the college-preparatory function of the high school. Eliot is to become one of the leaders of the social efficiency strand of progressive education.
1895	Alabama Tuskegee Institute's Booker T. Washington gives his "Atlanta Compromise Speech" at the Atlanta Exposition, arguing that Blacks should be more thrifty and industrious and should pursue vocational education to prepare them for work in the new southern industrial economy.

(Continued)

TABLE 3.1 *Continued*

Date	Event
1896	The Laboratory School at the University of Chicago is founded by John and Alice Chipman Dewey, ushering in the child-centered, developmental democratic strand of progressive education.
1896	In *Plessy* v. *Ferguson,* the U.S. Supreme Court rules that separate but equal facilities are constitutional. Justice John Marshall Harlan, the lone dissenter, argued that the Constitution is color-blind and that all citizens are equal before the law.
1903	W. E. B. DuBois, a Harvard Ph.D. and professor at Atlanta University, publishes *The Souls of Black Folk,* which criticizes Booker T. Washington's vocational approach to education as assimilationist. DuBois called for academic education and Civil Rights protest against institutional racism.
1918	The NEA's *Cardinal Principles of Secondary Education* argues for the broadening of the functions of the high school to include civic, vocational, and social responsibilities ushering in the life-adjustment period of U.S. education.
1920	The Nineteenth Amendment to the Constitution is ratified, giving women the right to vote.
1931	Jane Addams is the first woman recipient of the Nobel Peace Prize for her work, including founding the Women's Peace Party in 1915 and the Women's International League for Peace and Freedom in 1919.
1945	The GI Bill of Rights is passed, authorizing college tuition assistance for soldiers.
1950	After two years, Superintendent Willard Goslin is fired by the Pasadena (CA) School Board, after conservative forces protest his progressive policies and accuse him of being a Communist. The Goslin firing was part of the larger attack on "subversives" during the McCarthy Era, named after Wisconsin Joseph McCarthy, who led a congressional investigation of alleged Communists that resulted in blacklisting.
1950	In *Sweatt* v. *Painter* and in *McLaurin* v. *Board of Regents of the University of Oklahoma,* the U.S. Supreme Court rules that blacks must be admitted to segregated state law schools in Texas and Oklahoma, respectively.
1954	In *Brown* v. *The Topeka Board of Education,* the U.S. Supreme Court rules that separate but equal schools for black and white children is unconstitutional. The case consisted of separate cases in four states, *Briggs* v. *Elliot* (South Carolina), *Brown* v. *Board of Education of Topeka* (Kansas), *Davis* v. *School Board of Prince Edward County* (Virginia), *Belton* v. *Gebhart* and *Bulah* v. *Gebhart* (Delaware), and *Bolling* v. *Sharpe* (District of Columbia).
1956	Critics of progressive education, historians Arthur Bestor and Mortimer Smith establish the Council for Basic Education, committed to making intellectual training the primary focus of public education and the elimination of separating students by ability into different tracks.
1957	Arkansas Governor Orval Faubus sends in the state National Guard to prevent the desegregation of Little Rock Central High School; President Dwight D. Eisenhower sends in federal troops to implement the court order.
1957	The Soviet Union launches the first space satellite, *Sputnik,* resulting in U.S. efforts to improve mathematics and science education.
1958	The National Defense Education Act is passed, authorizing millions of dollars to mathematics, science, and gifted education.
1960	A. S. Neill's *Summerhill,* about a progressive English boarding school, begins the revival of child-centered progressive education in the United States.
1964	Congress passes the Civil Rights Act.
1964	Students for a Democratic Society (SDS) issue the *Port Huron Statement,* a radical critique of U.S. society and a call for action by U.S. students.
1964	The University of California, Berkeley, Free Speech Movement, led by Mario Savio, protests university rules limiting assembly and demonstrations on campus.
1965	The Elementary and Secondary School Act is passed.

TABLE 3.1 *Continued*

Date	Event
1967	Criticism of schools, and urban schools in particular, reaches a crescendo, with the publication of Jonathan Kozol's *Death at an Early Age* and Herbert Kohl's *36 Children.*
1968	African American students go on strike at San Francisco State University, resulting in the resignation of its president. Its new president, S. I. Hiyakawa, a law and order advocate, threatened to suspend anyone who interfered with the college. The strike ended after a number of months, with each side declaring victory.
1968	African American students take over Willard Straight Hall at Cornell University. Faced with threats to take over the entire university by the African-American Society (AAS) and SDS, President James Perkins agrees to consider their demands without reprimands.
1968	New York City police are called in to end the takeover of the Columbia University library. SDS-led students protesting the Vietnam War and the university's plan to build a gymnasium in the neighboring Morningside Heights section of Harlem are removed forcefully.
1969	City University of New York (CUNY) adopts its Open Admissions Policy, which offers a place for all New York City high school graduates in one of its senior colleges (for students with a high school average of above 80) or community colleges (for students with a high school average below 80). This policy results in the development of the largest remediation effort in U.S. higher education. Critics argue that it represents the downfall of the meritocratic ideal of higher education; proponents argue it represents higher education for all and the triumph of the democratic ideal of higher education.
1969	All-male Ivy League universities (Harvard, Yale, Princeton, Columbia, Brown, Pennsylvania and Dartmouth) begin to admit women.
1970	Charles Silberman publishes *Crisis in the Classroom,* a radical critique of U.S. public schools as "grim, joyless places," preoccupied with "order and control" and characterized by "banality and triviality."
1970	On May 4, four students at Kent State University, protesting the U.S. invasion of Cambodia, are killed by the Ohio National Guard called in by Governor James Rhodes after protestors burned down the Army ROTC building.
1970	Vassar College becomes coeducational, leading to other women's colleges such as Connecticut College for Women and Skidmore College admitting men. Coeducation will become the rule, with only some of the elite Seven Sisters (Smith, Mount Holyoke, Wellesley, and Bryn Mawr) and a few others remaining women's colleges in the year 2000.
1974	U.S. Federal Judge W. Arthur Garrity rules Boston School Committee is in violation of *Brown* v. *Board,* resulting in Boston school desegregation wars.
1975	During the New York City fiscal crisis, City University of New York initiates tuition, ending its more than century-long policy of free tuition.
1983	The National Commission for Excellence in Education, headed by U.S. Secretary of Education Terel Bell, releases *A Nation at Risk,* which argues that U.S. education is mediocre. The report results in the beginning of the education excellence movement and a repudiation of progressive education.
1986	National Governors Conference, headed by Governors Clinton of Arkansas, Alexander of Tennessee, and Riley of South Carolina, issues its report *A Time for Results,* calling for higher state standards in education.
1987	Chester Finn and Diane Ravitch's *What Do Our Seventeen Year Olds Know?* and E. D. Hirsch, Jr.'s *Cultural Literacy* provide a critique of U.S. students' lack of liberal arts and sciences knowledge and proposes the Core Curriculum movement.
1988	Minnesota becomes the first state to pass school choice legislation. As of 1992, 37 states have passed choice legislation.
1992	California becomes the second state (after Minnesota) to pass charter school legislation, allowing for state funding of schools independent of the public school system. By 1998, it has over 50,000 students

(Continued)

TABLE 3.1   *Continued*

Date	Event
	in charter schools—the most in the nation—and the second most charter schools (130), second only to Arizona (241).
1994	President William Jefferson Clinton's *Goals 2000: Educate America Act* becomes law, establishing national goals for content and performance; opportunity to learn standards; school-to-work opportunities; school, parent, and community support; teacher professional development; and safe and drug-free schools.
1995	Social psychologists David Berliner and Bruce D. Biddle publish *The Manufactured Crisis,* which argues that the empirical evidence does not support the conservative attack on U.S. public schools.
1998	The New Jersey Supreme Court issues the fifth of its historic decisions in *Abbott* v. *Burke* (1990), a landmark state school finance case.
2002	President George W. Bush signs into law the No Child Left Behind Act of 2001, the reauthorization of the Elementary and Secondary Education Act of 1965, aimed at eliminating student achievement gaps by 2014.
2002	In *Zelman* v. *Simmons-Harris,* the U.S. Supreme Court rules that the Constitution does not prohibit public funding of religious schools, at least in the form of Cleveland's school voucher program.
2003	In *Grutter* v. *Bollinger,* the U.S. Supreme Court rules that the University of Michigan Law School's use of racial preferences in student admissions did not violate the Equal Protection Clause of the Fourteenth Amendment or Title VI of the Civil Rights Act of 1964. In *Gratz* v. *Bollinger,* the Court adopts the same standard and finds that the university's undergraduate admissions system used race too mechanically and therefore did violate the Equal Protection Clause of the Fourteenth Amendment or Title VI of the Civil Rights Act of 1964.
2004	In *Williams* v. *State of California,* the plaintiffs argue that the state has failed to provide a minimally adequate education for low-income children. Governor Arnold Schwarzenegger settles the four-year-old case by agreeing to provide new state standards to ensure an adequate education for all children.
2004	A three-member panel appointed by New York Supreme Court Justice Leland DeGrasse recommends that the New York State legislature provide an additional $5.6 billion per year to the New York City public schools. As part of the final ruling in the decade-long Campaign for Fiscal Equity lawsuit, the Court rules that the state's funding formulas discriminated against New York City.

In order to evaluate the issues raised in this chapter, one must look at empirical evidence, including, but not limited to, the historical record. That is, to analyze the extent to which schools have provided opportunity and mobility or the extent to which standards have fallen requires data. As you will see, the sociological approach to education has been central to this endeavor. In the next chapter, we will explore this sociological approach in depth.

The following articles illustrate some of the major historical periods, writers, and reforms discussed in this chapter. The first selection, "Forgetting the Questions: The Problem of Educational Reform," written by education historian Diane Ravitch, looks at why educational reform has resulted in the decline of standards. Arguing that twentieth-century reforms centered on the sociological rather than the educational view, Ravitch, Assistant Secretary of Education for Research and Development in the Bush administration, criticizes the schools for ignoring their intellectual functions. Ravitch has been a severe critic of the revisionist historians.

The second selection, "Popular Schooling," written by the late historian of education Lawrence A. Cremin, discusses the historical dissatisfaction with U.S. education and the possibility of achieving the American dream of a quality education for all. This liberal version of education is illustrated through a historical analysis of popularization of the U.S. educational system and an alternative explanation from Ravitch.

Forgetting the Questions

The Problem of Educational Reform

DIANE RAVITCH

It would be difficult to find a sustained period of time in our history when Americans felt satisfied with the achievements of their schools. From the early nineteenth century on, it has been commonplace to find a fairly consistent recitation of complaints about the low state of learning, the poor training of teachers, the insufficient funding of education, the inadequacies of school buildings, and the apathy of the public. The temptation exists to attribute the concerns of the 1980s to this strain of despair about the historic gap between aspiration and reality, this sense that schools have always and will always fall short of their mission. But it would be wrong to do so, not only because it would encourage unwarranted complacency but because the educational problems of the present are fundamentally different from those of the past.

One important difference is that so much of the past agenda of educational reformers has been largely fulfilled. In one sense, the educational enterprise is the victim of its own successes, since new problems have arisen from the long-sought solutions to earlier problems. Idealistic reformers, eager to improve the schools and to extend their promise to all children, sought the appropriate lever of change. If only teachers had college degrees and pedagogical training; if only teachers would band together to form a powerful teachers' union; if only there were federal aid to schools; if only all children were admitted to school regardless of race or national origin; if only all students of high ability were admitted to college; if only colleges could accommodate everyone who wanted to attend; if only students had more choices and fewer requirements in their course work; if only schools were open to educational experimentation; if only there were a federal department of education. . . The "if only" list could be extended, but the point should be clear by now. All these "if onlies" have been put into effect, some entirely and others at least partially, and rarely have the results been equal to the hopes invested.

In reality, many present complaints are reactions to hard-won reforms of the past. Though the educational preparation of teachers is more extensive than ever, at least when measured by degrees and years of formal schooling, the education of teachers is still a subject of intense criticism. The realization has dawned in many quarters that a credential from a state university or a school of education is no guarantee that its bearer knows how to teach or what to teach, loves teaching or loves learning. Nor are today's critics delighted by the undeniable power of teachers' unions.

From *The Schools We Deserve* by Diane Ravitch. Copyright © 1985 by Diane Ravitch. Reprinted by permission of Basic Books, a member of Perseus Books, L.L.C.

True, the unions have used their political clout to improve teachers' salaries and to win vastly enlarged federal education expenditures, but unionization has not produced the educational changes that some of its advocates had anticipated. Similarly, the sense of achievement that should have followed the removal of racial barriers to higher education quickly gave way to concerns about social stratification, vocationalization, and declining quality. The reforms of the 1960s were effective, though not in the way that reformers had hoped. Now everyone who wants to go to college can go to some college, though not necessarily that of his first choice. By 1980, at least one-third of all institutions of higher education admitted everyone who applied, more than one-half accepted most or all of those who met their qualifications, and less than 10 percent were "competitive," that is, accepted only a portion of qualified applicants. As college enrollments decline, the number of competitive colleges will grow fewer. Curricular reforms have broken down the coherence of the liberal arts curriculum, both in high school and college, so that students have a wide degree of choice and few requirements. And a federal department of education has at last been established, though with what benefits or burdens for schools and children it is too soon to say.

Yet having won so many victories, some of truly historic dimension, American education is still embattled, still struggling to win public support and approval, and, perhaps worse, still struggling to find its own clear sense of purpose. Paradoxically, the achievements of the recent past seem to have exhausted the usually ready stock of prescriptions for school reform and to have raised once again the most basic questions of educational purpose.

Like other major institutions in our society, the schools are continually judged by today's demands and today's performance, and no credit is extended by clients or critics for yesterday's victories. Which is as it should be. School criticism, as I noted earlier, is nothing new. Behind any criticism, however, are assumptions about what schools should and can do, and criticisms have shifted as assumptions about the goals and potentialities of schools have changed. Since the early nineteenth century, the tenor of school criticism has been essentially optimistic; no matter how despairing the critic, his working assumption has been that schools are valuable institutions, that they have within them the power to facilitate social, moral, and political regeneration, and that more money, or more public concern, or better teachers could extend the promise of schooling to everyone. If more people had more schooling, critics have contended, and if schools were amply financed and well staffed, there would be enormous benefit to the individual, the society, the economy, and the body politic. With relatively little dissent, Americans have believed in schooling—not because of a love of the hickory stick and the three Rs, or (as some latter-day critics would have it) because of the schools' ability to make children docile workers, but because Americans are deeply committed to self-improvement and the school is an institutionalized expression of that commitment.

Participation in formal schooling has grown sharply in recent decades. The proportion of seventeen-year-olds who graduated from high school grew from about 50 percent in 1940 to about 75 percent in the late 1960s. Similarly, the proportion of young people who entered college climbed from about 16 percent in 1940 to about 45 percent in 1968, at which time it leveled off. In no other country in the world does participation in formal schooling last as long, for so many people, as in the United States. To understand why this broad democratization of educational participation occurred, as well as why the 1980s began on a note of disillusionment, it is useful to consider some of the expectations we have attached to formal schooling.

Until well into the twentieth century, only a small minority of Americans attended college. College was not only expensive but exclusive. Many, perhaps most, colleges maintained quotas for some groups (like Jews and Catholics) and excluded others altogether (blacks). After World War II, more than 2 million veterans attended college, crowding and sometimes overwhelming America's campuses. The GI Bill launched the world's first experiment in universal access to higher education. While most veterans did not use their benefits to attend college, the experience of those who did benefited the individuals, the institutions, and the economy. In light of the success and popularity of the GI program, the conviction that college should be a right rather than a privilege gained broad support.

While demand for expanded access to higher education grew steadily in the states and nation, other political forces combined to advance the role of education as a weapon against poverty. The notion that knowledge is power was certainly not novel, nor was the very American belief that schooling is an antidote to crime, poverty, and vice. The school promoters of the early nineteenth century repeatedly argued that schooling would give people the means to improve themselves and thereby break the cycle of poverty. During the early 1960s, this traditional rhetoric was given new life by scholars and policymakers. Educational programs burgeoned as an integral part of the federal government's war on poverty. Jacob Riis had written in 1892, "the more kindergartens, the fewer prisons"; in 1965 Lyndon Johnson predicted that the lives of children in the Head Start summer program would be spent "productively and rewardingly rather than wasted in tax-supported institutions or in welfare-supported lethargy." The hope of eliminating poverty and inequality provided the major rationale not only for Operation Head Start but for general federal aid to education as well.

By the time the period of educational expansion reached a high tide in the middle 1960s, much was expected by a variety of publics. It was hoped that more education would:

- Reduce inequality among individuals and groups by eliminating illiteracy and cultural deprivation.
- Improve the economy and economic opportunity by raising the number of intelligent and skilled individuals.
- Spread the capacity for personal fulfillment by developing talents, skills, and creative energies.
- Prove to be an uplifting and civilizing influence in the nation's cultural life by broadly diffusing the fruits of liberal education.
- Reduce alienation and mistrust while building a new sense of community among people of similar education and similar values.
- Reduce prejudice and misunderstanding by fostering contact among diverse groups.
- Improve the quality of civic and political life.

These hopes and expectations were a heavy burden for the schools to bear. Perhaps predictably, they did not accomplish all that was asked of them. Most of the problems that were laid at the schools' doors remained just as problematic years later (and some critics would argue that the provision of more schooling had produced the opposite effect in every instance). Poverty and inequality did not disappear; their roots were elsewhere, and the schools were not able to cure deep-seated social and economic ills. While the disadvantaged received more schooling, so did the advantaged. Many poor youths entered the middle class by using educational opportunity, but others remained as poor as their parents. The value of a high school diploma declined not only because its possession became nearly universal but also, and most important, because high school graduates were not necessarily literate—mainly because of the well-intended effort to keep as many youths in school for as long as possible and to deny no one a diploma, regardless of his educational development. Society's investment in education probably did spur economic development, but it did not prevent the emergence of skepticism about the desirability of economic growth; in fact, it was precisely among the educated (and the advantaged) that economic growth became suspect because of its association with the bureaucratization, centralization, and depersonalization of modern economic life. It is impossible to gauge the effects of increased schooling on popular culture or high culture. Television, which invariably seeks the largest possible audience, undoubtedly has more power to shape popular culture than schools do (a mixed blessing, since television disperses both sitcom pap and major cultural events to mass audiences). Participation in popular culture and high culture has surely been broadened, yet it is arguable whether the quality of either has been elevated during recent decades. Nor is it possible to demonstrate that increased educational participation has eliminated distrust between groups or contributed to a new sense of community. On the contrary, educational institutions have become settings for expression of militant particularism along racial, religious, ethnic, sexual, cultural, and linguistic lines. Very likely the differences among groups have been accentuated in the past twenty years. But again, it would be difficult to hold the schools directly responsible for these trends. More likely, it appears, the schools are the stage on which such issues are acted out rather than the cause of their appearance. Nor can the schools claim to have improved the quality of political life, since political participation has waned along with public regard for political institutions. But once again, it was not the schools that were responsible for the apparent ebbing of civic commitment and the surge of political apathy, nor could they even serve as a counterforce against such attitudes. The same attitudes of distrust, skepticism, hostility, and apathy eroded the schools' own status in the social order. The same confusions that pervaded the social atmosphere also pervaded the schools. If they failed to teach citizenship, it was at least in part because teachers and parents were confused about what a good citizen was and whether "citizenship" could be taught without imposing a partisan interpretation. In short, a society that is confused and contentious cannot look to its schools to straighten things out, for the schools will reflect the same confusion and contention.

In retrospect, it was folly to have expected the schools to transform society or to mold a new kind of person. The schools are by nature limited institutions, not total institutions. They do not have full power over their students' lives (even total institutions, like prisons, have discovered the difficulty of shaping or reshaping the lives and minds of those they fully control). Schools are not fully independent in their dealings with students; they are interrelated with, and dependent on, families, churches, the media, peer groups, and other agencies of influence. Nor can schools be considered as if they were machines, all operating in the same predictable manner. Teachers vary, administrators vary, students vary, communities vary, and therefore schools vary. The schools, being complex human institutions composed of actors with different goals, different interests, and different capacities, cannot be treated as if they were all interchangeable.

As it became clear that more schooling would not provide any magical solutions, the utopian hopes once focused on the schools dissipated. Having briefly been the repository of grand and even grandiose dreams of human betterment, the schools became a scapegoat for all the wide-ranging problems they had failed to solve. Having revealed that they were but fallible instruments of social change and that any change they promoted would only be incremental, the schools became the object of rage and scorn. They were portrayed as intractable, bureaucratic, even malevolent barriers to social change. But just as it was unrealistic to believe that the schools had the power to remake society by molding those who passed through their doors, it was equally unrealistic to assert that they were powerless, meaningless, superfluous institutions with no purpose other than the care and feeding of their own employees.

Nonetheless, when the dream of a school-led social revolution faded, school criticism shifted in tone. The voices of liberal critics—those who believed that men and women of goodwill might work together to improve schools by using this program or that curriculum—diminished to mere whispers. They were drowned out by critics who believed that only radical changes in teaching or in governing schools could "save" them; by those who believed that the public schools were beyond redemption and ought to be replaced by "free" schools; and by those who advocated

the abolition of compulsory schooling and the "deschooling" of society. For a time in the late 1960s and early 1970s, bookstore shelves fairly bulged with apocalyptic predictions about the imminent demise of schooling. One book, playing on the then current phrase "God is dead," was titled *School Is Dead.* While some of the writing of this period contained sharp and telling portraits of insensitive teachers and uncaring bureaucrats, others gave vent to undisguised anti-intellectualism in their attacks on academic standards, discipline, science, and rationality. In the larger culture—and, alas, especially in academic institutions—a great revival seemed to sweep the land, casting aside "old" doctrines of deferred gratification, structured learning, and professionalism while espousing mysticism, Eastern religions, the occult, astrology, and whatever else promised to touch the spontaneous, untrained inner spirit.

These trends had curricular and programmatic consequences. In colleges, students demanded, and usually won, the abolition of course requirements, the adoption of pass-fail grading, the de-emphasis of competition and testing, and extensive choice in selecting their own programs of study. As requirements for admission to college were relaxed, high schools soon succumbed to many of the same pressures that had changed the colleges: Course requirements were eased, new courses proliferated, academic standards dropped, homework diminished, and adults generally relinquished their authority to direct student learning. At all levels, both in college and high school, educational administrators reduced, to the extent possible, the schools' role as *in loco parentis.* To some extent, this period of student assertiveness and adult retreat was the educational side of the movement against the war in Vietnam, which provoked youthful revolt against authority in many parts of the society and the culture. But even after the war ended, there remained a lingering hostility to science, technology, and reason—as though these were the root causes of the hated war.

As the 1980s opened, it appeared that this wave of anti-intellectualism had spent itself, for complaints about the schools suggested entirely different concerns. The well-publicized decline in Scholastic Aptitude Test (SAT) scores created a context for worrying about a national deterioration in the quality of education. Not that the SAT scores were important in themselves, but they provided a sense of a pattern in the carpet that had not previously been discernible. For several years college officials had reported a steady increase in the number of freshmen who read poorly and wrote atrociously; the phenomenon of remedial reading and remedial writing classes spread throughout higher education, even to elite institutions. The apparent explanation, at first, was that so many new students from poor families had begun to attend college, but analysis of the SAT drop showed that the score decline continued long after the socioeconomic profile of the college-going population had stabilized. Bits and pieces of evidence from other sources began to fit together. Other standardized measures of academic ability reported score declines paralleling the SATs. National newsmagazines discovered a writing crisis and a literacy crisis. Educational malpractice suits were filed by disgruntled parents because their children had received a high school diploma in spite of being "functionally illiterate." The Council for Basic Education, a lonely voice for liberal education since its founding in 1958, found itself back in the educational mainstream, while still a lonely voice for liberal education. Demands for minimum competency tests seemed to spring up spontaneously in almost every state, though no national organization existed to promote or coordinate the movement. As concern for educational standards spread in the middle 1970s, demands for testing grew—not only minimum competency tests for high school graduation but tests at critical checkpoints in the lower grades and tests for would-be teachers. Reaction against those demands was not long in coming. The assault upon standardized testing was led by consumer activist Ralph Nader and the National Education Association. Nader released a lengthy attack on the credibility of the SAT, the most widely used college admission test, and lobbied successfully in New York State and elsewhere for passage of a "truth-in-testing" law.

While it did generate controversy, the dispute over testing was superficial, for tests were neither a cause of nor a remedy for the underlying malaise in American education. Nearly all the educational controversies of the 1970s—whether over bilingualism or sex education or testing or open admissions or busing—dealt with some aspect of the educational process that was of great importance to some constituency, but none directly raised these questions: What does it mean to be an educated person? What knowledge is of most worth? Are the graduates of our schools educated people?

The very absence of such questioning suggests a failure in educational thinking. Educators and, most especially, educational policymakers have fallen into the habit of analyzing school issues almost entirely in sociological and economic terms. In recent years it has been customary to think of schooling as a quantifiable economic good to be distributed in accordance with principles of equity or in response to political demands. The sociological-economic perspective has come to dominate educational discussion and has informed public policy. Without doubt it has contributed to necessary changes in patterns of schooling, by redirecting resources in a fair manner and by opening up access to educational opportunities. But the functionalist perspective became dysfunctional when it crowded substantive educational concerns off the policymakers' agenda, when the desire to keep students in school was unaccompanied by interest in what they would learn while they stayed in school. What I am suggesting here is not a conflict between the functionalist perspective and the educational perspective, but the danger of analyzing the schools through only one of the two prisms. There has been a fairly persistent tendency, I would argue, to neglect the role of schools as educational institutions, to treat them as sociological cookie cutters without regard to the content of their educational program. When I consider why this is so, I conclude that there are several possible explanations.

First, the sociological perspective has become dominant because it relies on quantifiable data that are accessible. It is far easier to gain information about years of educational attainment and socioeconomic status than it is to ascertain the conditions of learning in any given school. Educators cannot agree on how to assess the educational climate or even on what should be learned. Thus it becomes irresistible to deal with, perhaps even become the captive of, data that are both available and measurable.

Second, the sociological perspective is a useful adjunct to the concept of the school as a tool of social reform. By measuring which groups are in school and how their social background relates to their choice of occupation, we can attempt to monitor how educational resources are allocated and whether schooling is contributing to social progress. While it is neither new nor unusual to regard the school as a lever of social reform, it is unusual and perhaps unwise to see the school *solely* as a tool of social reform and *solely* as a resource to be redistributed. One consequence is that the school's diploma is confused with the learning that it is supposed to represent. In recent years, policymakers have sought to equalize educational attainment (years-of-schooling) without regard to the quality of education. This is like putting people on a diet of 1,800 calories a day without caring whether they are consuming junk food or nutritious food. Years-of-schooling, or a diploma, has been treated as an end in itself. Thus we have seen courts require school districts to present a diploma to students who could not meet minimum state standards of literacy, as if it were the diploma itself they needed rather than the learning that the diploma is supposed to signify. When school reformers in the nineteenth century advocated universal education as a way of improving society, they meant a broad diffusion of knowledge and wisdom, not a broad diffusion of diplomas.

Third, educational analysts have relied on the sociological perspective because it is easier to raise the level of educational attainment than it is to raise the level of educational quality. Staying in school, not dropping out, and getting a diploma represents a clear, unambiguous goal that everyone can understand without quarrel. As soon as school officials begin to define what should be taught and learned during those years, disagreements arise, which are best settled by making the schools all things for all people.

For these reasons and others, educational policymakers have tended to view schooling as an instrument to achieve some other goal, only rarely as an end in itself. To the extent that they do so, they rob schooling of the very attributes that give it power. If a young man or woman has a high school diploma but can scarcely read or write, then the diploma is worthless. When a diploma, either at the high school or college level, represents a certificate of time served but not of the systematic development of intelligence and skill, then it is difficult to know why it should have any inherent value. And of course it does not.

An educational critique of schooling should have as its starting point, I believe, the idea that the essential purpose of schooling is to develop the powers of intelligence: thinking, knowing, reflecting, observing, imagining, appreciating, questioning, and judging. Beyond that, schooling has many additional purposes, both for the student and for society. Educational literature teems with lists of the many ways in which schools should meet individual and social needs. But the schools' first purpose is to encourage and guide each person in the cultivation of intelligence and the development of talents, interests, and abilities. Schools do many other things as well: They may provide food, social services, psychological services, medical care, and

career guidance. But no matter how well or how poorly they fulfill these functions, the schools must be judged in the first instance by how well they do those things that only they can do. We expect the schools to teach children command of the fundamental skills that are needed to continue learning—in particular, the ability to read, write, compute, speak, and listen. Once they have command of these skills, they should progress through a curriculum designed to enlarge their powers. Such a curriculum would contain, for every student, history and social studies, language and literature, mathematics, science, and the arts. Students need to learn these skills and disciplines in school because, except for those individuals who can educate themselves without a teacher, they are unlikely to have an another chance to do so.

The schools are responsible both for preserving a sense of the past and for providing the ability to think about, and function in, the present and the future. More than any other educational agency, they ought to have an intelligent understanding of the inexorable connection between past, present, and future. Certainly there is disagreement about the meaning of the past and how it relates to the present and the future, and awareness of such disagreement is often invoked to justify educational aimlessness. But much of what seems to be dissension is a chimera; democratic debate ought not to be confused with chaos, nor should pluralistic politics be confused with anarchy. Education proceeds from widely shared values, and we do, in fact, have widely shared values. We may not agree about how democracy is to be achieved and about whether we have too much or too little of it, but few would question the idea that each person has the right as a citizen to participate in the shaping of public issues. We believe in the idea of self-government and in the greatest possible involvement of citizens as voters, as volunteers in community organizations, as members of interest groups, and as spokesmen for different views. While we may differ over particular educational issues, there is general support for the idea that schooling is a necessary mechanism for achieving society's goals: to prepare the younger generation to be thoughtful citizens; to enable each person to appreciate and contribute to the culture; to sharpen the intellectual and aesthetic sensibilities for lifelong enjoyment; to develop readiness for the educational, occupational, and professional choices that each person will confront; to kindle a sense of responsibility for others and a sense of integrity; to teach children how to lead and how to follow; and to acquaint young people with the best models of achievement in every field while encouraging them to strive to realize their own potential.

If these are widely shared educational aims, and I believe they are, then none of them should be left to chance. The curriculum should be designed so that every student has the fullest opportunity to develop his powers, intelligence, interests, talent, and understanding. Every student needs to know how to form and articulate his own opinions. To do so, he must learn how to read critically, how to evaluate arguments, how to weigh evidence, and how to reach judgments on his own. Every student, to understand the world in which he will be a participant, should be knowledgeable about history; should master some other language as well as his own; should discover the pleasures of literature, especially its power to reach across time and cultures and to awaken our sense of universality; should study science and technology, both as a citizen who will be asked to comprehend complex issues and as an individual who must live with constant change. Since we believe that everyone should be equally concerned about the problems of our society, then we must believe that everyone, every student, should be schooled in a way that meets his need to know history, science, mathematics, language, the arts, literature, and so on. And yet it is not simply on the grounds of utility, relevance, and political value that the case for liberal education rests. We do not *need* to know how to read Shakespeare; we can be good citizens without any knowledge of Athenian civilization, even though our concept of citizenship is based on the very period of which we are ignorant. We must concern ourselves with the survival of history, philosophy, literature, and those other humanistic disciplines that may lack immediate utility because without them ours would be an intellectually impoverished and spiritually illiterate civilization.

To some people, all this is so self-evident that it ought not be necessary to plead for the value of an education of substance and content. Yet it is necessary, because of the widespread disarray in high school and college curricula. In the face of changes that have occurred in the past decade or so, many educators seem unable to remember how to justify or defend or champion liberal education. The proposition that all students should be subject to curricular requirements that define the essentials of a good education has become controversial, rather than a starting point in defining the nature of a good curriculum.

Confronted with conflicting demands from those who want reduced requirements and those who want curricular substance, many schools have resolved the dilemma by reducing requirements while expanding electives. Thus students may take "history" courses to meet their minimal graduation requirement, but those so-called history courses may be little more than classes in current events or pop sociology. Or they may meet their English requirement by reading popular fiction, mystery stories, or science fiction. There is no harm in what is included; from the perspective of a liberal education, what is unfortunate is the wide body of knowledge that is excluded when course proliferation and lax requirements are joined together. Professors regularly encounter students who are ignorant of anything that happened before the Civil War as well as anything that happened, or was written, outside the United States. They may have *heard* of Plato and Aristotle in a survey course, but they have never read anything written by either and have only a dim notion (usually wrong) of what they "stood for." Mention Dickens, Tolstoy, Conrad, or Melville, and perhaps they have heard of them too, but they "didn't take that course." Some professors who teach literature have been astonished to find students who know nothing of mythology or the Bible allusions to Job or Icarus must be explained to those who have no intellectual furniture in their minds, no stock of literary or historical knowledge on which to draw beyond their immediate experience. In the April 11, 1980, issue of *Commonweal,* J. M. Cameron soberly observed that if Freud attended school today, he might not be able to think up the Oedipus theory because he would not have enough mythology in his head to do so. We seem now to turn to television or the movies to teach the history and literature that were neglected in school. To permit knowledge to be fragmented, as we have, by serving it up cafeteria-style, with each person choosing whether to be minimally literate or to be a specialist, contributes to the diminution and degradation of the common culture.

Popular Schooling

LAWRENCE A. CREMIN

Every nation, and therefore every national system of education, has the defects of its qualities.—Sir Michael Sadler, "Impressions of American Education"

The popularization of American schools and colleges since the end of World War II has been nothing short of phenomenal, involving an unprecedented broadening of access, an unprecedented diversification of curricula, and an unprecedented extension of public control. In 1950, 34 percent of the American population twenty-five years of age or older had completed at least four-years of high school, while 6 percent of that population had completed at least four years of college. By 1985, 74 percent of the American population twenty-five years of age or older had completed at least four years of high school, while 19 percent had completed at least four years of college. During the same thirty-five year period, school and college curricula broadened and diversified tremendously, in part because of the existential fact of more diverse student bodies with more diverse needs, interests, abilities, and styles of learning; in part because of the accelerating growth of knowledge and new fields of knowledge; in part because of the rapid development of the American economy and its demands on school systems; and in part because of the transformation of America's role in the world. The traditional subjects could be studied in a greater range of forms; the entry of new subjects into curricula provided a greater range of choice; and the effort to combine subjects into new versions of general education created a greater range of requirements. Finally, the rapid increase in the amount of state and federal funds invested in the schools and colleges, coupled with the rising demand for access on the part of segments of the population traditionally held at the margins, brought a corresponding development of the instruments of public oversight and control—local community boards, state coordinating boards, court-appointed masters and monitors, and federal attorneys with the authority to enforce federal regulations. In the process, American schools became at the same time both more centralized and more decentralized.[1]

It was in many ways a remarkable achievement, of which Americans could be justifiably proud. Yet it seemed to bring with it a pervasive sense of failure. During the 1970s, there was widespread suspicion that American students were failing behind in international competition, that while more people were going to school for ever longer periods of time, they were learning less and less. And in the 1980s, that suspicion seemed to be confirmed by the strident rhetoric of the National Commission on Excellence in Education. Recall the commission's charges in *A Nation at Risk:*

> We report to the American people that while we can take justifiable pride in what our schools and colleges have historically accomplished and contributed to the United States and the well-being of its people, the educational foundations of our society are presently being eroded by a rising tide of mediocrity that threatens our very future as a Nation and a people. What was unimaginable a generation ago has begun to happen—others are matching and surpassing our educational attainments.
>
> If an unfriendly power had attempted to impose on America the mediocre educational performance that exists today, we might well have viewed it as an act of war. As it stands, we have allowed this to happen to ourselves.[2]

Now, there have always been critics of the schools and colleges. From the very beginning of the public school crusade in the nineteenth century, there were those who thought that popular schooling was at best a foolish idea and at worst a subversive idea. The editor of the Philadelphia *National Gazette* argued in the 1830s that free universal education was nothing more than a harebrained scheme of social radicals, and claimed that it was absolutely illegal and immoral to tax one part of the community to educate the children of another. And beyond such wholesale opposition, even those who favored the idea of universal education thought that the results were unimpressive. The educa-

Excerpts from *Popular Education and Its Discontents* by Lawrence A. Cremin. Copyright © 1990 by Lawrence A. Cremin. Reprinted by permission of HarperCollins Publishers, Inc.

tor Frederick Packard lamented that the schools were failing dismally in even their most fundamental tasks. He charged on the basis of personal visits to classrooms that nine out of ten youngsters were unable to read a newspaper, keep a simple debit and credit account, or draft an ordinary business letter. The writer James Fenimore Cooper was ready to grant that the lower schools were developing a greater range of talent than was the case in most other countries, but he pointed to what he thought was the superficiality of much of the work of the colleges and bemoaned the absence of genuine accomplishment in literature and the arts. And the French commentator Alexis de Tocqueville, echoing the English critic Sydney Smith, observed that America had produced few writers of distinction, no great artists, and not a single first-class poet. Americans were a practical people, he concluded, but not very speculative. They could boast many lawyers but no jurists, many good workers but few imaginative inventors.[3]

By the early years of the twentieth century, as some elementary education was becoming nearly universal and as secondary education was beginning to be popularized, the critisism became broader and sharper. A writer in *Gunton's Magazine* charged that as schooling had spread it had been made too easy and too entertaining. "The mental nourishment we spoonfeed our children," he observed, "is not only minced but peptonized so that their brains digest it without effort and without benefit and the result is the anaemic intelligence of the average American schoolchild." And a Maryland farmer named Francis Livesey became so outraged at the whole idea of free universal education that he organized a society called the Herbert Spencer Education Club with two classes of membership—one for those seeking the complete abolition of public schooling and one for those willing to settle for the repeal of all compulsory attendance laws.[4]

With respect to secondary and higher education, critics such as Irving Babbitt, Abraham Flexner, and Robert Hutchins leveled blast after blast against the relaxation of language requirements, the overcrowding of curricula with narrow technical courses, and the willingness to permit students to work out their own programs of study. The spread of educational opportunity in the United States, they observed, reflected less a spirit of democratic fairness than a willingness to prolong adolescence. The result was an inferior educational product at every level—high school programs were too watered down and fragmented; the colleges were graduating men and women unable to write and

spell a decent English and pitifully ignorant of mathematics, the sciences, and modern languages; and the graduate schools were crowded with students of mediocre ability who lacked the slightest appreciation of higher culture.[5]

Even those foreign observers who were prone to admire the American commitment to popular schooling wrung their hands at what they saw as the widespread absence of high intellectual expectations, particularly at the high school and college levels. Thus, Sir Michael Sadler, the director of the Office of Special Inquiries and Reports of the British government, and a great friend of the United States, noted an absence of intellectual discipline and rigor in American schools—too much candy and ice cream, he liked to say, and not enough oatmeal porridge. And Erich Hylla, a member of the German ministry of education who had spent a year in residence at Teachers College, Columbia University, and who translated Dewey's *Democracy and Education* into German, lamented what he perceived as the disjointedness and superficiality of secondary and undergraduate study and the resultant poor achievement of American students.[6]

As popularization advanced at every level of schooling after World War II, the drumbeat of dissatisfaction grew louder. Arthur Bestor and Hyman Rickover argued during the 1950s and 1960s that popular schooling had been literally subverted by an interlocking directorate of education professors, state education officials, and professional association leaders; they charged that the basics had been ignored in favor of a trivial curriculum parading under the name of Life Adjustment Education and that as a result American freedom was in jeopardy. Robert Hutchins continued his mordant criticisms of the 1930s, contending that the so-called higher learning purveyed by the colleges and universities was neither higher nor learning but rather a collection of trade school courses intended to help young people win the material success that Americans prized so highly. And again, even those foreign observers who were disposed to admire the American commitment to popular education now made it something of a litany to comment on what they perceived to be the low standards and mediocre achievements of American students. The English political economist Harold Laski noted the readiness of American parents to expect too little of their youngsters and the readiness of the youngsters to see interest in abstract ideas as somewhat strange at best, with the result that American college graduates seemed to him to be two to three years less intellectually mature than their English or French counterparts. And the Scottish political scientist D. W. Brogan was quite prepared to grant that the American public school had been busy Americanizing immigrants for several generations at least—he liked to refer to the public school as "the formally unestablished national church of the United States"—but he saw the price of that emphasis on social goals as an insufficient attention to intellectual goals. For all their talk of preparing the young for life, Brogan maintained, Americans were not being realistic about what life would actually demand during the second half of the twentieth century.[7]

Within such a context, Paul Copperman's allegations of the late 1970s that Americans of that generation would be the first whose educational skills would not surpass or equal or even approach those of their parents, which the National Commission on Excellence in Education quoted approvingly in *A Nation at Risk,* and Allan Bloom's assertions of the late 1980s that higher education had failed democracy and impoverished the souls of American students were scarcely surprising or even original. Why all the fuss, then? How, if at all, did the criticisms of the 1980s differ from those that had come before? I believe they differed in three important ways: they were more vigorous and pervasive; they were putatively buttressed by data from cross-national studies of educational achievement; and, coming at a time when Americans seemed to be feeling anxious about their place in the world, they gave every indication of being potentially more dangerous and destructive.[8] . . .

The 1980s brought another shift in the climate of educational opinion, this one exemplified by the two reports that have already been alluded to, the reports of the National Commission on Excellence in Education entitled *A Nation at Risk,* and of the Study Group on the State of Learning in the Humanities in Higher Education entitled *To Reclaim a Legacy.*

The National Commission had been created in 1981 by President Reagan's first secretary of education, Terrel Bell—the same Terrel Bell, incidentally, who in the 1970s had introduced the report of the USOE's National Panel on High School and Adolescent Education with a glowing foreword referring to the report as a major contribution to the public discussion of secondary education. The membership of the commission included educators, scientists, businesspeople, and politicians, with David P. Gardner, president of the University of Utah, as chair (Gardner

subsequently became president of the University of California) and Yvonne W. Larsen, immediate past president of the San Diego school board, as vice-chair. The commission held hearings, took testimony, and visited schools in various parts of the country through much of 1982 and then reviewed various quite different drafts of the report during the first months of 1983. The final report—terse, direct, and unqualified in its assertions—was largely the work of the scientists on the panel. In effect, it put forward a severe indictment of American education and proposed a fundamental set of reforms. The report cited rates of adult illiteracy (as many as 23 million functionally illiterate Americans), declining scores on the Scholastic Aptitude Test (an almost unbroken decline from 1963 to 1980), and deficiencies in knowledge on the part of seventeen-year-olds as revealed by international tests of achievement (American students never ranked first or second on any of nineteen academic tests). From this and other "dimensions of the risk before us," the commission concluded that "the educational foundations of our society are presently being eroded by a rising tide of mediocrity that threatens our very future as a Nation and a people."[9]

As remedies, the commission put forward five recommendations: (1) that, as a minimum, all students seeking a high school diploma be required to complete during the four years of high school the following work in the "new basics"—four years of English, three years of mathematics, three years of science, three years of social studies, and a half year of computer science; (2) that schools, colleges, and universities adopt higher expectations of their students and that four-year colleges and universities raise their requirements for admission; (3) that significantly more time be devoted to teaching and learning the new basics, and that this be achieved through more effective use of the existing school day, a lengthened school day, or a lengthened school year; (4) that the preparation of teachers be strengthened and teaching be made a more rewarding and more respected profession; and (5) that citizens throughout the nation require their elected officials to support these reforms and to provide the money necessary to achieve them. Interestingly, the report mentioned a role for the federal government in defining the national interest in education, but it assigned to state and local officials the primary responsibility for initiating and carrying out the recommendations. Beyond that, it ended with a word to parents and students, asking the parents to raise their expectations of their children, and asking students to work harder in school.[10]

During the next few years there followed in the wake of *A Nation at Risk* a score of reports on the problems of the schools, each putting forth its own particular agenda for reform. A task force organized by the Twentieth Century Fund stressed the need for English as the language of schooling, through the grades and across the country. A commission organized by the National Science Board stressed the need for all young Americans to have a firm grounding in mathematics, science, and technology. A task force organized by the Education Commission of the States stressed the relationship of more intense schooling to the maintenance of America's economic competitiveness in the world. A panel organized by the National Academy of Sciences stressed the need for academic competence in the kind of workplace that was coming into being in the United States. A task force organized by the Committee for Economic Development stressed the need for businesspeople to be interested and involved in the work of the schools. And Ernest Boyer, writing on behalf of the Carnegie Foundation for the Advancement of Teaching, stressed the need for a coherent curriculum core at the heart of any worthy secondary education. All in one way or another re-sounded the themes of *A Nation at Risk*—the need for emphasis on a new set of basics, the need for a more intensive school experience for all young people, and the need for a better trained teaching profession in the nation's schools.[1]

In addition, several major reports dealing with higher education also followed the publication of *A Nation at Risk,* notably, William J. Bennett's report on behalf of the National Endowment for the Humanities Study Group, entitled *To Reclaim a Legacy;* the report of a Select Committee of the Association of American Colleges, entitled *Integrity in the College Curriculum;* and a report of Ernest Boyer, again writing on behalf of the Carnegie Foundation for the Advancement of Teaching, entitled *College: The Undergraduate Experience in America.* All three lamented the absence of a clear vision of the educated person at the heart of undergraduate education, one that would call for all students to undertake fundamental studies in the humanities (Bennett), the natural sciences, and the social sciences (the AAC Select Committee and Boyer); all three lamented the concentration on research and the inattention to teaching in the preparation and careers of college professors; all three called for a renewed effort to develop an integrated core of required subjects that would be taught to all candidates for the bachelor's degree, whatever their majors or professional goals; and

all three called for a new emphasis on imaginative and informed teaching in the nation's colleges and universities.[12]

Yet again, let us examine the grand story implicit and explicit in these reports, the ideas they present about how education works, why it goes wrong, and how it can be set right. For the various commissions of the early 1980s, the popularization of education has been an utter and complete failure, because popularization has brought with it declension and degradation. For the National Commission on Excellence in Education, the educational foundations of society are being eroded by a rising tide of mediocrity; in the National Commission's view, Paul Copperman is correct in his assertion that for the first time in the history of the United States the educational achievement of the present generate on will not surpass, equal, or even approach the educational achievement of its parents. For the AAC Select Committee, a century-long decline of undergraduate education into disarray and incoherence has accompanied the rise of academic specialization associated with the research universities, and that decline has been accelerated by the upsurge of higher education enrollments since World War II. In effect, the decline and degradation have occurred because education is essentially the study of the liberal arts—what Conant called general education, what the National Commission called the new basics, what Ernest Boyer called the integrated core. The liberal arts were at the heart of education during the nineteenth and early twentieth centuries, and popularization has brought a vitiation of their formative power in favor of narrow specialization and crass vocationalism. How can education be set right? By requiring study of the liberal arts of all students, and by popularizing education without permitting it to be vulgarized, that is, by universalizing precisely the education that was formerly preserved for the few and making it mandatory for all. The popularization of education involves an increase in the size of the clientele, not a transformation in the nature of the curriculum.

Nowhere was the grand story of the early 1980s more dramatically presented than in Allan Bloom's *The Closing of the American Mind.* The educational and political crisis of twentieth-century America is essentially an intellectual crisis, Bloom asserted. It derives, he continued, from the university's lack of central purpose, from the students' lack of fundamental learning, from the displacement of the traditional classical humanistic works that long dominated the curriculum—the works of Plato and Aristotle and Augustine and Shakespeare and Spinoza and Rousseau—by specialized electives and courses in the creative arts, and from the triumph of relativism over perennial humanistic values. How can the crisis be resolved? Clearly, by a restoration of true learning in the schools and colleges through the traditional disciplines and the works of the Western canon. Could that restoration be compatible with further popularization of higher education? Almost certainly not!

My friend Richard Heffner once asked me on his television program, *The Open Mind,* whether the ideal of popular education was not an impossible ideal, whether it not only was not working but in the end could not work. I maintained that no ideal is ever completely achievable; if it is, it is not an ideal. What an ideal does hold out is a goal, which people can then approach more or less successfully. And I argued that the ideal of popular education, at least as it had developed in the United States, was one of the most radical ideals in the Western world, that we had made great progress in moving toward the ideal, but that the attainment had been wanting in many domains, and that the institutions we had established to further that attainment had been flawed in many respects. We had, to be blunt, a long way to go, but it was worth trying to get there.

After we were off the air, I asked Heffner if he was not really asking whether the phrase popular education is an oxymoron, a contradiction, in its very nature flawed and unachievable. He protested not. But I think many people believe that the contradiction is there, that education in its true meaning is an elite phenomenon, just as such people would argue that culture in its true meaning is an elite phenomenon, and that as soon as education begins to be transformed by popularization—by popular interest, popular demand, popular understanding, and popular acceptance—it is inevitably vulgarized. In essence, these people would argue that there is no more possibility of a popular education than there is of a popular culture. What results when education is popularized is an educational version of what the critic Dwight Macdonald once labeled "masscult" or "midcult." I believe this is the explicit message of Allan Bloom's book. And I would trace the most fundamental and abiding discontent with popular education in the United States to the sense that it is not only an impossible ideal but in the end a hopeless contradiction.[13]

To argue in favor of popular education is not to deny the tremendous difficulties inevitably involved in achieving it. On the one side, there are the inescapable political problems of determining the nature, content, and values of popular education. Legislators want the schools to teach the advantages of patriotism and the dangers of substance abuse: parents want the schools to teach character and discipline; employers want the schools to teach diligence and the basic skills; arts advocates want the schools to teach painting, drama, music, and dance; academics want the schools to teach more of what they know—historians want more history, mathematicians more mathematics, and economists more economics; students want the schools to equip them to go on to college if they wish, to prepare them to obtain and hold a job with a future, and to offer them opportunities to enjoy sports, hobbies, and a decent social life; and a host of organized citizens' groups want the schools to attend to their special concerns, which range from civil liberties to fire prevention. Out of a process that involves all three branches of government at the state and federal levels as well as thousands of local school boards, a plethora of private interests ranging from publishers to accrediting agencies, and the variety of professionals who actually operate the schools emerges what we call the curriculum, with its requirements, its electives, its informal activities, and its unacknowledged routines. It is that curriculum, in various versions, that is supposed to be offered to all the children of all the people. On the other side, there are the demands of the children, with their almost infinite variety of needs, wants, and values, deriving from extraordinary differences in their family backgrounds, their rates and patterns of development, their learning styles, and their social, intellectual, and vocational aspirations.

The resulting dilemmas are as difficult philosophically as they are insistent politically. Will the increased stringency of academic requirements stimulated by the report of the National Commission on Excellence in Education create a rise in the dropout rate at the same time that it encourages more capable students to higher levels of academic performance? The dropout rate has indeed gone up, but we do not know whether that testifies to the inability (or unwillingness) of students to master the newly required material or the difficulties teachers face in teaching the newly required material with sufficient versatility, or both. However that may be, the loss to the American polity, economy, and society, and to the individual youngsters who drop out, is prodigious. Meanwhile, the Japanese, though admittedly a less heterogeneous people than the Americans, are mandating even more difficult material for their high school students, with a lower dropout rate. Will the effort to advance racial integration by insisting upon comprehensive high schools cause white flight that in the end leads to increased segregation and lower academic performance? There are those who say that it will, and there are communities where the effort to maintain comprehensive high schools has been correlated with white flight, increased segregation, and lower academic performance. Meanwhile, the Swedes seem to be managing to maintain comprehensive high schools in an increasingly heterogeneous society without lowering academic performance. Do the traditions of competitive individualism lead American parents, teachers, and students to assume that some young people must inevitably fall? The data from John Goodlad's study of schooling provide evidence that such assumptions are rampant. Yet there have long been experimental schools in the United States and abroad in which the school class as a whole has been made responsible for the performance of individual members, with the result that students end up helping one another to succeed. In sum, does the success of popular education ultimately depend upon the values of the society it is meant to nurture and sustain, which in the American case involves a penchant for utility, an ambivalence toward book learning, and a preoccupation with individual success? Do such values by their very nature compromise the success of popular education?[14]

Furthermore, there are the patent flaws in the system of institutions Americans have created to realize the ideal of popular education. One might note in the first place the undetermined number of children in the United States who are simply not in school at any given time for one reason or another and who are not even known to be not in school. When the Children's Defense Fund did its pioneering study of *Children Out of School in America* during the early 1970s, it found, quite beyond the United States census statistic of nearly two million children between the ages of seven and seventeen out of school, thousands of children who had been expelled or suspended for disciplinary reasons, countless truants who had managed to elude census enumerators and attendance officers, and undetermined numbers of children who had fallen through the cracks of the system for reasons of pregnancy, poverty, mental retardation, or emotional disability. In addition, it found even greater numbers of children who were technically in school but who might just as well have been counted as out of school—youngsters of recent immi-grant families sitting uncomprehendingly in classrooms conducted in English, youngsters misdiagnosed as retarded who were really deaf, youngsters so alienated by real or perceived indifference, condescension, or prejudice that they had long since stopped profiting from anything the schools had to offer.[15]

One might go on to note the flaws in individual institutions—elementary schools where children do not learn to read because they are not taught; high schools where young men and women from working-class backgrounds are denied access to the studies of languages and mathematics that would make it possible for them to become engineers or scientists; junior colleges where recent immigrants with aspirations to undergraduate degrees cannot find the guidance they require to choose the proper academic courses and hence end up locked into narrow occupational programs; and four-year colleges where students graduating with a melange of "gut" courses find themselves with a worthless credential and few prospects of decent employment. One might note, too, the flaws in whole systems of schooling, especially the overbureaucratized and underfinanced systems of many of our central cities, heavily populated by the poor, the nonwhite, and the recently arrived, those most in need of carefully and expertly delivered educational services and least likely to receive them.

Popular education, then, is as radical an ideal as Americans have embraced. It is by its very nature fraught with difficulty, and the institutions we have established to achieve it are undeniably flawed. Yet it is important to be aware of what has been accomplished in the movement toward popular education and of the possibilities for the future. I believe the predicament of American schooling during the early 1980s was not nearly so dire as the report of the National Commission suggested. As Lawrence Stedman and Marshall Smith pointed out in a detailed examination of the evidence cited in the report, the academic achievement of young Americans in the early 1980s was far more mixed than the commission alleged. There were definite improvements in the performance of younger children, reflecting, I believe, the additional educational services made available by Title I/Chapter I federal funds. These were coupled with a patently uneven performance on the part of adolescents, a performance marked by relatively good showings in literature and the social studies and rather poor showings in foreign languages, mathematics, and the natural sciences as well as in the development of the higher order skills associated with critical thinking. Everyone agreed that the results should have been better—in fact, there were data in John Goodlad's study of schooling suggesting that significant numbers of the students themselves believed they might have been working harder and more effectively. Moreover, given the extraordinary percentage of young Americans who were continuing on to postsecondary education, the results would likely have been better in comparison with other countries had the tests been administered at age nineteen or twenty instead of seventeen or eighteen. However that may be, there was surely no evidence to support the commission's affirmation of Paul Copperman's claim that the present generation would be the first in American history whose educational skills would not equal or even approach those of its parents.[16]

Furthermore, we know that standardized tests measure at best only a fraction of what young people have learned in school, and they measured that imperfectly, so that if one were to venture past the test scores to examine what was actually happening in the schools of the early 1980s, a cluster of studies by scholars like John Goodlad, Philip Jackson, Sara Lawrence Lightfoot, Mary Haywood Metz, Vito Perrone, Arthur Powell, and others revealed a far more complex picture of what was going on. They indicated that, overall, there was strong emphasis in school curricula on the English language and literature; that considerable importance was being placed on social studies, mathematics, the natural sciences, the arts, physical education, and, in the upper grades, so-called career education but that foreign languages were receiving limited attention at best; that teachers were mindful of their responsibility to inculcate discipline and nurture civic and social skills; that most schools were orderly places where teachers and students went about the diurnal business of education in a systematic and mutually respectful fashion; that many schools were contending thoughtfully and effectively with the prodigious problems of integrating vastly diverse clienteles into the American polity and economy; that students in general were learning what their parents and teachers thought it was important for them to learn; and that there were significant numbers of students who excelled, by any reasonable standard, in literature, the sciences, the fine and performing arts, and athletics. But they also indicated that students spent less time in school each year and less time at home doing schoolwork than their counterparts in a number of other countries; that teachers, particularly at the elementary level, were poorly

trained in mathematics and the natural sciences and that their poor training was a key factor in the relatively low achievement of students in those subjects; that far too much teaching was uninspired and unimaginative, with consistent overreliance on lectures, drills and workbooks and underreliance on a wide range of alternative pedagogies and technologies; that teachers felt severely constrained in their daily work by bureaucratic rules and procedures; and, most important, that the greatest failures and most serious unsolved problems of the system were those relating to the education of poor children from minority populations in the schools of the central cities.[17]

The reports on higher education during the 1980s, with their emphasis on the loss of an integrated core in undergraduate education and the deleterious effects of that loss, were also at best distorted in their diagnosis of the current situation. Whatever core there might have been in the liberal arts institutions of the seventeenth and eighteenth centuries had already begun to disintegrate in the nineteenth century in the face of rising enrollments and expanding commitments, and with the exception of its presence in a few elite colleges and universities, that core as traditionally defined has not been much seen in the twentieth century. The explosion of knowledge that marked the rise of the research university necessitated not only the extensive choice embodied in the elective system but also the kind of continuing redefinition of any integrated core by college and university faculties that would inevitably lead to various versions of general and liberal education. Allan Bloom's Western canon is one of those versions, but only one. There are other versions that derive from different definitions of the educated person.

That variety of definitions holds the key, it seems to me, to the current situation in American education. Americans have traditionally assigned a wide range of responsibilities to their schools and colleges. They want the schools and colleges to teach the fundamental skills of reading, writing, and arithmetic; to nurture critical thinking; to convey a general fund of knowledge; to develop creativity and aesthetic perception; to assist students in choosing and preparing for vocations in a highly complex economy; to inculcate ethical character and good citizenship; to develop physical and emotional well-being; and to nurture the ability, the intelligence, and the will to continue on with education as far as any particular individual wants to go. And this catalogue does not even mention such herculean social tasks as taking the initiative in racial desegregation and informing the population about the dangers of drug abuse and AIDS. Americans have also maintained broad notions of the active intellect and informed intelligence required to participate responsibly in the affairs of American life. One associates these notions with the inclusive definitions of literacy that make the role of literacy in everyday life central and with the plural definitions of intelligence that embrace musical and kinesthetic intelligence as well as logical, linguistic, and mathematical intelligence—the sorts of definitions that Howard Gardner has advanced in *Frames of Mind* (1983). And they have not only countenanced but urged a wide-ranging curriculum that goes far beyond the "new basics" or the "integrated core" or the "Western canon" of the recent policy reports—those are at best somewhat narrow, academicist versions of American education. As with all latitudinarianism, such definitions can permit triviality to enter the curriculum, and triviality is not difficult to find in American schools and colleges. But on balance I believe such broad definitions have served the American people well.[18]

If there is a crisis in American schooling, it is not the crisis of putative mediocrity and decline charged by the recent reports but rather the crisis inherent in balancing this tremendous variety of demands Americans have made on their schools and colleges—of crafting curricula that take account of the needs of a modern society at the same time that they make provision for the extraordinary diversity of America's young people; of designing institutions where well-prepared teachers can teach under supportive conditions, and where *all* students can be motivated and assisted to develop their talents to the fullest; and of providing the necessary resources for creating and sustaining such institutions. These tough problems may not make it into the headlines or onto television, and there is no quick fix that will solve them; but in the end they constitute the real and abiding crisis of popular schooling in the United States.

In thinking about the search for solutions, it is well to bear in mind that there remain some 15,000 school districts in the United States that sponsor about 59,000 elementary schools and 24,000 secondary schools, and that there are also almost 21,000 private elementary schools and 8,000 private secondary schools. In addition, there are around 3,000 institutions of higher education, of which fully a third are two-year community colleges. Given this multitude of institutions organized into fifty state systems—some highly centralized, some

loosely decentralized—programs of education will differ, and local as well as cosmopolitan influences will prevail. For all the centralizing tendencies in American schooling—from federal mandates to regional accrediting association guidelines to standardized tests and textbooks—the experience students have in one school will differ from the experience they have in another, whatever the formal curriculum indicates might be going on; and the standards by which we judge those experiences will derive from local realities, clienteles, faculties, and aspirations as well as from cosmopolitan knowledge, norms, and expectations. The good school, as Sara Lightfoot has argued, is good in its context.[19]

It is that point, I believe, that the high school reports of the 1970s were trying to make, when they recommended the further differentiation of curricula and the brokering by the schools of educational opportunities for youngsters in libraries, museums, workplaces, government agencies, and community organizations. It is that point, too, that the Carnegie Commission was trying to make when it recommended a vast expansion of enrollments and a further diversification of curricula in the first two years of postsecondary education. Where I would quarrel with the Carnegie Commission (and later the Carnegie Council on Policy Studies in Higher Education) would be in its insistence on confining the expansion and diversification to the junior college and on protecting the four-year colleges from the demands and effects of popularization. In my own view, the commission drew far too great a distinction between the programs of two-year and four-year colleges and invested far too much energy in trying to preserve the imagined distinctions. For one thing, there is tremendous overlap in the character of the two kinds of institutions. For another, both need adjustment to facilitate the easy transfer of students from the former to the latter, which was envisioned by President Truman's Commission on Higher Education, but which has not come to pass.

More important, however, I believe there is need for a far greater sense of unity in the American school system, one that envisions the system whole, extending from nursery schools through the so-called doctorate-granting institutions, with individuals making their way through the system according to their own lights and aspirations and institutions creating their clienteles competitively, much as they do today. I would abandon the constraint the Carnegie Commission preached when it expressed the hope that the two-year colleges would be discouraged from trying to become four-year undergraduate institutions. Sir Eric Ashby, who prepared the immensely incisive monograph *Any Person, Any Study* for the Carnegie Commission—the title bespoke Sir Eric's sense of the openness of American higher education—observed that while the Soviet Union maintained a diversity of higher education institutions stratified according to subjects the United States maintained a diversity of higher education institutions stratified according to quality. He defined quality, of course, in terms of what Martin Trow had called the "autonomous" functions of higher education—with the elite universities devoted primarily to research at the top, with the comprehensive universites dividing their efforts between research and teaching at a somewhat lower status, and with the colleges and universites devoting their efforts primarily to teaching occupying an even lower status. I would alter Ashby's aphorism to argue that while the Soviet Union maintains a diversity of higher education institutions stratified according to subjects the United States maintains a diversity of higher education institutions organized according to missions, missions that vary considerably. And I think that kind of organization is part of the genius of American education—it provides a place for everybody who wishes one, and in the end yields one of the most educated populations in the world.[20]

Notes

1. Thomas D. Snyder, *Digest of Education Statistics, 1987* (Washington, D.C.: Government Printing Office, 1987), 13.

2. National Commission on Excellence in Education. *A Nation at Risk: The Imperative for Educational Reform* (Washington, D.C.: GPO, 1983), 5.

3. Philadelphia *National Gazette,* July 10, 1830, 2; [Frederick Adolphus Packard], *The Daily Public School in the United States* (Philadelphia: Lippincott, 1866), 10–11; J. F. Cooper, *Notions of the Americans* (2 vols.; London: Henry Colburn, 1828), 2:122, 127; and Alexis de Tocqueville, *Democracy in America,* edited by Phillips Bradley (2 vols.; New York: Knopf, 1945), 1:315.

4. Lys d'Aimée, "The Menace of Present Educational Methods," *Gunton's Magazine,* 19 (September 1900):263; and Lawrence A. Cremin and Robert M. Weiss, "Yesterday's School Critic," *Teachers College Record,* 54 (November 1952):77–82.

5. Irving Babbitt, *Literature and the American College: Essays in Defense of the Humanities* (Boston: Houghton Mifflin, 1908), chap. 3; Abraham Flexner, *A Modern College and a Modern School* (Garden City, N.Y.: Doubleday, 1923); *Do Americans Really Value Education?* (Cambridge, Mass.: Harvard University Press, 1927); and *Universities: American, English, German* (New York: Oxford University Press, 1930); and Robert Maynard Hutchins, *The Higher Learning in America* (New Haven: Yale University Press, 1936).

6. Michael E. Sadler, "Impressions of American Education," *Educational Review,* 25 (March 1903):228; and Erich Hylla, *Die Schule der Demokratie, Ein Aufriss des Bildungswesens der Vereinigten Staaten* (Langensalza: Verlag von Julius Beltz, 1928), chap. 3.

7. Arthur Bestor, *The Restoration of Learning: A Program for Redeeming the Unfulfilled Promise of American Education* (New York: Knopf, 1955); H. G. Rickover, *Education and Freedom* (New York: Dutton, 1959); Hutchins, *Higher Learning in America;* Harold J. Laski, *The American Democracy: A Commentary and an Interpretation* (New York: Viking, 1948), chap. 8; and D. W. Brogan, *The American Character* (New York: Knopf, 1944), 137.

8. Paul Copperman, *The Literacy Hoax: The Decline of Reading, Writing, and Learning in the Public Schools and What We Can Do About It* (New York: Morrow, 1978), and "The Achievement Decline of the 1970's," *Phi Delta Kappan,* 60 (June 1979): 736–739; National Commission on Excellence in Education, *A Nation at Risk,* 11; and Allan Bloom, *The Closing of the American Mind* (New York: Simon and Schuster, 1987).

9. *National Commission on Excellence in Education, A Nation at Risk,* 8–11, 5.

10. *Ibid.,* 24–33.

11. Twentieth Century Fund Task Force on Federal Elementary and Secondary Education Policy, *Making the Grade* (New York: The Twentieth Century Fund, 1983); National Science Board Commission on Precollegiate Education in Mathematics, Science, and Technology, *Educating Americans for the 21st Century: A Plan of Action for Improving Mathematics, Science, and Technology Education for All American Elementary and Secondary Students So That Their Achievement Is the Best in the World by 1995* (Washington, D.C.: National Science Foundation, 1983); Education Commission of the States, Task Force on Education for Economic Growth, *Action for Excellence: A Comprehensive Plan to Improve Our Nation's Schools* (Washington, D.C.: Education Commission of the States, 1983); National Academy of Sciences, Committee on Science, Engineering, and Public Policy, Panel on Secondary School Education for the Changing Workplace, *High Schools and the Changing Workplace: The Employers' View* (Washington, D.C.: National Academy Press, 1984); Committee for Economic Development, Research

and Policy Committee, *Investing in Our Children: Business and the Public Schools* (New York: Committee for Economic Development, 1985); and Ernest L. Boyer, *High School: A Report on Secondary Education in America* (New York: Harper & Row, 1983).

12. William J. Bennett, *To Reclaim a Legacy: A Report on the Humanities in Higher Education* (Washington, D.C.: National Endowment for the Humanities, 1984); Association of American Colleges, Project on Defining the Meaning and Purpose of Baccalaureate Degrees, *Integrity in the College Curriculum: A Report to the Academic Community* (Washington, D.C.: Association of American Colleges, 1985); and Ernest L. Boyer, *College: The Undergraduate Experience in America* (New York: Harper & Row, 1987).

13. Dwight Macdonald, *Against the American Grain* (New York: Random House, 1962), part 1.

14. With respect to the prodigious costs of continuing high dropout rates, one might note the argument of Margaret D. LeCompte and Anthony Gary Dworkin: "Given the indirect link between education and poverty, we believe that a significant measure of the success of an educational innovation, whether enriching or compensatory, is not whether the student test scores rise, but whether it improves the retention of an entire cohort of students and faculty," in "Educational Programs: Indirect Linkages and Unfulfilled Expectations," in Harrell R. Rodgers, Jr., ed., *Beyond Welfare: New Approaches to the Problem of Poverty in America* (Armonk, N.Y.: Sharpe, 1988), 136. For some of the Goodlad evidence, see Kenneth A. Tye, *The Junior High: School in Search of a Mission* (Lankam, Md.: University Press of America, 1985), 1–2.

15. Children's Defense Fund, *Children out of School in America* (Washington, D.C.: Children's Defense Fund, 1974).

16. Lawrence C. Stedman and Marshall S. Smith, "Recent Reform Proposals for American Education," *Contemporary Education Review,* 2 (Fall 1983): 85–104. See also Ralph W. Tyler, "The U.S. vs. the World: A Comparison of Educational Performance," *Phi Delta Kappan,* 62 (January 1981): 307–310; Gilbert R. Austin and Herbert Garber, eds., *The Rise and Fall of National Test Scores* (New York: Academic Press, 1982); and, for a later summary of the test data, U.S. Congress, Congressional Budget Office, *Trends in Educational Achievement* (April 1986) and *Educational Achievement: Explanations and Implications of Recent Trends* (August 1987); John I. Goodlad, *A Place Called School Prospects for the Future* (New York: McGraw-Hill, 1984), chap. 3 and

passim; and Barbara Benham Tye, *Multiple Realities: A Study of 13 American High Schools* (Lanham, N.Y.: University Press of America, 1985), chap. 4 and *passim.*

17. Goodlad, *A Place Called School;* Stephen R. Graubard, ed., "America's Schools: Portraits and Perspectives." *Daedalus,* 110 (Fall 1981); Sara Lawrence Lightfoot, *The Good High School: Portraits of Character and Culture* (New York: Basic Books, 1983); Mary Haywood Metz, *Different by Design: The Context and Character of Three Magnet School*s (New York: Routledge & Kegan Paul, 1986); Jeannie Oakes, *Keeping Track: How Schools Structure Inequality* (New Haven: Yale University Press, 1985); Vito Perrone et al., *Portraits of High Schools* (Princeton, N.J.: The Carnegie Foundation for the Advancement of Teaching, 1985); Barbara Benham Tye, *Multiple Realities;* Kenneth A. Tye, *The Junior High,* and Arthur G. Powell, Eleanor Farrar, and David K. Cohen, *The Shopping Mall High School: Winners and Losers in the Educational Marketplace* (Boston: Houghton Mifflin, 1985).

For an early warning against using the international studies of education achievement as some kind of "international contest," see Torsten Husen, ed., *International Study of Achievement in Mathematics: A Comparison of Twelve Countries* (2 vols.; New York: Wiley, 1967), 2:288, and *passim.* For a review of the uses and limitations of standardized paper-and-pencil tests as instruments for assessing what is learned in school, see Bernard R. Gifford. ed., *Test Policy and Test Performance: Education, Language, and Culture* (Boston: Kluwer, 1989), Bernard R. Gifford and M. Catherine O'Connor, eds., *New Approaches to Testing: Rethinking Aptitude, Achievement, and Assessment* (Boston: Kluwer, 1990), and other publications reporting the work of the National Commission on Testing and Public Policy.

18. The list of responsibilities assigned to the schools and colleges is based on John I. Goodlad's study of schooling, as reported in *What Schools Are For* (Bloomington, Ind.: Phi Delta Kappa Educational Foundation, 1979) and *A Place Called School* and Ernest L. Boyer's study of the undergraduate experience, as reported in *College.*

19. Lightfoot, *The Good High School.*

20. Eric Ashby, *Any Person, Any Study: An Essay on Higher Education in the United States* (New York: McGraw-Hill, 1971); and Martin Trow, "Reflections on the Transition from Mass to Universal Higher Education," *Daedalus,* 99 (Winter 1970):1–7.

4 | The Sociology of Education

Many years ago, the famous philosopher Alfred North Whitehead was asked, "Which is more important, facts or ideas?" He reflected for a while and said, "Ideas about facts." At its very core, sociological inquiry is about ideas and how they shape people's understandings of society. The desire to know and to transform society is not unique to sociologists; in fact, social curiosity has played a key role in humans' adaptive capacity. In one sense, sociology is simply a method for bringing social aspirations and fears into focus by forcing people to ask sharp and analytic questions about the societies and cultures in which they live. The tools of sociology can be thought of as empirical and conceptual. Sociology is empirical because most sociologists gather facts about society. Facts, however, do not speak for themselves; without arranging them into meaningful patterns, facts are virtually useless. Trying to uncover the underlying patterns that give facts to their larger meaning is the purpose of making social theories. Often, teachers think that social theories are of little use in teaching children. Nothing could be further from the truth.

Without some idea of how the major elements in society fit together, teachers are at a loss in understanding the relation between school and society, how their own profession has evolved, and why students behave the way they do in school and outside of school. An understanding of society is essential if teachers are to develop as reflective practitioners. In a society that is becoming increasingly multiethnic and multiracial, the need for a sociological perspective among educators is urgent. In this chapter, we will explore some of the main elements of the sociology of education; these elements include theories about the relation between school and society, whether or not schooling makes a significant difference in individuals' lives, how schools influence social inequalities, and an examination of how school processes affect the lives of children, teachers, and other adults who are involved in the educational enterprise.

In her book, *Education and Inequality* (1977), Persell provided a model for analyzing the relationship between school and society through four interrelated levels of sociological analysis (see Figure 4.1). The *societal* level includes the most general structures of a society, including its political and economic systems, its level of development, and its system of social stratification (or institutionalized levels of inequality). The *institutional* level includes a society's major institutions, such as the family, school, churches and synagogues, business and government, and the media, all of which play an important role in socialization. The *interpersonal* level includes the processes, symbols, and interactions that occur within such institutional settings. These include language, dress, face-to-face interactions, gestures, and rituals, all of which comprise everyday life. The *intrapsychic* level includes individual thoughts, beliefs,

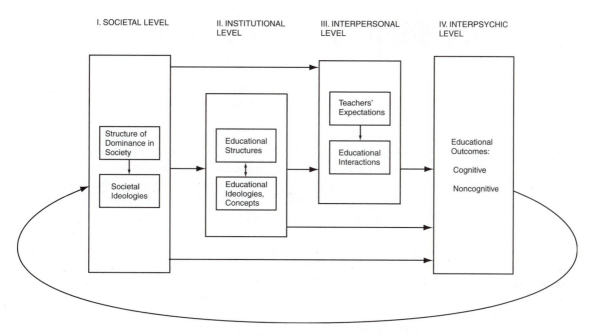

FIGURE 4.1   **Theoretical Model of Relevant Variables and Their Interrelationships**

Source: Reprinted with the permission of The Free Press, a division of Simon & Schuster Adult Publishing Group, from *Education and Inequality: A Theoretical Empirical Synthesis* by Caroline Hodges Persell. Copyright © 1977 by The Free Press. All rights reserved.

values, and feelings, which are to a large degree shaped by the society's institutions and interactions.

For sociologists, the issue of whether the individual actions are determined by external forces (*determinism;* called *behaviorism* in psychology) or whether individuals are capable of freely shaping the world (*voluntarism;* called *existentialism* in philosophy) is a crucial one. A sociological perspective, while recognizing human capacity for free will, emphasizes the power that external forces have on individual choices and how these are often related to group differences within the social stratification system.

As you will see, functionalism is concerned with the ways that societal and institutional forces create, in Durkheim's terms, a collective conscience (society internalized in the individual) based on shared values. Conflict theory is concerned with the ways in which differences among groups at the societal level produce conflict and domination that may lead to change.

The Uses of Sociology for Teachers

How can people create schools that are more effective environments for children to grow and learn? What is the relation between school and the larger society? Can schools produce more social and economic equality? These questions and many more have sparked the imaginations of generations of educators and those noneducators who have a deep interest in academic achievement, the welfare of children, and a more just, more open society. The kind of answers that are found to these questions will shape education and society for years. Without clear thinking, good information, and honest assessments, education as an institution is bound to move into the future like a ship without a rudder, floundering, directionless, and in danger of sinking. Before better educational programs can be designed, educators must know what works and what does not. The empirical and conceptual tools of sociology are ideally suited to this task because they guide one toward systematic thinking and realism about what is actually possible. There are those who would argue sociology is not fully scientific, but compared to other ways of problem solving, sociology utilizes the principles and methods of science and, moreover, sociologists are self-critical. Because of the standards of the discipline, the work of sociologists must bare the scrutiny of other sociologists and the public at large.

Sociologists, then, are in a good position to view schools with a dispassionate eye and a critical awareness that simple solutions to complex educational problems are almost bound to fail and can be counterproductive. From these observations, it should be evident that teachers can learn a great deal from the sociology of education; for example, sociological research helps pinpoint the characteristics of schools that enable them to become effective learning environments. These characteristics include vigorous instructional leadership; a principal who makes clear, consistent, and fair decisions; an emphasis on discipline and a safe and orderly environment; instructional practices that focus on basic skills and academic achievement; collegiality among teachers who believe that students can and will learn; and frequent review of student progress.

To take another example, it is known that interactions in the classroom shape the learning experiences of the child. Sociologists have developed many techniques for understanding classroom interactions. One of the best known is Ned Flanders's Interaction Analysis Scale (Amidon & Flanders, 1971). This method involves the use of observers who watch classroom interactions and note these interactions on a standard scale. This process gives observers a thorough and objective measure of what really goes on in classrooms. Flanders hypothesized that student performance and learning is greatest when teacher influence is indirect—that is, when there were other classroom interactions besides "teacher talk." The hypothesis was upheld when observations showed that students in indirect teacher classrooms learned more and were more independent than students in classrooms where most, if not all, instructional activities were directed by the teacher.

As teachers, sociology provides you with a special analytic lens on education and school that, when you learn to use it, will give you greater insight and coherence in your approach to studying education. We hope that this clarity will help you improve your pedagogical practices and promote your professional growth. Part of becoming a professional is developing an intellectual and experiential frame of reference that is sufficiently sophisticated. It is our belief that this intellectual sophistication will help you integrate the world of education into its larger social context. This last observation leads to our first major issue in exploring how sociology can help us understand education in the "big picture." What is the relation between school and society?

The Relation between School and Society

Have you ever wondered why schools are the way they are? Why do teachers teach what they teach in the way they do? Can schools change society, or must society change if schools are to become different? Obviously, there are no simple answers to these questions; yet struggling to find answers, even for complex questions, is in itself a process of clarification. Sociologists of education often ask big questions about the relation between school and society because they believe that educators cannot really understand how schools operate, or why they operate as they do, without a working idea of how schools and society interact. To help them in this complex intellectual and empirical process, sociologists almost always have a theory about the organization of society and how it shapes the education of children. In particular, sociologists take an interest in how schools act as agents of cultural and social transmission.

Schools—as well as parents, churches and synagogues, and other groups—shape children's perceptions of the world by processes of *socialization.* That is, the values, beliefs, and norms of society are internalized within children so that they come to think and act like other members of society. In this sense, schools socially and cultur-ally reproduce the existing society through the systematic socialization of its youngest members. Think of such a simple ritual as pledging allegiance to the flag. Through this culturally approved ritual, young children learn something about citizenship and patriotism.

Socialization processes can shape children's consciousness profoundly. Schools, for instance, wittingly or unwittingly, promote gender definitions and stereotypes when they segregate learning and extracurricular activities by gender, or when teachers allow boys to dominate class discussions and activities. Not only do schools shape students' perceptions and consciousness but they also act as important, perhaps the most impor-tant, sorters and selectors of students. Schools, through such practices as tracking, aca-demically stratify students by curricular placement, which, in turn, influences the long-term social, economic, and cultural destinies of children. In effect, schools play a major role in determining who will get ahead in society and who will not.

How do schools select some students for educational mobility? Is it on the basis of merit or is it primarily on the basis of students' ascriptive characteristics, such as class, race, or gender? Or is it a combination of merit and social position that ex-plains who gets into the educational "fast track" and who gets "cooled out"? The con-cept of equal educational opportunity is a key element in the belief system that maintains that the United States is a land of opportunity where hard work is re-warded. Is this belief based on real social facts or is it simply a myth that confuses people and leads them to believe that their relative social and economic failure is caused by personal inadequacies?

At an even deeper level, one might wonder why people study the subjects and ma-terials they do. Who selects what people teach and learn, and why? Is knowledge value free or socially constructed? Can ideas ever be taken out of their contexts? For instance, history texts have traditionally overlooked the role of minorities and women in shap-ing U.S. society. How has this influenced people's perceptions of what is really his-torically significant and what is not?

Theoretical Perspectives

From these remarks, it should be apparent to you that the sociology of education is a contentious field and that the questions sociologists ask about the relation between school and society are fundamental and complex. Because the scope of these questions is so large, sociologists usually begin their studies with an overall picture of how society looks in its most basic form. This is where theory comes in. A good definition of *theory* is "an integration of all known principles, laws, and information pertaining to a specific area of study. This structure allows investigators to offer explanations for relative phenomenon and to create solutions to unique problems" (Woolfolk, 1990, p. 585). Theory is like an x-ray machine; it allows one to see past the visible and obvious and examine the hidden structure. Unlike x-ray pictures, however, theoretical pictures of society are seldom crystal clear or easy to interpret. Why is this? Partly this is because people are members of society (i.e., people have been socialized by society) and it is very difficult to be objective or disinterested in the analysis of people. Theoretical pictures of society are created by human beings and interpreted by them. Thus, knowledge of the social world cannot be totally separated from one's personal and social situation. Still, should you let the fact that all knowledge is socially generated and interpreted discourage you from exploring those issues that shape your life? Obviously not. Without the struggle for objectivity and honesty, there is little hope that people can create a productive and just society.

Theory, then, as inadequate as it is, is one's best conceptual guide to understanding the relation between school and society because it gives one the intellectual scaffolding from which to hang empirical findings. Essentially, there are three major theories about the relation between school and society: functional, conflict, and interactional.

Functional Theories

Functional sociologists begin with a picture of society that stresses the *interdependence* of the social system; these researchers often examine how well the parts are integrated with each other. Functionalists view society as a kind of machine, where one part articulates with another to produce the dynamic energy required to make society work. Perhaps the earliest sociologist to embrace a functional point of view about the relation of school and society was Emile Durkheim (1858–1917), who virtually invented the sociology of education in the late nineteenth and early twentieth centuries. His major works include *Moral Education* (1962), *The Evolution of Educational Thought* (1977), and *Education and Sociology* (1956). While Durkheim recognized that education had taken different forms at different times and places, he believed that education, in virtually all societies, was of critical importance in creating the moral unity necessary for social cohesion and harmony. For Durkheim, moral values were the foundation of society.

Durkheim's emphasis on values and cohesion set the tone for how present-day functionalists approach the study of education. Functionalists tend to assume that consensus is the normal state in society and that conflict represents a breakdown of shared values. In a highly integrated, well-functioning society, schools socialize students into the appropriate values and sort and select students according to their abilities. Educational reform, then, from a functional point of view, is supposed to create structures, programs, and curricula that are technically advanced, rational, and encourage social unity. It should be evident that most U.S. educators and educational reformers implicitly base their reform suggestions on functional theories of schooling. When, for example, *A Nation at Risk* was released in 1983, the argument was made by the authors of the report that schools were responsible for a whole host of social and economic problems. There was no suggestion that perhaps education might not have the power to overcome deep, social, and economic problems without changing other aspects of U.S. society.

Conflict Theories — Social reproduction theory.

Not all sociologists of education believe that society is held together by shared values alone. Some sociologists argue that the social order is not based on some collective agreement, but on the ability of dominant groups to impose their will on subordinate groups through force, cooptation, and manipulation. In this view, the glue of society is economic, political, cultural, and military power. Ideologies or intellectual justifications created by the powerful are designed to enhance their position by legitimizing inequality and the unequal distribution of material and cultural goods as an inevitable outcome of biology, or history. Clearly, conflict sociologists do not see the relation between school and society as unproblematic or straightforward. Whereas functionalists emphasize cohesion in explaining social order, conflict sociologists emphasize struggle. From a conflict point of view, schools are similar to social battlefields, where students struggle against teachers, teachers against administrators, and so on. These antagonisms, however, are most often muted for two reasons: the authority and power of the school and the achievement ideology. In effect, the achievement ideology convinces students and teachers that schools promote learning and sort and select students according to their abilities and not according to their social status. In this view, the achievement ideology disguises the real power relations within the school, which, in turn, reflect and correspond to the power relations within the larger society (Bowles & Gintis, 1976).

Although Karl Marx (1818–1883) did not write a great deal about education specifically, he is the intellectual founder of the conflict school in the sociology of education. His analytic imagination and moral outrage were sparked by the social conditions found in Europe in the mid-nineteenth century. Industrialization and urbanization had produced a new class of workers—the proletariat—who lived in poverty, worked up to 18 hours a day, and had little, if any, hope of creating a better life for their children. Marx believed that the class system, which separated owners from workers and workers from the benefits of their own labor, made class struggle inevitable. He believed that, in the end, the proletariat would rise up and overthrow the capitalists, and, in doing so, establish a new society where men and women would no longer be alienated from their labor.

Marx's powerful and often compelling critique of early capitalism has provided the intellectual energy for subsequent generations of liberal and leftist thinkers who believe that the only way to a more just and productive society is the abolition or modification of capitalism and the introduction of socialism. Political economists Bowles and Gintis, in their book *Schooling in Capitalist America* (1976), used a Marxist perspective for examining the growth of the U.S. public school. To their minds, there is a direct correspondence between the organization of schools and the organization of society, and, until society is fundamentally changed, there is little hope of real school reform. It has been argued by other conflict sociologists of education, however, that traditional Marxism is too deterministic and overlooks the power of culture and human agency in promoting change.

An early conflict sociologist who took a slightly different theoretical orientation when viewing society was Max Weber (1864–1920). Like Marx, Weber was convinced that power relations between dominant and subordinate groups structured societies, but unlike Marx, Weber believed that class differences alone could not capture the complex ways human beings form hierarchies and belief systems that make these hierarchies seem just and inevitable. Thus, Weber examined status cultures as well as class position as an important sociological concept, because it alerts one to the fact that people identify their group by what they consume and with whom they socialize.

Weber also recognized that political and military power could be exercised by the state, without direct reference to the wishes of the dominant classes. Moreover, Weber had an acute and critical awareness of how bureaucracy was becoming the dominant type of authority in the modern state and how bureaucratic ways of thinking were bound to shape educational reforms. Weber made the distinction between the "specialist" and the "cultivated" man. What should be the goal of education—training individuals for employment or for thinking? Or are these two goals compatible?

The Weberian approach to studying the relation between school and society has developed into a compelling and informative tradition of sociological research. Researchers in this tradition tend to analyze school organizations and processes from the point of view of status competition and organizational constraints. One of the first U.S. sociologists of education to use these concepts was Willard Waller. In *The Sociology of Teaching* (1965), Waller portrayed schools as autocracies in a state of "perilous equilibrium." Without continuous vigilance, schools would erupt into anarchy because students are essentially forced to go to school against their will. To Waller's mind, rational models of school organization only disguise the inherent tension that pervades the schooling process. Waller's perspective is shared by many contemporary conflict theorists who see schools as oppressive and demeaning and portray student noncompliance with school rules as a form of resistance.

Another major research tradition that has emerged from the Weberian school of thought is represented by Randall Collins (1971, 1979), who has maintained that educational expansion is best explained by status group struggle. He argued that educational credentials, such as college diplomas, are primarily status symbols rather than indicators of actual achievement. The rise of credentialism does not indicate that society is becoming more expert, but that education is increasingly used by dominant groups to secure more advantageous places for themselves and their children within the occupation and social structure.

A recent variation of conflict theory that has captured the imagination of some U.S. sociologists began in France and England during the 1960s. Unlike most Marxists who tend to emphasize the economic structure of society, cultural reproduction theorists, such as Bourdieu and Passeron (1977), examined how "cultural capital"—knowledge and experiences related to art, music, and literature—and "social capital"—social networks and connections—are passed on by families and schools. The concepts of cultural and social capital are important because they suggest that, in understanding the transmission of inequalities, one ought to recognize that the cultural and social characteristics of individuals and groups are significant indicators of status and class position.

A growing body of literature suggests that schools pass on to graduates specific social identities that either enhance or hinder their life chances. For example, a graduate from an elite prep school has educational and social advantages over many public school graduates in terms of college attendance and occupational mobility. This advantage has very little to do with what prep school students learn in school, and a great deal to do with the power of their schools' reputations for educating members of the upper class. The theories of Bourdieu and Passeron extend the work of other sociologists who have argued persuasively that human culture cannot be understood as a isolated and self-contained object of study but must be examined as part of a larger social and cultural structure. To understand the impact of culture on the lives of individuals and groups, one must understand the meanings that are attributed to cultural experiences by those who participate in them (Mannheim, 1952).

The conflict perspective, then, offers important insights about the relation between school and society. As you think about schools and education, we hope that you will utilize functional and conflict theoretical perspectives as a way of organizing your readings and perceptions. Before we turn from theory to more empirical issues about students and schools, there is a theoretical perspective that ought not to be overlooked.

Interactional Theories

Interactional theories about the relation of school and society are primarily critiques and extensions of the functional and conflict perspectives. The critique arises from the observation that functional and conflict theories are very abstract and emphasize structure and process at a very general (macrosociological) level of analysis. Although this level of analysis helps in understanding education in the "big picture," macrosociological theories hardly provide an interpretable snapshot of what schools are like on an everyday level. What do students and teachers actually do in school? Interactional theories attempt to make the commonplace strange by turning on their heads everyday taken-for-granted behaviors and interactions between students and students, and between students and teachers. It is exactly what one does not question that is most problematic at a deep level. For example, the processes by which students are labeled gifted or learning disabled are, from an interactional point of view, important to analyze, because such processes carry with them many implicit assumptions about learning and children. By examining the microsociological or the interactional aspects of school life, people are less likely to create theories that are logical and eloquent, but without meaningful content.

Some of the sociology of education's most brilliant theorists have attempted to synthesize the macro- and microsociological approaches. Basil Bernstein (1990), for instance, has argued that the structural aspects of the educational system and the interactional aspects of the system reflect each other and must be viewed wholistically. He has examined how speech patterns reflect students' social class backgrounds and how students from working class backgrounds are at a disadvantage in the school setting be-cause schools are essentially middle-class organizations. Bernstein has combined a class analysis with an interactional analysis, which links language with educational processes and outcomes.

In this section, we have tried to give you a sense of how theory can be used to ex-plain the relation between school and society. These theories provide background metaphors and analytic focuses for the work of sociologists. We turn now to some spe-cific areas of research that have interested sociologists of education for many years.

Effects of Schooling on Individuals

Do schools matter? This provocative question is one that most people feel they have al-ready answered. It is safe to say that most Americans believe that schools have a sig-nificant impact on learning and on social and economic mobility. In this section, we examine some of the effects of schooling on individuals to see what the relative im-portance of schooling is in terms of what people learn, employment, job performance, income, and mobility.

Knowledge and Attitudes

It may be surprising to you to learn that sociologists of education disagree strongly about the relative importance of schooling in terms of what knowledge and attitudes young people acquire in school. Nobody argues that schools have no impact on student development, but there are sharp divisions among researchers about how significant school effects are, when taking into account students' social class background. Gener-ally, it is found that the higher the social class background of the student, the higher his or her achievement level. According to such researchers as Coleman and colleagues (1966) and Jencks and colleagues (1972), differences between schools account for very little of the differences in student achievement. Is this true? Does this finding make sense out of the world as we know it? Does it make no difference whether a stu-dent attends a school in a wealthy suburb or in underfinanced, overcrowded school in the inner city?

Actually, other research indicates that differences between schools in terms of their academic programs and policies do make differences in student learning. One of the first researchers to show that differences in schools are directly related to differ-ences in student outcomes was Ron Edmonds (1979a, 1979b), the pioneer of the ef-fective schools movement. As mentioned earlier, the effective schools research demonstrates that academically oriented schools do produce higher rates of learning. More recent research, which compares public and private schools, also indicates that in schools where students are compelled to take academic subjects and where there is con-sistent discipline, student achievement levels go up. An important study by Heyns (1978) found that sixth- and seventh-grade students who went to summer school, used the library, and read a great deal in the summer made greater gains in knowledge than pupils who did not study in the summer. Moreover, it has been found that the actual amount of time students spend in school is directly related to how much students learn.

Other research has indicated that the more education individuals receive, the more likely they are to read newspapers, books, and magazines, and to take part in politics and public affairs. More highly educated people are also more likely to be liberal in their political and social attitudes. Education is also related to individuals' sense of well-being and self-esteem. Thus, it is clear that, even taking into account the importance of individual social class background when evaluating the impact of education, more years of schooling leads to greater knowledge and social participation.

Employment

Most students believe that graduating from college will lead to greater employment opportunities, and they are right. In 1986, about 54 percent of the 8 million college graduates in the United States entered professional and technical jobs. Research has shown that large organizations, such as corporations, require high levels of education for white-collar, managerial, or administrative jobs (Collins, 1971). In fact, as we discussed earlier, credential inflation has led to the expectation among employers that their employees will have an ever-increasing amount of formal education. But do well-educated employees actually do a better job? Surprisingly, most research has shown that the amount of education is only weakly related to job performance. Berg (1970), for instance, studied factory workers, maintenance workers, department store clerks, technicians, secretaries, bank tellers, engineers, industrial research scientists, military personnel, and federal civil service employers and found that the level of education was essentially unrelated to job performance. From this evidence, it seems clear that schools act as gatekeepers in determining who will get employed in high-status occupations, but schools do not provide significant job skills for their graduates. People learn how to do their jobs by doing them, which is not so surprising.

The economic and social worth of an academic credential, however, cannot be fully measured by examining its effects on job performance. Perhaps because academic credentials help individuals to obtain higher-status jobs early in their careers, possession of a college degree is significantly related to higher income. In 2003, high school graduates earned, on average, $30,084; college graduates earned $53,356 (U.S. Bureau of the Census, 2003a). Among household heads who were women at all levels of education, women earn less than men. Women with professional degrees, on average, earn considerably less than men with college degrees. These differences are due to occupational segregation by sex, pay discrimination, and the fact that women, more than men, take time off or work part time due to family commitments.

These general findings, however, mask a great deal of variation when examining the relation between educational level and income level. According to some research, young African American males who are highly educated earn as much as their white male counterparts, but whether this remains true across the life course remains to be seen. Many other factors besides education affect how much income people earn in their lifetimes; these include type of employer, age, union membership, and social class background. In fact, even the most thorough research cannot demonstrate that more than one-third of income is directly attributable to level of education. So, getting a college and professional degree is important for earning more money, but education alone does not fully explain differences in levels of income.

Education and Mobility

The belief that occupational and social mobility begin at the schoolhouse door is a critical component of the American ethos. As part of what might be termed *civil religion,* there is an abiding faith among most Americans that education is the great equalizer in the "great status race." Of course, not everybody subscribes to this faith. In a fascinating study, MacLeod (1995) found that working class boys often reject the prevailing "attainment through education" ethos by emphasizing their relative lack of economic and social mobility through cultural values that glorify physical hardness, manual labor, and a certain sense of fatalism. In general, however, most Americans believe that more education leads to economic and social mobility; individuals rise and fall based on their merit. Turner (1960) called this *contest* mobility. He compared *contest* mobility in the United States to *sponsored* mobility in the United Kingdom, where students are selected at an early age for academic and university education and where social class background is very important in determining who will receive academic or vocational training.

In this regard, keep in mind another important distinction when thinking of education and mobility. Hopper (1971) has made the point that there is a difference between educational *amount* and educational *route.* That is, the number of years of education is one measure of educational attainment, but *where* people go to school also affects their mobility. Private and public school students may receive the same amount of education, but a private school diploma may act as a "mobility escalator" because it represents a more prestigious educational route (Cookson & Persell, 1985).

The debate as to whether the public school is really the great equalizer has not been resolved. For some groups, such as the middle class, increased education may be directly linked to upward occupational mobility; for the poor and rich, education may have little to do with mobility. An educational degree alone cannot lift many people out of poverty, and upper-class individuals do not lose their social class position if they fail to achieve a high-status educational degree. In general, the data do not support the belief that education alone provides individuals with great amounts of economic and social mobility.

Rosenbaum (1976) has offered one suggestion as to why this may be the case. He likened mobility to *tournament selection,* where winners are allowed to proceed to the next round of competition, and losers are dropped from the competition. Players (students) can be eliminated, but winners must still continue to compete. The problem with this tournament, however, is that the criteria for winning and losing include a great many variables that are related to students' social class, race, and gender characteristics, as well as merit variables, such as grade-point average and SAT scores. The complex interplay between merit and privilege creates a tournament where the rules are not entirely even-handed and not everyone has the opportunity to set the rules. Without a doubt, the relation between education and mobility will continue to be debated among scholars and policy makers. The popular belief that education opens the doors of opportunity, however, is likely to remain firmly embedded in the American ethos.

Inside the Schools

How can the sociology of education help one to understand schools in terms of their objectives, cultures, and how they shape students' perceptions and expectations? In other words, how do sociologists look at schools from an organizational point of view? How do such organizational characteristics as curricula, teacher behaviors, and student peer groups shape learning and social growth? Since most people are apt to think about learning and growth from a psychological perspective, it is illuminating to stand back and speculate how school structures can also influence student outcomes. Think of something as simple as school size. Larger schools can offer students more in the way of facilities, but large schools are also more bureaucratic and may restrain initiative. Smaller schools may allow more student and teacher freedom, but small schools often lack resources. In general, schools are getting larger, if for no other reason than they are cost effective. Whether schools are large or small, however, the content of what they teach is a topic of important study.

Curriculum expresses culture. The question is, Whose culture? For some time, sociologists of education have pointed out that curricula are not value free; they are expressions of certain groups' ideas, beliefs, and prejudices. Knowing something about the bias and viewpoints of those who write curricula awakens one to the relativity of knowledge and its social and cultural context.

As you know, not all students study the same curriculum. It is also a fact that curriculum placement within schools has a direct impact on the probabilities of students attending college. In 2000, approximately 47 percent of public high school students took what is called a college preparatory course of study, which includes such subjects as English, history, science, math, and foreign language; 10 percent took a vocational program; and approximately 43 percent enrolled in a general program, which combines such courses as English with accounting and clerical courses (U.S. Department of Education, National Center for Education Statistics, 2000a). In private school, virtually all students are enrolled in an academic curriculum. Research has shown that curricular placement is the single biggest determinant of college attendance (Lee & Bryk, 1989; Bryk, Lee, & Holland, 1993). For example, in 1992, there were significant differences among white, African American, Hispanic American, and Asian American high school students with regard to track placement. Some 46 percent of white students were in the college track, compared to 35 percent of African American students, 31 percent of Hispanic American students, 51 percent of Asian American students, and 23 percent of American Indian students. Some 11 percent of white students were in the vocational track; compared to 15 percent of African American students, 13 percent of Hispanic American students, 9 percent of Asian American students, and 17 percent of American Indian students. Some 43 percent of white students were in the general track, compared to 49 percent of African American students, 56 percent of Hispanic American students, 40 percent of Asian American students, and 61 percent of American Indian students (U.S. Department of Education, National Center for Educational Statistics, 1997a). In 1996, 133 per 1,000 white twelfth-graders took Advanced Placement Examinations (AP), compared to 32 per 1,000 African American twelfth-graders and 74 per 1,000 Hispanic Americans (U.S. Department of Education, National Center for Educational

Statistics, 1998). We will have a great deal to say about curriculum later in this book, but for now, it may be useful to underscore the importance of curriculum when studying schools from a sociological perspective, especially in terms of cultural transmission and the selective channelling of opportunity.

Teacher Behavior

It may seem obvious, but teachers have a huge impact on student learning and behavior. Jackson (1968) found that teachers have as many as 1,000 interpersonal contacts each day with children in their classrooms. Teachers are extremely busy people; they must also wear many different occupational hats: instructor, disciplinarian, bureaucrat, employer, friend, confidant, educator, and so on. Ingersoll (2004) supports these findings. These various roles sometimes are compatible with each other, and sometimes they are not. This can lead to *role strain,* where such conflicting demands are placed on teachers that they cannot feel totally comfortable in any role. Could this be a cause of teacher burnout?

Clearly, teachers are models for students and, as instructional leaders, teachers set standards for students and influence student self-esteem and sense of efficacy. In a fascinating study conducted by Rosenthal and Jacobsen (1968), teachers' expectations of students were found to directly influence student achievement. The researchers told some teachers in a California elementary school that children in their classes were likely to have a mental growth spurt that year. In reality, the intelligence test that the children had taken revealed nothing about their potential achievement level. The students had been placed in their classes randomly. At the end of the year, the researchers returned to school and gave another test to see which children had improved. Although all the children improved somewhat, those labeled "spurters" made significantly greater achievement gains than other children, especially in the first and second grades. Thus, the labels that teachers apply to children can influence actual performance. This form of *self-fulfilling prophecy* indicates that teachers' expectations play a major role in encouraging or discouraging students to work to their full potential.

Persell (1977) found that when teachers demanded more from their students and praised them more, students learned more and felt better about themselves. Research indicates that many teachers have lower expectations for minority and working class students; this suggests that these students may be trapped within a vicious cycle of low expectation–low achievement–low expectation. In part, this cycle of failure may be responsible for high dropout rates and failure to achieve at grade level. Of course, teachers cannot be held responsible for all the failures of education; there are many nonpedagogic reasons why U.S schools are failing to educate so many children. Teachers should not be scapegoated for society's problems, but the findings on teacher expectations do indicate that the attitudes of teachers toward their students may have a significant influence on student achievement and perceptions of self. Also, it is important not to overlook the fact that there are many outstanding teachers who are dedicated and inspirational and who have helped motivate students to do their best.

Student Peer Groups and Alienation

When you reflect on your high school and junior high experiences, you undoubtedly have strong memories of your fellow students and the various social groups that they created. Almost nobody wants to be labeled a "nerd," and in most schools, the student culture idealizes athletic ability, looks, and that detached style that indicates "coolness." In a sense, the adult culture of the teachers and administrators is in conflict with the student culture. This conflict can lead to alienation and even violence.

Stinchcombe (1964) found, for instance, that students in vocational programs and headed toward low-status jobs were the students most likely to join a rebellious subculture. In fact, student violence continues to be a problem. Students are not only attacking each other in increasing numbers but they are also assaulting teachers. The number of beatings, rapes, and even murders that are perpetrated against teachers has become something of a national scandal, but compared to what students do to each other, the danger for teachers is minimal. Some argue that school violence is increasing because teachers are underpaid and classes are too large. This may explain some of the violence, but it certainly does not explain all of it. A hundred years ago, teachers taught for little money and had class sizes double or triple present-day standards and there was little school violence. In today's culture, violence is far more acceptable, even glorified in the popular media. Being "bad" is misconstrued as being tough and smart. School children are bombarded with imaginary and actual violence in their homes, in their schools, and on the streets. It has been estimated that by the time the average child is 12 years old, he or she has been exposed to 18,000 television murders.

Student subcultures continue to be important after high school. There are four major types of college students: careerists, intellectuals, strivers, and unconnected. *Careerists* generally came from middle- and upper middle-class backgrounds, won few academic honors, lost confidence during college, and were not intellectually motivated by their experience. *Intellectuals* usually came from highly educated families, studied in the humanities, were politically involved, and earned many academic honors. *Strivers* very often had a working-class background, came from ethnic or racial minorities, worked hard, often did not have a high grade-point average, but graduated with a real sense of accomplishment. The *unconnected* came from all backgrounds, participated in few extracurricular activities, and were the least satisfied among all the groups with their college experience.

It should be evident, then, that student cultures play an important role in shaping students' educational experiences. We also hope that it is evident to you that looking within school from a sociological perspective can be very illuminating. Schools are far more than mere collections of individuals; they develop cultures, traditions, and restraints that profoundly influence those who work and study within them. They socialize and sort and select students and, in doing so, reproduce society. In the next section, we examine an issue of critical importance: How do schools reproduce social, cultural, and economic inequalities?

Education and Inequality

Suppose we asked you to draw a picture of American society. How would it look? Like a circle? A square? A shapeless blob? Let's rephrase this question a bit. In terms of the distribution of income, power, and property, would you say that the shape of American society is flat? Probably not. Most of us know that income, power, and property are unevenly distributed in society. There are the "haves" and the "have-nots." Thinking figuratively again, most of us would agree that the economic and social structure of the U.S. population resembles a triangle where most of the people can be found at the base.

In the United States, there are essentially five classes: the *upper class,* with 1 to 3 percent of the total U.S. population; the *upper middle class,* with 10 to 15 percent of the population; the *lower middle class,* with 25 percent of the population; the *working class,* with 40 percent of the population; and the *lower or underclass,* with 20 percent of the population. The distribution of income, power, and property among these classes is highly uneven. The top fifth of the U.S. population owns three-fourths of the nation's wealth, whereas the remaining four-fifths own only one-fourth of the wealth (U.S. Bureau of the Census, 1998, 2003a). The bottom fifth own less than 0.2 percent of the nation's wealth. In 1987, the top fifth of U.S. families earned 43.7 percent of all income, whereas the bottom fifth earned 4.6 percent of the income. Moreover, by 1998, income differences became wider and the United States increasingly became a bipolar society of great wealth, great poverty, and an ever-shrinking middle class (U.S. Bureau of the Census, 1998, 2003a).

Social class differences are not only reflected in differences in income but in other social characteristics such as education, family and child-rearing practices, occupation, place of residence, political involvement, health, consumer behavior, and religious belief. In short, if you know a family's or individual's class position, you have a good idea about their life-style and life chances. Moreover, class influences what people think, by shaping the way in which they think. Class position creates selective perception which, in turn, creates a world view that "explains" inequalities. Ideology, then, grows out of the class system and reinforces the class system through beliefs that justify or condemn the status quo. Those who are oppressed by the class system may resist and revolt and those who benefit usually cooperate with and defend the current form of *social stratification.*

People, however, are not just stratified by class; they are also stratified by race, ethnicity, age, and gender. In short, Americans live in a hierarchical society where mobility is blocked because of structural inequalities that have little or nothing to do with individuals' merits or abilities.

For some time, sociologists have speculated and argued about whether schools mitigate social inequalities by providing opportunities for those who would not normally have them. Can schools create a more open society? This is a topic of immense importance and complexity. In later chapters, we will examine this issue in depth; for now, however, it might be useful to review some of the major ways schools help transmit social and economic inequalities.

Inadequate Schools

Perhaps the most obvious way that schools reproduce inequalities is through inadequate schools. We have already discussed the crisis in U.S. education and how numerous critics of contemporary schooling have pointed out that the way in which children are educated today will not prepare them for productive and fulfilling lives in the future. Urban education, in particular, has failed to educate minority and poor children. Moreover, differences between schools and school systems reinforce existing inequalities. Students who attend suburban schools and private schools get a better educational experience than other children (Coleman, Hoffer, & Kilgore, 1982). Students who attend the most elite private schools obtain substantial educational benefits, both in terms of their actual educational experience and the social value of their diplomas (Cookson & Persell, 1985).

Tracking

There is compelling evidence that within-school tracking has a critical impact on student mobility (Lucas, 2002; Oakes, 1985). In principle, *tracking* refers to the placement of students in curricular programs based on students' abilities and inclinations. In reality, it has been found in many thorough studies that tracking decisions are often based on other criteria, such as students' class or race. By and large, working class students end up in vocational tracks and middle-class students in academic tracks. Studies have shown that students placed in "high-ability" tracks spend more time on actual teaching and learning activities; are able to use more interesting materials; and consistently receive better teachers, better laboratory facilities, and more extracurricular activities than do their lower-track peers (Oakes, 1985; Goodlad, 1984). Moreover, track placement directly affects cognitive development (Rosenbaum, 1976). Students in lower tracks experience more alienation and authoritarian teachers than high-track students.

De Facto Segregation

Another important way schools reinforce (even create) inequalities, particularly racial and ethnic inequalities, is through *de facto* segregation. In the previous chapter, we discussed in some depth the effects of segregated schools on student achievement, not to mention the issue of basic rights and equities. Although this issue is far from resolved, most of the evidence indicates that racially mixed schools benefit minorities and do *not* suppress white achievement. One study found that African Americans from low-income communities who attended racially mixed schools were more likely to graduate from high school and college than similar African American children who attended segregated schools. Moreover, African American students who attended integrated schools were less likely to be arrested by the police, more likely to live in desegregated neighborhoods, and women were less likely to have a child before the age of 18. Thus, racial integration at the school level seems to be beneficial to minority students, and there is no conclusive evidence that majority students are harmed by integration.

The issue of segregation, or resegregation, will be with society for a long time, if for no other reason than most people live in racially segregated neighborhoods. Groups and individuals who believe that students should be allowed to choose the schools they wish to attend argue that school choice will break down the barriers to integration created by racially segregated neighborhoods. Whether school choice would really end segregation is still very debatable; certainly, the historical evidence from the South during the 1960s and 1970s is not reassuring. During this period, white families set up their own academies in order to avoid racially integrated public schools.

Gender

Another way schools reproduce inequalities is through gender discrimination. Men and women do not share equally in U.S. society. Men are frequently paid more than women for the same work, and women, in general, have fewer occupational opportunities than men. Although this gender gap has been somewhat reduced for middle- and upper-middle-class women in the last decade, inequalities persist, particularly for working class and lower-class women. How do schools perpetuate this problem?

Although girls usually start school cognitively and socially ahead of boys, by the end of high school, girls have lower self-esteem and lower aspirations than do boys. Somewhere during the high school years, in particular, girls begin to show signs of not living up to their potentials. Is it the gender composition of the faculty and staff that influences girls to lower their aspirations? Most teachers are female, whereas most administrators are male; could this be sending a subliminal message to girls that they are somehow subordinate to men? Do teachers treat boys and girls differently by stereotyping them by behavior? Are girls supposed to be "nice" and "feminine" while boys are allowed to act out and gain the center of attention? Studies do show that boys get more teacher attention (good and bad) than girls.

Traditionally, textbooks have been biased against women by ignoring their accomplishments and social contributions. Until very recently, there was little discussion in textbooks of sexism or gender bias. Discrimination need not always be overt. Often, gender bias is subtle; for instance, women go to college at higher rates than men, but they often go to two-year colleges or to less academically prestigious institutions.

Thus, schools are active organizational agents in recreating gender inequalities. However, schools alone should not be held accountable for gender discrimination. This form of social stratification is rooted in the values and organization of society; schools in some ways only reflect these societal problems. This is not to say that educators *intend* to reproduce class, ethnic, racial, and gender inequalities, but the *consequences* of certain school policies and processes may reproduce these inequalities. Moreover, there is some evidence that for middle-class students, schooling does provide a "channel of attainment." In the main, however, the best evidence indicates that schools, despite educators' best intentions, tend to reproduce social inequalities. A major aspect of any meaningful reform movement must address this issue if schools are really to open doors to equal opportunity.

Sociology and the Current Educational Crisis

To grasp the magnitude of the current crisis in U.S. education, it is essential to recognize that at least one-third of the nation's children are at risk at failing in school, even before they enter kindergarten. Demographer Harold Hodgkinson (1991) described the condition of U.S. children in stark and poignant terms. Since 1987, one-fourth of all preschool children in the United States live in poverty. In 1990, approximately 350,000 children were born to mothers who were addicted to cocaine during pregnancy. Some 15 million children are being reared by single mothers whose family income averages about $11,400 a year. At least 2 million school-age children have no adult supervision after school, and every night between 50,000 and 200,000 children have no home. By

2004, these figures indicated an increase in these measures of poverty. How can schools help children to become productive and happy adults when so many children begin life with such severe disadvantages?

The sociological imagination helps one understand what is and what can be when one tries to imagine schools and school systems that meet the challenges that are facing today's children and young adults. The current educational crisis is complex, and solutions to the pressing problems are difficult to find. But people should not despair; we need to begin the work of reconstructing U.S. education. Sociologists ask the tough questions about schools and they search for answers by collecting data. Sometimes the data support preconceived beliefs, sometimes they do not. In either case, sociologists are committed to finding out the truth about the relationship between school and society, and it is this truth-seeking activity that is most likely to lead to meeting the challenges facing education today.

The following selections illustrate the sociological imagination applied to educational problems. The articles address important issues concerning the relationship between school and society and illustrate Persell's model of the levels of sociological analysis. The first article, "Japanese Education: A Durkheimian Ideal Type?, by anthropologist Roger Goodman, applies Dukheim's functionalist theory of education to the Japanese educational system. Goodman demonstrates the ways in which the Japanese schools illustrate functionalist theory and the ways in which they contradict it.

The second selection, written by sociologist Ray C. Rist, "On Understanding the Processes of Schooling: The Contributions of Labeling Theory," provides an illustration of the interpretive or interactionist perspective. Rist demonstrates how labeling theory provides a useful tool for understanding what goes on inside schools. The interactionist perspective, as Rist suggests, is an alternative to the more structural approaches of functionalism and conflict theory.

The third selection, "The Politics of Culture: Understanding Local Political Resistance to Detracking in Racially Mixed Schools," written by sociologist Amy Stuart Wells and Irene Serna, examines how affluent parents resist detracking policies. This article illustrates the ways in which conflict theory and interaction theory, used together, help us understand how power and privilege affect school practices and policies.

Japanese Education

A Durkheimian Ideal Type?

ROGER GOODMAN

Introduction

As has often been pointed out (see Karabel and Halsey 1977: 87), Emile Durkheim was the only one of the great thinkers of classical sociology who offered an analysis of education—both in its formal and informal sense—as an integral part of his general theory of society. It is perhaps surprising, therefore, that such little use has been made of Durkheim's work in the sociology of education, since so much of what he described a century ago would appear to be clearly pertinent to our understanding and analysis of contemporary systems. Durkheim's writing on education is as much a blueprint for how educational systems should develop as an analysis of how historically they have developed. On a first reading, few contemporary systems would appear to fit his ideal model as well as the Japanese system which is the focus for this particular discussion. If, for example, we extract from Durkheim's work ten prerequisites for a modern educational system, then it is interesting to see how Japan's model appears to measure up to them. The ten that follow are offered in no particular order.

1. Formal Education Should Not Be Separated from General Socialization (see Durkheim 1922a/t.1956a: 71)

In Japan formal educational institutions such as schools are seen as the prime locus for the socialization of the whole child. Few in Japan would argue other than that this has been achieved very effectively and many would assert that it is the formal educational system that has allowed Japan to develop its enviable combination of social cohesion and economic competitiveness. Even Japan's most ardent critics no longer subscribe to the view that its so-called economic miracle was built solely on unfair trade practices, and few still maintain that it can be found mainly in its management and labour practices. Instead, since the early 1980s, there has been a constant stream of visitors examining the Japanese educational system which has been held up as the key to its social and economic success, at least until very recently (for an overview of this debate see Goodman 1997).

2. The School Is the Correct Place for Such Socialization (see Durkheim 1925a/t.1961a: 230–1)

Durkheim's view here is well known: the church relies too heavily on revelation, and the family is too self-indulgent to be allowed to play the major role in the socialization of children. Instead, the school must perform this task. Such certainly is the case in Japan. Since the American occupation following the Second World War, there has been strict separation of church and state in Japan, nowhere more so than in the classroom. Schoolchildren receive no religious education at all, and only an hour or so of so-called 'moral education' (*dōtoku kyōiku*) which, being outside the normally tightly prescribed curriculum and usually in the hands of left-wing teachers, tends towards general discussions about 'good' behaviour. Often it is used as time to catch up with other classes. Children in the school system, therefore, learn very little about Buddhism, Shintoism or Confucianism, except possibly for a few dates during history classes. Even in schools set up as private Christian foundations, Christian education is minimal, in part because the national curriculum leaves very little room for such extra subjects (Holmes 1989: 212).

The role of the family in the socialization of children is clearly secondary, even if complementary, to that of the schools. An interesting example of how out of line Japan now is with other OECD countries can be seen in a recent OECD project that was based on the assumption that parents influence practices in schools and not the other way around as in Japan.[1] In Japan, the

From Roger Goodman, "Japanese Education: A Durkheimian Ideal Type?" in G. Walford and W. S. F. Pickering (eds.), *Durkheim and Modern Education* (Hampshire, England: Routledge). Reprinted by permission.

'authority' of the teacher extends to the child's home. All parents of children at state elementary and junior high schools (97 per cent of the total cohort) receive home visits from their teachers who also advise parents via notes on how they should look after their children at home. When children are in trouble with, say, the police, it is likely that their form teachers as well as their parents will be requested to visit the police station to discuss any issues that arise from the bad behaviour. Teachers are treated with enormous respect by parents and there is little culture of parental influence within the school environment.

3. If Neither the Church nor the State Should Be the Architects of the Educational System, then Responsibility Must Lie with the State (see Giddens 1986: 73)

Ever since the start of the Meiji period (1868), the architects of the Japanese educational system have been industry and the state. The modernization of the educational system was seen as the key to preventing colonization though rapid modernization by earning the respect of prospective Western colonizers. The state and business have remained the architects of the educational system until today. When a blue-ribbon committee on educational reform was convened in the 1980s its main representatives were bureaucrats, educationalists and industrial leaders (see Schoppa 1991). Teachers and parents, at least *qua* teachers and parents, were given only token representation. The state's goals, however, have always been broad public goals and not those serving only narrow interests which is something else on which Durkheim would have insisted.

4. Education Should Be Based on a Meritocratic Ideal (see Durkheim 1893b/t. 1984a: 313)

Durkheim believed passionately in a meritocratic, though not necessarily an egalitarian, educational system. He was not a socialist who believed that rewards should be shared out equally, but a meritocrat who believed that they should go to those who deserved them. Like any meritocrat, Durkheim believed in the power of nurture over nature and held a *tabula rasa* view of the human mind. As Ronald Dore (1976) pointed out over twenty years ago in *The Diploma Disease,* few countries have as strong a meritocratic educational ideology as Japan. Great efforts are expended to ensure the maintenance of the belief in equal opportunities in the system.

Efforts at making the Japanese educational system seem egalitarian can be seen in a wide variety of contexts. All examinations, right up and including university, are reduced to a multiple-choice formula which reduces subjectivity in marking. School buildings are built on a uniform design to prevent those who go to new institutions having an advantage over those in older ones. Children are taught as a class as opposed to as individuals; indeed individual education is minimized to reduce charges of favouritism. Even such minor detail as what children are given to eat is uniformly dictated: two noodle-based, two rice-based and two bread-based school lunches a week, and no individual choice.

The ideology of egalitarianism is underpinned by a strong social ideology of classlessness and ethnic homogeneity that is reinforced by the state both via the annual publication of a national survey suggesting that over 90 per cent of Japanese see themselves as members of some amorphous middle class (see Ishida 1993) and the denial of the existence of any minority groups (Weiner 1997). As a result, the state can maintain the ideology that everyone has an equal chance in the educational system — if they are prepared to put in the effort. The underlying pedagogical ideology is that hard work rather than ability leads to educational success. School reports draw on a vocabulary of spirit (*seisbin*), effort (*dōryoku*) and perseverance (*gaman*) rather than on one of ability and potential (for more detail on this, see Goodman 1989).

The apparent social rewards for effort are very clear in the Japanese system. Educational success is measured by both how far one can go in the educational system and which particular university one can enter. The further one goes and the better the institution one enters, then the larger the company in which one will be able to find employment, with greater job security, a better income package and higher social status.

5. Knowledge Should Be Transmitted Uniformly to All Children

As we have seen above, the Japanese educational system since the Meiji period has been highly centralized. This is not only something of which Durkheim would have approved, but indeed a model he would have recognized since it was largely copied from the French system of the 1870s. Between 1871 and 1873 in one of the most amazing stories in recent modern history, virtually the entire Japanese government under the leadership of Prince Iwakura Tomomi travelled throughout

North America and Western Europe picking up blue-prints for the modernization of the country (see, Jansen 1965, 1980; Soviak 1971). For its educational system, it picked up from North America concepts of vocational training, from Germany a system of higher education built around a few elite public universities, and from France the idea of a centralized authority and a strong emphasis on state-run normal schools (Hurst 1984: 3). Today, the uniformity of the educational system is not, however, uncontroversial. The ministry of education sets a core curriculum and screens textbooks for use in school. While in theory schools have some latitude for choosing between different books, in reality choice is very limited. The screening of history textbooks and their account of the Japanese involvement in the Second World War has been particularly controversial; the Japanese government has always defended its position, however, with the argument for the need to teach only verifiable facts that can be uniformly taught and uniformly tested (see Ienaga 1970; Pyle 1983). In short, all students learn the same facts at virtually the same time and at the same pace in practically the same fashion in identical buildings with identical timetables.

6. Knowledge Must Be Scientifically Passed On (see Lukes 1973: 390)

Durkheim believed strongly that collective ideas needed to be passed on to the child in a scientific manner; the mind was to be trained in a scientific manner through the acquisition of knowledge. This again accords with the model of teaching that is dominant in Japan: all subjects have been reduced to a form which can be learnt as facts that must be taught in the correct sequence and which can be tested by multiple-choice questions (for more on the philosophy behind this, see Cummings 1980). While it is easy to see why North American and Western European educationalists might understand this approach in the case of the hard sciences, they are less likely to perceive its significance in the arts and humanities. But the same principles apply here. Indeed, in Japan one can find multiple-choice art examinations. The principles here are important: there is no such thing in Japan as an inartistic individual, only someone who has not learnt how to draw. Art has been reduced to basic principles of shape, perspective and form which, if taught properly and in the right sequence, can be learnt by anyone prepared to put in the effort. The results, as with music where similarly there is no concept of the unmusical individual, can by Western standards be staggering.[2]

7. Schools Must Teach Children Boundaries (see Durkheim 1923a/t. 1961a)

Durkheim was much concerned to see educational institutions develop moral values, which are the foundation of social order. In particular, he asked what *function* the classroom should play in the process of developing social order and social cohesion. As is well known, he responded to these questions by observing that the role of the classroom is to construct boundaries for children and to teach them what would happen if they transgressed those boundaries. For children who can understand what constitutes good and bad behaviour knowledge of these boundaries is essentially a *liberation* (Wilson 1973: xv). In Japan, as many ethnographers have described, early socialization in the formal educational sphere is very largely learning symbolic and ritual boundaries and correct forms of behaviour which depend on context (see Hendry 1986; Lewis 1995; Peak 1992; Tobin 1992). In Japan, behavioural codes are very explicit, rules are precise, life courses are clearly laid out and much of the socialization process, up to and including socialization in the work place, is about mastering the correct ritual codes.

8. The Individual Must Learn to Subsume Their Identity within That of the Collective

Durkheim believed strongly that excessive individualism in the educational sphere could lead to what he termed 'personal defeat' and 'social chaos'. Moral education was the means of preventing this.

As is well known, the idea that Japan is a group society, where individual identity is expressed through and emanates from the collective, is widely expressed in a large number of ways. Linguistically, the word for Western-style individualism (*kojinshugi*) is the same as the word for selfishness (Moeran 1984); the word for different (*chigau*) is the same as the word for wrong. Group education in Japan is practised implicitly in all schools and explicitly in many. Individuals are taught to think of themselves not as individuals but in the group context (see Peak 1992). The best-known version of this style of teaching is the *han seido,* where a class of, say, forty-eight is divided into six groups of eight, with a boy and girl leader of each (co-education is the norm in Japan) who liaise on behalf of the team leader with the teacher. Leaders are rotated, which means that individuals follow requests of the leaders knowing that they will require similar support when they become leaders themselves. If a member of the group does well, then it is the whole group which receives praise; if a member does something bad, then it is also the whole group which is brought together to discuss how the individual can be helped to be better in future. Groups in the classroom are encouraged to be competitive with one another, so that the stronger members of the group are supposed (and indeed often do) help the weaker members with their work so as to bring the average level of the group up. Even in what might appear to be such inherently individualistic competitive activities, such as school sports days, elementary schools in Japan reduce the competition to between two groups (marked by which side of their reversible caps — red or white — are on display) with just one prize. As a result, even the slowest boy in the school has his part to play, since his one point for completing his event may make the crucial difference between the two teams (Hendry 1986: 142–3).

The use of groups is clearly more complicated than the simple picture outlined above. Children are simultaneously members of many groups — the *han,* the class, the grade, the school as a whole — and the group context that it invoked, say in disciplining children, depends on the individuals involved. Should members of different classes in one grade be involved in bad behaviour, then it will be all the members of all those classes in that grade who will be called together to discuss the behaviour of the miscreants. Moreover, group membership is flexible. At the beginning of each school year, children are purposefully moved around within and between classes (there is no streaming in Japanese classes) so that, as they themselves remark, they need to say 'good-bye' to their friends of the previous year at the end of the school year in March since, when the next school year starts in April, they will have new 'friends.' Thus groups provide more than just a working context but also a social one; children are expected to socialize with members of their groups, though they will probably be able to distinguish these relations (known as *tsukiai*) from those of friendship and kinship (though the categories of course may well overlap) (see Atsumi 1982).[3]

9. Punishment Is to Reinforce the Moral Code Rather than to Uphold Authority (see Giddens 1986: 74–6)

The ideologies of groupism as described above fit neatly with Durkheim's idea that to act morally is to act in the interests of the group. This implies, of course, a certain degree of what sociologists have sometimes called particularistic or contextual ethics. It is an ethos

which contrasts with Judaeo-Christian ideologies of universalistic ethics where internalized ideas of right and wrong must always be placed before contingent concerns. Both sets of values are of course ideologies—it is as nonsensical to suggest that guilt does not exist in Japan as it is to suggest that shame does not exist in Judaeo-Christian societies. But Durkheim's views on this subject are interesting to the extent to which they overlap with Japanese ideas of punishment. The severest form of punishment in Japan is often maintained to be that of ostracism (*murahachibu*) since an individual outside a group finds it very hard to function in Japanese society. In theory physical punishment is prohibited in Japanese schools and the threat of ostracism and shaming are meant to be the main forms of obtaining compliance. For bad behavior there should be an apology, and if this is done correctly the individual can quickly be rehabilitated into the group since there is a strong belief in the essential goodness (*seizensetsu*) of the individual. This is in contrast to ideologies of original sin that exist in Judaeo-Christian traditions.[4]

10. Teachers Should Be Moral Exemplars Who Educate through Their Demeanour as Well as through Their Instruction (Giddens 1986: 74)

The Japanese verb *manabu* (to learn) has its roots in the word *maneru* (to imitate) and it has been suggested that this summarizes the major difference in Japanese pedagogy from Western traditions where the verb 'to educate' comes from the Latin *educare,* 'to draw out' (Seward 1983: 30). Similarly the Japanese noun, *sensei* (teacher), literally means 'one who comes before' with connotations that the teacher provides a model for behavior rather than being simply an 'educator' of it. Teaching in Japan has always been a high status profession, and the word *sensei,* though perhaps overused, still carries much of the connotation of 'doctor' in Western societies. As we have already seen, teaching is a 24-hour job, and teachers are expected and indeed required by the local community to demonstrate the same standards of behavior outside the school environment as inside it.

Japanese Education: The Ideal and the Real

It would appear from the above account that the Japanese educational system fits closely Durkheim's general prescription. Unfortunately, however, the account we have given above is far from problematic. It is, however, widespread and to a certain extent such an account of the system, as with Durkheim's views of society, tell us as much about the ideological beliefs and concerns of those who support such a view, as they do about the educational system itself. Interestingly, for our discussion of Durkheim's influence on the sociology of education, the weaknesses of the above account are also, in many ways, the weaknesses in Durkheim's analysis not only of education but of other social systems as well.

The problem with the account offered above of the Japanese education is that it ignores the fact that individuals in Japan live in a democracy and, as in all democracies, class interests emerge which can, and frequently are, defended via the educational system. As Bourdieu among many others has demonstrated, education is a very effective means for the construction and the dissemination of class capital. In many societies, such as the UK, this defence of class cultural capital is substantiated most clearly by sending children to private institutions which are financially out of the reach of poorer families. In Japan, however, since the state has been so instrumental in designing the modern educational system and in utilizing it to create an effective work force, it has generally been the case that state education has had higher status than private education, though there have always been exceptions, especially at the tertiary level (such as Keio and Waseda Universities) which have mirrored the British experience.

In Japan (and also indeed South Korea and Taiwan) family investment in education has been not so much through private mainstream education as through payment for supplementary education. In Japan this comes in a variety of forms. Perhaps best known are the *juku* (commonly known as cram schools) which are attended by virtually all boys living in urban environments for two or three times a week from the age of 12 onwards. As they get older, attendance rates (and costs) go up. This supplementary education may itself be supplemented by home tutors (*katei kyōshi*). These are normally university students who are tutoring in order to pay their way through university. The most expensive form of supplementary education, however, is also the most intensive, and that is the system of full-time cram schools, known as *yobikō*. These are attended by those who either failed to get into any university at the first attempt or the university of their first choice, and who wish to spend another year, after the end of senior high school, in

full-time education preparing to retake their exams. Students who go to *yobikō* are known as *rōnin* which refers to the masterless samurai of the feudal period who, like the *rōnin* students of today, have no master institution which is responsible for them and to which they need to show undivided loyalty.

Since the ministry of education officially refuses to recognize the existence of supplementary education in Japan, it is difficult to get accurate figures on the background of students who attend these institutions. It is clear however, with the often large sums of money involved in attendance, that there must be disparities of access and certainly one survey of those attending high-quality *yobikō* suggests that over four times the national average of fathers had both managerial jobs and university education (30 per cent and 35 per cent against national averages of 7 per cent and 8 per cent respectively). The same survey showed that 85 per cent of those attending were male, reinforcing earlier surveys that parents invest considerably more in their sons than in their daughters when it comes to educational costs (Tsukada 1988).

The results of this expenditure on supplementary education are largely responsible for the disparities of wealth of those entering university. Already by the early 1970s, the average family income of those who won places at Tokyo University (the country's most elite institution) was almost double that of the national average. Those from the top 20 per cent in terms of family income were three times as likely to go to university than those from the bottom 20 per cent (James and Benjamin 1988: chapter 7). There is, of course, nothing startling in these figures when compared to Western European and North American statistics.[5] The problem is that the ideology of the Japanese system is rooted in its egalitarian ideals and yet inequalities have been growing at a very fast rate since the 1960s (Rohlen 1977).

One of the major ironies of the supplementary educational system and the fact that state education generally has higher status than private education is that the higher the family income generally the lower the expenditure on formal education (Takeuchi 1991). The result, of course, is that in examining education in contemporary Japan, one has to think of it in terms essentially of two parallel systems: a formal system based on ideologies of harmony, equality and homogeneity (in essence a Durkheimian ideal type of education) and an informal one based on realities of self-investment, conflict and the maintenance of class interests (in essence a Weberian or even a Marxist perception of education).

The decision to emphasize one model over the other is, as we go on to explore, more a political one than an academic one.

Critical Perspectives on Japanese Education

The vast majority of commentaries on the Japanese educational system coming from inside, but particularly outside Japan, concentrate on the first picture of the system that has been outlined above. They portray a system built on social values of homogeneity, classlessness, harmony, meritocracy, transparency and rewards for effort. In this sense, such accounts can be best described as functionalist, static and Durkheimian. As we have seen, we need to question the empirical validity of such accounts. We also need, however, to examine the political implications of taking such a position in describing any educational system, since there is a sense in which those who have written about Japanese education in such terms may have been helping to construct and legitimate such a system, as much as actually describing and analyzing it. Durkheimian accounts, as much as Marxist ones, are not constructed in a vacuum but express important (generally conservative) interests.

In order to understand the implications of the work-place on Japanese education, we need to situate them in a broader sociology of work in Japanese society. At the time when the modern Japanese educational system was being developed in the Meiji period, great efforts were being expended on the construction of a Japanese national identity. Indeed, a centralized and government-controlled educational system was seen as perhaps the most effective means of constructing and disseminating such an identity. It was at this stage that many of the features of what came to be seen as Japanese identity began to be constructed, notably the emphasis on homogeneity and harmony. Further it was often in historical and environmentally deterministic terms (see Gluck 1985: chapter 5). Such ideologies of national identity continue to retain a powerful presence in contemporary Japan and can be seen most clearly in the genre of literature widely known as *Nibonjinron* (literally Theories of Japaneseness). These accounts, as critics in the 1980s began to make clear, were essentially ahistorical, static, functionalist and, one could say, Durkheimian, and contained assumptions about the nature of the relationship between society and the individual. Such models are presaged on a view of society as essentially based on consensus and where conflict is seen as the abnormal (see Mouer and Sugimoto 1986;

Dale 1986). Some have suggested that they thereby reflected ideologies that served the interests of elites whose main desire was to deflect attention away from apparent lines of conflict within societies—in terms of gender, class, regionalism, ethnicity etc. Here was the guise of the Japanese having always been a 'naturally' harmonious, consensus-seeking, homogeneous, unitary race. Accounts of the educational system that also ignore the realities of class interests further serve to bolster those who want to hide such interests from public scrutiny. All accounts of the Japanese educational system, therefore, as with those of any other system, need to be placed in a political as well as a sociological context.

Similarly, as Parkin (1992: 71–2) notes, one must lay similar charges against Durkheim's approach to education in his work. As Steven Lukes (1973: 132) has pointed out, Durkheim never questioned exactly how it was that the states which needed to be socialized into the child by the political society as a whole were in fact determined by and serve the interests of particular groups within society. It may be that Durkheim's lack of discussion of class in education reflected the fact that class was virtually irrelevant in the context in which he was writing, where almost all children simply attended the local school. It was Durkheim's intellectual successors, however, most notably Bourdieu with his ideas of habitus and cultural capital and Basil Bernstein with his work on language codes who most effectively introduced concepts of class into a Durkheimian framework. So far, however, such approaches have had little effect in Japan, where the dominant paradigm of the educational system as essentially egalitarian and consensual remains very much in place.

Notes

1. Interestingly, the OECD researchers were unable to take on board the Japanese assumptions because of fears voiced by US and New Zealand representatives that examine the extent to which schools should inform practices in homes might be seen as patronizing to minority communities within those societies. No such debate exists in Japan, mainly because of the denial that there actually exist any minority groups.
2. I once looked over 120 still-life pictures done by a grade of 12-year-olds and was able to recognize, without difficulty, the picture each was trying to draw since every child had followed the basic principles of outline, shape, perspective, etc. Of course, similar ideas are becoming increasingly popular in the West where art, music and singing classes for adults who

were told at school that they had no natural talent in these areas are becoming increasingly popular.

3. It is worth pointing out in passing that exactly the same concepts of different categories of friendship and the need to transfer personal loyalties on being moved between groups also pertain in the Japanese workplace.
4. In Japan, very few (around 2 per cent) of those found guilty of crimes are sent to prison, as opposed to over 40 per cent in the US.
5. A recent, large-scale comparative project of class mobility in eleven capitalist and former communist countries, including the US and the UK, suggests that the odds ratio in Japan of moving from the working to the middle class is actually one of the lowest (Marshall, Swift and Roberts 1997: 52–3).

References

Atsumi, R. (1982) 'Patterns of personal relationships: a key to understanding Japanese thought and behaviour', in Sugimoto, Yoshio and Mouer, Ross (eds.), *Japanese Society: Reappraisals and New Directions, Social Analysis* (Special Edition), Nos. 5/6, 63–78.

Cummings, W. (1980) *Education and Equality in Japan,* Princeton: Princeton University Press.

Dale, P. (1986) *The Myth of Japanese Uniqueness,* London: Nissan Institute/Routledge Japanese Studies Series.

Dore, R. P. (1976) *The Diploma Disease: Education, Qualification and Development,* London: George Allen and Unwin.

Durkheim, E. (1893b) *De la division du travail social: étude sur l'organisation des sociétés supérieures,* Paris: Alcan.

_____ (1984a) by W. D. Halls, *The Division of Labour in Society,* with an introduction by L. Coser, London: Macmillan.

_____ (1922a) *Education et sociologie,* Paris: Alcan.

_____ (t.1956a) by S. D. Fox, *Education and Sociology,* Chicago: Free Press.

_____ (1925a) *L'Education morale,* Paris: Alcan.

_____ (t.1961a) by E. K. Wilson and H. Schnurer, *Moral Education,* New York: Free Press.

Giddens, A. (1986) *Durkheim,* London: Fontana Press.

Gluck, C. (1985) *Japan's Modern Myths: Ideology in the Late Meiji Period,* Princeton: Princeton University Press.

Goodman, R. (1989) 'Japanese education: a model to emulate?', in *The Pacific Review,* 2/1, 24–37.

_____ (1997) 'A model for all seasons? East Asian education and the problem of drawing lessons from other societies', in Yishay Yafeh et al. (eds), *Japan and East Asia: Lessons for the Development of the Middle East in the Era of Peace,* The Truman Institute, Jerusalem.

Hendry, J. (1986) *Becoming Japanese: The World of the Pre-School Child,* Manchester: Manchester University Press.

Holmes, B. (1989) 'Japan: private education' in Walford, Geoffrey (ed.), *Private Schools in Ten Countries: Policy and Practice,* London and New York: Routledge.

Hurst, G. C. (1984) *Japanese Education: Trouble in Paradise?* Asia, University Field Staff International Reports, No. 40.

Ienaga, S. (1970) 'The historical significance of the Japanese textbook lawsuit', *The Bulletin of Concerned Asian Scholars,* 2: 2–12.

Ishida, H. (1993) *Social Mobility in Contemporary Japan: Educational Credentials, Class and the Labour Market in a Cross-National Perspective,* Basingstoke: St Antony's/Macmillan.

James, E. and Benjamin, G. (1988) *Public Policy and Private Education,* Basingstoke: Macmillan.

James, M. B. (ed.) (1965) *Changing Japanese Attitudes toward Modernisation,* Princeton, NJ: Princeton University Press.

_____ (ed.) (1980) *Japan and Its World: Two Centuries of Change,* Princeton, NJ: Princeton University Press.

Karabel, J. and Halsey, A. H. (1977) 'Educational research: a review and an interpretation' in Karabel, Jerome and Halsey, A. H. (eds), *Power and Ideology in Education,* New York: Oxford University Press.

Lewis, C. C. (1995) *Educating Hearts and Minds: Reflections on Japanese Preschool and Elementary Education,* Cambridge: Cambridge University Press.

Lukes, S. (1973) *Emile Durkheim: His Life and Work: A Historical and Critical Study,* Harmondsworth: Penguin.

Marshall, G., Swift, A. and Roberts, S. (1997) *Against the Odds? Social Class and Social Justice in Industrial Societies,* Oxford: Clarendon Press.

Moeran, B. (1984) 'Individual, group and *Seisbin:* Japan's internal cultural debate', *Man,* 19/2: 252–66.

Mouer, R. and Sugimoto, Y. (1986) *Images of Japanese Society: A Study in the Structure of Social Reality,* London: KPI.

Parkin, F. (1992) *Durkheim,* Oxford: Oxford University Press.

Peak, L. (1992) *Learning to go to School in Japan: The Transition from Home to Preschool Life,* Berkeley: University of California Press.

Pyle, K. (1983) 'Japan besieged: the textbooks controversy', *Journal of Japanese Studies,* 9: 297–300.

Rohlen, T. P. (1977) 'Is Japanese education becoming less egalitarian? Notes on high school stratification and reform', *Journal of Japanese Studies* 3: 37–70.

Schoppa, L. (1991) *Education Reform in Japan: A Case of Immobilist Politics,* London: Nissan Institute/Routledge Japanese Studies Series.

Seward, J. (1983) *Japanese in Action* (rev. edn), New York and Tokyo: Weatherhill.

Soviak, E. (1971) 'On the nature of Western progress: The Journal of the Iwakura Embassy', in David H. Shiveley (ed.), *Tradition and Modernisation in Japanese Culture,* Princeton NJ: Princeton University Press.

Takeuchi, Y. (1991) 'Myth and reality in the Japanese selection system', *Comparative Education,* 27/1: 101–12.

Tobin, J. (1992) 'Japanese preschools and the pedagogy of selfhood' in Rosenberger, N. R. (ed.) *Japanese Sense of Self,* Cambridge: Cambridge University Press.

Tsukada, M. (1988) 'Institutionalised supplementary education in Japan: the Yobiko and Ronin student adaptations', *Comparative Education,* 24/3: 285–303.

Weiner, M. A. (1997) *Japan's Minorities: The Illusion of Homogeneity,* London: Sheffield Centre for Japanese Studies/Routledge.

Wilson, E. K. (1973) 'Editor's introduction' to Durkheim, Emile, *Moral Education: A Study of the Theory and Application of the Sociology of Education,* translated by Everett K. Wilson and Herman Schnurer, New York: The Free Press.

On Understanding the Processes of Schooling

The Contributions of Labeling Theory

RAY C. RIST

There have been few debates within American education which have been argued with such passion and intensity as that of positing causal explanations of success or failure in schools.[1] One explanation which has had considerable support in the past few years, particularly since the publication of *Pygmalion in the Classroom* by Rosenthal and Jacobson (1968), has been that of the "self-fulfilling prophecy." Numerous studies have appeared seeking to explicate the mechanisms by which the teacher comes to hold certain expectations of the students and how these are then operationalized within the classroom so as to produce what the teacher had initially assumed. The origins of teacher expectations have been attributed to such diverse variables as social class, physical appearance, contrived test scores, sex, race language patterns, and school records. But from the flurry of recent research endeavors, there has emerged a hiatus between this growing body of data and any larger theoretic framework. The concept of the self-fulfilling prophecy has remained simply that—a concept. The lack of a broader conceptual scheme has meant that research in this area has become theoretically stymied. Consequently, there has evolved instead a growing concern over the refinement of minute methodological nuances.

The thrust of this [article] is to argue that there is a theoretical perspective developing in the social sciences which can break the conceptual and methodological logjam building up on the self-fulfilling prophecy. Specifically, the emergence of *labeling theory* as an explanatory framework for the study of social deviance appears to be applicable to the study of education as well. Among the major contributions to the development of labeling theory are Becker, 1963, 1964; Broadhead, 1974; Lemert, 1951, 1972, 1974; Douglas, 1971, 1972; Kitsuse, 1964; Loffland, 1969; Matza, 1964, 1969; Scheff, 1966; Schur, 1971; Scott and Douglas, 1972; and Rubington and Weinberg, 1973.

If the labeling perspective can be shown to be a legitimate framework from which to analyze social processes influencing the educational experience and

From "On Understanding the Processes of Schooling: The Contributions of Labeling Theory" by Ray Rist, from *Power and Ideology in Education,* edited by Jerome Karabel and A. H. Halsey, copyright © 1977 by Oxford University Press, Inc. Used by permission of Oxford University Press, Inc.

the contributions of such processes to success or failure in school, there would then be a viable *interactionist* perspective to counter both biological and cultural determinists' theories of educational outcomes. While the latter two positions both place ultimate causality for success or failure *outside* the school, the labeling approach allows for an examination of what, in fact, is happening *within* schools. Thus, labeling theory would call our attention for example, to the various evaluative mechanisms (both formal and informal) operant in schools, the ways in which schools nurture and support such mechanisms, how students react, what the outcomes are for interpersonal interaction based on how these mechanisms have evaluated individual students, and how, *over time*, the consequences of having a certain evaluative tag influence the options available to a student within a school. What follows first is a summary of a number of the key aspects of labeling theory as it has been most fully developed in the sociological literature; second is an attempt to integrate the research on the self-fulfilling prophecy with the conceptual framework of labeling theory. Finally, the implications of this synthesis are explored for both future research and theoretical development.

I. Becoming Deviant: The Labeling Perspective

Those who have used labeling theory have been concerned with the study of *why* people are labeled, and *who* it is that labels them as someone who has committed one form or another of deviant behavior. In sharp contrast to the predominant approaches for the study of deviance, there is little concern in labeling theory with the motivational and characterological nature of the person who committed the act.

Deviance is understood, not as a quality of the person or as created by his actions, but instead as created by group definitions and reactions. It is a social judgment imposed by a social audience. As Becker (1963:9) has argued:

The central fact of deviance is that it is created by society. I do not mean this in the way it is ordinarily understood, in which the causes of deviance are located in the social situation of the deviant, or the social factors, which prompted his action. I mean, rather, that social groups create deviants by making the rules whose infraction constitutes deviance, and by applying those rules to particular people and labeling them as outsiders. From this point of view, *deviance is not the quality of the act the person commits, but rather a consequence of the application by others of rules and sanctions to an "offender." This de-*

viant is one to whom the label has been successfully applied. Deviant behavior is behavior that people so label. (emphasis added)

The labeling approach is insistent on the need for a shift in attention from an exclusive concern with the deviant individual to a major concern with the *process* by which the deviant label is applied. Again citing Becker (1964:2):

The labeling approach sees deviance always and everywhere as a process and interaction between at least two kinds of people: those who commit (or who are said to have committed) a deviant act, and the rest of the society, perhaps divided into several groups itself. . . . One consequence is that we become much more interested in the process by which deviants are defined by the rest of society, than in the nature of the deviant act itself.

The important questions, then, for Becker and others, are not of the genre to include, for example: Why do some individuals come to act out norm-violating behavior? Rather, the questions are of the following sort: Who applied the deviant label to whom? Whose rules shall prevail and be enforced? Under what circumstances is the deviant label successfully and unsuccessfully applied? How does a community decide what forms of conduct should be singled out for this kind of attention? What forms of behavior do persons in the social system consider deviant, how do they interpret such behavior, and what are the consequences of these interpretations for their reactions to individuals who are seen as manifesting such behavior? (See Akers, 1973.)

The labeling perspective rejects any assumption that a clear consensus exists as to what constitutes a norm violation—or for that matter, what constitutes a norm—within a complex and highly heterogeneous society. What comes to be determined as deviance and who comes to be determined as a deviant is the result of a variety of social contingencies influenced by who has the power to enforce such determinations. Deviance is thus problematic and subjectively given. The case for making the societal reaction to rulebreaking a major independent variable in studies of deviant behavior has been succinctly stated by Kitsuse (1964:101):

A sociological theory of deviance must focus specifically upon the interactions which not only define behaviors as deviant, but also organize and activate the application of sanctions by individuals, groups, or agencies. For in modern society, the socially significant differentiation of deviants from the nondeviant population is increasingly contingent upon circumstances of situation, place social and personal biography, and the bureaucratically organized activities of agencies of social control.

Traditional notions of who is a deviant and what are the causes for such deviance are necessarily reworked. By emphasizing the processual nature of deviance, any particular deviant is seen to be a product of being caught, defined, segregated, labeled, and stigmatized. *This is one of the major thrusts of the labeling perspective—that forces of social control often produce the unintended consequence of making some persons defined as deviant even more confirmed as deviant because of the stigmatization of labeling. Thus, social reactions to deviance further deviant careers.* Erikson (1966) has even gone so far as to argue that a society will strive to maintain a certain level of deviance within itself as deviance is functional to clarifying group boundaries, providing scapegoats, creating out-groups who can be the source of furthering ingroup solidarity, and the like.

The idea that social control may have the paradoxical effect of generating more of the very behavior it is designed to eradicate was first elaborated upon by Tannenbaum. He noted (1938:21):

> The first dramatization of the "evil" which separates the child out of his group . . . plays a greater role in making the criminal than perhaps any other experience. . . . He now lives in a different world. He has been tagged. . . . The person becomes the thing he is described as being.

Likewise, Schur (1965:4) writes:

> The societal reaction to the deviant, then, is vital to an understanding of the deviance itself and a major element in—if not the cause of—the deviant behavior.

The focus on outcomes of social control mechanisms has led labeling theorists to devote considerable attention to the workings of organizations and agencies which function ostensibly to rehabilitate the violator or in other ways draw him back into conformity. Their critiques of prisons, mental hospitals, training schools, and other people-changing institutions suggest that the results of such institutions are frequently nearly the opposite of what they were theoretically designed to produce. These institutions are seen as mechanisms by which opportunities to withdraw from deviance are sealed off from the deviant, stigmatization occurs, and

a new identity as a social "outsider" is generated. There thus emerges on the part of the person so labeled a new view of himself which is one of being irrevocably deviant.

This movement from one who has violated a norm to one who sees himself as a habitual norm violator is what Lemert (1972:62) terms the transition from a primary to a secondary deviant. A primary deviant is one who holds to socially accepted roles, views himself as a nondeviant, and believes himself to be an insider. A primary deviant does not deny that he has violated some norm, and claims only that it is not characteristic of him as a person. A secondary deviant, on the other hand, is one who has reorganized his social-psychological characteristics around the deviant role. Lemert (1972:62) writes:

> Secondary deviation refers to a special class of socially defined responses which people make to problems created by the societal reaction to their deviance. These problems. . . become central facts of existence for those experiencing them. . . . Actions, which have these roles and self-attitudes as their referents make up secondary deviance. The secondary deviant . . . is a person whose life and identity are organized around the facts of deviance.

A person can commit repeated acts of primary deviation and never come to view himself or have others come to view him as a secondary deviant. Secondary deviation arises from the feedback whereby misconduct or deviation initiates social reaction to the behavior which then triggers further misconduct. Lemert (1951:77) first described this process as follows:

> The sequence of interaction leading to secondary deviation is roughly as follows: 1) primary deviation; 2) societal penalties; 3) further primary deviation; 4) stronger penalties and rejections; 5) further deviations, perhaps with hostilities and resentments beginning to focus upon those doing the penalizing; 6) crisis reached in the tolerance quotient, expressed in formal action by the community stigmatizing of the deviant; 7) strengthening of the deviant conduct as a reaction to the stigmatizing and penalties; and 8) ultimate acceptance of deviant social status and efforts at adjustment on the basis of the associated role.

Thus, when persons engage in deviant behavior they would not otherwise participate in and when they develop social roles they would not have developed save for the application of social control measures, the outcome is the emergence of secondary deviance. The fact of having been apprehended and labeled is the critical element in the subsequent construction of a deviant identity and pursuit of a deviant career.

II. The Origins of Labeling: Teacher Expectations

Labeling theory has significantly enhanced our understanding of the process of becoming deviant by shifting our attention from the deviant to the judges of deviance and the forces that affect their judgment. Such judgments are critical, for a recurrent decision made in all societies, and particularly frequent in advanced industrial societies, is that an individual has or has not mastered some body of information, or perhaps more basically, has or has not the capacity to master that information. These evaluations are made periodically as one moves through the institution of school and the consequences directly affect the opportunities to remain for an additional period. To be able to remain provides an option for mastering yet another body of information, and to be certified as having done so. As Ivan Illich (1971) has noted, it is in industrial societies that being perceived as a legitimate judge of such mastery has become restricted to those who carry the occupational role of "teacher." A major consequence of the professionalization of the role of teacher has been the ability to claim as a near exclusive decision whether mastery of material has occurred. Such exclusionary decision-making enhances those in the role of "teacher" as they alone come to possess the authority to provide certification for credentials (Edgar, 1974).

Labeling theorists report that in making judgments of deviance, persons may employ information drawn from a variety of sources. Further, even persons within the same profession (therapists, for example) may make divergent use of the same material in arriving at an evaluative decision on the behavior of an individual. Among the sources of information available to labelers, two appear primary: first-hand information obtained from face-to-face interaction with the person they may ultimately label, and second-hand information obtained from other than direct interaction.

The corollary here to the activities of teachers should be apparent. Oftentimes, the evaluation by teachers (which may lead to the label of "bright," "slow," etc.) is based on first-hand information gained through face-to-face interaction during the course of the time the teacher and student spent together in the classroom. But a goodly amount of information about the student which informs the teacher's evaluation is second-hand information. For instance, comments from other teachers, test scores, prior report cards, permanent records, meetings with the parents, or evaluations from welfare agencies and psychological clinics are all potential informational sources. In a variation of the division between first-hand and second-hand sources of information, Johnson (1973) has suggested that there are three key determinants of teacher evaluations: student's prior performance, social status characteristics, and present performance. Prior performance would include information from cumulative records (grades, test scores, notes from past teachers or counselors, and outside evaluators) while social status and performance would be inferred and observed in the ongoing context of the classroom.

What has been particularly captivating about the work of Rosenthal and Jacobson (1968) in this regard is their attempt to provide empirical justification for a truism considered self-evident by many in education: School achievement is not simply a matter of a child's native ability, but involves directly and inextricably the teacher as well. Described succinctly, their research involved a situation where, at the end of a school year, more than 500 students in a single elementary school were administered the "Harvard Test of Inflected Acquisition." In actuality this test was a standardized, relatively nonverbal test of intelligence, Flanagan's (1960) Test of General Ability (TOGA). The teachers were told that such a test would, with high predictive reliability, sort out those students who gave strong indication of being intellectual "spurters" or "bloomers" during the following academic year. Just before the beginning of school the following fall, the teachers were given lists with the names of between one and nine of their students. They were told that these students scored in the top twenty percent of the school on the test, though, of course, no factual basis for such determinations existed. A twenty percent subsample of the "special" students was selected for intensive analysis. Testing of the students at the end of the school year offered some evidence that these selected children did perform better than the nonselected. The ensuing debate as to the validity and implications of the findings from the study will be discussed in the next section.

The findings of Deutsch, Fishman, Kogan, North, and Whiteman (1964); Gibson (1965): Goslin and Glass (1967); McPherson (1966); and Pequignot

(1966) all demonstrate the influence of standardized tests of intelligence and achievement on teacher's expectations. Goaldman (1971), in a review of the literature on the use of tests as a second-hand source of information for teachers, noted: "Although some of the research has been challenged, there is a basis for the belief that teachers at all levels are prejudiced by information they receive about a student's ability or character." Mehan (1971, 1974) has been concerned with the interaction between children who take tests and the teachers who administer them. He posits that testing is not the objective use of a measurement instrument, but the outcome of a set of interactional activities which are influenced by a variety of contingencies which ultimately manifest themselves in a reified "test score." Mehan suggests (1971):

> Standardized test performances are taken as an unquestioned, non-problematic reflection of the child's underlying ability. The authority of the test to measure the child's real ability is accepted by both teachers and other school officials. Test results are accepted without doubt as the correct and valid document of the child's ability.

Characteristics of children such as sex and race are immediately apparent to teachers. Likewise, indications of status can be quickly inferred from grooming, style of dress, need for free lunches, information on enrollment cards, discussion of family activities by children, and visits to the school by parents. One intriguing study recently reported in this area is that by two sociologists, Clifford and Walster (1973:249). The substance of their study was described as follows:

> Our experiment was designed to determine what effect a student's physical attractiveness has on a teacher's expectations of the child's intellectual and social behavior. Our hypothesis was that a child's attractiveness strongly influences his teachers' judgments; the more attractive the child, the more biased in his favor we expect the teachers to be. The design required to test this hypothesis is a simple one: Teachers are given a standardized report card and an attached photograph. The report card includes an assessment of the child's academic performance as well as of his general social behavior. The attractiveness of the photos is experimentally varied. On the basis of this information, teachers are asked to state their expectations of the child's educational and social potential.

Based on the responses of 404 fifth grade teachers within the state of Missouri, Clifford and Walster concluded (1973:255):

There is little question but that the physical appearance of a student affected the expectations of the teachers we studied. Regardless of whether the pupil is a boy or girl, the child's physical attractiveness has an equally strong association with his teacher's reactions to him.

The variables of race and ethnicity have been documented, by Brown (1968), Davidson and Lang (1960), Jackson and Cosca (1974), and Rubovits and Maehr (1973), among others, as powerful factors in generating the expectations teachers hold of children. It has also been documented that teachers expect less of lower-class children than they do of middle-class children (cf. Becker, 1952; Deutsch, 1963; Leacock, 1969; Rist, 1970, 1973; Stein, 1971; Warner, Havighurst, and Loeb, 1944; and Wilson, 1963). Douglas (1964), in a large scale study of the tracking system used in British schools, found that children who were clean and neatly dressed in nice clothing, and who came from what the teachers perceived as "better" homes, tended to be placed in higher tracks than their measured ability would predict. Further, when placed there they tended to stay and perform acceptably. Mackler (1969) studied schools in Harlem and found that children tended to stay in the tracks in which they were initially placed and that such placement was based on a variety of social considerations independent of measured ability. Doyle, Hancock, and Kifer (1971) and Palardy (1969) have shown teacher expectations for high performance in elementary grades to be stronger for girls than boys.

The on-going academic and interpersonal performance of the children may also serve as a potent source of expectations for teachers. Rowe (1969) found that teachers would wait longer for an answer from a student they believed to be a high achiever than for one from a student they believed to be a low achiever. Brophy and Good (1970) found that teachers were more likely to give perceived high achieving students a second chance to respond to an initial incorrect answer, and further, that high achievers were praised more frequently for success and criticized less for failure.

There is evidence that the expectations teachers hold for their students can be generated as early as the first few days of the school year and then remain stable over the months to follow (Rist, 1970, 1972, 1973; Willis, 1972). For example, I found during my three-year longitudinal and ethnographic study of a single, *de facto* segregated elementary school in the black community of St. Louis, that after only eight days of kindergarten, the teacher made permanent seating arrangements based on what she assumed were variations in academic capability. But no formal evaluation of the children had taken place. Instead, the assignments to the three tables were based on a number of socio-economic criteria as well as on early interaction patterns in the classroom. Thus, the placement of the children came to reflect the social class distinctions in the room—the poor children from public welfare families all sat at one table, the working class children sat at another and the middle class at the third. I demonstrated how the teacher operationalized her expectations of these different groups of children in terms of her differentials of teaching time, her use of praise and control, and the extent of autonomy within the classroom. By following the same children through first and second grade as well, I was able to show that the initial patterns established by the kindergarten teacher came to be perpetuated year after year. By second grade, labels given by another teacher clearly reflected the reality each of the three groups experienced in the school. The top group was called the "Tigers," the middle group the "Cardinals," and the lowest group, the "Clowns." What had begun as a subjective evaluation and labeling by the teacher took on objective dimensions as the school proceeded to process the children on the basis of the distinctions made when they first began.

Taken together, these studies strongly imply that the notion of "teacher expectations" is multi-faceted and multi-dimensional. It appears that when teachers generate expectations about their students, they do so not only for reasons of academic or cognitive performance, but for their classroom interactional patterns as well. Furthermore, not only ascribed characteristics such as race, sex, class, or ethnicity are highly salient, interpersonal traits are also. Thus, the interrelatedness of the various attributes which ultimately blend together to generate the evaluation a teacher makes as to what can be expected from a particular student suggests the strength and tenacity of such subsequent labels as "bright" or "slow" or "trouble-maker" or "teacher's little helper." It is to the outcomes of the student's having one or another of these labels that we now turn.

III. An Outcome of Labeling: The Self-Fulfilling Prophecy

W. I. Thomas, many years ago, set forth what has become a basic dictum of the social sciences when he ob-

served, "If men define situations as real, they are real in their consequences." This is at the core of the self-fulfilling prophecy. An expectation which defines a situation comes to influence the actual behavior within the situation so as to produce what was initially assumed to be there. Merton (1968:477) has elaborated on this concept and noted: "The self-fulfilling phase is, in the beginning, a *false* definition of the situation evoking a new behavior which makes the originally false conception come true." (emphasis in the original)

Here it is important to recall a basic tenet of labeling theory—that an individual does not become deviant simply by the commission of some act. As Becker (1963) stressed, deviance is not inherent in behavior *per se,* but in the application by others of rules and sanctions against one perceived as being an "offender." Thus, the only time one can accurately be termed a "deviant" is after the successful application of a label by a social audience. Thus, though many persons may commit norm violations, only select ones are subsequently labeled. The contingencies of race, class, sex, visibility of behavior, age, occupation, and who one's friends are all influence the outcome as to whether one is or is not labeled. Scheff (1966), for example, demonstrated the impact of these contingencies upon the diagnosis as to the severity of a patient's mental illness. The higher one's social status, the less the willingness to diagnose the same behavioral traits as indicative of serious illness in comparison to the diagnosis given to low status persons.

The crux of the labeling perspective lies not in whether one's norm violating behavior is known, but in whether others decide to do something about it. Further, if a label is applied to the individual, it is posited that this in fact causes the individual to become that which he is labeled as being. Due to the reaction of society, the change in the individual involves the development of a new socialized self-concept and social career centered around the deviant behavior. As Rubington and Weinberg (1973:7) have written:

> The person who has been typed, in turn, becomes aware of the new definition that has been placed upon him by members of his groups. He, too, takes this new understanding of himself into account when dealing with them. . . . When this happens, a social type has been ratified, and a person has been socially reconstructed.

As noted, Rosenthal and Jacobson's *Pygmalion in the Classroom* (1968) created wide interest in the notion of the self-fulfilling prophecy as a concept to explain differential performance by children in classrooms. Their findings suggested that the expectations teachers created about the children randomly selected as "intellectual bloomers" somehow caused the teachers to treat them differently, with the result that the children really did perform better by the end of the year. Though the critics of this particular research (Snow, 1969; Taylor, 1970; Thorndike, 1968, 1969) and those who have been unsuccessful in replicating the findings (Claiborn, 1969) have leveled strong challenges to Rosenthal and Jacobson, the disagreements are typically related to methodology, procedure, and analysis rather than to the proposition that relations exist between expectations and behavior.

The current status of the debate and the evidence accumulated in relation to it imply that teacher expectations are *sometimes* self-fulfilling. The early and, I think, overenthusiastic accounts of Rosenthal and Jacobson have obscured the issue. The gist of such accounts have left the impression, as Good and Brophy (1973:73) have noted, that the mere existence of an expectation will automatically guarantee its fulfillment. Rather, as they suggest:

> The fact that teachers' expectations can be self-fulfilling is simply a special case of the principle that any expectations can be self-fulfilling. This process is not confined to classrooms. Although it is not true that "wishing can make it so," our expectations do affect the way we behave in situations, and the way we behave affects how other people respond. In some instances, our expectations about people cause us to treat them in a way that makes them respond just as we expect they would.

Such a position would be borne out by social psychologists who have demonstrated that an individual's first impressions of another person do influence subsequent interactions (Dailey, 1952; Newcomb, 1947) and that one's self-expectations influence one's subsequent behavior (Aronson and Carlsmith, 1962; Brock and Edelman, 1965; and Zajonc and Brinkman, 1969).

The conditionality of expectations related to their fulfillment is strongly emphasized by labeling theorists as well. Their emphasis upon the influence of social contingencies on whether one is labeled, how strong the label, and if it can be made to stick at all, points to a recognition that there is a social process involved where individuals are negotiating, rejecting, accepting, modifying, and reinterpreting the attempts at labeling. Such interaction is apparent in the eight stages of the development of secondary deviance outlined above by

Lemert. Likewise, Erikson (1964:17), in his comments on the act of labeling as a rite of passage from one side of the group boundary to the other, has noted:

> The common assumption that deviants are not often cured or reformed, then, may be based on a faulty premise, but this assumption is stated so frequently and with such conviction that it often creates the facts which later "prove" it to be correct. If the returning deviant has to face the community's apprehensions often enough, it is understandable that he, too, may begin to wonder whether he has graduated from the deviant role—and *so respond to the uncertainty by resuming deviant activity.* In some respects, this may be the only way for the individual and his community to agree as to what kind of person he really is, for it often happens that the community is only able to perceive his "true colors" when he lapses, momentarily into some form of deviant performance. (emphasis added)

Explicit in Erikson's quote is the fact of the individual's being in interaction with the "community" to achieve some sort of agreement on what the person is "really" like. Though Erikson did not, in this instance, elaborate upon what he meant by "community," it can be inferred from elsewhere in his work that he sees "community" as manifesting itself in the institutions persons create in order to help organize and structure their lives. Such a perspective is clearly within the framework of labeling theory, where a major emphasis has been placed upon the role of institutions in sorting, labeling, tracking, and channeling persons along various routes depending upon the assessment the institution has made of the individual.

One pertinent example of the manner in which labeling theory has been applied to the study of social institutions and their impact upon participants has been in an analysis of the relation of schooling to juvenile delinquency. There have been several works which suggest as a major line of argument that schools, through and because of the manner in which they label students, serve as a chief instrument in the creation of delinquency (Hirschi, 1969; Noblit and Polk, 1975; Polk 1969; Polk and Schafer, 1972; Schafer and Olexa, 1971). For example, Noblit and Polk (1975:3) have noted:

> In as much as the school is the primary institution in the adolescent experience—one that promises not only the future status available to the adolescent, but also that gives or denies status in adolescence itself—it can be expected that its definitions are of particular significance for the actions of youth. That is, the student who has been reported

from success via the school has little reason to conform to the often arbitrary and paternalistic regulations and rules of the school. In a very real sense, this student has no "rational constraints" against deviance. It is through the sorting mechanisms of the school, which are demanded by institutions of higher education and the world of work, that youth are labeled and thus sorted into the situation where deviant behavior threatens little while providing some alternative forms of status.

It is well to reiterate the point—interaction implies behavior and choices being made by both parties. The person facing the prospect of receiving a new label imputing a systemic change in the definition of his selfhood may respond in any of a myriad number of ways to this situation. Likewise, the institutional definition of the person is neither finalized nor solidified until the end of the negotiation as to what precisely that label should be. But, in the context of a single student facing the authority and vested interests of a school administration and staff, the most likely outcome is that over time, the student will increasingly move towards conformity with the label the institution seeks to establish. Good and Brophy (1973:75) have elaborated upon this process within the classroom as follows:

1. The teacher expects specific behavior and achievement from particular students.
2. Because of these different expectations, the teacher behaves differently toward the different students.
3. This teacher treatment tells each student what behavior and achievement the teacher expects from him and affects his self-concept, achievement motivation, and level of aspiration.
4. If this teacher treatment is consistent over time, and if the student does not actively resist or change it in some way, it will tend to shape his achievement and behavior. High-expectation students will be led to achieve at high levels, while the achievement of low-expectations students will decline.
5. With time, the student's achievement and behavior will conform more and more closely to that originally expected of him.

The fourth point in this sequence makes the crucial observation that teacher expectations are not automatically self-fulfilling. For the expectations of the teacher to become realized, both the teacher and the student must move towards a pattern of interaction where expectations are clearly communicated and the behavioral response is consonant with the expected patterns. But as Good and Brophy (1973:75) also note:

> This does not always happen. The teacher may not have clear-cut expectations about a particular student, or his expectations may continually change. Even when he has consistent expectations, he may not necessarily communicate them to the student through consistent behavior. In this case, the expectation would not be self-fulfilling even if it turned out to be correct. Finally, the student himself might prevent expectations from becoming self-fulfilling by overcoming them or by resisting them in a way that makes the teacher change them.

Yet, the critique of American education offered by such scholars as Henry (1963), Katz (1971), Goodman (1964), or Reimer (1971) suggests the struggle is unequal between the teacher (and the institution a teacher represents) and the student. The vulnerability of children to the dictates of adults in positions of power over them leaves the negotiations as to what evaluative definition will be tagged on the children more often than not in the hands of the powerful. As Max Weber himself stated, to have power is to be able to achieve one's ends, even in the face of resistance from others. When that resistance is manifested in school by children and is defined by teachers and administrators as truancy, recalcitrance, unruliness, and hostility, or conversely defined as a lack of motivation, intellectual apathy, sullenness, passivity, or withdrawal, the process is ready to be repeated and the options to escape further teacher definitions are increasingly removed.

Postscript: Beyond the Logjam

This paper has argued that a fruitful convergence can be effected between the research being conducted on the self-fulfilling prophecy as a consequence of teacher expectations and the conceptual framework of labeling theory. The analysis of the outcomes of teacher expectations produces results highly similar to those found in the study of social deviance. Labels are applied to individuals which fundamentally shift their definitions of self and which further reinforce the behavior which had initially prompted the social reaction. The impact of the self-fulfilling prophecy in educational research is comparable to that found in the analysis of mental health clinics, asylums, prisons, juvenile homes, and other people-changing organizations. What the labeling perspective can provide to the study of educational outcomes as a result of the operationalization of teacher expectations is a model for the study of the *processes* by which the outcomes are produced. The detailing over time of the interactional patterns which lead to changes in self-definition and behavior within classrooms is sadly lacking in almost all of the expectation research to date. A most glaring example of this omission is the study by Rosenthal and Jacobson themselves. Their conclusions are based only on the analysis of a pre- and post-test. To posit that teacher expectations were the causal variable that produced changes in student performances was a leap from the data to speculation. They could offer only suggestions as to how the measured changes in the children's performance came about, since they were not in the classrooms to observe how assumed teacher attitudes were translated into subsequent actual student behavior.

To extend the research on the educational experiences of those students who are differentially labeled by teachers, what is needed is a theoretical framework which can clearly isolate the influences and effects of certain kinds of teacher reactions on certain types of students, producing, certain typical outcomes. The labeling perspective appears particularly well-suited for this expansion of both research and theoretical development on teacher expectations by offering the basis for analysis at either a specific or a more general level. With the former, for example, there are areas of investigation related to 1) types of students perceived by teachers as prone to success or failure; 2) the kinds of reactions, based on their expectations, teachers have to different students; and 3) the effects of specific teacher reactions on specific student outcomes. At a more general level, fruitful lines of inquiry might include 1) the outcomes in the post-school world of having received a negative vs. a positive label within the school; 2) the influences of factors such as social class and race on the categories of expectations teachers hold; 3) how and why labels do emerge in schools as well as the phenomenological and structural meanings that are attached to them; and 4) whether there are means by which to modify or minimize the effects of school labeling processes on students.

Labeling theory provides a conceptual framework by which to understand the processes of transforming attitudes into behavior and the outcomes of having done so. To be able to detail the dynamics and influences within schools by which some children come to see themselves as successful and act as though they were, and to detail how others come to see themselves as failures and act accordingly, provides in the final analysis an opportunity to intervene so as to expand the numbers of winners and diminish the numbers of losers. For that reason above all others, labeling theory merits our attention.

Endnote

1. The preparation of this paper has been aided by a grant (GS-41522) from the National Science Foundation—Sociology Program. The views expressed here are solely those of the author and no official endorsement by either the National Science Foundation or the National Institute of Education is to be inferred.

References

Akers, R. L. *Deviant Behavior: A Social Learning Approach.* Belmont, Cal.: Wadsworth, 1973.

Aronson, E., and Carlsmith, J. M. "Performance Expectancy as a Determinant of Actual Performance." *Journal of Abnormal and Social Psychology* 65 (1962):179–182.

Becker, H. S. "Social Class Variations in the Teacher-Pupil Relationship." *Journal of Educational Sociology* 25 (1952):451–465.

Becker, H. S. *Outsiders.* New York: The Free Press, 1963.

Becker, H. S. *The Other Side.* New York: The Free Press, 1964.

Broadhead, R. S. "A Theoretical Critique of the Societal Reaction Approach to Deviance." *Pacific Sociological Review* 17 (1974):287–312.

Brock, T. C., and Edelman, H. "Seven Studies of Performance Expectancy as a Determinant of Actual Performance." *Journal of Experimental Social Psychology* 1 (1965):295–310.

Brophy, J., and Good, T. "Teachers' Communications of Differential Expectations for Children's Classroom Performance: Some Behavioral Data." *Journal of Educational Psychology* 61 (1970):365–374.

Brown, B. *The Assessment of Self-Concept among Four Year Old Negro and White Children: A Comparative Study Using the Brown IDS Self-Concept Reference Test.* New York: Institute for Developmental Studies, 1968.

Claiborn, W. L. "Expectancy Effects in the Classroom: A Failure to Replicate." *Journal of Educational Psychology* 60 (1969):377–383.

Clifford, M. M., and Walster, E. "The Effect of Physical Attractiveness on Teacher Expectations." *Sociology of Education* 46 (1973):248–258.

Dailey C. A. "The Effects of Premature Conclusion upon the Acquisition of Understanding of a Person." *Journal of Psychology* 33 (1952):133–152.

Davidson, H. H., and Lang, G. "Children's Perceptions of Teachers' Feelings toward Them." *Journal of Experimental Education* 29 (1960):107–118.

Deutsch, M. "The Disadvantaged Child and the Learning Process," in *Education in Depressed Areas,* edited by H. Passow. New York: Teachers College Press, 1963.

Deutsch, M.; Fishman, J. A.; Kogan, L.; North, R.; and Whiteman, M. "Guidelines for Testing Minority Group Children." *Journal of Social Issues* 20 (1964):129–145.

Douglas, J. *The Home and the School.* London: MacGibbon and Kee, 1964.

Douglas, J. *The American Social Order.* New York: The Free Press, 1971.

Douglas, J. (ed.). *Deviance and Respectability.* New York: Basic Books, 1972.

Doyle, W.; Hancock, G.; and Kifer, E. "Teachers' Perceptions: Do They Make a Difference?" Paper presented at the meeting of the American Educational Research Association, 1971.

Edgar, D. E. *The Competent Teacher.* Sydney, Australia: Angus & Robertson, 1974.

Erikson, K. T. "Note on the Sociology of Deviance," in *The Other Side,* edited by H. S. Becker. New York: The Free Press, 1964.

Erikson, K. T. *Wayward Puritans.* New York: Wiley, 1966.

Flanagan, J. C. *Test of General Ability: Technical Report.* Chicago: Science Research Associates, 1960.

Gibson, G. "Aptitude Tests." *Science* 149 (1965):583.

Goaldman, L. "Counseling Methods and Techniques: The Use of Tests," in *The Encyclopedia of Education,* edited by L. C. Deighton. New York: Macmillan, 1971.

Good, T., and Brophy, J. *Looking in Classrooms.* New York: Harper and Row, 1973.

Goodmam, P. *Compulsory Mis-Education* New York: Random House, 1964.

Goslin, D. A., and Glass, D. C. "The Social Effects of Standardized Testing on American Elementary Schools." *Sociology of Education* 40 (1967): 115–131.

Henry, J. *Culture Against Man.* New York: Random House, 1963.

Hirschi, T. *Causes of Delinquency.* Berkeley: University of California Press, 1969.

Illich, I. *Deschooling Society.* New York: Harper and Row, 1971.

Jackson, G., and Cosca, C. "The Inequality of Educational Opportunity in the Southwest: An Observational Study of Ethnically Mixed Classrooms." *American Educational Research Journal* 11 (1974):219–229.

Johnson, J. *On the Interface between Low income Urban Black Children and Their Teachers during the Early School Years: A Position Paper.* San Francisco: Far West Laboratory for Educational Research and Development, 1973.

Katz, M. Class, *Bureaucracy and Schools.* New York: Praeger, 1971.

Kitsuse, J. "Societal Reaction to Deviant Behavior: Problems of Theory and Method," in *The Other Side,* edited by H. S. Becker. New York: The Free Press, 1964.

Leacock, E. *Teaching and Learning in City Schools.* New York: Basic Books, 1969.

Lemert, E. *Social Pathology.* New York: McGraw-Hill, 1951.

Lemert, E. *Human Deviance, Social Problems and Social Control.* Englewood Cliffs, N.J.: Prentice-Hall, 1972.

Lemert, E. "Beyond Mead: The Societal Reaction to Deviance." *Social Problems* 21 (1974):457–468.

Lofland, J. *Deviance and Identity.* Englewood Cliffs, N.J.: Prentice-Hall, 1969.

Mackler, B. "Grouping in the Ghetto." *Education and Urban Society* 2 (1969):80–95.

Matza, D. *Delinquency and Drift.* New York: Wiley, 1964.

Matza, D. *Becoming Deviant.* Englewood Cliffs, N.J.: Prentice-Hall, 1969.

McPherson, G. H. *The Role-set of the Elementary School Teacher: A case study.* Unpublished Ph.D. dissertation, Columbia University, New York, 1966.

Mehan, H. B. *Accomplishing Understanding in Educational Settings.* Unpublished Ph.D. dissertation, University of California, Santa Barbara, 1971.

Mehan, H. B. *Ethnomethodology and Education.* Paper presented to the Sociology of Education Association conference, Pacific Grove, California, 1974.

Merton, R. K. "Social Problems and Social Theory," in *Contemporary Social Problems,* edited by R. Merton and R. Nisbet. New York: Harcourt, Brace and World, 1968.

Newcomb, T. M. "Autistic Hostility and Social Reality." *Human Relations* 1 (1947):69–86.

Noblit, G. W., and Polk, K. *Institutional Constraints and Labeling.* Paper presented to the Southern Sociological Association meetings, Washington, D.C., 1975.

Palardy, J. M. "What Teachers Believe—What Children Achieve." *Elementary School Journal,* 1969, pp. 168–169 and 370–374.

Pequignot, H. "L'équation Personnelle du Juge." In *Semaine des Hopitaux* (Paris), 1966.

Polk, K. "Class, Strain, and Rebellion and Adolescents." *Social Problems* 17 (1969):214–224.

Polk, K., and Schafer, W. E. *Schools and Delinquency.* Englewood Cliffs, N.J.: Prentice-Hall, 1972.

Reimer, E. *School Is Dead.* New York: Doubleday, 1971.

Rist, R. C. "Student Social Class and Teachers' Expectations: The Self-fulfilling Prophecy in Ghetto Education." *Harvard Educational Review* 40 (1970):411–450.

Rist, R. C. "Social Distance and Social Inequality in a Kindergarten Classroom: An Examination of the 'Cultural Gap' Hypothesis." *Urban Education* 7 (1972):241–260.

Rist, R. C. *The Urban School: A Factory for Failure.* Cambridge, Mass.: The M.I.T. Press, 1973.

Rosenthal, R., and Jacobson, L. "Teachers' Expectancies: Determinants of Pupils' IQ Gains." *Psychology Reports* 19 (1966):115–118.

Rosenthal, R., and Jacobson, L. *Pygmalion in the Classroom.* New York: Holt, Rinehart and Winston, 1968.

Rowe, M. "Science, Silence and Sanctions." *Science and Children* 6 (1969):11–13.

Rubington, E., and Weinberg, M. S. *Deviance: The Interactionist Perspective.* New York: Macmillan, 1973.

Rubovits, P., and Maehr, M. L. "Pygmalion Black and White." *Journal of Personality and Social Psychology* 2 (1973):210–218.

Schafer, W. E., and Olexa, C. *Tracking and Opportunity.* Scranton, Pa.: Chandler, 1971.

Scheff, T. *Being Mentally Ill.* Chicago; Aldine, 1966.

Schur, E. *Crimes without Victims.* Englewood Cliffs, N.J.: Prentice-Hall, 1965.

Schur, E. *Labeling Deviant Behavior.* New York: Harper and Row, 1971.

Scott, R. A., and Douglas, J. C. (eds.). *Theoretical Per-* *spectives on Deviance.* New York: Basic Books, 1972.

Snow, R. E. "Unfinished Pygmalion." *Contemporary Psychology* 14 (1969):197–199.

Stein, A. "Strategies for Failure." *Harvard Educational Review* 41 (1971):158–204.

Tannenbaum, F. *Crime and the Community.* New York: Columbia University Press, 1938.

Taylor, C. "The Expectations of Pygmalion's Creators." *Educational Leadership* 28 (1970):161–164.

Thorndike, R. L. "Review of Pygmalion in the Classroom." *Educational Research Journal* 5 (1968): 708–711.

Thorndike, R. L. "But Do You Have to Know How to Tell Time?" *Educational Research Journal* 6 (1969):692.

Warner, W. L.; Havighurst, R.; and Loeb, M.B. *Who Shall be Educated?* New York: Harper and Row, 1944.

Willis, S. *Formation of Teachers' Expectations of Student Academic Performance.* Unpublished Ph.D. dissertation, University of Texas, Austin, Texas, 1972.

Wilson, A. B. "Social Stratification and Academic Achievement," in *Education in Depressed Areas,* edited by H. Passow. New York: Teachers College Press, 1963.

Zajonc, R. B., and Brinkman, P. "Expectancy and Feedback as Independent Factors in Task Performance." *Journal of Personality and Social Psychology* 11 (1969):148–150.

The Politics of Culture

Understanding Local Political Resistance to Detracking in Racially Mixed Schools

AMY STUART WELLS

IRENE SERNA

Research on tracking, or grouping students into distinct classes for "fast" and "slow" learners, has demonstrated that this educational practice leads to racial and socioeconomic segregation within schools, with low-income, African American, and Latino students frequently placed in the lowest level classes, even when they have equal or higher test scores or grades (see Oakes, 1985; Oakes & Welner, 1995). Furthermore, being placed in the low track often has long-lasting negative effects on these students, as they fall further

From Amy Stuart Wells and Irene Serna, "The Politics of Culture: Understanding Local Political Resistance in Racially Mixed Schools," *Harvard Educational Review,* 66:1 (Spring 1996), pp. 93–118. Copyright © 1996 by the President and Fellows of Harvard College. All rights reserved.

and further behind their peers and become increasingly bored in school. Partly in response to this research and partly in response to their own uneasiness with the separate and unequal classrooms created by tracking, educators across the country are beginning to respond by testing alternatives to tracking, a reform we call "detracking."

Over the last three years, our research team studied ten racially and socioeconomically mixed schools undergoing detracking reform, and attempted to capture the essence of the political struggles inherent in such efforts.[1] We believe that an important aspect of our qualitative, multiple case study is to help educators and policymakers understand the various manifestations of local political resistance to detracking—not only who instigates it, but also the ideology of opposition to such reforms and the political practices employed (see Oaken & Wells, 1995).

This article focuses on how forces outside the school walls shaped the ability of educators to implement "detracking reform"—to question existing track structures and promote greater access to challenging classes for all students. More specifically, we look at those actors whom we refer to as the "local elite"—those with a combination of economic, political, and cultural capital that is highly valued within their particular school community.[2] These elites are most likely to resist detracking reform because their children often enjoy privileged status in a tracked system. The capital of the elites enables them to engage in political practices that can circumvent detracking reform.

In order to understand the influence of local elites' political practices on the tracking reform, we examine their ideology of entitlement, or how they make meaning of their privilege within the educational system and how others come to see such meanings as the way things "ought to be." According to Gramsci (cited in Boggs 1984), insofar as ruling ideas emanating from elites are internalized by a majority of individuals within a given community, they become a defining motif of everyday life and appear as "common sense"—that is, as the "traditional popular conception of the world" (p. 161).

Yet we realize that the high-status cultural capital—the valued tastes and consumption patterns—of local elites and the resultant ideologies are easily affected by provincial social contexts and the particular range of class, race, and culture at those sites (Bourdieu, 1984). In a study of social reproduction in postmodern society, Harrison (1993) notes that "the task is

not so much to look for the global correspondences between culture and class, but to reconstruct the peculiarly local and material micrologic of investments made in the intellectual field" (p. 40). Accordingly, in our study, we particularize the political struggles and examine the specific ideologies articulated at each school site. Because we were studying ten schools in ten different cities and towns, we needed to contextualize each political struggle over detracking reform within its local school community. These local contexts are significant because the relations of power and domination that affect people most directly are those shaping the social contexts within which they live out their everyday lives: the home, the workplace, the classroom, the peer group. As Thompson (1990) states, "These are the contexts within which individuals spend the bulk of their time, acting and interacting, speaking and listening, pursuing their aims and following the aims of others" (p. 9).

Our research team used qualitative methods to examine technical aspects of detracking—school organization, grouping practices, and classroom pedagogy—as well as cultural norms and political practices that legitimize and support tracking as a "commonsense" approach to educating students (Oakes & Wells, 1995). Our research question was, What happens when someone with power in a totally mixed secondary school decides to reduce tracking? Guided by this question, we selected ten sites—six high schools and four middle schools—from a pool of schools that were undergoing detracking reform and volunteered to be studied. We chose these particular schools because of their diversity and demonstrated commitment to detracking. The schools we studied varied in size from more than three thousand to less than five hundred students. One school was in the Northeast, three were in the Midwest, one in the South, two in the Northwest, and three in various regions of California. Each school drew from a racially and socioeconomically diverse community and served significant but varied mixes of White, African American, Latino, Native American/Alaska Native, and/or Asian students. We visited each school three times over a two-year period. Data collection during our site visits included in-depth, semi-structured tape-recorded interviews with administrators, teachers, students, parents, and community leaders, including school board members. In total, more than four hundred participants across all ten schools were interviewed at least once. We also observed classrooms, as well as faculty, PTA, and school board meetings. We reviewed documents and wrote field notes about our observations within the schools and the communities. Data were compiled extensively from each school to form the basis of cross-case analysis. Our study ran from the spring of 1992 through the spring of 1995.[3]

Descriptions of "Local Elites"

The struggles over tracking and detracking reforms are, to a large extent, concerned with whose culture and life-style is valued, and, thus, whose way of knowing is equated with "intelligence." Traditional hierarchical track structures in schools have been validated by the conflation of culture and intelligence. When culturally biased "truths" about ability and merit confront efforts to "detrack," political practices are employed either to maintain the status quo or to push toward new conceptions of ability that would render a rigid and hierarchical track structure obsolete (see Oakes, Lipton, & Jones, 1995).

While we acknowledge that many agents contribute to the maintenance of a rigid track structure, this article examines the political practices of local elites in the school communities we studied. The elites discussed here had children enrolled in the detracking schools and thus constitute the subgroup of local elites active in shaping school policies. Their practices were aimed at maintaining a track structure, with separate and unequal educational opportunities for "deserving" elite students and "undeserving" or non-elite students. Our analysis of elite parents' ideology of privilege and the resultant political practices therefore includes an examination of "corresponding institutional mechanisms" (Bourdieu & Wacquant, 1992, p. 188) employed to prevent structural change that would challenge their status and privilege.

Our intention is not to criticize these powerful parents in an unsympathetic manner. Yet, we believe that too often the cultural forces that shape such parents' agency as they try to do what is best for their children remain hidden from view and thus unquestioned. Our effort to unpack the "knapsack" of elite privilege will expose the tight relationship between the "objective" criteria of the schools and the cultural forces of the elite (McIntosh, 1992).

Detracking, or the process of moving schools toward a less rigid system of assigning students to classes and academic programs, is a hotly contested educational reform. In racially mixed schools, the controversy surrounding detracking efforts is compounded by

beliefs about the relationship among race, culture, and academic ability. In virtually all racially mixed secondary schools, tracking resegregates students, with mostly White and Asian students in the high academic tracks and mostly African American and Latino students in the low tracks (Oakes, 1985; Oakes, Oraseth, Bell, & Camp, 1990). To the extent that elite parents have internalized dominant, but often unspoken, beliefs about race and intelligence, they may resist "desegregation" within racially mixed schools—here defined as detracking—because they do not want their children in classes with Black and Latino students.

Efforts to alter within-school racial segregation via detracking, then, are generally threatening to elites, in that they challenge their position at the top of the hierarchy. The perceived stakes, from an elite parent's perspective, are quite high. They argue, for instance, that their children will not be well served in detracked classes. And while these stakes are most frequently discussed in academic terms—for example, the dumbing down of the curriculum for smart students—the real stakes, we argue, are generally not academics at all, but, rather, status and power. For example, if a school does away with separate classes for students labeled "gifted" but teachers continue to challenge these students with the same curriculum in a detracked setting, the only "losses" the students will incur are their label and their separate and unequal status. Yet in a highly stratified society, such labels and privileged status confer power.

In looking at the ability of the upper strata of society to maintain power and control, Bourdieu (1977) argues that economic capital—that is, income, wealth, and property—is not the only form of capital necessary for social reproduction. He describes other forms of capital, including political, social, and cultural (Bourdieu & Wacquant, 1992). In our analysis of resistance to detracking reforms, we focus on cultural capital and its relationship to dominant ideologies within our school communities because of the explicit connections between cultural capital and educational achievement within Bourdieu's work. According to Bourdieu (1984), cultural capital consists of culturally valued tastes and consumption patterns, which are rewarded within the educational system. Bourdieu discusses "culture" not in its restricted, normative sense, but rather from a more anthropological perspective. Culture is elaborated in a "taste" for refined objects, which is what distinguishes the culture of the dominant class or upper social status from that of the rest of society. In order for elites to employ their cultural capital to maintain power, emphasis must be placed on subtleties of taste—for example, form over function, manner over matter. Within the educational system. Bourdieu argues, students are frequently rewarded for their taste, and for the cultural knowledge that informs it. For instance, elite students whose status offers them the opportunity to travel to other cities, states, and countries on family vacations are often perceived to be more "intelligent" than other students, simply because the knowledge they have gained from these trips is reflected in what is valued in schools. When high-status, elite students' taste is seen as valued knowledge within the educational system, other students' taste and the knowledge that informs it is devalued (Bourdieu & Passeron, 1979). In this way, high-status culture is socially constructed as "intelligence"—a dubious relationship that elites must strive to conceal in order to legitimize their merit-based claim to privileged status. In other words, what is commonly referred to as "objective" criteria of intelligence and achievement is actually extremely biased toward the subjective experience and ways of knowing of elite students. Similarly, Delpit (1995) describes the critical role that power plays in our society and educational system, as the worldviews of those in privileged positions are "taken as the only reality, while the worldviews of those less powerful are dismissed as inconsequential" (p. xv). The education system is the primary field in which struggles over these cultural meanings take place and where, more often than not, high-status cultural capital is translated into high-status credentials, such as academic degrees from elite institutions (Bourdieu & Passeron, 1977).

Thus, socially valuable cultural capital—form and manner—is the property many upper class and, to a lesser extent, middle-class families transmit to their offspring that substitutes for, or supplements, the transmission of economic capital as a means of maintaining class, status, and privilege across generations (Bourdieu, 1973). Academic qualifications and high-status educational titles are to cultural capital what money and property titles are to economic capital. The form and manner of academic qualifications are critical. Students cannot simply graduate from high school; they must graduate with the proper high-status qualifications that allow them access to the most selective universities and to the credentials those institutions confer.

Through the educational system, elites use their economic, political, and cultural capital to acquire symbolic capital—the most highly valued capital in a given society or local community. Symbolic capital signifies culturally important attributes, such as status, authority, prestige, and, by extension, a sense of honor. The social construction of symbolic capital may vary from one locality to another, but race and social class consistently play a role, with White, wealthy, well-educated families most likely to be at the top of the social strata (Harrison, 1993).

Because the cultural capital of the elite is that which is most valued and rewarded within the educational system, elite status plays a circular role in the process of detracking reform: parents with high economic, political, and cultural capital are most likely to have children in the highest track and most prestigious classes, which in turn gives them more symbolic capital in the community. The elite parents can then employ their symbolic capital in the educational decision-making arena to maintain advantages for their children. Educational reforms that, like detracking, challenge the advantages bestowed upon children of the elite are resisted not only by the elites themselves, but also by educators and even other parents and community members who may revere the cultural capital of elite families. The school and the community thus bestow elite parents with the symbolic capital, or honor, that allows them political power.

The status of the local elites in the ten school communities we studied derived in part from the prestige they and their children endowed to public schools simply by their presence. The elite are the most valued citizens, those the public schools do not want to lose, because the socially constructed status of institutions such as schools is dependent upon the status of the individuals attending them. These are also the families most likely to flee public schools if they are denied what they want from them. For example, at Grant High School, an urban school in the Northwest, the White, upper-middle-class parents who sent their children to public schools held tremendous power over the district administration. Many of them were highly educated and possessed the economic means to send their children to private schools if they so chose.

While the elites at each of the schools we studied held economic, social, and political capital, the specific combination of these varied at each site in relation to the cultural capital valued there. Thus, who the elites were and their particular rationale for tracking varied among locations, based on the distinctive mix of race, class, and culture. For instance, at Liberty High School, located in a West Coast city, many of the White parents were professors at a nearby university. As "professional intellectuals," they strongly influenced the direction of Liberty High; although they were generally not as wealthy as business executives, they were nevertheless imbued with a great deal of high-status cultural capital. Meanwhile, educators and White parents at Liberty noted that most of the Black and Latino students enrolled in the school came from very low-income families. Many of the people we interviewed said there was a sizable number of middle-class Black families in this community, but that they did not send their children to public schools. This school's social class divide, which some educators and Black students argued was a caricature, allowed White parents to blame the school's resegregation through tracking on the "family backgrounds" of the students, rather than on racial prejudice.

In the midwestern town of Plainview, the local White elites worked in private corporations rather than universities. Here, the high-status cultural capital was, in general, far more conservative, pragmatic, and less "intellectual" than at Liberty. Nonetheless, the elite parents here and at each of the schools we studied strove for the same advantages that the elite parents at Liberty High demanded for their children.

The African American students in Plainview comprised two groups—those who lived in a small, working-class Black neighborhood in the district and those who transferred into Plainview from the "inner city" through an inter-district desegregation plan. At this site, however, the social class distinctions between the two groups of Black students were blurred by many White respondents, particularly in their explanations of why Black students from both groups were consistently found in the lowest track classes. For instance, teachers could not tell us which Black students lived in Plainview and which rode the bus in from the city. Some teachers also spoke of Black students'—all Black students'—low levels of achievement as the result of their families culture of poverty, and not the result of what the school offered them. Despite the relative economic advantages of many African American students who lived in the Plainview district as compared to those who lived in the city, all Black students in this mostly White, wealthy suburban school were doing quite poorly. While African Americans constituted 25 percent of the student population, less than 5 percent of the students in the highest level courses were Black. Furthermore, a district task force on Black achievement

found that more than half of the Black students in the high school had received at least one D or F over the course of one school year.

In other schools, the interplay between race and class was more complex, especially when the local elite sought to distinguish themselves from other, lower income Whites. For instance, in the small midwestern Bearfield School District, which is partly rural and partly suburban, wealthy, well-educated, White suburban parents held the most power over the educational system because they possessed more economic and highly valued cultural capital than rural Whites or African Americans. When a desegregation plan was instituted in the 1970s, it was Black and poor rural White children who were bused. As the Bearfield Middle School principal explained, "As our business manager/superintendent once told me, the power is neither Black nor White; it's green—as in money. And that's where the power is. Rich people have clout. Poor people don't have clout."

Still, the less wealthy and less educated rural Whites in Bearfield, while not as politically powerful as the suburban Whites, remained more influential than the African American families. When the two middle schools in the district were consolidated in 1987, Whites—both wealthy suburban and poor rural—were able to convince the school board to close down the newly built middle school located in the African American community and keep open the older middle school on the White side of the town.

Although the interplay between class and culture within a racially mixed community is generally defined along racial lines, we found that was not always the case. For example, King Middle School, a magnet school in a large northeastern city, was designed to attract students of many racial groups and varied socioeconomic status. A teacher explained that the parents who are blue-collar workers do not understand what's going on at the school, but the professional and middle-class parents frequently call to ask for materials to help their children at home. Educators at King insisted that middle-class and professional parents were not all White, and that there was very little correlation between income and race at the school, with its student body composed of more than twenty racial/ethnic groups, including Jamaican, Chinese, Armenian, Puerto Rican, African American, and various European ethnic groups. While we found it difficult to believe that there was no correlation between race/ethnicity and income in the city with relatively poor African

American and Latino communities, it is clear that not all of the local elites at King were White.

Thus, the layers of stratification in some schools were many, but the core of the power elite in all ten communities consisted of a group of parents who were more White, wealthy, and well-educated relative to others in their community. They were the members of the school communities with the greatest economic and/or high-status cultural capital, which they have passed on to their children. The schools, in turn, greatly rewarded the children of these elite for their social distinctions, which were perceived to be distinctions of merit (DiMaggio, 1979).

The Political Ideology of Tracking and Detracking: "Deserving" High-Track Students

Bourdieu's concepts of domination and social reproduction are particularly useful in understanding the education system, because education is the field in which the elite both "records and conceals" its own privilege. Elites "record" privilege through formal educational qualifications, which then serve to "conceal" the inherited cultural capital needed to acquire them. According to Harrison (1993), "What is usually referred to as equality of opportunity or meritocracy is, for Bourdieu, a "sociodicy"; that is, a sacred story that legitimates the dominant class' own privilege" (p. 43).

The political resistance of the local elite to detracking reforms cannot, therefore, be understood separately from the "sociodicy" or ideology employed to legitimize the privileged place elites and their children hold in the educational system. Ideology, in a Gramscian sense, represents ideas, beliefs, cultural preferences, and even myths and superstitions, which possess a certain "material" reality of their own (Gramsci, 1971). In education, societal ideas, beliefs, and cultural preferences of intelligence have found in tracking structures their own material reality. Meanwhile, tracking reinforces and sustains those ideas, beliefs, and cultural preferences.

According to Thompson (1990), ideology refers to the ways in which meaning serves, in particular circumstances, to establish and sustain relations of power that are systematically asymmetrical. Broadly speaking, ideology is *meaning in the service of power.* Thompson suggests that the study of ideology requires researchers to investigate the ways in which meaning is constructed and conveyed by symbolic forms of various kinds, "from everyday linguistic utterances to complex images and texts; it requires us to investigate the social contexts within which symbolic forms are employed and deployed" (p. 7).

The ideology of the local elites in the schools we studied was often cloaked in the "symbolic form" that Thompson describes. While the symbols used by politically powerful people to express their resistance to detracking differed from one site to the next, race consistently played a central, if not explicit, role. Although local elites expressed their dissatisfaction with detracking reform in overtly racial terms, their resistance was couched in more subtle expressions of the politics of culture that have clear racial implications. For example, they said they liked the concept of a racially mixed school, as long as the African American or Latino students acted like White, middle-class children, and their parents were involved in the school and bought into the American Dream. At Central High, a predominately Latino school on the West Coast with a 23 percent White student body, the local elite consisted of a relatively small middle class of mostly White and a few Latino families. No real upper middle class existed, and most of the Latino students came from very low-income families; many were recent immigrants to the United States. A White parent whose sons were taking honors classes explained her opposition to detracking efforts at Central, exposing her sense of entitlement this way:

> I think a lot of those Latinos come and they're still Mexicans at heart. They're not American. I don't care what color you are, we're in America here and we're going for this country. And I think their heart is in Mexico and they're with that culture still. It's one thing to come over and bring your culture and to use it, but it's another thing to get into that . . . and I'm calling it the American ethic. They're not into it and that's why they end up so far behind. They get in school, and they are behind.

This construct of the "deserving minority" denies the value of non-White students' and parents' own culture or of their sometimes penetrating critique of the American creed (see Yonesawa, Williams, & Hirshberg, 1995), and implies that only those students with the cultural capital and underlying elite ideology deserve to be rewarded in the educational system. Yet because the political arguments put forth by powerful parents in the schools we studied sounded so benign, so "American," the cultural racism that guided their perspective was rarely exposed. Consequently, both the racial segregation within the schools and the actions of parents to maintain it were perceived as natural.

We found many instances in which elite parents attempted to distance their children from students they considered to be less deserving of special attention and services. For instance, at Rolling Hills Middle School, located in a southeastern metropolitan area with a large, county-wide desegregation plan, one wealthy White parent said she and her husband purchased a home in the nearby neighborhood because Rolling Hills and its feeder high school are two of the handful of schools in the district that offer an "advanced program." She said several people had told her that in the advanced program the curriculum was better, fewer behavior problems occurred in the classes, and students received more individualized attention from teachers. She also said that had her children not been accepted into the advanced program, she and her family would not have moved into this racially mixed school district, but would have purchased a home in one of the Whiter suburbs east of the county line. Interestingly enough, this parent did not know whether or not the White suburban schools offered an advanced program. Also of interest in this district is the creation of the advanced program in the same year as the implementation of the desegregation plan.

The White, well-educated parents at Grant High School often stated that the racial diversity of the student body was one characteristic they found most appealing about the school; They said that such a racially mixed environment better prepared their children for life in "the real world." One parent noted that "the positive mixing of racial groups is important to learning to live in society." But some teachers argued that while these parents found Grant's diversity acceptable—even advantageous—their approval was conditioned by their understanding that "their children [would] only encounter Black students in the hallways and not in their classrooms." Grant's assistant principal noted that "many upper class, professional parents hold occupational positions in which they work toward equity and democracy, but expect their children to be given special treatment at Grant."

This ideology of "diversity at a distance" is often employed by White parents at strategic moments when the privileged status of their children appears to be threatened (Lareau, 1989). In our study, the parents of honors students at Grant successfully protested the school effort to eliminate the "tennis shoe" registration process by which students and teachers jointly negotiated access to classes.[4] Some of the faculty had proposed that the school switch to a computer registration

program that would guarantee Black and Latino students greater access to high-track classes. The parents of the honors students stated that they were not protesting the registration change because they were opposed to having their children in racially mixed classes, but because "they [felt] that their children [would] learn more in an environment where all students are as motivated to learn as they are—in a homogeneous ability classroom."

Respondents at Grant said that parents assumed that if any student was allowed into an honors class, regardless of his or her prior track, it must not be a good class. The assumption here was that if there was no selectivity in placing students in particular classes, then the learning and instruction in those classes could not be good. Parents of the most advanced students "assumed" that since the language arts department had made the honors and regular curriculum the same and allowed more students to enroll in honors, the rigor of these classes had probably diminished, despite the teachers' claims that standards had remained high.

At Liberty High School, where the intellectual elite were more "liberal" than the elite in most of the other schools, parents also frequently cited the racial diversity of the school as an asset. For instance, one parent commented that it was the racial and cultural mix—"the real range of people here"—that attracted her to Liberty High. She liked the fact that her daughter was being exposed to people of different cultures and different socioeconomic backgrounds: "We took her out of private school, where there's all these real upper middle-class White kids." Yet, despite this espoused appreciation for diversity among White liberal parents at Liberty, they strongly resisted efforts to dismantle the racially segregated track system. According to another White parent of a high-track student at Liberty:

> I think the one thing that really works at Liberty High is the upper track. It does. And to me, I guess my goal would be for us to find a way to make the rest of Liberty High work as well as the upper track. But it's crucial that we not destroy the upper track to do that, and that can happen . . . it really could. . . . I feel my daughter will get an excellent education if the program continues the way it is, if self-scheduling continues so that they aren't all smoothed together.

In all of the schools we studied, the most interesting aspect of elites' opposition to detracking is that they based their resistance on the symbolic mixing of high "deserving" and low "undeserving" students, rather than on information about what actually happens in detracked classrooms. For instance, an English teacher at Plainview High School who taught a heterogeneous American Studies course in which she academically challenged all her students said that the popularity of the Advanced Placement classes among the elite parents was in part based upon a "myth" that "they're the only classes that offer high standards, that they're the only courses that are interesting and challenging. And the myth is that that's where the best learning takes place. That's a myth."

At Explorer Middle School, located in a mid-sized northwestern city, the identified gifted students—nearly all White, despite a school population that was 30 percent American Indian—were no longer segregated into special classes or teams. Rather, "gifted" students were offered extra "challenge" courses, which other "non-gifted" students could choose to take as well. The day after a grueling meeting with parents of the "gifted" students, the designated gifted education teacher who works with these and other students in the challenge classes was upset by the way in which the parents had responded to her explanation of the new challenge program and the rich educational opportunities available in these classes:

> And they didn't ask, "well what are our kids learning in your classes?" Nobody asked that. I just found that real dismaying, and I was prepared to tell them what we do in class and here's an example. I had course outlines. I send objectives home with every class, and goals and work requirements, and nobody asked me anything about that . . . like they, it's . . . to me it's like I'm dealing with their egos, you know, more than what their kids really need educationally.

What this and other teachers in our study told us is that many elite parents are more concerned about the labels placed on their children than what actually goes on in the classroom. This is a powerful illustration of what Bourdieu (1984) calls "form over function" and "manner over matter."

Notions of Entitlement

Symbols of the "deserving," high-track students must be juxtaposed with conceptions of the undeserving, low-track students in order for strong protests against detracking to make sense in a society that advocates equal opportunity. Bourdieu argues that "impersonal domination"—the sociocultural form of domination found in free, industrial societies where more coercive methods of domination are not allowed—entails the rationalization of the symbolic. When symbols of domination are rationalized, the *entitlement* of the upper strata of society is legitimized, and thus this impersonal domination is seen as natural (Harrison, 1993, p. 42).

In our study, we found that elite parents rationalized their children's entitlement to better educational opportunities based upon the resources that they themselves brought to the system. For instance, parents from the White, wealthy side of Bearfield Middle School's attendance zone perceived that the African American students who attended the school and lived on the "other" side of town benefited from the large tax burden shouldered by the White families. One White parent noted, "I don't feel that our school should have, you know, people from that far away coming to our school. I don't think it's right as far as the taxes we pay. . . . They don't pay the taxes that we pay, and they're at our schools also. Um, I just don't feel they belong here, no." According to the superintendent of the school district, this statement reflects the widely held belief among Whites that they are being taxed to pay for schools for Black students, "and therefore the White community . . . should make the decisions about the schools . . . because they are paying the bill." These perspectives explain in part why the consolidation of the district's two middle schools resulted in the closing of the mostly Black but much more recently built school, and favored the old, dilapidated Bearfield building as the single middle school site.

At the same time, these parents balked at the suggestion that their own social privilege and much of their children's advantages had less to do with objective merit or intellectual ability than it had to do with their families' economic and cultural capital. Harrison (1993) expands upon Bourdieu's notion that culture functions to deny or disavow the economic origins of capital by gaining symbolic credit for the possessors of economic and political capital. Harrison argues that the seemingly legitimate and meritocratic basis upon which students "earn" academic credentials is an important aspect of the dominant class's denial of entitlement as a process in which inherited economic and political power receives social consecration. In other words, the elite parents must convince themselves and others that the privileges their children are given in the educational system were earned in a fair and meritocratic way, and are not simply a consequence of the parents' own privileged place in society. "The demonstration that the belief of merit is a part of the process of social consecration in which the dominant class's power is both acknowledged and misrecognized, is at the core of Bourdieu's analysis of culture" (Harrison, 1993, p. 44).

There is strong evidence from the schools we studied that students frequently end up in particular tracks and classrooms more on the basis of their parents' privilege than of their own "ability." A school board member in the district in which Rolling Hills Middle School is located explained that students are placed in the advanced program depending on who their parents happen to know. Because the advanced program was implemented at the same time as the countywide desegregation plan, it has become a sophisticated form of resegregation within racially mixed schools supported by conceptions of "deserving" advanced students. The school board member said that parents of the advanced students are very much invested in labels that their children acquire at school. When children are labeled "advanced" it means their parents are "advanced," as well. In fact, said the board member, some of these parents refer to themselves as the "advanced parents": "There is still an elitist aspect as far as I am concerned. I also think it is an ego trip for parents. They love the double standard that their children are in Advanced Placement programs."

Similarly, several elite parents of students in the advanced program at Grant High School expressed regret that the school had such a poor vocational education department for the "other" students—those who were not advanced. Their lament for vocational education related to their way of understanding the purpose of the high school in serving different students. One of these parents, for example, stated that the role of the honors classes was to groom students to become "managers and professionals" and that something else should be done for those kids who would grow up to be "workers."

According to Harrison (1993), the elite seek to deny the arbitrary nature of the social order that culture does much to conceal. This process, which he calls "masking," occurs when what is culturally arbitrary is "essentialized, absolutized or universalized" (p. 45). Masking is generally accomplished via symbols—culturally specific as opposed to materially specific symbols (Bourdieu & Wacquant, 1992). For example, standardized test scores become cultural symbols of intelligence that are used to legitimize the track structure in some instances while they are "masked" in other instances.

An example of this "masking" process was revealed to us at Grant High School, where elite parents of the most advanced students approved of using test scores as a measure of students' intelligence and worthiness to enroll in the highest track classes. But when children of the elite who were identified as "highly able" in elementary school did not make the test score cutoffs for high school honors classes, the parents found ways to get their children placed in these classes anyway, as if the tests in that particular instance were not valid. The educators usually gave in to these parents' demands, and then cited such instances as evidence of a faulty system. The so-called faults within the system, however, did not lead to broad-based support among powerful parents or educators to dismantle the track structure.

Similarly, at Explorer Middle School, where the wealthy White "gifted" students were all placed in regular classes and then offered separate challenge classes along with other students who chose to take such a class, the principal collected data on the achievement test scores for the identified gifted students and other students in the school. She found huge overlaps in the two sets of scores with some identified "non-gifted" students scoring in the 90th percentile and above, and some "gifted" students ranking as low as the 58th percentile. Yet, when the mostly White parents of children identified by the district as "gifted" were presented with these data, they attributed the large number of low test scores among the pool of gifted students to a handful of non-White students participating in that program, although the number of non-White "gifted" students was far lower than the number of low test scores within the gifted program. The White parents simply would not admit that any of their children did not deserve a special label (and the extra resources that come with it). According to the teacher of the challenge classes, one of the most vocal and demanding "gifted" parents was the mother of a boy who was not even near the top of his class: "I still can't figure out how he got in the gifted program; he doesn't perform in any way at that high a level. . . . She is carrying on and on and on. . . ."

Despite evidence that the "gifted" label may be more a form of symbolic capital than a true measure of innate student ability, the parents of students who had been identified as gifted by this school district maintained a strong sense of entitlement. For instance, a Whiter upper middle-class father of two so-called gifted boys told us he was outraged that the "gifted and talented" teacher at Explorer spent her time teaching challenge classes that were not exclusively for gifted students. This father was adamant that the state's special funding for gifted and talented (G/T) programs should be spent exclusively on identified G/T students. He noted that at the other middle school in the district, the G/T teacher worked with a strictly G/T class, "whereas at Explorer, the G/T teacher works with a class that is only 50 percent G/T." In other words, "precious" state resources for gifted and talented students were being spent on "non-deserving" students—many of whom had higher middle school achievement test scores than the students who had been identified by the school district as gifted many years earlier.

At Plainview High School, the English teacher who created the heterogeneous American Studies class began reading about the social science research on intelligence, and concluded that our society and education system do not really understand what intelligence is or how to measure it. When the principal asked her to present her research to parents at an open house, her message was not well received, particularly by those parents whose children were in the Advanced Placement classes. According to this teacher, "If you were raised under the system that said you were very intelligent and high achieving, you don't want anyone questioning that system, OK? That's just the way it is." She said that what some of the parents were most threatened by was how this research on intelligence was going to be used and whether the high school was going to do away with Advanced Placement classes. She recalled, "I used the word 'track' once and debated whether I could weave that in because I knew the power of the word, and I didn't want to shut everyone down. It was very interesting."

Political Practices: How the Local Elite Undermined Detracking

The ideology and related symbols that legitimate local elites' sense of entitlement are critical to educational policy and practice. As Harrison (1993) and Harker (1984) note, Bourdieu's work is ultimately focused on the strategic practices employed when conflicts emerge. In this way, Bourdieu identifies "practices"—actions that maintain or change the social structures—within strategically oriented forms of conflict. These strategic actions must be rooted back into the logic or sense of entitlement that underlies these practices. In other words, we examined political practices that are intended to be consistent with an ideology of "deserv-

ing" high-track students. These practices were employed by elite parents when educators posed a threat to the privileged status of their children by questioning the validity and objectivity of a rigid track structure (Useem, 1990).

According to Bourdieu, when seemingly "objective" structures, such as tracking systems, are faithfully reproduced in the dispositions or ways of knowing of actors, then the "arbitrary" nature of the existing structure can go completely unrecognized (Bourdieu & Wacquant, 1992). For instance, no one questions the evidence of the separate and unequal "gifted and talented" or "highly advanced" program for children of the local elites, despite the fact that the supposedly "objective" measures that legitimize these programs—standardized tests scores—do not always support the somewhat "arbitrary" nature of student placement. This arbitrary placement system is more sensitive to cultural capital than academic "ability."

In the case of tracking, so-called objective and thus non-arbitrary standardized tests are problematic on two levels. First, the tests themselves are culturally biased in favor of wealthy, White students, and therefore represent a poor measure of "ability" or "intelligence." Second, scores on these exams tend to count more for some students than others. Elite students who have low achievement test scores are placed in high tracks, while non-White and non-wealthy students with high test scores are bound to the lower tracks (see Oakes et al., 1995; Welner & Oakes, 1995). Still, test scores remain an undisclosed and undisputed "objective" measure of student track placement and thus a rationale for maintaining the track structure in many schools.

When these undisclosed or undisputed parts of the universe are questioned, conflicts arise that call for strategic political practices on the part of elites. As Harrison (1993) states, "Where the fit can no longer be maintained and where, therefore, the arbitrary nature of the objective structure becomes evident, the dominant class must put into circulation a discourse in which this arbitrary order is misrecognized as such" (p. 41). When the arbitrary nature of the "objective" tracking structure becomes evident, detracking efforts are initiated, often by educators who have come to realize the cultural basis of the inequalities within our so-called meritocratic educational system.

Within each of our ten schools, when educators penetrated the ideology that legitimizes the track structure (and the advantages that high-track students have within it), elite parents felt that their privileges were threatened. We found that local elites employed four practices to undermine and co-opt meaningful detracking efforts in such a way that they and their children would continue to benefit disproportionately from educational policies. These four overlapping and intertwined practices were threatening flight, co-opting the institutional elites, soliciting buy-in from the "not-quite elite," and accepting detracking bribes.

Threatening Flight

Perhaps nowhere in our study was the power of the local elite and their ideology of entitlement more evident than when the topic of "elite flight" was broached, specifically when these parents threatened to leave the school. Educators in the ten schools we studied were acutely aware that their schools, like most institutions, gain their status, or symbolic capital, from the social status of the students who attend (Wells & Crain, 1992). They know they must hold onto the local elites in order for their schools to remain politically viable institutions that garner broad public support. As a result, the direct or indirect threat of elite flight can thwart detracking efforts when local elite parents have other viable public or private school options.

At Liberty High School, the liberal ideals and principles that are the cornerstone of this community were challenged when local elites were asked to embrace reforms that they perceived to be removing advantages held by their children. In fact, discussions and implementation of such reforms—for example, the creation of a heterogeneous ninth-grade English/social studies core—caused elite parents to "put into circulation a discourse" that legitimized their claim to something better than what other students received. Without this special attention for high-track students, elite parents said, they had little reason to keep their children at Liberty. As one parent of a high-track student noted in discussing the local elite's limits and how much of the school's equity-centered detracking reforms they would tolerate before abandoning the school:

> I think it happens to all of us; when you have children, you confront all your values in a totally different way. I mean, I did all this work in education, I knew all these things about it, and it's very different when it's your own child cause when it's your own child your real responsibility is to advocate for that child. I mean, I might make somewhat different decisions about Liberty High, though probably not terribly different, because as I say, I would always have in mind the danger of losing a big chunk of kids, and

with them the community support that makes this school work well.

The power of the threat of elite flight is evident in the history of the creation of tracking structures in many of our schools, where advanced and gifted programs began to appear and proliferate at the same time that the schools in these districts were becoming more racially mixed, either through a desegregation plan or demographic shifts. This shift toward more tracking as schools became increasingly racially mixed follows the long history of tracking in the U.S. educational system. Tracking became more systematized at the turn of the century, as non-Anglo immigrant students enrolled in urban high schools (Oakes, 1985). At Grant High School, which is located in a racially diverse urban school district surrounded by separate Whiter and more affluent districts, the highly advanced and "regular" advanced programs were started shortly after desegregation at the insistence of local elite parents who wanted separate classes for their children. One teacher noted that the advanced programs were designed to respond to a segment of the White community that felt, "Oh, we'll send our kids to public school, but only if there's a special program for them."

At Grant, the chair of the language arts department, an instigator of detracking reforms efforts, said that the parents of the "advanced" students run the school district:

> They scare those administrators the same way they scare us. They're the last vestiges of middle-class people in the public schools in some sense. And they know that. And they flaunt that sometimes. And they scare people with that. And the local media would spit [the deputy superintendent] up in pieces if she did something to drive these parents out of the school district. So, yeah, I'm sure she's nervous about anything we're doing.

Similarly, at Rolling Hills Middle School, where the Advanced Program began in the late 1970s, shortly after the county-wide desegregation plan was implemented, the mother of two White boys in the program noted, "If I heard they were going to eliminate the Advanced Program, I would be very alarmed, and would seriously consider if I could afford a private school." She indicated that she thought that most parents of students at Rolling Hills felt this way.

At Central High School, White flight consistently paralleled the influx of Latino immigrant students into the school. Administrators said they hoped that the relocation of the school to a new site in a more middle-class area of the district would allow Central to maintain its White population. But many educators said they felt that what keeps White students at Central is the honors program, which would have been scaled back under detracking reform. This reform effort has been almost completely derailed by political roadblocks from both inside the school and the surrounding community.

Suburban, midwestern Plainview High School was the school in which we perhaps noted the *perceived* threat of elite flight to be most powerful. There, the concept of "community stability" was foremost on the minds of the educators. Many of the teachers and administrators in the Plainview district, particularly at the high school, came to Plainview from the nearby Hamilton School District, which experienced massive White flight two decades earlier. Essentially, the population of the Hamilton district shifted from mostly White, upper middle class to all Black and poor in a matter often years—roughly between 1968 and 1978. According to these educators and many other respondents in Plainview, the status of the Hamilton district and its sole high school plummeted, as each incoming freshman class became significantly darker and poorer. Once regarded as the premier public high school in the metropolitan area, Hamilton suddenly served as a reminder of the consequences of White flight. The large numbers of White residents and educators who came to Plainview after fleeing Hamilton kept the memory of White flight alive, and used Hamilton as a symbol of this threat.

Of all the educators in the district, it was the Plainview High School principal, Mr. Fredrick, who appeared most fixated on issues of community "stability" and the role of the schools in maintaining it:

> Here's my problem, what I'm doing at Plainview High School is essentially trying to make it stable enough so that other people can integrate the neighborhood. Now if other people aren't integrating the neighborhood, I'm not doing it either. I'm not out there working on that, I don't have time to be out there working on that, I've got to be making sure that what we're doing in Plainview High School is strong, we're strong enough, and have the reputation of, so that as we integrate, which I'm hoping is happening, that Whites won't get up and flee . . . when they come in and say, I hope you're here in eight years, that is a commitment those White people are gonna be there in eight years.

Fredrick argues that an academically strong high school led by a principal who maintains a good relationship with the community will help stabilize the whole community. As he explains, "I believe we can keep stability in Plainview while still being out in front of education. Now that's what I feel my job is." Fredrick's goal of maintaining racial stability in the community is noble in many respects, but we learned during our visits to Plainview that his focus on White flight has resulted in intense efforts to please the elite White parents. These efforts to cater to elite parents have consistently worked against detracking reform in the school. While some of the teachers and other administrators continued to push for more innovative grouping and instructional strategies, Fredrick has advocated more Advanced Placement courses and encouraged more students to take these classes. In this way, the threat of White elite flight has helped maintain the hierarchical track structure and an Advanced Placement curriculum that many teachers, students, and less elite parents argue is not creative or instructionally sound.

Co-opting the Institutional Elites

The threat of flight is one of the ways in which local elites provoke responses to their institutional demands. This threat, and the fear it creates in the hearts of educators, is related to the way in which the "institutional elites"—that is educators with power and authority within the educational system—become co-opted by the ideology of the local elites. Both Domhoff (1983, 1990) and Mills (1956) write about institutional elites as "high-level" employees in institutions (either private corporations or governmental agencies, such as the U.S. Treasury Department) who see their roles as serving the upper, capitalist-based class. At a more micro or local level, we find that the institutional elites are the educational administrators who see their roles as serving the needs and demands of the local elites. Indeed, in most situations, their professional success and even job security depend on their ability to play these roles.

For instance, in small-town Bearfield, the new superintendent, who is politically very popular with elite parents and community members, has developed a less than positive impression of detracking efforts at the middle school. Yet his view is based less on first-hand information about the reform through visits to the school or discussions with the teachers than on the input he has received from White parents who have placed their children in private schools. To him, the educators at Bearfield Middle School have "let the academics slide just a little bit." Because of the superintendent's sense of commitment to the powerful White, wealthy parents, the principal of Bearfield indicated that he feels intense pressure to raise standardized test scores and prove that academics are not sliding at the school. Thus, some degree of "teaching to the test" has come at the expense of a more creative and innovative curriculum that facilitates detracking efforts by acknowledging, for example, different ways of knowing material. In a symbolic move, the teaching staff has rearranged the Black History Month curriculum to accommodate standardized test prepping in the month of February.

The relationship among the institutional elites at urban Grant High School, its school district office, and the local elite parents, however, demonstrates one of the most severe instances of "co-optation" that we observed. At the district's main office and at the high school, many of the educational administrators are African American. Still, these administrators frequently have failed to push for the kinds of reforms that would benefit the mostly African American students in the lowest track classes. Several respondents noted that Black educators who have been advocates for democratic reform have not survived in this district, and that those who cater to the demands of powerful White parents have been promoted within the system.

At the end of the 1993–1994 school year, the African American principal of Grant, Mr. Phillips, rejected the language arts department's proposal to detrack ninth-grade English by putting "honors" and "regular" students together in the same classes and offering honors as an extra credit option for all students. The principal claimed that it was not fair to do away with separate honors classes when the proposal had not been discussed with parents. His decision, he explained, was based on frequent complaints he received from the mostly White parents of high-track students that changes were being made at the school, particularly in the language arts department, without their prior knowledge or consent. According to the language arts department chair, when her department detracked twelfth-grade electives, it "really pissed people off." Also, when these elite parents were not consulted about the proposal to change the school schedule to an alternative four-period schedule, they protested and were successful in postponing the change.

Furthermore, a recent attempt by Grant's history department to do away with separate honors classes at the request of some students was thwarted by the parents of honors students, who, according to one teacher, "went through the roof." Some of the teachers in other departments indicated that they suspected the history department's move to eliminate honors classes was not sincere, but rather a political tactic designed to generate support among powerful elite parents for the honors program. In fact, the history department chair, who opposes detracking, noted that his only recourse to stop the detracking reform was to go to the parents and get them upset "because they had the power to do things at school."

At Grant, administrators at the district office have historically been very responsive to the concerns of White parents, and thus regularly implement policies designed to retain the White students. For instance, the district leadership convened an all-White "highly capable parent task force" to examine issues surrounding the educational advanced programs for "highly capable" students. The task force strongly recommended self-contained classrooms for advanced students, making detracking efforts across the district more problematic. According to one of the teachers at Grant, school board members would not talk about the elitism around this program because they were "feeling under siege."

At several schools in our study, educational administrators, especially principals, have lost their jobs since detracking efforts began, in part because they refused co-optation and advocated detracking. At Liberty High School, despite the principal's efforts to make detracking as politically acceptable to the elite parents as possible, in the end he was "done in" by the institutional elites at the district office who would not give him the extra resources he needed to carry out detracking in a manner local elites would have considered acceptable.

Buy-In of the "Not-Quite Elite"

In an interesting article about the current political popularity of decentralized school governance and growth of school-site councils with broad decision-making power, Beare (1993) writes that the middle class is a very willing accomplice in the strategy to create such councils and "empower" parents to make important decisions about how schools are run. He notes that it is the middle-class parents who put themselves forward for election to such governing bodies. Yet he argues that in spite of this new-found participatory role for middle-class parents, they actually have little control over the course of their children's schools, because such courses are chartered by a larger power structure. As Beare states, "In one sense, then, participative decision-making is a politically diversionary tactic, a means of keeping activist people distracted by their own self-inflicted, busy work. The middle class are willing accomplices, for they think they are gaining access to the decision-making of the power structures" (p. 202).

The ideology of the local elite's entitlement is so pervasive and powerful that the elites do not necessarily have to be directly involved in the decision-making processes at schools, although they often are. But between the local elites' threats to flee, co-optation of institutional elites, and ability to make their privilege appear as "common sense," such school-site councils will most likely simply reflect, as Beare (1993) points out, the broader power structure. In this way, the "self-inflicted busy work" of the not-quite elites, which, depending on the context of the schools, tend to be the more middle- or working-class parents, is just that— busy work that helps the schools maintain the existing power relations and a highly tracked structure. This is what Gramsci (1971) would refer to as the "consensual" basis of power, or the consensual side of politics in a civil society (see Boggs, 1984; Gramsci, 1971).

We saw a clear example of how this co-optation plays out at Plainview High School, where a group of about thirty predominantly White parents served on the advisory board for the most visible parent group, called the Parent-Teacher Organization, or PTO (even though there were no teachers in this organization). The PTO advisory board met with the principal once a month to act as his "sounding board" on important school-site issues, particularly those regarding discipline. We found through in-depth interviews with many of the parents on the PTO Board that these parents were not the most powerful or most elite parents in the one-high-school district. In fact, as the former president of the advisory board and the mother of a not-quite-high-track student explained, "The Advanced Placement parents don't run the president of the PTO. As a matter of fact, I'm trying to think when the last time [was] we had a president of the PTO whose kids were on the fast track in Advanced Placement. I don't think we've had one in quite a few years."

She did note, however, that there were "a lot of parents on the [district-wide] school board whose kids are in the Advanced Placement classes." Interestingly, in the Plainview school district, the school board, and the central administration, and not the school-site councils such as the PTO advisory board, have the power to change curricular and instructional programs—the areas most related to detracking reform— in the schools.

Furthermore, despite the past president's assertion that the Advanced Placement parents do not run the PTO advisory board, the board members we interviewed told us they were unwilling to challenge the pro-Advanced Placement stance of the principal. Still, several of the PTO board members said they believed there was too much emphasis on Advanced Placement at Plainview, and that they were at times uncomfortable with the principal's constant bragging about the number of Advanced Placement classes the school offers, the number of students taking Advanced Placement exams, and the number of students who receive 3's, 4's, or 5's on these exams. Some of these parents said that, in their opinion, a heavy load of Advanced Placement classes is too stressful for high school students; others said the curriculum in the Advanced Placement classes is boring rote memorization: But none of these parents had ever challenged the principal in his effort to boost the number of Advanced Placement classes offered and students enrolling in them. According to one mother on the PTO board:

> I think parents have seen that there are so many pressures in the world, they realize that this is a high school and they're fed up with all the competition. At the same time they know you have to play the game, you know. . . . And again, it's hard to evaluate with some of the top, top students, you know, what's appropriate. . . . I think a lot of this has to do with Plainview as a community, too. Now, for example, where I live right here is in Fillburn, and that is a more upscale community [within the Plainview district]. Two houses from me is the Doner school district, which is a community of wealthier homes, wealthier people, many of whom have children in private schools.

During interviews, most of the not-quite-elite parents at all of the schools in our study discussed their awareness of the demands that families with high economic and cultural capital placed on the schools. They cited these demands as reasons why they themselves did not challenge the push for more Advanced Placement or gifted classes and why they were not supporters of detracking efforts—even when they suspected that such changes might be beneficial for their own children. For instance, at Grant High School, the chair of the language arts department formed a parent support group to focus on issues of tracking and detracking. This group consisted mostly of parents of students in the regular and honors classes, with only a handful of parents of very advanced students in the highest track. The department chair said she purposefully postponed "the fight" with more of the advanced parents. "We thought if we could get a group of parents who are just as knowledgeable . . . as we were, they should be the ones that become the advocates with the other parents. So that's probably our biggest accomplishment this year is getting this group of parents that we have together." But one of the few parents of advanced students left the group because she said her concerns were not being addressed and the advisory group disbanded the following spring.

We saw other examples of "not-quite-elite" buy-in at schools where middle-class minority parents had become advocates of tracking practices and opponents of detracking efforts, despite their lament that their children were often the only children of color in the high-track classes. For instance, a Black professional parent at Rolling Hills Middle School, whose two children were in the advanced program, noted that a growing number of African American parents in the district were upset with the racial composition of the nearly all-White "advanced" classes and the disproportionately Black "comprehensive" tracks within racially mixed schools. He said, "So you have segregation in a supposedly desegregated setting. So what it is, you have a growing amount of dissatisfaction within the African American community about these advanced programs that are lily White." Despite his dissatisfaction, this father explained that he is not against tracking per se. "I think tracking has its merits. I just think they need to be less rigid in their standards."

Similarly, at Green Valley High School, a rural West Coast school with a 43 percent White and 57 percent Latino student population, a professional, middle-class Latino couple who had sent their children to private elementary and middle schools before enrolling them in the public high school said that the students at Green Valley should be divided into three groups: those at the top, those in the middle, and those at the bottom. The father added that those students in the middle should be given more of a tech prep education, and that an alternative school might be good for a lot of kids who won't go to college.

Detracking Bribes

Another political practice employed by local elites in schools that are attempting detracking reforms is their use of symbolic capital to bribe the schools to give them some preferential treatment in return for their willingness to allow some small degree of detracking to take place. These detracking bribes tend to make detracking reforms very expensive and impossible to implement in a comprehensive fashion.

Bourdieu (in Harrison, 1993) would consider such detracking bribes to be symbolic of the irreversible character of gift exchange. In exchange for their political buy-in to the detracking efforts, elite parents must be assured that their children are still getting something more than other children. In the process of gift exchange, according to Bourdieu, gifts must be returned, but this return represents neither an exchange of equivalents nor a case of cash on delivery:

> What is returned must be both different in kind and deferred in time. It is within this space opened up by these two elements of non-identity [of the gifts] and temporality [deferred time] that strategic actions can be deployed through which either one actor or another tries to accumulate some kind of profit. The kind of profit accumulated is, of course, more likely to be either symbolic or social, rather than economic. (p. 39)

In the case of the detracking bribes, the elite parents tend to profit at the expense of broad-based reform and restructuring. Yet, detracking bribes take on a different shape and character in different schools, depending upon the bargaining power of the local elite parents and the school's resources. As Bourdieu notes, in the case of the gift exchange, it is the agent's sense of honor that regulates the moves that can be made in the game (Harrison, 1993).

For instance, at King Middle School, located in a large northeastern city, the bribe is the school itself—a well-funded magnet program with formal ties to a nearby college and a rich art program that is integrated into the curriculum. Because King is a school of choice for parents who live in the surrounding area of the city, it is in many ways automatically perceived to be "better than" regular neighborhood schools, where students end up by default. Still, an administrator noted that King must still work at getting elite parents to accept the heterogeneous grouping within the school: "The thing is to convince the parents of the strong students that [heterogeneous grouping] is a good idea and not to have them pull children out to put them in a gifted program. It is necessary to really offer them a lot. You need parent education, along with offering a rich program for the parents so that they don't feel their children are being cheated."

At Rolling Hills Middle School, where African American students are bused to this otherwise White, wealthy school, the detracking bribe comes in the form of the best sixth-grade teachers and a "heterogeneous" team of students, which is skewed toward a disproportionate number of advanced program students. For instance, the heterogeneous team is comprised of 50 percent "advanced" students, 25 percent "honors" students, and 25 percent "regular" students, while the sixth grade as a whole is only about one-third "advanced" students and about one-half "regular" students. Thus, detracking at Rolling Hills is feasible when it affects only one of four sixth-grade teams, and that one team enrolls a disproportionate number of advanced students and is taught by the teachers whom the local elite consider to be the best. The generosity of the "gifts" that the school gives the elite parents who agree to enroll their children in the heterogeneous team are such that this team has become high status itself. The "parent network" of local elites at this school now promotes the heterogeneous team and advises elite mothers of incoming sixth-graders to choose that team. According to one wealthy White parent, "the heterogeneous team is 'hand-picked'." Another White parent whose daughter is on the heterogeneous team noted, "It's also been good to know that it's kind of like a private school within a public school. And that's kind of fair, I hate to say that, but it's kind of a fair evaluation."

Of course, Rolling Hills does not have enough of these "gifts" to bribe all of the local elite parents to place their children on a heterogeneous team. In other words, Rolling Hills will never be able to detrack the entire school as long as the cost of the bribe remains so high and the elite parental profit is so great. By definition, the "best" teachers at any given school are scarce; there are not enough of them to go around. In addition, the number of Advanced Placement students in the school is too small to assure that more heterogeneous teams could be created with the same skewed proportion of advanced, honors, and comprehensive tracks.

At Grant High School, the bribe for detracking the marine science program consists of this unique science offering, coupled with the school's excellent science and math departments and one of the two best music programs in the city. These are commodities that elite parents cannot get in other schools—urban or suburban. As one teacher explained, "So what options do these parents have? Lift their kids out of Grant, which they love? They can't get a science program like this anywhere else in the city." Although the school itself is highly tracked, especially in the history department, the marine science classes enroll students from all different tracks. A marine science teacher noted that parents of the advanced students never request that their kids be placed in separate classes because curricula in this program are both advanced and unique.

Interestingly, the detracking bribe at Liberty High, as the school moved toward the ninth-grade English/social studies core classes, was to be smaller class sizes and ongoing staff development. Unfortunately, the district administration withheld much of the promised funding to allow the school to deliver these gifts to the parents of high-track students. Whether or not these parents were ever committed to this bribe—whether they thought the school was offering them enough in return—is not really clear. What we do know is that the principal who offered the gift was, as we mentioned, recently "let go" by the district. His departure may have been the ultimate bribe with the local elites, because, as Bourdieu (in Harrison, 1993) argues, the kind of profit accumulated is, of course, more likely to be either symbolic or social, rather than economic.

Conclusions

When our research team began this study in 1992, we initially focused on what was happening *within* the racially mixed schools we were to study. Yet as we visited these schools, it became increasingly evident to us that the parents had a major impact on detracking reform efforts. Over the course of the last three years, we came to appreciate not only the power of this impact but its subtleties as well. In turning to the literature on elites and cultural capital, we gained a deeper understanding of the barriers educators face in their efforts to detrack schools.

As long as elite parents press the schools to perpetuate their status through the intergenerational transmission of privilege that is based more on cultural capital than "merit," educators will be forced to choose between equity-based reforms and the flight of elite parents from the public school system.

The intent of this article is not simply to point fingers at the powerful, elite parents or the educators who accommodate them at the ten schools we studied. We understand that these parents are in many ways victims of a social system in which the scarcity of symbolic capital creates an intense demand for it among those in their social strata. We also recognize the role that the educational system—especially the higher education system—plays in shaping their actions and their understanding of what they must do to help their children succeed.

Still, we hope that this study of ten racially mixed schools undertaking detracking reform is helpful to educators and policymakers who struggle to understand more clearly the political opposition to such reform efforts. Most importantly, we have learned that in a democratic society, the privilege, status, and advantage that elite students bring to school with them must be carefully deconstructed by educators, parents, and students alike before meaningful detracking reforms can take place.

Endnotes

1. Our three-year study of ten racially mixed secondary schools that are detracking was funded by the Lilly Endowment. Jeannie Oakes and Amy Stuart Wells were coprincipal investigators. Research associates were Robert Cooper, Amanda Datnow, Diane Hirshberg, Martin Lipton, Karen Ray, Irene Serna, Estella Williams, and Susie Yonezawa.
2. By "school community," we mean the broad and diverse network of students, parents, educators, and other citizens who are connected to these schools as institutions.
3. For a full description of the study and its methodology, see Oakes & Wells (1995).
4. During the "tennis shoe" registration, teachers set up tables in the gymnasium with registration passes for each of the classes they will be offering. Students have an allocated time slot in which they are allowed into the gym to run from teacher to teacher and ask for passes for classes they want. Under this system, teachers are able to control who gets into their classes, and the children of the elite, who hold more political power in the school, are more likely to get the high-track classes that they want.

References

Beare, H. (1993). Different ways of viewing school-site councils: Whose paradigm is in use here? In H. Beare & W. L. Boyd (Eds.), *Restructuring schools: An international perspective on the movement to transform the control and performance of schools* (pp. 200–214). Washington, DC: Falmer Press.

Boggs, C. (1984). *The two revolutions: Gramsci and the dilemmas of western Marxism.* Boston: South End Press.

Bourdieu, P. (1973). Cultural reproduction and social reproduction. In R. Brown (Ed.), *Knowledge, educations, and cultural change* (pp. 487–501). New York: Harper & Row.

Bourdieu, P. (1977). *Outline of a theory of practice.* Cambridge, Eng.: Cambridge University Press.

Bourdieu, P. (1984). *Distinction: A social critique of the judgement of taste.* Cambridge, MA: Harvard University Press.

Bourdieu, P., & Passeron, J. C. (1977). *Reproduction in education, society and culture.* Beverly Hills, CA: Sage.

Bourdieu, P., & Passeron, J. C. (1979). *The inheritors: French students and their relation to culture.* Chicago: University of Chicago Press

Bourdieu, P., & Wacquant, I. J. D. (1992). *An invitation to reflexive sociology.* Chicago, IL: University of Chicago Press.

Delpit, L. (1995). *Other people's children: Cultural conflict in the classroom.* New York: New Press.

DiMaggio, P. (1979). Review essay: On Pierre Bourdieu. *American Journal of Sociology, 84,* 1460–1472.

Domhoff, W. G. (1983). *Who rules America now? A view for the 80s.* Englewood Cliffs, NJ: Prentice-Hall.

Domhoff, W. G. (1990). *The power elite and the state: How polity is made in America.* New York: A. deGruyter.

Gramsci, A. (1971). *Selections from the prison notebooks.* New York: International Publishers.

Harker, K. (1984). On reproduction, habitus and education. *British Journal of Sociology of Education, 5*(2), 117–127.

Harrison, P. R. (1993). Bourdieu and the possibility of a postmodern sociology. *Thesis Eleven, 35,* 36–50.

Lareau, A. (1989). *Home advantage.* London: Falmer Press.

McIntosh, P. (January/February, 1992). White privilege: Unpacking the invisible knapsack. *Creation Spirituality,* pp. 33–35.

Mills, C. W. (1956). *The power elite.* London: Oxford University Press.

Oakes, J. (1985). *Keeping track: How schools restructure inequalities.* New Haven, CT: Yale University Press.

Oakes, J., Oraseth, T., Bell, R., & Camp, P. (1990). *Multiplying inequalities: The effects of race, social class, and tracking on opportunities to learn mathematics and science.* Santa Monica, CA: Rand.

Oakes, J., Lipton, M., & Jones, M. (1995, April). *Changing minds: Deconstructing intelligence in detracking schools.* Paper presented at the annual meeting of the American Educational Research Association, San Francisco.

Oakes, J., &. Wells, A. S. (1995, April) *Beyond sorting and stratification: Creative alternatives to tracking in racially mixed secondary schools.* Paper presented at the annual meeting of the American Educational Research Association, San Francisco.

Thompson, J. B. (1990). *Ideology and modern culture.* Stanford, CA: Stanford University Press.

Useem, E. (1990, April). *Social class and ability group placement in mathematics in transition to seventh grade: The role of parental involvement.* Paper presented at the annual meeting of the American Educational Research Conference, Boston.

Wells, A. S., & Crain, R. L. (1992). Do parents choose school quality or school status? A sociological theory of free-market education. In P. W. Cookson (Ed.), *The choice controversy* (pp. 65–82). Newbury Park, CA: Corwin Press.

Welner, K., & Oakes, J. (1995, April). *Liability grouping: The new susceptibility of school tracking systems to legal challenges.* Paper presented at the annual meeting of the American Educational Research Association, San Francisco.

Yonesawa, S., Williams, E., & Hirshberg, D. (1995, April). *Seeking a new standard: Minority parent and community involvement in detracking schools.* Paper presented at the annual meeting of the American Educational Research Association, San Francisco.

An earlier version of this article was presented at the American Educational Research Association's 1995 Annual Meeting in San Francisco.

5 | The Philosophy of Education and Its Significance for Teachers

In Chapter 1, we argued that Americans place a great deal of faith in education, and particularly that Americans view schools as the great panacea for the multitude of problems that plague both individuals and society as a whole. In this chapter, we point out that the study of philosophy of education as an integral part of the foundations perspective will allow prospective teachers to reflect on educational issues from a particular perspective—the perspective of philosophy. This perspective encourages logical, systematic thinking. It stresses the importance of ideas and allows—indeed, encourages—the act of reflection on every aspect of practice. Thus, philosophy acts as the building block for the reflective practitioner.

The Perspective of Philosophy of Education

Practitioners often argue, as do students in schools of education, that although philosophy of education may add another dimension to the way in which they view schools, nevertheless, they haven't the time for a discipline that does not offer tangible results. Rather, they wish to learn *what* to do, not *why* to do it. For too many practitioners and students of education, the practice of teaching is reduced to action devoid of a rationale or justification.

We believe that the practice of teaching cannot be separated from a philosophical foundation. Philosophy, as applied to education, allows practitioners and prospective practitioners to apply systematic approaches to problem solving in schools and illuminates larger issues of the complex relationship of schools to the social order.

What Is Philosophy of Education?

Philosophy of education differs from philosophy, as we have stated in Chapter 1. Philosophy of education is firmly rooted in practice, whereas philosophy, as a discipline, stands on its own with no specific end in mind. Given this difference, it is necessary to consider for a moment how a particular philosophy might affect practice.

All teachers, regardless of their action orientation, have a personal philosophy of life that colors the way in which they select knowledge; order their classrooms; interact with students, peers, parents, and administrators; and select values to emphasize within their classrooms. Engaging in philosophy helps teachers and prospective teachers to *clarify* what they do or intend to do and, as they act or propose to act, to *justify* or explain why they do what they do in a logical, systematic manner. Thus, the activity of doing philosophy aids teachers in understanding two very important notions: (1) who they are or intend to be and (2) why they do or propose to do what they do. Furthermore, through the action of clarification and justification of practice, teachers and prospective teachers think about practice and acquire specific information, which lends authority to their decision making.

The Meaning of Philosophical Inquiry

Although people exist as individuals, they also exist within the greater context of their culture. Through interactions with the norms common to the culture, people form attitudes, beliefs, and values, which are then transmitted to others. As people go about this process of acquiring cultural norms, they may accept norms wholeheartedly, accept norms partially, or, in certain instances, totally reject them. Whatever people choose to embrace, if their choices are made in a logical, rational manner, they are engaged in the process of "doing philosophy."

To proceed in doing philosophy, certain key questions are posed that can be divided into three specific areas of philosophical inquiry. The first is called *metaphysics,* a branch of philosophy that concerns itself with questions about the nature of reality. The second is called *epistemology,* a branch of philosophy that concerns itself with questions about the nature of knowledge. Last is *axiology,* a branch of philosophy that concerns itself with the nature of values.

We believe that these distinctions in philosophy are important for prospective teachers to know, since ideas generated by philosophers about education usually fall under a particular branch of philosophy, such as epistemology. Furthermore, the ideas generated by philosophers interested in particular questions help people to clarify their own notions of existence, knowledge, and values—in sum, one's personal philosophy of life. Moreover, this philosophy of life, as one comes to understand it, becomes the foundation upon which people construct pedagogic practice.

Particular Philosophies of Education

In the following pages, we will discuss several leading schools of philosophy that have influenced and continue to influence the way people view educational practice. We have included both classical philosophies and modern philosophies which, in our opinion, have made the most impact on the ways in which people think about schools. Many of the ideas overlap; many of the distinctions we make are artificial and, at times, arbitrary. Most important, we hope that you will appreciate the fact that all successful practitioners borrow from many schools of thought.

Idealism

We begin our discussion of particular schools of philosophy that have influenced educational thought with *idealism,* the first systematic philosophy in Western thought. Idealism is generally thought to be the creation of the Greek philosopher, Plato (427–347 B.C.), the pupil of Socrates, a famous Greek teacher and philosopher who lived in Athens (c. 469–399 B.C.). Socrates never wrote anything down; rather, he taught through establishing oral dialogues with his students or those he wished to engage in philosophical questions. Socrates saw himself, as Plato stated in *The Apology (The Defense),* as "the gadfly of Athens." Through questioning, he forced his fellow Athenians to consider their life choices, and, in many instances, made them uncomfortable or often provoked them to anger. In 399 B.C., Socrates was executed for his beliefs. He was officially charged with corrupting the minds of the youth of Athens.

Plato wrote down Socrates' ideas and his method, which was the dialogue. While doing so, he probably added to Socrates' ideas, since he was only 28 years old when Socrates was executed, and he continued to write Socratic dialogue long after Socrates' death. Scholars concur with the idea that Plato augmented Socrates' beliefs, since it is generally held that Plato was far more sophisticated in his thinking than Socrates (Guthrie, 1969). Nevertheless, it is difficult for the uninitiated to distinguish between Socrates' and Plato's work. Thus, we will refer to this combination as *Platonic philosophy.*

Generic Notions.   Philosophers often pose difficult, abstract questions that are not easily answered. Plato helped to initiate this tradition through his concern for the search for *truth.*

Plato distrusted the world of matter; he believed that it was in a constant state of flux. Therefore, matter was an inaccurate measurement of truth since it was constantly changing. Plato also believed that the senses were not to be trusted, as they continually deceive us. Because truth for Plato was perfect and because truth is eternal, it was not to be found in the world of matter: "The unchanging realities we can apprehend by the mind only: the senses can show us only transient and imperfect copies of reality" (Kitto, 1951, p. 194).

The only constant for Plato was the field of mathematics, since $1 + 1 = 2$ will never change. In fact, it is eternal. The problem, however, with all of this is that mathematics is only one field of inquiry and so individuals must look to other modes of inquiry in the quest for truth. For Plato, this was the task of the philosopher.

Plato's method of doing philosophy was to engage another individual in a dialogue and, through the dialogue, question that individual's point of view. This questioning was done in a systematic, logical examination of both points of view. Ultimately, both parties would reach a synthesis of viewpoints that would be acceptable to both. This approach, called the *dialectic,* was used by Plato to move individuals from the world of matter to the world of ideas. Perhaps, as some philosophers suggest, Plato's philosophy should be called "ideaism" rather than idealism, since, for Plato, ideas were what mattered above all.

Plato thought education, in particular, was important as a means of moving individuals collectively toward achieving the *good.* He believed that the state should play an active role in education and that it should encourage the brighter students to follow a curriculum that was more abstract and more concerned with ideas rather than with concrete matter. Thus, he would have brighter students focusing on ideas and assign data collecting to the less able. Plato's "tracking system" was gender free; however, he proposed that those students who functioned on a more concrete level should assume roles necessary for maintaining the city-state, such as craftsmen, warriors, and farmers. Those who functioned on a more abstract level should rule. In fact, Plato put forth the idea of a philosopher-king: an individual who would lead the state to discover the ultimate *good*. Thus, Plato believed that rulers were individuals of thought, action, and obligation.

Since Plato's time, people have seen the state become a major force in determining the system of education. People have also witnessed how increasingly the school and tracking, in particular, determine the life chances of students. Additionally, people still cling to the importance Plato attached to education as the instrument that will enlighten rulers and aid them in achieving the highest *good*. Perhaps naively, people still believe that evil comes through ignorance, and that if only the rulers are educated, evil will be obliterated. Unfortunately, modern history has yet to validate this view.

Modern Idealists.   Since Plato, there has been a series of philosophers who have augmented Plato's original notions. For example, St. Augustine (354–430 A.D.) added religion to classical idealism; later philosophers, such as Rene Descartes (1596–1650), Immanuel Kant (1724–1804), and George Wilhelm Friedrich Hegel (1770–1831), added their particular visions to Platonic idealism.

Goal of Education.   Educators who subscribe to idealism are interested in the search for truth through ideas rather than through the examination of the false shadowy world of matter. Teachers encourage their students to search for truth as individuals. However, with the discovery of truth comes responsibility—responsibility of those who achieve realization of truth to enlighten others. Moreover, idealists subscribe to the notion that education is transformation: Ideas can change lives.

Role of the Teacher.   It is the teacher's responsibility to analyze and discuss ideas with students in order for students to move to new levels of awareness so that ultimately students can be transformed. Teachers should deal with abstract notions through the dialectic method but should aim to connect analysis with action as well.

In an idealist's classroom, the teacher plays an active role in discussion, posing questions, selecting materials, and establishing an environment, all of which ensure the teacher's desired outcome. An idealist teacher subscribes to the doctrine of *reminiscence,* described in the *Meno,* an important Platonic dialogue, which states that the role of the teacher is to bring out that which is already in the student's mind. Additionally, an idealist teacher supports moral education as a means of linking ideas to action. Last, the idealist teacher sees herself or himself as a role model in the classroom, to be emulated by students.

Methods of Instruction.   Idealist teachers take an active part in their students' learning. Although they lecture from time to time, perhaps to fill in background material not covered in the reading, they predominately use the dialectic approach described by Plato. Through questioning, students are encouraged to discuss, analyze, synthesize, and apply what they have read to contemporary society. Students are also encouraged to work in groups or individually on research projects, both oral and written.

Curriculum.   Idealists place great importance on the study of classics (i.e., great literature of past civilizations that illustrated contemporary concerns). For idealists, all contemporary problems have their roots in the past and can best be understood by examining how previous individuals dealt with them. A good example of an idealist curriculum would be the Great Books curriculum at Saint John's University, in Annapolis, Maryland. During their four years in college, students read, analyze, and apply the ideas of classical works to modern life. For elementary school-age children, there is a Great Books course promoted by individuals in the private sector and there exists as well a grass-roots movement to institute a core curriculum in elementary and junior high schools throughout the nation.

An interesting proposal that has not taken root is Mortimer Adler's *Paideia Proposal* (1982), which advocates great literature for children of all abilities. Adler proposed that elementary school children read great literature that would contain issues of relevance to all. Adler emphasized both content and process through the actual readings, much like the current whole-language movement.

Many idealists also support a back-to-basics approach to education, which emphasizes the three Rs. Such an approach became popular among educational conservatives, such as President Reagan's Secretary of Education, William Bennett, in the 1980s.

Realism

Realism is a philosophy that follows in the same historical tradition as idealism. Realism is associated with both Plato and Aristotle, although philosophers tend to view Aristotle as the leading proponent of realism. Aristotle (384–322 B.C.), a student of Plato's, was the son of a physician. He studied at Plato's Academy in Athens until Plato's death in 347 B.C. Aristotle also lived in Asia Minor and in Macedonia, where he was tutor to King Philip of Macedonia's son, Alexander. Aristotle's pupil later became Alexander the Great and a lover of all things Greek, thanks to Aristotle's influence.

In 355 B.C., Aristotle returned to Athens and started a school in the Lyceum, a public grove. Aristotle's career as a great teacher was cut short by the death of Alexander, his protector. The Athenians charged Aristotle with "impiety" and thus Aristotle was forced to leave Athens and settle in Euboea, where he remained until his death. Aristotle is particularly important because he was the first philosopher who developed a systematic theory of logic.

Generic Notions.   In our discussion of idealism, we noted that Plato argued for the centrality of ideas. Aristotle, however, believed that only through studying the material world was it possible for an individual to clarify or develop ideas. Thus, realists reject the Platonic notion that only ideas are real, and argue instead that the material world or matter is real. In fact, realists hold that matter exists, independent of ideas. Aristotle might have, in fact, argued that a triangle exists whether or not there is a thinking human being within range to perceive it.

If Plato were to study the nature of reality, he would begin with ideas, since he believed that the world of matter was shadowy and unreliable (see *The Allegory of the*

Cave). Aristotle, however, in his quest for the nature of reality, would begin with the world of matter. It is important to note that both Plato and Aristotle subscribed to the importance of ideas but each philosopher dealt with them very differently.

Since the classical realism of Aristotle, many forms of realism have evolved. These range from the religious realism of Thomas Aquinas (1225–1274) to the modern realism of individuals such as Francis Bacon (1561–1626) and John Locke (1632–1704) to the contemporary realism of Alfred North Whitehead (1861–1947) and Bertrand Russell (1872–1970).

Aristotle's Systematic Theory of Logic.   Aristotle is particularly important because he was the first philosopher to develop a rational, systematic method for testing the logic of statements people make. Aristotle began his process with empirical research; then, he would speculate or use dialectic reasoning, which would culminate in a syllogism. A *syllogism* is a system of logic that consists of three parts: (1) a major premise, (2) a minor premise, and (3) a conclusion. A famous example of a syllogism, used by many philosophers is as follows:

> All men are mortal
> Socrates is a man
> therefore, Socrates is mortal. (Ozmon & Craver, 1990, p. 43)

For a syllogism to work, all of the parts must be correct. If one of the premises is incorrect, the conclusion will be fallacious. Basically, Aristotle used syllogisms to systematize thinking. The problem, however, with this method is that Aristotle never made it clear where the syllogism was to be placed in his schema or framework. Thus, subsequent philosophers may have misinterpreted Aristotelian logic, grossly misusing the syllogism.

As you may have concluded by now, philosophers have been posing questions concerned with "the good life" or "the importance of reason" from the Greeks through the present (and probably long before the Greeks, considering that recorded history began in 3500 B.C. in Sumer). Aristotle, as did his contemporaries, stressed the importance of moderation in all things—the importance of achieving balance in leading one's life. Reason, concluded Aristotle, was the instrument individuals could employ to achieve the proper balance or moderation in their lives. Education, therefore, became particularly important in achieving moderation since education would introduce individuals to the process of systematic, rigorous thought. Through education, individuals would learn to reason and thus become able to choose the path of moderation in their lives. Since Aristotle, there have been important subsequent developments in this school of philosophy.

Neo-Thomism.   Aristotle was never clear about the place of the syllogism in his schema, although classical scholars believe that the syllogism was to be the culmination of his system rather than the starting point (Bowder, 1982). Many medieval thinkers, however, used Aristotle's syllogism to begin their logical proofs and *deduced* from generalizations to specific conclusions.

Thomas Aquinas (1225–1274) was an important medieval authority on the works of Aristotle. A school of philosophy, Neo-Thomism, is derived from Aquinian thought based on Aristotle. Basically, Aquinas affected a synthesis of pagan ideas and Christian beliefs, employing reason as a means of ascertaining or understanding truth. Aquinas thought that God could be understood through reasoning but reasoning based on the *material world.* Thus, Aquinas and Aristotle both emphasized matter and ideas in their particular philosophical investigations.

Aquinas's philosophy became known as Neo-Thomism in the latter part of the nineteenth century when it was revived by the Vatican as a way of resolving the conflict between the natural sciences and the Catholic church. In particular, the church, through Neo-Thomism, could argue that there was no conflict between science and religion since scientific inquiry ultimately led to belief in God. Aquinas's influence on contemporary educational practice is especially profound in Catholic schools, that base their educational goals on balancing the world of faith with the world of reason.

Modern Realism. Modern realism dates from the Renaissance, particularly with the work of Francis Bacon (1561–1626), who developed the inductive or scientific method of learning. Bacon was troubled by the reliance of classical realists on a prior or preconceived notion upon which thinkers deduced truths. Based on Aristotle's use of observable data, Bacon was able to develop a method starting with observations, that might culminate in a generalization, which then might be tested in specific instances for the purpose of verification.

John Locke (1632–1704), continuing in the scientific tradition established by Bacon, attempted to explain how people know things from the *empirical* point of view. He, too, chafed at the notion of *a priori ideas,* stating that the mind was a blank page, or *tabula rasa,* and what humans know is based on information gathered through the senses and through experience. Locke thought that the human mind ordered sense data and experience and then *reflected* on it.

Contemporary Realists. Contemporary realists, or realists in modern times, have tended to focus on science and philosophy—in particular, on scientific issues that have philosophical dimensions. For example, Alfred North Whitehead came to philosophy through the discipline of mathematics and was concerned with the search for "universal patterns" (Ozmon & Craver, 1990, p. 50).

Bertrand Russell studied both mathematics and philosophy as a student at Trinity College and Cambridge University, and coauthored with Whitehead the important book, *Principia Mathematica.* Both men believed that the universe could be characterized through universal patterns; however, Russell proposed that these patterns could be verified and classified through mathematics. Both were interested in education. Whitehead confined his interests to writing about education—in particular, advocating (like Plato) the primacy of ideas. Nevertheless (like Aristotle), he recognized the necessity of grounding ideas within the context of the living world. Russell actually founded a school called Beacon Hill, in which he sought to put into practice some of his notions of education, particularly the idea of employing knowledge to social problems in order to create a better world.

Goal of Education.   Both Plato and Aristotle believed that important questions concerning such notions as the good life, truth, beauty, and so on could be answered through the study of ideas, using the dialectical method. They differed, however, in their studying points. Plato emphasized only the study of ideas to understand ideas. Aristotle believed that it was possible to understand ideas through studying the world of matter. For Plato, the real world was shadowy and deceptive; for Aristotle, the real world was the starting point in the quest for understanding philosophical concerns.

For contemporary realists, the goal of education is to help individuals understand and then apply the principles of science to help solve the problems plaguing the modern world. Again, the leading notion of realists is that through basic disciplines—and in particular, science—individuals will be able to fathom what philosophers have been debating since the beginning of their discipline: existence of the good life, but thanks to Aristotle, how it can be encouraged through science.

Role of the Teacher.   Teachers, according to contemporary realists, should be steeped in the basic academic disciplines in order to transmit to their students the knowledge necessary for the continuance of the human race. They should have a solid grounding in science, mathematics, and the humanities. Additionally, teachers must present ideas in a clear and consistent manner and demonstrate that there are definitive ways to judge works of art, music, poetry, and literature. From this point of view, it is the role of the teacher to enable students to learn objective methods of evaluating such works (Ozmon & Craver, 1990, p. 63).

Methods of Instruction.   Realists would support a number of methods—in particular, lecture and question and answer. Additionally, since realists believe in objective criteria for judging the value of artistic and literary works, they would support the lecture as a method of instruction in order to give students the knowledge necessary to make these evaluations. Finally, many realists support competency-based assessment as a way of ensuring that students learn what they are being taught (Osmon & Craver, 1990, p. 63). Remember that realists believe that the material world holds the key to the ideal world; therefore, realists would encourage questions that would help students in the classroom grasp the ideal through specific characteristics of particular manifestations.

Curriculum.   Curriculum for realists would consist of the basics: science and math, reading and writing, and the humanities. Realists believe that there is a body of knowledge that is essential for the student to master in order to be part of society. Indeed, as stated previously, this body of knowledge is viewed as being essential for the survival of society.

Recent debates have centered on various groups questioning whether, in fact, there is an essential core of knowledge and, if so, what it might consist of. In particular, the debate about cultural literacy, sparked by the work of E. D. Hirsch, and the championing of the primacy of history and geography in social studies curricula proposed by Diane Ravitch, Chester Finn, and Paul Gagnon (see the Bradley Commission, 1988, for a detailed discussion of these proposals) support the notion of specific knowledge that helps students better understand their culture. Those who might question just what "culture" consists of and support a curriculum that truly reflects the multiplicity of U.S. society are scholars of curriculum, such as James Banks (1988).

Pragmatism

Pragmatism is generally viewed as an American philosophy that developed in the latter part of the nineteenth century. Generally speaking, the founders of this school of thought are George Sanders Peirce (1839–1914), William James (1842–1910), and John Dewey (1859–1952). However, there are European philosophers from earlier periods who might also be classified as pragmatists, such as Frances Bacon, John Locke, and Jean-Jacques Rousseau.

Pragmatism comes from the Greek word *pragma,* meaning work. Both George Sanders Peirce and William James are credited with having described pragmatism in part through the Biblical phrase, "By their fruits ye shall know them." James specifically makes such a reference in his book, *Varieties of Religious Experience* (James, 1978). That is, pragmatism is a philosophy that encourages people to find processes that work in order to achieve their desired ends. Although pragmatists do study the past, they generally are more interested in contemporary issues and in discovering solutions to problems in present-day terms. Pragmatists are action oriented, experientially grounded, and will generally pose questions such as What will work to achieve my desired end? A pragmatic schema might look like this:

problem → speculative thought → action → results

Pragmatists might then ask Do the results achieved solve the problem? If the question is answered in the affirmative, then the solution may be judged as valid.

Pragmatism's roots, as well as modern realism's roots, may be traced to the English philosopher and scientist, Francis Bacon (1561–1626), who we have previously discussed. Troubled with the Aristotelian legacy of deductive reasoning through the syllogism, Bacon sought a way of thinking in which people might be persuaded to abandon the traditions or "idols" of the past for a more experiential approach to the world. Because Bacon emphasized experience posited firmly within the world of daily existence, he can be thought of as a pioneer in the pragmatic school of philosophy. Furthermore, the method of reasoning he emphasized was *inductive,* which became the foundation of observational method in educational research.

Another modern realist, political philosopher John Locke (1632–1704), also followed in the pragmatic tradition. Locke was particularly interested in the ways in which people come to know things. He believed that the mind was a *tabula rasa,* a blank tablet, and that one acquires knowledge through one's senses (in opposition to Plato who, centuries earlier, had supported the notion of innate ideas). Locke believed that people can have ideas, that people can obtain these ideas through their senses but that they never verify them through the material or natural world. Locke's emphasis on the world of experience is particularly important for later developments in the philosophy of education.

Jean-Jacques Rousseau (1712–1778), a French philosopher, wrote mainly in France during the years preceding the French Revolution. Rousseau believed that individuals in their primitive state were naturally good and that society corrupted them. Society was harmful, for it led people away from pure existences. For Rousseau, the good life meant, simply stated, "back to nature." Thus, the Queen of France, Marie Antoinette, and her court at Versailles, influenced by Rousseau's ideas, attempted to return to nature by dressing as milk maids, shepherds, and shepherdesses.

Rousseau placed an important emphasis on *environment* and *experience,* which makes him important to subsequent pragmatic thinkers. He is mainly known to educators for his book *Emile,* which centers on a young boy who is removed from society to the country and learns experientially, through his environment, with the help of a tutor. Two points of interest are (1) Emile does not read books until he reaches 12 years of age and (2) there is little regard for the education of women in Rousseau's scheme other than two chapters on Sophie, who eats sweets and cakes and plays with dolls, and whose *raison d'etre* is to be Emile's companion.

Rousseau is thought to be a romantic due to his preoccupation with individuals in their natural state. Nevertheless, his emphasis on experience and on the child in a state of nature, constantly growing and changing, paved the way for thinkers such as John Dewey.

John Dewey (1859–1952), intellectually, was heir to Charles Darwin, the British naturalist, whose theory of natural selection emphasized the constant interaction between the organism and its environment, thus challenging the Platonic and Aristotelian notions of fixed essences. Unlike the static, ordered world of the eighteenth-century philosophers, nineteenth-century pragmatists saw the world as dynamic and developing. Although Dewey acknowledged his intellectual debt to Hegel, an early nineteenth-century idealist, the idea of the dynamic quality of life was, to Dewey, of overriding importance. It could not have existed without the work of Charles Darwin.

Dewey, originally from Vermont, taught philosophy at the Universities of Minnesota, Michigan, Chicago, and Columbia. During this time, he formulated his own philosophy, introducing the terms *instrumentalism* and *experimentalism.* Instrumentalism refers to the pragmatic relationship between school and society; experimentalism refers to the application of ideas to educational practice on an experimental basis. While at the University of Chicago, he opened the Laboratory School (with his wife Alice Chapman Dewey), in which his ideas about education were applied.

Dewey's philosophy of education was the most important influence on what has been termed *progressive education.* Actually, progressive education from Dewey to the present has included a number of different approaches. Historically, the two most important have been child-centered progressivism, influenced by Dewey, and social reconstructionism, a radical interpretation of Dewey's work. Social reconstructionists, such as George Counts (1932) and Theodore Brameld (1956), viewed the schools as vehicles for improving and changing society. As we will suggest in Chapter 7, although social reconstructionists had some effect on curriculum, it has been Dewey's work that had the most profound intellectual and practical influence on U.S. progressive education. Our discussion of the progressive educational philosophy based on pragmatism therefore concentrates on Dewey's work.

Dewey's Pragmatism: Generic Notions.   Dewey's form of pragmatism—instrumentalism and experimentalism—was founded on the new psychology, behaviorism, and the philosophy of pragmatism. Additionally, his ideas were influenced by the theory of evolution and by an eighteenth-century optimistic belief in progress. For Dewey, this meant the attainment of a better society through education. Thus, the school became an "embryonic community" where children could learn skills both experientially as well as from books, in addition to traditional information, which would enable them to work cooperatively in a democratic society.

Dewey's ideas about education, often referred to as *progressive,* proposed that educators start with the needs and interests of the child in the classroom, allow the child to participate in planning his or her course of study, employ project method or group learning, and depend heavily on experiential learning.

Dewey's progressive methodology rested on the notion that children were active, organic beings, growing and changing, and thus required a course of study that would reflect their particular stages of development. He advocated both freedom and responsibility for students, since those are vital components of democratic living. He believed that the school should reflect the community in order to enable graduating students to assume societal roles and to maintain the democratic way of life. Democracy was particularly important for Dewey. He believed that it could be more perfectly realized through education that would continually reconstruct and reorganize society.

Goal of Education.   Dewey's vision of schools was rooted in the social order; he did not see ideas as separate from social conditions. He fervently believed that philosophy had a responsibility to society and that ideas required laboratory testing; hence, he stressed the importance of the school as a place where ideas can be implemented, challenged, and restructured, with the goal of implementing students with the knowledge of how to improve the social order. Moreover, he believed that school should provide "conjoint, communicated experience"—that it should function as preparation for life in a democratic society.

In line with the progressive political atmosphere of the turn of the century, Dewey viewed the role of the school within the larger societal conditions of which it was a part. As such, Dewey's vision of schooling must be understood as part of the larger project of social progress and improvement. Although Dewey was certainly concerned with the social dimensions of schooling, he also was acutely aware of the school's effects on the individual. Thus, Dewey's philosophy of education made a conscious attempt to balance the social role of the school with its effects on the social, intellectual, and personal development of individuals. In other words, Dewey believed that the schools should balance the needs of society and community on the one hand and the needs of the individual on the other. This tension, or what the philosopher of education Maxine Greene (1988) termed the "dialectic of freedom," is central to understanding Dewey's work.

Dewey, like his contemporary, the French sociologist Emile Durkheim, saw the effects of modernization and urbanization on the social fabric of Western society. The rapid transformation in the nineteenth century from a traditional, agrarian world to a modern industrial one shattered the traditional bonds of solidarity and cohesion that held people together. Combined with the mass immigration to the United States in the late nineteenth century, the urban worlds of Chicago and New York City where Dewey spent his adult life were often fragmented and, in Durkheim's words, *anomic* (without norms). For both Durkheim and Dewey, the schools had to play a key role in creating a modern form of cohesion by socializing diverse groups into a cohesive democratic community.

The key to Dewey's vision is his view that the role of the school was to integrate children into not just any type of society, but a democratic one. Therefore, Dewey's view of integration is premised on the school as an embryonic democratic society where cooperation and community are desired ends. Dewey did not believe, however, that the school's role was to integrate children into a nondemocratic society. Rather, he believed that if schools instilled democratic and cooperative values in children, they would be prepared as adults to transform the social order into a more democratic one. Although he located this central function of schools, he never adequately provided a solution to the problem of integrating diverse groups into a community without sacrificing their unique characteristics. This is a problem still hotly debated.

For Dewey, the primary role of education was growth. In a famous section of *Democracy and Education,* Dewey stated that education had no other goals than growth—growth leading to more growth. As Lawrence Cremin (1990) noted,

> John Dewey liked to define the aim of education as growth, and when he was asked growth toward what, he liked to reply, growth leading to more growth. That was his way of saying that education is subordinate to no end beyond itself, that the aim of education is not merely to make parents, or citizens, or workers, or indeed to surpass the Russians or Japanese, but ultimately to make human beings who will live life to the fullest, who will continually add to the quality and meaning of their experience and to their ability to direct that experience, and who will participate actively with their fellow human beings in the building of a good society. (p. 125)

Historian of education Diane Ravitch (1983, pp. 43–80) noted that Dewey's philosophies of education were often misunderstood and misapplied. As we discussed in Chapter 3, it was often misapplied as "life adjustment education" and learning through experience as vocational education; it was often misapplied with regard to freedom, with individual freedom often confused with license and becoming far more important than other processes; and it was often totally distorted by providing social class appropriate education (i.e., vocational education for the poor). Despite these distorted applications, Dewey's philosophy of education, often referred to as *progressive education,* was central to all subsequent educational theory. For Dewey, the role of the school was to be "a lever of social reform"—that is, to be the central institution for societal and personal improvement and to do so by balancing a complex set of processes.

Role of the Teacher.   In a progressive setting, the teacher is no longer the authoritarian figure from which all knowledge flows; rather, the teacher assumes the peripheral position of facilitator. The teacher encourages, offers suggestions, questions, and helps plan and implement courses of study. The teacher also writes curriculum and must have a command of several disciplines in order to create and implement curriculum.

Methods of Instruction.   Dewey proposed that children learn both individually and in groups. He believed that children should start their mode of inquiry by posing questions about what they want to know. Today, we refer to this method of instruction as the *problem-solving* or *inquiry method.* Books, often written by teachers and students together, were used; field trips and projects, that reconstructed some aspect of the child's course of study, were also an integral part of learning in Dewey's laboratory school. These methods in turn became the basis for other progressive schools founded in the Deweyan tradition.

Formal instruction was abandoned. Traditional blocks of time for specific discipline instruction were eliminated. Furniture, usually nailed to the floor, was discarded in favor of tables and chairs that could be grouped as needed. Children could converse quietly with one another, could stand up and stretch if warranted, and could pursue independent study or group work. What at first glance to the visitor used to formal pedagogy might appear as chaotic was a carefully orchestrated classroom with children going about learning in nontraditional yet natural ways. Lockstep, rote memorization of traditional schools was replaced with individualized study, problem solving, and the project method.

Curriculum. Progressive schools generally follow Dewey's notion of a core curriculum, or an integrated curriculum. A particular subject matter under investigation by students, such as whales, would yield problems to be solved using math, science, history, reading, writing, music, art, wood or metal working, cooking, and sewing—all the academic and vocational disciplines in an integrated, interconnected way. Progressive educators support starting with contemporary problems and working from the known to the unknown, or what is now called in social studies education, the curriculum of *expanding environments.* Progressive educators are not wedded to a fixed curriculum either; rather, curriculum changes as the social order changes and as children's interests and needs change.

There is some controversy over Dewey's ideas about traditional discipline-centered curriculum. Some contemporary scholars (Egan, 1992, pp. 402–404) have stated that Dewey's emphasis on the need for the curriculum to be related to the needs and interests of the child suggests he was against traditional subject matter and in favor of a child-centered curriculum based on imagination and intuition. Others, including Howard Gardner (1992, pp. 410–411), felt that Dewey proposed a balance between traditional disciplines and the needs and interests of the child. We concur with Gardner's reading of Dewey and believe that Dewey thought that an integrated curriculum provided the most effective means to this balance.

Existentialism and Phenomenology

Like pragmatism, existentialism is a rather modern philosophy. Although its roots can be traced back to the Bible, as a philosophy that has relevance to education, one may date existentialism as beginning with the nineteenth-century European philosopher Soren Kierkegaard (1813–1855). More recent philosophers who work in this school include Martin Buber (1878–1965), Karl Jaspers (1883–1969), Jean Paul Sartre (1905–1986), and the contemporary philosopher Maxine Greene.

Phenomenology was primarily developed by Edmund Husserl (1859–1935), Martin Heidegger (1889–1976), and Maurice Merleau-Ponty (1908–1961). Since both existentialism and phenomenology have much in common, and since many phenomenologists are existentialists as well, we have chosen to combine our discussion of these two schools here.

Generic Notions.   Because existentialism is an individualistic philosophy, many of its adherents argue that it is not a particular school of philosophy at all. However, there are certain notions to which a majority of existentialists adhere. So, for our purposes, we will consider it as a particular philosophical movement that has important implications for education.

Unlike traditional philosophers, such as Plato and Aristotle, who were concerned with posing questions about epistemology, axiology, and metaphysics, existentialists pose questions as to how their concerns impact on the lives of individuals. Phenomenologists focus on the phenomena of consciousness, perception, and meaning, as they arise in a particular individual's experiences.

Basically, existentialists believe that individuals are placed on this earth alone and must make some sense out of the chaos they encounter. In particular, Sartre believed that "existence precedes essence"—that is, people must create themselves, and they must create their own meaning. This is done through the choices people make in their lives. Thus, individuals are in a state of constantly becoming, creating chaos and order, creating good and evil. The choice is up to the individual. The amount of freedom and responsibility people have is awesome, since they can, according to Sartre, make a difference in a seemingly absurd world. Although Sartre rejected the idea of the existence of God, other existentialists, especially its founder Soren Kierkergaard, were devout Christians who, while attacking contemporary Christianity, proposed "a great leap to faith" through which individuals might accept the existence of God. Whereas Kierkergaard was rallying against the scientific, objective approach to existence, Sartre was attempting to sort out meaning in a world that supported gross inhumane behavior—in particular, World War II and the Holocaust.

Phenomenologists are concerned with the way in which objects present themselves to people in their consciousness, and how people order those objects. Hermeneutics, an outgrowth of phenomenology, seeks to discover how people give objects meaning. Language is important here, since language is used to describe the various phenomena in life.

Goal of Education.   Existentialists believe that education should focus on the needs of individuals, both cognitively and affectively. They also believe that education should stress individuality; that it should include discussion of the nonrational as well as the rational world; and that the tensions of living in the world—in particular, anxiety generated through conflict—should be addressed. Existential phenomenologists go further; they emphasize the notion of *possibility,* since the individual changes in a constant state of becoming. They see education as an activity liberating the individual from a chaotic, absurd world.

Role of the Teacher.   Teachers should understand their own "lived worlds" as well as that of their students in order to help their students achieve the best "live worlds" they can. Teachers must take risks; expose themselves to resistant students; and work constantly to enable their students to become, in Greene's (1978) words, "wide awake." Introspection is useful in order to enable students to become in touch with their worlds and to empower them to choose and to act on their choices. Thus, the role of the teacher is an intensely personal one that carries with it a tremendous responsibility.

Methods of Instruction.   Existentialists and phenomenologists would abhor "methods" of instruction as they are currently taught in schools of education. They view learning as intensely personal. They believe that each child has a different learning style and it is up to the teacher to discover what works for each child. Martin Buber, an existentialist, wrote about an I-thou approach, whereby student and teacher learn cooperatively from each other in a nontraditional, nonthreatening, "friendship." The teacher constantly rediscovers knowledge, the student discovers knowledge, and together they come to an understanding of past, present, and future, particularly a future ripe with possibilities. Thus, the role of the teacher is to help students understand the world through posing questions, generating activities, and working together.

Curriculum.   Existentialists and phenomenologists would choose curriculum heavily biased toward the humanities. Literature especially has meaning for them since literature is able to evoke responses in readers that might move them to new levels of awareness, or, in Greene's (1978) words, "wide awakeness." Art, drama, and music also encourage personal interaction. Existentialists and phenomenologists believe in exposing students at early ages to problems as well as possibilities, and to the horrors as well as accomplishments humankind is capable of producing.

Neo-Marxism

Neo-Marxist philosophies of education are those approaches that trace their intellectual roots and theoretical assumptions to the nineteenth-century economist and philosopher Karl Marx (1818–1883). Based on the radical critique of capitalism, these theories argue that the role of education in capitalist society is to reproduce the ideology of the dominant class and its unequal economic outcomes; and conversely, that the role of education ought to be to give students the insight to demystify this ideology and to become agents of radical educational and social change.

The neo-Marxist perspective is more an overall theory of society than a particular philosophy of education. That is, while its proponents suggest specific philosophical approaches to educational issues, they are a part of the longer critique of capitalist society and capitalist education. The neo-Marxist approach includes the political-economic analysis of education, such as the works of Samuel Bowles and Herbert Gintis (1976), the curriculum theories of Michael Apple (1978, 1979a, 1982a, 1982b), the pedagogical work of Paulo Freire (1972), and the critical educational theory of Henry Giroux (1983b). To understand the neo-Marxist philosophy of education, it is important to first understand some basic background issues.

Generic Notions.   The intellectual, theoretical, and methodological foundations of neo-Marxism are all found in the works of Karl Marx. Marx was an economist, sociologist (before the discipline of sociology was officially founded), and philosopher who left his native Germany in 1842, first for Paris and then to London, where he spent the remainder of his life. Marx is usually associated with the worldwide movement he inspired—communism—but his writings were the foundation for a radical critique of capitalism throughout the twentieth century.

Although critics have pointed to problems with his theories (e.g., that socialism always proceeds out of the collapse of capitalism, which it has not; that capitalism is destined to collapse, which it has not), it is unfair to blame the problems and apparent failures of communist and socialist societies (e.g., in the former Soviet Union and Eastern Europe) on Marx himself, for he wrote very little on what socialism would look like. Rather, the bulk of his voluminous life's work concerned the understanding of capitalism.

Marx's works may be divided into two periods. The early philosophical works, including *The Economic and Philosophical Manuscripts of 1844* (1844), *The German Ideology* (1846), and *The Communist Manifesto* (1848) (the later two written with his lifetime friend and collaborator Frederick Engels), were concerned with philosophical and political issues such as alienation, freedom, ideology, and revolution. His later economic works, including the three volumes of *Das Kapital* (1867–1894), are concerned with the economic laws of capitalism and the contradictions (a Marxian term meaning irreconcilable differences) that make its collapse inevitable.

Marx's theories are far too complex to do justice to in these brief pages. However, it is necessary to understand those parts of his theories that form the basis of neo-Marxist philosophies of education. Simply stated, Marx believed that the history of civilization was defined by class struggle—the struggle between the dominant economic group and subordinate economic groups. Although every society defined such groups according to its own economic system (e.g., under feudalism, the serfs and the nobility; under capitalism, the proletariat [workers] and the bourgeoisie [the capitalist owners]), it was the domination of subordinate economic groups by those who controlled the economy (or means of production) that marked each historical period and the revolution by subordinate groups that marked the collapse of an outmoded economic system and its replacement by a new and superior one.

For Marx, each new economic system moved civilization closer to his ideal: a society that would produce sufficient economic resources to allow all of its citizens to live productive and decent lives. Capitalism, for Marx, with its vast productive capacity, would have the potential to render economic scarcity and human misery obsolete. The problem, however, is that Marx believed that the laws of capitalist accumulation that give the bulk of its productive resources to those who own the means of production (capitalists) would make such a just society impossible. Therefore, Marx asserted that it was necessary for those who produced the resources (the workers) to recognize that it is in their collective interest to change the system to what he saw as the next logical stage in history: socialism, a society where the means of production are owned by the state in trust for the entire public. Marx believed that the laws of capitalism would lead to increasing economic crises (e.g., inflation, recession, depression), increasing poverty of the working class side by side with increasing wealth on the part of the small capitalist class. Thus, Marx believed that the working class would unite (class consciousness) and rebel (class struggle) to create a more just socialist society.

Numerous historical problems are evident with this theory. For instance, Marx did not foresee the rise of the welfare state to partially ameliorate such social problems, nor the success of labor unions in working within the system to gain significant economic rewards for workers. Theoretical problems also abound, such as the view of dominant and subordinate groups in narrow economic terms, rather than in broader social, political, and cultural terms. However, the general conflict theory of society (discussed more fully in Chapter 4) is central to understanding modern neo-Marxist philosophies of education.

The key component to this conflict theory is Marx's theory of social order and change. Although Marx indeed believed that economic laws are the foundation of any society, it is people, through conflict and struggle, who make history. Thus, the dominant group in any society must preserve order either through force and coercion, that is inherently unstable, or by convincing the subordinate groups that the system is fair and legitimate. For Marx, this is accomplished through *ideology,* or the ideas or belief system of the ruling class (Marx & Engels, 1848). Conversely, in order for change to take place, the subordinate group must see through this ideology and become conscious of its own interests (to change society). Thus, the subordinate groups must demystify the illusions of the dominant ideology and work toward change. It is education's role in transmitting this dominant ideology and its potential in allowing students to demystify it that is the main thrust of neo-Marxist philosophies of education.

Goal of Education.   Modern neo-Marxist theories include what may be termed *reproduction theories* (Bowles & Gintis, 1976) and *resistance theories* (Freire, 1978; Giroux, 1983b). Reproduction theories argue that the role of education in capitalist societies is to reproduce the economic, social, and political status quo. More specifically, the school through its ideology and curriculum (Apple, 1978, 1979a, 1982a, 1982b) and pedagogic practices (McLaren, 1989) transmits the dominant beliefs to children and serves to legitimate the capitalist order. Resistance theories, while agreeing that schools often reproduce the dominant ideology, state they also have the potential to empower students to question it.

Therefore, resistance theories question the overly deterministic view of reproduction theories and state that such approaches deny what they call "human agency"—that is, the power of individuals to shape their own world and to change it. In this respect, resistance theories have a great deal in common with existentialists, as they believe that the process of education contains the tools to enable individuals both to understand the weaknesses in the dominant ideology and to construct alternative visions and possibilities. Further, what are termed *postmodernist* (Cherryholmes, 1988; Giroux, 1991) and *feminist* (Ellsworth, 1989; Laird, 1989; Lather, 1991; Martin, 1987) theories of education are closely related to this aspect of neo-Marxism, although not all postmodernists and feminists are neo-Marxists.

What all of these theorists have in common is the view that education should transform the dominant culture (for a complete discussion of postmodernism and feminism, see Giroux, 1991, and Sadovnik, 1995b). Postmodernists and feminists disagree with neo-Marxists about who exactly comprises the dominant culture. Feminists argue that male domination is the problem; postmodernists are skeptical of any one theory that explains domination and therefore rejects the neo-Marxist emphasis on economic domination as too one dimensional (Lyotard, 1984).

The Role of the Teacher.   The neo-Marxist philosophy of education concentrates on the teacher and student as part of a critical pedagogical process. The teacher, from this vantage point, must become a "transformative intellectual" (Giroux, 1988) whose role is to engage his or her students in a critical examination of the world. The student thus becomes part of an educational process that seeks to examine critically the society and its problems and to seek radical alternatives.

In some respects, this view of education is similar to the existential phenomenology of Greene (1978, 1988) in that it views the purpose of education as "wide awakeness." The difference is that Greene is less committed to an objective truth that constitutes such a state (that is, one reality that is true), whereas neo-Marxists believe that "wide awakeness" requires an objective truth that includes a critique of capitalism. Such a conclusion is open to considerable debate, even among those sympathetic to neo-Marxism. However, its idea that education ought to result in critical awareness of self and society is a view that goes well beyond neo-Marxist philosophy and is shared by many of the other philosophies discussed here, including pragmatism, existentialism, phenomenology, postmodernism, and feminism.

Methods of Instruction.   Given their emphasis on education as transformation, neo-Marxists favor a dialectical approach to instruction, with the question-and-answer method designed to move the student to new levels of awareness and ultimately to change. Through rigorous analysis of the taken-for-granted aspects of the world, the goal of instruction is to reveal underlying assumptions of society and to help students see alternative possibilities.

Curriculum.   The neo-Marxist view of curriculum is that the curriculum is not objective or value free but is socially constructed (Apple, 1978, 1979a, 1982a, 1982b; Young, 1971). This view suggests that the curriculum is the organized and codified representation of what those with the power to shape it want the children to know. Such a critical stance requires that teachers understand the ways in which curriculum represents a particular point of view and to become critical curriculum constructors—that is, individuals who can reshape the curriculum to represent a fairer view of the world (although for neo-Marxists, this fairer view of the world means a curriculum that is critical of capitalism).

As we will discuss in Chapter 7, this view of the curriculum is shared by feminist curriculum theorists (Macdonald & Macdonald, 1981; Miller, 1982; Mitrano, 1979) and postmodern theorists (Giroux, 1991). The difference, however, is that feminists and postmodernists often disagree about whose interests the curriculum represents. Feminists, for example, argue that it is patriarchal interests rather than capitalist interests that affect the curriculum. The view of curriculum shared by these theorists leads them to support more multicultural and feminist curricula, which emphasize those social groups who are not in power.

Postmodernist and Critical Theory

Generic Notions.   Postmodernism developed out of a profound dissatisfaction with modernism. Beginning with the poststructural writings of Derrida (1981, 1982) and Baudrillard (1981, 1984), social theorists, particularly in France, questioned the appropriateness of modernist categories for understanding what they saw as a postmodern world—a world that transcended the economic and social relations of the industrial world that modernist thought sought to understand. In particular, the work of Lyotard (1984) rejected the Marxist project as well as the Enlightenment and modernist assumptions underlying Marxist theory and sought to create a different theory of the late twentieth century.

There is a vast body of literature on the definition of *postmodernist theory* (Aronowitz & Giroux, 1991; Giroux, 1991; Harvey, 1989; Jameson, 1982; Jencks, 1987; Lyotard, 1984), as well as a growing body of literature on postmodern approaches to education (Aronowitz & Giroux, 1991; Cherryholmes, 1988; Ellsworth, 1989; Giroux, 1988, 1991; Lather, 1991; McLaren, 1991; McLaren & Hammer, 1989; Wexler, 1987).

Modernist social theory, in both sociology and philosophy, traces its intellectual heritage to the Enlightenment. From the classical sociological theory of Marx (1971), Marx and Engels (1947), and Durkheim (1938/1977, 1947), to the pragmatist philosophy of Dewey (1916, 1927/1984), and to the social theory of Habermas (1979, 1981, 1982, 1983, 1987), what is usually referred to as modernist theories had a number of things in common. First, the theories were based on the belief in progress through science and technology, even if they were skeptical of positivist social science. Second, they emphasized the Enlightenment belief in reason. And third, they stressed Enlightenment principles such as equality, liberty, and justice.

Postmodernist thought consists of many interrelated themes:

1. Postmodernism insists on what Lyotard (1984) has labeled the rejection of all metanarratives. By this, Lyotard meant that the modernist preoccupation with grand, total, or all-encompassing explanations of the world needs to be replaced by localized and particular theories.
2. Postmodernism stresses the necessary connection between theory and practice as a corrective to the separation of them in much modernist thought.
3. Postmodernism stresses the democratic response to authoritarianism and totalitarianism. In particular, Aronowitz and Giroux (1991), Giroux (1991), and McLaren and Hammer (1989) call for a democratic, emancipatory, and antitotalitarism theory and practice, with schools seen as sites for democratic transformation.
4. Postmodernism sees modernist thought as Eurocentric and patriarchal. Giroux (1991), Lather (1991), Ellsworth (1989) and others provide an important critique of the racism and sexism in some modernist writings and the failure of modernism to address the interests of women and people of color.
5. Postmodernist theorists believe that all social and political discourse is related to structures of power and domination.
6. Postmodernism stresses what Burbules and Rice (1991) term "dialogue across differences." Recognizing the particular and local nature of knowledge, postmodern

theorists call for the attempt to work through differences, rather than to see them as hopelessly irreconcilable.

Thus, postmodern theories of education call for teachers and students to explore the differences between what may seem like inherently contradictory positions in an effort to achieve understanding, respect, and change.

Although much of postmodern theory developed as a critical theory of society and a critique of modernism, it quickly became incorporated into critical writings on education, often called *critical theory*. Educational theory—which over the past two decades has involved an interdisciplinary mixture of social theory, sociology, and philosophy—has been profoundly affected by postmodernist thought. In particular, critical theories of education, which, from the late 1970s, attempted to provide an antidote to the overdeterminism of Bowles and Gintis (1976), by the 1980s regularly incorporated postmodern language and concerns. There have been numerous postmodern theories of education or applications of postmodernism to education. Critical and postmodern theories of education often draw heavily on the work of the Brazilian educator Paolo Freire (1972, 1985, 1987), whose influential work, *Pedagogy of the Oppressed* (1972) became the foundation for critical educational theory in the United States (Kincheloe & Steinberg, 1998; Macedo, 1990).

The Role of the Teacher, Methods of Instruction, and Curriculum.   Postmodern and critical theories of education are similar to neo-Marxist theory with respect to curriculum and pedagogy. Critical pedagogy (Kincheloe & Steinberg, 1998, Chapter 1) stresses the classroom as a site for political action and teachers as agents of change.

Of all the postmodern writing in the United States, Henry Giroux's represents the most sustained effort to develop a postmodern theory of education and to connect it to previous critical theories, including neo-Marxism, critical theory, and resistance theory. Giroux (1991, pp. 47–59) outlined principles of critical pedagogy, which he stated are based on the insights of modernism, postmodernism, and feminism. Thus, he provided a synthesis of three of the important theoretical systems in the twentieth century and from these he developed a critical pedagogy, whose function is to transform teachers, schools, and ultimately society:

1. Giroux has argued that education must be seen not only as producing knowledge, but political subjects as well (1991, p. 47). Thus, schooling must be linked to a critical pedagogy aimed at the development of democratic education.
2. Giroux has indicated that ethics need to be a central concern of postmodern theories of education and critical pedagogy.
3. Critical pedagogy should focus on postmodern concerns with difference in a politically transformative manner. According to Giroux, students need to understand the social construction of different voices and identities, how these are related to historical and social forces, and how they can be used as the basis for change. The incorporation of different voices into the curriculum and student reflection on these voices need to be connected to the conception of a democratic community.

4. The concern for difference needs to be translated into a critical language that allows for competing discourses and that rejects any master narratives or curriculum canons.

5. Critical pedagogy needs to create new forms of knowledge out of analysis of competing discourses and from voices historically absent from traditional canons and narratives. Thus, pedagogic practice is seen as a political activity, with curriculum development no longer a technocratic exercise concerned with educational goals and objectives, but rather with providing students with new forms of knowledge rooted in a pluralistic and democratic vision of society.

6. Building on his earlier work, Giroux suggested that a postmodern critical pedagogy must provide a sense of alternatives through a "language of critique and possibility" (1991, p. 52). Critical pedagogy as a critique of what exists and a development of what is possible is central to a project of social transformation.

7. Critical pedagogy must be related to a view of teachers as transformative intellectuals. In his work on postmodernism, Giroux developed a theme central to his earlier work and has connected it to a view of democratic public life. Giroux calls for teachers to be involved not only within schools, but to connect their voices to democratic politics in their communities and within society, in general. Critical pedagogy needs to engage students and teachers in the systematic discovery of alternatives to institutional racism, classism, and sexism through the inclusion of the voices of marginalized groups. Such an enterprise should not be, Giroux has warned, merely exercises in giving voice to the voiceless, but needs to connect their voices to political strategies aimed at social change.

Sadovnik (1995b) has pointed out a number of problems with postmodern and critical theories of education. First, postmodern theories of education are often written in a language that is difficult to understand. While this is problematic for all academic work, it is more so for a theory that purports to provide an agenda for critique and change in the school. Second, postmodern theories usually eschew empirical methods to study schools. Thus, they are sometimes long on assertion and short on evidence. Finally, and most importantly, postmodernist theories of education often fail to connect theory to practice in a way that practitioners find meaningful and useful. Although this does not suggest that postmodernists write exclusively for practitioners, if one of the stated aims of theorists such as Giroux is to develop teachers as transformative intellectuals and to provide a critical pedagogy for school transformation, then the problem of language use is of central importance. How can there be dialogues across difference if teachers are excluded from the dialogue?

Conclusion

In this chapter, we have presented some of the major philosophies of education. Through a discussion of how each school of philosophy views the goal of education, the role of the teacher, methods of instruction, and the curriculum, we have presented how philosophers of education view important educational issues. These schools of philosophy often overlap. As a teacher, you will, more often than not, make use of several approaches. It is important that you develop, clarify, and justify your own particular philosophical approach to teaching, as it will form the foundation of your practice. Moreover, as we suggest in Chapter 10, the successful school reforms at schools such as Central Park East in New York City are based on a sound philosophical foundation. Thus, school improvement depends on both teachers and schools having a clear sense of purpose, and a philosophy of education provides the basis for such a purpose.

The following selections illustrate some of the philosophies of education discussed in this chapter. In the first selection, "My Pedagogic Creed," John Dewey presents the central aspects of the "new" or progressive education. Written in 1897, Dewey discusses his definition of education, the school, the curriculum, pedagogy, and the role of the school in social progress, and proposes a pragmatist philosophy of education.

In the second selection, "Wide-Awakeness and the Moral Life," philosopher of education Maxine Greene presents an existentialist philosophy of education. Greene passionately argues for teachers to become critically aware of the world around them and to help students better understand their own lives. This understanding, according to Greene, is a necessary condition for social improvement.

"The Ideal of the Educated Person," written by feminist philosopher of education Jane Roland Martin, examines what an educated person ought to be. Martin argues that traditional conceptions of the "educated man" have been gender biased.

My Pedagogic Creed

JOHN DEWEY

Article I—What Education Is

I believe that all education proceeds by the participation of the individual in the social consciousness of the race. This process begins unconsciously almost at birth, and is continually shaping the individual's powers, saturating his consciousness, forming his habits, training his ideas, and arousing his feelings and emotions. Through this unconscious education the individual gradually comes to share in the intellectual and moral resources which humanity has succeeded in getting together. He becomes an inheritor of the funded capital of civilization. The most formal and technical education in the world cannot safely depart from this general process. It can only organize it or differentiate it in some particular direction.

I believe that the only true education comes through the stimulation of the child's powers by the demands of the social situations in which he finds himself. Through these demands he is stimulated to act as a member of a unity, to emerge from his original narrowness of action and feeling, and to conceive of himself from the standpoint of the welfare of the group to which he belongs. Through the responses which others make to his own activities he comes to know what these mean in social terms. The value which they have is reflected back into them. For instance, through the response which is made to the child's instinctive bab-

From "My Pedagogic Creed" by John Dewey. In Martin Dworkin (Ed.), *Dewey on Education.* New York: Teachers College Press, 1959. Reprinted by permission..

blings the child comes to know what those babblings mean; they are transformed into articulate language and thus the child is introduced into the consolidated wealth of ideas and emotions which are now summed up in language.

I believe that this educational process has two sides—one psychological and one sociological; and that neither can be subordinated to the other or neglected without evil results following. Of these two sides, the psychological is the basis. The child's own instincts and powers furnish the material and give the starting point for all education. Save as the efforts of the educator connect with some activity which the child is carrying on of his own initiative independent of the educator, education becomes reduced to a pressure from without. It may, indeed, give certain external results, but cannot truly be called educative. Without insight into the psychological structure and activities of the individual, the educative process will, therefore, be haphazard and arbitrary. If it chances to coincide with the child's activity it will get a leverage; if it does not, it will result in friction, or disintegration, or arrest of the child nature.

I believe that knowledge of social conditions, of the present state of civilization, is necessary in order properly to interpret the child's powers. The child has his own instincts and tendencies, but we do not know what these mean until we can translate them into their social equivalents. We must be able to carry them back into a social past and see them as the inheritance of previous race activities. We must also be able to project them into the future to see what their outcome and end will be. In the illustration just used, it is the ability to see in the child's babblings the promise and potency of a future social intercourse and conversation which enables one to deal in the proper way with that instinct.

I believe that the psychological and social sides are organically related and that education cannot be regarded as a compromise between the two, or a superimposition of one upon the other. We are told that the psychological definition of education is barren and formal—that it gives us only the idea of a development of all the mental powers without giving us any idea of the use to which these powers are put. On the other hand, it is urged that the social definition of education, as getting adjusted to civilization, makes of it a forced and external process, and results in subordinating the freedom of the individual to a preconceived social and political status.

I believe that each of these objections is true when urged against one side isolated from the other. In order to know what a power really is we must know what its end, use, or function is; and this we cannot know save as we conceive of the individual as active in social relationships. But, on the other hand, the only possible adjustment which we can give to the child under existing conditions, is that which arises through putting him in complete possession of all his powers. With the advent of democracy and modern industrial conditions, it is impossible to foretell definitely just what civilization will be twenty years from now. Hence it is impossible to prepare the child for any precise set of conditions. To prepare him for the future life means to give him command of himself; it means so to train him that he will have the full and ready use of all his capacities; that his eye and ear and hand may be tools ready to command, that his judgment may be capable of grasping the conditions under which it has to work, and the executive forces be trained to act economically and efficiently. It is impossible to reach this sort of adjustment save as constant regard is had to the individual's own powers, tastes, and interests—say, that is, as education is continually converted into psychological terms.

In sum, I believe that the individual who is to be educated is a social individual and that society is an organic union of individuals. If we eliminate the social factor from the child we are left only with an abstraction; if we eliminate the individual factor from society, we are left only with an inert and lifeless mass. Education, therefore, must begin with a psychological insight into the child's capacities, interests, and habits. It must be controlled at every point by reference to these same considerations. These powers, interests, and habits must be continually interpreted—we must know what they mean. They must be translated into terms of their social equivalents—into terms of what they are capable of in the way of social service.

Article II—What the School Is

I believe that the school is primarily a social institution. Education being a social process, the school is simply that form of community life in which all those agencies are concentrated that will be most effective in bringing the child to share in the inherited resources of the race, and to use his own powers for social ends.

I believe that education, therefore, is a process of living and not a preparation for future living.

I believe that the school must represent present life—life as real and vital to the child as that which he carries on in the home, in the neighborhood, or on the playground.

I believe that education which does not occur through forms of life, or that are worth living for their own sake, is always a poor substitute for the genuine reality and tends to cramp and to deaden.

I believe that the school, as an institution, should simplify existing social life; should reduce it, as it were, to an embryonic form. Existing life is so complex that the child cannot be brought into contact with it without either confusion or distraction; he is either overwhelmed by the multiplicity of activities which are going on, so that he loses his own power of orderly re-action, or he is so stimulated by these various activities that his powers are prematurely called into play and he becomes either unduly specialized or else disintegrated.

I believe that as such simplified social life, the school life should grow gradually out of the home life; that it should take up and continue the activities with which the child is already familiar in the home.

I believe that it should exhibit these activities to the child, and reproduce them in such ways that the child will gradually learn the meaning of them, and be capable of playing his own part in relation to them.

I believe that this is a psychological necessity, because it is the only way of securing continuity in the child's growth, the only way of giving a background of past experience to the new ideas given in school.

I believe that it is also a social necessity because the home is the form of social life in which the child has been nurtured and in connection with which he has had his moral training. It is the business of the school to deepen and extend his sense of the values bound up in his home life.

I believe that much of present education fails because it neglects this fundamental principle of the school as a form of community life. It conceives the school as a place where certain information is to be given, where certain lessons are to be learned, or where certain habits are to be formed. The value of these is conceived as lying largely in the remote future; the child must do these things for the sake of something else he is to do; they are mere preparation. As a result they do not become a part of the life experience of the child and so are not truly educative.

I believe that the moral education centers upon this conception of the school as a mode of social life, that the best and deepest moral training is precisely that which one gets through having to enter into proper relations with others in a unity of work and thought. The present educational system, so far as they destroy or neglect this unity, render it difficult or impossible to get any genuine, regular moral training.

I believe that the child should be stimulated and controlled in his work through the life of the community.

I believe that under existing conditions far too much of the stimulus and control proceeds from the teacher, because of neglect of the idea of the school as a form of social life.

I believe that the teacher's place and work in the school is to be interpreted from this same basis. The teacher is not in the school to impose certain ideas or to form certain habits in the child, but is there as a member of the community to select the influences which shall affect the child and to assist him in properly responding to these influences.

I believe that the discipline of the school should proceed from the life of the school as a whole and not directly from the teacher.

I believe that the teacher's business is simply to determine on the basis of larger experience and riper wisdom, how the discipline of life shall come to the child.

I believe that all questions of the grading of the child and his promotion should be determined by reference to the same standard. Examinations are of use only so far as they test the child's fitness for social life and reveal the place in which he can be of the most service and where he can receive the most help.

Article III—The Subject-Matter of Education

I believe that the social life of the child is the basis of concentration, or correlation, in all his training or growth. The social life gives the unconscious unity and the background of all his efforts and of all his attainments.

I believe that the subject-matter of the school curriculum should mark a gradual differentiation out of the primitive unconscious unity of social life

I believe that we violate the child's nature and render difficult the best ethical results, by introducing the child too abruptly to a number of special studies of reading, writing, geography, etc., out of relation to this social life.

I believe, therefore, that the true center of correlation on the school subjects is not science, nor literature, nor history, nor geography, but the child's own social activities. . . .

I believe that literature is the reflex expression and interpretation of social experience; that hence it must follow upon and not precede such experience. It, therefore, cannot be made the basis, although it may be made the summary of unification.

I believe once more that history is of educative value in so far as it presents phases of social life and growth. It must be controlled by reference to social life. When taken simply as history it is thrown into the distant past and becomes dead and inert. Taken as the record of man's social life and progress it becomes full of meaning. I believe, however, that it cannot be so taken excepting as the child is also introduced directly into social life.

I believe accordingly that the primary basis of education is in the child's powers at work along the same general constructive lines as those which have brought civilization into being.

I believe that the only way to make the child conscious of his social heritage is to enable him to perform those fundamental types of activity which make civilization what it is. . . .

I believe that there is, therefore, no succession of studies in the ideal school curriculum. If education is life, all life has, from the outset, a scientific aspect, an aspect of art and culture, and an aspect of communication. It cannot, therefore, be true that the proper studies for one grade are mere reading and writing, and that at a later grade, reading, or literature, or science, may be introduced. The progress is not in the succession of studies but in the development of new attitudes towards, and new interests in, experience.

I believe finally, that education must be conceived as a continuing reconstruction of experience; that the process and the goal of education are one and the same thing.

I believe that to set up any end outside of education, as furnishing its goal and standard, is to deprive the educational process of much of its meaning and tends to make us rely upon false and external stimuli in dealing with the child. . . .

Wide-Awakeness and the Moral Life

MAXINE GREENE

"Moral reform," wrote Henry David Thoreau, "is the effort to throw off sleep." He went on:

> Why is it that men give so poor an account of their day if they have not been slumbering? They are not such poor calculators. If they had not been overcome with drowsiness they would have performed something. The millions are awake enough for physical labor; but only one in a million is awake enough for effective intellectual exertion, only one in a hundred million to a poetic or divine life. To be awake is to be alive. I have never yet met a man who was quite awake. How could I have looked him in the face? We must learn to reawaken and keep ourselves awake, not by mechanical aids, but by an infinite expectation of the dawn, which does not forsake us in our soundest sleep. I know of no more encouraging fact than the unquestionable ability of man to elevate his life by a conscious endeavor.[1]

It is of great interest to me to find out how this notion of wide-awakeness has affected contemporary thought, perhaps particularly the thought of those concerned about moral responsibility and commitment in this difficult modern age. The social philosopher Alfred Schutz has talked of wide-awakeness as an achievement, a type of awareness, "a plane of consciousness of highest tension originating in an attitude of full attention to life and its requirements."[2] This attentiveness, this *interest* in things, is the direct opposite

From "Wide-Awakeness and the Moral Life" by Maxine Greene. In *Landscapes for Learning*. New York: Teachers College Press, 1978. Reprinted by permission.

of the attitude of bland conventionality and indifference so characteristic of our time.

We are all familiar with the number of individuals who live their lives immersed, as it were, in daily life, in the mechanical round of habitual activities. We are all aware how few people ask themselves what they have done with their own lives, whether or not they have used their freedom or simply acceded to the imposition of patterned behavior and the assignment of roles. Most people, in fact, are likely to go on in that fashion, unless—or until—"one day the 'why' arises," as Albert Camus put it, "and everything begins in that weariness tinged with amazement." Camus had wide-awakeness in mind as well; because the weariness of which he spoke comes "at the *end* of the acts of a mechanical life, but at the same time it inaugurates the impulse of consciousness."[3]

The "why" may take the form of anxiety, the strange and wordless anxiety that occurs when individuals feel they are not acting on their freedom, not realizing possibility, not (to return to Thoreau) elevating their lives. Or the "why" may accompany a sudden perception of the insufficiencies in ordinary life, of inequities and injustices in the world, of oppression and brutality and control. It may accompany, indeed it may be necessary, for an individual's moral life. The opposite of morality, it has often been said, is indifference—a lack of care, an absence of concern. Lacking wide-awakeness, I want to argue, individuals are likely to drift, to act on impulses of expediency. They are unlikely to identify situations as moral ones or to set themselves to assessing their demands. In such cases, it seems to me, it is meaningless to talk of obligation; it may be futile to speak of consequential choice.

This is an important problem today in many countries of the world. Everywhere, guidelines are deteriorating; fewer and fewer people feel themselves to be answerable to clearly defined norms. In many places, too, because of the proliferation of bureaucracies and corporate structures, individuals find it harder and harder to take initiative. They guide themselves by vaguely perceived expectations; they allow themselves to be programmed by organizations and official schedules or forms. They are like the hero of George Konrad's novel, *The Case Worker*. He is a social worker who works with maltreated children "in the name," as he puts it, "of legal principles and provisions." He does not like the system, but he serves it: "It's law, it works, it's rather like me, its tool. I know its ins and outs. I simplify and complicate it, I slow it down and speed it up. I adapt myself to its needs or adapt it to my needs, but this is as far as I will go."[4] Interestingly enough, he says (and this brings me back to wide-awakeness) that his highest aspiration is to "live with his eyes open" as far as possible; but the main point is that he, like so many other clerks and office workers and middle management men (for all their meaning well), is caught within the system and is not free to choose.

I am suggesting that, for too many individuals in modern society, there is a feeling of being dominated and that feelings of powerlessness are almost inescapable. I am also suggesting that such feelings can to a large degree be overcome through conscious endeavor on the part of individuals to keep themselves awake, to think about their condition in the world, to inquire into the forces that appear to dominate them, to interpret the experiences they are having day by day. Only as they learn to make sense of what is happening, can they feel themselves to be autonomous. Only then can they develop the sense of agency required for living a moral life.

I think it is clear that there always has to be a human consciousness, recognizing the moral issues potentially involved in a situation, if there is to be a moral life. As in such great moral presentations as *Antigone, Hamlet,* and *The Plague,* people in everyday life today have to define particular kinds of situations as moral and to identify the possible alternatives. In *Antigone,* Antigone defined the situation that existed after her uncle forbade her to bury her brother as one in which there were alternatives: she could indeed bury her brother, thus offending against the law of the state and being sentenced to death, or (like her sister Ismene) submit to the men in power. In *Hamlet,* the Danish prince defined the situation in Denmark as one in which there were alternatives others could not see: to expose the murderer of his father and take the throne as the true king or to accept the rule of Claudius and his mother and return as a student to Wittenberg. In *The Plague,* most of the citizens of Oran saw no alternative but to resign themselves to a pestilence for which there was no cure; but Dr. Rieux and Tarrou defined the same situation as one in which there were indeed alternatives: to submit—or to form sanitary squads and, by so doing, to refuse to acquiesce in the inhuman, the absurd.

When we look at the everyday reality of home and school and workplace, we can scarcely imagine ourselves taking moral positions like those taken by a Hamlet or a Dr. Rieux. One reason has to do with the overwhelming ordinariness of the lives we live. Another is our tendency to perceive our everyday reality as a given—objectively defined, impervious to change. Taking it for granted, we do not realize that reality, like all others, is an interpreted one. It presents itself to us as it does because we have learned to understand it in standard ways.

In a public school, for instance, we scarcely notice that there is a hierarchy of authority; we are so accustomed to it, we forget that it is man-made. Classroom teachers, assigned a relatively low place in the hierarchy, share a way of seeing and of talking about it. They are used to watching schedules, curricula, and testing programs emanate from "the office." They take for granted the existence of a high place, a seat of power. If required unexpectedly to administer a set of tests, most teachers (fearful, perhaps, irritated or sceptical) will be likely to accede. Their acquiescence may have nothing at all to do with their convictions or with what they have previously read or learned. They simply see no alternatives. The reality they have constructed and take for granted allows for neither autonomy nor disagreement. They do not consider putting their objections to a test. The constructs they have inherited do not include a view of teachers as equal participants. "That," they are prone to say, "is the way it is."

Suppose, however, that a few teachers made a serious effort to understand the reasons for the new directive. Suppose they went out into the community to try to assess the degree of pressure on the part of parents. Suppose that they investigated the kinds of materials dispatched from the city or the state. Pursuing such efforts, they would be keeping themselves awake. They might become increasingly able to define their own values with regard to testing; they might conceivably see a moral issue involved. For some, testing might appear to be dehumanizing; it might lead to irrelevant categorizing; it might result in the branding of certain children. For others, testing might appear to be miseducative, unless it were used to identify disabilities and suggest appropriate remedies. For still others, testing might appear to be a kind of insurance against poor teaching, a necessary reminder of what was left undone. Discussing it from several points of view and within an understood context, the teachers might find themselves in a position to act as moral agents. Like Dr. Rieux and Tarrou, they might see that there are indeed alternatives: to bring the school community into an open discussion, to consider the moral issues in the light of overarching commitments, or to talk about

what is actually known and what is merely hypothesized. At the very least, there would be wide-awakeness. The members of the school community would be embarked on a moral life.

Where personal issues are concerned, the approach might be very much the same. Suppose that a young person's peer group is "into" drugs or alcohol or some type of sexual promiscuity. Young persons who are half asleep and who feel no sense of agency might well see no alternative to compliance with the group, when the group decides that certain new experiences should be tried. To such individuals, no moral situation exists. They are young; they are members; whether they want to particularly or not, they can only go along.

Other young persons, just as committed to the group, might be able to realize that there are indeed alternatives when, say, some of their comrades go out to find a supply of cocaine. They might be able to ponder those alternatives, to play them out in their imagination. They can accompany their friends on their search; they might even, if they are successful, get to sniff a little cocaine and have the pleasure such sniffs are supposed to provide. They can, on the other hand, take a moment to recall the feelings they had when they first smoked marijuana—the nervousness at losing touch with themselves, the dread about what might happen later. They can consider the fact that their friends are going to do something illegal, not playful, that they could be arrested, even jailed. They can confront their own reluctance to break the law (or even to break an ordinary rule), imagine what their parents would say, try to anticipate what they would think of themselves. At the same time, if they decide to back away, they know they might lose their friends. If they can remember that they are free, after all, and if they assess their situation as one in which they can indeed choose one course of action over another, they are on the way to becoming moral agents. The more considerations they take into account, the more they consider the welfare of those around, the closer they will come to making a defensible choice.

A crucial issue facing us is the need to find ways of educating young persons to such sensitivity and potency. As important, it seems to me, is the matter of wide-awakeness for their teachers. It is far too easy for teachers, like other people, to play their roles and do their jobs without serious consideration of the good and right. Ironically, it is even possible when they are using classroom manuals for moral education. This is partly due to the impact of a vaguely apprehended relativism, partly to a bland carelessness, a shrugging off (sometimes because of grave self-doubt) of responsibility, I am convinced that, if teachers today are to initiate young people into an ethical existence, they themselves must attend more fully than they normally have to their own lives and its requirements; they have to break with the mechanical life, to overcome their own submergence in the habitual, even in what they conceive to be the virtuous, and ask the "why" with which learning and moral reasoning begin.

"You do not," wrote Martin Buber, "need moral genius for educating character; you do need someone who is wholly alive and able to communicate himself directly to his fellow beings. His aliveness streams out to them and affects them most strongly and purely when he has no thought of affecting them. . . ."[5] This strikes me as true; but I cannot imagine an aliveness streaming out from someone who is half-asleep and out of touch with herself or himself. I am not proposing separate courses in moral education or value clarification to be taught by such a teacher. I am, rather, suggesting that attentiveness to the moral dimensions of existence ought to permeate many of the classes taught, that wide-awakeness ought to accompany every effort made to initiate persons into any form of life or academic discipline.

Therefore, I believe it important for teachers, no matter what their specialty, to be clear about how they ground their own values, their own conceptions of the good and of the possible. Do they find their sanctions in some supernatural reality? Are they revealed in holy books or in the utterances of some traditional authority? Do they, rather, depend upon their own private intuitions of what is good and right? Do they decide in each particular situation what will best resolve uncertainty, what works out for the best? Do they simply refer to conventional social morality, to prevailing codes, or to the law? Or do they refer beyond the law—to some domain of principle, of norm? To what extent are they in touch with the actualities of their own experiences, their own biographies, and the ways in which these affect the tone of their encounters with the young? Teachers need to be aware of how they personally confront the unnerving questions present in the lives of every teacher, every parent: What shall we teach them? How can we guide them? What hope can we offer them? How can we tell them what to do?

The risks are great, as are the uncertainties. We are no longer in a situation in which we can provide character-training with the assurance that it will make our children virtuous and just. We can no longer use systems of rewards and punishments and feel confident they will make youngsters comply. We recognize the futility of teaching rules or preaching pieties or presenting conceptions of the good. We can no longer set ourselves up as founts of wisdom, exemplars of righteousness, and expect to have positive effects. Children are active; children are different at the various stages of their growth. Engaged in transactions with an environment, each one must effect connections within his or her own experience. Using whatever capacities they have available, each one must himself or herself perceive the consequences of the acts he or she performs. Mustering their own resources, each one must embark—"through choice of action," as Dewey put it[6]—upon the formation of a self.

Moral education, it would seem, must be as specifically concerned with self-identification in a community as it is with the judgments persons are equipped to make at different ages. It has as much to do with interest and action in concrete situations as it does with the course of moral reasoning. It has as much to do with consciousness and imagination as it does with principle. Since it cannot take place outside the vital contexts of social life, troubling questions have to be constantly confronted. How can indifference be overcome? How can the influence of the media be contained? How can the young be guided to choose reflectively and compassionately, even as they are set free?

The problem, most will agree, is not to tell them what to do—but to help them attain some kind of clarity about how to choose, how to decide what to do. And this involves teachers directly, immediately—teachers as persons able to present themselves as critical thinkers willing to disclose their own principles and their own reasons as well as authentic persons living in the world, persons who are concerned—who care.

Many teachers, faced with demands like these, find themselves in difficult positions, especially if they are granted little autonomy, or their conceptions of their own projects are at odds with what their schools demand. Today they may be held accountable for teaching predefined competencies and skills or for achieving objectives that are often largely behavioral. At once, they may be expected to represent both the wider culture and the local community, or the international community and the particular community of the individual child. If teachers are not critically conscious, if they are not awake to their own values and commitments (and to the conditions working upon them), if they are not personally engaged with their subject matter and with the world around, I do not see how they can initiate the young into critical questioning or the moral life.

I am preoccupied, I suppose, with what Camus called "the plague"—that terrible distancing and indifference, so at odds with commitment and communion and love. I emphasize this because I want to stress the connection between wide-awakeness, cognitive clarity, and existential concern. I want to highlight the fact that the roots of moral choosing lie at the core of a person's conception of herself or himself and the equally important fact that choosing involves action as well as thought. Moral action, of course, demands choosing between alternatives, usually between two goods, not between good and bad or right and wrong. The problem in teaching is to empower persons to internalize and incarnate the kinds of principles that will enable them to make such choices. Should I do what is thought to be my duty and volunteer for the army, or should I resist what I believe to be an unjust war. Should I steal the medicine to save my mother's life, or should I obey the law and risk letting her die?

These are choices of consequence for the self and others; and they are made, they can only be made in social situations where custom, tradition, official codes, and laws condition and play upon what people think and do. We might think of Huck Finn's decision not to return Jim to his owner or of Anna Karenina's decision to leave her husband. These are only morally significant in relation to a particular fabric of codes and customs and rules. Think of the Danish king's wartime decision to stand with Denmark's Jewish citizens, Daniel Ellsberg's decision to publish the Pentagon Papers, or Pablo Casals' refusal to conduct in fascist Spain. These decisions too were made in a matrix of principles, laws, and ideas of what is considered acceptable, absolutely, or conditionally good and right. To be moral involves taking a position towards that matrix, thinking critically about what is taken for granted. It involves taking a principled position of one's own (*choosing* certain principles by which to live) and speaking clearly about it, so as to set oneself on the right track.

It is equally important to affirm that it is always the individual, acting voluntarily in a particular situation at a particular moment, who does the deciding. I do not mean that individuals are isolated, answerable only to themselves. I do mean that individuals, viewed as participants, as inextricably involved with other peo-

ple, must be enabled to take responsibility for their own choosing, must not merge themselves or hide themselves in what Soren Kierkegaard called "the crowd."[7] If individuals act automatically or conventionally, if they do only what is expected of them (or because they feel they have no right to speak for themselves), if they do only what they are told to do, they are not living moral lives.

Indeed, I rather doubt that individuals who are cowed or flattened out or depressed or afraid can learn, since learning inevitably involves a free decision to enter into a form of life, to proceed in a certain way, to do something because it is right. There are paradigms to be found in many kinds of teaching for those interested in moral education, since teaching is in part a process of moving people to proceed according to a specified set of norms. If individuals are wide-awake and make decisions consciously to interpret a poem properly, to try to understand a period in English history, or to participate in some type of social inquiry, they are choosing to abide by certain standards made available to them. In doing so, they are becoming acquainted with what it means to choose a set of norms. They are not only creating value for themselves, they are creating themselves; they are moving towards more significant, more understandable lives.

Consider, with norms and self-creation in mind, the case of Nora in Ibsen's *The Doll's House.* If she simply ran out of the house in tears at the end, she would not have been engaging in moral action. Granting the fact that she was defying prevailing codes, I would insist that she was making a decision in accord with an internalized norm. It might be called a principle of emancipation, having to do with the right to grow, to become, to be more than a doll in a doll's house. If asked, Nora might have been able to generalize and talk about the right of *all* human beings to develop in their own fashion, to be respected, to be granted integrity.

Principles or norms are general ideas of that kind, arising out of experience and used by individuals in the appraisal of situations they encounter as they live—to help them determine what they ought to do. They are not specific rules, like the rules against stealing and lying and adultery. They are general and comprehensive. They concern justice and equality, respect for the dignity of persons and regard for their points of view. They have much to do with the ways in which diverse individuals choose themselves; they are defined reflectively and imaginatively and against the backgrounds of biography. When they are incarnated in a person's life, they offer him or her the means for analyzing particular situations. They offer perspectives, points of view from which to consider particular acts. The Golden Rule is such a principle, but, as Dewey says, the Golden Rule does not finally decide matters just by enabling us to tell people to consider the good of others as they would their own. "It suggests," he writes, "the necessity of considering how our acts affect the interests of others as well as our own; it tends to prevent partiality of regard. . . . In short, the Golden Rule does not issue special orders or commands; but it does clarify and illuminate the situations requiring intelligent deliberation."[8] So it was with the principle considered by Ibsen's Nora; so it is with the principle of justice and the principles of care and truth-telling. Our hope in teaching is that persons will appropriate such principles and learn to live by them.

Now it is clear that young people have to pass through the stages of heteronomy in their development towards the degree of autonomy they require for acting on principle in the way described. They must achieve the kind of wide-awakeness I have been talking about, the ability to think about what they are doing, to take responsibility. The teaching problem seems to me to be threefold. It involves equipping young people with the ability to identify alternatives, and to see possibilities in the situations confront. It involves the teaching of principles, possible perspectives by means of which those situations can be assessed and appraised, *as well as* the norms governing historical inquiry, ballet dancing, or cooperative living, norms that must be appropriated by persons desiring to join particular human communities. It also involves enabling students to make decisions of principle, to reflect, to articulate, and to take decisive actions in good faith.

Fundamental to the whole process may be the building up of a sense of moral directedness, of oughtness. An imaginativeness, an awareness, and a sense of possibility are required, along with the sense of autonomy and agency, of being present to the self. There must be attentiveness to others and to the circumstances of everyday life. There must be efforts made to discover ways of living together justly and pursuing common ends. As wide-awake teachers work, making principles available and eliciting moral judgments, they must orient themselves to the concrete, the relevant, and the questionable. They must commit themselves to each person's potentiality for overcoming helplessness and submergence, for looking through his or her own eyes at the shared reality.

I believe this can only be done if teachers can identify themselves as moral beings, concerned with defining their own life purposes in a way that arouses others to do the same. I believe, you see, that the young are most likely to be stirred to learn when they are challenged by teachers who themselves are learning, who are breaking with what they have too easily taken for granted, who are creating their own moral lives. There are no guarantees, but wide-awakeness can play a part in the process of liberating and arousing, in helping people pose questions with regard to what is oppressive, mindless, and wrong. Surely, it can help people— all kinds of people—make the conscious endeavors needed to elevate their lives.

Camus, in an essay called "The Almond Trees," wrote some lines that seem to me to apply to teachers, especially those concerned in this way. He was talking about how endless are our tasks, how impossible it is to overcome the human condition—which, at least, we have come to know better than ever before:

We must mend "what has been torn apart, make justice imaginable again—give happiness a meaning once more. . . . Naturally, it is a superhuman task. But superhuman is the term for tasks men take a long time to accomplish, that's all. Let us know our aims, then, holding fast to the mind. . . . The first thing is not to despair.[9]

Endnotes

1. Henry David Thoreau, *Walden* (New York: Washington Square Press, 1963), pp. 66–67.
2. Alfred Schutz, ed. Maurice Natanson, *The Problem of Social Reality,* Collected Papers I (The Hague: Martinus Nijhoff, 1967), p. 213.
3. Albert Camus, *The Myth of Sisyphus* (New York: Alfred A. Knopf, 1955), p. 13.
4. George Konrad, *The Case Worker* (New York: Harcourt Brace Jovanovich, 1974), p. 168.
5. Martin Buber, *Between Man and Man* (Boston: Beacon Press, 1957), p. 105.
6. John Dewey, *Democracy and Education* (New York: Macmillan Company, 1916), p. 408.
7. Soren Kierkegaard, "The Individual," in *The Point of View for My Work as an Author* (New York: Harper & Row, 1962), pp. 102–136.
8. Dewey, *Theory of the Moral Life* (New York: Holt, Rinehart and Winston, 1960), p. 142.
9. Camus, "'The Almond Trees," in *Lyrical and Critical Essays* (New York: Alfred A. Knopf, 1968), p. 135.

The Ideal of the Educated Person

JANE ROLAND MARTIN

R. S. Peters calls it an ideal.[1] So do Nash, Kazemias and Perkinson who, in their introduction to a collection of studies in the history of educational thought, say that one cannot go about the business of education without it.[2] Is it the good life? the responsible citizen? personal autonomy? No, it is the educated man.

The educated man! In the early 1960s when I was invited to contribute to a book of essays to be entitled *The Educated Man,* I thought nothing of this phrase. By the early 1970s I felt uncomfortable whenever I came across it, but I told myself it was the thought not the words that counted. It is now the early 1980s. Peters's use of the phrase "educated man" no longer troubles me for I think it fair to say that he intended it in a gender-neutral way.[3] Despite one serious lapse which indicates that on some occasions he was thinking of his educated man as male, I do not doubt that the ideal he set forth was meant for males and females alike.[4] Today my concern is not Peters's language but his conception of the educated man—or person, as I will henceforth say. I will begin by outlining Peters's ideal for you and will then show that it does serious harm to women. From there I will go on to argue that Peters's ideal is inadequate for men as well as women and, furthermore, that its inadequacy for men is intimately connected to the injustice it does women. In conclusion I will explore some of the requirements an adequate ideal must satisfy.

Let me explain at the outset that I have chosen to discuss Peters's ideal of the educated person here because for many years Peters has been perhaps the dominant figure in philosophy of education. Moreover, although Peters's ideal is formulated in philosophically sophisticated terms, it is certainly not idiosyncratic. On the contrary, Peters claims to have captured our concept of the educated person, and he may well have done so. Thus, I think it fair to say that the traits Peters

claims one must possess to be a truly educated person and the kind of education he assumes one must have in order to acquire those traits would, with minor variations, be cited by any number of people today if they were to describe their own conception of the ideal. I discuss Peters's ideal, then. because it has significance for the field of philosophy of education as a whole.

I. R. S. Peters's Educated Person

The starting point of Peters's philosophy of education is the concept of the educated person. While granting that we sometimes use the term "education" to refer to any process of rearing, bringing up, instructing, etc., Peters distinguishes this very broad sense of "education" from the narrower one in which he is interested. The concept of the educated person provides the basis for this distinction: whereas "education" in the broad sense refers to any process of rearing, etc., "education" in the narrower, and to him philosophically more important, sense refers to the family of processes which have as their outcome the development of an educated person.[5]

Peters set forth his conception of the educated person in some detail in his book, *Ethics and Education.*[6] Briefly, an educated person is one who does not simply possess knowledge. An educated person has a body of knowledge and some kind of conceptual scheme to raise this knowledge above the level of a collection of disjointed facts which in turn implies some understanding of principles for organizing facts and of the "reason why" of things. Furthermore, the educated person's knowledge is not inert: it characterizes the person's way of looking at things and involves "the kind of commitment that comes from getting on the inside of a form of thought and awareness"; that is to say, the educated person cares about the standards of evidence

From "The Ideal of the Educated Person" by Jane Roland Martin, Spring 1981, *Educational Theory, 31*(2), pp. 97–109. Copyright 1982 by the Board of Trustees of the University of Illinois. Copyright permission for this article has been granted by the Board of Trustees of the University of Illinois and the editor of *Educational Theory.*

implicit in science or the canons of proof inherent in mathematics. Finally, the educated person has cognitive perspective. In an essay entitled "Education and the Educated Man" published several years later, Peters added to this portrait that the educated person's pursuits can be practical as well as theoretical so long as the person delights in them for their own sake, and that both sorts of pursuits involve standards to which the person must be sensitive.[7] He also made it clear that knowledge enters into his conception of the educated person in three ways, namely, depth, breadth and knowledge of good.

In their book, *Education and Personal Relationships,* Downie, Loudfoot and Telfer presented a conception of the educated person which is a variant on Peters's.[8] I cite it here not because they too use the phrase "educated man," but to show that alternate philosophical conceptions of the educated person differ from Peters's only in detail. Downie, Loudfoot and Telfer's educated person has knowledge which is wide ranging in scope, extending from history and geography to the natural and social sciences and to current affairs. This knowledge is important, relevant and grounded. The educated person understands what he or she knows, knows how to do such things as history and science, and has the inclination to apply this knowledge, to be critical and to have curiosity in the sense of a thirst for knowledge. Their major departure from Peters's conception—and it is not, in the last analysis, very major—is to be found in their concern with knowledge by acquaintance: the educated person must not merely have knowledge *about* works of art—and, if I understand them correctly, about moral and religious theories—but must know these as individual things.

Consider now the knowledge, the conceptual scheme which raises this knowledge above the level of disjointed facts and the cognitive perspective Peters's educated person must have. It is quite clear that Peters does not intend that these be acquired through the study of cooking and driving. Mathematics, science, history, literature, philosophy—these are the subjects which constitute the curriculum for his educated person. In short, his educated person is one who has had—and profited from—a liberal education of the sort outlined by Paul Hirst in his famous essay, "Liberal Education and the Nature of Knowledge." Hirst describes what is sought in a liberal education as follows:

first, sufficient immersion in the concepts, logic and criteria of the discipline for a person to come to know the

distinctive way in which it "works" by pursuing these in particular cases; and then sufficient generalization of these over the whole range of the discipline so that his experience begins to be widely structured in this distinctive manner. It is this coming to look at things in a certain way that is being aimed at, not the ability to work out in minute particulars all the details that can be in fact discerned. It is the ability to recognize empirical assertions or aesthetic judgments for what they are, and to know the kind of consideration on which their validity will depend, that matters.[9]

If Peters's educated person is not in fact Hirst's liberally educated person, he or she is certainly its identical twin.

Liberal education, in Hirst's view, consists in an initiation into what he calls the forms of knowledge. There are, on his count, seven of them. Although he goes to some lengths in his later writings on the topic to deny that these forms are themselves intellectual disciplines, it is safe to conclude that his liberally educated person, and hence Peters's educated person, will acquire the conceptual schemes and cognitive perspectives they are supposed to have through a study of mathematics, physical science, history, the human sciences, literature, fine arts, philosophy. These disciplines will not necessarily be studied separately: an interdisciplinary curriculum is compatible with the Peters-Hirst ideal. But it is nonetheless their subject matter, their conceptual apparatus, their standards of proof and adequate evidence, their way of looking at things that must be acquired if the ideal is to be realized.

II. Initiation into Male Cognitive Perspectives

What is this certain way in which the educated person comes to look at things? What is the distinctive manner in which that person's experience is structured? A body of literature documenting the many respects in which the disciplines of knowledge ignore or misrepresent the experience and lives of women has developed over the last decade. I cannot do justice here to its range of concerns or its sophisticated argumentation. Through the use of examples, however, I will try to give you some sense of the extent to which the intellectual disciplines incorporate a male cognitive perspective, and hence a sense of the extent to which Hirst's liberally educated person and its twin—Peters's educated person—look at things through male eyes.

Let me begin with history. "History is past politics" was the slogan inscribed on the seminar room wall at Johns Hopkins in the days of the first doctoral program.[10] In the late 1960s the historian, Richard Hofstadter, summarized his field by saying: "Memory is the thread of personal identity, history of public identity." History has defined itself as the record of the public and political aspects of the past; in other words, as the record of the productive processes—man's sphere—of society. Small wonder that women are scarcely mentioned in historical narratives! Small wonder that they have been neither the objects nor the subjects of historical inquiry until very recently! The reproductive processes of society which have traditionally been carried on by women are excluded *by definition* from the purview of the discipline.

If women's lives and experiences have been excluded from the subject matter of history, the works women have produced have for the most part been excluded from literature and the fine arts. It has never been denied that there have been women writers and artists, but their works have not often been deemed important or significant enough to be studied by historians and critics. Thus, for example, Catherine R. Stimpson has documented the treatment accorded Gertrude Stein by two journals which exert a powerful influence in helping to decide what literature is and what books matter.[11] Elaine Showalter, pursuing a somewhat different tack, has documented the double standard which was used in the nineteenth century to judge women writers: all the most desirable aesthetic qualities—for example, power, breadth, knowledge of life, humor—were assigned to men; the qualities assigned to women, such as refinement, tact, precise observation, were not considered sufficient for the creation of an excellent novel.[12]

The disciplines are guilty of different kinds of sex bias. Even as literature and the fine arts exclude women's works from their subject matter, they include works which construct women according to the male image of her. One might expect this tendency to construct the female to be limited to the arts, but it is not. Naomi Weisstein has shown that psychology constructs the female personality to fit the preconceptions of its male practitioners, clinicians either accepting theory without evidence or finding in their data what they want to find.[13] And Ruth Hubbard has shown that this tendency extends even to biology where the stereotypical picture of the passive female is projected by the male practitioners of that field onto the animal kingdom.[14]

There are, indeed, two quite different ways in which a discipline can distort the lives, experiences and personalities of women. Even as psychology constructs the female personality out of our cultural stereotype, it holds up standards of development for women to meet which are derived from studies using male subjects.[15] Not surprisingly, long after the source of the standards is forgotten, women are proclaimed to be underdeveloped and inferior to males in relation to these standards. Thus, for example, Carol Gilligan has pointed out that females are classified as being at Stage 3 of Kohlberg's six stage sequence of moral development because important differences in moral development between males and females are ignored.[16]

In the last decade scholars have turned to the study of women. Thus, historical narratives and analyses of some aspects of the reproductive processes of society—of birth control, childbirth, midwifery, for example—have been published.[17] The existence of such scholarship is no guarantee, however, of its integration into the mainstream of the discipline of history itself, yet this latter is required if initiation into history as a form of knowledge is not to constitute initiation into a male cognitive perspective. The title of a 1974 anthology on the history of women, *Clio's Consciousness Raised,* is unduly optimistic.[18] Certainly, the consciousness of some historians has been raised, but there is little reason to believe that the discipline of history has redefined itself so that studies of the reproductive processes of society are not simply tolerated as peripherally relevant, but are considered to be as central to it as political, economic and military narratives are. Just as historians have begun to study women's past, scholars in literature and the fine arts have begun to bring works by women to our attention and to reinterpret the ones we have always known.[19] But there is still the gap between feminist scholarship and the established definitions of literary and artistic significance to be bridged, and until it is, the initiation into these disciplines provided by a liberal education will be an initiation into male perspectives

In sum, the intellectual disciplines into which a person must be initiated to become an educated person *exclude* women and their works, *construct* the female to the male image of her and *deny* the truly feminine qualities she does possess. The question remains of whether the male cognitive perspective of the disciplines is integral to Peters's ideal of the educated person. The answer to this question is to be found in Hirst's essay, "The Forms of Knowledge Revisited."[20] There he presents the view that at any given time a liberal education consists in an initiation into *existing* forms of knowledge. Hirst acknowledges that new forms can develop and that old ones can disappear. Still, the analysis he gives of the seven distinct forms which he takes to comprise a liberal education today is based, he says on our present conceptual scheme. Thus, Peters's educated person is not one who studies a set of ideal, unbiased forms of knowledge; on the contrary, that person is one who is initiated into whatever forms of knowledge exist in the society at that time. In our time the existing forms embody a male point of view. The initiation into them envisioned by Hirst and Peters is, therefore, one in male cognitive perspectives.

Peters's educated person is expected to have grasped the basic structure of science, history and the like rather than the superficial details of content. Is it possible that the feminist critique of the disciplines therefore leaves his ideal untouched? It would be a grave misreading of the literature to suppose that this critique presents simply a surface challenge to the disciplines. Although the examples I have cited here may have suggested to you that the challenge is directed at content alone, it is in fact many pronged. Its targets include the questions asked by the various fields of inquiry and the answers given them: the aims of those fields and the ways they define their subject matter; the methods they use, their canons of objectivity, and their ruling metaphors. It is difficult to be clear on precisely which aspects of knowledge and inquiry are at issue when Hirst speaks of initiation into a form of knowledge. A male bias has been found on so many levels of the disciplines, however, that I think we can feel quite confident that it is a property also of the education embodied in Peters's ideal.

III. Genderized Traits

The masculinity of Peters's educated person is not solely a function of a curriculum in the intellectual disciplines, however. Consider the traits or characteristics Peters attributes to the educated person. Feelings and emotions only enter into the makeup of the educated person to the extent that being committed to the standards of a theoretical pursuit such as science, or a practical one such as architecture, counts as such. Concern for people and for interpersonal relationships has no role to play: the educated person's sensitivity is to the standards immanent in activities, not to other human beings; an imaginative awareness of emotional atmosphere and interpersonal/relationships need be no part of this person's makeup, nor is the educated person thought to be empathic or supportive or nurturant. Intuition is also neglected. Theoretical knowledge and what Woods and Barrow—two more philosophers who use the phrase "educated man"—call "reasoned understanding" are the educated person's prime characteristics:[21] even this person's practical pursuits are to be informed by some theoretical perspectives; moreover, this theoretical bent is to be leavened neither by imaginative nor intuitive powers, for these are never to be developed.

The educated person as portrayed by Peters, and also by Downie, Loudfoot and Telfer, and by Woods and Barrow, coincides with our cultural stereotype of a male human being. According to that stereotype men are objective, analytic, rational; they are interested in ideas and things; they have no interpersonal orientation; they are neither nurturant nor supportive, empathetic or sensitive. According to the stereotype, nurturance and supportiveness, empathy and sensitivity are female attributes. Intuition is a female attribute too.[22]

This finding is not really surprising. It has been shown that psychologists define moral development, adult development and even human development in male terms and that therapists do the same for mental health.[23] Why suppose that philosophers of education have avoided the androcentric fallacy?[24] Do not misunderstand! Females can acquire the traits and dispositions which constitute Peters's conception of the educated person; he espouses an ideal which, if it can be attained at all, can be by both sexes.[25] But our culture associates the traits and dispositions of Peters's educated person with males. To apply it to females is to impose on them a masculine mold. I realize that as a matter of fact some females fit our male stereotype and that some males do not, but this does not affect the point at issue, which is that Peters has set forth an ideal for education which embodies just those traits and dispositions our culture attributes to the male sex and excludes the traits our culture attributes to the female sex.

Now it might seem that if the mold is a good one, it does not matter that it is masculine; that if the traits which Peters's educated person possesses are desirable, then it makes no difference that in our society they are associated with males. Indeed, some would doubtless argue that in extending to women cognitive virtues which have long been associated with men and which education has historically reserved for men, Peters's theory of education strikes a blow for sex equality. It does matter that the traits Peters assigns the educated person are considered in our culture to be masculine, however. It matters because some traits which males and females can both possess are *genderized;* that is, they are appraised differentially according to sex.[26]

Consider aggressiveness. The authors of a book on assertive training for women report that in the first class meetings of their training courses they ask their students to call out the adjectives which come to mind when we say "aggressive woman" and "aggressive man." Here is the list of adjectives the women used to describe an aggressive man: "masculine," "dominating," "successful," "heroic," "capable," "strong," "forceful," "manly." Need I tell you the list of adjectives they used to describe an aggressive woman?: "harsh," "pushy," "bitchy," "domineering," "obnoxious," "emasculating," "uncaring."[27]

I submit to you that the traits Peters attributes to the educated person are, like the trait of aggressiveness, evaluated differently for males and females. Imagine a woman who is analytical and critical, whose intellectual curiosity is strong, who cares about the canons of science and mathematics. How is she described? "She thinks like a man," it is said. To be sure, this is considered by some to be the highest accolade. Still, a woman who is said to think like a man is being judged to be masculine, and since we take masculinity and femininity to lie at opposite ends of a single continuum, she is thereby being judged to be lacking in femininity.[28] Thus, while it is possible for a woman to possess the traits of Peters's educated person, she will do so at her peril: her possession of them will cause her to be viewed as unfeminine, i.e., as an unnatural or abnormal woman.

IV. A Double Bind

It may have been my concern over Peters's use of the phrase "educated man" which led me to this investigation in the first place, but as you can see, the problem is not one of language. Had Peters consistently used the phrase "educated person" the conclusion that the ideal he holds up for education is masculine would be unaffected. To be sure, Peters's educated person can be male or female, but he or she will have acquired male cognitive perspectives and will have developed traits which in our society are genderized in favor of males.

I have already suggested that Peters's ideal places a burden on women because the traits constituting it are evaluated negatively when possessed by females. The story of Rosalind Franklin, the scientist who con-

tributed to the discovery of the structure of DNA, demonstrates that when a woman displays the kind of critical, autonomous thought which is an attribute of Peters's educated person, she is derided for what are considered to be negative unpleasant characteristics.[29] Rosalind Franklin consciously opted out of "woman's sphere" and entered the laboratory. From an abstract point of view the traits she possessed were quite functional there. Nonetheless she was perceived to be an interloper, an alien who simply could not be taken seriously in relation to the production of new, fundamental ideas no matter what her personal qualities might be.[30]

But experiencing hostility and derision is the least of the suffering caused women by Peters's ideal. His educated person is one who will know nothing about the lives women have led throughout history and little if anything about the works or art and literature women have produced. If his educated person is a woman, she will have been presented with few female role models in her studies whereas her male counterpart will be able to identify with the doers and thinkers and makers of history. Above all, the certain way in which his educated man and woman will come to look at the world will be one in which men are perceived as they perceive themselves and women are perceived as men perceive them.

To achieve Peters's ideal one must acquire cognitive perspectives through which one sex is perceived on its own terms and one sex is perceived as the Other.[31] Can it be doubted that when the works of women are excluded from the subject matter of the fields into which they are being initiated, students will come to believe that males are superior and females are inferior human beings? That when in the course of this initiation the lives and experiences of women are scarcely mentioned, students will come to believe that the way in which women have lived and the things women have done throughout history have no value? Can it be doubted that these beliefs do female students serious damage? The woman whose self-confidence is bolstered by an education which transmits the message that females are inferior human beings is rare. Rarer still is the woman who, having been initiated into alien cognitive perspectives, gains confidence in her own powers without paying the price of self-alienation.

Peters's ideal puts women in a double bind. To be educated they must give up their own way of experiencing and looking at the world, thus alienating themselves from themselves. To be unalienated they must remain uneducated. Furthermore, to be an educated person a female must acquire traits which are appraised negatively when she possesses them. At the same time, the traits which are evaluated positively when possessed by her—for example, being nurturant and empathetic—are excluded from the ideal. Thus a female who has acquired the traits of an educated person will not be evaluated positively for having them, while one who has acquired those traits for which she will be positively evaluated will not have achieved the ideal. Women are placed in this double bind because Peters's ideal incorporates traits genderized in favor of males and excludes traits genderized in favor of females. It thus puts females in a no-win situation. Yes, men and women can both achieve Peters's ideal. However, women suffer, as men do not, for doing so.

Peters's masculine ideal of the educated person harms males as well as females, however. In a chapter of the 1981 NSSE Yearbook I argued at some length that Hirst's account of liberal education is seriously deficient.[32] Since Peters's educated person is to all intents and purposes Hirst's liberally educated person, let me briefly repeat my criticism of Hirst here. The Peters-Hirst educated person will have knowledge about others, but will not have been taught to care about their welfare, let alone to act kindly toward them. That person will have some understanding of society, but will not have been taught to feel its injustices or even to be concerned over its fate. The Peters Hirst educated person is an ivory tower person: a person who can reason yet has no desire to solve real problems in the real world; a person who understands science but does not worry about the uses to which it is put; a person who can reach flawless moral conclusions but feels no care or concern for others.

Simply put, quite apart from the burden it places on women, Peters's ideal of the educated person is far too narrow to guide the educational enterprise. Because it presupposes a divorce of mind from body, thought from action, and reason from feeling and emotion, it provides at best an ideal of an educated *mind,* not an educated *person.* To the extent that its concerns are strictly cognitive however, even in that guise it leaves much to be desired.

V. Education for Productive Processes

Even if Peters's ideal did not place an unfair burden on women it would need to be rejected for the harm it does

men, but its inadequacy as an ideal for men and the injustice it does women are not unconnected. In my Yearbook essay I sketched in the rough outlines of a new paradigm of liberal education, one which would emphasize the development of persons and not simply rational minds; one which would join thought to action, and reason to feeling and emotion. I could just as easily have called it a new conception of the educated person. What I did not realize when I wrote that essay is that the aspects of the Peters-Hirst ideal which I found so objectionable are directly related to the role, traditionally considered to be male, which their educated person is to play in society.

Peters would vehemently deny that he conceives of education as production. Nonetheless, he implicitly attributes to education the task of turning raw material, namely the *un*educated person, into an end product whose specifications he sets forth in his account of the concept of the educated person. Peters would deny even more vehemently that he assigns to education a societal function. Yet an examination of his conception of the educated person reveals that the end product of the education he envisions is designed to fit into a specific place in the social order; that he assigns to education the function of developing the traits and qualities and to some extent the skills of one whose role is to use and produce ideas.[33]

Peters would doubtless say that the production and consumption of ideas is everyone's business and that an education for this is certainly not an education which fits people into a particular place in society. Yet think of the two parts into which the social order has traditionally been divided. Theorists have put different labels on them, some referring to the split between work and home, others to the public and private domains and still others to productive and reproductive processes.[34] Since the public/ private distinction has associations for educators which are not germaine to the present discussion while the work/home distinction obscures some important issues, I will speak here of productive and reproductive processes. I do not want to make terminology the issue, however. If you prefer other labels, by all means substitute them for mine. My own is only helpful, I should add, if the term "reproduction" is construed broadly. Thus I use it here to include not simply biological reproduction of the species, but the whole process of reproduction from conception until the individual reaches more or less independence from the family.[35] This process I take to include not simply childcare and rearing, but the related activities of keeping house, running the household and serving the needs and purposes of all the family members. Similarly, I interpret the term "production" broadly to include political, social and cultural activities and processes as well as economic ones.

Now this traditional division drawn within the social order is accompanied by a separation of the sexes. Although males and females do in fact participate in both the reproductive and productive processes of society, the reproductive processes are considered to constitute "woman's sphere" and the productive processes "man's sphere." Although Peters's educated person is ill-equipped for jobs in trades or work on the assembly line, this person is tailor-made for carrying on certain of the productive processes of society, namely those which require work with heads, not hands. Thus his educated person is designed to fill a role in society which has traditionally been considered to be male. Moreover, he or she is not equipped by education to fill roles associated with the reproductive processes of society, i.e., roles traditionally considered to be female.

Once the functionalism of Peters's conception of the educated person is made explicit, the difficulty of including it in the ideal feelings and emotions such as caring and compassion, or skills of cooperation and nurturance, becomes clear. These fall under our culture's female stereotype. They are considered to be appropriate for those who carry on the reproductive processes of society but irrelevant, if not downright dysfunctional, for those who carry on the productive processes of society. It would therefore be irrational to include them in an ideal which is conceived of solely in relation to productive processes.

I realize now, as I did not before, that for the ideal of the educated person to be as broad as it should be, the two kinds of societal processes which Peters divorces from one another must be joined together.[36] An adequate ideal of the educated person must give the reproductive processes of society their due. An ideal which is tied solely to the productive processes of society cannot readily accommodate the important virtues of caring and compassion, sympathy and nurturance, generosity and cooperation which are genderized in favor of females.

To be sure, it would be possible in principle to continue to conceive of the educated person solely in relation to the productive processes of society while rejecting the stereotypes which produce genderized

traits. One could include caring and compassion in the ideal of the educated person on the grounds that although they are thought to be female traits whose home is in the reproductive processes of society, they are in fact functional in the production and consumption of ideas. The existence of genderized traits is not the only reason for giving the reproductive processes of society their due in an ideal of the educated person, however. These processes are themselves central to the lives of each of us and to the life of society as a whole. The dispositions, knowledge, skills required to carry them out well are not innate, nor do they simply develop naturally over time. Marriage, childrearing, family life: these involve difficult, complex, learned activities which can be done well or badly. Just as an educated person should be one in whom head, hand and heart are integrated, he or she should be one who is at home carrying on the reproductive processes of society, broadly understood, as well as the productive processes.

Now Peters might grant that the skills, traits, and knowledge necessary for carrying on reproductive processes are learned—in some broad sense of the term, at least—but argue that one does not require an education in them for they are picked up in the course of daily living. Perhaps at one time they were picked up in this way, and perhaps in some societies they are now. But it is far from obvious that, just by living, most adults in our society today acquire the altruistic feelings and emotions, the skills of childrearing, the understanding of what values are important to transmit and which are not, and the ability to put aside one's own projects and enter into those of others which are just a few of the things required for successful participation in the reproductive processes of society.

That education is needed by those who carry on the reproductive processes is not in itself proof that it should be encompassed by a conception of the educated person however, for this conception need not be all-inclusive. It need not be all inclusive but, for Peters, education which is not guided by his ideal of the educated person scarcely deserves attention. Moreover, since a conception of the educated person tends to function as an ideal, one who becomes educated will presumably have achieved something worthwhile. Value is attached to being an educated person: to the things an educated person knows and can do; to the tasks and activities that person is equipped to perform. The exclusion of education for reproductive processes from the ideal of the educated person thus carries with it an unwarranted negative value judgment about the tasks and activities, the traits and dispositions which are associated with them.

VI. Redefining the Ideal

An adequate ideal of the educated person must give the reproductive processes of society their due, but it must do more than this. After all, these processes were acknowledged by Rousseau in Book V of *Emile*.[37] There he set forth two distinct ideals of the educated person, the one for Emile tied to the productive processes of society and the one for Sophie tied to the reproductive processes. I leave open here the question Peters never asks of whether we should adopt one or more ideals of the educated person.[38] One thing is clear, however. We need a conception which does not fall into the trap of assigning males and females to the different processes of society, yet does not make the mistake of ignoring one kind of process altogether. We all participate in both kinds of processes and both are important to all of us. Whether we adopt one or many ideals, a conception of the educated person which is tied only to one kind of process will be incomplete.

An adequate ideal of the educated person must also reflect a realistic understanding of the limitations of existing forms or disciplines of knowledge. In my Yearbook chapter I made a case for granting them much less "curriculum space" than Hirst and Peters do. So long as they embody a male cognitive perspective, however, we must take into account not simply the amount of space they occupy in the curriculum of the educated person, but the hidden messages which are received by those who are initiated into them. An ideal of the educated person cannot itself rid the disciplines of knowledge of their sex bias. But it can advocate measures for counteracting the harmful effects on students of coming to see things solely through male eyes.

The effects of an initiation into male cognitive perspectives constitute a hidden curriculum. Alternative courses of action are open to us when we find a hidden curriculum and there is no reason to suppose that only one is appropriate. Let me say a few words here, however, about a course of action that might serve as at least a partial antidote to the hidden curriculum transmitted by an education in male biased disciplines.[39] When we find a hidden curriculum we can show it to its recipients; we can raise their consciousness, if you will, so that they will know what is hap-

pening to them. Raising to consciousness the male cognitive perspective of the disciplines of knowledge in the educated person's curriculum is no guarantee, of course, that educated females will not suffer from a lack of self-confidence and from self-alienation. Yet knowledge can be power. A curriculum which, through critical analysis, exposes the biased view of women embodied in the disciplines and which, by granting ample space to the study of women shows how unjust that view is, is certainly preferable to a curriculum which, by its silence on the subject, gives students the impression that the ways in which the disciplines look at the world are impartial and unbiased.

Now it might seem to be a relatively simple matter both to give the reproductive processes of society their due in an ideal of the educated person and to include in that ideal measures for counteracting the hidden curriculum of an education in the existing disciplines of knowledge. Yet given the way philosophy of education conceives of its subject matter today, it is not. The productive-reproductive dualism is built not simply into Peters's ideal but into our discipline.[40] We do not even have a vocabulary for discussing education in relation to the reproductive processes of society, for the distinction between liberal and vocational education which we use to cover the kinds of education we take to be philosophically important applies within productive processes: liberal and vocational education are both intended to fit people to carry on productive processes, the one for work with heads and the other for work with hands. The aims of education we analyze—critical thinking, rationality, individual autonomy, even creativity—are also associated in our culture with the productive, not the reproductive, processes of society. To give the reproductive processes their due in a conception of the educated person we will have to rethink the domain of philosophy of education.

Given the way we define our subject matter it is no more possible for us to take seriously the hidden curriculum I have set before you than the reproductive processes of society. Education, as we conceive of it, is an intentional activity.[41] Teaching is too.[42] Thus, we do not consider the unintended outcomes of education to be our concern. Moreover, following Peters and his colleagues, we draw a sharp line between logical and contingent relationships and treat the latter as if they were none of our business even when they are the *expected* outcomes of educational processes.[43] In sum, we leave it to the psychologists, sociologists and historians of education to worry about hidden curricula, not because we consider the topic unimportant—although perhaps some of us do—but because we consider it to fall outside our domain.

The redefinition of the subject matter of philosophy of education required by an adequate ideal of the educated person ought not to be feared. On the contrary, there is every reason to believe that it would ultimately enrich our discipline. If the experience and activities which have traditionally been considered to belong to women are included in the educational realm, a host of challenging and important issues and problems will present themselves for study. If the philosophy of education tackles questions about childrearing and the transmission of values, if it develops accounts of gender education to inform its theories of liberal education, if it explores the forms of thinking, feeling and acting associated with childrearing, marriage and the family, if the concepts of coeducation, mothering and nurturance become fair game for philosophical analysis, philosophy of education will be invigorated.

It would also be invigorated by taking seriously contingent as well as logical relationships. In divorcing educational processes from their empirical consequences and the mental structures which are said to be intrinsically related to knowledge from the empirical consequences of having them, we forget that education is a practical endeavor. It is often said that philosophy of education's concerns are purely conceptual, but the conclusion is inescapable that in analyzing such concepts as the educated person and liberal education we make recommendations for action. For these to be justified the contingent relationships which obtain between them and both the good life and the good society must be taken into account. A redefinition of our domain would allow us to provide our educational theorizing with the kind of justification it requires. It would also allow us to investigate the particularly acute and very challenging value questions that arise in relation to hidden curricula of all kinds.

Conclusion

In conclusion I would like to draw for you two morals which seem to me to emerge from my study of Peters's ideal of the educated person. The first is that Plato was wrong when, in Book V of the *Republic,* he said that sex is a difference which makes no difference.[44] I do not mean by this that there are inborn differences which suit males and females for separate and unequal roles in society. Rather, I mean that identical

educational treatment of males and females may not yield identical results so long as that treatment contains a male bias. There are sex differences in the way people are perceived and evaluated and there may well be sex differences in the way people think and learn and view the world. A conception of the educated person must take these into account. I mean also that the very nature of the ideal will be skewed. When sex or gender is thought to make no difference, women's lives, experiences, activities are overlooked and an ideal is formulated in terms of men and the roles for which they have traditionally been considered to be suited. Such an ideal is necessarily narrow for it is rooted in stereotypical ways of perceiving males and their place in society.

For some time I assumed that the sole alternative to a sex-biased conception of the educated person such as Peters set forth was a gender-free ideal, that is to say an ideal which did not take sex or gender into account. I now realize that sex or gender has to be taken into account if an ideal of the educated person is not to be biased. To opt at this time for a gender-free ideal is to beg the question. What is needed is a *gender-sensitive* ideal, one which takes sex or gender into account when it makes a difference and ignores it when it does not. Such an ideal would truly be gender-just.

The second moral is that *everyone* suffers when an ideal of the educated person fails to give the reproductive processes of society their due. Ideals which govern education solely in relation to the productive processes of society will necessarily be narrow. In their failure to acknowledge the valuable traits, dispositions, skills, traditionally associated with reproductive processes, they will harm both sexes although not always in the same ways.[45]

Endnotes

1. R. S. Peters, "Education and the Educated Man," in R. F. Dearden, P. H. Hirst, and R. S. Peters, eds., *A Critique of Current Educational Aims* (London: Routledge & Kegan Paul, 1972), pp. 7, 9.
2. Paul Nash, Andreas M. Kazemias, and Henry J. Perkinson, eds., *The Educated Man: Studies in the History of Educational Thought* (New York: John Wiley & Sons, 1965), p. 25.
3. For a discussion of "man" as a gender neutral term see Janice Moulton, "The Myth of the Neutral 'Man'," in Mary Vetterling-Braggin, Frederick A. Elliston, and Jane English, eds., *Feminism and Philosophy* (Totowa, NJ: Littlefield, Adams, 1977), pp.

124–137. Moulton rejects the view that "man" has a gender-neutral use.

4. Peters, "Education and the Educated Man," p. 11. Peters says in connection with the concept of the educated man: "For there are many who are not likely to go far with theoretical enquiries and who are unlikely to develop much depth or breadth of understanding to underpin and transform their dealings as workers, *husbands* and *fathers*" (emphasis added).

5. Ibid., p. 7.

6. R. S. Peters, *Ethics and Education* (London: George Allen & Unwin, 1966).

7. Peters, "Education and the Educated Man," pp. 9–11.

8. R. S. Downie, Eileen M. Loudfoot, and Elizabeth Telfer, *Education and Personal Relationships* (London: Methuen & Co., 1974), p. 11ff.

9. In Paul Hirst, *Knowledge and the Curriculum* (London: Routledge & Kegan Paul, 1974), p. 47.

10. Nancy Schrom Dye, "Clio's American Daughters," in Julia A. Sherman and Evelyn Torton Beck, eds., *The Prism ot Sex* (Madison: University of Wisconsin Press, 1979), p. 9.

11. Catherine R. Stimpson, "The Power to Name," in Sherman and Beck, eds., *Prism,* pp. 55–77.

12. Elaine Showalter, "Women Writers and the Double Standard," in Vivian Gornick and Barbara Moran, eds., *Women in Sexist Society* (New York: Basic Books, 1971), pp. 323–343.

13. Naomi Weisstein, "Psychology Constructs the Female" in Gornick and Moran, eds., *Women in Sexist Society,* pp. 133–146.

14. Ruth Hubbard, "Have Only Men Evolved?" in Ruth Hubbard, Mary Sue Henifin, and Barbara Fried, eds., *Women Look at Biology Looking at Women* (Cambridge: Schenkman Publishing Co., 1979), pp. 7–35.

15. Carol Gilligan, "Women's Place in Man's Life Cycle," *Harvard Educational Review* 49, 4 (1979): 431–446.

16. Carol Gilligan, "In a Different Voice: Women's Conceptions of Self and of Morality," *Harvard Educational Review* 47, 4 (1979): 481–517.

17. See, for example, Linda Gordon, *Woman's Body, Woman's Right: A Social History of Birth Control in America* (New York: Viking, 1976); Richard W. Wertz and Dorothy C. Wertz, *Lying-In* (New York: Free Press, 1977); Jean Donnison, *Midwives and Medical Men: A History of Interprofessional Rivalries and Women's Rights* (New York: Schocken Books, 1977).

18. Mary Hartman and Lois W. Banner, eds., *Clio's Consciousness Raised* (New York: Harper & Row, 1974).

19. See, for example, Carolyn G. Heilbrun, *Toward a Recognition of Androgyny* (New York: Alfred A. Knopf, 1973); Patricia Meyer Spacks, *The Female Imagination* (New York: Avon, 1975); Ellen Moers, *Literary Women* (New York: Anchor Books, 1977); Elaine Showalter, *A Literature of Their Own: British Women Novelists from Bronte to Lessing* (Princeton: Princeton University Press, 1977): Ann Sutherland Harris and Linda Nochlin, *Women Artists: 1550–1950* (New York: Alfred A. Knopf, 1976); Elsa Honig Fine, *Women and Art: A History of Women Painters and Sculptors from the Renaissance to the Twentieth Century* (Montclair and London: Allanheld & Schram/Prior, 1978); and Karen Peterson and J. J. Wilson, *Women Artists: Recognition and Reappraisal from the Early Middle Ages to the Twentieth Century* (New York: New York University Press, 1976).

20. In Paul Hirst, *Knowledge and the Curriculum,* p. 92.

21. R. G. Woods and R. St. C. Barrow, *An Introduction to Philosophy of Education* (Methuen & Co., 1975), Ch. 3.

22. For discussions of our male and female stereotypes see, e.g., Alexandra G. Kaplan and Joan P. Bean, eds., *Beyond Sex-role Stereotypes* (Boston: Little, Brown, 1976); and Alexandra G. Kaplan and Mary Anne Sedney, *Psychology and Sex Roles* (Boston: Little, Brown, 1980).

23. Carol Gilligan, "Women's Place"; I. Broverman, D. Broverman, F. Clarkson, P. Rosencrantz and S. Vogel, "Sex-role Stereotypes and Clinical Judgements of Mental Health," *Journal of Consulting and Clinical Psychology* 34 (1970): 1–7; Alexandra G. Kaplan, "Androgyny as a Model of Mental Health for Women: From Theory to Therapy," in Kaplan and Bean, eds., *Beyond Sex-role Stereotypes,* pp. 353–362.

24. One commits the androcentric fallacy when one argues from the characteristics associated with male human beings to the characteristics of all human beings. In committing it one often commits the naturalistic fallacy because the traits which are said to be natural to males are held up as ideals for the whole species.

25. I say *if* it can be attained by all, because it is not entirely clear that the ideal can be attained by *anyone* insofar as it requires mastery of Hirst's seven forms of knowledge.

26. See Elizabeth Beardsley, "Traits and Genderization," in Vetterling-Braggin, et al., eds., *Feminism and Philosophy,* pp. 117–123. Beardsley uses the term "genderization" to refer to language while I use it here to refer to traits themselves.

27. Lynn Z. Bloom, Karen Coburn, Joan Pearlman, *The New Assertive Woman* (New York: Delacorte Press, 1975), p. 12.

28. For discussion of the assumption that masculinity-femininity is a bipolar dimension see Anne Constantinople, "Masculinity-Femininity: An Exception to a Famous Dictum"; and Sandra L. Bern, "Probing the

Promise of Androgyny" in Kaplan and Bean, eds., *Beyond Sex-role Stereotypes.*

29. Anne Sayre, *Rosalind Franklin & DNA* (New York: W. W. Norton & Co., 1975). See also James D. Watson, *The Double Helix* (New York: Atheneum, 1968); and Horace Freeland Judson, *The Eighth Day of Creation* (New York: Simon and Schuster, 1979).

30. It is important to note, however, that some colleagues did take her seriously as a scientist; see Sayre, ibid. Adele Simmons cites historical evidence of the negative effects of having acquired such traits on women who did not opt out of "woman's sphere" in "Education and Ideology in Nineteenth-Century America: The Response of Educational Institutions to the Changing Role of Women," in Berenice A. Carroll, ed., *Liberating Women's History* (Urbana, IL: University of Illinois Press, 1976), p. 123. See also Patricia Meyer Spacks, *The Female Imagination* (New York: Avon Books, 1976), p. 25.

31. See Simone de Beauvoir, *The Second Sex* (New York: Bantam Books, 1961) for an extended discussion of woman as the Other.

32. Jane Roland Martin, "Needed: A Paradigm for Liberal Education," in Jonas F. Soltis, ed., *Philosophy and Education* (Chicago: National Society for the Study of Education, 1981), pp. 37–59.

33. For an account of education as production see Jane Roland Martin, "Sex Equality and Education: A Case Study," in Mary Vetterling-Braggin, ed., *"Femininity," "Masculinity," and "Androgyny"* (Totowa, N. J.: Littlefield, Adams, 1982). It should be noted that an understanding of the societal role for which Peters's educated person is intended illuminates both the sex bias and the class bias his ideal embodies.

34. For an interesting discussion and criticism of the two-sphere analysis of society, see Joan Kelly, "The Doubled Vision of Feminist Theory: A Postscript to the 'Women and Power' Conference," *Feminist Studies* 5, 1 (1979): 216–227. Kelly argues that a two-sphere analysis distorts reality and that feminist theory should discard it. I use it here as a convenient theoretical device.

35. I am indebted here to Lorenne M. G. Clark, "The Rights of Women: The Theory and Practice of the Ideology of Male Supremacy," in William R. Shea and John King-Farlow, eds., *Contemporary Issues in Political Philosophy* (New York: Science History Publications, 1976), pp. 49–65.

36. In saying that an adequate conception of the educated person must reject a sharp separation of productive and reproductive processes I do not mean that it must be committed to a specific philosophical theory of the relationship of the two. An adequate conception of the educated person should not divorce mind and body, but it does not follow from this that it must be committed to a specific view of the mind-body relationship; indeed, the union of mind and body in a theory of education is quite compatible with a dualistic philosophical account of the relationship between the two. Similarly, a theory of the educated person must not divorce one kind of societal process from the other even if the best account of the relationship of productive to reproductive processes should turn out to be dualistic.

37. Jean-Jacques Rousseau, *Emile* (New York: Basic Books, 1979, Allan Bloom, trans.). See also Lynda Lange, "Rousseau: Women and the General Will," in Lorenne M. G. Cark and Lynda Lange, eds., *The Sexism of Social and Political Theory* (Toronto: University of Toronto Press, 1979), pp. 41_52; Susan Moller Okin, *Women in Western Political Thought* (Princeton: Princeton University Press, 1979); and Jane Roland Martin, "Sophie and Emile: A Case Study of Sex Bias in the History of Educational Thought," *Harvard Educational Review* 51, 3 (1981): 357–372.

38. I also leave open the question of whether any ideal of the educated person should guide and direct education as a whole.

39. For more on this question see Jane Roland Martin, "What Should We Do with a Hidden Curriculum When We Find One?" *Curriculum Inquiry* 6, 2 (1976): 135–151.

40. On this point see Jane Roland Martin, "Excluding Women from the Educational Realm."

41. See, for example, Peters, *Ethics and Education.*

42. See, for example, Israel Scheffler, *The Language of Education* (Springfield, IL: Charles C. Thomas, 1960), Chs. 4, 5.

43. For a discussion of this point see Jane Roland Martin, "Response to Roemer," in Jerrold R. Coombs, ed., *Philosophy of Education 1979* (Normal, IL: Proceedings of the 35th Annual Meeting of the Philosophy of Education Society, 1980).

44. This point is elaborated on in Jane Roland Martin, "Sex Equality and Education: A Case Study."

45. I wish to thank Ann Diller, Carol Gilligan, Michael Martin and Janet Farrell Smith for helpful comments on earlier versions of this address which was written while I was a Fellow at the Mary Ingraham Bunting Institute of Radcliffe College.

6 Schools as Organizations and Teacher Professionalization

In this chapter, we explore the organizational characteristics of U.S. elementary and secondary education, school cultures, and the vocation of teaching. These topics are tied together by one underlying issue—the parameters and possibilities inherent in creating better schools. How can schools be distinguished organizationally, and why are some schools more effective learning environments than others? You undoubtedly have strong memories of the schools you attended, but have you ever wondered why these memories are so vivid? Why is it that schools create such powerful organizational cultures that deeply influence one's life and one's approach to learning? The schools that an individual attends shape not only his or her life chances but his or her perceptions, attitudes, and behaviors. Of course, schools operate in conjunction with families and society. No school is an island unto itself. Still, schools are powerful organizations that profoundly affect the lives of those children and adults who come in contact with them. It seems logical, therefore, that knowing more about schools' organizational characteristics is a first step in understanding their impact on students, teachers, and the society at large.

Education in the United States is one of the nation's largest businesses. According to the U.S. Department of Education (U.S. Department of Education, National Center for Educational Statistics, 1997a), elementary and secondary education was a $273 billion enterprise, serving 50 million students in 50 states and the District of Columbia. Understanding the complexity and enormity of the educational enterprise is a difficult task because it contains so many different elements. Just feeding all the youngsters who attend school every day is a substantial undertaking. The New York City Board of Education, for instance, serves more meals per day than Friendly's Restaurants. Supplying schools with equipment, textbooks, and such consumable items as paper and pencils is in itself a big business. Obviously, one could go on in this vein, but the point should be clear. To understand education, one must look beyond the classroom itself and the interaction between teachers and pupils to the larger world where different interest groups compete with each other in terms of ideology, finances, and power.

Clearly, any one of the preceding topics would be worthy of a book itself. In this chapter, we provide an overview of some of the basic elements of the organization of U.S. education so that you will be able to make increasingly informed decisions about the nature of education and how you as a teacher can grow professionally. In that sense, the purpose of this chapter is to create a broad frame of reference that grounds the perceptions of education in their organizational and social realities. To this end, we have included a section of this chapter that deals with the structure of U.S. education and compares that structure briefly to the structure of education in Great Britain, France, the former Soviet Union, Japan, and Germany.

We then turn to what is often called *school processes;* that is, we examine the way in which school cultures are created and maintained. Accordingly, we discuss such elements of school culture as authority structures and the significance of bureaucracy. These observations naturally lead to questions concerning the nature of teaching and the need for greater teacher professionalization. Good teaching will always be at the core of learning. Creating the conditions where teachers can use and improve their craft should be a major objective of those who believe that education is a cornerstone for a better society.

The Structure of U.S. Education

The organization of U.S. schools is complex on several levels. In this section, we examine the nation's elementary and secondary school system from the point of view of governance, size, degree of centralization, student composition, and its relative "openness." We also examine the duality of the U.S. school system; that is, in the United States, we have public and private educational systems that sometimes work in tandem and sometimes in opposition. The purpose of discussing the organization of schools should be clear—without a sense of structure, one has little way of grasping it as a whole. If one was to paint a landscape of elementary and secondary education in the United States, it would require a picture of almost infinite complexity and subtlety. It is the product of ideology, pragmatism, and history. It is unlike virtually any other educational system because the U.S. system is so decentralized and so dedicated to the concept of equal educational opportunity. We turn now to the issue of who is legally responsible for education in the United States.

Governance

When the Constitution of the United States was written, its authors indicated that those powers that were not mentioned explicitly as belonging to the federal government were retained by individual states. Because the federal government made no claims concerning its authority relative to education, the states retained their authority and responsibility for education. Thus, the United States has 50 separate state school systems. This picture is made even more complex by the fact that there is also a private school system within each state. There are few countries with this degree of decentralization. But this is just the beginning of the story, because most U.S. public schools are paid for by the revenue that is raised by local property taxes. As a consequence, tax payers within particular school districts have a substantial stake in the schools within their districts and they are able to make their voices heard through community school boards.

What this means, in effect, is that the U.S. public school system is, in large part, decentralized right down to the school district level. It is true that the state may mandate curriculum, qualifications for teaching, and safety codes, but the reality is that these mandates must be carried out not by agents of the state but by citizens of a particular school district. Is it any wonder that top-down reform in the United States is difficult to achieve?

Since the Civil Rights movement of the 1960s, the federal government has entered the educational policy field originally through the enforcement of students' civil rights. The role of the federal government in creating educational policy has increased since that time. This expansion of the federal role in education is perhaps best symbolized by the founding of the United States Department of Education in the late 1970s. During the era of Presidents Reagan and Bush, the U.S. Department of Education served primarily as a "bully-pulpit" for Secretaries of Education who helped to define the crisis in U.S. education and to provide blueprints for the resolutions of these crises. In actual fact, however, the Secretary of Education has relatively little authority when it comes to the governance of public schools.

Size and Degree of Centralization

As indicated earlier, the elementary and secondary school system in the United States is extremely large. It is estimated that more than 50 million youngsters are enrolled in kindergarten through the twelfth grade and that the cost of educating these children is over $230 billion annually. Interestingly enough, at the same time that the school system has been growing, it has been simultaneously becoming more centralized, presumably for reasons of efficiency. For instance, in the early 1930s, there were approximately 128,000 public school districts in the United States. By the late 1980s, this number had been reduced to slightly less than 16,000. Part of this consolidation process has been by virtue of elimination of single-teacher schools. In the early 1930s, there were approximately 143,000 such schools and by 2004, there were 14,404 (www.proximity one.com).

As a consequence of this consolidation, the average number of pupils per elementary public school rose from 91 in the early 1930s to 450 in the late 1980s. Public high schools expanded from 195 students per school in the early 1930s to 513 in the late 1980s (Witte, 1990, p. 15). At the same time schools are becoming larger, the number of pupils per teacher is decreasing. Today, the average public elementary school classroom averages 19 students, whereas 50 years ago, there were nearly 34 students per teacher. At the high school level, the average number of pupils per teacher is 16, whereas 50 years ago, it was 22.

What these statistics reveal is that there has been a considerable amount of consolidation and centralization in the last 50 years in U.S. public education. Although this trend may be cost effective, it may also have an negative impact on the diversity of schools that students may attend. Usually, large institutions are more bureaucratic than smaller ones and a high degree of centralization diminishes the amount of democratic participation. For example, because school districts have become larger, superintendents have become more powerful, and as a consequence teachers have had fewer opportunities to make fewer decisions regarding curriculum, conditions of employment, and school policy.

Student Composition

By the 1990s, 71 percent of the students in primary and secondary schools were white. This percent, however, masks a great deal of variation in terms of racial composition between states and school districts. Of the 50 states and the District of Columbia, 9 have less than 50 percent of white students, and over a dozen states have almost no minority students. Some large states such as California, Texas, and New York are extremely mixed racially. Many urban school districts enroll mostly minority students. For instance, in 2003, in New York City, 84 percent of the students were nonwhite; in Los Angeles, the figure was 90 percent; and in Detroit, 95 percent of the system's students were from minority backgrounds. In effect, nonminority families have moved out of the cities and into the suburbs, leading to a high degree of residential segregation. In some cities, less than 5 percent of the suburban population is minority.

What this means is that the student composition of U.S. schools is becoming more diverse at the same time that there has been a trend toward increasing residential segregation. Another way of expressing this is that *de jure* segregation has been replaced by *de facto* segregation (see Harvard Civil Rights Project, 2004). Student composition can also be viewed along other dimensions such as gender, class, ethnicity, and even ability. Later on, we will discuss how these characteristics of students can affect not only the student composition of schools but are related to educational and life outcomes. For example, we might wonder why it is that although approximately half the students in U.S. education are female, so few of them choose to pursue technological or scientific careers. Schools are also segregated or stratified according to the wealth and income of their student bodies. Students who attend schools in wealthy school districts, for instance, are more likely to have more curriculum options, better teachers, and more extracurricular activities than are students who attend relatively poor school districts. We will have a great deal more to say about these issues in subsequent chapters.

Degree of "Openness"

Public schools in the United States are organized as elementary, junior high or middle school, and high school. Elementary school usually encompasses kindergarten through grades 5 or 6; junior high, grades 7 through 9; middle school, grades 6 through 8; and high school, grades 9 through 12. Usually, children enter kindergarten at age 5 and graduate from high school at age 18. A key element to understanding the U.S. school system is that there are relatively few academic impediments placed before students if they choose to graduate from high school. Indeed, there may be many social and personal impediments that keep students from graduating from high school, but the school system is designed to give students many opportunities for advancement.

In this sense, the U.S. school system is quite open. All youngsters are entitled to enroll into public schools and to remain in school until they graduate. There is a powerful democratic ethos underlining the belief in the "common school." From a structural point of view, this means that there are multiple points of entry into the school system and there are few forced exits. When this openness is compared to other school systems, you will see that this is unusual, although most Americans would agree that schools should be as democratic as possible.

Private Schools

There are approximately 28,000 elementary and secondary private schools in the United States, enrolling 5.6 million students. Private schools constitute 25 percent of all elementary and secondary schools and educate 12 percent of the student population (Cookson, 1989, p. 61). The mean student enrollment of private schools is 234; only 7 percent of private schools enroll more than 600 students. Unlike the public sector, which has been consolidating over the last 50 years, there has been a remarkable growth of private schools. In the early 1930s, for instance, there were fewer than 10,000 private elementary schools in the United States; 50 years later, there were nearly 17,000 such schools. In 1999, there were 16,530 private elementary schools in the United States (U.S. Department of Education, National Center for Education Statistics, 2003).

There is a tremendous amount of diversity in the private sector, although most private schools are affiliated with religious organizations. Private school researcher Donald Erickson (1986, p. 87) has noted 15 major categories of private schools: Roman Catholic, Lutheran, Jewish, Seventh Day Adventist, Independent, Episcopal, Greek Orthodox, Quaker, Mennonite, Calvinist, Evangelical, Assembly of God, Special Education, Alternative, and Military. It should also be mentioned that in the United States there is very little regulation of private education by state authorities. The separation of church and state ensures the relative autonomy of private schools as long as they do not violate safety regulations and the civil rights of students. Each state has slightly different regulations, but in the main, it is safe to say that the autonomy of private schools is protected by a series of decisions made by the United States Supreme Court.

Most private schools are located on the east and west coasts. Connecticut has the highest percent of private school students and Wyoming has the least. Even though the percent of students who attend private schools has remained relatively steady when compared to the public sector, there has been significant shift in the private sector in terms of enrollment patterns. Clearly, Roman Catholic schools are experiencing a decline in enrollment. In the period between 1965 and 1983, there was a 46 percent drop in the number of students who attended Roman Catholic schools. During the same period, virtually every other type of private school experienced a great growth in terms of students and number of schools. Other religious schools doubled and tripled in size. This trend continued throughout the early twenty-first century. Private schools tend to attract students from families that are relatively affluent and who have a commitment to education.

Throughout the 1980s and 1990s, numerous studies seemed to indicate that private schools were more effective learning environments than were public schools. Various researchers claimed that private schools are communities and, because they compete for students, they are less bureaucratic than public schools, and as a consequence, they are more innovative. As you will see, there has been growing movement among some educational reformers to allow students to choose between public and private schools.

It is difficult to know whether in fact this kind of school choice will lead to school improvement or whether allowing students to choose private schools will lead to increased educational and social stratification. Many of these issues will be discussed in future chapters.

Conclusion

As this overview indicates, describing the U.S. elementary and secondary school system requires viewing the organization of schools from a variety of points of view. There is considerable diversity in the system despite the fact that there has been a trend toward centralization in the public sector. The authority structure of the public school system is diffuse; ultimately, it is the people who are responsible for the schools. This fact should not be minimized. Individuals, families, and groups are able to influence education by voting, by attending school district board meetings, and by paying for schools through taxes. This democratization gives the U.S. school system an unique egalitarian ethos. How does the U.S. system compare to other education systems? This is an important question to ask, because it is through comparison that one can see the unique features of the U.S. school system and those features that the U.S. system shares with the other national systems. This broadening frame of reference gives one greater understanding about the relationship between educational structure, processes, and outcomes.

International Comparisons

Countries vary considerably by how they organize their school systems. Few school systems are as complex as that in the United States; for instance, most countries have a National Ministry of Education or a Department of Education that is able to exert considerable influence over the entire educational system. Educational reforms can start from the top down with relative success because the state has the authority to enforce its decisions right down to the classroom level. Another dimension apparent in comparative analysis is the relative selectivity of systems. Education in the United States is fundamentally inclusive in its purposes; most other educational systems are not as inclusive. Individuals in other systems undergo a very rigorous academic rite of passage that is designed to separate the "academically talented" from the less gifted. The relative selectivity of a school system is an excellent indicator of its exclusiveness or inclusiveness.

What is the major purpose of the system? Is it to train an academic elite or to provide a broad-based educational experience for a wide segment of the population? Clearly, the relative openness of an educational system is related to the culture from which it originates. In this sense, educational systems are the expression of the values of the larger society. Educational systems can be located relative to each other by examining their degree of openness and the amount of authority that is exercised over the educational system by the national government. For instance, as we will see, France is a highly centralized educational system compared to the system in the United States.

Moreover, the educational system in France is designed to produce an academic elite compared to the system in the United States, where equality of educational opportunity for all children is a strong normative value.

Great Britain

Before the nineteenth century, the education of children in Great Britain was considered to be a responsibility of parents. All schools were private. For the children of very wealthy families, parents often hired tutors. For poor children, there was no schooling. During the nineteenth century, there was a system of charity schools for the poor. Most of these schools were operated by religious organizations. The establishment of a national educational system for all children in the early nineteenth century was opposed by the Church of England and Roman Catholics. The 1870 Education Act led to the beginnings of a national system, although the Church of England continued to maintain its own schools. This compromise between church and state led to the dual system of education that still exists in Great Britain, whereby state-run schools are controlled by Local Education Authorities (LEAs), while the church schools continue to operate, often funded by the state through the LEAs.

Although there were many attempts to reform this system, it was not until the 1944 Education Act that a truly national system of education was established as part of an "integrated public service welfare state" (Walford, 1992b). Free primary and secondary education was provided for all children. Despite the fact that the 1944 Education Act was designed to democratize Great Britain's school system, on the whole, the system recreated the class system by channeling students into different kinds of schools. Children from wealthy homes received academic training in grammar schools, and children from working class homes received vocational training. In short, Great Britain had a decentralized educational system that was fundamentally elitist.

During the 1960s, there was an effort to democratize Great Britain's educational system. When Margaret Thatcher was elected prime minister in 1979, however, she promised to reform the educational system. Throughout the 1980s, the conservative government, led by Thatcher, attempted to reform the educational system by privatizing public education, by encouraging greater parental choice, and by reorganizing the administrative structure of the state educational system. There were a series of legislative changes, culminating in the 1988 Reform Act. This reform established a national curriculum and set national assessment goals. Governing bodies of all secondary schools and many primary schools were given control over their own budgets. Parental choice was encouraged and a pilot network of City Technology Colleges was established. Also, state schools were given the right to opt out of local educational authority control. Thus, the 1988 Educational Reform Act was a radical challenge to the educational system that had been established in 1944.

Since 1988, England and Wales have implemented a highly centralized national curriculum and system of national assessment. Although teachers have been critical of the overly bureaucratic nature of these reforms, and the number of key curriculum areas has been narrowed, nonetheless, the 1988 Educational Reform Act has led to significant change (Walford, 1999).

The educational system in Great Britain is more open and less class stratified than it was a quarter century ago. However, despite a decrease in the school leaving rate to under 30 percent (from over 60 percent) (Brint, 1998) and an increase in university attendance to approximately 30 percent from under 10 percent, the educational system remains class stratified. It is also increasingly becoming race and ethnic stratified as Great Britain, especially London, has become increasingly multiracial and multiethnic, with a dramatic influx of immigrants from former colonial countries in Africa, the Caribbean, and Asia, including India and Pakistan. The inner-London schools are as multicultural as any urban school system in the United States, with some of the same problems experienced in U.S. urban schools.

The British educational system is no longer the highly stratified system in which students are sorted and selected by age 11 by examination, with achievement highly correlated to social class background. The national curriculum has also eliminated the comprehensive secondary school, which offered noncollege curriculum for its mostly working class students. Nonetheless, critics of the 1988 Education Reform Act argue that it has not significantly reduced educational stratification and to some degree has exacerbated it (Walford, 1999). Although some believe that with the election of Labor Party Prime Minister Tony Blair in the late 1990s, educational reform would become more concerned with equity than standards, to date this does not appear to have happened.

France

The educational system in France is quite centralized compared to the United States and Great Britain. The central government in France controls the educational system right down to the classroom level. Traditionally, there have been two public school systems—one for ordinary people and one for the elite. Efforts to end this dual system have been only partially successful, although throughout the last two decades or so, there has been an attempt to create one comprehensive system. The French educational system is highly stratified. For the academically talented, who usually come from the upper classes, there is a system of elementary, secondary, and postsecondary schools that is highly selective, highly academic, and socially elite. At the top of the system are the *grandes écoles,* which are small specialized institutions that produce members of the country's governmental and intellectual elite.

According to a noted authority on French education, George Male (1992), the French educational system is "excessively verbal." That is, French students are taught to frame ideas almost as an end unto itself, even as a matter of aesthetics. This sense of using language aesthetically is closely related to the importance placed on intellectual attainment within the French system. At one level, the objective of the French system is to produce a small number of highly qualified intellectuals. To identify this small group, the government has instituted a set of examinations that effectively, and one might even say ruthlessly, sort out the academically talented from the less academically gifted. The French believe, by and large, that this system of examinations is meritocratic, even though it is common knowledge that the system stratifies students by social class background. The French educational system is frankly competitive.

Efforts to democratize the system have not succeeded. Despite a number of re-forms associated with particular Ministers of Education, the French system continues to be centralized, competitive, and stratified. In 1984, the socialist government pro-posed to reduce state grants to private Catholic schools. The opposition to this proposal was so fierce that the plan was dropped, and since that time there have been few reform efforts, especially at the structural level.

In the past decade, the French educational system has become a little more demo-cratic. Approximately a third of 17- and 18-year-olds enroll in some form of higher ed-ucation, although only about 15 percent graduate from university. The majority complete some form of postsecondary occupational education. The top 10 percent of secondary students compete for the rare opportunity to enter the *grandes écoles,* which prepare students for prestigious civil service (Brint, 1998, p. 50). Entrance into the *grandes écoles,* although based on meritocratic selection, remains highly correlated with social class background.

The Former Soviet Union

In 1991, the Soviet Union as a single geographical and national entity dramatically and abruptly ceased to exist. The importance of this event cannot be underestimated. The end of the Soviet Union has affected the education of children in Russia and the other countries that have reemerged since the collapse of the Soviet system. It is interesting from a historical perspective how the Soviet educational system was organized, if for no other reason than as an example of how the best-planned educational policies will fail if they are unsupported by other cultural institutions.

The educational system that was established after the Bolshevik Revolution of 1917 was highly centralized, stratified, and deeply ideological. The purpose of the ed-ucational system was to create the "new Soviet man and woman." These new men and women were to become the leaders of the proletarian revolution that would transform the Soviet Union into a socialist paradise. Communist values were to be unquestioned and the educational system was conceived as being part of a planned economy that would produce a society where scarcity was virtually unknown. In reality, the Soviet system was quite stratified; that is, the children of high party members attended schools that taught foreign languages and prepared their students for university entrance, whereas the children of workers attended schools that were often underfunded and un-derequipped and produced graduates who took jobs in the Soviet factory system.

In the 1980s, it became increasingly clear to Soviet leaders and the Soviet people that the educational system was failing to educate Soviet students in the new skills that were required by technological change and international competition. Moreover, the system had become so rigid that it no longer provided significant opportunities for up-ward mobility. This situation led to a wave of educational reform in the Soviet Union. In the period between 1980 and 1985, a series of minor reforms attempted to change the system by finetuning it. For example, the age at which children were to start the first grade went from 7 years to 6 years. Teachers were paid slightly more and there was more emphasis on technical training. After the assent to power of Mikhail Gor-bachev, the Soviet educational system was transformed by a vision of education that al-lowed for decentralization, teacher initiative, and curriculum reform. As part of the policy of restructuring Soviet society *(perestroika),* education was to become more open, flexible, and responsive to the needs of students, parents, and communities. Naturally, such a huge change was difficult to implement. After all, teachers and administrators in the system had been trained under wholly different sets of values. The idea of creating an experimental school, more or less free of government control, was profoundly radical within the Soviet context.

Educational reform was made even more complex as the decade of the 1980s drew to a close and the 1990s began, because the Soviet Union's economy virtually collapsed and the very nature of the Soviet Union was in transition. Because the Soviet Union was composed of so many nationalities, there was little consensus between national groups, except that which had been imposed by the Soviet government. As the power of the Soviet government diminished, the demand for nationalistic autonomy increased. Social change exceeded the pace in which schools could be reformed. There is little doubt that education in the former Soviet Union has dramatically changed. Former Soviet citizens are still experimenting with new curricula, privatization, school choice, and new educational philosophies. Certainly, education in the former Soviet Union is dramatically different today than the education system that was established by the Bolshevik party in the beginning of the twentieth century.

Japan

During the late twentieth century, the educational system of Japan was thought by some experts as being exemplary when compared to the educational system in the United States (White, 1987). The Japanese educational system seemed to produce skilled workers and highly competent managers. In fact, Japan's economic rise in the 1980s represented a serious challenge to the international economic position of the United States. What is it about the Japanese system that makes it so distinctive?

The first national system of education in Japan was established in the 1880s under the central authority of the Ministry of Education, Science, and Culture. After World War II, the structure of schooling was changed when compulsory education was extended from six to nine years and democratic principles of equality of opportunity were suffused throughout the system. Parallel to the public system is a large and thriving private sector that plays an important role in providing educational opportunities at all levels of education. The Japanese system of education is highly competitive. To be admitted to a prestigious university, students are required to pass examinations that are extremely competitive. This emphasis on achievement and attainment is exemplified by the fact that Japanese students excel in every measured international standard up to the age of 17, both for the top students and for the 95 percent of students who graduate from high school.

What distinguishes the Japanese educational system from other educational systems in terms of its efficiency and effectiveness? Certainly, the educational system benefits by the work ethic that is so deeply entrenched in Japanese culture. Japanese parents have a high regard for the importance of education. The belief in education in Japan is so strong that it has led to the "double-schooling" phenomenon. In effect, many Japanese students are exposed to two educational systems. The first system is the traditional public schools and the second system is the nonformal schools that act as a national system of tutorial opportunities for students. The largest nonformal school system in Japan is the "study institution" *(Juku).* It is estimated that there are over 10,000 *Jukus* in Japan.

This love of education has made Japan a nation of strivers, but not without its own drawbacks. The Japanese have always placed a high value on moral education. Ethical dimensions of a moral education are not always easily compatible with the values inherent in competition. Thus, the debate over education in Japan has more to do with national character than it does with structural reform. Reconciling the cultural values of achievement and competition with those of cooperation and mutuality will be the hallmark of Japanese educational reform in the coming years.

Germany

The German educational system is significantly different from that of the United States. Through examinations, Germany selects and sorts its children at a relatively young age and tracks them into a tripartite system of secondary education (Mitter, 1992). The *Hauptschule* is designed for those destined for blue-collar and lower-level service positions; the *Realschule* is for lower-level white-collar and technical positions; the *Gymnasium* is for academic preparation for university and the intellectual and management professions (Brint, 1998, p. 41).

By the end of the lower-secondary years, students from the *Hauptschule* and *Realschule* enter the distinctive dual system of apprenticeship, where students spend part of the day working in apprenticeships in businesses and the other part in school. The close connection between business and schools in the training of workers is viewed as a model by many advocates of vocational educational reform in the United States. Students in the *Gymnasium* complete a rigorous academic curriculum that prepares them to take *Abitur,* the college entrance examination. About 25 percent qualify for university attendance, which is state supported and tuition free. Of these, more than half enroll in *Fachhochschulen,* or technical colleges. The remainder enter a four-year rigorous academic education in the arts and sciences, in universities that are similar to one another. Therefore, the rigid secondary school tracking system leads into a somewhat equal and undifferentiated system of higher education (Brint, 1998, p. 42). Less than 15 percent of German students complete this university education.

The German system is almost opposite of the U.S. system. Primary schools in the United States are relatively untracked, and secondary schools, although tracked, provide a relatively high degree of access to higher education. Higher education is open to large numbers of students, but also highly unequal and stratified, with technical and vocational programs and liberal arts and sciences in two-year community colleges, and a system of nonelite and elite four-year public and private colleges and universities. About 40 percent of U.S. students enter colleges and universities and another 20 percent enter community colleges, with approximately 30 percent completing a baccalaureate degree (U.S. Department of Education, National Center for Educational Statistics, 1997a).

German primary education sorts and selects students for a highly stratified and tracked secondary system, marked by a rigorous university preparatory track and two vocational and technical tracks, with a state-supported apprenticeship system. Although the system appears meritocratic, as placement is based on achievement, academic achievement is related to social class background (Mitter, 1992).

German reunification took place on October 3, 1990. Since then, the former East German system of communist education has been completely altered and replaced by the system of the Federal Republic of Germany (West Germany). Radical transformation of the curriculum to reflect a capitalist rather than communist ideology, and the transition to the highly stratified system just described, have taken place. Although it is too early to assess this transformation, some preliminary indications are that former East Germans may be having some difficulty adjusting to the more competitive system. Moreover, it will be interesting to see how those students who were socialized in the primary grades in the 1980s under communism and schooled in the 1990s in unified secondary schools are faring. The reunification of the German educational system is currently a fruitful avenue of educational research in Germany.

Conclusion

In sum, it is apparent from the preceding examples that educational systems and structures are in the process of change on an almost continuous basis. Educational systems are difficult to change because they are deeply embedded in their respective cultures. The values of a culture become institutionalized in an educational system. Every system is confronted with the same kinds of challenges. How many children shall be educated and what shall they learn? Every educational system attempts to select and sort students by their academic talent. The ethics and efficacy of any system is difficult to evaluate outside of its cultural context. Culture not only shapes structure but it also shapes school processes. Knowing the organization of a school or school system is a bit like knowing the architectural plans for a house. From a set of plans, one knows a house's dimensions and its form, but one does not know what it feels like to live in that structure. In the next section, we examine some of the key elements that underlie school processes.

School Processes and School Cultures

When you think back over your educational experiences, you undoubtedly have strong memories of the schools that you attended. You may remember particular teachers (for better or for worse), you may recall the students in your classes, and perhaps particular incidences stand out in your mind. Certainly, you remember the cafeteria. If you have strong powers of recall, you may remember the schools you attended more globally in terms of atmosphere, culture, and even smells. When one walks into a school, it is obvious that one is in a very particular place. Schools are unlike other organizations and because of this, they remain etched in one's memories for a lifetime. Thus, when one speaks of school processes, what we really are identifying are the powerful cultural qualities of schools that make them so potent in terms of emotional recall, if not in terms of cognitive outcomes.

Explaining school cultures is not easy because culture, by definition, is exactly that which one takes most for granted. Roughly 60 years ago, a sociologist of education, Willard Waller, attempted to understand the culture of schools. He later wrote, "The school is a unity of interacting personalities. The personalities of all who meet in the school are bound together in an organic relation. The life of the whole is in all its parts, yet the whole could not exist without any of its parts. The school is a social organism" (1965, p. 146). According to Waller (p. 147), schools are separate social organizations because:

1. They have a definite population.
2. They have a clearly defined political structure, arising from the mode of social interaction characteristics of the school, and influenced by numerous minor processes of interaction.
3. They represent the nexus of a compact network of social relationships.
4. They are pervaded by a "we feeling."
5. They have a culture that is definitely their own.

Waller went on to describe schools as despotisms in a state of perilous equilibrium (1965, p. 150). What is meant by this is that schools have authority structures that are quite vulnerable and that a great deal of political energy is expended every day, thus keeping the school in a state of equilibrium. In other words, school cultures are extremely vulnerable to disruption and that continuity is often maintained by the use of authority. Curiously, without the compliance of students, the exercise of authority within schools would be virtually impossible. Metz (1978) examined the use of authority in public schools and discovered that there was chronic tension within schools, in part because of conflicting goals. The teachers often have pedagogic goals that are difficult to reconcile with the social goals of the students. Administrators often have organizational goals that are shared neither by the teachers nor the students. Communities can exert tremendous pressure on schools and thus aggravate tensions within schools.

It is ironic that organizations that are formally dedicated to the goals of learning should be riddled with so many tensions and competing interests. However, this is the social reality within which many real schools operate. Schools are political organizations in which there are numerous competing interests. Thus, the culture of any one particular school is the product of the political compromises that have been created in order for the school to be viable. As a student, you experience these political compromises from a particular point of view. Individually, students generally have little power, but collectively they have a great deal of power in terms of whether they will accept the school's authority. Very often, this authority is represented in terms of the principal. Studies show that it is the principal who establishes the goals for the school, the level of social and academic expectations, and the effectiveness of the discipline (Persell & Cookson, 1982; Semel, 1992).

Because schools are so deeply political, effecting change within them is very difficult. Groups and individuals have vested interests. For example, teachers, represented through their unions, have a great deal to say about the conditions of their employment. Local school board members often struggle with the teachers in terms of pay, productivity, and professional standards. Many of these conflicts are resolved through negotiation. This is possible because schools, especially public schools, are bureaucracies.

Sociologist Max Weber (1976) suggested that bureaucracies are an attempt to rationalize and organize human behavior in order to achieve certain goals. In theory, bureaucracies are characterized by explicit rules and regulations that promote predictability and regularity in decision making and minimize the significance of personal relationships. Rules of procedure are designed to enforce fairness. As one knows, however, bureaucracies can become so complex, so rule oriented, and so insensitive that they suppress individualism, spontaneity, and initiative. Bureaucratic rationality can often suppress the creativity required for learning. Is it reasonable to suppose that learning best takes place in 40- or 50-minute segments that are marked by the ringing of bells or the mechanical rasp of buzzers? Is it reasonable to suppose that learning best takes place when every student reads the same textbook? Is it reasonable to suppose that learning is best measured by multiple-choice tests? In short, the demands of the bureaucracy can often be destructive to the very spontaneity and freedom that is required by teachers and students if they are to develop intellectually and personally.

Schools, as they are now organized, are shaped by a series of inherent contradictions that can develop cultures that are conflictual and even stagnant. Changing the cultures of schools requires patience, skill, and good will. Research on the effects of school-based management, for instance, indicate that it is not an easy task for teachers, administrators, parents, community members, and students to arrive at consensus.

An interesting example of how complex the restructuring of schools was is the "Schools of Tomorrow . . . Today" project, run by the New York City Teachers Center Consortium of the United Federation of Teachers. The purpose of this project was to create schools that were "more centered on learner's needs for active, experiential, cooperative, and culturally-connected learning opportunities supportive of individual talents and learning styles" (Lieberman, Darling-Hammond, & Zuckerman, 1991, p. ix). The aim of this project was to create schools that are "energized by collaborative inquiry, informed by authentic accountability, and guided by shared decision making." It was discovered that despite the best efforts of the restructuring participants within the schools, reform was difficult to achieve. Each of the 12 schools participating in the project had strikingly different approaches to change and experienced significantly different outcomes in terms of achieving the stated objectives.

The evaluators of this project identified four elements of change that applied to all the schools:

> Conflict is a necessary part of change. Efforts to democratize schools do not create conflicts, but they allow (and to be successful, *require*) previously hidden problems, issues, and disagreements to surface. Staff involvement in school restructuring must be prepared to elicit, manage, and resolve conflicts.

> New behaviors must be learned. Because change requires new relationships and behaviors, the change process must include building communication and trust, enabling leadership and initiative to emerge, and learning techniques of communication, collaboration, and conflict resolution.

> Team building must extend to the entire school. Shared decision making must consciously work out and give on-going attention to relationships within the rest of the school's staff. Otherwise, issues of exclusiveness and imagined elitism may surface, and perceived "resistance to change" will persist.

> Process and content are interrelated. The process a team uses in going about its work is as important as the content of educational changes it attempts. The substance of a project often depends upon the degree of trust and openness built up within the team and between the

team and the school. At the same time, the usefulness and the visibility of the project will influence future commitments from and the relationships among the staff and others involved. (Lieberman, Darling-Hammond, & Zuckerman, 1991, pp. ix–x)

As these quotes indicate, changing the culture of a school in order to make the school more learner centered requires time, effort, intelligence, and good will. Reflecting on the observations of Willard Waller, one can see that altering a particular school's culture is similar to diverting a river as it flows to the sea. Just as change is institutionalized, the institution itself changes. School processes are elusive and difficult to define, but all powerful nonetheless. This does not mean that planned change is not possible. It does mean that planned change requires new ways of thinking. It is our contention that teachers must be at the forefront of educational change and, therefore, the very definition of the profession must be redefined.

Teachers, Teaching, and Professionalization

In the prologue to his engaging and important book, *Horace's Compromise* (1984), Theodore Sizer describes Horace Smith, a 53-year-old, 28-year veteran of high school classrooms. Horace is an "old pro." He gets up at 5:45 A.M. in order to get to school before the first period of the day, which begins at 7:30 A.M. Horace puts in a long day, teaching English to high school juniors and seniors. In all, he will come in contact with 120 students. His days are long and demanding. Horace figures that by judiciously using his time, he is able to allot 5 minutes per week of attention on the written work of each student and an average of 10 minutes of planning for each 50-minute class. For this, he is paid $27,300. He earns another $8,000 a year working part time in a liquor store. Horace's daughter just graduated from law school and has her first job in a law firm. Her starting salary is $32,000 a year.

The story of Horace is by no means unusual. His loyalty, dedication, and hard work is repeated thousands of times by thousands of teachers every day. As this story indicates, there are numerous paradoxes related to the teaching profession. Teachers are expected to perform miracles with children but are seldom given the respect that professionals supposedly deserve. Teachers are asked to put in 60-hour weeks but are paid relatively small salaries. Teachers are expected to reform education, but are left out of the educational reform process. In short, teachers are the key players in education but their voices are seldom heard and their knowledge is terribly underutilized, and even devalued.

In this section we will briefly examine the nature of the teaching profession and the possibilities for further teacher professionalization. This topic is of utmost importance because we believe, as do John Goodlad and others, that teachers will be key players in educational reform in the future. After all, teachers are responsible for student learning. If they cannot assume responsibility for school improvement, how likely is it that schools will improve in terms of students learning?

Who Becomes a Teacher?

In 2001, 79 percent of all public school teachers in the United States were women. Their median age was 46; 73.1 percent were married, 15.2 percent were single, and

11.7 percent were widowed, divorced, or separated. Some 43.1 percent had a bachelor's degree, 56 percent had a master's degree, and less than 1 percent had a doctorate. Also, 31.7 percent would certainly teach if they had to do it over again; 28.7 percent probably would teach again; 18.4 percent said the chances were about even; 15.7 percent said they probably would not teach again; and 5.6 percent certainly would not teach again (U.S. Department of Education, National Center for Educational Statistics, 2003). With the aging of the teaching force and an attrition rate of approximately 40 percent in the first five years (Ingersoll, 2004), there will be increased demand for new teachers in the first decade of the twenty-first century.

Recently, there has been a great deal of discussion about the qualifications of those entering the teaching profession. In 1982, for instance, the national average Scholastic Aptitude Test (SAT) score was 893; the average score among students intending to major in education was 813 (Walker, Kozma, & Green, 1989, p. 26). Although SAT scores may not be accurate predictors of professional development, they do indicate that, on average, students entering the teaching profession are relatively weak academically. When top high school seniors are asked to indicate their future professions, less than 10 percent indicate that they are interested in becoming teachers. These data did not significantly change in the 1990s (National Commission on Teaching and America's Future, 1996). What is perhaps even more alarming is that the best students who enter the teaching profession are the ones that are most likely to leave the profession at an early date. Another concern is that there are few minority teachers. The United States is becoming an increasingly multicultural society. One wonders about the educational effectiveness of an aging white teaching force in the context of increasing racial and ethnic diversity.

Given the concerns about teacher qualifications and quality and the positive relationship between teacher quality and student achievement, especially in high-poverty schools (Education Trust, 1998), the No Child Left Behind Law mandates that states require all teachers to be highly qualified. According to NCLB, teachers are "highly qualified" when they meet three conditions:

1. A college degree.
2. Full certification or licensure, which specifically does not include any certification or licensure that has been "waived on an emergency, temporary, or provisional basis."
3. Demonstrable content knowledge in the subject they're teaching, or in the case of elementary teachers, in at least verbal and mathematics ability. This demonstration can come in various forms:
   - New elementary teachers must pass a state test of literacy and numeracy;
   - New secondary teachers must either pass a rigorous test in the subject area or have a college major;
   - Veteran teachers may either pass the state test, have a college major, or demonstrate content knowledge through some other uniformly applied process designed by the state (Education Trust, 2003).

Most states require that both elementary and secondary teachers pass a test in their subject area, such as the Educational Testing Services Praxis II examinations, which are given in each subject area. Although these processes have raised the entry-level qualifications of teachers, advocates for increased teacher quality, such as the Education Trust, argue that many states have set the bar for passing these examinations so low that teacher subject-level knowledge still needs improvement (Education Trust, 2003). Some states, such as New York, require that new teachers pass examinations in general liberal arts knowledge, teaching pedagogy, and pedagogical content knowledge and subject matter knowledge; other states, such as New Jersey, only test subject matter knowledge, permitting new teachers to enter the classroom with no examinations of teaching competence.

The majority of new teachers enter the profession after completing a university or college teacher education program, where they student teach for a semester prior to entering the classroom. Many states permit alternate route certification, where new teachers who pass subject matter examinations enter the classroom with little or no teacher education or student teaching. Teach for America (TFA), a national teacher corps that recruits liberal arts graduates for teaching in high-poverty urban and rural school districts, is an example of such an alternate route program. Although proponents of high-quality traditional teacher education, such as Linda Darling-Hammond, have been critical of TFA, saying that no other profession allows people to practice without years of training, defenders of TFA argue that their teachers are among the best and brightest in the country, are dedicated to teaching in areas that most new teachers do not want to teach, and have a positive effect on student achievement (Darling Hammond, Holtzman, Gatlin, & Vasquez, 2005; Decker, Mayer, & Glazerman, 2004).

The Nature of Teaching

Few professions are as demanding as teaching. Teachers must be skilled in so many areas of technical expertise and human relations. In their book, *The Complex Roles of the Teacher: An Ecological Perspective* (1984), Heck and Williams described the many roles that teachers are expected to play in their professional lives. These roles include colleague, friend, nurturer of the learner, facilitator of learning, researcher, program developer, administrator, decision maker, professional leader, and community activist. This is a daunting list and it leaves out the most important role of the teacher: the caring, empathetic, well-rounded person that can act as a role model to students, parents, and other professionals. Thus, on any single day, a teacher will be expected to wear many personal and professional "hats." This role switching is extremely demanding and may be one of the reasons for teacher burnout. It takes a great deal of emotional energy and imagination to maintain a sense of personal equilibrium in the face of meeting the needs of so many diverse groups.

Lieberman and Miller (1984) have explored what they call "the social realities of teaching." Through their research, they have been able to identify elements of the teaching experience that give it its unique flavor. According to Lieberman and Miller, the central contradiction of teaching is that "teachers have to deal with a group of students and teach them something and, at the same time, deal with each child as an individual. The teachers, then, have two missions: one universal and cognitive, and the other particular and affective" (p. 2). In order to reconcile this contradiction, teachers develop all kinds of classroom strategies that become highly personal and that evolve into a teaching style that is more akin to an artistic expression than it is to a technocratic or scientific resolution. Teachers, according to Lieberman and Miller, are best viewed as craftspeople and most of the craft is learned on the job. Teaching is a somewhat messy and personal undertaking.

There are other social realities of teaching that are significant. For instance, rewards are derived from students. Very often, the greatest and perhaps the only positive feedback that teachers receive is from their students. Seymour Sarason has written that teaching is a lonely profession. By this, he means that teachers get few opportunities to have professional interactions with their peers, and administrators seldom take the time or make the effort to give the kind of positive feedback teachers need.

Another element that gives teaching its unique characteristics is that very little is known about the links between teaching and learning. Researchers have only a marginal knowledge of whether or not what is taught is what is learned and what the nature of learning is. This means that the knowledge base of teaching is relatively weak compared to the knowledge base of other professions. Few teachers are experts in learning theory and many are only minimally qualified in some of the content areas they teach. What is key in teaching is the exercise of control. Control precedes instruction. Without control, there are few opportunities for learning, and yet control can stifle learning. Walking the razor's edge between social claustrophobia in the classroom and chaos in the classroom requires a high degree of self-understanding and understanding of group behavior. This is made more difficult by the fact that the goals of teaching are not always clear. There is a great deal of talk about holding teachers accountable for student learning. But the fact is classrooms are communities, where many needs need to be met. To be an effective teacher requires a sensitivity to individual and group dynamics.

Lieberman and Miller (1984) devoted a great deal of time discussing the "dailiness of teaching." There is a rhythm to the teacher's day. Thinking back to Horace in *Horace's Compromise* (Sizer, 1984), one can see that his day is punctuated by a set of rules, interactions, and feelings that are played out on a day-to-day basis with a certain predictability. Each day has a rhythm, weeks have rhythms, months have rhythms, and seasons have rhythms. For instance, fall is a time of high hopes and promise. As the fall winds down, energy winds down. By Thanksgiving, there is a great need for a break from the routine. Between Thanksgiving and Christmas, there is a frantic round of activities that culminate with the Christmas break. January can be brief, but February can seem never to end. It is in February that most teachers begin to think of other professions. By March, spirits begin to rise. This is accelerated by the spring break and the last-minute rush to fulfill the promises made in September by the closing of school in June. And then one day in June, school ends: No more routines, no more rituals, just memories of the year past.

Few professions are as simultaneously routinized and creative as teaching. Good teachers are creators. They take the dailiness of teaching and turn each day into a special event. A great teacher can turn a mundane lesson into an exciting intellectual voyage, and a poor teacher can make students reject learning altogether. There are few rules about what it takes to be a good teacher. Certainly, most good teachers genuinely like their students, have a commitment to their subject matter, are reasonably orderly in terms of their classroom organization, and have at least a working sense of humor. But these qualities are not professional qualities per se. How can one ensure that the teaching force will be staffed by people who are academically sound and pedagogically artistic? Given the condition of education today, it is important, even critical, that teachers be trained in new ways and redefine the nature of their professionalism.

Underqualified Teachers

A requirement of the No Child Left Behind (NCLB) Act is that all schools have highly qualified teachers in every classroom. This criterion highlighted the problem of unqualified teachers, many of whom were teaching out of their field of expertise. In the 1999–2000 school year, just prior to the enactment of NCLB, 99 percent of public school teachers held at least a bachelor's degree and almost half held a master's degree or higher. Moreover, about 92 percent of public school teachers held a regular or full teaching certificate.

Most teachers today meet the highly qualified standards of NCLB; however, the data indicate that significant numbers of classrooms are staffed by teachers who are not highly qualified in the particular subject taught. This is the result of the practice called *out-of-field teaching*—teachers being assigned to teach subjects that do not match their training or education. This is a crucial practice because highly qualified teachers may actually become highly unqualified if they are assigned to teach subjects for which they have little training or education. At the secondary school level, about one-fifth of classes in each of the core academic subjects (math, science, English, social studies) are taught by teachers who do not hold a teaching certificate in the subject taught. The data also show that some kinds of schools and classes have more out-of-field teaching than others. For example, low-income public schools have higher levels of out-of-field teaching than do schools in more affluent communities, and lower-track classes are more often taught by out-of-field teachers than are higher-track classes (Ingersoll, 2004).

According to Richard Ingersoll, a leading expert on issues relating to teacher staffing, the reasons for underqualified teachers have less to do with teacher shortages and more to do with organizational issues inside schools. Principals often find it easier to hire unqualified teachers than qualified ones, and the absence of status and professionalism in teaching leads to high dropout rates in the first five years of teaching. Therefore, districts are constantly replacing teachers on an ongoing basis, which has significant consequences, because it takes years to become an expert teacher. Rates of teacher attrition and misassignment are more prevalent in urban and high-poverty schools (Ingersoll, 1999, 2003, 2004). Ingersoll's research suggests that programs aimed at solving school staffing problems at the supply level through alternative teacher education programs—such as Teach for America, the New York City Teaching Fellows Program, and New Jersey's Alternative Certification Program (all of which allow college graduates with majors in their teaching field to enter teaching without traditional certification through a college teacher education program)—fail to address the organizational problems within schools that are responsible for high turnover rates (Ingersoll, 2004).

Teacher Professionalization

Thirty years ago, sociologist Dan Lortie (1975) pointed out that teaching, particularly elementary school teaching, is only partially professionalized. When he compared elementary school teachers to other professionals, he found that the prerequisites for professionalism among elementary school teachers were vaguely defined or absent altogether. For example, doctors have many clients, which means that they are not economically dependent on any single individual. This economic independence provides professional autonomy so that doctors need not always comply with the wishes of the client. Teachers are in a very different market situation. They receive their income from "one big client." There is little opportunity for teachers to teach independently of their school, and thus there is little opportunity for teachers to gain a reputation for excellence outside of their school or their school district. There is, in Lortie's words, "an incomplete subculture." Teacher socialization is very limited compared to other professions and there is little evidence that the socialization processes associated with becoming a teacher are highly professionalized or represent standards of behavior congruent with other professions. Lortie (1975, p. 213) concluded, "The general status of teaching, the teacher's role and the condition and transmission arrangements of its subculture point to a truncated rather than fully realized professionalization."

Educational researcher Linda M. McNeil (1988b) has written about what she calls the contradictions of control. She pointed out that "in theory, the bureaucratic design of schools frees teachers to teach by assigning to administrators and business managers the duties of keeping the school 'under control'" (p. 433). But as McNeil indicated, when so much attention is placed on keeping things under control, the educational purposes of the school can diminish in importance and teachers can begin to be part of a controlling process rather than an instructional one.

> As a result, teachers begin to take on the characteristics of the workers whose craft was splintered and recast when they became factory workers. When teachers see administrators emphasizing compliance with rules and procedures, rather than long term educational goals, teachers begin to structure their courses in ways that will elicit minimum participation from their students. When they see administrators run the schools according to impersonal procedures aimed at credentialing students, teachers begin to assert in their classrooms the authority they feel they are lacking in their schools as a whole. And when the complicated and often unpredictable task of educating a wide range of students is less valued than having quiet halls and finishing paperwork on time, teachers try to create in their own classrooms the same kind of efficiencies by which they are judged in the running of their schools. (McNeil, 1988b, p. 433)

Clearly, Lortie and McNeil are pointing to a set of conditions within the teaching profession that makes genuine professional autonomy a difficult goal to attain. On the one hand, teachers are expected to be autonomous, thoughtful experts in education. On the other hand, the conditions of their employment leave little scope for autonomy, thoughtfulness, or expertise. Perhaps none of this would really matter if the compromise between the norms of professionalism and the norms of bureaucracy did not lead to a kind of intellectual and moral paralysis among many teachers. Trying to be a professional and a bureaucrat, while at the same time trying to fulfill the many roles of a teacher, is a task that cannot be reasonably fulfilled by most people. Thus, in the teaching profession there is a tendency toward malaise, a lack of self-worth, and even cynicism. A visit to a teachers' lounge can be bracing and challenging to the idealist because teachers' lounges are notorious sites for gossip and back-stabbing. This is not to say that teaching is an impossible profession. There are many incredible teachers who overcome these obstacles and are inspirational to their students and even to their colleagues.

It is difficult to think of ways of educating inspirational teachers. After all, teaching is so personal. For educators such as John Goodlad, however, the time has come when society must find ways of better educating teachers. In the mid-1980s, Goodlad and two colleagues created the Center for Educational Renewal at the University of Washington. Using the Center as a base, they conducted a number of studies about teacher education in the United States. Goodlad's (1991, p. 5) findings included the following: "(1) A debilitating lack of prestige in the teacher education enterprise, (2) Lack of program coherence, (3) Separation of theory and practice, and (4) A stifling regulated conformity." These findings underscore what many already know. There is a crisis in teacher education. Goodlad suggested that there is a need for a complete redesign of teacher education programs and that a share of this redesign be conducted by policy makers, state officials, university administrators, and faculty members in the arts and sciences as well as in the schools of education. He also suggested that the redesign of teacher education include input from parents, teachers in schools, and the community at large.

Goodlad believes that a teacher education program should include a clearly articulated relationship between education and the arts and sciences. He believes that students should stay together with teams of faculty members throughout their period of preparation and that universities should commit enough resources to ensure first-rate teacher education programs. He is a strong believer that schools and universities should collaborate to operate joint educational projects as a way of preparing teachers for the real world of schools and as a way of revitalizing schools themselves. In short, Goodlad wants to raise the level of academic preparation for teachers, create a more cohesive curriculum, and professionalize teacher education by enlarging its clinical component.

Goodlad's ideas are far from radical. Many of them were incorporated into the recommendations of the National Commission on Teaching and America's Future (1996), which are summarized in Chapter 10. But if they are to be implemented, the way most teachers are prepared would have to be fundamentally altered. Clearly, there is a relationship between a higher level of preparation and professionalization. However, if teachers are to be truly professional, they must be able to share in the important decisions within the schools. School-based management, if it is to succeed, must empower teachers in terms of their decision-making capacities about curriculum, discipline, and other academic areas of importance. Whether or not school-based management will succeed as a reform will determine in no small degree the level of professionalization achieved by teachers. As one looks to the future, one can only hope that educational reformers will listen to teacher advocates such as John Goodlad who argue that without creating a new generation of teacher-leaders, there is little hope that schools will become more productive and just.

In this chapter we have discussed schools as organizations and teacher professionalization. Clearly, the many topics covered in this chapter deserve further discussion. The readings for this chapter touch on critical issues related to schools and teachers. The first selection, "Contradictions of Reform," written by educational researcher Linda M. McNeil, discusses the conflicting goals of U.S. high schools. The bureaucratic structure of the high schools is designed to control large numbers of students, while at the same time nurturing each student as an individual. Teachers are at the very center of this contradiction. McNeil argues that "standardized generic education" limits teachers' abilities to be creative and to take risks. Without true collaboration between teachers, administrators, and students, there is little hope for genuine reform.

The second selection, "The TIMSS Videotape Study," written by educational researchers James W. Stigler and James Hiebert, reports comparative findings on teaching mathematics in Germany, Japan, and the United States and relates differences in curriculum and teaching methods in achievement levels.

The third selection, "Is There Really a Teacher Shortage?" written by sociologist Richard M. Ingersoll, discusses whether or not there is a teacher shortage, the causes of the high turnover rate in teaching, the problem of underqualified teachers, and policy responses.

Contradictions of Reform

LINDA M. MCNEIL

If you can't teach at this school, you can't teach.
—Magnet high school teacher (spring 1984)

We're not teachers any more. We're workers now.
—Magnet high school teacher (spring 1986)

Ms. Watts is an extraordinary science teacher. She is one of the teachers who come to my mind when I think of Patricia Graham's recommendation that we recruit into the profession people who have a "passion for teaching," a passionate love of their subject and a deep commitment to bringing it to their students.

Ms. Watts' academic background includes degrees in science and engineering; she represents the level of professional knowledge and training for which schools are accustomed to being outbid by industry. She has taught in a predominately Hispanic high

school, and she now teaches in an integrated magnet school in which black students are the majority.

Ms. Watts begins her physics course with the reading of a play about the ethics of physics. Right from the start, her students learn that science is full of emotions, moral dilemmas, and personal involvement. She tries to organize all her courses around the concepts and processes that help students see science in the world around them. Ms. Watts is the kind of teacher who is both willing and expertly able to expend the time to build her lessons in ways that will involve her students in the scientific questions and procedures she finds so exciting.

Although she was very reluctant to leave her previous teaching position, Ms. Watts welcomed the chance to teach in a magnet program whose official purpose is to engage students in active learning. Within

From "The Contradictions of Control, Part 3: Contradictions of Reform" by Linda M. McNeil, *Phi Delta Kappan,* March 1988. Reprinted by permission.

such a program, she knew she would not only be allowed but required to create distinctive curricula in physics and physical science that would draw on her own "best" knowledge in these fields. In the company of other teachers developing active, engaging courses, she would be able to work on ways to structure classroom activities to link her students to the concepts and processes of the physical sciences.[1]

During Ms. Watts' first year of teaching, the district had pilot-tested a system of proficiency exams that, over a two-year period, would take both the choices of curriculum-building and the testing of students away from teachers like Ms. Watts and place them in the hands of consultants who design standardized tests. The content of Ms. Watts' courses would be divided into closely sequenced, numbered sections of factual content—"proficiencies." All of her lesson plans would need to be coded by number to show which element of the curriculum students were becoming "proficient" in during each lesson. The district office would supply her with a computer-gradable, multiple-choice final examination composed of the proficiencies recast as questions.

From her first year in the district, then, Ms. Watts' physical science course was proficiency-based. She was convinced that this format did a disservice to her students and an even greater disservice to science. "You have to spend a month on [the physics of] machines," she says. "You get to the end of it and the students hate it, and you hate it for what it does to them. They may be able to figure out the right answer on the proficiency test, but they don't know anything about machines."

The curriculum mandated by the district is heavily computational and assumes background in algebra that many students do not have (and are not required to have) when they enroll in the course. The curriculum (like the tests from which it derives) is not about machines and how they work; it is about calculation, about using formulas to describe the mechanics of machines. "The students aren't going to remember those formulas—never. They are only going to remember that it was a pain," Ms. Watts says. "And this will add to the general population of people out there who say, 'Science is hard. I don't want to do science.' This is not a conceptual course, an introductory course. It's a calculation and manipulation course. I'm not allowed and don't have time to give them a conceptual basis—to say, 'You can make a better machine.'" In her physics class, Ms. Watts has tried to preserve the links between student and content, links that she has seen the profi-

ciencies severing in the freshman physical science course. "If the district makes a proficiency test for physics," she says, "I will quit. That's it, period. I will not do it."

If Ms. Watts bases her physical science course on the district's numbered proficiencies and if 70% of her students make scores of 70% or better on the proficiency exams handed down from the district office, the district's reforms will be said to have worked. Ms. Watts' students will have "covered" the same chapter each week and will have worked the same computational problems as other high school freshmen in the district. They will have attained a minimum standard of knowledge in physical science.

In the process, according to Ms. Watts, they will have learned very little about what science is, about how to "do" science, about how science can be a part of their thinking. Her professional knowledge of science and her students' personal curiosities about the way the world works will have been set aside, while she and they meet in an exchange of "school science" that neither finds very meaningful. The institutional requirements will have been met, but Ms. Watts is fairly sure that any chance to learn real science will have been lost for her students.

The first two articles in this series suggested that behind the overt symptoms of poor quality in our schools lie very complicated organizational dynamics. The quality of the curriculum, the range of teaching styles, and the level of student commitment may not be what is "wrong" with schools. Each of these is an indication of the health (or lack of health) of the fundamental structure of the school. But an attempt to reform any one "problem" without giving attention to the underlying structural flaws may, as in the proficiencies imposed on Ms. Watts' courses, inadvertently make matters worse.

In Part 1 of this series, "Administrators and Teachers," I suggested that the American high school today embodies conflicting goals: educating individual students and at the same time processing large groups of students through to their credentials. The structure of the high school reflects this contradiction: school administration has evolved bureaucratic procedures to organize and control large numbers of students to insure that they are in the appropriate physical "place" and in the appropriate "place" on the path to a diploma. At the same time, the public expectation is that teachers will carry on the legacy of educating and caring for individual students—teaching course content and promoting learning.

As the most vulnerable of school employees, teachers stand at the point of conflict and must resolve the tension between these two contradictory purposes. The extensive classroom observations discussed in *Contradictions of Control: School Structure and School Knowledge* demonstrated that, when teachers feel that the administration and the school's reward structure subordinate educational goals to procedural controls, they will begin to treat their students in a similarly controlling manner. Feeling little sense of efficacy in the school as a whole, teachers will create their own efficiencies and establish their own authority in their classrooms by tightly controlling course content.

In Part 2, "Teachers, Students, and Curriculum," I described teachers who taught *defensively,* deliberately presenting simplified, fragmented bits of information to their students in the hope that students would comply with minimum requirements and leave the teacher in charge of the pacing of the course. These teachers often taught their most important content in the form of easily tested lists, they mystified complex topics, and they frequently omitted controversial or current material that might generate student discussion and thus disrupt the efficient "coverage" of the material.

Interviews with both students and teachers revealed that the "school knowledge" they dealt with in class bore little resemblance to the much more complex and sophisticated personal knowledge of the teachers. Students (and many school reformers) misread the dullness of lectures as a lack of teacher knowledge, and teachers mistook students' disappointment with this diluted content for apathy and a lack of curiosity. Although the students in the schools I studied did comply with course requirements in most cases, ironically they came to devalue what they learned at school. It seemed too divorced from the "real world" they knew from home and jobs and television. Indeed, "school knowledge" held little credibility for them.[2]

In my study of teachers' treatment of course content in a variety of school settings, one school demonstrated that, when the procedures, resources, and structures of the school are organized in support of academics (rather than in conflict with them), teachers feel supported to bring their best knowledge to their students.[3] In Chapter 6 of *Contradictions of Control* I describe Nelson High School's educational priorities, which helped encourage teachers to bring their best professional knowledge into their classrooms. Finding

that one school, where knowledge did not seem artificial, where teachers allowed their students to see them learning and asking questions (rather than tightly controlling all discussion), where scarce resources went first to instruction in a variety of imaginative ways, caused me to wonder what other structural arrangements might support the educational purposes of schools and overcome the organizational tendencies that reinforce defensive teaching.

Magnet Schools: Structured for Excellence

Nelson High School was an exception to the pervasive pattern of defensive teaching, student disengagement, and administrative attention to minimal compliance. This one school's building-level support for teaching and learning raised the issue of the difference that district level support might make in promoting the quality of education. More resources and policies originate at the district level than at the building level. If at the district level the tension between educating students and controlling them could be resolved in favor of the educational purposes of schooling, perhaps teachers would be even freer to bring their knowledge into the classroom.

A large urban district's system of magnet schools provided an opportunity to investigate this possibility. The district touts its magnet schools as "the best schools money can't buy." Organized as the district's response to court-ordered desegregation, the system of magnet schools promotes racial diversity by offering specialized curricula and excellent instruction. The district established specialized schools for such programs as engineering, fine arts, the health professions, gifted and talented students, law enforcement, aviation, computer science, and business. Teachers were hired according to their willingness and ability to create new courses and to work with colleagues to design distinctive programs. They were expected to teach so well that students all over the city would be willing to ride buses for an hour or more each day in order to attend these special schools.[4]

The federal court required reports on the programs and on student enrollments. District-level support for the magnet school program began with the efforts of the research and evaluation office in documenting enrollment statistics by race, but it also included the efforts of staff members in newly created administrative offices who worked with program development and provided support services in such areas as pupil transfers, transportation, and student recruitment. Although these supports centered first on equity, building-level magnet school coordinators were added as quasi-administrative staff to play leading roles in program development and daily oversight. In addition, some schools found added resources through corporate and foundation donations, state vocational funds for equipment purchases, and in participation from volunteers and school/community partnerships.

Months of daily classroom observations and interviews with teachers and students showed conclusively that teaching is very different in settings in which teachers do not have to choose between meeting minimum bureaucratic standards and teaching their students. When teachers do not have to teach in conflict with administrative policies, they are more likely to demand the best of their students, to learn along with their students, and to place few barriers between their professional knowledge and their classroom treatment of their subject.

Watching excellent, engaging teaching thrive in the supportive structures of these magnet schools and seeing the resulting engagement of students of widely ranging abilities affirmed the possibility that school organization need not stand in the way of "real teaching." These very positive observations and their implications for non-magnet schools were to have been the sole subject of my research.

However, my study took an unexpected turn when these teachers, who had been hired to specialize; came under the influence of centralized policies of "reform" that aimed to standardized teaching and the content of lessons. The contrast between their work as professionals in magnet schools and the new directives that required conformity to a centralized model of practice provides a dramatic story of the dangers of centralized school reforms and their power to create the very mediocrity that they are intended to eliminate.

Before the reforms, these magnet school teachers exhibited a high degree of professionalism in their work with colleagues and students. Several mentioned that they had chosen to work in the magnet schools not only because they cared about school integration but because the specialization of the magnet schools would permit them to function as curriculum developers in a state otherwise known for its statewide adoption of textbooks.

Teachers in the few magnet schools that required high entrance standards said that they felt ambivalent about teaching in "elite" public schools. They chose to remain because of their belief that "all students should be taught this way"—though in their district it was impossible to have the freedom to design courses anywhere except in a magnet school. "Teaching this way" meant first having the opportunity to collaborate with other teachers in developing the overall plan for the school. In a district in which faculty governance, even in the form of lively discussion in faculty meetings, is generally absent, magnet schools offer teachers a voice in shaping the program and a sense that a coherent educational program exists. Teachers in the magnet schools tended to develop a strong faculty culture, built around their commitment to desegregation, their participation in a specialized program, and their roles as professionals in schools aimed at excellence.

The magnet schools were not luxurious places in which to teach. In one school, teachers worked under asbestos-laden ceilings. Even at the science-specialty magnet school, science teachers rarely had adequate equipment for simple laboratory experiments. School libraries across the district were sparse, and they were no less so in most of the magnet schools. Some magnet schools had been placed as school-within-a-school programs in inner-city buildings whose declining enrollments needed a boost. Many of the school grounds were treeless, asphalt deserts that had long histories of neglect.

While more cheerful, better-equipped buildings and libraries would have made their teaching easier (and strained their personal pocketbooks less), these teachers found that the organizational support present in their magnet schools was a resource critical to their teaching. They managed to develop interesting courses and engaging teaching styles; they upheld a standard of excellence in a district historically known for the excellence of only a few schools in wealthier neighborhoods. They brought minority students into programs that would give them an opportunity to prepare for college, and they made science and engineering attractive fields for minority students and for girls. Their students spent hours riding buses and more hours reading literature, composing poetry, entering engineering design contests, discovering public and university libraries, and even asking questions in class.

The teaching in these magnet schools differed from school to school and from teacher to teacher. The common element seemed to be the teacher's ability to bring their "passion for teaching" into the classroom and to make classroom knowledge credible to students by making students participants in shaping it.

The teachers I reported on in *Contradictions of Control* had trivialized content by using it as a means of controlling students and by teaching defensively in order to gain at least minimal compliance from students and avoid unnecessary inefficiencies. The teachers in the magnet schools, on the other hand, did not feel that they were teaching in opposition to student apathy or administrative passion for efficiency. Their treatment of course content was almost exactly the opposite of defensive teaching.[5]

The midwestern teachers who taught defensively presented their most important course content in the form of lists of facts and fragments of information. They covered much material quickly, and their students knew what would be tested. The unintended consequence of their actions was the lack of credibility that such oversimplified, decontextualized information had for the students.

By contrast, teachers in the magnet schools tended to integrate rather than to fragment course content. They made—and allowed students to make—connections between lectures, readings, personal experience, current events, information from mentors in the community, and independent projects. Unlike the defensive presentation of the history of labor as a list of labor leaders and the dates of strikes, one teacher in a magnet school had her students stage a trial of robber barons. Through careful research and role-playing each student became a resource for the rest of the class on such matters as the competing interests of laborers, the survivors of workplace accidents, and the politicians, industrialists, journalists, and legal experts of the period. Her students debated "their" positions with fervor and were able to refer to issues and events they had studied long after the names and dates in a list-based lecture would have been forgotten.

The defensive practice of mystifying complex information rather than explaining it would itself have mystified most of these magnet school teachers. Rather than keep their lecture moving quickly by avoiding complex or controversial material, many of these teachers felt a direct commitment to demystify the world for their students. Exit polling after a federal election sent racially integrated teams of students into black, working-class white, and upper-class white neighborhoods to poll voters. Such terms as *interest group* and *social class* were no longer just vocabulary words in the government text.

A biology teacher knew that city children rarely think of being surrounded by nature. He required each student to build a collection of insects or leaves over the course of the semester, so that they could begin to appreciate the hundreds species around them and the purposes of scientific classification. The students also began to think about environments and habitats and to see themselves as gathers of information.

Mystification teaches children to "trust the experts" not to bother learning difficult things. Demystification begins to make the world theirs. When school knowledge incorporates personal dimensions, tools of inquiry—whether specialized vocabulary, steps in measurement in the laboratory, or ways of thinking—becomes useful to students for their own ends, rather that disconnected parts of "skill" units that teachers are compelled to teach.

The defensive teaching strategy that most offended the students I talked with in the *Contradictions of Control* study was the tendency of teachers to omit topics that were extremely current or controversial. Whether in sciences or in the humanities, limiting classroom knowledge to things about which experts had reached consensus maintained the teacher's authority over content and kept the students in the role of passive recipients.

The teachers in the magnet schools were much more likely to bring current issues and their own current reading and learning into their courses. A biology teacher attended summer institutes to learn more about biology and studied microbiology with a professor at a medical college. As a result, her courses were enriched, and she contributed to the districtwide curriculum in those areas. More important, her excitement for learning was never hidden from her students. The week a scientific journal carried dramatically new information about DNA, this teacher brought the journal—and her own genuine excitement—to her biology students.

When the time came for students to choose a subject and a teacher/advisor for their independent projects, many selected this teacher and a biological topic. Some even found mentors in the medical and industrial research communities as an additional resource. These students were willing to be fumbling amateurs in the company of experts because they had seen their teacher take similar risks and achieve good results. "School science" and the continually developing field of biology were not separate in the minds of these students. Similarly, two teachers developed active assignments for bringing students into the study of the stock market, and a history teacher skirted no controversies when she allowed a Hispanic student to talk to the class about proposed immigration laws in light of his own parents' status as undocumented aliens.

These magnet school teachers and others like them offered no apologies for the work they demanded of students; few settled for minimal, passive compliance. High school teachers whose courses were related to the health professions felt a special imperative to keep their courses up to date by dealing with the personal, scientific, and ethical demands that the students would face in their rotations through the labs and practice areas of local hospitals. In doing so, they demonstrated what both Fred Newmann and Theodore Sizer have termed *authentic* evaluation: the assessment of students' performance for a purpose beyond generating grades for the grade book.[6] To have made the work easy merely to avoid student complaints and potential resistance would have been to lay the groundwork for serious incompetence once these students reached the hospital. Instead, the students wore their lab coats and their new skills with great pride, as participants in their own learning, participants whose knowledge mattered.

These magnet school teachers rarely had the physical materials that they needed for their teaching. Many subsidized classroom resources out of their own pockets and taught in inelegant city schools, when they would have been in great demand in more comfortable suburban settings. They chose the magnets because in them they could work as professionals, empowered by the structure of the school to place their students and their subjects at the center of their teaching. They had avoided school settings in which they would be deskilled by state-adopted lists of textbooks and prescribed curricula. The results of their choice showed in teaching that kept school knowledge integrated with their personal knowledge, with their professional knowledge of their subjects, with the growing information and changing events around them, and with their students' capacities to become engaged in learning.

Meanwhile Downtown . . .

My study of magnet schools was to have ended with the documentation of the kinds of teaching and the resulting course content and levels of student involvement that characterized schools in which the tension between administrative controls and educational purposes was clearly resolved in favor of the latter. Many of the teachers in the magnet schools would be prime candidates for certification by the Carnegie Forum's

National Board or for positions as "lead teachers." The magnet schools in which they taught would have demonstrated within a traditional school structure excellent models of variations that empowered teachers.

However, when the school district and the state moved to enact "school reforms," these strong teachers were not distinguished from their weaker colleagues. They fell under the jurisdictions of two levels of reform, both of which aimed to improve teaching through tighter management of teachers. Both the state and the district aimed to bring up the lowest levels of educational quality, and both aimed to standardize teaching. *Both levels of reform significantly shifted the structural conditions of teaching and placed these engaging teachers squarely in conflict with new administrative controls over teaching and curriculum.* The district-level reforms removed the design of curriculum and of student assessments from the teachers' control. The state-level reforms dictated the teachers' role in the classroom and redefined teaching style as "teacher behaviors."

Proficiency-Based Curricula

The district-level reforms took the form of a proficiency system. Partly in response to the superintendent's anticipation that the state would soon impose a set of standardized tests on the schools and partly from genuine concern over such factors as the uneven quality of education, grade inflation in weak schools, and wide variations in teacher competence, the district staff sought a means for raising the quality of education in the schools most severely at risk.

Such an effort might have taken a very different direction had it arisen as a curriculum issue, an issue of oversight of principals, or even a staff development matter. In this district, however, the problem arose in the research and evaluation office, and the solution was thought to lie in better *testing*.

The research staff borrowed a test model previously used for assessing minimum levels of mastery of basic skills in an at-risk school. For reasons of cost and ready availability, the minimum competency test, rather than a "yardstick" of academic excellence from, for example, the district's stronger schools, became the model for the assessment of teaching.

Under this reform plan, the quality of teaching was to be assessed through the testing of students. Curriculum was to be reformed to achieve not academic quality but ease of testing. Staff members recall that curriculum was criticized as lacking "clarity," in the words of the testing office, the goals and purposes needed to be made "measurable." Up-to-dateness, comprehensibility for various groups of students, rigor of thought, use of high-quality resources, coherence of information, and variety of instructional activities were subordinated to measurability.

Curriculum committees (and this process remains mystified for the teachers) consisting of central office staff members, local graduate students, some teachers, and apparently some clerical assistants selected aspects of each course on which students were to become "proficient." The curriculum components were taken apart, sequenced, numbered, and sub-numbered in a manner reminiscent of the transformation of factories by "efficiency experts" early in the century.[7]

For each semester's work, a private testing firm designed tests of student outcomes that were multiple-choice and computer-gradable. A teacher who followed the prescribed curriculum in sequence, keeping pace with the district's guide, would "cover" the material in time for the test. All lesson plans were to be numbered to match appropriate proficiencies, and some principals required that the day's proficiencies be posted for students to see. Teacher merit pay, building principals' bonuses, and newspaper comparisons of school scores were all linked to student performance on the proficiencies.

A subject such as English, with an enormous range of content, was limited to proficiencies in the form of reading comprehension selections and grammar. Other subjects, such as social studies and science, were transformed into fragments of fact and bits of jargon, similar to the lectures typical of the defensive teaching I found in my earlier study. Although central office curriculum staff members were concerned about critical thinking and conceptual content, the reductionist format of the proficiency tests and related curriculum material reinforced convergent, consensus-based thinking, with the student in the role of recipient and rote learner rather than active participant. The teacher's role was reduced to that of monitor.

To blunt the effects of the proficiency-based curricula—which official district policy claimed to be the minimum standard, not the entire curriculum, but which in fact overwhelmed class time—the magnet school teachers began to deliver "double-entry" lessons. The biology teacher who was working with medical college researchers refused to dumb down her lessons to match the proficiencies: one day she wrote a simplified formula for photosynthesis on the board,

telling students to write it in their notebooks and learn it for the proficiency test. For the remaining two weeks' lessons, the teacher provided another, more complex version of the formula that the students helped derive through lab activities.

Frequently, the magnet school teachers would have to put their "real" lessons on hold for a few days in order to lecture on the proficiencies, or they would have to continually point out proficiencies during each lesson, so that students could keep them separate from the "real" information. The students were not unaware that often the "official" content contradicted the complicated interpretations and reflected only partial information and oversimplified processes.

It was ironic that the teachers in these magnet schools, whose teaching embodied an integration of their personal knowledge, their professional knowledge, their students' developing knowledge, and the knowledge they arrived at jointly in the classroom, were being required to cordon off their knowledge of their students and of their subject from the official "school knowledge."

Rather than call on these "best" teachers as models and resources the district reformers placed measurability ahead of substance. Like the administrators described in Part 1 of this series, they subordinated the educational purposes of the institution to the procedural ones. Unlike the defensive teachers, however, the magnet school teachers generally refused to be de-skilled by the proficiencies. Either they went to great lengths to overcome the inadequacies of the new system and took time out to "cover" proficiency material at the expense of other course activities (rather than transform the whole course into fragments and facts), or they helped students keep parallel sets of notes.

When proficiency scores began to be tied to teacher assessment and merit pay, these teachers began to talk of leaving the profession or at least the school district. When Ms. Watts said that she would refuse to teach physics under the proficiency system, she was speaking for many of her colleagues. When ways to work around the proficiencies and the administrative controls with which they were aligned became too confining, the magnet school teachers would not acquiesce in the de-skilling that these approaches represented.

Teacher Assessment

The state mechanism for assessing the classroom practice of teachers paralleled the district prescriptions for curriculum and student testing. Measurability was paramount, and the wisdom of teachers was discounted. Again, in the name of reform and in an effort to even out the quality of teaching across the state, an instrument was developed to standardize practice and hold teachers accountable to central management.

The assessment instrument, modeled perhaps unwittingly on the activity-analysis efficiency procedure for pacing assembly lines, transforms the tasks of the teacher into a set of *generic behaviors*. Derived from the language of classroom management and the narrowest applications of cognitive psychology, the list of 45 behaviors (55 in the first year it was used) enumerates such teacher actions as varying activities and waiting for student responses to questions. Providing "closure" at the end of class and using praise words are also among the behaviors that assessors look for.

The behaviors are meant to be scientifically derived from "research" on effective teachers (such studies are listed in a bibliography at the end of the teacher's guide to the assessment process). These "objective" measures include just three evaluation levels for the observer: "satisfactory," "needs improvement," and "exceptional quality"—the last a very subjective term for which little guidance is given either to the teachers or to the administrator/assessors.

The teacher assessment instrument is directly tied to teachers' progress through the career ladder and in fact was the cost teachers paid politically to have the state legislature approve a career ladder system of salary advancement. The assessment system leaves little to chance regarding its implementation: the frequency of the observations, the number of hours of training for assessors, the scores needed to advance on the career ladder are all carefully specified.

However, the educational aspects of teacher practice are not specified. The latest edition of the assessment form does have a place for the teacher's signature, but it still does not have a place for a teacher to explain *why* certain classroom activities were undertaken or how the teacher's role in the class that day related to his or her knowledge of the students' needs or to the purposes of the lesson.

Administrator/assessors are not required to have subject-matter expertise in the courses they observe. (After all, these behaviors are supposed to be generic.) Worst of all, the assessment instrument reinforces the extreme of teacher centered classroom practice. Many of the teachers described in Part 2 of this series as teaching defensively could have earned high scores on

the assessment instrument, even though their students found teacher controlled knowledge boring and trivial.

Decades of research on child development and the entire movement toward enhancing teachers' knowledge are ignored by this mandatory, statewide assessment system. Most teachers feel that to do the items listed on the form (enough of them to produce a high score) during one 50-minute class period would be to perform more as a marionette than as a teacher.

The teachers who want to hold onto a more personalized, professional teaching style must work around the assessment instrument, just as they must work around the proficiencies. Their students figure out quickly that class will be different on assessment days. A teacher who has developed writing workshops and is known for creative ways to relate writing assignments to literature says that when the assessor is due, she teaches a very traditional grammar lesson. "They would never understand our literature lesson," she asserts.

A 25-year veteran second-grade teacher reports that she has never felt politically motivated by a school policy before. But now "they have taken away my ability to do what I know my students need." A teacher of Advanced Placement courses reported using praise words during the class his assessor observed; later, the students who were accustomed to the teacher's probing questions and impatience with glibness, asked, "What were you *doing* in there today? Are you feeling all right?"

Teachers' views of administrative inability to link their best practice with the assessment instrument are not overstated. In a workshop devoted to placing students in the role of active workers in the classroom, a teacher asked how this could be reconciled with the teacher centered system of assessment. A principal stood up and said, "That's easy to figure out. When I go to assess a teacher and see the kids are working on projects or group activities, I just leave and come another day. It's like being there when the projector is running—you just come back some other time."

That principal and the designers and implementers of the assessment system have mistaken technique for teaching, classroom management for pedagogy. They are supported by a body of reductionist research and by political pressure for placing quality controls on public expenditures for education. It is little wonder that the magnet school teachers, who had chosen schools in which they could integrate their teaching style and course content and could continue developing their courses and their expertise, now feel like workers on assembly lines.

The Contradiction

The contradictions of control evident in these two reforms, the proficiencies and the generic assessment system, are even more serious than those I discussed in Parts 1 and 2 of this series. First, by leaping from symptoms (some weak teaching, some low achievement scores) to remedies, these top-down reforms not only ignore many of the dynamics that produce low-quality instruction, but they actually reinforce them. By applying across-the-board generic remedies, they are dumbing down the best teaching even as they try to raise the bottom. Disclaimers that these efforts establish "minimums" have little credibility when the best teachers are the ones who feel most alienated and who are talking of leaving the profession (several have done so since this research began).

Good teaching can't be engineered into existence. But an engineering approach to schooling can crowd out good teaching. Instead of holding up a variety of models for practice and learning from their strengths, these reforms continue our historically flawed search for "one best way" to run our schools. These reforms take a cynical view of teachers' ability to contribute constructively to schooling; they choose to make the content, the assessment of students, and the decisions about pedagogy all teacher-proof, so that a standardized model will become the norm.

Such reforms render teaching and the curriculum inauthentic. If we are to engage students in learning, we must reverse this process. When school knowledge is not credible to students, they opt out and decide to wait until "later" to learn "what you really need to know." Mechanical teaching processes knowledge in a way that guarantees it will be something other than credible. Centralized curricula, centralized tests of outcomes, and standardized teacher behaviors can only frustrate those teachers whose "passion for teaching" has shown students (and the rest of us) what education should be about.

The teachers in the magnet schools I studied now have a superintendent who thinks that teachers should participate in curriculum development. That superintendent is working with the school board to dismantle the proficiency system, perhaps in favor of a system of diagnostic tests (that will help teachers learn more about their students rather than control the curriculum)

and in favor of new curricula produced by groups of teachers.

Meanwhile, the state assessment system has been ratcheted into place in exchange for increased teacher pay. The resources for pay increments along the career ladder have dissolved with the state's economic problems, but the system remains in place nevertheless. The state school chief has deflected criticism by suggesting that critics who oppose the system may not understand school reform; he has also implied that only the weakest teachers would oppose it.

Despite a national effort to professionalize and board-certify teachers and to increase their latitude for leadership within schools, outcomes testing is now on the national agenda, in the form of congressional approval for extending the reach of the National Assessment of Educational Progress. Before the federal government increases its role in outcomes testing and before a centralized curriculum inevitably evolves, this experience in this state should serve as an example that, educationally speaking, the emperor of standardized, generic education wears no clothes. The effects of such standardized reforms contradict the rhetoric of their purpose and leave us more educationally impoverished than when we began. Genuine reform will have to address the structural tensions within schools and seek, not minimum standards, but models of excellence. Reforms that make schools educational will require not adversarial relations between administrators and teachers, but the best collaborative efforts of all who work in and for our schools.

Endnotes

1. Ms. Watts is a fictitious name, but the teacher I am describing is a very real, dedicated teacher who consented to be interviewed and quoted for my study of magnet schools.
2. See "Contradictions of Control, Part 1: Administrators and Teachers." *Phi Delta Kappan,* January 1988, pp. 333–39; and "Contradictions of Control, Part 2: Teachers, Students, and Curriculum," *Phi Delta Kappan,* February 1988, pp. 432–38.
3. See Linda M. McNeil, *Contradictions of Control: School Structure and School Knowledge* (New York: Methuen/Routledge & Kegan Paul, 1986), Ch. 6.
4. This ethnographic study of magnet high schools was funded by a grant from the National Institute of Education. See Linda M. McNeil, *Structuring Excellence and Barriers to Excellence* (Washington, DC: National Institute of Education/Office of Educational Research and Improvement, 1987).

5. See *Contradictions of Control,* Ch. 7.
6. Fred Newmann's project on alternative, "authentic" assessments has been profiled in a fall 1987 *Newsletter* of the National Center for Effective Secondary Schools, University of Wisconsin-Madison. Theodore Sizer's Coalition of Essential Schools aims for "exhibitions" of students' work, as advocated in his book, *Horace's Compromise* (New York: Houghton Mifflin, 1984).
7. See Raymond Callahan, *Education and the Cult of Efficiency* (Chicago: University of Chicago Press, 1962), which reminds us that school reforms are always born of good intentions and always have unintended consequences.

The TIMSS Videotape Study

JAMES W. STIGLER

JAMES HIEBERT

The video study that we conducted as a part of the Third International Mathematics and Science Study (TIMSS) collected samples of classroom instruction from 231 eighth-grade math classrooms in Germany, Japan, and the United States. It was the first time anyone had videotaped classroom instruction from nationally representative samples of teachers.

The study was a test run to allow us to see whether such a study would be feasible on a large scale. In the meantime, we hoped to get insight into what actually goes on inside the eighth-grade math classrooms in these three countries. It is relatively easy to gather data about classroom input by looking at curricula and textbooks and to get an idea about results from test scores. However, the classes themselves have been a black box; we have had little or no information about the process of teaching. Once coded and analyzed, the videotapes opened a new window on classroom practice. Furthermore, they revealed some fascinating national differences in a number of areas, including the following:

- The way the lessons are structured and delivered
- The kind of mathematics taught
- The kind of thinking students engage in during the lessons
- The way teachers view reform

Procedures

We videotaped each classroom one time, on a date convenient for the teacher. In order to discourage teachers from making special preparations for the videotaped lesson, we issued instructions telling them that our goal was to capture a typical lesson and that we wanted them to show us exactly what they would have done had we not been videotaping.

In addition to the data from the videotapes, we collected responses to a questionnaire and some supplementary materials—for example, copies of textbook pages or worksheets. The questionnaire asked teachers to describe the goal of the lesson, its place within the current sequence of lessons, how typical the lesson was, and whether teachers had used methods recommended by current reforms.

Lessons: Structure and Delivery

1. Lesson Goals

To evaluate a classroom mathematics lesson, you must first know what the teacher was trying to accomplish. We asked teachers, on the questionnaire, to tell us what they "wanted students to learn" from the lessons we videotaped. Most of the answers fell into one of two categories:

Reprinted with permission from the Winter 1998 issue of the *American Educator,* the quarterly journal of the American Federation of Teachers.

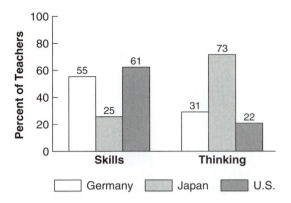

FIGURE 1 **Teachers' Descriptions of the Lesson Goal**

> Skills—These answers focused on students being able to *do* something: perform a procedure, solve a specific type of problem.
>
> Thinking—These answers focused on students being able to *understand* mathematical concepts or ideas.

As the graph indicates, Japanese teachers focused on thinking and understanding; German and U.S. teachers on skills. These different goals led Japanese teachers to construct their lessons in a different way from U.S. and German teachers.

2. Lesson Scripts

The videotaped lessons revealed a clear distinction between the "script"—the underlying pattern or template—used by Japanese teachers as they create a lesson and the scripts used by German and U.S. teachers. These different scripts follow from the different instructional goals, and they are probably based on different assumptions about the role of problem solving in the lesson, the way students learn from instruction, and what the proper role of the teacher should be.

U.S. and German lessons tend to have two phases. In the first or acquisition phase, the teacher demonstrates and/or explains how to solve a sample problem. The explanation might be purely procedural (this is what most often happens in the U.S.) or it might include developing concepts (this is more often the case in Germany). Still, the goal in both countries is to teach students a method of solving the sample problem. In the second or application phase, students practice solving similar examples on their own while the teacher helps individual students who are having difficulty.

Japanese lessons generally follow a different script. Problem solving comes first, followed by a time in which students share the methods for solving the problem that they have found on their own or in small groups. So while students in U.S. and German classrooms are expected to follow the teacher as she leads them through the solution of a sample problem or problems, Japanese students have a different job. They must invent their own solutions and then reflect together on those solutions in an attempt to increase their understanding of various ways to approach a problem.

3. Coherence

Students are more likely to make sense of a lesson that is coherent. When we compared U.S. lessons with those in Germany and Japan, we found the American to be less coherent by several criteria. First, American lessons contained significantly more topics than Japanese lessons, and significantly more topic segments than both Japanese and German lessons.

Second, when changing from one topic or segment to another, American teachers were less likely than Japanese teachers to make a transition linking the different parts of the lesson.

Third, American teachers devoted significantly more time during the lesson to irrelevant diversions such as discussing last night's rock concert or an upcoming field trip than German or Japanese teachers. Depending when these diversions occur, they can weaken the coherence of the lesson.

Finally, American lessons were more frequently interrupted by outside events, such as PA announcements or visitors. Lessons were halted by such inter-

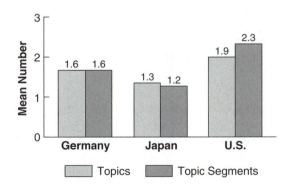

FIGURE 2 **Mean Number of Topics and Topic Segments per Lesson**

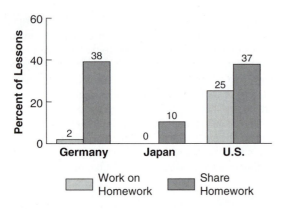

FIGURE 3   Percentage of Lessons in Which Class Worked on or Shared Homework

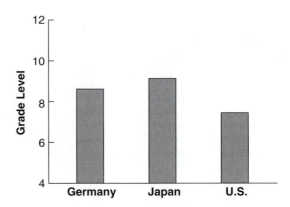

FIGURE 4   Average Grade-Level Content of Lessons

ruptions in 28 percent of American lessons, 13 percent of German lessons, and zero percent of Japanese lessons.

4. Homework during the Lesson

Another cross-national difference revealed by the videotaped lessons was in the role of homework. The graph [Figure 3] shows the percentage of lessons in which students reviewed and shared homework in class and the percentage in which they worked on their homework for the next day.

Japanese students never worked on the next day's homework during class and rarely shared homework results. Both German and American students shared homework frequently, but only American students commonly spent time in class working on the next day's homework. When we calculated the total percentage of time during the lesson that was devoted to assigning, working on, or sharing homework we got a similar result: Only 2 percent of lesson time in Japan involved homework in any way, compared with 8 percent in Germany and 11 percent in the United States.

The Kind of Mathematics Taught

1. Level of the Mathematics

Although it is not possible, a priori, to say that one mathematical topic is more complex than another, looking at where a topic appears in mathematics curricula around the world shows how advanced the topic is generally considered to be. This is what experts from forty-one countries did in order to establish a TIMSS math framework.

When we coded our videotapes, we used the TIMSS framework and were thus able to compare the topics taught with the international average. By international standards, the mathematical content of U.S. lessons was, on average, at a seventh-grade level, whereas German and Japanese lessons fell in the high eighth-grade or low ninth-grade levels.

2. Nature of the Mathematics

The videotaped lessons also revealed that the nature of the content differed across countries. For example, most mathematics lessons include some mixture of concepts and the application of those concepts to solving problems. How concepts are presented, however, varies a great deal. They might simply be stated, as in "the Pythagorean theorem states that $a^2 + b^2 = c^2$" or they might be developed and derived over the course of the lesson. The graph [Figure 5] shows the percentage of topics in each lesson that contained concepts that were developed and the percent that were only stated.

Although constructing proofs and reasoning deductively are important aspects of mathematics, American students lacked opportunities to engage in these kinds of activities. None of the U.S. lessons that we videotaped included proofs, whereas 10 percent of German lessons and 53 percent of the Japanese lessons included proofs.

3. Quality of Mathematical Content

As part of the video study, we asked an independent group of American college mathematics teachers to evaluate the quality of mathematical content in a repre-

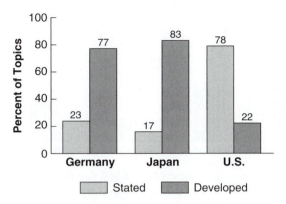

FIGURE 5 **Average Percentage of Topics per Lesson Containing Concepts That Were Stated and Concepts That Were Developed**

sentative selection of the video lessons. Basing their judgments on detailed written descriptions, they examined thirty lessons from each country. In order to decrease the likelihood of bias, we deleted information that might identify the country in which a lesson took place. The group's judgments are summarized in the graph [Figure 6].

Whereas 39 percent of the Japanese lessons and 28 percent of the German lessons received the highest rating, none of the U.S. lessons received the highest rating. Furthermore, 89 percent of U.S. lessons received the lowest rating, compared with 11 percent of Japanese lessons.

Students' Thinking

1. Tasks during Seatwork

When we examined the kind of work students engaged in during the lesson, we found a strong resemblance between Germany and the U.S. [Figure 7]. Three types of work were coded in the video study:

- Practicing routine procedures
- Applying concepts to novel situations
- Inventing new solution methods/thinking

Approximately 90 percent of student working time in Germany and the U.S. was spent in practicing routine procedures, compared with 41 percent in Japan. Japanese students spent nearly half their time inventing new solutions and attempting to grapple with mathematical concepts.

2. Alternative Methods for Solving Problems

We also were interested in the frequency with which students were exposed to alternative methods of solving problems. We distinguished two types of alternative methods—those presented by the teacher, and those generated by the students.

As shown on the graph [in Figure 8], 42 percent of Japanese lessons contained student-generated alternative methods, more than twice as many as German (14 percent) or U.S. (only 8 percent) lessons. The percentage of teacher-presented alternative methods did not differ significantly in the three countries.

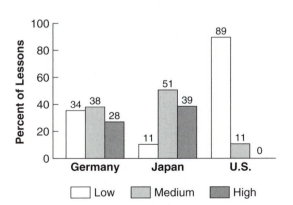

FIGURE 6 **Percentage of Lessons with Content of Low, Medium, or High Quality**

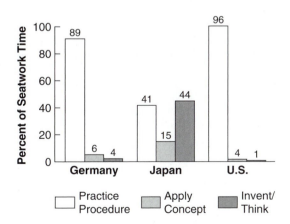

FIGURE 7 **Average Percentage of Seatwork Time Spent Working on Three Kinds of Tasks**

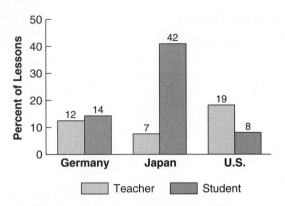

FIGURE 8 **Percentage of Lessons Including Teacher-Presented and Student-Generated Alternative Solution Methods**

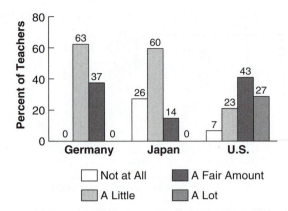

FIGURE 9 **Teachers' Ratings of Their Videotaped Lessons in Terms of Current Ideas**

Teachers' View of Reform

U.S. teachers believe that they are implementing current reform ideas in their classrooms. When asked specifically to evaluate their videotaped lesson, almost three-fourths of the American teachers rated it as reasonably in accord "a lot" or "a fair amount" with current ideas about the teaching and learning of mathematics. They were more than twice as likely to respond this way than either the Japanese or the German teachers.

Teachers who said that the videotaped lesson was in accord with current ideas about the teaching and learning of mathematics were asked to justify their responses. Although the range and variety of responses to this question were great, the vast majority of American teachers' responses pointed to surface features, such as the use of real-world problems, manipulatives, or cooperative learning, rather than to the deeper character-

istics of instruction such as the depth of understanding developed by their students.

The findings of the video study suggest that written reports that are disseminated to teachers may have little impact on practices in the classroom. One reason for this may be that teachers do not have widely shared understanding of what such terms as "problem solving" mean, leading to idiosyncratic interpretations in the classroom. Video examples of high-quality instruction tied to descriptions of what quality instruction should look like may help, in the future, to solve this problem.

Of course, not all teachers in these three countries follow the "script" sketched here, and not all lessons take the forms we have described. But what is striking, viewing the videotapes, is how many of the lessons display common national—or perhaps we should say cultural—patterns.

Is There Really a Teacher Shortage?

RICHARD M. INGERSOLL

Introduction

Few educational problems have received more attention in recent years than the failure to ensure that elementary and secondary classrooms are all staffed with qualified teachers. Severe teacher shortages, it is widely believed, are confronting our elementary and secondary schools. We have been warned repeatedly that "the nation will need to hire at least two million teachers over the next ten years" (e.g., National Commission on Teaching, 1997, p. 15–16), and our teacher training institutions are simply not producing sufficient numbers of teachers to meet the demand. At the root of this school staffing crisis, according to the conventional wisdom, are two converging macro demographic trends—increasing student enrollments and increasing teacher turnover due to a "graying" teaching force. The resulting shortfalls of teachers, the argument continues, force many school systems to resort to lowering standards to fill teaching openings, inevitably resulting in high levels of underqualified teachers and lower school performance.

The prevailing policy response to these school staffing problems has been to attempt to increase the supply of teachers. In recent years a wide range of initiatives have been implemented to recruit new candidates into teaching. Among these are career-change programs, such as "troops-to-teachers," designed to entice professionals into mid-career switches to teaching and Peace Corps-like programs, such as Teach for America, designed to lure the "best and brightest" into understaffed schools. Some school districts have resorted to recruiting teaching candidates from overseas. Many states have instituted alternative certification programs, whereby college graduates can postpone formal education training and begin teaching immediately. Financial incentives, such as signing bonuses, student loan forgiveness, housing assistance, and tu-

ition reimbursement have all been instituted to aid teacher recruitment (Hirsch, Koppich & Knapp 2001; Feistritzer, 1997; Kopp, 1992). The "No Child Left Behind Act" passed in winter 2002 provides extensive federal funding for such initiatives.

Teacher shortages and subsequent teacher recruitment initiatives are not new to the K–12 education system. In the early and mid 1980s a series of highly publicized reports trumpeted an almost identical series of diagnoses and prescriptions (see, e.g., National Commission on Excellence in Education, 1983; Darling-Hammond, 1984; National Academy of Sciences, 1987; for reviews of this issue, see Boe & Gilford, 1992). Indeed, teacher shortages have been a cyclic threat for decades (Weaver, 1983).

Concern over teacher shortages in turn has spurred interest in empirical research on these issues, but until the past decade such efforts were limited by a lack of data. It was partly in order to address these data shortcomings that the U.S. Department of Education's National Center for Education Statistics conceived the Schools and Staffing Survey (SASS) and its supplement, the Teacher Followup Survey (TFS), beginning in the late 1980s (Haggstrom et al., 1988). This is now the largest and most comprehensive data source available on the staffing, occupational, and organizational aspects of schools.

Over the past decade I have undertaken a series of research projects using SASS/TFS to examine a range of issues concerned with teacher supply, demand, and quality (e.g., Ingersoll, 1995, 1999, 2001a, 2003b). In this report I will summarize what these data tell us about the realities of school staffing problems and teacher shortages. The theoretical perspective I adopt in my research is drawn from organizational theory and the sociology of organizations, occupations, and work. My operating premise is that in order to fully understand the causes and consequences of these social prob-

From Richard M. Ingersoll, "Is There Really a Teacher Shortage?" A Research Report Co-Sponsored by the Center for the Study of Teaching and Policy and the Consortium for Policy Research in Education. Reprinted by permission.

lems it is necessary to examine them from the perspective of the organizations—the schools and districts—where these processes happen and within which teachers work. Employee supply, demand, and turnover are central issues in organizational theory and research. However, there have been few efforts to apply this theoretical perspective to understanding school staffing problems and policy. As I will show, by "bringing the organization back in," these school staffing problems are reframed from macro-level issues, involving inexorable societal demographic trends, to organizational issues, involving manipulable and policy-amenable aspects of particular schools. A close look at the data from this perspective, I argue, shows that the conventional wisdom concerning teacher shortages is largely a case of a wrong diagnosis and a wrong prescription.

The Data

As mentioned, the primary data source for this research is the nationally representative Schools and Staffing Survey (SASS) and its supplement, the Teacher Followup Survey (TFS), both conducted by the National Center for Education Statistics of the U.S. Department of Education. To date, four independent cycles of SASS have been completed: 1987–1988; 1990–1991; 1993–1994; 1999–2000. SASS is an unusually large survey. Each cycle of SASS administers survey questionnaires to a random sample of about 53,000 teachers, 12,000 principals, and 4,500 districts, representing all types of teachers, schools, districts and all 50 states. In addition, one year later, the same schools are contacted again, and all those in the original teacher sample who had moved from or left their teaching jobs are given a follow-up second questionnaire to obtain information on their departures. This latter group, along with a representative sample of those who stayed in their schools, comprise the Teacher Followup Survey. The TFS sample contains about 7,000 teachers. Unlike most previous data sources on teacher turnover, the TFS is large, comprehensive, nationally representative, and includes the reasons teachers themselves give for their departures and a wide range of information on the characteristics and conditions of elementary and secondary schools. It is also unusual in that it does not solely focus on a particular subset of total separations, but includes all turnover: voluntary, involuntary, transfers, quits, retirements, etc. In this report, I present data from all four cycles of SASS and TFS. (As of summer

2003, the 2000–2001 TFS had only been partially released by NCES and data presented here from that cycle are preliminary estimates.)

Demand for Teachers Has Risen

What do the data tell us about school staffing problems and teacher shortages? The data show that the conventional wisdom on teacher shortages is correct in some respects. Consistent with shortage predictions, data from SASS and other NCES data sources show that demand for teachers has indeed increased in recent years. Since 1984, student enrollments have increased, most schools have had job openings for teachers, and the size of the teaching workforce (K–12) has increased, although the rate of these increases began to decline slightly in the late 1990s (Gerald & Hussar, 1998; Snyder & Hoffman, 2001, p. 11). Most importantly, many schools with teaching openings have experienced difficulties with recruitment. Overall, the data show that in the 1999–2000 school year, 58% of all schools reported at least some difficulty filling one or more teaching job openings, in one or more fields. However, the data also show that in any given field less than half of the total population of schools actually experienced recruitment problems (see Figure 1). For instance in 1999–2000, 54% of secondary schools had job openings for English teachers and about one-half of these indicated they had at least some difficulty filling these openings—representing one-quarter of all secondary schools. Similarly, 54% of secondary schools had job openings for math teachers and about four-fifths of these indicated they had at least some difficulty filling these math openings—representing about 40% of all secondary schools. Likewise, 45% of secondary schools had job openings for special education teachers and about three-quarters of these indicated they had at least some difficulty filling these openings—representing 34% of secondary schools.[1]

How Adequate Is the Supply of Teachers?

While demand has increased and many schools have had hiring difficulties, the data do not show, contrary to the conventional wisdom, that there is overall an insufficient supply of teachers being produced. National data on the overall supply of teachers trained, licensed, and certified each year are difficult to obtain. One source is NCES' Integrated Postsecondary Educational Data System (IPEDS). This source collects data on the

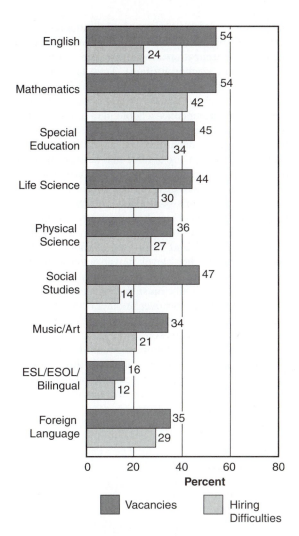

FIGURE 1   Percent Secondary Schools with Vacancies and Percent with Difficulties Filling Those Vacancies, 1999–2000

numbers of post-secondary degree completions by field and by year. The IPEDS data indicate that, for example, at the end of the 1998–99 academic year there were over 220,000 new recipients of education degrees at the undergraduate and graduate levels (IPEDS, 2001). But, the SASS data show that only about 86,000 of those hired for the following school year were drawn from this group of recent college graduates. Indeed,

large proportions of those who train to become teachers do not ever become teachers. For example, data from the nationally representative 1993 Baccalaureate and Beyond Survey show that, of new recipients of bachelor's of education degrees who graduated in 1993, after one year out of college only 42% had taught and after four years out of college only 58% had taught. Many of those who decided not to pursue teaching indicated that they needed more education, or wanted another occupation (for a more detailed presentation of the B&B data, see Henke et al., 2000).

In short, the data appear to indicate that, overall, there are more than enough prospective teachers produced each year in the U.S. But, there are also some important limitations to these data. An overall surplus of newly trained teachers does not, of course, mean there are sufficient numbers of graduates produced in each field. A large proportion of education degree completions are in elementary education. The data are unclear on whether a sufficient quantity of teachers are produced each year in such fields as math, science, and special education.

But, on the other hand, the IPEDS database on degree completions underestimates the supply of newly qualified teachers because it does not include recipients of non-education undergraduate degrees who also completed the requirements for certification. Moreover, newly qualified candidates, as counted in the IPEDS data, are only one source of new hires in schools. Far more of those newly hired into schools each year are from what is often referred to as the "reserve pool." These include delayed entrants—those who completed teacher training in prior years, but who have never taught, and re-entrants—former teachers who left teaching for a period to later return. The addition of these other types and sources of teachers could well mean that there are more than enough teachers produced each year.

However, from an organizational perspective, the key question is not whether the overall national supply of teachers is adequate or inadequate, instead it is which schools have staffing problems and teacher supply and demand imbalances? Even in the same jurisdiction, the degree of staffing problems varies greatly among different types of schools, and sites ostensibly drawing from the same teacher supply pool can have significantly different staffing scenarios. Some analysts have found, for example, that in the same metropolitan area in the same year some schools have extensive waiting lists of qualified candidates for their teaching job openings, while other nearby schools have great difficulty filling their teaching job openings with qualified candidates (National Commission on Teaching, 1997). Consistent with this, I have found in an analysis of variance of the SASS data that the variation in school hiring difficulties is far greater within, than between, states.[2] This suggests that to be fully understood imbalances between demand and supply must be examined at the level of the organization—an issue to which I return.

The Importance of Teacher Turnover for School Staffing Problems

There is another problem with the conventional wisdom on shortages. The data show that the demand for new teachers and subsequent staffing difficulties are not primarily due to student enrollment and teacher retirement increases, as widely believed, but these are largely due to teacher turnover—teachers moving from or leaving their teaching jobs—and most of this turnover has little to do with a graying workforce.

The TFS data show that teaching has a relatively stable annual turnover rate: 14.5% in 1988–89; 13.2% in 1991–92; 14.3% in 1994–95; 15.7% in 2000–2001. (See Figure 2.) There are two types of total turnover included in Figure 2: movers—those who move to teaching jobs in other schools (often and hereafter referred to as teacher migration)—and leavers—those who leave the teaching occupation altogether (often and hereafter referred to as teacher attrition). Total teacher departures are fairly evenly split between them. Much of the existing research on teacher turnover does not include the former. Teacher cross-school migration is a form of turnover that does not decrease the overall supply of teachers because departures are simultaneously new hires. As a result, many assume that teacher migration does not contribute to the problem of staffing schools and to overall shortages. From a macro and system level of analysis, this is probably correct and for this reason educational researchers have often de-emphasized or excluded movers. However, from an organizational perspective and from the viewpoint of those managing at the school-level, movers and leavers have the same effect—in either case it results in a decrease in staff, which usually must be replaced. Hence, research on employee turnover in other occupations and organizations almost always includes both movers and leavers—and for this reason I include them here. As illustrated in Figure 2, adopting a system-level or an organizational-level of analysis makes a difference—if one excludes cross-school moves, total turnover would appear far less than it is—from the viewpoint of those managing schools.

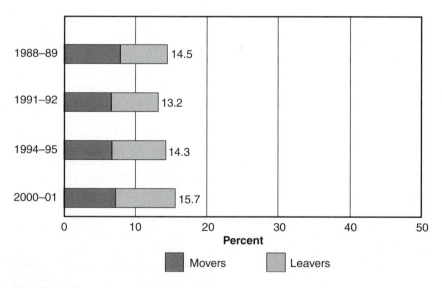

FIGURE 2   Percent Annual Teacher Turnover

One question that naturally arises concerns how rates of teacher turnover from schools compare to those in other organizations, occupations, and industries. There has never been much empirical research on this issue. In earlier work I compared the TFS data with data from one of the better known sources of information on employee turnover in a range of occupations and organizations, the Bureau of National Affairs (2002). This comparison showed that teaching has a slightly higher annual turnover rate than the nationwide level for total employee departures—which over the past decade averaged 11.9% annually (Ingersoll, 2001a). But, this comparison provided only a crude benchmark. The BNA data represent an organizational rate of employee turnover, which ostensibly includes the whole range of employees on the payroll—from clerical staff to senior management—within a given organization. Far more informative would be comparisons of *occupational* rates of turnover, i.e., how do rates of teacher turnover compare to those in other occupations? But, such data are difficult to obtain and suffer from serious issues of measure comparability (Price, 1977, 1997).[3] In more recent work I have found that, as one might expect, teaching has higher turnover than some higher-status professions (professors at 9.3%; technology and scientific professionals from 3.6% to 9.2%), about the same as other female semi-professions (nurses at 18%) and less turnover than

some lower-status, lower-skill occupations (federal clerical workers at 30%).[4]

But, from an organizational perspective the key question is not whether teaching has higher or lower turnover than other occupations, but rather is teacher turnover a problem for schools themselves. The data indicate it is. There is a strong link between teacher turnover and the difficulties schools have adequately staffing classrooms with qualified teachers—as shown in Table 1 which presents data on the flows in and out of schools from all four cycles of the SASS/TFS data.

Reading down the column for the 1993–94 school year, for example, Table 1 indicates there were just under three million teachers in the K–12 education system that year, including both public and private schools. About 377,135 of these teachers entered their schools at the beginning of the 1993–94 school year. Of these, 192,550 had not taught the prior year. This latter group included newly qualified candidates fresh out of college, delayed entrants who had completed their training in a prior year but had not previously taught, and re-entrants who had taught previously, stopped for a while and then returned. Another 184,585 of these hires to schools had moved from another school. By the following school year, 417,588 teachers had moved from or left their school jobs. Just under half of these departures—204,680—moved to other schools to teach. Another 212,908 left

TABLE 1 Trends in Teacher Flows In and Out of Schools

	1987–88 School Year	1990–91 School Year	1993–94 School Year	1999–00 School Year
1.) Total Teaching Force—during school year	2,630,335	2,915,774	2,939,659	3,451,316
2.) Total Hires—at beginning of school year	361,649	387,807	377,135	534,861
A.) Entrants	178,344	191,179	192,550	232,232
B.) Movers from other schools	183,305	196,628	184,585	302,629
3.) Total Departures—by following school year	390,731	382,879	417,588	539,778
A.) Movers to other schools	218,086	208,885	204,680	252,408
B.) Leavers from occupation	172,645	173,994	212,908	287,370
Retirees	35,179	47,178	50,242	NA

Notes:
- Entrants: includes new, delayed, and re-entrants. This refers to those who did not teach the prior year; some did teach in the past.
- These data are calculated at the level of the school. Hence, "hires" and "departures" refer to those newly entering or departing a particular school. "Movers" includes transfers among schools within districts. Reassignments within a school are not defined as hires or as departures.
- As of summer 2003, teacher retirement data for the 2000 school year were not yet available.

the occupation altogether. Of the latter, 50,242 were retirees.

Table 1 documents two important points. First, the data show that the demand for new teachers is not primarily due to student enrollment increases, nor to teacher retirement increases, but to pre-retirement teacher turnover. That is, most of the hiring of new teachers is simply to fill spots vacated by teachers who just departed. For instance, about 191,000 individuals entered teaching at the beginning of the 1990–91 school year. However, by the following school year 12 months later, about 174,000 teachers (equivalent to 91% of those just hired) left the occupation altogether. At the beginning of the 1993–94, three years later, about 192,500 teachers entered teaching, but by the following school year, about 213,000 (equivalent to 110% of those just hired) left the occupation. At the beginning of the 1999–00, six years later, about 232,000 teachers entered teaching, but by the following school year, about 287,000 (equivalent to 124% of those just hired) left the occupation.

Second, although teacher retirements have increased in recent years, they account for only a small portion of the above total turnover. For example, from 1994 to 1995 there were about 50,000 retirees, accounting for only 24% of the 213,000 leavers and only 12% of the total turnover of 417,588 during that period. In sum, the data show that the demand for new teachers, and subsequent staffing difficulties, is not primarily due to student enrollment increases, nor to teacher retirement increases, but to pre-retirement teacher turnover. That is, most of the hiring of new teachers is simply to fill spots vacated by teachers who just departed. And, most of those departing are not doing so because of gray hair.

The Revolving Door

It is also important to note that teaching is a relatively large occupation—it represents 4% of the entire civilian workforce. There are, for example, over twice as many K–12 teachers as registered nurses and five times as many teachers as either lawyers or professors (U.S. Bureau of the Census, 2002).[5] The sheer size of the teaching force combined with its relatively high annual turnover means that there are large flows in, through, and out of schools each year. The image that these data suggest is one of a "revolving door"—which I have tried to capture in Figure 3. It shows that for the 1999–2000 school year, 534,861 teachers entered

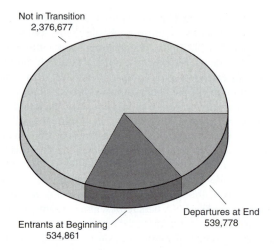

Not in Transition
2,376,677

Departures at End
539,778

Entrants at Beginning
534,861

FIGURE 3   Numbers of Teachers in Transition Before, During, and After the 1999–2000 School Year

schools, while by the following school year an even larger number—539,778—had moved from or left their schools.[6] Hence, in a 12-month period over one million teachers—almost a third of this relatively large workforce—were in job transition into, between, or out of schools. This revolving door is a major factor behind school staffing problems.

Table 1 and Figure 3 also provide a context to interpret the widely used statistic, introduced earlier, that the nation "will need to hire at least two million teachers over the next 10 years." This statistic was drawn from an NCES analysis (Gerald & Hussar, 1998; Hussar, 1998) that projected the numbers of teachers that would need to be hired from 1998 to 2008 in order to replace those who had left teaching and to account for student enrollment increases. These analyses themselves did not examine supply, nor changes in hiring needs over time. But, a wide variety of commentators, researchers, and policy makers have interpreted this statistic to mean that hiring two million new teachers is an unusually large number and assumed to be evidence that we face an alarmingly inadequate supply of new teachers being produced. A close look at the data reveals that neither is the case.

The Importance of Teacher Turnover for Organizations

Of course, not all teacher turnover is detrimental. There is an extensive research literature on employee turnover conducted by those who study organizations and occupations in general (e.g., Price, 1977, 1989; Mueller & Price, 1990; Bluedorn, 1982; Halaby & Weakliem, 1989; Hom & Griffeth, 1995; Kalleberg & Mastekaasa, 1998; March & Simon, 1958; Mobley, 1982; Steers & Momday, 1981). On the one hand, researchers in this tradition have long held that a low level of employee turnover is normal and efficacious in a well-managed organization. Too little turnover of employees is tied to stagnancy in organizations; effective organizations usually both promote and benefit from a limited degree of turnover by eliminating low-caliber performers and bringing in "new blood" to facilitate innovation. Moreover, some job and career changes are, of course, normal and inevitable in any occupation. On the other hand, researchers in this tradition have also long held that high levels of employee turnover are both cause and effect of performance problems in organizations.

Organizational analysts have also noted that the consequences of employee turnover vary among different types of employees and among different types of organizations. Labor process analysts, for instance, have argued that a major issue, from the viewpoint of organizational management, is the extent to which the organization is, or is not, dependent on particular types of employees and, hence, vulnerable to the disruption caused by their turnover (e.g. Braverman, 1974; Burawoy, 1979; Edwards, 1979). For just this reason the issue of employee "substitutability," or the ease with which organizations can replace employees, is a central concern in organizational management and a central theme in organizational research. In this perspective, employee turnover is especially consequential for work that involves uncertain and non-routine technologies and which requires extensive interaction among participants. Such organizations are often unusually dependent upon the commitment and cohesion of employees and, hence, especially vulnerable to turnover (e.g., Burns & Stalker, 1961; Kanter, 1977; Likert, 1967; Porter, Lawler & Hackman, 1975; Turner & Lawrence, 1964; Walton, 1980).

Schools are an example of this type of organization. Education theory and research have long shown that, while education is a mass "industry" involving large complex formal organizations, in important ways schools do not fit standard input-output, economic-production models in either theory or practice (Bidwell, 1965; Lortie, 1975; Ingersoll, 2003a). The "raw materials" in schools are children and youth; the "technology" of teaching and learning is often uncertain,

ambiguous, and non-routine; and the "product" is youngsters' growth. As a result while schools in some ways resemble economic-production organizations, in other ways they resemble another kind of institution altogether—the family. Student test outcomes are one of the important output functions of school production. But not surprisingly, similar to families the presence of a positive sense of community, belongingness, communication, and cohesion among members has long been held by education theory and research to be one of the most important indicators and aspects of effective schools (e.g., Durkheim, 1925/1961; Waller, 1932; Parsons, 1959; Grant, 1988; Coleman & Hoffer, 1987; Kirst, 1989; Rosenholtz, 1989).

Hence, from an organizational perspective, some teacher turnover, especially of ineffective teachers, is necessary and beneficial. But from this perspective, turnover of teachers from schools is of concern not simply because it may be an indicator of sites of potential staffing problems and so-called teacher shortages, but because of its relationship to school cohesion and, in turn, performance. Moreover, from this perspective this relationship runs both directions. That is, high rates of teacher turnover are of concern not only because they may be an outcome indicating underlying problems in how well schools function, but also because they can be disruptive, in and of themselves, for the quality of school community and performance.

Some of these costs and consequences of turnover are more easily measured and quantified than others. In contrast to the corporate sector, however, there has been very little attention paid to the costs and consequences of employee turnover in education. One notable exception was a recent attempt to quantify the costs of teacher turnover in Texas—this study concluded these costs run into the hundreds of millions of dollars each year to the state (Texas Center for Educational Research, 2000).

Teacher and School Differences in Turnover

The data also show that the revolving door varies greatly among different kinds of teachers and different kinds of schools. As found in previous research (Murnane et al., 1991; Huling-Austin, 1990; Hafner & Owings, 1991), the SASS data show that teaching is an occupation that loses many of its newly trained members very early in their careers—long before the retirement years. I used these data to provide a rough estimate of the cumulative attrition of beginning teachers from the occupation in their first several years of teaching. The data suggest that after just five years, between 40 and 50% of all beginning teachers have left teaching altogether. (See Figure 4.)[7] Of course, not all of this attrition results in a permanent loss of teachers. One form of this revolving door is represented by temporary attrition—teachers who leave teaching but return in later years, as discussed earlier (also see Murnane et al., 1991). But again, from the viewpoint of those managing at the school-level, temporary and permanent attrition have the same effect—in either case it results in an immediate decrease in staff, which usually must be replaced.

Annual teacher turnover also varies according to the teachers' main field. Math, science, and elementary special education teachers have higher rates of turnover, and social studies and English have lower rates (see Figure 5). Moreover, a number of studies have found that teachers with higher ability, as measured by test scores such as the SAT, the National Teacher Exam, and teacher licensure tests, are more likely to turn over (e.g., Weaver, 1983; Murnane et al., 1991; Schlecty & Vance, 1981; Stinebrickner, 2001; Henke et al., 2000).

The data also show that the revolving door varies greatly among different kinds of schools, as illustrated in Figure 6.[8] For example, high-poverty public schools have far higher turnover rates than do more affluent public schools. Urban public schools have slightly more turnover than do suburban and rural public schools. Private schools have higher turnover rates than public schools, but there are also large differences among private schools. On one end of the continuum lie larger private schools with among the lowest average turnover rate—about 13.5%. On the other end of the continuum lie smaller private schools with among the highest average levels—about 22%.

The Sources of Teacher Turnover

These data raise another important set of questions: why do teachers depart at relatively high rates and why are these rates so dramatically different among schools? To answer these questions I conducted multivariate statistical analyses of data from different cycles of SASS/TFS to determine which characteristics of teachers and schools are associated with the likelihood of teacher turnover, after controlling for background

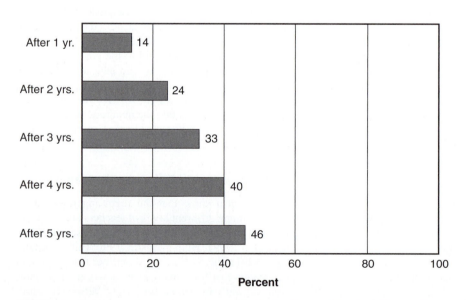

FIGURE 4   Beginning Teacher Attrition (Cumulative Percent Teachers Having Left Teaching Occupation, by Years of Experience)

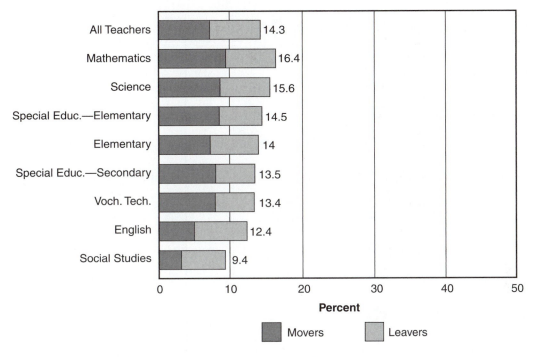

FIGURE 5 **Percent Annual Teacher Turnover, by Field (1994–95)**

factors (Ingersoll, 2001b). I also examined data on the reasons teachers themselves give for their turnover. Such self-report data are useful because those departing are, of course, often in the best position to know the reasons for their turnover. But, such self-report data are also retrospective attributions, subject to bias and, hence, warrant caution in interpretation. Nevertheless, I found a great deal of consistency among these different types of data and from different cycles of the survey. The following section summarizes my principal findings. Along with the annual rates of turnover, Table 2 presents self-report data on teachers' reasons for both migration and attrition. In addition, for all teachers who departed because of job dissatisfaction, the bottom portion of the table presents data on the reasons for their dissatisfaction.[9]

Contrary to conventional wisdom, retirement is not an especially prominent factor. The latter was listed by only 25% of leavers and 13% of total departures. School staffing cutbacks due to lay-offs, terminations, school closings, and reorganizations account for a larger pro-

portion of turnover than does retirement. These staffing actions more often result in migration to other teaching jobs rather than leaving the teaching occupation altogether. But, the data also show that, overall, staffing actions, like retirement, account for only a small portion of total turnover from schools—about 20%.

A third category of turnover—that for personal reasons—includes departures for pregnancy, child rearing, health problems, and family moves. These account for more turnover than either retirement or staffing actions and they are probably common to all occupations and all types of organizations. The two final sets of reasons are directly related to the organizational conditions of teaching. Individually each of these categories accounts for more turnover than does retirement. Together these are the most prominent source of turnover. Almost half of all departures report as a reason either job dissatisfaction or the desire to pursue a better job, another career, or to improve career opportunities in or out of education.

Of those who depart because of job dissatisfaction, most often link their turnover to low salaries, lack

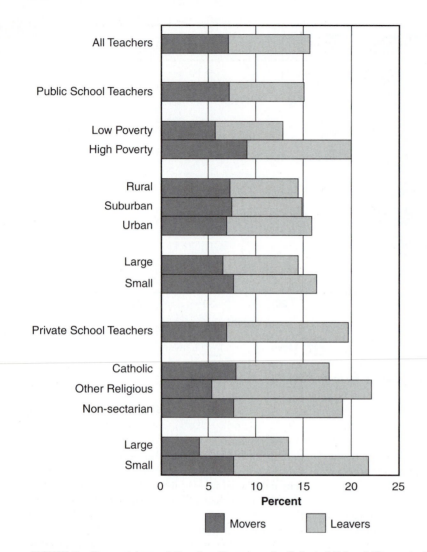

FIGURE 6   **Percent Annual Teacher Turnover, by Selected School Characteristics (2000–2001)**

of support from the school administration, student discipline problems, poor student motivation, and lack of teacher influence over decision-making. In general, similar kinds of dissatisfactions lie behind both teacher migration and teacher attrition. Interestingly, several factors stand out as *not major reasons* behind turnover, according to those who departed: large class sizes, intrusions on classroom time, and lack of planning time.

In sum, the data indicate that teachers depart their jobs for a variety of reasons. Retirement accounts for a relatively small number of total departures, a moderate number of departures are due to school staffing actions, a large proportion indicate they depart for personal reasons, and a large proportion also report they depart either because they are dissatisfied with their jobs or in order to seek better jobs or other career opportunities. I

TABLE 2 Percent Teacher Turnover and Percent Teachers Giving Various Reasons for Their Turnover, 1994–95

	All	**Movers**	**Leavers**
Rates of Turnover	14.3	7	7.3
Reasons for Turnover			
Retirement	13	–	25
School Staffing Action	20	34	8
Family or Personal	40	36	44
To Pursue Other Job	27	29	25
Dissatisfaction	29	32	25
Reasons for Dissatisfaction			
Poor Salary	54	49	61
Poor Administrative Support	43	51	32
Student Discipline Problems	23	22	24
Lack of Faculty Influence & Autonomy	17	18	15
Poor Student Motivation	15	12	18
No Opportunity for Professional Advancement	6	8	5
Inadequate Time to Prepare	6	5	6
Intrusions on Teaching Time	7	5	11
Class Sizes Too Large	7	3	11

have found these reasons for turnover to be highly consistent across different types and cycles of the data, across different kinds of schools, and across different subsets of teacher turnover. These findings are important because of their policy implications. Unlike explanations that focus on external demographic trends "out there," these findings suggest there is a role "in here" for the internal organization and management of schools.

Implications for Policy

It is widely believed that shortfalls of teachers resulting primarily from two converging demographic trends—increasing student enrollments and increasing teacher retirements—are leading to problems staffing schools with qualified teachers and will, in turn, lower educational performance. In response school districts, states, and the federal government have developed a variety of recruitment initiatives designed to recruit more candidates into teaching.

However worthwhile these efforts may be, the data suggest that, alone, they will not solve school staffing problems. The data suggest that school staffing problems are not solely or even primarily due to teacher shortfalls resulting from either increases in student enrollment or increases in teacher retirement. In

contrast, the data suggest that school staffing problems are to a large extent a result of a "revolving door"—where large numbers of teachers depart teaching for reasons other than retirement. From the framework of supply and demand theory, the data show that the problem is not primarily shortages, in the sense of an insufficient supply of teachers being recruited and trained. Some economists would still call this a shortage—in the technical sense that there is an inadequate quantity of teachers supplied—those willing to continue to offer their services at a given wage and given working conditions in given schools. This diagnostic and terminological distinction has crucial implications for prescription. It is also a distinction that is almost always overlooked in research and policy on the teacher shortage.

Supply and demand theory holds that where the quantity of teachers demanded is greater than the quantity of teachers supplied, there are two basic policy remedies: increase the quantity supplied or decrease the quantity demanded. The first approach—the traditionally dominant approach—is to increase the quantity of teachers supplied through recruitment. However, this analysis cautions that recruitment programs alone will not solve the staffing problems of schools if they do not also decrease turnover. States such as California, where class size reductions have strained the supply of new teachers pose exceptions. But, for just these reasons, California, like other states, must pay close attention to retention. In short, recruiting more teachers will not solve the teacher crisis if 40 to 50% of such teachers then leave within five years. The image that comes to mind is a bucket rapidly losing water because of holes in the bottom. Pouring more water into the bucket will not be the answer if the holes are not first patched.

Recruitment and other supply-side solutions may not only fail to solve the problem but could also make the situation worse. If recruitment strategies involve lowering teacher standards, or if the effect of increasing teacher supply is to deflate salaries or erode working conditions, then these measures may simply exacerbate the root factors behind school staffing problems.

This situation is analogous to aspects of management-labor conflict in industry. Critics of business practice argue that industrialists have long used labor supply recruitment as a strategy to undermine worker and union efforts to improve working conditions and wages (e.g., Braverman, 1974; Burawoy, 1979; Edwards, 1979). For example, by bringing in immigrant laborers from eastern and southern Europe at the turn of the 19th century, industrialists, the critics hold, were able to keep wages down, undermine union power, and increase profits. One of the downsides with this strategy, from a management perspective, is that it can decrease employee quality and increase employee turnover. Hence, one of the objectives behind the design of the assembly-line model of production used in industry was to increase the ease of substitutability and, hence, insulate the organization from disruption caused by employee turnover.

Similarly, social scientists have long characterized K–12 teaching as a lower status, easy-in/easy-out, high turnover occupation that has relied historically on recruitment, and not retention, to solve its staffing problems (e.g., Tyack, 1974; Lortie, 1975). Since the inception of the public school system in the late 19th century, teaching was socially defined and treated as a temporary line of work suitable for women, prior to their "real" career of child rearing. For men, teaching was socially defined as a stepping stone, prior to their "real" career in one of the male-dominated skilled blue-collar occupations or white-collar professions. Indeed, historically there was an ambivalence toward persistors in teaching, especially males—who had to account for why they continued to be "merely" a teacher. Low

pre-service training standards and requirements, relatively unselective entry criteria, and front-loaded salaries that paid newcomers relatively high salaries compared to veterans all tended to favor recruitment over retention. Moreover, low pay, isolated job conditions, little professional autonomy, and a faint sense of a career ladder all undermined longer-term commitment to teaching as a career and profession. Attempts to upgrade the status of the occupation through more rigorous training and licensing standards or more selective entry gates often resulted in decreases in male entrants to teaching, who were more attracted to occupations with better rewards attached to rigorous standards (Strober & Tyack, 1980).

It appears that school districts continue to favor teacher recruitment strategies for many of the same reasons and with many of the same consequences. By widening the entry gate and increasing the quantity of teachers supplied, districts are able to control labor costs and, hence, control local property taxes. The downside of this strategy in schools, as in industry, is that it can decrease employee quality and increase employee turnover. Treating workers as interchangeable, expendable, low-skill workers cuts some expenses, but it is not cost-free. If turnover is at the root of school staffing problems and if the quality of the teaching job is a large factor behind turnover, then policies that further erode the low status of teaching, that undermine salary increases, or that undermine working conditions may simply backfire by increasing turnover.

In short, the data suggest that school staffing problems are rooted in the way schools are organized and the way the teaching occupation is treated and that lasting improvements in the quality and quantity of the teaching workforce will require improvements in the quality of the teaching job.

Conclusion: What Is to Be Done?

How do schools improve the teaching job? Teachers themselves have offered some ideas. The 1994–95 TFS asked teachers who had moved from or left their teaching jobs since the prior year to suggest possible steps schools might take to encourage teachers to remain in teaching. Their responses are summarized in Figure 7.[10]

One strategy suggested by departed teachers to aid retention is *increasing salaries,* which are, not surprisingly, strongly linked to teacher turnover rates. But, salaries are not the only issue, which is important from

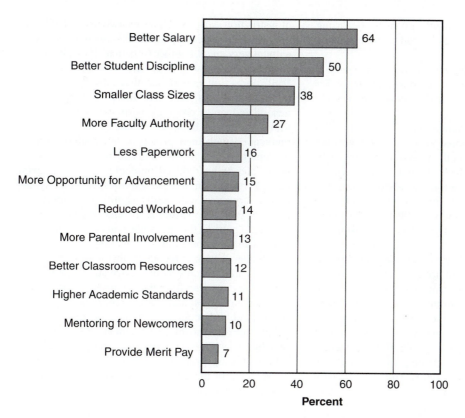

FIGURE 7   Of Those Teachers Who Moved from or Left Their Jobs, Percent Giving Various Steps Schools Might Take to Encourage Teachers to Remain in Teaching, 1994–95

a policy perspective because increasing overall salaries is expensive given the sheer size of the occupation.

Reduction of *student discipline problems* is a second factor frequently suggested by departed teachers. Multivariate analysis of the data also document that this factor is strongly tied to the rates of teacher turnover; again, not surprisingly, schools with more student misbehavior problems have more teacher turnover (Ingersoll, 2001b). But, the data also tell us that, regardless of the background and poverty levels of the student population, schools vary dramatically in their degree of student misbehavior.

One of the factors tied to both student discipline and teacher turnover is how much *decision-making in-fluence* teachers themselves have over school policies that affect their jobs, especially those concerned with student behavioral rules and sanctions. In a separate multivariate analysis of data from SASS, I have found that, on average, teachers have little say in many of the key decisions that concern and affect their work, but schools where teachers are allowed more input into issues, such as student discipline in particular, have less conflict between staff and students and less teacher turnover (Ingersoll, 2003a). Increasing teacher decisionmaking power and authority is also, not surprisingly, suggested by teachers as a step to aid retention.

Class size reduction was also frequently suggested by teachers as a step to increase retention, although interestingly, it was not frequently given by departing teachers as one of the sources behind turnover related to dissatisfaction (Table 2).

Also surprising in Figure 7 is how few teachers suggested increasing support, such as *mentoring,* for new teachers as one of the main steps necessary for retention.

In a separate multivariate analysis of the 1999–2000 SASS data, we explored the impact of mentoring and induction programs on the turnover of new teachers. After controlling for the background characteristics of teachers and schools, we found a strong link between participation by beginning teachers in induction and mentoring programs and their likelihood of moving or leaving after their first year on the job (Smith & Ingersoll, 2003). The data showed that the predicted probability of turnover of first year, newly hired, inexperienced teachers, who did not participate in any induction and mentoring programs was 40% (see Figure 8). In contrast, after controlling for the background characteristics of teachers and schools, the turnover probability of beginning teachers who received what I labeled as "some" induction (had a helpful mentor from their same field; had common planning time with other teachers in their subject area; and had regularly scheduled collaboration with other teachers on issues

of instruction) was 28%. Twenty-two percent of beginning teachers received just these three components. Finally, a very small number (less than 1% of beginning teachers in 1999–00) experienced what I label as a "full" induction experience that included the above three components, plus five more: participated in a general induction program; participated in a seminar for beginning teachers; had regular or supportive communication with their principal, other administrators, or department chair; participated in an external network; and had a reduced number of course preparations. Participation in these activities, collectively, had a very large and statistically significant impact—the probability of a departure at the end of their first year for those getting this package was less than half of those who participated in no induction activities.

It is important to recognize that none of these data suggests adopting any of the above steps will be inexpensive or easy. But, from the perspective of this analysis, the data suggest that schools are not simply victims of inexorable demographic trends and that there is a significant role for the management and organization of schools in both the genesis of, and the solution to, school staffing problems. The data suggest that improvements in the above aspects of the teaching job would contribute to lower rates of turnover, in turn, di-

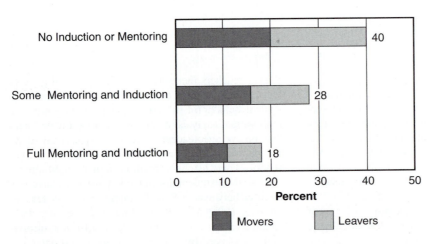

FIGURE 8   Percent Turnover After First Year of Newly Hired, Inexperienced Teachers, According to Whether They Participated in Induction and Mentoring Programs, 2000–01

Source: Adapted from Smith and Ingersoll (2003).

minish school staffing problems and, hence, ultimately, aid the performance of schools.

Endnotes

1. The data on school hiring difficulties from the 1999–2000 SASS school questionnaire asked school officials "how difficult or easy it was to fill the vacancies for this school year" in each field. I counted as having "difficulty filling teaching vacancies" all those schools reporting either: "somewhat difficult," "very difficult," or "could not fill."

2. Using a one-way random effects ANOVA model, the data show that the variance component within states was 44 times the size of the variance component between states. Intraclass correlation = .022.

3. One example of a cross-occupational comparison that appears to have measurement shortcomings is an analysis of Baccalaureate and Beyond data by Henke et al. (2001). This analysis looked at beginning teacher attrition in comparison to other recent college grads. It followed 1993 grads who became teachers in the 1993–1994 year and then calculated how many of them were gone by April 1997. The analysis found a 18% rate of new teacher attrition for the three year span from April 1994 to April 1997. But the analysis did not appear to count all types of attrition. It appears that it only counted as attrition those who moved to full-time, non-teaching careers and jobs. It did not count those who went back to college, or those who left the workforce to, for example, do family caregiving. But other data, such as the SASS/TFS, tell us these other flows are substantial and are certainly counted as attrition in existing research. Not including them would make the overall attrition look smaller than it really is. Indeed, elsewhere in that report it appeared that 12% of new teachers left the full-time workforce for these other things; adding this 12% to the 18% attrition, the analysis did count, brings the B&B 3 year attrition rate to something close to 30% after three years—which is quite consistent with many other studies on beginning teacher attrition. It is unclear what this undercounting might mean for the cross-occupation comparisons made in the report, but it certainly casts doubt on them.

4. Data for professors are from a study sponsored by the American Association for University Professors (1989) and represent annual averages for the period from 1972 to 1989 (Ehrenberg et al., 1991). Data on technology and science professionals, such as engineers, research scientists, and software designers represent the 2000 year and are from Kochanski and Ledford (2001). Data for nurses are from the March 2000 National Sample Survey of Registered Nurses

conducted by the American Hospital Association. Data for federal employees are from the Office of Personnel Management (2003).

5. The most recent data from the US Census Bureau are from 2001: 5,473,000 teachers/135,073,000 total workforce = 4.05%. "Teachers" include all Pre-K, K, Elementary, Secondary and Special education teachers. College and university instructors and professors are not counted as teachers. Counselors and librarians are not counted as teachers.

6. As in Table 1, the data in Figure 3 are calculated at the level of the school. Hence "hires" and "departures" refer to those newly entering or departing a particular school. "Movers" includes transfers among schools within districts. Reassignments within a school are not defined as hires or as departures.

7. I calculated these cumulative rates of beginning teacher attrition using preliminary data from the 2000–2001 TFS. The results are similar to what I've found using each of the other three cycles of the TFS—1988–89; 1991–92; 1994–95. It should be recognized that the data shown in Figure 4 are only a rough approximation. The SASS/TFS data do not follow a particular cohort of newly hired teachers to ascertain how many remain in teaching after five years. Instead I approximated the cumulative loss of beginning teachers by multiplying together the probabilities of staying in teaching for teachers with experience from 1 to 5 years. (i.e., yr. 1 probability of staying in teaching $\times$ yr. 2 probability $\times$ yr. 3 probability $\times$ yr. 4 probability $\times$ yr. 5 probability). These cumulative estimates also do not account for those who later re-enter teaching—which has been found to be as much as 25%.

8. In Figure 6, large schools are defined as those with 600 or more students; small schools are those with fewer than 300 students. High-poverty refers to schools with a poverty enrollment of 80% or more; low-poverty refers to schools with a poverty enrollment below 10%. Middle categories of size and poverty are omitted in the figure.

9. The data in Table 2 are from the 1994–95 TFS because the relevant data from the 2000–2001 TFS were not released as of summer 2003. Note that the column segments in Table 2 displaying percentages reporting various reasons for turnover each add up to more than 100%, because respondents could indicate up to three reasons for their departures. The same applies to the column segments displaying reasons for dissatisfaction.

10. The data in Figure 7 are from the 1994–95 TFS because the relevant data from the 2000–2001 TFS were not released as of summer 2003. Note that the estimates add up to more than 100%, because respondents could indicate up to three steps.

References

American Association of University Professors. (1989). The annual report on the economic status of the profession, 1988–89. *Academe, 75*(2), 3–74.

Bidwell, C. (1965). The school as a formal organization. In J. March (Ed.), *Handbook of organizations* (pp. 973–1002). Chicago: Rand McNally.

Bluedorn, A. C. (1982). A unified model of turnover from organizations. *Human Relations, 35,* 135–153.

Boe, E., & Gilford, D. (1992). *Teacher supply, demand and quality.* Washington, DC: National Academy Press.

Braverman, Harry. (1974). *Labor and monopoly capitalism.* New York: Monthly Review Press.

Burawoy, Michael. (1979). *Manufacturing consent: Changes in the labor process under monopoly capitalism.* Chicago: University of Chicago Press.

Bureau of National Affairs. (2002). BNAs quarterly report on job absence and turnover. *Bulletin to Management.* Washington DC: Bureau of National Affairs.

Burns, T., & Stalker, G. M. (1961). *The management of innovation.* London: Tavistock.

Coleman, J., & Hoffer, T. (1987). *Public and private schools: The impact of communities.* New York: Basic.

Darling-Hammond, L. (1984). *Beyond the commission reports: The coming crisis in teaching.* Santa Monica, CA: Rand Corporation.

Durkheim, E. (1961/1925). *Moral education: A study in the theory and application of the sociology of education,* translated by E. K. Wilson and H. Schnurer. NewYork: Free Press.

Edwards, Richard. (1979). *Contested terrain.* New York: Basic Books.

Ehrenberg, R., Kasper, H., & Rees, D. (1991). Faculty turnover at American colleges and universities: analyses of AAUP data. *Economics of Education Review, 10*(2) 99–110.

Feistritzer, E. (1997). *Alternative teacher certification: A state-by-state analysis (1997).* Washington, DC: National Center for Education Information.

Gerald, D., & Hussar, W. (1998). *Projections of education statistics to 2008.* Washington, DC: National Center for Education Statistics.

Grant, G. (1988). *The world we created at Hamilton High.* Cambridge, MA: Harvard University Press.

Hafner, A., & Owings, J. (1991). *Careers in teaching: Following members of the high school class of 1972 in and out of teaching* (NCES Report No. 91–470). Washington, DC: U.S. Department of Education, National Center for Education Statistics.

Haggstrom, G. W., Darling-Hammond, L., & Grissmer, D. (1988). *Assessing teacher supply and demand.* Santa Monica, CA: Rand Corporation.

Halaby, C., & Weakliem, D. (1989). Worker control and attachment to the firm. *American Journal of Sociology, 95,* 549–591.

Henke, R., Chen, X., & Geis, S. (2000). *Progress through the pipeline: 1992–93 college graduates and elementary/secondary school teaching as of 1997.* Washington, DC: National Center for Education Statistics.

Henke, R., Zahn, L., & Carroll, D. (2001). *Attrition of new teachers among recent college graduates.* Washington, DC: National Center for Education Statistics.

Hirsch, E., Koppich, J., & Knapp, M. (2001). *Revisiting what states are doing to improve the quality of teaching: An update on patterns and trends.* Center for the Study of Teaching and Policy, University of Washington.

Hom, P., & Griffeth, R. (1995). *Employee turnover.* Cincinnati: South-Western Publishing.

Huling-Austin, L. (1990). Teacher induction programs and internships. In W. R. Houston (Ed.), *Handbook of research on teacher education.* Reston, VA: Association of Teacher Educators.

Hussar, W. (1998). *Predicting the need for newly hired teachers in the United States to 2008–09.* Washington, DC: National Center for Education Statistics.

Ingersoll, R. (1995). *Teacher supply, teacher qualifications and teacher turnover.* Washington, DC: National Center for Education Statistics.

Ingersoll, R. (1999). The problem of underqualified teachers in American secondary schools. *Educational Researcher, 28,* 26–37.

Ingersoll, R. (2001a). *Teacher turnover, teacher shortages and the organization of schools.* Center for the Study of Teaching and Policy, University of Washington.

Ingersoll, R. (2001b). Teacher Turnover and Teacher Shortages: An Organizational Analysis. *American Educational Research Journal, 38*(3), 499–534.

Ingersoll, R. (2003a) *Who controls teachers' work?: Power and accountability in America's schools.* Cambridge, MA: Harvard University Press. www.hup.harvard.edu/catalog/INGWHO.html.

Ingersoll, R. (2003b) Is there a shortage among mathematics and science teachers? *Science Educator 12*(1), 1–9.

Ingersoll, R., & Smith, T. (2003). The wrong solution to the teacher shortage. *Educational Leadership 60*(8), 30–33.

Integrated Postsecondary Educational Data System (IPEDS). (2001). *Data File.* Washington, DC: National Center for Education Statistics.

Kalleberg, A., & Mastekaasa, A. (1998). Organizational size, layoffs and quits in Norway. *Social Forces, 76,* 1243–73.

Kanter, R. (1977). *Men and women of the corporation.* New York: Basic.

Kirst, M. (1989). Who should control the schools? In T. J. Sergiovanni & J. Moore (Eds.), *Schooling for tomorrow*. Boston: Allyn and Bacon.

Kochanski, J., & Ledford, G. (2001). How to keep me—Retaining technical professionals. *Research-Technology Management,* May–June: 31–38.

Kopp, W. (1992). Reforming schools of education will not be enough. *Yale Law and Policy Review, 10,* 58–68.

Likert, R. (1967). *The human organization.* New York: McGraw-Hill.

Lortie, D. (1975). *School teacher.* Chicago: University of Chicago Press.

March, J., & Simon, H. (1958). *Organizations.* New York: Wiley.

Mobley, W. (1982). *Employee turnover: Causes, consequences and control.* Reading, MA: Addison-Wesley.

Mueller, C., & Price, J. (1990). Economic, psychological and sociological determinants of voluntary turnover. *Journal of Behavioral Economics, 19,* 321–335.

Murnane, R., Singer, J., Willett. J., Kemple, J., & Olsen, R. (Eds.). (1991). *Who will teach?: Policies that matter.* Cambridge, MA: Harvard University Press.

National Academy of Sciences. (1987). *Toward understanding teacher supply and demand.* Washington, DC: National Academy Press.

National Commission on Excellence in Education. (1983). *A nation at risk: The imperative for educational reform.* Washington, DC: Government Printing Office.

National Commission on Teaching and America's Future. (1997). *Doing what matters most: Investing in quality teaching.* New York: NCTAF.

Office of Personnel Management. (2003). *Central Personnel Data File (CPDF).* Washington, DC: OPM. www.opm.gov/feddata/index.asp.

Parsons, Talcott. (1959). The school class as a social system: Some of its functions in American society. *Harvard Educational Review 29,* 297–318.

Porter, L. W., Lawler, E. E., & Hackman, J. R. (1975). *Behavior in organizations.* New York: McGraw-Hill.

Price, J. (1977). *The study of turnover.* Ames, IA: Iowa State University Press.

Price, J. (1989). The impact of turnover on the organization. *Work and Occupations, 16,* 461–473.

Price, J. (1997). Handbook of organizational measurement. *International Journal of Manpower, 18,* 4–6.

Rosenholtz, S. (1989). *Teacher's workplace: The social organization of schools.* New York: Longman.

Schlecty, P., & Vance, V. (1981). Do academically able teachers leave education? The North Carolina case. *Phi Delta Kappan, 63,* 105–112.

Smith, T., & Ingersoll, R. (2003). Reducing teacher turnover: What are the components of effective induction? Paper presented at the annual meeting of the American Educational Research Association, Chicago.

Snyder, T., & Hoffman, C. (2001). *The digest of education.* Washington, DC: U.S. Department of Education, National Center for Education Statistics.

Steers, R. M., & Momday, R. T. (1981). Employee turnover and the post-decision accommodation process. In B. M. Shaw & L. L. Cummings (Eds.), *Research in organizational behavior.* Greenwich: JAI Press.

Stinebrickner, T. R. (2001). A dynamic model of teacher labor supply. *Journal of Labor Economics, 19*(1), 196–230.

Strober, M., & Tyack, D (1980). Why do women teach and men manage? *Signs, 5,* 499–500.

Texas Center for Educational Research. (2000). *The cost of teacher turnover.* Austin, TX: Texas State Board for Educator Certification.

Turner, A. N., & Lawrence, P. R. (1964). *Industrial jobs and the worker.* Cambridge, MA: Harvard University Press.

Tyack, D. (1974). *The one best system.* Cambridge, MA: Harvard University Press.

U.S. Bureau of the Census. (2002). *Statistical abstract* (117th Edition). Washington, DC: U.S. Department of Commerce.

Waller, W. (1932). *The sociology of teaching.* New York: Wiley.

Walton, R. E. (1980). Establishing and maintaining high commitment work systems. In J. Kimberly & R. Miles (Eds.), *The organization life cycle.* San Francisco: Jossey-Bass.

Weaver, T. (1983). *America's teacher quality problem: Alternatives for reform.* New York: Praeger Publishers.

7 | Curriculum, Pedagogy, and the Transmission of Knowledge

In Chapter 6, we looked at the organization and structure of U.S. schools. In this chapter, we will examine what goes on inside of the schools by focusing on curriculum and teaching practices. As we argued in Chapter 4, sociologists of education suggest that schools produce important cognitive and noncognitive results and affect students' lives in significant ways. The important question, however, is how do the schools do this? The answer, in part, lies in what the schools teach and how they teach it. This chapter explores these issues in detail.

What Do the Schools Teach?

Teachers and students in teacher education programs too often think in very simplistic terms about what the schools teach. Their answer to the question is that the schools teach a specific curriculum, one that is mandated by the state education department and implemented in an organized manner within the schools. This view defines the curriculum as an objective and organized body of knowledge to be transmitted to students. Unfortunately, such a view simplifies the complexity of the curriculum and ignores the social and political dimensions of what is taught in schools.

Traditional approaches to the curriculum have been concerned with the science of the curriculum. These approaches view the curriculum as objective bodies of knowledge and examine the ways in which this knowledge may be designed, taught, and evaluated. Using a technical-rational model, traditional curriculum theorists and curriculum planners are not concerned with why the curriculum looks as it does, but rather with how it can be effectively designed and transmitted to students. Students in teacher education programs, from this perspective, are taught to design curriculum using goals and objectives and to evaluate it in terms of the effectiveness of student learning. Although there may be some practical merit for prospective teachers to understand how to develop curriculum strategies, these traditional approaches eschew important political, sociological, historical, and philosophical questions about what is taught in schools. The effects of such teacher education practices is that teachers look at the curriculum from this "objectivist" perspective and therefore seldom question critically the central component of what they do on a daily basis: transmit knowledge and values to students.

Beginning in the 1960s and 1970s, sociologists of education and curriculum began to challenge the traditional theories of curriculum. Rather than viewing curriculum as an objective body of knowledge, they suggested that the curriculum is an organized body of knowledge that represents political, social, and ideological interests. The "new sociology of education" ushered in by the works of Michael F. D. Young (1971) and Basil Bernstein (1973a, 1973b, 1977) in Britain looked critically at the curriculum as a reflection of the dominant interests in society and suggested that what is taught in schools is a critical component of the effects of schooling.

Drawing on the insights of the sociology of knowledge (Berger & Luckmann, 1967; Durkheim, 1947, 1954; Mannheim, 1936; Marx & Engels, 1947), the new sociology did not view the curriculum as value neutral, but rather as the subject for critical and ideological analysis. Although the new sociology certainly had a radical flavor to it and inspired what has been labeled "critical curriculum theory" (Apple, 1978, 1982a, 1982b; Giroux, 1981, 1983a, 1983b), the insights of the sociology of curriculum do not always have a radical perspective. What is important about the sociological approach to the curriculum is that it rejects the view that the curriculum is objective and instead insists that the curriculum be viewed as subjectively reflecting particular interests within a society. What these interests are and how the curriculum reflects them is a question of ideological debate as well as for empirical investigation.

We will return to sociological studies of the curriculum later in this chapter. First, we will examine the historical and philosophical dimensions of the curriculum. Whereas the sociology of curriculum analyzes what is taught in schools, the history of the curriculum examines what was taught, the politics of the curriculum examines the battles and conflicts over what is and should be taught, and the philosophy of the curriculum examines what ought to be taught and why.

The History and Philosophy of the Curriculum

The history of the curriculum helps explain why the curriculum looks as it does today. Kliebard (1986), in his book *The Struggle for the American Curriculum: 1893–1958,* outlines four different types of curriculum in the twentieth century: humanist, social efficiency, developmentalist, and social meliorist, each of which had a different view of the goals of schooling.

The *humanist curriculum* reflects the idealist philosophy that knowledge of the traditional liberal arts is the cornerstone of an educated citizenry and that the purpose of education is to present to students the best of what has been thought and written. Traditionally, this curriculum focused on the Western heritage as the basis for intellectual development, although some who support this type of curriculum argue that the liberal arts need not focus exclusively on the Western tradition. This curriculum model dominated nineteenth-century and early twentieth-century U.S. education and was codified in the National Education Association's Committee of Ten report issued in 1893, "which recommended that all secondary students, regardless of whether they intended to go to college, should be liberally educated and should study English, foreign languages, mathematics, history, and science" (Ravitch, 1983, p. 47).

Although the view that a Western liberal arts curriculum for all secondary students did not remain the dominant model of secondary schooling in the twentieth century, conservative critics have called for a return to the humanist curriculum. As we noted earlier, critics such as Bennett (1988), Hirsch (1987), and Ravitch and Finn (1987) have argued that U.S. students do not know enough about their cultural heritage because the school curriculum has not emphasized it for all students. They have proposed that the schools should return to a traditional liberal arts curriculum for all students and that this curriculum should focus, although not necessarily exclusively, on the Western tradition. Bennett (1988), as Secretary of Education during the Reagan administration, took an activist posture in promoting such curriculum reform. In his proposals for a model elementary and secondary curriculum, he emphasized the need for a traditional core of subjects and readings that would teach all students a common set of worthwhile knowledge and an array of intellectual skills.

From a functionalist perspective, the conservative curriculum reformers of the 1980s and 1990s believed that the purpose of schooling was to transmit a common body of knowledge in order to reproduce a common cultural heritage. As we noted earlier, the problem with this view, from a conflict perspective, is that it assumed a common culture. It is this disagreement about the role of schools in transmitting a common culture that was at the heart of disagreements over curriculum in the twentieth century.

The *social efficiency curriculum* was a philosophically pragmatist approach developed in the early twentieth century as a putatively democratic response to the development of mass public secondary education. As we suggested in Chapter 3, the introduction of the comprehensive high school was marked by the processes of differentiated curriculum, scientific management of the schools and the curriculum, and standardized testing of students for placement into ability groups and/or curriculum tracks (Oakes, 1985, Chapter 2; Powell, Farrar, & Cohen, 1985, Chapter 5). Rather than viewing the need for a common academic curriculum for all students, as with the humanist tradition, the social efficiency curriculum was rooted in the belief that different groups of students, with different sets of needs and aspirations, should receive different types of schooling. Although this perspective emerged from the progressive visions of Dewey about the need for individualized and flexible curriculum, many critics (Cremin, 1961; Hofstadter, 1966; Sadovnik, 1991a; Tyack, 1974) believe that the social efficiency curriculum was a distortion of his progressive vision.

The publication of the *Cardinal Principles of Secondary Education* in 1918 by the National Education Association's Commission on the Reorganization of Secondary Schools represented a direct contrast to the humanist tradition of the Committee of Ten. This report ushered in what Ravitch (1983, p. 48) termed *pedagogical progressivism* and stressed the relationship between schooling and the activities of adults within society. Given the stratified nature of adult roles, the school curriculum was tailored to prepare students for these diverse places in society. The result, as we argued in Chapter 3, was that students often received very different curricula, based on their race, class, and gender. In criticizing the distortion of early progressivism, Ravitch (1983, p. 48) wrote, "The social efficiency element of the *Cardinal Principles,* which inverted Dewey's notion of the school as a lever of social reform into the school as a mechanism to adjust the individual to society, became the cornerstone of the new progressivism." It is important to note the distinction made between this new progressivism and its social efficiency bent and the principles of Dewey, that we believe were profoundly distorted by this view of curriculum.

The development of the social efficiency curriculum in the twentieth century was related to the scientific management of the schools. Based on the writings of Frederick Taylor about the management of the factory system, the administration of schools began to mirror this form of social organization, with its emphasis on efficiency, time on task, and a social division of labor (see Callahan, 1962; Tyack, 1974; Tyack & Hansot, 1982). The scientific management of the curriculum involved both the division of knowledge into strictly defined areas and its transmission into scientifically defined goals and objectives, as well as the division of students into different aspects of the curriculum, based on ability. Beginning in the early twentieth century, the definition of ability became increasingly based on performance on standardized tests.

The development of standardized testing was inextricably related to the differentiation of the curriculum. At the elementary school level, intelligence tests and reading tests were used to assign students to ability groups and ability-grouped classes. At the secondary level, standardized tests, as well as previous school achievement (and other factors not related to ability), were used to place students into different curriculum tracks: academic, for college-bound students; vocational, to prepare students directly for the postsecondary world of work; and general, which usually was an academic curriculum taught at a lower level. These practices, which will be discussed later in this chapter, became a defining characteristic of U.S. education. The important point, however, is that the development of standardized testing became the process by which students were placed in different curriculum tracks, putatively in a fair and meritocratic manner. The extent to which such placement has been meritocratic (i.e., based on ability) has been a controversial and hotly debated issue. It will be discussed in Chapter 9.

Putting the fairness of curriculum placement aside for the moment, the basic assumption of the social efficiency curriculum that different groups of students should receive different curricula has come increasingly under criticism from both conservatives and radicals. Conservatives argue that the separation of the curriculum into different tracks has led to the denigration of the traditional purpose of schooling—to pass on a common culture to all citizens. Radicals argue that the placement into curriculum tracks has been based on race, class, and gender and thus has limited the life chances of minority, working class, and female students, who, because they are often more likely to elect or wind up in general or vocational tracks, are less likely to go on to college. These are empirical questions that will be discussed in Chapter 9.

The important point is that the curriculum tracking associated with the social efficiency curriculum is a subject of considerable research and debate. Moreover, many critics question the moral basis of providing different students with such radically different school experiences. This issue returns us to the very nature and purpose of schooling in a complex and diverse society: Should it be the same for everyone or should it be variable and flexible, given the diverse nature of the social division of labor?

The *developmentalist curriculum* is related to the needs and interests of the student rather than the needs of society. This curriculum emanated from the aspects of Dewey's writings related to the relationship between the child and the curriculum (Dewey, 1902), as well as developmental psychologists such as Piaget, and it emphasized the process of teaching as well as its content. This philosophically progressive approach to teaching was student centered and was concerned with relating the curriculum to the needs and interests of each child at particular developmental stages. Thus, it stressed flexibility in both what was taught and how it was taught, with the emphasis on the development of each student's individual capacities. Moreover, the developmental curriculum stressed the importance of relating schooling to the life experiences of each child in a way that would make education come alive in a meaningful manner. The teacher, from this perspective, was not a transmitter of knowledge but rather a facilitator of student growth.

Although school and curriculum historians (Kliebard, 1986; Spring, 1989) pointed out that the developmental curriculum model was not very influential in the U.S. public schools, they also noted that it has been profoundly influential in teacher education programs, as well as an important model in independent and alternative schools. It was in the private, independent sector that this view of curriculum and pedagogy first became dominant, with Dewey's progressive principles implemented in a number of independent progressive schools, such as Bank Street (Antler, 1987), City and Country (Pratt, 1924), Dalton (Semel, 1992), Putney (Lloyd, 1987), and Shady Hill (Yeomans, 1979).

Furthermore, in the 1960s and 1970s, the reemergence of what Ravitch (1983, pp. 239–256) called *romantic progressivism* occurred, placing its philosophical allegiance squarely within this form of curriculum and pedagogy. Among its most radical proponents was the British psychoanalyst and educator A. S. Neill, whose boarding school Summerhill had no required curriculum and became a prototype of the "open" and "free" schools of the period.

Although the influence of the developmental curriculum has been marginal in the public schools (Cuban, 1984) and its advocacy waned in the conservative era of the 1980s and 1990s, there are still remnants of it in both the public and private sectors. In the private sector, many of the early progressive schools still exist and in varying degrees still reflect their early progressive character. Some, such as Bank Street and City and Country, remain faithful to their founders' visions; others, such as Dalton, have been transformed considerably into a more traditional humanist model (Semel, 1992). In the public sector, the whole-language movement for teaching reading and writing is developmental in its approach. Rather than teaching reading and writing through traditional basal readers, it relates literacy instruction to the experiences and developmental stages of children (Bennett & LaCompte, 1990, p. 186).

The *social meliorist curriculum,* which was philosophically social reconstructionist (the radical wing of progressive education), developed in the 1930s, both out of the writings of Dewey, who was concerned with the role of the schools in reforming society (James, 1995; Semel & Sadovnik, 1999), as well as a response to the growing dominance of the social efficiency curriculum. Two of the most influential of the social meliorists were two Teachers College (Columbia University) professors, George Counts and Harold Rugg, who radicalized Dewey's philosophy into an explicit theory that the schools should change society, or, at the least, help solve its fundamental problems. In books such as Counts's *Dare the Schools Build a New Social Order?* (1932) and Rugg's writings on curriculum, these critics proposed that the school curriculum should teach students to think and to help solve societal problems, if not to change the society itself.

Although this view of curriculum never challenged the dominance of the social efficiency model, it has continued to influence curriculum theory in the United States and elsewhere. The social meliorist tradition is the precursor to what is called *contemporary critical curriculum theory,* with Apple and Giroux's work the most important examples. Additionally, philosophers such as Maxine Greene and Paulo Freire, discussed in Chapter 5, adopt a consciously social meliorist view of curriculum, which stresses the role of the curriculum in moving students to become aware of societal problems and to become active in changing the world. Although these writings are sometimes presented to prospective teachers in teacher education programs, the effects of the social meliorist model in public schools is minimal. For the most part, it has been the social efficiency curriculum, much more than the other three models, that is responsible for what is taught in U.S. schools.

The social efficiency curriculum resulted in the organization of the curriculum into distinct tracks. Although we will discuss the stratification of the curriculum later in this chapter, it is important to note that the degree of overlap between various segments of the curriculum varied according to the type of school and its philosophy of curriculum. Bernstein (1977) argued that curriculum may be either strongly classified (i.e., where there is a strong distinction between academic subjects such as mathematics, science, history, literature, music, art, etc.) or weakly classified (i.e., where there is integration and overlap between academic subjects, such as mathematics and science, social studies, humanities—including history, literature, art, music, etc.). Additionally, in the social efficiency curriculum there may be strong classification between academic and vocational curricula, with students taking the majority of their courses in one area or the other, or weak classification, with students taking courses in both areas. There have been both philosophical and sociological factors in the organization of the curriculum.

From a philosophical vantage point, traditionalists (conservatives) supported the humanist curriculum model and the strong classification between academic subjects. This was necessary, they argued, to properly transmit the traditional cultural knowledge. Progressives tended to support a more integrative curriculum, discouraging the separation of subjects. In many of the early progressive schools, such as the Lincoln School in New York City, an integrative core curriculum revolving around common themes rather than subjects was favored. This approach is now reappearing in the contemporary whole-language movement and in the thematic core curriculum at New York City's Central Park East School, a public progressive school.

From a sociological vantage point, the organization of the curriculum has been stratified according to the social class composition of the school. Elite private schools, for example, have always had a humanist curriculum with strong classification between academic subjects. Public high schools have had a social efficiency curriculum with strong classification between academic and vocational subjects. Within the public system, the degree to which the academic track has mirrored the humanist curriculum has varied, often in relation to the social class composition of the students. Progressive private and public schools have had a weakly classified academic curriculum that reflected their particular philosophy of education, but as Bernstein (1977) suggested, this philosophy reflected their particular middle- and upper middle-class preferences. Thus, the organization of the curriculum has not been and is not now a simple matter. It relates to philosophical, sociological, and political factors. We now turn to the sociological and political dimensions.

The Politics of the Curriculum

The politics of curriculum analyzes the struggles over different conceptions of what should be taught. As we have noted, the history of the U.S. curriculum may be understood in terms of different models of school knowledge. Throughout the twentieth century, various groups, both inside and outside the schools, fought to shape and control the schools' curriculum. Labeling these groups and determining their degree of control is still the subject of debate. For example, functionalists, subscribing to a pluralist democratic model of schooling, believe that the curriculum represents a democratic consensus about what should be taught. Neo-Marxist conflict theorists believe that the dominant capitalist class controls what is taught in school. Non-Marxist conflict theorists believe that many groups struggle over the curriculum, with different groups winning and losing at different historical periods.

Ravitch (1983) has documented the long and conflictual struggles that have marked U.S. educational history. Her history of education in the twentieth century reveals a pattern of conflict between various groups about the purpose and goals of the schools. Within this context, the curriculum became contested terrain—the subject of heated controversy and disagreements. Earlier in this chapter, we presented the four curriculum models that predominated in the twentieth century; in this section, we will discuss the politics of curriculum and how various groups attempt to shape the curriculum to reflect their own interests and ideologies.

The central question in the politics of the curriculum is: *Who shapes the curriculum?* As the new sociology of education suggests, the curriculum is not a value-neutral, objective set of information to be transmitted to students; rather, it represents what a culture wants its students to know. From this perspective, curriculum represents culturally valued knowledge. The question remains, however: Whose values are represented and how do groups manage to translate their values into the subjects that are taught in school?

These questions are first and foremost related to power. The ability to shape the curriculum requires that groups have the power to affect the selection of instructional materials and textbooks. There are two models of political power used by political scientists. The first, the pluralist model (Dahl, 1961), argues that the political system in the United States is not controlled by any one group; rather, the decisions are made through the input of many groups, each attempting to exercise influence and control. The second, the political elite model (Domhoff, 1967, 1983; Mills, 1956), argues that a small number of powerful groups (i.e., those with wealth and political influence) dominate the political landscape and have disproportionate control over political decision making.

Although the controversy over which of the two views is correct has not been settled, we believe that the reality, as in most controversies, lies somewhere in the middle. The U.S. political system allows for participation from many groups, but it also requires a great deal of money and power to successfully affect political decisions. On this level, the political elite model finds considerable support. Nonetheless, the evidence does not support the view that less powerful groups cannot win some of the time or that a ruling elite manages to control the political arena. For example, the ability of a coalition of community groups in New York City to defeat the proposed Westway Project (to rebuild the collapsed West Side Highway), which was supported by the most powerful and wealthy interests in the city, is an example of the ability of the less powerful to sometimes emerge victorious. Thus, political decision making is a complex, conflictual process in which many groups vie for advantage, with those with more wealth and power having distinct advantages but not total domination. In the educational arena, these conflicts are certainly apparent.

Conflicts over curriculum are more likely to occur in the public schools than in the private ones. The reason for this is fairly clear. Parents who send their children to private or parochial schools do so, in part, because they support the particular school's philosophy. Where there are conflicts in the private sector, it is usually about disagreements within a particular philosophical or religious tradition, as opposed to between two or more different philosophies. In the public sector, however, there is rarely agreement about educational matters and thus the curriculum, like other aspects of the educational system, is the focus of considerable debate. In a society with diverse cultural groups, it is inevitable that what the schools teach will not be the product of consensus. The questions are: How do all of the groups affect what is taught in classrooms, and which groups are successful in accomplishing this task?

Kirst (1984, p. 114) has outlined the different levels of influence on the school curriculum in Table 7.1. As the table indicates, there are multiple factors that influence

TABLE 7.1 Influences on Curriculum Policy Making

	National	**State**	**Local**
General Legislative	Congress	State Legislature	City Council (usually has no influence)
Educational Legislative	U.S. House Committee on Education & Labor	State School Board	Local School Board
Executive	President	Governor	Mayor (usually has no influence)
Administrative School	U.S. Department of Education	State Department of Education	Superintendent
Bureaucratic	National Science Foundation (Division of Curriculum Improvement)	State Department of Education (Division of Instruction)	Department Chairmen, Teachers
Professional Association	National Testing Agencies such as Educational Testing Services (ETS)	Accrediting Associations; State Subject Matter Affiliates, National Education Association	County Association of Superintendents
Private Interests	Foundations & Business Corporations, Political & Service Organizations		

Source: Wirt and Kirst (1972).

curriculum policy making at the national, state, and local levels. Curriculum decisions occur through a number of different channels, including the legislative and executive branches of government; the levels of the school system; and other interests, including professional associations, bureaucratic interests, and private interests (such as business and parent groups). As we discussed in Chapter 6, unlike many countries where there is governmental control of education and thus a national curriculum, education in the United States is controlled at the state and local levels. Therefore, curriculum policy making is, for the most part, a state and local matter, although in the last decade the federal government has taken an increasingly activist role in education. Nonetheless, the federal government, through its Department of Education or through the president himself, is one part of the process, not the determining factor.

Although each of these political actors just listed has input into the curriculum, it is evident that all do not have equal input. If there is any one group with more influence than the others, it is the education profession itself, consisting of state-level educational bureaucrats, administrators at the district and school levels, and teachers. The traditional humanist curriculum and the social efficiency curriculum, which have dominated U.S. education to a large degree, reflect the values and interests of professional educators. Moreover, as Ravitch (1983) and Kliebard (1986) noted, the struggle over the U.S. curriculum has involved primarily educators and has revolved around different philosophies of education.

Although there is no denying that there have been influences from outside the educational establishment—including students, parents, and politicians—their influence has not been nearly as significant. The U.S. curriculum has reflected the professional values of educators. Additionally, it mirrored the increased power of expertise in the twentieth century. As Collins (1979) argued, the rise of professions has led to the use of professional expertise as a means of influence. In the case of the curriculum, professional educators have made valuable use of their expertise as a means to legitimate their control over the curriculum.

Despite the dominance of professional educators in determining the curriculum, other groups have sought control with varying degrees of success. More often than not, conflicts over the curriculum have symbolized significant political and cultural conflicts. For example, in 1925, amidst the fundamentalist religious movements of the period, the Scopes Trial reflected the tensions between schooling and particular groups opposed to the official curriculum. More importantly, the trial represented the role of the school in reflecting the values of a modern society and the opposition of those still faithful to traditional societal values.

This trial involved the prosecution of a Tennessee biology teacher, John Scopes, who violated the state law prohibiting the teaching of evolution and requiring the teaching of creationism. In the decades following the publication of Darwin's *On the Origin of the Species* (1859), conflict between secular theories of evolution and religious theories of creationism raged on. Backed by the American Civil Liberties Union, Scopes used a biology textbook that taught evolution and was arrested. The trial, which literally became a circus and a symbol of the conflict between the old and the new, involved two important individuals in U.S. political and legal history: William Jennings Bryan, the populist leader and fundamentalist crusader, who assisted the prosecution, and Clarence Darrow, the liberal legal crusader, who represented the defendant. In

Tennessee, where fundamentalism was widely accepted, and with a judge who was clearly biased against Scopes (Garraty, 1985, p. 430), the defendant was found guilty and fined $100.

This case represented the battle between the values of the secular modern world and the values of the traditional religious world. Despite the belief of the majority of educators that evolution was the correct scientific interpretation, the power of a conservative state legislature to shape the curriculum won out, at least temporarily. Over the years, however, the professional expertise of scientists has been dominant. Today, fundamentalists are still trying to eliminate the teaching of evolution or to include creationism as a viable alternative theory.

In the 1940s and 1950s, controversies over curriculum were widespread. As part of the intellectual attack on progressive education, a number of educational and cultural critics argued that progressivism had watered down the traditional curriculum and replaced it with a social efficiency curriculum. Critics such as Arthur Bestor (1953) called for a return to the classical humanist curriculum and to an emphasis on the intellectual functions of schooling.

Whereas many of these critiques were based on academic and intellectual grounds, some of the conflicts revolved around blatantly political issues. With the rise of anticommunism during the McCarthy Era (where alleged Communists were brought before the House on Un-American Activities Committee and a Senate Investigative Committee chaired by Senator Joseph McCarthy of Wisconsin), the school curriculum became the subject of political turmoil. Anti-Communist groups pressured school districts to eliminate textbooks and instructional materials that they believed to be Communist. Moreover, progressive education, as a whole, was seen as part of a Communist conspiracy and labeled REDucation (Ravitch, 1983, p. 105). During this period, books by noted progressive educators such as Harold Rugg were banned in many districts, teachers at both the K–12 and university levels were required to take loyalty oaths, and many teachers and professors were dismissed as Communists or Communist sympathizers. This was a period in which conservatives actively sought to control what was taught in school, both by controlling the curriculum and the faculty.

One of the best examples of the politics of schooling during this period occurred in Pasadena, California. In 1948, Willard Goslin, a celebrated progressive educator, was hired as superintendent. As Cremin (1990, pp. 87–88) noted, for the next two years, a strongly organized group of conservatives attacked the superintendent's policies, the school curriculum, and its teaching methods. In 1950, under considerable pressure and amidst continual conflict, Superintendent Goslin was forced to resign. Cremin has suggested that this case is a prime example of the historical tendency for Americans to use politics as a means for controlling education, with political disagreements often a key aspect of the fight for control.

Although this period was a shameful era in U.S. history, Ravitch (1983) pointed out that the incidents of book banning were by no means the rule. Many districts successfully battled the book-banning activists. Moreover, by the 1950s, the tide began to turn, with both the legislative and judicial branches reacting against McCarthyism. However, during this time, conscious efforts were made to control what was taught in schools, and the wounds inflicted did not easily heal.

During the past 20 or so years, new controversies surrounding the curriculum have emerged. In the 1970s through the 1990s, conservative groups argued that many books—including Ken Kesey's (1977) *One Flew Over the Cuckoo's Nest,* Richard Wright's (1969) *Native Son,* and Joseph Heller's (1985) *Catch* 22—were unsuitable for use in public schools. In some districts, books were banned and taken off reading lists and library shelves.

Although the cases of book banning are the most sensational examples of the attempt to control curriculum, the struggle over what is conveyed to students occurs in more routine ways, such as in the selection of textbooks. Kirst (1984, pp. 118–122) provided an illuminating discussion of the factors affecting textbook adoptions. He suggested that a number of forces—including the economics of publishing, the dominance of those states such as Texas and California with statewide adoption policies, the clout of political pressure groups, the guidelines of professional associations, and the input of educators—all combine to create a complex and politically charged process. The attempt to meet the demands of such a complex and often contradictory set of pressure groups leads to what many critics suggest are textbooks with little controversy and less life (Sewall, 1991). According to Kirst, although textbook publishers are constantly concerned with which group they will offend and thus risk losing market share, they are unfortunately less concerned with such significant issues as content and presentation.

The difficulties in textbook publishing are part of a larger curricular issue—that is: What is the appropriate content of the curriculum? In the 1980s, the question of what should be taught became a difficult and controversial subject. Beginning with the conservative claim that U.S. students know very little because the schools have abandoned their traditional role in transmitting the nation's cultural heritage, questions about the definition of the cultural heritage became central to curriculum debates. While conservatives such as Finn and Hirsch argued that the school curriculum should consist largely of the Western tradition, liberals and radicals countered that this tradition unfairly ignored the important traditions of non-Western groups, people of color, women, and other minority groups.

This controversy affected both the K–12 level and the postsecondary level. At the K–12 level in New York state, a commission was appointed in 1990 by Commissioner of Education Thomas Sobel to revise the social studies curriculum in light of the demands of some groups for a more multicultural curriculum and the counterclaims by other groups that such demands were both racist and encouraged historical inaccuracies. On the one hand, supporters of multicultural curriculum charged that the traditional curriculum was ethnocentric and reinforced the low self-esteem of minority groups because they rarely were presented with historical role models. On the other hand, conservative critics responded that in order to give equal time to all groups, the teaching of history would be revised in a distorted and inaccurate manner (Ravitch, 1989).

The conflict between parental values and the curriculum was clearly illustrated in New York City in 1992 when District 24 in Queens objected to the New York City Board of Education's new multicultural curriculum. This curriculum was titled "Children of the Rainbow" and it called for the teaching of tolerance for homosexual families to elementary school children. Outraged parents and community leaders, first in

District 24 and then throughout New York City, challenged the curriculum, arguing that schools do not have the right to teach "immoral" values to children. Proponents of the curriculum argued that the intent behind the curriculum was to foster tolerance and respect for all groups and that the schools were the appropriate place for such an education.

Some of the curriculum's optional teaching materials, including "Heather Has Two Mommies" and "Daddy Has a Roommate," became the focus of heated conflict between New York City Chancellor Joseph Fernandez and a number of local school boards. The Chancellor suspended the District 24 Community School Board for refusing to comply with the curriculum or to offer a suitable alternative; the Board of Education reinstated the community school board and called on all parties to reach a compromise that would maintain the integrity of the multicultural curriculum. Although the conflict has yet to be resolved fully, the issue has revealed strong feelings about homosexuality and the fact that significant numbers of parents are strongly opposed to schools teaching what parents consider values to their children. It also underscores the political dimension of the curriculum and how the often moral aspects of such political conflict become educational issues. In the aftermath of this conflict, the New York City Board of Education did not renew Fernandez's contract.

At the postsecondary level, debates about the need for a core curriculum for all students and what that core should be have raged from campus to campus. At Stanford University, for example, the requirement that all undergraduates take a core curriculum stressing Western civilization was abolished after considerable controversy and was replaced with requirements stressing multiculturalism. At Columbia University, where undergraduates have for decades taken a core curriculum stressing Western civilization, the curriculum has been retained despite vigorous criticism. However, the University of Chicago has recently decided to revise its curriculum.

By the early 1990s, the term *politically correct* became part of the popular culture. It referred to definitions of what is construed as acceptable language, curriculum, and ideas. It was initially coined by campus conservatives who argued that universities were dominated by radicals who conspired to alter the traditional curriculum and who "censor" all ideas that they deem offensive (e.g., see D'Souza, 1991; Kimball, 1990). Critics responded that the university has always reflected the dominant interests of society and that the curriculum is in dire need of revision in a more democratic and representative manner.

Although there have been serious debates on many campuses on the important philosophical issues underlying these disagreements—such as the purpose of higher education and the nature of a literary canon, or whether one exists—to a large degree, the media has simplified the issue of political correctness in such a way that it has become a symbol not for the critical questions it raises but for the putative silliness of university life. More importantly, the conflicts over curriculum correctness and free speech (that is, do individuals have the right to say offensive things, and who decides what is and what is not offensive?) have raised the specter of McCarthyism and all the ugliness that it represented.

What is clear from these examples is that curriculum debates are hotly contested because they represent fundamental questions about the purposes of schooling. The transmission of knowledge, as we have suggested, is never objective or value neutral.

Rather, it represents what particular interest groups believe students should know. Because there is little agreement about this, it is no surprise that there is significant conflict over the content of the curriculum. We have also suggested that the shaping of the curriculum is a complex process with many groups having input; but if there is one dominant group in this process, it is professional educators, whose expertise enables them to justify their claims. However, professional educators are not a cohesive interest group, so many of the most heated curriculum debates involve disagreements within this group about the nature and purpose of the curriculum.

The Sociology of the Curriculum

Sociologists of curriculum have focused on not only what is taught but why it is taught. As we have mentioned, sociologists of curriculum reject the objectivist notion that curriculum is value neutral; rather, they view it as a reflection of particular interests within a society. Additionally, sociologists believe that the school curriculum includes both what is formally included as the subject matter to be learned—the formal curriculum—as well as the informal or hidden curriculum. The hidden curriculum includes what is taught to students through implicit rules and messages, as well as through what is left out of the formal curriculum. For example, very few undergraduate or graduate students can list more than one nineteenth-century American feminist. In fact, many do not know that there was a feminist movement in the nineteenth century (for a complete discussion, see Leach, 1980). Why is this the case? We believe it is because the history of women has never been a part of the school curriculum. Certain ideas, people, and events are not part of the curriculum because those who formulate it do not deem them important enough. From the standpoint of the formal curriculum, this is a political and social statement; in terms of the hidden curriculum, students receive a message that these things are just not important, which ultimately is a powerful force in shaping human consciousness. The sociology of curriculum, as the following discussion will illuminate, is concerned with both the formal and informal curriculum.

The sociology of the curriculum concentrates on the function of what is taught in schools and its relationship to the role of schools within society. As we stated in Chapter 4, functionalist and conflict theories of school and society differ about the roles of schools in U.S. society. Functionalists believe the role of the schools is to integrate children into the existing social order—a social order that is based on consensus and agreement. Conflict theorists believe that the role of schools is to reproduce the existing social order—a social order that represents the dominant groups in society. Based on these differences, the two theories have different perspectives on the school curriculum.

Functionalists argue that the school curriculum represents the codification of the knowledge that students need to become competent members of society. From this perspective, the curriculum transmits to students the cultural heritage required for a cohesive social system. Thus, the role of the curriculum is to give students the knowledge, language, and values to ensure social stability, for without a shared common culture social order is not possible.

The general functionalist theory, derived by the work of Emile Durkheim (1962, 1977) in the late nineteenth and early twentieth centuries, was concerned with the role of schools in combating the social and moral breakdown initiated by modernization. As the processes of industrialization, secularization, and urbanization weakened the bonds between people and the rituals that traditionally gave people a sense of community, Durkheim argued that the schools had to teach students to fit into the less cohesive modern world.

Modern functionalist theory, developed in the United States through the works of Talcott Parsons (1959) and Robert Dreeben (1968), stressed the role of the schools in preparing students for the increasingly complex roles required in a modern society. This society, according to functionalists, is a democratic, meritocratic, and expert society (Hurn, 1993, pp. 44–47) and the school curriculum is designed to enable students to function within this type of society. According to Hurn (pp. 193–194), functionalists believe that in the twentieth century, the curriculum had to change to meet the new requirements of the modern world. In this respect, the schools began to move away from the teaching of isolated facts through memorization to the general task of teaching students how to learn. Thus, for functionalists, the specific content of the curriculum, such as history or literature, is less important than the role of the schools in teaching students how to learn—a skill vital in an increasingly technocratic society.

In addition to teaching general cognitive skills, functionalists believe that the schools teach the general values and norms essential to a modern society. According to Parsons (1959) and Dreeben (1968), the modern society is one where individuals are rewarded based on achievement and competence. This meritocratic system is reflected in the way schools operate, with the norm of universalism (that people are treated according to universal principles of evaluation) rather than particularism (that people are treated according to individual characteristics, such as family background, personality, etc.) the basis for evaluation.

Finally, functionalists believe that schools teach students the values that are essential to a modern society. According to this theory, modern society is a more cosmopolitan and tolerant one than traditional society, and schools teach students to respect others, to respect differences, and to base their opinions on knowledge rather than tradition. Such attitudes are necessary in a society where innovation and change are the foundation of technological development, and schools teach students these vitally important things. In summary, the functionalist theory is a positive view of the role of the schools and suggests that what schools teach are the general norms, values, and knowledge required for the maintenance and development of modern society.

According to conflict theorists, who provide a far more radical view of the roles of schools in society, the functionalist perspective of what is taught in schools is more a reflection of ideology than empirical reality. Conflict theorists do not believe that the schools teach liberal values and attitudes such as tolerance and respect. Rather, they believe that the schools' hidden curriculum teaches the attitudes and behaviors required in the workplace and that the formal curriculum represents the dominant cultural interests in society.

As we pointed out in Chapter 4, neo-Marxists, such as Bowles and Gintis (1976), believe that the hidden curriculum of the school teaches the character traits, behaviors, and attitudes needed in the capitalist economy. According to their correspondence theory, school organization and processes reflect the social needs of the economic division of labor, with the schools preparing students to fit into the economic order. From this perspective, the hidden curriculum differentially prepares students from different social class backgrounds with the type of personality traits required in the workplace. For example, working class children attend working class schools where the values of conformity, punctuality, and obedience to authority are relayed through the hidden curriculum; middle-class children attend middle-class schools where the hidden curriculum is more likely to teach the values of initiative and individual autonomy; upper-class children attend elite private schools where the hidden curriculum rewards independence, creativity, and leadership. Thus, working class students are prepared for working class jobs, middle-class students are prepared for middle-class jobs, and upper-class students are prepared for leadership positions in the corporate and political arenas. Although, as we will argue later in this chapter, this view of schooling is far too neat and rational, there are significant social class-related differences between schools. We will also show that there are significant curriculum and pedagogical differences *within* schools and that these differences may be as important as the ones *between* different schools.

Whereas neo-Marxists such as Bowles and Gintis emphasize the importance of the hidden curriculum in the shaping of values, other conflict theorists stress the effects of the formal and hidden curriculum on the reproduction of consciousness (Hurn, 1993, p. 197). According to these social reproduction theorists, such as Apple and Bourdieu, the role of the curriculum is to shape the way people think and in doing so to reproduce the dominant interests of society. Thus, for Apple (1978, 1979a, 1979b, 1982a, 1982b) the school curriculum represents the dominant class, cultural, and gender interests within society, and students internalize these interests as they go through schools. Bourdieu (1973) and Bourdieu and Passeron (1977) argued that the school curriculum represents a form of cultural capital, which separates different groups within the system of social stratification. This cultural capital symbolizes the "high culture" of the dominant groups within society as opposed to the popular culture of the masses.

Since the school system, according to conflict theorists, is highly stratified according to social class, and because students from different social class backgrounds learn different things in school, the cultural capital required for membership in the dominant groups is not universally learned but is acquired by children whose families already possess such knowledge. The system is not completely closed, however, as the system of curriculum tracking teaches at least some students in all secondary schools this high-status knowledge. The important point is that through the cultural capital transmitted through the school curriculum, the class differences in society are reflected not merely in terms of economic wealth and income but through cultural differences. Thus, through a subtle yet complex process, the schools transmit both a common body of knowledge to all students, usually at the elementary school level, and a stratified body of knowledge to students, usually at the secondary level. According to conflict theorists, this process allows for societal reproduction on the one hand and for class and cultural stratification on the other hand.

Hurn (1993, pp. 197–198) suggested that these forms of radical conflict theory are far more ideological than they are empirical. Although they point to a number of important functions of the curriculum, they do not provide sufficient evidence about the nature of the curriculum or curriculum change to support their assertions. Additionally, in arguing that school curriculum both reproduces the overall interests of the dominant groups in society by reflecting their interests and separates groups based on differential access to such a curriculum, the theory never fully explains how this is possible. If the school curriculum functions both as a means of societal reproduction and cultural separation, specifically how does it accomplish this herculean task? Moreover, the theory needs to document empirically the ways in which the curriculum reproduces social stratification between dominant and subordinate groups by looking at the curriculum and teaching practices in different schools serving different groups. To date, this has not been accomplished sufficiently.

A different variety of conflict theory, which we discussed in Chapter 4, is the neo-Weberian conflict theory of Randall Collins. For Collins, both functionalist and neo-Marxist conflict theory are far too rational. These theories, according to Collins (1979), posit too cohesive a link between the economy, the workplace, and the schools. If the role of the curriculum is truly to give students the knowledge and skills needed in the workplace, then how does one explain the relatively weak relationship between schooling and work-related skills? Collins has argued that most work skills are learned on the job, not in schools. Further, he has suggested that schools transmit a cultural currency (Hurn, 1993, pp. 198–199) to students through a credentialing process, and that the actual content of what is learned in schools is less relevant than the credential. Thus, it is not that the specific content of the curriculum is functionally related to the workplace, but it is that the credential given by schools reflects the ability of some groups to attain it and the failure of other groups to do so.

For Collins, the link between the school curriculum and the skills required in the workplace is very weak. Moreover, he has stated that the curriculum reflects the interests of various groups rather than one dominant group. If anything, the traditional school curriculum, with its emphasis on the liberal arts and sciences, reflects the cultural beliefs of those who shape the curriculum—the middle-class professional educators who have primary input into curricular matters. It is their cultural values that are represented in schools as much as the values of the upper class.

Finally, this view demonstrates that what is taught in schools must be understood as part of the larger process of cultural conflict and stratification, with school knowledge important not so much for its functional value but for its value in attaining access to specific occupations. It is this belief that the credential is related to occupational performance rather than the fact that it actually is that makes it so important. To the contrary, Collins has suggested that the actual knowledge and skills learned in acquiring a credential do not correlate highly with the actual requirements of most occupations. Therefore, Collins has provided a more cynical and skeptical view of what is taught in schools and has suggested that a more multidimensional view of conflict is required to understand the complexities of the curriculum.

Multicultural Education

The conflict perspective is illustrated nicely by the debates over multicultural education. Beginning in the 1980s, critics of the humanist curriculum argued that the traditional curriculum was Eurocentric and male dominated. They argued that the curriculum had to be transformed to represent the varied voices of the groups that make up the United States.

James Banks (1993; Banks & McGee Banks, 1995) has been the premier writer on multicultural education over the past three decades. Banks (Banks & McGee Banks, 1995) has made it clear that there is no one definition of multiculturalism and, more importantly, that multicultural approaches are by no means new, but must be traced back to the end of the nineteenth century. He has presented a typology of five dimensions of multiculturalism: content integration, knowledge construction, prejudice reduction, equity pedagogy, and empowering school culture.

Geneva Gay (1995) provided one of the best and most comprehensive discussions of multicultural curriculum theory available. Gay argued that "a high degree of consensus exists among multiculturalists on the major principles, concepts, concerns, and directions for changing educational institutions to make them more representative of and responsive to the cultural pluralism that exists in the United States and the world" (p. 40) and that "educational equity and excellence for all children in the United States are unattainable without the incorporation of cultural pluralism in all aspects of the educational process."

A related component of multicultural education is termed *culturally relevant pedagogy*. Proponents of culturally relevant pedagogy (Foster, 1995, pp. 570–581; Ladson-Billings, 1994) have described a number of characteristics of successful teachers of African American students, including having high self-esteem and a high regard for others; seeing themselves as part of the community; believing that all students can succeed; helping students make connections between their community, national, and global identities; and seeing teaching as "pulling knowledge out" (Ladson-Billings, 1994, p. 34). Further, Ladson-Billings (1994, p. 55) described the social relations of cultural relevant pedagogy in the following way: (1) The teacher/student relationship is fluid, extending to interactions beyond the classroom and into the community; (2) The teacher demonstrates a connectedness with all students; (3) The teacher encourages a "community of learners"; and (4) The teacher encourages students to learn collaboratively. Students are expected to teach each other and be responsible for each other.

Conservative critics of multicultural education (see Sleeter, 1995, for an overview) argued that it threatened the foundation of Western civilization and the role of schooling in transmitting this culture. Even liberals such as historian Arthur Schlesinger, Jr., suggested that multicultural education might lead to the breakdown of social order (Schlesinger, 1992). Supporters of multicultural education also raised questions (Semel, 1996). If curriculum and pedagogy, as multiculturalists suggest, need to be culture centered to meet the needs of each group, how does one construct a truly multicultural curriculum out of the diverse and different needs of all the groups that make up this nation's society? If an Afrocentric curriculum is the appropriate culture-centered curriculum for African Americans, do schools need separate, culture-specific curricula for Asian Americans, Puerto-Ricans, Mexican Americans, or White Americans (or for specific white ethnic groups, as well)? Based on their unique histories, problems, and cultures (Takaki, 1993, 1998a, 1998b), the more appropriate question seems to be: How does one revise and expand the curriculum to include multiple culture-centered approaches? If the goal of multiculturalism is rather to produce multiple, but separate, curricula, each tailored to specific groups, then educators may be in danger of what Schlesinger (1992) terms a "disuniting of America." The problem with the conservative critique of multiculturalism that argues for the superiority of the Western canon is that it calls for an either/or stance and assumes a unity that has never existed; however, many multiculturalists (Gordon, 1995; King, 1995) appear to call for the same either/or position (Eurocentric or Afrocentric). Given the diversity of ethnic, race, class, and gender groups in U.S. society, the problem of developing a multicultural curriculum that is both culture centered and not separatist remains one of the greatest challenges in education (see Semel, 1996, for a detailed analysis of multiculturalism).

Curriculum Theory and Practice: The Reconceptualization of Curriculum Studies

For most of the twentieth century, the field of curriculum studies was concerned with relating the study of curriculum to classroom practice. From the child-centered and social-reconstructionist strands of progressive education in the first half of the century (Semel & Sadovnik, 1999) to the professionalization of teacher education (Labaree, 1996), the subject of curriculum studies has often been more concerned with practice than theory and has viewed classroom practice within the narrow confines of schools. Beginning in the 1970s, critical curriculum theorists both in the United States and England questioned the assumptions of curriculum studies and argued that school knowledge represented the socially constructed interests of dominant groups in society (Apple, 1979a, 1992, 1993; Sadovnik, 1991a; Young, 1971).

From the 1970s onward, William Pinar has been the preeminent figure in the reconceptualization of curriculum studies into the field of curriculum theory (Pinar, 1975, 1978a, 1978b, 1979, 1988; Pinar et al., 1995). Building on the critical curriculum theory of Apple and others, Pinar integrated both psychoanalytic and postmodern approaches to the curriculum. His approach called for the separation of theory and practice, rather than its traditional integration. Pinar suggested that this separation was necessary for curriculum theorists to have the necessary distance to understand the complex factors that affect practice. However, he also indicated that eventually theory and practice had to be reconnected. He also connected the personal (autobiographical) to the study of schools by relating experience to theory. By the 1990s, reconceptualized curriculum theory had become a dominant voice in the field, with its own national conference.

In the 1990s, amid the calls for teacher education reform that criticized university-based schools of education for failing to adequately connect theory to practice and involve education professors in school improvement (Holmes Group, 1995; Labaree, 1996; National Commission on Teaching and America's Future, 1996), curriculum theory came under fire. Wraga (1997, 1999) argued that the reconceptualization of curriculum studies into curriculum theory has resulted in a false dichotomy between theory and practice, eschewed the historic roles of universities from the 1862 Morrill Act (see Chapter 3) onward to provide practical knowledge for social policy, and created an elitism in education characteristic of the split in the sciences between pure and applied science. Wraga has called for the reestablishment of a Deweyan vision that educational theory must be tested in real-life schools (Wraga, 1999).

The Wraga-Pinar debate reflects much of the educational debate of the 1990s by reducing complex issues to either/or poles. As Dewey noted in *Experience and Education* (1938), both sides of either/ors are usually equally misinformed. Critical curriculum studies and reconceptualized curriculum theory have provided an important corrective to traditional approaches by demanding that scholars examine the social, political, and economic forces outside schools that affect classroom discourse and practice. These approaches have made important contributions to the knowledge of how schools contribute to social inequalities. However, curriculum theorists have often been so detached from the everyday life of teachers and students that they have had little impact on school reform and improvement. As we begin the new millennium, the field of curriculum studies needs to integrate the rich findings of curriculum theory into a more pragmatic approach to school improvement. Such a vision is consistent with Dewey's pragmatism, which stressed the need to balance theory, research, and practice.

Pedagogic Practices: How the Curriculum Is Taught

Thus far in this chapter, we have focused on what is taught in schools and why it is taught. As students, you are aware that how something is taught is as important as, and at times more important than, the content. On the most simplistic level, how something is taught is important to you because it can make the difference between learning the material or not learning it. Moreover, we have all sat in classes with teachers who certainly knew their subject matter but did not have the ability or teaching skills to convey it to the class. Conversely, the ability to teach something without the requisite knowledge of the subject matter is equally problematic. Thus, the relationship between curriculum, the content of education, and pedagogy (the process of teaching) is an interdependent one, with each being a necessary but insufficient part of the act of teaching.

On a more complex level, the process of teaching, like the curriculum, is not an objective skill agreed on by all practitioners; rather, it is also the subject of disagreements over what constitutes appropriate teaching practices. Additionally, sociologists of education (Bernstein, 1990; Sadovnik, 1991a) suggest that different pedagogic practices, like different curricula, are differentially offered to different groups of students, often based on class, racial, ethnic, and gender differences.

The Philosophy of Teaching: Differing Views on Pedagogic Practices

Philip Jackson, in his insightful book, *The Practice of Teaching* (1986), provided a thoughtful discussion of the philosophical dimensions of teaching. He suggested that there have been different views about teaching—some see it as an art or craft while others see it as a scientific enterprise with distinct and testable methodological principles.

Although the scope of this chapter does not permit us to go into this in detail, this section will outline some of the salient features of the major philosophical viewpoints on teaching practices.

Jackson (1986, pp. 115–145) has distinguished between the two dominant traditions of teaching: the mimetic and the transformative. In Chapters 2, 3, and 5, we referred to progressive and traditional (conservative) models in U.S. education. Using these terms, the mimetic tradition loosely coincides with the traditional (conservative) model and the transformative with the progressive model.

The *mimetic* tradition is based on the viewpoint that the purpose of education is to transmit specific knowledge to students. Thus, the best method of doing this is through what is termed the *didactic method,* a method that commonly relies on the lecture or presentation as the main form of communication. At the heart of this tradition is the assumption that the educational process involves the relationship between the knower (the teacher) and the learner (the student), and that education is a process of transferring information from one to the other. Based on the belief that the student does not possess what the teacher has, the mimetic model stresses the importance of rational sequencing in the teaching process and assessment of the learning process (i.e., a clear statement of learning goals and a clear means to assess whether students have acquired them). The emphasis on measurable goals and objectives has become a central component of many teacher education programs, with the attempt to create a science of teaching often viewed as the key to improving educational achievement.

The *transformative* tradition rests on a different set of assumptions about the teaching and learning process. Although learning information makes the student different than he or she was before, this model defines the function of education more broadly and, according to some, more ambiguously. Simply put, proponents of this tradition believe that the purpose of education is to change the student in some meaningful way, including intellectually, creatively, spiritually, and emotionally. In contrast to the mimetic tradition, transformative educators do not see the transmission of knowledge as the only component of education and thus they provide a more multidimensional theory of teaching. Additionally, they reject the authoritarian relationship between teacher and student and argue instead that teaching and learning are inextricably linked.

Thus, the process of teaching involves not just the didactic transfer of information but the conversation between teacher and student in such a way that the student becomes an integral part of the learning process. Although the lecture may be used in this tradition, the dialectical method, which involves the use of questioning, is at the core of its methodology. Derived from the teaching methods of Socrates, as presented in the dialogues of Plato, and given philosophical grounding in the works of John Dewey, transformative educators believe that all teaching begins with the active participation of the student and results in some form of growth. Exactly what type of growth is desired varies with the specific goals of the classroom, but given the broader spectrum of goals outlined by transformative educators, it is more difficult to assess and measure educational outcomes. Moreover, the transformative tradition tends to reject the scientific model of teaching and instead views teaching as an artistic endeavor.

Dewey was somewhat ambiguous about what he believed to be the goals of education, saying that the goal of education was simply growth leading to more growth (Cremin, 1990, p. 125). However, the transformative tradition has often defined growth within a radical critique of the status quo. Critical theorists such as Freire (1972, 1977, 1978) and Giroux (1983a, 1983b, 1988, 1991), existential phenomenologists such as Greene (1978, 1988), and feminist theorists such as Belenky (Belenky et al., 1986), Laird (1989), and Martin (1987) believe that the purpose of education is to change human consciousness and in doing so begin to change society. These perspectives view teaching as a political activity; its goal is to transform students' minds as the first step in radical social transformation.

For example, feminist theorists (Macdonald & Macdonald, 1981; Miller, 1982; Mitrano, 1979) believe that traditional curriculum and pedagogy reproduce the dominant patriarchal relations of society and reinforce male domination. They teach competition and sexism, rather than cooperation and gender equality. Therefore, feminists suggest that a curriculum and pedagogy that teach caring and that are explicitly anti-sexist is required.

Critical theorists, who are political radicals, argue that traditional curriculum and pedagogy reproduce the consciousness required in a competitive, capitalist society. They suggest that a critical pedagogy is required—one that enables students to critique the dominant ideologies of society and that is explicitly concerned with democratic and egalitarian principles. Thus, for the radical wing of the transformative tradition, growth leading to more growth is unacceptable, as the definition of growth is left at the level of the individual student. What is necessary, they argue, is individual growth that leads to social change. It should be noted also that these contemporary educational theories are examples of the social meliorist tradition outlined earlier in this chapter.

A major difference between the mimetic (traditional) and transformative (progressive) models of teaching relates to the question of authority relations in the classroom. Given the fact that the traditional model views the teacher as the knowledgeable authority in the classroom, traditional classrooms usually have explicit authority relations, with teachers in charge and students in a subservient position. The lesson is usually teacher directed, with students speaking when spoken to and in response to direct questions. The progressive model usually has less authoritarian authority relations in the classroom, with authority internalized within the student rather than in direct response to the teachers' higher authority. Although there are differences in authority, they are often less explicitly structured. Additionally, students usually have more input in their education and the classroom is often more child centered than teacher directed.

It is important to point out that these two models of teaching are ideal types, and that most classrooms are neither totally one nor totally the other. Most teachers combine different methods of teaching and most classrooms are neither totally authoritarian nor totally unstructured. Nonetheless, most classrooms, schools, and teachers lean in one direction or the other, based on philosophical and sociological factors. On a philosophical level, the belief in one model over the other is an essential determinant of classroom practice; on a sociological level, the use of different models appears to correlate with class differences.

For example, Bernstein's (1990) work on pedagogic practices has indicated that the looser authority relations of what he calls invisible pedagogy (usually found in progressive education) are found in schools with middle- and upper middle-class populations; the more authoritarian relations of what he calls visible pedagogy (usually found in traditional education) are found in schools with poor and working class populations as well as in schools with upper-class populations. Although the poor and the working class seem to receive the same form of pedagogic practices, they receive a very different form of curriculum from the upper class, with the upper class receiving a classical humanist curriculum and the poor and working class receiving a social efficiency curriculum (that often is vocationally based). Bernstein argued that these class differences in pedagogic practices are the result of the different functions of schooling for different groups.

The important point here is that different teaching practices are not the result of philosophical preferences only, nor are they randomly distributed between schools in a nonrational manner. They are also related to sociological factors and may be important in understanding differences in academic achievement between groups. We will explore this in more detail in our discussion of the stratification of the curriculum and again in Chapter 9, when we discuss explanations of unequal educational achievement among different groups.

The Stratification of the Curriculum

As we have noted, the social efficiency curriculum has been the dominant model in U.S. public education since the 1920s. From this period onward, U.S. schools offered a stratified curriculum to students, with some students receiving an academic curriculum and others receiving a vocational or general curriculum. Curriculum stratification (i.e., the division of the curriculum), usually at the secondary school level, is not the only form of differentiation in U.S. schools. Ability grouping, or the separation of students into groups based on putative ability (usually based on standardized tests), is another important form of stratification. Ability grouping begins at the elementary school level with reading and mathematics groups within the same classroom, and is often extended in the upper elementary and middle school levels with separate classes with the same curriculum but different ability levels. These ability groups are often directly related to high school curriculum tracks (different curricula and different abilities) or ability groups (similar curricula and different abilities).

It is important to note that ability grouping and curriculum tracking are related aspects of the curriculum stratification system. Students, from elementary school through college, may be separated according to ability, curriculum, or both. For example, there are a number of different ways that schools organize the curriculum. First, some schools require all students to learn the same curriculum and therefore group students without regard to ability (heterogeneous grouping). Second, other schools require all students to learn the same curriculum and thus group students based on ability (homogeneous grouping). Third, other schools stratify students based on both ability and the curriculum, with high-ability students at the secondary level enrolled in an academic curriculum and low-ability students enrolled in a vocational or general curriculum. Finally, although these differences are found within schools, there are also important differences between schools, both public and private, in terms of their curriculum and pedagogy.

These differences between schools are often based on the social class differences of the students who attend them. They are found at all levels of education through the university, where the U.S. system provides different types of postsecondary education based on both curriculum and ability (e.g., from vocational education and liberal arts education at the community colleges, to liberal arts education at selective elite private colleges and universities, to variations of both at other public and private colleges and universities).

The factors affecting ability group and/or curricula track placement, as well as the outcomes of such placement, have been the subject of considerable debate in the sociology of education. For example, the degree to which track placement is based on meritocratic criteria and actually reflect ability—or the degree to which it is based on nonmeritocratic criteria such as race, class, and gender—are important empirical questions. Additionally, the effects of such placement on the life chances and educational careers of groups of students are likewise crucial to understanding the relationship between schooling and inequalities. These issues will be explored in detail in Chapter 9, which discusses explanations of educational inequality. At this point it is important to understand that the U.S. schools are stratified by curriculum and ability, and these differences are reflected both between schools at all levels (e.g., differences between public and private schools at all levels and differences between public schools at all levels) and within schools through tracking and ability grouping. Further, it is important to understand why such practices exist.

The rationales for curriculum tracking and ability grouping are complex, as they speak to some of the most fundamental questions concerning teaching and learning. First, should all students learn the same things or should different groups of students learn different things, depending on their needs, interests, and future plans? Second, is there a common body of knowledge that all students, regardless of their future plans, should learn? Third, if all students should learn the same things, at least for a part of their education, should they learn them in heterogeneous groups or homogeneous ability groups? That is, given individual differences in ability, can students of different abilities learn the same material at the same pace, without some students falling behind or others being held back? Or is it more effective to teach students of different abilities at different paces in order to ensure that they all eventually learn the same material?

Debates about these questions have been central to U.S. education since the 1920s. In terms of the curriculum, the dominant social efficiency model has accepted the view that all students should not be required to take the same curriculum and that the secondary school curriculum should meet the different aspirations of different groups of students. In terms of ability grouping, the separation of students into homogeneous ability groups, beginning at the elementary level, has been a salient feature of U.S. education from about the same time (e.g., see Oakes, 1985). Moreover, there is often a strong relationship between elementary school ability grouping and secondary school track placement (Hurn, 1993; Oakes, 1985).

According to Oakes (1985), ability grouping and tracking have been based on four rationales. The first is that students learn more effectively in homogeneous groups and that students with different abilities require different and separate schooling. The second is that "slower" students develop a more positive self-image if they do not have to compete with "brighter" students. The third is that placement procedures accurately reflect students' academic abilities and prior accomplishments. The last rationale is that homogeneous groups are easier to manage and teach. Oakes argued that each of these are myths that cannot be supported by empirical evidence and that ability grouping and curriculum tracking have unfairly limited the lives of students from lower socioeconomic backgrounds who are far more likely to be placed in lower tracks. In Chapter 9, we will review the evidence on the effects of these processes; for now, it is important to understand that they have been significant organizational processes in the stratification of curriculum and pedagogy.

The Effects of the Curriculum: What Is Learned in Schools?

Thus far in this chapter, we have discussed the organization of the curriculum and its effect on what is taught in schools. It is important to note, however, that what is taught in schools is not necessarily equivalent to what is learned in schools. Much of the discussion about curriculum assumes that the curriculum is important precisely because it affects student consciousness, values, and so on. This is true only to the extent that the school curriculum is actually internalized by students; if it is not (i.e., if the students do not actually learn what is taught or what is in the curriculum), then the claim that schooling transmits important knowledge to students and that it has important social functions may be more ideological than real.

Hurn (1993, pp. 199–201) pointed out that there are a number of methodological problems in studying school effects, in general, and what students learn cognitively and noncognitively, in particular. First, it is difficult to separate school effects from more general processes of childhood and adolescent development. To what extent the increased knowledge of children as they get older is due to schooling and to what extent it is due to developmental patterns and maturation is difficult to ascertain. Second, it is difficult to separate the effects of schooling from other variables, including social class and cultural factors. For example, one may be able to ascertain that students with more education have more academic knowledge than those with lower levels of education or that they may have more liberal political values. However, it is not easy to demonstrate that these differences have been caused by the independent effects of schooling rather than the effects of social class or cultural differences external to the processes of schooling.

Despite these difficulties, some things are known about the effects of schooling that suggest that schools have some important effects on students. First, the evidence indicates that students who have higher levels of educational attainment do know more about school subjects than those with lower levels of attainment. Research on school effects (Hurn, 1993, pp. 201–204) suggests that schooling does increase knowledge; that there is a strong correlation between formal schooling and tests of cognitive skills, such as reasoning, mathematics, and so on; and that evidence from the United States and other societies (Hurn, 1993, pp. 206–216) shows that schools have powerful effects on cognitive development. This evidence suggests that the cynical view of conflict theorists such as Collins (that little is really learned in school and that schooling is mostly a credentialing process) is not fully supported by empirical evidence. This does not refute Collins's claim that school knowledge is not necessary for the workplace (this is a different question), but it does demonstrate that schools do teach things to students (whether it is valuable or not is as much an ideological as it is an empirical question).

A second issue related to the effects of schooling regards the effects of different schools and different tracks within schools. This is a very controversial question, with proponents of the effective school movement arguing that there are specific school characteristics that correlate highly with learning. At the same time, however, there is evidence (Hurn, 1993) to suggest that school characteristics, independent of other factors such as the social class background of students, make little difference in student learning.

Although we will review these disagreements more fully in Chapter 9 in our discussion of education and inequality, it is important to note here that some research on curriculum tracking does provide an important piece of the puzzle. If students in different curriculum tracks within the same school—or more importantly, within different ability groups with similar curricula within the same school—have substantially different educational experiences and this results in vastly different educational learning outcomes, then one may conclude that schooling does have important effects. Oakes's (1985) research on tracking and ability grouping suggested such a process. Although we will suggest in Chapter 9 that these findings are not universally accepted (as it is difficult to rule out the independent effects of outside factors such as family), they do provide some support for the argument that schools affect different groups of students in significantly different ways.

Another important aspect of what students learn in school concerns the noncognitive effects of schooling. Since both functionalists (Dreeben, 1968) and conflict theorists (Bowles & Gintis, 1976) believe that schools teach important societal values and beliefs to students (albeit they disagree about whose values and what they are), it is important to empirically document the actual effects in this area. The empirical evidence is incomplete and inconclusive, but there are some conclusions that may be drawn. First, there is some evidence (Hurn, 1993, p. 205) that increased levels of education lead to greater tolerance, greater openness, and less authoritarianism. Further, the evidence does not support the radical view that schools in capitalist societies teach conformity, docility, and obedience to authority as the only values; the effects of schooling are more complicated. Finally, given the multiple influences on values, including the role of the family and the media, it is difficult to isolate the independent role of schooling. Hurn (1993, p. 218) has suggested, "Students in contemporary society are exposed to a wide variety of *competing values and ideals* both within and in the wider environment, and many of these implicit and explicit messages cancel each other out. Thus although *particular* and *unusual* schools may have quite powerful effects on some students, schooling in *general* cannot be said to have enduring or important effects on one set of attitudes and values rather than another."

Although we agree that the effects of schooling on values and attitudes has been exaggerated by both functionalists and Neo-Marxists, the fact that some schools do have powerful effects on student attitudes, that students in different curriculum tracks are often taught and learn different attitudes, and that students with more education have different attitudes and values does suggest that schools do have some effects on students. That it is difficult, as Hurn points out, to disentangle these effects from other societal institutions demonstrates the complex relationship between schooling and other educating institutions; it does not suggest that schooling is unimportant.

Conclusion

This chapter has discussed the content and process of schooling: curriculum and pedagogy. We have suggested that curriculum and pedagogy are not objective phenomena, but rather must be understood within the context of their sociological, philosophical, political, and historical roots. The curriculum represents what particular groups think is important and, by omission, what they believe is not important. What is included and excluded is often the subject of debate and controversy. Teachers too often are excluded from such decisions, but as we argued in Chapter 1, you, as teachers, must be part of these debates. Only through an understanding of the complex issues involved can you become active and critical curriculum makers rather than passive reproducers of a curriculum into which you have no input.

Most importantly, we have pointed out that what is taught and how it is taught are complex matters with profound consequences, both for individuals and society. Although there are differences of opinion concerning the effects of curriculum organization and pedagogic practices, it is evident that differences in these areas are not random; they affect different groups of students in different ways. In the next chapters (8 and 9), we will explore the broader question of schooling and inequality and examine how both factors within the schools, such as curriculum and pedagogy, as well as outside the school, such as family, neighborhood, economics, and other variables, are related to unequal educational attainment and achievement.

The following articles examine issues relating to curriculum and pedagogy. The first article, "The Politics of a National Curriculum," written by curriculum theorist Michael W. Apple, examines the politics of curriculum through an analysis of a national curriculum. Apple argues that the curriculum represents the dominant interests in society, and therefore curriculum decisions are always political and conflictual. Although Apple is not necessarily against a national curriculum, he points out that its proponents represent a particular curriculum ideology.

The second article, "The Mimetic and the Transformative: Alternative Outlooks on Teaching," written by educational theorist and researcher Philip W. Jackson, compares two different models of teaching: the mimetic and the transformative. Through an examination of their basic premises and methods, Jackson demonstrates how each model has been a significant part of the way teachers teach.

The third article, "The Silenced Dialogue: Power and Pedagogy in Educating Other People's Children," written by educator Lisa D. Delpit, analyzes the concept of *culturally relevant pedagogy,* and questions whether one form of pedagogic practice is appropriate for all children.

The Politics of a National Curriculum

MICHAEL W. APPLE

Introduction

Education is deeply implicated in the politics of culture. Its curriculum is never simply a neutral assemblage of knowledge, somehow appearing in the texts and classrooms of a nation. It is always part of a *selective tradition,* and is someone's selection, some group's vision of legitimate knowledge. It is produced out of the cultural, political, and economic conflicts, tensions, and compromises that organize and disorganize a society. As I argue in *Ideology and Curriculum* (Apple 1990) and *Official Knowledge* (Apple 1993), the decision to define some groups' knowledge as the most legitimate, as official, while other groups' knowledge hardly sees the light of day, says something extremely important about who has power in a society.

Consider social studies texts that continue to speak of the "Dark Ages" rather than using the historically more accurate and much less racist phrase "the age of African and Asian Ascendancy." Or consider books that treat Rosa Parks as merely a naive African-American woman who was simply too tired to go to the back of the bus rather than discussing her training in organized civil disobedience at the Highlander Folk School. The realization that teaching, especially at the elementary school level, has in large part been defined as women's work—with its accompanying struggles over autonomy, pay, respect, and deskilling—also documents the connections between curriculum and teaching and the history of gender politics (Apple 1988b). Thus, whether we like it or not, differential power intrudes into the very heart of curriculum, teaching, and evaluation. What *counts* as knowledge, the ways in which knowledge is organized, who is empowered to teach it, what counts as an appropriate display of having learned it, and—just as critically—who is allowed to ask and answer all of these questions are part and parcel of how dominance and subordination are reproduced and altered in this society (Bernstein 1977; Apple 1988a). There is, then, always a *politics* of offi-cial knowledge, a politics that embodies conflict over what some regard as simply neutral descriptions of the world and what others regard as elite conceptions that empower some groups while disempowering others.

Speaking in general about how elite culture, habits, and tastes function, Pierre Bourdieu (1984, p. 7) puts it this way:

> The denial of lower, coarse, vulgar, venal, servile—in a word, natural—enjoyment, which constitutes the sacred sphere of culture, implies an affirmation of the superiority of those who can be satisfied with the sublimated, refined, disinterested, gratuitous, distinguished pleasures forever closed to the profane. That is why art and cultural consumption are predisposed, consciously and deliberately or not, to fulfill a social function of legitimating social difference.

As he goes on to say, these cultural forms, "through the economic and social conditions which they presuppose . . . are bound up with the systems of dispositions (habitus) characteristic of different classes and class fractions" (Bourdieu 1984, pp. 5–6). Thus, cultural form and content function as markers of class (Bourdieu 1984, p. 2). The granting of sole legitimacy to such a system of culture through its incorporation within the official centralized curriculum, then, creates a situation in which the markers of taste become the markers of people. The school becomes a class school.

The contemporary tradition of scholarship and activism has been based on exactly these insights: the complex relationships between economic capital and cultural capital; the role of the school in reproducing and challenging the multitude of unequal relations of power (which go well beyond class, of course), and the roles that content and organization of the curriculum, pedagogy, and evaluation all play.

It is exactly now that these kinds of issues must be considered most seriously. This is a period—which we can call the *conservative restoration*—when conflict over the politics of official knowledge is severe. At

Copyright © 1995 from "The Politics of a National Curriculum" by Michael W. Apple in *Transforming Schools* (pp. 345–370) by P. W. Cookson and B. Schneider (Eds.). Reprinted by permission of Routledge/Taylor & Francis Books, Inc.

stake is the very idea of public education and a curriculum that responds to the cultures and histories of large and growing segments of the American population. Even with a "moderate" Democratic administration now in Washington, many of this administration's own commitments embody the tendencies addressed below.

I intend to instantiate these arguments through an analysis of the proposals for a national curriculum and national testing. But in order to understand these issues, we must think *relationally,* and connect these proposals to the larger program of the conservative restoration. I intend to argue that behind the educational justification for a national curriculum and national testing is a dangerous ideological attack, the effects of which will be truly damaging to those who already have the most to lose. I shall first present a few interpretive cautions. Then I shall analyze the general project of the rightist agenda. Third, I shall show the connections between the national curriculum and national testing and the increasing focus on privatization and "choice" plans. And, finally, I want to discuss the pattern of differential benefits that will likely result.

The Question of a National Curriculum

Where should those of us who count ourselves a part of the long progressive tradition in education stand in relationship to the call for a national curriculum?

At the outset, I wish to make clear that I am not opposed in principle to a national curriculum. Nor am I opposed in principle to the idea or practice of testing. Rather, I wish to provide a more conjunctural set of arguments based on my claim that at this time—given the balance of social forces—there are very real dangers which are important to recognize. I shall confine myself largely to the negative case here, and my task is to raise serious questions about the implications of these developments in a time of conservative triumphalism.

We are not the only nation where a largely rightist coalition has put such proposals on the educational agenda. In England, a national curriculum, first introduced by the Thatcher government, is now mostly in place. It consists of "core and foundation subjects" such as mathematics, science, technology, history, art, music, physical education, and a modern foreign language. Working groups to determine the standard goals, "attainment targets," and content in each subject have already brought forth their results. This curriculum is accompanied by a national system of achievement testing—one that is both expensive and time-consuming—for all students in state-run schools at the ages of seven, eleven, fourteen, and sixteen (Whitty 1992, p. 24).

The assumption in many quarters in the United States is that we must follow nations such as Britain and especially Japan or we shall be left behind. Yet it is crucial that we understand that we *already* have a national curriculum, which is determined by the complicated nexus of state textbook adoption policies and the market in textbook publishing (Apple 1988b; Apple and Christian-Smith 1991). Thus, we have to ask whether a national curriculum—one that will undoubtedly be linked to a system of national goals and nationally standardized instruments of evaluation—is *better* than an equally widespread but somewhat more covert national curriculum established by textbook adoption states such as California and Texas, which control 20 to 30 percent of the market in textbooks (Apple 1993). Whether or not such a covert national curriculum already exists, however, there is a growing feeling that standardized national curricular goals and guidelines are essential to "raise standards" and to hold schools accountable for their students' achievement.

We can concede that many people representing an array of educational and political positions are involved in the call for higher standards, more rigorous curricula at a national level, and a system of national testing. Yet we must ask the question: which group is in the leadership of these "reform" efforts? This leads to another, broader question: who will benefit or lose as a result of all this? I contend that, unfortunately, rightist groups are setting the political agenda in education and that, in general, the same pattern of benefits that has characterized nearly all areas of social policy—in which the top 20 percent of the population reap 80 percent of the benefits (Apple 1989; Danziger and Weinberg 1986; Burtless 1990)—will be reproduced here.

We need to be very cautious of the genetic fallacy, the assumption that *because* a policy or a practice originates within a distasteful position it is fundamentally determined, in all its aspects, by its origination within that tradition. Take Edward Thorndike, one of the founders of educational psychology in the United States, for instance. The fact that his social beliefs were often repugnant—as evidenced by his participation in the popular eugenics movement and his notions of racial, gender, and class hierarchies—does not necessarily destroy every aspect of his research on learning. While I am not at all a supporter of this paradigm of research (its epistemological and social implications continue to demand major criticism),[1] this requires a different kind of argument than one based on origin. (Indeed, one can find some progressive educators turning to Thorndike for support for some of their claims about what needed to be transformed in our curriculum and pedagogy.)

It is not only those who are identified with the rightist project who argue for a national curriculum. Others who have historically been identified with a more liberal agenda have attempted to make a case for it (Smith, O'Day, and Cohen 1990).

Smith, O'Day, and Cohen suggest a positive, if cautionary, vision for a national curriculum. A national curriculum would involve the invention of new examinations, a technically, conceptually, and politically difficult task. It would require the teaching of more rigorous content and thus would require teachers to engage in more demanding and exciting work. Teachers and administrators, therefore, would have to "deepen their knowledge of academic subjects and change their conceptions of knowledge itself." Teaching and learning would have to be seen as "more active and inventive." Teachers, administrators, and students would need "to become more thoughtful, collaborative, and participatory" (Smith, O'Day, and Cohen 1990, p. 46).

In Smith, O'Day, and Cohen's (1990) words:

> Conversion to a national curriculum could only succeed if the work of conversion were conceived and undertaken as a grand, cooperative learning venture. Such an enterprise would fail miserably if it were conceived and organized chiefly as a technical process of developing new exams and materials and then "disseminating" or implementing them. (p. 46)

And they go on to say:

> A worthwhile, effective national curriculum would also require the creation of much new social and intellectual connective tissue. For instance, the content and pedagogy of teacher education would have to be closely related to the content of and pedagogy of the schools' curriculum. The content and pedagogy of examinations would have to be tied to those of the curriculum and teacher education. Such connections do not now exist. (p. 46)

The authors conclude that such a revitalized system, one in which such coordination would be built, "will not be easy, quick, or cheap," especially if it is to preserve variety and initiative. "If Americans continue to want educational reform on the cheap, a national curriculum would be a mistake" (Smith, O'Day, and Cohen 1990, p. 46). I could not agree more with this last point.

Yet they do not sufficiently recognize that much of what they fear is already taking place in the very linkage they call for. Even more importantly, what they do not pay sufficient attention to—the connections between a national curriculum and national testing and the larger rightist agenda—constitutes an even greater danger. It is this I wish to focus on.

Between Neoconservatism and Neoliberalism

Conservatism by its very name announces one interpretation of its agenda: it conserves. Other interpretations are possible, of course. One could say, somewhat more wryly, that conservatism believes that nothing should be done for the first time (Honderich 1990, p. 1). Yet in many ways, in the current situation, this is inaccurate. For with the Right now in ascendancy in many nations, we are witnessing a much more activist project. Conservative politics now are very much the politics of alteration—not always, but clearly the idea of "Do nothing for the first time" is not a sufficient explanation of what is happening either in education or elsewhere (Honderich 1990, p. 4).

Conservatism has in fact meant different things at different times and places. At times it involves defensive actions; at other times it involves taking the initiative against the status quo (Honderich 1990, p. 15). Today we are witnessing both.

Thus, it is important to set out the larger social context in which the current politics of official knowledge operates. There has been a breakdown in the accord that guided a good deal of educational policy since World War II. Powerful groups within government and the economy and within "authoritarian populist" social movements have been able to redefine—often in very retrogressive ways—the terms of debate in education, social welfare, and other areas of social policy. What education is *for* is being transformed (Apple 1993). No longer is education seen as part of a social alliance which combines many "minority"[2] groups, women, teachers, community activists, progressive legislators and government officials, and others who act together to propose (limited) social democratic policies for schools (e.g., expanding educational opportunities, limited attempts at equalizing outcomes, developing special programs in bilingual and multicultural education, and so on). A new alliance has been formed, one that has increasing power in educational and social policy. This new power bloc combines neoliberal elements of business with the New Right and with neoconservative intellectuals. Its interests are less in increasing the life opportunities of women, people of color, and labor than in providing the educational conditions believed necessary both for increasing international competitiveness, profit, and discipline and for returning us to a romanticized past of the "ideal" home, family, and school (Apple 1993).

The power of this alliance can be seen in a number of educational policies and proposals: (1) programs for voucher plans and tax credits to make schools operate like the thoroughly idealized free-market economy; (2) the movement at national and state levels to "raise standards" and mandate both teacher and student "competencies" and basic curricular goals and knowledge, increasingly through the implementation of statewide and national testing; (3) the increasingly effective attacks on the school curriculum for its antifamily and anti–free enterprise "bias," its secular humanism, its lack of patriotism, and its supposed neglect of the knowledge and values of the "Western tradition" and of "real knowledge"; and (4) the growing pressure to make the perceived needs of business and industry into the primary goals of the school (Apple 1988b; Apple 1993).

In essence, the new alliance in favor of this conservative restoration has integrated education into a wider set of ideological commitments. The objectives in education are the same as those which serve as a guide to its economic and social welfare goals. These include the expansion of the "free market," the drastic reduction of government responsibility for social needs (though the Clinton Administration intends to mediate this in not very extensive—and not very expensive—ways), the reinforcement of intensely competitive structures of mobility, the lowering of people's expectations for economic security, and the popularization of what is clearly a form of Social Darwinist thinking (Bastian et al. 1986).

As I have argued at length elsewhere, the political Right in the United States has been very successful in mobilizing support *against* the educational system and its employees, often exporting the crisis in the economy onto the schools. Thus, one of its major achievements has been to shift the blame for unemployment and underemployment, for the loss of economic competitiveness, and for the supposed breakdown of traditional values and standards in the family, education, and paid and unpaid workplaces from the economic, cultural, and social policies and effects of dominant groups to the school and other public agencies. "Public" now is the center of all evil; "private" is the center of all that is good (Apple 1985).

In essence, then, four trends have characterized the conservative restoration in both the United States and Britain—privatization, centralization, vocationalization, and differentiation (Green 1991, p. 27). These trends are actually largely the results of differences within the most powerful wings of this alliance—neoliberalism and neoconservatism.

Neoliberalism has a vision of the weak state. A society that lets the "invisible hand" of the free market guide all aspects of its forms of social interaction is seen as both efficient and democratic. On the other hand, neoconservatism is guided by a vision of the strong state in certain areas, especially over the politics of the body and gender and race relations, over standards, values, and conduct, and over what kind of knowledge should be passed on to future generations (Hunter 1988).[3] These two positions do not easily sit side by side in the conservative coalition.

Thus, the rightist movement is contradictory. Is there not something paradoxical about linking all of the feelings of loss and nostalgia to the unpredictability of the market, "in replacing loss by sheer flux"? (Johnson 1991a, p. 40).

The contradiction between neoconservative and neoliberal elements in the rightist coalition are "solved" through a policy of what Roger Dale has called *conservative modernization.* Such a policy is engaged in

> simultaneously "freeing" individuals for economic purposes while controlling them for social purposes; indeed, in so far as economic "freedom" increases inequalities, it is likely to increase the need for social control. A "small, strong state" limits the range of its activities by transferring to the market, which it defends and legitimizes, as much welfare [and other activities] as possible. In education, the new reliance on competition and choice is not all pervasive; instead, "what is intended is a dual system, polarized between . . . market schools and minimum schools." (quoted in Edwards, Gewirtz, and Whitty forthcoming, p. 22)

That is, there will be a relatively less regulated and increasingly privatized sector for the children of the better-off. For the rest—whose economic status and racial composition will be thoroughly predictable—the schools will be tightly controlled and policed and will continue to be underfunded and unlinked to decent paid employment.

One of the major effects of the combination of marketization and the strong state is "to remove educational policies from public debate." That is, the choice is left up to individual parents and "the hidden hand of unintended consequences does the rest." In the process, the very idea of education being part of a *public* political sphere in which its means and ends are publicly debated atrophies (Education Group II 1991, p. 268).

There are major differences between democratic attempts at enhancing people's rights over the policies and practices of schooling and the neoliberal emphasis on marketization and privatization. The goal of the former is to *extend politics,* to "revivify democratic practice by devising ways of enhancing public discussion, debate, and negotiation." It is based inherently on a vision of democracy as an educative practice. The latter, on the other hand, seeks to *contain politics.* It wants to *reduce all politics to economics,* to an ethic of "choice" and "consumption" (Johnson 1991a, p. 68). The world in essence becomes a vast supermarket.

Enlarging the private sector so that buying and selling—in a word, competition—is the dominant ethic of society involves a set of closely related propositions. This position assumes that more individuals are motivated to work harder under these conditions. After all, we "already know" that public servants are inefficient and slothful, while private enterprises are efficient and energetic. It assumes that self-interest and competitiveness are the engines of creativity. More knowledge and more experimentation are created and used to alter what we have now. In the process, less waste is created. Supply and demand remain in a kind of equilibrium. A more efficient machine is thus created, one which minimizes administrative costs and ultimately distributes resources more widely (Honderich 1990, p. 104).

This ethic is not meant to benefit simply the privileged few. However, it is the equivalent of saying that you have the right to climb the north face of the Eiger or scale Mount Everest, provided, of course, that you are very good at mountain climbing and have the necessary institutional and financial resources (Honderich 1990, pp. 99–100).

Thus, in a conservative society, access to a society's private resources (and remember, the attempt is to make nearly *all* of society's resources private) is largely dependent on one's ability to pay. And this is dependent on one's being a person of an *entre-preneurial or efficiently acquisitive class type.* On the other hand, society's public resources (that rapidly decreasing segment) are dependent on need (Honderich 1990, p. 89). In a conservative society, the former is to be maximized, the latter is to be minimized.

However, the conservatism of the New Right does not merely depend in large portion on a particular view of human nature—the view of human nature as primarily self-interested. It has gone further; it has set out to degrade human nature, to force all people to conform to what at first could only be claimed to be true. Unfortunately, in no small measure it has succeeded. Perhaps blinded by their own absolutist and reductive vision of what it means to be human, many of our political leaders do not seem to be capable of recognizing what they have done. They have set out, aggressively, to drag down the character of a people (Honderich 1990, p. 81), while at the same time attacking the poor and the disenfranchised for their supposed lack of values and character.

Curriculum, Testing, and a Common Culture

As Whitty reminds us, what is striking about the rightist coalition's policies is its capacity to connect the neoconservative emphasis on traditional knowledge and values, authority, standards, and national identity with the neoliberal emphasis on the extension of market-driven principles (also embraced by Clinton) into all areas of society (Whitty 1992, p. 25). Thus, a national curriculum—coupled with rigorous national standards and a system of testing that is performance driven—is able at one and the same time to be aimed at "modernization" of the curriculum and the efficient "production" of better "human capital" *and* represent a nostalgic yearning for a romanticized past (Whitty 1992, p. 25). When tied to a program of market-driven policies such as voucher and choice plans, such a national system of standards, testing, and curriculum—while perhaps internally inconsistent—is an ideal compromise within the rightist coalition.

But one could still ask, won't a national curriculum coupled with a system of national achievement testing contradict in practice the concomitant emphasis on privatization and school choice? Can it really simultaneously achieve both? I maintain that this apparent contradiction may not be as substantial as one might expect. One long-term aim of powerful elements within the conservative coalition is not necessarily to transfer power from the local level to the center, although for some neoconservatives who favor a strong state in the area of morality, values, and standards, this may indeed be the case. Rather, these elements would prefer to decentralize such power altogether and redistribute it according to market forces, thus tacitly disempowering those who already have less power while employing a rhetoric of empowering the consumer. In part, both a national curriculum and national testing can be seen as "necessary concessions in pursuit of this long term aim" (Green 1991, p. 29).

In a time of a loss of legitimacy in government and a crisis in educational authority, the government must be seen to be doing something about raising educational standards. After all, this is exactly what it promises to offer to "consumers" of education. This is why a national curriculum is crucial. Its major value does not lie in its supposed encouragement of standardized goals and content and of levels of achievement in what are considered the most important subject areas. This concern with achievement, of course, should not be totally dismissed. However, the major role of a national curriculum is rather in providing the framework within which national testing can function. It enables the establishment of a procedure that can supposedly give consumers "quality tags" on schools so that "free market forces" can operate to their fullest extent. If we are to have a free market in education in which the consumer is presented with an attractive range of choices, both a national curriculum and especially national testing then act as a "state watchdog committee" to control the "worst excesses" of the market (Green 1991, p. 29).[4]

However, let us be honest about our own educational history here. Even with the supposed emphasis of some people on student portfolios and other more flexible forms of evaluation, there is no evidence at all to support the idea that what will ultimately be installed—even if only because of time and expense—will be anything other than a system of mass standardized paper-and-pencil tests.

Yet we must also be clear about the social function of such a proposal. A national curriculum may be seen as a device for accountability that will help us establish benchmarks so that parents can evaluate schools. But it also puts into motion a system in which children themselves will be ranked and ordered as never before. One of its primary roles will be to act as "a mechanism for differentiating children more rigidly against fixed norms, *the social meanings and derivation of which are not available for scrutiny*" (Johnson 1991a, p. 79).

Thus, while the proponents of a national curriculum may see it as a means to create social cohesion and to give all of us the capacity to improve our schools by measuring them against objective criteria, the effects will be the reverse. The criteria may seem objective, but the results will not be, given existing differences in resources and class and race segregation. Rather than cultural and social cohesion, differences between "us" and the "others" will be generated even more strongly, and the attendant social antagonisms and cultural and economic destruction will worsen.

Richard Johnson helps us understand the social processes at work here.

> This nostalgia for "cohesion" is interesting, but the great delusion is that all pupils—black and white, working class, poor, and middle class, boys and girls—will receive the curriculum in the same way. Actually, it will be read in different ways, according to how pupils are placed in social relationships and culture. A common curriculum, in a heterogeneous society, is not a recipe for "cohesion," but for resistance and the renewal of divisions. Since it always rests on cultural foundations of its own, it will put pupils in their places, not according to "ability," but according to how their cultural communities rank along the criteria taken as the "standard." A curriculum which does not "explain itself," is not ironical or self-critical, will always have this effect. (Johnson 1991a, pp. 79–80)

These are significant points, especially the call for all curricula to *explain themselves.* In complex societies like ours, which are riven with differential power, the only kind of cohesion that is possible is one in which we overtly recognize differences and inequalities. The curriculum then should not be presented as "objective." Rather, it must constantly *subjectify* itself. That is, it must "acknowledge its own roots" in the culture, history, and social interests out of which it arose. It will accordingly neither homogenize this culture, history, and social interest, nor will it homogenize the students. The "same treatment" by sex, race and ethnicity, or class is not the same at all. A democratic curriculum and pedagogy must begin with a recognition of "the different social positionings and cultural repertoires in the classrooms, and the power relations between them." Thus, if we are concerned with "really equal treatment"—as I think we must be—we must base a curriculum on a recognition of those differences that empower and disempower our students in identifiable ways (Johnson 1991a, p. 80; Ellsworth 1989).

Foucault reminds us that if you wish to understand how power works, you should examine the margins, look at the knowledge, self-understandings, and struggles of those whom powerful groups in this society have cast off as "the other" (Best and Kellner 1991, pp. 34–75). The New Right and its allies have created entire groups of "others"—people of color, women who refuse to accept external control of their lives and bodies, gays and lesbians, the poor (and the list could go on). It is in the recognition of these differences that curriculum dialogue can occur. Such a national dialogue should begin with the concrete and public exploration of how we are differently positioned in society and culture. What the New Right embargoes—the knowledge of the margins, of how culture and power are indissolubly linked—becomes a set of indispensable resources for this task (Johnson 1991b, p. 320).

The proposed national curriculum of course would recognize some of these differences. But, as Linda Christian-Smith and I argue in *The Politics of the Textbook,* the national curriculum serves both to partly acknowledge difference and at the same time to recuperate it within the supposed consensus that exists about what we should teach (Apple and Christian-Smith 1991; see also Apple 1993). It is part of an attempt to recreate hegemonic power that has been partly fractured by social movements.

The very idea of a common culture upon which a national curriculum—as defined by neoconservatives—is to be built is itself a form of cultural politics. In the immense linguistic, cultural, and religious diversity that makes up the constant creativity and flux in which we live, it is the cultural policy of the Right to override such diversity. Thinking it is reinstituting a common culture, it is instead *inventing* one, in much the same way as E. D. Hirsch (1987) has tried to do in his self-parody of what it means to be literate (Johnson 1991b, p. 319). A uniform culture never truly existed in the United States, only a selective version, an invented tradition that is reinstalled (though in different forms) in times of economic crisis and a crisis in authority relations, both of which threaten the hegemony of the culturally and economically dominant.

The expansion of voices in the curriculum and the vehement responses of the Right become crucial here. Multicultural and antiracist curricula present challenges to the program of the New Right, challenges that go to the core of their vision. In a largely monocultural national curriculum (which deals with diversity by centering the always ideological "we" and usually then simply mentioning "the contributions" of people of color, women, and "others"), the maintenance of existing hierarchies of what counts as official knowledge, the revivifying of traditional Western standards and values, the return to a "disciplined" (and one could say largely masculine) pedagogy, and so on, are paramount. A threat to any of these becomes a threat to the entire worldview of the Right (Johnson 1991a, p. 51; Rose 1988).

The idea of a common culture—in the guise of the romanticized Western tradition of the neoconservatives (or even as expressed in the longings of some socialists)—does not give enough thought, then, to the immense cultural heterogeneity of a society that draws its cultural traditions from all over the world. The task of defending public education as *public,* as deserving of widespread support "across an extremely diverse and deeply divided people, involves a lot more than restoration" (Education Group II 1991, p. x).

The debate in England is similar. A national curriculum is seen by the Right as essential to prevent relativism. For most of its proponents, a common curriculum must transmit both the common culture and the high culture that has grown out of it. Anything else will result in incoherence, no culture, merely a "void." Thus, a national culture is "defined in exclusive, nostalgic, and frequently racist terms" (Johnson 1991a, p. 71).

Richard Johnson's (1991a) analysis documents its social logic.

> In formulations like these, culture is thought of as a homogeneous way of life or tradition, not as a sphere of difference, relationships, or power. No recognition is given to the real diversity of social orientations and cultures within a given nation-state or people. Yet a selective version of a national culture is installed as an absolute condition for any social identity at all. The borrowing, mixing and fusion of elements from different cultural systems, a commonplace everyday practice in societies like [ours], is unthinkable within this framework, or is seen as a kind of cultural misrule that will produce nothing more than a void. So the "choices" are between . . . a national culture or no culture at all. (p. 71)

The racial subtext here is perhaps below the surface but is still present in significant ways.[5]

The national curriculum is a mechanism for the political control of knowledge (Johnson 1991a, p. 82). Once it is established, there will be little chance of turning back. It may be modified by the conflicts that its content generates, but it is in its very establishment that its politics lies. Only by recognizing its ultimate logic of false consensus and, especially, its undoubted hardening in the future as it becomes linked to a massive system of national testing can we fully understand this. When this probable future is connected to the other parts of the rightist agenda—marketization and privatization—there is reason to make us pause, especially given the increasingly powerful conservative gains at local, regional, and state levels (Apple 1993).

Who Benefits?

Since leadership in such efforts to "reform" our educational system and its curriculum, teaching, and evaluative practices is largely exercised by the rightist coalition, we need always to ask, "Whose reforms are these?" and "Who benefits?"

A system of national curricula and national testing cannot help but ratify and exacerbate gender, race, and class differences in the absence of sufficient resources both human and material. Thus, when the fiscal crisis in most of our urban areas is so severe that classes are being held in gymnasiums and hallways, when many schools do not have enough funds to stay open for the full 180 days a year, when buildings are disintegrating before our very eyes (Apple 1993), when in some cities three classrooms must share one set of textbooks at the elementary level (Kozol 1991)—I could go on—it is simply a flight of fantasy to assume that more standardized testing and national curriculum guidelines are the answer. With the destruction of the economic infrastructure of these same cities through capital flight, with youth unemployment at nearly 75 percent in many of them, with almost nonexistent health care, with lives that are often devoid of hope for meaningful mobility because of what might simply be called the pornography of poverty, to assume that establishing curricular benchmarks based on problematic cultural visions and more rigorous testing will do more than affix labels to poor students in a way that is seemingly more neutral is to totally misunderstand the situation. It will lead to more blame being placed on students and poor parents and especially to the schools that they attend. It will also be very expensive. Enter voucher plans with even wider public approval.

Basil Bernstein's analysis of the complexities of this situation and of its ultimate results is more than a little useful here. He says, "the pedagogic practices of the new vocationalism [neoliberalism] and those of the old autonomy of knowledge [neoconservatism] represent a conflict between different elitist ideologies, one

based on the class hierarchy of the market and the other based on the hierarchy of knowledge and its class supports" (Bernstein 1990, p. 63). Whatever the oppositions between market- and knowledge-oriented pedagogic and curricular practices, present racial, gender, and class-based inequalities are likely to be reproduced (Bernstein 1990, p. 64).

What he calls an "autonomous visible pedagogy"—one that relies on overt standards and highly structured models of teaching and evaluation—is justified by referring to its intrinsic worthiness. The value of the acquisition of say, the Western tradition, lies in its foundational status for "all we hold dear" and by the norms and dispositions that it instills in the students. "Its arrogance lies in its claim to moral high ground and to the superiority of its culture, its indifference to its own stratification consequences, its conceit in its lack of relation to anything other than itself, its self-referential abstracted autonomy" (Bernstein 1990, p. 87).

Its supposed opposite—one based on the knowledge, skills, and dispositions "required" by business and industry and one that seeks to transform schooling around market principles—is actually a much more complex ideological construction:

> It incorporates some of the criticism of the autonomous visible pedagogy . . . criticism of the failure of the urban school, of the passivity and inferior status [given to] parents, of the boredom of . . . pupils and their consequent disruptions of and resistance to irrelevant curricula, of assessment procedures which itemize relative failure rather than the positive strength of the acquirer. But it assimilates these criticisms into a new discourse: a new pedagogic Janus. . . . The explicit commitment to greater choice by parents . . . is not a celebration of participatory democracy, but a thin cover for the old stratification of schools and curricula. (Bernstein 1990, p. 87)

Are Bernstein's conclusions correct? Will the combination of national curricula, testing, and privatization actually lead away from democratic processes and outcomes? Here we must look not to Japan (where many people unfortunately have urged us to look) but to Britain, where this combination of proposals is much more advanced.

In Britain, there is now considerable evidence that the overall effects of the various market-oriented policies introduced by the rightist government are *not* genuine pluralism or the "interrupting [of] traditional modes of social reproduction." Far from this. They may instead largely provide "a legitimating gloss for the perpetuation of long-standing forms of structured inequality" (Whitty 1991, pp. 20–21). The fact that one of its major effects has been the disempowering and deskilling of large numbers of teachers is not inconsequential either (Apple 1993).

Going further, Edwards, Gewirtz, and Whitty have come to similar conclusions. In essence, the rightist preoccupation with "escape routes" diverts attention from the effects of such policies on those (probably the majority) who will be left behind (Edwards, Gewirtz, and Whitty forthcoming, p. 23).

Thus, it is indeed possible—actually probable—that market-oriented approaches in education (even when coupled with a strong state over a system of national curriculum and testing) will exacerbate already existing and widespread class and race divisions. Freedom and choice in the new educational market will be for those who can afford them. "Diversity" in schooling will simply be a more polite word for the condition of educational apartheid (Green 1991, p. 30; see also Karp 1992 and Lowe 1992).

Afterthoughts by Way of Conclusion

I have been more than a little negative in my appraisal here. I have argued that the politics of official knowledge—in this case surrounding proposals for a national curriculum and for national testing—cannot be fully understood in an isolated way. A national curriculum and national testing needs to be situated within larger ideological dynamics in which we are seeing an attempt by a new hegemonic bloc to transform our very ideas of what education is. This transformation involves a major shift—one that Dewey would have shuddered at—in which democracy becomes an economic, not a political, concept and where the idea of the public good withers at its very roots.

But perhaps I have been too negative. Perhaps there are good reasons to support national curricula and national testing even as currently constituted precisely *because* of the power of the rightist coalition.

It is possible, for example, to argue that only by establishing a national curriculum and national testing can we stop the fragmentation that will accompany the neoliberal portion of the rightist project. Only such a system would protect the very idea of a public school, would protect teachers' unions which in a privatized and marketized system would lose much of their power, would protect poor children and children of color from the vicissitudes of the market. After all, it is

the free market that created the poverty and destruction of community that they are experiencing in the first place.

It is also possible to argue, as Geoff Whitty has in the British case, that the very fact of a national curriculum encourages both the formation of intense public debate about what knowledge should be declared official and the creation of progressive coalitions against such state-sponsored definitions of legitimate knowledge.[6] It could be the vehicle for the return of the political which the Right so wishes to evacuate from our public discourse and which the efficiency experts wish to make into merely a technical concern.

Thus, it is quite possible that the establishment of a national curriculum could have the effect of unifying oppositional and oppressed groups. Given the fragmented nature of progressive educational movements today, and given a system of school financing and governance that forces groups to focus largely on the local or state level, one function of a national curriculum could be the coalescence of groups around a common agenda. A national movement for a more democratic vision of school reform could be the result.

In many ways—and I am quite serious here—we owe principled conservatives (and there are many) a debt of gratitude. It is their realization that curriculum issues are not only about techniques that has helped to stimulate the current debate. When many women, people of color, and labor organizations fought for decades to have society recognize the selective tradition in official knowledge, these movements were often (though not always) silenced, ignored, or recuperated into dominant discourses (Apple 1993; Apple and Christian-Smith 1991). The power of the Right—in its contradictory attempt to establish a national common culture, to challenge what is now taught, and to make that culture part of a vast supermarket of choices and thus to purge cultural politics from our sensibilities—has now made it impossible for the politics of official knowledge to be ignored.

Should we then support a national curriculum and national testing to keep total privatization and marketization at bay? Under current conditions, I do not think it is worth the risk—not only because of its extensive destructive potential in the long and short run but also because I think it misconstrues and reifies the issues of a common curriculum and a common culture.

Here I must repeat the arguments I made in the second edition of *Ideology and Curriculum* (Apple 1990). The current call to return to a common culture in which all students are to be given the values of a specific group—usually the dominant group—does not in my mind concern a common culture at all. Such an approach hardly scratches the surface of the political and educational issues involved. A common culture can never be the general extension to everyone of what a minority means and believes. Rather, and crucially, it requires not the stipulation of the facts, concepts, skills, and values that make us all "culturally literate," but the creation of the conditions necessary for all people to participate in the creation and recreation of meanings and values. It requires a democratic process in which all people—not simply those who are the intellectual guardians of the Western tradition—can be involved in the deliberation over what is important. This necessitates the removal of the very real material obstacles—unequal power, wealth, time for reflection—that stand in the way of such participation (Williams 1989, pp. 35–36). As Raymond Williams (1989) so perceptively puts it:

> The idea of a common culture is in no sense the idea of a simply consenting, and certainly not of a merely-conforming society. [It involves] a common determination of meanings by all the people, acting sometimes as individuals, sometimes as groups, in a process which has no particular end, and which can never be supposed at any time to have finally realized itself, to have become complete. In this common process, the only absolute will be the keeping of the channels and institutions of communication clear so that all may contribute, and be helped to contribute. (pp. 37–38)

In speaking of a common culture, then, we should not be talking of something uniform, something to which we all conform. Instead what we should be asking is precisely, for that free, contributive and common *process* of participation in the creation of meanings and values. It is the very blockage of that process in our institutions that must concern all of us.

Our current language speaks to how this process is being defined during the conservative restoration. Instead of people who participate in the struggle to build and rebuild our educational, cultural, political, and economic relations, we are defined as consumers (of that "particularly acquisitive class type"). This is truly an extraordinary concept, for it sees people as either stomachs or furnaces. We use and use up. We don't create—someone else does that. This is disturbing enough in general, but in education it is truly disabling. Leave it to the guardians of tradition, the efficiency and

accountability experts, the holders of "real knowledge," or to the Christopher Whittles of this world who have given us commercial television in the classroom and intend to franchise "schools of choice" for the generation of profit (Apple 1993). Yet we leave it to these people at great risk, especially to those students who are already economically and culturally disenfranchised by our dominant institutions.

As I noted at the outset, we live in a society with identifiable winners and losers. In the future we may say that the losers made poor "consumer choices" and that's the way markets operate. But is this society really only one vast market?

As Whitty reminds us, in a time when so many people have found out from their daily experiences that the supposed "grand narratives" of progress are deeply flawed, is it appropriate to return to yet another grand narrative, the market? (Whitty 1992). The results of this narrative are visible every day in the destruction of our communities and environment, in the increasing racism of society, in the faces and bodies of our children, who see the future and turn away.

Many people are able to disassociate themselves from these realities. There is almost a pathological distancing among the affluent (Kozol 1991). Yet how can one not be morally outraged at the growing gap between rich and poor, the persistence of hunger and homelessness, the deadly absence of medical care, the degradations of poverty. If this were the (always self-critical and constantly subjectifying) centerpiece of a national curriculum (but then how could it be tested cheaply and efficiently, and how could the Right control its ends and means?), perhaps such a curriculum would be worthwhile. But until such a time, we can take a rightist slogan made popular in another context and apply it to their educational agenda—"Just say no."

Notes

A draft of this chapter was presented as the John Dewey Lecture, jointly sponsored by the John Dewey Society and the American Educational Research Association, San Francisco, April 1992. I would like to thank Geoff Whitty, Roger Dale, James Beane, and the Friday Seminar at the University of Wisconsin, Madison, for their important suggestions and criticism. An extended version will appear in *Teachers College Record*.

1. See, e.g., Gould (1981). Feminist criticisms and reconstructions of science are essential to this task. See, for example, Haraway (1989), Harding and Barr (1987), Tuana (1981), and Harding (1991).

2. I put the word "minority" in quotation marks here to remind us that the vast majority of the world's population is composed of persons of color. It would be wholly salutary for our ideas about culture and education to bear this fact in mind.

3. Neoliberalism doesn't ignore the idea of a strong state, but it wants to limit it to specific areas (e.g., defense of markets).

4. I am making a "functional," not necessarily an "intentional," claim here. See Liston (1988). For an interesting discussion of how such testing programs might actually work against more democratic efforts at school reform, see Darling-Hammond (1992).

5. For a more complete analysis of racial subtexts in our policies and practices, see Omi and Winant (1986).

6. Geoff Whitty, personal communication. Andy Green, in the English context, argues as well that there are merits in having a broadly defined national curriculum but goes on to say that this makes it even more essential that individual schools have a serious degree of control over its implementation, "not least so that it provides a check against the use of education by the state as a means of promoting a particular ideology" (Green 1991, p. 22).

References

Apple, M. W. 1985. *Education and Power.* New York: Routledge.

_____. 1988a. Social Crisis and Curriculum Accords. *Educational Theory* 38: 191–201.

_____. 1988b. *Teachers and Texts: A Political Economy of Class and Gender Relations in Education.* New York: Routledge.

_____. 1989. American Realities: Poverty, Economy, and Education. In *Dropouts from School,* ed. Lois Weis, Eleanor Farrar, and Hugh Petrie, 205–223. Albany: State University of New York Press.

_____. 1990. *Ideology and Curriculum.* 2d. ed. New York: Routledge.

_____. 1993. *Official Knowledge: Democratic Education in a Conservative Age.* New York: Routledge.

Apple, M. W., and L. Christian-Smith, eds. 1991. *The Politics of the Textbook.* New York: Routledge.

Bastian, A., N. Fruchter, M. Gittell, C. Greer, and K. Haskins. 1986. *Choosing Equality.* Philadelphia: Temple University Press.

Bernstein, B. 1977. *Class, Codes and Control.* Vol. 3. New York: Routledge.

_____. 1990. *The Structuring of Pedagogic Discourse.* New York: Routledge.

Best, S., and D. Kellner. 1991. *Postmodern Theory: Critical Interrogations.* London: Macmillan.

Bourdieu, P. 1984. *Distinction.* Cambridge: Harvard University Press.

Burtless, G., ed. 1990. *A Future of Lousy Jobs?* Washington, DC: Brookings Institution.

Danziger, S., and D. Weinberg, eds. 1986. *Fighting Poverty.* Cambridge: Harvard University Press.

Darling-Hammond, L. 1992. Bush's Testing Plan Undercuts School Reforms. *Rethinking Schools* 6 (March/April): 18.

Education Group II, eds. 1991. *Education Limited.* London: Unwin Hyman.

Edwards, T., S. Gewirtz, and G. Whitty. Forthcoming. Whose Choice of Schools? In *Sociological Perspectives on Contemporary Educational Reforms,* ed. Madeleine Arnot and Len Barton. London: Triangle Books.

Ellsworth, E. 1989. Why Doesn't This Feel Empowering? *Harvard Educational Review* 59: 297–324.

Gould, S. J. 1981. *The Mismeasure of Man.* New York: Norton.

Green, A. 1991. The Peculiarities of English Education. In *Education Limited,* ed. Education Group II, 6–30. London: Unwin Hyman.

Haraway, D. 1989. *Primate Visions.* New York: Routledge.

Harding, S. 1991. *Whose Science, Whose Knowledge?* Ithaca: Cornell University Press.

Harding, S., and J. Barr, eds. 1987. *Sex and Scientific Inquiry.* Chicago: University of Chicago Press.

Hirsch, E. O. Jr. 1987. *Cultural Literacy.* New York: Vintage.

Honderich, T. 1990. *Conservatism.* Boulder, CO: Westview Press.

Hunter, A. 1988. *Children in the Service of Conservatism.* Madison: University of Wisconsin Law School, Institute for Legal Studies.

Johnson, R. 1991a. A New Road to Serfdom. In *Education Limited,* ed. Education Group II, 31–86. London: Unwin Hyman.

_____. 1991b. Ten Theses on a Monday Morning. In *Education Limited,* ed. Education Group II, 306–321. London: Unwin Hyman.

Karp, S. 1992. Massachusetts "Choice" Plan Undercuts Poor Districts. *Rethinking Schools* 6 (March/April): 4.

Kozol, J. 1991. *Savage Inequalities.* New York: Crown.

Liston, D. 1988. *Capitalist Schools.* New York: Routledge.

Lowe, R. 1992. The Illusion of "Choice." *Rethinking Schools* 6 (March/April): 1, 21–23.

Omi, M., and H. Winant. 1986. *Racial Formation in the United States.* New York: Routledge.

Rose, S. 1988. *Keeping Them Out of the Hands of Satan.* New York: Routledge.

Smith, M., J. O'Day, and D. Cohen. 1990. National Curriculum, American Style: What Might It Look Like. *American Educator* 14: 10–17, 40–47.

Tuana, N., ed. 1989. *Feminism and Science.* Bloomington: Indiana University Press.

Whitty, G. 1991. Recent Education Reform: Is It a Post-modern Phenomenon? Paper presented at the conference on Reproduction, Social Inequality, and Resistance, University of Bielefeld, Germany.

_____. 1992. *Education, Economy, and National Culture.* Milton Keynes, England: Open University Press.

Williams, R. 1989. *Resources of Hope.* New York: Verso.

The Mimetic and the Transformative

Alternative Outlooks on Teaching

PHILIP W. JACKSON

The Greek sophist Protagoras allegedly claimed that on every subject two opposite statements could be made, each as defensible as the other. Whether or not he was right in a universal sense is something for logicians and rhetoricians to decide. However, insofar as the affairs of everyday life are concerned, he seems to have hit upon a fundamental truth, for we encounter daily all manner of "opposite statements," each with its share of supporters and critics.

As might be expected, education as a field of study is no exception to the rule. There too, differing outlooks, poles apart at first glance, are as common as elsewhere. Who, for example, is unfamiliar with the many verbal exchanges that have taken place over the years between "traditional" educators on the one side and their "progressive" opponents on the other, debates in which the merits of "child-centered" practices are pitted against those considered more "subject-centered"?

This [reading] introduces a dichotomy that encompasses the differences just named as well as others less familiar, though it is not usually talked about in the terms I will employ here. Indeed, the names of the two outlooks to be discussed have been purposely chosen so as to be *un*familiar to most followers of today's educational discussions and debates. My reason for this is not to introduce novelty for its own sake, much less to

add glitter by using a pair of fancy terms. Instead, it is to avoid becoming prematurely embroiled in the well-known controversies associated with phrases like "child-centered" and "subject-centered," controversies that too often degenerate into mud-slinging contests which reduce the terms themselves to little more than slogans and epithets. A similar fate may well await the pair of terms to be introduced here. But for the time being the fact that they are rather new, or at least newly employed within an educational context, should prevent that.

In brief, I contend in this [reading] that two distinguishably different ways of thinking about education and of translating that thought into practice undergird most of the differences of opinion that have circulated within educational circles over the past two or three centuries. Framed within an argument, which is how they are usually encountered, each of these two outlooks seeks to legitimate its own vision of how education should be conducted. It does so by promoting certain goals and practices, making them seem proper and just, while ignoring others or calling them into question.

These dichotomous orientations are not the exact opposites of which Protagoras spoke, though they are often presented that way by people propounding one or the other. How they *are* related to each other is a ques-

From "The Mimetic and the Transformative" in *The Practice of Teaching* by Philip W. Jackson (New York: Teachers College Press, 1986). Reprinted by permission.

tion I will consider in some detail in the second half of this [reading]. For now, however, it will suffice to call their relationship enigmatic. Most of the time their challengers and defenders are depicted at swords' points, but there is a perspective from which the two outlooks appear complementary and interdependent. Indeed, there are angles of vision from which what originally seemed to be two diametrically opposed orientations suddenly appear to be one.

What shall we name these two points of view? As the chapter title already reveals, I recommend they be called the "mimetic" and the "transformative." I also propose we think of them not simply as two viewpoints on educational matters but as two traditions within the domain of educational thought and practice. Why *traditions?* Because each has a long and respectable history going back at least several hundred years and possibly beyond. Also, each is more than an intellectual argument. Each provokes feelings of partisanship and loyalty toward a particular point of view; each also entails commitment to a set of related practices. In short, each comprises what might be called (following Wittgenstein[1]) a "form of life," a relatively coherent and unified way of thinking, feeling, and acting within a particular domain—in this instance, the sphere of education. The term "traditions" stands for that complexity. Its use reminds us that each outlook stretches back in time, and that each has a "lived" dimension that makes it something much more than a polemical argument.

The Mimetic Tradition

We turn to the "mimetic" tradition first not because it is any older or any more important than the one called "transformative," but principally because it is the easier of the two to describe. In addition, it is closer to what most people today seem to think education is all about. Thus, presenting it first has the advantage of beginning with the more familiar and moving to the less familiar. Third, it is more harmonious with all that is thought of as "scientific" and "rigorous" within education than is its competitor. To all who rank that pair of adjectives highly, as I reservedly do myself, therein lies an additional reason for putting it first.

This tradition is named "mimetic" (the root term is the Greek word *mimesis,* from which we get "mime" and "mimic") because it gives a central place to the transmission of factual and procedural knowledge from one person to another, through an essentially *imitative*

process. If I had to substitute another equally unfamiliar word in its place, with which to engage in educational debate, I would choose "epistemic"—yet another derived from the Greek, this from *episteme,* meaning knowledge. The first term stresses the *process* by which knowledge is commonly transmitted, the second puts its emphasis on the *content* of the transaction. Thus we have the "mimetic" or the "epistemic" tradition; I prefer the former if for no other reason than that it places the emphasis where I believe it belongs, on the importance of *method* within this tradition.

The conception of knowledge at the heart of the mimetic tradition is familiar to most of us, though its properties may not always be fully understood even by teachers committed to this outlook on teaching. For this reason it seems essential to say something about its properties.

First of all, knowledge of a "mimetic" variety, whose transmission entails mimetic procedures, is by definition identifiable in advance of its transmission. This makes it secondhand knowledge, so to speak, not in the pejorative sense of that term, but simply in that it has to have belonged to someone first before it can belong to anyone else. In short, it is knowledge "presented" to a learner, rather than "discovered" by him or her.[2]

Such knowledge can be "passed" from one person to another or from a text to a person; we can thus see it as "detachable" from persons *per se,* in two ways. It is detachable in the first place in that it can be preserved in books and films and the like, so that it can "outlive" all who originally possessed it. It is detachable, secondly, in the sense that it can be forgotten by those who once knew it. Though it can be "possessed," it can also be "dispossessed" through memory loss. Moreover, it can be "unpossessed" in the sense of never having been "possessed" in the first place. A correlate of its detachability is that it can be "shown" or displayed by its possessor, a condition that partially accounts for our occasional reference to it as "objective" knowledge.

A crucial property of mimetic knowledge is its reproducibility. It is this property that allows us to say it is "transmitted" from teacher to student or from text to student. Yet when we speak of it that way we usually have in mind a very special kind of process. It does not entail handing over a bundle of some sort as in an actual "exchange" or "giving." Rather, it is more like the transmission of a spoken message from one person to another or the spread of bacteria from a cold-sufferer to a new victim. In all such instances both parties wind up possessing what was formerly possessed by only one of them. What has been transmitted has actually been "mirrored" or "reproduced" without its ever having been relinquished in the process.

The knowledge involved in all transmissions within the mimetic tradition has an additional property worth noting: It can be judged right or wrong, accurate or inaccurate, correct or incorrect on the basis of a comparison with the teacher's own knowledge or with some other model as found in a textbook or other instructional materials. Not only do judgments of this sort yield a measure of the success of teaching within this tradition, they also are the chief criterion by which learning is measured.

My final remark about knowledge as conceived within the mimetic tradition may already be obvious from what has been said. It is that mimetic knowledge is by no means limited to "bookish" learning, knowledge expressible in words alone. Though much of it takes that form, it also includes the acquisition of physical and motor skills, knowledge to be *performed* in one way or another, usually without any verbal accompaniment whatsoever. "Knowing that" and "knowing how" is the way the distinction is sometimes expressed.[3]

Here then are the central epistemological assumptions associated with the mimetic tradition. The key idea is that some kind of knowledge or skill can be doubly possessed, first by the teacher alone (or the writer of the textbook or the computer program), then by his or her student. In more epigrammatic terms, the slogan for this tradition might well be: "What the teacher (or textbook or computer) knows, that shall the student come to know."

How might the goal of this tradition be achieved? In essence, the procedure for transmitting mimetic knowledge consists of five steps, the fourth of which divides in two alternate routes, "a" or "b," dependent on the presence or absence of student error. The series is as follows:

Step One: *Test.* Some form of inquiry, either formal or informal, is initiated to discover whether the student(s) in question already knows the material or can perform the skill in question. This step is properly omitted if the student's lack of knowledge or skill can be safely assumed.

Step Two: *Present.* Finding the student ignorant of what is to be learned, or assuming him or her to be so, the teacher "presents" the material, either discur-

sively—with or without the support of visual aids—or by modeling or demonstrating a skillful performance or some aspect thereof.

Step Three: *Perform/Evaluate.* The student, who presumably has been attentive during the presentation, is invited or required to repeat what he or she has just witnessed, read, or heard. The teacher (or some surrogate device, such as a test scoring machine) monitors the student's performance, making a judgment and sometimes generating a numerical tally of its accuracy or correctness.

Step Four (A): (Correct performance) *Reward/Fix.* Discovering the performance to be reasonably accurate (within limits usually set in advance), the teacher (or surrogate device) comments favorably on what the student has done and, when deemed necessary, prescribes one or more repetitions in order to habituate or "fix" the material in the student's repertoire of things known or skills mastered.

Step Four (B): (Incorrect performance) *Enter Remedial Loop.* Discovering the student's performance to be wrong (again within limits usually established in advance), the teacher (or surrogate) initiates a remedial procedure designed to correct the error in question. Commonly this procedure begins with a diagnosis of the student's difficulty followed by the selection of an appropriate corrective strategy.

Step Five: *Advance.* After the unit of knowledge or skill has been "fixed" (all appropriate corrections having been made and drills undertaken), the teacher and student advance to the next unit of "fresh" instruction, returning to Step One, if deemed necessary by the teacher, and repeating the moves in sequential order. The sequence of steps is repeated until the student has mastered all the prescribed knowledge or until all efforts to attain a prescribed level of mastery have been exhausted.

In skeletal form, this is the way instruction proceeds within the mimetic tradition. Readers familiar with cybernetic models will readily recognize the five steps outlined as an instance of what is commonly referred to as a "feedback loop" mechanism, an algorithmic device equipped with "internal guidance circuitry."[4]

Which teachers teach this way? Almost all do so on occasion, yet not all spend an equal amount of time at it. Some teachers work within the mimetic tradition only on weekends, figuratively speaking, about as often as a "do-it-yourself-er" might wield a hammer or turn a wrench. Others employ the same techniques routinely on a day-to-day basis, as might a professional carpenter or mechanic.

Which do which? That question will be treated at some length later in this [reading], where I will take up the relationship between the two traditions. For now it will suffice to observe in passing what is perhaps obvious, that teachers intent upon the transmission of factual information, plus those seeking to teach specific psychomotor skills, would more likely use mimetic procedures than would those whose conception of teaching involved educational goals less clearly epistemic in nature.

What might the latter category of goals include? To answer that question we must turn to the second of the two dominant outlooks within educational thought and practice, which I have chosen to call:

The Transformative Tradition

The adjective "transformative" describes what this tradition deems successful teaching to be capable of accomplishing: a transformation of one kind or another in the person being taught—a qualitative change often of dramatic proportion, a metamorphosis, so to speak. Such changes would include all those traits of character and of personality most highly prized by the society at large (aside from those having to do solely with the possession of knowledge *per se*). They also would include the eradication or remediation of a corresponding set of undesirable traits. In either case, the transformations aimed for within this tradition are typically conceived of as being more deeply integrated and ingrained within the psychological makeup of the student—and therefore as perhaps more enduring—than are those sought within the mimetic or epistemic outlook, whose dominant metaphor is one of "adding on" to what already exists (new knowledge, new skills, etc.) rather than modifying the would-be learner in some more fundamental way.

What traits and qualities have teachers working within the transformative tradition sought to modify? Our answer depends on when and where we look. Several centuries ago, for example, when the mission of schools was primarily religious, what was being sought was nothing other than students' salvation through preparing them for Bible reading and other religiously oriented activities. Such remains the goal of much religious instruction today, though the form of its expression may have changed somewhat.

Over the years, as schooling became more widespread and more secular in orientation, educators began to abandon the goal of piety *per se,* and focused instead upon effecting "transformation" of character, morals, and virtue. Many continue to speak that way today, though it is more common to name "attitudes," "values," and "interests" as the psychological traits many of today's teachers seek to modify.

However one describes the changes sought within the transformative tradition, it is interesting that this undertaking is usually treated as more exalted or noble than the more mimetic type of teaching. Why this should be so is not readily apparent, but the different degrees of seriousness attached to the two traditions are apparent in the metaphors associated with each of them.

As I have already said, within the mimetic tradition knowledge is conceived of as something akin to material goods. Like a person materially wealthy, the possessor of knowledge may be considered "richer" than his ignorant neighbor. Yet, like the materially rich and poor, the two remain fundamentally equal as human beings. This metaphor of knowledge as coins in one's purse is consonant with the concomitant belief that it is "detachable" from its owner, capable of being "shown," "lost," and so forth. A related metaphor, one often used to lampoon the mimetic tradition, depicts the learner as a kind of vessel into which knowledge is "poured" or "stored." What is important about all such metaphors is that the vessel in question remains essentially unchanged, with or without its "contents."

The root image within the transformative tradition is entirely different. It is much closer to that of a potter working with clay than it is to someone using the potter's handiwork as a container for whatever contents such a vessel might hold. The potter, as we know, not only leaves her imprint on the vessel itself in the form of a signature of some kind, she actually molds and shapes the object as she creates it. All who later work with the finished product have a different relationship to it entirely. They may fill it or empty it to their hearts' content. They may even break it if they wish. But all such actions accept the object in question as a "given," something whose essence is fundamentally sacrosanct.

The metaphor of teacher-as-artist or teacher-as-creator gives the transformative tradition an air of profundity and drama, perhaps even spirituality, that is largely lacking within the mimetic tradition, whose root metaphor of mere addition of knowledge or skill is much more prosaic. But metaphors, as we know, are mere figures of speech. No matter how flattering they might be, they don't tell us whether such flattery is deserved. They leave us to ask whether teachers working within the transformative tradition actually succeed in doing what they and others sometimes boast they can do. And that's not all they leave unanswered. Beyond the question of whether transformative changes due to pedagogical interventions really occur at all there awaits the more practical question of *how* they happen. What do teachers do to bring them about? As we might guess, it is easier to answer the former question than the latter.

Fictional accounts of teachers who have had enduring effects on their students of the kind celebrated within the transformative tradition are familiar enough to be the stock in trade of the pedagogical novel. *Goodbye, Mr. Chips* and *The Prime of Miss Jean Brodie*[5] are but two of such works that come to mind most readily. Each exemplifies a teacher who has a profoundly transformative influence on his or her students. But what of real life? Do teachers *there* make a difference of the same magnitude as do the fictional Chipses and Brodies?

An answer to that question which I find quite convincing is contained in a study undertaken by Anne Kuehnle, a student of mine a few years back. In preparation for her term paper in a course on the analysis of teaching, work which later became the basis of her master's thesis, Kuehnle distributed questionnaires to 150 friends and neighbors in her hometown of Elmhurst, Illinois; she asked them to write a paragraph or two about the teachers they remembered most vividly. The results were striking. Not only did most respondents comply enthusiastically with the request, their descriptions yielded literally scores of vignettes showing the transformative tradition in action. Here are but three of them, chosen almost at random.

> He moved the learning process from himself to us and equipped us to study independently. We were able to see such mundane concepts as money supply, price mechanism, supply and demand, all around us. We became interested. We actually talked economics after class! In Eckstein's class I became aware that I was there to evaluate, not ingest, concepts. I began to discriminate . . .

> She was, to me, a glimpse of the world beyond school and my little town of 800 people. She was beautiful, vivacious, witty, and had a truly brilliant mind. Her energy knew no limit—she took on all the high school English classes, class plays, yearbook, began interpretive reading

and declamatory contests, started a library in the town, and on and on. *She* was our town's cultural center.

> His dedication rubbed off on nearly all of us. I was once required to write him a 12-page report, and I handed in an 84-page research project. I always felt he deserved more than the minimum.[6]

These three examples are quite representative of the protocols quoted throughout Kuehnle's report. So if we can trust what so many of her respondents told us—and I am inclined to do so, for had I been asked I would have responded much as they did—there seems no shortage of testimonial evidence to support the conclusion that at least some teachers do indeed modify character, instill values, shape attitudes, generate new interests, and succeed in "transforming," profoundly and enduringly, at least some of the students in their charge. The question now becomes: How do they do it? How are such beneficial outcomes accomplished?

As most teachers will readily testify, the answer to that question will disappoint all who seek overnight to become like the teachers described in Kuehnle's report. It seems there *are* no formulas for accomplishing these most impressive if not miraculous feats of pedagogical skill. There are neither simple instructions for the neophyte nor complicated ones for the seasoned teacher. There is not even an epigram or two to keep in mind as guides for how to proceed, nothing analogous to the ancient "advice" that tells us to feed a cold and starve a fever.

And yet that last point is not quite as accurate as were the two that came before it. For if we look carefully at what such teachers do and listen to what others say about their influence, we begin to see that they *do* have some characteristic ways of working after all, "modes of operation" that, even if they can't be reduced to recipes and formulas, are worth noting all the same. The three of these modes most readily identifiable seem to me to be:

1. *Personal modeling.* Of the many attributes associated with transformative teaching, the most crucial ones seem to concern the teacher as a person. For it is essential to success within that tradition that teachers who are trying to bring about transformative changes personify the very qualities they seek to engender in their students. To the best of their ability they must be living exemplars of certain virtues or values or attitudes. The fulfillment of that requirement achieves its apex in great historical figures, like Socrates and

Christ, who epitomize such a personal model; but most teachers already know that no attitude, interest, or value can be taught except by the teacher who himself or herself believes in, cares for, or cherishes whatever it is that he or she holds out for emulation.

2. *"Soft" suasion.* Among teachers working toward transformative ends, the "showing" and "telling" so central to the mimetic tradition (actions contained in Step Two: *Present* of the methodological paradigm outlined above) are replaced by less emphatic assertions and by an altogether milder form of pedagogical authority. The teaching style is rather more forensic and rhetorical than it is one of proof and demonstration. Often the authority of the teacher is so diminished by the introduction of a questioning mode within this tradition that there occurs a kind of role reversal, almost as though the student were teaching the teacher. This shift makes the transformative teacher look humbler than his or her mimetic counterpart, but it is by no means clear that such an appearance is a trustworthy indicator of the teacher's true temperament.

3. *Use of narrative.* Within the transformative tradition "stories" of one kind or another, which would include parables, myths, and other forms of narrative, play a large role. Why this should be so is not immediately clear, but it becomes so as we consider what is common to the transformations that the schools seek to effect. The common element, it turns out, is their moral nature. Virtues, character traits, interests, attitudes, values—as educational goals all of them fall within the moral realm of the "right" or "proper" or "just." Now when we ask about the function or purpose of narrative, one answer (some might say the only one) is: to moralize.[7] Narratives present us with stories about how to live (or how not to live) our lives. Again, Socrates and Christ come readily to mind as exemplars of the teacher-as-storyteller as well as the teacher about whom stories are told.

The examples of Socrates and Christ as both transformative models and as storytellers help us to realize that differences in the conception of teaching within the two traditions go far beyond the question of what shall be taught and how it shall be done. They extend to the psychological and epistemological relationship between the teacher and his or her students.

Within the mimetic tradition the teacher occupies the role of expert in two distinct ways. He or she supposedly is in command of a specifiable body of knowl-

edge or set of skills whose properties we have already commented upon. Such knowledge constitutes what we might call *substantive* expertise. At the same time the teacher is thought to possess the know-how whereby a significant portion of his or her substantive knowledge may be "transmitted" to students. The latter body of knowledge, whose paradigmatic contours have also been sketched, constitutes what we might call the teacher's *methodological* expertise. The students, by way of contrast, might be described as doubly ignorant. They neither know what the teacher knows, substantively speaking, nor do they know how to teach it in methodological terms. This dual condition of ignorance places them below the teacher epistemologically no matter where they stand regarding other social attributes and statuses.

Within the transformative tradition, the superiority of the teacher's knowledge, whether substantive or methodological, is not nearly so clear-cut. Nor is the teacher's status in general vis-à-vis his or her students. Instead, the overall relationship between the two is often vexingly ambiguous if not downright upsetting to some students; it can even become so at times to teachers themselves. Nowhere are many of these ambiguities portrayed more dramatically than in the early Socratic dialogues of Plato.[8] In the person of Socrates we witness perhaps the most famous of all transformative teachers in action. He is also a teacher whose actions are often as puzzling as they are edifying.

Does Socrates know more than his students? Well of course he does, says commonsense, why else would so many seek him out for advice and confront him with the most profound of questions? Yet, as we know, Socrates rarely if ever answers the questions he is asked, often professing to know less about the answer than does the questioner himself. Is he feigning ignorance when he behaves that way? It is not always easy to tell, as we can gather from the frequent expressions of puzzlement on the part of those conversing with him. And what about his method? How canny is he as a teacher? Does he really know what he is doing every step of the way or is he more or less bumbling along much of the time, never quite sure of where he is going or of how to get there? Again, it is hard to say for sure. There are times when he seems completely in control of the situation, but other times when he seems utterly confused about what to say or do next; he even goes so far as to say so. Finally, what shall we make of the social relationship between Socrates and his fellow Athenians? Where do they stand in relation to each other?

That too is a difficult question to answer definitively. Certainly he was greatly revered by many of his followers—Plato, of course, chief among them. But he was just as obviously envied by some and actively disliked by others.

A fuller treatment of the complexities and ambiguities of the Socratic method is beyond the scope of this work.[9] However, the little I have already said should make the point that ambiguities like those in the Socratic dialogues are common to the transformative tradition within teaching wherever it may be found. They are so because all such teachers are engaged in what is fundamentally *a moral undertaking* much like that of Socrates, whether they acknowledge it or not. Moreover, it is also a *philosophic* undertaking. That too is not always recognized by those actually engaged in such an enterprise.

What does it mean to speak of transformative teaching in these terms? In what sense is it either a moral or a philosophic undertaking? It is moral in that it seeks moral ends. Teachers working within the transformative tradition are actually trying to bring about changes in their students (and possibly in themselves as well) that make them better persons, not simply more knowledgeable or more skillful, but better in the sense of being closer to what humans are capable of becoming—more virtuous, fuller participants in an evolving moral order.

It is philosophic in that it employs philosophical means. No matter how else they might describe their actions, teachers working within the transformative tradition seek to change their students (and possibly themselves as well) by means neither didactic nor dogmatic. Instead, they use discussion, demonstration, argumentation. Armed only with the tools of reason, the transformative teacher seeks to accomplish what can be attained in no other way. Here is how one student of the process describes its operation within philosophy proper.

> We have discovered philosophy to be the sum total of those universal rational truths that become clear only through reflection. To philosophize, then, is simply to isolate these rational truths with our intellect and to express them in general judgments. . . .
>
> The teacher who seriously wishes to impart philosophical insight can aim only at teaching the art of philosophising. He can do no more than show his students how to undertake, each for himself, the laborious regress that alone affords insight into basic principles. If there is such a thing at all as instruction in philosophy, it

can only be instruction in doing one's own thinking; more precisely, in the independent practice of the art of abstraction.[10]

Another commentator on the same subject sums up the difference by referring to himself as "a philosopher, not an expert." "The latter," he goes on to explain, "knows what he knows and what he does not know: the former does not. One concludes, the other questions—two very different language games."[11]

But talk of teachers being engaged in a moral and philosophic enterprise has its difficulties. For one thing, it sounds rather pretentious, especially when we consider some of the more mundane aspects of the average teacher's work—the routines of giving assignments, grading papers, taking attendance, keeping order in the classroom, and so on. Little of such activity deserves to be called either moral or philosophical. Moreover, teachers themselves do not seem to talk that way about what they do. Least of all do those who do it best, like Socrates.

The way out of these difficulties is to deny neither the moral and philosophical dimensions of teaching nor the prosaic nature of much that teachers actually do. Rather it requires that we acknowledge the compatibility of both viewpoints, seeing them as complementary rather than mutually exclusive. In short, nothing save a kind of conceptual narrow-mindedness keeps us from a vision of teaching as both a noble and a prosaic undertaking. Erasmus approached that insight several centuries ago when he remarked that "In the opinion of fools [teaching] is a humble task, but in fact it is the noblest of occupations."[12] Had he been a trifle more charitable he might have added that the fools were not totally wrong. Their trouble was that they were only half right.

Teachers themselves often overlook the moral dimensions of their work, but that failing must be treated as a problem to be solved, rather than as evidence of the amorality of teaching itself. There is no doubt that one can teach without giving thought to the transformative significance of what he or she is doing. But whether it should be so performed is another question entirely. Moreover, though the teacher may pay no attention whatsoever to such matters, we must ask if they are thereby eliminated as a class of outcomes. The well-known phenomenon of *unintended consequences,* sometimes referred to as "incidental learnings" when they take place within the context of a classroom, leads us to suspect that the delivery of moral messages and actions of transformative significance may often take place whether the teacher intends them to or not. Indeed, it is far more interesting to ask whether such outcomes are inevitable, which is equivalent to asking whether all teachers are ultimately working within the transformative tradition whether they realize it or not.

Endnotes

1. Ludwig Wittgenstein, *Philosophical Investigations* (Oxford: Basil Blackwell, 1968), p. 9e.
2. Aristotle once remarked that "All instruction given or received by way of argument proceeds from pre-existent knowledge." (*Posterior Analytic, Book* I, 71a). By this he meant that we must begin with major and minor premises whose truth is beyond dispute before we can move to a novel conclusion. This is not quite the same as claiming that all knowledge is second-hand, but it does call attention to how much of the "known" is properly described as having been "transmitted" or "passed along" to students from teachers or teacher surrogates, such as textbooks or computers.
3. For a well-known discussion of that distinction, see Gilbert Ryle, *The Concept of Mind* (New York: Barnes and Noble, 1949).
4. See, for example, G. A. Miller, E. Galanter, and K. H. Pribham, *Plans and the Structure of Behavior* (New York: Holt, 1960).
5. James Hilton, *Goodbye Mr. Chips* (Boston: Little, Brown and Co., 1934) and Muriel Spark, *The Prime of Miss Jean Brodie* (Philadelphia: Lippincott, 1961).
6. Anne Kuehnle, "Teachers remembered," unpublished master's thesis, University of Chicago, June 1984.
7. See Hayden White, "The value of narrativity in the representation of reality," in W. J. T. Mitchell (ed.), *On Narrative* (Chicago: University of Chicago Press, 1981), 1–24. Also, John Gardner, *On Moral Fiction* (New York: Basic Books, 1978). Gardner points out that "the effect of great fiction is to temper real experience, modify prejudice, humanize" (p. 114).
8. See Edith Hamilton and Huntington Cairns (eds.), *The Collected Dialogues of Plato* (Princeton, New Jersey: Princeton University Press, 1961). See especially the *Charmides, Laches, Euthydemus, Protagoras, Gorgias, and Meno.*
9. For a fuller treatment of these and other ambiguities having to do with Socrates' teaching style see Gregory Vlastos, "Introduction: The paradox of Socrates," in Gregory Vlastos (ed.), *The Philosophy of Socrates* (Notre Dame, Indiana: University of Notre Dame Press, 1980), 1–21. Several other essays in that volume treat specialized aspects of the subject, such as Socrates' use of the technique of *elenchus.* See also, W. K. C. Guthrie, *Socrates* (Cambridge: Cambridge University Press, 1971), especially "The ignorance of Socrates," pp. 122–129. Also, Gerasimos Xenophon Santas, *Socrates* (Boston: Routledge & Kegan Paul, 1979). An unusually enlightening essay on the Socratic method is contained in Leonard Nelson, *Socratic Method and Critical Philosophy* (New York: Dover Publications, 1965), 1–40.
10. Nelson, *Socratic Method,* 10–11.
11. Jean-Francois Lvotard, *The Postmodern Condition: A Report on Knowledge* (Minneapolis: University of Minnesota Press, 1984), xxv.
12. Claude M. Fuess and Emory S. Basford (eds.), *Unseen Harvests: A Treasury of Teaching* (New York: Macmillan, 1947), v.

The Silenced Dialogue

Power and Pedagogy in Educating Other People's Children

LISA D. DELPIT

A black male graduate student who is also a special education teacher in a predominantly black community is talking about his experiences in predominantly white university classes:

> There comes a moment in every class where we have to discuss "The Black Issue" and what's appropriate education for black children. I tell you, I'm tired of arguing with those white people, because they won't listen. Well, I don't know if they really don't listen or if they just don't believe you. It seems like if you can't quote Vygotsky or something, then you don't have any validity to speak about your *own* kids. Anyway, I'm not bothering with it anymore, now I'm just in it for a grade.

A black woman teacher in a multicultural urban elementary school is talking about her experiences in discussions with her predominantly white fellow teachers about how they should organize reading instruction to best serve students of color:

> When you're talking to white people they still want it to be their way. You can try to talk to them and give them examples, but they're so headstrong, they think they know what's best for *everybody,* for *everybody's* children. They won't listen; white folks are going to do what they want to do *anyway.*
>
> It's really hard. They just don't listen well. No, they listen, but they don't *hear*—you know how your mama used to say you listen to the radio, but you *hear* your mother? Well they don't *hear* me.
>
> So I just try to shut them out so I can hold my temper. You can only beat your head against a brick wall for so long before you draw blood. If I try to stop arguing with them I can't help myself from getting angry. Then I end up walking around praying all day "Please Lord, remove the bile I feel for these people so I can sleep tonight." It's funny, but it can become a cancer, a sore.
>
> So, I shut them out. I go back to my own little cubby, my classroom, and I try to teach the way I know will

work, no matter what those folk say. And when I get black kids, I just try to undo the damage they did.

> I'm not going to let any man, woman, or child drive me crazy—white folks will try to do that to you if you let them. You just have to stop talking to them, that's what I do. I just keep smiling, but I won't talk to them.

A soft-spoken Native Alaskan woman in her forties is a student in the Education Department of the University of Alaska. One day she storms into a black professor's office and very uncharacteristically slams the door. She plops down in a chair and, still fuming, says, "Please tell those people, just don't help us anymore! I give up. I won't talk to them again!"

And finally, a black woman principal who is also a doctoral student at a well-known university on the West Coast is talking about her university experiences, particularly about when a professor lectures on issues concerning educating black children:

> If you try to suggest that's not quite the way it is, they get defensive, then you get defensive, then they'll start reciting research.
>
> I try to give them my experiences, to explain. They just look and nod. The more I try to explain, they just look and nod, just keep looking and nodding. They don't really hear me.
>
> Then, when it's time for class to be over, the professor tells me to come to his office to talk more. So I go. He asks for more examples of what I'm talking about, and he looks and nods while I give them. Then he says that that's just *my* experience. It doesn't really apply to most black people.
>
> It becomes futile because they think they know everything about everybody. What you have to say about your life, your children, doesn't mean anything. They don't really want to hear what you have to say. They wear blinders and earplugs. They only want to go on research they've read that other white people have written.

From Lisa D. Delpit, "The Silenced Dialogue: Power and Pedagogy in Educating Other People's Children," *Harvard Educational Review,* 58:3 (August 1988), pp. 280–298. Copyright © 1988 by the President and Fellows of Harvard College. All rights reserved.

It just doesn't make any sense to keep talking to them.

Thus was the first half of the title of this text born: "The Silenced Dialogue." One of the tragedies in this field of education is that scenarios such as these are enacted daily around the country. The saddest element is that the individuals that the black and Native Alaskan educators speak of in these statements are seldom aware that the dialogue *has* been silenced. Most likely the white educators believe that their colleagues of color did, in the end, agree with their logic. After all, they stopped disagreeing, didn't they?

I have collected these statements since completing a recently published article, a somewhat autobiographical account entitled "Skills and Other Dilemmas of a Progressive Black Educator," in which I discuss my perspective as a product of a skills-oriented approach to writing and as a teacher of process-oriented approaches.[1] I described the estrangement that I and many teachers of color feel from the progressive movement when writing process advocates dismiss us as too "skills oriented." I ended the article suggesting that it was incumbent upon writing process advocates, or indeed, advocates of any progressive movement, to enter into dialogue with teachers of color, who may not share their enthusiasm about so-called new, liberal, or progressive ideas.

In response to this article, which presented no research data and did not even cite a reference, I received numerous calls and letters from teachers, professors, and even state school personnel from around the country, both black and white. All of the white respondents, except one, have wished to talk more about the question of skills versus process approaches—to support or reject what they perceive to be my position. On the other hand, *all* of the nonwhite respondents have spoken passionately on being left out of the dialogue about how best to educate children of color.

How can such complete communication blocks exist when both parties truly believe they have the same aims? How can the bitterness and resentment expressed by the educators of color be drained so that the sores can heal? What can be done?

I believe the answer to these questions lies in ethnographic analysis, that is, in identifying and giving voice to alternative worldviews. Thus, I will attempt to address the concerns raised by white and black respondents to my article "Skills and Other Dilemmas." My charge here is not to determine the best instructional

methodology; I believe that the actual practice of good teachers of all colors typically incorporates a range of pedagogical orientations. Rather, I suggest that the differing perspectives on the debate over "skills" versus "process" approaches can lead to an understanding of the alienation and miscommunication, and thereby to an understanding of the "silenced dialogue."

In thinking through these issues, I have found what I believe to be a connecting and complex theme: what I have come to call "the culture of power." There are five aspects of power I would like to propose as given for this presentation:

1. Issues of power are enacted in classrooms.
2. There are codes or rules for participating in power; that is, there is a "culture of power."
3. The rules of the culture of power are a reflection of the rules of the culture of those who have power.
4. If you are not already a participant in the culture of power, being told explicitly the rules of that culture makes acquiring power easier.
5. Those with power are frequently least aware of—or least willing to acknowledge—its existence. Those with less power are often most aware of its existence.

The first three are by now basic tenets in the literature of the sociology of education, but the last two have seldom been addressed. The following discussion will explicate these aspects of power and their relevance to the schism between liberal educational movements and that of non-white, non-middle-class teachers and communities.[2]

1. *Issues of power are enacted in classrooms.* These issues include: the power of the teacher over the students; the power of the publishers of textbooks and of the developers of the curriculum to determine the view of the world presented; the power of the state in enforcing compulsory schooling; and the power of an individual or group to determine another's intelligence or "normalcy." Finally, if schooling prepares people for jobs, and the kind of job a person has determines her or his economic status and, therefore, power, then schooling is immediately related to that power.

2. *There are codes or rules for participating in power; that is, there is a "culture of power."* The codes or rules I'm speaking of relate to linguistic forms, communicative strategies, and presentation of self; that is, ways of talking, ways of writing, ways of dressing, and ways of interacting.

3. *The rules of the culture of power are a reflection of the rules of the culture of those who have power.* This means that success in institutions—schools, workplaces, and so on—is predicated upon acquisition of the culture of those who are in power. Children from middle-class homes tend to do better in school than those from nonmiddle-class homes because the culture of the school is based on the culture of the upper and middle classes—of those in power. The upper and middle classes send their children to school with all the accoutrements of the culture of power; children from other kinds of families operate within perfectly wonderful and viable cultures but not cultures that carry the codes or rules of power.

4. *If you are not already a participant in the culture of power, being told explicitly the rules of that culture makes acquiring power easier.* In my work within and between diverse cultures, I have come to conclude that members of any culture transmit information implicitly to co-members. However, when implicit codes are attempted across cultures, communication frequently breaks down. Each cultural group is left saying, "Why don't those people say what they mean?" as well as, "What's wrong with them, why don't they understand?"

Anyone who has had to enter new cultures, especially to accomplish a specific task, will know of what I speak. When I lived in several Papua New Guinea villages for extended periods to collect data, and when I go to Alaskan villages for work with Native Alaskan communities, I have found it unquestionably easier, psychologically and pragmatically, when some kind soul has directly informed me about such matters as appropriate dress, interactional styles, embedded meanings, and taboo words or actions. I contend that it is much the same for anyone seeking to learn the rules of the culture of power. Unless one has the leisure of a lifetime of "immersion" to learn them, explicit presentation makes learning immeasurably easier.

And now, to the fifth and last premise:

5. *Those with power are frequently least aware of—or least willing to acknowledge—its existence. Those with less power are often most aware of its existence.* For many who consider themselves members of liberal or radical camps, acknowledging personal power and admitting participation in the culture of power is distinctly uncomfortable. On the other hand, those who are less powerful in any situation are most likely to recognize the power variable most acutely. My guess is that the white colleagues and instructors of those previously quoted did not perceive themselves to have power over the nonwhite speakers. However, either by virtue of their position, their numbers, or their access to that particular code of power of calling upon research to validate one's position, the white educators had the authority to establish what was to be considered "truth" regardless of the opinions of the people of color, and the latter were well aware of that fact.

A related phenomenon is that liberals (and here I am using the term "liberal" to refer to those whose beliefs include striving for a society based upon maximum individual freedom and autonomy) seem to act under the assumption that to make any rules or expectations explicit is to act against liberal principles, to limit the freedom and autonomy of those subjected to the explicitness.

I thank Fred Erickson for a comment that led me to look again at a tape by John Gumperz on cultural dissonance in cross-cultural interactions.[3] One of the episodes showed an East Indian interviewing for a job with an all-white committee. The interview was a complete failure, even though several of the interviewers appeared to really want to help the applicant. As the interview rolled steadily downhill, these "helpers" became more and more indirect in their questioning, which exacerbated the problems the applicant had in performing appropriately. Operating from a different cultural perspective, he got fewer and fewer clear clues as to what was expected of him, which ultimately resulted in his failure to secure the position.

I contend that as the applicant showed less and less aptitude for handling the interview, the power differential became ever more evident to the interviewers. The "helpful" interviewers, unwilling to acknowledge themselves as having power over the applicant, became more and more uncomfortable. Their indirectness was an attempt to lessen the power differential and their discomfort by lessening the power-revealing explicitness of their questions and comments.

When acknowledging and expressing power, one tends towards explicitness (as in yelling at your ten-year-old, "Turn that radio down!"). When deemphasizing power, there is a move toward indirect communication. Therefore, in the interview setting, those who sought to help, to express their egalitarianism with the East Indian applicant, became more and more indirect—and less and less helpful—in their questions and comments.

In literacy instruction, explicitness might be equated with direct instruction. Perhaps the ultimate expression of explicitness and direct instruction in the primary classroom is Distar. This reading program is based on a behaviorist model in which reading is taught through the direct instruction of phonics generalizations and blending. The teacher's role is to maintain the full attention of the group by continuous questioning, eye contact, finger snaps, hand claps, and other gestures, and by eliciting choral responses and initiating some sort of award system.

When the program was introduced, it arrived with a flurry of research data that "proved" that all children—even those who were "culturally deprived"—could learn to read using this method. Soon there was a strong response, first from academics and later from many classroom teachers, stating that the program was terrible. What I find particularly interesting, however, is that the primary issue of the conflict over Distar has not been over its instructional efficacy—usually the students did learn to read—but the expression of explicit power in the classroom. The liberal educators opposed the methods—the direct instruction, the explicit control exhibited by the teacher. As a matter of fact, it was not unusual (even now) to hear of the program spoken of as "fascist."

I am not an advocate of Distar, but I will return to some of the issues that the program, and direct instruction in general, raises in understanding the differences between progressive white educators and educators of color.

To explore those differences, I would like to present several statements typical of those made with the best of intentions by middle-class liberal educators. To the surprise of the speakers, it is not unusual for such content to be met by vocal opposition or stony silence from people of color. My attempt here is to examine the underlying assumptions of both camps.

"I want the same thing for everyone else's children as I want for mine."

To provide schooling for everyone's children that reflects liberal, middle-class values and aspirations is to ensure the maintenance of the status quo, to ensure that power, the culture of power, remains in the hands of those who already have it. Some children come to school with more accoutrements of the culture of power already in place—"cultural capital," as some

critical theorists refer to it[4]—some with less. Many liberal educators hold that the primary goal for education is for children to become autonomous, to develop fully who they are in the classroom setting without having arbitrary, outside standards forced upon them. This is a very reasonable goal for people whose children are already participants in the culture of power and who have already internalized its codes.

But parents who don't function within that culture often want something else. It's not that they disagree with the former aim, it's just that they want something more. They want to ensure that the school provides their children with discourse patterns, interactional styles, and spoken and written language codes that will allow them success in the larger society.

It was the lack of attention to this concern that created such a negative outcry in the black community when well-intentioned white liberal educators introduced "dialect readers." These were seen as a plot to prevent the schools from teaching the linguistic aspects of the culture of power, thus dooming black children to a permanent outsider caste. As one parent demanded, "My kids know how to be black—you all teach them how to be successful in the white man's world."

Several black teachers have said to me recently that as much as they'd like to believe otherwise, they cannot help but conclude that many of the "progressive" educational strategies imposed by liberals upon black and poor children could only be based on a desire to ensure that the liberals' children get sole access to the dwindling pool of American jobs. Some have added that the liberal educators believe themselves to be operating with good intentions, but that these good intentions are only conscious delusions about their unconscious true motives. One of the black anthropologist John Gwaltney's informants in *Drylongso* reflects this perspective with her tongue-in-cheek observation that the biggest difference between black folks and white folks is that black folks *know* when they're lying!

Let me try to clarify how this might work in literacy instruction. A few years ago I worked on an analysis of two popular reading programs, Distar and a progressive program that focused on higher-level critical thinking skills. In one of the first lessons of the progressive program, the children are introduced to the names of the letters *m* and *e*. In the same lesson they are then taught the sound made by each of the letters, how to write each of the letters, and that when the two are blended together they produce the word *me*.

As an experienced first-grade teacher, I am convinced that a child needs to be familiar with a significant number of these concepts to be able to assimilate so much new knowledge in one sitting. By contrast, Distar presents the same information in about forty lessons.

I would not argue for the pace of Distar lessons—such a slow pace would only bore most kids—but what happened in the other lesson is that it merely provided an opportunity for those who already knew the content to exhibit that they knew it, or at most perhaps to build one new concept onto what was already known. This meant that the child who did not come to school already primed with what was to be presented would be labeled as needing "remedial" instruction from day one; indeed, this determination would be made before he or she was ever taught. In fact, Distar was "successful" because it actually *taught* new information to children who had not already acquired it at home. Although the more progressive system was ideal for some children, for others it was a disaster.

I do not advocate a simplistic "basic skills" approach for children outside of the culture of power. It would be (and has been) tragic to operate as if these children were incapable of critical and higher-order thinking and reasoning. Rather, I suggest that schools must provide these children the content that other families from a different cultural orientation provide at home. This does not mean separating children according to family background, but instead, ensuring that each classroom incorporate strategies appropriate for all the children in its confines.

And I do not advocate that it is the school's job to attempt to change the homes of poor and nonwhite children to match the homes of those in the culture of power. That may indeed be a form of cultural genocide. I have frequently heard schools call poor parents "uncaring" when parents respond to the school's urging, saying, "But that's the school's job." What the school personnel fail to understand is that if the parents were members of the culture of power and lived by its rules and codes, then they would transmit those codes to their children. In fact, they transmit another culture that children must learn at home in order to survive in their communities.

"Child-centered, whole language, and process approaches are needed in order to allow a democratic state of free, autonomous, empowered adults, and because research has shown that children learn best through these methods."

People of color are, in general, skeptical of research as a determiner of our fates. Academic research has, after all, found us genetically inferior, culturally deprived, and verbally deficient. But beyond that general caveat, and despite my or others' personal preferences, there is little research data supporting the major tenets of process approaches over other forms of literacy instruction, and virtually no evidence that such approaches are more efficacious for children of color.[5]

Although the problem is not necessarily inherent in the method, in some instances adherents of process approaches to writing create situations in which students ultimately find themselves held accountable for knowing a set of rules about which no one has ever directly informed them. Teachers do students no service to suggest, even implicitly, that "product" is not important. In this country, students will be judged on their product regardless of the process they utilized to achieve it. And that product, based as it is on the specific codes of a particular culture, is more readily produced when the directives of how to produce it are made explicit.

If such explicitness is not provided to students, what it feels like to people who are old enough to judge is that there are secrets being kept, that time is being wasted, that the teacher is abdicating his or her duty to teach. A doctoral student of my acquaintance was assigned to a writing class to hone his writing skills. The student was placed in the section led by a white professor who utilized a process approach, consisting primarily of having the students write essays and then assemble into groups to edit each other's papers. That procedure infuriated this particular student. He had many angry encounters with the teacher about what she was doing. In his words:

> I didn't feel she was teaching us anything. She wanted us to correct each other's papers and we were there to learn from her. She didn't teach anything, absolutely nothing.
>
> Maybe they're trying to learn what black folks knew all the time. We understand how to improvise, how to express ourselves coercively. When I'm in a classroom, I'm not looking for that, I'm looking for structure, the more formal language.
>
> Now my buddy was in [a] black teacher's class. And that lady was very good. She went through and explained and defined each part of the structure. This [white] teacher didn't get along with that black teacher. She said that she didn't agree with her methods. But *I* don't think that white teacher *had* any methods.

When I told this gentleman that what the teacher was doing was called a process method of teaching writing, his response was, "Well, at least now I know that she *thought* she was doing *something*. I thought she was just a fool who couldn't teach and didn't want to try."

This sense of being cheated can be so strong that the student may be completely turned off to the educational system. Amanda Branscombe, an accomplished white teacher, recently wrote a letter discussing her work with working-class black and white students at a community college in Alabama. She had given these students my "Skills and Other Dilemmas" article to read and discuss, and wrote that her students really understood and identified with what I was saying. To quote her letter:

> One young man said that he had dropped out of high school because he failed the exit exam. He noted that he had then passed the GED without a problem after three weeks of prep. He said that his high school English teacher claimed to use a process approach, but what she really did was hide behind fancy words to give herself permission to do nothing in the classroom.

The students I have spoken of seem to be saying that the teacher has denied them access to herself as the source of knowledge necessary to learn the forms they need to succeed. Again, I tentatively attribute the problem to teachers' resistance to exhibiting power in the classroom. Somehow, to exhibit one's personal power as expert source is viewed as disempowering one's students.

Two qualifiers are necessary, however. The teacher cannot be the only expert in the classroom. To deny students their own expert knowledge *is* to disempower them. Amanda Branscombe, when she was working with black high school students classified as "slow learners," had the students analyze rap songs to discover their underlying patterns. The students became the experts in explaining to the teacher the rules for creating a new rap song. The teacher then used the patterns the students identified as a base to begin an explanation of the structure of grammar, and then of Shakepeare's plays. Both student and teacher are expert at what they know best.

The second qualifier is that merely adopting direct instruction is not the answer. Actual writing for real audiences and real purposes is a vital element in helping students to understand that they have an important voice in their own learning processes. E. V. Siddle ex-

amines the results of various kinds of interventions in a primarily process-oriented writing class for black students.[6] Based on readers' blind assessments, she found that the intervention that produced the most positive changes in the students' writing was a "mini-lesson" consisting of direct instruction about some standard writing convention. But what produced the *second* highest number of positive changes was a subsequent student-centered conference with the teacher. (Peer conferencing in this group of black students who were not members of the culture of power produced the least number of changes in students' writing. However, the classroom teacher maintained—and I concur—that such activities are necessary to introduce the elements of "real audience" into the task, along with more teacher-directed strategies.)

"It's really a shame but she (that black teacher upstairs) seems to be so authoritarian, so focused on skills and so teacher directed. Those poor kids never seem to be allowed to really express their creativity. (And she even yells at them.)"

This statement directly concerns the display of power and authority in the classroom. One way to understand the difference in perspective between black teachers and their progressive colleagues on this issue is to explore culturally influenced oral interactions.

In *Ways with Words*, Shirley Brice Heath quotes the verbal directives given by the middle-class "townspeople" teachers:[7]

- "Is this where the scissors belong?"
- "You want to do your best work today."

By contrast, many black teachers are more likely to say:

- "Put those scissors on that shelf."
- "Put your name on the papers and make sure to get the right answer for each question."

Is one oral style more authoritarian than another?

Other researchers have identified differences in middle-class and working-class speech to children. Snow and others, for example, report that working-class mothers use more directives to their children than do middle- and upper-class parents.[8] Middle-class parents are likely to give the directive to a child to take his bath as, "Isn't it time for your bath?" Even though the utterance is couched as a question, both child and adult understand it as a directive. The child may respond with "Aw, Mom, can't I wait until . . .," but whether or not negotiation is attempted, both conversants understand the intent of the utterance.

By contrast, a black mother, in whose house I was recently a guest, said to her eight-year-old son, "Boy, get your rusty behind in that bathtub." Now, I happen to know that this woman loves her son as much as any mother, but she would never have posed the directive to her son to take a bath in the form of a question. Were she to ask, "Would you like to take your bath now?" she would not have been issuing a directive but offering a true alternative. Consequently, as Heath suggests, upon entering school the child from such a family may not understand the indirect statement of the teacher as a direct command. Both white and black working-class children in the communities Heath studied "had difficulty interpreting these indirect requests for adherence to an unstated set of rules."[9]

But those veiled commands are commands nonetheless, representing true power, and with true consequences for disobedience. If veiled commands are ignored, the child will be labeled a behavior problem and possibly officially classified as behavior disordered. In other words, the attempt by the teacher to reduce an exhibition of power by expressing herself in indirect terms may remove the very explicitness that the child needs to understand the rules of the new classroom culture.

A black elementary school principal in Fairbanks, Alaska, reported to me that she has a lot of difficulty with black children who are placed in some white teachers' classrooms. The teachers often send the children to the office for disobeying teacher directives. Their parents are frequently called in for conferences. The parents' response to the teacher is usually the same. "They do what I say; if you just *tell* them what to do, they'll do it. I tell them at home that they have to listen to what you say." And so, does not the power still exist? Its veiled nature only makes it more difficult for some children to respond appropriately, but that in no way mitigates its existence.

I don't mean to imply, however, that the only time the black child disobeys the teacher is when he or she misunderstands the request for certain behavior. There are other factors that may produce such behavior. Black children expect an authority figure to act with authority. When the teacher instead acts as a "chum," the message sent is that this adult has no authority, and the children react accordingly. One reason that is so, is that black people often view issues of power and au-

thority differently than people from mainstream middle-class backgrounds.[10] Many people of color expect authority to be earned by personal efforts and exhibited by personal characteristics. In other words, "the authoritative person gets to be a teacher because she is authoritative." Some members of middle-class cultures, by contrast, expect one to achieve authority by the acquisition of an authoritative role. That is, "the teacher is the authority because she is the teacher."

In the first instance, because authority is earned, the teacher must consistently prove the characteristics that give her authority. These characteristics may vary across cultures, but in the black community they tend to cluster around several abilities. The authoritative teacher can control the class through exhibition of personal power; establishes meaningful interpersonal relationships that garner student respect; exhibits a strong belief that all students can learn; establishes a standard of achievement and "pushes" the students to achieve that standard; and holds the attention of the students by incorporating interactional features of black communicative style in his or her teaching.

By contrast, the teacher whose authority is vested in the role has many more options of behavior at her disposal. For instance, she does not need to express any sense of personal power because her authority does not come from anything she herself does or says. Hence, the power she actually holds may be veiled in such questions/commands as "Would you like to sit down now?" If the children in her class understand authority as she does, it is mutually agreed upon that they are to obey her no matter how indirect, soft-spoken, or unassuming she may be. Her indirectness and soft-spokenness may indeed be, as I suggested earlier, an attempt to reduce the implication of overt power in order to establish a more egalitarian and nonauthoritarian classroom atmosphere.

If the children operate under another notion of authority, however, then there is trouble. The black child may perceive the middle-class teacher as weak, ineffectual, and incapable of taking on the role of being the teacher; therefore, there is no need to follow her directives. In her dissertation, Michelle Foster quotes one young black man describing such a teacher:

> She is boring, boring. She could do something creative. Instead she just stands there. She can't control the class, doesn't know how to control the class. She asked me what she was doing wrong. I told her she just stands there like she's meditating. I told her she could be mediating for all I know. She says that we're supposed to know what to do.

I told her I don't know nothin' unless she tells me. She just can't control the class. I hope we don't have her next semester.[11]

But of course the teacher may not view the problem as residing in herself but in the student, and the child may once again become the behavior-disordered black boy in special education.

What characteristics do black students attribute to the good teacher? Again, Foster's dissertation provides a quotation that supports my experience with black students. A young black man is discussing a former teacher with a group of friends:

> We had fun in her class, but she was mean. I can remember she used to say, "Tell me what's in the story, Wayne." She pushed, she used to get on me and push me to know. She made us learn. We had to get in the books. There was this tall guy and he tried to take her on, but she was in charge of that class and she didn't let anyone run her. I still have this book we used in her class. It has a bunch of stories in it. I just read one on Coca-Cola again the other day.[12]

To clarify, this student was *proud* of the teacher's "meanness," an attribute he seemed to describe as the ability to run the class and pushing and expecting students to learn. Now, does the liberal perspective of the negatively authoritarian black teacher really hold up? I suggest that although all "explicit" black teachers are not also good teachers, there are different attitudes in different cultural groups about which characteristics make for a good teacher. Thus, it is impossible to create a model for the good teacher without taking issues of culture and community context into account.

And now to the final comment I present for examination:

> *"Children have the right to their own language, their own culture. We must fight cultural hegemony and fight the system by insisting that children be allowed to express themselves in their own language style. It is not they, the children, who must change, but the schools. To push children to do anything else is repressive and reactionary."*

A statement such as this originally inspired me to write the "Skills and Other Dilemmas" article. It was first written as a letter to a colleague in response to a situation that had developed in our department. I was teaching a senior-level teacher education course. Students were asked to prepare a written autobiographical document for the class that would also be shared with their placement school prior to their student teaching.

One student, a talented young Native American woman, submitted a paper in which the ideas were lost because of technical problems—from spelling to sentence structure to paragraph structure. Removing her name, I duplicated the paper for a discussion with some faculty members. I had hoped to initiate a discussion about what we could do to ensure that our students did not reach the senior level without getting assistance in technical writing skills when they needed them.

I was amazed at the response. Some faculty implied that the student should never have been allowed into the teacher education program. Others, some of the more progressive minded, suggested that I was attempting to function as gatekeeper by raising the issue, and had internalized repressive and disempowering forces of the power elite to suggest that something was wrong with a Native American student just because she had another style of writing. With few exceptions, I found myself alone in arguing against both camps.

No, this student should not have been denied entry to the program. To deny her entry under the notion of upholding standards is to blame the victim for the crime. We cannot justifiably enlist exclusionary standards when the reason this student lacked the skills demanded was poor teaching at best and institutionalized racism at worst.

However, to bring this student into the program and pass her through without attending to obvious deficits in the codes needed for her to function effectively as a teacher is equally criminal—for though we may assuage our own consciences for not participating in victim blaming, she will surely be accused and convicted as soon as she leaves the university. As Native Alaskans were quick to tell me, and as I understood through my own experience in the black community, not only would she not be hired as a teacher, but those who did not hire her would make the (false) assumption that the university was putting out only incompetent Natives and that they should stop looking seriously at any Native applicants. A white applicant who exhibits problems is an individual with problems. A person of color who exhibits problems immediately becomes a representative of her cultural group.

No, either stance is criminal. The answer is to *accept* students but also to take responsibility to *teach* them. I decided to talk to the student and found out she had recognized that she needed some assistance in the technical aspects of writing soon after she entered the university as a freshman. She had gone to various members of the education faculty and received the same two kinds of responses I met with four years later: faculty members told her either that she should not even attempt to be a teacher, or that it didn't matter and that she shouldn't worry about such trivial issues. In her desperation, she had found a helpful professor in the English Department, but he left the university when she was in her sophomore year.

We sat down together, worked out a plan for attending to specific areas of writing competence, and set up regular meetings. I stressed to her the need to use her own learning process as insight into how best to teach her future students those "skills" that her own schooling had failed to teach her. I gave her some explicit rules to follow in some areas; for others, we devised various kinds of journals that, along with readings about the structure of the language, allowed her to find her own insights into how the language worked. All that happened two years ago, and the young woman is now successfully teaching. What the experience led me to understand is that pretending that gatekeeping points don't exist is to ensure that many students will not pass through them.

Now you may have inferred that I believe that because there is a culture of power, everyone should learn the codes to participate in it, and that is how the world should be. Actually, nothing could be further from the truth. I believe in a diversity of style, and I believe the world will be diminished if cultural diversity is ever obliterated. Further, I believe strongly, as do my liberal colleagues, that each cultural group should have the right to maintain its own language style. When I speak, therefore, of the culture of power, I don't speak of how I wish things to be but of how they are.

I further believe that to act as if power does not exist is to ensure that the power status quo remains the same. To imply to children or adults (but of course the adults won't believe you anyway) that it doesn't matter how you talk or how you write is to ensure their ultimate failure. I prefer to be honest with my students. I tell them that their language and cultural style is unique and wonderful but that there is a political power game that is also being played, and if they want to be in on that game there are certain games that they too must play.

But don't think that I let the onus of change rest entirely with the students. I am also involved in political work both inside and outside of the educational system, and that political work demands that I place myself to influence as many gatekeeping points as possible. And it is there that I agitate for change, pushing gatekeepers to open their doors to a variety of styles and codes. What I'm saying, however, is that I do not believe that political change toward diversity can be effected from the bottom up, as do some of my colleagues. They seem to believe that if we accept and encourage diversity within classrooms of children, then diversity will automatically be accepted at gatekeeping points.

I believe that will never happen. What will happen is that the students who reach the gatekeeping points—like Amanda Branscombe's student who dropped out of high school because he failed his exit exam—will understand that they have been lied to and will react accordingly. No, I am certain that if we are truly to effect societal change, we cannot do so from the bottom up, but we must push and agitate from the top down. And in the meantime, we must take the responsibility to *teach*, to provide for students who do not already possess them, the additional codes of power.[13]

But I also do not believe that we should teach students to passively adopt an alternate code. They must be encouraged to understand the value of the code they already possess as well as to understand the power realities in this country. Otherwise they will be unable to work to change these realities. And how does one do that?

Martha Demientieff, a masterful Native Alaskan teacher of Athabaskan Indian students, tells me that her students, who live in a small, isolated, rural village of less than two hundred people, are not aware that there are different codes in English. She takes their writing and analyzes it for features of what has been referred to by Alaskan linguists as "Village English," and then covers half a bulletin board with words or phrases from the students' writing, which she labels "Our Heritage Language." On the other half of the bulletin board she puts the equivalent statements in "Standard English," which she labels "Formal English."

She and the students spend a long time on the "Heritage English" section, savoring the words, discussing the nuances. She tells the students, "That's the way we say things. Doesn't it feel good? Isn't it the absolute best way of getting that idea across?" Then she turns to the other side of the board. She tells the students that there are people, not like those in the village, who judge others by the way they talk or write.

We listen to the way people talk, not to judge them, but to tell what part of the river they come from. These other people are not like that. They think everybody needs to talk like them. Unlike us, they have a hard time hearing what people say if they don't talk exactly like them. Their way of talking and writing is called "Formal English."

We have to feel a little sorry for them because they have only one way to talk. We're going to learn two ways to say things. Isn't that better? One way will be our Heritage way. The other will be Formal English. Then, when we go to get jobs, we'll be able to talk like those people who only know and can only really listen to one way. Maybe after we get the jobs we can help them to learn how it feels to have another language, like ours, that feels so good. We'll talk like them when we have to, but we'll always know our way is best.

Martha then does all sorts of activities with the notions of Formal and Heritage or informal English. She tells the students,

In the village, everyone speaks informally most of the time unless there's a potlatch or something. You don't think about it, you don't worry about following any rules—it's sort of like how you eat food at a picnic—nobody pays attention to whether you use your fingers or a fork, and it feels *so* good. Now, Formal English is more like a formal dinner. There are rules to follow about where the knife and fork belong, about where people sit, about how you eat. That can be really nice, too, because it's nice to dress up sometimes.

The students then prepare a formal dinner in the class, for which they dress up and set a big table with fancy tablecloths, china, silverware. They speak only Formal English at this meal. Then they prepare a picnic where only informal English is allowed.

She also contrasts the "wordy" academic way of saying things with the metaphoric style of Athabaskan. The students discuss how book language always uses more words, but in Heritage language, the shorter way of saying something is always better. Students then write papers in the academic way, discussing with Martha and with each other whether they believe they've said enough to sound like a book. Finally, students further reduce the message to a "saying" brief enough to go on the front of a T-shirt, and the sayings are put on little paper T-shirts that the students cut out and hang throughout the room. Sometimes the students reduce other authors' wordy texts to their essential meanings as well.

The following transcript provides another example. It is from a conversation between a black teacher and a Southern black high school student named Joey,

who is a speaker of Black English. The teacher believes it very important to discuss openly and honestly the issues of language diversity and power. She has begun the discussion by giving the student a children's book written in Black English to read.

TEACHER: What do you think about that book?

JOEY: I think it's nice.

TEACHER: Why?

JOEY: I don't know. It just told about a black family, that's all.

TEACHER: Was it difficult to read?

JOEY: No.

TEACHER: Was the text different from what you have seen in other books?

JOEY: Yeah. The writing was.

TEACHER: How?

JOEY: It uses more of a southern-like accent in this book.

TEACHER: Uhm-hmm. Do you think that's good or bad?

JOEY: Well, uh, I don't think it's good for people down this-a-way, cause that's the way they grow up talking anyway. They ought to get the right way to talk.

TEACHER: Oh. So you think it's wrong to talk like that?

JOEY: Well. . . {Laughs}

TEACHER: Hard question, huh?

JOEY: Uhm-hmm, that's a hard question. But I think they shouldn't make books like that.

TEACHER: Why?

JOEY: Because they are not using the right way to talk and in school they take off for that, and li'l chirren grow up talking like that and reading like that so they might think that's right, and all the time they getting bad grades in school, talking like that and writing like that.

TEACHER: Do you think they should be getting bad grades for talking like that?

JOEY: {Pauses, answers very slowly} No. . .no.

TEACHER: So you don't think that it matters whether you talk one way or another?

JOEY: No, not long as you understood.

TEACHER: Uhm-hmm. Well, that's a hard question for me to answer, too. It's, ah, that's a question that's come up in a lot of schools now as to whether they should correct children who speak the way we speak all the time. Cause when we're talking to each other we talk like that even though we might not talk like than when we get into other situations, and who's to say whether it's—

JOEY: {Interrupting} Right or wrong.

TEACHER: Yeah.

JOEY: Maybe they ought to come up with another kind of. . .maybe Black English or something. A course in Black English. Maybe Black folks would be good in that cause people talk, I mean black people talk like that, so. . . but I guess there's a right way and wrong way to talk, you know, not regarding what race. I don't know.

TEACHER: But who decided what's right or wrong?

JOEY: Well that's true. . .I guess white people did. {Laughter. End of tape.}

Notice how throughout the conversarion Joey's consciousness has been raised by thinking about codes of language. This teacher further advocates having students interview various personnel officers in actual workplaces about their attitudes toward divergent styles in oral and written language. Students begin to understand how arbitrary language standards are, but also how politically charged they are. They compare various pieces written in different styles, discuss the impact of different styles on the message by making translations and back translations across styles, and discuss the history, apparent purpose, and contextual appropriateness of each of the technical writing rules presented by their teacher. *And* they practice writing different forms to different audiences based on rules appropriate for each audience. Such a program not only "teaches" standard linguistic forms, but also explores aspects of power as exhibited through linguistic forms.

Tony Burgess, in a study of secondary writing in England by Britton, Burgess, Martin, McLeod, and Rosen, suggests that we should not teach "iron conventions . . .imposed without rationale or grounding in communicative intent," but "critical and ultimately cultural awareness."[14] Courtney Cazden calls for a two-pronged approach:

1. Continuous opportunities for writers to participate in some authentic bit of the unending conversation . . .thereby becoming part of a vital community of talkers and writers in a particular domain, and
2. Periodic, temporary focus on conventions of form, taught as cultural conventions expected in a particular community.[15]

Just so that there is no confusion about what Cazden means by a focus on conventions of form, or about

what I mean by "skills," let me stress that neither of us is speaking of page after page of "skill sheets" creating compound words or identifying nouns and adverbs, but rather about helping students gain a useful knowledge of the conventions of print while engaging in real and useful communicative activities. Kay Rowe Grubis, a junior high school teacher in a multicultural school, makes lists of certain technical rules for her eighth graders' review and then gives them papers from a third grade to "correct." The students not only have to correct other students' work, but also tell them why they have changed or questioned aspects of the writing.

A village teacher, Howard Cloud, teaches his high school students the conventions of formal letter writing and the formulation of careful questions in the context of issues surrounding the amendment of the Alaska Land Claims Settlement Act. Native Alaskan leaders hold differing views on this issue, critical to the future of local sovereignty and land rights. The students compose letters to leaders who reside in different areas of the state seeking their perspectives, set up audioconference calls for interview/debate sessions, and, finally, develop a videotape to present the differing views.

To summarize, I suggest that students must be *taught* the codes needed to participate fully in the mainstream of American life, not by being forced to attend to hollow, inane, decontextualized subskills, but rather within the context of meaningful communicative endeavors; that they must be allowed the resource of the teacher's expert knowledge, while being helped to acknowledge their own "expertness" as well; and that even while students are assisted in learning the culture of power, they must also be helped to learn about the arbitrariness of those codes and about the power relationships they represent.

I am also suggesting that appropriate education for poor children and children of color can only be devised in consultation with adults who share their culture. Black parents, teachers of color, and members of poor communities must be allowed to participate fully in the discussion of what kind of instruction is in their children's best interest. Good liberal intentions are not enough. In an insightful 1975 study entitled "Racism without Racists: Institutional Racism in Urban Schools," Massey, Scott, and Dornbusch found that under the pressures of teaching, and with all intentions of "being nice," teachers had essentially stopped attempting to reach black children.[16] In their words: "We have shown that oppression can arise out of warmth, friendliness, and concern. Paternalism and a lack of challenging standards are creating a distorted system of evaluation in the schools." Educators must open themselves to, and allow themselves to be affected by, these alternative voices.

In conclusion, I am proposing a resolution for the skills/process debate. In short, the debate is fallacious; the dichotomy is false. The issue is really an illusion created initially not by teachers but by academics whose worldview demands the creation of categorical divisions—not for the purpose of better teaching, but for the goal of easier analysis. As I have been reminded by many teachers since the publication of my article, those who are most skillful at educating black and poor children do not allow themselves to be placed in "skills" or "process" boxes. They understand the need for both approaches, the need to help students establish their own voices, and to coach those voices to produce notes that will be heard clearly in the larger society.

The dilemma is not really in the debate over instructional methodology, but rather in communicating across cultures and in addressing the more fundamental issue of power, of whose voice gets to be heard in determining what is best for poor children and children of color. Will black teachers and parents continue to be silenced by the very forces that claim to "give voice" to our children? Such an outcome would be tragic, for both groups truly have something to say to one another. As a result of careful listening to alternative points of view, I have myself come to a viable synthesis of perspectives. But both sides do need to be able to listen, and I contend that it is those with the most power, those in the majority, who must take the greater responsibility for initiating the process.

To do so takes a very special kind of listening, listening that requires not only open eyes and ears, but open hearts and minds. We do not really see through our eyes or hear through our ears, but through our beliefs. To put our beliefs on hold is to cease to exist as ourselves for a moment—and that is not easy. It is painful as well, because it means turning yourself inside out, giving up your own sense of who you are, and being willing to see yourself in the unflattering light of another's angry gaze. It is not easy, but it is the only way to learn what it might feel like to be someone else and the only way to start the dialogue.

There are several guidelines. We must keep the perspective that people are experts on their own lives. There are certainly aspects of the outside world of which they may not be aware, but they can be the only authentic chroniclers of their own experience. We must

not be too quick to deny their interpretations, or accuse them of "false consciousness." We must believe that people are rational beings, and therefore always act rationally. We may not understand their rationales, but that in no way militates against the existence of these rationales or reduces our responsibility to attempt to apprehend them. And finally, we must learn to be vulnerable enough to allow our world to turn upside down in order to allow the realities of others to edge themselves into our consciousness. In other words, we must become ethnographers in the true sense.

Teachers are in an ideal position to play this role, to attempt to get all of the issues on the table in order to initiate true dialogue. This can only be done, however, by seeking out those whose perspectives may differ most, by learning to give their words complete attention, by understanding one's own power, even if that power stems merely from being in the majority, by being unafraid to raise questions about discrimination and voicelessness with people of color, and to listen, no, to *hear* what they say. I suggest that the results of such interactions may be the most powerful and empowering coalescence yet seen in the educational realm—for *all* teachers and for *all* the students they teach.

Notes

1. See chapter 1 of this [original] volume, "Skills and Other Dilemmas of a Progressive Black Educator."
2. Such a discussion, limited as it is by space constraints, must treat the intersection of class and race somewhat simplistically. For the sake of clarity, however, let me define a few terms: "black" is used herein to refer to those who share some or all aspects of "core black culture" (see John Gwaltney, *Drylongso,* New York: The New Press, 1993), that is, the mainstream of black America—neither those who have entered the ranks of the bourgeoisie nor those who are participants in the disenfranchised underworld. "Middle-class" is used broadly to refer to the predominantly white American "mainstream." There are, of course, nonwhite people who also fit into this category; at issue is their cultural identification, not necessarily the color of their skin. (I must add that there are other nonwhite people, as well as poor white people, who have indicated to me that their perspectives are similar to those attributed herein to black people.)
3. *Multicultural Britain: "Crosstalk,"* National Centre of Industrial Language Training, Commission for Racial Equality, London, England, John Twitchin, producer.

4. See, for example, M. W. Apple, *Ideology and Curriculum* (Boston: Routledge and Kegan Paul, 1979).

5. See E. V. Siddle, "A Critical Assessment of the Natural Process Approach to Teaching Writing," unpublished qualifying paper, Harvard University, 1986.

6. See E. V. Siddle, "The Effect of Intervention Strategies on the Revisions Ninth Graders Make in a Narrative Essay," unpublished doctoral dissertation, Harvard University, 1988.

7. Shirley Brice Heath, *Ways with Words* (Cambridge, Eng.: Cambridge University Press, 1983), p. 280.

8. C.E. Snow, A. Arlman-Rup, Y. Hassing, J. Josbe, J. Joosten, and J. Vorster, "Mother's Speech in Three Social Classes," *Journal of Psycholinguistic Research* 5(1976), pp. 1–20.

9. Heath, *Ways with Words,* p. 280.

10. I would like to thank Michelle Foster, who is presently planning a more in-depth treatment of the subject, for her astute clarification of the idea.

11. Michelle Foster, "'It's Cookin Now': An Ethnographic Study of the Teaching Style of a Successful Black Teacher in a White Community College," unpublished doctoral dissertation, Harvard University, 1987, pp. 67–68.

12. Ibid., p. 68.

13. B. Bernstein makes a similar point when he proposes that different educational frames cannot be successfully institutionalized in the lower levels of education until there are fundamental changes at the postsecondary levels (see "Class and Pedagogies: Visible and Invisible," in B. Bernstein, *Class, Codes, and Control,* vol. 3 [Boston: Routledge and Kegan Paul, 1975]).

14. J. Britton, T. Burgess, N. Martin, A. McLeod, and H. Rosen, *The Development of Writing Abilities* (London: Macmillan Education for the Schools Council, and Urbana, Ill.: National Council of Teachers of English, 1975/1977), p. 54.

15. Ibid., p. 20.

16. G.C. Massey, M.V. Scott, and S. M. Dornbusch, "Racism without Racists: Institutional Racism in Urban Schools," *The Black Scholar* 73 (1975), pp. 2–11.

8 Equality of Opportunity and Educational Outcomes

The evolution of the U.S. education system is a story that is profoundly moving because it is a narrative of struggle. From the founding of the Republic, there has been a deep belief on the part of the American people in equality of opportunity. Echoing throughout the Declaration of Independence and the Constitution of the United States are the voices of people who demand to be treated with respect, dignity, and equality. From its inception, public education has been conceived of as a social vehicle for minimizing the importance of class and wealth as a determinant of who shall get ahead. Before the word *meritocracy* was invented, Americans believed that hard work, thrift, and a little bit of luck should determine who receives the economic and social benefits that the society has to offer. To some degree, education has helped to make this dream come true. Yet, there is an underside to this story. The United States has only been partially successful in developing an educational system that is truly meritocratic and just.

In this chapter, we examine this belief in equal opportunity in the context of the social realities of life in the United States. We ask very fundamental questions: To what degree do schools mitigate the significance of such ascriptive characteristics as class, race, and gender in determining who shall receive the benefits of education? Do differences between schools make a difference in who gets ahead? What is the relationship between education and economic outcomes? And last, is it reasonable to characterize the U.S. educational system as meritocratic or does the educational system simply reproduce existing social and economic inequalities?

In 1842, Horace Mann said, "Education, then, beyond all other devices of human origin, is the great equalizer of the conditions of men—the balance wheel of the social machinery" (Walker, Kozma, & Green, 1989, p. 133). From the viewpoint of the year 2000, can one say with certainty that Horace Mann's dream has become a reality? The answer to this question requires empirical investigation. To determine the relationship between education and equality is a complex intellectual task. Interpreting these facts is also complex. Perhaps you remember from Chapter 2 our discussion of the three fundamental points of view: conservative, liberal, and radical. Nowhere are the differences between these three groups more clearly drawn than in their rivaling interpretations of the empirical facts concerning the degree of equality in the United States. There is, so to speak, a set of calculations that could be called life arithmetic. But there is also a set of interpretations that accompany this arithmetic that are shaded by the shadow of ideology. We do not, nor could we, definitively resolve these debates. However, based on the data that are available, we would be less than candid if we did not admit that, to our way of thinking, U.S. society is deeply stratified by class, race, and gender. These forms of stratification negatively impact on the mobility of certain individuals and groups. Throughout the 1980s, the emphasis on educational reform focused on competition and excellence. In a society that is increasingly multicultural, we believe that reform must also focus on cooperation and equity.

Calculating Educational and Life Outcomes

Most people are aware that society is stratified—there are rich people, poor people, and people in between. People are discriminated against on the basis of gender and race. Curiously, the significance of these issues is often muted by public perceptions that in the United States, individuals, through their own efforts, can overcome the effects of stratification—that is, educational and social mobility are matters of individual life experiences. Although it is true that certain individuals do become upwardly mobile because of their success in business or because they possess an unusual talent, the stark fact is that the overwhelming number of individuals will remain in the social class into which they were born. Social stratification is a structural characteristic of societies. Human differences do not cause social stratification; social stratification causes human differences.

Sociologist Daniel Rossides (1976, p. 15) defined *social stratification* as follows: "Social stratification is a hierarchical configuration of families (and in industrial societies in recent decades, unrelated individuals) who have differential access to whatever is of value in the society at a given point and over time, primarily because of social, not biopsychological, variables." He went on to point out that "a full system of social stratification emerges only when parents can see to it that their children inherit or acquire a social level equal or superior to their own regardless of innate ability" (p. 16). In other words, parents attempt to roll the dice of life chances in favor of their children so that they may be successful in terms of material comfort, security, personal fulfillment, and occupation.

Rossides (1976) described three basic forms of social stratification. *Caste stratification* occurs in agrarian societies where social level is defined in terms of some strict ascriptive criteria such as race and/or religious worth. *Estate stratification* occurs in agrarian societies where social level is defined in terms of the hierarchy of family worth. *Class stratification* occurs in industrial societies that define social level in term of a hierarchy of differential achievement by individuals, especially in economic pursuits. Within each one of these major forms of stratification there can be other hierarchies (i.e., patriarchal distinctions between men and women) and the three major forms of stratification can overlap within any given society. For example, in the United States, individuals can experience caste stratification because of their race, while simultaneously experiencing class stratification because of their occupation and lack of property.

With this discussion as a prelude, one can begin to look at the United States in terms of social stratification. There can be little doubt that the population of the United States is stratified by class. Very briefly, approximately 1 to 3 percent of Americans are members of the upper class, approximately 15 percent of Americans are upper middle class, another 25 percent belong to the lower middle class, 40 percent are working class, and 20 percent belong to what has been called the under class. Each of these classes have a somewhat different relationship to the economy. The upper class derives most of its wealth through the possession of property; the upper middle class is essentially a professional and managerial class; the lower middle class are likely to be semi-professionals such as school teachers and small business owners; the working class derive their income directly from their labor and are often paid an hourly wage; and the under class are marginal to the economy and are often extremely poor.

In the last 20 years, the upper and upper middle classes in the United States have become increasingly wealthy while the other classes have experienced a relative decline in terms of their economic security and income. In fact, the United States is the most unequal industrial country in terms of the distribution of income. According to Phillips (1990, p. 11), "America's top 420,000 households alone accounted for 26.9 percent of U.S. family net worth—in essence, 26.9 percent of the nation's wealth. The top 10 percent of households, meanwhile, controlled approximately 68 percent." In 1988, approximately 1.3 million Americans were millionaires, which is double the number of millionaires in 1980. In 1953, there were only 27,000 millionaires in the United States. It was not since the latter part of the nineteenth century that the United States has experienced such an upsurge of wealth into the upper classes. In 1999, the number of millionaires dramatically increased, with over 400,000 in New York City alone (Koch, 1999). Moreover, during the 1990s, as the number of millionaires skyrocketed, due, in part, to an incredible rise in the stock market (especially Internet stocks), the number of poor also increased (Wilson, 1999).

Again, according to Phillips (1990), the "downside of the American dream" is that individuals in the lower middle class, the working class, and the under class have suffered a decline in terms of their incomes when income is adjusted for inflation. To cite one example, in 1972, weekly per worker income was $366.00. In 1987, the weekly per worker income was $312.00, when adjusted for inflation. These data indicate that when calculating the effects of class in determining an individual's or group's life arithmetic, one must not fail to take into account the increasing significance of class. These inequalities increased in the 1990s and at the beginning of the twenty-first century, with the top decile of income earners experiencing significant gains in income and wealth and the bottom decile experiencing significant declines (Andersen, 1999; Anyon, 2005; Wilson, 1999).

Clearly, connecting the linkages between class and other forms of stratification and educational outcomes is extremely complex. In Chapter 4, we presented Persell's model for analyzing the relationship of what she called "the societal structure of dominance" and educational outcomes. By analyzing the relationship between the societal, institutional, interactional, and intrapsychic levels, you can see that there is a set of interrelated social and school variables that create the context for the production of educational outcomes. In brief, economic and political resources directly influence the selectivity of schools and the authority structures within schools, which, in turn, influence the climate of expectations and patterns of interactions within schools.

To illustrate these relationships, imagine a public school located in a wealthy white suburb and a public school located in an urban neighborhood. The suburban school will differ significantly from the urban school in terms of its resources, its ability to monitor students' progress, its discipline, its climate of expectations, and its culture. In effect, the suburban school is similar to a private school in that it can provide better educational opportunities for its students than the urban school, which has very few resources and educates students who come to school with few advantages.

Sociologists of education have studied the relationship between education and mobility in great detail. Sometimes the study of mobility is referred to as the *status-attainment process.* Summarizing this literature is virtually impossible since there is no consensus about how much education influences attainment. Clearly, the number of years of education an individual possesses is directly linked to occupation and income. For example, individuals who attain managerial and professional statuses are very likely to have a bachelor's degree from college and to have attended some graduate school. Laborers and individuals in the service fields are, on average, likely to have a high school diploma. In terms of wages, individuals with a high school diploma are paid, on average, $7.00 per hour for their work, whereas individuals who possess advanced degrees are paid approximately $11.00 per hour for their labor.

To complicate matters further, other forms of stratification also influence income. In 2003, a man age 25 or over with a college degree earned $65,151 a year on average, whereas a woman with the same educational qualifications earned $40,201 a year. If minorities and nonminorities are compared in terms of how much they earn, one discovers that, as in the case of gender, nonminority individuals earn considerably more money than do minority individuals (U.S. Bureau of the Census, 2003a).

Shortly, we will discuss the effects of race and gender on educational attainment, but for now, the central point to be made is that there is a relationship between education and attainment, although it is certainly not an open contest, as was alleged by Turner (1960) some 45 years ago. You may recall from Chapter 4 that we discussed the work of Rosenbaum (1976), who suggested that educational mobility was similar to what he called "tournament selection." In this form of competition, winners are allowed to proceed to the next round and losers are dropped. Some students are eliminated, but "winning" students must still continue to compete. Unfortunately, from the point of view of equality of opportunity, this tournament is not played on a truly level field. Privilege can tilt the field to the advantage of whites, males, and the wealthy. The empirical results of this tilting are discussed next.

Class

Students in different social classes have different kinds of educational experiences. There are several factors that can influence these class-based experiences. For instance, education is extremely expensive. The longer a student stays in school, the more likely he or she needs parental financial support. Obviously, this situation favors wealthier families. Families from the upper class and the middle class are also more likely to expect their children to finish school, whereas working class and under-class families often have lower levels of expectation for their children. From a cultural point of view, schools represent the values of the middle and upper classes.

Studies show that the number of books in a family's home is related to the academic achievement of its children. Middle and upper middle-class children are more likely to speak "standard" English. Clearly, the ability to use this standard English is an educational asset. Teachers have been found to think more highly of middle-class and upper middle-class children than they are of working class and under-class children because working class and under-class children do not speak middle-class English. This phenomenon leads to labeling children, ostensibly according to their abilities, but covertly according to their social class backgrounds. Also, data show that peer groups have a significant influence on students' attitudes toward learning. In a school that enrolls many middle-class students, there is a high likelihood that more emphasis is placed on high academic achievement than in a school where there are few middle-class children.

It is little wonder, then, that class is directly related to achievement and to educational attainment; there is a direct correlation between parental income and children's performance on achievement tests, as well as placement in ability groups and curriculum track in high school. Study after study shows that class is related to achievement on reading tests and basic skills tests. Children from working class and under-class families are more likely to underachieve, drop out, and resist the curriculum of the school. In terms of going on to college, there is little doubt that the higher an individual's social class, the more likely he or she is to enroll in college and to receive a degree. The more elite the college, the more likely the college is to enroll upper-class and upper middle-class students. In sum, social class and level of educational attainment are highly correlated. This finding represents a challenge to those who believe in equality of opportunity.

Race

Despite the Civil Rights legislation of the 1960s, U.S. society is still highly stratified by race. An individual's race has a direct impact on how much education he or she is likely to achieve. Among 18-year-olds, for instance, roughly 12 percent of white students drop out of school, whereas 15 percent of African American students and 27 percent of Hispanic American students are likely to drop out of school. Among 17-year-olds, 89 percent of white students will be able to read at the intermediate level, which includes the ability to search for specific information, interrelate ideas, and make generalizations about literature, science, and social studies materials. However, 66 percent of African American students have reached that level of reading proficiency and 70 percent of Hispanic American students are reading at the intermediate level (U.S. Department of Education, National Center for Education Statistics, 2003). It is not surprising, therefore, that these lower levels of proficiency are reflected by the fact that minorities have, on average, lower SAT scores than white students. As you know, there is a direct link between SAT scores and admission to college. There is also a link between SAT scores and being awarded scholarships for study in postsecondary institutions.

That race is related to educational outcomes is undeniable, although, given the nature of U.S. society, it is extremely difficult to separate race from class. In a society as segregated as that in the United States, it is not surprising that minority students receive fewer and inferior educational opportunities than white students. Explanations as to why minorities underachieve compared to whites vary. But, at one level, the answer is not terribly complex. Minorities do not receive the same educational opportunities as whites, and their rewards for educational attainment are significantly less.

Gender

Historically, an individual's gender was directly related to his or her educational attainment. Even though women are often rated as being better students than men, in the past they were less likely to attain the same level of education. Today, females are less likely to drop out of school than males and are more likely to have a higher level of reading proficiency than males. The same is true for writing. The one area that males outperform females is in mathematics proficiency. There are numerous explanations as to why males do better than females in mathematics, the most convincing of which is related to the behavior of classroom teachers who tend to assume that females will not do as well as males in mathematics. Overall, males are more likely to score higher on the SATs than females. It should be added that more women are now attending postsecondary institutions than men, although it is true that many of the postsecondary institutions that women attend are less academically and socially prestigious than those postsecondary institutions attended by men (Persell, Catsambis, & Cookson, 1992).

In the last 20 years, gender differences between men and women, in terms of educational attainment, have been reduced. Recent data from the United States, the United Kingdom, Canada, and Australia indicate that not only have girls caught up to boys in almost all measures of academic achievement, policy makers are now discovering the "boy problem" (Arnot, David, & Weiner, 1999; Datnow & Hubbard, 2002; Riordan, 1999). Liberals argue that these increases demonstrate the success of educational reforms aimed at improving achievement; conservatives argue that the decline in male achievement and attainment is a result of the "feminizing" of the classroom. There are still significant advantages for men when competing for the most prestigious academic prizes, however. Whether men receive preferential treatment within schools is an issue that will be discussed in the next chapter. There is little doubt that society discriminates against women occupationally and socially. Given this, one might wonder about the relationship between educational attainment and occupational attainment for women. Are these two forms of attainment highly correlated or, in fact, is there only a weak relationship between educational attainment and occupational attainment for women?

Educational Achievement and Attainment of African American, Hispanic American, and Women Students

The academic achievement of students from different backgrounds is an important aspect of sociological research on education. The National Center for Education Statistics publishes yearly statistical reports, including *The Condition of Education,* which provides important statistical data on a variety of educational issues. The following discussion and data rely heavily on *The Condition of Education, 2004* (2004).

Figures 8.1 through 8.4 (pages 320–324) indicate these achievement gaps among whites, blacks, and Hispanics; they also show that achievement goes up in relation to parental level of education. Figures 8.5 through 8.8 (pages 325–329) indicate the achievement gaps with respect to gender. Females achieve at higher levels in reading at ages 9, 13, and 17; females achieve at slightly lower levels in mathematics and science at ages 9, 13, and 17.

(text continues on page 330)

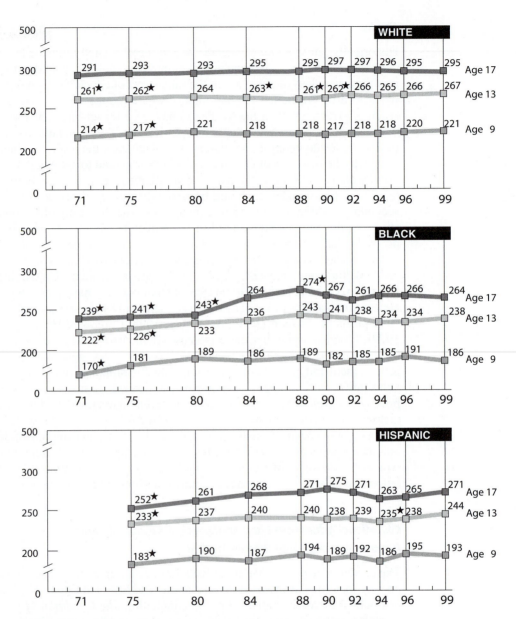

FIGURE 8.1   Trends in Average Reading Scale Scores by Race/Ethnicity
*Significantly different from 1999.

Source: National Center for Education Statistics, National Assessment of Educational Progress (NAEP), 1999 Long-Term Trend Assessment.

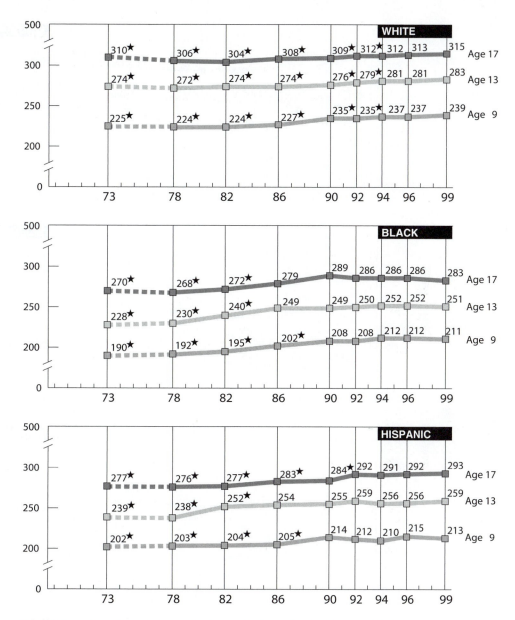

FIGURE 8.2 **Trends in Average Mathematics Scale Scores by Race/Ethnicity**
*Significantly different from 1999.

Note: Dashed lines represent extrapolated data.

Source: National Center for Education Statistics, National Assessment of Educational Progress (NAEP), 1999 Long-Term Trend Assessment.

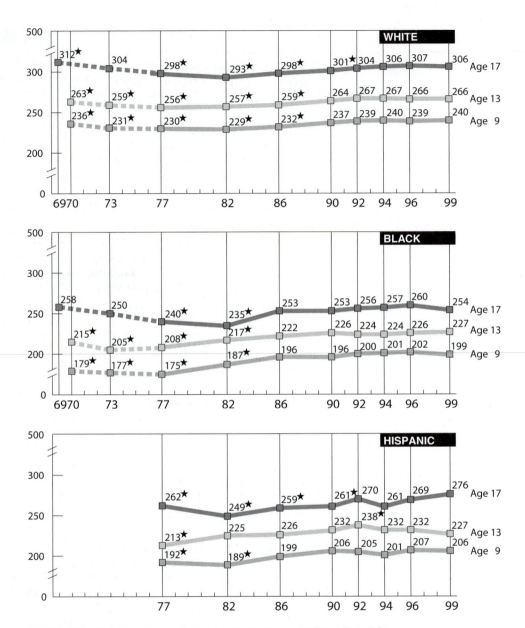

FIGURE 8.3   Trends in Average Science Scale Scores by Race/Ethnicity

*Significantly different from 1999.

Note: Dashed lines represent extrapolated data.

Source: National Center for Education Statistics, National Assessment of Educational Progress (NAEP), 1999 Long-Term Trend Assessment.

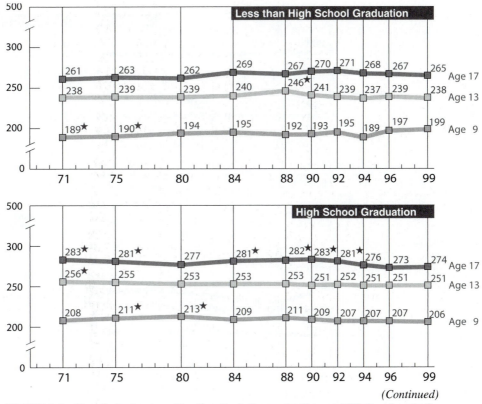

FIGURE 8.4   Trends in Average Reading Scale Scores by Parents' Highest Level of Education

*Significantly different from 1999.

Note: "Graduated College" Is not available as a separate category for reading results.

Source: National Center for Education Statistics, National Assessment of Educational Progress (NAEP), 1999 Long-Term Trend Assessment.

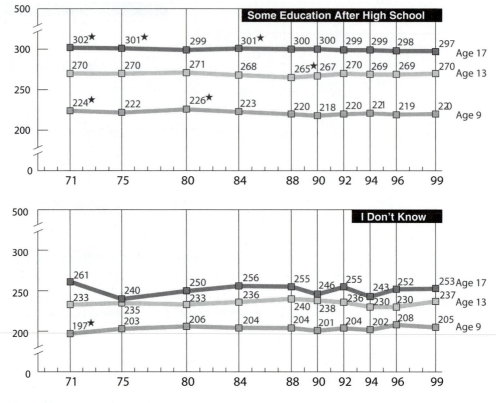

FIGURE 8.4 (Continued)

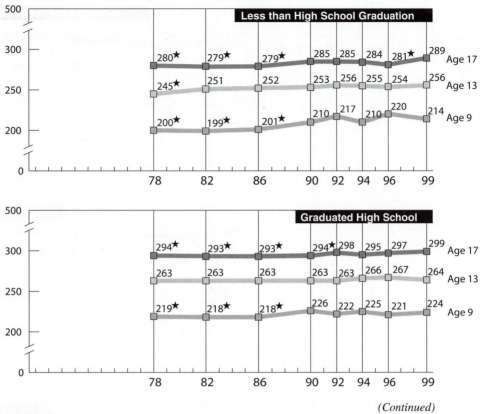

FIGURE 8.5   Trends in Average Mathematics Scale Scores by Parents' Highest Level of Education

*Significantly different from 1999.

Source: National Center for Education Statistics, National Assessment of Educational Progress (NAEP), 1999 Long-Term Trend Assessment.

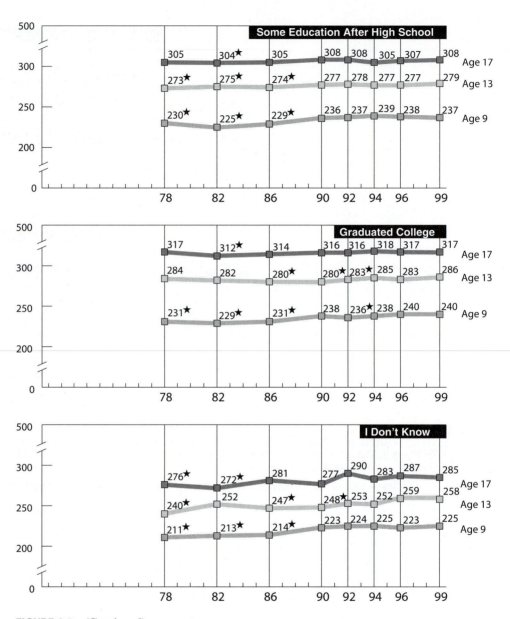

FIGURE 8.5 (Continued)

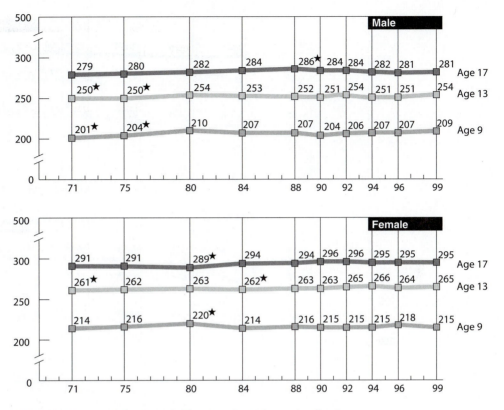

FIGURE 8.6 **Trends in Average Reading Scale Scores by Gender**
*Significantly different from 1999.

Source: National Center for Education Statistics, National Assessment of Educational Progress (NAEP), 1999 Long-Term Trend Assessment.

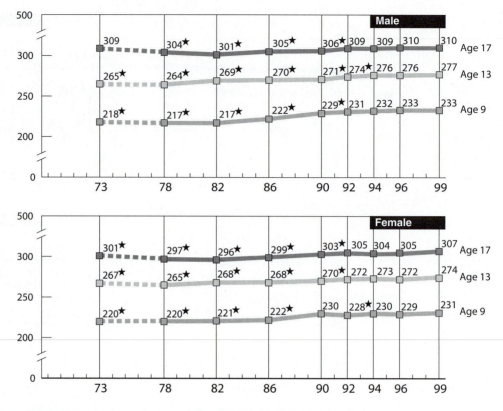

FIGURE 8.7 **Trends in Average Mathematics Scale Scores by Gender**

*Significantly different from 1999.

Note: Dashed lines represent extropolated data.

Source: National Center for Education Statistics, National Assessment of Educational Progress (NAEP), 1999 Long-Term Trend Assessment.

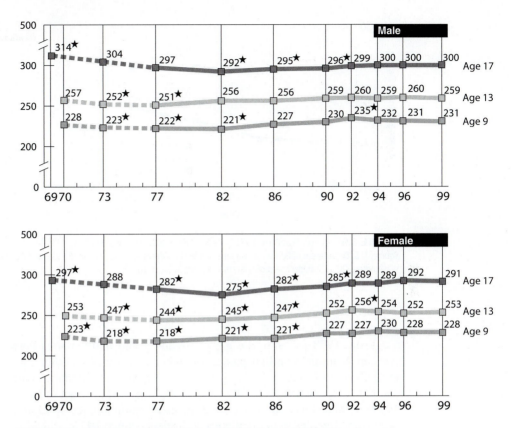

FIGURE 8.8 **Trends in Average Science Scale Scores by Gender**
*Significantly different from 1999.

Note: Dashed lines represent extrapolated data.

Source: National Center for Education Statistics, National Assessment of Educational Progress (NAEP), 1999 Long-Term Trend Assessment.

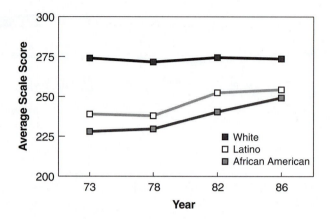

FIGURE 8.9   Gaps Narrow 1973–86 NAEP Math Scores, 13-Year-Olds
Source: U.S. Department of Education, National Center for Education Statistics. *NAEP 1999 Trends in Academic Progress.* Washington, DC: U.S. Department of Education, August 2000, p. 108.

From 1973 to 1986, the gaps in reading and mathematics between 13-year-old African Americans and Hispanics and whites narrowed and then increased from 1986 to 1999; for 17-year-olds, the gaps in reading and mathematics narrowed until 1988 and then increased from 1988 to 1999 (National Assessment of Educational Progress, 1999). Females have outperformed males in reading since 1973 and males have outperformed females in mathematics and science since 1973.

Although the achievement gaps have decreased since the 1970s, a closer examination reveals that much of the progress occurred until 1988. Since then, the gaps have widened. According to data reported by the Education Trust (2004b), the gaps between African Americans and Hispanics on the one hand, and whites on the other have increased in reading and mathematics since 1988 (see Figures 8.9 through 8.12 on pages 330–332). This has occurred despite federal legislation aimed at reducing these gaps, including Goals 2000 and NCLB. There appear to be a number of explanations for these trends, including the significant effects of early federal policies in the 1960s and 1970s, including programs such as Head Start and the long-term effects of the crack cocaine epidemic of the 1980s, with many minority and poor children born addicted to cocaine and showing cognitive deficits in the 1990s.

The rationale for preschool programs such as Head Start or the mandate in New Jersey under *Abbott* v. *Burke* for free preschool for all 3- and 4-year-olds in the low-income, urban districts, is that these gaps begin well before kindergarten (Lynch, 2004/2005). Figures 8.13 and 8.14 (pages 333 and 334) illustrate that blacks enter kindergarten with lower reading and mathematics skills than whites. These differences persist at all income levels, and will be discussed further in Chapter 9.

Attainment.   These gaps in achievement are reflected in attainment gaps among groups. For persons of both sexes 25 years old or older, 89.4 percent of whites gradu-

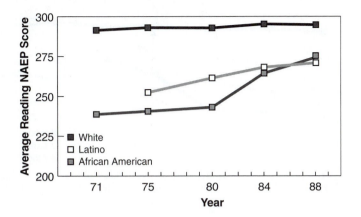

FIGURE 8.10   Gaps Narrow 1970–88 NAEP Reading, 17-Year-Olds
Source: U.S. Department of Education, National Center for Education Statistics. *NAEP 1999 Trends in Academic Progress.* Washington, DC: U.S. Department of Education, August 2000, p. 107.

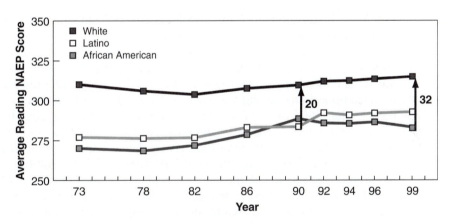

FIGURE 8.11   Gaps Narrow, Then Hold Steady or Widen: NAEP Math Scores, 17-Year-Olds
Source: U.S. Department of Education, National Center for Education Statistics. *NAEP 1999 Trends in Academic Progress.* Washington, DC: U.S. Department of Education, August 2000, p. 108.

ated from high school and 30 percent received a bachelor's degree; 80 percent of African Americans graduated from high school and 17.3 percent received a bachelor's degree; 87.6 percent of Asian Americans graduated from high school and 49.8 percent received a bachelor's degree; 57 percent of Hispanic Americans graduated from high school and 11.4 percent received a bachelor's degree. Also, 84.1 percent of males graduated from high school and 28.9 percent received a bachelor's degree; 85 percent

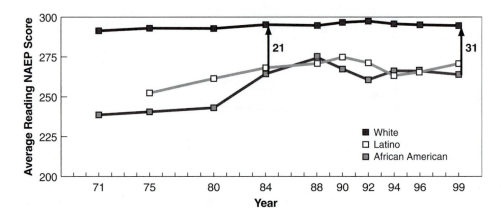

FIGURE 8.12 **After 1988, Gaps Mostly Widen: NAEP Reading, 17-Year-Olds**
Source: U.S. Department of Education, National Center for Education Statistics. *NAEP 1999 Trends in Academic Progress.*
Washington, DC: U.S. Department of Education, August 2000, p. 107.

of females graduated from high school and 25.7 percent received a bachelor's degree (U.S. Bureau of the Census, 2003a, 2003b).

The Scholastic Aptitude Test (SAT) has become the unofficial college entrance examination in the United States. Began as a utopian experiment to create a meritocratic aristocracy of talent in the 1930s by Henry Chauncey, the president of the newly founded Educational Testing Service (ETS), and Harvard president James Bryant Conant, by the 1990s, the SAT became a high-stakes test that appeared to serve the affluent and white at the expense of the poor and nonwhite (Lemann, 1999). Rather than providing a fair, meritocratic process giving the best and brightest, regardless of family background, a chance to attain the Jeffersonian ideal of mobility, the examination has advantaged the already advantaged, with some exceptions. *The Digest of Educational Statistics* (U.S. Department of Education, National Center for Education Statistics, 2002) indicates that white students outperform all other students, with the exception of Asian American students; and male students continue to outperform female students. Lemann (1999), in his history of the SAT, argues that in part through the use of private preparation services such as Stanley Kaplan and Princeton Review, affluent families have managed to use the SATs to their advantage. The case of Asian Americans, however, provides an important exception—one that will be explored in the next chapter.

These data indicate that despite improvements by minority students, African American and Hispanic American students still lag behind white students in educational achievement and attainment. Female students, however, outperform male students in most categories, with the exception of mathematics and science, where they have made some gains. The problem, however, with these data is that *The Condition of Education* does not include measures of socioeconomic status and social class background in order to provide similar analyses of the relationship between social class and

A. Reading Skills at Start of Kindergarten

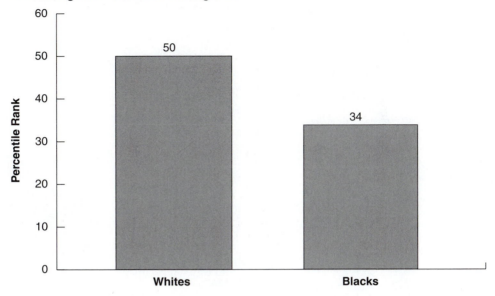

B. Reading Skills on Entering Kindergarten by Race and Socioeconomic Status

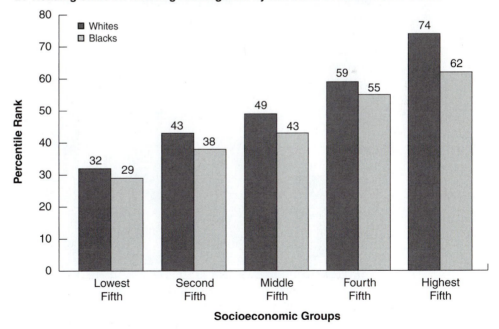

FIGURE 8.13 **Kindergarten Reading Skills**

Note: The reading performance of black students has been normalized to the reading performance of white students.

Source: Lee and Burkam (2002).

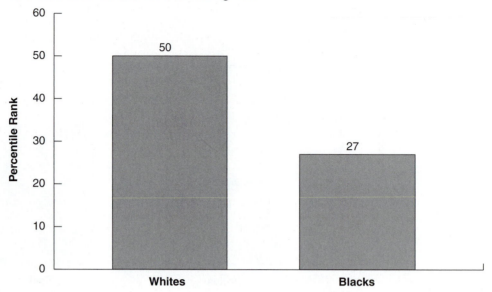

A. Mathematics Skills at Start of Kindergarten

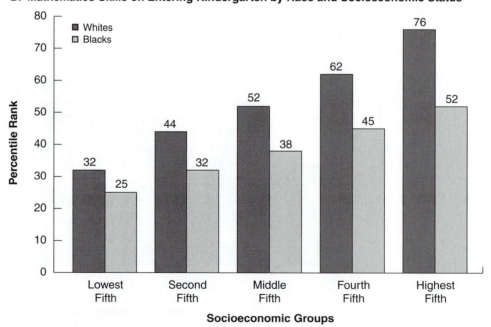

B. Mathematics Skills on Entering Kindergarten by Race and Socioeconomic Status

FIGURE 8.14 Kindergarten Mathematics Skills

Note: The mathematics performance of black students has been normalized to the mathematics performance of white students.

Source: Lee and Burkam (2002).

educational achievement and attainment. More importantly, these data do not control for the independent effects of social class with respect to racial, ethnic, and gender differences—that is, to what degree do race, ethnic, and gender differences begin to disappear when social class is controlled? Much research indicates that social class is strongly and independently related to educational attainment and achievement (Bowles & Gintis, 1976; Hurn, 1993; Riordan, 1997). Recent data from *The Digest of Educational Statistics* (U.S. Department of Education, National Center for Education Statistics, 1997) support this relationship. For example, although the digest does not control for income or social class, it does have measures of parental level of education, which is one indicator of socioeconomic status. Using this measure, we see that reading proficiency is both highly correlated with race, ethnicity, and parental level of education, with higher level of education predicting higher reading proficiency.

The significant sociological question is how to explain the reasons why these differences exist and persist. As the following section and Chapter 9 indicate, race, ethnicity, and socioeconomic levels are also highly correlated with curriculum track placement, with working class and minority students more likely to be in lower tracks and white and affluent students more likely to be in higher tracks. In addition (see Figures 8.15 to 8.20 on pages 336–341), low-income and minority students are more likely to have less challenging curricula, less likely to be in advanced placement classes, more likely to have underqualified and less experienced teachers, more likely to be in larger classes, more likely to change schools, and less likely to have their parents participate in school activities than affluent and white students (Barton, 2003, 2004).) In the next chapter, we will explore various explanations of these educational inequalities more fully.

Students with Special Needs

The field of special education has mirrored the debates about equality of educational opportunity and the concern with the appropriate placement of students with special educational needs. Beginning in the late 1960s, parents of children with special needs (including physical and learning disabilities) began to put pressure on the educational system to serve their children more appropriately and effectively. Arguing that their children were often treated as invisible and not given appropriate services, or in some cases excluded entirely from schools, parent groups demanded legislation to ensure that their children receive an appropriate and adequate education (Budoff, 1975; Gartner & Lipsky, 1987; Milofsky, 1974; Weatherly & Lipsky, 1977).

In 1975, Congress passed the Education of All Handicapped Children Law (EHA) (PL 94-142), which included six basic principles: (1) the right of access to public education programs; (2) the individualization of services; (3) the principle of "least restrictive environment"; (4) the scope of broadened services to be provided by the schools and a set of procedures for determining them; (5) the general guidelines for identifying disability; and (6) the principles of primary state and local responsibilities (Gartner & Lipsky, 1987 in Hehir & Latus, 1992, p. 126). The purpose of the law was to guarantee that children with special needs were properly identified and placed in appropriate classes, defined as the "least restrictive environment." This meant that students should be placed in specially designated classes if they required such a placement

(text continues on page 342)

A. Percentage of High School Graduates with Substantial Credits in Academic Courses, 1982 and 1998

Percentage with four years of English, three years each of social studies and mathematics, and two years of a foreign language

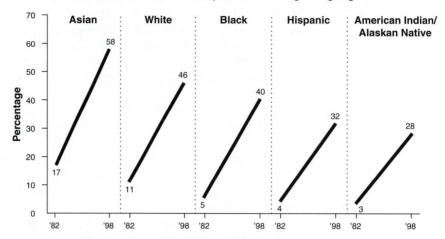

B. Distribution of Advanced Placement Examinations Compared with the Distribution of the High School Population, by Race/Ethnicity, 1999/2002*

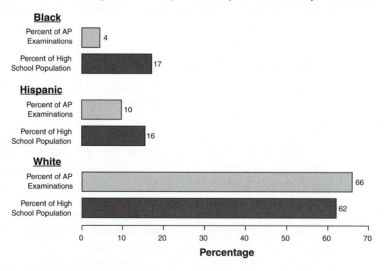

FIGURE 8.15   Rigor of Curriculum

Source for 8.15A: National Center for Education Statistics, *Digest of Education Statistics 2001,* Table 143. Original data from National Center for Education Statistics, *High School Transcript Study.*

*AP examinations are for 2002; high school population data are for 1999.

Source for 8.15B: AP data are from the College Board; high school population data are from National Center for Education Statistics, *Digest of Education Statistics 2001,* Table 42.

A. Percentage of Secondary-Level Core Academic Courses Taught by a Teacher without at Least a Minor in the Subject, 1999–2000

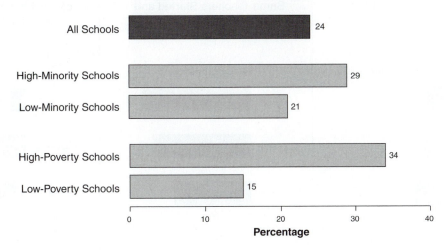

B. Percentage of Eighth Graders Whose Math Teachers Lack Certification in Middle/Junior High School or in Secondary School Mathematics, by Race/Ethnicity and Poverty, 1996-2000

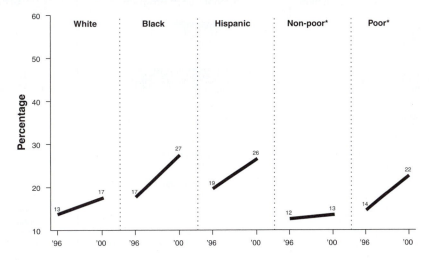

FIGURE 8.16   Teacher Preparation

Note for 8.16A: High-minority schools contain 50 percent or more minority students; low-minority schools contain 15 percent or fewer minority students. High-poverty schools contain 50 percent or more poor students; low-poverty schools contain 15 percent or fewer poor students.

Source for 8.16A: Craig D. Jerald (data analysis by Richard M. Ingersoll), *All Talk, No Action: Putting an End to Out-of-Field Teaching,* Education Trust, August 2002.

*As measured by whether eligible or ineligible for free/reduced school lunch.

Source for 8.16B: http://nces.ed.gov/nationsreportcard/naepdata.

338   CHAPTER 8

Percentage of Teachers with Three or Fewer Years of Experience, 1998

Level of Minority Enrollment

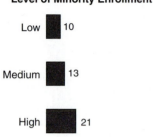

Level of Low Income Enrollment

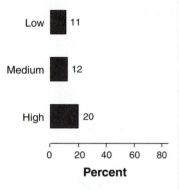

Percentage of Fourth-Grade Students in Schools Where Same Teachers Started and Ended the Year, 2000

Race/Ethnicity

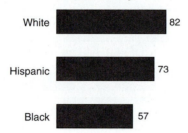

School Lunch Program

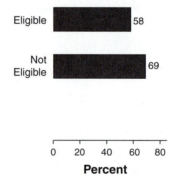

Percentage of Twelfth-Grade Students Where 6 to 10 Percent of Teachers Are Absent on Average Day, 2000

Race/Ethnicity

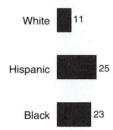

School Lunch Program

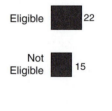
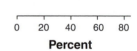

Note: Low, medium, and high are defined as the schools in the bottom quartile, the middle two quartiles, and the top quartile, respectively. Low income is defined as the percent of students eligible for free or reduced-price lunch.

Source: From Mayer et al., 2000, which cites the Fast Response Survey System's *Teacher Survey on Professional Development and Training,* NCES, 1998.

Source: http://nces.ed.gov/ nationsreportcard/ naepdata/getdata.asp, 1/12/03. Data are for public schools.

Source: http://nces.ed.gov/ nationsreportcard/ naepdata/getdata.asp, 1/12/03. Data are for public schools.

FIGURE 8.17   **Teacher Experience and Attendance**

By the Percent of Minority Students

Less than 10	22*
10 to 24	25
25 to 49	22
50 to 75	26
More than 75	31

By the Percent of Students Eligible for School Lunch Program

Less than 15	27
15 to 29	25
30 to 49	19
50 to 74	23
75 to 100	26

By the Percent of Students with Limited-English Proficiency

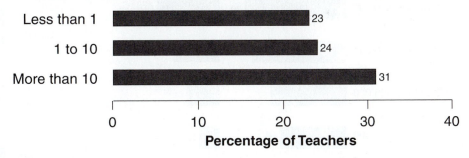

Less than 1	23
1 to 10	24
More than 10	31

0   10   20   30   40
Percentage of Teachers

FIGURE 8.18 **Percentage of Teachers with Classes of 25 or More Students, 1999–2000**
*In classes with less than 10 percent minority students, 22 percent of the teachers have 25 or more students in their classes.

Source: National Center for Education Statistics, *School and Staffing Survey (SASS), 1999–2000.*

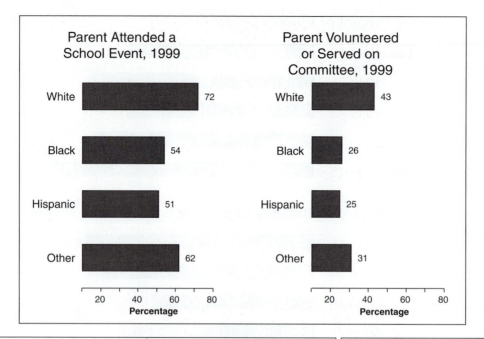

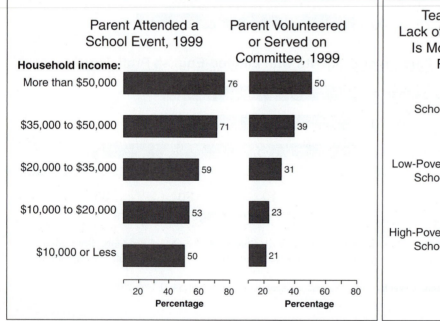

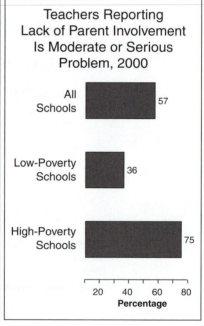

FIGURE 8.19 Parent Participation

Sources: Child Trends Data Base (original source–NCES, *The Condition of Education, 2001*) and *Education Week,* "Quality Counts," 2003, p. 62.

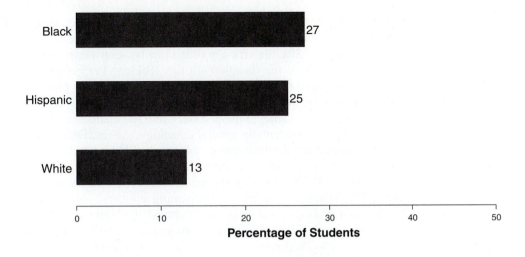

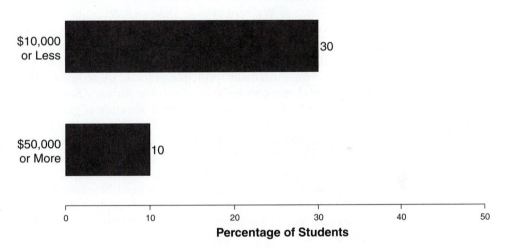

FIGURE 8.20 Percentage of Third-Graders Who Changed Schools Three Times or More Since First Grade, by Race/Ethnicity and Income, 1990–1991
Source: U.S. General Accounting Office, *Elementary School Children: Many Change Schools Frequently, Harming Their Education,* February 1994, pp. 27–28. Percentages for race/ethnicity are interpolated from bar chart.

and in regular classes with assistance, if they could function in the mainstream. The law was reauthorized in 1996 as the Individuals with Disabilities Education Act (IDEA).

By the mid-1980s, the efficacy of the law became a critical issue for policy makers and advocates of the disabled. Critics (Biklen, 1985; Gartner & Lipsky, 1987; Lytle, 1988) argued that despite its good intentions, the law produced adverse effects, such as the overidentification of students with handicapping conditions, the failure of special education students to make it back into the mainstream, and the overrepresentation of minority students in special education classes. Defenders (Singer & Butler, 1987) countered that despite some problems, the EHA provided significant increases in the quality of services for children with disabilities.

In the late 1980s, critics of special education pushed the *regular education initiative (REI),* which called for mainstreaming children with disabilities into regular classes. The REI called for *inclusion* of almost all children into the mainstream, which many critics argued would result in chaos and the inability to educate mainstream children effectively. Proponents of REI argued that democratic principles require that all students be educated together and that special education placement had not proven effective for most students (Gartner & Lipsky, 1987; Lilly, 1986; Pugach & Lilly, 1984; Reynolds, Wang, & Walberg, 1987; Stainback & Stainback, 1989). Critics of REI (Kaufman, 1989) countered that inclusion of the majority of students with special needs was unfair to both "regular" and special students, neither of whom would be served effectively. They indicated that special education reform should ensure that the "least restrictive environment" principle of the EHA be more fully implemented.

Skrtic (1991), in a comprehensive essay in *Harvard Educational Review,* analyzed the relationship between the organizational structure of public education and the bureaucratization of special education since 1975. Arguing that the organizational procedures of special education had resulted in a system that was often concerned more with its own perpetuation than with the needs of students, Skrtic argued for reform of the entire system to ensure proper placement and education. Skrtic placed the special education system in the larger context of educational bureaucracy and suggested that it needed to be understood as part of the more general system of testing and tracking. He concluded that special education be reformed within a democratic overhaul of public education.

Today, the field of special education remains in conflict. The controversies over REI and EHA continue. As we move ahead in the twenty-first century, it is imperative that educational researchers provide empirical evidence to inform placement decisions. It is clear that far too many students have been labeled and placed into special education classes and, that for many, these classes have resulted in lifetime sentences that have limited their educational opportunities. It is also clear that minority students have been overrepresented in special education placements. However, it is not clear that all students with special needs will benefit from inclusion, nor that students in the mainstream will not be harmed academically from wholesale mainstreaming. What is needed is a flexible system that provides appropriate placements for students with special needs: an inclusion class for those who can function within it and a special class for students whose needs require a separate placement. Unfortunately, too often the politics of special education has been more important than the needs of children. As you will see in Chapter 9, this has been true of tracking in general.

Conclusion

In this section, we have examined the relationship between social stratification and educational outcomes. We have made a strong case that the ideal of equal opportunity is somewhat tarnished by the reality that an individual's origin has a significant impact on his or her destination. Education is related to mobility, but this relationship is made complex by the fact that education cannot erase the effects of inequality. Class and race, in particular, continue to haunt the egalitarian ideal that all children should be treated equally. Thinking in terms of life arithmetic, one might say that in the equation of educational outcomes, who you are is almost as significant a factor as what you know. Critics of this position might argue that effective schools can make a difference in terms of providing equality of opportunity. In the next section, we examine the issue of whether school differences have a significant impact on educational outcomes.

School Differences and Educational Outcomes

There is now a great controversy as to whether differences between schools lead to significant differences in terms of student outcomes. This may surprise you. After all, it seems only common sense that the better the school, the greater its positive impact on students. A deep faith in the power of education to overcome ignorance and inequality virtually requires one to believe that there is a close and powerful relationship between the characteristics of schools and their effects on students. Untangling this issue is a complex intellectual challenge.

The essential problem can be stated as follows: To what degree can student outcomes, whether they be cognitive or affective, be attributed directly to the organizational characteristics of schools? How can family influences, maturation, and peer influences be separated from the organizational influences of schools on students? Obviously, this is not an either/or proposition—hence, the complexity of the problem. This problem is compounded by the fact that schools have direct and indirect effects on students' lives. For example, one direct effect is the amount of cognitive growth that can be attributed to years of schooling. Indirect effects are more difficult to measure but, nonetheless, are very significant because they relate to the social consequences of having attended certain types of schools. Thus, the graduate of a socially elite private school may have gone to school the same number of years as the graduate of an inner-city public school, but the social marketability of their degrees are quite different. The higher the social status of a school, the more likely the school will be able to increase the social statuses of its graduates. Considering what is known about the class system, this should not be totally surprising, even though it may be somewhat repugnant. This issue was raised briefly in Chapter 4, when we discussed the difference between educational amount and educational route.

There are two major rivaling hypotheses concerning the relationship between school characteristics and student outcomes. The first hypothesis states that there is a strong, positive correlation between school quality and student achievement. Curiously, conservatives, liberals, and radicals all seem to subscribe to this hypothesis. Conservatives and liberals see this positive correlation as an expression of meritocracy, whereas radicals see this correlation as an expression of oppression. The second hypothesis is not popular in the educational community or with the public at large. This hypothesis states that there is a very weak relationship between school characteristics and student outcomes. That is, the organizational characteristics of schools are not strong enough to undo the cognitive and social consequences of class background. In other words, degrees simply credentialize students; the actual content of what they have learned is not terribly significant (Meyer, 1977; Collins, 1975). Testing these rivaling hypotheses is a demanding empirical task.

In this section, we examine the issues raised by the preceding rivaling hypotheses. Not all of the evidence is in; therefore, hard and fast conclusions cannot be drawn. But the debate is significant because in the balance lie significant policy decisions.

The Coleman Study (1966)

If you were to pick up almost any textbook on education, you would most likely read that differences among schools account for a variety of student outcomes. Almost everybody in education and in the public at large is committed to the civil religion that education is meritocratic and transformative. Most educational reform movements rest on this assumption. To say that differences among schools do not really matter that much in terms of student cognitive outcomes is close to civil heresy. Up until the 1960s, no one really challenged the assumption that school characteristics were extremely important in determining student outcomes. It seemed common sense that the more books a school had and the more degrees the teachers had, the more the students would learn.

With the advent of computers, large-scale survey analysis became possible by the mid-1960s. Researchers could collect huge amounts of national data and analyze the data relatively rapidly. On the forefront of this type of research was the sociologist James Coleman. During this period, Coleman received an extremely large grant to study the relationship between the organizational characteristics of schools and student achievement. The motivation behind this grant was to demonstrate that African American students and white students had fundamentally different schooling experiences. It was hoped by policy makers that Coleman's study would provide the rationale for federally funding those schools that were primarily attended by minority students.

The results of Coleman's study were shocking because what he found, in essence, was that the organizational differences between schools were not particularly important in determining student outcomes when compared to the differences in student-body compositions between schools. On average, students who attended schools that were predominantly middle class were more likely to do better on tests of achievement than students who attended school where middle-class students were not a majority. Peer group association could be more important than the number of books in the library. It should not surprise you at this point that Coleman's findings caused a tremendous controversy. After all, if differences among schools are only weakly related to student outcomes, what did this say about the power of education to overcome inequalities?

Responses to Coleman: Round One.   There were two major responses to Coleman's findings. On the one hand, other sociologists examined and reexamined Coleman's data. On the other hand, a group of minority scholars, led by Ron Edmonds of Harvard

University, set about the task of defining those characteristics of schools that made them effective. Edmonds argued strongly that all students could learn and that differences between schools had a significant impact on student learning. We will discuss in some depth the "effective school" movement in Chapters 9 and 10.

Within the sociological community, the debate concerning Coleman's findings produced a number of studies that, when all the dust settled, more or less substantiated what Coleman and his colleagues had found. Despite the nation's best intentions, differences among schools are not powerful predictors of differences in student outcomes. After an extensive review of the literature, McDill (1978, p. 2) concluded:

> In the past twelve years a body of empirical knowledge has accumulated, beginning with the *Equality of Educational Opportunity* survey (Coleman et al., 1966), and based on both cross-sectional and longitudinal studies, which unequivocally indicates that, overall, between school differences in any measurable attribute of institutions are only modestly related to a variety of outcome variables.

In other words, where an individual goes to school has little effect on his or her cognitive growth or educational mobility. This seems to be a case where the data and common sense separate. Can it be true that the characteristics of an academically elite school are relatively insignificant in terms of student outcomes? Clearly, the implications of these findings would lead one to believe that the road to equality of opportunity does not go through the schoolhouse door. The political nature of these findings were explosive. After all, if student-body composition has such a major effect on student learning, then the policy implication is clearly that poor students should go to school with middle-class students in order to equalize their educational opportunities. This assumption was the foundation that justifies busing students between schools and between school districts.

During the 1970s, this debate continued and some researchers began to examine the effects of magnet schools on student learning, arguing that schools that were innovative, learner centered, and mission driven could make a difference in what students learned and how they learned it. These studies were intriguing and provided a ray of research hope for those optimists who still believed in the efficacy of education to provide equal opportunities for all children. Still, from a research point of view, these findings were not terribly convincing. At this point, James Coleman and his colleagues at the University of Chicago reentered the debate.

The Coleman Study (1982)

In 1982, James Coleman, Thomas Hoffer, and Sally Kilgore published *High School Achievement: Public, Catholic, and Private Schools Compared.* Like the first Coleman report, this book set off a firestorm of controversy. Coleman and his associates found that when they compared the average test scores of public school and private school sophomores, there was not one subject in which public school students scored higher than private school students. In reading, vocabulary, mathematics, science, civics, and writing tests, private school students outperformed public school students sometimes by a wide margin. Coleman and his associates (1982, p. 177) concluded:

In the examination of effects on achievement, statistical controls on family background are introduced, in order to control on those background characteristics that are most related to achievement. The achievement differences between the private sectors and the public sector are reduced (more for other private schools than for Catholic schools) but differences remain.

In other words, differences among schools do make a difference. The Coleman findings of 1966 were challenged by the Coleman findings of 1982. Coleman and his colleagues argued that private schools were more effective learning environments than public schools because they place more emphasis on academic activities and because private schools enforce discipline in a way that is consistent with student achievement. In short, private schools demand more from their students than do public schools. As in 1966, the more recent Coleman findings were challenged by a number of sociologists and other scholars. And, as in 1966, Coleman's findings essentially withstood the criticisms leveled at them. However, the interpretations of these findings are still a matter of debate.

Responses to Coleman: Round Two.   The debate over the *High School Achievement* findings has centered on the interpretations attached to the magnitude of the findings. What Coleman and his associates saw as significant, others saw as nearly insignificant. For example, Jencks (1985) used Coleman's findings to compute the estimated yearly average achievement gain by public and Catholic school students. He estimated that the annual increment attributable to Catholic schooling was tiny. To put it simply, the differences that do exist between public and Catholic schools are statistically significant, but in terms of significant differences in learning, the results are negligible. The interpretation was echoed by Alexander and Pallas (1983, p. 122):

> What then of Coleman, Hoffer, Kilgore's claim that Catholic schools are educationally superior to public schools? If trivial advantage is what they mean by such a claim, then we suppose we would have to agree. But judged against reasonable benchmarks, there is little basis for this conclusion.

Subsequent studies that have compared public and private schools have also found that private schools seem to "do it better," particularly for low-income students (Chubb & Moe, 1990; Bryk, Lee, & Holland, 1993). The same criticisms that have been directed at Coleman and his colleagues, however, can be directed at Chubb and Moe. Yes, private schools seem to have certain organizational characteristics that are related to student outcomes, but are these relationships as significant as some researchers claim? This debate is not resolved, and one can expect that more research and more controversy will surface. For example, a recent article by Baker and Riordan argued that Catholic schools in the 1990s have become more elite, belying the argument that they are modern common schools (Bryk, Lee, & Holland, 1993; Greeley, 1982). In a scathing response, sociologist and priest Andrew Greeley argued that Baker and Riordan's evidence ignores the past two decades of findings that support a democratic view of Catholic schools. It appears that there is evidence to support parts of both views. Catholic schools seem to advantage low-income minority students, especially in urban areas. However, they are also becoming more elite and like suburban public schools. Given this trend, it will be interesting to see if they continue to serve the poor.

Conclusion

Do school differences make a difference in terms of student outcomes? At this point, probably the best answer to this question is a highly qualified and realistic yes. Schools that are less bureaucratic and more academically oriented are better learning environments for students. But, and this is a big *but,* these findings should not be interpreted to mean that private schools are substantially superior to public schools and therefore the public system should be privatized. On a related note, if people think of school organizations and student outcomes within the class structure, it is quite likely that differences among schools matter for middle-class children because they are the beneficiaries of the meritocratic scramble for educational advantage. For very wealthy students, the schools they attend bear almost no relationship to the money they will inherit, and for very poor students, their economic and social disadvantages are so profound that schools have little hope of altering their life chances.

The relationship between social class, race, and achievement is a complex one. Although higher social class is correlated with higher achievement, the degree to which this is due to factors inside or outside schools is the subject of significant research.

Tables 8.1 and 8.2 (about Long Island, New York) and Figures 8.21 through 8.28 (about New Jersey, pages 350–353) present a simple and at the same time complex view of equality of educational opportunity and educational inequalities. First, these data suggest that although funding is important, the socioeconomic level of communities is the most powerful explanation of unequal performance, often independent of funding. Second, they indicate that because race is so strongly correlated with socioeconomic level, race is also strongly associated with achievement, but not always independent of social class. Third, although schools with lower socioeconomic levels clearly have lower academic achievement, there are enough examples of schools (Abington Avenue, Ann Street, North Star Academy Charter School, and Robert Trent Academy Charter School, all in Newark, New Jersey) to suggest that schools have the ability to overcome the external nonschool factors and make a significant difference (see Figures 8.23 through 8.28).

New Jersey's public schools and public charter schools provide excellent examples. Newark (under state takeover since 1995), all other low-income urban Abbott districts, and the I and J highest wealth districts illustrate the relationship among race, ethnicity, social class, and academic achievement. As a result of New Jersey's *Abbott* v. *Burke* decision that has mandated that the states high-need, low-income urban districts are funded at the average of the state's highest socioeconomic districts, New Jersey's urban Abbott districts receive more money than all but the highest-income districts. As these data indicate (see Figures 8.21 and 8.22 on page 350), even with equal spending, students in low-income districts still perform at significantly lower levels, although there have been significant improvements, especially at the fourth-grade level (Education Law Center, 2005). However, in Newark, there are sometimes significant achievement differences among schools with similar socioeconomic, race, and ethnic characteristics, with some schools having high achievement and others much

TABLE 8.1   School Wealth, Funding, and Achievement in Nassau County, Long Island, Eastern Suburbs of New York City (Funding Figures Are for the 2001–2002 School Year; Regents Data Are for the 2002–2003 School Year)

Contiguous Districts[1]	District Wealth Ratio[2]	Spending per Student (General Education, Excluding Special Education)	% Pass English Regents[3]	% Regents Diploma	% Graduates of 4-Year Colleges	% Graduates of 2-Year Colleges
Freeport	0.807	$8,360	75%	49%	36%	40%
Baldwin	1.292	$8,167	92%	76%	66%	27%
Roosevelt	0.588	$6,997	78%	18%	36%	47%
Bellmore-Merrick	1.408	$8,352	97%	91%	73%	23%
Carle Place	1.673	$9,849	89%	76%	58%	33%
East Williston	2.674	$11,760	100%	87%	80%	16%
Hempstead	0.676	$9,026	71%	14%	32%	15%
Garden City	2.889	$9,824	97%	91%	87%	7%
Glen Cove	1.665	$8,857	90%	63%	52%	36%
North Shore	2.977	$10,562	97%	78%	75%	20%

[1]The grouped districts border each other.

[2]District wealth ratio compares each district's wealth to the state average, which is defined as 1.0. Wealthier districts have a ratio higher than 1.0, while poorer districts are below 1.0.

[3]Regents examinations are statewide tests in New York State required to graduate with a Regents diploma. State standards will require that all students take and pass five regents examinations in order to graduate.

Notes on School Districts

Freeport is an racially-mixed community on the South Shore of Long Island, which is lower middle to middle class. Baldwin is a majority white community contiguous to Freeport, which is middle class.

Roosevelt is a predominantly African American community in the middle of Nassau County on Long Island, which is predominantly poor and lower middle class. The Roosevelt School District was taken over by the New York State Education Department in the mid-1990s due to poor academic performance and is currently being managed by the State Education Department. Bellmore-Merrick is a predominately white community contiguous to Roosevelt. It is a central secondary school district, with feeder elementary schools from Bellmore and Merrick. Its three high schools serve a population that ranges from lower middle class to upper middle class.

Carle Place is a predominantly white middle-class community on the middle of Nassau County. East Williston is a predominantly white upper middle-class district contiguous (north) of Carle Place.

Hempstead is a predominantly African American community, which ranges from poor to middle class. Garden City is a predominantly white upper middle-class community contiguous (immediately northwest) of Hempstead.

Glen Cove is a mixed-racial community on the North Shore of Nassau County (Long Island), which ranges from lower middle class to upper middle-class. North Shore is a predominately white, upper middle-class community contiguous (southeast) of Glen Cove.

Source: New York State Department of Education, as cited in "School by School Report Card" (2004).

lower achievement. This is true for both public and charter schools (Barr, 2004a, 2004b). At the high school level, the major differences are between selective magnet schools, where students are admitted based on test scores, and comprehensive schools, where all students are admitted. However, the achievement scores of a number of non-selective schools in Newark that are at or above the state, district, and districts with

TABLE 8.2 School Wealth, Funding, and Achievement on Long Island (Nassau and Suffolk Counties) by Social Class and Race

	District Wealth Ratio	Spending per Student 2001–2002 (General Education, Excluding Special Education)	% Pass English Regents (2002–2003)	% Regents Diploma (2002–2003)	% Graduates to 4-Year Colleges (2002–2003)	% Graduates to 2-Year Colleges (2002–2003)
North Shore Districts (>80% White and Asian; High SES)						
Great Neck	3.600	$10,858	96%	89%	79%	10%
Jericho	3.643	$11,303	100%	100%	90%	7%
Locust Valley	3.349	$10,569	99%	88%	78%	20%
Manhasset	3.469	$12,683	99%	85%	83%	10%
Roslyn	2.945	$12,137	97%[1]	89%	90%	10%
"Urban"-like Suburban Districts (>80% African American or Hispanic; Low SES)						
Amityville	1.153	$8,031	84%	37%	51%	25%
Hempstead	0.676	$9,026	71%	14%	32%	15%
Roosevelt	0.588	$6,997	78%	18%	36%	47%
Uniondale	1.049	$10,211	81%	37%	40%	38%
Wyandanch	0.396	$12,142	82%	30%	48%	30%

Note: The North Shore of Long Island is considered the metropolitan area's *gold coast,* made famous in F. Scott Fitzgerald's *The Great Gatsby.* The term *"urban"-like suburban districts* is used to describe districts that are demographically similar to the urban districts described in Kozol's *Savage Inequalities,* as well as to illustrate that these inequalities are not limited to urban-suburban differences, but are found within suburbs, as well. As we noted in Chapter 1, rural schools often mirror the problems found in many urban schools. See Singer (1999) for a detailed analysis of Long Island school districts and educational inequality.
[1]2001–2002; data not available for 2002–2003.
Source: New York State Department of Education, as cited in "School by School Report Card" (2004).

similar socioeconomic level (District Factor Groups DFG) average (Figures 8.23 through 8.28 on pages 351–353) demonstrate that schools can make a difference independent of the social class, race, and ethnicity of their students (www.just4kids.org, New Jersey Department of Education, 2004). In the final analysis, in New Jersey—ranked by the Education Trust (www.edtrust.org) as one of the most equitable states with respect to funding of low- income schools—social class, race, and ethnicity remain powerful predictors of academic success. The complex intersection among social class, race, and ethnicity, as well as how school and nonschool factors affect achievement, are the subject of the next chapter.

(text continues on page 354)

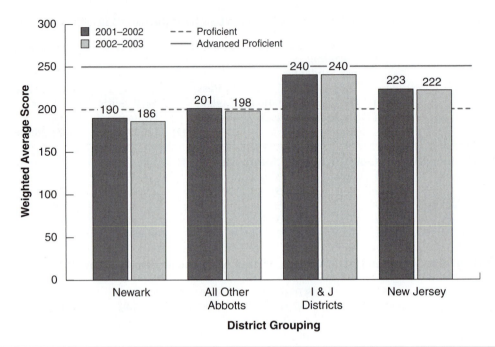

FIGURE 8.21   HSPA Math Average Scores by District Grouping, 2001–02 to 2002–03

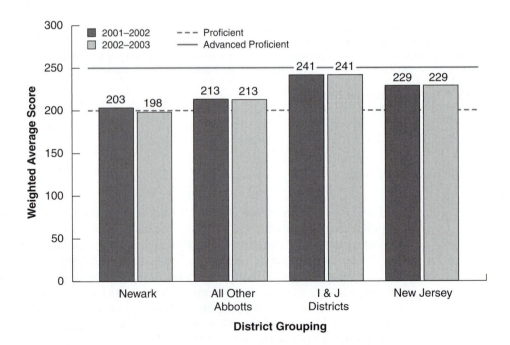

FIGURE 8.22   HSPA Language Arts Learning Average Scores by District Grouping, 2001–02 to 2003–04

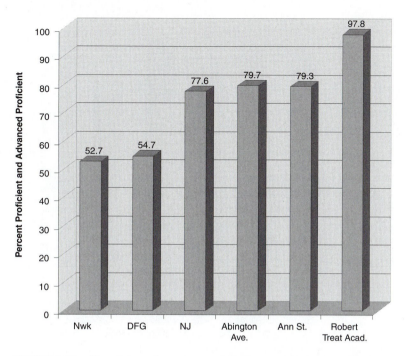

FIGURE 8.23 New Jersey Assessment of Skills and Knowledge (NJASK4) 2002–2003: Language Arts Literacy

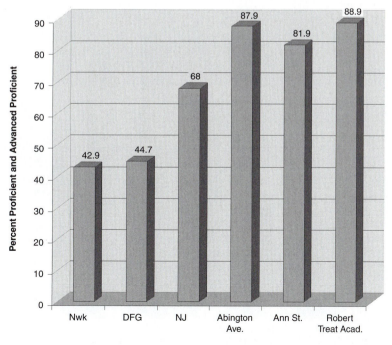

FIGURE 8.24 New Jersey Assessment of Skills and Knowledge (NJASK4) 2002–2003: Math

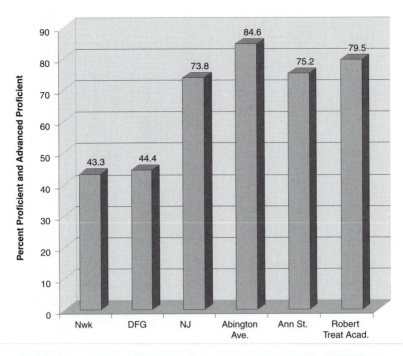

FIGURE 8.25   Grade Eight Proficiency Assessment (GEPA) 2002–2003: Language Arts Literacy

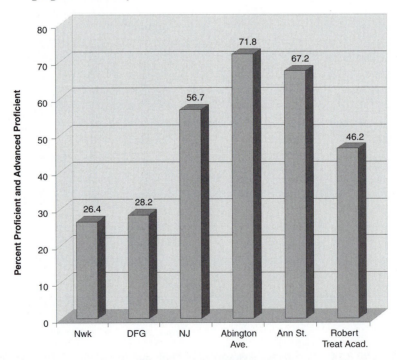

FIGURE 8.26   Grade Eight Proficiency Assessment (GEPA) 2002–2003: Math

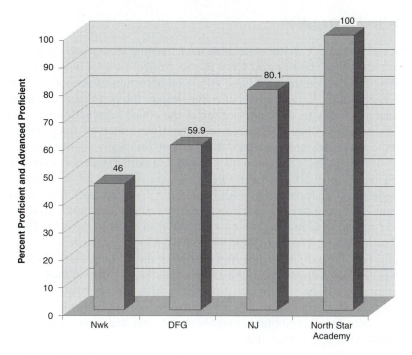

FIGURE 8.27   High School Proficiency Assessment (HSPA) 2002–2003: Language Arts Literacy

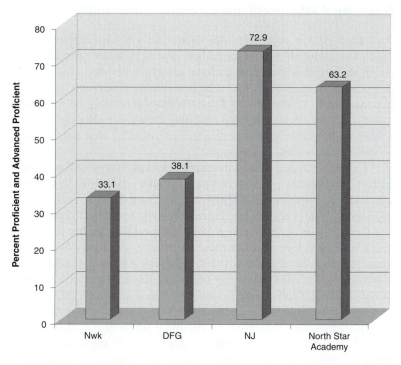

FIGURE 8.28   High School Proficiency Assessment (HSPA) 2002–2003: Math

School Segregation

As we noted in Chapter 4, schools have become increasingly segregated over the past two decades. The Harvard Civil Rights Project (www.civilrightsproject.harvard.edu) provides data on the racial and ethnic composition of school districts throughout the United States. Research indicates that despite the fact that schools are less segregated than 40 years ago, the degree of racial and ethnic segregation is increasing.

Although there is disagreement about the effects of integration on achievement, there is considerable evidence that students in highly segregated schools have lower achievement and graduation rates and that minority students in integrated schools have higher levels of achievement (Orfield & Lee, 2004, pp. 24–25). Even though there was widespread dissatisfaction with busing for desegregation, there is evidence that students attending integrated schools received educational and social benefits. In a study of students who attended desegregated high schools in the early 1980s in five cities—Austin, Texas; Charlotte; North Carolina; Montclair, New Jersey; Pasadena, California; and Topeka, Kansas—20 years after their graduation, Wells, Holme, Tijerina Revilla, and Korantemaa (2004) found that the majority of these students looked back favorably at their experiences, despite the difficulties of being the ones to integrate formerly segregated schools. Moreover, the majority of both whites and blacks stated that they now live in segregated neighborhoods and that their children attend more segregated schools than they did.

Educational Attainment and Economic Achievement

As we saw earlier, college graduates are likely to earn higher salaries than high school graduates, and it should be noted here that high school graduates are likely to be paid more per hour than people who have not graduated from high school. Jencks and colleagues (1979, p. 230) wrote, "The best readily observable predictor of a young man's eventual status or earnings is the amount of schooling he has had. This could be because schooling is an arbitrary rationing devise for allocating scarce jobs; or because schooling imparts skills, knowledge, or attitudes that employers value; or because schooling alters men's aspirations."

That education is related to employment and economic achievement is undeniable. In 1987, for instance, a man 25 years or older, with three to five years of high school, was likely to earn roughly $22,000 a year. From then on, each increment in educational attainment (four years of high school, one to three years of college, four years of college, and five years or more of college) is associated with higher income. In 1987, for example, a man with five years or more of college was likely to earn $45,000 a year. The same pattern holds true for women, only for each level of educational attainment, they earn roughly $10,000 less a year than men. Looking at the relationship between educational attainment and economic achievement in another light, one can see is a strong inverse relationship between unemployment and educational attainment. That is, the more highly educated an individual is, the more unlikely it is that he or she will be unemployed. As the labor market creates more high-skill jobs and fewer manufacturing jobs, the economic value of a college education will become even more pronounced.

From our previous discussion, you are aware of the fact that educational attainment alone does not explain economic achievement. Class background is a powerful predictor of economic achievement. The higher an individual's class background, the more likely he or she is to earn more money than individuals from other classes. Moreover, the higher the prestige of the occupation, the more likely it is to be filled with people with relatively high academic credentials. In surveys of occupational prestige, the professions are consistently rated to be more prestigious than other occupations, and to become a professional usually requires a great deal of education.

Not withstanding this discussion, it is not clear what it is about education that makes it so economically valuable. Jencks and associates (1979) posed three possible explanations for the close relationship between educational attainment and economic achievement. It could be that education is simply a sorting device. That is, educational credentials signal to employers the market value of a prospective employee, with little reference to what the employee actually knows. Another possible explanation for why education is related to economic achievement is that educated people actually know something that is valuable to employers. The employer hires the individual with more education because he or she is more expert. The third explanation that Jencks offered concerning the relationship between education and economic achievement is that there is an interaction between years of schooling and aspirations. That is, motivated people stay in school and staying in school motivates people to achieve. There is, among some people, a hunger for education that far exceeds the rational need for a marketplace credential. After all, most college professors make relatively small amounts of money when compared to their years of education. Some people simply enjoy learning.

Sociologists have tested these rivaling explanations. Collins (1971), for instance, asked employers why they hired college graduates for managerial jobs. Did employers actually inquire into what prospective employees knew? Was there a test of potential employees' expertise? Or was it simply the credential that seemed to matter in the decision-making process? You may remember our discussion of the differences between functional and conflict theorists in Chapter 2. Collins was testing the relative efficacy of these two theories. If employers made employment decisions based on what prospective employees knew, this would substantiate the functionalist perspective because it would support the argument that the amount of schooling was a reliable index for expertise. On the other hand, if employers made employment decisions simply on the basis of a prospective employees' paper credentials, then this would be an argument for the conflict perspective. In effect, employers would be hiring individuals based on the social status of possessing a credential, rather than on the individuals' knowledge and expertise.

Collins found that, on balance, the conflict perspective was supported. Employers seldom even knew what prospective employees had studied in school, nor did they consider such knowledge to be particularly relevant in making their employment decisions. A businessman who saw education primarily as an initial screening devise said:

> Industry places a high value on the college degree, not because it is convinced that four years of schooling insure that individuals acquire maturity and technical competence, but rather because it provides an initial point of division between those more trained and those

less trained; those better motivated and those less motivated; those with more social experience and those with less. (cited in Persell, 1977, p. 159)

In his book *Education and Jobs: The Great Training Robbery* (1970), Ivar Berg found that years of schooling are generally related (and sometimes negatively related) to job performance ratings. That is, his findings were very similar to those of Collins: Education counts but mostly as a social credential and not as an academic indicator of presumed expertise. Berg (1970, p. 185) wrote:

> Educational credentials have become the new property in America. Our nation, which has attempted to make the transmission of real and personal property difficult, has contrived to replace it with an inheritable set of values concerning degrees and diplomas which will most certainly reinforce the formidable class barriers that remain, even without the right within families to pass benefits from parents to their children.

It seems that from the available evidence, one can conclude that although educational attainment is directly related to economic achievement, the reason for this relationship has very little to do with technical competence but a great deal to do with social acceptability. These findings may surprise you—even shock you. Nobody maintains that the intrinsic value of an education is of no economic or social value. What is being said is that in a class system, educational credentials are valuable assets in the great status race, above and beyond their intrinsic intellectual value.

Education and Inequality: Mobility or Reproduction?

In this chapter, we have put to the test the American belief in equality of educational opportunity and found that this belief is based partly on reality and partly on blind faith. The amount of education an individual receives is directly related to his or her life chances. But life chances are also directly related to where an individual is located in the class structure. Life chances are also directly related to race and, to a somewhat lesser degree, gender. Organizational characteristics of schools do have a slight impact on student outcomes such as achievement, but these differences are quite small. The larger truth is that differences between the organizational characteristics of schools only marginally affect the life chances of students, especially if social class is held constant. Although educational credentials are good predictors of economic achievement, the reason for this relationship has less to do with the amount of learning that has taken place than it has to do with the power of credentials to send social signals of respectability.

From this account, it should be clear that although education provides a method of economic and social mobility, in the main, education reproduces the existing class structure. Marxist scholars, such as Bowles and Gintis (1976), have argued that there is a direct correspondence between the class system and the educational system. Although we do not subscribe to a deterministic or mechanical view of the relationship between school and society, it does appear that educational opportunities are closely related to one's social class position and that for the overwhelming majority of people, there is little likelihood that their educational credentials will lift them out of their social class of origin.

The issues that have been raised in this chapter are so fundamental and so related to the concept of democracy that they will continue to shape U.S. educational policy for the foreseeable future. The passionate belief of Americans that education can resolve economic and social problems will be put to the test in the years ahead. Although one's heart wants to believe that, through education, the United States can achieve equality of opportunity, one's head must remain skeptical. The empirical evidence indicates that the United States is a long way away from achieving equal educational opportunity.

In this chapter, we have touched on many important issues regarding the relationship between education, occupation, and the reproduction of social inequalities. We include three articles that highlight some of the issues that have been discussed in this chapter. The first article, "Class and the Classroom: Even the Best Schools Can't Close the Race Achievement Gap," written by journalist Richard Rothstein, analyzes the black–white achievement gap and the limits and possibilities of schools in reducing them.

The second article, "Chartering and Bartering: Elite Education and Social Reproduction," written by sociologists Caroline Hodges Persell and Peter W. Cookson, Jr., illuminates the relationship between college counselors in elite U.S. boarding schools and U.S. colleges and universities that are academically selective. This article documents the process by which informal personal relationships bind institutions together. These relationships have little or nothing to do with the maintenance of a meritocracy but have a great deal to do with the transmission of privilege.

The third article, "College-for-All: Do Students Understand What College Demands?" written by sociologist James E. Rosenbaum, provides an analysis of the opposite side of U.S. education than the one explored by Persell and Cookson. Rosenbaum examines the effects of the "college-for-all" ideology, which states that college education is a right for everyone, especially for disadvantaged students. This ideology discourages students from working hard in high school and leaves many unable to handle the demands of a college education, often resulting in failure and dropping out.

Class and the Classroom

Even the Best Schools Can't Close the Race Achievement Gap
RICHARD ROTHSTEIN

The achievement gap between poor and middle-class black and white children is widely recognized as our most important educational challenge. But we prevent ourselves from solving it because of a commonplace belief that poverty and race can't "cause" low achievement and that therefore schools must be failing to teach disadvantaged children adequately. After all, we see many highly successful students from lower-class backgrounds. Their success seems to prove that social class cannot be what impedes most disadvantaged students.

Yet the success of some lower-class students proves nothing about the power of schools to close the achievement gap. In every social group, there are low achievers and high achievers alike. On average, the achievement of low-income students is below the average achievement of middle-class students, but there are always some middle-class students who achieve below typical low-income levels. Similarly, some low-income students achieve above typical middle-class levels. Demography is not destiny, but students' family characteristics are a powerful influence on their relative average achievement.

Widely repeated accounts of schools that somehow elicit consistently high achievement from lower-class children almost always turn out, upon examination, to be flawed. In some cases, these "schools that beat the odds" are highly selective, enrolling only the most able or most motivated lower-class children. In other cases, they are not truly lower-class schools—for example, a school enrolling children who qualify for subsidized lunches because their parents are graduate students living on low stipends. In other cases, such schools define high achievement at such a low level that all students can reach it, despite big gaps that remain at more meaningful levels.

It seems plausible that if some children can defy the demographic odds, all children can, but that belief reflects a reasoning whose naiveté we easily recognize in other policy areas. In human affairs where multiple causation is typical, causes are not disproved by exceptions. Tobacco firms once claimed that smoking does not cause cancer because some people smoke without getting cancer. We now consider such reasoning specious. We do not suggest that alcoholism does not cause child or spousal abuse because not all alcoholics are abusers. We understand that because no single cause is rigidly deterministic, some people can smoke or drink to excess without harm. But we also understand that, on average, these behaviors are dangerous. Yet despite such understanding, quite sophisticated people often proclaim that the success of some poor children proves that social disadvantage does not cause low achievement.

Partly, our confusion stems from failing to examine the concrete ways that social class actually affects learning. Describing these may help to make their influence more obvious—and may make it more obvious why the achievement gap can be substantially narrowed only when school improvement is combined with social and economic reform.

The Reading Gap

Consider how parents of different social classes tend to raise children. Young children of educated parents are read to more consistently and are encouraged to read more to themselves when they are older. Most children whose parents have college degrees are read to daily before they begin kindergarten, but few children whose parents have only a high school diploma or less benefit from daily reading. And, white children are more likely than black children to be read to in their prekindergarten years.

From Richard Rothstein, "Class and the Classroom: Even the Best Schools Can't Close the Race Achievement Gap," *American School Board Journal,* 191, no. 10, October 2004. Reprinted by permission.

A 5-year-old who enters school recognizing some words and who has turned the pages of many stories will be easier to teach than one who has rarely held a book. The second child can be taught, but with equally high expectations and effective teaching, the first will be more likely to pass an age-appropriate reading test than the second. So the achievement gap begins.

If a society with such differences wants all children, irrespective of social class, to have the same chance to achieve academic goals, it should find ways to help lower-class children enter school having the same familiarity with books as middle-class children have. This requires rethinking the institutional settings in which we provide early childhood care, beginning in infancy.

Some people acknowledge the impact of such differences but find it hard to accept that good schools should have so difficult a time overcoming them. This would be easier to understand if Americans had a broader international perspective on education. Class backgrounds influence relative achievement everywhere. The inability of schools to overcome the disadvantage of less-literate homes is not a peculiar American failure but a universal reality. The number of books in students' homes, for example, consistently predicts their test scores in almost every country. Turkish immigrant students suffer from an achievement gap in Germany, as do Algerians in France, as do Caribbean, African, Pakistani, and Bangladeshi pupils in Great Britain, and as do Okinawans and low-caste Buraku in Japan.

An international reading survey of 15-year-olds, conducted in 2000, found a strong relationship in almost every nation between parental occupation and student literacy. The gap between the literacy of children of the highest-status workers (such as doctors, professors, and lawyers) and the lowest-status workers (such as waiters and waitresses, taxi drivers, and mechanics) was even greater in Germany and the United Kingdom than it was in the United States.

After reviewing these results, a U.S. Department of Education summary concluded that "most participating countries do not differ significantly from the United States in terms of the strength of the relationship between socioeconomic status and literacy in any subject." Remarkably, the department published this conclusion at the same time that it was guiding a bill through Congress—the No Child Left Behind Act—that demanded every school in the nation abolish social class differences in achievement within 12 years.

Urging less-educated parents to read to children can't fully compensate for differences in school readiness. Children who see parents read to solve their own problems or for entertainment are more likely to want to read themselves. Parents who bring reading material home from work demonstrate by example to children that reading is not a segmented burden but a seamless activity that bridges work and leisure. Parents who read to children but don't read for themselves send a different message.

How parents read to children is as important as whether they do, and an extensive literature confirms that more educated parents read aloud differently. When working-class parents read aloud, they are more likely to tell children to pay attention without interruptions or to sound out words or name letters. When they ask children about a story, the questions are more likely to be factual, asking for names of objects or memory of events.

Parents who are more literate are more likely to ask questions that are creative, interpretive, or connective, such as, "What do you think will happen next?" "Does that remind you of what we did yesterday?" Middle-class parents are more likely to read aloud to have fun, to start conversations, or as an entree to the world outside. Their children learn that reading is enjoyable and are more motivated to read in school.

The Conversation Gap

There are stark class differences not only in how parents read but in how they converse. Explaining events in the broader world to children at the dinner table, for example, may have as much of an influence on test scores as early reading itself. Through such conversations, children develop vocabularies and become familiar with contexts for reading in school. Educated parents are more likely to engage in such talk and to begin it with infants and toddlers, conducting pretend conversations long before infants can understand the language.

Typically, middle-class parents ask infants about their needs, then provide answers for the children. ("Are you ready for a nap now? Yes, you are, aren't you?") Instructions are more likely to be given indirectly: "You don't want to make so much noise, do you?" This kind of instruction is really an invitation for a child to work through the reasoning behind an order and to internalize it. Middle-class parents implicitly begin academic instruction for infants with such indirect guidance.

Yet such instruction is quite different from what policy-makers nowadays consider "academic" for young children: explicit training in letter and number recognition, letter-sound correspondence, and so on. Such drill in basic skills can be helpful but is unlikely to close the social class gap in learning.

Soon after middle-class children become verbal, their parents typically draw them into adult conversations so the children can practice expressing their own opinions. Being included in adult conversations this early develops a sense of entitlement in children; they feel comfortable addressing adults as equals and without deference. Children who ask for reasons, rather than accepting assertions on adult authority, develop intellectual skills upon which later academic success in school will rely. Certainly, some lower-class children have such skills and some middle-class children lack them. But, on average, a sense of entitlement is based on one's social class.

Parents whose professional occupations entail authority and responsibility typically believe more strongly that they can affect their environments and solve problems. At work, they explore alternatives and negotiate compromises. They naturally express these personality traits at home when they design activities in which children figure out solutions for themselves. Even the youngest middle-class children practice traits that make academic success more likely when they negotiate what to wear or to eat. When middle-class parents give orders, the parents are more likely to explain why the rules are reasonable.

But parents whose jobs entail following orders or doing routine tasks show less sense of efficacy. They are less likely to encourage their children to negotiate over clothing or food and more likely to instruct them by giving directions without extended discussion. Following orders, after all, is how they themselves behave at work. Their children are also more likely to be fatalistic about obstacles they face, in and out of school.

Middle-class children's self-assurance is enhanced in after-school activities that sometimes require large fees for enrollment and almost always require parents to have enough free time and resources to provide transportation. Organized sports, music, drama, and dance programs build self-confidence and discipline in middle-class children. Lower-class parents find the fees for such activities more daunting, and transportation may also be more of a problem. Organized athletic and artistic activities may not be available in their neighborhoods, so lower-class children's sports are more informal and less confidence-building, with less opportunity to learn teamwork and self-discipline. For children with greater self-confidence, unfamiliar school challenges can be exciting. These children, who are more likely to be from middle-class homes, are more likely to succeed than those who are less self-confident.

Homework exacerbates academic differences between these two groups of children because middle-class parents are more likely to help with homework. Yet homework would increase the achievement gap even if all parents were able to assist. Parents from different social classes supervise homework differently. Consistent with overall patterns of language use, middle-class parents—especially those whose own occupational habits require problem solving—are more likely to assist by posing questions that break large problems down into smaller ones and that help children figure out correct answers. Lower-class parents are more likely to guide children with direct instructions. Children from both classes may go to school with completed homework, but middle-class children are more likely to gain in intellectual power from the exercise than lower-class children.

Twenty years ago, Betty Hart and Todd Risley, two researchers from the University of Kansas, visited families from different social classes to monitor the conversations between parents and toddlers. Hart and Risley found that, on average, professional parents spoke more than 2,000 words per hour to their children, working-class parents spoke about 1,300, and welfare mothers spoke about 600. So by age 3, the children of professionals had vocabularies that were nearly 50 percent greater than those of working-class children and twice as large as those of welfare children.

Deficits like these cannot be made up by schools alone, no matter how high the teachers' expectations. For all children to achieve the same goals, the less advantaged would have to enter school with verbal fluency that is similar to the fluency of middle-class children.

The Kansas researchers also tracked how often parents verbally encouraged children's behavior and how often they reprimanded their children. Toddlers of professionals got an average of six encouragements per reprimand. Working-class children had two. For welfare children, the ratio was reversed—an average of one encouragement for two reprimands. Children whose initiative was encouraged from a very early age are more likely, on average, to take responsibility for their own learning.

The Role Model Gap

Social class differences in role modeling also make an achievement gap almost inevitable. Not surprisingly, middle-class professional parents tend to associate with, and be friends with, similarly educated professionals. Working-class parents have fewer professional friends. If parents and their friends perform jobs requiring little academic skill, their children's images of their own futures are influenced. On average, these children must struggle harder to motivate themselves to achieve than children who assume, on the basis of their parents' social circle, that the only roles are doctor, lawyer, teacher, social worker, manager, administrator, or businessperson.

Even disadvantaged children usually say they plan to attend college. College has become such a broad rhetorical goal that black eighth-graders tell surveyors they expect to earn college degrees as often as white eighth-graders do. But despite these intentions, fewer black than white eighth-graders actually graduate from high school four years later; fewer enroll in college the following year; and fewer still persist to get bachelor's degrees.

This discrepancy is not due simply to the cost of college. A bigger reason is that while disadvantaged students say they plan to go to college, they don't feel as much parental, community, or peer pressure to take the courses or to get the grades they need to become more attractive to college admission offices. Lower-class parents say they expect children to get good grades, but they are less likely to enforce these expectations, for example with rewards or punishments. Teachers and counselors can stress doing well in school to lower-class children, but such lessons compete with children's own self-images, formed early in life and reinforced daily at home.

As John Ogbu and others have noted, a culture of underachievement may help explain why even middle-class black children often don't do as well in school as white children from seemingly similar socioeconomic backgrounds. On average, middle-class black students don't study as hard as white middle-class students and blacks are more disruptive in class than whites from similar income strata.

This culture of underachievement is easier to understand than to cure. Throughout American history,

many black students who excelled in school were not rewarded for that effort in the labor market. Many black college graduates could find work only as servants or Pullman car porters or, in white-collar fields, as assistants to less-qualified whites. Many Americans believe that these practices have disappeared and that blacks and whites with similar test scores now have similar earnings and occupational status. But labor market discrimination continues to be a significant obstacle—especially for black males with high school educations.

Evidence for this comes from employment discrimination cases, such as the prominent 1996 case in which Texaco settled for a payment of $176 million to black employees after taped conversations of executives revealed pervasive racist attitudes, presumably not restricted to executives of this corporation alone. Other evidence comes from studies that find black workers with darker complexions have less success in the labor market than those with identical education, age, and criminal records but lighter complexions.

Still more evidence comes from studies in which blacks and whites with similar qualifications are sent to apply for job vacancies; the whites are typically more successful than the blacks. In one recent study where young, well-groomed, and articulate black and white college graduates, posing as high school graduates with identical qualifications, submitted applications for entry-level jobs, the applications of whites with criminal records got positive responses more often than the applications of blacks with no criminal records.

So the expectation of black students that their academic efforts will be less rewarded than the efforts of their white peers is rational for the majority of black students who do not expect to complete college. Some will reduce their academic efforts as a result. We can say that they should not do so and, instead, should redouble their efforts in response to the greater obstacles they face. But as long as racial discrimination persists, the average achievement of black students will be lower than the average achievement of whites, simply because many blacks (especially males) who see that academic effort has less of a payoff will respond rationally by reducing their effort.

The Health and Housing Gaps

Despite these big race and social class differences in child rearing, role modeling, labor market experiences, and cultural characteristics, the lower achievement of lower-class students is not caused by these differences alone. Just as important are differences in the actual social and economic conditions of children.

Overall, lower-income children are in poorer health. They have poorer vision, partly because of pre-natal conditions and partly because, even as toddlers, they watch too much television, so their eyes are poorly trained. Trying to read, their eyes may wander or have difficulty tracking print or focusing. A good part of the over-identification of learning disabilities for lower-class children may well be attributable to undiagnosed vision problems that could be easily treated by op-tometrists and for which special education placement then should be unnecessary.

Lower-class children have poorer oral hygiene, more lead poisoning, more asthma, poorer nutrition, less-adequate pediatric care, more exposure to smoke, and a host of other health problems. Because of less-adequate dental care, for example, they are more likely to have toothaches and resulting discomfort that affects concentration.

Because low-income children live in communities where landlords use high-sulfur home heating oil and where diesel trucks frequently pass en route to indus-trial and commercial sites, they are more likely to suf-fer from asthma, leading to more absences from school and, when they do attend, drowsiness from lying awake at night, wheezing. Recent surveys in Chicago and in New York City's Harlem community found one of every four children suffering from asthma, a rate six times as great as that for all children.

In addition, there are fewer primary-care physi-cians in low-income communities, where the physi-cian-to-population ratio is less than a third the rate in middle-class communities. For that reason, disadvan-taged children—even those with health insurance—are more likely to miss school for relatively minor prob-lems, such as common ear infections, for which mid-dle-class children are treated promptly.

Each of these well-documented social class differ-ences in health is likely to have a palpable effect on academic achievement; combined, their influence is probably huge.

The growing unaffordability of adequate housing for low-income families also affects achievement. Children whose families have difficulty finding stable housing are more likely to be mobile, and student mo-bility is an important cause of failing student perfor-mance. A 1994 government report found that 30 percent of the poorest children had attended at least

three different schools by third grade, while only 10 percent of middle-class children had done so. Black children were more than twice as likely as white chil-dren to change schools this often. It is hard to imagine how teachers, no matter how well trained, can be as ef-fective for children who move in and out of their class-rooms as they can be for those who attend regularly.

Differences in wealth are also likely to be impor-tant determinants of achievement, but these are usually overlooked because most analysts focus only on an-nual family income to indicate disadvantage. This makes it hard to understand why black students, on av-erage, score lower than whites whose family incomes are the same. It is easier to understand this pattern when we recognize that children can have similar fam-ily incomes but be of different economic classes. In any given year, black families with low income are likely to have been poor for longer than white families with similar income in that year.

White families are also likely to own far more as-sets that support their children's achievement than are black families at the same income level, partly because black middle-class parents are more likely to be the first generation in their families to have middle-class status. Although the median black family income is about two-thirds the median income of white families, the assets of black families are still only 12 percent those of whites. Among other things, this difference means that, among white and black families with the same middle-class incomes, the whites are more likely to have savings for college. This makes white chil-dren's college aspirations more practical, and therefore more commonplace.

Narrowing the Gaps

If we properly identify the actual social class charac-teristics that produce differences in average achieve-ment, we should be able to design policies that narrow the achievement gap. Certainly, improvement of in-structional practices is among these, but a focus on school reform alone is bound to be frustrating and ulti-mately unsuccessful. To work, school improvement must combine with policies that narrow the social and economic differences between children. Where these differences cannot easily be narrowed, school should be redefined to cover more of the early childhood, after-school, and summer times, when the disparate in-fluences of families and communities are now most powerful.

Because the gap is already huge at age 3, the most important new investment should no doubt be in early childhood programs. Prekindergarten classes for 4-year-olds are needed, but they barely begin to address the problem. The quality of early childhood programs is as important as the existence of such programs themselves. Too many low-income children are parked before television sets in low-quality day-care settings. To narrow the gap, care for infants and toddlers should be provided by adults who can create the kind of intellectual environment that is typically experienced by middle-class infants and toddlers. This requires professional caregivers and low child-adult ratios.

After-school and summer experiences for lower-class children, similar to programs middle-class children take for granted, would also be needed to narrow the gap. This does not mean remedial programs where lower-class children get added drill in math and reading. Certainly, remediation should be part of an adequate after-school and summer program, but only a part. The advantage that middle-class children gain after school and in summer comes from the self-confidence they acquire and the awareness of the world outside that they develop through organized athletics, dance, drama, museum visits, recreational reading, and other activities that develop inquisitiveness, creativity,

self-discipline, and organizational skills. After-school and summer programs can be expected to narrow the achievement gap only by attempting to duplicate such experiences.

Provision of health-care services to lower-class children and their families is also required to narrow the achievement gap. Some health services are relatively inexpensive, such as school vision and dental clinics. A full array of health services will cost more, but it cannot be avoided if we truly intend to raise the achievement of lower-class children.

The connection between social and economic disadvantage and an academic achievement gap has long been well known. Most educators, however, have avoided the obvious implication: Improving lower-class children's learning requires ameliorating the social and economic conditions of their lives. School board members—who are often the officials with the closest ties to public opinion—cannot afford to remain silent about the connection between school improvement and social reform. Calling attention to this link is not to make excuses for poor school performance. It is only to be honest about the social support schools require if they are to fulfill the public's expectation that the achievement gap will disappear.

Chartering and Bartering

Elite Education and Social Reproduction

CAROLINE HODGES PERSELL

PETER W. COOKSON, JR.

The continuation of power and privilege has been the subject of intense sociological debate. One recurring question is whether the system of mobility is open or whether relationships of power and privilege are reproduced from one generation to the next. If reproduction occurs, is it the reproduction of certain powerful and privileged families or groups (cf. Robinson, 1984)? Or, does it involve the reproduction of a structure of power and privilege which allows for replacement of some members with new recruits while preserving the structure?

The role of education in these processes has been the subject of much dispute. Researchers in the status

Copyright © 1986 by The Society for the Study of Social Problems. Reprinted from *Social Problems,* Vol. 33, No. 2, December 1985, pp. 114–129, by permission.

attainment tradition stress the importance for mobility of the knowledge and skills acquired through education thereby emphasizing the meritocratic and open basis for mobility (e.g., Alexander and Eckland, 1975; Alexander et al., 1975; Blau and Duncan, 1967; Haller and Portes, 1973; Otto and Haller, 1979; Kerckhoff, 1984; Sewell et al., 1969, 1970; Wilson and Portes, 1975). On the other hand, theorists such as Bowles and Gintis (1976) suggest education inculcates certain noncognitive personality traits which serve to reproduce the social relations within a class structure; thus they put more emphasis on non-meritocratic features in the educational process.

Collins (1979) also deals with non-meritocratic aspects when he suggests that educational institutions develop and fortify status groups, and that differently valued educational credentials protect desired market positions such as those of the professions. In a related vein, Meyer (1977) notes that certain organizational "charters" serve as "selection criteria" in an educational or occupational marketplace. Meyer defines "charter" as "the social definition of the products of [an] organization" (Meyer, 1970: 577). Charters do not need to be recognized formally or legally to operate in social life. If they exist, they would create structural limitations within a presumably open market by making some people eligible for certain sets of rights that are denied to other people.

Social observers have long noted that one particular set of schools is central to the reproduction and solidarity of a national upper class, specifically elite secondary boarding schools (Baltzell, 1958, 1964; Domhoff, 1967, 1970, 1983; Mills, 1956). As well as preparing their students for socially desirable colleges and universities, traditionally, such schools have been thought to build social networks among upper class scions from various regions, leading to adult business deals and marriages. Although less than one percent of the American population attends such schools, that one percent represents a strategic segment of American life that is seldom directly studied. Recently, Useem and Karabel (1984) reported that graduates of 14 elite boarding schools were much more likely than non-graduates to become part of the "inner circle" of Fortune 500 business leaders. This evidence suggests that elite schools may play a role in class reproduction.

Few researchers have gained direct access to these schools to study social processes bearing on social re-

production. The research reported here represents the first systematic study of elite secondary boarding schools and their social relations with another important institution, namely colleges and universities.

The results of this research illustrate Collins' view that stratification involves networks of "persons making bargains and threats . . . [and that] the key resource of powerful individuals is their ability to impress and manipulate a network of social contacts" (1979: 26). If such were the case, we would expect to find that upper class institutions actively develop social networks for the purpose of advancing the interests of their constituencies.

By focusing on the processes of social reproduction rather than individual attributes or the results of intergenerational mobility, our research differs from the approaches taken in both the status attainment and status allocation literature. Status attainment models focus on individual attributes and achievements, and allocation models examine structural supports or barriers to social mobility; yet neither approach explores the underlying processes. Status attainment models assume the existence of a relatively open contest system, while reproduction and allocation models stress that selection criteria and structural barriers create inequalities, limiting opportunities for one group while favoring another (Kerckhoff, 1976, 1984). Neither attainment nor allocation models show how class reproduction, selection criteria, or structural opportunities and impediments operate in practice.

Considerable evidence supports the view that structural limitations operate in the labor market (e.g., Beck et al., 1978; Bibb and Form, 1977; Stolzenberg, 1975) but, with the exception of tracking, little evidence has been found that similar structural limitations exist in education. Tracking systems create structural impediments in an open model of educational attainment (Oakes, 1985; Persell, 1977; Rosenbaum, 1976, 1980), although not all research supports this conclusion (e.g., Alexander et al., 1978; Heyns, 1974).

In this [reading] we suggest that there is an additional structural limitation in the key transition from high school to college. We explore the possibility that special organizational "charters" exist for certain secondary schools and that a process of "bartering" occurs between representatives of selected secondary schools and some college admissions officers. These processes have not been clearly identified by prior research on education and stratification, although there has been some previous research which leads in this direction.

Empirical Literature

Researchers of various orientations concur that differences between schools seem to have little bearing on student attainment (Averch et al., 1972; Jencks et al., 1972; Meyer, 1970, 1977). Indeed, Meyer (1977) suggests the most puzzling paradox in the sociology of American education is that while schools differ in structure and resources, they vary little in their effects because all secondary schools are assumed to have similar "charters." Meyer believes that no American high school is specially chartered by selective colleges in the way, for instance, that certain British Public Schools have been chartered by Oxford and Cambridge Universities. Instead, he suggests that "all American high schools have similar status rights, (and therefore) variations in their effects should be small" (Meyer, 1977: 60).

Kamens (1977: 217–218), on the other hand, argues that "schools symbolically redefine people and make them eligible for membership in societal categories to which specific sets of rights are assigned." The work of Alexander and Eckland (1977) is consistent with this view. These researchers found that students who attended high schools where the social status of the student body was high also attended selective colleges at a greater rate than did students at other high schools, even when individual student academic ability and family background were held constant (Alexander and Eckland, 1977). Their research and other work finding a relationship between curricular track placement and college attendance (Alexander et al., 1978; Alexander and McDill, 1976; Jaffe and Adams, 1970; Rosenbaum, 1976, 1980) suggest that differences between schools may affect stratification outcomes.

Research has shown that graduation from a private school is related to attending a four-year (rather than a two-year) college (Falsey and Heyns, 1984), attending a highly selective college (Hammack and Cookson, 1980), and earning higher income in adult life (Lewis and Wanner, 1979). Moreover, Cookson (1981) found that graduates of private boarding schools attended more selective colleges than did their public school counterparts, even when family background and Scholastic Aptitude Test (SAT) scores were held constant. Furthermore, some private colleges acknowledge the distinctive nature of certain secondary schools. Klitgaard (1985: Table 2.2) reports that students from private secondary schools generally had an advantage for admission to Harvard over public school graduates, even when their academic ratings were comparable. Karen (1985) notes that applications to Harvard from certain private boarding schools were placed in special colored dockets, or folders, to set them apart from other applications. Thus, they were considered as a distinct group. Not only did Harvard acknowledge the special status of certain schools by color-coding their applicants' folders, attendance at one of those schools provided an advantage for acceptance, even when parental background, grades, SATS, and other characteristics were controlled (Karen, 1985).

Networks and the Transmission of Privilege

For these reasons we believe it is worth investigating whether certain secondary schools have special organizational charters, at least in relation to certain colleges. If they do, the question arises, how do organizational charters operate? Network analysts suggest that "the pattern of ties in a network provides significant opportunities and constraints because it affects the relative access of people and institutions to such resources as information, wealth and power" (Wellman, 1981: 3). Furthermore, "because of their structural location, members of a social system differ greatly in their access to these resources" (Wellman, 1981: 30). Moreover, network analysts have suggested that class-structured networks work to preserve upper class ideology, consciousness, and life style (see for example Laumann, 1966: 132–36).

We expect that colleges and secondary schools have much closer ties than has previously been documented. Close networks of personal relationships between officials at certain private schools and some elite colleges transform what is for many students a relatively standardized, bureaucratic procedure into a process of negotiation. As a result, they are able to communicate more vital information about their respective needs, giving selected secondary school students an inside track to gaining acceptance to desired colleges. We call this process "bartering."

Sample and Data

Baltzell (1958, 1964) noted the importance of elite secondary boarding schools for upper class solidarity.

However, he was careful to distinguish between those boarding schools that were truly socially elite and those that had historically served somewhat less affluent and less powerful families. He indicates that there is a core group of eastern Protestant schools that "set the pace and bore the brunt of criticism received by private schools for their so-called 'snobbish,' 'undemocratic' and even 'un-American' values" (Baltzell, 1958: 307–308). These 16 schools are: Phillips (Andover) Academy (MA), Phillips Exeter Academy (NH), St. Paul's School (NH), St. Mark's School (MA), Groton School (MA), St. George's School (RI), Kent School (CT), The Taft School (CT), The Hotchkiss School (CT), Choate Rosemary Hall (CT), Middlesex School (MA), Deerfield Academy (MA), The Lawrenceville School (NJ), The Hill School (PA), The Episcopal High School (VA), and Woodberry Forest School (VA). We refer to the schools on Baltzell's list as the "select 16."[1]

In 1982 and 1983, we visited a representative sample of 12 of the select 16 schools. These 12 schools reflect the geographic distribution of the select 16 schools. In this time period we also visited 30 other "leading" secondary boarding schools drawn from the 1981 *Handbook of Private Schools'* list of 289 "leading" secondary boarding schools. This sample is representative of leading secondary boarding schools nationally in location, religious affiliation, size, and the sex composition of the student body. These schools are organizationally similar to the select 16 schools in offering only a college preparatory curriculum, in being incorporated as non-profit organizations, in their faculty/student ratios, and in the percent of boarders who receive financial aid. They differ somewhat with respect to sex composition, average size, the sex of their heads, and number of advanced placement courses (see Table 1). However, the key difference between the select 16 schools and the other "leading" schools is that the former are more socially elite than the latter. For instance, in one of the select 16 boarding schools in 1982, 40 percent of the current students' parents were listed in *Social Register.*[2]

All 42 schools were visited by one or both of the authors. Visits lasted between one and five days and included interviews with administrators, teachers and students. Most relevant to this study were the lengthy interviews with the schools' college advisors. These interviews explored all aspects of the college counseling process, including the nature and content of the advisors' relationships with admissions officers at various colleges. At a representative sample of six of the select 16 schools and a representative sample of 13 of the other "leading" schools a questionnaire was administered to seniors during our visits.[3] The questionnaire contained more than 50 items and included questions on parental education, occupation, income, number of

TABLE 1 Comparison of Population and Two Samples of Boarding Schools

	Total Population (N = 289)	**Other Boarding School Sample** (N = 30)	**Select 16 Sample** (N = 12)
Percent with college preparatory curriculum	100	100	100
Percent with no religious affiliation	65	70	67
Percent incorporated, not-for-profit	83	90	83
Average faculty/student ratio	0.17	0.15	0.15
Average percent of boarders aided	15	16	18
Percent of schools which are all-boys	28	17	33
Percent of schools which are all-girls	17	28	0
Percent coeducational schools	55	55	67
Percent with male heads	92	73	100
Average number of advanced courses	3.5	4.8	6.7
Average size	311	322	612

Note: Computed from data published in the *Handbook of Private Schools* (1981).

books in the home, family travel, educational legacies as well as many questions on boarding school life and how students felt about their experiences in school. Overall, student survey and school record data were collected on 687 seniors from the six select 16 schools and 658 seniors from other leading schools. Although not every piece of data was available for every student, we did obtain 578 complete cases from six select 16 schools and 457 cases from ten leading schools.[4] School record data included student grade point averages, Scholastic Aptitude Test (SAT) scores, class rank, names of colleges to which students applied, names of colleges to which students were accepted, and names of colleges students will attend. This material was supplied by the schools after the seniors graduated, in the summer or fall of 1982 and 1983. With this population actual enrollment matches school reports with high reliability. The record data have been linked with questionnaire data from the seniors and with various characteristics of the college. The colleges students planned to attend, were coded as to academic selectivity, Ivy League, and other characteristics not analyzed here.[5]

Chartering

Historical evidence shows that the select 16 schools have had special charters in relation to Ivy League colleges in general, and Harvard, Yale, and Princeton in particular. In the 1930s and 1940s, two-thirds of all graduates of 12 of the select 16 boarding schools attended Harvard, Yale, or Princeton (Karabel, 1984). But, by 1973, this share had slipped noticeably to an average of 21 percent, although the rate of acceptance between schools ranged from 51 percent to 8 percent (Cookson and Persell, 1978: Table 4). In the last half century, then, the proportion of select 16 school graduates who attended Harvard, Yale or Princeton dropped substantially.

This decrease was paralleled by an increase in the competition for admission to Ivy League colleges. According to several college advisors at select 16 boarding schools, 90 percent of all applicants to Harvard in the 1940s were accepted as were about half of those in the early 1950s. In 1982, the national acceptance rate for the eight Ivy League schools was 26 percent, although it was 20 percent or less at Harvard, Yale and Princeton (*National College Data Bank,* 1984).

The pattern of Ivy League college admissions has changed during this time. Ivy League colleges have

begun to admit more public school graduates. Before World War II at Princeton, for example, about 80 percent of the entering freshmen came from private secondary schools (Blumberg and Paul, 1975: 70). In 1982, 34 percent of the freshman class at Harvard, 40 percent of Yale freshmen, and 40 percent of Princeton freshmen were from nonpublic high schools (*National College Data Bank,* 1984).

This shift in college admissions policy, combined with increased financial aid and an inflationary trend in higher education that puts increased emphasis on which college one attends, contributes to the large number of applications to certain colleges nationally. Thus, while in the past decade the number of college age students has declined, the number of students applying to Ivy League colleges has increased (Mackay-Smith, 1985; Maeroff, 1984; Winerip, 1984).

In view of these historical changes, is there any evidence that the select 16 schools still retain special charters in relation to college admissions? When four pools of applications to the Ivy League colleges are compared, the acceptance rate is highest at select 16 schools, followed by a highly selective public high school, other leading boarding schools, and finally the entire national pool of applications (Table 2).[6]

While we do not have comparable background data on all the applicants from these various pools, we do know that the students in the highly selective public high school have among the highest academic qualifications in the country.[7] Their combined SAT scores, for example, average at least 150 points higher than those of students at the leading boarding schools. On that basis they might be expected to do considerably better than applicants from boarding schools: which they do at some colleges but not at Harvard, Yale or Princeton.

The most revealing insights into the operation of special charters, however, are provided by a comparison between select 16 boarding schools and other leading boarding schools—the most similar schools and the ones on which we have the most detailed data.

Students from select 16 schools apply to somewhat different colleges than do students from other leading boarding schools. Select 16 school students were much more likely to apply to one or more of the eight Ivy League and at least one of the other highly selective colleges than were students from other leading boarding schools (Table 3). Among those who applied, select 16 students were more likely to be accepted than were students from other boarding schools, and, if accepted, they were slightly more likely to attend.

TABLE 2   Percent of Applications That Were Accepted at Ivy League Colleges from Four Pools of Applications

College Name	Select 16 Boarding Schools[1] (1982–83)	Other Leading Boarding Schools[2] (1982–83)	Selective Public High School[3] (1984)	National Group of Applicants[4] (1982)
Brown University				
Percent accepted	35	20	28	22
Number of applications	95	45	114	11,854
Columbia University				
Percent accepted	66	29	32	41
Number of applications	35	7	170	3,650
Cornell University				
Percent accepted	57	36	55	31
Number of applications	65	25	112	17,927
Dartmouth College				
Percent accepted	41	21	41	22
Number of applications	79	33	37	8,313
Harvard University				
Percent accepted	38	28	20	17
Number of applications	104	29	127	13,341
Princeton University				
Percent accepted	40	28	18	18
Number of applications	103	40	109	11,804
University of Pennsylvania				
Percent accepted	45	32	33	36
Number of applications	40	19	167	11,000
Yale University				
Percent accepted	40	32	15	20
Number of applications	92	25	124	11,023
Overall percent accepted	42	27	30	26
Total number of applications	613	223	960	88,912

Notes:
[1]Based on school record data on applications of 578 seniors.
[2]Based on school record data on the applications of 457 seniors.
[3]Based on data published in the school newspaper.
[4]Based on data published in the *National College Data Bank* (1984).

Before we can conclude that these differences are due to a school charter, we need to control for parental SES[8] and student SAT scores.[9] This analysis is shown in Table 4. One striking finding here is the high rate of success enjoyed by boarding school students in general. At least one-third and as many as 92 percent of the students in each cell of Table 4 are accepted. Given that the average freshman combined SAT score is more than 1175 at these colleges and universities, it is par-

ticularly notable that such a large proportion of those with combined SAT scores of 1050 or less are accepted.

In general, high SAT scores increase chances of acceptance, but the relationship is somewhat attenuated under certain conditions. Students with low SAT scores are more likely to be accepted at highly selective colleges if they have higher SES backgrounds, especially if they attend a select 16 school. These students seem to

TABLE 3 Boarding School Students' College Application, Chances of Acceptance, and Plans to Attend

	Ivy League Colleges % (N)	Highly Selective Colleges % (N)
A. Percent of boarding school samples who applied		
Select 16 boarding schools	61 (353)	87 (502)
Other leading boarding schools	28 (129)	61 (279)
B. Percent of applicants who were accepted		
Select 16 boarding schools	54 (191)	84 (420)
Other leading boarding schools	36 (47)	64 (178)
C. Percent of acceptees who plan to attend		
Select 16 boarding schools	79 (151)	81 (340)
Other leading boarding schools	53 (25)	77 (137)

have relatively high "floors" placed under them, since two thirds of those from select 16 schools and more than half of those from other schools were accepted by one of the most selective colleges.[10]

The most successful ones of all are relatively low SES students with the highest SATs attending select 16 schools—92 percent of whom were accepted. Students from relatively modest backgrounds appear to receive a "knighting effect" by attending a select 16 school. Thus, select 16 schools provide mobility for some individuals from relatively less privileged backgrounds. To a considerable degree all students with high SATs, regardless of their SES, appear to be "turbo-charged" by attending a select 16

school compared to their counterparts at other leading schools.

At every level of SATs and SES, students' chances of acceptance increase if they attend a select 16 school. Such a finding is consistent with the argument that a chartering effect continues to operate among elite educational institutions. The historical shifts toward admitting more public school students on the part of Ivy League colleges and the increased competition for entry, described above, have meant that more effort has been required on the part of select 16 schools to retain an advantage for their students. We believe that certain private boarding schools have buttressed their charters by an increasingly active bartering operation.

TABLE 4 Percent of Students Who Applied to the Most Highly Selective Colleges Who Were Accepted, SAT Scores, SES, and School Type Held Constant

	Student Combined SAT Scores					
	High (1580–1220)		*Medium (1216–1060)*		*Low (1050–540)*	
Student Socioeconomic Status	*Select 16 Schools % (N)*	*Other Leading Boarding Schools % (N)*	*Select 16 Schools % (N)*	*Other Leading Boarding Schools % (N)*	*Select 16 Schools % (N)*	*Other Leading Boarding Schools % (N)*
High	87 (93)	70 (33)	80 (73)	64 (36)	65 (34)	53 (30)
Medium	89 (100)	71 (28)	85 (66)	76 (46)	44 (18)	35 (51)
Low	92 (72)	72 (25)	78 (51)	69 (32)	55 (33)	33 (49)

Note: Based on student questionnaires and school record data on 1035 seniors for whom complete data were available.

Bartering

Normally, we do not think of the college admissions process as an arena for bartering. It is assumed that colleges simply choose students according to their own criteria and needs. Few students and no high schools are thought to have any special "leverage" in admissions decisions. Our research revealed, however, that select 16 boarding schools—perhaps because of their perennial supply of academically able and affluent students—can negotiate admissions cases with colleges. The colleges are aware that select 16 schools attract excellent college prospects and devote considerable attention to maintaining close relationships with these schools, especially through the college admissions officers. Secondary school college advisors actively "market" their students within a context of tremendous parental pressure and increasing competition for admission to elite colleges.

Select 16 College Advisors and Ivy League Admissions Directors: The Old School Tie

Of the 11 select 16 school college advisors on whom data were available, 10 were graduates of Harvard, Yale, or Princeton. Of the 23 other leading boarding school college advisors on whom data were available, only three were Ivy League graduates, and none of them was from Harvard, Yale, or Princeton. College advisors are overwhelmingly white men. At the select 16 schools only one (an acting director) was a woman, and at other schools five were women. Some college advisors have previously worked as college admissions officers. Their educational and social similarity to college admissions officers may facilitate the creation of social ties and the sharing of useful information. Research shows that the exchange of ideas most frequently occurs between people who share certain social attributes (Rogers and Kincaid, 1981).

College advisors at select 16 schools tend to have long tenures—15 or more years is not unusual. On the other hand, college advisors at other schools are more likely to have assumed the job recently. A college advisor at one select 16 school stressed the "importance of continuity on both sides of the relationship." Thus, it is not surprising that select 16 schools hold on to their college advisors.

Select 16 college advisors have close social relationships with each other and with elite college admissions officers that are cemented through numerous face-to-face meetings each year. All of the select 16

schools are on the east coast, whereas only 70 percent of the other leading boarding schools are in that region. However, even those leading boarding schools on the east coast lack the close relationships with colleges that characterize the select 16 schools. Thus, geography alone does not explain these relationships.

The college advisors at most of the boarding schools we studied have personally visited a number of colleges around the country. Boarding schools often provide college advisors with summer support for systematic visits, and a number of geographically removed colleges offer attractive incentives, or fully paid trips to their region (e.g., Southern California). These trips often take place during bitter New England winters, and include elegant food and lodging as well as a chance to see colleges and meet admissions officers.

However, the college advisors at select 16 schools are likely to have visited far more schools (several mentioned that they had personally visited 60 or 70 schools) than college advisors at other schools (some of whom had not visited any). They are also much more likely to visit regularly the most selective and prestigious colleges.[11]

Numerous college admissions officers also travel to these boarding schools to interview students and meet the college advisors. The select 16 schools have more college admissions officers visit than do other schools: more than 100 in any given academic year is not unusual. College advisors have drinks and dinner with selected admissions officers, who often stay overnight on campus. As one college advisor noted, "We get to establish a personal relationship with each other." Moreover, Ivy League colleges bring students from select 16 schools to their campus to visit for weekends.

By knowing each other personally, college advisors and admissions officers "develop a relationship of trust," so that they can evaluate the source as well as the content of phone calls and letters. We observed phone calls between college advisors and admissions officers when we were in their offices. Several college advisors mentioned, "It helps to know personally the individual you are speaking or writing to," and one college advisor at a select 16 school said, "I have built up a track record with the private colleges over the years."

Virtually all of the select 16 school college advisors indicated that in the spring—before colleges have finished making their admissions decisions—they take their application files and drive to elite colleges to discuss "their list." They often sit in on the admissions deliberations while they are there. In contrast, the other schools' college advisors generally did not make such trips. Such actions suggest the existence of strong social networks between select 16 school college advisors and elite college admissions officers.

How the System Works: "Fine Tuning" the Admissions Process

Bartering implies a reciprocal relationship, and select 16 schools and elite colleges have a well-developed system of information exchange. Both sides have learned to cooperate to their mutual benefit. College advisors try to provide admissions officers with as much information about their students as possible to help justify the acceptance of a particular applicant. Select 16 schools have institutionalized this process more than other schools. The most professional operation we found was in a select 16 school where about half the graduating class goes to Harvard, Yale or Princeton. There, the college advisor interviews the entire faculty on each member of the senior class. He tape records all their comments and has them transcribed. This produces a "huge confidential dossier which gives a very good sense of where each student is." In addition, housemasters and coaches write reports. Then the college advisor interviews each senior, dictating notes after each interview. After assimilating all of these comments on each student, the college advisor writes his letter of recommendation, which he is able to pack with corroborative details illustrating a candidate's strengths. The thoroughness, thought, and care that goes into this process insures that anything and everything positive that could be said about a student is included, thereby maximizing his or her chances for a favorable reception at a college.[12]

Information also flows from colleges to the secondary schools. By sitting in on the admissions process at colleges like Harvard, Princeton, and Yale, select 16 school college advisors say they "see the wealth and breadth of the applicant pool." They get a first-hand view of the competition their students face. They also obtain a sense of how a college "puts its class together," which helps them to learn strategies for putting forward their own applicants.

By observing and participating in the admissions process, select 16 school college advisors gain an insider's view of a college's selection process. This insider's knowledge is reflected in the specific figures select 16 advisors mentioned in our conversations with

them. One select 16 school college advisor said that a student has "two and one half times as good a chance for admission to Harvard if his father went there than if he did not." Another said, "while 22 percent in general are admitted to Ivy League colleges, 45 percent of legacies are admitted to Ivy League colleges." In both cases, they mentioned a specific, quantified statement about how being a legacy affected their students' admissions probabilities.[13] Similarly, several select 16 school college advisors mentioned the percentages of the freshman class at Harvard and Yale that were from public and private schools, and one even mentioned how those percentages have changed since 1957. College advisors at other schools do not lace their conversations with as many specific figures nor do they belong to the special organization that some of the select 16 schools have formed to share information and strategies.

The special interest group these schools have formed is able to negotiate with the colleges to their students' advantage. For instance, the college advisors explained that select 16 school students face greater competition than the average high school student and carry a more rigorous course load.[14] Therefore, this group persuaded the colleges that their students should not receive an absolute class rank, but simply an indication of where the students stand by decile or quintile. Colleges may then put such students in a "not ranked" category or report the decile or quintile rank. No entering student from such a secondary school is clearly labeled as the bottom person in the class. To our knowledge, only select 16 schools have made this arrangement.

Armed with an insider's knowledge of a college's desires, select 16 school college advisors seek to present colleges with the most appropriate candidates. As one select 16 school college advisor said, "I try to shape up different applicant pools for different colleges," a process that has several components. First, college advisors try to screen out hopeless prospects, or as one tactfully phrased it, "I try to discourage unproductive leads." This is not always easy because, as one said, "Certain dreams die hard." College advisors in other schools were more likely to say that they never told students where they should or should not apply.

One select 16 school requires students to write a "trial college essay" that helps the college advisor ascertain "what kind of a student this is." From the essay he can tell how well students write, determine whether they follow through and do what they need to do on time, and learn something about their personal and family background. With faculty and student comments in hand, college advisors can begin to assemble their applicant pools. One thing they always want to learn is which college is a student's first choice, and why. This is useful information when bartering with colleges.

Some college advisors are quite frank when bartering, for example, the select 16 college advisor who stressed, "I am candid about a student to the colleges, something that is not true at a lot of schools where they take an advocacy position in relation to their students. . . . We don't sell damaged goods to the colleges." College advisors at other schools did not define their role as one of weeding out candidates prior to presenting them to colleges, although they may do this as well. It would seem then that part of the gate-keeping process of admission to college is occurring in select 16 secondary schools. College advisors, particularly those with long tenures at select 16 schools, seem quite aware of the importance of maintaining long-term credibility with colleges, since credibility influences how effectively they can work for their school in the future.

While the children of certain big donors (so-called "development cases") may be counseled with special care, in general the college advisors have organizational concerns that are more important than the fate of a particular student. Several select 16 school college advisors spoke with scorn about parents who see a rejection as the "first step in the negotiation." Such parents threaten to disrupt a delicate network of social relationships that link elite institutions over a considerable time span.

At the same time, college advisors try to do everything they can to help their students jump the admissions hurdle. One select 16 school college advisor said:

I don't see our students as having an advantage (in college admissions). We have to make the situation unequal. We do this by writing full summary reports on the students, by reviewing the applicants with the colleges several times during the year, and by traveling to the top six colleges in the spring. . . . [Those visits] are an advocacy proceeding on the side of the students. The colleges make their best decisions on our students and those from [another select 16 school] because they have the most information on these students.

Another select 16 college advisor said. "We want to be sure they are reading the applications of our students fairly, and we lobby for our students." A third se-

lect 16 college advisor made a similar statement, "When I drive to the [Ivy League] colleges, I give them a reading on our applicants. I let them know if I think they are making a mistake. There is a lobbying component here."

Select 16 college advisors do not stop with simply asking elite college admissions officers to reconsider a decision, however. They try to barter, and the colleges show they are open to this possibility when the college admissions officer says, "Let's talk about your group." One select 16 college advisor said he stresses to colleges that if his school recommends someone and he or she is accepted, that student will come. While not all colleges heed this warranty, some do.

One select 16 college advisor said, "It is getting harder than it used to be to say to an admissions officer, 'take a chance on this one,' especially at Harvard which now has so many more applications." But it is significant that he did not say that it was impossible. If all else fails in a negotiation, a select 16 college advisor said, "we lobby for the college to make him their absolute first choice on the waiting list." Such a compromise represents a chance for both parties to save face.

Most public high school counselors are at a distinct disadvantage in the bartering process because they are not part of the interpersonal network, do not have strategic information, and are thus unable to lobby effectively for their students. One select 16 advisor told us about a counselor from the Midwest who came to an Ivy League college to sit in on the admissions committee decision for his truly outstanding candidate—SATs in the 700s, top in his class, class president, and star athlete. The select 16 college advisor was also there, lobbying on behalf of his candidate—a nice undistinguished fellow (in the words of his advisor, "A good kid") with SATs in the 500s, middle of his class, average athlete, and no strong signs of leadership. After hearing both the counselors, the Ivy League college chose the candidate from the select 16 school. The outraged public school counselor walked out in disgust. Afterwards, the Ivy League college admissions officer said to the select 16 college advisor, "We may not be able to have these open meetings anymore." Even in the unusual case where a public school counselor did everything that a select 16 boarding school college advisor did, it was not enough to secure the applicant's admission. Despite the competitive environment that currently surrounds admission to elite colleges, the admissions officers apparently listen more closely to advisors from select 16 boarding schools than to public school counselors.

Conclusions and Implications

The graduates of certain private schools are at a distinct advantage when it comes to admission to highly selective colleges because of the special charters and highly developed social networks these schools possess. Of course, other factors are operating as well. Parental wealth (which is not fully tapped by a measure of SES based on education, occupation, and income), preference for the children of alumni, Advanced Placement (AP) coursework, sports ability especially in such scarce areas as ice hockey, crew or squash, and many other factors also influence the process of college admission. Elite boarding schools are part of a larger process whereby more privileged members of society transmit their advantages to their children. Attendance at a select 16 boarding school signals admissions committees that an applicant may have certain valuable educational and social characteristics.

Significantly, neither the families nor the secondary schools leave the college admissions process to chance or to formal bureaucratic procedures. Instead, they use personal connections to smooth the process, and there is reason to believe that those efforts affect the outcomes. The "knighting effect" of select 16 schools helps a few low SES, high SAT students gain admission to highly selective colleges, evidence of sponsored mobility for a few worthy youngsters of relatively humble origins. Our findings are consistent with Kamens' (1974) suggestion that certain schools make their students eligible for special social rights. Furthermore, the interaction between social background, SATs, and select 16 school attendance suggests that both individual ability and socially structured advantages operate in the school-college transition.

These results illustrate Collins' (1979) view that stratified systems are maintained through the manipulation of social contacts. They show one way that networks and stratification processes are interconnected. College access is only one aspect of the larger phenomenon of elite maintenance and reproduction. Elite boarding schools no doubt contribute as well to the social contacts and marriage markets of their graduates. What this instance shows is that reproduction is not a simple process. It involves family and group reproduction as well as some structural replacement with carefully screened new members. There is active personal

intervention in what is publicly represented as a meritocratic and open competition. The internal processes and external networks described here operate to construct class privileges as well as to transmit class advantages, thereby helping to reproduce structured stratification within society.

If this example is generalizable, we would expect that economically and culturally advantaged groups might regularly find or create specially chartered organizations and brokers with well-developed networks to help them successfully traverse critical junctures in their social histories. Such key switching points include the transition from secondary school to college, admission to an elite graduate or professional school, obtaining the right job, finding a mentor, gaining a medical residency at a choice hospital (Hall, 1947, 1948, 1949) getting a book manuscript published (Coser et al., 1982), having one's paintings exhibited at an art gallery or museum, obtaining a theatrical agent, having one's business considered for venture capital or bank support (Rogers and Larsen, 1984), being offered membership in an exclusive social club, or being asked to serve on a corporate or other board of directors (Useem, 1984).

In all of these instances, many qualified individuals seek desired, but scarce, social and/or economic opportunities. Truly open competition for highly desired outcomes leaves privileged groups vulnerable. Because the socially desired positions are finite at any given moment, processes that give an advantage to the members of certain groups work to limit the opportunities of individuals from other groups.[15] In these ways, dominant groups enhance their chances, at the same time that a few worthy newcomers are advanced, a process which serves to reproduce and legitimate a structure of social inequality.

Endnotes

We wish to thank E. Digby Baltzell, Steven Brint, Kevin Dougherty, Eliot Freidson, Kathleen Gerson, David Greenberg, Wolf Heydebrand, Herbert Menzel, John Meyer, Karen Miller, Richard R. Peterson, Edwin Schur, Susan Shapiro, Beth Stevens, and a number of anonymous reviewers for their thoughtful reactions to this paper.

1. Others besides Baltzell have developed lists of elite private schools, including Baird (1977), Domhoff (1967, 1970, 1983), and McLachlan (1970).
2. We were not able to compute the percent of students in *Social Register* for every school because most schools do not publish the names of their students.

Hence, we were not able to look their families up in *Social Register.* We do know that less than .000265 percent of American families are listed in *Social Register.* See Levine (1980) for an historical discussion of the social backgrounds of students at several of the select 16 schools.

3. We asked to give the student questionnaires at nine of the 12 select 16 schools and six of those nine schools agreed. At the other leading schools, we asked to give the questionnaires at 15 and 13 schools agreed.

4. Three leading schools did not supply the college data.

5. Following Astin et al. (1981: 7), we measured selectivity with the average SAT scores of the entering freshmen.

6. The entire national applicant pool includes the relatively more successful subgroups within it. If they were excluded, the national acceptance rate would be even lower.

7. Students admitted to this selective public high school must be recommended by their junior high school to take a competitive entrance exam, where they must score very well. The school was among the top five in the nation with respect to the number of National Merit Scholarships won by its students, and each year a number of students in the school win Westinghouse science prizes. This school was selected for purposes of comparison here because academically it is considered to be among the very top public schools in the nation. However, it does not have the social prestige of the select 16 boarding schools.

8. SES was measured by combining father's education, father's occupation, and family income into a composite SES score. These SES scores were then standardized for this population, and each student received a single standardized SES score.

9. The combined verbal and mathematics scores were used.

10. We performed separate analyses for boys and girls to see if sex was related to admission to a highly selective college when type of boarding school, SATs, and SES were held constant, and generally it was not. Girls who attend either select 16 or other leading boarding schools do as well: or better in their admission to college as do their male counterparts, with the single exception of girls at select 16 schools in the top third on their SATs and SES. In that particular group, 92 percent of the boys but only 77 percent of the girls were accepted at the most highly selective colleges. Since that is the only exception, boys and girls are discussed together in the text of the paper.

11. Our field visits and interviews with college advisors at two highly selective public high schools and three open admissions public high schools show that college advisors at even the most selective public high schools generally do not personally know the admissions officers at colleges, particularly at the most selective and Ivy League colleges, nor do they talk with them over the phone or in person prior to their admissions decisions.

12. Such a procedure requires considerable financial and personnel resources. Select 16 schools have more capital intensive and professional office services supporting their college admissions endeavor than other schools. Most of them have word processors, considerable professional staff, and ample secretarial and clerical help.

13. We did not ask students what colleges their parents attended so we could not control for college legacy in our analysis. Future research on the admissions process should do so.

14. One way select 16 schools establish their reputations as rigorous schools is through the numbers of their students who succeed on the Advanced Placement (AP) Exams given by the College Entrance Examination Board. Compared to other secondary schools, select 16 schools offer larger numbers of advanced courses (Table 1), encourage more students to take them, coach students very effectively on how to take the test, and maintain contacts with the people who design and read AP exams so that they know what is expected and can guide students accordingly. (See Cookson and Persell, 1985, for more discussion of these processes.) Other schools are much less likely than select 16 ones to have teachers who have graded AP exams or to know people who have helped to write the tests.

15. See Parkin (1979) for a discussion of social closure as exclusion and usurpation.

References

Alexander, Karl L., Martha Cook and Edward L. McDill 1978 "Curriculum tracking and educational stratification: some further evidence." American Sociological Review 43:47–66.

Alexander, Karl L. and Bruce K. Eckland 1975 "Contextual effects in the high school attainment process." American Sociological Review 40:402–16.

_____ 1977 "High school context and college selectivity: institutional constraints in educational stratification." Social Forces 56:166–88.

Alexander, Karl L., Bruce K. Eckland and Larry J. Griffin 1975 "The Wisconsin model of socioeconomic achievement: a replication." American Journal of Sociology 81:324–42.

Alexander, Karl L. and Edward L. McDill 1976 "Selection and allocation within schools: some causes and consequences of curriculum placement." American Sociological Review 41:963–80.

Astin, Alexander W., Margo R. King, and Gerald T. Richardson 1981 The American Freshman: National Norms for Fall 1981. Los Angeles: Laboratory for Research in Higher Education, University of California.

Averch, Harvey A., Steven J. Carroll, Theodore S. Donaldson, Herbert J. Kiesling, and John Pincus 1972 How Effective is Schooling? A Critical Review and Synthesis of Research Findings. Santa Monica, CA: The Rand Corporation.

Baird, Leonard L. 1977 The Elite Schools. Lexington, MA: Lexington Books.

Baltzell, E. Digby 1958 Philadelphia Gentlemen. New York: Free Press.

_____ 1964 The Protestant Establishment. New York: Random House.

Beck, E. M., Patrick M. Horan, and Charles M. Tolbert II 1978 "Stratification in a dual economy." American Sociological Review 43:704–20.

Bibb, Robert C. and William Form 1977 "The effects of industrial, occupational and sex stratification on wages in blue-collar markets." Social Forces 55:974–96.

Blau, Peter and Otis D. Duncan 1967 The American Occupational Structure. New York: Wiley.

Blumberg, Paul M. and P. W. Paul 1975 "Continuities and discontinuities in upper-class marriages." Journal of Marriage and the Family 37:63–77.

Bowles, Samuel and Herbert Gintis 1976 Schooling in Capitalist America. New York: Basic Books.

Collins, Randall 1979 The Credential Society. New York: Academic Press.

Cookson, Peter Willis, Jr. 1981 "Private secondary boarding school and public suburban high school graduation: an analysis of college attendance plans." Unpublished Ph.D. dissertation, New York University.

Cookson, Peter W., Jr. and Caroline Hodges Persell 1978 "Social structure and educational programs: a comparison of elite boarding schools and public education in the United States." Paper presented at the annual meeting of the American Sociological Association, San Francisco.

_____ 1985 Preparing for Power: America's Elite Boarding Schools. New York: Basic Books.

Coser, Lewis A., Charles Kadushin, and Walter W. Powell 1982 Books: The Culture & Commerce of Publishing. New York: Basic Books.

Domhoff, G. William 1967 Who Rules America? Englewood Cliffs: Prentice-Hall.

_____ 1970 The Higher Circles. New York: Vintage.

_____ 1983 Who Rules America Now? Englewood Cliffs: Prentice-Hall.

Falsey, Barbara and Barbara Heyns 1984 "The college channel: private and public schools reconsidered." Sociology of Education 57:111–22

Hall, Oswald 1946 "The informal organization of the medical profession." Canadian Journal of Economics and Political Science 12:30–41.

_____ 1948 "The stages of a medical career." American Journal of Sociology 53:327–36.

_____ 1949 "Types of medical career." American Journal of Sociology 55:243–53.

Haller, Archibald O. and Alejandro Portes 1973 "Status attainment processes." Sociology of Education 46:51–91.

Hammack, Floyd M. and Peter W. Cookson, Jr. 1980 "Colleges attended by graduates of elite secondary schools." The Educational Forum 44:483–90.

Handbook of Private Schools 1981 Boston: Porter Sargent Publishers, Inc.

Heyns, Barbara 1974 "Social selection and stratification within schools." American Journal of Sociology 79:1434–51.

Jaffe, Abraham and Walter Adams 1970 "Academic and socio-economic factors related to entrance and retention at two- and four-year colleges in the late 1960s." New York: Bureau of Applied Social Research, Columbia University.

Jencks, Christopher, Marshall Smith, Henry Acland, Mary Jo Bane, David Cohen, Herbert Gintis, Barbara Heyns, and Stephan Michelson 1972 Inequality. New York: Basic Books.

Kamens, David 1974 "Colleges and elite formation: the case of prestigious American colleges." Sociology of Education 47:354–78.

_____ 1977 "Legitimating myths and educational organization: the relationship between organizational ideology and formal structure." American Sociological Review 42:208– 19.

Karabel, Jerome 1984 "Status-group struggle, organizational interests, and the limits of institutional autonomy: the transformation of Harvard, Yale, and Princeton 1918–1940." Theory and Society 13:1–40.

Karen, David 1985 "Who gets into Harvard? Selection and exclusion." Unpublished Ph.D. dissertation. Department of Sociology, Harvard University.

Kerckhoff, Alan C. 1976 "The status attainment process: socialization or allocation?" Social Forces 55:368–81.

_____ 1984 "The current state or social mobility research." Sociology Quarterly 25:139–53.

Klitgaard, Robert 1985 Choosing Elites. New York: Basic Books.

Laumann, Edward O. 1966 Prestige and Association in an Urban Community: An Analysis of an Urban Stratification System. Indianapolis: Bobbs-Merrill.

Levine, Steven B. 1980 "The rise of American boarding schools and the development of a national upper class." Social Problems 28:63–94.

Lewis, Lionel S. and Richard A. Wanner 1979 "Private schooling and the status attainment process." Sociology of Education 52:99–112.

Mackay-Smith, Anne 1985 "Admissions crunch: top colleges remain awash in applicants despite a smaller pool." Wall Street Journal (April 2):1,14.

Maeroff, Gene I. 1984 "Top Eastern colleges report unusual rise in applications." New York Times (February 21):A1,C10.

McLachlan, James 1970 American Boarding Schools: A Historical Study. New York: Charles Scribner's Sons.

Meyer, John 1970 "The charter: Conditions of diffuse socialization in school." Pp. 564–78 in W. Richard Scott (ed.), Social Processes and Social Structure. New York: Holt, Rinehart.

_____ 1977 "Education as an institution." American Journal of Sociology 83:55–77.

Mills, C. Wright 1956 The Power Elite. London: Oxford University Press.

National College Data Bank 1984 Princeton: Peterson's Guides, Inc.

Oakes, Jeannie 1985 Keeping Track: How Schools Structure Inequality. New Haven: Yale University Press.

Otto, Luther B. and Archibald O. Haller 1979 "Evidence for a social psychological view of the status attainment process: four studies compared." Social Forces 57:887–914.

Parkin, Frank 1979 Marxism Class Theory: A Bourgeois Critique. New York: Columbia University Press.

Persell, Caroline Hodges 1977 Education and Inequality. New York: The Free Press.

Robinson, Robert V. 1984 "Reproducing class relations in industrial capitalism." American Sociological Review 49:182–96.

Rogers, Everett M. and D. Lawrence Kincaid 1981 Communications Networks: Toward a New Paradigm for Research. New York: The Free Press.

Rogers, Everett M. and Judith K. Larsen 1984 Silicon Valley Fever: The Growth of High-Tech Culture. New York: Basic Books.

Rosenbaum, James E. 1976 Making Inequality: The Hidden Curriculum of High School Tracking. New York: Wiley.

_____ 1980 "Track misperceptions and frustrated college plans: an analysis of the effects of tracks and track perceptions in the national longitudinal survey." Sociology of Education 53:74–88.

Sewell, William H., Archibald O. Haller, and Alejandro Portes 1969 "The educational and early occupational attainment process." American Sociological Review 34:82–91.

Sewell, William H., Archibald O. Haller, and George W. Ohlendorf 1970 "The educational and early occupational status achievement process: Replication and revision." American Sociological Review 35:1014–27.

Social Register 1984 New York: Social Register Association.

Stolzenberg, Ross M. 1975 "Occupations labor markets and the process of wage attainment." American Sociological Review 40:645–65.

Useem, Michael 1984 The Inner Circle: Large Corporations and the Rise of Business Political Activity in the U.S. and U.K. New York: Oxford University Press.

Wellman, Barry 1981 "Network analysis from method and metaphor to theory and substance." Working Paper Series 1B, Structural Analysis Programme, University of Toronto.

Wilson, Kenneth L. and Alejandro Portes 1975 "The Educational attainment process: Results from a national sample." American Journal of Sociology 81:343–63.

Winerip, Michael 1984 "Hot colleges and how they get that way." New York Times Magazine. (November 18):68ff.

College-for-All

Do Students Understand What College Demands?[3]

JAMES E. ROSENBAUM

Sociology has long tried to discover the ways disadvantaged backgrounds harm youth. While human capital theory in economics attributes such problems to deficiencies in individuals' ability or motivation, sociology looks at the ways societal factors block opportunity. However, reality is likely to be more complex. Societal factors do sometimes pose explicit barriers; but explicit barriers are relatively ineffective because they are so obviously unjust, readily seen, and easily attacked. Ambiguous opportunities and unclear requirements may be far more important in blocking mobility than explicit barriers (Cicourel and Kitsuse, 1963; Rosenbaum, 1978, 1989). Clark (1960) showed that the ambiguous mission of community colleges seemed to offer access to four-year colleges when, in fact, these institutions "cooled out" aspirations as students gradually realized that college was not appropriate for their abilities.

In the decades since Clark's study, community colleges have grown enormously. While four-year college enrollment roughly doubled between 1960 and 1990, public community college enrollment increased five-fold in the same period—from 200,000 to over 1,000,000 (U.S. Department of Health, Education, and Welfare, 1992, Table 169). In turn, college opportunities have dramatically increased. While 45.1% of high school graduates entered some postsecondary institution in 1960, over 62% did in 1993. Moreover, community colleges initiated open-admissions policies and remedial courses to reduce the academic barriers to college; and the Associate of Arts (AA) degree has increased in value in the labor market so that students do not need a BA to get an economic benefit from attending community college (Brint and Karabel, 1989; Grubb, 1992, 1993, 1995). Community colleges have increased access to an economically valued degree.

Have these changes created an easy route to college success, or do they merely confuse students so that they fail to prepare themselves appropriately? Studies since Clark's have continued to find substantial college attrition (Grubb, 1989) and have focussed on the factors that redirect students' plans (Karabel, 1986). Yet, rather than focus on the cooling-out process in community colleges, one must remember that "cooling out" is just the institutional mechanism for dealing with failure—not the original cause.

Clark took the term "cooling out" from Goffman's (1952) analysis of confidence swindles. The key to a swindle is to give "marks" confidence that they will gain a valuable reward at very little cost and then lure them to an "easy success" strategy. That is why a "mark" willingly hands over something of value to a swindler, and people pay for "snake oil" remedies that offer high expectations for a small price. Marks only realize that their expectations were mistaken at a later time, after the person who encouraged the expectation is no longer present.

This paper contends that the high level of community-college dropout arises because high schools offer vague promises of open opportunity for college but fail to specify the actual requirements for successful degree completion. Like Goffman's confidence schemes, students are promised college for very little effort. Lured by the prospect of easy success, students choose easy curricula and low efforts. Just as some high schools implicitly offer students an undemanding curriculum in return for nondisruptive behavior (Sedlak, Wheeler, Pullin, and Cusick, 1986), many high schools enlist students' cooperation by telling them that college is the only respectable goal and that it is easily attainable by all. Rather than community-college failure arising from an overt barrier in community colleges, the seeds of failure in community colleges may arise much earlier—when youth are still in high school.

In the current era, many high schools encourage the "college-for-all" norm which states that all students

From *Social Psychology of Education*, 2 (1): 55–80, 1997, "College for All: Do Students Understand What College Demands?" by James E. Rosenbaum, © 1997 Springer Science and Business Media. Reprinted with kind permission from Springer Science and Business Media.

can and should attend college but which fails to tell students what they must do to attain this goal (Rosenbaum, Miller, and Krei, 1996). The college-for-all norm (CFA) is a variant of "the contest mobility norm" which says that opportunity for upward mobility should always stay open (Turner, 1960). This norm encourages youth to retain ambitions of advancement as long as possible, but it ignores barriers that limit youths' careers (Rosenbaum, 1975, 1976, 1986).

Americans are rightly proud of the CFA norm. It discourages schools from tracking students prematurely, and it encourages high expectations in youth. It argues for better instruction in schools, especially schools serving low-income youth. Without this norm, society might give up on raising the educational achievement of the most disadvantaged youth.

While it is not meant to be deceptive, the CFA norm can inadvertently encourage a deception that hurts many youth, including the disadvantaged youth it is meant to help. The CFA norm encourages all students to plan on college regardless of their past achievement. To avoid discouraging students, the CFA norm avoids focussing on requirements; but, in the process, it fails to tell students what steps they should take and does not warn them when their low achievements make their college plans unlikely to be attained. While such encouragement helps younger children, it may mislead students in their later years of high school.

Thus, while 70.9% of high school seniors in the class of 1982 planned to get college degrees, half of 12th-grade students lacked basic 9th-grade math and verbal skills (Murnane and Levy, 1997), and only about half of college entrants completed a college degree (Resnick and Wirt, 1996). The completion rate from two-year colleges is even worse. For the 1980 graduates enrolled full time in two-year public colleges in October 1980, less than 40% (38.8%) completed any degree (AA or higher) by 1986, and the rates were only 15.2% for the substantial numbers (about 25%) who were enrolled part time (U.S. Department of Health, Education, and Welfare, 1992, Table 287). Students rarely attain their college plans. For the 1980 graduates who planned less than four years of college (but more than a certificate), less than 20% (19.9%) attained a college degree (AA or higher) in the next six years (U.S. Department of Health, Education, and Welfare, 1992, Table 286).

This has not always been true. The dropout rate from public two-year colleges increased sharply after 1972 (49.6% in 1980 vs. 36.0% in 1972, Grubb, 1989,

Table 2). One reason for these disappointing outcomes is that school officials do not warn students about potential problems. Rather than acting as gatekeepers as they did in earlier decades (Rosenbaum, 1976), guidance counselors now urge all students to attend college but rarely warn poorly prepared students that they will have difficulty completing a degree (Rosenbaum, Miller, and Krei, 1996). Rather than hurting students by posing obstacles to their plans, counselors may now be hurting students by not informing them of potential obstacles they will face later on.

Contrary to Karabel's (1986) interpretation of community colleges as institutions which mislead students, Goffman's model suggests that deception is earlier, more subtle, and often in a different location. Indeed, "marks" go along with a swindle because their hopes are initially "heated up" to unrealistic expectations, and "cooling out" is only done late in the process. Thus, rather than focus on the "cooling out" process, one needs to examine why youth have unrealistically high expectations—the precipitating conditions for why "cooling out" is required.

This paper asserts that information is central to this process. If high school students are informed that they are poorly prepared for community college, they can either increase their efforts to prepare themselves or revise their plans to be more realistic. In either case, "cooling out" is unneeded, and youths' plans will be less likely to fail.

High schools probably do not intentionally deceive students. Rather, many schools have well-intentioned practices of raising students' expectations; but these practices may have unintended consequences. High schools encourage college plans for all students, even poorly achieving students whose subsequent failure is highly predictable even before they enter community colleges. Yet, students do not anticipate their probable failure, and they do not take actions to prepare themselves for their goals.

Such a mechanism is more subtle than the one Karabel describes. Poor information allows many students to have high hopes, to use their high school experiences poorly, and thus to seem to be personally responsible for their failures—in precisely the way that human capital theory describes. By the time students enter community college, their eventual outcomes are largely determined. Community colleges cannot be blamed for the poor preparation of their entrants. Yet, the high schools which poorly convey information about requirements are not a visible target. Indeed, they are praised for encouraging students to have "high expectations."

The above description suggests that students' perceptions of college requirements are key to their efforts in high school and to their college attainments. It can be posed as a model with several elements:

1. Many seniors believe they can attain college plans with low high school achievement.
2. Students with these beliefs, including college-bound students, exert little effort in high school.
3. Such beliefs are partly correct—students can enter college even if they have low achievement.
4. High school achievement predicts degree completion, but students' plans do not anticipate this relationship.
5. High school achievement predicts much of the lower attainment and disappointed plans of disadvantaged students.
6. Students with low high school achievement get less economic payoff for college degrees.

This paper takes these contentions as hypotheses and presents analyses to test them empirically. The analyses support these hypotheses and pose serious challenges to current practices. This paper concludes that shielding high school seniors from the realities of college demands and allowing them to hold unrealistic plans is not a kindness. It is a deception which prevents students from taking actions to improve their achievement or to revise their plans and make better use of high school. Students with unrealistic plans should be so informed. They should be encouraged to increase their efforts or to develop backup plans and preparation.

Data and Methods

This report is based on three kinds of data. First, students' perceptions are described using detailed interviews of a nonrandom sample of high school seniors in two high schools. Second, students' views are systematically analyzed using a survey administered to a random sample of 2,091 seniors classes in 12 high schools across the Chicago metropolitan area during 1992–94. The schools and sample are diverse in ethnicity and SES backgrounds and are described in detail elsewhere (Rosenbaum and Roy, 1996).

Third, students' outcomes are assessed using the recent release of the 12-year follow-up of the High

School and Beyond 1980 sophomores (National Center for Educational Statistics, 1983). This national sample was first surveyed in 1980 (when respondents were sophomores) and subsequently resurveyed in 1982, 1984, 1986, and 1992. Of the original 14,825 sophomores in 1980, the survey obtained responses from 95.1% in 1982 (n = 14,102), and 85.3% in 1992 (n = 12,640). This survey provides a unique opportunity for a long-term study of the determinants of educational attainments. This paper studies the outcomes for the individuals responding in both the 1982 and 1992 surveys.

Many Seniors Believe They Can Attain College Plans with Low High School Achievement

Economic theory is a good model of our rational common sense assumptions. For instance, human capital theory explains students' achievement using two factors: students' inherent capabilities and their efforts to invest in themselves. The theory says students will invest in themselves and exert effort in school because they know there is a societal payoff.

While it is widely assumed that students believe that school efforts have a payoff, this assumption is rarely examined. Do students believe that school effort and achievement are relevant and helpful in improving their future careers? Of course teachers tell this to students, but it is clearly in teachers' own self-interest to convince students of their own importance. As parents and teachers often notice, one of the less convenient aspects of adolescence is the cognitive capacity that enables them to doubt what they are told.

Stinchcombe (1965) hypothesized that many students believed that school was not relevant to their future careers and that students' school efforts were determined, not only by their internal motivation, but also by their perceptions of schools' future relevance. While economists assume that incentives exist and are seen, Stinchcombe suggests this may not be true for work-bound students. Unfortunately, while Stinchcombe provided an intriguing model, his small sample and bivariate analyses (on a card sorter in the precomputer age) were too simple for a convincing test.

To examine these ideas, a nonrandom sample of 50 students was interviewed about how they thought about the relevance of school. Consistent with the dictum, "the more things change, the more they stay the same," these interviews in 1993 found similar sentiments to those Stinchcombe found 30 years previously. Many students reported that school was not relevant to their future careers. Yet something had changed. While Stinchcombe found that only work-bound students expressed these beliefs in 1960, these sentiments were also expressed by college-bound students in 1993. Many students who planned to attend college reported that high school achievement was not relevant to their future careers. Their comments suggested that the vast expansion of community colleges over the past 30 years contributed to their views. One student noted, "High school doesn't really matter . . ., because . . . junior college is not such a big deal to get into" (#42). Another said, "If you could apply yourself [in junior college], you'd get better grades" [regardless of how you did in high school] (#27). Many students agreed with the student who saw the "two-year college as another chance for someone who's messed up in high school" (#39). This second chance was also viewed as making high school effort less relevant. As one student said in explaining why he does not try hard in high school, "I think college is much more important than high school" (#16).

To examine Stinchcombe's hypotheses more systematically, survey items were constructed which reflected two aspects of individuals' perceptions of schools' relevance: whether students believed that high school education had relevance for their future success (hereafter "future relevance") and whether students believed that there was no penalty if they had poor school performance (hereafter "no penalty" attitude). The first variable refers to students' belief that high school can help their future careers; the second refers to beliefs that bad school performance (even if possibly relevant) is not necessarily a barrier to attaining their future careers.[1]

Surveys were recently administered to 2,091 high school seniors enrolled in 12 city and suburban high schools in a large, Midwestern metropolitan area. Just as Stinchcombe found, the survey found that many students doubted school's future relevance. This was not only true for work-bound students. Almost as many college-bound students held such beliefs. On five-point scales ranging from "strongly agree" to "strongly disagree," our analyses found that 30–40% of students did not agree with such statements as, "My courses give me useful preparation I'll need in life" (39.3% for whole sample, for college-bound respondents, 37.2%), "School teaches me valuable skills" (29.7%, college 28.2%), and "Getting a good job depends on how well you do at school" (36.6%, college 36.5%). We summed to create a scale for "future relevance."

Similar patterns appear for items concerned with lack of penalty for poor high school grades. Almost 46% of students agree with the item "Even if I do not work hard in high school, I can still make my future plans come true" (45.9%, college 44.3%). While educators want students to believe that students with bad grades rarely get college degrees or good jobs, many students disagree with the first point (regarding graduation from two-year colleges, 40.7% for whole sample, college 41.2%) and almost as many disagree with the second (getting good jobs after high school, 37.9%, college 32.9%). Most surprisingly, despite many campaigns against dropping out of high school, over 40% of seniors do not disagree with the statement "People can do OK even if they drop out of high school" (43.7%, college 40.8%). Apparently, many students see no penalty to their planned careers if they do not have high school diplomas, good grades, and work hard in school. We summed these latter items to create a scale for "no penalty."

The two scales of "future relevance" and "no penalty" are correlated, but the correlation is far from perfect (r = .30). Students who plan to get a college degree have a somewhat higher sense of schools' "future relevance," and a lesser sense that there is "no penalty" if they do poorly in high school, than students without college plans, but the difference is small (about 1/3 of a standard deviation). Moreover, these beliefs vary substantially within such groups, and the variation is similar within both groups (standard deviations of .61–.65).

Students with These Beliefs Exert Little Effort in High School

While there is nothing wrong with students having optimistic hopes, we would be concerned if students responded to these beliefs by reducing their efforts. This section examines: what factors may determine future relevance and no penalty beliefs, what factors may determine students' school efforts, and whether these beliefs mediate the potential influence of other factors on students' school efforts and may have independent influences on students' school efforts.

The antecedents of future relevance and no penalty beliefs are first examined. The survey asked three or more items relating to locus of control, parent support, teacher help, school help, peer pro-school influences, and peer anti-school (rebellion) influences. Items were factor analyzed and scales were constructed. All had alpha coefficients over .70. The survey also asked about respondents' race, ethnicity, parents' education and occupation, and gender (for details, see Rosenbaum and Roy, 1996).

First, OLS regression analyses show that both future relevance and no-penalty are strongly explained by parent support for school, teacher help, and personal locus of control. Peers and low-SES studies also have significant coefficients but gender and being Black do not (Table 1, columns 1 and 2).

Second, we examine the antecedents of students' school effort. Effort is measured by a scale combining students' reports of their behaviors (how much time they spend on homework) and three other items: I just do enough to pass my classes, I try to do my best in school, I only work in school if I'm worried about failing (each coded on a five-point scale from "strongly agree" to "strongly disagree").

As in previous research (Kandel and Lesser, 1972), these analyses find that students' school efforts are explained by parent, peer, and school variables (Table 1, column 3). Males and having low-SES have negative coefficients, but ethnicity has no influence. Students' locus of control has a large and significant effect.

However, when future relevance and no-penalty are added to the analysis, we find that they mediate much of the potential influence of parents, school help, teacher help, and locus of control and reduce the negative coefficient of SES to nonsignificance. In contrast,

their addition has relatively little effect on the influence of the two peer variables (see column 4). After controlling for other factors, future relevance and no-penalty also have significant independent effects on effort (standardized coefficients of .155 for future relevance, −.145 for "no penalty," column 4). Thus, these beliefs have significant and independent associations with effort, perhaps indicating strong effects in reducing students' school efforts.

These findings have implications for theory and practice. Theoretically, this study supports Stinchcombe's hypothesis. Students vary in whether they see school as relevant to their future lives, and this variable is strongly associated with their school efforts. In addition, this study identifies a second measure—the "no penalty" belief—and shows that both beliefs have significant, independent relationships with school effort.

These results imply that some youth have misread the American emphasis on opportunity. While Americans want society to provide "second chances" to youth, Stevenson and Stigler (1992) warn that youth might misinterpret this to mean that school failures never matter and effort is not needed. This study finds that many youth see little penalty to avoiding school work and little payoff to high school, and these beliefs may justify their poor effort in high school.

Of course, it is possible that causality goes in the other direction—that individuals rationalize their poor

TABLE 1 Determinants of Future Relevance, No Penalty, and Effort (Standardized Coefficients)

	Future Rel.	No Penalty	Effort (Step 1)	Effort (Step 2)
Parental support for school	.1702**	−.2786**	.2795**	.2128**
Rebellious peers	−.0576*	.0943**	−.1369**	−.1143**
Pro-school peers	.0949**	−.0217	.1157**	.0979**
Locus of control	.1253**	−.1655**	.2060**	.1627**
Female	−.0411	−.0149	.1051**	.1094**
Low SES	−.0439*	.0828**	−.0554*	−.0366
Black	.0344	−.0202	.0006	−.0076
Hispanic	.0526*	−.0391	−.0370	−.0510*
Asian	.0660**	−.0030	−.0043	−.0149
Teacher help	.2822**	.0510*	.0893**	.0530*
School help	.1310**	−.0441	.0564**	.0300
Future relevance				.1550**
No penalty belief				−.1448**
R-squared (adjusted)	.2446	.1710	.2947	.3393

n = 2.091, * = p < .05, ** = p < .01

effort by denying future relevance. However, these views, whether beliefs or rationalizations, are held by 40% of students so they are not just the problems of a few individuals. Indeed, since guidance counselors do not challenge these beliefs, part of the problem arises from school practices (Rosenbaum, Miller, and Krei, 1996). Even if these views arise as rationalizations, they are not effectively challenged by schools and represent misconceptions that encourage a continuing cycle of further low effort.

Students Can Enter College Even if They Have Low Achievement

Are students wrong when they say school achievement is not relevant to their futures? Community colleges are frequently seen as "second chance" institutions for those who have done poorly before, offering open admissions, low tuition, and remedial courses. In some community college departments, remedial courses may be 40% of the courses offered. Over 40% of freshmen at public two-year colleges take one or more years of remedial coursework just to acquire the same skills they did not learn in high school (National Center for Educational Statistics, 1995).

Although sociologists have produced extensive research showing that grades are strongly related to college attendance (e.g., Kerckhoff and Campbell 1977; Porter, 1974), much of this research is based on studies from the 1960s and 1970s. Yet, college admissions have changed a great deal since 1960. As noted, the five-fold growth of community colleges has dramatically increased opportunities to go to college, and fewer students are likely to face barriers to access to college.

Moreover, community colleges have initiated open-admissions policies and remedial courses to reduce the academic barriers to college. In the past, college admission standards compelled lower-achieving students to confront their unrealistic college plans. While college admission standards were a severe barrier to college for low-achieving students in 1960, admission standards are now practically nonexistent in community colleges. For example, Illinois high school graduates can attend a community college even if they have Ds and no college-prep courses (after age 21, even a diploma is not required). In addition, a full array of remedial courses have been devised to provide high-school-level curricula in the community colleges in order to improve students' chances of success (Brint and Karabel, 1989; Dougherty, 1994; Grubb and

Kalman, 1994). Open admissions policies and remedial courses have removed some academic barriers to college entrance.

Are students correct in the belief that high school performance is not relevant to their educational outcomes? The High School and Beyond data indicate that poor high school performance does not prevent college attendance. Even students with low grades (Cs or lower) can attend college. Indeed, 27% of students enrolling in two-year colleges had low grades in high school. That is only slightly less than the proportion of students with low grades who did not enroll in any postsecondary education (30%). Obviously, low grades are not a barrier to enrolling in two-year colleges. College-bound students who think high school effort is irrelevant to their future plans are partly correct—high school grades are not an obstacle to enrollment in two-year colleges.

High School Achievement Predicts Degree Completion, but Students' Plans Do Not Anticipate This Relationship

Having found that many students believe high school achievement is not relevant and, indeed, that many students with low grades can enter two-year colleges, one must wonder whether these students are correct that high school achievement is not relevant to college attainment. Or do these beliefs lead students to make plans which they will be unable to realize? This section of the paper addresses these questions with simple percentages, and the next section uses multivariate analyses.

These analyses emphasize grades because all students know their grades, so students could use this knowledge if they chose to do so. But do they choose to do so? Because most people have had a few teachers who gave arbitrary or unfair grades, grades are often dismissed as erroneous and irrelevant. Yet, knowledge of scale construction suggests that averaging grades eliminates random idiosyncracies and might make grade averages a meaningful indicator. This section examines whether students' cumulative grade point averages in high school predict college outcomes.

Our analyses of the High School and Beyond data find that many students with college plans fail to attain college degrees, and high school grades strongly predict which students fail at their college plans. Of the 12,475 seniors with complete information on plans, grades, and educational attainment, 8,795 (70.5%) planned to get a college degree (AA or higher) in their senior year in high school. Many seniors (4,103 of the 12,475) had low grades (Cs or lower), yet 50.8% of those with low grades still planned to get a college degree (n = 2,086).

However, low grades have a strong impact on actual educational attainment. Among all seniors with college plans, 40.3% succeed in getting a college degree (AA or higher) in the 10 years after high school (Table 2a). By comparison, low high school grades cut students' chances in half—only 19.6% of seniors with low grades attained their college plans.

Of all the seniors planning to get a BA or higher (n = 5,528), 49.5% succeed in getting that degree (Table 2b). However, students with As have a 70.7% chance of getting as BA or higher, and those with Bs have a 46.6% chance. Students planning BAs who have a C average or less (n = 916) achieve BA degrees at less than half the rate of all students with BA plans (49.5%–> 20.5%). It might also be noted that 73% of those with poor grades do little homework—less than an hour per week, and low homework time decreases their BA chances to only 11%.

Since the AA is a shorter and perhaps easier degree than a BA, one might expect that students plan-

ning to get AA degrees are more likely to be successful. That is not the case. Seniors who plan to get an AA degree succeed less often than those planning a BA. Of the 3,267 seniors who plan to get an AA degree, only 23.9% succeed in getting a college degree (AA or higher) in the next 10 years; and of those with low grades (Cs or lower), only 12.6% do (Table 2c). The success rates are even lower for those with low grades who did little homework (n = 248; p = 8%). Recall that these tables report students' college-degree outcomes, based only on their high school grades, and giving youth 10 years to attain any college degree (AA or higher).

Why do over half of seniors with low grades believe they can attain college degrees? Perhaps "social promotion" practices in high schools, which automatically promote students each year to the next grade regardless of their achievement, may encourage this belief. Similarly, open admissions at community colleges may contribute to this belief. Seeing these two practices, which award attainments without requiring academic achievement, students may infer a similar view of college degrees—as an award for putting in time that does not require academic achievement. This

TABLE 2 Percentage of Seniors with College Plans Who Complete College Degrees within 10 Years

Table IIa. Percentage of Seniors with College Plans (AA or higher) Who Complete at Least an AA

Average high school grades	As	Bs	Cs or lower	Total
Percent attaining AA or higher	69.5	43.2	19.6	40.3
N	2007	4702	2086	8795

Table IIb. Percentage of Seniors with BA Plans Who Succeed in Completing at Least a BA Degree

Average high school grades	As	Bs	Cs or lower	Total
Percent attaining BA or higher	70.7	46.6	20.5	49.5
N	1668	2944	916	5528

Table IIc. Percentage of Seniors with AA Plans Who Succeed in Completing at an AA

Average high school grades	As	Bs	Cs or lower	Total
Percent attaining AA or higher	46.6	27.1	12.6	23.9
N	339	1758	1170	3267

Note: The data displayed represent 1992 degree attainment figures for "High School and Beyond" respondents who were seniors in 1982.

may also suggest that students view school as a credentialing process rather than a human-capital-building process.

Ironically, although colleges offering AA degrees are more accessible than BA colleges to students with low grades, the AA degree is not necessarily more available to them. Students with AA plans have lower success rates than students with BA plans, both because students with AA plans are twice as likely to have low grades and because their chances of getting the degree are very slim if they have low grades (12.6%). Multivariate analyses indicate that grades and homework time explain most of this differential success rate between those with BA and AA plans (Rosenbaum and Miller, 1998).

Newspaper stories sometimes report that students who got As in high school actually lack the academic skills to do well in college. This may explain our findings that only half (49.5%) of students with As in high school complete an AA degree or higher (although low SES seems to be more important than low test scores in explaining these failures). Yet, newspapers rarely consider the other issue, that students with Cs in high school have very little chance of completing a college degree, and their plans do not seem to recognize these risks.

In sum, many students report that they plan to get a college degree even though they have poor academic achievement. Yet, in fact, low grades predict much lower chances of attaining a degree. Within the High School and Beyond data, over 80% of students with low grades who planned to get a college degree failed to do so, and the failures were even greater for those planning an AA degree. Even without making any causal inferences, the strong predictive power of high school grades is important—it tells seniors how to place their bets. While students are correct that they can enter a college with low grades, they are usually mistaken in thinking that they can complete the degree. Their poor success rates make these outcomes a real long shot, not something students should be counting on.

High School Achievement Predicts Much of the Lower Attainment and Disappointed Plans of Disadvantaged Students

While the strong predictive power of high school grades tells seniors how to place their bets, do grades really predict educational attainment after controlling for other factors? If students want to raise their chances, they need to know whether to focus on improving grades, homework time, or track placement; and they may be worried that their future attainment is predestined by their social background (SES, ethnicity, gender) or intelligence (as test scores are sometimes interpreted). Policy makers also need to know to what extent grades or other factors predict the lower outcomes and disappointed plans of disadvantaged students.

Regression analysis is a good way to examine these issues. It allows researchers to look at simple gross associations between background characteristics and attainment and then to examine the mediating and independent predicting power of other factors such as high school achievement. We ran a series of OLS regressions on the High School and Beyond cohort who graduated in 1982 and were followed through 1992. The survey had 8,969 respondents who provided information for all variables in our model.

Our basic analyses made use of five dependent variables: students' cumulative grade point averages (Grades), tested achievement (Test), homework time (HW), educational plans (EdPlan), and educational attainment (EdYears). The first four were based on information gathered in the students' senior year, 1982; educational attainment constituted the number of years of students' educational attainments in 1992. Our independent variables included social background variables (Black, Hispanic, female, and a cumulative index of parents' SES computed in the High School and Beyond file), region of the U.S. (South, West, and Northeast regions, with the Midwest as the comparison), and school variables (private school, general, and vocational tracks, with college track as the comparison). Subsequent analyses concerned with plans and educational attainment added grade point average, tested achievement, and homework time as additional independent variables.

These analyses revealed several effects. First, Blacks, Hispanics, and low-SES students have lower grades and achievement test scores (Table 3, columns 1 and 3). If these coefficients indicate influences, they are partly mediated by track and private schools (columns 2 and 4). But even after controls are entered, Blacks, Hispanics, and low SES youth have lower grades and test scores.

Second, SES and being Black are associated with homework time, although in different directions (column 5), and the SES relationship is only partly diminished after controls are entered (column 6). While low-SES youth spend less time on homework than

TABLE 3 Regression Analyses for the Predictions of Grades, Tests, Homework, Educational Plans and Attainment

	1 Grades	2 Grades	3 Test	4 Test	5 HW	6 HW	7 EdPlan	8 EdPlan	9 EdPlan	10 EdYears	11 EdYears	12 EdYears
SES	.207*	.163*	.368*	.295*	.223*	.164*	.450*	.378*	.240*	.386*	.324*	.201*
Black	−.141*	−.150*	−.212*	−.202*	.055*	.060*	.096*	.094*	.159*	−.023*	−.026*	.050*
Hispanic	−.110*	−.115*	−.201*	−.187*	−.007	.002	−.013	−.008	.060*	−.059*	−.045*	.024*
Female	.178*	.176*	−.037*	−.041*	.179*	.174*	.035*	.031*	−.014	.013	.007	−.040*
South		.020		−.055*		−.060*		−.014*	.012		−.023*	−.008
West		.047*		−.007		−.017		.014	.013		−.058*	−.064*
NE		−.073*		.037*		.002		−.015	−.017		.038*	.045*
Private		−.021		.059*		.092*		.061*	.028*		.075*	.056*
Vocational		−.164		−.221*		−.119*		−.206*	−.098*		−.176*	−.075*
General		−.173		−.178*		−.172*		−.211*	−.104*		−.184*	−.085*
Test									.288*			.236*
GPA									.126*			.221*
HW									.200*			.105*
R2 (adj)%	12.2	16.1	27.2	33.5	7.8	12.1	19.6	25.3	41.2	16.5	22.1	36.3
n	8969	8969	8969	8969	8969	8969	8969	8969	8969	8969	8969	8969

Note: Standardized coefficients are presented. * = p < .05

high-SES youth, Blacks spend significantly more time on homework than Whites (Hispanics spend about the same as Whites). Despite potential concerns because homework time is self-reported, Fordham and Ogbu's (1986) findings would predict that Blacks would underreport school effort (to avoid being seen as "acting White"), and these analyses find the opposite (Fordham and Ogbu's prediction was also not supported in Cook and Ludwig's, 1997, analysis). If homework time turns out to be an important predictor of educational attainment, then it may account for problems of low-SES students but is not likely to do so for Blacks.

Third, low-SES youth have lower educational plans, but Blacks have higher plans than Whites (column 7). These results remain after controls are entered for track and private schools (column 8). The SES relationship declines after controlling for grades, tests, and homework time, but the positive association for Blacks increases (column 9). Blacks have even higher plans than others with similar achievement, as previous research has noted (Jencks et al., 1972).

Fourth, Black, Hispanic, and low-SES youth have lower educational attainment (column 10). These relationships are only slightly altered after controls for track and private schools (column 11). However, these relationships are largely mediated by grades, test scores, and homework time. Indeed, when grades, test scores, and homework time are added to the analysis, the SES relationship declines substantially (from .324 to .201), although it remains statistically significant and the Black and Hispanic coefficients actually reverse and become significantly positive (column 12). Thus, students' grades, homework time, and tested achievement explain a significant part of the lower attainment of low-SES students, and Black and Hispanic students have higher attainments than Whites with similar achievement.

Finally, by adding seniors' plans to the regression, the analyses can discover which high school information predicts the disappointing attainments of disadvantaged students many years later (see Table 4). Since a few students (8.4%) attained more than they planned, they are removed from the analyses in Table 4, leaving 8,117 students in the analyses.[2] As a result. Table 4 shows the factors predicting which students' attainments fall short of their plans—explaining discrepancies between the 31.5% of students who attained their senior-year plans and the 60.1% who attained one or more years less than they planned. The analyses found that low-SES, Black, and Hispanic students had signif-

icantly lower attainments than they had planned (Table 4, column 1). However, when variables for school achievement and effort were added, the ethnic variables became insignificant and the SES coefficient became smaller (Table 4, column 3). Apparently, the disappointments of Black and Hispanic students are entirely predictable from their lower achievement and effort in high school.

Indeed, students' plans do not take sufficient account of their achievement. Over 58% (.142/.244) of the relationship between test scores and attainment and 78% (.173/.221) of the relationship between grades and attainment remain after controlling for plans (Table 4, columns 2 and 3). Less than half of these relationships are mediated by plans. Thus, consistent with the cross-tabular analyses (displayed in Table 2), we conclude that, even after controls, seniors' college plans vastly underestimate how much their grades and test scores predict their ultimate educational outcomes.

It is noteworthy that the female coefficient on educational attainment, which is virtually zero in the early regressions (Table 3, column 10), becomes significantly negative after controlling for achievement (column 12). Apparently, women have roughly the same educational attainments as males, but their attainments are still below what they would be if their previous achievement were the only determinant. Females have higher grades and homework time than males (but slightly lower test scores, see Table 3, columns 1–6), so there should be some concern about why their attainments are lower than their achievement would predict.

Finally, while the above analyses look at simple additive effects of ethnicity, one might still wonder if some of the factors in our model have different coefficients for Blacks and Whites. One indication of bias is when Blacks get less benefit from their achievements than Whites. In the 1970s, Porter (1974) found that Blacks received less gain in educational attainment from their high school grades than did Whites. Our regression analyses for educational attainment run separately for Whites and Blacks find that grades have about the same coefficients for both (Table 4, columns 4 and 6—betas .224 and .214), and the same is true for test scores (.228 and .227) but slightly larger coefficients for Whites than for Blacks (.114 vs .071) when it comes to homework.[3] Thus, Blacks get roughly the same gain in attainment for increases in their test scores and grades as Whites, although they get slightly less gain for increases in their homework time. Apparently, the old pattern of discrimination in which Blacks got

TABLE 4 Regression Analyses for the Predictions of Educational Attainment: All Students, Whites and Blacks

	1 EdYears	2 EdYears	3 EdYears	Whites		Blacks	
				4 EdYears	5 EdYears	6 EdYears	7 EdYears
SES	.154*	.211*	.127*	.213*	.113*	.225*	.190*
Black	−.072*	.050*	−.008				
Hispanic	−.035*	.032*	.011				
Female	.002	−.032*	−.025*	−.048*	−.031*	.055*	.024
South	−.006	.002	−.002	−.002	−.003	−.073	−.076*
West	−.060*	−.059*	−.064*	−.066*	−.069*	−.040	−.037
NE	.041*	.041*	.046*	.046*	.052*	.012	.011
Private	.031*	.045*	.031*	.047*	.033*	.019	.008
Vocational	−.083*	−.083*	−.044*	−.089*	−.047*	−.012	.000
General	−.089*	−.093*	−.052*	−.097*	−.052*	−.044	−.024
Test		.244*	.142*	.227*	.118*	.228*	.175*
Grades		.221*	.173*	.214*	.170*	.224*	.196*
HW		.119*	.050*	.114*	.040*	.071*	.043
Plans	.483*		.354*		.383*		.201*
R2 (adj) %	40.3	38.3	45.4	38.1	46.0	27.2	30.0
n	8117	8117	8117	5014	5014	996	996

Note: Standardized coefficients are presented. * = p < .05 Analyses based on cases where EdYears is less than or equal to EdPlans.

lower attainment benefits for increasing their grades is no longer the case. Indeed, SES, test scores, and grades are somewhat stronger predictors of attainment for Blacks than for Whites (Table 4, columns 5 and 7).

In sum, these results indicate that SES, ethnicity, private schools, and track are related to attainment; but grades, test scores, and homework time also have effects which tend to mediate much of the relationship between disadvantaged backgrounds and attainment. However, there are indications that many students do not realize how much high school achievement predicts future attainment. While all students probably know their grades, their plans underestimate the extent that their grades predict their later attainment—and this is true for both Black and White students. Indeed, grades are the single best predictor of the ways attainment falls short of plans, and this predictability is somewhat larger for Blacks than for Whites. If students could focus on changing one set of attributes in high school to make their plans come true, they should improve those associated with their grades.[4],[5]

Thus, these analyses suggest that students are overly complacent about the ease of getting a college degree. Many students have plans that have little chance of succeeding because their plans underestimate the relationship between high school achievement and later attainment. This is particularly true for Blacks, Hispanics, and low-SES students whose attainments fall short of their plans. These disappointments are largely predicted by their high school achievements (Table 4, columns 1 and 3). It seems likely that these students might work harder if they realized the future relevance of their high school achievement.

Students with Low High School Achievement Get Less Economic Payoff to College Degrees

Despite these odds, some students with low high school grades get college degrees. Do they get the same earnings payoff from college as students with better grades? While Murnane, Willett, and Levy (1995) have shown additive wage payoffs of educational attainment and achievement (measured by test scores), the present analyses examine whether college degrees have lower payoffs for those with lower achievement, which is operationalized by high school grades since it more clearly indicates achievement (rather than ability) and is known by all students. The above model is used to explain the 1991 earnings of the same High School and Beyond cohort, adding dummy variables for educational attainment (AA representing those who had received the AA but no higher; BA representing those who had earned the BA but no higher degree; and MA representing those who had earned an MA or higher degrees). By taking the log of annual earnings as the dependent variable, unstandardized coefficients can be interpreted as percentage increases in earnings, so these tables report unstandardized coefficients. Thus, in the first step of the analysis, the High School and Beyond data indicate that youth who earn AA and BA degrees report 10.1% and 14.5% higher earnings, respectively, than those without a degree (Table 5, column 1).

To see if students with low grades get the same benefits from those degrees, these analyses create a new dummy variable (AA-LoGPA) for people who got an AA degree and had low grades in high school (AA-LoGPA equals 1 if a person has an AA degree and high school grades of C or lower, 0 otherwise), and similar variables for BALoGPA and MA-LoGPA. Adding these three variables into the regression, the analyses find that youth who had low high school grades got less earnings advantage for their college degrees (Table 5, column 2). To figure the payoff to BAs for students with Cs, the coefficients for BA and BA-LoGPA are added, so the payoff to a BA degree is 4.3% (.166 − .123 = .043), and the payoff to an AA degree is −7.2%, less than if they had not gotten the degree (.155 − .227 = −.072). While the average student gets strong earnings benefits from BA and AA degrees, students with low grades get much smaller earnings benefits from a BA degree and lower earnings from an AA degree than from no degree.[6] Previous studies have found that poor grades predict lower earnings for young adults who have only a high school diploma (Miller, 1997; Rosenbaum, Miller, and Roy, 1996). These results indicate that low grades also substantially reduce the payoffs to college degrees (cf. also Rosenbaum and Miller, 1998).

TABLE 5   Regression Analyses for the Predictions of Earnings

	Ln (Earnings)	Ln (Earnings)
SES	.101*	.101*
Black	.040	.041
Hispanic	.026	.025
Female	−.299*	−.299*
South	−.032*	−.032*
West	−.036	−.036
NE	.097*	.099*
Private	.043*	.045*
Vocational	−.030	−.031
General	−.027	−.026
Test	.003*	.003*
Grades	.034*	.025*
HW	−.004	−.004
AA	.101*	.155*
BA	.145*	.166*
MA	.096*	−.112*
AALoGPA		−.227*
BALoGPA		−.123*
MALoGPA		.022
c	9.657	9.695
R2 (adj.) %	13.2	13.5

Note: Nonstandardized coefficients are presented. * = p < .05, N = 8,413

Conclusion

These analyses help elucidate the problem of disadvantaged youth. Simple gross analyses find that low-SES, Black, and Hispanic students have lower educational attainment. However, the SES coefficient declines, and the ethnic disadvantages actually reverse and become advantages when achievement variables are entered. Thus, Blacks and Hispanics have significantly higher educational attainment than Whites with the same level of high school achievement. In addition, high school grades and test scores predict many of the cases where disadvantaged youth have lower attainment than they had planned.

Looking at these results, some might blame disadvantaged youth for their failures; but another interpretation is more plausible. Students' plans are what they think they can expect in the future, and their plans are likely to influence their high school efforts. In finding that students' plans do not take sufficient account of the influence of grades on their ultimate educational attainment, one can infer that students do not realize how much high school achievement affects their actual prospects. This is consistent with the future relevance and "no penalty" beliefs noted earlier. These results may indicate that schools fail to provide clear information to these youth which is consistent with what is known about counselors' advising practices (Rosenbaum, Miller, and Krei, 1996).

What is the harm in letting students have "high expectations"? Perhaps these plans are just dreams that make students a little happier and do them little harm. As noted, guidance counselors say they do not want to disappoint young people and so they encourage all students to attend college, even students with low achievement.

Consistent with this interpretation, Manski (1989) has proposed that many youth begin community college as an "experiment," a low-cost way to discover whether they can make it in college. But is it really low cost? Manski analyzes the process from the viewpoint of a student who is already in a community college, noting that his analysis does not consider students before they enter college.

However, there are opportunity costs to any decision, and this "experiment" has some large opportunity costs to students while they are still in high school. Should students with more than an 80% chance of failing at college place *all* their bets on their college experiment? Or would it be prudent for such students to hedge their college bets?

A first opportunity cost of the college-for-all norm is that students' high expectations may inadvertently encourage them to see high school as irrelevant and thus to make poor use of high school. Our interviews and survey of high school seniors indicate that 40% of students with college plans believe that high school is irrelevant. Postponing the key test for whether one is "college-bound" until after high school may inadvertently tell students that high school achievement is not important.

A second opportunity cost of the college-for-all norm is that it may lead to a lack of effort. Human capital theory posits that people invest effort in improving their capabilities if they believe better outcomes will result. But if they believe they can get the same outcomes without added effort, they will not make the effort. If students realize that their low high school grades will be associated with blocked college plans, they might increase their efforts in high school. Yet High School and Beyond data indicate that a large majority (78.0%) of poorly achieving high school students with college plans do less than an hour a day of homework, and many (25.3%) do less than an hour in a whole week. These High School and Beyond students exert little effort, even though they have low grades (which predict an 80% failure rate). Moreover, guidance counselors let these students hold unrealistic plans because they wish to encourage "high expectations" and "second chances" (Rosenbaum, Miller, and Krei,

1996). Students are not told what level of high school achievement is needed to succeed in community college, and they are lulled into a complacency that leaves them unprepared for getting college degrees.

The third opportunity cost of the college-for-all norm is that students with little prospect for getting a college degree will fail to get vocational training. Encouraging poorly achieving students to delay their work preparation until they see the results of their college "experiment" makes it likely that they will make poor use of vocational preparation in high school, which has been shown to improve earnings (Campbell, Basinger, Dauner, and Parks, 1986; Kang and Bishop, 1986; Rosenbaum, 1996). Indeed, students with poor grades are less likely to be in vocational courses if they have college plans than if they are not planning college (Rosenbaum, unpublished analyses), and many students with low probability of success in college have no backup plans or training. Similarly, many public schools (such as those in Chicago) have reduced or ended their vocational programs because they expect all students to delay their vocational decisions until they get to college.

Although Manski did not consider it, there is an even more inexpensive experiment to help students infer their readiness for college—high school. If the CFA norm did not focus so much on getting everyone into college, then high schools could tell students their realistic chances of attaining college degrees. If students realized that high school achievement is the first "experiment," and this "experiment" has strong predictive power, then students with poor grades would either revise their plans downwards, or they might try to correct bad habits that lead to poor achievements.

Protecting students' high expectations when they are unwarranted is not a kindness; it is a deception. Failing to challenge students to examine the plausibility of their college plans has serious opportunity costs—it prevents them from seeing the importance of high school, it prevents them from taking the additional efforts that might make their plans more likely to come true, and it prevents them from preparing for alternative outcomes. When some seniors have high school records that make their college plans highly likely to fail, schools' protection of their "high expectations" is not a kind gesture. It looks a lot more like the confidence scheme that Goffman describes, distracting the "mark" from taking other constructive actions.

Unfortunately, students understand very well the *short-term* consequences of their high school efforts—

they are minor. But they assume that this means that high school achievement and effort are irrelevant and that there will be no penalty if they do badly in high school. They believe they can postpone their efforts until they get into college, and their plans will work out fine.

Students' misperceptions may arise from their limited knowledge about older cohorts. High school students can see the college enrollment of last year's seniors more easily than the college completion of much older students, and they can more easily identify with the students a year older than themselves who enter college than with the 28-year-olds who never finished the degree. As a result, perceptions are likely to be distorted. Students easily perceive college enrollment, for which high school achievements are irrelevant, but they have difficulty seeing college completion, for which high school achievements are highly relevant. Under such circumstances, students' perceptions will not improve unless policy action is taken.

Policy Implications

The community college system and its open admissions policies are rightfully a source of pride. They have created new opportunities for large numbers of youth. However, open admissions may inadvertently contribute to students' complacency. Students with low grades may not realize that they have very poor prospects of getting a degree or earnings benefits from that degree.

High schools are partly responsible for such delusions. Our research suggests that high school guidance counselors believe that open admission means that they do not have to discourage students' college expectations. They believe that "high expectations" should be encouraged, and they report that they get complaints from parents and principals if they try to discourage unrealistically high plans (Rosenbaum, Miller, and Krei, 1996). Counselors' practices may help explain why students hold these views.

While policy has focussed on opening college admissions, it has not devoted similar effort to providing clear information about community colleges (Orfield, 1997; Paul, 1997, Rosenbaum, Miller, and Krei, 1997). Indeed, many schools push the college-for-all (CFA) norm, which lulls students into a complacency, which ultimately is unwarranted. High school grades could inform students about their likelihood of attaining a college degree, but this fact is hidden from students' awareness, and perhaps even teachers' and counselors' awareness.

To return to Goffman's model, the CFA norm is highly misleading and does great harm to youth. It offers big promises to students without warning that few low-achieving students will get a college degree. Indeed, it leaves many youth worse off than before, keeping them in the dark about actual requirements so they fail to take suitable actions to prepare themselves to accomplish their plans. It also harms youth as they waste time, energy, and money on a college experience they are ill prepared to handle and that is likely to lead to failure, low self-esteem, and misused opportunities in high school. While high school counselors brag about their college enrollment rates, students will blame themselves for the failure that they did not anticipate but which was highly predictable.

The CFA norm also has big impact on policies and practices in schools. An example can be seen in the Chicago public schools in the early 1990s when Superintendent Argie Johnson urged all of the city's high schools to stress college goals. She closed or withdrew resources from many vocational programs. Even the famous Chicago Vocational School began stressing that its goal was no longer vocational, but college. Meanwhile, the Chicago schools had low achievement levels, many of their graduates lacked the academic skills needed to take college-credit courses in the city college, and the degree completion rates at the city colleges were very low. The superintendent's urging that more students attend college was politically popular because it fit the CFA norm. It stressed "high expectations," but it may have led to increased failure.

This is not to urge that one abandon "high expectations" entirely or scrap open admissions policies. But three other reforms are warranted.

First, high schools should provide more complete information on community college success rates as a function of students' grades, test scores, and homework time. This could be aided by a universally recognized test of achievement (not aptitude or intelligence), either statewide (such as Illinois's IGAP achievement test) or national (such as Clinton's proposal for national proficiency examinations). Even if such tests are not available, grades can be used. While the grades from individual teachers are highly imperfect, grade point averages have strong predictive power. Schools and society should be stressing their importance to students.

Students need to realize that "open admissions" does not mean that high school achievement is irrelevant.

Second, linkages between high schools and colleges may help improve high school students' understanding of college requirements. By seeing that many college students must repeat high school classes, high school students will learn that they can work hard now, or next year they can repeat the same class and pay tuition for it. Several recent reforms seek to improve coordination of high school and college programs which may help students see the future relevance of their current courses (e.g., tech-prep, 2 + 2 programs, and career academies; see Berryman and Bailey, 1992; Stern, Finkelstein, Stone, Latting, and Dornsife, 1995).

Finally, students must be prepared for backup career options if their college plans are unlikely to succeed. While schools can encourage all students to aim for college, this should not be an excuse to cut vocational programs. Research indicates that after controls for test scores, vocational education graduates are 10–15% more likely to be in the labor force and are paid 8–9% more than graduates of academic programs (Campbell et al., 1986; Kang and Bishop, 1986; Rosenbaum, 1996).[7] Even if students plan to attend community college, low success rates at these colleges suggest that backup plans would be prudent, particularly for students with low grades. Over 80% of such students fail to get a degree and lose time, tuition, and self-confidence in the process. After they drop out of college, they enter the labor market without the vocational skills or preparation that they might have gotten if they had not been taken in by the college-for-all rhetoric.

Notes

1. Somewhat similar beliefs have been shown to influence students' achievements (Mickelson, 1990); but since achievement is influenced by many factors besides motivation, this study has chosen to focus on the determinants of effort (cf. also Steinberg, 1996, for an excellent overview).
2. Since one would not be concerned about the disappointment of very high plans, analyses were also run using recoded versions of plans and attainments in which values higher than BA were recoded to be the same as BA = 16. This recode does not alter results very much so those results are not reported.
3. Similar results are obtained on the full sample of 8,969 individuals not shown here.
4. What determines grades? Bowles and Gintis (1976) have suggested noncognitive components which are not supported in some other studies (Bills, 1983;

Rosenbaum and Kariya, 1989, 1991). Miller and Rosenbaum (1998) pursue this question in greater detail.
5. Logit analyses were also run to see the determinants of who got AA or higher versus the high school graduates who got less than an AA. Using the same independent variables as the regression, the results indicate virtually the same conclusions as the above linear regression: grades, test scores, and homework all have significant influences, with grades having the largest influence. Grades have even larger influence than test scores in explaining disappointed plans. Similar findings occur in explaining who got BA or higher, although the grade influence is even greater. These tables are not reported because the results are virtually the same as those reported here.
6. Youth who did not complete high school are removed from this analysis so the constant represents all youth with high school diplomas but no college degrees. Note that the Malogpa coefficient is not significant and only 22 (4%) of MA students had low high school grades.
7. Kane and Rouse (1995) find that students get some economic benefit from the college credits they earn, even if they do not complete college degrees. However, these benefits may depend on whether the courses were vocational and in particular fields (Grubb, 1995). If the economic benefits of college courses (without a degree) arise from the vocational preparation they offer, then vocational courses in high schools or nondegree programs could possibly provide similar benefits. It is possible that the economic value of isolated college credits comes because individuals seek specific job-relevant courses, perhaps because of a job they already hold or one they know is available. Employers in some fields (tool and die, machining, etc.) require employees to obtain a few specific courses but not a certificate or degree (Rosenbaum and Binder, 1996).

Moreover, for many students, the economic benefits of some colleges are negligible. Kane and Rouse (1995, p. 602) found that "40% [of two-year college dropouts] completed fewer than a semester's worth of credits" and a large number completed none, so the economic benefits of college entry were minimal for these students. Given that most of these students probably expected to get college degrees, they surely got much less academic and economic benefit from college than they anticipated and experienced relatively large psychological costs.

I am grateful to Tom Bailey, Regina Deil, Maureen Hallinan, Jens Ludwig, Aaron Pallas, Shazia Miller, and Bruce Biddle for thoughtful comments on earlier drafts of this paper. Support for this work was provided by the Spencer

Foundation, the community College Research Center at Columbia University, and the Institute for Policy Research at Northwestern University. Of course, the opinions expressed here are solely those of the author. Correspondence concerning this article should be sent to James E. Rosenbaum, Institute for Policy Research and School of Education and Social Policy, Northwestern University, 2040 Sheridan Road, Evanston, IL 60208 U.S.A. Tel: 847-491-3795; Fax: 847-491-9916; E-mail:J-Rosenbaum@nwu.edu

References

Berryman, Susan E. and Bailey, Thomas R. (1992). *The double helix: Education and the economy.* New York: Teachers College Press.

Bills, David (1983). Social reproduction and the Bowles-Gintis thesis of a correspondence between school and work settings. *Research in sociology of education and socialization.* Greenwood, CT: JAI.

Bowles, Samuel and Gintis, Herbert (1976). *Schooling in capitalist America.* New York: Basic Books.

Brint, Steven and Karabel, Jerome (1989). *The diverted dream.* New York: Oxford University Press.

Campbell, Paul B., Basinger, K. S., Dauner, M. B., and Parks, M. A. (1986). *Outcomes of vocational education.* Columbus, OH: Ohio State University, National Center for Research in Vocational Education.

Cicourel, Aaron V. and Kitsuse, John I. (1963). *The educational decision-makers.* Indianapolis: Bobbs Merrill.

Clark, Burton (1960). The "cooling out" function in higher education. *American Journal of Sociology, 65,* 569–576.

Cook, Philip J. and Ludwig, Jens (1997). Weighing the burden of "acting White": Are there race differences in attitudes toward education? *Journal of Policy Analysis and Management, 16*(2), 256–278.

Dougherty, Kevin J. (1994). *The contradictory college.* Albany, NY: SUNY Press.

Fordham, Signithia and Ogbu, John (1986). Black students' school success: Coping with the burden of "acting White." *The Urban Review, 18*(3), 176–206.

Goffman, Erving (1952, November). Cooling the mark out: Some aspects of adaptation to failure. *Psychiatry, 15,* 451–463.

Grubb, W. Norton (1989). Dropouts, spells of time, and credits in postsecondary education. *Economics of Education Review, 8*(1), 49–67.

Grubb, W. Norton (1992). Postsecondary education and the sub-baccalaureate labor market. *Economics of Education Review, 11*(3), 225–248.

Grubb, W. Norton (1993). The varied economic returns of postsecondary education. *Journal of Human Resources, 28*(2), 265–282.

Grubb, W. Norton (1995). Response to comment. *Journal of Human Resources, 30*(1), 222–228.

Grubb, W. Norton and Kalman, Judy (1994, November). Relearning to earn. *American Journal of Education, 103,* 54–93.

Jencks, Christopher L., Smith, Smith, Acland, Henry, Bane, Mary Jo, Cohen, David K., Gintis, Herbert, Heyns, Barbara, and Michaelson, Stephan (1972). *Inequality.* New York: Basic Books.

Kandel, Denise and Lesser, Gerald (1972). *Youth in two worlds: United States and Denmark.* New York: Jossey-Bass.

Kane, Thomas and Rouse, Cecilia E. (1995). Labor-market returns to two- and four-year college. *American Economic Review, 85*(3), 600–614.

Kans, Suk and Bishop, John (1986). The effect of curriculum on labor market success. *Journal of Industrial Teacher Education,* 133–148.

Karabel, Jerome (1986). Community colleges and social stratification in the 1980s. In L.S. Zwerling (Ed.), *The community college and its critics.* San Francisco: Jossey-Bass, pp. 13–30.

Kerckhoff, Alan C. and Campbell, Richard T. (1977). Black-White differences in the educational attainment process. *Sociology of Education, 50*(1), 15–27.

Manski, Charles F. (1989). Schooling as experimentation. *Economics of Education Review, 8*(4), 305–312.

Mickelson, Roslyn. (1990, January). The attitude-achievement paradox among Black adolescents. *Sociology of Education, 63,* 44–61.

Miller, Shazia (1997). *Shortcut: High school grades as a signal of human capital.* Paper presented at the annual meeting of the American Sociological Association, Toronto.

Miller, Shazia and Rosenbaum, James (1998). *What do grades mean?* Unpublished manuscript, Northwestern University, Institute for Policy Research.

Murnane, Richard, Willett, John B., and Levy, Frank (1995). The growing importance of cognitive skills in wage determination. *Review of Economics and Statistics, 77*(2), 251–266.

Murnane, Richard and Levy, Frank (1997). *Teaching the new basic skills.* New York: The Free Press.

National Center for Educational Statistics. (1983). *High school and beyond: 1980 senior cohort first follow-up (1982): Datafile user's manual.* Chicago: National Opinion Research Center.

National Center for Educational Statistics (1983). *High school and beyond: Data file user's manual.* Chicago: National Opinion Research Center.

National Center for Educational Statistics (1995). *Remedial education at higher education institutions.* Washington, DC: U.S. Department of Education.

Orfield, Gary (1997). Going to work: Weak preparation, little help. In Kenneth K. Wong (Ed.), *Advances in educational policy* (Vol. 3). Greenwood, CT: JAI Press, pp. 3–32.

Paul, Faith (1997). Negotiated identities and academic program choice. In Kenneth K. Wong (Ed.), *Advances in educational policy* (Vol. 3). Greenwood, CT: JAI Press, pp. 53–78.

Porter, James N. (1974, June). Race, socialization and mobility in educational and early occupational attainment. *American Sociological Review, 39,* 303–316.

Resnick, Lauren B. and Wirt, John G. (1996). The changing workplace. In Lauren B. Resnick and John G. Wirt (Eds.), *Linking school and work.* San Francisco: Jossey Bass, pp. 1–22.

Rosenbaum, James E. (1975). The stratification of socialization processes. *American Sociological Review, 40*(1), 48–54.

Rosenbaum, James E. (1976). *Making inequality.* New York: Wiley.

Rosenbaum, James E. (1978). The structure of opportunity in school. *Social Forces, 57,* 236–256.

Rosenbaum, James E. (1986). Institutional career structures and the social construction of ability. In G. Richardson (Ed.), *Handbook of theory and research for the sociology of education.* Westport, CT: Greenwood Press, pp. 139–171.

Rosenbaum, James E. (1989). Organizational career systems and employee misperceptions. In Michael Arthur, Douglas T. Hall, and Barbara Lawrence (Eds.), *Handbook of career theory.* New York: Cambridge University Press, pp. 329–353.

Rosenbaum, James E. (1996, Summer). Policy uses of research on the high school-to-work transition. *Sociology of Education,* Summer, pp. 102–122.

Rosenbaum, James E. and Kariya, Takehiko (1989). From high school to work: Market and institutional mechanisms in Japan. *American Journal of Sociology, 94*(6), 1334–1365.

Rosenbaum, James E. and Kariya, Takehiko (1991). Do school achievements affect the early jobs of high school graduates in the United States and Japan? *Sociology of Education, 64,* 78–95.

Rosenbaum, James E. and Binder, Amy (1997, January). Do employers really need more educated youth? *Sociology of Education, 70,* 68–85.

Rosenbaum, James E. and Miller, Shazia (1998). The earnings payoff to college degrees for youth with poor high school achievement. *Unpublished manuscript, Northwestern University, Institute for Policy Research.

Rosenbaum, James E., Miller, Shazia, and Krei, Melinda (1996, August). Gatekeeping in an era of more open gates. *American Journal of Education, 104,* 257–279.

Rosenbaum, James E., Miller, Shazia, and Krei, Melinda (1997). What role should counselors have? In Kenneth K. Wong (Ed.), *Advances in educational policy* (Vol. 3). Greenwood, CT: JAI Press, pp. 79–92.

Rosenbaum, James E. and Roy, Kevin (1996, April). Trajectories for success in the transition from school to work. Paper presented at the annual meeting of the American Educational Research Association, New York.

Rosenbaum, James E., Miller, Shazia, and Roy, Kevin (1996, August). Long-term effects of high school grades and job placements. Paper presented at the annual meeting of the American Sociological Association, New York.

Sedlak, Michael W., Wheeler, Christopher W., Pullin, Diane C., and Cusick, Phillip A. (1986). *Selling students short.* New York: Teachers College Press.

Steinberg, Lawrence (1996). *Beyond the classroom.* New York: Simon and Shuster.

Stern, David, Finkelstein, Neal, Stone, James, Latting, John, and Dornsife, Carolyn (1995). *School to work: Research on programs in the United States.* Washington and London: Falmer Press.

Stevenson, Harold W., and Stigler, James W. (1992). *The learning gap.* New York: Simon and Shuster.

Stinchcombe, Arthur L. (1965). *Rebellion in a high school.* Chicago: Quadrangle.

Turner, Ralph (1960). Sponsored and contest mobility and the school system. *American Sociological Review, 25,* 855–867.

U.S. Department of Health, Education, and Welfare (1992). *Digest of educational statistics.* Washington, DC: U.S. Government Printing Office.

Explanations of Educational Inequality

In Chapter 8, we explored unequal educational outcomes among various groups in U.S. society. The data suggest that there are significant differences in educational achievement and attainment based on social class, race, gender, and other ascriptive characteristics. Further, such unequal outcomes call into question the country's ideology of equality of educational opportunity and the ethos that schooling provides an important mechanism for social mobility. Although the data indicate that there has been mobility for individuals and that schooling has become increasingly tied to the labor market as a credentialing process, they do not support the democratic-liberal faith that schooling provides mobility for entire groups. In fact, the data indicate that the relationship between family background and economic outcomes has been fairly consistent, with family background exerting a powerful effect on both educational achievement and attainment and economic outcomes.

Given the persistent inequalities of educational outcomes—especially those based on race, class, and gender (although as we noted in the previous chapter, social class remains the most powerful factor in explaining educational inequalities)—the next step is to explain these unequal outcomes of the schooling process. In a society that is at least ideologically committed to the eradication of educational inequality, why do these differences continue to persist, often in the face of explicit social policies aimed at their elimination?

In this chapter, we will review the complex explanations of the problem. As you will see, there are numerous conflicting theories of educational inequality. We will present an overview of each and then offer our own multidimensional approach to understanding this most difficult situation. Let us note at the outset that there are no simple explanations and no simple solutions, despite experts' claims to the contrary. More often than not, the literature on educational inequality is filled with ideological explanations devoid of evidence. It is incumbent, however, to sift through the polemics and examine the research in order to reach reasonable conclusions. Given the complexity of the problem, this is no easy task; given the enormity and gravity of the problem, there is no choice but to continue to attempt to solve it.

Explanations of Unequal Educational Achievement

The two major sociological theories of education provide a general understanding of the problem, although from very different directions. Both theories are also concerned about the existence of profound and persistent inequalities, albeit from different vantage points. Functionalists believe that the role of schools is to provide a fair and meritocratic selection process for sorting out the best and brightest individuals, regardless of family background. The functionalist vision of a just society is one where individual talent and hard work based on universal principles of evaluation are more important than ascriptive characteristics based on particularistic methods of evaluation.

Functionalists expect that the schooling process will produce unequal results, but these results ought to be based on individual differences between students, not on group differences. Thus, although there is a persistent relationship between family background and educational outcomes, this does not in and of itself mean that the system fails to provide equality of opportunity. It is possible that even with equality of opportunity there could be these patterns of unequal results, although most functionalists would agree that this is highly unlikely. Therefore, functionalists believe that unequal educational outcomes are the result, in part, of unequal educational opportunities. Thus, for functionalists, it is imperative to understand the sources of educational inequality so as to ensure the elimination of structural barriers to educational success and to provide all groups a fair chance to compete in the educational marketplace. This perspective has been the foundation of liberal educational policy in the United States since the 1960s.

Conflict theorists are not in the least bit surprised by the data. Given that conflict theorists believe that the role of schooling is to reproduce rather than eliminate inequality, the fact that educational outcomes are to a large degree based on family background is fully consistent with this perspective. Nonetheless, conflict theorists are also concerned with inequality and its eradication. Whereas functionalists focus on the attempts to provide equality of opportunity and to ensure a meritocratic system, conflict theorists are concerned with both equality of opportunity and results. That is, conflict theorists, who usually fall into the more radical political category, do not believe that equality of opportunity is a sufficient goal.

A system that could guarantee equitable and fair treatment to all would not necessarily produce equal results, as individual differences (rather than group differences) would still play an important role in creating significant inequalities. Although most radicals do not believe that complete equality of results is possible or even desirable, they do want to reduce significantly the degree of educational, social, and economic inequalities. Thus, conflict theorists call for more radical measures to reduce inequality; also, they are far more skeptical than functionalists that the problem can be solved.

Despite these differences, both functionalists and conflict theorists agree that understanding educational inequality is a difficult task. Further, it is clear that the third sociological approach, interactionist theory, is necessary to grasp fully the problem. Interactionism suggests that one must understand how people within institutions such as families and schools interact on a daily basis in order to comprehend the factors explaining academic success and failure. Thus, in addition to studying empirical data on school outcomes, which often explains what happens, one must also look into the lives and worlds of families and schools in order to understand why it happens. Many of the research studies of educational inequality that are discussed in this chapter use an interactionist approach based on field work in order to examine what goes on in families and schools.

The next step is to explain race-, class-, and gender-based inequalities of educational attainment and achievement. Researchers have posed two different sets of explanations. The first is centered on factors outside of the school, such as the family, the community, the culture of the group, the peer group, and the individual student. These explanations are often termed *student-centered* (Dougherty & Hammack, 1990, p. 334) or *extra-school* (Hurn, 1993, p. 161) *explanations.* The second is centered on factors within the school, such as teachers and teaching methods, curriculum, ability grouping and curriculum tracking, school climate, and teacher expectations. These explanations are often termed *school-centered* (Dougherty & Hammack, 1990, p. 334) or *within-school* (Hurn, 1993, p. 162) *explanations.*

Although there is merit in both approaches, the dichotomy between what are inexorably linked spheres is somewhat shortsighted. As Hurn (1993, pp. 161–162) has pointed out, functionalists tend to support extra-school explanations because these provide support for the view that the schooling process is somewhat meritocratic and that educational inequalities are caused by factors outside the schooling process. Conflict theorists, although not denying the deleterious impact of extra-school factors such as poverty, believe that schools play an important role in reproducing the problems. The attempt to pigeon hole the explanation into one explanatory system denies the connection between schooling and other societal institutions.

We prefer a more multidimensional approach, such as the one outlined by Persell (1977), which argues that educational inequality is the product of the relationship between societal, institutional, interactional, and intrapsychic variables. Thus, in order to understand education and inequality, one must explore not only what goes on within society and its institutions (such as the family and the school) but also the connections between them and their effects on individuals and groups. In the following sections, we outline the major student-centered and school-centered explanations and then propose a more multidimensional synthesis of these explanations.

Before we begin, it is important to discuss briefly the interconnection between race, class, gender, and ethnicity. As we noted in Chapter 8, individuals have more than one ascriptive status. For example, in terms of gender, men and women belong to different social classes and races, and come from different ethnic groups. In terms of race and ethnicity, members of different racial and ethnic groups may belong to different socioeconomic classes. Thus, there are differences in educational attainment and achievement between working class and middle-class women or men, between working class and middle-class blacks or whites, and between different ethnic groups based on social class position.

Sociological research on educational outcomes attempts to separate the independent effects of these variables, although their relationship is often difficult to distinguish. It is clear, however, that although gender, race, and ethnicity have independent effects, and that women, African Americans, and other ethnic groups are often negatively affected by societal and school processes, social class background has the most powerful effect on educational achievement and attainment. This is not to say that women or African Americans as groups may not be disadvantaged in schools, independent of social class background—only that social class appears to be the more powerful explanatory variable in explaining educational attainment and achievement.

On the one hand, given the powerful relationship between social class and educational attainment and achievement, much of the sociological research on educational outcomes has focused on class issues. On the other hand, given the significant relationship between social class and race, the problems of African Americans' achievement, and the important political movements aimed at ameliorating conditions of African American poverty and improving African American educational performance, this research has also focused on the relationship between race and education. In the following sections, we do not treat issues of race and class separately. Rather, we look at research that sometimes examines race as a separate category, sometimes looks at class as a separate category, and sometimes looks at them together. The following discussion assumes that groups that do not fare well in school do so because of their subordinate position in society, with race, class, gender, and ethnicity important components of a group's position. As the bulk of research concentrates on race and class, the following discussion concentrates on these studies.

We are not implying that gender and ethnicity are unimportant. A growing body of literature is interested in the educational performance of different ethnic groups, including Asians, Italians, Latinos, and others (Doran & Weffer, 1992; Lomawaima, 1995; Nieto, 1995; Pang, 1995; Wong-Fillmore & Valdez, 1986). Additionally, the problems faced by students whose first language is not English are increasingly the subject of educational research (Hakuta & Garcia, 1989; Nieto, 1995; Pang, 1995; Thornburg & Karp, 1992; Wong-Fillmore & Valdez, 1986). The following discussions of student-centered and school-centered explanations, although not directly related to particular ethnic groups, assumes that the student- and school-related processes that affect working class and black students also affect other ethnic groups in a similar manner.

The research on gender and education is crucial for understanding how schooling affects particular groups (American Association of University Women, 1992). Unlike the research on ethnicity, this research cannot be easily subsumed under the student- or school-centered rubric. As we noted in Chapter 8, although there are some differences in the educational attainment and achievement of men and women, these differences are less than those based on race and class. Women do better in the humanities and men do better in math and science. However, the key difference is not in education but rather in economic outcomes, with women, despite somewhat equal levels of education, doing significantly less well economically. Part of the reason for this is related to labor market issues and gender discrimination in the workplace. Some of it is due to the different occupational choices made by men and women, with traditionally female positions rewarded less well than those occupied by men. Why women select different career paths, many of which pay less well than those selected by men, is an important question. It can be examined through the research on gender and education, which looks specifically at the ways schools socialize men and women differently.

Whereas much of the research on education and inequality focuses on the cognitive outcomes of schooling and concentrates on educational attainment and achievement, research on gender and education also focuses on the noncognitive outcomes of schooling. Thus, this research looks at the ways in which schooling affects the manner in which men and women come to view themselves, their roles, and society. Feminist scholarship on schooling examines questions of unequal opportunity for women, the differential socialization processes for boys and girls in schools, and the ways in which the hidden curriculum unequally affects women. Although feminists argue that these differential socialization patterns begin in the family and that girls bring cultural differences to the school, the bulk of educational research focuses on school-related processes. Hence, in the subsequent discussions of student-centered and school-centered explanations, we discuss gender inequalities under the school-centered rubric.

Student-Centered Explanations

In the 1960s, sociologists of education interested in educational inequality often worked from a set of liberal political and policy assumptions about why students from lower socioeconomic backgrounds often did less well in school than students from higher socioeconomic backgrounds. The conventional wisdom of the time suggested that economically disadvantaged students attended inferior schools—schools that spent less money on each student, schools that spent less money on materials and extracurricular activities, and schools that had inferior teachers. The argument continued that if school differences and financing were responsible for the problem, then the solution was simply to pump resources and money into schools with children from lower socioeconomic backgrounds.

A number of research studies in the 1960s and 1970s demonstrated, however, that the conventional liberal wisdom was far too simplistic and that solutions were far more complex. Coleman and colleagues (1966), in *Equality of Educational Opportunity,* commonly referred to as the Coleman Report, argued that school differences were not the most significant explanatory variable for the lower educational achievement of working class and nonwhite students. Rather, the report suggested, it was the differences among the groups of students that had a greater impact on educational performance. Additionally, research by Jencks and colleagues (1972) indicated that the differences between schools in privileged areas and in economically disadvantaged areas had been exaggerated. Moreover, where significant differences did exist, they did not sufficiently explain the inequalities of educational performance.

This research suggested that there were far more significant differences in academic performance among students in the same school than among students in different schools. This latter finding on what is termed *within-school differences* (as opposed to *between-school differences*) does not rule out the possibility that schools affect educational inequality, as it is possible that differences in the school such as ability grouping and curriculum tracking may explain these differences. Nevertheless, the research by Coleman and by Jencks casted doubt on the claim that differences between schools explained the performance gap among students from different socioeconomic or racial backgrounds. We will return to the question of school differences later in this chapter, but for now, it is important to discuss the consequences of these findings.

If school differences and financing did not explain unequal educational performance, then perhaps the schools themselves were not the most important factor. Based on the Coleman Report, educational researchers and policy makers concluded that the reason students from lower socioeconomic backgrounds did less well in school had more to do with the students themselves, their families, their neighborhood and communities, their culture, and perhaps even their genetic makeup. These student-centered explanations became dominant in the 1960s and 1970s and are still highly controversial and politically charged.

Genetic Differences

The most controversial student-centered explanation is the genetic or biological argument. From a sociological and anthropological perspective, biological explanations of human behavior are viewed as limited because social scientists believe that environmental and social factors are largely responsible for human behavior. Recent advances in the understanding of mental illnesses such as schizophrenia, however, suggest that there may be biochemical and genetic causes. This research indicates that although social and psychological factors are crucial, biological factors cannot be ruled out entirely. Having said this, the question remains as to whether there is evidence to support the argument that differences in school performance among groups of students are due to genetic differences among these groups, particularly in intelligence.

The argument that unequal educational performance by working class and non-white students is due to genetic differences in intelligence was offered by psychologist Arthur Jensen in a highly controversial article in the *Harvard Educational Review* (1969). Jensen indicated that compensatory programs (i.e., programs aimed at improving the educational performance of disadvantaged students) were doomed to failure because they were aimed at changing social and environmental factors, when the root of the problem was biological. Jensen, based on sophisticated statistical analyses, argued that African Americans, genetically, are less intelligent than whites and therefore do less well in school, where intelligence is an important component of educational success. Given these data and his conclusions, Jensen was pessimistic about the likelihood that the academic performance of African Americans could be substantially improved.

Hurn (1993, pp. 142–152) provided a detailed and balanced assessment of the IQ controversy. Given the sensitivity of the subject, more often than not, the debate about Jensen's work consisted of polemical attacks accusing him of being a racist and dismissed his claim that there is a biological basis of intelligence, rather than carefully considering his arguments. Hurn demonstrated through a careful analysis of Jensen's thesis that although there is evidence that a genetic component to human intelligence exists, and that although a small percentage of the social class differences in intelligence may be attributed to genetic factors, the most significant factor affecting intelligence is social. Moreover, he argued that there is no persuasive evidence that social class and racial differences in intelligence are due to genetic factors. Additionally, Hurn and others have indicated that these differences in intelligence are in part due to the cultural bias of IQ test questions, the conditions under which they are given, and cultural and family differences (Bowles & Gintis, 1976, Chapter 4; Kamin, 1974; Persell, 1977, pp. 58–75). In the 1990s, the genetic argument reemerged with the publication of *The Bell Curve* (1994) by Richard Herrnstein and Charles Murray. This book presented many of the same arguments made in the 1960s by Jensen and was greeted with similar criticism (Kincheloe, Steinberg, & Gressom, 1996).

Given the weakness of the genetic argument, how does one explain unequal educational performance by working class and nonwhite students? As we stated earlier, as a result of the Coleman and Jencks studies, researchers looked to the family and the culture of the students for answers. Cultural deprivation and cultural difference theories have been two related approaches. Although these theories are more widely accepted by social scientists, because they view social and cultural factors as essential, they have been no less controversial.

Cultural Deprivation Theories

In light of the Coleman Report's findings that school differences and resources did not adequately explain unequal performance by working class and nonwhite students, some educational researchers argued that these students came to school without the requisite intellectual and social skills necessary for school success. Cultural deprivation theory, popularized in the 1960s, suggests that working class and nonwhite families often lack the cultural resources, such as books and other educational stimuli, and thus arrive at school at a significant disadvantage.

Moreover, drawing on the thesis advanced by anthropologist Oscar Lewis (1966) about poverty in Mexico, cultural deprivation theorists assert that the poor have a deprived culture—one that lacks the value system of middle-class culture. According to this perspective, middle-class culture values hard work and initiative, the delay of immediate gratification for future reward, and the importance of schooling as a means to future success. The culture of poverty eschews delayed gratification for immediate reward, rejects hard work and initiative as a means to success, and does not view schooling as the means to social mobility. According to cultural deprivation theorists such as Deutsch (1964), this deprivation results in educationally disadvantaged students who achieve poorly because they have not been raised to acquire the skills and dispositions required for satisfactory academic achievement (Dougherty & Hammack, 1990, p. 341).

Based on this etiology, policy makers sought to develop programs aimed not at the schools but rather at the family environment of working class and nonwhite students. Compensatory education programs such as Project Head Start—a preschool intervention program for educationally and economically disadvantaged students—are based on the assumption that because of the cultural and familial deprivation faced by poor students, the schools must provide an environment that makes up for lost time. If these students are not prepared for school at home, then it is the role of the preschool to provide the necessary foundation for learning. Further, programs such as Head Start attempt to involve parents in their children's schooling and to help them develop parenting and literacy skills necessary for their children's academic development.

Cultural deprivation theory was attacked vociferously in the 1960s and 1970s by social scientists who believed it to be paternalistic at best and racist at worst. Critics argue that it removes the responsibility for school success and failure from schools and teachers and places it on families. Further, they suggest that it blames the victims of poverty for the effects of poverty rather than placing the blame squarely where it belongs: on the social and economic processes that produce poverty (Baratz & Baratz, 1970; Dougherty & Hammack, 1990, p. 341; Ryan, 1971).

Another criticism of cultural deprivation theory concerned the relative failure of many of the compensatory education programs that were based on its assumptions about why disadvantaged children have lower levels of achievement than more advantaged children. Although Project Head Start has received mixed evaluations (with early findings somewhat negative and later research providing more positive results; cf. Weikert & Schweinhart, 1984), compensatory programs, as a whole, have not improved significantly the academic performance of disadvantaged students. Given these criticisms and the weakness of the geneticist argument, a third student-centered explanation emerged: cultural difference theory.

Cultural Difference Theories

Cultural difference theorists agree that there are cultural and family differences between working class and nonwhite students and white middle-class students. Working class and nonwhite students may indeed arrive at school with different cultural dispositions and without the skills and attitudes required by the schools. This is not due to deficiencies in their home life but rather to being part of an oppressed minority. The key difference in this perspective is that although cultural difference theorists acknowledge the impact of student differences, they do not blame working class and nonwhite families for educational problems. Rather, they attribute cultural differences to social forces such as poverty, racism, discrimination, and unequal life chances.

There are a number of different varieties of cultural difference theory. First, researchers such as anthropologist John Ogbu (1978, 1979, 1987) argue that African American children do less well in school because they adapt to their oppressed position in the class and caste structure. Ogbu argued that there is a "job ceiling" for African Americans in the United States, as there is for similar caste-like minorities in other countries, and that African American families and schools socialize their children to deal with their inferior life chances rather than encourage them to internalize those values and skills necessary for positions that will not be open to them. Although this is a complex, and at times a hidden, process, the results are lower educational attainment and performance.

Ogbu's later work (Fordham & Ogbu, 1986) suggests that school success requires that African American students deny their own cultural identities and accept the dominant culture of the schools, which is a white middle-class model. African American students thus have the "burden of acting white" in order to succeed (Fordham, 1997). This explanation, as we will see later in this chapter, rejects the argument that school-centered explanations are unimportant, and proposes the interaction of school and student variables to explain educational achievement. The view that there are cultural differences between the culture of the school and the culture of working class and nonwhite students has resulted in calls for changes in school curriculum and pedagogy to more adequately represent the cultures of minority children. As we stated in Chapter 7, the demand for multicultural curricula is rooted in the belief that the schools need to reflect the cultures of all the students who attend, not just the culture of dominant social groups.

Ogbu's macrosociological perspective is similar to those of Bowles and Gintis (1976), whose correspondence theory suggests that working class students adapt to the unequal aspects of the class structure, and to Bourdieu and Passeron (1977) and Bernstein (1977), whose theories point out the ways in which class and cultural differences are reflected in the schools. Bernstein, in particular, has often been accused of being a cultural deprivation theorist because of his theory that working class students in England have a different language and communication code, which disadvantages them in the schools. Bernstein (1990) has consistently denied that working class language is deficient. Rather, he has stated that cultural and class differences are a product of an unequal economic system and that the schools reward middle-class communication codes, not working class codes. This viewpoint is a complex one, as it sees educational inequality as a product of the relationships between the economic system, the family, and the schools, with cultural differences turned into deficits by the schooling process. As with Ogbu's theories, Bernstein's theory insists on looking at the schools as sources of educational inequality, not just the culture or families of working-class students.

Bourdieu's concepts of social and cultural capital are also important in understanding how cultural differences affect educational inequality (Swartz, 1997). More affluent families give their children access to cultural capital (e.g., visits to museums, concerts, travel, etc.) and social capital (e.g., networks for access to educational resources, college admissions, parental involvement, etc.). Although Bourdieu recognizes that economic capital (income and wealth) are still paramount in providing affluent families with an educational advantage, social and cultural capital are more subtle ways that social class advantages reproduce educational inequalities. Lareau (1989, 2003) uses Bourdieu's concepts to examine social class differences in the relationship between family and schools.

Ogbu's research also examines the relationship between language and educational achievement among low-income, inner-city African American students (Ogbu, 1999). Based on an extensive ethnographic study of a low-income community in Oakland, California, Ogbu documents the tensions between the standard English required for school success and the "slang-English" (Black English) used in the community. Consistent with Bernstein's analysis of restricted (working class) and elaborated (middle-class) codes, Ogbu argues that although African American students and parents believe it is important that schools teach standard English for educational and occupational mobility, they are ambivalent about its use within the community. Such ambivalence results in difficulties in using standard English and is an important factor in explaining educational inequalities for these students.

Just as Bernstein does not see British working class language as inferior, Ogbu does not see African American linguistic codes as culturally deficient. Black English is a different dialect that is defined as deficient by the dominant linguistic codes of schooling and society. The question is how low-income African American students can be successfully bidialectic—that is, be able to use standard English for academic and occupational mobility and not feel they are committing cultural or racial suicide. The film, *Educating Rita,* illustrates this problem for a British working class woman who enrolls in the Open University. Eventually, she must choose between continuing her education or losing her husband, who rejects her new use of middle-class codes. Ultimately, she leaves her husband and working class community and attains academic success. The question is: Is the price of losing one's culture too high a price to pay?

Ogbu's article appeared after the Oakland School District's 1996 Ebonics (Black English) controversy. The Oakland School Board voted (and subsequently rescinded) a policy to teach Ebonics as a second language as a way of promoting standard English language literacy. The policy resulted in a national controversy in which many African American leaders, including Jesse Jackson, stressed the importance of standard

English. Ogbu's work demonstrates that the issue is far more complex than telling low-income African American students to simply learn standard English. Rather, linguistic codes are at the heart of unequal power relations between dominant and subordinate groups and represent one's definition of cultural identity. Clearly, standard English is necessary for academic and occupational success; internalizing and acting on this is a more difficult social psychological problem.

Ogbu's last book, completed shortly before his death in 2003, examined the persistence of the black–white achievement gap in middle and upper–middle-class communities. Asked by the African American parents in Shaker Heights, Ohio, to help them understand why their children were performing at lower levels than their white classmates, Ogbu spent a year studying the community and its schools. He concluded that although there were school-based reasons for unequal achievement, especially the underrepresentation of African American students in honors and advanced placement classes and their overrepresentation in regular classes, the main reasons had to do with student, parental, and community cultures. African American students studied less, watched more television, and had lower aspirations than their white classmates. They were also more likely to be affected by an antischool culture and received less pressure from their parents to excel in school. Ogbu did not discount school factors, but argued that they are related to powerful cultural differences (Ogbu, 2003).

A second type of cultural difference theory sees working class and nonwhite students as resisting the dominant culture of the schools. From this point of view, these students reject the white middle-class culture of academic success and embrace a different, often antischool culture—one that is opposed to the culture of schooling as it currently exists. Research by Willis (1981) on working class boys in England shows that these students explicitly reject middle-class values and enthusiastically embrace a working class culture, which eschews the values of schooling. They consciously reject schooling and resist academic success. This resistance results in dropping out of school and into the world of work—that is, the world of the factory floor, which they romanticize as the proper place for men.

A study of suburban life in the New York–New Jersey metropolitan area (Gaines, 1991) documents the antischool culture of working class suburban adolescents, for whom heavy metal, rock and roll music, and "souped-up" automobiles are the symbols of adolescent culture, with the academic life of schooling consciously rejected and scorned. According to this type of cultural difference theory, these cultural norms are not inferior to middle-class norms, only different. Thus, the fact that society and its schools demand middle-class cultural norms places these students at a distinct disadvantage. Cultural difference theorists, such as Ogbu, suggest that subordinate groups often see little reason to embrace the culture of schooling, as they do not believe it will have value for them. Given the labor market barriers to these groups, Ogbu has argued that this type of resistance may in fact be a form of cultural adaptation to the realities of economic life.

The problem with cultural difference theory, according to Hurn (1993, pp. 154–155), is that it is too culturally relativistic. That is, in its insistence that all cultures are equally valid and that all values and norms are acceptable in the context of the culture that generated them, cultural difference theorists too often deny cultural problems and dysfunction. Although it is fair to acknowledge that cultural deprivation theorists are often ethnocentric and biased, and that the culture of schooling often alienates students from working class and nonwhite families, it is apparent that cultural patterns may negatively affect school performance. That these patterns are often caused by social and economic forces does not eliminate them nor reduce their negative impact on academic achievement. As Hurn (1993, p. 154) stated:

> The claim that lower-class environments are not deficient in their provision of resources for intellectual growth but reflect differential valuations of ideal family forms is also problematic. While we may grant some of the characterizations of lower-class family life as pathological are ethnocentric and insensitive to cultural differences, much research has shown that poverty and unemployment make it extremely difficult for lower-class families to maintain relationships *they define* as satisfactory. Among poor black families, for example, over 50% of the households are headed by women, and illegitimacy rates exceed 60 percent. There is little evidence that blacks regard such families as desirable, and indeed there is increasing evidence that in the 1980s the black community began to define this situation as a crisis in the black family. The causes of that crisis undoubtedly lie in the legacy of discrimination and in poverty and unemployment. But it is hard to deny that the instability of family life in many lower-class black households makes for an unpropitious environment for the development of intellectual skills.

Lemann (1991), in his journalistic history of the black migration from the Mississippi Delta to Chicago in the post–World War II years, chronicled the cycles of poverty, hopelessness, and despair that mark life in the public housing projects of Chicago. Although he argued that economic transformations and conditions are the root causes of poverty, and that racism and discrimination exacerbate the problems, he nonetheless pointed out that the culture of the projects—with their rampant violence, drug abuse, and hopelessness—are part of the problem. Although it is important not to blame the poor for their situation and to understand that what Lemann described is a result of poverty, it is equally important to acknowledge that such life-styles should not be celebrated as "resistance." Rather, as Lemann noted, public policy must simultaneously address the elimination of the social and economic conditions responsible for poverty and the behaviors that serve to reproduce it.

In Chapter 8, we presented data on the academic success of Asian American students. Recent political decisions in California to eliminate affirmative action in college admissions to state universities and to end bilingual education have placed Asian American achievement in a national spotlight. With respect to bilingual education, why do Asian Americans do better than other students whose first language is not English? With respect to affirmative action, ending affirmative action in California has resulted in a significant increase in the percentage of Asian Americans attending the state's flagship institutions such as Berkeley and UCLA, with over 60 percent of Berkeley's first-year classes now comprised of Asian Americans; and a subsequent decline in the percentage of African American and Hispanic American students (Orfield & Miller, 1998). Sociologists disagree about the causes of Asian American academic success. One explanation is that as voluntary immigrants (Ogbu, 1999), Asian Americans come to the United States willing to adapt to the dominant culture in order to succeed. Another explanation is that a large number of Asian Americans come from the educated middle classes of their native countries and already possess the skills and dispositions necessary for academic success. A third is that Asian Americans possess family values that place enormous emphasis on educational achievement and have high expectations for their children. Critics of cultural theories argue that blaming poor people for their problems is "blaming the victim" (Ryan, 1971). They argue that poor people suffer dramatically from the ravages of poverty, which affects their academic performance. Richard Rothstein (2004b) argues that poor people suffer from significant health problems, including high rates of asthma, exposure to lead paint, smoking and alcohol use, poor vision and nutrition, lower birth weight, and inadequate health care. These poverty-related health problems can have significant effects on academic achievement. For example, exposure to lead paint or to smoking, alcohol, or drugs can lower IQ and limit cognitive development. Rothstein argues that investments in improving the health of low-income children will significantly reduce the achievement gaps based on income. Although some may see this explanation as cultural deprivation theory in reverse, it is difficult to ignore the relationship between family beliefs in the importance of academic success and Asian American academic achievement. Lew (2005a, 2005b, 2005c), however, argues that the "model minority" explanation of Asian American student success overlooks the variation among these students. According to Lew there are significant numbers of failing Asian American students. Successful Asian American students are more likely to come from more affluent families and to make use of social capital, including community networks that help them navigate the academic world. Stanton-Salazar's (2001) research on Mexican American students supports the importance of social capital for immigrant students.

It is important to transcend the often emotional and political arguments that accompany discussions of cultural deprivation and differences. Too often, those who point to the negative impact of cultural differences on academic achievement are accused of class and racial bias, when such ethnocentrism is not part of their analysis. Clearly, the poor should not be blamed for their problems, as the causes of poverty are more social and economic then they are cultural. Neither should the cultural differences related to school success and failure be denied. The key is to move past the ideological and to eliminate the social and educational barriers to school success for working class and nonwhite students. Perhaps more importantly, one must recognize that unequal educational achievement cannot be explained by looking at students and their families alone; one must also look at the schools themselves.

School-Centered Explanations

Earlier in this chapter, we reviewed the early research of Coleman and of Jencks on the relationship between school quality and resources and unequal academic attainment. Although their research questioned the conventional wisdom that between-school differences are the key factor in explaining differences in student performance between groups, it did not exclude the possibility that schools have significant effects on students. Although Coleman's early work concluded that student differences were more important than school differences, a conclusion that his subsequent work on public and private schools rejects (Coleman, Hoffer, & Kilgore, 1982; Coleman & Hoffer, 1987), and Jencks concluded that school effects were minimal, both researchers found that there are significant within-school differences that suggested schools may indeed make a difference.

For example, how does one explain differences in academic performance among groups of students within the same school? A completely individualistic explanation states that these differences are the result of individual differences in intelligence or initiative. Another student-centered explanation sees these differences as the result of student differences prior to entering school. School-centered explanations, however, suggest that school processes are central to understanding unequal educational performance. In the 1980s, educational researchers examined carefully the myriad processes within schools that explain the sources of unequal academic achievement. This school-centered research focused on both between- and within-school processes.

School Financing

Jonathan Kozol (1991), in his muckraking book *Savage Inequalities,* compared public schools in affluent suburbs with public schools in poor inner cities. He documented the vast differences in funding between affluent and poor districts and called for equalization in school financing. In Chapter 8, we presented recent data on differences in funding between affluent and poor school districts. As these data indicated, in 1995–1996, significant differences between affluent suburban and poorer urban districts remain, with New York City schools receiving less than $10,000 per student and affluent Long Island schools receiving over $15,000 per student (see Table 9.1). These differences have remained consistent in most states through 2004, with the exception of a number of states, including Delaware, Kentucky, Massachusetts, Minnesota, and New Jersey. In order to comprehend why these inequalities exist, it is important to understand the way in which public schools are financed in the United States.

Public schools are financed through a combination of revenues from local, state, and federal sources. However, the majority of funds come from state and local taxes, with local property taxes a significant source. Property taxes are based on the value of property in local communities and therefore is a proportional tax. Since property values are significantly higher in more affluent communities, these communities are able to raise significantly more money for schools through this form of taxation than poorer communities with lower property values. Additionally, since families in more affluent communities have higher incomes, they pay proportionately less of their incomes for their higher school taxes.

Thus, more affluent communities are able to provide more per-pupil spending than poorer districts, often at a proportionately less burdensome rate than in poorer communities. This unequal funding has been the subject of considerable legal attack by communities that argue that funding based on local property taxes is discriminatory under the Equal Protection Clause of the Fourteenth Amendment and that it denies equality of opportunity.

In *Serrano* v. *Priest* (1971), the California Supreme Court ruled the system of unequal school financing between wealthy and poor districts unconstitutional. It did not, however, declare the use of property taxes for school funding illegal. Five other state courts (in Arizona, Minnesota, New Jersey, Texas, and Wyoming) rendered similar rulings within the next year. However, in 1973, the U.S. Supreme Court in *San Antonio*

TABLE 9.1   School Funding in New York City and Selected Long Island Districts: 1995–96 School Year

District	Wealth Ratio (higher = more wealth)	Spending per Pupil (Including Special Education Students)
New York City (Bronx, King's, New York, Queen's, and Richmond Counties)	N/A	$ 9,782
Nassau County		
Baldwin	1.292	$10,283
Bellmore-Merrick	1.568	$12,876
East Williston	2.674	$15,483
Franklin Square	1.414	$ 9,417
Freeport	0.807	$ 9,970
Garden City	2.889	$13,150
Hempstead	0.676	$11,590
Long Beach	1.590	$13,404
Malverne	1.227	$12,140
Manhasset	3.469	$17,560
New Hyde Park	1.721	$ 8,780
Oyster Bay	3.966	$15,867
Roosevelt	0.588	$12,013
Roslyn	2.945	$15,045
Suffolk County		
Amagansett	11.651	$21,796
Amityville	1.153	$11,793
Central Islip	0.630	$13,468
Copiague	0.882	$ 9,431
Hauppauge	1.656	$13,831
Huntington	1.795	$13,290
Miller Place	0.907	$ 9,572
Northport	1.895	$12,957
Quogue	12.234	$19,277
Rocky Point	0.817	$ 9,902
South Huntington	1.351	$11,869
Shoreham-Wading River	4.478	$15,797
West Islip	1.083	$10,794
Wyandanch	0.396	$12,142

Note: Nassau County is directly east of New York City's borough of Queens and stretches approximately 30 miles to the Suffolk County border. Nassau County includes the wealthy *Gold Coast* made famous by F. Scott Fitzgerald in the *Great Gatsby;* Jones Beach, planned by famous planner Robert Moses; Levittown, one of the first planned communities built for GIs returning from WWII; Roosevelt Field, one of the first and still among the largest shopping malls in the country; and Mitchell Field, the departure site of Charles Lindberg's historic cross-Atlantic flight. The county has communities of great wealth, great poverty, and many middle-income communities. Although western Suffolk County is suburban, it becomes more rural the further east you go. It has numerous farms and vineyards, as well as the famous beach resort areas of Fire Island and the Hamptons. It, too, has communities of great wealth, great poverty, and many middle-income communities. For a more detailed analysis, see Singer (1999).
Source: New York State Department of Education, as cited in "School by School Report Card" (1998).

(Texas) Independent School District v. *Rodriguez* reversed a lower-court ruling and up-held the use of local property taxes as the basis for school funding. In a 5–4 opinion, the Court ruled that this method of funding, although unjust, was not unconstitutional. Justice Thurgood Marshall, in a dissenting opinion, stated that the decision represented a move away from a commitment to equality of opportunity (Johnson, 1991, p. 308).

Although the Supreme Court decision has made it unlikely that the federal government will intervene in local financing of public schools, individual states have taken on the responsibility of attempting to decrease inequalities in school financing. The Kentucky, Texas, Arkansas, California, Connecticut, Montana, New Jersey, New York, Washington, West Virginia, and Wyoming state courts have ruled against their states' system of school financing. The Kentucky decision called for a shift to state funding of schools to ensure equality of educational opportunity. In *Abbott* v. *Burke* (1990), the New Jersey Supreme Court ruled that the funding differences between rich and poor districts was unconstitutional. This resulted in the Quality Education Act (QEA), which was implemented (Anyon, 1997; Firestone, Goertz, & Natriello, 1997). As a result of *Abbott V* (1998), New Jersey's 31 urban districts receive the highest per-pupil funding anywhere in the country (> $15,000 per student). In the future, it appears that more states will begin to use state funding to close the gap between rich and poor districts. The use of foundation state aid programs, which seeks to make sure all districts receive a minimum standard of funding, with more state aid going to poorer districts in order to enable poorer districts to meet this minimum level, is one way of providing equality of opportunity. Although wealthier districts are still able to go above this minimum by taxing themselves at higher rates through property taxes, the use of foundation aid programs, at the very least, attempts to guarantee that all districts have the minimum necessary to provide a quality education (Johnson, 1991, pp. 314–320).

The use of federal aid to equalize school funding is a controversial issue. Proponents argue that such aid has occurred historically, as in the Elementary and Secondary Education Act of 1965. They also argue that it is the fairest and most progressive system of school financing, as it would guarantee equality of opportunity regardless of residence. Advocates of a federal system of financing, such as Kozol (1991), believe that schools should be financed through federal income taxes. Critics, however, believe that, under the Tenth Amendment to the Constitution, education is a state and local matter and that federal financing would threaten local decision making.

It is clear that the present reliance on local property taxes and state aid has not reduced inequalities of financing. Thus, children from lower socioeconomic backgrounds do not receive equality of opportunity, at least in terms of funding. Although, as we note in the next sections, differences in academic achievement among students from different social classes cannot be understood in terms of funding alone, there is a moral as well as educational question at issue. Even if, as some researchers suggest (e.g., see Jencks et al., 1972), equalization of funding would not reduce inequalities of achievement among groups, is it fair that some students have significantly more money spent on them than others?

Critics of school financing believe equalization is a moral imperative, but there is not widespread agreement on this matter. For example, when New York Governor Mario Cuomo, faced with severe budgetary shortfalls during the recession in 1991, cut state aid to education more severely in affluent suburbs than in poorer cities, such as

New York City, the hue and cry in the suburbs was extraordinary. Affluent suburban districts—faced with dramatic reductions in state aid, which resulted in teacher layoffs and cutbacks in services—argued that such proportionate cutbacks threatened their ability to maintain their academic excellence. Governor Cuomo responded that state aid should be cut in districts spending sometimes over twice as much per pupil than in city districts. Thus, the question of funding is not a moral issue alone; it is a political issue, as different communities struggle to give their children what they consider the best possible education. In doing so, however, critics maintain that affluent communities continue to defend their advantages over poorer communities. In 2004, New York state's highest court mandated an additional $5.6 billion for the New York City public schools in its ruling in the decade-long Campaign for Fiscal Equity lawsuit. Governor Pataki and a divided state legislature, however, still have been unable to enact a funding formula to meet the court's mandate. In the same year, Governor Arnold Schwarzenegger settled the *Williams* v. *State of California* case by agreeing to set new state standards to ensure an adequate education to all the state's children.

Although the question of the morality of unequal school financing is an important one, its effects on unequal achievement is equally important. There is disagreement over the extent to which school financing affects unequal academic achievement, but it is clear that school factors other than financing have an important impact on achievement. Nonetheless, there is increasing evidence that school financing matters (Firestone, Goertz, & Natriello, 1997; Hedges, Laine, & Greenwald, 1994). Six years after the broad-based mandates of *Abbott V,* in New Jersey, including in all 31 poor urban districts (Abbott districts), results include the following: (1) parity funding equal to the state's highest wealth districts, (2) full-day preschool for all 3- and 4-year-olds, (3) comprehensive whole school reform, (4) supplemental funding for school health and other student needs, and (5) a multi-billion-dollar school facilities and construction plan. New Jersey's latest school achievement results demonstrate significant improvements in the Abbott districts at the fourth-grade level. Some of these are surely a result of the *Abbott* reforms. Although improvements have been slower at the higher grades, there is evidence to suggest that improvement will follow if the state continues its historic commitment to its poorest children. In the next sections, we explore some of these factors.

Effective School Research

The findings of Coleman and Jencks that differences in school resources and quality do not adequately explain between-school differences in academic achievement was viewed by teachers as a mixed blessing. On the one hand, if student differences are more important than school differences, then teachers cannot be blamed for the lower academic performance of nonwhite and working class students. On the other hand, if schools' effects are not significant, then schools and, more specifically, teachers can do little to make a positive difference. Although Jencks's admonition that societal change was necessary to improve schools may have made teachers feel less directly responsible for problems that were often beyond their control, it also left teachers with a sense of hopelessness that there was little if anything they could do to improve schooling from inside the schools. Critics of the student-centered findings went further. They argued that this research took the responsibility away from schools and teachers and placed it on communities and families. Common sense, they believed, suggested that there were differences between good and bad schools, and between good and incompetent teachers. These differences certainly had to have some effects on students. The difficult empirical task, however, is to untangle the ways in which school processes affect student learning.

The concern with unequal educational performance of nonwhite and working class students is at the heart of such inquiry. The finding that within-school differences are as or more significant than between-school differences raised questions about the common-sense argument that students from lower socioeconomic backgrounds do poorly simply because they attend inferior schools. Ronald Edmonds (1979a), an African American former school superintendent and Harvard professor, suggested that comparing schools in different socioeconomic communities was only part of the puzzle. He argued that researchers needed to compare schools within lower socioeconomic communities, as well. If all schools in such neighborhoods produce low educational outcomes, and these lower outcomes could not be explained in terms of school differences in comparison to schools in higher socioeconomic communities, then the student-centered findings could be supported. Conversely, if there are significant differences in student performance between schools within lower socioeconomic neighborhoods, then there have to be school effects. That is, how is it possible that homogeneous groups of students (i.e., in terms of race and socioeconomic class) in a lower socioeconomic community perform differently depending on the school that they attend? Student-centered explanations would suggest that the factors outside the schools that affect nonwhite and working class students are the same in different schools within the same neighborhood. Thus, if students from the same racial and socioeconomic backgrounds attending different schools within the same community perform at significantly different rates, then something within the schools themselves must be affecting student performance.

Based on this logic, Edmonds and other effective school researchers (Austin & Garber, 1985; Brookover et al., 1979) examined schools that produced unusually positive academic results given what would be expected, based on the socioeconomic composition of the school and/or schools that are unusually effective in general. *The effective school literature,* as it is termed, suggests that there are characteristics of unusually effective schools that help to explain why their students achieve academically. These characteristics include the following (Stedman, 1987):

- A climate of high expectations for students by teachers and administrators
- Strong and effective leadership by a principal or school head
- Accountability processes for students and teachers
- The monitoring of student learning
- A high degree of instructional time on task, where teachers spend a great deal of their time teaching and students spend a great deal of their time learning
- Flexibility for teachers and administrators to experiment and adapt to new situations and problems.

These phenomena are more likely found in effective schools than ineffective ones, independent of the demographic composition of the students in the school. Given the differences between students in schools in lower and higher socioeconomic neighborhoods, these findings may suggest that there are a higher number of schools with these characteristics in higher socioeconomic communities. Or, given the extra-school factors in these neighborhoods, it is easier for schools in higher socioeconomic communities to develop such characteristics within their schools. More importantly, these findings suggest that there are things that schools can do to positively affect student achievement in lower socioeconomic communities (Thernstrom & Thernstrom, 2003; The Education Trust, 2004a).

The effective school research suggests that there are school-centered processes that help to explain unequal educational achievement by different groups of students. It supports the later work of Coleman and his colleagues (Coleman, Hoffer, & Kilgore, 1982; Coleman & Hoffer, 1987) that argues that Catholic schools produce significantly better levels of academic achievement because of their more rigorous academic curriculum and higher academic expectations. Ironically, Coleman has thus moved full circle from his earlier work, which stated that students—not schools—were the most significant explanatory variable, to his recent work, which states that schools make a significant difference independent of the students who attend. Critics of Coleman's recent work (see Chapter 8), however, suggest that he has insufficiently controlled for student and parental effects and that such extra-school differences may be more important than the differences between public and Catholic schools. What these ongoing debates indicate is that school and student effects cannot be isolated and that the interaction between these factors must be addressed more completely. We will return to this point later in this chapter.

Although the effective school literature has attracted much support from policy makers and is often cited in the educational reform literature as the key to school improvement (Stedman, 1987), the road from research to implementation is not a clear one. The effective school researchers do not provide clear findings on implementation, nor do they provide answers to how effective schools are created. Additionally, some critics of the effective school movement argue that its definition of effective schools is based on narrow and traditional measures of academic achievement, such as standardized test scores, and that such a perspective defines educational success from a traditional back-to-basics perspective. Such a view may result in school reform that emphasizes success on standardized tests and overlooks other nontraditional and progressive measures of school success, which may emphasize artistic, creative, and noncognitive goals as well (cf. Cuban, 1983; Dougherty & Hammack, 1990, p. 339; Stedman, 1985, 1987). In order to respond to these criticisms, effective school researchers are attempting to replicate their findings in numerous schools (see www.edtrust.org, www.just4kids.org).

Between-School Differences: Curriculum and Pedagogic Practices

The effective school research points to how differences in what is often termed *school climates* affect academic performance. Much of this research looked at differences between schools in inner-city, lower socioeconomic neighborhoods in order to demonstrate that schools can make a difference in these communities. Although there are problems with the research, most researchers agree that its findings support the argument that schools do affect educational outcomes, at times, independent of extra-school factors.

Nonetheless, one is still faced with the task of explaining why a larger proportion of students who attend schools in higher socioeconomic communities achieve well in school. Is it because a larger proportion of schools in these communities have school climates conducive to positive academic achievement? This is a difficult question and the data are insufficient to support unequivocally such a claim. A number of theorists, however, argue that there are significant differences between the culture and climate of schools in lower socioeconomic and higher socioeconomic communities.

Bernstein (1990), examining the situation in England, suggested that schools in working class neighborhoods are far more likely to have authoritarian and teacher-directed pedagogic practices and to have a vocationally or social efficiency curriculum at the secondary level. Schools in middle-class communities are more likely to have less authoritarian and more student-centered pedagogic practices and to have a humanistic liberal arts college preparatory curriculum at the secondary level. Upper-class students are more likely to attend elite private (in England, they are called *public schools*) schools, with authoritarian pedagogic practices and a classical-humanistic college preparatory curriculum at the secondary level. Bernstein's theory is similar to Bowles and Gintis's view that the type of schooling corresponds to the social class of students in a particular school, with such differences a vehicle for socializing students from different social class backgrounds to their different places in society. Anyon's (1980) research on U.S. schools supports these findings.

Although Bernstein's work is theoretical and needs further empirical support, especially as it relates to U.S. education, there is a growing research literature that supports the existence of class-based school differences. Rist's (1970, 1973) work on urban schools, Fine's (1991) ethnography of urban school dropouts, MacLeod's (1995) description of urban schooling, Cookson and Persell's (1985) analysis of elite boarding schools, Powell, Farrar, and Cohen's (1985) descriptions of U.S. secondary schools, and Lightfoot's (1983) portraits of urban, suburban, and elite high schools all document important class-related differences in school climate, curriculum, and pedagogic practices. Moreover, journalistic portraits—including Freedman's (1990) description of a New York City high school, Kidder's (1989) discussion of a Massachusetts elementary school, and Sachar's (1991) portrait of a New York City middle school—further support the existence of these differences.

What this research does not explain is why these differences exist and precisely how they affect the different academic achievement of their students. Do schools reflect differences in student cultures that exist prior to entry into school, thus supporting student-centered explanations? Or do students respond to the different curricula, pedagogic practices, and expectations that exist in different types of schools? Finally, is there sufficient evidence to support the argument that differences in academic achievement are caused by the differences in curricula, pedagogic practices, and expectations in the different schools? These are important questions. Unfortunately, there is conflicting evidence concerning these overall conclusions. There is, however, reason to conclude that these school differences are part of the complex explanation of unequal educational achievement.

For example, a high school student at a "select 16" boarding school, such as Groton, St. Paul's, Hotchkiss, or Andover (for a complete list of the select 16, see Cookson & Persell, 1985), attends a school with a large campus in a bucolic country like setting. His or her parents pay a hefty tuition (over $21,000 per year) to support small class size, extracurricular activities, the latest in technological and curricular innovations, and support services, including counseling, tutoring, and college advisement. A high school student in an upper middle-class suburb attends a school with many of these features, although he or she lives at home, not at school. His or her parents pay high school taxes to support the level of funding necessary to provide these types of services. A high school student in a poor urban neighborhood attends a school that is often overcrowded, with large classes, a student/counselor ratio of sometimes 400 to 1, and without the latest in technology and curricula innovations.

In his book *Savage Inequalities* (1991), Jonathan Kozol portrayed these significant differences in per-student spending between suburban and urban schools. Cookson, Persell, and Catsambis (1992) documented the achievement differences between boarding schools, private day and parochial schools, and public schools. Although sociologists of education differ as to whether these achievement differences are caused by school differences, independent of student background factors, school differences must play a significant role.

The 17-year-old sitting on the ninth green on the Hotchkiss Golf Course, looking at the fall foliage on the rolling hills of Connecticut, sees a very different set of possibilities than the 17-year-old sitting on the schoolyard at Seward Park High School in New York City (the subject of Freedman's book *Small Victories*). Of course, these different life chances begin with their different class backgrounds, but their different school environments teach them to dream a different set of dreams. Research on the relationship between schooling and life expectations (Cicourel & Kitsuse, 1963; MacLeod, 1995; Ogbu, 1978; Rosenbaum, 1976) suggests that schooling can elevate or limit student aspirations about the future. It seems obvious that these two students receive very different sets of aspirations from their schooling—aspirations that more often than not translate into educational achievement, college choices, and eventual occupational destinations. Whether schooling is the causal factor is beside the point—that it is part of the process seems evident.

Within-School Differences: Curriculum and Ability Grouping

As we have stated, not only are there significant differences in educational achievement between schools but within schools, as well. The fact that different groups of students in the same schools perform very differently suggests that there may be school characteristics affecting these outcomes. As we argued in Chapter 7, ability grouping and curriculum grouping (often referred to as *tracking by ability* or *curriculum tracking*) is an important organizational component of U.S. schooling.

At the elementary school level, students are divided into reading groups and separate classes based on teacher recommendations, standardized test scores, and sometimes ascriptive characteristics such as race, class, or gender. For the most part, elementary students receive a similar curriculum in these different groups, but it may be taught at a different pace, or the teachers in the various groups may have different expectations for the different students. At the secondary school level, students are divided both by ability and curriculum, with different groups of students often receiving considerably different types of education within the same school.

There is considerable debate among educators and researchers about the necessity, effects, and efficacy of tracking. From a functionalist perspective, tracking is viewed as an important mechanism by which to separate students based on ability and to ensure that the "best and brightest" receive the type of education required to prepare them for society's most essential positions. For functionalists, the important thing is to ensure that track placement is fair and meritocratic—that is, based on ability and hard work rather than ascriptive variables. Conflict theorists, conversely, suggest that tracking is a mechanism for separating groups, often based on ascriptive characteristics, and that it is an important mechanism in reproducing inequalities.

Debates concerning the pedagogical necessity of ability and curriculum grouping abound. Many teachers and administrators argue that heterogeneous groups are far more difficult to teach and result in teaching to the middle. This results in losing those with lower abilities and boring those with higher abilities. Critics of tracking (Oakes, 1985; Sadovnik, 1991b) suggest that homogeneous grouping results in unequal education for different groups, with differences in academic outcomes often due to the differences in school climate, expectations, pedagogic practices, and curriculum between tracks.

Echoing this view, Albert Shanker (1991) stated that education in the United States assumes that students in the lower tracks are not capable of doing academic work and thus schools do not offer them an academically challenging curriculum. When these students do not perform well on examinations measuring their skills and knowledge, it confirms those expectations. The problem, Shanker suggested, is that students cannot learn what they have not been taught. Further, he pointed out that these students are capable of far more than teachers realize, and suggested that if teachers demanded and expected more, students would meet the raised expectations. Hallinan (1994b) argued that although tracking does produce inequalities based on curriculum differences, it need not do this. She suggested that tracks with equally demanding curriculum need not produce such negative results.

Much of the debate concerning tracking is emotional and ideological. Moreover, proponents of each view often lack sound empirical evidence to support their claims. It is important, then, to explore what the research states about ability and curriculum grouping by asking four important questions. First, is there evidence to support the claim that there are significant differences between tracks? Second, are there significant differences in educational attainment by students in different tracks? Third, are track placements based on discriminatory practices founded on ascriptive characteristics or are they founded on meritocratic selection mechanisms? Fourth, do the differences in the tracks explain the differences in academic attainment between tracks?

With respect to differences between tracks, many researchers (Braddock, 1990a, 1990b; Catsambis, 1994; Dougherty, 1996; Gamoran, 1987, 1993; Lucas, 1999; Oakes, 1985, 1990; Oakes, Gamoran, & Page, 1992; Sadovnik, 1991b) stated that there are significant differences in the curricula and pedagogic practices of secondary school curriculum groups. Oakes (1985) suggested that the lower tracks are far more likely to have didactic, teacher-directed practices, with rote learning and fact-based evaluation. Higher tracks are more likely to have more dialectical, student-centered practices, with discussion and thinking-based evaluation. These differences hold even when the tracks are based on ability rather than curriculum (i.e., when students in different ability tracks learn the same material, it is usually taught in a very different manner in the lower tracks). When the tracking is based on different curricula, students in different curriculum groups receive essentially different educations within the same school.

With respect to the effects of tracking and track placement, tracking has a significant effect on educational attainment at both the elementary and secondary levels. Although the effects appear to be larger for elementary school ability grouping than for high school tracking, most researchers agree that tracking affects educational attainment and achievement, independent of student characteristics (Alexander & Cook, 1982; Catsambis, 1994; Dougherty, 1996; Oakes, 1985, 1990, 1994b). Additionally, track placement is associated with student race and social characteristics, with working class and nonwhite students more likely to be assigned to lower tracks (Alexander & Cook, 1982; Dreeben & Gamoran, 1986; Hallinan, 1984; Oakes, Gamoran, & Page, 1992; Rosenbaum, 1980a, 1980b). There is insufficient evidence, however, to prove that track placement is based on discriminatory rather than meritocratic practices.

Although some researchers (Oakes, 1985) argue that the race and social class based composition of tracks is evidence of discrimination, Hurn (1993, pp. 165–167) has contended that high school tracking placement, as well as its effects, is a far more complex process. He suggested that the evidence on track placement and outcomes is mixed, but that, on the whole, track placement is based more on previous ability and aspirations than on discriminatory practices. Although this may suggest that student characteristics prior to schooling or to high school placement are important factors, it also suggests that ability is an important part of high school track assignment. Hurn pointed out, however, that high school track placement may be dependent on elementary school processes, including ability grouping and teacher expectations, which may be far less meritocratic.

Research on the self-fulfilling prophecy of teacher expectations (Rist, 1970; Rosenthal & Jacobson, 1968) and of elementary school ability groups and reading groups (Eder, 1981; Felmlee & Eder, 1983; McDermott, 1977) point to the impact of teacher expectations and ability grouping on student aspirations and achievement at the elementary school level. Persell (1977), in her review of the teacher expectations literature, argued that teacher perceptions of students and their abilities have an impact on what is taught, how it is taught, and, ultimately, student performance. Although more research is needed to determine clearly the extent to which these different expectations are based on ascriptive rather than meritocratic factors, there is reason to believe that such processes are not entirely meritocratic (Rist, 1970).

Finally, research indicates that differences in tracks help to explain the variation in academic achievement of students in different tracks. Some researchers argue that discrepancies in the amount of instruction are responsible for these differences (Barr & Dreeben, 1983; Dreeben & Gamoran, 1986); others point to differences in the quality of instruction (McDermott, 1977; Oakes, 1985; Persell, 1977); still others point to both (Lucas, 1999; Spade, Columba, & Vanfossen, 1997). It seems clear that differences in the curriculum and pedagogic practices between tracks are partly responsible for the diverse academic achievement of students in different tracks. Given that more working class and nonwhite students are placed in the lower tracks, it is evident that such school-related practices have a significant effect on their lower academic achievement. What is not entirely clear is the degree to which such placement is unfair and discriminatory or meritocratically based on ability or on characteristics such as ability and aspirations brought by students to the school. This brings you full circle to the question of student-centered versus school-centered explanations. As we have noted, neither one, by itself, is sufficient to explain unequal educational performance. What is needed is a more integrated and multidimensional approach.

Gender and Schooling

In October 1991, during the confirmation hearing of Supreme Court Justice nominee Clarence Thomas, Anita Hill, a law professor at the University of Oklahoma, charged that Judge Thomas sexually harassed her when he was her supervisor at the Department of Education and later at the EEOC (the Equal Employment Opportunity Commission). The charges and subsequent Senate Judiciary Committee hearings on the allegations pointed to significant differences between how men and women see the world. When the all-male, 14-member committee originally voted to pass the nomination onto the Senate without investigating Professor Hill's charges, women throughout the country were outraged, charging that "men just don't get it" (meaning that they do not take sexual harassment seriously). This episode pointed to a much larger question: If men and women see the world differently, why does this occur? Feminist scholarship on gender differences, in general, and gender and schooling, in particular, has concentrated on this issue.

Although the feminist movement in the United States dates back at least to the mid-nineteenth century (cf. Leach, 1980), the second wave of feminism began in the 1960s. Influenced by the French feminist Simone de Beauvoir (1952) and reacting to the narrowly defined gender roles of the 1950s, feminists in the 1960s and 1970s—including Betty Friedan, Gloria Steinem, Ellen Willis, Germaine Greer, and Kate Millett—challenged the view that biology is destiny. Vivian Gornick (1987), in her poignant essay, "The Next Great Moment in History Is Theirs," argued that differences between men and women are cultural, not biological, and that women deserve equality in the public and private spheres of life (the family and the workplace). Thus, the feminist movement challenged unequal treatment of women in all aspects of society and worked actively to change both attitudes and laws that limited the life chances of women.

Feminist scholarship on schooling has attempted to understand the ways in which the schools limit the educational and life chances of women. It has focused on achievement differences (Fennema, 1974; Sadker & Sadker, 1985), on women and school administration (Shakeshaft, 1986, 1987), on the history of coeducation (Tyack & Hansot, 1990), on the relationship between pedagogy and attitudes and knowledge (Belenky et al., 1986), and other related issues. A significant aspect of this literature concerns gender differences in how men and women see the world, their cultural causes, and the role of schools in perpetuating or eliminating them.

Carol Gilligan, a psychologist at Harvard's Graduate School of Education, has been one of the most influential feminist scholars working in the area of gender differences. In her book, *In a Different Voice* (1982), she criticized the view asserted by the psychologist Lawrence Kohlberg that there is a developmental hierarchy in moral decision making. Kohlberg placed a justice orientation to moral reasoning (based on universal principles) on a higher plane than a caring orientation (based on interpersonal feelings). Gilligan argued that women are more likely to adopt a caring orientation, in part because they are socialized to do so, and that Kohlberg's hierarchical categories judged women unfairly. She continued that women do reason in a different voice and that this female voice as an important component of the human experience should not be devalued. Gilligan's work pointed to the differences and their relation to gender socialization and how society rewards men for "male" behavior and negatively affects women for "female" behavior.

Gilligan's work has been extremely controversial among feminists. Many scholars have adopted her concept of caring as a part of female psychology and argue that the schools devalue connectedness and caring in favor of male behaviors such as competition (Martin, 1987; Noddings, 1984). Many feminists argue that schools should revise their curricula and pedagogic practices to emphasize caring and connectedness (Belenky et al., 1986; Laird, 1989). Other feminists (Epstein, 1990) are troubled by the conservative implications of Gilligan's work, which they argue reinforces traditional gender differences by attributing behaviors as typically female and male. The argument that women are more caring and connected and men more competitive and intellectual may reproduce sexist stereotypes that historically justified the domestic roles of women. These feminists believe that traditional male and female characteristics are part of the full range of human possibilities and that schools should socialize both boys and girls to be caring and connected.

Despite these differences, feminists agree that schooling often limits the educational opportunities and life chances of women in a number of ways. For example, boys and girls are socialized differently through a variety of school processes. First, curriculum materials portray men's and women's roles often in stereotypical and traditional ways (Hitchcock & Tompkins, 1987). Second, the traditional curriculum, according to Bennett and LeCompte (1990) "silences women" by omitting significant aspects of women's history and women's lives from discussion. As with other groups calling for multicultural curriculum, feminists call for a more gender-fair curriculum. Third, the hidden curriculum reinforces traditional gender roles and expectations through classroom organization, instructional practices, and classroom interactions (Bennett & LeCompte, 1990, pp. 234–237). For example, research demonstrates that males dominate classroom discussion (Brophy & Good, 1970; Martin, 1972) and receive more attention from teachers (LaFrance, 1985; Lippitt & Gold, 1959; Sikes, 1971), and that teachers are more likely to assist males with a task but to actually do the task for female students (Sadker & Sadker, 1985).

A fourth way that schooling often limits the educational opportunities and life chances of women is that the organization of schools reinforces gender roles and gender inequality. For example, the fact that women are far more likely to teach elementary grades and men secondary grades gives the message to children that women teach children and men teach ideas. The fact that men are far more likely to be administrators, despite recent advances in this area, reinforces the view that men hold positions of authority. Although some research on single-sex and coeducation indicates that females do better in single-sex schools (Datnow & Hubbard, 2002; Shakeshaft, 1987; Tyack & Hansot, 1990) and are given more leadership opportunities in women's colleges (Miller-Bernal, 1993, 2000), recent research does not support the conclusion that females do better in single-sex schools (American Association of University Women, 1998; Datnow & Hubbard, 2000; Shmurak, 1998), with the exception of females from lower socioeconomic backgrounds (Riordan, 1994, 1998). Nonetheless, legal scholar Rosemary Salomone (2003) argues that although "the research as a whole does not refute or support single-sex schooling . . . voluntary single-sex schooling is a legally acceptable option, especially for disadvantaged children" (Publishers Weekly, 2003). These unequal processes help to explain both gender differences in attitudes and academic achievement.

Given the role schools play in reproducing gender inequalities, feminists argue that school organization, curriculum, and pedagogic practices need to be changed to more adequately address the needs of females. For example, Gilligan's study of the Emma Willard School (Gilligan et al., 1990), a private girls school in Troy, New York, concludes that by adolescence, girls receive an education that devalues their inner voice and limits their opportunities. That this occurs in a single-sex school devoted to the education of females suggests that females face more significant problems of educational opportunity in coeducational institutions.

Interestingly, recent research in Great Britain (Arnot, 2002; Arnot, David, & Weiner, 1999; Arnot & Dillabough, 2000) and the United States (American Association of University Women, 1998; Riordan, 1999) indicates that the gender gap in achievement has diminished greatly, if not disappeared. In both countries, females outperform males in almost all academic areas (with the exception of secondary chemistry and physics) and females have higher high school graduation rates and higher levels of college attendance and graduation, and boys are significantly overrepresented in special education classes. In both countries, educational policy makers have begun to analyze the "boy problem" in order to understand the reasons boys have begun to lag behind girls.

Do Schools Reproduce Inequality?

The research on educational inequality, as you have read, is quite complex and perplexing. There is a significant difference of opinion as to the role of the school in affecting student performance, with school-centered explanations stressing the role of schools and student-centered explanations stressing the importance of what students bring to school. Additionally, the research is conflicting concerning the central hypotheses of functionalism and conflict theory. Some researchers believe that the schools unfairly perpetuate social inequalities and thus confirm conflict theorists' belief that schools advantage the dominant groups in society. Other researchers believe that there is insufficient evidence to support much of conflict theory, at least in regard to school processes, and that some of the evidence supports the functionalist view that school selection processes are meritocratic (Hurn, 1993).

How does one reconcile these apparent contradictions? First, we suggest that school-centered and student-centered explanations are not diametrically opposed, but rather need to be incorporated into a multidimensional theory of education and inequality. Second, we suggest that although there is evidence to support some of the functionalists' hypotheses, on the whole, there is more evidence to support conflict theorists' claim that schools help to reproduce inequality. Schools are only part of this process, and must be seen within the context of a larger set of institutional forces affecting social stratification.

Persell's (1977) model for understanding education and inequality, presented in Chapter 4, outlines the relationship between four levels of sociological analysis: the societal level, the institutional level, the interactional level, and the intrapsychic level. The social stratification system, at the societal level, produces structures of domination and societal level ideologies. The structures of domination affect the institutions within a society, including the family, the schools, the churches and synagogues, the media, and others. The important point is that different social groups, based on their position in the societal hierarchy, have different institutional experiences, and are affected in different ways by the social structure. Thus, families from lower socioeconomic backgrounds face different problems and have different life chances than families from higher socioeconomic backgrounds. Much of the student-centered literature focuses on these processes. Children from different classes also attend different types of schools, which often vary in terms of school climate, quality, and outcomes. Much of the school-centered literature focuses on these processes.

The relationships between families and schools at the institutional level, and what goes on within schools at the interactional levels, are not isolated from each other but are dialectically intertwined. Clearly, students from lower socioeconomic backgrounds face significantly different problems in their communities due to factors such as racism, poverty, and other societal and institutional processes. To argue whether they are different or deficient is beside the point; that they negatively impact on children is the point. Children from lower socioeconomic backgrounds thus have significantly lower life chances before they enter schools. Once they enter, they often attend schools that are inferior and have significantly less funding, and encounter school processes that limit their educational chances. That the evidence does not overwhelmingly support the view that school funding and climate are independently responsible for their lower achievement does not eliminate these as part of the problem. It only means that there are other nonschool variables that also affect educational performance. It is clear that at the intrapsychic level, students from different social class backgrounds leave school with different educational outcomes, both cognitive (in terms of learning) and noncognitive (in terms of values and self-esteem). Research on within- and between-school differences demonstrate how school processes may affect such outcomes.

Student-centered theories suggest that these unequal outcomes are the result of differences at the societal and institutional levels, but that families and communities are more important than schools. School-centered theories stress the importance of schooling in reproducing inequality. Persell's (1977) model suggests that society, communities, families, and schools cannot be separated from each other. Societal forces unequally affect families and schools. The result is a complex process through which students from lower socioeconomic backgrounds have lower levels of educational attainment and achievement.

Research that attempts to connect the four levels of sociological analysis is needed to more clearly understand the role of schooling in the reproduction of inequality. Studies by Annette Lareau (1989, 2003) on social class differences in the relationship between family and school documents the importance of both family and schools. She also demonstrates how the differences in schooling for working class and middle-class students is an important factor in unequal outcomes. Using Bourdieu's concept of cultural capital (the cultural symbols and resources a group has), Lareau demonstrated that those with cultural capital have significant advantages in the schooling process. More ethnographic research of this type—which explores the processes within schools, families, and communities, and their relationship to educational outcomes—is needed.

Do schools reproduce inequality? Based on the evidence reviewed in this chapter, our conclusion is they do not, solely by themselves. Schools are part of a larger complex process in which social inequalities are transmitted across generations. Although there is evidence of social mobility for individuals through schooling and of a degree of meritocracy within schools, there is insufficient evidence to support the functionalist argument that schools are a means for the meritocratic selection of individuals based on talent and hard work. Rather, there is more powerful evidence to support the conflict view that schools are part of the process through which dominant groups maintain their advantages.

The first article, "Keeping Track, Part 1: The Policy and Practice of Curriculum Inequality," written by educational researcher Jeannie Oakes, argues against curriculum tracking and ability grouping. Oakes, one of the strongest advocates of heterogeneous grouping, examines a number of myths that support tracking and proposes its elimination. She analyzes how school organization and processes contribute to educational inequality.

The second article, "Females + Mathematics = A Complex Equation," written by educational researcher Karen Karp, provides an overview of the explanations for gender differences in mathematics achievement. Based on the available research, Karp recommends a number of policies to address discrimination against women in the field of mathematics and argues that change must begin in teacher education programs and in elementary schools.

The third article, "Social Class Differences in Family-School Relationships: The Importance of Cultural Capital," written by sociologist Annette Lareau, analyzes the relationship between family and school. Applying Pierre Bourdieu's concept of cultural capital, Lareau argues that middle-class parents, who possess more cultural capital than working class parents, have distinct advantages in advancing their children's educational achievement. Based on an ethnographic study of two schools, one with working class children and one with middle-class children, Lareau explores how each group of families interacts with their children's schools. She concludes that family differences between working class and middle-class parents are part of the reason why middle-class children are more successful in school.

The fourth article, "A Black Student's Reflection on Public and Private Schools," written by Imani Perry, provides a poignant analysis of an African American student's struggle with issues of race and schooling. Written when she was a high school student, Perry discusses the differences between her education at both public and private schools and the miseducation of African Americans in U.S. society.

Keeping Track, Part 1

The Policy and Practice of Curriculum Inequality

JEANNIE OAKES

The idea of educational equality has fallen from favor. In the 1980s policy makers, school practitioners, and the public have turned their attention instead to what many consider a competing goal: excellence. Attempts to "equalize" schooling in the Sixties and Seventies have been judged extravagant and naive. Worse, critics imply that those well-meant efforts to correct inequality may have compromised the central mission of the schools: teaching academics well. And current critics warn that, given the precarious position of the United States in the global competition for economic, technological, and military superiority, we can no longer sacrifice the quality of our schools to social goals. This view promotes the judicious spending of limited educational resources in ways that will produce the greatest return on "human capital." Phrased in these economic terms, special provisions for underachieving poor and minority students become a bad investment. In short, equality is out; academic excellence is in.

On the other hand, many people still argue vociferously that the distinction between promoting excellence and providing equality is false, that one cannot be achieved without the other. Unfortunately, whether "tight-fisted" conservatives or "fuzzy-headed" liberals are in the ascendancy, the heat of the rhetoric surrounding the argument largely obscures a more serious problem: the possibility that the unquestioned *assumptions* that drive school practice and the *basic features of schools* may themselves lock schools into

patterns that make it difficult to achieve *either* excellence *or* equality.

The practice of tracking in secondary schools illustrates this possibility and provides evidence of how schools, even as they voice commitment to equality and excellence, organize and deliver curriculum in ways that advance neither. Nearly all schools track students. Because tracking enables schools to provide educational treatments matched to particular groups of students, it is believed to promote higher achievement for all students under conditions of equal educational opportunity. However, rather than promoting higher achievement, tracking contributes to mediocre schooling for *most* secondary students. And because it places the greatest obstacles to achievement in the path of those children least advantaged in American society—poor and minority children—tracking forces schools to play an active role in perpetuating social and economic inequalities as well. Evidence about the influence of tracking on student outcomes and analyses of how tracking affects the day-to-day school experiences of young people support the argument that such basic elements of schooling can*prevent* rather than *promote* educational goals.

What Is Tracking?

Tracking is the practice of dividing students into separate classes for high-, average-, and low-achievers; it lays out different curriculum paths for students headed

From "Keeping Track, Part 1: The Policy and Practice of Curriculum Inequality" by Jeannie Oakes. *Phi Delta Kappan,* September 1986. Reprinted by permission of Dr. Jeannie Oakes.

for college and for those who are bound directly for the workplace. In most senior high schools, students are assigned to one or another *curriculum track* that lays out sequences of courses for college-preparatory, vocational, or general track students. Junior and senior high schools also make use of *ability grouping*—that is, they divide academic subjects (typically English, mathematics, science, and social studies) into classes geared to different "levels" for students of different abilities. In many high schools these two systems overlap, as schools provide college-preparatory, general, and vocational sequences of courses and also practice ability grouping in academic subjects. More likely than not, the student in the vocational curriculum track will be in one of the lower ability groups. Because similar overlapping exists for college-bound students, the distinction between the two types of tracking is sometimes difficult to assess.

But tracking does not proceed as neatly as the description above implies. Both curriculum tracking and ability grouping vary from school to school in the number of subjects that are tracked, in the number of levels provided, and in the ways in which students are placed. Moreover, tracking is confounded by the inflexibilities and idiosyncrasies of "master schedules," which can create unplanned tracking, generate further variations among tracking systems, and affect the courses taken by individual students as well. Elective subjects, such as art and home economics, sometimes become low-track classes because college-preparatory students rarely have time in their schedules to take them; required classes, such as drivers' training, health, or physical education, though they are intended to be heterogeneous, become tracked when the requirements of other courses that *are* tracked keep students together for large portions of the day.

Despite these variations, tracking has common and predictable characteristics:

- The intellectual performance of students is judged, and these judgments determine placement with particular groups.
- Classes and tracks are labeled according to the performance levels of the students in them (e.g., advanced, average, remedial) or according to students' postsecondary destinations (e.g., college-preparatory, vocational).
- The curriculum and instruction in various tracks are tailored to the perceived needs and abilities of the students assigned to them.

- The groups that are formed are not merely a collection of different but equally-valued instructional groups. They form a hierarchy, with the most advanced tracks (and the students in them) seen as being on top.
- Students in various tracks and ability levels experience school in very different ways.

Underlying Assumptions

First, and clearly most important, teachers and administrators generally assume that tracking promotes overall student achievement—that is, that the academic needs of all students will be better met when they learn in groups with similar capabilities or prior levels of achievement. Given the inevitable diversity of student populations, tracking is seen as the best way to address individual needs and to cope with individual differences. This assumption stems from a view of human capabilities that includes the belief that students' capacities to master schoolwork are so disparate that they require different and separate schooling experiences. The extreme position contends that some students cannot learn at all.

A second assumption that underlies tracking is that less-capable students will suffer emotional as well as educational damage from daily classroom contact and competition with their brighter peers. Lowered self-concepts and negative attitudes toward learning are widely considered to be consequences of mixed-ability grouping for slower learners. It is also widely assumed that students can be placed in tracks and groups both accurately and fairly. And finally, most teachers and administrators contend that tracking greatly eases the teaching task and is, perhaps, the *only* way to manage student differences.

The Record of Tracking

Students clearly differ when they enter secondary schools, and these differences just as clearly influence learning. But separating students to better accommodate these differences appears to be neither necessary, effective, nor appropriate.

Does Tracking Work?

At the risk of oversimplifying a complex body of research literature, it is safe to conclude that *there is little evidence to support any of the assumptions about tracking.* The effects of tracking on student outcomes have been widely investigated, and the bulk of this work *does not* support commonly-held beliefs that tracking increases student learning. Nor does the evidence support tracking as a way to improve students' attitudes about themselves or about schooling.[1] Although existing tracking systems *appear* to provide advantages for students who are placed in the top tracks, the literature suggests that students at all ability levels can achieve at least as well in heterogeneous classrooms.

Students who are *not* in top tracks—a group that includes about 60% of senior high school students—suffer clear and consistent disadvantages from tracking. Among students identified as average or slow, tracking often appears to retard academic progress. Indeed, one study documented the fact that the lowered I.Q. scores of senior high school students followed their placement in low tracks.[2] Students who are placed in vocational tracks do not even seem to reap any benefits in the job market. Indeed, graduates of vocational programs may be less employable and, when they do find jobs, may earn lower wages than other high school graduates.[3]

Most tracking research does not support the assumption that slow students suffer emotional strains when enrolled in mixed-ability classes. Often the opposite result has been found. Rather than helping students feel more comfortable about themselves, tracking can reduce self-esteem, lower aspirations, and foster negative attitudes toward school. Some studies have also concluded that tracking leads low-track students to misbehave and eventually to drop out altogether.[4]

The net effect of tracking is to exaggerate the initial differences among students rather than to provide the means to better accommodate them. For example, studies show that senior high school students who are initially similar in background and prior achievement become *increasingly* different in achievement and future aspirations when they are placed in different tracks.[5] Moreover, this effect is likely to be cumulative over most of the students' school careers, since track placements tend to remain fixed. Students placed in low-ability groups in elementary school are likely to continue in these groups in middle school or junior high school; in senior high school these students are typically placed in non-college-preparatory tracks. Studies that have documented increased gaps between initially comparable high school students placed in different tracks probably capture only a fraction of this effect.

Is Tracking Fair?

Compounding the lack of empirical evidence to support tracking as a way to enhance student outcomes are compelling arguments that favor exposing all students to a common curriculum, *even if differences among them prevent all students from benefiting equally.* These arguments counter both the assumption that tracking can be carried out "fairly" and the view that tracking is a legitimate means to ease the task of teaching.

Central to the issue of fairness is the well-established link between track placements and student background characteristics. Poor and minority youngsters (principally black and Hispanic) are disproportionately placed in tracks for low-ability or non-college-bound students. By the same token, minority students are consistently underrepresented in programs for the gifted and talented. In addition, differentiation by race and class occurs within vocational tracks, with blacks and Hispanics more frequently enrolled in programs that train students for the lowest-level occupations (e.g., building maintenance, commercial sewing, and institutional care). These differences in placement by race and social class appear regardless of whether test scores, counselor and teacher recommendations, or student and parent choices are used as the basis for placement.[6]

Even if these track placements are ostensibly based on merit—that is, determined by prior school achievement rather than by race, class, or student choice—they usually come to signify judgments about supposedly fixed abilities. We might find appropriate the disproportionate placements of poor and minority students in low-track classes if these youngsters were, in fact, known to be innately less capable of learning than middle- and upper-middle-class whites. But that is not the case. Or we might think of these track placements as appropriate *if* they served to remediate the obvious educational deficiencies that many poor and minority students exhibit. If being in a low track prepared disadvantaged students for success in higher tracks and opened future educational opportunities to them, we would not question the need for tracking. However, this rarely happens.

The assumption that tracking makes teaching easier pales in importance when held up against the abundant evidence of the general ineffectiveness of tracking and the disproportionate harm it works on poor and minority students. But even if this were not the case, the assumption that tracking makes teaching easier would stand up *only if* the tracks were made up of truly homogeneous groups. In fact, they are not. Even within tracks, the variability of students' learning speed, cognitive style, interest, effort, and aptitude for various tasks is often considerable. Tracking simply masks the fact that instruction for any group of 20 to 35 people requires considerable variety in instructional strategies, tasks, materials, feedback, and guidance. It also requires multiple criteria for success and a variety of rewards. Unfortunately, for many schools and teachers, tracking deflects attention from these instructional realities. When instruction fails, the problem is too often attributed to the child or perhaps to a "wrong placement." The fact that tracking *may* make teaching easier for some teachers should not cloud our judgment about whether that teaching is best for any group of students—whatever their abilities.

Finally, a profound ethical concern emerges from all the above. In the words of educational philosopher Gary Fenstermacher, "[U]sing individual differences in aptitude, ability, or interest as the basis for curricular variation denies students equal access to the knowledge and understanding available to humankind." He continues, "[I]t is possible that some students may not benefit equally from unrestricted access to knowledge, but this fact does not entitle us to control access in ways that effectively prohibit all students from encountering what Dewey called 'the funded capital of civilization.'"[7] Surely educators do not intend any such unfairness when by tracking they seek to accommodate differences among students.

Why Such Disappointing Effects?

As those of us who were working with John Goodlad on A Study of Schooling began to analyze the extensive set of data we had gathered about 38 schools across the U.S., we wanted to find out more about tracking.[8] We wanted to gather specific information about the knowledge and skills that students were taught in tracked classes, about the learning activities they experienced, about the ways in which teachers managed instruction, about the classroom relationships, and about how involved students were in their learning. By studying tracked classes directly and asking over and over whether such classes differed, we hoped to begin to understand why the effects of tracking have been so disappointing for so many students.

We wanted to be able to raise some reasonable hypotheses about the ways in which the good intentions of practitioners seem to go wrong.

We selected a representative group of 300 English and mathematics classes. We chose those subjects because they are most often tracked and because nearly all secondary students take them. Our sample included relatively equal numbers of high-, average-, low-, and mixed-ability groups. We had a great deal of information about these classes because teachers and students had completed extensive questionnaires, teachers had been interviewed, and teachers had put together packages of materials about their classes, including lists of the topics and skills they taught, the textbooks they used, and the ways in which the evaluated student learned. Many teachers also gave us sample lesson plans, worksheets, and tests. Trained observers recorded what students and teachers were doing and documented their interactions.

The data gathered on these classes provided some clear and consistent insights. In the three areas we studied—curriculum content, instructional quality, and classroom climate—we found remarkable and disturbing differences between classes in different tracks. These included important discrepancies in student access to knowledge, in their classroom instructional opportunities, and in their classroom learning environments.

Access to Knowledge

In both English and math classes, we found that students had access to considerably different types of knowledge and had opportunities to develop quite different intellectual skills. For example, students in high-track English classes were exposed to content that can be called "high-status knowledge." This included topics and skills that are required for college. High-track students studied both classic and modern fiction. They learned the characteristics of literary genres and analyzed the elements of good narrative writing. These students were expected to write thematic essays and reports of library research, and they learned vocabulary that would boost their scores on college entrance exams. It was the high-track students in our sample who had the most opportunities to think critically or to solve interesting problems.

Low-track English classes, on the other hand, rarely, if ever, encountered similar types of knowledge. Nor were they expected to learn the same skills. Instruction in basic reading skills held a prominent place in low-track classes, and these skills were taught mostly through workbooks, kits, and "young adult" fiction. Students wrote simple paragraphs, completed worksheets on English usage, and practiced filling out applications for jobs and other kinds of forms. Their learning tasks were largely restricted to memorization or low-level comprehension.

The differences in mathematics content followed much the same pattern. High-track classes focused primarily on mathematical concepts; low-track classes stressed basic computational skills and math facts.

These differences are not merely curricular adaptations to individual needs, though they are certainly thought of as such. Differences in access to knowledge have important long-term social and educational consequences as well. For example, low-track students are probably prevented from *ever* encountering at school the knowledge our society values most. Much of the curriculum of low-track classes was likely to lock students into a continuing series of such bottom-level placements because important concepts and skills were neglected. Thus these students were denied the knowledge that would enable them to move successfully into higher-track classes.

Opportunities to Learn

We also looked at two classroom conditions known to influence how much students will learn: instructional time and teaching quality. The marked differences we found in our data consistently showed that students in higher tracks had better classroom opportunities. For example, all our data on classroom time pointed to the same conclusion: students in high tracks get more; students in low tracks get less. Teachers of high-track classes set aside more class time for learning, and our observers found that more actual class time was spent on learning activities. High-track students were also expected to spend more time doing homework, fewer high-track students were observed to be off-task during class activities, and more of them told us that learning took up most of their class time, rather than discipline problems, socializing, or class routines.

Instruction in high-track classes more often included a whole range of teacher behaviors likely to enhance learning. High-track teachers were more enthusiastic, and their instruction was clearer. They used strong criticism or ridicule less frequently than did teachers of low-track classes. Classroom tasks were more various and more highly organized in high-

track classes, and grades were more relevant to student learning.

These differences in learning opportunities portray a fundamental irony of schooling: those students who need more time to learn appear to be getting less; those students who have the most difficulty learning are being exposed least to the sort of teaching that best facilitates learning.

Classroom Climate

We were interested in studying classroom climates in various tracks because we were convinced that supportive relationships and positive feelings in class are more than just nice accompaniments to learning. When teachers and students trust one another, classroom time and energy are freed for teaching and learning. Without this trust, students spend a great deal of time and energy establishing less productive relationships with others and interfering with the teacher's instructional agenda; teachers spend their time and energy trying to maintain control. In such classes, less learning is likely to occur.

The data from A Study of Schooling permitted us to investigate three important aspects of classroom environments: relationships between teachers and students, relationships among the students themselves, and the intensity of student involvement in learning. Once again, we discovered a distressing pattern of advantages for high-track classes and disadvantages for low-track classes. In high-track classes students thought that their teachers were more concerned about them and less punitive. Teachers in high-track classes spent less time on student behavior, and they more often encouraged their students to become independent, questioning, critical thinkers. In low-track classes teachers were seen as less concerned and more punitive. Teachers in low-track classes emphasized matters of discipline and behavior, and they often listed such things as "following directions," "respecting my position," "punctuality," and "learning to take a direct order" as among the five most important things they wanted their class to learn during the year.

We found similar differences in the relationships that students established with one another in class. Students in low-track classes agreed far more often that "students in this class are unfriendly to me" or that "I often feel left out of class activities." They said that their classes were interrupted by problems and by arguing in class. Generally, they seemed to like each other less. Not surprisingly, given these differences in relationships, students in high-track classes appeared to be much more involved in their classwork. Students in low-track classes were more apathetic and indicated more often that they didn't care about what went on or that failing didn't bother most of their classmates.

In these data, we found once again a pattern of classroom experience that seems to enhance the possibilities of learning for those students already disposed to do well—that is, those in high-track classes. We saw even more clearly a pattern of classroom experience likely to inhibit the learning of those in the bottom tracks. As with access to knowledge and opportunities to learn, we found that those who most needed support from a positive, nurturing environment got the least.

Although these data do show clear instructional advantages for high-achieving students and clear disadvantages for their low-achieving peers, other data from our work suggest that the quality of the experience of *average* students falls somewhere between these two extremes. Average students, too, were deprived of the best circumstances schools have to offer, though their classes were typically more like those of high-track students. Taken together, these findings begin to suggest *why* students who are not in the top tracks are likely to suffer because of their placements: their education is of considerably lower quality.

It would be a serious mistake to interpret these data as the "inevitable" outcome of the differences in the students who populate the various tracks. Many of the mixed-ability classes in our study showed that high-quality experiences are very possible in classes that include all types of students. But neither should we attribute these differences to consciously mean-spirited or blatantly discriminatory actions by schoolpeople. Obviously, the content teachers decide to teach and the ways in which they teach it are greatly influenced by the students with whom they interact. And it is unlikely that students are passive participants in tracking processes. It seems more likely that students' achievements, attitudes, interests, perceptions of themselves, and behaviors (growing increasingly disparate over time) help produce some of the effects of tracking. Thus groups of students who, by conventional wisdom, seem less able and less eager to learn are very likely to affect a teacher's ability or even willingness to provide the best possible learning opportunities. The obvious conclusion about the effects of these track-specific differences on the ability of the schools to achieve academic excellence is that students who are exposed to less content and lower-quality teaching are unlikely to get the full benefit out of their schooling. Yet this less-fruitful experience seems to be the norm when average- and low-achieving students are grouped together for instruction.

I believe that these data reveal frightening patterns of curricular inequality. Although these patterns would be disturbing under any circumstances (and though many white, suburban schools consign a good number of their students to mediocre experiences in low-ability and general-track classes), they become particularly distressing in light of the prevailing pattern of placing disproportionate numbers of poor and minority students in the lowest-track classes. A self-fulfilling prophecy can be seen to work at the institutional level to prevent schools from providing equal educational opportunity. Tracking appears to teach and reinforce the notion that those not defined as the best are *expected* to do less well. Few students and teachers can defy those expectations.

Tracking, Equality, and Excellence

Tracking is assumed to promote educational excellence because it enables schools to provide students with the curriculum and instruction they need to maximize their potential and achieve excellence on their own terms. But the evidence about tracking suggests the contrary. Certainly students bring differences with them to school, but, by tracking, schools help to widen rather than narrow these differences. Students who are judged to be different from one another are separated into different classes and then provided knowledge, opportunities to learn, and classroom environments that are vastly different. Many of the students in top tracks (only about 40% of high-schoolers) do benefit from the advantages they receive in their classes. But, in their quest for higher standards and superior academic performance, schools seem to have locked themselves into a structure that may *unnecessarily* buy the achievement of a few at the expense of many. Such a structure provides but a shaky foundation for excellence.

At the same time, the evidence about tracking calls into question the widely held view that schools provide students who have the "right stuff" with a neutral environment in which they can rise to the top (with "special" classes providing an extra boost to those who might need it). Everywhere we turn we find that the differentiated structure of schools throws up barriers to achievement for poor and minority students. Measures of talent clearly seem to work against them, which leads to their disproportionate placement in groups identified as slow. Once there, their achievement seems to be further inhibited by the type of knowledge they are taught and by the quality of the learning opportunities they are afforded. Moreover, the social and psychological dimensions of classes at the bottom of the hierarchy of schooling seem to restrict their chances for school success even further.

Good intentions, including those of advocates of "excellence" and of "equity," characterize the rhetoric of schooling. Tracking, because it is usually taken to be a neutral practice and a part of the mechanics of schooling, has escaped the attention of those who mean well. But by failing to scrutinize the effects of tracking, schools unwittingly subvert their well-meant efforts to promote academic excellence and to provide conditions that will enable all students to achieve it.

Endnotes

1. Some recent reviews of studies on the effects of tracking include: Robert C. Calfee and Roger Brown, "Grouping Students for Instruction," in *Classroom Management* (Chicago: 78th Yearbook of the National Society for the Study of Education, University of Chicago Press, 1979); Dominick Esposito, "Homogeneous and Heterogeneous Ability Grouping: Principal Findings and Implications for Evaluating and Designing More Effective Educational Environments," *Review of Educational Research,* vol. 43, 1973, pp. 163–79; Jeannie Oakes, "Tracking: A Contextual Perspective on How Schools Structure Differences," *Education Psychologist,* in press; Caroline H. Persell, *Education and Inequality: The Roots and Results of Stratification in American's Schools* (New York: Free Press, 1977); and James E. Rosenbaum,

"The Social Implications of Educational Grouping," in David C. Berliner, ed., *Review of Research in Education, Vol. 8* (Washington, D.C.: American Educational Research Association, 1980), pp. 361–401.

2. James E. Rosenbaum, *Making Inequality: The Hidden Curriculum of High School Tracking* (New York: Wiley, 1976).

3. See, for example, David Stern et al., *One Million Hours a Day: Vocational Education in California Public Secondary Schools* (Berkeley: Report to the California Policy Seminar, University of California School of Education, 1985).

4. Rosenbaum, "The Social Implications. . ." and William E. Shafer and Carol Olexa, *Tracking and Opportunity* (Scranton, Pa.: Chandler, 1971).

5. Karl A. and Edward L. McDill, "Selection and Allocation Within Schools: Some Causes and Consequences of Curriculum Placement," *American Sociological Review,* vol. 41, 1976, pp. 969–80; Karl A. Alexander, Martha Cook, and Edward L. McDill, "Curriculum Tracking and Educational Stratification: Some Further Evidence," *American Sociological Review,* vol. 43, 1978, pp. 47–66; and Donald A. Rock et al., *Study of Excellence in High School Education: Longitudinal Study, 1980–82* (Princeton, N.J.: Educational Testing Service, Final Report, 1985).

6. Persell, *Education and Inequality. . .*; and Jeannie Oakes, *Keeping Track: How Schools Structure Inequality* (New Haven, Conn.: Yale University Press, 1985).

7. Gary D. Fenstermacher, "Introduction," in Gary D. Fenstermacher and John I. Goodlad, eds., *Individual Differences and the Common Curriculum* (Chicago: 82nd Yearbook of the National Society for the Study of Education, University of Chicago Press, 1983), p. 3.

8. John I. Goodlad, *A Place Called School* (New York: McGraw-Hill, 1984).

Females + Mathematics = A Complex Equation

KAREN KARP

The well-known British author, Margaret Drabble, reflecting on her own recollections of mathematics instruction, stated:

> I dropped mathematics at 12, through some freak in the syllabus. . . . I cannot deny that I dropped math with a sigh of relief, for I had always loathed it, always felt uncomprehending even while getting tolerable marks, didn't like subjects I wasn't good at, and had no notion of this subject's appeal or significance.
>
> The reason, I imagine, was that, like most girls I had been badly taught from the beginning: I am not really as innumerate as I pretend, and suspect there is little wrong with the basic equipment but I shall never know.
>
> . . . And that effectively, though I did not appreciate it at the time, closed most careers and half of culture to me forever. (1975, p. 16)

Margaret Drabble's story is not unique. The fact is that many women in all walks of life could relate episodes of their skillful navigation around mathematics coursework during their years of schooling. Some report these tales with a twinge of regret, while others, possibly as a defense mechanism, take perverse pride in using humor to diminish the significance of these events. Regardless of their interpretation, the reality of mathematics avoidance is that women are often bound by the ensuing limitations on their professional qualifications, and may be barred from careers requiring mathematical knowledge.

Problem

Despite voluminous research efforts on gender issues in education over the past 20 years, stubborn patterns of inequitable practices and beliefs continue to persist. Although there has been some measurable progress, the challenge to overcome chronic inequities is formidable. Even though discrimination on the basis of sex in any federally funded educational program became illegal in 1972, the initial promise of Title IX legislation has fallen short of expectations. Charged with eliminating sex bias, creating equal opportunities, encouraging females to enter male-dominated careers (with a hope that a reduction of pay differential would follow), and given the funding to support such activities, schools began to enact piecemeal remedies. Yet, recent data reveal the following:

- Within a large group of high school seniors who scored above the 90th percentile on the mathematics portion of the SAT, females were only two-thirds as likely as males to indicate plans for pursuing a career in science or engineering (Matyas & Dix, 1992).
- Females are still outscored by an average of approximately 40 points on the mathematics component of the SAT (36 points on the recentered scale) (College Board, 1997).
- Females in the workforce earn only a fraction of the salaries of males (U.S. Department of Education, 1997), unless they have earned eight or more mathematics credits in college (Adelman, 1991).

These statistics raise issues about school practices and stimulate particular inquiries as to why the improvement of females' mathematics performance has proceeded at such an uneven pace.

Mathematics has long been noted as the "critical filter" (Sells, 1978). For example, when students enter college with less than the full complement of high school mathematics classes, they often miss essential prerequisites and can suffer the de facto elimination of 82 potential career paths (Toronto Board of Education, 1989). This fact is especially compelling when linked with the recognition that the rank ordering of the best jobs in the United States for the twenty-first century results in most of the top 10 occupations relating directly to mathematics (Krantz, 1995). Yet, over three times as many males as females who have taken physics and

This article was written expressly for this book and is used with permission from the author.

calculus select college majors relating to mathematics and science (Dick & Rallis, 1991). When these data are correlated with the reality that males comprise more than 90 percent of the employment force in professions relating to mathematics and science, the results are no longer surprising. In actuality, many females are still confined to a range of professions that are, in general, poorly paid.

Another barrier in the complex intersection of schooling and future career goals is the Scholastic Aptitude Test: "In a world where test scores translate into scholarships and admission to college, and college in turn leads to high-paying jobs, the failure of high school girls to score as well as boys on college-entrance examinations has led to widespread concern" (Goleman, 1987, p. 42). Although research has established that gender differences in spatial and mathematical ability have all but been eliminated, differential performance on the mathematics portion of the scholastic aptitude test lingers as a painful exception (Linn & Hyde, 1989).

In the period between 1987 and 1997, females scored an average of 43 points less than males on the SAT mathematics section. For example, in 1994, males outscored females by 501 to 460 on the SAT-M (College Board, 1995). Although scores of both males and females increase in linear correspondence with the number of years of mathematics they have taken, surprisingly the greatest gap occurs between the select group of students who have more than four years of mathematics coursework.

In addition, in the population of students designated as "high scorers" (having scores between 750 and 800), the male-to-female ratio as reported by College Board's 1995 profile is approximately 3:1. That ratio translates into 11,618 males as compared to 4,294 females—clearly a compelling statistic. Such differences in SAT scores translate into serious consequences for females. Young women are at risk of losing out academically through rejection from competitive postsecondary institutions; psychologically, as they are more apt than males to deem the SAT as an accurate assessment of their intelligence, leaving them without the confidence to apply to colleges requesting higher test scores; and financially, through scholarships that are bound directly or indirectly to the SAT-M score. Several years ago, New York State's granting of Regents and Empire State Scholarships that were awarded solely on the basis of SAT scores was ruled unconstitutional. Up to that time, males captured 72 percent of the awards. A similar case based in the gender discrepancies resulting from the allocation of National Merit Scholarships, which were based on the related PSAT exam, also yielded changes in the scholarship selection process (FairTest, 1996).

In contrast to SAT-M results, the grades high school females earn in class are comparable to or in some cases higher than those of males (Riordan, 1999). This dichotomy between classroom performance and summative testing results has enormous impact on female students as well as the public mind, for the results of national testing, not student report cards, are what is shared in public forums, thereby reinforcing images of inadequate performance.

Despite outstanding academic records, fewer females are admitted to the most prestigious colleges and universities as a result of SAT-M scores. This situation continues to exist despite an awareness that testing materials may be patently unfair to females. Certain common testing practices such as biased problem contexts and sexist language have been so often and so consistently shown to discriminate against females that knowledge of them is public; however, many of these patterns still exist.

In evaluating 74 different psychological and educational test items for gender-related content, references to males outnumbered those to females 2 to 1. On items in which people of accomplishment were described, males outnumbered females 8 to 1 (Selkow, 1984). In response, the Educational Testing Service (ETS) has been vigilant in attempting to eliminate overt and subtle biases in their testing instruments. They have utilized elaborate and complex statistical analyses to locate and eliminate gender bias in either problem context or content that may favor one group over another.

Regardless of changes in testing materials, males may have an advantage over females in their speed of response. SAT preparation courses commonly claim to boost overall scores by teaching students to make rapid assessments of problems and then produce quick guesses rather than employ lengthy computations (Robinson & Katzman, 1986). Indeed, if males are more confident in their mathematics ability (Hyde, Fennema, Ryan, Frost, & Hopp, 1990), then they may be more inclined to trust intuitive thinking and holistic examinations of problems. On the other hand, females who have frequently found themselves rewarded for rule-compliance behavior are less likely to employ swift inspections of problems and revert to lengthy but reliable formulas (Gallagher & DeLisi, 1994).

The tendency is for males to exhibit more confidence in their mathematics abilities than females, even when both groups perform equally well (Linn & Hyde, 1989). This confidence gap is only one explanation commonly used to account for females' performance in mathematics. The following sections examine some other factors and discuss possible means for fostering improved mathematics performance in female students.

Biological Factors

In 1980, Benbow and Stanley conducted what initially seemed to be critical research supporting the genetic inferiority of females in terms of mathematics ability. In an effort to control for previous methodological concerns regarding differential course-taking behaviors of males and females, they administered the SAT mathematics component to gifted seventh- and eighth-graders presumably at a point where they had all taken the same mathematics courses. The results suggested "huge and significant differences" favoring males over females. The researchers concluded that males had superior innate mathematics ability and that this ability naturally shaped the selection of advanced mathematics courses.

According to the study, there were about 13 male math geniuses in seventh grade for every female. In general, females were described as not being able to understand the material and, as a consequence, "women would be better off accepting the differences" (Benbow, 1980, p. 1235). Unfortunately, only after this study received tremendous publicity and media attention did other researchers move to the forefront with questions and serious concerns regarding the methods and conclusions of the investigation (Alexander & Pallas, 1983; Egelman, Alper, Leibowitz, Beckwith, Levine, & Leeds, 1981).

These researchers demanded more details as to how Benbow and Stanley equated SAT-M performance with innate mathematics ability (no biological data were collected), how they reconciled the inherent bias against females in the testing instrument, what impact the overwhelmingly large percentage of males in the sample had on the results, how the socioeconomic status of the students may have skewed outcomes (most came from family backgrounds where financial support for a summer program for gifted students was possible), how the findings of research with a highly select sample could be generalized to an entire popula-

tion, and whether the schooling experience up to that point had in reality been the same for males and females. The answers raised serious doubts. Although the Benbow and Stanley study originally heralded the belief that there were causative biological factors, the early support this hypothesis garnered has disappeared. Unfortunately, misguided authors still report the conclusions of the study as statements of fact in articles and textbooks for readers ranging from parents to college students (Brandt, 1989; Christen, 1995).

Another biogenetic theory relating to brain lateralization has also attracted interest. In the maturing human fetus, exposure to the male sex hormone, testosterone, slows development of the left hemisphere of the brain. As a result, the right hemisphere is thought to compensate by increasing dominance and enhancing the components of intelligence under its control (i.e., spatial sense) (Ramey, 1987). Most believe that these developmental differences exist, but direct linkages to mathematical abilities has not been proven.

Declining differences between males and females in both mathematics and spatial skills suggest that a biological causation is not probable (Halpern, 1989). In the words of Rosenthal and Rubin (1982), such changes in gender differences are happening "faster than the gene can travel" (p. 711). Few researchers today would posit that biogenetic theories provide a worthwhile explanation for gender differences in mathematics ability. Most would concur instead with the premise that gender expectations and differential performance remain enmeshed in environmental and cultural variables.

Differential Ability

Rather than an observed continuity of poor performance, researchers identify a discontinuity in females' mathematics achievement. Usually no performance differences are identified until the age of 10 (Dossey, Mullis, Lindquist, & Chambers, 1988) but, interestingly, when differences are found in the early years, they are inclined to favor females (Brandon, Newton, & Hammond, 1987). In the middle school years, the data reveal a mixture of results, but during the high school years, differences in favor of males are common (Carpenter, Lindquist, Mathews, & Silver, 1983; Ramist & Arbeiter, 1986).

One area of disparate ability that initially attracted a good share of attention was differences in spatial ability. A recent meta-analysis reveals that these differences are declining to the point where they no longer exist (Linn & Hyde, 1989).

One domain where differences are still marked is in the skill component of mental rotation, which is the ability to flip and turn a geometric figure in space (Thomas & Kail, 1991). These differences are seemingly in speed rather than accuracy, which may suggest that practice will impact favorably on improving this ability (Gallagher & Johnson, 1992). Although measured variance in performance may be slight or even nil, we must be cautious in dismissing this area as rectified, as females' mathematics ability seems to be more inexorably linked to spatial abilities.

Fortunately, spatial skills have proven to respond well to training (Linn & Hyde, 1989; Baenninger & Newcombe, 1989). Baenninger and Newcombe further question why such training in spatial skills is omitted from the regular school curriculum if significant improvement has been demonstrated by both genders when such practice is provided. We must ask why there are so many intervention programs for reading problems (which are mainly populated by male students) and yet such little attention devoted to the remediation of spatial skills. Frequently, female students must manifest greater deficiencies than males prior to receiving special services (Vogel, 1990).

School Effects

Researchers overwhelmingly report that mathematics learning is largely a function of mathematics teaching (Fennema, 1990; Karp, 1991). Although mathematics terms may be used outside of school, the classroom remains the central site for instruction. Yet, school is clearly a place of uneven opportunities for females. A comprehensive report undertaken by the American Association for University Women Foundation (1992) states that their research findings debunk "another myth—that boys and girls receive equal education. The wealth of statistical evidence must convince even the most skeptical that gender bias in our schools is shortchanging girls—and compromising our country" (McKee, 1992 p. A1). Over the years, researchers have identified that the "shortchanging" females experience unfolds in various forms.

Classroom Interactions

Sadker and Sadker found that "at all grade levels, in all communities (urban, suburban and rural) and in all subject areas, boys dominated classroom communication.

Boys participated in more interactions than girls did, this participation becoming greater as the year went on" (1980, p. 165). Males receive more verbal contact with teachers, both positive and negative (Spender, 1982). They are called on more frequently, asked more complex and open-ended questions, and are more often engaged in inquiries that involve abstract reasoning (Jones, 1989).

Conversely, interactions between teachers and female students often include rewards for following rules, conformity, neatness, silence, and appearance (Sadker & Sadker, 1994). For instance, while observing in a nursery school classroom in England, Walden and Walkerdine (1985) observed two students approach the teacher with a drawing. One was told, "Well done, John, that's a good drawing"; the other was told, "You do look pretty today, Alice." Females are asked more basic recall questions and are often given correct answers when they cannot produce them. Serbin and O'Leary (1975) found that teachers are more likely to encourage learned helplessness by performing a task for a female student who is having difficulty but will give males eight times more information on how to solve the problem themselves. Thus, the crux of the problem regarding disparities between treatment of males and females in classroom discourse lies in the content of student/teacher interactions rather than the number of interactions.

Parent Expectations

Consistent with stereotypical expectations from the past, a recent investigation yielded the predictable results that parents of males held more positive beliefs regarding their child's mathematics performance and more frequently identified the need for their child to continue in upper-level mathematics than parents of females (Eccles, Flanagan, Goldsmith, Jacobs, Jayaratne, Wigfield, & Yee, 1987). Upon closer examination of the sample, this finding becomes more surprising, as the female students were matched with the males precisely for equivalent performance on both formal mathematics tests and in classroom grades. Parents of a subset of the females in the study rated their daughters' abilities in language arts as higher than their mathematics abilities, even though their daughters had identical grades in both subjects. Parents of males with identical grades in these subjects gave a higher rating to their sons' mathematical abilities.

Parental influence is a more potent factor in affecting mathematics performance than originally thought. Parents' beliefs about their child's abilities and their expectations for the child's future success have a stronger influence on a child's future than his or her grades in school (Eccles et al., 1987; Jacobs & Eccles, 1992). Other studies confirm that parents are the strongest influence on their child's career selection as well as their course-taking decisions (Bender, 1994), particularly when the choices involve science or engineering (Dick & Rallis, 1991). Girls also tend to revert to more traditional careers if they do not receive consistent support from their parents (Bender, 1994).

In a study examining the United States, Japan, and China, Stevenson (1987) found that differential parental expectations were evidenced as early as the first grade. For example, both children and their mothers tended to believe that males had superior mathematics ability and that females excelled in reading. Even prior to entering first grade, Japanese females said they preferred reading, while males stated that they preferred mathematics. Although enormous differences in mathematics achievement were identified among the countries, interestingly, only a few significant gender differences in performance were reported but numerous gender differences in attitude toward mathematics (males having more positive attitudes) were identified.

Subtle messages sent by parents to children may be an element in the trend for females to not perform as well in mathematics in the higher grades and for them to opt out of advanced mathematics and mathematically oriented careers.

Gender Role Socialization Factors

Factors impacting on gender role socialization encompass a variety of behaviors, feelings, attitudes, and interests designated by society as appropriate for females or males. They are learned through interactions with parents, peers, teachers, books, toys, and the media. In addition, participation in social events and encounters with social institutions shape the child's reality.

Sometimes, pressures for children to conform to social definitions of suitable behavior for their sex are great. Even from the moment after a baby's birth where "Is the baby a boy or girl?" is the most commonly asked question (Intons-Peterson & Reddel, 1984), patterns for orchestrating the world around the child as male oriented or female oriented begin. When given an opportunity to play with a baby, adults have engaged in different activities, depending on whether they were told the infant was a male or a female (Will, Self, & Datan, 1976).

Similarly, the first playthings purchased often reflect societal beliefs. Males are frequently supplied with objects that encourage moving, building, and taking things apart and putting them back together. They are apt to be taught at a very young age how to catch a ball and keep score. On the other hand, females are inclined to be given toys that involve relationships with people. Therefore, when males and females first enter school, socialization patterns previously established in the home promote the continuation of play with items and settings that are familiar. In this way, through what is described as the "practice component," the children avoid classroom activities about which they are unfamiliar or less confident (Greenberg, 1985). Hence, the role established in the home environment takes on increased potency.

After exposure to conventional societal expectations, males tend to "judge themselves by what they are able to do" and females "portray their worth in terms of their physical appearance" (Harris & Pickle, 1992, p. 12). This culture-bound, systematic conditioning of humans into patterns of performance is referred to as the "social construction of gender." Undoubtedly, these are the most complex variables to consider as well as the most difficult to unravel. Yet, change in this domain has the potential to generate the greatest effect.

Curriculum

Both in content and in organization, curriculum explicitly and implicitly reflects culture. Critical sociologists (e.g., Apple, 1979) have considered the "hidden curriculum" of schools as including the nonacademic but significant outcomes of schooling that are rarely explicitly expressed. These are often assumptions that underlie what is taught and often result in the replication of culture, class, and gender expectations. Although linkages between the school's culture and society are expected, critical sociologists ask why access to educational experiences differs for some groups and why some individuals are able to resist such forces?

For example, in many classrooms the methodology frequently incorporates debate, argument, and challenge, all of which center on the drive to win (Belenky, Clinchy, Goldberger, & Tarule, 1986; Lewis, 1991; Tannen, 1991). Yet, initially through informal groupings and now more formally through structuring by teachers, the ever-increasing incorporation of cooperative learning groups in mathematics sends messages contrary to the usual competitive model. Cooperative learning attempts to balance members' contributions while increasing the focus on group dynamics and encouraging cohesiveness. Females have consistently responded more favorably, through measured increases in academic performance, to the use of cooperative groupings (as compared to competitive) (Isaacson, 1990). Perhaps this propensity to function well in groupings that combine academic growth with the development of relationships relates to the development of the "ethic of care" (Noddings, 1992), which may be a passive form of resistance to traditional mathematics lessons.

Directions for the Future

Given what is known about cultural and environmental variables, the examination must shift to actions that educators can take to reduce or eliminate these obstacles. One collaborative effort, funded by the Ford Foundation and charged with the improvement of mathematics education nationwide, has generated propositions to assist agents of change. They are:

1. Expect high achievement and hold high expectations for all students, particularly those who have been previously underrepresented. Assume everyone can meet with success and develop instructional strategies that will build students' confidence in learning mathematics.
2. Provide access to mathematical concepts, real-world applications, and linkages to students' cultural frameworks.
3. Move away from dependence on standardized tests to more authentic formats that align the learning and assessment processes. Improved observation skills will enable teachers to formally analyze what happens in their classroom during mathematics instruction. Forms of data collection, such as interviewing students and having students keep journals about their experiences in mathematics, promise to reveal much that would not be evident from previous types of assessment, mostly tests.
4. Develop pre-service and in-service teachers' abilities through better preparation in effective methods to teach mathematics. Teachers need to be made familiar with research on equity issues as they relate to classroom teaching practices.
5. Develop pre-service and in-service teachers' knowledge of mathematics curriculum, particularly in light of the recent development of national standards in mathematics.
6. Create a supportive environment for efforts relating to school restructuring, including increased teacher input in curricular decisions, allocation of resources, and selection of appropriate professional development activities. (Urban Mathematics Collaborative, 1991, pp. 5–6)

In the discussion that follows, more specific elements that overlap several of the Urban Collaborative's recommendations and suggest other routes to pursue are examined in greater depth. Educational institutions should be responsive to needed support systems for females, the creation of positive learning environments, the promise of alternative models of assessment, revised paradigms of teacher education, and the necessity for administrators to be educated on equity issues.

Support Systems

Female students who have entered the fields of mathematics, science, and technology repeatedly report the crucial impact their teachers' encouragement had on their career choices. Occasionally, these women have indicated that support came from women who were working in the field and acted as role models. These were connections commonly made through special summer school or after-school programs for females with interests in mathematics and science (AAUW, 1992). Such programs were crucial in building the confidence of young females. This confidence is critical because, as females' confidence in their mathematics ability dwindles, so does their performance. The all-female cohorts assembled for these programs also reduce the isolation often expressed by female students with a predilection to mathematics. Such opportunities to identify others with like interests initiate subsequent support structures and networks.

Guidance counselors need to be an integral part of the support system for females. Many have now received training in equity issues and are therefore less likely to steer females away from upper-level mathematics courses (even if their cumulative average might go down). In the past, counselors were frequently guilty of this "coercive inducement" (Isaacson, 1988) wherein females make choices "because of a system of rewards and approvals which act as inducements and which are so powerful that they come to be a kind of coercion" (p. 17).

Methodology and the Classroom Learning Environment

The fundamental template of mathematics instruction must face the necessity for alterations. The recently revised standards envisioned and developed by the National Council of Teachers of Mathematics (1998) in both curriculum and methodology promise to be a paradigm of inclusive instruction. The suggested avoidance of lock-step applications of procedures and the recommended incorporation of understanding, estimation, testing for reasonableness, and identification of patterns are attempts to provide all students with power in mathematics. A positive learning environment can be employed to build confidence and problem-solving abilities through discussion of strategies and thinking processes, demonstrations that mathematics is relevant, nurturing of cooperative efforts, and emphasis on more authentic assessment models. Mathematics teachers at all levels must renounce teaching methods that encourage learned helplessness in students (Karp, 1991).

Research reported by AAUW (1992) suggests that when teachers become aware of their gender biases, they are willing to change. Therefore, teachers require the kind of in-service and pre-service training that will keep them apprised of the current theories and suggested practices in promoting gender equity. This knowledge can result in an increased alertness to gender bias and stereotyping in textbooks, software, audiovisual materials, and course titles, as well as choices of speakers, field trips, and mentoring or job shadowing programs.

Additionally, teachers must terminate the silence in school environments when students or faculty demonstrate behaviors that are biased or discriminatory. Such passive behaviors further entrench attitudes and actions that are harmful to those who are subjected to them. Only active confrontation can encourage the awareness and attitudinal change necessary to promote fairness to all groups. Institutions of teacher education have the responsibility of preparing teachers to assume leadership roles when faced with these challenges.

Teacher Education

In 1980, Sadker and Sadker evaluated the three best-selling texts in mathematics education and found that they did not contain any content related to either gender differences or the contributions of women to mathematics. In a more recent examination of 25 extant texts in mathematics education, which included the three most popular texts (as reported in Pedersen, Beal, Con-

nelly, Klespis, Leitzel, & Tayeh, 1991), similar patterns of invisibility exist (Karp, 1992). Only four of the texts made specific mention of gender-related equity issues or techniques that could be incorporated to improve the performance of female students. Although one text had comprehensive coverage, with 21 pages exploring research on gender differences, the other texts each had less than 2 pages of information. Sadker and Sadker stated that pre-service teaching candidates "are being prepared with textbooks more likely to promote and reinforce sex bias than to reduce and eliminate such prejudice" (1980, p. 550).

Apparently not much has changed. Current texts provide future teachers with neither the recent research on the issues nor the curricular resources and methodologies to combat sexism or encourage the models proven to be most successful with females. "Teacher education in most institutions of higher learning reinforces the already existing sexist attitudes of many undergraduates" (O'Reilly & Borman, 1984, p. 110).

To end the reproduction of teachers who are unaware of the challenges engendered by gender inequities in mathematics education, teacher education programs need to aggressively respond. As already implemented by professors of elementary mathematics education courses, readings and discussions on equity issues can and should be supplementary components to any textbook that does not provide adequate information. More importantly, professors must model methods and discourse that are likely to nurture the same gender-balanced behaviors in their students.

Assessment

Culture-practice theorists examine the gender differences question from another lens. They weigh heavily the value of examining "context specificity," an assumption that constitutes the framework of this theory. They suggest that when the context in which a problem is posed is relevant to the culture of the individual, previous differences in cognition cease to be identified (Laboratory of Comparative Human Cognition, 1983). For example, Liberian children were given a group of geometric shapes and asked to group them according to an attribute of their choice. When they were unable to accomplish this task successfully, they were deemed weak in classification skills. However, when they were asked to group rice, they demonstrated skill in this ability far beyond the performance of U.S. participants (Irwin, Schafer, & Feiden, 1974).

The question, thus, becomes: In what contexts other than those traditionally used in school settings can females best display their mathematics skills? Answers may lie in the diverse options presented by alternative forms of assessing mathematical ability. Formats such as portfolios, performance tasks, or interviews may provide the best forum for unveiling the mathematics skills females possess.

School Restructuring and Administration

In addition to the dissemination of awareness information to teachers, administrators need to acquire fine-tuned observation skills that encourage sensitivity to gender inequities (Schmuck & Schubert, 1986). Yet, in particular, women administrators have to be seen as more than just focusing on gender-related issues to avoid losing their job (Shakeshaft, 1987). Shakeshaft (1990) further suggests that her research findings confirm that women's ways of managing are aligned with research on effective schools and that schools and educational administration programs should be restructured to profit from females' strengths.

To best organize a school restructuring effort that includes equity concerns on its agenda, educational institutions should conduct formal assessments of gender equity. From basic statistics on course enrollments and participation in extracurricular activities to elaborate observational evaluations, patterns of inequities need to be identified. The ensuing analyses might result in the development and implementation of administrative and curricular policies to ensure equity in classroom interactions and curricula and school management. As a first step, knowledge about equity laws and research that counteracts sex biases might be reflected in the comments and suggestions generated by supervisors' observations of lessons.

Conclusion

Schools remain sources of cultural reproduction; therefore, awareness of students' developing roles and values is critical. By tolerating an environment of gender bias, females and males are exposed to behaviors and attitudes that corrupt their overall growth.

Males who excel over females in this environment constitute a small percentage. Not enough students of either gender attain the high levels of mathematics thinking realized by students in other nations. Fortunately, there is not a zero-sum relationship to the nurturing of females' mathematics abilities. Classroom

strategies that create an environment where females can be successful do not disadvantage males and in many instances have been beneficial to them. Gender inequities do not just harm females; they have an impact on everyone.

The answers we seek in creating an environment that encourages females to welcome mathematical experiences and consider possible careers in the discipline are still being generated. In fact, we may need to think of other questions. The key may lie in the more subtle or complex constructs we have not yet investigated, such as those referred to by Tyack and Hansot (1988) when they suggest the "need to be aware of the importance of the dog that did not bark" (p. 34).

References

Adelman, C. (1991). *Women at thirty something: Paradoxes of attainment.* Washington, DC: U.S. Department of Education.

Alexander, K., & Pallas, A. (1983). Reply to Benbow and Stanley. *American Educational Research Journal, 20,* 475–477.

American Association of University Women. (1992). *How schools shortchange girls.* Washington, DC: AAUW Educational Foundation and National Education Association.

Apple, M. (1979). *Ideology and curriculum.* London: Routledge & Kegan Paul.

Baenninger, M., & Newcombe, N. (1989). The role of experience in spatial test performance: A meta-analysis. *Sex Roles, 20,* 327–344.

Belenky, M., Clinchy, B., Goldberger, N., & Tarule, J. (1986). *Women's ways of knowing: The development of self, voice, and mind.* New York: Basic Books.

Benbow, C. (1980). In G. B. Kolata, Math and sex: Are girls born with less ability? *Science, 210,* 1234–1235.

Benbow, C., & Stanley, J. (1980). Sex differences in mathematical ability: Fact or artifact? *Science, 210,* 1262–1264.

Bender, S. (1994). *Female student career aspirations in science* (SSTA Research Centre Report No. 94-04, SSTA research in Brief). Regina, Saskatchewan: Saskatchewan School Trustees Association.

Brandon, P., Newton, B., & Hammond, O. (1987). Children's mathematics achievement in Hawaii: Sex differences favoring girls. *American Educational Research Journal, 24,* 437–461.

Brandt, A. (1989, December/January). Sex and the facts of math. *Parenting,* 122–124, 127.

Carpenter, P., Lindquist, M., Mathews, W., & Silver, E. (1983). Results of the third NAEP mathematics assessment: Secondary school. *Mathematics Teacher, 76,* 652–659.

Christen, Y. (1995). Brain structure explains male/female differences. In D. Bender & B. Leone (Eds.), *Male/female roles: Opposing viewpoints* (pp 48–56). San Diego, CA: Greenhaven Press.

College Board. (1994, 1995, 1997). *Profile of SAT and achievement test takers.* Princeton, NJ: College Entrance Examination Board.

Conlan, G. (1990). Text and context reading comprehension and the mechanics of meaning. *College Board Review, 157,* 18–25.

Dick, T. P., & Rallis, S. F. (1991). Factors and influences on high school students' career choices. *Journal for Research in Mathematics Education, 22,* 281–292.

Dossey, J., Mullis, I., Lindquist, M., & Chambers, D. (1988). *The mathematics report card: Are we measuring up? Trends and achievement based on the 1986 national assessment.* Princeton, NJ: Educational Testing Service.

Drabble, M. (1975, August 5). Interview. *The Guardian* (London), p. 16.

Eccles, J., Flanagan, C., Goldsmith, R., Jacobs, J., Jayaratne, T., Wigfield, A., & Yee, D. (1987). *Parents as socializers of achievement attitudes.* Paper presented at the Society for Research in Child Development, Baltimore.

Egelman, E., Alper, J., Leibowitz, L., Beckwith, J., Levine, R., & Leeds, A. (1981). Letter to the editor. *Science, 212,* 116.

FairTest. (Fall, 1996). FairTest complaint will lead to millions more for girls. *FairTest Examiner,* 1–3.

Fennema, E. (1990). Justice, equity, and mathematics education. In E. Fennema & G. Leder (Eds.), *Mathematics and gender* (pp. 1–9). New York: Teachers College Press.

Gallagher, A. M., & DeLisi, R. (1994). Gender differences in scholastic aptitude tests—Mathematics problem solving among high-ability students. *Journal of Educational Psychology, 86,* 204–211.

Gallagher, S., & Johnson, E. (1992). The effects of time limits on performance of mental rotations by gifted adolescents. *Gifted Child Quarterly, 36* (l), 19–22.

Gilligan, C. (1982). *In a different voice.* Cambridge, MA: Harvard University Press.

Goleman, D. (1987, August 2). Girls and math: Is biology really destiny? *New York Times: Educational Supplement,* 42–46.

Greenberg, S. (1985). Educational equity in early childhood environments. In S. Klein (Ed.), *Handbook for achieving sex equity through education.* Baltimore: Johns Hopkins University Press.

Gross, S. (1988). *Participation and performance of women and minorities in mathematics (E-4).* Rockville, MD: Department of Educational Accountability.

Halpern, D. (1989). The disappearance of cognitive gender differences: What you see depends on where you live. *American Psychologist, 44,* 1156–1157.

Harris, M., & Pickle, J. (1992). Creating an equitable environment: Gender equity in Lincoln, Nebraska. *The Educational Forum, 57* (l), 12–17.

Hyde, J., Fennema, E., Ryan, M., Frost, L., & Hopp, C. (1990). Gender comparisons of mathematics ability and affect: A meta-analysis. *Psychology of Women Quarterly, 14* (1990): 299–324.

Intons-Peterson, M., & Reddel, M. (1984). What do people ask about a neonate? *Developmental Psychology, 20* (3), 358–359.

Irwin, M., Schafer, G., & Feiden, C. (1974). Emic and unfamiliar category sorting of Mano farmers and U.S. undergraduates. *Journal of Cross-Cultural Psychology, 5* (4), 407–423.

Isaacson, Z. (1988). Of course you could be an engineer, dear, but wouldn't you rather be a nurse or teacher or secretary? In P. Ernest (Ed.), *The social context of mathematics teaching* (pp. 17–25). Exeter, UK: Exeter University Publishing.

Isaacson, Z. (1990). "They look at you in absolute horror": Women writing and talking about mathematics. In L. Burton (Ed.), *Gender and mathematics: An international perspective* (pp. 20–28). New York: Cassell Education.

Jacobs, J., & Eccles, J. (1992). The impact of mothers' gender-role stereotypic belief on mothers' and children's ability perceptions. *Journal of Personality and Social Psychology, 63,* 932–944.

Jones, G. (1989). Gender bias in classroom interactions. *Contemporary Education, 60,* 216–222.

Karp, K. (1991). Elementary school teachers' attitudes toward mathematics: The impact on students' autonomous learning skills. *School Science and Mathematics, 91* (6), 265–270.

Karp, K. (1992). Mathematics and science education texts: Do they examine the issue of gender equity? Unpublished paper.

Krantz, L. (1995). *The jobs rated almanac.* New York: Ballantine Books.

Laboratory of Comparative Human Cognition. (1983). Culture and cognitive development. In P. Mussen & W. Kessen (Eds.), *Handbook of child psychology (4th ed.) Volume I: History, theory, and methods* (pp. 295–356). New York: Wiley and Sons.

Lewis, A. (1991). Taking women seriously. *Phi Delta Kappan, 73* (4), 268–269.

Linn, M., & Hyde, J. (1989). Gender mathematics, and science. *Educational Researcher, 12,* 17–19, 22–27.

Matyas, M., & Dix, L. (1992). *Science and engineering programs: On target for women?* Washington, DC: National Academy Press.

McKee, A. (1992, February 12). In S. Chira, Bias against girls is found rife in schools, with lasting damage. *New York Times,* pp. A1, A23.

National Commission on Working Women. (1989). *Women, work and the future.* Washington, DC: Wider Opportunities for Women.

National Council of Teachers of Mathematics. (1998). *Principles and standards for school mathematics.* Reston, VA: NCTM.

Noddings, N. (1992). The gender issue. *Educational Leadership, 49* (4), 65–70.

O'Reilly, P., & Borman, K. (1984). Sexism and sex discrimination in education. *Theory into Practice, 23* (2), 110–116.

Pedersen, K., Beal, S., Connelly, R., Klespis, M., Leitzel, J., & Tayeh, C. (1991). *How is mathematics education reform affecting teacher education programs?* Presentation at the National Council of Supervisors of Mathematics, New Orleans.

Ramey, E. (1987). *Sex hormones and science ability.* Paper presented at the Annual Meeting of the National Science Teachers' Association, Washington, DC.

Ramist, L., & Arbeiter, S. (1986). *Profiles of college-bound seniors: 1985.* New York: College Entrance Examination Board.

Robinson, A., & Katzman, J. (1986). *Cracking the system.* New York: Villard.

Rosenthal, R., & Rubin, D. (1982). Further meta-analytic procedures for assessing cognitive gender differences. *Journal of Educational Psychology, 74,* 708–712.

Sadker, M., & Sadker, D. (1980). Sexism in teacher education texts. *Harvard Educational Review, 50,* 36–46.

Sadker, M., & Sadker, D. (1994). *Failing at fairness: How our schools cheat girls.* New York: Simon & Schuster.

Sadker, M., Sadker, D., & Klein, S. (1991). The issue of gender in elementary and secondary education. In G. Grant (Ed.), *Review of the research in education, 17,* 269–334. Washington, DC: American Educational Research Association.

Schmuck, P., & Schubert, J. (1986). *Women administrators' views on sex equity: Exploring issues of information, identity, and integration.* Paper presented at the annual meeting of the American Education Research Association, Washington, DC.

Selkow, P. (1984). *Assessing sex bias in testing: A review of the issues and evaluations of 74 psychological and educational tests.* Westport, CT: Greenwood.

Sells, L. (1978). Mathematics—A critical filter. *The Science Teacher, 45,* 28–29.

Serbin, L., & O'Leary, K. (1975 December). How nursery schools teach girls to shut up. *Psychology Today, 55.*

Shakeshaft, C. (1987). *Women in educational administration.* Newbury Park, CA: Sage.

Shakeshaft, C. (1990). Administrative preparation for equity. In H. P. Baptiste, H. C. Waxman, J. Walker de Felix, & J. E. Anderson (Eds.), *Leadership, equity, and school effectiveness* (pp. 213–223). Newbury Park, CA: Sage.

Spender, D. (1982). *Invisible women: The schooling scandal.* London: Writers and Readers.

Stevenson, H. (1987). America's math problems. *Educational Leadership, 45* (2), 4–10.

Tannen, D. (1991). How men and women use language differently in their lives and in the classroom. *Education Digest, 57* (6), 3–4.

Thomas, H., & Kail, R. (1991). Sex differences in speed of mental rotation and the X-linked genetic hypothesis. *Intelligence, 15* (1), 17–31.

Toronto Board of Education. (1989). *Dropping math? Say good-bye to 82 jobs.* Toronto, Canada: Mathematics Department of the Toronto Board of Education.

Tyack, D., & Hansot, E. (1988). Silence and policy talk: Historical puzzles about gender and education. *Educational Researcher,* 33–41.

Urban Mathematics Collaborative. (1991). Math equity in the classroom: A vision of reform from the urban mathematics collaboratives. *Women's Educational Equity Act Digest.* Newton, MA: Women's Educational Equity Act Publishing Center.

U.S. Department of Education. (1997). *Digest of education statistics.* Washington, DC: Office of Educational Research and Improvement.

Vogel, S. (1990). Gender difference in intelligence, language, visual-motor abilities, and academic achievement in students with learning disabilities: A review of the literature. *Journal of Learning Disabilities, 23,* 44–52.

Walden, R., & Walkerdine, V. (1985). *Girls and mathematics: From primary to secondary schooling* (Bedford Way Papers, No. 24). London: Institute of Education, London University.

Will, J., Self, P., & Datan, N. (1976). Maternal behavior and perceived sex of infant. *American Journal of Orthopsychiatry, 46* (1), 135–139.

Social Class Differences in Family-School Relationships

The Importance of Cultural Capital

ANNETTE LAREAU

The influence of family background on children's educational experiences has a curious place within the field of sociology of education. On the one hand, the issue has dominated the field. Wielding increasingly sophisticated methodological tools, social scientists have worked to document, elaborate, and replicate the influence of family background on educational life chances (Jencks et al. 1972; Marjoribanks 1979). On the other hand, until recently, research on this issue focused primarily on educational *outcomes;* very little attention was given to the *processes* through which these educational patterns are created and reproduced.

Over the past fifteen years, important strides have been made in our understanding of social processes inside the school. Ethnographic research has shown that classroom learning is reflexive and interactive and that language in the classroom draws unevenly from the sociolinguistic experiences of children at home (Bernstein 1975, 1982; Cook-Gumperez 1973; Heath 1982, 1983; Labov 1972; Diaz, Moll, and Mehan 1986; Mehan and Griffin 1980). Studies of the curriculum, the hidden curriculum, the social organization of the classroom, and the authority relationships between teachers and students have also suggested ways in which school processes contribute to social reproduction (Aggleton and Whitty 1985; Anyon 1981; Apple 1979; Erickson and Mohatt 1982; Gearing and Epstein 1982; Gaskell 1985; Taylor 1984; Valli 1985; Wilcox 1977, 1982).

Surprisingly, relatively little of this research has focused on parental involvement in schooling. Yet, quantitative studies suggest that parental behavior can be a crucial determinant of educational performance (Epstein 1984; Marjoribanks 1979). In addition, increasing parental participation in education has become a priority for educators, who believe it promotes educational achievement (Berger 1983; Seeley 1984; National Education Association 1985; Robinson 1985; Trelease 1982; Leichter 1979).

Those studies that have examined parental involvement in education generally take one of three major conceptual approaches to understanding variations in levels of parental participation. Some researchers subscribe to the culture-of-poverty thesis, which states that lower-class culture has distinct values and forms of social organization. Although their interpretations vary, most of these researchers suggest that lower-class and working-class families do not value education as highly as middle-class families (Deutsch 1967). Other analysts trace unequal levels of parental involvement in schooling back to the educational institutions themselves. Some accuse schools of institutional discrimination, claiming that they make middle-class families feel more welcome than working-class and lower-class families (Lightfoot 1978; Ogbu 1974). In an Australian study of home-school relationships, for example, Connell et al. (1982) argue that working-class parents are "frozen out" of schools. Others maintain that institutional differentiation, particularly the role of teacher leadership, is a critical determinant of parental involvement in schooling (Epstein and Becker 1982; Becker and Epstein 1982).

A third perspective for understanding varying levels of parental involvement in schooling draws on the work of Bourdieu and the concept of cultural capital. Bourdieu (1977a, 1977b; Bourdieu and Passeron 1977) argues that schools draw unevenly on the social and cultural resources of members of the society. For example, schools utilize particular linguistic structures, authority patterns, and types of curricula; children from higher social locations enter schools already familiar with these social arrangements. Bourdieu maintains that the cultural experiences in the home facilitate children's adjustment to school and academic achievement, thereby transforming cultural resources into what he calls cultural capital (Bourdieu 1977a, 1977b).

This perspective points to the structure of schooling and to family life and the dispositions of individu-

From *Sociology of Education* (April 1987): 73–85. Reprinted by permission of the American Sociological Association.

als (what Bourdieu calls habitus [1977b, 1981]) to understand different levels of parental participation in schooling. The standards of schools are not neutral; their requests for parental involvement may be laden with the social and cultural experiences of intellectual and economic elites. Bourdieu does not examine the question of parental participation in schooling, but his analysis points to the importance of class and class cultures in facilitating or impeding children's (or parents') negotiation of the process of schooling (also see Baker and Stevenson 1986; Connell et al. 1982; Joffee 1977; Ogbu 1974; Rist 1978; McPherson 1972; Gracey 1972; Wilcox 1977, 1982).

In this paper I argue that class-related cultural factors shape parents' compliance with teachers' requests for parental participation in schooling. I pose two major questions. First, what do schools ask of parents in the educational experience of young children? Are there important variations in teachers' expectations of parental involvement in elementary schooling? Second, how do parents respond to schools' requests? In particular, how does social class influence the process through which parents participate in their children's schooling? The analysis and conclusions are based on an intensive study of home-school relationships of children in the first and second grades of a white working-class school and an upper-middle-class school.

I begin the discussion with a very brief review of historical variations in home-school relationships. Then, I describe the research sites and methodology. In the third section, I examine teachers' views of family involvement in schooling. This is followed by a description of family-school interactions in the working-class and middle-class communities. Finally, I analyze the factors contributing to social class variations in home-school relationships and review the implications for future research.

Historical Variations in Family-School Relationships

Families and schools are dynamic institutions: both have changed markedly in the last two centuries. Not surprisingly, family-school interactions have shifted as well. Over time, there has been a steady increase in the level of parental involvement in schooling. At least three major stages of family-school interaction can be identified. In the first period, parents in rural areas provided food and shelter for the teacher. Children's education and family life were intertwined, although

parents evidently were not involved in the formal aspects of other children's cognitive development (Overstreet and Overstreet 1949). In the second period, marked by the rise of mass schooling, parents provided political and economic support for the selection and maintenance of school sites. Parents were involved in school activities and classroom activities, but again, they were not fundamentally involved in their children's cognitive development (Butterworth 1928; Hymes 1953; National Congress of Parents and Teachers 1944). In the third and current period, parents have increased their efforts to reinforce the curriculum and promote cognitive development at home. In addition, parents have played a growing role in monitoring their children's educational development, particularly in special education programs, and have moved into the classroom as volunteers (Berger 1983; Levy, Meltsner, and Wildavsky 1974; Mehan, Hertweck, and Meihls 1986).

These changes in family-school interactions do not represent a linear progression. Nor is there only one form of relationship at any given time. Many factors—e.g., parents' educational attainment, the amount of nonwork time parents can invest in their children's schooling—affect the kind and degree of parental involvement. Family-school relationships are socially constructed and are historically variable. Home-school partnerships, in which parents are involved in the cognitive development of their children, currently seem to be the dominant model, but there are many possible types of family-school relationships (Baker and Stevenson 1986). As in other social relationships, family-school interactions carry the imprint of the larger social context: Acceptance of a particular type of family-school relationship emerges as the result of social processes.

These aspects of family-school relationships are routinely neglected in social scientists' discussions of parental involvement (Epstein 1983, 1984; Seeley 1984). When home-school relationships are evaluated exclusively in terms of parental behavior, critical questions are neither asked nor answered. The standards of the schools must be viewed as problematic, and further, the researcher must ask what kinds of social resources are useful in complying with these standards.

Research Methodology

The research presented here involved participant-observation of two first-grade classrooms located in two different communities. Also, in-depth interviews of parents, teachers, and principals were conducted while the children were in first and second grade. Following other studies of social class differences in family life (Rubin 1976; Kohn 1977), I chose a white working-class community and a professional middle-class community. I sought a working-class community in which a majority of the parents were high school graduates or dropouts, employed in skilled or semiskilled occupations, paid an hourly wage, and periodically unemployed. For the professional middle-class school, I sought a community in which a majority of the parents were college graduates and professionals who had strong career opportunities and who were less vulnerable to changes in the economy. The two communities described here met these criteria.

Colton School (fictitious name) is located in a working-class community. Most of the parents of Colton students are employed in semiskilled or unskilled occupations (see Table 1). School personnel report that most of the parents have a high school education; many are high school dropouts. The school has about 450 students in kindergarten, first grade, and second grade. Slightly over one half of the children are white, one third are Hispanic, and the remainder are black or Asian, especially recent Vietnamese immigrants. About one half of the children qualify for free lunches under federal guidelines.

Prescott School (fictitious name) is in an upper-middle-class suburban community about 30 minutes from Colton. Most of the parents of Prescott students are professionals (Table 1). Both parents in the family are likely to be college graduates, and many of the children's fathers have advanced degrees. The school enrolls about 300 students from kindergarten to fifth grade. Virtually all the students are white, and the school does not offer a lunch program, although the Parents' Club sponsors a Hot Dog Day once a month.

For a six-month period, January to June 1982, I visited one first-grade classroom at each school. My visits averaged once or twice a week per school and lasted around two hours. During this time, I observed the classroom and acted as a volunteer in the class, passing out paper and helping the children with math and spelling problems.

At the end of the school year, I selected six children in each class for further study. The children were selected on the basis of reading-group membership; a boy and a girl were selected from the high, medium, and low reading groups. To prevent the confounding effects of race, I chose only white children. I interviewed one single mother in each school; the remaining households had two parents. In both of the schools, three of the mothers worked full time or part time, and three were at home full time. All of the Colton mothers, however, had worked in recent years, when their children were younger. The Prescott mothers had worked prior to the birth of their children but had not been in the labor force since that time.

When the children finished first grade, I interviewed their mothers individually. When they finished second grade, I interviewed their mothers for a second time, and in separate sessions, I interviewed most of their fathers. I also interviewed the first- and second-grade teachers, the school principals, and a resource specialist at one of the schools. All the interviews were semistructured and lasted about two hours. The interviews were tape recorded, and all participants were promised confidentiality.

TABLE 1 The Percentages of Parents in Each Occupational Category, by School

Occupation	Colton	Prescott
Professionals, executives, managers	1	60
Semiprofessionals, sales, clerical workers, and technicians	11	30
Skilled and semiskilled workers	51	9
Unskilled workers (and welfare recipients)	23	1
Unknown	20	—

Note: The figures for the Prescott school are based on the principal's estimation of the school population.
Source: California Department of Education, 1983.

Teachers' Requests for Parental Involvement

The research examined the formal requests from the teachers and school administrators asking parents to participate in schooling, particularly surrounding the issue of achievement. It also studied the quality of interaction between teachers and parents on the school site. Although there were some variations among the teachers in their utilization of parents in the classrooms, all promoted parental involvement and all believed there was a strong relationship between parental involvement (particularly reading to children) and academic performance. At both schools, the definition of the ideal family-school relationship was the same: a partnership in which family life and school life are integrated.

In the course of the school year, teachers in both schools actively promoted parental involvement in schooling in several ways. For example, newsletters were used to notify families of school events and to invite them to attend. Teachers also reminded children verbally about school events to which parents had been invited and encouraged the children to bring their parents to classroom and schoolwide events.

In their interactions with parents, educators urged parents to read to their children. The principal at Prescott school, for example, told the parents at Back to School Night that they should consider reading the child's homework. In every class at Colton school, there was a Read at Home Program, in which the teacher kept track of the number of hours a child read to an adult at home or was read to by a sibling or adult. A chart posted in the classroom marked hours of reading in 15-minute intervals. A child could choose a free book after eight hours of reading at home. This emphasis on reading also surfaced in the routine interactions between parents and teachers and between teachers and children. In the classroom, the teachers suggested that children check out library books, read to their parents, or have their parents read to them at home. At parent-teacher conferences, teachers suggested that parents read to their child at home. In one 20-minute parent-teacher conference, for example, the teacher mentioned five times the importance of reading to the child at home.

Other requests of parents were made as well. Teachers encouraged parents to communicate any concerns they had about their child. In their meetings with parents, teachers also expressed a desire for parents to review and reinforce the material learned in class (e.g., to help their children learn their spelling words). Generally, teachers at both schools believed that the relationship between parental involvement and academic performance was important, and they used a variety of approaches to encourage parents to participate in education.

Teachers and administrators spoke of being "partners" with parents, and they stressed the need to maintain good communication, but it was clear that they desired parents to defer to their professional expertise. For example, a first-grade teacher at Prescott did not believe in assigning homework to the children and did not appreciate parents communicating their displeasure with the policy by complaining repeatedly to the principal. Nor did principals welcome parents' opinions that a teacher was a bad teacher and should be fired. Teachers wanted parents to support them, or as they put it, to "back them up."

Although generally persuaded that parental involvement was positive for educational growth, some teachers, particularly in the upper-middle-class school, were ambivalent about some types of parental involvement in schooling. The Prescott teachers were very concerned that some parents placed too much pressure on their children. Parental involvement could become counterproductive when it increased the child's anxiety level and produced negative learning experiences. As one Prescott teacher put it,

> It depends on the parent. Sometimes it can be helpful, sometimes it creates too much pressure. Sometimes they learn things wrong. It is better for them to leave the basics alone . . . and take them to museums, do science, and other enrichment activities.

As Becker and Epstein (1982) have found, there was some variation among the teachers in the degree to which they took leadership roles in promoting parental involvement in schooling, particularly in the area of classroom volunteers. Although all the teachers in the study requested parents to volunteer and had parents in the classroom, there were other teachers in the school who used parents more extensively. Teachers also varied in how they judged parents. While the extreme cases were clear, the teachers sometimes disagreed about how supportive parents were or about how much pressure they were putting on their children. For example, the first-grade teacher at Prescott thought one boy's father placed too much pressure on him, but the second-grade teacher judged the family to be supportive and helpful. Thus, there were variations in teachers' styles as well as in the way they implemented the model of home-school partnerships.

This study does not, however, support the thesis that the different levels of parental involvement can be traced to institutional differentiation or institutional discrimination, i.e., to teachers' pursuit of different kinds of relationships with working-class and middle-class families (Connell et al. 1982; Epstein and Becker 1982). All of the first- and second-grade teachers in the study made similar requests to parents. In both schools, teachers made clear and repeated efforts to promote parental involvement in the educational process.

Educational Consequences of Family-School Relationships

Parents who agreed with the administrators' and teachers' definition of partnership appeared to offer an educational advantage to their children; parents who turned over the responsibility of education to the professional could negatively affect their child's schooling.

Teachers' methods of presenting, teaching, and assessing subject matter were based on a structure that presumed parents would help children at home. At Colton, for example, spelling words were given out on Monday and students were repeatedly encouraged to practice the words at home with their parents before the test on Friday. Teachers noticed which children had practiced at home and which children had not and believed it influenced their performance.

This help at home was particularly important for low achievers. At Prescott, teachers encouraged parents of low achievers to work with them at home. In one case, a girl missed her spelling lessons because she had to meet with the reading resource teacher. Rather than fall behind in spelling, she and her mother did her spelling at home through most of the year. Colton teachers also tried to involve parents in the education of low achievers. One Colton teacher arranged a special conference at a student's home and requested that the parents urge the student to practice reading at home. The teacher complained that the girl didn't "get that much help at home." The teacher believed that if the parents had taken an active role in schooling, the child would have been promoted rather than retained.

In other instances, the initiative to help children at home came from parents. For example, at Prescott, one mother noticed while volunteering in the classroom that her son was somewhat behind in his spelling. At her request, she and her son worked on his spelling every day after school for about a month, until he had advanced to the lesson that most of the class was on. Prior to the mother's actions, the boy was in the bottom third of the class in spelling. He was not, however, failing spelling, and it was unlikely that the teacher would have requested the parent to take an active role. After the mother and son worked at home, he was in the top third of the class in his spelling work. The teacher was very impressed by these efforts and believed that the mother's active involvement in schooling had a positive effect on her son's performance:

> She is very supportive, very committed. If she didn't work in the class [volunteering] her boys wouldn't do too well. They are not brilliant at all. But they are going to do well. She is just going to see that they are going to get a good foundation. A child like that would flounder if you let him.

Not all parental involvement in schooling was so positive, however. There is a dark side to the partnership, which is not usually addressed in the literature aimed at increasing parental participation in education (Epstein and Becker 1982; Seeley 1984). Particularly in the upper-middle-class school, teachers complained of the pressure parents placed on teachers and children for academic performance. One mother reported that her son had been stealing small objects early in first grade, a pattern the pediatrician and the mother attributed to the boy's "frustration level" in schooling. A girl in the lowest reading group began developing stomach aches during the reading period in first grade. Teachers at Prescott mentioned numerous cases in which parental involvement was unhelpful. In these cases, parents had usually challenged the professional expertise of the teachers.

Generally, however, the teachers believed that the relationship between parental participation and school performance was positive. These results provide indications that teachers take *parental performance* in schooling very seriously. Teachers recall which parents participate and which parents fail to participate in schooling. They believe that their requests of parents are reasonable and that all parents, regardless of social position, can help their children in first and second grade.

Parents' Involvement in Schooling

Although teachers at both schools expressed a desire for parental participation in schooling, the amount of contact varied significantly between the sites. The response of parents to teachers' requests was much higher at the upper-middle-class school than at the working-class school.

Attendance at School Events

As Table 2 shows, the level of attendance at formal school events was significantly higher at Prescott than at Colton. Virtually all Prescott parents attended the parent-teacher conferences in the fall and spring, but only 60 percent of Colton parents attended. Attendance at Open House was almost three times higher at Prescott than at Colton.

The difference between the two schools was apparent not only in the quantity of interaction but in the quality of interaction. Although teachers at both schools asked parents to communicate any concerns they had about their children, Colton parents rarely initiated contact with teachers. When Colton parents did contact the school, they frequently raised nonacademic issues, such as lunchboxes, bus schedules, and playground activities. One of the biggest complaints, for example, was that children had only 15 minutes to eat lunch and that slower eaters were often unable to finish.

At Colton, the interactions between parents and teachers were stiff and awkward. The parents often showed signs of discomfort: nervous shifting, blushing, stuttering, sweating, and generally looking ill at ease. During the Open House, parents wandered around the room looking at the children's pictures. Many of the parents did not speak with the teacher during their visit. When they did, the interaction tended to be short, rather formal, and serious. The teacher asked the parents if they had seen all of their children's work, and she checked to see that all of the children had shown their desk and folder of papers to their parents. The classrooms at Colton often contained only about

10 adults at a time, and the rooms were noticeably quiet.

At Prescott, the interactions between parents and teachers were more frequent, more centered around academic matters, and much less formal. Parents often wrote notes to the teacher, telephoned the teacher at school, or dropped by during the day to discuss a problem. These interactions often centered around the child's academic progress; many Prescott parents monitored their children's education and requested additional resources for them if there were problems. Parents, for example, asked that children be signed up to see the reading resource teacher, be tested by the school psychologist, or be enrolled in the gifted program. Parents also asked for homework for their children or for materials that they could complete at home with their children.

The ease with which Prescott parents contacted the school was also apparent at formal school events. At the Open House, almost all of the parents talked to the teacher or to the teacher's aide; these conversations were often long and were punctuated by jokes and questions. Also, many of the parents were friends with other parents in the class, so there was quite a bit of interaction between families. In inviting me to the Open House, the teacher described the event as a "cocktail party without cocktails." The room did indeed have the noisy, crowded, and animated atmosphere of a cocktail party.

In sum, Colton parents were reluctant to contact the school, tended to intervene over nonacademic matters, and were uncomfortable in their interactions in the school. In contrast, although Prescott parents varied in the level of supervision and scrutiny they gave their child's schooling, they frequently contacted teachers to discuss their child's academic progress.

Parents' attendance at school activities and their contact with teachers enabled the teachers to directly assess parents' compliance with requests for involvement. However, Prescott teachers had difficulty estimating the number of children whose parents read to them at home regularly. The teachers believed that a majority of children were read to several times per week and that many children spent time reading to themselves. Among the six families interviewed, all of the parents said that they read to their children almost every day, usually before bedtime. Colton teachers used the Read at Home Program to evaluate the amount of reading that took place at home. During the participant-observation period, only three or four children in

TABLE 2 Percentage of Parents, Participating in School Activities, by School, First Grade Only, 1981–1982

Activity	Colton ($n = 34$)	Prescott ($n = 28$)
Parent-teacher conferences	60	100
Open house	35	96
Volunteering in classroom	3	43

the class of 34 brought back slips every day or every few days demonstrating that they had read at home for it least 15 minutes. Some children checked out books and brought back slips less frequently. The majority of the class earned only two books in the program, indicating that they had read at home an average of 16 hours during the 180 days of school, or between two and four minutes a day.

The Read at Home Program was actively promoted by Colton teachers. Children were brought to the front of the class for applause every time they earned a book, and the teachers encouraged children to check out books and read at home. Nevertheless, in the interviews, only half of the parents said that they read to their children every day; the remainder read to their children much more irregularly. Colton parents clearly did not read to their children as often as the upper-middle-class parents at Prescott.

In addition, Prescott parents played a more active role in reinforcing and monitoring the school work of their children. Colton parents were asked by teachers to help review and reinforce the material at school, particularly spelling words. Though a few parents worked with their children, Colton teachers were disappointed in the response. Colton parents were also unfamiliar with the school's curriculum and with the specific educational problems of their children. Parents of children with learning disabilities, for example, knew only that their children's grades "weren't up to par" or that their children "didn't do too well" in school. Moreover these parents were unaware of the teacher's specific efforts to improve their child's performance.

Prescott parents, on the other hand, carefully followed their children's curriculum. They often showed children the practical applications of the knowledge they gained at school, made up games that strengthened and elaborated children's recently acquired knowledge, and reviewed the material presented in class with their children. Parents of low achievers and children with learning problems were particularly vigorous in these efforts and made daily efforts to work with children at home. Parents knew their child's specific problems and knew what the teacher was doing to strengthen their child's performance. Parents' efforts on behalf of their children were closely coordinated with the school program.

There were some variations in parents' response to teachers' requests in the two school communities. Notably, two of the Colton parents (who appeared to be upwardly mobile) actively read to their children at home, closely reviewed their children's school work, and emphasized the importance of educational success. The teachers were very impressed by the behavior of these parents and by the relatively high academic performance of their children. At Prescott, parents differed in how critically they assessed the school and in their propensity to intervene in their children's schooling. For example, some parents said that they "felt sorry for teachers" and believed that other parents in the community were too demanding. The child's number of siblings, birth order, and temperament also shaped parental intervention in schooling. There was some variation in the role of fathers, although in both schools, mothers had the primary responsibility for schooling.

There were important differences, then, in the way in which Colton and Prescott parents responded to teachers' requests for participation. These patterns suggest that the relationship between families and schools was *independent* in the working-class school, and *interdependent* in the middle-class school.

Factors Structuring Parents' Participation

Interviews and observations of parents suggested that a variety of factors influenced parents' participation in schooling. Parents' educational capabilities, their view of the appropriate division of labor between teachers and parents, the information they had about their children's schooling, and the time, money, and other material resources available in the home all mediated parents' involvement in schooling

Educational Capabilities

Parents at Colton and Prescott had different levels of educational attainment. Most Colton parents were high school graduates or high school dropouts. Most were married and had their first child shortly after high school. They generally had difficulties in school as children; several of the fathers, for example, had been held back in elementary school. In interviews, they expressed doubts about their educational capabilities and indicated that they depended on the teacher to educate their children. As one mother stated,

> I know that when she gets into the higher grades, I know I won't be able to help her, math especially, unless I take a refresher course myself. . . . So I feel that it is the teacher's

job to help her as much as possible to understand it, because I know that I won't be able to.

Another mother, commenting on her overall lack of educational skills, remarked that reading preschool books to her young son had improved her reading skills:

I graduated from high school and could fill out [job] applications, but when I was nineteen and married my husband, I didn't know how to look up a word in the dictionary. When I started reading to Johnny, I found that *my* reading improved.

Observations of Colton parents at the school site and in interviews confirmed that parents' educational skills were often wanting. Prescott parents' educational skills, on the other hand, were strong. Most were college graduates and many had advanced degrees.

Parents in the two communities also divided up the responsibility between home and school in different ways. Colton parents regarded teachers as "educated people." They turned over the responsibility for education to the teacher, whom they viewed as a professional. As one mother put it,

My job is here at home. My job is to raise him, to teach him manners, get him dressed and get him to school, to make sure that he is happy. Now her [the teacher's] part, the school's part, is to teach him to learn. Hopefully, someday he'll be able to use all of that. That is what I think is their part, to teach him to read, the writing, any kind of schooling.

Education is seen as a discrete process that takes place on the school grounds, under the direction of a teacher. This mother's role is to get her son to school; once there, his teacher will "teach him to learn."

This mother was aware that her son's teacher wanted him to practice reading at home, but neither she nor her husband read to their son regularly. The mother's view of reading was analogous to her view of work. She sent her children to school to learn for six hours a day and expected that they could leave their schooling (i.e., their work) behind them at the school site, unless they had been given homework. She believed that her seven-year-old boy's afternoons and evenings were time for him to play. In this context, her son's reading at home was similar to riding his bike or to playing with his truck. The mother did not believe that her child's academic progress depended upon his activities at home. Instead, she saw a separation of spheres.

Other parents had a different conception of their role in schooling. They believed education was a shared responsibility: They were *partners* with teachers in promoting their children's academic progress. As one mother stated,

I see the school as being a very strong instructional force, more so than we are here at home. I guess that I am comfortable with that, from what I have seen. It is a three-to-one ratio or something, where out of a possible four, he is getting three quarters of what he needs from the school, and then a quarter of it from here. Maybe it would be better if our influence was stronger, but I am afraid that in this day and age it is not possible to do any more than that even if you wanted to.

Prescott parents wanted to be involved in their child's educational process in an important way. In dividing up the responsibility for education, they described the relationship between parents and teachers as a relationship between equals, and they believed that they possessed similar or superior educational skills and prestige. One Prescott father discussed his relationship with teachers in this way:

I don't think of teachers as more educated than me or in a higher position than me. I don't have any sense of hierarchy. I am not higher than them, and they are not higher than me. We are equals. We are reciprocals. So if I have a problem I will talk to them. I have a sense of decorum. I wouldn't go busting into a classroom and say something. . . . They are not working for me, but they also aren't doing something I couldn't do. It is more a question of a division of labor.

Prescott parents had not only better educational skills and higher occupational status than Colton parents but also more disposable income and more flexible work schedules. These material resources entered into the family-school relationships. Some Colton mothers, for example, had to make a series of complicated arrangements for transportation and child care to attend a school event held in the middle of the afternoon. Prescott parents, on the other hand, had two cars and sufficient resources to hire babysitters and housecleaners. In addition, Prescott parents generally had much greater flexibility in their work schedules than Colton parents. Material resources also influenced the educational purchases parents made. Colton parents reported that most of the books they bought for their children came from the flea market. Prescott parents had the financial flexibility to purchase new books if they desired, and many of the parents of low achievers hired tutors for their children during the summer months.

Information about Schooling

Colton parents had only limited information about most aspects of their children's experience at school; what they did know, they learned primarily from their children. For example, the Colton mothers knew the names of the child's teacher and the teacher's aide, the location of the classroom on the school grounds, and the name of the janitor, and they were familiar with the Read at Home Program. They did not know details of the school or of classroom interaction. The amount of information Colton parents had did not seem to vary by how much contact they had with the school.

In the middle-class community, parents had extensive information about classroom and school life. For example, in addition to knowing the names of their child's current classroom teacher and teacher's aide, the mother knew the names and academic reputations of most of the other teachers in the school. The mothers also knew the academic rankings of children in the class (e.g., the best boy and girl in math, the best boy and girl in reading). Most of the mothers knew the composition of their child's reading group, the math and spelling packet the child was working on, and the specific academic problems to which the child was being exposed (e.g., adding single-digit numbers). Other details of the classroom experience were also widely known, including the names of children receiving the services of the reading resource specialist, occupational therapist, and special education teacher. Although a few fathers had very specific information about the school, most depended on their wives to collect and store this information. The fathers were, however, generally apprised of the reputations of teachers and the dissatisfactions that some parents had with particular teachers.

Much of the observed difference between the schools in parents' information about schooling may be traced to differences in family life, particularly in social networks and childrearing patterns. Prescott families saw relatively little of their relatives; instead, many parents socialized with other parents in the school community Colton parents generally had very close ties with relatives in the area, seeing siblings or parents

three times per week or more. Colton parents had virtually no social contact with other parents in the school, even when the families lived on the same street. The social networks of the middle-class parents provided them with additional sources of information about their child's school experience; the networks of working-class parents did not (see Bott 1971; Litwack and Szeleny 1971).

The childrearing patterns of the two groups also differed, particularly in the leisure time activities they encouraged. At Colton, children's after-school activities were informal: bike riding, snake hunting, watching television, playing with neighbor children, and helping parents with younger siblings. Prescott children were enrolled in formal socialization activities, including swimming lessons, soccer, art and crafts lessons, karate lessons, and gymnastics. All the children in the classroom were enrolled in at least one after-school activity, and many were busy every afternoon with a lesson or structured experience. The parents took their children to and from these activities. Many stayed to watch the lesson, thus providing another opportunity to meet and interact with other Prescott parents. Discussions about schools, teachers' reputations, and academic progress were frequent. For many parents, these interactions were a major source of information about their children's schooling, and parents believed that the discussions had an important effect on the way in which they approached their children's schooling.

Discussion

Teachers in both schools interpreted parental involvement as a reflection of the value parents placed on their children's educational success (see Deutsch 1967; Strodbeck 1958). As the principal at Prescott commented,

> This particular community is one with a very strong interest in its schools. It is a wonderful situation in which to work. Education is very important to the parents and they back that up with an interest in volunteering. This view that education is important helps kids as well. If parents value schooling and think it is important, then kids take it seriously.

The teachers and the principal at Colton placed a similar interpretation on the lack of parental participation at the school. Speaking of the parents, the principal remarked,

They don't value education because they don't have much of one themselves. [Since] they don't value education as much as they could, they don't put those values and expectations on their kids.

Interviews and observations of parents told a different story, however. Parents in both communities valued educational success; all wanted their children to do well in school, and all saw themselves as supporting and helping their children achieve success at school. Middle and working-class parents' aspirations differed only in the level of achievement they hoped their children would attain. Several Colton parents were high school dropouts and bitterly regretted their failure to get a diploma. As one mother said, "I desperately want her to graduate. If she can do that, that will satisfy me." All of the Prescott parents hoped that their children would get a college diploma, and many spoke of the importance of an advanced degree.

Although the educational values of the two groups of parents did not differ, the ways in which they promoted educational success did. In the working-class community, parents turned over the responsibility for education to the teacher. Just as they depended on doctors to heal their children, they depended on teachers to educate them. In the middle-class community, however, parents saw education as a shared enterprise and scrutinized, monitored, and supplemented the school experience of their children. Prescott parents read to their children, initiated contact with teachers, and attended school events more often than Colton parents.

Generally, the evidence demonstrates that the level of parental involvement is linked to the class position of the parents and to the social and cultural resources that social class yields in American society. By definition, the educational status and material resources of parents increase with social class. These resources were observed to influence parental participation in schooling in the Prescott and Colton communities. The working-class parents had poor educational skills, relatively lower occupational prestige than teachers, and limited time and disposable income to supplement and intervene in their children's schooling. The middle-class parents, on the other hand, had educational skills and occupational prestige that matched or surpassed that of teachers: they also had the necessary economic resources to manage the child care, transportation, and time required to meet with teachers, to hire tutors, and to become intensely involved in their childrens' schooling.

These differences in social, cultural, and economic resources between the two sets of parents help explain differences in their responses to a variety of teacher requests to participate in schooling. For example, when asked to read to their children and to help them at home with school work, Colton parents were reluctant to comply because they felt that their educational skills were inadequate for these tasks. Prescott parents, with their superior educational skills, felt more comfortable helping their children in these areas. Parents at Colton and Prescott also differed in their perceptions of the appropriate relationship between parents and teachers. Prescott parents conceived of schooling as a partnership in which parents have the right and the responsibility to raise issues of their choosing and even to criticize teachers. Colton parents' inferior educational level and occupational prestige reinforced their trust in and dependence on the professional expertise of educators. The relatively high occupational position of Prescott parents contributed to their view of teachers as equals.[1] Prescott parents occasionally had more confidence in their right to monitor and to criticize teachers. Their occupational prestige levels may have helped both build this confidence and demystify the status of the teacher as a professional.

Finally, more straightforward economic differences between the middle- and working-class parents are evident in their different responses to requests to attend school events. Attendance at parent-teacher conferences, particularly those held in the afternoon, requires transportation, child care arrangements, and flexibility at the workplace—all more likely to be available to Prescott parents than to Colton parents.

The literature on family life indicates that social class is associated with differences in social networks, leisure time, and childrearing activities (Bott 1971; Kohn 1977; Rubin 1976). The observations in this study confirm these associations and, in addition, indicate that social class differences in family life (or class cultures) have implications for family-school relationships. Middle-class culture provides parents with more information about schooling and promotes social ties among parents in the school community. This furthers the interdependence between home and school. Working-class culture, on the other hand, emphasizes kinship and promotes independence between the spheres of family life and schooling.

Because both schools promote a familyschool relationship that solicits parental involvement in schooling and that promotes an interdependence between family and school, the class position and the class culture of middle-class families yield a social profit not available to working-class families. In particular, middle-class culture provides parents with more information about schooling and also builds social networks among parents in the school community. Parents use this information to build a family-school relationship congruent with the schools' definition of appropriate behavior. For example, they may request additional educational resources for their children, monitor the behavior of the teacher, share costs of a tutor with other interested parents, and consult with other parents and teachers about their children's educational experience.

It is important to stress that if the schools were to promote a different type of family-school relationship, the class culture of middle-class parents might not yield a social profit. The data do not reveal that the social relations of middle-class culture are intrinsically better than the social relations of working-class culture. Nor can it be said that the family-school relationships in the middle-class are objectively better for children than those in the working class. Instead, the social profitability of middle-class arrangements is tied to the schools' definition of the proper family-school relationship.

Future research on parental participation in education should take as problematic the standards that schools establish for parental involvement in schooling and should focus on the role of class cultures in facilitating and impeding compliance with these standards. In addition, research might profitably examine the role of social class in structuring the conflict between the universalistic concerns of the teacher and the particularistic agenda of parents (Waller 1932; McPherson 1972). Parents and teachers may be "natural enemies" (Waller 1932) and may face enduring problems of negotiating "boundaries" between their "territories" (Lightfoot 1978). Social class appears to influence the educational, status, monetary, and informational resources that each side brings to that conflict.

Family-School Relationships and Cultural Capital

These results suggest that social class position and class culture become a form of cultural capital in the school setting (Bourdieu 1977a; Bourdieu and Passeron 1977). Although working-class and middle-class parents share a desire for their children's educational success in first and second grade, social location leads them to construct different pathways for realizing that

success. Working-class parents' method—dependence on the teacher to educate their child—may have been the dominant method of promoting school success in earlier periods within the middle class. Today, however, teachers actively solicit parents' participation in education. Middle-class parents, in supervising, monitoring, and overseeing the educational experience of their children, behave in ways that mirror the requests of schools. This appears to provide middle-class children with educational advantages over working-class children.

The behavior of parents in this regard is not fully determined by their social location. There are variations within as well as between social classes. Still, parents approach the family-school relationship with different sets of social resources. Schools ask for very specific types of behavior from all parents, regardless of their social class. Not all cultural resources are equally valuable, however, for complying with schools' requests. The resources tied directly to social class (e.g., education, prestige, income) and certain patterns of family life (e.g., kinship ties, socialization patterns, leisure activities) seem to play a large role in facilitating the participation of parents in schools. Other aspects of class and class cultures, including religion and taste in music, art, food, and furniture (Bourdieu 1984) appear to play a smaller role in structuring the behavior of parents, children, and teachers in the family-school relationship. (These aspects of class cultures might, of course, influence other dimensions of schooling.)

These findings underline the importance of studying the significance of cultural capital within a social context. In recent years, Bourdieu has been criticized for being overly deterministic in his analysis of the role of cultural capital in shaping outcomes (Giroux 1983; Connell et al. 1982). Connell et al., for example, argue that cultural capital

> practically obliterates the person who is actually the main constructor of the home/school relationship. The student is treated mainly as a bearer of cultural capital, a bundle of abilities, knowledges and attitudes furnished by parents. (p. 188)

Moreover, Bourdieu has focused almost exclusively on the social profits stemming from high culture. Although he is quite clear about the arbitrary character of culture, his emphasis on the value of high culture could be misinterpreted. His research on cultural capital of elites may be construed as suggesting that the culture of elites is intrinsically more valuable than that of the working class. In this regard, the concept of cultural capital is potentially vulnerable to the same criticisms that have been directed at the notion of the culture of poverty (Valentine 1968).

This study highlights the need for more extensive research in the area of cultural capital. It would be particularly useful for future research to take into account historical variations in definitions of culture capital. Family-school relationships have changed over time; what constitutes cultural capital at one point in time may or may not persist in a future period. Historical studies help reveal the way in which cultural resources of social groups are unevenly valued in a society; these studies help illustrate the dynamic character of these value judgments. Historical work on definitions of cultural capital can also shed light on the arbitrariness of the current social standards.

In addition, research on cultural capital could fruitfully expand its focus to include more social groups. The research on high culture (Bourdieu 1977a, 1977b; DiMaggio and Useem 1982; Cookson and Persell 1985) has made a useful contribution to the field (see also Lamont and Lareau 1987). This study, however, suggests that middle-class families have cultural resources that become a form of cultural capital in specific settings. In moving beyond studies of elites, it might be useful to recognize that all social groups have cultural capital and that some forms of this capital are valued more highly by the dominant institutions at particular historical moments. As Samuel Kaplan (pers. comm. 1986) points out, members of the working class have cultural capital as well, but it is only rarely recognized by dominant social institutions. During World War II, for example, the dangerous and difficult task of the marksman was usually filled by working-class youths; only rarely was it assigned to a college boy. Marksman skills and, more generally, compliance with the expectations of supervising officers are important in the military. Here, the childrearing values of working-class parents (e.g., obedience, conformity) may advantage working-class youths; the values of middle-class families (e.g., self-direction, autonomy, and pemissiveness) may disadvantage middle-class youth (Kohn 1977; Kohn and Schooler 1983).

Implications for Further Research

Educators and policymakers may seek to increase parental involvement in schooling by boosting the ed-

ucational capabilities and information resources of parents. For sociologists interested in family, schools, and social stratification, a somewhat different task is in order. Families and schools, and family-school relationships, are critical links in the process of social reproduction. For most children (but not all), social class is a major predictor of educational and occupational achievement. Schools, particularly elementary and secondary schools, play a crucial role in this process of social reproduction; they sort students into social categories that award credentials and opportunities for mobility (Collins 1979, 1981c). We know relatively little about the stages of this process.

The concept of cultural capital may help by turning our attention to the structure of opportunity and to the way in which individuals proceed through that structure (see also Collins 1981a, 1981b; Knorr-Cetina and Cicourel 1981). Moreover, the concept does not overlook the importance of the role of the individual in constructing a biography within a social structure. Class provides social and cultural resources, but these resources must be invested or activated to become a form of cultural capital. Analyzing the role of cultural capital in structuring family-school relationships, particularly parental participation in education, provides a rich setting for analyzing the linkages between micro and macro levels of analysis.

Endnote

1. Some Prescott parents, however, did report that they felt intimidated by a teacher on some occasions.

References

Aggleton, Peter J., and Geoff Whitty. 1985. "Rebels Without a Cause? Socialization and Subcultural Style among the Children of the New Middle Classes." *Sociology of Education* 58:60–72.

Anyon, Jean. 1981. "Social Class and School Knowledge." *Curriculum Inquiry* 11:1–42.

Apple, Michael W. 1979. *Ideology and Curriculum.* London: Routledge and Kegan Paul.

Baker, David, and David Stevenson. 1986. "Mothers' Strategies for School Achievement: Managing the Transition to High School." *Sociology of Education* 59:156–66.

Becker, Henry Jay, and Joyce L. Epstein. 1982. "Parent Involvement: A Survey of Teacher Practices." *Elementary School Journal* 83:85–102.

Berger, Eugenia H. 1983. *Beyond the Classroom: Parents as Partners in Education.* St. Louis: C. V. Mosby.

Bernstein, Basil. 1975. *Class, Codes and Control.* Vol. 3. London: Routledge and Kegan Paul.

_____. 1982. "Codes, Modalities and the Process of Cultural Reproduction: A Model." Pp. 304–55 in *Cultural and Economic Reproduction in Education,* edited by Michael W. Apple. London: Routledge and Kegan Paul.

Bott, Elizabeth. 1971. *Family and Social Networks.* New York: Free Press.

Bourdieu, Pierre, 1977a. "Cultural Reproduction and Social Reproduction." Pp. 487–511 in *Power and Ideology in Education,* edited by J. Karabel and A. H. Halsey. New York: Oxford University Press.

_____. 1977b. *Outline of a Theory of Practice.* Cambridge: Cambridge University Press.

_____. 1981. "Men and Machines." Pp. 304–17 in *Advances in Social Theory: Toward an Integration of Micro- and Macro-Sociologies,* edited by K. Knorr-Cetina and A. V. Cicourel. Boston, Routledge and Kegan Paul.

_____. 1984. *Distinction: A Social Critique of the Judgment of Taste.* Translated by Richard Nice. Cambridge, MA: Harvard University Press.

Bourdieu, Pierre, and Jean-Claude Passeron. 1977. *Reproduction in Education, Society and Culture.* Translated by Richard Nice. Beverly Hills: Sage.

Butterworth, Julian E. 1928. *The Parent-Teacher Association and Its Work.* New York: Macmillan.

California Department of Education. 1983. *California Assessment Program 1981–1982.* Sacramento: California Department of Education.

Collins, Randall. 1979. *The Credential Society.* New York: Academic Press.

_____. 1981a. "Micro-Translation as a Theory-Building Strategy." Pp. 81–108 in *Advances in Social Theory: Toward an Integration of Micro- and Macro-Sociologies,* edited by K. Knorr-Cenna and A. V. Cicourel. Boston: Routledge and Kegan Paul.

_____. 1981b. "On the Micro-Foundations of Macro-Sociology." *American Journal of Sociology* 86:984–1014.

_____. 1981c. *Sociology Since Midcentury: Essays in Theory Cumulation.* New York: Academic Press.

Connell, R. W., D. J. Ashendon, S. Kessler, and G. W. Dowsett. 1982. *Making the Difference: Schools, Families and Social Division.* Sydney: George Allen and Urwin.

Cook-Gumperez, Jenny. 1973. *Social Control and Socialization: A Study of Class Difference in the Language of Maternal Control.* Boston: Routledge and Kegan Paul.

Cookson, Peter W., Jr., and Caroline H. Persell. 1985. *Preparing for Power: America's Elite Boarding Schools.* New York: Basic Books.

Deutsch, Martin. 1967. "The Disadvantaged Child and the Learning Process." Pp. 39–58 in *The Disadvantaged Child,* edited by M. Deutsch. New York: Basic Books.

Diaz, Stephan, Luis C. Moll, and Hugh Mehan. 1986. "Sociocultural Resources in Instruction: A Context-Specific Approach." Pp. 187–230 in *Beyond Language: Social and Cultural Factors in Schooling Language Minority Students,* edited by the Bilingual Education Office. Los Angeles: California State University, Evaluation, Dissemination, and Assessment Center.

DiMaggio, Paul, and Michael Useem. 1982. "The Arts in Cultural Reproduction." Pp. 181–201 in *Cultural and Economic Reproduction in Education,* edited by Michael W. Apple. London: Routledge and Kegan Paul.

Epstein, Joyce. 1983. "Effect on Parents of Teacher Practices of Parent Involvement." Report No. 346. Baltimore: Johns Hopkins University, Center for the Social Organization of Schools.

_____. 1984. "Effects of Teacher Practices and Parent Involvement on Student Achievement." Paper presented at the annual meetings of the American Educational Research Association, New Orleans.

Epstein, Joyce, and Henry Jay Becker. 1982. "Teachers' Reported Practices of Parent involvement: Problems and Possibilities." *Elementary School Journal* 83:103–13.

Erickson, Frederick, and Gerald Mohatt. 1982. "Cultural Organization of Participation Structures in Two Classrooms of Indian Students." Pp. 132–75 in *Doing the Ethnography of Schooling,* edited by G. Spindler. New York: Holt, Rinehart and Winston.

Gaskell, Jane. 1985. "Course Enrollment in the High School: The Perspective of Working-Class Females." *Sociology of Education* 58:48–59.

Gearing, Frederick, and Paul Epstein. 1982. "Learning to Wait: An Ethnographic Probe into the Operation of an Item of Hidden Curriculum." Pp. 240–67 in *Doing the Ethnography of Schooling,* edited by G. Spindler. New York: Holt, Rinehart and Winston.

Giroux, Henry A. 1983. *Theory and Resistance in Education.* South Hadley, MA: Bergin and Harvey.

Gracey, Harry L. 1972. *Curriculum or Craftsmanship.* Chicago: University of Chicago Press.

Heath, Shirley B. 1982. "Questioning at Home and at School: A Comparative Study." Pp. 102–31 in *Doing the Ethnography of Schooling,* edited by G. Spindler. New York: Holt, Rinehart and Winston.

_____. 1983. *Ways with Words.* London: Cambridge University Press.

Hymes, James L., Jr. 1953. *Effective Home-School Relations.* New York: Prentice-Hall.

Jencks, Christopher et al. 1972. *Inequality.* New York: Basic Books.

Joffee, Carol. 1977. *Friendly Intruders.* Berkeley: University of California Press.

Knorr-Cetina, Karin, and Aaron V. Cicourel. 1981. *Advances in Social Theory: Toward an Integration of Micro- and Macro-Sociologies.* Boston: Routledge and Kegan Paul.

Kohn, Melvin L. 1977. *Class and Conformity.* Chicago: University of Chicago Press.

Kohn, Melvin L., and Carmi Schooler. 1983. *Work and Personality: An Inquiry into the Impact of Social Stratification.* Norwood, NJ: Ablex.

Labov, William. 1972. *Sociolinguistic Patterns.* Philadelphia: University of Pennsylvania Press.

Lamont, Michele, and Annette Lareau. 1987. "Cultural Capital in American Research: Problems and Possibilities." Working Paper No. 9. Chicago: Center for Psychosocial Studies.

Leichter, Hope Jensen. 1979. "Families and Communities as Educators: Some Concepts of Relationships." Pp. 3–94 in *Families and Communities as Educators,* edited by H. J. Leichter. New York: Teachers College Press.

Levy, Frank, Arnold J. Meltsner, and Aaron Wildavsky. 1974. *Urban Outcomes.* Berkeley: University of California Press.

Lightfoot, Sara Lawrence. 1978. *Worlds Apart.* New York: Basic Books.

Litwack, Eugene, and I. Szeleny. 1971. "Kinship and Other Primary Groups." Pp. 149–63 in *Sociology of the Family,* edited by M. Anderson. Middlesex, England: Penguin.

Majoribanks, Kevin. 1979. *Families and Their Learning Environments: An Empirical Analysis.* London: Routledge and Kegan Paul.

McPherson, Gertrude H. 1972. *Small Town Teacher.* Cambridge, MA: Harvard University Press.

Mehan, Hugh, and Peg Griffin. 1980. "Socialization: The View from Classroom Interactions." *Social Inquiry* 50:357–98.

Mehan, Hugh, Alma L. Hertweck, and J. L. Meihls. 1986. *Handicapping the Handicapped.* Stanford: Stanford University Press.

National Congress of Parents and Teachers. 1944. *The Parent-Teacher Organization, Its Origins and Development.* Chicago: National Congress of Parents and Teachers.

National Education Association. 1985. "Teacher-Parent Partnership Program, 1984–1985 Status Report." Unpublished paper. Washington, DC: National Education Association.

Ogbu, John. 1974. *The Next Generation.* New York: Academic Press.

Overstreet, Harry, and Bonaro Overstreet. 1949. *Where Children Come First.* Chicago: National Congress of Parents and Teachers.

Rist, Ray C. 1978. *The Invisible Children.* Cambridge, MA: Harvard University Press.

Robinson, Sharon. 1985. "Teacher-Parent Cooperation." Paper presented at the annual meetings of the American Educational Research Association, Chicago.

Rubin, Lillian B. 1976. *Worlds of Pain.* New York: Basic Books.

Seeley, David. 1984. "Home-School Partnership." *Phi Delta Kappan* 65:383–93.

Strodbeck, F. L. 1958. "Family Interaction, Values, and Achievement." Pp. 131–91 in *Talent and Society,* edited by D. D. McClelland. New York: Van Nostrand.

Taylor, Sandra. 1984. "Reproduction and Contradiction in Schooling: The Case of Commercial Studies." *British Journal of Sociology of Education* 5:3–18.

Trelease, James. 1982. *The Read-Aloud Handbook.* New York: Penguin.

Valentine, Charles A. 1968. *Culture and Poverty.* Chicago: University of Chicago Press.

Valli, Linda. 1985. "Office Education Students and the Meaning of Work." *Issues in Education* 3:31–44.

Waller, Willard. 1932. *The Sociology of Teaching.* New York: Wiley.

Wilcox, Kathleen A. 1977. "Schooling and Socialization for Work Roles." Ph.D. diss., Harvard University.

———. 1982. "Differential Socialization in the Classroom: Implications for Equal Opportunity." Pp. 269–309 in *Doing the Ethnography of Schooling,* edited by G. Spindler. New York: Holt, Rinehart and Winston.

A Black Student's Reflection on Public and Private Schools

IMANI PERRY

My name is Imani Perry. I am a fifteen-year-old Black female who has experienced both private and public education. These experiences have led me to believe there are significant differences between the two types of education that deserve to be acknowledged and resolved by society as a whole.

After ten years in private schools I made the decision to attend a public school. I left because I felt isolated as a person of color. I yearned to have a large, strong Black community be a part of my development. I believed that I would find such a community in the public high school of my city, which is a fairly urban school with approximately 2,600 students, 20 percent of whom are Black.

Despite the fact that I had never been in a traditional public school environment, when I decided to go to one I had certain expectations about the teaching. I assumed that the teaching philosophy would be similar to that of the private schools I had attended. I expected that any teaching differences that did exist would be limited to less sophisticated reading, or a less intense work load. As I quickly learned, the differences were more substantial.

I believe the differences I found in the teaching between the private and public schools that I attended would best be illustrated by several examples of what I encountered. My initial realization of this difference began with an argument I had with a math teacher over a point value on a test. I felt that he should give partial credit for problems with computational errors rather than procedural errors or conceptual misunderstanding. I presented this point to the math teacher, who responded by saying math is computation and the theories and concepts of math are only used to compute. I was astonished by this statement. Coming from a school where the teachers' stated goal for freshman math was to begin to teach you how to become a "theoretical mathematician," my entire perception of math

was different. Perhaps that emphasis of theoretical math was also extreme; nevertheless, I believe that a good math teacher believes that computation in math should be used to assist in the organization of theories. Computation is a necessary but not sufficient step toward math knowledge. I felt this teacher was probably the product of schooling that did not emphasize the artistic qualities of math. While I could sympathize with his position, I felt that all I loved about math—new ideas, discussing unproved theorems, and developing personal procedures—was being ignored. I withdrew from this course only to find the ideological differences emerged again in my advanced English class at the public school, particularly in essay writing.

In this class, once we wrote a paper—mind you, with no assistance from the teacher—the process ended. We did not discuss papers, receive constructive criticism, or improve them through rewriting. Despite the fact that there was no proofreading assistance offered, 10 percent of the grade was taken off for sentence errors. It seemed as if the teacher assumed we no longer needed to continue developing our writing skills.

In my last school, which had an abundance of excellent essayists, my English teacher would have a detailed description of what he felt about each paper. At points where he felt one deserved praise or criticism, he would make comments in the margin. He would not neglect to correct punctuation errors—such as commas instead of semicolons—but these errors were not the sole criteria for our grades, especially if the writing was good. The emphasis was upon improving intellectual and organizational skills to raise the quality of the writing.

These examples illustrate my belief that my learning environment had changed from a place where thought and theory were emphasized to a place where form and precision were emphasized. The teaching sys-

From Imani Perry, "A Black Student's Reflection on Public and Private Schools," *Harvard Educational Review,* 58:3 (August 1988), pp. 332–336. Copyright © 1988 by the President and Fellows of Harvard College. All rights reserved.

tem at the public school appears to assume that at some point in our education, learning and thinking are no longer important. Schooling in this situation becomes devoted to making things look correct. This is in sharp contrast to my private schools, where proper form was something I learned was necessary, but secondary in importance to the content and organization of what is produced.

Because of this difference in the concept of teaching and learning, there is also a difference in what and who teachers consider intelligence. The teaching at the public school has less to do with thinking and processing ideas, and more to do with precision and detail in appearance. Therefore, students who are considered intelligent by the public school faculty possess different skills than those at the private schools I have attended. In the public school a student is considered intelligent if he or she is well-behaved and hard working. The ability to grasp a subject in its entirety—from theory to practice—is not valued.

For example, in the fall of 1987 there was an academic contest, where my school was competing against other public schools. All the teachers I encountered were very enthusiastic about it. The students who were selected to participate were raised on a pedestal. These students, most of whom were clean-cut and apparently straight-laced, were to serve as our models of very intelligent students. They were drilled in formulas, book plots, and other information for several days a week. It seemed as if the teachers were not concerned with whether the students digested the depth of these subjects and resources as long as the students completed all the reading, memorized the facts, and could repeat the information. The contest was more a demonstration of a memory function than anything else. In my opinion there is nothing wrong with such a contest, but it should be recognized for what it is and is not. One thing it is not is a true measure of knowledge and ability. This was never recognized by the school.

Another example of how a different view of intelligence is manifested in this public school is the school's view of two students whom I know. I will identify them as Student A and Student B. Student B is an intellectual. She reads, is analytical in her discussions and is knowledgeable. Student A is very precise with his homework, answers the patronizing questions the teachers ask ('What color was the horse?" "Black with a white spot!" "Correct!"), and is very "all-American" in behavior and appearance. Student A is considered more intelligent at this public school because he displays skills that are considered signs of intelligence at this school. The intelligence criteria at this school are more related to superficial qualities such as appearance, knowing facts, etc., rather than the intellectual qualities that student B possesses. Student B displays an ability to learn and write in creative and analytical formats. I left a school where the criterion for intelligence was the student's thought process resulting from the information, for a school where the information was the measure of intelligence.

In reflecting on schooling it is important to realize that all people, including teachers, have biases based on the physical appearances of other people. On the train most people are more likely to sit next to the clean-shaven Harvard freshman than next to the Mohawked, multiple-earringed punk-rocker. In teachers, however, these biases should diminish as they begin to know a student. Unfortunately, in the public school there is an absence of teacher-student contact. Because of this lack of contact there are no criteria by which intelligence can be determined, besides grades, appearance, and behavior. As I mentioned before, the grading system at this school often reflects one's ability to memorize and not one's thinking and analytical abilities. Moreover, since people are biased in their acceptance of different appearances, students who look different are judged differently. The only way they can make up for this difference is to be "well behaved," and, as I will mention later, the definition of well-behaved is arbitrary.

All these issues I have discussed have very negative effects for students from minority groups, more specifically the Black and Hispanic youths who make up a large percentage of most urban schools. It is those Black and Hispanic students who retain strong cultural characteristics in their personalities who are most negatively acted by teachers' emphasis on behavior, appearance, and respect for authority.

Public schools' emphasis on the teaching of form merely trains students for low-powered or menial jobs that do not require analytical thought. It is evident when most students are discussing what they intend to be that their goals are most often focused toward areas and professions about which they have some idea or knowledge. If in class you've never spoken about how language and colloquialisms are reflections of the society you are studying, you definitely will not be thinking of being a linguist. And if you are only asked to type a paper summarizing the book, rather than writing an analysis of it, the primary skill shown is typing. This should not be the main skill which is emphasized.

The neglect of intellectual development also occurs in higher-level classes, but at least the resources, books, etc., available to students are not altogether lacking in intellectual value. Occasionally these resources will have depth and content, be philosophical, or insightful. But in lower-level classes, where minority students are most often found and where bad textbooks are used without outside resources, the reading has less content, and the point of reading is to perfect reading skills, not to broaden thinking skills or gain knowledge of how the subject is currently affecting us. It is often not possible to broaden your thinking skills or knowledge with the books used in lower-level classes, which are more often stripped of any content. In an upper-level class, if you have a parent who wants you to know the subject in depth, and to think about it, it is possible to do that detached from the school environment, because the subject matter may have content, or have some meaning beyond the words. My high-level sophomore English class read *Moby Dick* as an outside reading. We didn't discuss the symbolism or religious qualities of it, but I am aware of them because I read critical essays and discussed them with my mother. If one is reading a book which has been stripped of meaningful content, it is not helpful to do outside research, because it is lacking in meaning.

Many students from minority groups are being trained only in form and not in creative ways of thinking. This I believe causes disenchantment among students. Upper-class students are not as affected, because of their social class, and their "social responsibility" to be achievers. This is especially true of upper-class students in a public school whose social-class peers are in private schools. But instead of striving to be true learners, they quickly learn how to be good students by being well-behaved. What well-behaved means is always taking the teacher's word as absolute truth and never questioning the teacher's authority. This definition of well-behaved is of course culturally based and can be in opposition to cultures of Black and Hispanic students.

In Black and Hispanic cultures, respect and obedience come and develop with the relationship. Rather than being automatic, respect must be earned. For example, one will occasionally hear a Black child say to a stranger, "You can't tell me what to do, you're not my mother." But at the same time, often one will see Black kids following the orders and rules of an adult friend of the family, whom they would under no circumstances disrespect. In addition, in Black and His-

panic cultures it appears that adult and child cultures are more integrated than those of other ethnic groups. For example, parties in the Hispanic community will often have an age range from toddler to elderly. Children are often present in the conversation and socializing of adults and are not treated as separate, as they may be in other cultures.

When this relationship is not made between teacher and student, it is not an acceptable educational situation, because the Black and Hispanic students are now expected to respect someone in a different manner than their culture has socialized them to. Often students are not aware of the fact that the demands being placed on them by the relationship conflict with those of their culture. They then show signs of what a teacher views as a lack of the respect that he/she deserves. The student might feel it is just a sign that they do not know the teacher and have no obligation to him or her. Many times I have seen a dumbstruck student of color sent to detention; when asked what he or she did, the student will seriously say that he or she has no idea; perhaps that he or she sucked his or her teeth in dismay, or something of that sort.

Black and Hispanic students have less of a chance at building strong relationships with any teachers because their appearance and behavior may be considered offensive to the middle-class White teachers. These students show signs of what White teachers, and some teachers of color, consider disrespect, and they do not get the nurturing relationships that develop respect and dedication. They are considered less intelligent, as can be seen in the proportion of Blacks and Hispanics in lower-level as opposed to upper-level classes. There is less of a teacher-student contact with "underachievers," because they are guided into peer tutoring programs. Perhaps this is understandable, because the teachers have less of a vested interest in the achievement of students that are not of their community, or have less of an idea of how to educate them. Public school teachers are no longer part of the same community as the majority of their students. The sad part of the situation is that many students believe that this type of teaching is what academic learning is all about. They have not had the opportunity to experience alternative ways of teaching and learning. From my experience in public school, it appears that many minority students will never be recognized as capable of analytical and critical thinking.

In the beginning of this article I spoke about my decision to leave my private school because of feeling isolated. After three months at a large urban public school I found myself equally isolated—intellectually as well as racially. My thinking process has gradually affected my opinions and character. I am in upper-level classes in which there are barely any kids of color, except Asians. Black and Hispanic students have been filtered down into lower-level classes. Most of the students I meet are kind, interesting people whom I like and respect. However, because the environment of the school is one in which ideas are not valued or fostered, I find it difficult to discuss issues with them, because my thoughtfulness has flourished, while others have been denied an opportunity to explore their intellectual development. I am now at a point of deciding which isolation is worse, cultural/racial or intellectual-opinion-based and slightly racial. This is a decision many Black students who have attended private schools at some time are wrestling to make, a decision that will affect their development, knowledge, and viewpoint of education, and their relationships to educators—those supposed possessors of greater knowledge than themselves.

Afterword

Since the writing of this article I have returned to a private school with the feeling that one's educational development is too much to sacrifice. I now attend a private high school with a strong unified Black community, as well as academic merit. Even though I did not remain at the urban public school, I valued my experience there, mostly because through it I learned one of the most blatant forms of oppression and inequity for lower-class students in American society, and I appreciate the opportunities with which I have been blessed.

10 Educational Reform and School Improvement

In Chapter 2, we presented conservative, liberal, and radical perspectives on educational problems. Throughout this book, we have examined a number of educational problems from the foundations perspective. This chapter looks at the most significant educational problems and the role of teachers and schools in solving them. To what extent do teachers and schools make a difference? To what degree can they make a difference? Most importantly, to what extent are teachers and schools limited in their ability to solve educational and social problems, without significant changes outside the schools?

In Chapter 1, we related the stories of two teachers. The first, memorialized by the late *New York Times* education writer Fred Hechinger, was a beloved teacher who made a significant impact on the lives of her students. The second, a veteran teacher in an urban school district, retired from teaching because of the difficult problems she faced. We asked to what extent do the structural problems faced by teachers limit their ability to affect meaningful change and, conversely, to what degree do talented, enthusiastic, and excellent teachers have the ability to affect educational change in spite of the significant problems that they face. Although there is no easy answer to this question, it is clear that teachers work within social and organizational environments that indeed have profound effects on them and often limit their ability to affect meaningful change. It is also clear that teachers can and do make a difference, often in spite of what may seem like intractable problems.

Thus, although teachers can and do make a difference, the research indicates that solutions to educational problems cannot rely on the talent, energy, and hard work of teachers alone, but must reform the social and organizational conditions of schooling (Sizer, 1992). Before we examine ways in which educational reforms have attempted to do this, let us first look at some examples of how individual teachers make a difference.

Effective Teachers

Jessica Siegel taught high school English and journalism at Seward Park High School, on New York City's lower east side, for 10 years. Samuel Freedman's *Small Victories* (1990) poignantly chronicles Jessica's struggles, triumphs, and defeats as she attempted to teach her students, most of them poor and immigrants, to value an education and to make their dreams a reality. Teaching in a neighborhood long a haven for immigrants and their children—first for East European Jews and Italians at the turn of the twentieth century, and now for Asians, Dominicans, and other Latinos—Jessica battles against the effects of poverty, drugs, gangs, homelessness, family violence and abuse, and language difficulties to give her students an opportunity to succeed in school and in life.

As the advisor to the Seward Park student newspaper, she uses journalism as a vehicle to involve students in the learning experience. Freedman captures the daily struggles, the long hours, and the selfless dedication of a teacher committed to making a difference in the lives of her students. He also captures the bureaucratic nonsense, the petty collegial jealousies, the social problems, and the school conditions that make success difficult, if not impossible. Jessica encourages students to go to college, she helps them with their applications, and she even drives them to college interviews. For every student she helps succeed and who gets into college, there are many others with talent and dreams who do not graduate.

After 10 years of heroic and successful teaching, Jessica decides to leave teaching and return to her first career as a journalist. In part, she leaves because she wants to be a journalist; in part, she leaves because to be a successful teacher required too much personal sacrifice, with too little reward. Freedman's book portrays the limits and possibilities of good teaching—that teachers like Jessica make an important difference, but that without reform of schools, teachers like Jessica may leave teaching. In her review of the book, Johnson (1991, p. 184) stated:

> Freedman leaves us with admiration for Jessica Siegel, respect for many of her colleagues, compassion for her students, anger at a seemingly impersonal school bureaucracy, and remorse for a society that values cash more than children. . . . Yet it is clear that much more can be done to support exemplary teachers like Jessica Siegel. The moral of *Small Victories* is sobering and unequivocal: If we do not change schools to support good teaching, many good teachers will leave schools.

The film *Stand and Deliver* chronicles the work of Jaime Escalante at Garfield High School in East Los Angeles, a poor neighborhood of African Americans, Mexican Americans, and other Latino Americans. Jaime Escalante refuses to accept the stereotype that students from low-income neighborhoods cannot succeed at high-level academic work. He came to Garfield as a computer teacher after a successful career as a computer analyst in the corporate world and immediately instituted an Advanced Placement (AP) Calculus program, despite the objections of the chairperson of the Mathematics Department, a woman who did not want to set the students up for failure.

Stand and Deliver portrays the heroic efforts of Jaime Escalante to teach his student advanced mathematics. He demonstrates what positive expectations can do and how hard work and dedication on the part of teachers and students can often overcome the pernicious effects of poverty, racism, and social problems. Despite a shortage of materials, the accusation of the Educational Testing Service (ETS) that his students cheated on the AP test (according to ETS, because they had many of the same wrong answers; according to Jaime Escalante, because they did too well for students from their backgrounds), and numerous personal hurdles that students had to overcome, all 18 students passed the AP examination the first year of the program. Within four years, over 85 students passed the AP calculus examination.

The film demonstrates a number of important points. First, a talented and dedicated teacher can make a difference. Second, if teachers expect all students to learn and excel, they can and do. Third, it is possible to institutionalize the effective teaching of one teacher into an overall school philosophy, as Garfield High School had to do in order to serve as many students as it now does. Despite these positive lessons, however, there has been a tendency to romanticize the work of Jaime Escalante, or worse to use his success as an example that all that is necessary to improve schools in low-income neighborhoods is to raise expectations. The fact is that although Jaime Escalante did make a difference, students at schools like Garfield High School still have significantly fewer opportunities than students at more affluent high schools. Furthermore, teachers like Jaime Escalante cannot eliminate the negative effects of poverty and other social problems.

These two stories of wonderful teachers can be supplemented by your own recollections of wonderful teachers who have influenced your lives. Unfortunately, they can also be countered by your own stories of terrible teachers and ineffective schools. Our point in telling these stories is to indicate that, as teachers, you can make a difference. However, they also demonstrate that wonderful teachers alone cannot ameliorate societal and school problems, and that wonderful teachers in ineffective schools are severely limited in what they can accomplish. The foundations perspective enlightens one to the importance of changing structures, not just individuals, if the educational system is to improve. For the past decade, there have been a number of significant reform efforts aimed at doing just this. The following section explores some of these efforts.

Educational Reform from the 1980s to 2005

The 1980s and 1990s and into the twenty-first century were periods of significant debate and reform in U.S. education. Beginning in 1983, with the National Commission on Educational Excellence's report *A Nation at Risk,* government leaders, educational reformers, teacher organizations, administrators, and various other interest groups attempted to improve the quality of U.S. schools. Although the decades included two specific waves of reform, the first beginning in 1983 and the second beginning in 1985 and continuing through 2005, the period must be understood as a conservative response to the progressive reforms of the 1960s and 1970s, if not the entire progressive agenda of the twentieth century.

In the 1980s, the major reform actors shifted from the federal to the state to the local levels. In the 1990s, President Clinton's *Goals 2000* and President Bush's *No Child Left Behind* placed the federal government back at the forefront of educational policy. From the outset, the federal government, through the Department of Education, attempted to balance its ideological belief that education is not a federal governmental matter, with its commitment to providing the impetus for change. First, through its influential report *A Nation at Risk,* written during the tenure of Secretary Terrel Bell, and second, through his successor William Bennett's use of his office as a "bully pulpit," the U.S. Department of Education played a significant role in keeping the pressure on states and localities to improve educational outcomes, which for Secretary Bennett defined the goals of educational reform. Finally, NCLB placed accountability at the fore-front of reforms aimed at reducing the achievement gap.

The educational reforms from the 1980s to today consisted of two waves of reform (Bacharach, 1990; Passow, 1989). The first wave, marked by the reports of the early and mid-1980s and the educational initiatives directly responding to them, were concerned primarily with the issues of accountability and achievement (Dougherty, 1990, p. 3). Responding to the call for increased academic achievement, many states increased graduation requirements, toughened curriculum mandates, and increased the use of standardized test scores to measure student achievement.

By the mid to late 1980s, however, it became increasingly clear that such top-down reform would be ineffective in dealing with the schools' myriad problems. Although raising achievement standards for students and implementing accountability measures for evaluating teachers had some positive effects, many (including the National Governors Association, which took a leading role in reform) believed that educational reform had to do more than provide changes in evaluation procedures. The second wave of reform, then, was targeted at the structure and processes of the schools themselves, placing far more control in the hands of local schools, teachers, and communities. Whereas the first wave was highly centralized at the state level, the second wave was more decentralized to the local and school levels. What they had in common, however, was what the Governors Conference emphasized as the "triple theme of achievement, assessment, and accountability" (Bacharach, 1990, p. 8). By the mid-1990s, however, the first and second waves began to overlap, with top-down federal and state mandates defining the goals and standards of education, but leaving it to local districts to implement them.

Despite the second wave's insistence that locally based reforms were central to success, many critics (including teacher organizations and unions) argued that the reforms were highly bureaucratic and aimed primarily at assessment procedures. Significant reforms, they suggested, had to emphasize both changes within schools and changes that involved teachers, students, and parents as part of the reform process, not merely as objects of it. From the latter part of the 1980s through the end of the 1990s, reforms that emphasized teacher empowerment, school-based management, and school choice, charter schools, and tuition vouchers became the most important ones under consideration.

To summarize, the first wave of reform reports stressed the need for increased educational excellence though increased educational standards and a reversal of the rising tide of mediocrity. Passow (1989, p. 16) stated the following themes as essential to the first wave of educational reform:

1. The need to attain the twin goals of excellence and equity
2. The need to clarify educational goals, unburdening schools from responsibilities they cannot or should not fill
3. The need to develop a common core curriculum (not unlike the standard college-bound curriculum) with few or no electives, little or no curricular differentiation, but only pedagogical differentiation
4. The need to eliminate tracking programs so that students could tackle the common core courses in a common curriculum in different ways

5. The need for major changes in vocational education: in the student populations served, the curricula provided, and the sites of such education if offered
6. The need for education to teach about technology, including computer literacy, and to become involved in the technological revolution
7. The need to "increase both the duration and intensity of academic learning," lengthening the school day and the school year
8. The need to recruit, train, and retain more academically able teachers, to improve the quality of teaching, and to upgrade the professional working life of teachers
9. The need to redefine the principal's role and put the "principal squarely in charge of educational quality in each school"
10. The need to forge new partnerships between corporations, business, and the schools

Typifying the second wave of educational reform were the recommendations of the State Governor's Conference. Governor Lamar Alexander, in *Time for Results: The Governor's 1991 Report on Education* (1986), summarized the Governor's Association's year-long analysis of a variety of issues, including teaching, leadership and management, parental involvement and choice, readiness, technology, school facilities, and college quality, with (among others) the following recommendations:

1. Now is the time to work out a fair, affordable Career Ladder salary system that recognizes real differences in function, competence, and performance of teachers.
2. States should create leadership programs for school leaders.
3. Parents should have more choice in the public schools their children attend.
4. The nation—and the states and local districts—need report cards about results, and about what students know and can do.
5. School districts and schools that do not make the grade should be declared bankrupt, taken over by the state, and reorganized.
6. It makes no sense to keep closed half a year the school buildings in which America has invested a quarter of a trillion dollars while we are undereducated and overcrowded.
7. States should work with four- and five-year-olds from poor families to help them get ready for school and decrease the chances that they will drop out later.
8. Better use of technologies through proper planning and training for use of videodiscs, computers, and robotics is an important way to give teachers more time to teach.
9. States should insist that colleges assess what students actually learn while in college. (cited in Passow, 1989, p. 23)

During both waves of educational reform, a number of programs and initiatives received considerable attention. Among these are school choice, charter schools, tuition vouchers, school-business partnerships, privatization, school-to-work programs, school-based management, reform of teacher education, the effective school movement, state intervention in local districts, and school finance litigation.

School Choice, Charter Schools, and Tuition Vouchers

During the 1980s and 1990s, many educational researchers and policy analysts indicated that most public schools were failing in terms of student achievement, discipline, and morality. At the same period, some researchers were investigating private schools and concluding that they were more effective learning environments than public schools. Private schools were reputed to be accountable, efficient, and safe. Moreover, the work of Coleman, Hoffer, and Kilgore (1982) seemed to prove that private school students learned more than their public school counterparts. Other research on *magnet schools* (schools with special curricula and student bodies) seemed to indicate that public schools that operated independently of the public school bureaucracy were happier, healthier, and more academically productive than zone schools where students were required to attend based on their residence.

As the 1980s came to a close, some researchers reasoned that magnet schools and private schools were superior to neighborhood public schools because schools of choice reflected the desires and needs of their constituents and were thus sensitive to change. For several decades, the idea of school choice had been on the fringes of the educational policy world in the form of voucher proposals. Essentially, voucher proponents argued that if families, rather than schools, were funded, it would allow for greater parental choice and participation. Moreover, by voting with their dollars, parents would reward good schools and punish bad schools. A voucher system, in effect, would deregulate the public school system. That a voucher system might also privatize the public school system was a muted issue.

By the late 1980s, however, school choice was at the forefront of the educational reform movement. Presidents Reagan and Bush supported choice and one influential White House report enumerated a number of reasons why choice was the right reform for the times (Paulu, 1989). In essence, choice was a panacea that was nonbureaucratic, inexpensive, and fundamentally egalitarian because it allowed market forces to shape school policy rather than subjecting educators to the heavy hand of the educational bureaucracy. A very influential book by John E. Chubb and Terry M. Moe, *Politics, Markets, and America's Schools* (1990), seemed to provide empirical evidence that unregulated school choice policies, in and of themselves, would produce a structural reform in U.S. education.

Congressional support for greater school choice was expressed in a bill that was passed by the House of Representatives in the summer of 1990, which, among other things, provided direct federal support for open enrollment experiments. Needless to say, all this political activity stirred up a great deal of controversy and confusion. Choice is controversial because it is deeply political and rests on a set of assumptions about educational marketplaces and private schools that are questionable. It is confusing because choice is a rubric that covers a wide variety of policies that are quite different, except that they include an element of student and parental choice. Next, we briefly touch on some of the major types of school choice plans that have been recently implemented in the United States (see Cookson, 1994, for a complete discussion).

Intersectional choice plans include public and private schools. For example, the cities of Milwaukee and Cleveland provided tuition vouchers to students who attended private neighborhood schools. The inclusion of private schools in choice plans stirred a great deal of debate among policy makers because there are fundamental issues of constitutionality and equity inherent in any public policy that transfers funds from the public sector to the private sector. In the United States, there is a constitutionally protected division between church and state that forbids the establishment of any state religion and thus forbids state support of any particular religion. Because an overwhelming number of private schools in the United States are religiously affiliated, this issue is critical. However, in 2002, the U.S. Supreme Court in *Zelman* v. *Simmons-Harris* ruled that the Cleveland voucher program did not violate the First Amendment separation of church and state, making future voucher programs more likely. Additionally, equity issues arise from the fact that some private schools are believed to contribute to the maintenance of social inequalities. The most elite secondary schools in the United States, for instance, are private. A public policy that would transfer funds to these schools would clearly raise issues of equal educational opportunity.

Intrasectional school choice policies include only public schools. States, such as Minnesota, permit students to attend school in any public school district in the state, so long as the nonresident school district is willing, has space, and the transfer does not upset racial balance. Statewide choice plans, such as Minnesota's, have been adopted by a number of other states. Most choice plans, however, are more limited geographically. The most common form of intrasectional choice plans permit students to attend schools outside of their community school district. These interdistrict choice plans commonly allow urban students to cross district lines and attend suburban schools and vice versa. In St. Louis, for example, minority students from the inner city are able to attend suburban schools that are located in relatively affluent white neighborhoods. In theory, students from the suburbs are supposed to be drawn into the inner city by some outstanding magnet schools, but, in fact, only a handful of white students have traveled into the inner city to attend school.

Intradistrict choice plans refer to any option available to students within a given public school district. These options range from a choice of curriculum within a particular school to allowing students to attend any school in the district. One particular intradistrict choice plan that has gained a great deal of recognition is *controlled choice*. In this type of plan, students choose a school anywhere in a district or within some zones within a district. The key to this policy is that student choices are not allowed to upset racial balances. In effect, some students may not be able to enroll in their first-choice schools if it would mean increased districtwide racial segregation. Often, other factors are also taken into consideration, such as whether an applicant has a sibling already in his or her school of choice. There are several successful controlled choice districts in the United States, including Cambridge (Massachusetts), Montclair (New Jersey), and District 4 located in the borough of Manhattan in New York City. District 4 also allows students outside its boundaries to attend schools within the district, thus combining intradistrict and interdistrict features.

Boston initiated a controlled choice plan that may serve as a test of whether these types of plans can be successfully implemented on a citywide basis. According to Charles L. Glenn, executive director of the Office of Educational Equity in the Massachusetts Department of Education, the choice plan in Boston appears to be operationally successful, although "vulnerable schools" (i.e., those with declining student populations) need extra assistance to remain open and to provide services to the students who attend them. According to Glenn (1991, p. 43), "Public school choice will not produce overnight miracles, and the Boston experience—like that of Soviet-bloc economies—shows how very difficult it can be to reform an entrenched institution with a monopoly position and a tradition of top-down decision making."

Throughout the 1990s, public school choice, tuition vouchers for private schools, and charter schools (schools that are publicly funded by state charters but independent of many school district mandates) have been key educational reforms. Powers and Cookson (1999) summarized the available evidence on school choice and concluded that (1) market-driven choice programs increase stratification within school districts; (2) choice programs increase the educational opportunities for minority students, who, without these programs, would be limited to their neighborhood public schools; (3) choice parents tend to be more involved in their children's education; (4) choice parents tend to be more satisfied with their children's education; and (5) there is disagreement among researchers about the effect of choice on student achievement. For example, using the same data on Milwaukee Parental Choice Program (MPCP), Witte (1996; Witte, Sterr, & Thorn, 1995; Witte et al., 1994) argued that the effect of choice has been inconsistent; Greene and Peterson (1996) argued that MPCP has resulted in significant achievement gains; and Rouse's (2002) findings are in the middle.

A longitudinal study of the Cleveland Scholarship Program concluded that there were no significant differences between voucher students and students in the Cleveland public schools, when controlling for race and income of the students. Ladd (2002), in a balanced and exhaustive review of the literature, concluded:

> Contrary to the claims of many voucher advocates, widespread use of school vouchers is not likely to generate substantial gains in the productivity of the U.S. K–12 education system. Any gains in overall student achievement are likely to be small at best. Moreover, given the tendency of parents to judge schools in part by the characteristics of students in the school, a universal voucher system would undoubtedly harm large numbers of disadvantaged students. Although small means-tested voucher programs might provide a helpful safety valve for some children, policymakers should be under no illusion that such programs will address the fundamental challenge of providing an adequate education to the large numbers of disadvantaged students in many of our large cities. At the same time, there are good arguments for giving families, especially those who are economically disadvantaged, more power to choose the schools their children attend. The challenge for policymakers is to find ways to expand parental choices without excessively privileging the interests of individual families over the social interests that justify the funding of K–12 education.

The choice movement resulted in the development of charter schools and tuition vouchers for private schools. Whereas conservatives became the major proponents of tuition vouchers, advocates of charter schools often came from all sides of the political spectrum. Wells and colleagues (1998) summarized the claims by charter school advocates: charter schools (1) are more accountable for student outcomes; (2) have greater autonomy and thus are empowered to better serve their students; (3) are more efficient; (4) provide greater choice to more families; (5) create a competitive market and will force public schools to change; and (6) are more innovative.

The UCLA Charter School Study of 10 California school districts (Wells et al., 1998) reported the following findings:

1. California Charter Schools (CCS) are most often not held accountable for increased student achievement.
2. School boards are ambivalent about monitoring CCS.
3. CCS are accountable to multiple constituencies.

4. CCS vary greatly in their autonomy.
5. CCS funding varies widely between and within districts.
6. Private resources are needed for CCS to survive.
7. CCS differ greatly in their ability to raise private funds.
8. CCS depend on strong leadership.
9. CCS have significant control over the types of students they admit.
10. The requirement that CCS reflect the racial/ethnic makeup of their districts has not been enforced.
11. Teachers in CCS welcome their freedom, small-class size, and collegiality, but note their heavy workloads.
12. Although it is not required, most CCS have state-credentialed teachers.
13. Teachers in schools converted to CCS continue to belong to unions, but teachers in new CCS do not.
14. There are few formal ways for public schools and CCS to learn from each other.
15. Public school educators believe that CCS have an unfair advantage that limits competition.

The UCLA study indicates that charter schools in California have not fulfilled many of their advocates claims and suggests that charter schools may continue to advantage already advantaged families. However, since the study did not include an empirical investigation of achievement outcomes, it is still premature to reach any overall conclusions about the efficacy of charter schools, particularly for children from lower socioeconomic backgrounds.

In a recent study by the U.S. Department of Education, researchers found that students in district public schools had higher achievement than comparable students in charter schools (*Education Week,* 2005). Tractenberg, Sadovnik, and Liss (2004) found that the performance of New Jersey's charter schools has been mixed at best, and Barr (2004a) found that there were no overall significant differences between New Jersey's public and charter schools, when controlling for student background. He also found that charter schools are among some of the highest- and lowest-performing schools in New Jersey. Hoxby (2004a, 2004b), however, in a study comparing students in charter schools with those who applied through lotteries, but were put on waiting lists and stayed in public schools, found that charter school students had higher achievement. Hill (2005) and Miron and Nelson (2004), in looking at the disagreements over charter school achievement, have cautioned that difficulties in study designs make it hard to reach reliable conclusions.

Clearly, it is too early to tell whether school choice will lead to the revitalization of public education in the United States. It may well be that choice is a method of school improvement, but cannot by itself resolve many of the fundamental problems associated with public education. Moreover, choice plans usually involve complex and volatile issues of constitutionality, equity, and feasibility. For instance, how will already impoverished school districts pay for the increased transportation costs required by many choice plans? In sum, there is evidence that school choice can lead to improvement in individual schools, but there is little convincing evidence that choice will result in the overall improvement of U.S. education.

School-Business Partnerships

During the 1980s, business leaders became increasingly concerned that the nation's schools were not producing the kinds of graduates necessary for a revitalization of the U.S. economy. Several school-business partnerships were formed, the most notable of which was the Boston Compact begun in 1982. These partnerships have been formed in other cities. For instance, in 1991, the Committee to Support Philadelphia Public Schools pledged management assistance and training to the Philadelphia School District to restructure and implement a site-based management plan. In return, the city promised that by 1995 it would raise the test scores of its graduates and improve grade promotion rates. Other school-business partnerships include scholarships for poor students to attend college and programs where businesses "adopt" a school.

However, despite the considerable publicity that surrounds these partnerships, the fact is that in the 1980s, only 1.5 percent of corporate giving was to public primary and secondary public schools (Reich, 1991, p. 43). In fact, corporate and business support for public schools has fallen dramatically since the 1970s. School-business partnerships have attracted considerable media attention, but there is little convincing evidence that they have significantly improved schools or that, as a means of reform, school-business partnerships will address the fundamental problems facing U.S. education.

Privatization

From the 1990s, the traditional distinction between public and private education became blurred, with private education companies increasingly becoming involved in public education in a variety of ways. First, for-profit companies, such as the Edison Company, took over the management of failing schools and districts. The Philadelphia Public Schools, taken over by the state of Pennsylvania in 2003 due to low student achievement, hired for-profit companies, including Edison, as well as local universities, including Penn and Temple to manage its schools. Second, for-profit companies, such as Kaplan and Sylvan Learning Centers, have the majority of contracts for supplemental tutoring under NCLB. It is too early to assess the efficacy of such privatization, but it is clear that corporations see the multi-billion-dollar education industry as a lucrative market.

School-to-Work Programs

In the 1990s, school-business partnerships became incorporated into school-to-work programs. Their intent was to extend what had been a vocational emphasis to non-college-bound students regarding skills necessary for successful employment and to stress the importance of work-based learning.

On May 4, 1994, President Bill Clinton signed the School-to-Work Opportunities Act of 1994. This law provided seed money to states and local partnerships of business, labor, government, education, and community organizations to develop school-to-work systems. The law did not create a new program, but allowed states and their partners to bring together efforts at education reform, worker preparation, and economic development to create a system—a system to prepare youth for the high-wage, high-skill careers of today's and tomorrow's global economy.

Using federal seed money, states and their partnerships were encouraged to design the school-to-work system that made the most sense for them. While these systems were different from state to state, each was supposed to provide every U.S. student with the following:

- Relevant education, allowing students to explore different careers and see what skills are required in their working environment
- Skills, obtained from structured training and work-based learning experiences, including necessary skills of a particular career as demonstrated in a working environment
- Valued credentials, establishing industry-standard benchmarks and developing education and training standards that ensure that proper education is received for each career

Every state and locally created school-to-work system had to contain three core elements: (1) school-based learning (classroom instruction based on high academic and business-defined occupational skill standards); (2) work-based learning (career exploration, work experience, structured training and mentoring at job sites); and (3) connecting activities (courses integrating classroom and on-the-job instruction, matching students with participating employers, training of mentors, and the building of other bridges between school and work).

Although the school-to-work programs were well intentioned, researchers (Charner, 1996; Mortimer, 1996) have suggested that these programs often failed to fulfill their promise. The U.S. system of vocational education remains a "second-class" educational track, which often does not equip students with a sound liberal arts foundation and is not adequately connected to career opportunities. Unlike other nations, such as Japan and Germany, U.S. students who do not wish to go on to postsecondary education are not given adequate career paths.

School-Based Management and Teacher Empowerment

In part, the history of education in the United States can be characterized as a struggle between the rivaling traditions of decentralization and centralization. Generally, the educational system, as a whole, is decentralized because the ultimate authority for educational policy rests with the individual states and not with the federal government. Yet, within states and school districts, there has been a long-term tendency to centralize decision making in state agencies, elected and appointed school boards, and superintendents' offices. Throughout the 1980s and 1990s, there were repeated calls for the exercise of local and community authority in educational decision making. After all, the argument runs, who knows best what the children in any one particular school need—administrators and teachers or state and local bureaucrats?

School-based management is a decentralizing policy that has captured the imagination of many U.S. educators and much of the public. Joseph Fernandez, former school chancellor for New York City, for instance, is a powerful advocate for school-based management because it enables those who interact with students every day to oversee budgets and set curricula most relevant to the needs of students. He believes in giving schools more decision-making discretion "because generally they will make better decisions" ("Do Poor Kids Deserve Poor Schools?" 1991).

Major school-based management reforms have been put in place in New York City; Dade County, Florida; San Diego, California; Rochester, New York; Louisville, Kentucky; and Chicago, Illinois. Perhaps the most dramatic of these reforms has been in Chicago, where locally elected councils—composed of six parents, two community residents, two teachers, and the principal—have been put in charge of each of the city's 541 public schools. Evidence from the Chicago school reform suggests that school-based management by parents and teachers has not been particularly effective in reforming urban education or significantly raising achievement levels (Bryk et al., 1993; Hess, 1995). Although all of the legal issues surrounding this reform have not been settled, there is little doubt that school-based management reforms will continue to enjoy support among many policy makers, some teachers, and some local communities.

The notion that local decision making will automatically make schools better learning environments and more collegial may ignore some of the problems implicit in extreme decentralization. For example, how can the tension between providing teachers with more decision-making authority while simultaneously providing for administrative action and initiative be resolved? There is considerable research that suggests that principals play a key role in creating effective schools.

Moreover, some actions that may be required to make schools more effective may run counter to teachers' desires or self-perceived interests. If teachers and parents are to successfully formulate and implement policy, they need to be given training and related technical assistance. And unless teachers are given substantial amounts of time to plan, implement, monitor, and change their initiatives, there is little reason to expect that school-based reforms will be successful. This issue is becoming more acute in states where budgetary shortfalls have resulted in teacher layoffs and increased teaching workloads. Finally, school-based management requires that some rules and regulations be waived by federal, state, and local authorities as well as teachers' unions. To some extent, these negotiations may mean that school-based reforms may be slowly and partially implemented, and thus their effectiveness may be diminished.

Clearly, school-based management implies teacher empowerment. Without providing teachers with the professional opportunities and responsibilities that come with decision making, many school-level reforms will wither. Yet, what does *teacher empowerment* really mean? How much power should teachers have in policy making and how much power do teachers want? It is becoming increasingly common for principals to establish faculty councils or committees that, in effect, administer the school. These committees and councils may have actual power or they may be thought of more in an advisory capacity.

It is far too early to tell if the teacher empowerment movement will reshape the authority systems within elementary and secondary schools in the United States. In particular, if there is no basic redefinition of teachers' roles within schools, there is little likelihood that teachers will have the opportunity, time, or support to implement change. It is not entirely clear that all teachers want to be policy makers. Definitions of professional responsibilities are not universally agreed upon. Undoubtedly, each school and school district will arrive at a definition of what constitutes teachers' roles and responsibilities in the coming decade. In some schools and school districts, teachers may gain real authority, while in others, principals and superintendents may retain most of the decision-making power. However, if the movement toward school-based management continues, it is likely that teachers will be increasingly empowered and given authority to make professional decisions regarding school management, school curriculum, and pedagogy.

Teacher Education

The emergence and development of teacher education as an educational problem was a response to the initial debates concerning the failure of the schools (Labaree, 1992a, 1992b, 1996). If the schools were not working properly, then teachers and teaching–perhaps the most important piece in the puzzle–had to be looked at critically. In addition, teacher organizations such as the National Education Association (NEA) and the American Federation of Teachers (AFT), fearing the scapegoating of their members, took an active role in raising the debate as the opportunity to both recognize and improve the problematic conditions under which, from their perspective, most of their members work.

Finally, if teachers and teaching were indeed part of the problem, then perhaps the education and training of teachers was a good starting point for analysis. Thus, teacher education and schools and colleges of education, long the object of critical scrutiny within universities, became the subject of intensive national investigation. By 1986, at least five major reports (by the National Commission on Excellence in Teacher Education, the California Commission on the Teaching Profession, the Holmes Group, the Southern Regional Education Board, and the Carnegie Report of the Task Force on Teaching as a Profession) outlined major problems in teacher education and the professional lives of teachers, and proposed a large-scale overhaul of the system that prepares teachers. Although the reports differed in some respects, there was widespread agreement about the nature of the problem. The debate revolved around three major points:

1. The perceived lack of rigor and intellectual demands in teacher education programs
2. The need to attract and retain competent teacher candidates
3. The necessity to reorganize the academic and professional components of teacher education programs at both the baccalaureate and post baccalaureate levels (Teacher Education Project, 1986).

Although all five reports contributed to the ongoing discussions, the Carnegie and Holmes reports attracted the most public response and became symbolic of the teacher education reform movement. (Perhaps this was because they represented two of the major interest groups in teacher education–in the case of Carnegie, major political and educational leaders, and for Holmes, the Deans of Education from the major research universities.) Therefore, this section will analyze the Carnegie and Holmes reports as representative of the current attempts to improve the training of teachers (see Labaree, 1992a, 1992b, for a detailed discussion).

The Carnegie Report, entitled *A Nation Prepared: Teachers for the 21st Century* (1986) and prepared by its Task Force on Teaching as a Profession (including representatives from corporations, the NEA and AFT, school journalists and administrators, legislators, the Governor of New Jersey, and a Dean of Education of a major research university), focused on the necessity of educational quality for a competitive U.S. economy and the value of education in a democratic political system. Building on the critique offered by *A Nation at Risk,* the Carnegie Report suggested that improvements in teacher education were necessary preconditions for improvements in education.

In addition to this underlying democratic-liberal model of education, the report argued that the decline in traditional low-wage jobs in the U.S. economy and the corresponding increase in high-technology and service positions would require the schools to better prepare its students for this "new" economic reality. In this regard, also, the Carnegie Report stressed the centrality of better prepared teachers to meet the challenges of the twenty-first century. Echoing this political-economic perspective, the report stated:

> If our standard of living is to be maintained, if the growth of a permanent underclass is to be averted, if democracy is to function effectively [in the twenty-first] century, our schools must graduate the vast majority of their students with achievement levels long thought possible for only the privileged few. The American mass education system, designed in the early part of the century for a mass production economy, will not succeed unless it not only raises but redefines the essential standards of excellence and strives to make quality and equality of opportunity compatible with each other. (1986, p. 3)

In order to accomplish these democratic-liberal goals, the Carnegie Report (1986, p. 3) called for "sweeping changes in educational policy," which would include the restructuring of schools and the teaching profession, the elimination of the undergraduate education major, the recruitment of minorities into the teaching profession, and the increase of standards in teacher education and in teaching.

The Holmes Group, on the other hand, avoided explicit political-economic goals, but focused on the relationship between university-based teacher education, the professional lives of teachers, and the structure of the schools themselves. Arguing that their role as teacher educators gave a unique and also perhaps subjective perception of these issues, the Holmes Report, entitled *Tomorrow's Teachers* (1986), outlined a set of five goals and proposals for the improvement of teacher education. Michael Sedlak, one of the original coauthors of the report, introduced his brief summary of the document by stressing that "the Holmes Group is dedicated not just to the improvement of teacher education but to the construction of a genuine profession of teaching" (1987, p. 315). The goals of the report included raising the intellectual soundness of teacher education, creating career ladders for teachers, developing entry-level requirements into the profession, linking schools of education at the university level to schools, and improving schools for students and teachers.

In two subsequent reports, *Tomorrow's Schools* (1990) and *Tomorrow's Schools of Education* (1995), the Holmes Group advocated systemic changes in professional development and radically altering schools of education with an emphasis on school-university partnerships and professional development schools (PDS). Critics of the Holmes Group (Labaree, 1992a, 1992b, 1996) argued that its proposals represented a "disabling vision" for schools of education, as they limit their roles to teacher education only, while deemphasizing their other important roles in research and education in broader societal and psychological contexts.

Despite differences in tone and some minor differences in emphasis, both the Carnegie and Holmes Reports focus on the same general concerns:

1. They agree that overall problems in education cannot be solved without corresponding changes in teacher education.
2. Teacher education programs must be upgraded in terms of their intellectual rigor and focus, their need to emphasize the liberal arts, their need to eliminate undergraduate teacher education programs and, like other professions (i.e., psychology, social work, law, medicine), move professional training and certification to the graduate level.
3. Rigorous standards of entry into the profession must be implemented, and systematic examinations to monitor such entry must be developed.
4. University teacher education programs and schools must be connected in a more systematic and cooperative manner.
5. Career ladders that recognize differences in knowledge, skill, and commitment must be created for teachers.
6. Necessary changes must be made in the schools and the professional lives of teachers in order to attract and retain the most competent candidates for the profession.

John Goodlad, in *Teachers for Our Nation's Schools* (1990), proposed a radical transformation of the way teachers are prepared, requiring an overhaul of university-based teacher preparation. Echoing many of the recommendations of the Carnegie Commission and the Holmes Group on school-university cooperation, Goodlad stressed the importance of rewarding teacher-educators for their work, rather than relegating them, as is currently the case, to the bottom rung of the university status hierarchy.

In the 1990s, teacher education and professionalization continued to be significant issues. Talbert (1996) argued that both teacher education and professional development programs have been inadequate for equipping prospective teachers and teachers to fulfill their myriad responsibilities. Most teachers receive one-shot professional development workshops that have little effect on their performance. She argued that long-term systemic professional development is needed.

As head of the National Commission on Teaching and America's Future, Linda Darling-Hammond (1996b) has been one of the recent leaders of the teacher education reform. The commission report indicated that the criticisms presented by the Carnegie and Holmes reports in the 1980s had not been adequately addressed. It pointed out that "school reform cannot succeed unless it focuses on creating the conditions in which teachers can teach, and teach well" (p. vi) and it identified the following barriers to improving teacher education development: (1) low expectations for student performance, (2) unenforced standards for teachers, (3) major flaws in teacher preparation, (4) slipshod teacher recruitment, (5) inadequate induction for beginning teachers, (6) lack of professional development and rewards for knowledge and skill, and (7) schools that are structured for failure rather than success. Therefore, the Commission recommended the following:

1. Get serious about standards, for both students and teachers.
2. Reinvent teacher preparation and professional development.
3. Fix teacher recruitment and put qualified teachers in every classroom.
4. Encourage and reward teacher knowledge and skill.
5. Create schools that are organized for student and teacher success. (National Commission on Teaching and America's Future, 1996, pp. vi–vii)

Representative of the second wave of educational reforms, the effective school movement's recommendations, as well as those of the Carnegie, Holmes, and National Commission on Teaching and America's Future reports, emphasized the processes of teaching and learning, the school environment, and especially the need to improve the professional lives and status of teachers.

The Effective School Movement

In response to *A Nation at Risk* and other reports criticizing the effectiveness of U.S. public schools, the school effectiveness movement emerged and suggested that there were characteristics in good schools that could be used as models for improving educational effectiveness. The late Ron Edmonds, one of the early leaders of this movement, argued that educational reform and improvement must consider problems of both equity and quality. Based on Edmonds's work on effective schools for disadvantaged students (Edmonds, 1979a), research on school effectiveness sought to identify the characteristics of effective schools (Brookover et al., 1979, 1982).

The school effectiveness research points out five key factors that define successful schools: (1) high expectations for all students, and staff acceptance of responsibility for student learning; (2) instructional leadership on the part of the principal; (3) a safe and orderly environment conducive to learning; (4) a clear and focused mission concerning instructional goals shared by the staff; and (5) frequent monitoring of student progress (Gartner & Lipsky, 1987, p. 389).

Based on this research, educational policy makers focused on how to build the capacity in districts, schools, and classrooms to improve student achievement and to reduce the achievement gaps. Research suggests that districts have a specific role to play in assisting schools to build the necessary capacity to improve student achievement. Districts can assist schools in developing organizational/structural and instructional capacity. Research provides advice to districts about how they can build organizational capacity, and suggests a focus on the following five dimensions:

1. Vision and leadership
2. Collective commitment and cultural norms
3. Knowledge or access to knowledge
4. Organizational structures and management
5. Resources (Goertz et al., 1995, p. 3)

Research also argues that the reform process itself is instrumental in building capacity, and indicates four strategies for building the capacity for standards-based reforms:

1. Articulating a reform vision
2. Providing instructional guidelines
3. Restructuring governance and organizational structures
4. Establishing evaluation and accountability mechanisms (Goertz et al., 1995, p. 4)

In other words, it is incumbent on districts to do the following:

- Assist schools in using achievement data as a baseline for targeted improvement.
- Provide districtwide professional development aimed at improving teacher knowledge and skills.
- Help schools align their curriculum and instruction to state learning standards and assessments.
- Target those students and schools with the most need for districtwide help.

Efforts aimed at capacity building must start with a vision of what an effective school should look like. After all, it is at the school level—more than at the district—that student achievement is most directly impacted. There is general agreement in the research conducted on the effective practices of high-performing, high-poverty schools. These schools (American Federation of Teachers, 1998, 1999; American Institutes for Research, 1999; Carter, 2000; Connell, 1999; Haycock, 1999; Johnson et al., 1999; Lein et al., 1997; U.S. Department of Education, 1998, 2001):

- Set high standards and develop curriculum and assessment tools based on those standards.
- Hold teachers and school administrators accountable for student performance and meeting goals.
- Create a safe and orderly academic environment.
- Employ teachers who are experienced and qualified to teach their subject matter and have access to quality professional development and school administrators who are committed to education
- Encourage parental and community involvement.
- Enjoy administrative flexibility in making decisions involving curriculum, personnel, and school budgets.

Research from the U.S. Department of Education, National Center for Education Statistics (2000b) summarized the key components of school quality as follows:

- Teacher quality and experience, including the academic skills of teachers, teachers who are teaching in their field of preparation, teacher experience, professional development
- Classroom climate, including course content and alignment with learning standards, technology, class size, pedagogy
- School context, including school leadership, goals, professional community, discipline, academic environment

In order to be more specific about school capacity, it is useful to look at what the research says about the characteristics of effective schools and classrooms, and also about effective teachers. The characteristics described encompass structural issues, broad school and classroom-culture issues, and specific instructional issues.

The National Center for Educational Statistics (U.S. Department of Education, 2000b) concluded that there are five characteristics of effective schools that have a positive effect on student learning:

1. School leadership that provides direction, guidance, and support;
2. School goals that are clearly identified, communicated, and enacted;
3. A school faculty that collectively takes responsibility for student learning;
4. School discipline that establishes and orderly atmosphere conducive to learning;
5. School academic organization and climate that challenges and supports students toward higher achievement (p. 36)

At the level of the classroom, research indicates that a variety of factors—including course content, pedagogy, technology and class size—have an impact on student achievement. However, without effective teachers, these factors mean little. Research indicates that at the classroom level, effective instructional practices, implemented by knowledgeable teachers, are a prerequisite for school improvement (Darling-Hammond, Holtzman, Gatlin, & Vasquez-Helig, 2005).

Research reveals a lot about the characteristics of effective teachers. What this research means on a practical level is that the state must partner with districts and schools to build an infrastructure that will increase the likelihood that every teacher possesses the characteristics listed below. According to the research, the most qualified teachers possess the following characteristics (Ingersoll, 2003):

- Strong academic skills
- Teaching within the individual's field of expertise—having an equivalent of a major in the field
- At least three years of teaching experience
- Participation in high-quality professional development programs

Class size is another component of effective schools, especially for low-income students. A Tennessee class size study provides important evidence on the value of small classes (Krueger, 1998; Mosteller, 1995; Sanders & Rivers, 1996). Based on a random assignment experiment, this study indicated that there were significant achievement gains made by students in the smaller classes, when controlling for all other factors. Further, the greatest gains were made by black students in the early grades. Further studies confirmed that the largest gains were made by black, disadvantaged students (Achilles, 1996; Finn, J. D., 1998; Grissmer, Flanagan, & Williamson, 1998; Hanuschek, 1998; Krueger, 1998; Mosteller, Light, & Sachs, 1996; U.S. Department of Education, 1998). A report by the National Center for Educational Statistics (2000b) suggests that reductions in class size have the potential for helping all students in the primary grades (U.S. Department of Education, 2000b, p. 35). Based on the Tennessee evidence, it appears that for disadvantaged students the gains are especially strong. Beginning in the 1990s, a number of nonprofit organizations developed models for school improvement, based on the research evidence on effective schools. These include Success for All, a highly structured and scripted program founded by Robert Slavin at Johns Hopkins University; Accelerated Schools, a program that provides rigorous curriculum for students at risk, founded by Henry Levin at Stanford and now at Teachers College, Columbia University; the Coalition of Essential Schools, a progressive school reform program, founded by Theodore Sizer at Brown University; a capacity building model founded by the Hudson Institute; the Comer School Development Program, a program based on school–family partnerships, founded by James Comer at Yale Medical Schools; Core Knowledge, a program based on "traditional" core knowledge, founded by E. D. Hirsch at the University of Virginia; and America's Choice, a program based on standards and assessments, aligned instructional systems, focus on literacy and mathematics, leadership, and professional learning communities, founded by the National Center for Education and the Economy (for a complete list see www.nwrel.org/scpd/catalog/modellist.asp).

Federal funds are available for comprehensive school reform programs in low-income schools. However, the programs must demonstrate that the school reform program integrates all eleven of the components outlined in the *Comprehensive School Reform (CSR) program guidance* (www.csrclearinghouse.org/index.cgi?l=csr_program_components):

1. Proven methods and strategies based on scientifically based research
2. Comprehensive design
3. Professional development
4. Measurable goals and benchmarks
5. Support within the school
6. Support for teachers and principals
7. Parental and community involvement
8. External technical support and assistance
9. Annual evaluation
10. Coordination of resources
11. Strategies that improve academic achievement—The program must meet one of the following requirements:
    a. the program has been found, through scientifically based research, to significantly improve the academic achievement of participating students
    or
    b. the program has been found to have strong evidence that it will significantly improve the academic achievement of participating children.

The evidence on the success of these programs has been the subject of considerable debate, particularly Success for All (SFA). Pogrow (1996, 1999, 2000) has argued that SFA has not significantly improved its schools, whereas Slavin (1997, 1999) has argued that there is considerable scientific evidence to demonstrate his program's effectiveness. More recent research by the American Institutes for Research (Aladjem et al., 2002) demonstrates differences in effectiveness among 24 programs, but also indicates that many programs improve low-income schools. A 2004 study by the Consortium on Policy Research in Education (May, Supovitz, & Perda, 2004) showed significant achievement gains in schools using America's Choice in Rochester, New York. Borman and colleagues (2003) have provided a meta-analysis of the studies on the effects of CSR and conclude that comprehensive school reforms have the potential for improving schools and reducing the achievement gaps.

The evidence suggests that these types of reforms have the potential for improving low-income, high-minority schools. The Education Trust (2005) provided examples of many high-performing, low-income, high-minority schools. Further, it argued that there are some districts (e.g., Aldine and El Paso, Texas) and some states (e.g., Delaware, Illinois, Massachusetts, North Carolina, and Texas) that have significantly reduced the race, ethnic, and social class achievement gaps through the types of educational policies outlined in this chapter. However, sometimes such reforms fail to improve consistently failing schools and more drastic action is taken.

State Intervention in Local School Districts*

For several decades at least, school accountability has been a prominent issue on the national education scene. Accountability has taken many forms, often involving state regulation or oversight. It has included state certification of school personnel and of school districts; statewide testing and assessment of pupils; state monitoring of local fiscal, management, and educational practices; local districts reporting to the state; state dissemination of report cards and other district- and school-specific information to the public; and state intervention in the operation of local districts when problems were identified and solutions were determined to be beyond the local capacity.

Virtually all state accountability systems focus on rewards and sanctions. State policy makers increasingly are directing their attention to how to reward schools and districts that perform well and how to sanction those that do not. Currently, 38 states have some form of rewards or sanctions in place: 8 states reward school districts, 20 reward schools, 29 impose sanctions on school districts, and 32 impose sanctions on schools. Three states (Delaware, Oklahoma, and Texas) do all four. For an excellent description and analysis of the accountability structures in each state, see CPRE (Consortium for Policy Research on Education), *State Assessment & Accountability Systems: 50 State Profiles* (2000).

Some systems include school or district takeover as ultimate accountability measures. Currently, 23 states have enacted statutes authorizing their state education agencies to take control of school districts from local authorities: Alabama, Arkansas, California, Connecticut, Illinois, Iowa, Maryland, Massachusetts, Michigan, Mississippi, Missouri, New Jersey, New Mexico, New York, North Carolina, Ohio, Oklahoma, Pennsylvania, Rhode Island, South Carolina, Tennessee, Texas, and West Virginia. Most of those statutes provide for a succession of increasingly severe sanctions imposed on underperforming districts, leading to takeover as a last resort, whereas some provide only for takeover; some indicate a preference for assistance to

*This section is adapted from P. Tractenberg, M. Holzer, G. Miller, A. R. Sadovnik, and B. Liss (2002), *Developing a Plan for Reestablishing Local Control in the State-Operated School Districts*. Newark, NJ: Institute on Education Law and Policy, Rutgers University (http://ielp.rutgers.edu).

local boards and administrators, again with takeover a last resort; and still others indicate no such preference. Most provide for systems of assessment or accreditation of schools and districts statewide, whereas others target a single troubled school district. As to the basis for takeover, most statutes authorize action on the basis of poor academic performance; others refer to district governance and management as well as academics. Most provide for replacement of administrative personnel with a state-appointed administrator, and some provide for a "receiver," or transfer of control to municipal officials, or annexation into a neighboring school district.

In short, there appears to be no standard method of imposing or implementing state control of local school districts, and there appears to be no standard method of returning control to local authorities. The experience with state takeovers is still relatively limited and fragmentary, but it has led to some perceived advantages and disadvantages. Among the advantages are the following:

- Takeover is, in appropriate cases, a necessary expression of a state's constitutional responsibility for public education.
- Properly done, takeover can provide a good opportunity for state and local decision makers to combine resources and knowledge to improve children's learning.
- Takeover can allow a competent executive staff to guide an uninterrupted and effective implementation of school improvement efforts.
- Takeover can help create a healthy environment in which the local community can address a school district's problems.
- Takeover can make possible more radical changes in low-performing school districts than the customary regimen.
- Takeover, by its relatively extreme and dramatic nature, can put school boards throughout the state on notice that personal agendas, nepotism, and public bickering can have severe consequences.
- If the state carefully collects and analyzes pupil achievement and other data in state-operated districts and schools, it can lead to improvements in statewide accountability efforts.

The perceived disadvantages of state takeover include the following:

- Takeover may be seen as a thinly veiled attempt to reduce local control over schools and to increase state authority over school districts, especially if state government is dominated by one political party and urban districts by another.
- The very concept of state takeover suggests that some local communities lack the capacity to operate effective public schools, and that the state has ready answers and personnel capable of turning around poor performance of the most educationally disadvantaged students.
- State takeover might place poorly prepared state-selected officials in charge, with little possibility of any meaningful change occurring in the classroom.
- Takeover tends to rely on narrow learning measures (i.e., standardized test scores) as the primary criterion for takeover decisions.

- No matter what triggers takeover, it usually focuses, at least initially, on cleaning up petty corruption and incompetent administration and does not get at the root problems impeding the learning of disadvantaged students in urban school districts.
- By fostering a negative image of school board members, administrators, teachers, students, and parents in urban districts, takeover tends to undermine their self-esteem and capacity to improve their performance.
- Takeover that largely supplants local responsibility for the schools inevitably leads to frictions and confrontations between state and local officials that slow the overhaul of management practices, drain resources from educational reforms, and reinforce community resentments.

There is very little research on the effects of state takeovers. For the most part, the studies suggest that takeover has yielded more gains in central office activities than in classroom instructional practices. Illustratively, state takeovers are credited with the following:

- Reducing nepotism within a school district's decision-making process
- Improving a school district's administrative and fiscal management practices
- Removing the threat of teachers' strikes within a school district
- Upgrading the physical condition of schools
- Implementing innovative programs within a school district, such as small schools programs and cooperative arrangements between schools and social service agencies

Unfortunately, however, the limited research suggests that under state takeover, student achievement gains often have fallen short of expectations.

Nevertheless, several states, including California, Connecticut, Kentucky, and West Virginia, have intervention schemes that have resulted in improvements in failing school districts. What they have in common is their focus on improving the local school district's capacity to correct its own problems and to operate a successful educational program. Both the literature and the reported experience of states that have the highest rated state intervention programs suggest that local capacity building must be the cornerstone of successful state involvement. New Jersey, which took over its three largest school districts—Jersey City in 1987, Paterson in 1991, and Newark in 1995—has been less successful, with all three districts still under state control (Tractenberg et al., 2002). Unlike New Jersey, where a command and control approach did little to improve failing districts, California's approach in the Compton Unified School District provides an example of how state intervention may be successful. Through the County Office Fiscal Crisis and Management Assistance Team's (FCMAT) capacity building approach, the Compton District was returned to local control in four years. Currently, FCMAT is working in the Oakland School District, which was taken over by the state in 2004.

The types of reforms, including state intervention, cost money, and low-income–high-minority schools often have significantly less money to spend, despite the availability of federal Title 1 funds. These funding disparities have been the subject of considerable legal actions.

School Finance Litigation

Since the *Brown* decision in 1954, the courts have been an important part of educational reform. After the Supreme Court's decision in *Milliken* v. *Bradley* in 1974, which prohibited interdistrict busing for school desegregation, educational lawyers turned to school finance litigation as a means for bringing about equality of opportunity. With the Supreme Court's decision in *San Antonio, Texas, School District* v. *Rodriguez* that there is no constitutional right to an equal education, cases were filed at the state level, using state provisions for equal education as the basis for these claims. Over the past 30 years, the courts have moved from providing equity, in terms of funding and services, to adequacy, in terms of providing funding for an adequate education for all children.

In New Jersey, *Robinson* v. *Cahill* (1973) and *Abbott* v. *Burke* (1990) are the best examples of equity cases, with the New Jersey Supreme Court ruling that in order to provide all children with its constitutionally mandated thorough and efficient education, the state had to provide its low-income urban districts with funding at the level of its highest-spending districts. It also mandated that the state fund specific programs, such as whole school reform, mandatory preschool for 3- and 4-year-olds, supplementary programs in health and counseling, and new school construction for the 30 Abbott districts.

Although there is evidence of significant improvement in achievement at the fourth-grade level in the Abbott districts, achievement continues to lag at the eighth- and eleventh-grade levels (Education Law Center, 2004). Furthermore, although New Jersey ranks very high in the Education Trust's ranking of states that have reduced the spending gap between rich and poor districts, it ranks low in *Education Week*'s ranking of state funding equity (*Education Week*, 2005). The reason for this is that Abbott equalized spending between rich and poor districts, but did little for those in the middle, resulting in significant disparities between the high-income districts and low-income urban Abbott districts on the one hand, and the middle-, lower-middle-, and low-income rural districts on the other. There are ongoing debates about how to address these issues, given limited state resources, in a way that does not violate the *Abbott* decisions.

New York and California are examples of adequacy cases. In the Campaign for Fiscal Equity Case (CFE) filed over a decade ago, New York's highest court ruled in 2004 that the state must provide an additional $5.6 billion per year to New York City to ensure its constitutional guarantee for a sound and basic education. The court used a number of studies on how much funding would be required to ensure an adequate education for children in New York City who were not receiving a fair share of state funding. The court defined "adequate" as an education that would prepare students to meet the state's rigorous high school graduation requirements. As of the beginning of 2005, the New York state legislature has yet to approve a new funding formula to meet the court's decision, and how the decision will affect the funding of the state's other cities and its many low-income rural districts remains to be determined.

In *Williams* v. *the State of California,* filed in 2000, Governor Arnold Schwarzenegger agreed to a multi-billion-dollar settlement in order to provide the state's low-income districts with the funds to provide an adequate education for its children. The question remains as to how the state with huge deficits will finance this decision.

Although these cases, along with the Kentucky case in the late 1980s, represented monumental victories for advocates of school funding reform, it is less clear that they will reduce the achievement gaps, because, as we argued in the last chapter, the causes are far more complicated and often lie outside of the schools. Nevertheless, school finance adequacy, if not equity, should be part of reform efforts aimed at reducing the achievement gaps.

Although all of these educational reforms have demonstrated the potential to improve schools for low-income and minority children, especially in urban areas, by themselves they are limited is reducing the achievement gaps (Anyon, 2005; Rothstein, 2004b; Tractenberg, Sadovnik, & Liss, 2004) unless they also address the factors outside of schools responsible for educational inequalities. In addition to school-based programs, such as early childhood programs, summer programs, and after-school programs, Rothstein (2004b, pp. 129–150) calls for economic programs to reduce income inequality and to create stable and affordable housing, and the expansion of school-community clinics to provide health care and counseling. He also warns that although school finance suits are necessary to ensure that all children receive an adequate education, without addressing the economic forces outside of schools they will not be sufficient. Rothstein, a liberal, and Anyon, a radical, both conclude that school reform is necessary but insufficient to reduce the achievement gaps without broader social and economic policies aimed at addressing the pernicious effect of poverty.

Federal Involvement in Education

By the early 1990s, it was still unclear as to whether school reforms would begin to produce some of the improvements they promised. In 1990, President G. H. W. Bush—with the support of the National Governor's Association—announced six national goals for U.S. education:

1. Goal 1: By the year 2000, all children will start school ready to learn.
2. Goal 2: By the year 2000, the high school graduation rate will increase to at least 90 percent.
3. Goal 3: By the year 2000, American students will leave grades 4, 8, and 12 having demonstrated competency in challenging subject matter, including English, mathematics, science, history, and geography, and every school in America will ensure that all students learn to use their minds well, so they may be prepared for responsible citizenship, further learning, and productive employment in our modern economy.
4. Goal 4: By the year 2000, U.S. students will be first in the world in mathematics and science achievement.
5. Goal 5: By the year 2000, every adult American will be literate and will possess the skills necessary to compete in a global economy and exercise the rights and responsibilities of citizenship.

6. Goal 6: By the year 2000, every school in America will be free of drugs and violence and will offer a disciplined environment conducive to learning. ("Text of Statement of Goals Adopted by the Governors," 1990, pp. 16–17)

Until 1993, President Bush's educational reform proposal *America 2000,* based on these national goals, was in the implementation stage. *America 2000* built on four related themes:

1. Creating better and more accountable schools for today's students;
2. Creating a New Generation of American Schools for tomorrow's students;
3. Transforming America into a nation of students; and
4. Making our communities places where learning will happen. (*America 2000,* 1991)

Within each of the objectives, *America 2000* proposed a number of specific goals:

- Creating better and more accountable schools for today's students:
   1. World Class Standards in Five Core Subjects (English, mathematics, science, history, and geography).
   2. A system of voluntary national examinations.
   3. Schools as the site of reform.
   4. Providing and promoting school choice.
   5. Promoting outstanding leadership by teachers and principals.
- Creating a New Generation of American Schools for tomorrow's students:
   1. The development of Research and Development teams, funded by the business community, to develop these schools.
   2. The creation of at least 535 New American Schools that "break the mold" of existing school designs.
   3. The development of leadership at all levels, federal, state, and local.
   4. The commitment of families and children devoted to learning.
- Transforming America into a nation of students:
   1. Strengthening the nation's education effort for yesterday's students, today's workers.
   2. Establishing standards for job skills and knowledge.
   3. Creating business and community skill clinics.
   4. Enhancing job training opportunities.
   5. Mobilizing a "nation of students," by transforming a "Nation at Risk" into a "Nation of Students."
- Making our communities places where learning will happen:
   1. Developing greater parental involvement.
   2. Enhancing program effectiveness for children and communities.

When President Clinton was elected in November 1992, he already had a great deal of experience as an educational reformer. As Governor of Arkansas, he led a statewide campaign for teacher accountability, higher academic standards for students, and public school choice. In the late 1980s, he was Chair of the National Governor's Association and led the governors in establishing a national agenda for educational improvement. As president, Clinton promised to revitalize education and to pay close attention to issues of equity and community service. To this end, he initiated legislation for national service and legislation that would make college student loans easier to obtain and at a lower interest level. His *Goals 2000* bill formally recognized the national goals and provided a framework for what is referred to as "systemic" reform. *Systemic reform* is the coordination of reform efforts at the local, state, and federal levels. It is top-down support for bottom-up reform. An important component to systemic reform is the creation of national standards; panels of experts are currently creating content standards, performance standards, and new forms of assessment. A key issue in the development of national standards is the degree to which government is responsible for providing students with equal opportunities to learn if they are to be held to high standards. The reauthorization of the Elementary and Secondary Education Act provided an opportunity for the Clinton administration to fulfill its promise for greater education equity because the ESEA is the federal government's largest compensatory education program.

Goals 2000: Building on a Decade of Reform

Goals 2000 was a direct outgrowth of the state-led education reform agenda of the 1980s, which included increasing high school graduation requirements, particularly in math and science, instituting statewide testing programs, offering more Advanced Placement courses, promoting the use of technology in the classroom, and instituting new teacher evaluation programs.

Unlike the piecemeal approach favored during the Reagan-Bush years, the systemic approach to educational reform was comprehensive and focused on coordinating state policy with restructured governance. The objective of systemic reform was to create coherent educational policy. Systemic reform gave the Clinton educational agenda a set of organizing principles that were unique in U.S. educational history. Supporters of systemic reform like to describe it as "top-down support for bottom-up reform." By creating a coherent plan for reform, the Clinton administration had been unusually successful in winning bipartisan support prior to the November 1994 elections. This support resulted in the passage of several bills, including Direct Government Student Loans, National Service, the Safe Schools Act, the reauthorization of the Office of Educational Research and Improvement, the School-to-Work Opportunities Act of 1994, the Improving America's Schools Act of 1993, and the overall reauthorization of the Elementary and Secondary Education Act.

The key intellectual element of the administration's effort was *Goals 2000.* This law provides the framework of reform that shaped the educational ethos of the Clinton administration. Title I codified the original six National Education Goals concerning school readiness, school completion, student academic achievement, leadership in math and science, adult literacy, and safe and drug-free schools, and added two new goals related to parental participation and professional development. Title II established the National Education Goals Panel, which built public support for the goals, reported on the nation's progress on meeting the goals, and reviewed the voluntary national content, student performance, and voluntary learning standards. Title III provided a state grant program to support, accelerate, and sustain state and local education improvement efforts. Title IV established a new program to create parent information and resource centers. Title V created a National Skills Board to serve as a catalyst in stimulating the development and adoption of a voluntary national system of occupational skills standards. Rather than seeing the federal government as an educational safety net, the authors of *Goals 2000* saw the federal government, despite the rhetoric of volunteerism, as crafting, shaping, and, to some degree, controlling education throughout the 50 states. There can be little doubt that issues of school autonomy and authority have been dramatically altered by the passage of the bill.

Borman and colleagues (1996) provided a comprehensive sociological analysis of *Goals 2000* in the following areas: (1) systemic reform; (2) national standards for content and performance; (3) opportunity-to-learn standards; (4) school-to-work standards; (5) school, parent, and community support; (6) professional development; (7) safe, disciplined, and drug-free schools; and (8) implications of the *Goals 2000* legislation. The authors indicated that although there have been some significant gains in each of the areas, *Goals 2000* is insufficient to provide significant systemic reform of U.S. schools. As sociologists of education, the authors concluded that systemic reform requires significant reforms outside of the educational context, which federal legislation has not mandated.

The bulk of educational reforms with respect to standards and assessments were initiated at the state level. By the end of the decade, 48 states had tested their students, 40 states had standards in all core subjects, and many states increased standards for teachers ("Text of Statement of Goals Adopted by the Governors," 1999, p. 5). Assessments to measure achievement continue to be controversial (pp. 11, 15–17). What is clear is that the 1990s became defined as the decade of standards, often imposed top-down by federal mandates and state initiatives. While the educational reforms implemented by President Clinton are significant, we believe that genuine reform must include issues of teacher empowerment, diversity, and creating schools that are communities. In the final section, we will propose a more systematic approach to educational reform.

No Child Left Behind

The *No Child Left Behind Act (NCLB)* is a landmark and controversial piece of legislation that may have far-reaching consequences for education in the United States. Already there is talk of spreading similar accountability efforts to higher education in the next reauthorization of the Higher Education Act. And, of course, state governments have been busily pushing accountability requirements for K–12 and higher education for years now. No Child Left Behind is the centerpiece of President George W. Bush's educational policy. A logical progression of the standards movement initiated in 1983 by *A Nation at Risk* and in federal legislation under Presidents G. H. W. Bush *(America 2000)* and W. J. Clinton *(Goals 2000),* NCLB is the most comprehensive federal legislation governing state and local educational policies in U.S. history.

No Child Left Behind represented a logical extension of a standards movement that tossed the left's critique of U.S. education back on itself. Based on the critique that U.S. education has historically underserved low-income and minority children through curriculum tracking, poor instruction, and low-quality teachers in urban schools, NCLB mandates the uniform standards for all students in order to reduce and eventually eliminate the social class and race achievement gap by 2014.

The key components of NCLB are:

- Annual testing is required of students in grades 3 through 8 in reading and math plus at least one test in grades 10 through 12; science testing to follow. Graduation rates are used as a secondary indicator for high schools.
- States and districts are required to report school-by-school data on student test performance, broken out by whether the student is African American, Hispanic American, Native American, Asian American, white non-Hispanic, special education, limited english proficiency (LEP), and/or low income.
- States must set adequate yearly progress (AYP) goals for each school. In order to meet AYP, not only must each subgroup make progress in each year in each grade in each subject but there must also be 95 percent participation of each subgroup as well. The increments in AYP should be arranged so that 100 percent of students reach proficiency by 2014.
- Schools that don't meet AYP for two years are labeled "In Need of Improvement" (INOI). Initially, this means that schools must offer students the option to go to another public school and/or to receive federally funded tutoring. Funds would also be made available for teacher professional development. In the absence of meeting future AYP targets, schools would be subject to "restructuring" (firing teachers and principal; state takeover; private company takeover; etc.).
- Schools must have "highly qualified" teachers for the "core academic subjects" (English, reading or language arts, math, science, foreign languages, civics and government, economics, arts, history and geography) by 2005–2006.

Advocates of NCLB, including progressive organizations such as the Education Trust, argue that its annual testing and disaggregation requirements will force states to ensure that low-income students who continue to lag far behind higher-income students will meet the same standards, and thus reduce the achievement gap by 2014. Critics from both the academic and political worlds argue that however noble the goal of eliminating the achievement gap, NCLB does not provide sufficient funds to improve failing schools and, more importantly, is heavy on punishment and light on building school capacity. Liberal and radical critics argue that NCLB fails to acknowledge the social and economic foundation of unequal schooling and is a backdoor to the implementation of publicly funded school vouchers and the dismantling of public education in the United States. Finally, assessment experts argue that since the types of tests and definitions of adequate yearly progress vary by state, there is no uniform definition of "proficiency," and since the assessments evaluate schools rather than students, schools with high mobility rates are punished for such a high turnover, most of the time outside of their control. In addition, because the assessments are based on a zero-sum definition of proficiency rather than a value-added one, schools whose students show significant progress but are still below proficiency are labeled as failures rather than rewarded for their progress.

Conclusion

Educational reform in the United States from the 1980s to 2005 has emphasized the excellence side of the excellence and equity equation. Although federal, state, and local reforms have resulted in some improvement in achievement, critics (Berliner & Biddle, 1995) have pointed out that the U.S. educational system was never as problematic as its conservative critics suggested. They suggest that the real problem in U.S. education has been, and continues to be, that it works exceptionally well for children from higher socioeconomic backgrounds and exceptionally poorly for those from lower socioeconomic backgrounds. Despite the efforts of school choice and charter school programs to address these inequalities, particularly those in urban schools, the available evidence does not overwhelmingly support the claims of their advocates for a reduction in educational inequality. As the nation moves further into the new millennium, educational equity needs to be put back on the front burner of educational reform.

A Theory of Educational Problems and Reforms

In Chapters 1 and 2, we examined a number of pressing educational problems and the ways in which conservatives, liberals, and radicals defined and approached them. Throughout the book, we have looked at how anthropologists, historians, philosophers, political scientists, sociologists, and educators have analyzed a variety of issues and problems.

For the past decade, the dominant political definition of educational problems has been a conservative one, with the crisis in education defined in terms of the decline of standards and authority, and the putative mediocrity of U.S. schools and students. From the *Nation at Risk* report in 1983 through President Clinton's educational reform proposal *Goals 2000* in 1994 and G. W. Bush's No Child Left Behind, the question of how to improve schools has centered on definitions of academic excellence. Although we certainly believe there is some merit to the conservative claims about the need to raise standards for all U.S. students, the preoccupation with excellence has unfortunately obscured other significant educational problems, most particularly those related to issues of equity. Despite NCLB's emphasis on reducing the achievement gaps, equity still has been less important than raising standards.

Furthermore, the emphasis on standards has defined educational problems narrowly, looking primarily on the intellectual and skills function of schooling to the exclusion of the social and psychological functions. Schools, in addition to teaching children skills and knowledge, also should provide students from all backgrounds the opportunity to succeed in U.S. society, as well as to develop their individual potential. The Deweyan conception that schools should have integrative, developmental, and egalitarian functions has been lost in the past decade, with the latter two almost fully overlooked.

Thus, school improvement ought to be aimed at all three aspects of schooling. In the *integrative realm,* schools do need to improve their effectiveness in teaching basic skills and knowledge. Although the conservative claim that the decline in educational standards is the cause of U.S. economic decline is overstated, the nation's students too often graduate from high school without the requisite skills or knowledge for postsecondary education. In part, this is due to the erosion of the academic function of schooling in the twentieth century and the belief that all students cannot handle an academically rigorous curriculum. On the one hand, to the extent that curriculum tracking and ability grouping has limited access to an academic curriculum to working class and nonwhite students, the erosion of standards has been significantly undemocratic.

On the other hand, since academic standards and performance appear to have declined across social class, race, gender, and ethnic lines, the problem of mediocrity is a problem for U.S. education in general.

Where we part company with conservatives is with regard to their preoccupation with standards as the most significant educational problem and with their emphasis on academic standards as either ends in themselves or as they relate to technological and economic imperatives. The reason a society should want a literate and skilled citizenry is not just because these traits are necessary for the economic system. They are also, as Dewey argued, the cornerstone of a democracy, where intelligent and informed citizens take an active role in their community. Thus, education is not an end in and of itself but is instrumental in the life of a democratic society.

In the *developmental realm,* schools need to become more humane institutions where students develop as complete human beings. The conservative emphasis on academic standards and the life of the mind is too shortsighted. Although the life of the mind is important, so too is the life of the heart. Schools need to emphasize, as well, values such as caring, compassion, and cooperation, as feminist educators have correctly pointed out (Laird, 1989; Noddings, 1984). Moreover, schools ought to be places that nurture the creative and spiritual (spiritual need not connote religious) lives of children and enable them to develop a thirst for active learning and creative endeavor. In far too many of this nation's schools, student creativity and imagination is stifled rather than developed.

What is wrong with U.S. schools in this regard is not new. It has been the subject of criticism from Dewey's progressive call for child-centered schools that would emphasize community and development, to the romantic progressive critiques of schooling in the 1960s as authoritarian and stifling, to current calls for educational reform from a variety of individuals and groups. All of these emphasize the need to create schools to educate children in all aspects of life—the social, psychological, emotional, moral, and creative—not just the intellectual. These efforts have included feminist educators with their concern with caring and cooperation, holistic educators with their concern for creative and spiritual dimensions, radical educators with their concern with transformative and liberating dimensions, and progressive educators with their concern for community, democracy, and the need to connect students' lives to the curriculum. These educators encompass both the liberal and radical political spectrum and continue to define educational problems more broadly than do conservatives, and to define solutions that are aimed at making schools places where children want to be.

Perhaps the most overlooked aspect of schooling during the past decade of conservative ascendancy has been the *egalitarian realm* of schooling. Although many of the reports on the crisis in education have stressed the need to balance equity and excellence, the role of schooling in providing equality of opportunity and possibilities for social mobility has taken a backseat. As we argued in Chapters 8 and 9, inequalities of educational opportunity and achievement have remained persistent problems. Jonathan Kozol, in his book *Savage Inequalities* (1991), pointed to the profound inequalities in funding between schools in poor urban areas and affluent suburban districts. In a muckraking style, Kozol placed the issue of equity back on the nation's front burner and demonstrated how current conditions belie the democratic and egalitarian ethos of U.S. schooling.

In a report on Kozol's book, *Time Magazine* (October 14, 1991) chronicled the political controversies over unequal funding of public schools based on property taxes. Although many child advocacy groups have called for the elimination of property taxes in educational financing because they are an advantage to affluent neighborhoods with higher property values, there is often strong opposition from parents in affluent neighborhoods against a "Robin Hood" plan, which would redistribute funds from affluent to poor districts. Kozol, who is interviewed in the article, stated that it is not that affluent parents do not care in the abstract about poor children, but that in the concrete they care more about giving their own children the best education they can afford. They believe that their tax dollars should support their own schools and that redistribution would lead to across-the-board mediocrity.

Although these conflicts point to the sharp divisions and perhaps ambivalence Americans feel about equity issues, they also point out the difficulty of ameliorating problems of educational inequality. Nonetheless, the fact seems clear that in the twenty-first century, the divisions between rich and poor and in the schooling they receive is becoming more glaring than ever. The solutions to these problems will not be easy, and certainly cannot be addressed through school reform alone, but it is apparent that the issue of equity has been relegated to the back burner for too long. Thus, efforts at school improvement must consider equity issues as central to their agenda.

What we are suggesting is that educational reform needs to be aimed at creating schools that teach students the basic skills and knowledge necessary in a technological society—where students have the opportunity to develop their emotional, spiritual, moral, and creative lives; where concern and respect for others is a guiding principle; where caring, cooperation, and community are stressed; where students from different social classes, races, genders, and ethnic groups have equality of opportunity; and where inequalities of class, race, gender, and ethnicity are substantially reduced. These goals, which have been the cornerstone of progressive education for almost a century, are goals that progressives (both liberals and radicals) have too often felt obliged to apologize for, as they have been viewed as either politically naive or utopian. They are neither, although they certainly will be difficult to achieve.

At the beginning of this chapter, we discussed some effective teachers and suggested that effective teaching is necessary but not sufficient to solve educational problems. Without reforms aimed at societal problems, many educational dilemmas will remain unsolved. At the school level, unless schools are restructured to support good teaching and learning, teachers will continue to swim upstream against the current of school improvement.

There are, however, examples of schools that are succeeding. Central Park East Secondary School (CPESS) is a school in East Harlem, which is part of the Center for Collaborative Education (CCE) in New York City. The Center consists of elementary, middle, and high schools and is affiliated with the Coalition for Essential Schools. CPESS is a progressive urban public secondary school that subscribes to the CCE's 12 principles of education:

1. Schools that are small and personalized in size
2. A unified course of study for all students

3. A focus on helping young people use their minds well
4. An in-depth, intradisciplinary curriculum respectful of the diverse heritages that encompass U.S. society
5. Active learning with student-as-worker/student-as-citizen and teacher-as-coach
6. Student evaluation by performance-based assessment methods
7. A school tone of unanxious expectation, trust, and decency
8. Family involvement, trust, and respect
9. Collaborative decision making and governance
10. Choice
11. Racial, ethnic, economic, and intellectual diversity
12. Budget allocations targeting time for collective planning

Under the leadership of Deborah Meier until the late 1990s and a committed and talented faculty, CPESS provided an alternative to the failing comprehensive high schools for urban students. Fine (1991) used CPESS to demonstrate the possibilities for change and described it "as an example of what can be" (p. 215). Unfortunately, there is reason to believe that since Meier's departure, the school has gone downhill. Nonetheless, many of its successful features are now part of the small schools movement operated by New Visions for Public Schools in New York City and funded by the Gates Foundation, which has shown promise.

David Berliner and Bruce Biddle (1995, pp. 282–336), two eminent educational researchers, outlined 10 principles toward the improvement of education consistent with our views of educational reform:

1. Schooling in the United States can be improved by according parents more dignity and their children more hope.
2. Schooling in the United States can be improved by making certain that all schools have funds needed to provide a decent education for their students. This will require more fairness in school funding.
3. Schooling in the United States can be improved by reducing the size of the nation's largest schools.
4. Schooling in the United States can be improved by enlarging the goals of the curricula. This will require thoughtful learning environments where the emphasis is on skills needed for membership in a democratic society.
5. Schooling in the United States can be improved by adopting innovative teaching methods that serve enlarged curricular aims.
6. Schooling in the United States can be improved by adjusting the content of the curriculum. This will require deemphasizing the tie between schooling and employment and by expanding curricula tied to the productive use of leisure.
7. Schooling in the United States can be improved by rethinking and redesigning the system for evaluating student achievement.
8. Schooling in the United States can be improved by changing the ways in which schools manage heterogeneity. This change will mean abandoning the age-graded classroom and finding alternatives for ability groups and tracks.
9. Schooling in the United States can be improved by strengthening the ties between communities and their schools. Such ties can be promoted through programs that

encourage more active roles for parents, more contacts between parents and teachers, and expanded visions for the responsibilities of schools.

10. Schooling in the United States can be improved by strengthening the professional status of teachers and other educators.

We began this book with the conviction that the foundations perspective (i.e., the use of the politics, history, sociology, and philosophy of education) is an important tool in understanding and solving educational problems. Throughout the book, through text and readings, we have provided an analysis of many educational problems and a look at some of the proposed solutions. We end it with the conviction that teachers can make a difference, that schools can and must be restructured, and that the types of reforms discussed here are possible. They will not happen, however, unless people make them happen. School improvement is thus a political act. As prospective teachers and teachers, you must be a part of the ongoing struggle to improve this nation's schools. As Maxine Greene (1988, p. 23) stated:

> [I am] not the first to try to reawaken the consciousness of possibility . . . or to seek a vision of education that brings together the need for wide-awakeness with the hunger for community, the desire to know with the wish to understand, the desire to feel with the passion to see. I am aware of the ambivalences with respect to equality and justice as well. Fundamentally, perhaps, I am conscious of the tragic dimension in every human life. Tragedy, however, discloses and challenges; often it provides images of men and women on the verge. We may have reached a moment in our history when teaching and learning, if they are to happen meaningfully, must happen on the verge. Confronting a void, confronting nothingness, we may be able to empower the young to create and re-create a common world—and, in cherishing it, in renewing it, discover what it signifies to be free.

We believe that as teachers, you will have the opportunity to contribute to the improvement of this nation's schools. As we have attempted to indicate throughout this book, solutions to educational problems are by no means easy, as the problems are complex and multidimensional. Teachers, alone, will not solve these problems. However, they must be part of the solution. We encourage you to accept the challenge.

The following articles examine issues relating to educational reform and school improvement. The first article, "The Politics of School Choice," written by sociologists Jeanne M. Powers and Peter W. Cookson, Jr., reviews the empirical evidence on school choice in the 1990s and its effect on reducing educational inequality, especially for low-income students.

The second article, "Reinventing Teaching," written by educator Deborah Meier, analyzes the changes that will be required in schools to assure that good teaching can take place. Based on her ground-breaking work as principal of Central Park East Secondary School in East Harlem, New York City, Meier proposes significant changes in the structure of schools and underscores the importance of good teaching.

The third article, "A Level Playing Field" by journalist Catherine Gewertz, examines the effects of the historic New Jersey *Abbott* v. *Burke* school equity decision on schools in that state. *Abbott* v. *Burke* was named as one of the most important state court decisions in the last 50 years of the twentieth century.

The Politics of School Choice Research

Fact, Fiction, and Statistics

JEANNE M. POWERS

PETER W. COOKSON, JR.

For most educational reformers, statistical analyses are an afterthought; a reading program is evaluated years after its implementation, school-based management is examined after the reform has lost its momentum, a desegregation plan is researched a decade after students have been bused. Data wars are usually academic skirmishes, professional arrows flung across academic journals with little or no policy or political impact. This is not the case with school choice. The deregulation of public education stirs deep passions often fueled by data analyses that more resemble manifestos than policy memorandums or research reports. Within this context, school choice is best understood as a social movement (Cookson, 1994; Henig, 1994), led by politicians, policy advocates, and public personalities rather than educators and the traditional allies of public education. School choice encompasses a wide range of policies, programs, and ways of organizing schooling ranging from alternative schools to charter schools and voucher programs. The latest—and perhaps most prominent—iteration of proposals for increased choice in schooling is best characterized as market-driven choice programs.

Although the choice debate cannot easily be broken into two sides of heroes and villains or black hats and white hats, it can be roughly divided into two policy camps. On the one hand is a loose coalition of business groups, market theorists, policy advocates, religious groups, and entrepreneurs who believe that the public school establishment is monolithic, rigid, unaccountable, and failing America's children. For members of this coalition, market-driven choice will usher in a series of positive changes at the individual and institutional levels (Chubb & Moe, 1990; Finn, Manno, Bierlein, & Vanourek, 1997; Little Hoover Commission, 1996; Moe, 1995). Students and parents, unhappy with the existing system of public education—which is often characterized as a monopoly—will not only be more satisfied with chosen schools, but students will also experience gains in academic achievement (Chubb, 1988; Viteritti, 1996). Likewise, choice programs will radically change the organization of schooling by essentially forcing schools to reform; schools will improve out of necessity because they will have to compete for students. Those schools that do not improve will lose clients as parents and students "vote with their feet," and the most recalcitrant schools will ultimately be forced "out of business." Thus, the competition and entrepreneurship unleashed by "uncompromised" market-driven choice plans will result in institutional changes in schooling that will ultimately enhance student achievement; the end result will be a system of streamlined and efficient schools that effectively serve their consumers (Moe, 1995; Peterson & Noyes, 1996).

On the other hand is the public school establishment—teachers' unions, many school boards, school administrators, some policy advocates, liberal foundations, and academics—who see public education as the cornerstone of democracy and are less sanguine about the effects of market-driven choice programs on public schooling. Although they often agree that parents and students are more satisfied with chosen schools, they also note that the evidence for achievement gains as a result of choice is less clear. For some, what are at best minimal achievement gains may come at the cost of increasing stratification within the educational system; the positive effects of participating in choice programs for individual students have to be balanced against the possible negative effects of choice on a school district

From Jeanne M. Powers and Peter W. Cookson, Jr., "The Politics of School Choice Research: Fact, Fiction, and Statistics," January and March, 1999, *Educational Policy, 13* (1 and 2), pp. 104–122. Copyright © 1999 Corwin Press, Inc. Reprinted by permission of Corwin Press.

(Witte, 1996a). Many of these analysts also question the attendant claims that the public schools are too bureaucratic and/or have a monopoly on education (e.g., Cookson, 1994, pp. 23–26). Moreover, they note that although the increased options for parents as a result of choice are positive, they also see choice as one policy that can promote change within schools but will not by itself solve the problems of public schooling. Similarly, in instances where the expansion of choice has been accompanied by other reforms, it is difficult to identify clear causal links between choice and school improvement. For these observers, it is not choice per se that is important; the critical factor in determining whether or not a choice program works is how it is implemented in a particular setting. In truth, both sides tend to oversimplify and we should not underestimate the strength of vested interest in shaping the research about choice.

These observations are only meant to set the scene for this article. Our task is not to analyze in depth choice as a political movement but to examine the research studies that have been pivotal in shaping the debate. We aim to touch on those points that are most critical in shaping scholarly perception and public awareness. Obviously, in a short article such as this we can only highlight some of the major studies that have influenced the school choice debate. It should also be pointed out that the school choice literature is not strong, although choice studies have become more and more prevalent and sophisticated; there may be a time when we can draw some genuine conclusions from the research.

From Alum Rock to Chubb and Moe

The earliest systematic attempt to evaluate school choice occurred in Alum Rock, California. This experiment was funded by the federal government as a way of determining the educational and social effects a voucher plan would have on a school system (Bridge & Blackman, 1978). Conducted by the Rand Corporation, the study revealed that socially advantaged families were better informed about school choice options, though over time information was shared more broadly in the community. Following the Alum Rock study, there was research on magnet schools as a form of choice (Blank, 1989; Metz, 1986). This line of research, however, did not develop into a robust body of findings. In the mid-1980s, research was conducted by the Manhattan Institute concerning choice in East Harlem, New York City (Domanico, 1989; Fliegel,

1990). Domanico and Fliegel examined achievement data from District 4 and found that there was a high correlation between the introduction of school choice and improvement in reading and math scores. These data were echoed at the 1989 White House workshop on choice and education. The workshop issued a report, "Improving Schools and Empowering Parents: Choice in American Education" (Paulu, 1989). That report made claims for school choice including higher reading and math scores, lower rates of school violence, and higher attendance rates. Much of this research was nonsystematic and therefore the results are questionable (Cookson, 1994).

These analyses paralleled the work of James Coleman and his associates (Coleman & Hoffer, 1987; Coleman, Hoffer, & Kilgore, 1982) who, after analyzing the "High School and Beyond" data set, claimed that private schools are dramatically more effective than public schools in producing achievement even when controlling for the class backgrounds of students. In particular, Coleman and his associates claimed that Catholic education was academically superior to public education. This research paved the way for choice advocates who argue that the private sector is more educationally effective than the public sector. Not incidentally, this line of argument has provided intellectual support to the voucher movement.

Perhaps a defining moment in the choice debate came with the publication of John E. Chubb and Terry M. Moe's *Politics, Markets and America's Schools* (1990). In this book, the authors make large claims concerning the superiority of market-sensitive schools (i.e., private) to state-controlled schools (i.e., public). This book, which was supported by the Brookings Institution and the Olin Foundation, has had a huge impact. Although subsequently Chubb and Moe's research has been widely critiqued (Cookson, 1994; Henig, 1994), over the years it has provided—and continues to provide—considerable political ammunition for those who believe that markets are superior to democracy in creating more just and more productive school systems (Viteritti, 1996).

In recent years, there have been a steadily increasing number of studies about choice programs that allow us to draw some preliminary conclusions. This growing body of empirical work includes, but is not limited to, two edited collections of analyses of choice programs, one on privately funded voucher programs (Moe, 1995) and the other on publicly funded choice programs ranging from local elementary schools to national college-level programs (Fuller, Elmore, & Orfield, 1996; see also Fowler, 1996; Greene, Peterson, & Du, 1997; Greene, Howell, & Peterson, 1997; Rofes, 1998; Rouse, 1998, in press). However, it should also be noted that for the most part, these more recent studies share the preoccupation with educational outcomes that characterize earlier studies of school choice. Despite the often sweeping claims that have been made about the effect of choice on school systems, few analyses of choice programs have systematically examined how much, if at all, choice programs can be linked to broader processes of school reform.

Recent Empirical Evidence: Overview of Samples and Methodologies

As noted above, the central questions of most choice studies focus on the effect of choice on families and students: What are the characteristics of families participating in choice programs, and how does participating in a choice program affect parent and student satisfaction and/or student achievement? Methodologically, most empirical studies of choice programs have used survey research.[1] One of the earliest of these was John Witte's evaluation of the Milwaukee Parental Choice Program (MPCP); his survey has since become a model for subsequent evaluations of other voucher programs (Beales & Wahl, 1995; Heise, Colburn, & Lamberti, 1995; Martinez, Godwin, & Kemerer, 1995). In some cases, survey research is combined with other sources of data such as case studies of schools (Witte, 1996a[2]), information from student transcripts (Witte, 1996a), and parental requests to transfer into a district's magnet school system (Henig, 1996).

Most of these studies compare participating students with one or more control groups: students who chose to participate in the program but were not admitted because of space limitations (Greene, Howell, & Peterson, 1997; Greene, Peterson, & Du, 1997; Heise et al., 1995), public school students that participate in a public school choice program (Martinez et al., 1995), nonchoosers who remain in the public school system (Hill, 1995; Martinez et al., 1995, 1996; Wells, 1996; Witte, 1996a), and students participating in other choice programs (Beales & Wahl, 1995; Martinez et al., 1995). A handful of studies have examined student attrition from choice programs (Beales & Wahl, 1995; Greene, Howell, & Peterson, 1997; Wells, 1996; Witte, 1996a). Analyses of survey results range from univariate analyses comparing results for choice participants

and the control group on some combination of background variables (e.g., race and parental education), responses to survey questions, achievement test scores, and graduation rates (Beales & Wahl, 1995; Greene, Howell, & Peterson, 1997; Heise et al., 1995; Hill, 1995) to multivariate analyses with participation in a choice program (Martinez et al., 1995, 1996) or achievement (Greene, Peterson, Du, Boeger, & Frazier, 1996; Greene, Peterson, & Du, 1997; Rouse, 1997, 1998; Witte, 1996a) as the dependent variable. In addition to the studies described above, a few qualitative studies combine data from interviews with school superintendents and other school personnel with information gleaned from document analyses to examine how choice programs have affected educational systems at the district level (Fowler, 1996; Jimerson, 1998; Rofes, 1998).

What Do We Know about Market-Driven Choice?

Who Is Participating?

Because market-driven choice has been highly touted as an answer to the educational crisis in inner-city schools (Moe, 1995), we examine the evidence closely in this area and assess whether these programs fulfill claims associated with market-driven choice in practice. Market-driven choice is premised on a relatively simple idea: The market model is the best way to reform the educational system because it introduces principles such as competition and accountability into how schools are organized; this also entails revisioning the recipients of the "products" of schooling—parents and students—as consumers. Although market-driven choice is certainly not new, it has been extraordinarily resilient. For more than 15 years, it has been a recurrent theme in educational policy making at the national, state, and local levels. Examples of market-driven choice include voucher programs, charter schools, and privatization; however, it should also be noted that it is often difficult to draw a clear boundary between market-driven choice and other forms of choice because an extraordinary array of programs have been linked to market-driven choice in political arguments for the expansion of choice programs (Henig, 1994). Likewise, familiar arguments for school reform, such as civil rights-influenced arguments for increasing equity within the school system, have also been used by advocates across the political spectrum to promote market-driven choice (Alves & Willie, 1987). Market-driven school reformers want nothing less than to "break the mold" of public education and replace it with a "leaner and meaner" system of quasi-public and private schools responsive to consumers.

Perhaps the most consistent effect of market-driven choice programs across the studies described below is that choice programs tend to have the effect of increasing stratification to one degree or another within school districts. This stratifying effect of choice has even been found in programs that specifically target low-income families. Although choice programs have been successful at providing otherwise unavailable educational opportunities to this population in the short term, the families that take advantage of these programs also tend to be the most advantaged within that group—choosers tend to come from smaller and more highly educated families than nonchoosers (Beales & Wahl, 1995; Heise et al., 1995[3]; Martinez et al., 1995, 1996; Wells, 1996; Witte, 1996a). In some instances, low-income choice families also tended to be advantaged in terms of employment (Wells, 1996) and income (Heise et al., 1995).[4]

The significance of these findings has been the subject of varying interpretations. Moe (1995) argues that although there is evidence of a "skimming effect" in choice programs, it is far less than the one embedded within the existing public school system where middle-class families are able to choose the best schools because they have more opportunities for geographic mobility. Moreover, Moe also implies that if choice programs provide increased educational options for some low-income families and reduce the overall degree of stratification, then the skimming effect of choice programs, although regrettable, is acceptable. Likewise, skimming can be mitigated by program design; however, the trade-off may be an undesirable increase in administrative rules and bureaucracy. In contrast, Fuller and Elmore (1996) argue that the current evidence is inconclusive regarding whether this stratification effect can be attributed to program design or whether it is a general outcome of choice programs. However, they find it significant that these patterns are found across choice programs—including those specifically targeted to economically disadvantaged families. For Fuller and Elmore, these findings suggest the need for increased government involvement in the operation of choice programs, which they note is at odds with the calls for deregulation that often accompany choice proposals (see also Henig, 1994).

In many of the choice programs described above, 50% or more of the participants are minority students, which is not surprising given the demographics of the inner cities in which they are located (Hill, 1995; Martinez et al., 1995, 1996; Witte, 1996a). However, a number of voucher programs award scholarships to students who are already attending private schools (Beales & Wahl, 1995; Greene, Howell, & Peterson, 1997; Heise et al., 1995). In two of these, there is a higher percentage of White participants in this population than the students transferring from public to private schools with vouchers (Greene, Howell, & Peterson, 1997; Heise et al., 1995).[5] From the available information, it is difficult to tell what impact these programs have on the racial composition of private schools. For example, although Beales and Wahl (1995) note that the Partners Advancing Values in Education (PAVE) program "makes it possible for proportionately more minority students to attend Catholic schools" than there would be without the program, the overall percentage of minority students in Milwaukee Catholic schools remains low—8% of the total Catholic school enrollment in 1993–94 (p. 48). Given that just under half of PAVE scholarships were awarded to White students and more than half—60%— of PAVE students attended Catholic schools in 1993–1994,[6] it is possible that PAVE could be increasing racial segregation in Milwaukee's private religious schools and particularly White flight to Catholic schools.

Choice parents tend to be more involved in their children's education than nonchoosers (Beales & Wahl, 1995; Martinez et al., 1996; Wells, 1996; Witte, 1996a); a few studies reported that choice parents also have higher educational expectations for their children (Martinez et al., 1995, 1996; Witte, 1996a).[7] There were less consistent patterns across choice programs on other characteristics of participants. For example, the MPCP participants tend to have lower preentry achievement scores than their public school counterparts (Witte, 1996a). In contrast, both public school and private school choosers in San Antonio had higher achievement test scores than nonchoosers—although the former is attributable to a performance-based admissions process (Martinez et al., 1995). Finally, the studies by Wells (1996) and Martinez et al. (1995) suggest that one important contrast that should be undertaken in any evaluation of choice programs—particularly in instances where choice is not required of all students but made available to a limited number of students—is that between choosers and nonchoosers. We need to know more about why families elect not to participate in choice programs.

Choice and Parental Satisfaction

Another consistent finding across studies of choice programs is that choice parents tend to be more satisfied with the educational experience offered their children (Beales & Wahl, 1995; Finn et al., 1997; Greene, Howell, & Peterson, 1997; Heise et al., 1995; Witte, 1996a). Likewise, a number of studies of voucher programs reported that choice parents also tend to be dissatisfied with public schools (Beales & Wahl, 1995; Heise et al., 1995). A few of these studies also provide a comparison group of public school parents to help place these particular findings in a broader context (Greene, Howell, & Peterson, 1997; Martinez et al., 1995; Witte, 1996a). In the latter two studies, choice parents reported being less satisfied with their children's prior schools than nonchoosing public school parents;[8] they were particularly dissatisfied with school discipline and how much their child was learning in public schools. Likewise, these parents also reported being much more satisfied with the private schools their children attended in addressing these key areas of concern.

Choice and Achievement

Presently, there is much debate but little conclusive evidence about the effect of choice on student achievement. Some studies suggest that choice students are outperforming their public school peers. For example, Beales and Wahl (1995) report that, on average, students participating in the Milwaukee PAVE program score higher on achievement tests than Milwaukee public school students. Likewise, Hill (1995) notes that students participating in the private voucher student-sponsorship program graduate from high school, take the SAT, and score higher on the SAT than New York City public high school students. However, we should also keep in mind that these are largely univariate comparisons of means and percentages, which make it difficult to definitively determine achievement effects of choice programs relative to other factors that also influence achievement, such as family background.

Similarly, in addition to evidence of achievement gains at individual charter schools based on a rise in the number of students performing above the national av-erage compared to previous tests, Finn et al. (1997) relate that both parents and students report "dramatic improvements" in students' academic performance as a result of their experiences with charter schools. Not only are these results consistent when the data are broken down by race and income level, but low-income students reported the highest achievement gains in charter schools. At the same time, given that the latter are self reported data, it is best understood and interpreted as perceptions of improved academic performance among participants rather than measured achievement gains. Finally, Martinez et al. (1996) report that participation in a selective multilingual public school choice program in San Antonio had a positive effect on students' math and reading scores after controlling for family background, prior test scores, and parental educational expectations (pp. 62–64). However, these results are based on only 1 year of test scores; it should also be noted that students who came from choosing families but were not admitted to the program also experienced a positive gain in test scores net of other factors.

One of the few evaluations of a choice program to collect detailed data on student achievement is John Witte's evaluation of MPCP. In operation since the fall of 1991, MPCP is one of two publicly funded voucher programs.[9] Over the course of five annual evaluations from 1991 to 1995, Witte and his colleagues have collected both qualitative and quantitative data on a wide range of outcomes of the program; however, his analysis of the effect of MPCP on achievement is the most highly contested of all his findings. Witte's data have been subsequently reanalyzed in separate analyses by Paul Peterson and Jay Greene and Cecilia Rouse. What is striking about the three analyses of the same data is the sharp divergence in results. Witte argues that the effect of choice on achievement has been inconsistent. In contrast, Greene and Peterson argue that MPCP has had significant long-term effects on student achievement; after 3 years in the program students gain on average 3 to 5 percentile points in reading and 5 to 12 percentile points in math (Greene et al., 1996, p. 4). Rouse's (in press) results fall somewhere in the middle. Although she found the effect of choice on reading scores to be inconsistent, she argues that being selected to attend a choice school increased students' math scores by 1.5 to 2.3 percentage points per year. Those students who actually attended choice schools demonstrated similar gains in math achievement scores.

Embedded in this apparent disagreement about the magnitude of the relationship between choice and achievement is a methodological debate about how to best assess the effects of choice. Although the often quite technical details of the debate are beyond the scope of this article, it boils down to two main points. First, what is the relevant control group with which to compare the academic performance of choice students? Should choice students be compared to other choosers who were not selected for the program or is it appropriate to compare them with Milwaukee Public School (MPS) students? Second, what is the appropriate method to control for student background characteristics?

Of the two, the former has been the most controversial. Witte argues that MPS students are the optimal control group; in contrast, Greene, Peterson, and their colleagues argue that the analysis should be limited to students who apply to the choice program because there are systematic differences between the MPS students and the choice students. For example, choice students were more likely to be Black or Hispanic, low income, from single-parent homes, and on welfare than the full sample of MPS students; however, it should be noted that on most of these characteristics the choice group and a sample of low-income MPS students also used by Witte as a comparison group are roughly comparable[10] (Witte, Thorn, Pritchard, & Clairborn, 1994). On the other hand, choice parents, and in particular mothers of choice students, tended to be more educated than both the low income and the full MPS samples.

It should also be noted that the sample employed by Greene and Peterson is not without problems. Greene and Peterson analyze the effect of choice on achievement using separate multiple regression models for the number of years of participation in the choice program; by 3 and 4 years, their samples consist of 309 and 108 students, respectively—choice participants and nonselected students combined.[11] Yet, these are also the years in the analysis that their conclusion—choice students are dramatically outperforming their peers—hinges on. Moreover, in their initial analysis, their results are hardly robust.[12] Nonetheless, they conclude that "the consistency of the estimated effects generated by the two analyses lends weight to the conclusion that enrolling in choice schools yields decidedly positive effects after a student's third and fourth years" (Greene et al., 1996, p. 11). In a subsequent analysis, Greene, Peterson, and Du (1997) reanalyze their data using a different technique to control

for background characteristics; although the coefficients for both reading and math are comparable to their previous results, the statistical significance increased substantially to conventionally accepted levels. To date, they have not substantively addressed the problems with their sample or with their model.

In contrast, Rouse (1998) differs with Witte in her method of controlling for student background characteristics. This comprises the second component of the methodological debate between these analysts, although it is considerably muted compared to the heated—and often public—exchanges between Peterson and Witte.[13] She argues that fixed-effect models are the optimal method for controlling for background characteristics including ability, whereas Witte controls for ability by including the previous year's test score in his models.[14] Using this analytical strategy, Rouse finds a positive and statistically significant effect of participating in the choice program; these results were consistent for both the sample of choosers only as well as a larger sample that includes MPS students.

Although in the analysis described above Rouse finds that choice schools on average outperform Milwaukee public schools, the results from a follow-up study suggest that aggregating the results for the Milwaukee public schools is problematic (Rouse, 1998). In this analysis, she divides the MPS schools into different types: regular attendance area schools, magnet schools, and "P-5" schools—attendance area schools that have smaller class sizes and receive additional funds from the state of Wisconsin. Rouse finds that the math achievement scores of students in the choice and P-5 schools increase at the same rate, which is higher than their peers attending magnet schools and the city-wide schools; moreover, the reading achievement scores of P-5 students increases faster than their peers attending the three other types of schools (pp. 14–15). Finally, Rouse turns her attention to why both choice and P-5 schools are outperforming other Milwaukee schools. Both choice and P-5 schools have substantially lower teacher-student ratios than either the regular attendance area schools and magnet schools. Because the achievement gains of choice students compared to all MPS students roughly parallels the achievement gains of students in MPS schools with low teacher-student ratios compared to those in schools with high teacher-student ratios, Rouse argues that there is indirect evidence that the observed achievement effects for math in choice schools may be partially attributable to lower class size (p. 17). Rouse's analysis underscores the need to look more carefully at the processes of schooling to understand what goes on within schools that may be driving achievement gains.

The Impact of Choice on School Districts and School Reform

As noted above, there are few systematic studies of the effects of school choice on school districts and broader processes of school reform. This is a significant gap in our knowledge about the effects of choice, particularly given the sweeping claims about the wonders of competition that often accompany calls for increased choice in schooling. Instead, what is available consists largely of anecdotal evidence. For example, both Peterson and Noyes (1997) and Witte (1996a) agree that the MPCP program has revitalized one of the private schools participating in the program, Bruce Guadalupe, which has had a positive impact on the surrounding community. Percy and Maier (1996) also note that in 1995, after the Wisconsin legislature expanded MPCP to include larger numbers of students and religious schools, the MPS board announced plans to revamp its school selection procedures to allow parents greater choice in selecting the schools their children will attend (p. 659). Likewise, in Cleveland, two private schools, the Hope schools, were formed in response to the voucher program, which may be seen as a positive outcome of the program to the extent that they offer parents increased educational options for their children. However, Witte (1996a) also speculates that MPCP may also have had a negative effect on the school district because choice parents tend to be more involved in their children's education than nonchoosing parents, which could mean that the district is in essence losing a group of parents that might otherwise start advocating for reform within the public schools.

However, there are a growing number of studies that give us glimmers of more definitive conclusions. In her study of the effects of the Minnesota choice program on rural school districts, Jimerson (1998) found that there were significant financial implications for districts strongly affected by the choice program through increasing or contracting enrollments. Districts that experienced a net gain in students were able to expand their educational and extracurricular programs, add additional staff, upgrade their technology, and decrease class sizes. Conversely, districts that experienced a decline in enrollments had to cut both programming and staff and increase class sizes. Moreover, districts that lost students also spent proportion-

ately more on special education (and thus less on regular education) and also tended to make up their losses in funding via an increase in local taxes through referendums. Jimerson argues that local residents in these latter districts were in essence subsidizing the negative consequences of the choice program for these districts and as a result—and ironically—experienced a loss of choice (Jimerson, 1998, p. 12).

In addition to the financial repercussions of choice, superintendents also reported other unintended consequences related to the tenets of accountability and competition embedded in the market model; however, they unfold in a far less straightforward manner than the model would imply. First, parents were using the threat of moving their children to another school to extract concessions from school districts that were not necessarily related to academic programming.[15] Second, the choice program certainly increased competition among school districts, which in theory is a positive outcome of market-driven choice. However, superintendents reported that the increased competition not only resulted in a loss of collegiality among their group but also that some of their group felt they had to spend more of their time and money on public relations and marketing their schools. Both of these examples suggest that accountability and competition in practice may not necessarily result in improvements in the academic quality of schools. In the case of the latter, competition appears to be diverting much needed resources from that goal—a troubling outcome of the market model.

Rofes's (1998) study of the impact of charter schools on school districts specifically addresses the effect of choice—here, charter schools—on processes of school reform. Not surprisingly, smaller (both urban and suburban) or rural school districts tend to experience the greatest impact from charter schools, whether in terms of district administrators' perception of the financial impact of charter schools or the degree that charter schools influenced reform within the school district (Rofes, 1998, p. 10). One of Rofes's more interesting findings was that, in general, school district personnel did not see charter schools as "educational laboratories" or sites where innovative educational programs could be generated and later transferred into traditional public schools. If anything, charter schools were seen primarily as providing a source of new ideas for educational management and governance.

According to Rofes, there are a number of barriers inhibiting this kind of exchange. Two are perhaps endemic to the early stages of any reform. First, many charter schools are still in the process of developing their curricula, which would preclude sharing ideas. This is compounded by the second. Charter school personnel often have little time—or inclination—to share innovations with other teachers and administrators. A third barrier might be understood as somewhat built into the charter school model. Because charter schools are often created outside of the control of school districts, charter schools may have hostile relationships with other schools in the school district and/or district administrators. This latter point is important because, as in Jimerson's (1998) study, it points to the possible negative effect of competition that we may be observing across different types of choice programs. To a certain extent, this amplifies her findings because it suggests that a breakdown of or a lack of collegiality as a result of competition can actually inhibit positive change (Rofes, 1998, p. 14).

Finally, some of Rofes's findings about charter schools parallel those of other researchers. For example, a number of the districts in his study had increased their own marketing and public relations efforts. As in Jimerson's study, many superintendents report spending an increasing amount of their time in this area, and in one case a school district hired a communications director (Rofes, 1998, p. 12). Once again, this raises questions about the degree that competition is stimulating change within school districts that is directed toward improving the academic component of schooling. Rofes's study also suggests that the increased choice via charter schools is allowing more active and vocal parents to opt out of traditional public schools rather than attempt to press for reform within their current schools. Many district administrators reported that these parents often try out charter schools and in many cases return to their former schools. Although some administrators saw charter schools as a way to relieve pressure on district schools, others, like Witte, saw the loss of these parents as potentially negatively affecting reform within district schools (Rofes, 1998, p. 7).

Conclusion

In July 1998, the *Wall Street Journal* published a study about the economist Milton Friedman. The story was about Friedman's early, vocal, and continuous support of vouchers. The title of the article was "The Next Big Free Market Thing." Presently, there are approximately 40 educational management organizations (EMOs)

traded on the New York Stock Exchange. This surge of corporate interest in deregulation, coupled with the recent Supreme Court decision regarding the appropriateness of public funds being given to private schools, indicates that public education as it has been known for more than 100 years is on the edge of becoming a system of quasi-public and private schools. These schools will be held together loosely by the demands of higher education, basic administrative regulations, and minimum standards of academic achievement.

Unlike most historic changes, however, the transition from a quasi-public system of education to a quasi-private system will be studied by all manner of investigators, serious and otherwise. As the title of this article suggests, separating fact from fiction and statistical findings from the extravagant claims of market theorists will not be an easy task. In essence, the politics of the school choice movement is a textbook case of how social science can be misused but also how it can be beneficially used; if the devil (or God) is in the details, social science can be of great service for looking below the surface of public debate and posturing. We hope that before privatization is embraced without question and at times without thought, enough good research will be generated to throw light across the opaque and uncharted waters of public school deregulation.

Notes

1. One of the rare qualitative studies of a choice program is Amy Stuart Wells's analysis of students in St. Louis that were affected by a voluntary school desegregation program that allowed inner-city students to transfer into suburban schools.
2. Witte (1996a) provides a summary of the main analyses presented in Witte et al. (1994) and Witte et al. (1995).
3. The latter study does not provide information on the family size of program participants.
4. Wells found that the parents of students participating in a voluntary desegregation program in St. Louis were more likely to be employed than nonchoosers and students who dropped out of the program, as well as more likely to have a job that took them out of the inner city. Likewise, in their study of the Golden Rule Program in Indianapolis, which targets half of its vouchers to families already in the private school system, Heise et al. (1995) found that these families tended to have higher incomes than those who transferred out of the public schools using the vouchers.
5. In the case of the Cleveland Scholarship and Tutoring Program, there is a statistically significant differ-

ence in the percentage of minority scholarship recipients already in private school and those that move from public to private schools (Greene, Howell, & Peterson, 1997, pp. 47, 61). Heise et al. (1995) do not provide tests of significance for this comparison in their analysis of the Golden Rule Program in Indianapolis. Likewise, Beale and Wahl (1995) report that 45% of PAVE scholarships in 1992–1993 were already attending private schools but do not provide a breakdown of these participants by race (p. 46).

6. Again, Scales and Wahl (1995) do not provide a breakdown of students who transfer from public to private schools as a result of the PAVE program by race and type of school.

7. Not all of the studies examined these characteristics of participants, making it harder to generalize across programs.

8. In Greene, Howell, and Peterson's (1997) evaluation of the Cleveland Scholarship and Tutoring Program, the comparison group are applicants to the program that either were not chosen for or did not participate in the program.

9. The second, the Cleveland Scholarship and Tutoring Program in Cleveland, began in January 1996.

10. Witte argues that the comparison between choice students and low-income MPS students is the most relevant because the full sample of MPS students contains high-income students who are less comparable to choice participants given the income restrictions on participation in MPCP.

11. There are three substantive problems with the Greene and Peterson analysis. First, their sample is quite small and the available evidence suggests that the sample of nonselected students may not be representative of this group (Rouse, 1998, in press; Witte, 1996b, 1997). Second, attrition from the program appears to have resulted in selection bias; both Rouse and Witte note that the students who remained with the program and therefore were included in the later models tended to be those who were doing better academically. Finally, their analysis and conclusions are highly dependent on their ability to model the random lottery process for selection into the program, and there are numerous places where there are possible mismatches (Rouse, 1998, in press; Witte, 1996b, 1997).

12. Using the commonly accepted standard for statistical significance ($p < .05$, using a two-tailed test), only the results for reading in the fourth year are significant. The significance levels for math do not even approach statistical significance at .16 and .25 for the third and fourth years, respectively (Greene et al., 1996, p. 32).

13. The fixed-effect methodology employed by Rouse, which controls for student characteristics that are time variant or that do not change over time, is driven by the assumption that selected students and unselected students (including MPS students) would have the same growth in test scores net of preexisting differences in ability before they applied to the program (Rouse, 1998, p. 25). In both this analysis and a subsequent analysis described below. Rouse does note, however, that in the case that choice students experience faster gains in test scores before applying to the choice program, this method will overestimate the effect of the choice program on achievement (Rouse, 1998, p. 9). At the same time, she argues that the available evidence would suggest that this is not the case and that the fixed-effect models are appropriate for the data. In contrast, one potential problem with Witte's approach—particularly with the models for the later years of the program—is that it would understate the effects of the choice program to the extent that a prior year's test scores are positively influenced by participation in the program (see also Davis, 1996; Fuller, 1997; Greene & Peterson, 1996a, 1996b; Peterson, 1997; Rouse, in press).

14. Jimerson notes this came up in a number of interviews but is largely anecdotal evidence and in need of further exploration. It is also unclear from Jimerson's analysis how widespread this phenomenon was, what range of demands these parents were making—the two examples cited were playing football and being named class valedictorian—and whether or not demands were met.

15. Rofes notes that this was particularly evident in states with strong or less restrictive charter laws that allow charter schools to be sponsored by people outside of the school district (Rofes, 1998, p. 12). Thus—and perhaps ironically—although sponsorship from outside the school system may encourage innovation, the laws governing charter schools in these states could institutionalize relationships that discourage diffusion.

References

Alves, M. J., & Willie, C. V. (1987). Controlled choice assignment: A new and more effective approach to school desegregation. *Urban Review, 19*(2), 67–87.

Beales, J. R., & Wahl, M. (1995). Private vouchers in Milwaukee: The PAVE program. In Terry M. Moe (Ed.), *Private vouchers* (pp. 41–73). Stanford, CA: Hoover Institution Press.

Blank, R. K. (1989). *Educational effects of magnet schools.* Madison: University of Wisconsin, National Center in Effective Secondary Schools, Wisconsin Center for Educational Research.

Bridge, R. G., & Blackman, J. (1978). *Family choice in American education: A study of alternatives in American education* (Vol. 4). Santa Monica, CA: RAND.

Chubb, J. E. (1988, Winter). Why the current wave of school reform will fail. *Public Interest, 90,* 28–49.

Chubb, J. E., & Moe, T. M. (1990). *Politics, markets and America's schools.* Washington, DC: Brookings Institution.

Coleman, J. S., & Hoffer, T. (1987). *Public and private high schools: The impact of communities.* New York: Basic Books.

Coleman, J. S., Hoffer, T., & Kilgore, S. (1982). *High school achievement: Public, Catholic, and private schools compared.* New York: Basic Books.

Cookson, P. W. Jr. (1994). *School choice: The struggle for the soul of American education.* New Haven, CT: Yale University Press.

Davis, B. (1996, October 11). Class warfare: Dueling professors have Milwaukee dazed over vouchers. *Wall Street Journal,* pp. Al, A7.

Domanico, R. (1989). *Model for choice: A report on Manhattan's District 4.* New York: Manhattan Institute Center for Educational Innovation.

Finn, C. E. Jr., Manno, B. V., Bierlein, L., & Vanourek, G. (1997, July). *Charter schools in action: Final report.* Washington, DC: Hudson Institute.

Fliegel, S. (1990). Creative non-compliance. In W. H. Clune & J. F. Witte (Eds.), *Choice and control in American education. Vol 2: The practice of choice, decentralization, and school restructuring* (pp. 199–216). New York: Falmer.

Fowler, F. C. (1996). Participation in Ohio's interdistrict open enrollment option: Exploring the supply-side of choice. *Educational Policy, 10*(4), 518–536.

Fuller, B., & Elmore, R. F. (1996). Empirical research on educational choice: What are the implications for policymakers? In B. Fuller, R. F. Elmore, & G. Orfield (Eds.), *Who chooses? Who loses? Culture, institutions and the unequal effects of school choice* (pp. 187–201). New York: Teachers College Press.

Fuller, B., Elmore, R. F., & Orfield, G. (Eds.). (1996). *Who chooses? Who loses? Culture, institutions and the unequal effects of school choice.* New York: Teachers College Press.

Fuller, H. L. (1997, January 21). New research bolsters case for school choice. *Wall Street Journal,* p. A18.

Greene, J. P., & Peterson, P. E. (1996a). *Methodological issues in evaluation research: The Milwaukee school choice plan.* Occasional Paper 96-4. Cambridge, MA: Harvard University, Program in Educational Policy and Governance.

Greene, J. P., & Peterson, P. E. (1996b, August 14). School choice data rescued from bad science. *Wall Street Journal,* p. A12.

Greene, J. P., Howell, W., & Peterson, P. E. (1997, September). *An evaluation of the Cleveland scholarship program.* Cambridge, MA: Harvard University, Program in Educational Policy and Governance.

Greene, J. P., Peterson, P. E., & Du, J. (1997, March). *Effectiveness of school choice: The Milwaukee experiment.* Occasional Paper 97-1. Cambridge, MA: Harvard University, Program in Educational Policy and Governance.

Greene, J. P., Peterson, P. E., Du, J., Boeger, L., & Frazier, C. L. (1996). *The effectiveness of school choice in Milwaukee: A secondary analysis of data from the program's evaluation.* Occasional Paper 96-3. Cambridge, MA: Harvard University, Program in Educational Policy and Governance.

Heise, M., Colburn K. D. Jr., & Lamberti, J. F. (1995). Private vouchers in Indianapolis: The Golden Rule program. In Terry M. Moe (Ed.), *Private vouchers* (pp. 100–119). Stanford, CA: Hoover Institution Press.

Henig, J. R. (1994). *Rethinking school choice: The limits of the market metaphor.* Princeton, NJ: Princeton University Press.

Henig, J. R. (1996). The local dynamics of choice: Ethnic preferences and institutional responses. In B. Fuller, R. F. Elmore, & G. Orfield (Eds.), *Who chooses? Who loses? Culture, institutions and the unequal effects of school choice* (pp. 95–117). New York: Teachers College Press.

Hill, P. T. (1995). Private vouchers in New York City: The Student-Sponsor Partnership program. In T. M. Moe (Ed.), *Private vouchers* (pp. 120–135). Stanford, CA: Hoover Institution Press.

Jimerson, L. (1998, April). *Hidden consequences of school choice: Impact on programs, finances, and accountability.* Paper presented at the annual meeting of the American Educational Research Association, San Diego, CA.

Little Hoover Commission. (1996, March). The charter movement: Educational reform school by school. Sacramento: Milton Marks Commission on California State Government Organization and Economy.

Martinez, V., Godwin, K., & Kemerer, F. R. (1995). Private vouchers in San Antonio: The CEO program. In T. M. Moe (Ed.), *Private vouchers* (pp. 74–99). Stanford, CA: Hoover Institution Press.

Martinez, V., Godwin, K., & Kemerer, F. R. (1996). Public school choice in San Antonio: Who chooses and with what effects? In B. Fuller, R. F. Elmore, & G. Orfield (Eds.), *Who chooses? Who loses? Culture, institutions and the unequal effects of school choice* (pp. 50–69). New York: Teachers College Press.

Metz, M. H. (1986). *Different by design.* New York: Routledge.

Moe, T. M. (Ed.). (1995a). *Private vouchers.* Stanford, CA: Hoover Institution Press.

Moe, T. M. (1995b). Private vouchers. In T. M. Moe (Ed.), *Private vouchers* (pp. 1–40). Stanford, CA: Hoover Institution Press.

Paulu, N. (1989). *Improving schools and empowering parents: Choice in American education.* Washington DC: Government Printing Office.

Percy, S. L., & Maier, P. (1996). School choice in Milwaukee: Privatization of a different breed. *Policy Studies Journal, 24*(4), 649–665.

Peterson, P. E. (1997, 28 July). Value of school choice. *Washington Post,* p. A18.

Peterson, P. E., & Noyes, C. (1996, Fall). School choice in Milwaukee. *Public Interest, 125,* 38–56.

Peterson, P. E., & Noyes, C. (1997). School choice in Milwaukee. In D. Ravitch & J. P. Viteritti (Eds.), *New schools for a new century: The redesign of urban education* (pp. 123–146). New Haven, CT: Yale University Press.

Rofes, E. (1998, April). *How are school districts responding to charter laws and charter schools?: A study of eight states and the District of Columbia.* Berkeley: Policy Analysis for California Education.

Rouse, C. E. (1998). *Schools and student achievement: More evidence from the Milwaukee Parental Choice Program.* Working Paper No. 396, Industrial Relations Section, Princeton University, Princeton, NJ.

Rouse, C. E. (1998). Private vouchers and student achievement: An evaluation of the Milwaukee Parental Choice Program. *Quarterly Journal of Economics., 113* (2), pp. 533–602.

Viteritti, J. (1996). Stacking the deck for the poor. The new politics of school choice. *Brookings Review, 14*(3), 10–13.

Wells, A. S. (1996). African American students' view of school choice. In B. Fuller, R. F. Elmore, & G. Orfield (Eds.), *Who chooses? Who loses? Culture, institutions and the unequal effects of school choice* (pp. 25–49). New York: Teachers College Press.

Witte, J. F. (1996a). Who benefits from the Milwaukee choice program. In B. Fuller, R. F. Elmore, & G. Orfield (Eds.), *Who chooses? Who loses? Culture, institutions and the unequal effects of school choice* (pp. 118–137). New York: Teachers College Press.

Witte, J. F. (1996b). Reply to Greene, Peterson, and Du: The effectiveness of school choice in Milwaukee: A secondary analysis of data from the program's evaluation. Department of Political Science and the Robert LaFollette Institute of Public Affairs, University of Wisconsin–Madison.

Witte, J. F. (1997, January). *Achievement effects of the Milwaukee voucher program.* Paper presented at the annual meeting of the American Economics Association, New Orleans, LA.

Witte, J. F., Steir, T. D., & Thorn, C. A. (1995). *Fifth-year report: Milwaukee Parental Choice Program.* Department of Political Science and the Robert LaFollette Institute of Public Affairs, University of Wisconsin–Madison.

Witte, J. P., Thorn, C. A., Pritchard, K. M., & Clairborn, M. (1994). *Fourth-year report: Milwaukee Parental Choice Program.* Department of Political Science and the Robert LaFollette Institute of Public Affairs, University of Wisconsin–Madison.

Reinventing Teaching

DEBORAH MEIER

Since I began teaching, some twenty-five years ago, I have changed the way I think about what it means to be a good teacher. Today it is clear that since we need a new kind of school to do a new kind of job, we need a new kind of teacher, too.

The schools we need require different habits of work and habits of mind on the part of teachers—a kind of professionalism within the classroom few teachers were expected to exhibit before. In addition, to get from where we are now to where we need to be will require teachers to play a substantially different role within their schools as well as in public discourse. Teachers need to relearn what it means to be good in-school practitioners, while also becoming more articu-

From Deborah Meier, *Teachers College Record,* 93 (4), Summer 1992. Oxford, England: Blackwell Publishing. Reprinted by permission.

late and self-confident spokespeople for the difficult and often anxiety-producing changes schools are expected to undertake. If teachers are not able to join in leading such changes, the changes will not take place. Politicians and policymakers at all levels may institute vast new legislated reforms; but without the understanding, support, and input of teachers, they will end up in the same dead end as such past reforms as "new math" or "open ed." For all the big brave talk, they will be rhetorical and cosmetic, and after a time they will wither away.

Four experiences over the past twenty-five years have influenced my thinking and led me to this conclusion. The first (and latest) is my experience on the National Board for Professional Teaching Standards, which has spent the past three years trying to define the qualities of excellent teaching. The effort we have spent has been well worth it (whether trying to test for it will be as successful I am not yet sure). The National Board has done a superb job of trying to describe the complex set of knowledge and skills that an experienced "master" of teaching must possess. It is a daunting description, but it tells us little about what might go into the making of such a teacher or how such a teacher can be an agent and shaper of the reforms the National Board argues must go hand-in-hand with such an upgraded concept of the profession. I urge you to read it over carefully: It is an important starting place.[11]

The other three experiences that have gradually shaped my thinking on this subject began, not surprisingly, with my own early experiences as a student—my elementary, secondary, and college education. My fortunate and favored personal history had the advantage of making me acutely aware of what distinguished America's best from its worst schools. It was, as a result, not until I started teaching in the Chicago public schools in my early thirties that I experienced what it meant to be treated with disrespect, both personally and intellectually. It was in the role of schoolteacher, not student, that I first had such an experience, and it hit me like a ton of bricks.

The next formative experience was working in the school system, as a kindergarten and Head Start teacher, then as a teacher "trainer," and finally as a teacher director and principal trying to shape a school environment. Twenty-five years of experience in urban public schools has not numbed me, but it has made me aware of the constraints on change, of the enormous difficulties under which my colleagues work, our students learn, and their parents labor—difficulties that

are profound, long-standing, and deeply imbedded in our system and our mind set.

Finally, my recent work with the Coalition of Essential Schools, in seeking ways to force-feed changes in a whole interrelated set of entrenched school practices, has required **me** to think about larger social policy questions as they affect school reform: How can we use "top-down" reform to influence what, in the end, must be "bottom-up" change?

In all these years, surprisingly, I have not spent a lot of time thinking about how schools of education could assist in this task of school reform. They never fit into my bottom-up or top-down agenda. Since I have thought about a lot of issues, this may take some explaining. It has probably been a by-product of the fact that I did not enter teaching through that route, nor have many of the teachers whose work I have known best. Perhaps it has also been influenced by the fact that while I was always a "good student," I have never enjoyed "student-hood." Unlike many of my friends, I have never taken a formal course voluntarily since I got my M.A. thirty-five years ago. Finally, I will admit that the courses I did have to take in education were not a sample of the best that could be found, but generally of the worst.

Above and beyond my personal educational history, and based on literally hundreds of in-depth experiences with new teachers, I have yet to see the best or worst schools of education exert much influence. The so-called better schools often attract "better" students, but it is hard for me to see what value has been added. The dominant educational impact—99 percent—had already happened. I am referring to the cumulative influence of their own schooling.

The lessons drawn from sixteen or more years of school experience as a student remain largely intact and dictate the way most people handle their role as teachers. This is hardly surprising. Many of those who enter teaching hope to do unto others what the teachers they knew and loved did unto them. In a few cases—and I tend to have a fondness, however short-lived, for these exceptions—teaching as a career attracts young people who did not like their schooling or were not naturally successful at it. They hope that as teachers they might be able to do unto others what they wished their teachers had done for them. They have come into teaching to change practice, not perpetuate it—to break a tradition, not carry it on. But such teachers often leave teaching quickly, when they discover that their students do not love them for being different, less authoritarian, more genial, smarter. They often leave with new ideas about what is wrong with "these" kids or the evils and stupidity ties of their fellow teachers—the ones who stayed. Some people, fortunately, enter teaching at a later age, not fresh out of school. They bring to their jobs a wider range of experience, and are accustomed to different kinds of institutional arrangements and ways of relating to colleagues. Sometimes they even come to teaching after they have had children, and if they are lucky, at least one of their children has not found school so easy. They are not quite so quick to judge parents at fault, and may have a special personal empathy for school losers. But in most cases the constraints of the job, plus old habits and a kind of societal nostalgia for what school "used to be like," make teachers part of the broader inertia that makes fundamental change hard to implement.

In short: The habits of schooling are deep, powerful, and hard to budge. No public institution is more deeply entrenched in habitual behavior than schools—and for good reason. Aside from our many years of direct experience as students, we have books, movies, television shows, advertisements, and myriad other activities, games, and symbols that reinforce our view of what school is "supposed" to be. Our everyday language and metaphors are built on a kind of prototype of schoolhouse and classroom, with all its authoritarian, filling-up-the-empty-vessel, rote-learning assumptions.

For example, the other night I watched a semi-documentary entitled "Yearbook." It purported to depict the life of a school by following a group of seniors during their last year in high school. We watch, with a kind of false nostalgia, the senior year so few of us truly had but believe we should have had: the selection of cheerleaders and homecoming queens in the fall, the pains of dating, the sports fields, the trivia of home economics classes, and so forth. There is not even a momentary bow to the intellectual purposes of high school. At Central Park East schools, we laugh sometimes about how our own students (and even our own children), many of whom have never attended any school but ours, still play "pretend school" in a traditional way—lining up the desks, and yelling at the children. Our Central Park East Secondary School (CPESS) high school students complain about not having lockers—that is where true high school life takes place, the absence of bells, passing time, proms, and so forth. They view these as essential rites of passage. My four-year-old granddaughter loves playing school with me—but I am required to be the mean principal who does awful things to bad children. She cannot wait until she gets to such a real school.

It is no easier to change such habits, built around age-old metaphors about teaching and learning, about getting ahead, than it is to change our personal habits (like giving up smoking), or our seemingly ingrained primitive ideas about the physical universe. It is current wisdom to recognize that despite all the correct information offered in physics and astronomy courses, including laboratory experiences and visits to the planetarium, the average citizen's real-life view of the universe remains amazingly heliocentric at best (and geocentric, if not New York-centric, at worst). We pile new theories on top of old conceptions rooted in childhood experience, language, and symbols, and they are absorbed in some odd commonsensical way. The sky remains up, as does the North Pole; we imagine looking up at the moon and therefore assume that the men on the moon must look down to see the Earth; we know that the moon is very far away—about halfway to Mars or Venus. This is now old-hat theory, yet few schools are successful in getting their students to see the world in post-Copernican terms. Habit and everyday common sense rule. So why should it be any different when it comes to teaching adults how to teach?

Until we are ready to engage students in a far different form of pedagogy, with far greater in-depth exploration, such commonsense habits will not be overcome in physics classes. Our graduates may be able to recite more modern ideas, but their understanding will remain paper-thin and school-bound. That may suffice for physics, because few have to base their future practices on a different view of the universe. In everyday life, in fact, the old pre-Copernican view works quite well.

So too with education courses, and pedagogical theories. As in physics, our habitual view of teaching as telling and learning as remembering is hard to dislodge. The difference is, of course, that we expect would-be teachers to overcome such views and then act on the basis of their new wisdom. We pretend that this can be so, despite the fact that we know that teaching, more than virtually any field (aside from parenting, perhaps), depends on quick instinctive habits, behaviors, and deeply held ways of seeing and valuing. Teachers are confronted with literally hundreds of decisions and unmonitored responses every hour they work, which cannot be mediated by cool calculation. Nothing is more unsettling in the presence of real-live students in real-live classrooms than an uncertain teacher, searching for the right response. A doctor can examine patients slowly and carefully, and look up the answers in books before being required to commit to action. Not so a teacher.

In short, we come to be teachers knowing all about teaching. We have been exposed to more teaching and teachers than to any other single phenomenon. Most of us have spent more time with teachers than with our parents. To make matters worse, what we learn from our parents in a more informal pedagogy is rarely even thought of as having been taught. In fact, the more "naturally" and "readily" we learn something, the less credit we give to those who taught us. Furthermore, our first exposure to teaching is done under the frequently scornful eye of experienced teachers who are quick to put down the green ambitions of innovators, whose early innovations are likely to be dismal failures.

If teaching and schooling are so entrenched, if our habits are so deeply rooted and so hard to change, is there no hope for school reform? The answer will depend on how serious we are about the need to change, and how long we are willing to stick with the effort to effect it.

At present, there is not a lot of evidence of a serious will to change. There is a desire, for sure, for youngsters to "do better," for much better results—especially on competitive test scores. But it should surprise no one, given the above analysis, that most people think improvement is a matter of all those involved trying harder—or even returning to former more didactic ways, which presumably we have mistakenly abandoned. Lots of people want parents and teachers to be more like they used to be in the good old days—if mothers would just stay home and teachers would just assign more homework, and so forth. More demanding, tougher, and more dedicated teachers might restore the high standards many of the critics suggest. Let the students face the consequences. Some suggest these nostrums will not work given the nature of "kids today" and some wonder about whether "those" children (read "nonwhite") are really able to meet high standards. But few see the problem the way the members of prestigious task forces do: as creating a different system to do a different job. Thus, the will thoroughly to restructure the institutions themselves, with all this implies in terms of resources for basic research and development, for massively retraining the educational work force, has little public backing.

Many things must be done if we are to alter this bleak picture. At the heart of it is the question of how teachers can be changed—even what it means to "retrain" the educational work force. The change that must take place among the work force involves three tough tasks: changing how teachers view teaching and learning, developing new habits to go with that new cognitive understanding, and simultaneously developing new habits of work—habits that are collegial and public in nature, not solo and private as has been the custom in teaching. Such changes cannot be "taught" in the best-designed retraining program and then imported into classroom practice. What is entailed is changing the daily experiences of teachers, substituting experiences that will require them to engage in new practices and support them in doing so.

If it were possible to escape the issue by somehow inculcating the next generation with a different set of habits, thus bypassing both teachers and their parents, it would be an attractive idea. Otherwise, this is a kind of pulling oneself-up-by-the-bootstraps problem. Every revolutionary ideology comes up against this same conundrum and, historically, most revolutionaries think they can resolve it only by totalitarian measures. Some try removing children from their families, sowing suspicion between generations, forcing prescriptive ideological training from infancy on up, or creating a network of "big brothers." They hope thus to breed a new generation that leaps over the weaknesses of the present misguided and corrupted generation. In a milder form, most school reform efforts are not so different in conception. It is the familiar design that rests on hopes for teacher-proof curriculum, reform by testing and monitoring, by penalties and threats. They will have no more luck.

One cannot impose such change—not because it is immoral or unpleasant, but because it does not work. And the price paid for trying to wipe out the past by fiat is enormous. Benign schemes for trying to do the same thing fail just as the obviously malign ones do. This is not surprising. It is illogical to imagine that we can produce thoughtful and critical thinkers by rote imposition or that we can build strong intellectual understanding through required amnesia. If the logic of it fails to impress, years and years of failed efforts to do so ought to. It is, at the very least, a great waste of time, a diversion of energy and resources that we can ill afford. We cannot pass on to a new generation that which we do not ourselves possess. That is the conundrum, the seemingly impossible paradox.

How might we approach such a riddle? We can change the schools so as to promote thoughtful and critical practices on the part of teacher practitioners, and in ways that undercut any need for teachers themselves to become lobbyists against change. Teachers must lead the way toward their own liberation.

Teachers were force-marched to the promised land of "new math," and the results should be a warning. Impatience for rapid improvement in math education following *Sputnik* produced a dud—and today, thirty years later, we are once again trying to introduce just such a math education. Had we been more patient thirty years ago we would be thirty years ahead of the game now.

The only route possible requires involving all parties to education in the process of reinventing schooling. Not, please note, revolution or reform, but reinvention is required. It is our mind set that needs changing, and the institutional arrangements that either support or impede the new mind set. However, you do not and should not fool with people's minds loosely. It requires the utmost respect, a stance that is not easy for us to assume. The changes needed are not changes in the solo acts teachers perform inside their classrooms, hard as that might be to accomplish. We are talking about creating a very different school culture, a new set of relationships and ideas. We are talking about changes that will affect not just teachers (although without them it is pointless), but also their constituents—parents and children. Given enough time—if we are not in too much of a hurry; if we allow for lapses and half-measures, and do not give up—we might begin to see changes. It is through collective co-ownership of new designs for schooling, in an atmosphere that allows for reflective examination and reshaping based on experience, that something new might emerge.

We can change teachers only by changing the environment in which teaching takes place. Teaching can be changed only by reinventing the institutions within which teaching takes place—schools. Reinvention has to be done by those who will be stuck in the reinvented schools. It cannot be force-fed—not to teachers, nor to parents and children. All three constituents can sabotage the best-laid plans. While parents and children will put up with some dissonance and anxiety, the mismatch between what they expect and what they experience cannot be ignored or evaded. Their willingness to participate in change is critical. While such willingness can be encouraged by various public policies, a thoroughly "converted" and committed faculty is a must.

When school people visit CPESS they often dismiss our achievements—which I believe to be modest compared with the achievements that lie ahead of us—on the basis that we, after all, had the opportunity to start from scratch, whereas they must reform an existing huge, sluggish institution, only some of whose members want to change. If we had your freedom, they suggest, we too could produce Central Park East's successes. I think they are right, so I suggest they be given precisely the same freedom we have had. That is what public policy can create.

Our visitors argue that we have the advantage of having a student and parent body who chose to come to our school. I propose that all schools be given precisely the same freedom: a student and parent body of those who choose to come to their school. (Note that by "school" I do not necessarily mean a building. A single building can contain many such reinvented schools of choice.) Visitors argue that we had a chance to select our staff, from among those who agree with us. It is much easier to carry out a collective policy when people agree on the policy, they complain. We propose that all schools should have this same freedom. Professionals should work in a school that they want to work in because they share its assumptions. Visitors complain that our work is not replicable because we have been given the freedom to organize our day, select our curriculum, and design our forms of assessment in the way we think best—and to change them whenever we find they do not work. We propose that all other schools be offered the same freedom, along with the same responsibilities we have accepted.

If these are the four freedoms that you envy, we tell our visitors, why not demand the same for yourselves? But you have to want such freedom and you have to accept the responsibility that goes with it. It will be exhausting, even at times frustrating. The thing we keep telling our colleagues in other schools is that it surely will not lead to "burn-out"—because people burn out when they are treated like appliances. This kind of teaching and schooling is, in contrast, never dehumanizing. It rests on intense human interaction and involvement.

You can only change people's habits, at best, when they have strong reasons to want to change and an environment conducive to it. That is the first requirement. For teachers, this means sufficient support from those they depend on—schools boards, administrators, parents—to take some risky first steps. They need, furthermore, the luxury of being able to waste money on ideas that will not work, rather than feeling obliged to pretend that everything they do is successful.

They need access to expertise without promising to follow expert advice. They need time. They need more time in a daily weekly, monthly sense—to reflect, examine, redo. They also need recognition of the other kind of time—the years it will take to see it through. These are the conditions we know work whenever we are really in a hurry to do something difficult: cure cancer, go to the moon, invent new technologies, or win a war.

The greater the desire for change on the part of teachers, parents, and children, the less it will cost. Unpaid volunteer armies can defend their homeland better than highly trained and equipped mercenary troops. Very eager and driven reformers are ready to exploit themselves, putting in endless hours and sleepless nights—although they often also exhaust themselves too soon. But the more timid, the less eager, the less confident and self-motivated, the more ideal the circumstances must be before we get the necessary sustained effort. Money (for extra personnel, financial incentives, paid time, equipment) compensates for zeal. We will not get large-scale school reform in the United States if we count only on zealots, but we would be foolish indeed not to promote such zeal, and give such ardent reformers the room and space to work their hearts out as we build up credibility for more ambitious national efforts.

The job of those in policymaking positions who want to improve the quality of teachers must be to change the conditions of teaching. They must offer incentives for change, and above all the resources (in this case the key is well-designed staff development time) to enable teachers to learn from their changed conditions. Unlike most industries, we cannot retool by closing down the factories and sending all the workers back to school. We need to do everything at once. It is driving while changing the tires, not to mention the transmission system.

Our schools must be labs for learning about learning. Only such labs can teach both children and their teachers simultaneously. They must create a passion for learning, not only among children, but also among their teachers. Both have become "passion-impaired." In the words of Ginny Stiles, a kindergarten teacher at Reek Elementary School in Wisconsin, "It's my job to find the passion, to open eyes and weave a web of intrigue and surprise." Indeed, she notes, too many teachers have themselves become what she calls passion-impaired. The motivator par our excellence is our heart's desire, our taste for "the having of wonder-

ful ideas," as Eleanor Duckworth calls it.[2] How better to impart such ideas than by engaging in the having of wonderful ideas oneself?

If I could choose five qualities to look for in prospective teachers they would be: (1) a self-conscious reflectiveness about how they themselves learn and, maybe even more, how and when they do not learn; (2) a sympathy toward others, an appreciation of their differences, an ability to imagine their "otherness"; (3) a willingness to engage in, better yet a taste for, collaborative work; (4) a desire to have others to share some of one's own interests; and (5) a lot of perseverance, energy, and devotion to getting things right.

Since we cannot count on finding enough teachers who already possess all five qualities, we need to create the kind of schools that will draw out these qualities. Of course, when I say we need schools that will encourage such characteristics, I include liberal arts colleges and schools of education as well as schools for children and adolescents. Nothing we have discovered lately about how the brain works is uniquely true for children versus adults, or would-be teachers versus would-be anything else. The kind of education that is best for teachers is one that is best for learners in all subjects and domains.

We will change American education only insofar as we make all our schools educationally inspiring and intellectually challenging for teachers, not just students. It is not enough to worry about some decontextualized quality called teacher "morale" or "job satisfaction." Those words, like "self-esteem," are not stand-alones. Neither happy teachers nor happy students are our goal. What we need is a particular kind of job satisfaction that has as its anchor intellectual growth. The school itself must be intellectually stimulating—organized to make it hard for teachers to remain unthoughtful. High teacher (or student) morale needs to be viewed as a by-product of the wonderful ideas that are being examined under the most challenging circumstances. During our first year at CPESS we went around muttering under our breath that our job was not to make the children happy but to make them strong. That goes for teacher education too.

Mindlessness as a habit may drive employers crazy, but it is a habit we have too often fostered in schools. The habit of failing back on excuses—"I had to," "that's the way it's supposed to be"—can be rooted out only by major surgery. It will be painful, and it will not all come out at once. Expecting teachers to take responsibility for the success of the whole school requires that they begin to accept responsibility for their own as well as their colleagues' teaching—surely no overnight task. At the very least, one must imagine schools in which teachers are in frequent conversation with each other about their work, have easy and necessary access to each other's classrooms, take it for granted that they should comment on each other's work, and have the time to develop common standards for student work. They need frequent and easy access to the kind of give-and-take with professionals from allied fields that is the mark of a true professional. They need opportunities to speak and write publicly about their work, attend conferences, read professional journals, and discuss something besides what they are going to do on Monday. There must be some kind of combination of discomfiture and support—focused always on what does and does not have an impact on children's learning.

What would be the role in such schools of administration and supervision? I do not think the answer is yet in regarding the nature of school governance best suited to faculty growth. Insofar as the faculty are prevented from blaming others for their problems, they are more likely to look to their own practice. So some form of work-place democracy is essential, but there are numerous possible candidates for the form and style that best frees teachers to work together on professional matters. What is certain is that this kind of collegiality works best in settings that are sufficiently small and intimate so that self-governance and staff-development schemes do not exhaust teachers' energies or divert them from their central task.

There are doubtless many models of how a university faculty could work with such restructured schools. It is easy to see how they could play critical roles, probably involving far less emphasis on running full-time education programs for would-be teachers. Most of the models I can envisage would take place primarily around the work site itself, although school people (like other professionals) need opportunities to "get away" from time to time for more distanced reflections, sometimes with people other than those they daily contend with. "Distance" can become an advantage. That goes for the distance that the university faculty bring to the work site, and the distance that teachers can experience when they go away from their work site. I can envisage countless ways in which an empowered and self-confident school faculty could use the expertise of university people. For example, university faculty could teach occasional mini-courses to

children under carefully observed and even videotaped conditions; they could meet with faculty to examine curriculum in their fields of expertise; they could observe classes and act as friendly critics; they could videotape instructional settings for teachers and act as guides in looking them over; they could read student papers and discuss ways to support better writing; they could lead reading groups on issues of pedagogical or school reform; they could give lectures on issues the faculty as a whole wants to learn more about, including lectures on particular literary texts, historical disputes, or mathematical discoveries, not just pedagogy; they could recommend important readings or circulate articles relevant to each school's situation. They could include "school teachers" of history in professional historical associations, acknowledging them in the brother- and sisterhood of historians. And, of course, they could teach differently in their own courses.

Above all, our university colleagues can commit themselves to the equally difficult task of taking teaching and learning seriously in their own institutions, to reinventing universities as educational institutions. They can observe each other, consider why and how their students are or are not learning what they intend to be teaching. They can provide models of a lively intellectual community for their students. They can team teach, creating courses that are contentious so that students are forced to deal with different viewpoints, make judgments between them, consider evidence, and ask questions.

Psycholinguist Frank Smith tells a story about a lecture he gave, attacking courses on "thinking skills." After the meeting, the superintendent of schools came up to him and said that he was in a quandary. The week before another speaker had presented just the opposite viewpoint. What should he do, he asked Smith. Well, said Smith, we cannot both be right can we? So you will just have to think about it and then make your own decision. That is what thinking is all about.

The world of schools has habituated us not only to teach children that there is always one "right" answer, but to think that way ourselves. Even where we have taken the giant step of considering that how we teach is worthy of serious intellectual thought, we rarely think about the impact the institutional arrangement of teaching and learning has on our lives and on the lives of our students. We do not imagine that thinking about that is part of our job as teacher educators.

Colleges and universities, not just public elementary and secondary schools, bear considerable responsibility for having given the vast majority of those we send out into schools as teachers the same mis-message that Frank Smith's superintendent labors under. The vast majority of those who enter teaching attended colleges that also rewarded mindlessness and rote learning. The thing that is wrong with prescriptive teaching is not that it does not "work"—it does work. It produces just the kind of miseducated people that society may once have been looking for, or in any case not seriously minded. But for the kind of educational purposes that are now being demanded, such mindlessness will not do.

Since the public at large plays such an important role in decisions about education, perhaps the only specific education requirement that all colleges should have is one directed at all its students, not just those considering teaching as a career. Reflecting on learning, becoming more sensitive to how human beings in general learn as well as how each of us individually learns—as well as addressing issues of schools as institutions—would be foundation courses at least as appropriate, if not more so, for liberal arts students as for would-be teachers. Maybe Ed 101 should be mandatory for all students, or its content woven into all courses.

The Central Park East schools were created, invented if you will, with all these considerations, plus a few more, in mind. They were efforts to imagine the kind of collegial setting in which adults could and would learn side by side with their students. We sought to create an intellectually transformative environment, a culture of mutual respect for others, a set of habits of mind that foster inquiry as well as responsibility. We based our work on some simple principles, familiar enough to those who work with young children, but less familiar to those who work with adolescents or adults. We started with the premise that there is far more in common between a five-year-old, a fifteen-year-old, and a fifty-year-old than there are differences. Our common humanity means we learn in much the same way. That was, in fact, our first principle. Good kindergarten practice is probably on target at any age, including the age of teachers.

For example, we knew that five-year-olds learn best when they feel relatively safe—physically as well as psychically. (Young children need to feel comfortable about going to the bathroom, for example. How about teenagers? How about teachers?) Feeling safe includes trusting at least some of those "in charge," not to mention being able to predict with some degree of ac-

curacy how the place works. The same is true for adults. For young children we know it also means that parents need to see the school as safe so that they can reassure their children that "those people are okay," "you can trust them to care for you," "they are not our enemies." It turns out that this is also critical for the development of fifteen-year-olds. They too suffer if they come to school carrying wary or hostile warnings from their families. The appropriate rebellion of adolescence cannot be carried out successfully in a setting in which the adults may truly be seen as dangerous. Healthy "testing out" rests on a basic trust that there are adults prepared to set limits. Is it so different at fifty? Do we not need a work place that is safe, predictable, and on our side, if we expect to do our best work?

A second principle, one at the heart of the Coalition of Essential Schools' "Nine Basic Principles," can be put succinctly: You cannot teach well if you do not know your students well. That means size and scale are critical. Even prisons, or army units, are not as huge, impersonal, and anonymous as many schools for young children, not to mention the average American high school. It is not just children who suffer from this depersonalization of work; adults do too. All but a few stars become lookers-on, admirers, or wallflowers, not active participants.

Our third principle is an old familiar one: You cannot use the coach or expert well if he or she is also judge and high executioner. As my son explained to me one day when I was trying to convince him to ask his teacher to explain something to him, "Mom, you don't understand. The last person in the world who I'd let know what I don't understand is my teacher." Schooling becomes a vast game in which teachers try to trick students into revealing their ignorance while students try to trick teachers into thinking they are not ignorant. Getting a good grade, after all, is getting the teacher to think you know more than you do. Is it so different for teachers, whose only source of help and support is precisely the person who rates and rules them? The metaphor "teacher as coach" is full of possibilities not only for the relationship between adults and children, but in all teaching/learning settings.

A fourth principle for an efficient learning environment is that we learn best when we are in a position to make sense of things—especially to make sense of things we are interested in. Human beings are by nature meaningmakers, trying to put the puzzle together. From the moment of birth until our death this is our preeminent mode. Schools rarely capitalize on it. A nursery school teacher uses the room itself to create interest and curiosity. She carefully sets up the environment so that it invites questions; and she spends her time moving about the room, prodding, inquiring, changing materials and tools so that curiosity is kept lively and current. She creates dissonances as well as harmonies; she creates confusion as well as serenity. Contradictions are accepted as natural. By the time students reach high school we have stripped the environment bare, and lessons are dry and "clear cut." No high school teacher (and surely not a college professor) worthy of her salt assumes the actual physical setting of the classroom is a relevant part of her job. The typical explanation for why we teach what we do is that it is required at the next grade level—or, at best, that it is required on a state-mandated exam. Teaching becomes simplified, focusing more and more on test-taking skill. Nor do teachers view the courses they are required to take to get a license or upgrade their status much differently. Teachers' own interests are often irrelevant, or sneaked into a high school schedule. A teacher with a love for physics and expertise in the field may teach biology because that is what is "needed." No wonder that the phrase "It's academic" means it is irrelevant.

Fifth, human beings by nature are social, interactive learners. We check out our ideas, argue with authors, bounce issues back and forth, ask friends to read our early drafts, talk together after seeing a movie, pass on books we have loved, attend meetings and argue out our ideas, share stories and gossip that extends our understanding of ourselves and others. Talk lies at the heart of our lives. This kind of exchange is never allowed in school, nor modeled there—not between children, nor between adults. Monthly faculty meetings are no better imitations of true discussion than the average so-called classroom discussion. The most powerful motivation for becoming learned—that we might influence others—is purposely removed from students and their teachers. No one among the powerful policymakers wonders, as they imagine the perfect curriculum, what it means to teach a subject year after year, based on someone else's design. We organize schools as though the ideal were an institution impervious to human touch.

If we intend dramatically to improve the education of American children we need to invent very different environments for them. Teachers must be challenged to invent schools they would like to teach in, organized around the principles of learning that we know matter.

That is the simple idea we put into practice at Central Park East.

What did we do? First, children stay with teachers for two years, so it is worth getting to know each other well—students, their families, and the teacher. Even high school students do not move around every forty-five minutes, do not change courses in midyear, and stay with the same faculty for two years. There are no pull-outs, and no seven-period days. In the high school most students see no more than two to three different teachers a day, including an advisor who spends an hour a day with a small group of his or her own fifteen advisees. Furthermore, each teacher teaches an interdisciplinary course: literature and history or math and science, for example.

A typical class is long enough (often two hours) to include whole-class seminars, small-group work, independent study, and one-on-one coaching by teachers and fellow students. Students do their writing and reading in school, not just as homework, so they can get feedback and insight into how to read and write more effectively. Teachers, furthermore, teach in collaborative settings; four to five teachers work in physically contiguous rooms and with the same set of students so that they can easily make decisions, alter plans, rearrange schedules, regroup students, share ideas, and observe each other at work.

Decisions are made as close to each teacher's own classroom setting as possible, although all decisions are ultimately the responsibility of the whole staff. The decisions are not merely on minor matters—length of classes or the number of field trips. The teachers collectively decide on content, pedagogy, and assessment as well. They teach what they think matters. The "whole staff" is not enormous—none of our Central Park East schools is larger than about 450 students, most are 200 to 300. That means a faculty that can sit in a circle in one room and get a chance to hear each other. Governance is simple. There are virtually no permanent standing committees. Finally, we work together to develop assessment systems for our students, their families, ourselves, and the broader public—systems that represent our values and beliefs in as direct a manner as possible. When we are asked "Does it work?" we have had a voice in deciding what "work" means. Our forms of assessment are constantly open to public review and what is open is direct evidence: Observers may visit our classrooms, read our students' work, examine our scoring grids, look at samples of graduation-level portfolios. We even invite experts to review our work and our students' performances, as a way to sharpen our insights and check our potentially overgenerous hearts.

The result: Our students succeed in far greater measure than their socioeconomic, ethnic, and racial background and prior academic skills would predict. We have not closed the gap between rich and poor, we have not sent all our graduates to prestigious colleges, nor made enough difference to ensure that none will fall through the cracks of the larger society. But in a city in which nearly half of all students fail to complete high school, about 90 percent of those who attend Central Park East schools do complete high school, even after only four to six years in our elementary schools. While the fact that half of those who graduate from our elementary schools go on to college is a promising piece of data, the numbers are much higher for those who attend our secondary school. We hope, over time, to prove that their capacity to stick it out in college and hold good jobs and be strong citizens will be even more convincing. Whether they leave us at twelve or eighteen, they are far better able to join society as productive and socially useful citizens than are their counterparts.

It is not enough. It never will be. But the fact that schools cannot do the job alone is a far cry from claiming that schools cannot do their job better if they take seriously what they know about teaching and learning and practice it at every age and grade level. Period.

Just as our student body is not exceptional, but reflects the general population of New York City schools, our faculty are by no means exceptionally well educated, more learned than the average teacher in New York City, and certainly no more experienced. Many had virtually no prior experience as teachers and some had taken no courses in teaching. Many started as interns with us, spending their first year in low-paid assistant teaching roles. Some came from other schools where they had been good but not exceptional teachers (the most exceptional often build comfortable niches for themselves and are hard to woo away). But they all came with a willingness to learn from each other, although often vulnerable, prickly, and defensive, and they have all grown incredibly in the process of becoming better teachers. Today many speak about our work all over the country, something we consciously committed ourselves as a faculty to help each other learn to do. Others write about our work, again something we have helped each other learn to do. They see

themselves first as the teachers of a particular group of youngsters, but then also see themselves as the governing body of a school and the carriers of an idea.

My colleague Ann Bussis claims that teaching is not so complex as to verge on the impossible or to defy conception at an abstract level, but it does defy concrete prescriptions for action—there is neither prescription for action nor a checklist for observation to assure intelligent and responsive teaching. All that can be offered is a guiding theory and abundant examples.

That is what schools must help us develop—guiding ideas and abundant examples, and then the opportunity to put such guiding ideas into practice and to learn from our abundant examples. It is hoped that someday, not too far in the future, we will have abundant enough examples of what such reinvented schools might be like for them to become the norm.

In summary, if we want schools for the twenty-first century to resemble schools of the twentieth century, we can afford to tinker a little and leave the structure pretty much intact. Then teacher-training institutions need only follow suit, tinkering too. But if we want the least of our citizens to know and be able to do the kinds of things that only those lucky few at the top of the ladder have ever achieved before, then we need to begin a slow and steady revolution in how and what teachers must know and know how to do. To do this means we have to learn how to drive while changing not only the tire but the whole mechanism! Impossible? No, but very, very hard. The place it will happen is in the schools themselves—not the schools as we now know them, but reinvented schools created by school people and their communities. And it does not come with guarantees.

(A version of this article was presented as the DeGarmo Lecture for the Society of Professors of Education at the annual meeting of the American Educational Research Association, April 4, 1991 in Chicago.)

Endnotes

1. National Board for Professional Teaching Standards, "What Teachers Should Know and Be Able to Do," in *Toward High and Rigorous Standards for the Teaching Profession. Initial Policies for the National Board for Professional Teaching Standards* (Detroit: NBPTS, 1991), pp. 13–32.
2. Eleanor Duckworth, *"The Having of Wonderful Ideas" and Other Essays on Teaching and Learning* (New York: Teachers College Press, 1987).

A Level Playing Field

CATHERINE GEWERTZ

To Joseph M. Ferraina, one need only cruise this humble seaside town, and then its hyper-posh neighbors, to understand why New Jersey desperately needed the school finance lawsuit that has delivered billions of dollars to the state's poorest districts. "Just look at that," he says as he steers his car past low-rise public-housing projects in Long Branch, where he has been the school superintendent for 10 years. Within minutes, he is passing the massive homes and manicured lawns of adjoining Deal. "It's a tale of two cities."

Ferraina, the Argentine-immigrant son of a custodian, sees the *Abbott* v. *Burke* case as justice for the most underprivileged of children. In just seven years, it has transformed his district, he says, by expanding the educational opportunities of a needy student population.

Five of Long Branch's nine schools are being replaced, and all have undergone millions of dollars in health- and safety-related upgrades. Ninety-four percent of the 3- and 4-year-olds in the district—more than 750 children—are taking advantage of the free full-day preschool program now available, and early test results suggest the program is boosting their skills in kindergarten and 1st grade.

Whole-school reform models, or schoolwide strategies to overhaul instruction and management, are in place in all Long Branch schools and seem to be improving test scores. In 2001, 74 percent of the district's 4th graders in general education passed the state's language arts test. In 2004, 85 percent passed, though that proportion still trailed the state average of 90 percent.

In one of 10 *Abbott* decisions, the New Jersey Supreme Court said that the state's poorest students need an education "beyond the norm." Ferraina believes that focus is well-placed. Seven in 10 of his 5,000 students come from poverty, which he believes justifies the elevated investment the state has been obligated to make in his district.

"These children need a better education more than the ones over here," Ferraina says, gesturing toward one of Long Branch's affluent neighbors. "The American dream is based on a good, free education, and the resources of *Abbott* can make that happen for these kids."

Policymakers and observers on all sides of school funding debates nationwide watch the *Abbott* case closely as a test of whether raising spending levels in poor districts to parity with the wealthiest can significantly improve achievement for students from low-income families. Activists also use it as a case study of how a court's deep involvement in schools' inner workings has benefits—or limits.

In response to a 1970 lawsuit known as *Robinson* v. *Cahill,* and to the 1981 *Abbott* case, the New Jersey Supreme Court struck down incarnations of the state's school finance formula four times from 1973 to 1997. In *Abbott,* the high court took the unique step of ordering the state to ensure that public schools in the poorest urban districts are able to spend at the same level as those in the wealthiest suburbs.

"No Excuse"

The court's 1998 blueprint also is unusual for being highly detailed and prescriptive.

The court mandated that all elementary schools adopt whole-school reform models, with Success for All as the presumptive model, though others were permitted. The court mandated full-day kindergarten and preschool, broad social-service programs, enhanced school security and technology, high school dropout programs, and smaller class sizes, as well as a major facilities program to overhaul subpar buildings.

Additional programs, such as summer school, could receive funding with demonstrated need, the court said.

From Gewertz, Catherine, "A Level Playing Field," Quality Counts, 2005. Reprinted with permission from Editorial Projects in Education.

"We must reach the point," the unanimous court wrote in 1998, "where it is possible to say with confidence that the most disadvantaged schoolchildren in the state will not be left out or left behind."

Few disagree that the 31 so-called *Abbott* districts need extra state help.

When the class action was filed on behalf of New Jersey schoolchildren, the state's poorest districts were spending 40 percent less than its wealthiest ones. Now, with huge infusions of court-required state aid, the *Abbott* districts are spending about $13,000 per pupil, very nearly what the richest districts spend.

That parity of spending, advocates and critics alike contend, can't help but yield results that will inform—or at least fuel—the national debate about how far money and state policy can go in closing the performance gap between privileged and underprivileged children.

"We have the resources, so there can be no excuse for not doing it. Period," says Gordon A. MacInnes, who in 2002 assumed the newly created post of assistant state commissioner of education for *Abbott* implementation.

Local administrators in Trenton say that providing all of their district's 14,000 children what they need is a work in progress.

Half the district's 24 buildings are being renovated, expanded, or replaced. Experimentation with seven models of whole-school reform has settled into a customized approach, in which schools employ the elements of the models they find useful. The experience has helped the district build school leadership and spark valuable critical thinking about curriculum and practice, says Superintendent James M. Lytle.

Elementary school students' performance has improved, and an extensive dropout-recovery program has raised Trenton's high school enrollment by 50 percent and tripled the graduation rate. But in middle school, performance has declined, leading to more soul-searching about what changes need to be made, Lytle says.

Lytle believes *Abbott* is making promising things possible in his district, though he and his staff know they have a longer road to travel.

"Is *Abbott* working? It's too early to tell," he says. "There is lots of strong evidence, and I'm praying the legislature and the New Jersey electorate hold the course. To my mind, this is the most important experiment in urban schooling, in trying to educate minority and poor students, that there has ever been."

Seven years into New Jersey's bid to put poor districts on a financial footing with the wealthy, the *Abbott* districts offer a mixture of promise and struggle.

Gauging Gains

The state's 4th grade language arts test for general education students shows those in *Abbott* districts improving at a faster rate than students statewide, and those in the worst-performing *Abbott* districts—where state administrators have been conducting intensive intervention in literacy skills—improving faster still.

Abbott districts improved their average passing rate on that test from 62.6 percent to 75.4 percent—nearly 13 percentage points—between 2001 and 2004, compared with the state's 5-percentage-point gain.

But *Abbott* districts' average passing rate still lags well below the state average of 90 percent.

Academic improvements in *Abbott* middle and high schools, at least as measured by test scores, have generally been more elusive. But officials note that the state supreme court's decisions focused heavily on elementary school remedies and said little about middle and high school.

The state is now engaged in designing reform plans to bolster achievement in *Abbott* districts at those levels.

Fred Carrigg, the state's special assistant commissioner for urban literacy, characterizes the *Abbott* districts' progress as promising and significant. Working intensively with students and districts that have long lacked the tools to succeed does not yield big results quickly, but builds crucial capacity, he says.

State officials and school advocates theorize that the 4th grade tests are the first evidence that the court's mandates on whole-school reform are beginning to pay off. But some experts say that because some schools and districts have had more success with whole-school improvement than others, and no state evaluation has been performed, ascertaining exactly what is working and why is tricky.

"We really don't know what elements hold the weight of this improvement. It's unbelievably difficult to figure this thing out," says Bari A. Erlichson, an education consultant and former Rutgers University professor of public policy who studies *Abbott*.

In one recent report, Erlichson found that implementation of whole-school reform models in *Abbott* districts was hampered by inadequate support from the models' developers and districts.

She also cited a flawed process at the school level that gave teachers too little information and voice in selecting reform models, and noted waning state support for the whole-school reform approach, among other factors. By June 2004, she found, scores of *Abbott* schools were terminating their contracts with developers of reform models.

Abbott's preschool mandates are changing the education landscape in many New Jersey districts. Preschool enrollment in the *Abbott* districts has more than doubled from 19,000 in the 1999-2000 school year, the year the program began, to a projected 43,000 in 2004–05, or more than 80 percent of the 3- and 4-year-olds in those districts. Some districts, such as Long Branch, have conceived their own programs, while others, such as Trenton, rely largely on community providers. Some use a mix.

Preschool Progress

Early-childhood experts say the court case has improved services in the *Abbott* districts by requiring all New Jersey preschool teachers to have a bachelor's degree and early-childhood certification. The state developed such a certification in response to the rulings, designed standards for program content and quality, and provided scholarships to preschool teachers so they could complete their college degrees.

It also took steps to ensure that teachers in private-provider preschool programs were paid on the same scale as those in district-run programs, though better benefits packages offered by district programs still tend to tilt employment scales their way.

More than 92 percent of the teachers in *Abbott* preschool programs now hold bachelor's degrees, a far better-qualified preschool workforce than is seen nationally. Only an estimated one-third to one-half of U.S. teachers in early-childhood programs are similarly educated, according to a study by Sharon Ryan and Debra J. Ackerman of the National Institute for Early Education Research, based at Rutgers University in New Brunswick, N.J.

"What's happened with preschool in New Jersey is merely revolutionary," says Cynthia Rice, a senior policy analyst with the Association for Children in New Jersey, a Newark-based advocacy group. "Before *Abbott,* anyone with a high school diploma could teach preschool."

Studies of the preschool program suggest that while quality varies, and the children's skills still do not match national averages when they enter kindergarten. New Jersey preschoolers have made great strides, especially in their oral-language and early-literacy skills.

Another major piece of the finance case was a court mandate that the state upgrade school facilities in *Abbott* districts.

The high court's requirement that all *Abbott* districts have safe buildings has produced $660 million in repairs, such as replacement of leaky roofs and removal of asbestos. More than 500 renovations, additions, or new buildings are planned, with more than 200 in some stage of approval, design, or construction.

A dozen projects have been completed so far. All 500-plus of the planned projects will be completely state-financed. The original law passed in 2000 to pay for the court mandate authorized $6 billion in spending in the *Abbott* districts, but experts believe the price tag could easily double by the time the projects are finished.

However grand the scale of New Jersey's attempt to improve the lot of urban schoolchildren, there are those who remain skeptical that it is the right path.

"Difficult Political Calculus"

Some observers point out that seven years of near-parity in spending between rich and poor districts has not yet closed the performance gap between them, and ask whether the supreme court's package of remedies, and intimate involvement, can do so.

"*Abbott* is the poster child for court-run schools," says Eric A. Hanushek, a senior scholar at Stanford University's Hoover Institution. "They've been doing this for 30 years, and what is the evidence that any of it has impacted student achievement?"

Some experts worry that support for the court-mandated remedies could erode because of the way the cost basis was determined—linking it to spending in the wealthiest districts, rather than calculating what it actually costs to provide the needed services.

"It falls to build support for the *Abbott* districts, and public understanding of what education costs," says Erlichson. "It looks like a huge gift to them, rather than a number based on need."

Even MacInnes, the assistant commissioner in charge of *Abbott* implementation and a former Democratic state senator, says that spending just over half the state's annual $8 billion pre-K–12 education budget on the *Abbott* districts—which enroll 22 percent of its 1.4

million schoolchildren—makes for "a difficult political calculus."

Craig A. Stanley, the Democratic chairman of the state Assembly's education committee, says New Jersey should overhaul funding statewide to reduce its reliance on property taxes to support schools. "We do it totally wrong," he says. "We look at what we have and divide it up, because we lack the political will to look at what we need and find out what it costs."

National experts in school finance note that the *Abbott* case was among the first to inquire into what services were required to mitigate the effects of poverty, and to outline how the money would be used, instead of focusing only on whether there was enough money. But they criticize the two-tiered funding system that it created: one for the 31 *Abbott* districts, another for the state's 562 other districts.

"It creates two groups of districts that vie with each other," says John G. Augenblick, a Denver-based consultant who has helped states redesign their financing formulas. "What you need is a unified, single system that would use the same procedures for each district to determine state aid."

Apart from divisions over the *Abbott* remedies, the way New Jersey finances schools has sparked anger and litigation.

A group of middle-wealth school districts sued the state in 1998, contending that the state formula demanded too high a local share for schools, and drove those districts' property taxes to unreasonable levels. A court dismissed the suit, saying such an action should be filed by taxpayers, not districts. But resentment about inequitable financing remains.

Ronald E. Bolandi, the superintendent of the East Windsor Regional schools, a central New Jersey, middle-income district of 4,700 students, says his community lacks the tax base of its wealthier counterparts, and doesn't get the added state aid that the *Abbott* districts do. As a result, the district had to raise property taxes by an average of $400 per homeowner last year.

Only 26 percent of Bolandi's budget comes from state funds, compared with 82 percent in Trenton, an *Abbott* district 10 miles away. East Windsor Regional spends $10,200 per pupil annually, compared with $13,500 in Trenton, the state capital. "Our parents need full-day preschool and kindergarten, too," Bolandi says. "*Abbott* districts have those things, but I can't afford them."

Low-income districts not classified as *Abbott* districts suffer from the inability to generate revenue, but also from their residents' severely limited ability to pay higher taxes, says Frederick A. Jacob, a lawyer for eight rural districts seeking to be designated as *Abbott* districts.

"Tooting Our Horn"

He complains that in defining "special needs" districts as urban, *Abbott* overlooks needs in rural areas that equal or exceed those in urban areas.

Jacob cites the example of Commercial Township, a district in southern New Jersey, which had $145,212 worth of taxable property per child in the 1999–2000 school year, compared with nearby Millville, an *Abbott* district, with $173,346.

"These districts are the poorest of the poor, with some of the highest poverty rates in the state," he says, "yet they're not getting the funds—so they don't have as good buildings, they lose faculty to other districts that can pay more, and many times their class sizes are horrible."

Gary W. Ritter, an associate professor of education and public policy at the University of Arkansas who has studied *Abbott's* financial impact on New Jersey districts, found that middle-income districts and low-income non-*Abbott* districts have higher tax rates than *Abbott* or wealthy districts, yet still end up with less money. The roots of the inequities, he says, lie not in the court mandates, but in the state's aid system.

"There continue to be 'winners' and 'losers' in the school finance scheme," said a 2001 paper he co-wrote on the subject for the *Journal of Education Finance*. "Only the faces have changed."

David G. Sciarra, the lead attorney for the schoolchildren in the *Abbott* case, agrees that the near future must hold a reckoning when the state stares down the inequities of its finance system and finds a way to provide for all children the same high-quality programs from which *Abbott* children are benefiting.

But he believes the state "ought to be celebrating, tooting our horn," for doing what few states have done: assuring adequate resources for children in the poorest districts. "We've almost done it," he says. "Now we have to finish the job, to become a state in which we can say that every kid, not just in the *Abbotts*, but everywhere, has what they need."

Appendix

Suggested Resources

Research Literatures

ERIC can be searched on-line to find research and reflections on a wide variety of educational topics:
http://www.eric.ed.gov
Jstor: http://www.jstor.org (Found at college and university libraries that subscribe.) Jstor contains
electronic versions of journal articles more than several years old in such journals as *Sociology of
Education, American Journal of Sociology, American Sociological Review,* and others.
National Library of Education: http://www.ed.gov/NLE/index.html

On-Line Journals and/or Abstracts

Anthropology and Education Quarterly: http://www.aaanet.org/cae/aeq
Black Issues in Higher Education: http://www.blackissues.com
Chronicle of Higher Education: http://chronicle.com/
Education Week: http://www.edweek.org
Educational Leadership: http://www.ascd.org/cms/index.cfm
Harvard Education Letter: http://www.edletter.org
Harvard Education Review: http://www.gse.harvard.edu/~hepg/her.html
Rethinking Schools: http://www.rethinkingschools.org
Teachers College Record at http://www.tcrecord.org
Sociological Research Online is at: http://www.socresonline.org.uk

On-Line News Sources

Boston Globe: http://www.boston.com
LA Times: http://www.latimes.com
New York Times: http://www.nytimes.com
Library of Congress: http://www.olc.gov
New York Public Library: http://www.nypl.org/

Professional Associations

Association of School Administrators: http://www.aasa.org
American Educational Research Association: http://www.aera.net
American Federation of Teachers: http://www.aft.org/index.html
American Sociological Association (ASA): http://www.asanet.org/

From Caroline Hodges Persell and Floyd M. Hammack, "Internet Resources: How Instructors Are Using the
World Wide Web in Teaching the Sociology of Education." A section within *Teaching the Sociology of Education: A Resource Manual,* 6th ed. (Washington DC: American Sociological Association, 2004). Reprinted by
permission.

Sociology of Education Section: http://www.asanet.org/sections/educat.html
Association for Supervision and Curriculum Development: http://www.ascd.org/
Council for Aid to Education: http://www.cae.org
Council of Chief State School Officers: http://www.ccsso.org
Council of Great City Schools: http://www.cgcs.org
Education Commission of the States: http://www.ecs.org/
National Library of Education: http://www.ed.gov/NLE/

On-Line Journals and/or Abstracts

National Board for Professional Teaching Standards: http://www.nbpts.org/
National Education Association: http://www.nea.org
Sociology of Education Section, ASA: http://www.asanet.org/soe

Research Organizations

AACTE Education Policy Clearinghouse: http://www.edpolicy.org
Center for Social Organization of Schools: http://www.csos.jhu.edu/
Consortium for Policy Research in Education: http://www.upenn.edu/gse/cpre
National Center for Research in Vocational Education: http://vocserve.berkeley.edu

National Research and Development Centers

National Science Foundation: http://www.nsf.gov
Office of Educational Research and Improvement: http://www.ed.gov/offices/OERI/index.html
Office of Postsecondary Education: http://www.ed.gov/about/offices/list/ope/index.html
RAND Organization: http://www.rand.org
U.S. Department of Education: http://www.ed.gov/index.jsp
White House Briefing Room, Education: http://www.whitehouse.gov/fsbr/education.html

Educational Reform Organizations and Information

Achieve: http://www.achieve.org/achieve/achievestart.nsf?opendatabase
AVID: http://www.avidcenter.org
Center on School, Family, and Community Partnerships: http://www.csos.jhu.edu/p2000/center.html
Coalition for Essential Schools: http://www.essentialschools.org
Comer School Development Program: http://info.med.yale.edu/comer
Edison Schools: http://www.edisonproject.com
New American Schools Network: http://www.naschools.org
Public Education Network: http://www.publiceducation.org
Success for All: http://www.successforall.net/

Testing: Test Preparation and Tutoring Organizations

ACT: http://www.act.org
Educational Testing Service (ETS): http://www.ets.org
Kaplan: http://www.kaplan.com
Kumon: http://www.kumon.com
National Assessment of Student Progress (Nation's Report Card):
        http://nces.ed.gov/nationsreportcard/site/home.asp
Princeton Review: http://www.princetonreview.com
Psychological Corporation: http://www.tpc-international.com/
Sylvan Associates: http://www.sylvanlearning.com/

Higher Education Resources

American Association of Colleges and Universities: http://www.aacu-edu.org
American Association of Community Colleges: http://www.aacc.nche.edu
Association for Institutional Research: http://www.airweb.org/
Association for the Study of Higher Education: http://www.ashe.ws/
Community College Web: http://www.mcli.dist.maricopa.edu/cc/
Educause (formerly Educom and CAUSE): http://www.educause.net
Fund for the Improvement of Postsecondary Education: http://www.ed.gov/about/offices/list/ope/fipse
Higher Education Resource Hub: http://www.higher-ed.org
League for Innovation in the Community College: http://www.league.org
National Center for Postsecondary Improvement: http://www.stanford.edu/group/ncpi/index.html
National Center for Public Policy and Higher Education: http://www.highereducation.org
Review of Higher Education: http://www.press.jhu.edu/journals/review_of_higher_education/; also try
        http://muse.jhu.edu/journals/rhe/
Society for College and University Planning: http://www.scup.org
Western Interstate Commission on Higher Education: http://www.wiche.edu/

International Materials

Digest of Educational Statistics: International Comparisons:
        http://nces.ed.gov/programs/digest/d03/list_tables4.asp#c6
International Association for Social Science Information Service & Technology:
        http://www.iassistdata.org/
International Bureau of Education: http://www.ibe.unesco.org
International Education Links: http://nces.ed.gov/partners/internat.asp
Swedish Social Science Data Service: http://www.ssd.gu.se/enghome.html
UNESCO: http://www.unesco.org

Data

Country and Data Book: http://www.census.gov/statab/www/ccdb.html
General Social Survey (GSS) is available on-line, and simple analyses may be conducted on-line at:
        http://www.webapp.icpsr.umich.edu/cocoon/ICPSR-SERIES/00028.xml
National Center for Educational Statistics (NCES): http://nces.ed.gov
NCES Encyclopedia of Education Statistics: http://nces.ed.gov/edstats
NCES Surveys: http://nces.ed.gov/surveys
Roper Center for Public Policy Research: http://www.ropercenter.uconn.edu
State Education Report Cards: http://measuringup2000.highereducation.org/
U.S. Census Bureau, Home Page: http://www.census.gov

References

Achilles, C. M. (1996). Response to Eric Hanushek: Students achieve more in smaller classes. *Educational Leadership, 76.*

Adler, M. (1982). *The paideia proposal: An educational manifesto.* New York: Macmillan.

Adler, M. (1990). *Reforming education: The opening of the American mind.* New York: Macmillan.

Aladjem, D., Shive, J., Fast, E. F.., Herman, R., Borman, K., Katzenmeyer, W., Hess, M., & Hoffer, T. (2002). *A large-scale mixed-methods approach to studying comprehensive school reform* (Available from the American Institutes for Research, 1000 Thomas Jefferson Street, NW, Washington, DC 20007).

Albjerg, P. G. (1974). *Community and class in American education, 1865–1918.* New York: John Wiley.

Alexandar, L. (1986). Chairman's summary. In *Time for results: The governor's 1991 report on education.* National Governor's Association Center for Policy Research and Analysis. Washington, DC: National Governor's Association.

Alexander, K., & Cook, M. (1982). Curriculum and coursework. *American Sociological Review, 47,* 626–640.

Alexander, K., & Pallas, A. M. (1983). Private schools and public policy: New evidence on cognitive achievement in public and private schools. *Sociology of Education, 56,* 170–182.

Alexander, K. A., Entwisle, D. R., & Dauber, S. L. (1994). *On the success of failure: A reassessment of the effects of retention in the primary grades.* New York: Cambridge University Press.

Allen, W. R. (1988). Black students in U.S. higher education: Toward improved access, adjustment and achievement. *Urban Review, 20,* 165–188.

Allen, W. R. (1992). The color of success: African American college student outcomes at predominantly white and historically Black public colleges and universities. *Harvard Educational Review, 62,* 26–44.

Allen, W. R., Epps, E. G., & Haniff, N. Z. (1991). *College in Black and White: African American students in predominantly White and historically Black public universities.* Albany: State University of New York Press.

Allison, C. (1998). *Teachers for the new South.* New York: Peter Lang.

Altbach, P. G., Kelly, G. P., Petrie, H. G., & Weis, L. (Eds.). (1991). *Textbooks in American society: Politics, policy, and pedagogy.* Albany: State University of New York Press.

Althusser, L. (1971). Ideology and ideological state apparatuses. In *Lenin and philosophy and other essays.* New York: Monthly Review Press.

America 2000. (1991). Washington, DC: The White House.

American Association of University Women. (1992). *How schools shortchange girls.* Washington, DC: AAUW Educational Foundation and National Education Association.

American Association of University Women. (1998). *Separated by sex: A critical look at single-sex education for girls.* Washington, DC: AAUW Foundation.

American Federation of Teachers. (1998). *Building on the best, learning from what works: Six promising schoolwide reform programs.* Washington DC: Author.

American Federation of Teachers. (1999). *Improving low-performing high schools: Ideas & promising programs for high schools.* Washington DC: Author.

American Institutes for Research. (1999). *An educator's guide to schoolwide reform.*

Amidon, E. J., & Flanders, N. A. (1971). *The role of the teacher in the classroom.* Minneapolis: Paul S. Amidon and Associates, Inc.

Ancess, J., & Wichterle Ort, S. (1999). *How the coalition campus schools have re-imagined high school: Seven years later.* New York: The National Center for Restructuring Education, Schools, and Teaching, Teachers College, Columbia University.

Andersen, J. (1988). *The education of blacks in the south, 1860–1935.* Chapel Hill: University of North Carolina Press.

Andersen, M. L. (1999). Restructuring for whom? Race, class, gender and the ideology of invisibility. Presidential Address, *Eastern Sociological Society,* March 5, Boston.

Antler, J. (1987). *Lucy Sprague Mitchell: The making of a modern woman.* New Haven, CT: Yale University Press.

Antler, J., & Biklen, S. K. (Eds.). (1990). *Changing education: Women as radicals and conservators.* Albany: State University of New York Press.

Anyon, J. (1980). Social class and the hidden curriculum of work. *Journal of Education, 162,* 67–92.

Anyon, J. (1983). Workers, labor and economic history, and textbook content. In M. W. Apple & L. Weis (Eds.), *Ideology and practice in schooling* (pp. 37–60). Philadelphia: Temple University Press.

Anyon, J. (1994a). The retreat of marxism and socialist feminism: Postmodern theories in education. *Curriculum Inquiry, 24,* 115–134.

Anyon, J. (1994b). Teacher development and reform in an inner city school. *Teachers College Record, 96*(1), 14–31.

Anyon, J. (1995a). Educational reform, theoretical categories, and the urban context. *Access: Critical Perspectives and Policy Studies in Education, 14*(1), 1–11.

Anyon, J. (1995b). Inner city school reform: Toward useful theory. *Urban Education, 30*(1), 56–70.

Anyon, J. (1997). *Ghetto schooling: A political economy of urban educational reform.* New York: Teachers College Press.

Anyon, J. (2005a). Radical possibilities: *Public policy urban education and a new social movement.* New York: Routledge.

Anyon, J. (2005b). What "counts" as educational policy? Notes toward a new paradigm. *Harvard Educational Review, 75,* 1: 65–88.

Apple, M. W. (1978). Ideology, reproduction, and educational reform. *Comparative Educational Review, 22*(3), 367–387.

Apple, M. W. (1979a). *Ideology and curriculum.* Boston: Routledge & Kegan Paul.

Apple, M. W. (1979b). The other side of the hidden curriculum: Correspondence theories and the labor process. *Journal of Education, 162,* 7–66.

Apple, M. W. (1982a). *Cultural and economic reproduction in education.* Boston: Routledge & Kegan Paul.

Apple, M. W. (1982b). *Education and power.* Boston: Routledge & Kegan Paul.

Apple, M. W. (1990). What reform talk does: Creating new inequalities. In S. Bacharach (Ed.), *Educational reform: Making sense of it all* (pp. 155–164). Boston: Allyn and Bacon.

Apple, M. W. (1992). The text and cultural politics. *Educational Researcher, 21*(7), 4–11, 19.

Apple, M. W. (1993). *Official knowledge: Democratic education in a conservative age.* New York: Routledge.

Apple, M. W., & Christian-Smith, L. K. (Eds.). (1991). *The politics of the textbook.* London: Routledge.

Archer, M. S. (1979). *Social origins of educational systems.* Beverly Hills: Sage.

Aries, P. (1962). *Centuries of childhood: A social history of family life.* New York: Vintage Books.

Aristotle. (1943). *Politics.* New York: Modern Library.

Armor, D. (1995). *Forced justice: School desegregation and the law.* New York: Oxford University Press.

Arnot, M. (2002). *Reproducing gender: Selected critical essays on educational theory and feminist politics.* London: Falmer.

Arnot, M., David, M., & Weiner, G. (1999). *Closing the gender gap: Postwar education and social change.* Cambridge: Polity.

Arnot, M., & Dillabough, J. (2000) *Challenging democracy: International perspectives on gender, education and citizenship.* New York: Routledge.

Arnot, M., & Weiler, K. (Eds.). (1993). *Feminism and social justice in education.* London: Falmer.

Arnove, R. F., Altbach, P. G., & Kelly, G. P. (Eds.). (1992). *Emergent issues in education: Comparative perspectives.* Albany: State University of New York Press.

Aronowitz, S. (1987/1988). Postmodernism and politics. *Social Text, 18,* 94–114.

Aronowitz, S., & Giroux, H. (1985). *Education under siege.* South Hadley, MA: Bergin and Garvey.

Aronowitz, S., & Giroux, H. (1991). *Postmodern education: Politics, culture and social criticism.* Minneapolis: University of Minnesota Press.

Arons, S. (1986). *Compelling belief: The culture of American schooling.* Amherst: University of Massachusetts Press.

Arsen, D., et al. (1999). *School choice policies in Michigan: The rules matter.* Education Policy Center at Michigan State University. www.epc.msu.edu/publications/rules/summary.pdf.

Arthur, J., & Shapiro, A. (Eds.). (1995). *Culture wars: Multiculturalism and the politics of difference.* Boulder, CO: Westview Press.

Atkinson, P. (1981). Bernstein's structuralism. *Educational Analysis, 3,* 85–96.

Atkinson, P. (1985). *Language, structure and reproduction: An introduction to the sociology of Basil Bernstein.* London: Methuen.

Atkinson, P., Davies, B., & Delamont, S. (1995). *Discourse and reproduction: Essays in honor of Basil Bernstein.* Cresskill, NJ: Hampton Press.

Attewell, P. (2001) The winner-take-all high school: Organizational adaptations to educational stratification. *Sociology of Education, 74,* 267–296.

Attewell, P. (2001). Comment: The first and second digital divides. *Sociology of Education, 74,* 252–259.

Austin, G. R. (Ed.). (1982). *The rise and fall of national test scores.* New York: Academic Press.

Austin, G. R., & Garber, H. (Eds.). (1985). *Research on exemplary schools.* Orlando, FL: Academic Press.

Bacharach, S. (1990). *Educational reform: Making sense of it all.* Boston: Allyn and Bacon.

Bailyn, B. (1960). *Education in the forming of American society.* Chapel Hill: University of North Carolina Press.

Baker, D. P. (1992). The politics of American catholic school expansion, 1870–1930. In B. Fuller & R. Rubinson (Eds.), *The political construction of education* (pp. 189–206). New York: Praeger.

Baker, D. P. (1993). Compared to Japan, the U.S. is a low achiever . . . really: New evidence and comment on Westbury. *Educational Researcher, 22,* 18–26.

Baker, D. P. (1994). In comparative isolation: Why comparative research has so little influence on American sociology of education. In A. M. Pallas (Ed.), *Research in sociology of education and socialization* (Vol. 10) (pp. 53–70). Greenwich, CT: JAI Press.

Baker, D. P., Ethnington, C., Sosniak, L., & Westbury, I. (Eds.). (1992). *In search of more effective mathematics education: Evidence from the Second International Mathematics Study.* Norwood, NJ: Ablex.

Baker, D. P., & Riordon, C. (1998, September). The "eliting" of the common American Catholic school and national education crisis. *Phi Delta Kappan,* pp. 16–23.

Baker, D. P., & Smith, T. (1997). Three trends in the condition of education in the United States. *Teachers College Record, 99*(1), 14–18.

Baker, D. P., & Stevenson, D. L. (1986). Mothers' strategies for children's school achievement: Managing the transition to high school. *Sociology of Education, 59,* 156–166.

Baker, D. P., & Stevenson, D. L. (1991). State control of the curriculum and classroom instruction. *Comparative Education Review, 64,* 1–10.

Banks, J. A. (1988). *Multiethnic education: Theory and practice* (2nd ed.). Boston: Allyn and Bacon.

Banks, J. A. (1993). Multicultural education: Historical development, dimensions, and practice. In L. Darling-Hammond (Ed.), *Review of research in education* (pp. 3–49). Washington, DC: American Educational Research Association.

Banks, J. A., & McGee Banks, C. (1995). *Handbook of research on multicultural education.* New York: Macmillan.

Baratz, S. S., & Baratz, J. C. (1970). Early childhood intervention: The social science base of institutional racism. *Harvard Educational Review, 40,* 29–50.

Barber, B. (1992). *An aristocracy of everyone: The politics of education and the future of America.* New York: Ballantine.

Barr, J. (2004a). *A statistical portrait of New Jersey's schools.* Newark, NJ: Cornwall Center for Metropolitan Studies.

Barr, J. (2004b). *A statistical portrait of Newark's schools.* Newark, NJ: Cornwall Center for Metropolitan Studies.

Barr, R., & Dreeben, R. (1983). *How schools work.* Chicago: University of Chicago Press.

Barton, P. (2003). *Parsing the achievement gap.* Princeton, NJ: Educational Testing Service.

Barton, P. (2004, November). Why does the gap still persist? *Educational Leadership,* 8–13.

Bastian, A., Fruchter, N., Gittell, M., Greer, C., & Haskins, K. (1985). *Choosing equality: The case for democratic schooling.* Philadelphia: Temple University Press.

Baudrillard, J. (1981). *For a critique of the political economy of the sign* (C. Levin, Trans.). St. Louis: Telos Press.

Baudrillard, J. (1984). The precession of simulacra. In B. Wallis (Ed.), *Art after modernism: Rethinking representation* (pp. 213–281). Boston: David Godine.

Bayles, E. (1966). *Pragmatism in education.* New York: Harper and Row.

Beauboeuf, T., & Augustine, D. S. (1996). *Facing racism in education.* Cambridge, MA: Harvard University Press.

Becker, G. (1964). *Human capital.* New York: National Bureau of Economic Research.

Becker, H. S. (1952). Social-class variations in the teacher-pupil relationship. *Journal of Educational Sociology, 25,* 451–465.

Beineke, J. (1998). *There were giants in the land: The life of William Heard Kilpatrick.* New York: Peter Lang.

Belenky, M. F., Clinchy, B. M., Goldberger, N. R., & Tarule, J. M. (1986). *Women's ways of knowing: The development of self, voice, and mind.* New York: Basic Books.

Belfield C. R., & Levin, H. M. (2001a). *The effects of competition on educational outcomes: A review of US evidence.* National Center for the Study of Privatization in Education, Columbia University. Available at http://ncspe.org.

Belfield C. R. (2001b). *Tuition tax credits: What do we know so far?* National Center for the Study of Privatization in Education, Columbia University. Available at http://ncspe.org.

Belfield, C. R., & Levin, H. M. (2002). The effects of competition between schools on educational outcomes: A review for the United States, 72. *Review of Education Research, 279.*

Bell, D. (Ed.). (1980). *Shades of brown: New perspectives on school desegregation.* New York: Teachers College Press.

Bennett, K. P., & LeCompte, M. D. (1990). *How schools work.* New York: Longman.

Bennett, W. (1984). *To reclaim a legacy.* Washington, DC: National Endowment for the Humanities.

Bennett, W. (1988). *James Madison High School.* Washington, DC: U.S. Office of Education.

Bensman, D. (2000). *Central park east and its graduates: Learning by heart.* New York: Teachers College Press.

Berends, M., Bodilly, S., & Kirby, S. (2002). Looking back over a decade of whole-school reform: The experience of new American schools. *Phi Delta Kappan, 84*(2), 168–175.

Berg, I. (1970). *Education and jobs: The great training robbery.* New York: Praeger.

Berger, P. L., & Luckmann, T. (1967). *The social construction of reality: A treatise in the sociology of knowledge.* New York: Anchor Books.

Berliner, D., & Biddle, B. (1995). *The manufactured crisis.* New York: Longman.

Berman, P., & Chambliss, D. (2000). *Readiness of low-performing schools for comprehensive reform.* Washington DC: RPP International.

Bernstein, B. (1973a). *Class, codes, and control* (Vol. 1). London: Paladin.

Bernstein, B. (1973b). *Class, codes, and control* (Vol. 2). London: Routledge & Kegan Paul.

Bernstein, B. (1977). *Class, codes, and control* (Vol. 3). London: Routledge & Kegan Paul.

Bernstein, B. (1990). *The structuring of pedagogic discourse: Volume IV: Class, codes and control.* London: Routledge.

Bernstein, B. (1996). *Pedagogy, symbolic control and identity: Theory, research, and critique.* London: Taylor and Francis.

Best, R. (1983). *We've all got scars.* Bloomington: Indiana University Press.

Bestor, A. (1953). *Educational wastelands.* Urbana, IL: University of Illinois Press.

Biddle, B., Good, T., & Goodson, I. (Eds.). (1996). *International handbook of teachers and teaching.* Amsterdam: Kluwer Academic Publishers.

Bidwell, C. (1965). The school as a formal organization. In J. G. March (Ed.), *Handbook of organizations* (pp. 994–1003). Chicago: Rand McNally.

Bidwell, C. E., Plank, S., & Muller, C. (1996). Peer social networks and adolescent career development. In A. C. Kerckhoff (Ed.), *Generating social stratification: Toward a new generation of research.* Denver: Westview Press.

Biklen, D. (1985). *Advancing the complete school: Strategies for effective mainstreaming.* New York: Columbia University Press.

Binder, A. J. (2000). Why do some curricular challenges work while others do not? The case of three afrocentric challenges. *Sociology of Education, 73,* 69–91.

Blau, P., & Duncan, O. D. (1967). *The American occupational structure.* New York: Wiley.

Bloom, A. (1987). *The closing of the American mind.* New York: Simon and Schuster.

Blount, J. (1998). *Destined to rule the schools: Women and the superintendency.* Albany: State University of New York Press.

Bluestone, B., & Harrison, B. (1982). *The de-industrialization of America.* New York: Basic Books.

Boli, J., & Ramirez, F. O. (1986). World culture and the institutional development of mass education. In J. G. Richardson (Ed.), *Handbook of theory and research in the sociology of education* (pp. 65–90). Westport, CT: Greenwood Press.

Boli, J., Ramirez, F. O., & Meyer, J. W. (1985). Exploring the origins and expansion of mass education. *Comparative Education Review, 29,* 145–170.

Bond, L. A., Roeber, E., & Braskamp, D. C. (1994). *The status of statewide student assessment programs in the United States.* Washington, DC: Council of Chief State School Officers.

Booth, A., & Dunn, J. (Eds.). (1995). *Family-school links: How do they affect educational outcomes.* Hillsdale, NJ: Erlbaum.

Borman, G., Hewes, G., Overman, L., & Brown, S. (2003). Comprehensive school reform and student achievement: A meta-analysis. *Review of Educational Research, 73*(2), 125–230.

Borman, K. (1992). *The first "real" job: A study of young workers.* Albany: State University of New York Press.

Borman, K., Cookson, P. W., Jr., Sadovnik, A. R., & Spade, J. Z. (1996). *Implementing educational reform: Sociological perspectives on educational policy.* Norwood, NJ: Ablex.

Borman, K., & Spring, J. (1984). *Schools in central cities.* New York: Longman.

Borman, K. M., Kersaint, G., Boydston, T., Lee, R., Cotner, B., Uekawa, K., Baber, G., Kromrey, J., & Katzenmeyer, W. (2004). *Meaningful urban education reform: Confronting the learning crises in mathematics and science.* Albany, NY: SUNY Press.

Boudon, R. (1974). *Education, opportunity, and social inequality: Changing prospects in Western society.* New York: Wiley.

Bourdieu, P. (1973). Cultural reproduction and social reproduction. In R. Brown (Ed.), *Knowledge, education, and cultural change* (pp. 71–112). London: Tavistock Publications.

Bourdieu, P. (1984). *Distinction: A social critique of the judgment of taste.* Cambridge, MA: Harvard University Press.

Bourdieu, P., & Passeron, J.-C. (1977). *Reproduction: In education, society, and culture.* Beverly Hills: Sage.

Bowder, D. (Ed.). (1982). *Who was who in the Greek world?* Oxford: Phaedon Press.

Bowen, W. G., & Bok, D. (1998). *The shape of the river: Long-term consequences of considering race in college and university admissions.* Princeton, NJ: Princeton University Press.

Bowles, S. (1977). Unequal education and the reproduction of the social division of labor. In J. Karabel & A. H. Halsey (Eds.), *Power and ideology in education* (pp. 137–152). New York: Oxford University Press.

Bowles, S., & Gintis, H. (1976). *Schooling in capitalist America: Educational reform and the contradictions of economic life.* New York: Basic Books.

Bowles, S., & Gintis, H. (1986). *Democracy and capitalism.* New York: Basic Books.

Boyer, E. (1983). *High school.* New York: Harper and Row.

Boyer, E. (1990). The new agenda for the nation's schools. In S. Bacharach (Ed.), *Education reform: Making sense of it all* (pp. 30–38). Boston: Allyn and Bacon.

Bracey, G. (1991). Why can't they be like we were? *Phi Delta Kappan, 72,* 106–121.

Braddock, J. H., II. (1990a). *Tracking: Implications for student race-ethnic subgroups.* Baltimore, MD: Johns Hopkins University, Center for Research on Effective Schooling for Disadvantaged Students.

Braddock, J. H., II. (1990b). Tracking the middle grades: National patterns of grouping for instruction. *Phi Delta Kappan, 71,* 445–449.

Braddock, J. H., II, & Dawkins, M. P. (1993). Ability grouping, aspirations, and attainments: Evidence from the national educational longitudinal study of 1988. *Journal of Negro Education, 62,* 324–336.

Braddock, J. H., II, & McPartland, J. M. (1990). Alternatives to tracking. *Educational Leadership, 47*(7), 76–79.

Braddock, J. H., II, & McPartland, J. M. (1992). *More effective education for disadvantaged students: A conceptual framework on learning environments and student motivation.* Baltimore, MD: Johns Hopkins University, Center for Research on Effective Schooling for Disadvantaged Students.

Bradley Commission. (1988). *Building a history curriculum.* Washington, DC: Educational Excellence Network.

Brameld, T. (1956). *Toward a reconstructed philosophy of education.* New York: Holt, Rinehart and Winston.

Brint, S. (1998). *Schools and societies.* Thousand Oaks, CA: Pine Forge Press.

Brint, S., & Karabel, J. (1989). *The diverted dream: Community colleges and the promise of educational opportunity in America, 1900–1985.* New York: Oxford University Press.

Bronfennbrenner, U. (1970). *Two worlds of childhood: U.S. and U.S.S.R.* New York: Russell Sage.

Brookover, W., et al. (1979). *School social systems and student achievement: Schools can make a difference.* New York: Praeger.

Brookover, W., et al. (1982). *Creating effective schools: An inservice program for enhancing school learning climate and achievement.* Holmes Beach, FL: Learning Publications.

Brophy, J. E., & Good, T. L. (1970). Teachers' communication of differential expectations for children's classroom performance: Some behavioral data. *Journal of Educational Psychology, 61,* 365–374.

Brown, D. K. (1995). *Degrees of control: A sociology of educational expansion and occupational credentialism.* New York: Teachers College Press.

Brown, L., & Gilligan, C. (1992). *Meeting at the crossroads: Women's psychology and girls' development.* Cambridge, MA: Harvard University Press.

Bryk, A. S., Easton, J. Q., Kerbow, D., Rollow, S. G., & Sebring, P. A. (1993). *A view from the elementary schools: The state of reform in Chicago.* Chicago: Consortium on Chicago School Research.

Bryk, A. S., Lee, V. E., & Holland, P. B. (1993). *Catholic schools and the common good.* Cambridge, MA: Harvard University Press.

Budoff, M. (1975). Engendering change in special education practices. *Harvard Educational Review, 45*(4). In T. Hehir & T. Latus (Eds.). (1992). *Special education at the century's end: Evolution of theory and practice since 1970* (pp. 69–88). Cambridge, MA: Harvard Educational Review.

Bulkley, K., & Fisher J. (2002). *A decade of charter schools: From theory to practice.* Consortium for Policy Research in Education. Available at www.cpre.org.

Bulkley, K., & Wohlstetter (Eds.). (2004). *Taking account of charter schools: What's happened and what's next.* New York: Teachers College Press.

Bulman R. C., & Kirp, D. L. (1999). The shifting politics of school choice. In Sugarman, S. D., & Kemerer, F.R. (Eds.), *School choice and social controversy: Politics, policy and law.* (pp. 36–67). Brookings Institution Press.

Burbules, N., & Rice, S. (1991). Dialogue across differences: Continuing the conversation. *Harvard Educational Review, 61*(4), 393–416.

Burbules, N., & Rice, S. (1992). Can we be heard? A reply to Leach. *Harvard Educational Review, 62*(2), 264–271.

Burris, B. (1983a). *No room at the top.* New York: Praeger.

Burris, V. (1983b, August). The social and political consequences of overeducation. *American Sociological Review, 48,* 454–467.

Buss, W. G. (1999). Teachers, teachers' unions, and school choice. In S. D. Sugarman & F. R. Kemerer (Eds.), *School choice and social controversy: Politics, policy and law* (pp. 300–331). Washington, DC: Brookings Institution Press.

Button, W. H., & Provenzano, E. E. (1989). *History of education and culture in America.* Englewood Cliffs, NJ: Prentice-Hall.

Butts, R. F. (1978). *Public education in the United States: From revolution to reform.* New York: Holt, Rinehart and Winston.

Butts, R. F., & Cremin, L. A. (1953). *A history of education in American culture.* New York: Holt.

Callahan, R. E. (1962). *Education and the cult of efficiency.* Chicago: University of Chicago Press.

Canada, K., & Pringle, R. (1995). The role of gender in college classroom interactions: A social context approach. *Sociology of Education, 68*(3), 161–186.

Carl, J. (1994). Parental choice as national policy in England and the United States. *Comparative Education Review, 38*(3), 294–322.

Carnegie Task Force on Teaching as a Profession. (1986). *A nation prepared: Teachers for the 21st century.* Washington, DC: Carnegie Forum on Education and the Economy.

Carnoy, M. (1974). *Education as cultural imperialism.* New York: McKay.

Carnoy, M. (Ed.). (1975). *Schooling in a corporate society.* New York: McKay.

Carnoy, M. (2001). *School vouchers: Examining the evidence.* Washington, DC: Economic Policy Institute.

Carnoy, M., & Levin, H. (Eds.). (1976). *The limits of educational reform.* New York: Longman.

Carnoy, M., & Levin, H. (1985). *Schooling and work in the democratic state.* Stanford, CA: Stanford University Press.

Carpenter, P. (1985). Single-sex schooling and girls' academic achievements. *Australian and New Zealand Journal of Sociology, 21,* 456–472.

Carpenter, P., & Hayden, M. (1987). Girls' academic achievements: Single-sex versus coeducational schools in Australia. *Sociology of Education, 60,* 156–167.

Carter, S. M. (2000). *No excuses: Lessons from 21 high-performing, high-poverty schools.* Washington DC: The Heritage Foundation.

Catsambis, S. (1994). The path to math: Gender and racial-ethnic differences in mathematics participation from middle school to high school. *Sociology of Education, 67,* 199–215.

Catsambis, S., Jordan, W. J., & McPartland, J. M. (1994). *Effects of program and course tracking on high school students' behaviors, attitudes, and aspirations.* Baltimore, MD: Johns Hopkins University, Center for Social Organization of Schools.

Cavallo, D. (1981). *Muscles and morals: Organized playgrounds and urban reform, 1880–1920.* Philadelphia: University of Pennsylvania Press.

Cavallo, D. (1999). *A fiction of the past: The sixties in America history.* New York: St. Martin's Press.

Center for Policy Research on Education (CPRE). (2000). *Assessment and accountability systems: 50 state profiles.* Philadelphia: CPRE, University of Pennsylvania.

Center on Education Policy. (2004). *From the capital to the classroom: Year 2 of the No Child Left Behind Act.* www.ctredpol.org/pubs/nclby2/cep_nclb_y2_full.pdf.

Center on Organization and Restructuring of Schools. (1995). *Bibliography on school restructuring.* Madison: University of Wisconsin-Madison, Wisconsin Center for Education Research.

Chabbot, C., & Ramirez, F. O. (2000). Development and education. In M. T. Hallinan (Ed.), *Handbook of sociology of education.* New York: Kluwer, 2000.

Chall, J. S., Jacobs, V. A., & Baldwin, L. E. (1990). *The reading crisis: Why poor children fall behind.* Cambridge, MA: Harvard University Press.

Chambliss, J. J. (Ed.). (1996). *Philosophy of education: An encyclopedia.* New York: Garland.

Charner, I. (1996). School-to-work opportunities: Prospects and challenges. In K. Borman, P. W. Cookson, Jr., A. R. Sadovnik, & J. Z. Spade (Eds.), *Implementing educational reform: Sociological perspectives on educational policy* (pp. 139–170). Norwood, NJ: Ablex.

Cherryholmes, C. (1988). *Power and criticism: Poststructural investigations in education.* New York: Teachers College Press.

Childs, J. L. (1931). *Education and the philosophy of experimentalism.* New York: Century.

Chubb, J. E. (2003). Real choice. In Paul E. Peterson (Ed.), *Our Schools Our Future . . . Are We Still at Risk?* (pp. 329–362), Stanford, CA: Hoover Institution.

Chubb, J. E., & Moe, T. M. (1990). *Politics, markets, and America's schools.* Washington, DC: Brookings Institution.

Cicourel, A. V., & Kitsuse, J. I. (1963). *The educational decision-makers.* New York: Bobbs-Merrill.

The Civil Rights Project, Harvard University. (2002). *The impact of racial and ethnic diversity on educational outcomes: Cambridge, MA School District,* www.civilrightsproject.harvard.edu/research/diversity/cambridge_diversity.php.

Clark, B. (1962). *Educating the expert society.* San Francisco: Chandler.

Clark, R. (1983). *Family life and school achievement: Why poor black children succeed or fail.* Chicago: University of Chicago Press.

Cohen, D., Raudenbush, S., & Ball, D. (2001). Resources, instruction, and research. In R. Boruch & F. Mosteller (Eds.), *Evidence matters: Randomized trials in education research.* Washington, DC: The Brookings Institution.

Cohen, D. K. (1995). What standards for national standards? *Phi Delta Kappan, 76,* 751–757.

Cohen, D. K., McLaughlin, M. W., & Talbert, J. E. (Eds.). (1993). *Teaching for understanding: Challenges for policy and practice.* San Francisco: Jossey-Bass.

Cohen, E. G. (1994a). *Designing groupwork: Strategies for the heterogeneous classroom.* New York: Teachers College Press.

Cohen, E. G. (1994b). Restructuring the classroom: Conditions for productive small groups. *Review of Educational Research, 64,* 1–35.

Cohen, E. G., Lotan, R., & Leechor, C. (1989). Can classrooms learn? *Sociology of Education, 62,* 75–94.

Coleman, J. S. (1961). *The adolescent society.* Glencoe, IL: The Free Press.

Coleman, J. S. (1965). *Adolescents and the schools.* New York: Basic Books.

Coleman, J. S. (1990). *Foundations of social theory.* Cambridge, MA: The Belknap Press of Harvard University Press.

Coleman, J. S., et al. (1966). *Equality of educational opportunity.* Washington, DC: U.S. Government Printing Office.

Coleman, J. S., & Hoffer, T. (1987). *Public and private schools: The impact of communities.* New York: Basic Books.

Coleman, J., Hoffer, T., & Kilgore, S. (1982). *High school achievement: Public, Catholic, and Private Schools Compared.* New York: Basic Books.

Collins, R. (1971). Functional and conflict theories of educational opportunity. *Harvard Educational Review, 38,* 7–32.

Collins, R. (1975). *Conflict sociology: Toward an explanatory science.* New York: Academic Press.

Collins, R. (1979). *The credential society.* New York: Academic Press.

Comer, J. (1988). Educating poor minority children. *Scientific American, 259*(5), 42–48.

Comer, J. (1996). *Rallying the whole village: The Comer process for reforming education.* New York: Teachers College Press.

Comer, J. (1993). The Yale school development program: Process, outcomes and policy implications. *Urban Education, 28,* 166–199.

Comer, J., & Haynes, N. M. (1991). Parent involvement in schools: An ecological approach. *Elementary School Journal, 91,* 271–277.

Conley, D. (2001). Capital for college: Parental assets and postsecondary schooling. *Sociology of Education, 74,* 59–71.

Connell, N. (1999). *Beating the odds: High-achieving elementary schools in high-poverty neighborhoods.* New York: Educational Priorities Panel.

Connell, R. W. (1993). Disruptions: Improper masculinities and schooling. In L. Weis & M. Fine (Eds.), *Beyond silenced voices* (pp. 191–208). Albany: State University of New York Press.

Cook, T. (2002). Randomized experiments in education: Why are they so rare? *Educational Evaluation and Policy Analysis, 24*(3), 175–200.

Cookson, P. W., Jr. (1989). United States of America: Contours of continuity and controversy in private schools. In G. Walford (Ed.), *Private schools in ten countries: Policy and practice.* London: Routledge.

Cookson, P. W., Jr. (1991). Politics, markets, and America's schools: A review. *Teacher College Record, 93,* 156–160.

Cookson, P. W., Jr. (1992). *The choice controversy.* Newbury Park, CA: Corwin Press.

Cookson, P. W., Jr. (1994). *School choice: The struggle for the soul of American education.* New Haven, CT: Yale University Press.

Cookson, P. W., Jr. (1995, Spring). Goals 2000: Framework for the new educational federalism. *Teachers College Record, 96*(3), 405–417.

Cookson, P. W., Jr., & Persell, C. H. (1985). *Preparing for power: America's elite boarding schools.* New York: Basic Books.

Cookson, P. W., Jr., Persell, C. H., & Catsambis, S. (1992). Differential asset conversion: Class and gendered pathways to selective colleges. *Sociology of Education, 65,* 208–225.

Cookson, P. W., Jr., Sadovnik, A. R., & Semel, S. F. (Eds.). (1992). *International handbook of educational reform.* Westport, CT: Greenwood Press.

Coons, J. E. (2001). *Rescuing school choice from its friends. America, 7,* 185.

Cooper, R., & Jordan, W. (2003). Cultural issues in comprehensive school reform. *Urban Education, 38*(4), 380–397.

Corwin, R. (1970). *Militant professionalism: A study of organizational conflict in high schools.* New York: Appleton-Century-Crofts.

Counts, G. S. (1932). *Dare the schools build a new social order?* New York: John Day.

Cremin, L. A. (1961). *The transformation of the school.* New York: Vintage Books.

Cremin, L. A. (1972). *American education: The colonial experience, 1607–1783.* New York: Harper and Row.

Cremin, L. A. (1977). *Traditions of American education.* New York: Basic Books.

Cremin, L. A. (1980). *American education: The national experience, 1783–1876.* New York: Harper and Row.

Cremin, L. A. (1988). *American education: The metropolitan experience, 1876–1980.* New York: Harper and Row.

Cremin, L. A. (1990). *Popular education and its discontents.* New York: Harper and Row.

Cross, Christopher T. (2004). *Political education: National policy comes of age.* New York: Teachers College Press.

Cuban, L. (1983, June). Effective schools: A friendly but cautionary note. *Phi Delta Kappan, 64,* 695–696.

Cuban, L. (1984). *How teachers taught: Constancy and change in American classrooms, 1890–1980.* New York: Longman.

Cuban, L. (1990a). Reforming again, again, and again. *Educational Researcher, 19*(1), 3–13.

Cuban, L. (1990b). Why do some reforms persist? In S. Bacharach (Ed.), *Education reform: Making sense of it all.* Boston: Allyn and Bacon.

Cubberly, E. P. (1934). *Public education in the United States: A study and interpretation of American educational history.* Boston: Houghton Mifflin.

Cuffaro, H. K. (1995). *Experimenting with the world.* New York: Teachers College Press.

Cummins, J. (1993). Empowering minority students: A framework for intervention. In L. Weis & M. Fine (Eds.), *Beyond silenced voices: Class, race, and gender in United States schools* (pp. 101–118). Albany: State University of New York Press.

Curti, M. (1959/1971). *The social ideas of American educators.* Totowa, NJ: Littlefield, Adams & Company.

Cusick, P. A. (1983). *The egalitarian ideal and the American high school.* New York: Longman.

D'Souza, D. (1991). *Illiberal education: The politics of race and sex on campus.* New York: The Free Press.

Dahl, R. A. (1961). *Who governs?* New Haven, CT: Yale University Press.

Darling-Hammond, L. (1984). *Beyond the commission reports: The coming crisis in teaching.* Santa Monica, CA: Rand.

Darling-Hammond, L. (1992). *Standards of practice for learner-centered schools.* New York: National Center for Restructuring Schools and Teaching.

Darling-Hammond, L. (1996a). The right to learn and the advancement of teaching: Research, policy, and practice for democratic education. *Peabody Journal of Education, 67*(3), 123–154.

Darling-Hammond, L. (1996b). Restructuring schools for high performance. In S. Fuhrman & J. O'Day (Eds.), *Rewards and reforms: Creating educational incentives that work* (pp. 144–194). San Francisco: Jossey-Bass.

Darling-Hammond, L. (1997). *The right to learn: A blueprint for creating schools that work.* San Francisco: Jossey-Bass.

Darling-Hammond. L. (2004). Inequality and the right to learn: Access to qualified teachers in California's public schools. *Teachers College Record, 106*(10), 1936–1966.

Darling-Hammond, L., Ancess, J., & Falk, B. (1995). *Authentic assessment in action: Studies of schools and students at work.* New York: Teachers College Press.

Darling-Hammond, L., Holtzman, D. J., Gatlin, S. J., & Vasquez-Helig, J. V. (2005). *Does teacher preparation matter? Evidence about teacher certification, Teach for America, and teacher effectiveness.* Palo Alto: Stanford University. Downloaded from www.schooldesign.net/binaries/(teachercert.pdf on May 27, 2005.

Darwin, C. (1982). *On the origin of the species.* New York: Penguin. (Original work published 1859)

Datnow, A., Borman, G., Stringfield, S., Overman, L., & Castellano, M. (2003). Comprehensive school reform in culturally and linguistically diverse contexts: Implementation and outcomes from a four-year study. *Educational Evaluation and Policy Analysis, 25*(2), 25–54.

Datnow, A., & Hubbard, L. (2002). *Gender in policy and practice.* New York: Routledge/Falmer.

Datnow, A., & Stringfield, S. (2000). Working together for reliable school reform. *Journal of Education for Students Placed at Risk, 5*(1 & 2), 183–204.

Dauber, S. L., & Epstein, J. L. (1993). Parents' attitudes and practices of involvement in inner-city elementary and middle schools. In N. Chavkin (Ed.), *Families and schools in a pluralistic society* (pp. 53–71). Albany: State University of New York Press.

Davies, S. (1995). Leaps of faith: Shifting currents in critical sociology of education. *American Journal of Sociology, 100*(6), 1448–1478.

de Beauvoir, S. (1989). *The second sex.* New York: Random House. (Original work published 1952)

Decker, P., Mayer, D. P., & Glazerman, S. (2004). *The effects of Teach for America on students: Evidence from a national evaluation.* Princeton, NJ: Mathematica.

Delamont, S. (1983). *Interaction in the classroom.* London: Routledge.

Delamont, S. (1989). *Knowledgeable women: Structuralism and the reproduction of elites.* New York: Routledge & Kegan Paul.

Delamont, S. (1990). *Sex roles and the school* (2nd ed.). London: Routledge.

Delamont, S. (1991). The hit list and other horror stories. *Sociological Review, 39*(2), 238–259.

DelFattore, J. (1992). *What Johnny shouldn't read: Textbook censorship in America.* New Haven, CT: Yale University Press.

Delpit, L. (1995). *Other people's children.* New York: The New Press.

Derrida, J. (1981). *Positions.* Chicago: University of Chicago Press.

Derrida, J. (1982). *Of grammatology.* Baltimore: Johns Hopkins University Press.

Deutsch, M., et al. (1964). *The disadvantaged child.* New York: Basic Books.

Dewey, J. (1897). My pedagogic creed. In M. S. Dworkin (Ed.), *Dewey on education* (pp. 19–32). New York: Teachers College Press.

Dewey, J. (1899). The school and society. In M. S. Dworkin (Ed.), *Dewey on education* (pp. 33–90). New York: Teachers College Press.

Dewey, J. (1902). The child and the curriculum. In M. S. Dworkin (Ed.), *Dewey on education* (pp. 91–111). New York: Teachers College Press.

Dewey, J. (1916). *Democracy and education: An introduction to the philosophy of education.* New York: Macmillan.

Dewey, J. (1927/1984). *The public and its problems.* In *John Dewey: The later works. Vol. 2: 1925–1927.* Carbondale and Edwardsville: Southern Illinois University Press. (Original work published 1927)

Dewey, J. (1938). *Experience and education.* New York: Macmillan.

DiMaggio, P. (1982, April). Cultural capital and school success: The impact of status culture participation on the grades of U.S. high school students. *American Sociological Review, 47,* 189–201.

DiMaggio, P., & Mohr, J. (1984). Cultural capital, educational attainment, and marital selection. *American Journal of Sociology, 90*(6), 1231–1261.

Do poor kids deserve poor schools? (1991, October 14). *Time Magazine,* pp. 60–61.

Domhoff, G. W. (1967). *Who rules America?* Englewood Cliffs, NJ: Prentice-Hall.

Domhoff, G. W. (1983). *Who rules America now?* Englewood Cliffs, NJ: Prentice-Hall.

Doran, B., & Weffer, W. (1992). Immigrant aspirations, high school process and academic outcomes. *American Education Research Journal, 29*(1), 163–181.

Dougherty, K. (1987, April). The effects of community colleges: Aid or hindrance to socioeconomic attainment? *Sociology of Education, 60,* 86–103.

Dougherty, K. (1988, Summer). Educational policymaking and the relative autonomy of the state: The case of occupational education in the community college. *Sociological Forum, 3,* 400–432.

Dougherty, K. (1990). *Quality, equality, and politics: The political sources of the current school reform wave.* Paper presented at the Annual Meeting of the American Sociological Association.

Dougherty, K. (1994). *The contradictory college: The conflicting origins, impacts, and futures of the community college.* Albany: State University of New York Press.

Dougherty, K. (1996). Opportunity-to-learn standards: A sociological critique. *Sociology of Education,* Extra Issue (Special Issue on Sociology and Educational Policy: Bringing Scholarship and Practice Together), 40–65.

Dougherty, K., & Hammack, F. (1990). *Education and society.* New York: Harcourt Brace Jovanovich.

Dougherty, K., & Sostre, L. (1992). Minerva and the market: The sources of the movement for school choice. *Educational Policy, 6,* 160–179.

Dreeben, R. (1968). *On what is learned in school.* Boston: Addison-Wesley.

Dreeben, R. (1994). The sociology of education: Its development in the United States. *Research in Sociology of Education and Socialization,* 10.

Dreeben, R., & Gamoran, A. (1986). Race, instruction, and learning. *American Sociological Review, 51,* 660–669.

Dryfoos, J. (1998). *Full service schools: A revolution in health and social services for children, youth and families.* San Francisco: Jossey-Bass.

Du Bois, W. E. B. (1935). Does the negro need separate schools? *Journal of Negro Education, 4,* 328–335.

Dumais, S. A. (2002). Cultural capital, gender, and school success: The role of habitus. *Sociology of Education, 77,* 44–68.

Durkheim, E. (1947). *The division of labor in society.* Glencoe, IL: The Free Press. (Original work published 1893)

Durkheim, E. (1954). *The elementary forms of religious life.* Glencoe, IL: The Free Press. (Original work published 1915)

Durkheim, E. (1956). *Education and sociology* (S. D. Fox, Trans.). New York: The Free Press.

Durkheim, E. (1962). *Moral education: A study of the theory and application of the sociology of education.* New York: The Free Press.

Durkheim, E. (1965). *The elementary forms of the religious life.* New York: The Free Press.

Durkheim, E. (1938/1977). *The evolution of educational thought* (P. Collins, Trans.). London: Routledge & Kegan Paul. (Original work published 1938)

Dworkin, A. G. (1985). *When teachers give up: Teacher burnout, teacher turnover, and their impact on children.* Austin, TX: Hogg Foundation for Mental Health and Texas Press.

Dworkin, A. G. (1987). *Teacher burnout in the public schools: Structural causes and consequences for children.* Albany: State University of New York Press.

Dworkin, A. G., Haney, C. A., Dworkin, R. J., & Telschow, R. L. (1990). Stress and illness behavior among urban public school teachers. *Educational Administration Quarterly, 26,* 59–71.

Dworkin, M. S. (Ed.). (1959). *Dewey on education.* New York: Teachers College Press.

Eder, D. (1981, July). Ability grouping as a self-fulfilling prophecy: A micro-analysis of teacher-student interaction. *Sociology of Education, 54,* 151–162.

Eder, D. (1995). *School talk.* New Brunswick, NJ: Rutgers University Press.

Eder, D., & Parker, S. (1987). The cultural reproduction of gender: The effect of extracurricular activities on peer-group culture. *Sociology of Education, 60,* 200–213.

Edmonds, R. (1979a). Effective schools for the urban poor. *Educational Leadership, 37*(1), 5–24.

Edmonds, R. (1979b, March–April). Some schools work and more can. *Social Policy,* 28–32.

Edmonds, R. (1982). Programs of school improvement: An overview. *Educational Leadership, 40,* 4–11.

Education Commission of the States. (1983). *Action for excellence: A comprehensive plan to improve our nation's schools.* Denver, CO: Author. (ERIC ED 235 588)

Education Commission of the States. (2004). *ECS report to the nation: State implementation of No Child Left Behind.* Denver: Education Commission of the States.

Education Law Center. (1996). *Wiping out disadvantages: The programs and services needed to supplement regular education for poor school children.* Newark, NJ: Author.

Education Law Center. (1998). *Transforming teaching and learning in special needs districts.* Newark, NJ: Education Law Center.

Education Law Center. (2005). *Abbott indicators report.* Newark, NJ: Education Law Center.

Education Trust. (1998). *Good teaching matters: How well-qualified teachers can close the gap.* Washington, DC: Author.

Education Trust. (2003). *Telling the whole truth (or not) about highly qualified teachers:* New state data. Washington, DC: Author.

Education Trust. (2004a). *Education watch: The nation.* Washington, DC: Author.

Education Trust. (2004b). *Education watch: Achievement gap summary tables.* Washington, DC: Author.

Education Trust. (2005). *Increasing achievement and closing gaps between groups.* Washington DC: Author. www2.edtrust.org/EdTrust/Product+Catalog/recent+presentations.htm. Retrieved on June 2, 2005.

Education Week. (2000). *Lessons of a century: A nation's schools comes of age.* Bethesda, MD: Author.

Education Week. (2005). No small change: Targeting money toward student performance. Quality counts, 2005. Bethesda, MD: *Education Week, 24,* 17.

Educational Priorities Panel. (1987). *A teacher for the apple: Why New York City can't staff its schools.* New York: Author.

Egan, K. (1992). Review of *The unschooled mind: How children think and how schools should teach,* by Howard Gardner. *Teachers College Record, 94*(2), 397–406.

Eisenmann, L. (1998). *Historical dictionary of women's education.* Westport, CT: Greenwood Press.

Eisner, E. W. (1995). Standards for American schools: Help or hindrance? *Phi Delta Kappan, 78,* 758–764.

Ellsworth, E. (1989). Why doesn't this feel empowering? Working through the repressive myths of critical pedagogy. *Harvard Educational Review, 59*(3), 297–324.

Elmore, R. (2004). *School reform from the inside out: Policy, practices and performance.* Cambridge, MA: Harvard.

Elmore, R. F. (1993). School decentralization: Who gains? Who loses? In J. Hannaway & M. Carnoy (Eds.), *Decentralization and school improvement: Can we fulfill the promise?* San Francisco: Jossey-Bass.

Elmore, R. F. (1994a). *Educational renewal: Better teachers, better schools.* San Francisco: Jossey-Bass.

Elmore, R. F. (1994b, December). Thoughts on program equity: Productivity and incentives for performance in education. *Educational Policy, 8*(4), 453–459.

Elmore, R. F., et al. (1990). *Reconstructing schools: The next generation of educational reform.* San Francisco: Jossey-Bass.

Ensminger, M. E., & Slusarcick, A. L. (1992). Paths to high school graduation or dropout: A longitudinal study of a first-grade cohort. *Sociology of Education, 65,* 95–113.

Entwisle, D. R., & Alexander, K. (1992). Summer setback: Race, poverty, school composition, a mathematics achievement in the first 2 years of school. *American Sociological Review, 57,* 72–84.

Entwisle, D. R., Alexander, K., & Gordon, L. S. (1997). *Children, schools and inequality.* Boulder, CO: Westview.

Epstein, C. F. (1990). *Deceptive distinctions: Sex, gender and the social order.* New Haven, CT: Yale University Press.

Epstein, J. (2001). *School, family and community partnerships: Preparing educators and improving schools.* Boulder, CO: Westview.

Epstein, J. L. (1986). Parents' reactions to teacher practices of parent involvement. *The Elementary School Journal, 86,* 277–294.

Epstein, J. L. (1987). Toward a theory of family-school connections: Teacher practices and parent involvement. In K. Hurrelmann, F. Kaufmann, & F. Losel (Eds.), *Social intervention: Potential and constraints* (pp. 121–136). New York: DeGruyter.

Epstein, J. L. (1990). School and family connections: Theory, research, and implications for integrating sociologies of education and family. In D. Unger & M. Sussman (Eds.), *Families in community settings: Interdisciplinary perspectives* (pp. 99–126). New York: Haworth Press.

Epstein, J. L. (1991a). Effects on student achievement of teacher practices of parent involvement. In S. Silvern (Ed.), *Advances in reading/language research, Vol. 5. Literacy through family, community and school interaction.* Greenwich, CT: JAI Press.

Epstein, J. L. (1991b, January). Paths to partnership: What we can learn from federal, state, district, and school initiatives. *Phi Delta Kappan, 72*(5), 344–349.

Epstein, J. L. (1992). School and family partnerships. In M. Alkin (Ed.), *Encyclopedia of educational research* (6th ed.) (pp. 1139–1151). New York: Macmillan.

Epstein, J. L. (1995). School/family/community partnerships: Caring for the children we share. *Phi Delta Kappan, 76,* 701–712.

Epstein, J. L., Sanders, M. G., Simon, B. S., Salinas, K. C., Jansorn, N. R., & Van Voorhis, F. L. (2002). *School, family, and community partner ships: Your handbook for action* (2nd ed.). Thousand Oaks, CA: Corwin.

Erickson, D. (1986). Choice and private schools: Dynamics of supply and demand. In D. C. Levy (Ed.), *Private education: Studies in choice and public policy* (pp. 82–109). New York: Oxford University Press.

Erickson, F. (1987). Transformation and school success: The politics and culture of educational achievement. *Anthropology and Education Quarterly, 18*(4).

Erlichson B. A., et al. (1999). *Implementing whole school reform in New Jersey: Year one in the first cohort.* New Brunswick, NJ: Center for Government Services, Rutgers University.

Erlichson, B. A., & Goertz, M. (2001). *Implementing whole school reform in New Jersey: Year two.* New

Brunswick, NJ: Center for Government Services, Rutgers University.

Farkas, G., et al. (1990). Cultural resources and school success: Gender, ethnicity, and poverty groups within an urban school district. *American Sociological Review, 55,* 127–142.

Fashola, O. S., & Slavin, R. E. (1998). Schoolwide reform models: What works? *Phi Delta Kappan, 370.*

Featherman, D. L., & Hauser, R. M. (1978). *Opportunity and change.* New York: Academic Press.

Feinberg, W. (1996). Affirmative action and beyond: A case for a backward-looking gender and race-based policy. *Teachers College Record, 97,* 362–399.

Felmlee, D., & Eder, D. (1983, April). Contextual effects in the classroom: The impact of ability groups on student attention. *Sociology of Education, 56,* 77–78.

Fennema, E. (1974). Mathematics learning and the sexes: A review. *Journal for Research in Mathematics Education, 5,* 126–139.

Fennema, E., & Leder, G. (1990). *Mathematics and gender.* New York: Teachers College Press.

Fine, M. (1986). Why urban adolescents drop into and out of public high school. *Teachers College Record, 87,* 393–409.

Fine, M. (1988). Sexuality, schooling and adolescent females. *Harvard Educational Review, 58*(1), 29–53.

Fine, M. (1991). *Framing dropouts: Notes on the politics of an urban public high school.* Albany: State University of New York Press.

Fine, M. (1993). [Ap]parent involvement: Reflections on parents, power, and urban public schools. *Teachers College Record, 94,* 682–708.

Fine, M. (Ed.). (1994). *Chartering urban school reform.* New York: Teachers College Press.

Finkelstein, B. (1989). *Governing the young: Teacher behavior in popular primary schools in 19th century United States.* London: Falmer Press.

Finkelstein, B. (1992). Education historians as mythmakers. In G. Grant (Ed.), *Review of research education* (pp. 255–297). Washington, DC: American Educational Research Association.

Finn, C. (1989). Presentation at *Forum on National Standards.* Teachers College, Columbia University.

Finn, J.D. (1998). *Class size and students at risk: What is known? What is next?* U.S. Department of Education. Washington, DC: Office of Educational Research and Improvement.

Firestone, W. A., Goertz, M. E., & Natriello, G. (1997). *From cashbox to classroom: The struggle for fiscal reform and educational change in New Jersey.* New York: Teachers College Press.

Fishman, S., & McCarthy, L. (1998). *John Dewey and the challenge of classroom practice.* New York: Teachers College Press.

FitzGerald, F. (1979). *America revised: History schoolbooks in the twentieth century.* Boston: Little, Brown.

Fordham, S. (1997). *Blacked out: Dilemmas of race, identity, and success at Capital High.* Chicago: University of Chicago Press.

Fordham, S., & Ogbu, J. (1986). Black students' school success: Coping with the "burden" of "acting white." *The Urban Review, 18*(3), 176–206.

Foster, M. (1995). African-American teachers and culturally relevant pedagogy. In J. A. Banks & C. McGee Banks (Eds.), *Handbook of research on multicultural education* (pp. 570–581). New York: Macmillan.

Frankenberg, E., & Lee, C. (2002). *Race in American public schools: Rapidly resegregating school districts.* Cambridge, MA: The Civil Rights Project, Harvard University Press.

Frankenberg, E., & Lee, C. (2003). *Charter schools and race: A lost opportunity for integrated education,* Cambridge, MA: The Civil Rights Project, Harvard University Press. www.civilrightsproject.harvard.edu/research/deseg/private_schools02.php.

Frankenberg, E., Lee, C., & Orfield, G. (2003). *A multiracial society with segregated schools: Are we losing the dream?* Cambridge, MA: The Civil Rights Project, Harvard University Press.

Franklin, B. M. (1995). *From backwardness to at risk: Childhood learning difficulties and the contradictions of school reform.* Albany: State University of New York Press.

Freedman, S. G. (1990). *Small victories.* New York: HarperCollins.

Freeman, R. (1976). *The overeducated American.* New York: Academic Press.

Freire, P. (1972). *Pedagogy of the oppressed.* New York: Herder and Herder.

Freire, P. (1977). *Education for critical consciousness.* New York: Seabury Press.

Freire, P. (1978). *Pedagogy in process.* New York: Seabury Press.

Freire, P. (1985). *The politics of education.* South Hadley, MA: Bergin and Garvey.

Freire, P. (1987). *A pedagogy for liberation.* South Hadley, MA: Bergin and Garvey.

Fullan, M. G., & Stiegelbauer, S. (1991). *The new meaning of educational change.* New York: Teachers College Press.

Fuller, B. (2000). *Inside charter schools.* Cambridge, MA: Harvard University Press.

Fuller, B., Elmore, R., & Orfield, G. (Eds.). (1996). *School choice: The cultural logic of families, the political rationality of schools. Who chooses? Who loses? Culture institutions and the unequal effects of school choice.* New York: Teachers College Press.

Fuller, B., & Rubinson, R. (Eds.). (1992). *The political construction of education: The state, school expansion, and economic change.* New York: Praeger.

Furstenberg, F., & Hughes, M. E. (1995). Social capital and successful development among at-risk youth. *Journal of Marriage and the Family, 57,* 580–592.

Futrell, M. H. (1990). Redefining national security: New directions for education reform. In S. Bacharach (Ed.), *Education reform: Making sense of it all* (pp. 259–268). Boston: Allyn and Bacon.

Gaines, D. (1991). *Teenage wasteland: Suburbia's dead end kids.* New York: Pantheon.

Gamarnikow, E., & Green, T. (1999). Developing social capital: Dilemmas, possibilities and limitations in education. In A. Hayton (Ed.), *Tackling disaffection and social exclusion* (pp. 46–64). London: Kogan Page.

Gamoran, A. (1986). Instructional and institutional effects of ability groupings. *Sociology of Education, 59,* 185–198.

Gamoran, A. (1987). The stratification of high school learning opportunities. *Sociology of Education, 60,* 135–155.

Gamoran, A. (1993). Alternative uses of ability grouping in secondary schools: Can we bring high-quality instruction to low-ability classes? *American Journal of Education, 101,* 1–22.

Gamoran, A. (1996a). Curriculum standardization and equality of opportunity in Scottish secondary education, 1984–1990. *Sociology of Education, 29,* 1–21.

Gamoran, A. (1996b). Student achievement in public magnet, public comprehensive, and private city high schools. *Educational Evaluation and Policy Analysis.*

Gamoran, A. (2001). American schooling and education inequality: A forecast for the 21st century. *Sociology of Education, 74,* Extra Issue, 135–153.

Gamoran, A. (2003). *Transforming teaching in math and science: How schools and districts can support change.* Sociology of Education Series, New York: Teachers College Press.

Gamoran, A., & Berends, M. (1987). The effects of stratification in secondary schools: A synthesis of survey and ethnographic research. *Review of Educational Research, 57,* 415–437.

Gamoran, A., & Dreeben, R. (1986). Coupling and control in educational organizations. *Administrative Science Quarterly, 31,* 612–632.

Gamoran, A., & Mare, R. D. (1989). Secondary school tracking and educational inequality: Compensation, reinforcement, or neutrality? *American Journal of Sociology, 94*(5), 1146–1183.

Gamoran, A., Nystand, M., Berends, M., & LePore, P. (1995). An organizational analysis of the effects of ability grouping. *American Educational Research Journal, 32,* 59–87.

Gardner, H. (1989). *To open minds: Chinese clues to the dilemma of contemporary education.* New York: Basic Books.

Gardner, H. (1991). *The unschooled mind: How children think and how schools should teach.* New York: Basic Books.

Gardner, H. (1992). A response. *Teachers College Record, 94*(2), 407–413.

Garet, M., Porter, A., Desimone, L., Birman, B., & Yoon, K. (2001). What makes professional development effective? Results from a national sample of teachers. *American Educational Research Journal, 38*(4), 915–945.

Garraty, J. A. (1985). *A short history of the American nation, Vol. B—Since 1865.* New York: Harper and Row.

Gartner, A., & Lipsky, D. K. (1987). Beyond special education: Toward a quality system for all students. *Harvard Educational Review, 57,* 367–395.

Gay, G. (1995). Curriculum theory and multicultural education. In J. A. Banks & C. McGee Banks (Eds.), *Handbook of research on multicultural education* (pp. 25–43). New York: Macmillan.

Gay, P. (Ed.). (1964). *John Locke on education.* New York: Teachers College Bureau of Publications.

Gewertz, C. (2005). A level playing field. *Education Week, 24,* 17, 41–45, 47–48.

Gibson, M., & Ogbu, J. (1992). *Minority status and schooling: A comparative study of immigrants and involuntary minorities.* New York: Garland.

Giddens, A. (1998). *The third way.* Cambridge: Polity.

Gill, B., et al. (2001). *Rhetoric vs. reality: What we know and what we need to know about vouchers and charter schools.* RAND Corporation.

Gilligan, C. (1982). *In a different voice.* Cambridge, MA: Harvard University Press.

Gilligan, C., et al. (1990). *Making connections: The relational worlds of adolescent girls at Emma Willard School.* Cambridge, MA: Harvard University Press.

Giroux, H. (1981). *Ideology, culture and the process of schooling.* Philadelphia: Temple University Press.

Giroux, H. (1983a). Theories of reproduction and resistance in the new sociology of education. *Harvard Educational Review, 53,* 257–293.

Giroux, H. (1983b). *Theory and resistance in education.* South Hadley, MA: Bergin and Garvey.

Giroux, H. (1988). *Teachers as intellectuals.* Granby, MA: Bergin and Garvey.

Giroux, H. (1991). *Postmodernism, feminism, and cultural politics: Redrawing educational boundaries.* Albany: State University of New York Press.

Glenn, C. L. (1991). Will Boston be the proof of the choice pudding? *Educational Leadership, 48,* 41–43.

Goertz, G., Floden, R., & O'Day. (1995). *Building capacity for education reform.* Consortium for Policy Research

Education (CPRE) Policy Briefs. Philadelphia: University of Pennsylvania, pp. 1–10.

Goodlad, J. I. (1979). *What schools are for.* Bloomington, IN: Phi Delta Kappa.

Goodlad, J. I. (1984). *A place called school: Prospects for the future.* New York: McGraw-Hill.

Goodlad, J. I. (1990). *Teachers for our nation's schools.* San Francisco: Jossey-Bass.

Goodlad, J. I. (1991, November). Why we need a complete redesign of teacher education. *Educational Leadership, 49,* 7–10.

Goodson, I. (1993). *School subjects and curriculum change* (3rd ed.). London: Falmer Press.

Goodwin, R. K., & Kemerer, F. R. (2002). *School choice tradeoffs: Liberty, equity & diversity.* Austin: University of Texas Press.

Gordon, B. (1995). Knowledge construction, competing theories, and education. In J. A. Banks & C. McGee Banks (Eds.), *Handbook of research on multicultural education* (pp. 184–199). New York: Macmillan.

Gordon, D. (1977). *Problems in political economy: An urban perspective.* Boston: D. C. Heath.

Gore, J. (1993). *The struggle for pedagogies: Critical and feminist discourses as regimes of truth.* New York: Routledge.

Gornick, V. (1987). The next great moment in history is theirs. In A. R. Sadovnik et al. (Eds.), *Exploring society* (pp. 260–266). New York: Harper and Row.

Goslin, D. (1965). *The school in contemporary society.* Atlanta: Scott, Foresman.

Government Accounting Office. *No Child Left Behind Act: Improvements needed in education's process for tracking states' implementation of key provisions.* www.gao.gov/cgi-bin/getrpt?GAO-04-734.

Grant, G. (1988). *The world we created at Hamilton High.* Cambridge, MA: Harvard University Press.

Grant, L., Horan, P. M., & Watts-Warren, B. (1994). Theoretical diversity in the analysis of gender and education. *Research in Socialization of Education and Socialization, 10,* 71–110.

Greeley, A. M. (1982). *Catholic schools and minority students.* New Brunswick, NJ: Transaction Books.

Greeley, A. M. (1998, September). The so-called failure of Catholic schools. *Phi Delta Kappan,* pp. 24–25.

Greene, J. P., et al. (1999). *Effectiveness of school choice: The Milwaukee experiment.* Education: Urban & Society, available at www.ksg.harvard.edu/pepg/other/mil.htm.

Greene, J., & Peterson, P. (1996). *Methodological issues in evaluation research: The Milwaukee school choice program.* Occasional Paper 96–4. Cambridge, MA: Harvard University Program in Educational Policy and Governance.

Greene, M. (1973). *Teacher as stranger: Educational philosophy for the modern age.* Belmont, CA: Wadsworth.

Greene, M. (1978). *Landscapes of learning.* New York: Teachers College Press.

Greene, M. (1988). *The dialectic of freedom.* New York: Teachers College Press.

Greene, M. (1989). The question of standards. *Teachers College Record, 94,* 9–14.

Greene, M. (1993). The passions of pluralism: Multiculturalism and the expanding community. *Educational Researcher, 22*(1), 13–18.

Greer, C. (1973). *The great school legend.* New York: Viking Press.

Grissmer, D., Flanagan, A., & Williamson, S. (1998). Why did the Black-White score gap narrow in the 1970s and 1980s? In C. Jencks & M. Phillips (Eds.), *The black/white test score gap.* Washington, DC: Brookings Institution Press.

Grissmer, D. W., et al. (2000). *Improving student achievement: What NAEP state test scores tell us.* RAND Corporation.

Gutek, G. (1991). *An historical introduction to American education* (2nd ed.). Prospect Heights, IL: Waveland Press.

Guthrie, W. K. (1969). *A history of Greek philosophy, Volume 3, Part 2: Socrates.* Cambridge: Cambridge University Press.

Gutmann, A. (1987). *Democratic education.* Princeton, NJ: Princeton University Press.

Habermas, J. (1979). *Communication and the evolution of society.* Boston: Beacon Press.

Habermas, J. (1981). Modernity versus postmodernity. *New German Critique, 8*(1), 3–18.

Habermas, J. (1982). The entwinement of myth and enlightenment. *New German Critique, 9*(3), 13–30.

Habermas, J. (1983). Modernity: An incomplete project. In H. Foster (Ed.), *The anti-aesthetic: Essays on postmodern culture* (pp. 3–16). Seattle: Bay Press.

Habermas, J. (1987). *The philosophical discourse of modernity* (F. Lawrence, Trans.). Cambridge, MA: MIT Press.

Hacker, A. (1992). *Two nations: Black and white, separate, hostile, unequal.* New York: Scribners.

Hakuta, K., & Garcia, E. (1989). Bilingualism and education. *American Psychologist, 53,* 374–379.

Hallinan, M. T. (1984). Summary and implications. In P. Peterson, L. C. Wilkinson, & M. Hallinan (Eds.), *The social context of instruction* (pp. 229–240). New York: Academic Press.

Hallinan, M. T. (1987). Ability grouping and student learning. In M. T. Hallinan (Ed.), *The social organization of schools: New conceptualizations of the learning process* (pp. 41–69). New York: Plenum.

Hallinan, M. T. (1990). The effects of ability grouping in secondary schools: A response to Slavin's Best-Evidence Synthesis. *Review of Educational Research, 60,* 501–504.

Hallinan, M. T. (1994a). Tracking: From theory to practice. *Sociology of Education, 67,* 79–84.

Hallinan, M. T. (1994b). School differences in tracking effects on achievement. *Social Forces, 72,* 799–820.

Hallinan, M. T. (2001). Sociological perspectives on Black-White inequalities in American schooling. *Sociology of Education, 74,* Extra Issue, 50–70.

Hallinan, M. T. (Ed.). (2000). *Handbook of sociology of education.* New York: Kluwer.

Hammack, F. M. (1986). Large school systems: Dropout reports: An analysis of definitions, procedures and findings. *Teachers College Record, 87,* 324–342.

Hannaway, J., & Carnoy, M. (1993). *Decentralization and school improvement: Can we fulfill the promise?* San Francisco: Jossey-Bass.

Hanushek, E. A. (1994). *Making schools work: Improving performance and controlling costs.* Washington, DC: The Brookings Institution.

Hanushek, E. A. (1998). *The evidence on class size.* Rochester, NY: University of Rochester, W. Allen Wallis Institute of Political Economy.

Harvard Civil Rights Project. (2004). www.civilrightsproject.harvard.edu/.

Harvey, D. (1989). *The condition of postmodernity: An inquiry into the origins of cultural change.* Cambridge, MA: Basil Blackwell.

Hatch, T. (2002). When improvement programs collide. *Phi Delta Kappan, 83*(8), 626–634, 639.

Hauser, R., & Featherman, D. (1976). Equality of schooling: Trends and prospects. *Sociology of Education, 49,* 99–119.

Haycock, K. (1999). *Dispelling the myth: High poverty schools exceeding expectations.* Washington, DC: The Education Trust.

Haynes, N., & Comer, J. P. (1993). The Yale school development program: Process, outcomes, and policy implications. *Urban Education, 28,* 166–199.

Hayton, A. (Ed.). (1999). *Tackling disaffection and social exclusion.* London: Kogan Page.

Hechinger, F. (1987, November 10). Gift of a great teacher. *New York Times.*

Heck, S. F., & Williams, C. R. (1984). *The complex roles of the teacher: An ecological perspective.* New York: Teachers College Press.

Hedges, L., Laine, R., & Greenwald, R. (1994). Does money matter? A meta-analysis of the effects of differential school inputs on student outcomes. *Educational Researcher, 23*(3), 5–14.

Hedges, L. V., Laine, R. D., & Greenwald, R. (1994). Does money matter? A meta-analysis of studies of the effects of differential school inputs on student outcomes. *Educational Researcher, 23,* 5–14.

Hehir, T., & Latus, T. (1992). *Special education at the century's end: Evolution of theory and practice since 1970.* Cambridge, MA: Harvard Educational Review.

Heller, J. (1985). *Catch 22.* New York: Dell.

Henig, J. (1994). *Rethinking school choice: Limits of the market metaphor.* Princeton, NJ: Princeton University Press.

Henig, J. R. (1995). *Rethinking school choice: Limits of the market metaphor.* Princeton, NJ: Princeton University Press.

Henig, J. R., & Sugarman, S. D. (1999). The nature and extent of school choice. In S. Sugarman & F. R. Kemerer (eds.), *School choice and social controversy: Politics, policy and law* (pp. 13–35). Washington, DC: Brookings Institution Press.

Herman, R., Aladjem, D., McMahon, P., O'Malley, A., Quinones, S., & Woodruff, D. (1999). *An educators' guide to schoolwide reform.* Washington, DC: American Institutes for Research.

Herrnstein, R. J. (1973). *IQ in the meritocracy.* Boston: Little, Brown.

Herrnstein, R. J., & Murray, C. (1994). *The bell curve: Intelligence and class structure in American life.* New York: The Free Press.

Hess, F. M. (2002). *Revolution at the margins: The impact of competition on urban school systems.* Washington, DC: Brookings Institution Press.

Hess, F. M. (Ed.). (2005). *Urban school reform: Lessons from San Diego.* Cambridge, MA: Harvard University Press.

Hess, F. M., Rotherham, A. J., & Walsh, K. (2004). *A qualified teacher in every classroom? Appraising old answers and new ideas.* Cambridge, MA: Harvard University Press.

Hess, G. A., Jr. (1991). *School restructuring, Chicago style.* Newbury Park, CA: Corwin Press.

Hess, G. A., Jr. (1994). Introduction: School-based management as a vehicle for school reform. *Education and Urban Society, 26,* 203–219.

Hess, G. A., Jr. (1995). *Restructuring urban schools: A Chicago perspective.* New York: Teachers College Press.

Heubert, J. P., & Hauser, R. M. (1999). *High stakes: Testing for tracking, promotion, and graduation.* Washington, DC: National Academy Press.

Heyns, B. (1978). *Summer learning and the effects of schooling.* New York: Academic Press.

Hildebrand, J. (1998, May 4). Winners, losers in a money game. *Newsday,* pp. A5, A26–A27.

Hill, P. T. (2005). Assessing student performance in charter schools: Why studies often clash and answers remain elusive. *Education Week, 24*(18), 33, 44.

Hill, P. T., et al. (2000). *It takes a city: Getting serious about urban school reform.* Washington, DC: Brooking Institution Press.

Hill, P. T., & Bonan, J. (1991). *Decentralization and accountability in public education.* Santa Monica, CA: Rand.

Hirsch, E. D., Jr. (1987). *Cultural literacy.* Boston: Houghton Mifflin.

Hirsch, E. D., Jr. (1988). *Cultural literacy: What every American needs to know.* New York: Random House.

Hitchcock, M. E., & Tompkins, G. E. (1987). Are basal reading textbooks still sexist? *The Reading Teacher, 41,* 288–292.

Hochschild, J. (1984). *The new American dilemma: Liberal democracy and school desegregation.* New Haven, CT: Yale University Press.

Hochschild, J. (1986). *What's fair? American beliefs about distributive justice.* Cambridge, MA: Harvard University Press.

Hochschild, J. (1995). *Facing up to the American dream: Race, class and the soul of the nation.* Princeton, NJ: Princeton University Press.

Hodgkinson, H. (1985). *All one system: Demographics of education, kindergarten through graduate school.* Washington, DC: Institute for Educational Leadership.

Hodgkinson, H. (1991, September). Reform versus reality. *Phi Delta Kappan,* 9–16.

Hoffer, T. (1992). Middle school ability grouping and student achievement in science and mathematics. *Educational Evaluation and Policy Analysis, 14,* 205–227.

Hoffer, T., Greeley, A. M., & Coleman, J. S. (1985, April). Achievement growth in public and Catholic schools. *Sociology of Education, 58,* 74–97.

Hofstadter, R. (1966). *Anti-intellectualism in American life.* New York: Rand.

Hogan, D. J. (1978). Education and the making of the Chicago working class, 1880–1930. *History of Education Quarterly, 18,* 227–270.

Hogan, D. J. (1985). *Class and reform: School and society in Chicago, 1880–1930.* Philadelphia: University of Pennsylvania Press.

Holmes Group. (1986). *Tomorrow's teachers.* East Lansing, MI: Author.

Holmes Group. (1990). *Tomorrow's schools.* East Lansing, MI: Author.

Holmes Group. (1995). *Tomorrow's schools of education.* East Lansing, MI: Author.

Honig, B. (1990). The key to reform: Sustaining and expanding upon initial success. In S. Bacharach (Ed.), *Education reform: Making sense of it all* (pp. 52–56). Boston: Allyn and Bacon.

Hopper, E. (1971). Stratification, education and mobility in industrial societies. In E. Hopper (Ed.), *Readings in the theory of educational systems.* London: Hutchinson.

Horn, J., & Miron, G. (2002a). *Evaluation of Connecticut charter schools and the charter school initiative: Final report.* Kalamazoo, MI: Evaluation Center Western Michigan University.

Horn, J., & Miron, G. (2002b). *An evaluation of the Michigan charter school initiative: performance, accountability, and impact.* Kalamazoo, MI: Evaluation Center Western Michigan University. www.wmich.edu/evalctr/.

Horowitz, H. L. (1984). *Alma mater: Design and experience in the women's colleges from their nineteenth century beginnings to the 1930s.* New York: Knopf. (Second edition published by University of Massachusetts Press in 1993)

Horvat, E. M. (2003). Reassessing the "Burden of 'Acting White'": The importance of peer groups in managing academic success. *Sociology of Education, 76,* 265–280.

Howell, W. G., & Peterson, P. E. (2002). *The education gap: Vouchers and urban schools.* Washington, DC: Brookings Institution Press.

Hoxby, C. M. (2000a). Does competition among public schools benefit students and taxpayers? *American Economic Review, 90,* 5.

Hoxby, C. M. (2000b). The effects of class size on student achievement: New evidence from population variation. *Quarterly Journal of Economics, 115,* 4.

Hoxby, C. M. (2001). All school finance equalizations are not created equal. *Quarterly Journal of Economics, 116,* 4.

Hoxby, C. M. (2004a). A straightforward comparison of charter schools and regular public schools in the United States. HIER Working Paper. http://post.economics.harvard.edu/faculty/hoxby/papers.html.

Hoxby, C. M. (2004b). Achievement in charter schools and regular public schools in the United States: Understanding the differences. HIER Working Paper. http://post.economics.harvard.edu/faculty/hoxby/papers.html.

Hoxby, C. M., & Rockoff, J. (2004). The impact of charter schools on student Achievement. HIER Working Paper. http://post.economics.harvard.edu/faculty/hoxby/papers.html.

Hunter, M. (1982). *Mastery teaching.* El Segundo, CA: TIP Publications.

Hurn, C. J. (1993). *The limits and possibilities of schooling* (3rd ed.). Boston: Allyn and Bacon.

Illich, I. (1970). *Deschooling society.* New York: Harper and Row.

Ingersoll, R. (1999). The problem of underqualified teachers in American secondary schools. *Educational Researcher, 28,* 26–37.

Ingersoll, R. (2001). Teacher turnover and teacher shortages. *American Educational Research Journal, 38*(3), 499–534.

Ingersoll, R. (2003). *Who controls teachers' work?: Power and accountability in America's schools.* Cambridge, MA: Harvard University Press.

Ingersoll, R. (2004). Why some schools have more underqualified teachers than others. In Diane Ravitch (Ed.), *Brookings papers on education policy.* Washington, DC: Brookings Institution Press.

Ingersoll, R. M. (1994). Organizational control in secondary schools. *Harvard Educational Review, 64,* 150–172.

Inkeles, A. (1979). National differences in scholastic performance. *Comparative Education Review, 23,* 386–407.

Jackson, P. (1968). *Life in classrooms.* New York: Holt, Rinehart and Winston.

Jackson, P. (1986). *The practice of teaching.* New York: Teachers College Press.

Jackson, P. (1997). *John Dewey and the lessons of art.* New Haven, CT: Yale University Press.

Jacobs, J. A. (1995). Gender and academic specialties: Trends among recipients of college degrees in the 1980s. *Sociology of Education, 68,* 81–98.

James, M. (Ed.). (1995). *Social reconstruction through education: The philosophy, history, and curricula of a radical ideal.* Norwood, NJ: Ablex.

James, M. (2005). *The conspiracy of the good: Civil rights and the struggle for community in two American cities, 1875–2000.* New York: Peter Lang.

James, W. (1978). *Varieties of religious experience.* New York: Norton.

Jameson, F. (1982). Postmodernism and consumer society. In H. Foster (Ed.), *The anti-aesthetic: Essays on postmodern culture* (pp. 11–125). Seattle: Bay Press.

Jencks, C. (1985). How much do high school students learn? *Sociology of Education, 58,* 128–135.

Jencks, C. (1987). *What is post-modernism?* New York: St. Martin's.

Jencks, C. (1992). *Rethinking social policy: Race, poverty, and the underclass.* New York: HarperPerennial.

Jencks, C., Bartlett, S., Corcoran, M., Crouse, J., Eaglesfield, D., Jackson, G., McClelland, K., Mueser, P., Olneck, M., Schwartz, J., Ward, S., & Williams, J. (1979). *Who gets ahead?* New York: Basic Books.

Jencks, C., Smith, M., Acland, H., Bane, M. J., Cohen, D., Gintis, H., Heyns, B., & Michelson, S. (1972). *Inequality.* New York: Basic Books.

Jensen, A. (1969). How much can we boost I.Q. and scholastic achievement? *Harvard Educational Review, 39,* 1–23.

Johnson, J. (1991). *Introduction to the foundations of American education* (8th ed.). Boston: Allyn and Bacon.

Johnson, J. F., Jr., et al. (1999). *Hope for urban education: A study of nine high-performing, high-poverty, urban elementary schools.* Austin: The Charles A. Dana Center, The University of Texas at Austin.

Johnson, S. M. (1990). *Teachers at work: Achieving success in our schools.* New York: Basic Books.

Johnson, S. M. (1991). Review of *Small victories* by Samuel G. Freedman. *Teachers College Record, 93*(1), 180–184.

Johnson, W. R. (1987). Empowering practitioners: Holmes, Carnegie, and the lessons of history. *History of Education Quarterly, 27,* 221–240

Johnson, W. R. (1989). Teachers and teacher training in the twentieth century. In D. Warren (Ed.), *American teachers: Histories of a profession at work* (pp. 237–256). New York: Macmillan.

Kaestle, C. F. (1973). *The evolution of an urban school system.* Cambridge, MA: Harvard University Press.

Kaestle, C. F. (1983). *Pillars of the republic: Common schools and American society, 1780–1860.* New York: Hill & Wang.

Kaestle, C. F. (1991). *Literacy in the United States: Readers and reading since 1800.* New Haven, CT: Yale University Press.

Kaestle, C. F., & Vinovskis, M. A. (1978). From apron strings to ABCs: Parents, children and schooling in nineteenth-century America. In J. Demos & S. S. Boocock (Eds.), *Turning points: Historical and sociological essays on the family* (pp. 39–80). Chicago: University of Chicago Press.

Kaestle, C. F., & Vinovskis, M. A. (1980). *Education and social change in nineteenth-century Massachusetts.* New York: Basic Books.

Kahlenberg, R. (2001). *All together now: Creating middle-class schools through public school choice.* Washington, DC: Brookings Institution Press.

Kamin, L. (1974). *The science and politics of I.Q.* Potomac, MD: Erlbaum.

Kaminsky, J. (1992). A pre-history of educational philosophy in the United States: 1861–1914. *Harvard Educational Review, 62*(2), 179–198.

Kantor, H., & Brenzel, B. (1992). Urban education and the truly disadvantaged: The historical roots of the contemporary crisis, 1945–1990. *Teachers College Record, 94*(2), 278–314.

Karabel, J. (1972). Community colleges and social stratification. *Harvard Educational Review, 42,* 521–562.

Karabel, J., & Halsey, A. H. (Eds.). (1977). *Power and ideology in education.* New York: Oxford University Press.

Karen, D. (1990). Toward a political-organizational model of gatekeeping: The case of elite colleges. *Sociology of Education, 63,* 227–240.

Karen, D. (1991a). Achievement and ascription in admission to an elite college: A political-organizational analysis. *Sociological Forum, 6,* 349–380.

Karen, D. (1991b). Politics of race, class, and gender: Access to higher education in the United States, 1960–1986. *American Journal of Education, 99,* 208–237.

Karen, D. (2002). Changes in access to higher education in the United States: 1980–1992. *Sociology of Education, 75,* 191–210.

Karier, C. (Ed.). (1976). *Shaping the American educational state.* New York: Free Press.

Karier, C., Violas, P., & Spring, J. (1973). *Roots of crisis: American education in the twentieth century.* New York: Rand McNally.

Katz, J. (1988). Unpublished commentary on New York City education.

Katz, M. B. (1968). *The irony of early school reform: Educational innovation in mid-nineteenth-century Massachusetts.* Cambridge, MA: Harvard University Press.

Katz, M. B. (1971a). *Class, bureaucracy, and schools: The illusion of educational change in America.* New York: Praeger.

Katz, M. B. (1971b). *School reform, past and present.* Boston: Little, Brown.

Katz, M. B. (1987). *Reconstructing American education.* Cambridge, MA: Harvard University Press.

Katz, M. B. (1990). *The undeserving poor: From the war on poverty to the war on welfare.* New York: Pantheon Books.

Katzman, L., Gandhi, A. G., Harbour, W. S., & LaRock, J. D. (Eds.). (2005). *Special education for a new century.* Cambridge, MA: Harvard University Press.

Katznelson, I., & Weir, M. (1985). *Schooling for all.* New York: Basic Books.

Kaufman, J. M. (1989). The regular-education initiative as Reagan-Bush education policy: A trickle-down theory of the hard to teach. *Journal of Special Education, 23*(3), 256–278.

Keddie, N. (1971). Classroom knowledge. In M. F. D. Young (Ed.), *Knowledge and control.* London: Collier.

Kelly, G. P. (1992). Women and higher education reforms: Expansion without equality. In P. W. Cookson, A. R. Sadovnik, & S. F. Semel (Eds.), *International handbook of educational reform* (pp. 545–559). Westport, CT: Greenwood Press.

Kerckhoff, A. C. (1986). The effects of ability grouping. *American Sociological Review, 51,* 842–858.

Kerckhoff, A. C. (1993). *Diverging pathways: Social structure and career deflections.* New York: Cambridge University Press.

Kerckhoff, A. C. (2001). Education and social stratification process in comparative perspective. *Sociology of Education, 74,* Extra Issue, 3–18.

Kerckhoff, A. C., & Everett, D. D. (1986). Sponsored and contest education pathways in Great Britain and the United States. In A. C. Kerckhoff (Ed.), *Research in sociology of education and socialization* (Vol. 6) (pp. 133–163). Greenwich, CT: JAI Press.

Kesey, K. (1977). *One flew over the cuckoo's nest.* New York: Penguin.

Kidder, T. (1989). *Among schoolchildren.* Boston: Houghton Mifflin.

Kilgore, S. (1991). The organizational context of tracking in schools. *American Sociological Review, 56,* 189–203.

Kimball, R. (1990). *Tenured radicals: How politics has corrupted higher education.* New York: Harper and Row.

Kincheloe, J., & Steinberg, S. (Eds.). (1998). *Unauthorized methods: Strategies for critical teaching.* New York: Routledge.

Kincheloe, J., Steinberg, S., & Gressom, A. (1996). *Measured lies: The bell curve examined.* New York: St. Martin's.

King, J. E. (1995). Culture-centered knowledge: Black studies, curriculum transformation, and social action. In J. A. Banks & C. McGee Banks (Eds.), *Handbook of research on multicultural education* (pp. 265–290). New York: Macmillan.

Kingston, P. W. (1986, Fall). Theory at risk: Accounting for the excellence movement. *Sociological Forum,* , 632–656.

Kingston, P. W. (2001). The unfulfilled promise of cultural capital theory. *Sociology of Education, 74,* Extra Issue, 88–99.

Kirp, D. L. (1982). *Just schools: The idea of racial equality in American education.* Berkeley, CA: University of California Press.

Kirst, M. W. (1984). *Who controls our schools?* New York: W. H. Freeman.

Kitto, H. D. F. (1951). *The Greeks.* New York: Penguin.

Kliebard, H. M. (1986). *The struggle for the American curriculum: 1893–1958.* Boston: Routledge & Kegan Paul.

Kluger, R. (1975). *Simple justice: The history of Brown v. Board of Education and black America's struggle for equality.* New York: Knopf.

Koch, E. (1999, December 3). Just arresting homeless is fruitless. *Newsday,* p. A57.

Kohl, H. (1967). *36 children.* New York: New American Library.

Kommarovsky, M. (1985). *Women in college.* New York: Basic Books.

Kozol, J. (1967). *Death at an early age.* New York: Houghton Mifflin.

Kozol, J. (1986). *Illiterate America.* New York: New American Library.

Kozol, J. (1991). *Savage inequalities.* New York: Crown.

Kraushaar, O. F. (1972). *American nonpublic schools: Patterns of diversity.* Baltimore, MD: Johns Hopkins University Press.

Krueger, A. B. (1998). *Experimental estimates of education production functions.* Princeton, NJ: Princeton University Industrial Relations Section.

Kurlaender, M., & Ma, J. (2003). *Educational benefits of racially and ethnically diverse schools.* Cambridge, MA: The Civil Rights Project, Harvard University.

Kurlaender, M., & Yun, J. (2003). *Fifty years after Brown: New evidence on the impact of school racial composition on student outcomes.* Cambridge, MA: The Civil Rights Project, Harvard University.

Labaree, D. F. (1986). Curriculum, credentials, and the middle class: A case study of a nineteenth-century high school. *Sociology of Education, 59,* 42–57.

Labaree, D. F. (1988). *The making of an American high school: The credentials market and the Central High*

School of Philadelphia, 1838–1939. New Haven, CT: Yale University Press.

Labaree, D. F. (1992a). Doing good, doing science: The Holmes group reports and the rhetorics of educational reform. *Teachers College Record, 93*(4), 628–640.

Labaree, D. F. (1992b). Power, knowledge, and the rationalization of teaching: A genealogy of the movement to professionalize teaching. *Harvard Educational Review, 62*(2), 123–155.

Labaree, D. F. (1996). A disabling vision: Rhetoric and reality in tomorrow's schools of education. *Teachers College Record, 97*(2), 166–205.

Labaree, D. F. (1997). *How to succeed in school without really learning: The credential race in American education.* New Haven, CT: Yale University Press.

Labaree, D. F., & Pallas, A. M. (1996). Dire straits: The narrow vision of the Holmes Group. *Educational Researcher, 25*(5), 25–28.

Labov, W. (1970). The logic of non-standard English. In F. Williams (Ed.), *Language and poverty* (pp. 153–189). Chicago: Markham.

Ladson-Billings, G. (1994). *The dreamkeepers.* San Francisco: Jossey-Bass.

Ladson-Billings, G. (2004). Landing on the wrong note: The price we paid for Brown. *Educational Researcher, 33*(7), pp. 3–13

Ladd, H. F. (2002). *Market-based reforms in urban education.* Washington, DC: Economic Policy Institute.

Ladd, H. F., & Fiske, E. B. (2003). The uneven playing field of school choice: Evidence from New Zealand. *Journal of Policy Analysis & Management, 43.*

LaFrance, M. (1985). The school of hard knocks: Nonverbal sexism in the classroom. *Theory Into Practice, 24,* 40–44.

Lagemann, E. C. (1979). *A generation of women: Education in the lives of progressive reformers.* Cambridge, MA: Harvard University Press.

Lagemann, E. C. (1989). *The politics of knowledge: The Carnegie Corporation, philanthropy, and public policy.* Hanover, NH: University Press of New England.

Laird, S. (1989). Reforming "Women's true profession": A case for "feminist pedagogy" in teacher education? *Harvard Educational Review, 58*(4), 449–463.

Lareau, A. (1989). *Home advantage: Social class and parental intervention in elementary education.* London: Falmer.

Lareau, A. (2003). *Unequal childhood: Class, race and family life.* Los Angeles: University of California Press.

Lareau, A., & Horvat, E. M. (1999). Moments of social inclusion and exclusion: Race, class, and cultural capital in family-school relationships. *Sociology of Education, 72,* 37–53.

Lasch, C. (1983). *The culture of narcissism.* New York: Norton.

Lather, P. (1991). *Getting smart: Feminist research and pedagogy within the postmodern.* New York: Routledge.

Lavin, D., Alba, R., & Silberstein, R. (1981). *Right versus privilege: The open admissions experiment at the City University of New York.* New York: The Free Press.

Lavin, D., & Hyllegard, D. (1996). *Changing the odds: Open admissions and the life chances of the disadvantaged.* New Haven, CT: Yale University Press.

Leach, M. (1992). Can we talk? A response to Burbules and Rice. *Harvard Educational Review, 62*(2), 257–263.

Leach, W. (1980). *True love and perfect union: The feminist reform of sex and society.* New York: Basic Books.

LeCompte, M. D. (1987). The cultural context of dropping out: Why remedial programs don't solve the problems. *Education and Urban Society, 19,* 232–249.

LeCompte, M. D., & Dworkin, A. G. (1991). *Giving up on school: Student dropouts and teacher burnouts.* Newbury Park, CA: Corwin.

Lee, C. D., & Slaughter-Defoe, D. T. (1995). Historical and sociocultural influences on African American education. In J. A. Banks & C. McGee Banks (Eds.), *Handbook of research on multicultural education* (pp. 348–371). New York: Macmillan.

Lee, G. (1961). *Crusade against ignorance: Thomas Jefferson on education.* New York: Teachers College Press.

Lee, V. E. (1985). *Access to higher education: The experience of Blacks, Hispanics, and low socio-economic status Whites.* Washington, DC: Division of Policy Analysis and Research, American Council on Education.

Lee, V. E., & Burkham, D. (2002). *Inequality at the starting gate: Social background differences in achievement as children begin school.* Washington DC: Economic Policy Institute.

Lee, V. E., & Bryk, A. (1986). Effects of single-sex and coeducational high schools on achievement, attitudes, behaviors, and sex differences. *Journal of Educational Psychology, 78,* 381–395.

Lee, V. E., & Bryk, A. (1988). Curriculum tracking as mediating the social distribution of high school achievement. *Sociology of Education, 61,* 78–94.

Lee, V. E., & Bryk, A. (1989). A multilevel model of the social distribution of high school achievement. *Sociology of Education, 62,* 172–192.

Lee, V. E., & Croninger, R. G. (1994). The relative importance of home and school in the development of literacy skills for middle-grade students. *American Journal of Education, 102*(2), 286–329.

Lee, V. E., Croninger, R. G., & Smith, J. B. (1994). Parental choice of schools and social stratification in education: The paradox of Detroit. *Educational Evaluation and Policy Analysis, 16*(4), 434–457.

Lee, V. E., Dedrick, R. F., & Smith, J. B. (1991). The effect of the social organization of schools on teachers' self-efficacy and satisfaction. *Sociology of Education, 64,* 190–208.

Lee, V. E., & Frank, K. A. (1990). Students' characteristics that facilitate the transfer from two-year to four-year colleges. *Sociology of Education, 63,* 178–193.

Lee, V. E., Mackie-Lewis, C., & Marks, H. M. (1993). Persistence to the baccalaureate degree for students who transfer from community college. *American Journal of Education, 120,* 80–114.

Lee, V. E., Marks, H. M., & Byrd, T. (1994). Sexism in single-sex and coeducational independent secondary school classrooms. *Sociology of Education, 67,* 92–120.

Lee, V. E., & Smith, J. B. (1995, October). Effects of high school restructuring and size on gains in achievement for early secondary school students. *Sociology of Education, 68*(4), 241–270.

Lein, L., et al. (1997). *Successful Texas schoolwide programs.* Austin: The Charles A. Dana Center, The University of Texas at Austin.

Legters, N. E., Balfanz, R., Jordan, W. J., & McPartland, J. M. (2002). *Comprehensive reform for urban high school.* New York: Teachers College Press.

Lemann, N. (1991). *The promised land.* New York: Vintage.

Lemann, N. (1999). *The big test: The secret history of the American meritocracy.* New York: Farrar, Straus and Giroux.

Lesko, N. (1988). *Symbolizing society: Stories, rites, and structure in a catholic high school.* New York: Falmer Press.

Lesko, N. (2001). *Act your age! A cultural construction of adolescence.* New York: Routledge.

Lever, J., & Schwartz, P. (1971). *Women at Yale: Liberating a college campus.* Indianapolis: Bobbs-Merrill.

Levine, D. U., & Havighurst, R. J. (1989). *Society and education* (7th ed.). Boston: Allyn and Bacon.

Levinson, D., Cookson, P. W., Jr., & Sadovnik, A. R. (2000). *Encyclopedia of the sociology of education.* New York: Falmer.

Levinson, D. L., Cookson, P. W., & Sadovnik, A. R. (2002). *Encyclopedia of education and sociology.* New York: Routledge.

Lew, J. (2005a). *Success and failure of Asian American youths in urban schools: A case of second-generation Korean Americans.* New York: Teachers College Press.

Lew, J. (2005b). The other story of model minorities: Korean American high school dropouts in urban context. *Anthropology and Education Quarterly.*

Lew, J. (2005c). *Success and failure among 1.5- and second-generation Korean American youths in urban schools: Significance of social class and school context.* New York: Teachers College Press.

Lewis, A. (2003). *Race in the schoolyard: Negotiating the color line in classrooms and communities.* New Brunswick, NJ: Rutgers University Press.

Lewis, C. (1995). *Educating mind and heart: Rethinking the roots of Japanese education.* London: Cambridge University Press.

Lewis, D., & Nakagawa, K. (1995). *Race and educational reform in the American metropolis: A study of school decentralization.* Albany: State University of New York Press.

Lewis, J. F. (1995). Saying no to vouchers: What is the price of democracy? *National Association of Secondary School Principals Bulletin, 79,* 41–51.

Lewis, O. (1966). The culture of poverty. *Scientific American, 215,* 19–25.

Lieberman, A. (Ed.). (1988). *Building a professional culture in schools.* New York: Teachers College Press.

Lieberman, A. (Ed.). (1995). *The work of restructuring schools: Building from the ground up.* New York: Teachers College Press.

Lieberman, A., Darling-Hammond, L., & Zuckerman, D. (1991, August). *Early lessons in restructuring schools.* New York: National Center for Restructuring Education, Schools, and Teaching.

Lieberman, A., & Miller, L. (1984). The social realities of teaching. In A. Lieberman & L. Miller (Eds.), *Teachers, their world, and their work.* Alexandria, VA: Association for Supervision and Curriculum Development.

Lightfoot, S. L. (1978). *Worlds apart.* New York: Basic Books.

Lightfoot, S. L. (1983). *The good high school.* New York: Basic Books.

Lilly, M. S. (1986, March). The relationship between general and special education. *Counterpoint, 6*(1), 10.

Lipman, P. (1998). *Race, class and power in school restructuring.* New York: State University of New York Press.

Lippitt, R., & Gold, M. (1959). Classroom social structure as a mental health problem. *Journal of Social Issues, 15,* 40–49.

Little, J. W. (1990). Conditions of professional development in secondary schools. In M. W. McLaughlin, J. E. Talbert, & N. Bascia (Eds.), *The contexts of teaching in secondary schools: Teachers realities* (pp. 187–223). New York: Teachers College Press.

Little, J. W. (1992). *Two worlds: Vocational and academic teachers in comprehensive high schools.* Berkeley, CA: National Center for Research in Vocational Education, University of California at Berkeley.

Little, J. W. (1993a). Professional community in comprehensive high schools: The two worlds of academic and vocational teachers. In J. W. Little & M. W. McLaughlin (Eds.), *Teachers work: Individuals, col-*

leagues, and contexts (pp. 137–163). New York: Teachers College Press.

Little, J. W. (1993b, Summer). Teachers professional development in a climate of educational reform. *Education Evaluation and Policy Analysis, 15*(2), 129–151.

Lloyd, S. M. (1987). *The Putney school: A progressive experiment.* New Haven, CT: Yale University Press.

Loewen, J. W. (1995). *Lies my teacher told me.* New York: New Press.

Lomawaima, K. T. (1995). Educating Native Americans. In J. A. Banks & C. McGee Banks (Eds.), *Handbook of research on multicultural education* (pp. 331–347). New York: Macmillan.

Lortie, D. (1975). *School teacher: A sociological study.* Chicago: University of Chicago Press.

Losen, D., & Orfield, G. (Eds.). (2002). *Racial inequity in special education.* Cambridge, MA: Harvard Education Publishing Group.

Lucas, S. R. (1999). *Tracking inequality: Stratification and mobility in American high schools.* New York: Teachers College Press.

Lucas, S. R. (2001). Race, class, and tournament track mobility. *Sociology of Education, 74,* 139–156.

Lucas, S. R. (2002). Sociodemographic diversity, correlated achievement, and de facto tracking. *Sociology of Education, 75,* 328–348.

Lukas, J. A. (1986). *Common ground.* New York: Vintage Books.

Luke, A. (1988). *Literacy, textbooks, and ideology.* London: Falmer Press.

Luke, C., & Jennifer, G. (Eds.). (1992). *Feminisms and critical pedagogy.* New York: Routledge.

Lynch, R. G. (2004/2005, Winter). Preschool pays: High-quality education would save billions. *American Educator, 26*–35.

Lyotard, J. F. (1984). *The postmodern condition* (G. Bennington & B. Massumi, Trans.). Minneapolis: University of Minnesota Press.

Lytle, J. H. (1988). Is special education serving minority students? A response to Singer and Butler. *Harvard Educational Review, 58*(1). In T. Hehir & T. Latus (1992). *Special education at the century's end: Evolution of theory and practice since 1970* (pp. 191–197). Cambridge, MA: Harvard Educational Review.

Macdonald, J., & Macdonald, S. (1981). Gender values and curriculum. *Journal of Curriculum Theorizing, 3*(1), 299–304.

Macedo, D. (1990). *Literacies of power: What Americans are not allowed to know.* Boulder, CO: Westview.

MacInnes, G. (1999). *Kids who pick the wrong parents and other victims of voucher scheme.* New York: The Century Foundation.

MacLeod, J. (1995). *Ain't no makin' it: Aspirations and attainment in low income neighborhood* (2nd ed.). Boulder, CO: Westview.

Maedus, G., & Clarke, M. (2001). The adverse impact of high-stakes testing on minority students: Evidence from one hundred years of test data. In G. Orfield and M. L. Kornhaber (Eds.), *Raising standards or raising barriers: Inequality and high-Stakes testing in public education* (pp. 85–106). New York: The Century Foundation Press.

Maeroff, G. I. (1988). *The empowerment of teacher: Overcoming the crisis of confidence.* New York: Teachers College Press.

Maher, F., & Tetrault, M. T. (1994). *The feminist classroom.* New York: Basic Books.

Male, G. A. (1992). Educational reform in France. In P. W. Cookson, Jr., A. Sadovnik, & S. Semel (Eds.), *International handbook of educational reform.* Westport, CT: Greenwood Press.

Malone, D., & Rauch, B. (1960). *Empire for liberty.* New York: Appleton-Century-Crofts.

Mannheim, K. (1936). *Ideology and Utopia: An introduction to the sociology of knowledge.* New York: Harcourt, Brace & World.

Mannheim, K. (1952). *Essays on the sociology of knowledge.* New York: Oxford University Press.

Marsh, H. W. (1989a). The effects of attending single-sex and coeducational high schools on achievement, attitudes, behaviors and on sex differences. *Journal of Educational Psychology, 81,* 70–85.

Marsh, H. W. (1989b). Effects of attending single-sex and coeducational high schools: A response to Lee and Bryk. *Journal of Educational Psychology, 81,* 651–653.

Marsh, H. W. (1991). Public, catholic single-sex, and catholic coeducational high schools: Their effects on achievement, affect, and behaviors. *American Journal of Education, 99,* 320–356.

Martin, J. R. (1987). Reforming teacher education, rethinking liberal education. *Teachers College Record, 88,* 406–409.

Martin, R. (1972). Student sex and behavior as determinants of the type and frequency of teacher-student contacts. *Journal of School Psychology, 10,* 339–347.

Martin-Kniep, G., & Kniep, W. M. (1992). Alternative assessment: Essential, not sufficient for systematic change. *Holistic Education Review, 9*(4), 4–13.

Marx, K. (1844/1964). *The economic and philosophical manuscripts of 1844.* New York: International Publishers.

Marx, K. (1867/1967). *Das Kapital, Volume I.* New York: International Publishers.

Marx, K. (1893/1967). *Das Kapital, Volume II.* New York: International Publishers.

Marx, K. (1894/1967). *Das Kapital, Volume III.* New York: International Publishers.

Marx, K. (1963). *The eighteenth brumaire of Louis Bonaparte.* New York: International Publishing Company. (Original work published 1852)

Marx, K. (1971). *The poverty of philosophy.* New York: International Publishers.

Marx, K., & Engels, F. (1846/1947). *The German ideology.* New York: International Publishers. (Original work published 1846)

Marx, K., & Engles, F. (1848/1983). *The communist manifesto.* New York: International Publishers.

Massell, D., & Fuhrman, S., with Kirst, M., Odden, A., Wohlstetter, P., Carver, C., & Yee, G. (1994). *Ten years of state education reform, 1983–1993: Overview with four case studies.* New Brunswick, NJ: Consortium for Policy Research in Education.

Massell, D., & Goertz, M. (1999). *Local strategies for building capacity: The district role in supporting instructional reform.* Philadelphia: CPRE, University of Pennsylvania.

Massey, D., & Denton, N. A. (1993). *American apartheid: Segregation and the making of the underclass.* Cambridge, MA: Harvard University Press.

Mattingly, D., Prislin, R., McKenzie, T., Rodriquez, J., & Kayzar, B. (2002). Evaluating evaluations: The case of parent involvement programs. *Review of Educational Research, 72*(4), 549–576.

May, H., Supovitz, J., & Perda. (2004). *A longintudinal study of the impact of America's Choice on student performance in Rochester, New York, 1998–2003.* Consortium for Policy Research on Education. Philadelphia: University of Pennsylvania.

Mazzeo, C. (2001). Frameworks of state: Assessment policy in historical perspective. *Teachers College Record, 103*(3), 367–397.

McCarthy, C. (1993). Beyond the poverty of theory in race relations: Nonsynchrony and social difference in education. In L. Weis & M. Fine (Eds.), *Beyond silenced voices: Class, race and gender in United States schools* (pp. 325–346). Albany: State University of New York Press.

McCarthy, C., & Criticheloe, W. (Eds.). (1993). *Race, identity and representation in education.* New York and London: Routledge.

McDermott, R. P. (1977). Social relations as contexts for learning. *Harvard Educational Review, 47,* 198–213.

McDermott, R. P., & Varenne, H. (1995). Culture as disability. *Anthropology and Education Quarterly, 26*(3), 324–348.

McDill, E. (1978). *An updated answer to the question: Do schools make a difference?* Paper presented at the National Institute of Education: International Conference on School Organization and Effect, San Diego, CA.

McLaren, P. (1989). *Life in schools.* New York: Longman.

McLaren, P. (1991). Schooling and the postmodern body: Critical pedagogy and the politics of enfleshment. In H. Giroux (Ed.), *Postmodernism, feminism, and cultural politics: Redrawing educational boundaries* (pp. 144–173). Albany: State University of New York Press.

McLaren, P. (1995). *Critical pedagogy and predatory culture: Oppositional politics in a postmodern era.* London and New York: Routledge.

McLaren, P., & Hammer, R. (1989). Critical pedagogy and the postmodern challenge: Toward a critical postmodernist pedagogy of liberation. *Educational Foundations, 3*(3), 29–62.

McLaughlin, M., Artiles, A., & Pullin, D. (2001). Challenges for the transformation of special education in the 21st century: Rethinking culture in school reform. *Journal of Special Education Leadership, 14*(2), 51–62.

McLaughlin, M., & Talbert, J. (2003). *Reforming districts: How districts support school reform.* Seattle, WA: Center for the Study of Teaching and Policy.

McLaughlin, M. W., & Little, J. W. (Eds.). (1993). *Teachers work: Individuals, colleagues, and contexts.* New York: Teachers College Press.

McLaughlin, M. W., & Talbert, J. E. (1993a). *Contexts that matter for teaching and learning.* Stanford, CA: Center for Research on the Context of Secondary School Teaching.

McLaughlin, M. W., & Talbert, J. E. (1993b). How the world of students and teachers challenges policy coherence. In S. H. Fuhrman (Ed.), *Designing coherent education policy: Improving the system.* San Francisco: Jossey-Bass.

McNeal, R. B., Jr. (1995). Extracurricular activities and high school dropouts. *Sociology of Education, 68,* 62–81.

McNeil, L. M. (1986). *Contradictions of control: School structure and school knowledge.* New York: Routledge.

McNeil, L. M. (1988a). Contradictions of control, Part I: Administrators and teachers. *Phi Delta Kappan, 69*(5), 333–339.

McNeil, L. M. (1988b). Contradictions of control, Part II: Teachers, students and curriculum. *Phi Delta Kappan, 69*(6), 432–438.

McNeil, L. M. (1988c). Contradictions of control, Part III: Contradictions of reform. *Phi Delta Kappan, 69*(7), 478–485.

McNeil, L. M. (1988d). *Contradictions of control: School structure and school knowledge.* New York: Routledge.

McNeil, L. M. (2000). *Contradictions of school reform: Educational costs of standardized testing.* New York: Routledge.

Mehan, H., Villanueva, I., Hubbard, L., & Lintz, A. (1996). *Constructing school success: The consequences of untracking low achieving students.* Cambridge: Cambridge University Press.

Meier, D. (1995). *The power of their ideas.* Boston: Beacon.

Metcalf, K. K. (1998). *Evaluation of the Cleveland scholarship program: Second year report 1997–98.* Bloomington: Indiana Center for Evaluation, Indiana University.

Metcalf, K. K., et al. (1999). *Evaluation of the Cleveland scholarship & tutoring grant program 1996–1999.* Bloomington: Indiana Center for Evaluation, Indiana University.

Metcalf, K. K., et al. (2001). *Cleveland Scholarship program evaluation 1998–2000.* Bloomington: Indiana Center for Evaluation, Indiana University.

Metcalf, K. K., et. al. (2003). *Evaluation of the Cleveland scholarship and tutoring program 1998–2001.* Bloomington: Indiana Center for Evaluation, Indiana University.

Metz, M. H. (1978). *Classrooms and corridors: The crisis of authority in desegregated secondary schools.* Berkeley, CA: University of California Press.

Metz, M. H. (1986). *Different by design: The context and character of three magnet schools.* New York: Routledge & Kegan Paul.

Metz, M. H. (1990). How social class differences shape teachers' work. In M. McLaughlin, J. Talbert, & N. Bascia (Eds.), *The contexts of teaching in secondary schools: Teachers' realities* (pp. 40–107). New York: Teachers College Press.

Meyer, J. W. (1977, July). The effects of education as an institution. *American Journal of Sociology, 83,* 55–77.

Meyer, J. W., Kamens, D., Benavot, A., Cha, Y. K., & Wong, S. Y. (1992). *School knowledge for the masses: World models and national primary curriculum categories in the twentieth century.* London: Falmer.

Meyer, J. W., Ramirez, F. O., Rubinson, R., & Boli, J. (1977). The world educational revolution, 1950–1970. *Sociology of Education, 50,* 242–258.

Meyer, J. W., & Rowan, B. (1977). The structure of educational organizations. In M. Meyer & Associates (Eds.), *Environments and organizations* (pp. 78–109). San Francisco: Jossey-Bass.

Meyer, J. W., & Rowan, B. (1978). Institutionalized organizations: Formal structure as myth and ceremony. *American Journal of Sociology, 83,* 340–363.

Meyer, J. W., Tyack, D., Nagel, J., & Gordon, A. (1979). Public education as nation-building in America. *American Journal of Sociology, 85,* 591–613.

Mickelson, R. A. (1990). The attitude-achievement paradox among black adolescents. *Sociology of Education, 63,* 44–61.

Mickelson, R. A. (1999). International business machinations: A case study of corporate involvement in local educational reform. *Teachers College Record, 100*(3), 476–512.

Mickelson, R. A. (2002). Subverting Swann: First and second generation segregation in the Charlotte-Mecklenburg schools. *American Education Research Journal, 38*(2), 215–252.

Mickelson, R. A. (2003). Gender Bourdieu, and the anomaly of women's achievement redux. *Sociology of Education, 75,* 373–375.

Mickelson, R. A., & Ray, C. A. (1994). Fear of falling from grace: The middle class, downward mobility, and school desegregation. *Research in Sociology of Education and Socialization, 10,* 207–238.

Mickelson, R. A., Ray, C. A., & Smith, S. S. (1993). The growth machine and the politics of urban educational reform: The case of Charlotte, North Carolina. In N. Stromquist (Ed.), *Education in the urban context.* New York: Praeger.

Miles, K. H. (2000). *Money matters: Rethinking school district spending to support Comprehensive School Reform.* Arlington, VA: New American Schools Issue Brief.

Miller, J. (1982). Feminist pedagogy: The sound of silence breaking. *Journal of Curriculum Theorizing, 4,* 5–11.

Miller-Bernal, L. (1980). Comment on Tidball's women's colleges and women's achievers revisited. *Signs, 6,* 342–345.

Miller-Bernal, L. (1989). College experiences and sex-role attitudes: Does a women's college make a difference? *Youth and Society, 20,* 363–387.

Miller-Bernal, L. (1993). Single sex versus coeducational environments: A comparison of women students' experiences at four colleges. *American Journal of Education, 102*(1), 23–54.

Miller-Bernal, L. (2000). *Separate by degree: Women students' experiences in single-sex and coeducational colleges.* New York: Peter Lang.

Miller-Bernal, L., & Poulson, S. (2004). *Going coed: Coeducation at formerly men's college, 1950–2000.* Nashville: Vanderbilt University Press.

Miller-Bernal, L., & Poulson, S. (2005). *Going coed: Coeducation at formerly women's colleges.* Nashville: Vanderbilt University Press.

Mills, C. W. (1956). *The power elite.* New York: Oxford University Press.

Mills, C. W. (1959). *The sociological imagination.* New York: Oxford University Press.

Milofsky, C. (1974). Why special education isn't special. *Harvard Educational Review, 44*(4). In T. Hehir & T. Latus. (1992). *Special education at the century's end: Evolution of theory and practice since 1970* (pp. 47–68). Cambridge, MA: Harvard Educational Review.

Mirel, J. E. (1993). *The rise and fall of an urban school system: Detroit, 1907–81.* Ann Arbor: University of Michigan Press.

Miron, G., & Nelson, C. (2001). *Autonomy in exchange for accountability: An initial study of Pennsylvania charter schools—Executive summary.* Kalamazoo, MI: The Evaluation Center, Western Michigan University. www,wmich.edu/evalctr/.

Miron, G., & Nelson, C. (2004). Student academic achievement in charter schools: What we know and why we know so little. In K. Bulkley & Wohlstetter (Eds.), *Taking account of charter schools: What's happened and what's next* (pp. 161–175). New York: Teachers College Press

Mitrano, B. (1979). Feminist theology and curriculum theory. *Journal of Curriculum Studies, 2,* 211–220.

Mitter, W. (1992). Germany. In P. W. Cookson, Jr., A. R. Sadovnik, & S. F. Semel (Eds.), *International handbook of educational reform* (pp. 209–228). Westport, CT: Greenwood Press.

Moe, T. M. (2001). *Schools, vouchers, and the American public.* Washington, DC: Brookings Institution Press.

Morris, V. C. (1966). *Existentialism in education.* New York: Harper and Row.

Mortenson, T. (1997). Research seminar on public policy analysis of opportunity for post secondary education. Education Trust website, www.edtrust.org. Retrieved May 25, 2005.

Mortimer, J. T. (1996). A sociological perspective on school-to-work opportunities: Response and rejoinder. In K. Borman, P. W. Cookson, Jr., A. R. Sadovnik, & J. Z. Spade (Eds.), *Implementing educational reform: Sociological perspectives on educational policy* (pp. 171–184). Norwood, NJ: Ablex.

Mortimore, P., & Whitty, G. (1999). School improvement: A remedy for social exclusion. In A. Hayton (Ed.), *Tackling disaffection and social exclusion* (pp. 80–94). London: Kogan Page.

Mosteller, F. (1995). The Tennessee study of class size in the early grades. *The Future of Children, 5*(2), 113–127.

Mosteller, F., Light, R. J., & Sachs, J. A. (1996). Sustained inquiry in education: Lessons from skill grouping and class size. *Harvard Education Review, 66*(4), 797–842.

Mosteller, F., & Moynihan, D. P. (1972). *On equality of educational opportunity.* New York: Vintage Books.

Muller, C. (1993). Parent involvement and academic achievement: An analysis of family resources available to the child. In B. Schneider & J. S. Coleman (Eds.), *Parents, their children, and schools* (pp. 77–114). Boulder, CO: Westview Press.

Muller, C., & Kerbow, D. (1993). Parent involvement in the home, school, and community. In B. Schneider & J. S. Coleman (Eds.), *Parents, their children, and schools* (pp. 13–42). Boulder, CO: Westview Press.

Murphy, J. (1991). *Restructuring schools: Capturing and assessing the phenomena.* New York: Teachers College Press.

Murphy, J., & Hallinger, P. (1993). *Restructuring schooling: Learning from ongoing efforts.* Newbury Park, CA: Corwin.

Murphy, J., & Louis, K. S. (1994). *Reshaping the principalship: Insights from transformational reform efforts.* Thousand Oaks, CA: Corwin.

Murray, C. (1989). *In pursuit of happiness and good government.* New York: Touchstone Books.

Myrdal, G. (1944). *An American dilemma.* New York: Harper and Ruthers.

Nassaw, D. (1979). *Schooled to order.* New York: Oxford University Press.

National Center for History in the Schools. (1994). *National standards for United States history: Exploring the American experience.* Los Angeles: Author.

National Center for Educational Statistics. (1997). *Monitoring school quality: An indicators report.* Washington, DC: U.S. Department of Education, Office of Educational Research

National Commission on Excellence in Education. (1983). *A nation at risk.* Washington, DC: U.S. Government Printing Office.

National Commission on Social Studies in Schools. (1989). *Charting a course: Social studies for the 21st century.* Washington, DC: Author.

National Commission on Teaching and America's Future. (1996). *What matters most: Teaching for America's future.* New York: Author.

National Council for the Social Studies. (1994). *Expectations of excellence: Curriculum standards for social studies.* Washington, DC: Author.

National Council of Teachers of Mathematics. (1989). *Curriculum and evaluation standards for school mathematics.* Reston, VA: Author.

National Education Goals Panel. (1988). *Restructuring the education system.* Washington, DC: Author.

National Education Goals Panel. (1989). *Restructuring in progress.* Washington, DC: Author.

National Education Goals Panel. (1991). *Measuring progress toward the national education goals.* Washington, DC: Author.

National Working Commission on Choice in K–12 Education. (2003). *School choice: doing it the right way makes a difference.* Washington, DC: The Brookings Institution, available at www.brookings.edu/gs/brown/20031116schoolchoicereport.pdf.

Natriello, G. (Ed.). (1986). *School dropouts: Patterns and policies.* New York: Teachers College Press.

Natriello, G. (Ed.). (1997). The state of American education: Special section. *Teachers College Record, 99*(1), 9–72.

Natriello, G., McDill, E., & Pallas, A. (1990). *Schooling disadvantaged students: Racing against catastrophe.* New York: Teachers College Press.

Neill, A. S. (1960). *Summerhill.* New York: Holt.

Network of Progressive Educators. (1991). Statement of principles. *Pathways, 7*(2), 3.

New Jersey Department of Education. (2004). School report cards. www.state.nj.us/education/. Retrieved December 18, 2004.

New York City Board of Education. (1989). *Human relations task force: Final report.* New York: Author.

New York City Department of Education. (2003). Student achievement reports. www.nycenet.edu/. Retrieved September 18, 2004.

New York State Board of Regents. (1998). *Teachers prepared. The Regents report on teacher education in New York state.* Albany: New York State Department of Education.

New York State Board of Regents. (1999). *Teaching to higher standards.* Albany: New York State Department of Education.

New York State Department of Education. (2004). School report cards. www.nysed.gov/. Retrieved January 30, 2005.

Newberg, N. A., & Cohen, B. J. (1991). *The Southwest Philadelphia educational complex: Report on a pilot project to create and manage a cluster of schools based on feeder patterns.* Philadelphia: Graduate School of Education, University of Pennsylvania.

Nieto, S. (1995). A history of the education of Puerto Rican students in U.S. mainland schools: "Losers," "outsiders," or "leaders." In J. A. Banks & C. McGee Banks (Eds.), *Handbook of research on multicultural education* (pp. 388–411). New York: Macmillan.

Noddings, N. (1984). *Caring: A feminine approach to ethics and moral education.* Berkeley: University of California Press.

Noddings, N. (1995). *Philosophy of education.* Boulder, CO: Westview.

Noguera, P. A. (2003). *City schools and the American dream: Reclaiming the promise of public education.* New York: Teachers College Press.

Noguera, P. A. (2004) Social capital and the education of immigrant students: Categories and generalizations. *Sociology of Education, 77,* 180–184.

O'Day, J., & Bitter, C. (2003). *Evaluation study of the immediate intervention/underperforming schools program and the high achieving/improving schools program of the P.S. Accountability Act of 1999.* Palo Alto, CA: American Institutes for Research.

O'Day, J. A., & Smith, M. S. (1992). Systemic reform and equal educational opportunity. In S. H. Fuhrman (Ed.), *Designing coherent education policy* (pp. 250–312). San Francisco: Jossey-Bass.

Oakes, J. (1985). *Keeping track: How schools structure inequality.* New Haven: Yale University Press.

Oakes, J. (1990). *Multiplying inequalities: The effects of race, social class, and tracking on opportunities to learn math and science.* Santa Monica, CA: Rand.

Oakes, J. (1994a). *Opportunity to learn: Can standards-based reform be equity-based reform?* Paper presented for Effects of New Standards and Assessment on High Risk Students and Disadvantaged Schools, a research forum for the New Standards Project, Harvard University, Cambridge, MA.

Oakes, J. (1994b). More than misapplied technology: A normative and political response to Hallinan. *Sociology of Education, 67,* 84–89.

Oakes, J. (2004). Investigating the claims in *Williams* v. *the State of California:* An unconstitutional denials of education's basic tools. *Teachers College Record, 106*(10), 1889–1906.

Oakes, J., Gamoran, A., & Page, R. N. (1992). Curriculum differentiation: Opportunities, outcomes, and meanings. In P. W. Jackson (Ed.), *Handbook of research on curriculum* (pp. 570–608). New York: Macmillan.

Oakes, J., & Guiton, G. (1995). Matchmaking: The dynamics of high school tracking decisions. *American Educational Research Journal, 32,* 3–33.

Odden, A. (2000). The costs of sustaining educational change through comprehensive school reform. *Phi Delta Kappan, 81*(6), 433–438.

Ogbu, J. (1978). *Minority education and caste.* New York: Academic Press.

Ogbu, J. (1979). Social stratification and the socialization of competence. *Anthropology and Education Quarterly, 10*(1).

Ogbu, J. (1987). Variability in minority school performance: A problem in search of an explanation. *Anthropology and Education Quarterly, 18,* 312–334.

Ogbu, J. (2003). *Black Americans students in an affluent suburb: A study of academic disengagement.* Mahwah, NJ: Erlbaum.

Ogbu, J. U. (1992). Low school performance as adaptation: The case of blacks in Stockton, California. In M. A. Gibson & J. U. Ogbu (Eds.), *Minority status and schooling: A comparative study of immigrants and involuntary minorities* (pp. 249–285). New York: Garland.

Ogbu, J. U. (1999, Summer). Beyond language: Ebonics, proper English, and identity in a Black-American speech community. *American Educational Research Journal, 36*(2), 147–184.

Olneck, M. R. (1993). Terms of inclusion: Has multiculturalism redefined equality in American education? *American Journal of Education, 101,* 234–260.

Olsen, L. (1999). Researchers rate whole-school reform models. *Education Week,* 14.

Orfield, G. (1992). Money, equity, and college access. *Harvard Educational Review, 62,* 337–372.

Orfield, G. (2004). *Dropouts in America: Confronting the graduate rate crisis.* Cambridge, MA: Harvard University Press.

Orfield, G., & Ashkinaze, C. (1991). *The closing door: Conservative policy and black opportunity.* Chicago: University of Chicago Press.

Orfield, G., & Eaton, S. (1996). *Dismantling desegregation: The quiet reversal of Brown v. Board of Education.* New York: New Press.

Orfield, G., & Lee, C. (2002). *Why segregation matters: Poverty and educational inequality.* Cambridge, MA: The Civil Rights Project, Harvard University Press.

Orfield, G., & Lee, J. (2004). *Brown at 50: King's dream or Plessy's nightmare?* www.civilrightsproject.harvard.edu/research/deseg/reseg_schools99.php.

Orfield, G., & Miller, E. (1998). *Chilling admissions: The affirmative action crisis and the search for alternatives.* Cambridge, MA: Harvard Education Publishing Group.

Orfield, G., & Yun, J. T. (1999). Resegregation in American schools. Cambridge, MA: The Civil Rights Project, Harvard University. www.civilrightsproject.harvard.edu/research/deseg/reseg_schools99.php.

Ozmon, H. A., & Craver, S. M. (1990). *Philosophical foundations of education.* Columbus, OH: Merrill.

Page, A. L., & Clelland, D. A. (1978, September). The Kanawha County textbook controversy. *Social Forces, 57,* 265–281.

Page, R. N. (1991). *Lower track classrooms: A curricular and cultural perspective.* New York: Teachers College Press.

Page, R. N., & Valli, L. (Eds.). (1990). *Curriculum differentiation: Interpretive studies in U.S. secondary schools.* Albany: State University of New York Press.

Pallas, A. M., Entwisle, D. R., Alexander, K. L., & Cadigan, D. (1987). Children who do exceptionally well in first grade. *Sociology of Education, 60,* 257–271.

Pallas, A. M., Entwisle, D. R., Alexander, K. L., & Stluka, M. F. (1994). Ability group effects: Instructional, social, or institutional. *Sociology of Education, 67,* 27–46.

Palmieri, P. (1987). From republican motherhood to race suicide: Arguments on the higher education of women in the United States, 1820–1920. In C. Lasser (Ed.), *Educating men and women together* (pp. 49–66). Champaign-Urbana: University of Illinois Press.

Palmieri, P. (1995). *In Adamless Eden.* New Haven, CT: Yale University Press.

Pang, V. O. (1995). Asian Pacific American students: A diverse and complex population. In J. A. Banks & C. McGee Banks (Eds.), *Handbook of research on multicultural education* (pp. 412–424). New York: Macmillan.

Pankratz, R. S., et al. (2000). In Roger S. Pankratz & Joseph M. Petrosko (Eds.), *All children can learn: Lessons from the Kentucky reform experience.* San Francisco: Jossey-Bass.

Parsons, T. (1959). The school class as a social system. *Harvard Educational Review, 29,* 297–318.

Passow, A. H. (1989). Present and future directions in school reform. In T. Sergiovanni & J. Moore (Eds.),

Schooling for tomorrow (pp. 13–39). Boston: Allyn and Bacon.

Passow, A. H., et al. (1976). *The national case study: An empirical comparative study of education in twenty-one countries.* New York: Wiley.

Patterson, J. T. (2002). *Brown v. Board of Education: A civil rights milestone and its troubled legacy.* New York: Oxford.

Paulu, N. (1989). *Improving schools and empowering parents: Choice in American education.* Washington, DC: U.S. Government Printing Office.

Perkinson, H. (1995). *The imperfect panacea: American faith in education, 1865–1968.* New York: McGraw-Hill.

Perlmann, J. (1988). *Ethnic differences: Schooling and social structure among the Irish, Italians, Jews, and Blacks in an American city, 1880–1935.* New York: Cambridge University Press.

Perlstein, D. (2004). *Justice, justice: School politics and the eclipse of liberalism.* New York: Peter Lang.

Persell, C. H. (1977). *Education and inequality.* New York: The Free Press.

Persell, C. H. (1990). *Understanding society.* New York: HarperCollins.

Persell, C. H., Catsambis, S., & Cookson, P. W., Jr. (1992). Family background, school type, and college attendance: A conjoint system of cultural capital transmission. *Journal of Research on Adolescence, 2,* 1–23.

Persell, C. H., & Cookson, P. W., Jr. (1982). *The effective principal in action.* Reston, VA: National Association of Secondary Principals.

Peshkin, A. (1986). *God's choice: The total world of a fundamentalist Christian school.* Chicago: University of Chicago Press.

Peters, R. S. (1965). *Ethics and education.* London: Allen and Unwin.

Peters, R. S. (Ed.). (1973). *The philosophy of education.* London: Oxford University Press.

Phillips, K. P. (1990). *The politics of rich and poor: Wealth and the American electorate in the Reagan aftermath.* New York: Random House.

Pickering, W. F., & Walford, G. (1998). *Durkheim on education.* London: Routledge.

Picus, L. (1995). *Does money matter in education? A policymaker's guide.* Selected Papers in School Finance. Washington, DC: National Center for Education Statistics.

Pinar, W. F. (1975). Currere: Toward reconceptualization. In W. F. Pinar (Ed.), *Curriculum theorizing: The reconceptualists* (pp. 396–414). Berkeley, CA: McCutchan.

Pinar, W. F. (1978a). Notes on the curriculum field 1978. *Educational Researcher, 7*(8), 5–12.

Pinar, W. F. (1978b). The reconceptualization of curriculum studies. *Journal of Curriculum Studies, 10*(3), 205–214.

Pinar, W. F. (1979). What is reconceptualization? *The Journal of Curriculum Theorizing, 1,* 93–104.

Pinar, W. F. (Ed.). (1988). *Contemporary curriculum discourses.* Scottsdale, AZ: Gorsuch Scarisbrick.

Pinar, W. F., Reynolds, W. M., Slattery, P., & Taubman, P. M. (1995). *Understanding curriculum.* New York: Peter Lang.

Pincus, F. L. (1980). The false promise of community colleges. *Harvard Educational Review, 50,* 332–360.

Pincus, F. L. (1985). From equity to excellence: The rebirth of educational conservatism. In B. Gross & R. Gross (Eds.), *The great school debate* (pp. 329–344). New York: Simon and Schuster.

Pink, W., & Noblit, G. W. (Eds.). (1995). *Continuity and contradiction: The futures of the sociology of education.* Creskill, NJ: Hampton Press.

Plato. (1945). *Republic.* New York: Oxford University Press.

Plato. (1971). *Meno.* New York: Macmillan.

Plato. (1986). *The dialogues of Plato.* New York: Bantam.

Pogrow, S. (1996). Reforming the wannabe reformers: Why education reforms almost always end up making things worse. *Phi Delta Kappan, 77*(10), 656–663.

Pogrow, S. (1999). Rejoinder: Consistent large gains and high levels of achievement are the best measures of program quality: Pogrow responds to Slavin. *Educational Researcher, 28*(8), 24–31.

Pogrow, S. (2000). The unsubstantiated Success of Success For All. *Phi Delta Kappan. 81*(8), 596–600

Powell, A. G., Farrar, E., & Cohen, D. K. (1985). *The shopping mall high school.* Boston: Houghton Mifflin.

Power, S., Warren, S., Gillborn, D., Clark, A., Thomas, S. & Coate, K. (2001). *Education in deprived areas.* London: Institute of Education University of London.

Powers, J. M., & Cookson, P. W., Jr. (1999). School choice as a political movement. *Educational Policy, 13*(1,2), 104–122.

Pratt, C. (1924). *Experimental practice in the city and country school.* New York: E. P. Dutton.

Publishers Weekly (2003). Review of Rosemary Salomone, *Same, different, equal: Rethinking single-sex schooling.* New York: Publishers Weekly, Reed Business Information.

Pugach, M., & Lilly, M. S. (1984). Reconceptualizing support services for classroom teachers: Implications for teacher education. *Journal of Teacher Education, 35*(5), 48–55.

Quality counts, 1999. (1999, January 11). *Education Week, 28*(17).

Ramirez, F. O., & Boli, J. (1987a). Global patterns of educational institutionalization. In G. M. Thomas et al. (Eds.), *Institutional structure: Constituting state, society, and the individual.* Newbury Park, CA: Sage.

Ramirez, F. O., & Boli, J. (1987b, January). The political construction of mass schooling: European origins and worldwide institutionalization. *Sociology of Education, 60,* 15.

Ravitch, D. (1974). *The great school wars, New York City, 1805–1973: A history of the public schools as battlefield of social change.* New York: Basic Books.

Ravitch, D. (1977). *The revisionists revised.* New York: Basic Books.

Ravitch, D. (1983). *The troubled crusade.* New York: Basic Books.

Ravitch, D. (1985). *The schools we deserve.* New York: Basic Books.

Ravitch, D. (1989). *Multiculturalism in the curriculum.* Presentation to the Manhattan Institute.

Ravitch, D. (1994). *Personal communication.* Author.

Ravitch, D. (2000). *Left back: A century of failed school reforms.* New York: Simon & Schuster.

Ravitch, D., & Finn C. E. (1987). *What do our seventeen year olds know?* New York: Basic Books.

Ray, C. A., & Mickelson, R. A. (1993). Restructured students for restructured work: The economy, school reform, and noncollegebound youth. *Sociology of Education, 66,* 1–23.

Ready, D. G., Lee, V. E., & Welner, K. (2004). Educational equity and social structure: School size, overcrowding, and school-within-schools. *Teachers College Record, 106*(10), 1989–2014.

Reardon, S. F. (2001). Suburban racial change and suburban school segregation: 1987–96. *Sociology of Education, 74,* 79–101.

Reese, W. J. (1986). *Power and the promise of school reform: Grassroots movements during the progressive era.* Boston: Routledge & Kegan Paul.

Reese, W. J. (1995). *The origins of the American high school.* New Haven, CT: Yale University Press.

Reich, R. B. (1990). Education and the next economy. In S. Bacharach (Ed.), *Education reform: Making sense of it all* (pp. 194–212). Boston: Allyn and Bacon.

Reich, R. B. (1991, January 20.) Succession of the successful. *The New York Times Magazine,* pp. 42–45.

Reynolds, M. C., Wang, M. C., & Walberg, H. J. (1987). The necessary restructuring of special and general education. *Exceptional Children, 53*(5), 391–398.

Riehl, C. (2001). Bridges to the future: Contributions of qualitative research to the sociology of education. *Sociology of Education, 74,* Extra Issue, 115–134.

Riordan, C. (1985). Public and catholic schooling: The effects of gender context policy. *American Journal of Education, 93,* 518–540.

Riordan, C. (1990). *Girls and boys in school: Together or separate?* New York: Teachers College Press.

Riordan, C. (1992). Single- and mixed-gender colleges for women: Educational, attitudinal, and occupational outcomes. *Review of Higher Education, 15,* 327–346.

Riordan, C. (1994). Single-gender schools: Outcomes for African and Hispanic Americans. *Research in Sociol-*

ogy of Education and Socialization, *10*(1994): 177–205.

Riordan, C. (1997). *Equality and achievement: An introduction to the sociology of education.* New York: Longman.

Riordan, C. (1998). The future of single-sex schools: In *Separated by sex: A critical look at single-sex education for girls* (pp. 53–62). Washington, DC: AAUW Foundation.

Riordan, C. (1999, November 17). The silent gender gap. *Education Week.*

Rist, R. C. (1970). Student social class and teacher expectations: The self-fulfilling prophecy in ghetto education. *Harvard Educational Review, 40,* 411–451.

Rist, R. C. (1973). *The urban school: A factory for failure.* Cambridge, MA: MIT Press.

Roeber, E. D. (2003). *Assessment models for No Child Left Behind.* Washington, DC: Education Commission of the States, www.ecs.org.

Rogers, D. (1968). *110 Livingston Street: Politics and bureaucracy in the New York City schools.* New York: Random House.

Rorty, R. (1980). *Philosophy and the mirror of nature.* Princeton, NJ: Princeton University Press.

Rosenbaum, J. E. (1976). *Making inequality: The hidden curriculum of high school tracking.* New York: Wiley.

Rosenbaum, J. E. (1980a). Social implications of educational grouping. In D. Berliner (Ed.), *Review of research in education* (pp. 361–401). Washington, DC: American Educational Research Association.

Rosenbaum, J. E. (1980b). Track misperceptions and frustrated college plans. *Sociology of Education, 53,* 74–87.

Rosenbaum, J. E. (1998). College-for-all: Do students understand what college demands? *Social Psychology of Education, 2,* 50–85.

Rosenbaum, J. E. (2001). *Beyond college for all: Career paths for the forgotten half.* New York: Russell Sage Foundation.

Rosenbaum, J. E., & Jones, S. A. (1995). Creating linkages in the high school-to-work transition: Vocational teachers' networks. In M. Hallinan (Ed.), *Making schools work.* New York: Plenum.

Rosenbaum, J. E., Stern, D., Hamilton, M. A., Hamilton, S. F., Berryman, S. E., & Kazis, R. (1992). *Youth apprenticeship in America: Guidelines for building an effective system.* Washington, DC: William T. Grant Foundation Commission on Youth and America's Future.

Rosenthal, R., & Jacobson, L. (1968). *Pygmalion in the classroom.* New York: Holt, Rinehart and Winston.

Rossi, R., & Stringfield, S. (1995). What we must do for students placed at risk. *Phi Delta Kappan, 77,* 73–76.

Rossides, D. W. (1976). *The American class system: An introduction to social stratification.* New York: Houghton Mifflin.

Rothstein, R. (2000). Equalizing resources on behalf of disadvantaged children. In R. D. Kahlenberg (Ed.), *A notion at risk: Preserving public education as an engine for social mobility* (pp. 21–92). New York: The Century Foundation Press.

Rothstein, R. (2004a). Class and the classroom. *American School Board Journal,* 17–21.

Rothstein, R. (2004b). *Class and schools: Using social, economic, and educational reform to close the Black-White achievement gap.* New York: Teachers College Press.

Rouse, C. E. (1997). *Private school vouchers and student achievement: An evaluation of the Milwaukee parental choice program.* Washington, DC: National Bureau of Economic Research, Working Paper No. 5964.

Rouse, C. E. (2002). Private vouchers and student achievement: More evidence from the Milwaukee parental choice program. Working paper No. 396, Industrial Relations Section, Princeton, University, Princeton, NJ.

Rousseau, J. J. (1979). *Emile* (A. Bloom, Trans.). New York: Basic Books.

Rowan, B., & Miracle, A. (1983). Systems of ability grouping and the stratification of achievement in elementary school. *Sociology of Education, 56,* 133–144.

Rubinson, R. (1986). Class formation, politics and institutions: Schooling in the United States. *American Journal of Sociology, 92,* 519–548.

Rumberger, R. W., & Gandara, P. (2004). Seeking equity in the education of California's English learners. *Teachers College Record, 106*(10), 2032–2056.

Rury, J. L. (1991). *Education and women's work: Female schooling and the division of labor in urban America, 1870–1930.* Albany: State University of New York Press.

Rury, J. L., & Mirel, J. E. (1997). The political economy of urban education. In M. Apple (Ed.), *Review of Research in Education, 22* (pp. 49–110). Washington, DC: AERA.

Russell, B. (1926). *Education and the good life.* New York: Boni and Liveright.

Rust, V. (1991). Postmodernism and its comparative education implications. *Comparative Education Review, 35*(4), 610–626.

Rutgers School of Law. Supreme Court Syllabus. *Raymond Abbott et al. v. Fred G. Burke et al.* (A-155-97). Available: http://lawlibrary.rutgers.edu/courts/supreme/a-155-97.opn.html.

Rutter, M., et al. (1979). *Fifteen thousand hours.* London: Open Books.

Ryan, J. E., & Heise, M. (2002). *The political economy of school choice. Yale Law Journal 111,* 2043.

Ryan, W. (1971). *Blaming the victim.* New York: Random House.

Sachar, E. (1991). *Shut up and let the lady teach.* New York: Poseidon Press.

Sadker, M., & Sadker, D. (1985, March). Sexism in the schoolroom of the '80's. *Psychology Today, 54–57.*

Sadker, M., & Sadker, D. (1994). *Failing at fairness: How America's schools cheat girls.* New York: Scribners.

Sadovnik, A. R. (1991a). Basil Bernstein's theory of pedagogic practice: A structuralist approach. *Sociology of Education, 64*(1), 48–63.

Sadovnik, A. R. (1991b). Derailing high school tracking: One beginning. *Pathways, 7*(2), 4–8.

Sadovnik, A. R. (1994). *Equity and excellence in higher education.* New York: Peter Lang.

Sadovnik, A. R. (Ed.). (1995a). *Knowledge and pedagogy: The sociology of Basil Bernstein.* Norwood, NJ: Ablex.

Sadovnik, A. R. (1995b). Postmodernism and the sociology of education: Closing the gap between theory, research and practice. In W. Pink & G. Noblit (Eds.), *Continuity and contradiction: The futures of the sociology of education* (pp. 309–326). Creskill, NJ: Hampton Press.

Sadovnik, A. R., Persell, C., Baumann, E., & Mitchell, R., Jr. (1987). *Exploring society.* New York: Harper and Row.

Sadovnik, A. R., & Semel, S. F. (Eds.), (2002). *Founding mothers and others: Women educational leaders during the progressive era.* New York: Palgrave.

Salomone, R. (2003). *Same, different, equal: Rethinking single-sex schooling.* New Haven, CT: Yale University Press.

Sanders, M. (1996). *School-family-community partnerships and the academic achievement of African-American urban adolescents.* Center Report. Baltimore: Center for Research on the Education of Students Placed at Risk, Johns Hopkins University.

Sanders, W. L., & Rivers, J. C. (1996). *Cumulative and residual effects of teachers on future student academic achievement.* Knoxville: University of Tennessee Value-Added Research and Assessment Center.

Sanjek, R. (1998). *The future of us all.* Ithaca NY: Cornell University Press.

Sarason, S. B. (1982). *The culture of the school and the problem of change.* Boston: Allyn and Bacon.

Sartre, J. P. (1974). *Existentialism and human emotions.* New York: Philosophical Library.

Scarr, S., & Weinberg, R. A. (1978). The influence of "family background" on intellectual attainment. *American Sociological Review, 43,* 674–692.

Scheffler, I. (1960). *The language of education.* Springfield, IL: Charles Thomas.

Schlesinger, A. M., Jr. (1992). *The disuniting of America.* New York: Norton.

Schneider, B., & Bryk, A. (1996). *Social trust: A moral resource for school improvement.* Chicago: Center for School Improvement.

Schneider, B., & Coleman, J. S. (1993). *Parents, their children, and schools.* Boulder, CO: Westview Press.

Schneider, B., Schiller, K. S., & Coleman, J. S. (1995). *Public school choice: Some evidence from the National Education Longitudinal Study of 1988.* Chicago: University of Chicago, Center for the Study of the Economy and the State, Working Paper Series No. 113.

Schön, D. A. (1983). *The reflective practitioner: How professionals think in action.* New York: Basic Books.

School by school report card: The state's second yearly look at Long Island's districts. (1998, March 15). *Newsday,* pp. H1–H11.

School choice: A guide to picking a public school in New York City. (1998). *Newsday,* special reprint.

Schorr, L. B., & Schorr, D. (1989). *Within our reach: Breaking the cycle of disadvantage.* New York: Doubleday.

Schwartz, F. (1981). Supporting or subverting learning: Peer group patterns in four tracked schools. *Anthropology and Education Quarterly, 12,* 99–121.

Sedlak, M. (1987). Tomorrow's teachers: The essential arguments of the Holmes Group Report. *Teachers College Record, 88*(3), 314–325.

Seller, M., & Weis, L. (1997). *Beyond black and white: New voices in U.S. schools.* Albany: State University of New York Press.

Semel, S. F. (1992). *The Dalton School: The transformation of a progressive school.* New York: Peter Lang.

Semel, S. F. (1996). Yes, but . . .: Multiculturalism and the reduction of educational inequality. *Teachers College Record, 98*(1), 153–177.

Semel, S. F., & Sadovnik, A. R. (1995, Summer). Lessons from the past: Individualism and community in three progressive schools. *Peabody Journal of Education, 70*(4), 56–85.

Semel, S. F., & Sadovnik, A. R. (1998). Durkheim, Dewey, and progressive education: Individualism and community in the history of American education. In W. F. Pickering & G. Walford (Eds.), *Durkheim on education.* London: Routledge.

Semel, S. F., & Sadovnik, A. R. (1999). *Schools of tomorrow, schools of today: What happened to progressive education?* New York: Peter Lang.

Sewall, G. (1991). Common culture and multiculture. *Social Studies Review, 7.*

Sewell, W., & Hauser, R. M. (1974). *Education, occupation, and earnings.* New York: Academic Press.

Sewell, W., & Hauser, R. M. (1976). Causes and consequences of higher education: Modes of the status attainment process. In W. H. Sewell, R. M. Hauser, & D. L. Featherman (Eds.), *Schooling and achievement in American society.* New York: Academic Press.

Sexton, P. C. (1961). *Education and income.* New York: Viking.

Shakeshaft, C. (1986). A gender at risk. *Phi Delta Kappan, 67,* 449–503.

Shakeshaft, C. (1987). *Women in educational administration.* Newbury Park, CA: Sage.

Shanker, A. (1991, October). Lecture at Adelphi University.

Shavit, Y., & Blossfeld, H. P. (Eds.). (1993). *Persistent inequalilty: Changing educational attainment in thirteen countries.* Boulder, CO: Westview Press.

Sherman, J. (1994). *The condition of education in rural schools.* U.S. Department of Education. Washington, DC: Federal Printing Office.

Shmurak, C. B. (1998). *Voices of hope: Adolescent girls of single-sex and coeducational schools.* New York: Peter Lang.

Sikes, J. (1971). *Differential behavior of male and female teachers with male and female students.* Unpublished Doctoral Dissertation, University of Texas, Austin.

Silberman, C. (1969). *Crisis in the classroom.* New York: Random House.

Simon, B. S. (2004). High school outreach and family involvement. *Social Psychology of Education, 7,* 185–209.

Singer, A. (1999). American apartheid: Race and the politics of school finance on Long Island, N.Y. *Equity and Excellence in Education, 32*(3), 25–36.

Singer, J. D., & Butler, J. A. (1987). The education for all handicapped children act: Schools as agents of social reform. *Harvard Educational Review, 57*(2). In T. Hehir & T. Latus (1992). *Special education at the century's end: Evolution of theory and practice since 1970* (pp. 159–190). Cambridge, MA: Harvard Educational Review.

Siskin, L. S. (1991). Departments as different worlds: Subject subcultures in secondary schools. *Educational Administration Quarterly, 27*(2), 134–160.

Siskin, L. S. (1994). *Realms of knowledge: Academic departments in secondary schools.* London: Falmer.

Siskin, L. S., & Little, J. W. (Eds.). (1995). *The subjects in question: Departmental organization and the high school.* New York: Teachers College Press.

Sizer, T. R. (1984). *Horace's compromise: The dilemma of the American high school.* Boston: Houghton Mifflin.

Sizer, T. R. (1985). *Horace's compromise: The dilemma of the American high school* (2nd ed.) Boston: Houghton Mifflin.

Sizer, T. R. (1992). *Horace's school: Redesigning the American high school.* Boston: Houghton Mifflin.

Sizer, T. R. (1996). *Horace's hope.* Boston: Houghton Mifflin.

Skinner, B. F. (1971). *Beyond freedom and dignity.* New York: Bantam.

Skocpol, T. (1995). *Social policy in the United States.* Princeton, NJ: Princeton University Press.

Skrtic, T. (1991). The special education paradox: Equity as a way to excellence. *Harvard Educational Review, 61*(2). In T. Hehir & T. Latus (1992). *Special education at the century's end: Evolution of theory and practice since 1970* (pp. 203–272). Cambridge, MA: Harvard Educational Review.

Slavin, R. E. (1983a). *Cooperative learning.* New York: Longman.

Slavin, R. E. (1983b). When does cooperative learning increase student achievement? *Psychological Bulletin, 94,* 429–445.

Slavin, R. E. (1987). Ability grouping and student achievement in elementary schools: A best evidence synthesis. *Review of Educational Research, 57,* 293–336.

Slavin, R. E. (1988, September). Synthesis of research on grouping in elementary and secondary schools. *Educational Leadership, 46,* 67–77.

Slavin, R. E. (1990a). Achievement effects of ability grouping in secondary schools: A best-evidence synthesis. *Review of Educational Research, 60,* 471–500.

Slavin, R. E. (1990b). *Cooperative learning: Theory, research and practice.* Englewood Cliffs, NJ: Prentice-Hall.

Slavin, R. E. (1991). Are cooperative learning and untracking harmful to the gifted? *Educational Leadership, 48*(6), 68–71.

Slavin, R. E. (1997a). Design competitions: A proposal for a new federal role in educational research and development. *Educational Researcher, 26*(1), 22–28.

Slavin, R. E. (1997b). Rejoinder: Design competitions and expert panels: Similar objectives, very different paths, *Educational Researcher, 26*(6), 21–22.

Slavin, R. E. (1999). Rejoinder: yes, control groups are essential in program evaluation: A response to Pogrow. *Educational Researcher, 28*(3), 36–38.

Sleeter, C. (1995). An analysis of the critiques of multicultural education. In J. A. Banks & C. McGee Banks (Eds.), *Handbook of research on multicultural education* (pp. 81–94). New York: Macmillan.

Solomon, B. M. (1985). *In the company of educated women.* New Haven, CT: Yale University Press.

Soltis, J. (Ed.). (1981). *Philosophy and education.* Eightieth Yearbook of the National Society for the Study of Education, Part I. Chicago: National Society for the Study of Education.

Sowell, T. (1977, March 27). New light on the black I.Q. controversy. *New York Times Magazine,* pp. 56–63.

Spade, J. Z., Columba, L., & Vanfossen, B. E. (1997). Thinking in mathematics and science: Courses and course-selection procedures. *Sociology of Education, 70*(2), 108–127.

Spillane, J. (1998). State policy and the nonmonolithic nature of the local school district: Organizational and professional considerations. *American Educational Research Journal, 35*(1), 33–63.

Spillane J., & Thompson, C. (1997). Reconstructing conceptions of local capacity: The local education agency's capacity for ambitious instructional reform. *Educational Evaluation and Policy Analysis, 19*(2), 185–203.

Spring, J. (1972). *Education and the rise of the corporate state.* Boston: Beacon Press.

Spring, J. (1986). *The American school: 1642–1985.* New York: Longman.

Spring, J. (1989). *American education* (4th ed.). New York: Longman.

Stainback, S., & Stainback, W. (1989). Integration of students with mild and moderate handicaps. In D. K. Lipsky & A. Gartner (Eds.), *Beyond special education: Quality education for all* (pp. 41–52). Baltimore, MD: Paul H. Brookes.

Stanton-Salazar, R. (2001). *Manufacturing hope and despair: The school and kin support networks of U.S. Mexican youth.* New York: Teachers College Press.

Stanton-Salazar, R. D., & Dornbusch, S. M. (1995). Social capital and the reproduction of inequality: Information networks among Mexican-origin high school students. *Sociology of Education, 68*(2), 116–135.

Stedman, L. C. (1985). A new look at the effective schools literature. *Urban Education, 20,* 295–326.

Stedman, L. C. (1987). It's time we changed the effective schools formula. *Phi Delta Kappan, 69,* 215–224.

Steinberg, S., & Kincheloe, J. (1998). *Changing multiculturalism.* London: Open University Press.

Stevens, F. I. (1993a). Applying an opportunity-to-learn conceptual framework to the investigation of the effects of teaching practices via secondary analysis of multiple case study summary data. *Journal of Negro Education, 62,* 232–248.

Stevens, F. I. (1993b). *Opportunity to learn: Issues of equity for poor and minority students.* Washington, DC: National Center for Education Statistics.

Stevens, F. I. (1993c). Opportunity to learn and other social contextual issues: Addressing the low academic achievement of African American students. *Journal of Negro Education, 62,* 227–231.

Stevenson, D., & Baker, D. (1991). State control of the curriculum and classroom instruction. *Sociology of Education, 64,* 1–10.

Stevenson, D. L., Schiller, K. S., & Schneider, B. (1994). Sequences of opportunities for learning. *Sociology of Education, 67,* 184–198.

Stinchcombe, A. (1964). *Rebellion in a high school.* Chicago: Quadrangle Books.

Stodolsky, S. S. (1993). A framework for subject matter comparisons in high schools. *Teaching and Teacher Education, 9,* 333–346.

Strain, J. P. (1975). Idealism: A clarification of an educational philosophy. *Educational Theory, 25,* 263–271.

Stringfield, S., et al. (1996). Bold plans for school restructuring: The New American Schools designs. In S. Stringfield et al. (Eds.). Hillsdale, NJ: Erlbaum.

Suarez-Orozco, M., & Qin-Hilliard, D. (Eds.). (2004). *Globalization: Culture and education in the new millennium.* Berkeley: University of California Press.

Sugarman, S. D. (1999). School choice and public funding. In S. D. Sugarman & F. R. Kemerer (Eds.), *School choice and social controversy: Politics, policy and law,* Washington, DC: Brookings Institution Press, pp. 111, 139.

Supovitz, J., & May, H. (2003). *The relationship between teacher implementation of America's choice and student learning in Plainfield, New Jersey.* Philadelphia, PA: Consortium for Policy Research in Education.

Swartz, D. (1997). *Culture and power: The sociology of Pierre Bourdieu.* Chicago: University of Chicago Press.

Swidler, A. (1979). *Organizations without authority: Dilemmas of social control in free schools.* Cambridge, MA: Harvard University Press.

Takaki, R. (1993). *A different mirror: A history of multicultural America.* Boston: Little, Brown.

Takaki, R. (1998a). *A larger memory: A history of our diversity, with voices.* Boston: Little, Brown.

Takaki, R. (1998b). *Strangers from a different shore: A history of Asian Americans.* Boston: Back Bay.

Talbert, J. E. (1992). *New strategies for developing our nation's teacher force and ancillary staff with a special emphasis on implications for Chapter 1.* Paper commissioned by the U.S. Department of Education.

Talbert, J. E. (1993). Constructing a schoolwide professional community: The negotiated order of a performing arts school. In J. W. Little & M. W. McLaughlin (Eds.), *Teachers' work: Individuals, colleagues, and contexts* (pp. 164–184). New York: Teachers College Press.

Talbert, J. E. (1995). Boundaries of teachers' professional communities in U.S. high schools: Power and precariousness of the subject department. In L. S. Siskin & J. W. Little (Eds.), *The subjects in question: Departmental organization and the high school* (pp. 68–94). New York: Teachers College Press.

Talbert, J. E. (1996). Primacy and promise of professional development in the nation's reform agenda: Sociological views. In K. Borman, P. W. Cookson, Jr., A. R. Sadovnik, & J. Z. Spade (Eds.), *Implementing educational reform: Sociological perspectives on educational policy* (pp. 283–312). Wesport, CT: Ablex.

Talbert, J. E., & McLaughlin, M. W. (1994, February). Teacher professionalism in local school context. *American Journal of Education, 102,* 123–153.

Task Force on the Common School. (2002). *Divided we fail: Coming together through public school choice.* New York: The Century Foundation.

Teacher Education Project. (1986). *A compilation of the major recommendations of teacher education.* Washington, DC: National Educational Project.

Teachers College Record. (1979, Winter). *81*(2), 127–248.

Teske, P., & Schneider, M. (2001). What research can tell policymakers about school choice. *Journal of Policy Analysis & Management, 20,* 609.

Text of statement of goals adopted by the governors. (1990, March 7). *Education Week, 9,* 16–17.

Thernstrom, A., & Thernstrom, S. (2003). *No excuses: Closing the racial gap in learning.* New York: Simon and Schuster.

Thomas, K. J., & Staiger, D. O. (2003). Unintended consequences of racial subgroup rules. In P. E. Peterson & M. R. West (Eds.), *No child left behind? The politics and practice of accountability.* Washington, DC: Brookings Institution Press.

Thornburg, D., & Karp, K. S. (1992). Lessons learned: Mathematics + science + higher order thinking × second language learning = ? *Journal of Language Minority Students, 10,* 159–184.

Thorne, B. (1993). *Gender play: Girls and boys in school.* New Brunswick, NJ: Rutgers University Press.

Tidball, E. (1973). Perspectives on academic women and affirmative action. *Journal of Higher Education, 54,* 130–135.

Tidball, E. (1980). Women's colleges and women's achievers revisited. *Signs, 5,* 504–517.

Tidball, E. (1985). Baccalaureate origins of entrants into American medical schools. *Journal of Higher Education, 56,* 385–402.

Tidball, E. (1986). Baccalaureate origins of recent natural science doctorates. *Journal of Higher Education, 57,* 606–620.

Tidball, E., et al. (1999). *Taking women seriously: Lessons and legacies for educating the majority.* Phoenix, AZ: American Council on Education/Onyx Press.

Toenjes, L. A., Dworkin, A. G., Lorence, J., & Hill, A. N. (2002). High-stakes testing, accountability, and student achievement in Texas and Houston. In J. E. Chubb & T. Loveless (Eds.), *Bridging the achievement gap* (pp. 109–130). Washington, DC: The Brookings Institution.

Tractenberg, P., Holzer, M., Miller, G., & Sadovnik, A. (2002). *Developing a plan for reestablishing local control in the state-operated districts.* Newark, NJ: Institute on Education Law and Policy, Rutgers University. www.ielp/rutgers.edu.

Tractenberg, P., Sadovnik, A., & Liss, B. (2004). *Tough choices: An informed discussion of school choice.* Newark, NJ: Institute on Education Law and Policy, Rutgers University. www.ielp/rutgers.edu.

Traub, J. (1994). *City on a hill: Testing the American dream at City College.* Reading, MA: Addison-Wesley.

Trow, M. (1961). The second transformation of American secondary education. *International Journal of Comparative Sociology, 2,* 144–166. In Karabel, J., & Halsey, A. H. (Eds.), *Power and ideology in education* (pp. 105–118). New York: Oxford University Press, 1977.

Trueba, H., Jacobs, L., & Kirton, E. (1990). *Cultural conflict and adaptation: The case of Hmong children in American society.* New York: Falmer.

Turner, R. H. (1960, October). Sponsored and contest mobility and the school system. *American Sociological Review, 25,* 855–867.

Tushnet, M. (1994). *Making civil rights law: Thurgood Marshall and the supreme court, 1936–1961.* New York: Oxford University Press.

Twentieth Century Fund Task Force on Federal Elementary and Secondary Education Policy. (1983). *Making the grade.* New York: Author. (ERIC ED 233 112)

Tyack, D. (1974). *The one best system.* Cambridge, MA: Harvard University Press.

Tyack, D. (1990). Restructuring in historical perspective: Tinkering toward utopia. *Teachers College Record, 92,* 170–191.

Tyack, D., & Cuban, L. (1995). *Tinkering toward utopia: A century of public school reform.* Cambridge, MA: Harvard University Press.

Tyack, D., & Hansot, E. (1982). *Managers of virtue: Public school leadership in America, 1820–1980.* New York: Basic Books.

Tyack, D., & Hansot, E. (1990). *Learning together: A history of coeducation in American public schools.* New Haven, CT: Yale University Press.

Tyson, K. (2003). Notes from the back of the room: Problems and paradoxes in the schooling of young Black students. *Sociology of Education, 76,* 326–343.

U.S. Bureau of the Census. (1998). *Statistical abstract of the United States, 1998.* Washington, DC: Government Printing Office.

U.S. Bureau of the Census. (2003a). *Current populations reports.* Washington, DC: Author.

U.S. Bureau of the Census. (2003b). *Annual demographic survey.* Washington, DC: Author.

U.S. Department of Education, National Center for Education Statistics. (1989a). *The condition of education, 1989 edition.* Washington, DC: Government Printing Office.

U.S. Department of Education, National Center for Education Statistics. (1989b). *The digest of education statistics, 1989.* Washington, DC: Government Printing Office.

U.S. Department of Education, National Center for Education Statistics. (1996). *NAEP 1994 trends in academic progress.* Washington, DC: Author.

U.S. Department of Education, National Center for Education Statistics. (1997a). *The digest of educational statistics.* Washington, DC: Author.

U.S. Department of Education, National Center for Education Statistics. (1997b). *Pursuing excellence: A study of U.S. fourth grade mathematics and science achievement in international context.* Washington, DC: Author.

U.S. Department of Education, National Center for Education Statistics. (1998). *The condition of education, 1998 edition.* Washington, DC: Author.

U.S. Department of Education, Office of Educational Research and Improvement. (1994). *School-to-work: What does research say about it?* Washington, DC: Author.

U.S. Department of Education, Office of Planning and Evaluation. (1998). *Turning around low-performing schools: A guide for state and local leaders.* Washington, DC: Author.

U.S. Department of Education, Office of Educational Research and Improvement. (1998a). *Tools for schools: School reform models supported by the National Institute on the Education of At-Risk Students.* Washington, DC: Author.

U.S. Department of Education, National Center for Education Statistics, Office of the Under Secretary and Office of Elementary and Secondary Education. (2000a). *The digest of educational statistics.* Washington, DC: Author.

U.S. Department of Education, Office of the Under Secretary and Office of Elementary and Secondary Education. (2001). *First annual school improvement report: Executive order on actions for turning around low-performing schools.* Washington, DC: Author.

U.S. Department of Education, National Center for Education Statistics, Office of Educational Research and Improvement. (2000b). *Monitoring school quality: An Indicators Report* (NCES 2001-030). Washington, DC: Author.

U.S. Department of Education, National Center for Educational Statistics, Office of the Under Secretary and Office of Elementary and Secondary Education. (2002). *The digest of educational statistics.* Washington DC: Author.

U.S. Department of Education, National Center for Educational Statistics, Office of the Under Secretary and Office of Elementary and Secondary Education. (2003). *The digest of educational statistics.* Washington DC: Author.

U.S. Department of Education, Office of the Under Secretary and Office of Elementary and Secondary Education. (2004). *Parental involvement, Title I, Part A: Non-regulatory guidance.* Washington DC: Author.

U.S. Department of Education, National Center for Educational Statistics, Office of the Under Secretary and Office of Elementary and Secondary Education. (2004). *The condition of education: National assessment of educational progress.* Washington DC: Author.

Useem, E. L. (1991). Student selection into course selection sequences in mathematics: The impact of parent involvement and school policies. *Journal of Research on Adolescence, 1,* 231–250.

Useem, E. L. (1992a). Getting on the fast track in mathematics: School organizational influences on math track assignment. *American Journal of Education, 100*(3), 325–353.

Useem, E. L. (1992b). Middle schools and math groups: Parents' involvement in children's placement. *Sociology of Education, 65,* 263–279.

Useem, E. L. (1994). *Renewing schools: A report on the Cluster Initiative in Philadelphia.* Philadelphia: PATHS/PRISM: The Philadelphia Partnership for Education.

Valentine, C. A. (1968). *Culture and poverty: Critique and counter proposals.* Chicago: University of Chicago Press.

Valentine, C. A. (1975). Deficit, difference and bicultural models of Afro-American behavior. In "Challenging the myths: The schools, the blacks and the poor." *Harvard Educational Review* (Reprint Series No. 5), 1–21.

Valenzuela, A. (1999). *Subtractive schooling: U.S. Mexican Youth and the politics of caring.* Albany: SUNY Press.

Vandenberg, D. (1971). *Being and education: An essay in existential phenomenology.* Englewood Cliffs, NJ: Prentice-Hall.

Van Dunk, E., & Dickman, E. (2003). *School choice and the question of accountability.* New Haven, CT: Yale University Press.

Vanfossen, B. E., Jones, J. D., & Spade, J. Z. (1987). Curriculum tracking and status maintenance. *Sociology of Education, 60,* 104–122.

Van Hook, J. (2002). Immigration and African American educational opportunity: The transformation of minority schools. *Sociology of Education, 75,* 169–189.

Van Voorhis, F. L. (2003). Interactive homework in middle school: Effects on family involvement and students' science achievement. *Journal of Educational Research, 96*(9), 323–339.

Velez, W. (1989). Why Hispanic students fail: Factors affecting attrition in high schools. In J. H. Ballantine (Ed.), *Schools and society: A unified reader* (2nd ed.). Palo Alto, CA: Mayfield.

Vergari, S. (2002). *The charter school landscape,* University of Pittsburgh Press.

Verstegen, D. (1993). Financing education reform: "Where did all the money go?" *Journal of Education Finance, 19,* 1–35.

Verstegen, D., & McGuire, C. K. (1991). The dialectic of reform. *Educational Policy, 5,* 386–411.

Viadero, D. (1999). Who's in, who's out. *Education Week,* 12.

Vinovskis, M. A. (1995). *Education, society, and economic opportunity: A historical perspective on persistent issues.* New Haven, CT: Yale University Press.

Viteritti, J. P. (1999). *Choosing equality.* Washington, DC: Brookings Institution Press.

Walford, G. (1992a). Educational choice and equity in Great Britain. *Educational Policy, 6,* 123–381.

Walford, G. (1992b). Educational reform in Great Britain. In P. W. Cookson, Jr., A. Sadovnik, & S. Semel (Eds.), *International handbook of educational reform.* Westport, CT: Greenwood Press.

Walford, G. (1999). Educational reform in England and Wales. In D. L. Levinson, P. W. Cookson, Jr., & A. R. Sadovnik (Eds.), *Encyclopedia of sociology and education.* New York: Garland.

Walker, J. H., Kozma, E. J., & Green, R. P., Jr. (1989). *American education: Foundations and policy.* St. Paul, MN: West.

Waller, W. (1965). *The sociology of teaching.* New York: Wiley.

Walters, P. B. (2001). Educational access and the State: Historical continuities and discontinuities in racial inequality in American education. *Sociology of Education, 74,* Extra Issue, 35–45.

Wasley, P. (1994). *Stirring the chalkdust: Tales of teachers changing classroom practice.* New York: Teachers College Press.

Weakliem, D., McQuillan, J., & Schauer, T. (1995). Toward meritocracy? Changing social-class differences in intellectual ability. *Sociology of Education, 68,* 271–287.

Weatherly, R. A., & Lipsky, M. (1977). Street-level bureaucrats and institutional innovation: Implementing special education reform. *Harvard Educational Review, 47*(2). In T. Hehir & T. Latus (1992). *Special education at the century's end: Evolution of theory and practice since 1970* (pp. 89–119). Cambridge, MA: Harvard Educational Review.

Weber, M. (1976). Types of authority. In L. A. Coser & B. Rosenberg (Eds.), *Sociological theory: A book of readings.* New York: Macmillan.

Wehlege, G. G., & Smith, G. A. (1992). Building new programs for students at risk. In F. M. Newmann (Ed.), *Student engagement and achievement in American secondary schools* (pp. 92–118). New York: Teachers College Press.

Weikert, D., & Schweinhart, L. J. (1984). *Changed lives: The effects of the Perry Preschool Program on youths through age 19.* Ypsilanti, MI: High Scope.

Weiler, K. (1988). *Women teaching for change.* South Hadley, MA: Bergin and Garvey.

Weiler, K. (1998). *Country schoolwomen: Teaching in rural California, 1850–1950.* Palo Alto, CA: Stanford University Press.

Weir, M., Orloff, A., & Skocpol, T. (1988). *The politics of social policy in the United States.* Princeton, NJ: Princeton University Press.

Weis, L. (1985). *Between two worlds: Black students in an urban community college.* Boston: Routledge & Kegan Paul.

Weis, L. (Ed.). (1988). *Class, race and gender in American education.* Albany: State University of New York Press.

Weis, L. (1992). *Working class without work.* Albany: State University of New York Press.

Weis, L. (1993). White male working-class youth: An exploration of relative privilege and loss. In L. Weis & M. Fine (Eds.), *Beyond silenced voices* (pp. 237–258). Albany: State University of New York Press.

Weis, L. (2004). *Class reunion: The remaking of the American white working class.* New York: Routledge.

Wells, A. S. (1991). Choice in education: Examining the evidence on equity. A symposium on politics, markets, and America's schools. *Teachers College Record, 93*(1), 137–155.

Wells, A. S. (1993a). The sociology of school choice: Why some win and others lose in the educational marketplace. In E. Rassell & R. Rothstein (Eds.), *School choice: Examining the evidence.* Washington, DC: The Economic Policy Institute.

Wells, A. S. (1993b). *Time to choose: America at the crossroads of school choice policy.* New York: Hill and Wang.

Wells, A. S. (1995). Reexamining social science research on school desegregation: Long- versus short-term effects. *Teachers College Record, 96,* 691–706.

Wells, A. S. (1996). African-American students' view of school choice. In B. Fuller, R. Elmore, & G. Orfield (Eds.), *School choice: The cultural logic of families, the political rationality of schools. Who chooses? Who loses? Culture institutions and the unequal effects of school choice.* New York: Teachers College Press.

Wells, A. S., Artiles, L., Carnochan, S., Cooper, C., Grutzik, C., Holme, J., Lopez, A., Scott, J., Slayton, J., & Vasuveda, A. (1998). *Beyond the rhetoric of charter school reform: A study of ten California districts.* Los Angeles: University of California, Los Angeles.

Wells, A. S., & Crain, R. L. (1992). Do parents choose school quality or school status? A sociological theory of free market education. In P. W. Cookson, Jr. (Ed.), *The choice controversy* (pp. 65–82). Newbury Park, CA: Corwin Press.

Wells, A. S., & Crain, R. L. (1997). *Stepping over the color line: African-American students in white suburban schools.* New Haven, CT: Yale University Press.

Wells, A. S., Holme, J. J., Tijerina Revilla, A., & Korantemaa Atanda, A. (2004). How desegregation changed us: The effects of racially mixed schools on students and society: A study of desegregated high schools and their class of 1980 graduates. www.tc.columbia.edu/faculty/documents.htm?facid=asw86. Forthcoming in *In search of Brown,* Harvard University Press, 2005.

Wells, A. S., & Serna, I. (1996). The politics of culture: Understanding local political resistance to detracking in racially mixed schools. *Harvard Educational Review, 66,* 93–118.

Wenglinsky, H. (1997). How money matters: The effect of school district spending on academic achievement. *Sociology of Education, 70,* 221–237.

Westbrook, R. B. (1991). *John Dewey and American democracy.* Ithaca, NY: Cornell University Press.

Wexler, P. (1976). *The sociology of education: Beyond equality.* Indianapolis, IN: Bobbs-Merrill.

Wexler, P. (1987). *Social analysis of education.* London: Routledge & Kegan Paul.

Wexler, P. (1992). *Becoming somebody.* London: Falmer.

Wexler, P. (1996). *Holy sparks: Social theory, education, and religion.* New York: St. Martin's.

White, M. (1987). *The Japanese educational challenge.* New York: The Free Press.

Whitehead, A. N. (1957). *The aims of education and other essays.* New York: The Free Press.

Whitty, G. (1985). *Sociology and school knowledge.* London: Metheun.

Whitty, G. (1997). Creating quasimarkets in education: A review of recent research on parental choice and school autonomy in three countries. *Review of Research in Education, 22,* 3–48.

William T. Grant Foundation Commission on Work, Family, and Citizenship. (1988). *The forgotten half: Pathways to success for America's youth and young families.* Washington, DC: William T. Grant Foundation.

Willis, P. (1981). *Learning to labor: How working class kids get working class jobs.* New York: Columbia University Press.

Wilson, W. J. (1998). The role of the environment in the Black-White test score gap. In C. Jencks & M. Phillips (Eds.), *The Black-White test score gap* (pp. 501–510). Washington, DC: Brookings Institution Press.

Wilson, W. J. (1987). *The truly disadvantaged: The inner city, the underclass, and public policy.* Chicago: University of Chicago Press.

Wilson, W. J. (1995). *When work disappears.* Cambridge, MA: Harvard University Press.

Wilson, W. J. (1999, March 6). Rising inequality and the case for multiracial coalition politics. Keynote address, Eastern Sociological Society, Boston.

Wirt, F., & Kirst, M. (1972). *Political and social foundations of education.* Berkeley, CA: McCutchan.

Wirt, F., & Kirst, M. (1982). *Schools in conflict.* San Francisco: McCutchan.

Witte, J. (1990). Choice and control: An analytical overview. In W. H. Clune & J. F. Witte (Eds.), *Choice and control in American education, Volume 1: The theory of choice and control in American education.* New York: Falmer.

Witte, J. (1996). Who benefits from the Milwaukee choice program. In B. Fuller, R. F. Elmore, & G. Orfield (Eds.), *Who chooses? Who loses? Culture institutions and the unequal effects of school choice* (pp. 118–137). New York: Teachers College Press.

Witte, J., Sterr, T. D., & Thorn, C. A. (1995). *Fifth-year report: Milwaukee parental choice program.* Department of Political Science and the Robert LaFollette Institute of Public affairs, University of Wisconsin–Madison.

Witte, J., Thorn, C. A., Pritchard, K. M., & Claiborn, M. (1994). *Fourth-year report: Milwaukee parental choice program.* Department of Political Science and the Robert LaFollette Institute of Public Affairs, University of Wisconsin–Madison.

Witte, J., & Walsh, D. J. (1990). A systematic test of the effective schools model. *Educational Evaluation and Policy Analysis, 12,* 188–212.

Witte, J. F. (2000). *The Market approach to education.* Princeton, NJ: Princeton University Press.

Wohlstetter, P., Malloy, C., Chau, D., & Polhemus, J. (2003). Improving schools through networks: A new approach to urban school reform. *Educational Policy, 17*(4), 399–430.

Wolk, R. (1998). Strategies for fixing failing public schools. *Education Week supplement,* 43.

Wong, S. L. (1991). Evaluating the content of textbooks: Public interests and professional authority. *Sociology of Education, 64*(1), 11–18.

Wong-Fillmore, L., & Valdez, C. (1986). Teaching bilingual children. In M. Wittrock (Ed.), *Handbook of research on teaching* (3rd ed.). New York: Macmillan.

Woolfolk, A. E. (1990). *Educational psychology* (4th ed.). Boston: Allyn and Bacon.

Wraga, W. G. (1997). Patterns of interdisciplinary curriculum organization and professional knowledge of the curriculum field. *Journal of Curriculum and Supervision, 12*(2), 98–117.

Wraga, W. G. (1999). "Extracting sun-beams out of cucumbers": The retreat from practice in reconceptualized curriculum studies. *Educational Researcher, 28*(1), 4–13.

Wright, L. B. (1957). *The cultural life of the American colonies.* New York: Harper & Brothers.

Wright, R. (1969). *Native son.* New York: Harper and Row.

Wrigley, J. (1982). *Class, politics and public schools: Chicago, 1900–1950.* New Brunswick, NJ: Rutgers University Press.

Wrigley, J. (Ed.). (1992). *Education and gender equality.* London: Falmer.

Yeomans, E. (1979). *The Shady Hill School: The first fifty years.* Cambridge, MA: Windflower Press.

Young, M. (1958). *The rise of the meritocracy, 1870–2033: An essay on education and equality.* London: Thames and Hudson.

Young, M. F. D. (1971). *Knowledge and control: New directions for the sociology of education.* London: Collier-Macmillan.

Zajda, J. I. (1980). *Education in the U.S.S.R.* New York: Pergamon.

Zelman v. Simmons-Harris, 122 S.Ct. 2460 (2002).

Zigler, E., & Muenchow, S. (1992). *Head Start: The inside story of America's most successful educational experiment.* New York: Basic Books.

Zigler, E., & Styfco, S. (1993). *Head Start and beyond: A national plan for extended childhood intervention.* New Haven, CT: Yale University Press.

Zigler, E., & Valentine, J. (Eds.). (1979). *Project Head Start: A legacy of the war on poverty.* New York: The Free Press.

Zweigenhaft, R. L., & Domhoff, G. W. (1991). *Blacks in the white establishment? A study of race and class in America.* New Haven, CT: Yale University Press.

Index

This page constitutes a continuation of the copyright page.

Permission credits: **pp. 2–3 quotation:** Reprinted by permission of the author. **pp. 3–4 quotation:** Copyright © 1987 by The New York Times Co. Reprinted with permission. **pp. 74–82, 458–464, 466–475 text:** Adapted from Susan F. Semel, Peter W. Cookson, Jr., and Alan R. Sadovnik, "United States," in Peter W. Cookson, Jr., Alan R. Sadovnik, and Susan F. Semel (Eds.), *International Handbook of Educational Reform* (pp. 445–469). © 1992 by Peter W. Cookson, Jr., Alan R. Sadovnik, and Susan F. Semel. Westport, CT: Greenwood Press, 1992, an imprint of Greenwood Publishing Group, Inc., Westport CT. Reprinted with permission. **pp. 181–183 text:** Adapted from *Continuity and Contradiction: The Future of the Sociology of Education,* G. Noblit and W. Pinks (Eds.), © 1995 Hampton Press, Inc., Cresskill, NJ. Reprinted with permission. **p. 263 Table 7.1:** From Frederick M. Wirt and Michael W. Kirst, *Political and Social Foundations of Education,* copyright 1972 by McCutchan Publishing Corporation, Berkeley, CA 94702. Permission granted by the publisher.